Learn the Bible
IN A YEAR

From Genesis to Revelation,
365 daily readings to help
you understand your Bible
in just 7 minutes a day!

Shane W. Houle, D.Min.

Bibles For
The World

Special Edition

Learn the Bible in a Year — by Shane W. Houle, D.Min.

Copyright © December 5th, 2017
Learn the Bible in a Year
Formerly, Bible in a Year to the World

Shane W. Houle
All rights reserved
shanehoule1@gmail.com
www.LearntheBibleinaYear.com
ISBN-13: 978-1532805943
Library of Congress Control Number: 2015904728.

CreateSpace Independent Publishing Platform, North Charleston, SC

No portion of this book may be reproduced or used in any form, or by any means, without prior written permission from the copyright owner.

Scripture passages taken from Holy Bible, New International Version (NIV), Copyright© 1973, 1978, 1984, 2011 by Biblica, Inc', Used by permission. All rights reserved worldwide.

Used by permission of Hodder & Stoughton Publishers, an Hachette UK company. All rights reserved worldwide. 'NIV' is a trademark of Biblica. UK trademark number 1448790. Reproduced by permission of Hodder and Stoughton Limited.

Used by permission of Zondervan. All rights reserved worldwide. WWW.ZONDERVAN.COM

The "NIV" and "New International Version" are trademarks registered in the United States Patent and Trademark Offices by Biblica, Inc. ™

This edition of *Learn The Bible In A Year* was produced by special arrangement with Bibles For The World, Colorado Springs, Colorado.

Author

Shane W. Houle earned his M.A. at Columbia Biblical Seminary, and his D.Min. at Trinity International University. He has been married to Julene for 30 years and lives in beautiful Colorado Springs, Colorado.

Dedication

This book is dedicated to my dear friends, Ed and Sharon Porter. Their generous support and constant encouragement made this project possible. [T]he Lord will reward each one for whatever good they do (Ephesians 6:8).

Disclaimer

I learned early as a preacher to gather thoughts, ideas, and illustrations from wherever I could. Many have found their way into this book but, in most cases, credit is not given because I have forgotten the source. I make no claim to originality and am thankful for all who have taught me.

Learn the Bible
IN A YEAR

Foreword

I first met Shane Houle upon the recommendation of two friends in Colorado, who said, "You have to meet with this man. What he's done is phenomenal." Suitably intrigued, I invited Shane to meet in my office at Bibles For The World. When he dropped his early edition of **Learn the Bible in a Year** on my desk the loud "THUD!" definitely got my attention.

As we chatted, I discovered a man who is, quite simply, in love with God's Word. A man who wants desperately for others to develop that same love. And a man who wants the people of the world to understand the power to transform lives that lies within the Bible's pages.

As our conversations continued, Shane realized that Bibles For The World has the same passion for the transformational power of God's Word. After all, the ministry founded by my father and mother in 1958 has provided the Bible and/or Scripture portions in dozens of languages to tens of millions of people in 122 nations of the world. We both began to realize that a partnership was inevitable. Our mutual passion to see God's Word be available to everyone, everywhere, is only exceeded by our desire that they understand its contents, the marvelous story of God's plan for humankind that culminates in the redemptive gift of Jesus Christ and the restoration of relationship with God the Father.

That desire is what has resulted in not only a partnership between Shane Houle and Bibles For The World, but also a conviction that the contents of this book can help <u>anyone</u> come to a full and complete understanding of the Bible. Together we're devoting our energies to helping people worldwide discover the timeless truths, the wonderful language and the real-world application of God's Story to their own lives.

How do I know that understanding God's Word can transform even the most hardened of hearts? Because my own grandfather — who belonged to a tribe of fierce headhunters in northeast India — was transformed through the message of the Gospel of John, a gift from a young Welsh missionary in 1910 who was determined to reach the headhunting tribes of that area. And not only my grandfather, but his entire tribe of more than 100,000 people was transformed from head-hunters to heart-hunters for Jesus Christ through the power of God's Word. [NOTE: You can watch the story of this transformation in a powerful motion picture presentation called "Beyond the Next Mountain." Visit <u>BiblesForTheWorld.org</u> for details]

As you work your way through **Learn the Bible in a Year**, I hope God uses the wonderful lessons Shane has created to transform your own life. May God bless you as you study His Word.

John L. Pudaite
President, Bibles For The World

Introduction

When Philip found the Ethiopian gentleman reading the prophet Isaiah, he asked him, Do you understand what you are reading? To this the man replied, How can I … unless someone explains it to me? (Acts 8:30-31). The Bible is a difficult book and a little explanation can be helpful.

The goal of Learn the Bible in a Year is to teach the whole Bible, in three hundred sixty-five lessons, in every language of the world, for free. We want everyone in the world to have access to quality Bible teaching that is both comprehensive and concise.

To cover the Bible more thoroughly, and to improve the quality, new editions of Learn the Bible in a Year are due to be released every year or so. This will help it attain an excellence that is worthy of a global audience. If you find the material helpful, please become a monthly supporter. Thank you for helping more and more people to Learn the Bible in a Year.

Overview

The Bible is the story of God's salvation, and can be surveyed in fifteen stages. What follows is a summary of each stage in its proper order. All dates are approximate.

Creation: In the beginning God created the heavens and the earth (Genesis 1:1), and all they contain. Then he made Adam and Eve in his image to have fellowship with him. The first couple enjoyed walking with God in the Garden of Eden when everything was good. This stage is difficult to date, and believing scholars disagree.

The Fall: Adam and Eve were free to eat from every tree in the garden except the tree of the knowledge of good and evil. Tragically, the devil convinced them to eat the forbidden fruit, and they brought God's curse on the world. As a result, all their offspring are born with a sinful nature, and everyone dies eventually.

The world soon became so corrupt that God sent a flood, killing everyone but Noah and his family. Then the world became corrupt again so God called Abraham (2091 BC) and promised to bless the world through him (Genesis 12:2-3). The rest of the Bible is the story of this man's family.

The Patriarchs: Abraham had a son named Isaac, Isaac had a son named Jacob, and Jacob had twelve sons. God changed Jacob's name to Israel and his sons became the twelve tribes of Israel. None of these men were perfect, but they believed in God and what he had promised them.

The Exodus: Jacob's son, Joseph, was sold by his brothers into Egyptian slavery (1898 BC). But God was with him, and he rose to prominence. When Israel numbered about seventy, Joseph brought them down to Egypt and cared for them. The family grew dramatically and, generations later, Pharaoh considered them a threat and made them his slaves. They were cruelly oppressed until Moses arrived and led them out of Egypt, through the Red Sea (1446 BC).

The Desert: After leaving Egypt, the Israelites camped at Mount Sinai where God gave them Ten Commandments, and many other laws. A year or two later they arrived at Canaan, the land God had promised to Abraham (Genesis 13:15). God told his people to take the land, but they refused because they feared the people who lived there, and wouldn't trust God to defeat them. As a result, God made them wander in the desert forty years, until most of the adults had died—even Moses.

The Conquest: Joshua led the next generation of Israelites into the Promised Land (1406 BC). As Moses had parted the Red Sea (Exodus 14:29), Joshua led them across the Jordan River on dry ground (Joshua 3:17). With God's help they took most of the land, but not all of it. The presence of enemy occupants would remain a serious problem for hundreds of years.

The Judges: Once in the Promised Land, the Israelites turned away from God. But when life became difficult, they turned back to him for help. God faithfully helped them by raising up leaders (called Judges) to defeat their enemies. But then they turned away from God again, until life became difficult again. This cycle repeated itself several times for hundreds of years.

The United Kingdom: Even though God was their king, Israel wanted an earthly king so they could be like the other nations. Saul was the first king of Israel (1043 BC) and, though he started well, he ended badly. David was the second king of Israel, and also its greatest king, because he defeated their enemies and led them to worship God. God even promised to establish the throne of his kingdom forever (2 Samuel 7:13). David's son Solomon was the third king of Israel, and brought the nation to its greatest height. But Solomon turned away from God and most of the people followed him. Due to his unfaithfulness, the nation soon broke apart.

The Divided Kingdom: After Solomon's death (931 BC) the nation split apart, north and south. The ten tribes to the north kept the name Israel. They adopted a false religion and, a couple centuries later, fell to the Assyrians (722 BC). The tribes to the south were called Judah (later known as the Jews). They served God occasionally, but not faithfully, and were conquered by the Babylonians (586 BC).

The Exile: The Babylonians took the conquered Jews back to Babylon where, once again, they turned back to God. Even if you have been banished to the most distant land under the heavens, from there the Lord your God will gather you and bring you back (Deuteronomy 30:4), wrote Moses. After several decades of Babylonian exile, that's exactly what happened.

The Return: When Babylon was defeated by the king of Persia, he allowed the Jews to go home (537 BC). Many stayed behind, but those who returned rebuilt the temple, and tried to follow God. They were a tiny fraction of what they used to be, and struggled in many ways. God sent a few prophets to encourage them, but then the prophetic voice ceased (430 BC).

The Silent Years: Like a dramatic pause, the Bible is silent for hundreds of years before the arrival of Christ. God's people were back in the Promised Land, but were under Persian rule. Then they were ruled by Greeks. Then they won their independence for about a hundred years. By the time of Christ they were under Roman rule, and longed to be free again.

The Christ: For God so loved the world that he gave his one and only Son, that whoever believes in him shall not perish but have eternal life (John 3:16). Jesus lived a perfect life, but was crucified those who hated him (AD 30). Then he was laid in a tomb, but he rose on the third day, showing he had conquered death. Through his life, death, and resurrection, Jesus reversed the curse of sin for all who believe in him.

The Mission: After Jesus rose from the dead he told his followers to make disciples of all nations (Matthew 28:19). Peter preached on the day of Pentecost, and three thousand believed (Acts 2:41). Paul's ministry was slightly less dramatic, but he took the gospel all the way to Rome (Acts 28:16). The church has continued to preach the gospel and, today, nearly a third of the people on earth claim to be Christians in some sense.

The Future: Jesus will return at an unexpected time to judge the living and the dead (1 Peter 4:5). To some he will say, Come, you who are blessed by my Father; take your inheritance, the kingdom prepared for you since the creation of the world (Matthew 25:34). To the rest he will say, Depart from me, you who are cursed, into the eternal fire prepared for the devil and his angels (Matthew 25:41).

This is the most amazing story ever written, and it just happens to be true.

Shane W. Houle, D.Min.

Lesson 1

Genesis 1:1 *In the beginning God created the heavens and the earth.*

The book of Genesis was written by Moses, for the people of God, around 1445 BC. He began with the best explanation of who God is: the creator of the universe.

Notice first, the universe began to exist. There was a time when the universe did not exist, and this is powerful evidence for the existence of God. If anything is clear to us, it's that something cannot come from nothing. If there was nothing more than a single grain of sand in the entire universe, it would still prove the existence of God because, *out of nothing, nothing comes.*

To avoid responsibility to their Maker, however, some have argued the universe is eternal. If it always existed, then it didn't need to be created—or so it is thought. But in the last century, scientists discovered the universe is expanding and, therefore, had a beginning.

If you play the movie of an expanding universe backward, you'll see it become smaller and smaller, until it no longer exists. And if you play the movie forward again, you'll see the universe pop into existence at a particular point in time. An expanding universe proves the universe is not eternal—but had a beginning—just as the Bible teaches.

Notice second, the greatness of God who exists outside time and space, and is the best explanation for both. When I was a child, I tried to imagine the beginning of time. I traveled back to the very first moment when everything began. But then I wondered, *What was before then?*

Then I traveled to the edge of space, where I could only imagine a massive brick wall. But then I wondered, *What's on the other side of that wall?* We can't imagine the beginning of time, or space, but we can easily think of the God who made them both, because that's how he designed us. Time and space find their source in God, and lead us back to him.

Notice third, nothing is impossible with God. Unbelievers scoff at biblical miracles like the virgin birth of Christ (Luke 1:35), and the resurrection of Christ (Matthew 28:1-7). This is understandable since, by their very nature, miracles are rare and hard to believe.

But if you accept the first and most spectacular miracle of the Bible—that God created everything out of nothing—then there's no reason to think he couldn't part the sea (Exodus 14:21-22), make the sun stand still (Joshua 10:13), or preserve a man inside a fish (Jonah 1:17). Nothing is logically impossible for a God who creates everything out of nothing.

Genesis 1:3 *God said, Let there be light, and there was light.*

But God didn't make the sun for another three days (Genesis 1:16), so we ought to think about where this light came from. The best explanation is that it came from God himself. *God is light; in him there is no darkness at all* (1 John 1:5), wrote John.

So after he made the world, God began to reveal himself. This he did progressively to Adam and Eve, Abraham, Moses, the prophets, and to many others. God revealed himself, more and more, until he came in the person of Jesus Christ who said, *I am the light of the world* (John 8:12). Isaiah didn't say it. Neither did Jeremiah, Ezekiel, or Daniel. Only Jesus Christ could say, *I am the light of the world*, because only Jesus Christ is divine.

And coming to Christ is like God turning on his light in our hearts. *For God, who said, Let light shine out of darkness, made his light shine in our hearts to give us the light of the knowledge of God's glory displayed in the face of Christ* (2 Corinthians 4:6), wrote Paul. We live in spiritual darkness until we understand the gospel. Then, suddenly, the light comes on.

Through Jesus Christ we come to know God, not by argument or inference, but directly and personally. There's excellent evidence for

Christianity, but we aren't Christians primarily because of the evidence. We are Christians because Jesus Christ revealed himself to us through the gospel.

Nor is he done revealing himself. *The city [of God] does not need the sun or the moon to shine on it, for the glory of God gives it light, and the Lamb is its lamp* (Revelation 21:23), wrote John.

Notice the progression: *God said, Let there be light, and there was light* (Genesis 1:3). Then he revealed himself, more and more, to Abraham, Moses, and the prophets. Then he came in the person of Jesus Christ who said, *I am the light of the world* (John 8:12). Then he *made his light shine in our hearts* (2 Corinthians 4:6). And, soon, we'll live in the city where God himself is the light (Revelation 21:23), because *God is light; in him there is no darkness at all* (1 John 1:5).

Genesis 1:16 *God made two great lights—the greater light to govern the day and the lesser light to govern the night. He also made the stars.*

Moses wrote for the Israelites who, after many years, came out of Egyptian slavery. In Egypt they learned about the sun god, the moon god, and many other gods. So Moses had to teach them that those gods don't exist. The God who just redeemed them created both the sun and the moon—and *He also made the stars.*

Credible estimates put the number of stars in the sky to be more than all the grains of sand on earth. *To whom will you compare me? Or who is my equal? says the Holy One. Lift up your eyes and look to the heavens: Who created all these? He who brings out the starry host one by one and calls forth each of them by name. Because of his great power and mighty strength, not one of them is missing* (Isaiah 40:25-26), wrote Isaiah.

But God was just getting started. After he made the stars, God created birds, fish, and every other creature (Genesis 1:20-25). Over a million species of life on earth has been catalogued, and that's probably only a tenth of what exists. If the name *BOB* written in the sand proves intelligence at work, how much more the world, and all its amazing creatures!

Hummingbirds are a fine example of God's intelligent design. They're the smallest birds in the world, and some weigh less than a penny. Their wings rotate a full circle, allowing them to fly forward, backward, sideways, and even upside-down. They fly about twenty-five miles an hour, and can dive up to sixty miles an hour. Some can fly over twenty hours, without rest, and migrate over two thousand miles. They breathe over two hundred times a minute, and their hearts beat over a thousand times a minute. They visit about a thousand flowers a day, and pollinate every flower they visit. *How many are your works, Lord! In wisdom you made them all* (Psalm 104:24), wrote the Psalmist.

For Reflection and Review

- *Why does the first miracle in the Bible make it easier to believe other miracles in the Bible?*
- *Why did Jesus claim to be the light of the world?*
- *How does creation prove the existence of God?*

Lesson 2

Genesis 1:11 *Let the land produce vegetation: seed-bearing plants and trees on the land that bear fruit with seed in it, according to their various kinds.*

In the beginning, God created everything out of nothing (Genesis 1:1). But, since then, he normally uses the means he built into creation. He could produce a million apples a day out of nothing, but prefers to use natural means instead. So after he made the fish and the birds he said, *Be fruitful and increase in number and fill the water in the seas, and let the birds increase on the earth* (Genesis 1:22). At first, God created animals according to their kinds (Genesis 1:25). But, since then, he uses the natural means he built into them.

God's two ways of working can be understood as *miracle* and *providence*. Jesus healed many people miraculously, but God heals most people providentially. Small cuts normally heal through the means God built into the body. He may also use medicine (which comes from creation) and doctors who've learned how the body works. This kind of healing is not technically *miraculous*, but *providential*.

Likewise, Jesus taught us to pray for our *daily bread* (Matthew 6:11), but it doesn't normally drop out of heaven. He normally gives us jobs, to earn money, so we can buy bread from the market. When Jesus fed the multitudes with *only five loaves of bread and two fish* (Matthew 14:17), he was providing miraculously. More often he uses soil, sun, rain, farmers, bakers, and merchants to provide.

When we understand that God works providentially, not just miraculously, we'll see his kindness in every plate of food, every healing, and every other need he meets. Miracles still occur, of course, but God is always working providentially. Miracle and providence, we could say, are the right and left hands of God.

Genesis 1:27 *God created mankind in his own image, in the image of God he created them; male and female he created them.*

This was important to the Israelites because, in Egypt, they were treated like beasts. They were Pharaoh's slaves and their primary job was to make bricks. And if they didn't make their quota, they were given a beating (Exodus 5:1-18). Whole generations lived and died under the hot Egyptian sun, working like beasts and considered little more.

But here we learn there is a qualitative difference between people and animals. People are made in the image of God, animals are not. It's not merely a matter of degree, but of kind, dignity, and worth. Without clarity on this point we'll treat people like animals, and animals like people. There are some countries, in fact, where cattle are treated with honor while people go hungry. This is one reason theology matters.

The image of God is also that which allows us to know God personally. You can't have a personal relationship with a turtle, because a turtle is too different from you. You can't have a meaningful conversation with a cat, because a cat is too different from you too. But you can know God more deeply than you know your spouse, because you were made in the image of God.

This is also why the Bible allows capital punishment in the case of murder. *Whoever sheds human blood, by humans shall their blood be shed; for in the image of God has God made mankind* (Genesis 9:6), wrote Moses. God sees murdering others as an attack on himself because every human being bears the image of God.

This is also why it's wrong to curse other people. *With the tongue we praise our Lord and Father, and with it we curse human beings, who have been made in God's likeness. . . . this should not be* (James 3:9-10), wrote James.

Before we curse another person, or make an obscene gesture, we should remember whose image they bear. The image of God is so basic to our humanity, and to the ordering of society, that it's found in the very first chapter of the Bible.

And the reason God created people in his image is because he planned to become one of us. When Christ came into the world, God took on our humanity, never to put it off again. For all eternity we'll relate to God through Jesus Christ, who is fully God and fully human.

Genesis 1:28 *God blessed them and said to them, Be fruitful and increase in number; fill the earth and subdue it.*

God gave Adam and Eve an important job to do: *fill the earth and subdue it*. From this we learn that God wants people to contribute to society through work and family. Raising children, building roads, creating art, and anything else that contributes to the good of society is actually serving God. This idea is reinforced by the Apostle Paul who wrote,

Whatever you do, work at it with all your heart, as working for the Lord. . . . It is the Lord Christ you are serving (Colossians 3:23-24).

Some people think the only way to serve God is through church, or some other religious means. It's true that every child of God has an essential role to play in the church (1 Corinthians 12:12-31), but the work we do for God in the world is equally important. Adam, for example, served God by gardening. *The Lord God took the man and put him in the Garden of Eden to work it and take care of it* (Genesis 2:15), wrote Moses. Gardening was Adam's service to God.

The work we do for the glory of God, and the good of others, is not merely a way to make money or raise a family. *It is the Lord Christ you are serving.* This gives meaning and significance to all we do, and should make our work an act of worship.

Genesis 1:31 *God saw all that he had made, and it was very good.*

God could've made the world an average place, but chose to make it very good. I was on my way to class, on a fall afternoon, when I passed a familiar tree. I'd seen it many times before, but this time was different. The lowering sun shone through the golden leaves and seemed to darken the branches. The tree itself was grand but, against the deep blue sky, it was art. I wanted to say to everyone, *Look at that!*

Before there was television, people went for long walks and called it *marveling.* They'd look at flowers, trees, and birds, and simply marvel at them. And, if we're willing to take the time, we can too. Creation reflects the glory of God (Isaiah 6:3), and he wants us to see it everywhere.

Genesis 2:3 *God blessed the seventh day and made it holy, because on it he rested from all the work of creating that he had done.*

After God created the world, we might imagine he was tired. But the amount of God's power he used to create the world was mathematically zero. God's power is infinite so, no matter how much power he uses, it's never at all diminished. God didn't rest because he was tired, but because resting is good. It's also good for us.

Come to me, all you who are weary and burdened, and I will give you rest (Matthew 11:28), said Jesus. Many are surprised to learn the way to heaven is not by working, but by resting. If all we had to do was a million good deeds, we'd all be very busy. Or if all we had to do was pay a million dollars, we'd all be working overtime. But the way to heaven isn't by working, or even by being good, but by resting in the finished work of Christ. *In repentance and rest is your salvation* (Isaiah 30:15), wrote Isaiah.

A little girl was hiking with her big brother when she twisted her ankle and couldn't go on. The only way home was to climb on her brother's back, and let him carry her. Likewise, we put all our weight on Christ, and trust him to carry us home.

For Reflection and Review

- *How is a miracle different from providence?*
- *How should the image of God affect how we treat others?*
- *What does the beauty of creation suggest about God?*

Lesson 3

Genesis 3:1 *Now the serpent was more crafty than any of the wild animals the Lord God had made.*

This is the first mention of Satan in the Bible and, though he's not on every page, he has a leading role. He's called the *Destroyer* (Revelation 9:11), *the enemy* (Luke 10:19), the *father of lies* (John 10:44), *a murderer* (John 8:44), *the evil one* (Matthew 5:37), and many other things.

Satan is God's enemy but, since he can't attack God directly, he attacks those who are made in God's image, and dearly loved by him. Satan knows his doom is sure, but he wants to take as many people down with him as he can.

Here the Bible says he's *crafty*. Other translations include *sneaky, clever, cunning, subtle, intelligent,* and *shrewd*. Satan is a clever devil, who's good at what he does. If you lived a thousand years, you could easily become an expert at something: music, math, philosophy, or any number of things. Satan has been around longer than that, and he's refined his craft to an art form.

He's so skillful, in fact, that he *leads the whole world astray* (Revelation 12:9), wrote John. We know how to split the atom and fly to the moon but, after thousands of years, there's still no consensus on who God is, what he requires, or even if he exists. Satan is an evil genius, and an expert at leading the world astray.

Genesis 3:1b *He said to the woman, Did God really say, You must not eat from any tree in the garden?*

This is the first temptation of a human being, and it's brilliant. If Satan can make us doubt God's word, then he's severed the relationship, and won the battle for our souls. That's why more books have been written against the Bible than any other book by far. The Bible is the most banned, burned, and blasphemed book in the world. Satan is serious about turning people away from God, and he starts by attacking God's word.

Satan hates the Bible and wants us to doubt it, but Jesus loves the Bible and wants us to trust it. *For truly I tell you, until heaven and earth disappear, not the smallest letter, not the least stroke of a pen, will by any means disappear from the Law until everything is accomplished* (Matthew 5:18), he said. By referring to the *smallest letter* and *least stroke of a pen*, Jesus showed that he believed the Bible right down to the spelling.

He also said *your word is truth* (John 17:17). He didn't say *your word is truthful,* or *your word contains truth,* but *your word is truth*. In fact, *All Scripture is God-breathed* (2 Timothy 3:16), wrote Paul. It's as though God himself breathed out every syllable of the Bible.

So when Jesus was tempted by the devil he didn't doubt the Bible—he quoted it. *It is written . . . . It is also written . . . . it is written* (Matthew 4:4, 7, 10), he said. The most trustworthy person in the world, believed the most trustworthy book in the world, and they bear witness to each other.

Our first parents were deceived by the devil because they doubted God's word. Jesus triumphed over the devil because he trusted God's word. Now the choice is ours: we can follow Jesus, or we can follow Satan.

Genesis 3:5 *God knows that when you eat from it your eyes will be opened, and you will be like God, knowing good and evil.*

Satan wanted Adam and Eve to doubt the goodness of God, so he focused on what God withheld. They were free to eat from every tree in the garden, except *the tree of the knowledge of good and evil* (Genesis 2:17). But if God was withholding something good from Adam and Eve, maybe he wasn't good after all. First the devil tempted them to doubt God's word, then he tempted them to doubt God's goodness.

This is still effective whenever we don't get something that we want (like someone to marry), or whenever we do get something that we don't want. A missionary served God for years, when his son was attacked by a swarm of bees that forced him to jump off a cliff to his death. Wouldn't a good God have kept that from happening? Adam and Eve were the first, but certainly not the last, to question the goodness of God.

Thankfully, God has proven his goodness, once and for all, through the death and resurrection of his Son. Before the death and resurrection of Jesus Christ, it was less clear what kind of God we were dealing with. But when *God so loved the world that he gave his one and only Son* (John 3:16), his goodness was displayed for all to see. Only a perfectly good God would give his Son for the sins of a world that hated him.

As soon as we believe that Jesus Christ died for our sins, we give up the right to question the goodness of God ever again. If the sacrificial death of Jesus Christ doesn't persuade us that God is good, nothing ever will. Every believer must settle this matter once and for all: *God is good all the time.* The devil hates this fact, and wants us to doubt it. But Jesus proved this fact, and wants us to trust it.

Genesis 3:6 *When the woman saw that the fruit of the tree was good for food and pleasing to the eye, and also desirable for gaining wisdom, she took some and ate it. She also gave some to her husband, who was with her, and he ate it.*

The first duty of a Christian husband is to protect his family from the devil, but Adam chose to use his wife as a guinea pig instead. If she fell over dead, he wouldn't have eaten the fruit. But, since she survived, he thought it might be safe.

Genesis 3:7 *Then the eyes of both of them were opened, and they realized they were naked; so they sewed fig leaves together and made coverings for themselves.*

This is how shame came into the world. Adam and Eve had nothing to hide before they sinned but, afterward, they wanted to cover themselves. So they gathered fig leaves and stitched them together in a desperate attempt to cover their shame. If you've ever dreamed of being naked in public, you know how they felt.

But even if we have no physical shame, everyone carries moral shame. If everything we've ever done became public information, we couldn't leave the house. One survey showed that fifty percent of adult males carry a secret so dark that, if it were exposed, it would destroy them.

Shame is a negative emotion, but it has a positive side. It means we're not as bad as we could be. As long as we have a sense of shame, we also have a conscience. The work of the Holy Spirit is to convict us of our sins (John 16:8), so that we can repent, and be restored to God.

For Reflection and Review

- *What did Satan want Adam and Eve to think about God?*
- *How does Jesus prove that God is perfect goodness?*
- *What is the best way to handle shame?*

Lesson 4

Genesis 3:8 *Then the man and his wife heard the sound of the Lord God as he was walking in the garden in the cool of the day, and they hid from the Lord God among the trees of the garden.*

This was a little desperate but, for all they knew, God was coming to kill them. *[W]hen you eat [of the tree] you will certainly die* (Genesis 2:17), he warned. God had given them life, and now he was free to take it away.

Like our first parents, we also hide from God. Some hide by putting God out of their minds. Others hide by neglecting his word. Others use religion to hide from God, instead of coming to God himself. Nothing comes more naturally to sinners than trying to hide from God.

Genesis 3:9 *But the Lord God called to the man, Where are you?*

This is God seeking man, not to kill him, but to restore him. The idea is so important that Jesus repeated it several times. The good shepherd searches for his one lost sheep (Luke 15:4). The distressed woman searches for her one lost coin (Luke 15:8). And the rejected Father looks down the road searching for his one lost son (Luke 15:20). *For the Son of Man came to seek and to save the lost* (Luke 19:10), said Jesus.

A little boy was separated from his father at the county fair. He was surrounded by the best stuff in the world, but couldn't enjoy it, because he didn't know where his father was. But after his father found him, the little boy enjoyed both the fair, and his father, more than ever. God is seeking lost people, not to punish them, but to restore them.

Genesis 3:15 *I will put enmity between you and the woman, and between your offspring and hers; he will crush your head, and you will strike his heel.*

This is God's solution to the problem of sin, which he spoke to the devil. It's a messianic prophecy that's remarkable for at least three reasons:

First, the solution to sin wouldn't be Adam or Eve, but someone else. We'd expect the first couple to pay for their own sin, but God promised to send another who'd *crush [the devil's] head*. This idea is further developed throughout the Old Testament, so the Promised One wouldn't be unexpected.

Second, the Promised One would be male. *He will crush your head*, not *She will crush your head*. In a single pronoun God eliminated half the human race from the pool of possible candidates. And throughout the Old Testament, the pool shrinks even further.

The Promised One would be descended from Abraham (Genesis 12:1-3), from the tribe of Judah (Genesis 49:10), born in Bethlehem (Micah 5:2), but minister in Galilee (Isaiah 9:1-2). If you put all the prophecies together, in fact, there's only one person who fulfilled them all perfectly. *These are the very Scriptures that testify about me* (John 5:39), said Jesus.

Third, the conflict between the serpent and the Promised One would likely include fatalities. If you step on a serpent's head, it will probably die. And, if it bites your heel, you could also die. The crucifixion of Jesus Christ was fatal in the sense that he actually died. But, through his resurrection, he dealt a fatal blow to Satan. It was a cosmic conflict of life and death. The rest of the Bible is the unfolding of this original promise.

Genesis 3:19 *By the sweat of your brow you will eat your food until you return to the ground, since from it you were taken; for dust you are and to dust you will return.*

Even though the Promised One would fix the problem of sin, there'd still be consequences for Adam and Eve, and their descendants. Mankind was made to tend the garden, but now they'd become part of the garden. Now we're all born with a terminal disease called *aging*, and are just at various stages.

If you get together with friends, whom you haven't seen for years, you'll be surprised by how much they've changed. Smooth skin may've become wrinkled. A full head of hair may've fallen out. And those who used to be thin may've put on weight. You'll be surprised by how much they've changed, and they'll be surprised by you. Then you'll have a contest to see who can act the least surprised. *Ashes to ashes, dust to dust, everyone sins and die we must.*

Genesis 3:21 *The Lord God made garments of skin for Adam and his wife and clothed them.*

The only way to get skin off an animal is to kill it, so this is the first animal sacrifice. Animals were likely tame before the fall, and may've been something like pets. Adam and Eve were vegetarians (Genesis 1:29, 9:3) and had never seen an animal die. But, naked and ashamed, they needed the animal's skin to cover their humiliation.

To make his point, God may've made them watch the slaughter of this innocent victim: throat slit, blood spilt, eyes wild, body trembling, life draining, lights out. It was a bloody object lesson to portray the wickedness of sin, and the terrible cost involved.

The Old Testament, in fact, is filled with the blood of sacrificial animals—sheep, goats, bulls, and more. But all the blood of all the animals ever sacrificed could *never take away sins* (Hebrews 10:11), says Hebrews. That required nothing less than the shed blood of Jesus Christ—God in human flesh.

Sin is man taking the place of God, and salvation is God taking the place of man. Adam and Eve were clothed with the skin of a beast, but all who believe are clothed with Jesus Christ. *[Y]ou who were baptized into Christ have clothed yourselves with Christ* (Galatians 3:27), wrote Paul. The first animal sacrifice pointed ahead to the sacrifice of Christ.

Genesis 3:24 *After he drove the man out, he placed on the east side of the Garden of Eden cherubim and a flaming sword flashing back and forth to guard the way to the tree of life.*

The opportunity to eat from the tree of life, and live forever, was apparently gone for ever. How sad it must've been for Adam and Eve to leave the garden, and venture into the untamed world. There they would die, and all their offspring would also die. This remains the worst day in the history of the world.

But, thankfully, the tree of life appears again at the end of the Bible. *On each side of the river stood the tree of life, bearing twelve crops of fruit* (Revelation 22:2), wrote John. The tree of life first appeared in the old paradise of Eden. But after the death of Christ it appears again in the new paradise of God's eternal kingdom.

This is helpful for understanding the Bible's overarching storyline. It's the record of paradise lost through sin, and regained through Jesus Christ. The cherubim mentioned above were later embroidered on the temple curtain (2 Chronicles 3:14), which kept people away from the presence of God. That curtain was torn from top to bottom when Jesus died on the cross (Matthew 27:51). This shows the way to God is now open to everyone who comes through faith in Christ.

For Reflection and Review

- *Why do people try to hide from God?*
- *How did sin change the world?*
- *What is the Bible's storyline?*

Lesson 5

Genesis 4:1-2 *Adam made love to his wife Eve, and she became pregnant and gave birth to Cain. . . . Later she gave birth to his brother Abel.*

Cain and Abel were the first two sons born to Adam and Eve. There weren't many career choices back then, so Cain grew up to be a farmer, and Abel kept flocks. As an offering to God, Cain brought some of his produce, and *Abel brought fat portions from some of the firstborn of his flock* (Genesis 4:4). This is how they honored God as the source of all they had.

Genesis 4:4-5 *The Lord looked with favor on Abel and his offering, but on Cain and his offering he did not look with favor.*

Not all offerings are equally pleasing to God. The text is not explicit, but Abel seems to have brought his best, while Cain bought something less. The real problem wasn't what they brought, however, but the attitude of their hearts. We learn elsewhere that Abel's heart was right with God (Hebrews 11:4), and Cain's heart was not (1 John 3:12). It's not enough to bring God our offerings, we must bring them with a good heart.

Genesis 4:5b *So Cain was very angry, and his face was downcast.*

Cain thought his offering was perfectly fine, and God was lucky to have it. He should've received God's favor, not his disapproval. What kind of God would disapprove of an offering anyway? Cain wasn't sure that he even liked God very much. *Then the Lord said to Cain, Why are you angry? Why is your face downcast? If you do what is right, will you not be accepted?* (Genesis 4:6-7).

Cain didn't understand worship at all. His offering showed a measure of compliance, but he wasn't even thankful. Giving to God seemed like a tax to Cain, not an expression of love. But God assured Cain that he would be accepted, if he'd only do what was right. *But if you do not do what is right, sin is crouching at your door; it desires to have you, but you must rule over it* (Genesis 4:7b), said God.

God described sin as a wild beast ready to pounce. Cain could do the right thing, and be accepted by God, or he could do as he pleased and be devoured by sin. But now it was time for Cain to choose: rule the beast, or be devoured.

Many face a similar choice at one time or another. Some choose to conquer lust, others are devoured. Some choose to conquer drugs, others are devoured. Some choose to conquer hate, others are devoured. Sin is not a paper tiger, but a ferocious beast hungry for souls.

Genesis 4:8 *Cain said to his brother Abel, Let's go out to the field.*

Cain led his brother far enough away that their parents wouldn't hear him scream. Cain probably gave some thought to the place, and how to dispose of the body. If his brother went missing, his parents would assume he was eaten by an animal, or that he was lost. So *While they were in the field, Cain attacked his brother Abel and killed him* (Genesis 4:8b).

Cain became the first murderer, and his brother became the first martyr. Cain wasn't merely jealous of his brother—he hated him for loving God. Cain hated God so much that he murdered his brother for loving God. *Do not be like Cain, who belonged to the evil one and murdered his brother* (1 John 3:12), wrote John.

Believers and unbelievers often get along, but when the devil gets involved we should expect the worst. *If they persecuted me, they will persecute you* (John 15:20), said Jesus. Abel was the first to die for his faith, but millions have followed him.

We should also notice that sin can have unintended consequences. When Adam and Eve ate the forbidden fruit, they hoped to elevate the human condition (Genesis 3:5). Instead, their natures were corrupted, and passed down to their children, so one killed the other. Even worse, their sinful natures were passed down to future generations producing a world of sin, sorrow, and death. If Adam and Eve could've foreseen the results of their sin, they wouldn't have sinned in the first place. Sadly, many can tell a similar story.

Genesis 4:9 *Then the Lord said to Cain, Where is your brother Abel? I don't know, he replied. Am I my brother's keeper?*

Cain's sarcastic reply showed he was completely unrepentant. He had no sorrow for sin, or any regret for what he'd done. He hardened his heart against the voice of God, and became a hardened killer. Even then, if Cain would've repented, God would've received him. *[A] broken and contrite heart you, God, will not despise* (Psalm 51:17), wrote David. But Cain preferred his sin over the mercy of God.

Genesis 4:10 *Listen! Your brother's blood cries out to me from the ground.*

Abel's parents didn't hear him scream, but God heard his blood crying out from the ground. *It is mine to avenge; I will repay* (Deuteronomy 32:25), said God. Whoever rejects God's mercy will have to face his justice.

As part of his punishment, Cain would become a *restless wanderer* (Genesis 4:12). His life would be an aimless journey, without meaning or direction, leading to the grave, and then to hell below. This sad path is chosen by many, but those who follow Christ journey to a better place. We can go with God, or we can go with the devil, but the destinations are as different as the paths we choose.

Genesis 4:25-26 *Adam made love to his wife again, and she gave birth to a son and named him Seth, saying, God has granted me another child in place of Abel, since Cain killed him. Seth also had a son, and he named him Enosh. At that time people began to call on the name of the Lord.*

Since Cain had rejected God, and his righteous brother was dead, true religion was in danger of vanishing altogether. But God gave Adam and Eve another son, and then a grandson. Having learned their family's history, they took God seriously, and *began to call on the name of the Lord.*

This idea repeats throughout the Bible along with a promise of salvation. *[E]veryone who calls on the name of the Lord will be saved* (Joel 2:32), wrote Joel. *[E]veryone who calls on the name of the Lord will be saved* (Acts 2:21), preached Peter. And *Everyone who calls on the name of the Lord will be saved* (Romans 10:13), wrote Paul.

A little girl fell into a hole that was, in fact, a very deep well. Rescue teams worked unceasingly, for over two days, while others watched and prayed. In what seemed to be a miracle, the little girl was finally saved from the pit of her destruction. Our pit is also deep, and leads to hell itself, but *Everyone who calls on the name of the Lord will be saved* (Romans 10:13).

For Reflection and Review

- *What kind of an offering pleases God?*
- *Why does God compare sin to a beast?*
- *What does it mean to call on the name of the Lord?*

Lesson 6

Genesis 6:5 *The Lord saw how great the wickedness of the human race had become on the earth, and that every inclination of the thoughts of the human heart was only evil all the time.*

Things went downhill rather quickly after Adam and Eve ate the forbidden fruit. Their first-born son Cain, murdered their second-born son Abel, in the first religious persecution (Genesis 4:8). Then Lamech corrupted God's pattern for marriage by introducing polygamy (Genesis 4:19). And, before long, *every inclination of the thoughts of the human heart was only evil all the time.*

This is one the clearest statements of human depravity in the Bible and, two chapters later, we read that *every inclination of the human heart is evil from childhood* (Genesis 8:21). We don't have to grow up to sin; it starts when we're kids.

I could tell of my own childhood sins, which were many and deadly, but I'll tell on my friends instead. We lived near a lake where there were plenty of frogs and, to pass the time, we'd catch them. Not content to let them go, however, my friends invented with ways to torture the frogs for their enjoyment. I could list the ways, but it's more disturbing than it's worth. Even in our youth we have more in common with devil than we do with Jesus Christ.

The Bible's main concern isn't how to have a wonderful life, or make the world a better place. It speaks to these, and other issues, but they're not the point. The Bible's main concern is sin, and what God has done to fix it through his Son Jesus Christ. Any other reading is a misinterpretation.

Genesis 6:6 *The Lord regretted that he had made human beings on the earth, and his heart was deeply troubled.*

Other translations say, *his heart was filled with pain* (NIRV), *he was heartbroken* (GW) and, *it broke his heart* (NLT). This is a little surprising because we don't expect an all-powerful God to be emotionally involved with his creatures. Unless, of course, he's also a heavenly Father who suffers deeply whenever his children go astray.

A friend of mine grew up in a good and godly home, and we went to the same school. He was normal in grade school, a little wild in middle school, but in high school he personified rebellion. He engaged in every form of destructive behavior until he disappeared. About a year later I saw his mother and was surprised by her appearance. She looked ten years older than the last time I saw her. I shudder to think how many times I broke my parents' hearts, not to mention my heavenly Father's heart.

Genesis 6:7 *So the Lord said, I will wipe from the face of the earth the human race I have created . . . for I regret that I have made them.*

The people God created turned out so badly that he had second thoughts. God is an all-powerful supreme being, complete in himself. But he's also a rejected Father with all the attending emotions. God is a real person, with real feelings, and our behavior affects his feelings.

Genesis 6:9 *Noah was a righteous man, blameless among the people of his time, and he walked faithfully with God.*

The world was filled with wickedness, but Noah was an exception. He preferred to be in step with God, and out of step with the world, than to be in step with the world, and out of step with God. Noah didn't care about the world's approval nearly as much as God's approval. Whether he had many friends or few, Noah would only have one best friend—the God who gave him life. So when God determined to judge the world with a flood, he commissioned Noah to build an ark in which he and his family would be saved.

Noah was also a preacher (2 Peter 2:5), so when people came to see the ark he likely gave them a sermon. We don't have a record of his words, but he probably told the people to repent, since God isn't *wanting anyone to perish, but everyone to come to repentance* (2 Peter 3:9), wrote Peter. This went on day after day, week after week, and year after year. But, apart from his family, Noah never won a single convert. Ministry can be hard sometimes.

Genesis 6:15 *The ark is to be three hundred cubits long, fifty cubits wide and thirty cubits high.*

Critics like to mock this story, but there are some interesting facts to support it. First, the ark was about four hundred fifty feet long, by seventy-five feet wide, by forty-five feet high. Imagine a building one and a half times the size of a football field, and four and a half stories high. It was a massive boat, but credible estimates show it was precisely the right size for the cargo.

Second, the ark was six times longer than it was wide. This is the same ratio that's used by modern ship builders. Ships built to these proportions are extremely stable and almost impossible to capsize. And, as far as we know, the ark was the first of its kind. It was engineered by God, and the pattern is still used today.

Third, there are extra-biblical accounts supporting the idea of a catastrophic flood. The two most famous are the Atra-Hasis Epic and the Gilgamesh Epic. Both were written before the biblical account, which suggests the story was passed down orally from Noah and his family, to later generations, until it was written down by Moses around 1446 BC. There are differences between the stories, but the biblical account is the most plausible one by far.

Genesis 7:13 *On that very day Noah and his sons, Shem, Ham and Japheth, together with his wife and the wives of his three sons, entered the ark.*

By this time the ark was fully loaded, and the rain was coming down. Of all the people on earth, only eight were saved (1 Peter 3:20). This is meant to shock us because we can barely imagine God only saving eight people. What about Aunt Edna, Uncle Roy, and Cousin Pete? When it came to being saved most people missed the boat—just like today. *[S]mall is the gate and narrow the road that leads to life, and only a few find it* (Matthew 7:13-14), said Jesus.

Like Noah and his family, Christians sense the approaching judgment of God and take action. As Noah and his family entered the ark, we enter into a saving relationship with Jesus Christ (John 5:24). We're despised by many, but would rather be in the boat with Jesus, than in the world without him.

For Reflection and Review

- *Are people sinners by nature or by choice?*
- *How does God feel about the wicked?*
- *Why didn't the people believe Noah?*

Lesson 7

Genesis 7:16 *Then the Lord shut him in.*

As the rain was pouring down, we can imagine people changing their minds about Noah. For years they heard him preach, and watched his godly behavior. At any time they could've picked up a hammer, or a saw, and come over to his side. But it was easier to be part of the godless majority, than part of a godly minority.

We can also imagine people standing around the ark saying, *We're sorry Noah. Can you open the door? Can you please, please, open the door?* But Noah couldn't open the door because Noah didn't close the door. The door had been closed by God.

And, as the water rose, we should imagine families on their housetops, and children asking their parents if they were going to die. We should imagine parents regretting their failure to raise their children for the Lord, and looking into their eyes with panic as they were being swept away.

This is so important, in fact, that Jesus used this story to teach about the end of the age. *As it was in the days of Noah, so it will be at the coming of the Son of Man. For in the days before the flood, people were eating and drinking, marrying and giving in marriage, up to the day Noah entered the ark; and they knew nothing about what would happen until the flood came and took them all away. That is how it will be at the coming of the Son of Man* (Matthew 24:37-39), he said.

And, *Once the owner of the house gets up and closes the door, you will stand outside knocking and pleading, Sir, open the door for us. But he will answer, I do not know you or where you come from* (Luke 13:25). According to Jesus, there will be people who planned to get in the kingdom of God, but put it off until it was too late. Then they'll plead with God, but he will say, *I do not know you.*

A few other parallels ought to be noticed: Building the ark seemed foolish to those who'd perish, and *the message of the cross is foolishness to those who are perishing* (1 Corinthians 1:18), wrote Paul. The ark was the only way to be saved, and *there is no other name under heaven . . . by which we must be saved* (Acts 4:12), said Peter. Those who heard Noah preach rejected the truth, and others *perish because they refused to love the truth and so be saved* (2 Thessalonians 2:10), wrote Paul. Salvation in Noah's day wasn't completely different than it is today.

Genesis 8:20 *Noah built an altar to the Lord [and] sacrificed burnt offerings on it. . . . a pleasing aroma to the Lord.*

Noah and his family were on the ark for three hundred seventy-eight days. Three hundred seventy-eight days in a floating zoo. Three hundred seventy-eight days with the same people. Three hundred seventy-eight days praying for the ark: Would it hold together? Did they use enough nails? Would it spring a leak?

Finally, the boat came to rest, the waters receded, and everyone got off. They were so happy, they probably kissed the dirt. Then they built an altar to worship God.

Hard times can make us thankful. When everything is wonderful, every single day, our appreciation begins to fade. But when God sends hardship, we learn how precious a normal day really is. Whenever the sun goes down on a normal day, we ought to thank God that we're not in a flood. And if we are in a flood, we ought to thank God that he will get us through.

Genesis 9:3 *Everything that lives and moves about will be food for you. Just as I gave you the green plants, I now give you everything.*

At first, God only allowed a vegetarian diet (Genesis 1:29) but, after the flood, he included meat. This is an important correction to false religious views that restrict the human diet. Whatever God has made should *be received with thanksgiving by those who believe and who know the truth* (1 Timothy 4:3), wrote Paul.

A young lady attended a Bible study where she argued for the equal sacredness of all living things. She was a vegetarian by conviction, and even thought it was wrong to swat a mosquito.

But, during the study, a bee crawled up her sleeve and, when it stung her, she killed it. And everyone saw what she did. False religions often confuse the created order. But the Bible makes sense of the world, and works in the world God created.

Genesis 9:13 *I have set my rainbow in the clouds, and it will be the sign of the covenant between me and the earth.*

The next time Noah saw a cloud he might've become nervous, and the next time it rained he might've panicked. So God gave him the sign of a rainbow to assure him that he'd never destroy the earth with a flood again (Genesis 9:15). Whenever we see a rainbow, we should thank God for preserving the world throughout the ages.

Genesis 9:20-21 *Noah, a man of the soil, proceeded to plant a vineyard. When he drank some of its wine, he became drunk and lay uncovered inside his tent.*

This is a little surprising since *Noah was a righteous man, blameless among the people of his time, and he walked faithfully with God* (Genesis 6:9), wrote Moses. Noah's preaching (2 Peter 2:5), and his building the ark, also speak to his noble character. Noah should be seen as one of the godliest people in the history of the world. But he wasn't perfect.

Life wasn't easy, after the flood, and Noah sought comfort in wine. But too much wine leads to drunkenness, which may also lead to immodesty. Noah may've disrobed because of the heat, or some other reason, but this story doesn't reflect well on him.

Genesis 9:22-23 *Ham, the father of Canaan, saw his father naked and told his two brothers outside. But Shem and Japheth took a garment and laid it across their shoulders; then they walked in backward and covered their father's naked body. Their faces were turned the other way so that they would not see their father naked.*

Ham should've protected his father's dignity by saying nothing at all. *[L]ove covers over a multitude of sins* (1 Peter 4:8), wrote Peter. But, instead of keeping quiet, Ham broadcast his father's indiscretion to his brothers. They could've joined in the ridicule, but showed proper respect by covering their father's shame. When Noah found out what happened, he blessed Shem and Japheth, and cursed the descendants of Ham (Genesis 9:24-27).

Other than Jesus Christ, there are no perfect people. Even righteous Noah had a moment of failure. We ought to keep this in mind when living with other sinners, and even for ourselves. Some sins need to be exposed, but most should be covered over. And, whenever we fail, we should take our sins to Jesus Christ, and be assured of his forgiveness (1 John 1:9).

For Reflection and Review

- Why didn't God save more people?
- What did Jesus think about this story?
- Are you surprised by Noah's failure?

Lesson 8

Genesis 10:1 *This is the account of Shem, Ham and Japheth, Noah's sons, who themselves had sons after the flood.*

For humanity to survive after the flood, Noah's sons had to reproduce, and here we find the names of their offspring. The Bible contains many genealogies and, though not always entertaining, they show we're part of a much larger story. Like those who've gone before us, we're born into the world, play a part, and then we die. Our lives are made up of the choices we make, and each day is a new page on which to write our story.

Genesis 10:7-12 *The sons of Cush:* Seba, Havilah, Sabtah, Raamah and Sabteka. *The sons of Raamah: Sheba and Dedan. Cush was the father of Nimrod. . . . The first centers of his kingdom were Babylon, Uruk, Akkad and Kalneh, in Shinar. From that land he went to Assyria, where he built Nineveh, Rehoboth Ir, Calah and Resen.*

Here we learn that Nimrod was a builder of civilizations. Whether he was good or evil isn't clear, but if we enjoy the benefits of an advanced civilization, we ought to be thankful for those who've helped to build it. This will include leaders, teachers, parents, artists, and ordinary workers. Great societies happen because people give their best. Our duty to God (Genesis 1:28), and to others, is to make the world a better place than if we hadn't been here.

Genesis 11:1 *Now the whole world had one language and a common speech.*

For many years communication flowed freely as the world enjoyed a single language. This helped people cooperate, and make cultural progress. Instead of using their social cohesion to glorify God, however, they used it to rebel against him. Instead of pursuing God's glory, they pursued their own.

Genesis 11:4 *Come, let us build ourselves a city, with a tower that reaches to the heavens, so that we may make a name for ourselves.*

Simply put, they wanted to be famous. They wanted to build a city with a magnificent tower that would distinguish them, and win the approval of others. They wanted to be well-known, and very well-respected. And we're not completely different.

How many people have built homes they couldn't afford, to impress people they didn't like? And how many have bought cars for the same reason? Our purpose on earth is not to bring glory to ourselves, however, but to the One who made us. *Not to us, Lord, . . . but to your name be the glory* (Psalm 115:1), wrote the Psalmist. This is a great relief, and a wonderful blessing, once we understand it.

Genesis 11:6 *The Lord said, If as one people speaking the same language they have begun to do this, then nothing they plan to do will be impossible for them.*

Nothing is impossible for God, of course. But here God says that nothing is impossible for us, under the right circumstances. This is the clearest statement of human potential in the Bible, and was spoken by God himself. When people work together on a common goal there is little they can't achieve.

This is more obvious today than ever before. Technological developments have produced better machines, medicines, and hospitals then ever before. The rate of progress is only getting faster, so it's hard to know where we'll be a hundred years from now. But unified people often produce a world opposed to God. The people in this story had little concern for God, and wanted to build a city without him.

Genesis 11:7-6 *Come, let us go down and confuse their language so they will not understand each other. So the Lord scattered them from there over all the earth, and they stopped building the city.*

How strange it must've been to go to work that day, and find so many people speaking other languages. The bosses couldn't communicate with the foremen, the foremen couldn't communicate with the laborers, and no one knew what to do. The community broke apart, as people went their ways, with whoever spoke their language.

The world still remains divided by over six thousand different languages. But after Jesus rose form the dead, God did something different. People from different countries were gathered in Jerusalem when the Spirit enabled the disciples to speak in languages the people could understand. *[W]e hear them declaring the wonders of God in our own tongues* (Acts 2:11), the people said.

God confused the human language, due to our sin, but he let us hear the gospel due to his grace. We still have different languages, but all who believe are united by faith in Jesus Christ. This is a greater unity than sharing a common language, and is based on the knowledge of God. God is reversing the curse of of this event through the gospel of Jesus Christ.

Genesis 11:9 *That is why it was called Babel—because there the Lord confused the language of the whole world.*

Babel and *confused* are similar in Hebrew, so the writer made a play on words. *Babylon* became a city opposed God, and was later destroyed. It stands for all civilizations opposed to God, which will also be destroyed. *[A] mighty angel picked up a boulder the size of a large millstone and threw it into the sea, and said: With such violence the great city of Babylon will be thrown down, never to be found again* (Revelation 18:21), wrote John.

God is not against cities, or progress, but the purpose of both are to glorify him. Human centered cities will come and go, but the city of God will last forever. *For here we do not have an enduring city, but we are looking for the city that is to come* (Hebrews 13:14), says Hebrews. *[That] city does not need the sun or the moon to shine on it, for the glory of God gives it light, and the Lamb is its lamp* (Revelation 21:23), wrote John. There we'll live forever, and never be confused again.

For Reflection and Review

- *Why are genealogies helpful?*
- *Is it wrong to want the approval of others?*
- *What does God think about cities?*

Lesson 9

Genesis 12:1 *The Lord had said to Abram, Go from your country, your people and your father's household to the land I will show you.*

This begins the story of how God built the nation of Israel, beginning with Abram (later called Abraham). Here the story shifts from God's relationship with the world in general, to God's relationship with Abraham and his offspring—the Israelites. Abraham wasn't chosen by God because he was better than anyone else, but simply because God chose him (Romans 9:15). He became so important to the Bible's story, however, that his name is mentioned over two hundred times.

Abraham was living in a pagan culture when God broke into his life, and told him to move to a Promised Land. After that, for much of his life, Abraham lived in a tent (Hebrews 11:9). He's an example to those who refuse to settle down in this world as they journey to the next. *For he was looking forward to the city with foundations, whose architect and builder is God* (Hebrews 11:10), says Hebrews.

Genesis 12:2-3 *I will make you into a great nation, and I will bless you; I will make your name great, and you will be a blessing. I will bless those who bless you, and whoever curses you I will curse; and all peoples on earth will be blessed through you.*

God kept this promise to Abraham by making him into a great nation, and by making him famous. In the previous chapter the people wanted to *make a name* for themselves (Genesis 11:4). But as Abraham followed God, God made a name for Abraham.

God also promised Abraham . . . *all peoples on earth will be blessed through you.* This anticipates the gospel of Jesus Christ (Galatians 3:7-9) who, two thousand years later, was Abraham's descendent (Matthew 1:1). Because the gospel of Jesus Christ has spread throughout the world, the world has been blessed through Abraham. The God of Abraham keeps his promises, and we can trust him.

Genesis 12:10 *Now there was a famine in the land, and Abram went down to Egypt to live there for a while because the famine was severe.*

Abraham probably hoped for great things in the Promised Land but, instead, he met with famine. Like many since, Abraham found that God's ways don't always make sense to us. The way of faith can be difficult even when we're exactly where God wants us to be.

Due to the famine, Abraham went down to Egypt where the food supply was stable, because of the Nile River. But he feared Pharaoh might kill him to take his beautiful wife Sarai (later called Sarah). *Say you are my sister, so that I will be treated well for your sake and my life will be spared because of you* (Genesis 12:13), he said to her.

Abraham's wife was, in fact, his half sister (Genesis 20:12). But this was still a deception, and a terrible thing to ask. Pharaoh did, in fact, take Sarah to be his wife. And while the text is not explicit, he seems to have slept with her (Genesis 12:19). This would've strained Abraham and Sarah's relationship, and compromised their walk with God. It's interesting how early in the story they failed.

Like others who try to follow God, Abraham and Sarah weren't perfect. Their confidence in God wasn't always strong and, under pressure, they failed more than once. The story of God and his people is about sin and grace, failure and forgiveness. The only one who never sinned, in fact, was Jesus Christ (1 Peter 2:22). He lived our life, and died our death, so that we could be saved through faith in him (Ephesians 2:8-9).

Genesis 12:20 *Then Pharaoh gave orders about Abram to his men, and they sent him on his way, with his wife and everything he had.*

God sent diseases on Pharaoh and his household to show his disapproval. They came to understand that this was due to Sarah, so Pharaoh gave her back to Abraham and sent them on their way. Here we see that God took care of Abraham and Sarah, even when they were sinning. They left Pharaoh's palace with *sheep and cattle, male and female donkeys, male and female servants, and camels* (Genesis 12:16), far more than what they came with.

Sin normally has negative consequences including discipline (Hebrews 12:6). But on occasion, God may bring us good even when we sin. Then we should praise him for not giving us what we deserve, but for giving us what we don't deserve. The biblical word for this is *grace* (Ephesians 2:8). Justice is getting what we deserve; mercy is not getting what we deserve; grace is getting what we don't deserve—the undeserved favor of God.

*****

Genesis 13:5 *Now Lot, who was moving about with Abram, also had flocks and herds and tents.*

Lot was Abraham's nephew, and they both became so wealthy the land couldn't support their families together. Both groups began to quarrel, so Abraham made peace by offering Lot whatever region he preferred. *If you go to the left, I'll go to the right; if you go to the right, I'll go to the left* (Genesis 13:9), he said.

This was a generous offer and reflects well on Abraham's character. As the elder of the clan, Abraham had the right to choose, but gave the choice to Lot. This allowed Abraham to be blessed by God even more. *A generous person will prosper* (Proverbs 11:25), says Proverbs. God applauds generosity, and is often pleased to reward it.

Genesis 13:10 *Lot looked around and saw that the whole plain of the Jordan toward Zoar was well watered, like the garden of the Lord, like the land of Egypt.*

Lot may've asked his wife, or made the decision himself. But he chose the best of the land, and left the rest to Abraham. The land he chose was close to Sodom, however, a town known for its wickedness (Genesis 13:13). But the region's wealth was enough to offset any concerns Lot may've had. Abraham made Lot a generous offer, and Lot made the most of it.

Lot chose to live near Sodom, but there was something he didn't know: Sodom would soon be destroyed by the judgment of God (Genesis 19:1-29). Lot would escape with his two daughters, but everything else would be lost.

Genesis 13:14-15 *The Lord said to Abram after Lot had parted from him, Look around from where you are, to the north and south, to the east and west. All the land that you see I will give to you and your offspring forever.*

Lot thought he chose the best, but it soon became the worst. Abraham settled for what was left, but it soon became the best. This is a helpful principle when it comes to making choices. Instead of grasping for what we want, it's often wise to let others go first. God knows what's best for us, and he also knows the future (Isaiah 46:10). Letting others choose first is a way of being generous, and trusting God to give us what is best.

For Reflection and Review

- *How does living in a tent illustrate the Christian life?*
- *How has God blessed the world through Abraham?*
- *What can we learn from Lot's choice to live near Sodom?*

Lesson 10

Genesis 14:14 *When Abram heard that his relative had been taken captive, he called out the 318 trained men born in his household and went in pursuit.*

A coalition of kings conquered Sodom and Gomorrah, and a few other towns in the region. Many were taken captive including Abrahams' nephew, Lot. When Abraham learned of this, he marshaled his personal army and went to the rescue.

Abraham's army shows he was a man of power and wealth. But if the battle went badly, he might become a prisoner of war. It's easy to be courageous from a distance, but when trouble comes near we must look to God. The little phrase, *Do not be afraid* occurs over fifty times in the Bible, and is often spoken by God himself.

Genesis 14:16 *[Abraham] recovered all the goods and brought back his relative Lot and his possessions, together with the women and the other people.*

Abraham's nighttime attack was so effective that all the opposing armies fled. He rescued those who were taken captive, and recovered their possessions. Everyone must've rejoiced as they returned safe and sound. Abraham was now a hero.

On the way home, Abraham was met by the king of Jerusalem, with whom he ate and drank. Abraham gave him ten percent of the booty, and the king gave him a blessing: *Blessed be Abram by God Most High, Creator of heaven and earth* (Genesis 14:19), he said.

This is a little surprising since most people didn't believe in the one true God. But this man was a godly king as well a godly priest. His name was *Melchizedek*, and he's only mentioned one other time in the Old Testament. *You are a priest forever, in the order of Melchizedek* (Psalm 110:4), wrote David.

King David was not a priest, but he foresaw a king who would be a priest. This was fulfilled by Jesus Christ the *King of kings* (1 Timothy 6:15) and *great high priest* (Hebrews 4:14). *He has become a high priest forever, in the order of Melchizedek* (Hebrews 6:20), says Hebrews.

Abraham acknowledged Melchizedek's greatness by giving him a tenth of the plunder, and by receiving his blessing. Likewise, we give offerings to Jesus Christ (Philippians 4:18), and are also blessed by him (Romans 10:12). The Old Testament foreshadows Jesus Christ in many ways, and Melchizedek is a fine example.

*****

Genesis 15:1 *After this, the word of the Lord came to Abram in a vision: Do not be afraid, Abram. I am your shield, your very great reward.*

After defeating a coalition of kings, Abraham may've feared retaliation. God responded by saying, *I am your shield*. Abraham also returned the booty, instead of keeping it for himself. God responded by saying, *I am . . . your very great reward*. God shields those who trust him (Psalm 18:30), and rewards those who serve him.

God is our shield, and very great reward. But whoever has God, gets everything else thrown in. *He who did not spare his own Son, but gave him up for us all—how will he not also, along with him, graciously give us all things?* (Romans 8:32), wrote Paul.

Jesus is the best of all possible kings, and his kingdom is the best of all possible worlds (Revelation 21:21). God has given us his Son and, with him, will give us everything else. Nothing needed for our happiness will ever be lacking in the age to come.

Genesis 15:2 *But Abram said, Sovereign Lord, what can you give me since I remain childless and the one who will inherit my estate is Eliezer of Damascus?*

Abraham would have his eternal reward, but wanted something else. He didn't have any children, and wasn't getting any younger. Unless God answered his prayer for a child, all he owned would go to one of his servants. Abraham was troubled by this, so he brought it to God's attention.

Genesis 15:4 *Then the word of the Lord came to him: This man will not be your heir, but a son who is your own flesh and blood will be your heir.*

Then God told him to count the stars and said, *So shall your offspring be* (Genesis 15:5). *Abram believed the Lord, and he credited it to him as righteousness* (Genesis 15:6), wrote Moses.

This verse is quoted three times by the Apostle Paul to show that salvation is by faith, not by works (Romans 4:3, Romans 4:23, Galatians 3:6). *The words it was credited to him were written not for him alone, but also for us, to whom God will credit righteousness—for us who believe in him who raised Jesus our Lord from the dead* (Romans 4:23-24), he wrote.

God didn't count Abraham righteous because he was good, but because he believed God's promise. And God doesn't count us righteous because we are good, but because we believe his promise of eternal life through his Son Jesus Christ. *For we maintain that a person is justified by faith* (Romans 3:28), wrote Paul. Other religions teach we get right with God by being good. Christianity teaches we get right with God by believing in Jesus Christ. *[T]he one who believes has eternal life* (John 6:47), said Jesus.

Genesis 15:7 *He also said to him, I am the Lord, who brought you out of Ur of the Chaldeans to give you this land to take possession of it.*

In addition to offspring, God promised Abraham the land of Canaan, and confirmed it with an oath. He told him to bring some animals and cut them in half. That evening *a smoking firepot with a blazing torch appeared and passed between the pieces* (Genesis 15:17). This is strange to us but, in effect, God was saying, *May I become like these severed animals if I don't keep my word.*

When God makes a promise to his people, he wants us to believe it. Since Abraham didn't have a Bible or a church to encourage his faith, God confirmed his promise with a bloody oath. This showed that God would rather die than break his word to Abraham.

We find something similar to this in the Lord's Supper. *For whenever you eat this bread and drink this cup, you proclaim the Lord's death* (1 Corinthians 11:26), said Paul. God made a bloody covenant with Abraham, and *This cup is the new covenant in my blood* (Luke 22:20), said Jesus.

God would rather die than break his word to Abraham, and God was willing to die to keep his word to us (Jeremiah 31:33, Isaiah 53:5). If Abraham believed God on the basis of severed animals, how much more should we believe God on the basis of his crucified Son, whom he also raised from the dead (Matthew 28:6). *The Lord is trustworthy in all he promises and faithful in all he does* (Psalm 145:13), wrote David.

For Reflection and Review

- *How does Melchizedek remind us of Jesus Christ?*
- *How do we get right with God?*
- *Why can we be sure that God will keep his word?*

Lesson 11

Genesis 16:1 *Now Sarai, Abram's wife, had borne him no children.*

Ten years passed since God promised Abraham he'd become a great nation (Genesis 12:1-4), but he still didn't have any children. Abraham's wife grew impatient and suggested they have children through Hagar, Sarah's slave. Abraham agreed, and Hagar conceived. But as soon as she knew she was pregnant tension developed in the family. As the mother of Abraham's child, Hagar felt superior to Sarah, and began to disrespect her. This made Sarah so angry she mistreated Hagar until she ran away. What started as a perfect plan ended in domestic strife.

Sometimes God will let us choose between two kinds of suffering: not getting what we want, and getting what we don't want. The sorrow of not getting what they wanted convinced Abraham and Sarah to act apart from God's will. Due to their impatience, they got what they didn't want—family conflict. Not getting what we want is usually better than getting what we don't want, so it's generally best to wait for God. But God is seldom in a hurry, so this can be a test of faith.

Genesis 16:7 *The angel of the Lord found Hagar near a spring in the desert.*

Hagar ran away from home, but didn't have a good place to go, so she ended up near a spring in the desert—pregnant and alone. There she encountered *the angel of the Lord* who spoke to her: *Hagar, slave of Sarai, where have you come from, and where are you going?* (Genesis 16:8).

Hagar was partly to blame for her trouble since she had provoked Sarah. If she had been more humble and respectful, things would've been different. God could've left her to the consequences of her misbehavior, but he sought her out when she was at her lowest.

This reminds us of Jesus who *came to seek and to save the lost* (Luke 19:10). When we make a mess of things Jesus comes with love and compassion. We may've put him off in the past, but desperation will often make us more willing to obey.

Genesis 16:9 *Then the angel of the Lord told her, Go back to your mistress and submit to her.*

This may've been the last thing Hagar wanted to hear. Sarah had treated her badly, and submitting wouldn't be easy. But submission to God often involves submitting to difficult people.

Wives, submit yourselves to your own husbands (Ephesians 5:22), wrote Paul. *Submit yourselves for the Lord's sake to every human authority* (1 Peter 2:13), wrote Peter. *Slaves, in reverent fear of God submit yourselves to your masters* (1 Peter 2:18), wrote Peter again. *In the same way, you who are younger, submit yourselves to your elders* (1 Peter 5:5), wrote Peter yet again. By submitting to those who are over us we show our submission to Christ. This brings glory to God, and is often the way to future blessing.

Genesis 16:10 *I will increase your descendants so much that they will be too numerous to count.*

God told Hagar to do a difficult thing, and promised to reward her. Large families were greatly desired, and Hagar's descendants would be too many to count. When following God seems difficult we should remember his promise: *the Lord will reward each one for whatever good they do* (Ephesians 6:8), wrote Paul.

The angel of the Lord told Hagar to call her son *Ishmael* (Genesis 16:11), meaning *God hears*. But she also had a name for God: *You are the God who sees me* (Genesis 16:13). When no one else can hear us, God does. When no one else can see us, God does. Whenever we're hurting or in trouble, he's the God who sees and hears us.

*****

Genesis 17:1 *When Abram was ninety-nine years old, the Lord appeared to him and said, I am God Almighty; walk before me faithfully and be blameless.*

It had been nearly twenty-five years since God promised Abraham that he'd become a great nation (Genesis 12:2). But Sarah still hadn't conceived, so God appeared again to reinforce his promise: *No longer will you be called Abram; your name will be Abraham, for I have made you a father of many nations.* (Genesis 17:5), he said.

Abram means *exalted father* and Abraham means *father of many*. God changed Abram's name to Abraham because he'd become the *father of many nations*. This was difficult for Abraham to believe but, eventually, God's fulfilled his promise.

Biologically, Abraham became the father of the Israelites, the Edomites (Genesis 36:1-43), and the Ishmaelites (Genesis 25:12-18). To be the father of three nations is a remarkable legacy, but it seems to fall short of God's promise to make him the father of *many nations*.

In addition to the biological fulfillment of God's promise, however, there's also a spiritual fulfillment. *Understand, then, that those who have faith are children of Abraham* (Galatians 3:7), wrote Paul. Eventually, this will include people from every nation on earth.

[T]here before me was a great multitude that no one could count, from every nation, tribe, people and language, standing before the throne and before the Lamb (Revelation 7:9), wrote John. This far exceeds anything Abraham could've imagined. God's promises take time to be fulfilled, but their fulfillment will surpass every expectation.

Genesis 17:10 *This is my covenant with you and your descendants after you, the covenant you are to keep: Every male among you shall be circumcised.*

In response to God's promise, Abraham and all his male offspring were to be circumcised. This symbolized the Abrahamic covenant as a wedding ring symbolizes the covenant of marriage. *Any uncircumcised male, who has not been circumcised in the flesh, will be cut off from his people* (Genesis 17:14), said God. Circumcision was the sign of God's covenant for hundreds of years.

It's no surprise, therefore, that a controversy developed in the early church about whether Gentile Christians should be circumcised. *The Gentiles must be circumcised and required to keep the law of Moses* (Acts 15:5), some argued. So the apostles gathered to discuss this issue, and concluded it wasn't necessary. *We believe it is through the grace of our Lord Jesus that we are saved* (Acts 15:11), said Peter.

The Apostle Paul later explained that our sinful natures are circumcised by Christ, and the sign of the new covenant is baptism. *Your whole self ruled by the flesh was put off when you were circumcised by Christ, having been buried with him in baptism, in which you were also raised with him* (Colossians 2:11-12), he said. Circumcision has been replaced by baptism as the mark of the new covenant (Jeremiah 31:31-34).

For Reflection and Review

- *What are two kinds of suffering from which we can often choose?*
- *Why does God require submission to others?*
- *Why is circumcision no longer necessary?*

Lesson 12

Genesis 19:1 *The two angels arrived at Sodom in the evening, and Lot was sitting in the gateway of the city.*

This is the account of the destruction of Sodom and Gomorrah by the judgment of God. The towns were given over to the sin of homosexuality, so God rained down burning sulfur on them (Genesis 19:24). Before he poured out his wrath, however, God sent two angels in human form to rescue Lot, Abraham's nephew.

Lot was *a righteous man, who was distressed by the depraved conduct of the lawless* (2 Peter 2:7), wrote Peter. Lot was a child of God who was trying to live in a godless culture. He'd settled down in Sodom and compromised his values. Lot would still be saved, but his choice to live in a godless culture would cost him dearly.

Genesis 19:8 *Look, I have two daughters who have never slept with a man. Let me bring them out to you, and you can do what you like with them.*

The men of Sodom surrounded Lot's house and demanded he send out the angelic visitors to be sexually molested. Lot tried to dissuade them by offering his daughters instead. It's hard to imagine a father making this kind of compromise unless he was already compromised. Spiritual compromise is a slippery slope that leads to ever-increasing compromise.

Living in a wicked culture will condition us to wickedness until we think that wickedness is normal. Living together before marriage used to be called *living in sin*, but now it's normal. Saving one's virginity for marriage used to be praised, but now it's often ridiculed. Homosexuality used to be unmentionable, but now it's mainstream. We can't escape our culture, but should be aware of how it's shaping us.

Genesis 19:14 *So Lot went out and spoke to his sons-in-law, who were pledged to marry his daughters. He said, Hurry and get out of this place, because the Lord is about to destroy the city! But his sons-in-law thought he was joking.*

The angels warned Lot of the coming judgment, so Lot tried to warn his sons-in-law. They were unconvinced, however, because Lot's lifestyle didn't reflect his faith. The more we live like the world, the less compelling our witness will be. The more we compromise our faith, the less we'll be believed.

Genesis 19:15 *Hurry! Take your wife and your two daughters who are here, or you will be swept away when the city is punished.*

The angels warned Lot to flee with his family, or be destroyed with the city. *Come out from them and be separate, says the Lord. Touch no unclean thing, and I will receive you* (2 Corinthians 6:17), wrote Paul. There are some places Christians shouldn't be, and some people they shouldn't be with. This doesn't mean we should avoid the ungodly altogether, but that we should be careful about our associations (1 Corinthians 15:33).

Genesis 19:24-25 *Then the Lord rained down burning sulfur on Sodom and Gomorrah—from the Lord out of the heavens. Thus he overthrew those cities and the entire plain, destroying all those living in the cities.*

Sodom and Gomorrah were located near the south end of the Dead Sea. The burning sulfur may've come from an earthquake that ejected sulfur, gases, and asphalt still found in this region. If ignited by lighting, they could result in the catastrophic destruction this passage describes.

Genesis 19:26 *Lot's wife looked back, and she became a pillar of salt.*

This was a fatal mistake since the angel had warned them clearly: *Don't look back* (Genesis 19:17). But Lot's wife was leaving everything she owned, and nearly everyone she loved. She nearly escaped the doom of the city but, when she looked back, she became a pillar of salt. Lot's wife was almost saved.

Looking back often leads to going back, so if we look back on what we've left for Christ, we'll find an opportunity to return. *Let your eyes look straight ahead; fix your gaze directly before you* (Proverbs 4:25), says Proverbs. The doom of Lot's wife reveals the foolishness of looking back on the world we've left behind.

This idea is so important that Jesus applied it to his return. *On that day no one who is on the housetop, with possessions inside, should go down to get them. Likewise, no one in the field should go back for anything. Remember Lot's wife!* (Luke 17:31-32), he said. When Christ returns we shouldn't look back on what we're leaving behind, but fix our eyes firmly on him.

Jesus' brother, Jude, also referred to this episode. *Sodom and Gomorrah . . . . serve as an example of those who suffer the punishment of eternal fire* (Jude 1:7), he wrote. We shouldn't think of hell as anything less than the misery of being burned alive forever. This is a graphic illustration of the fate of all who prefer their sin over the Savior. Hell is not a mild discomfort, but a terrible agony that will never end.

The primary sin for which Sodom and Gomorrah were destroyed was flagrant homosexuality. This is clearly condemned by Scripture, along with other sins. *Neither the sexually immoral nor idolaters nor adulterers nor men who have sex with men nor thieves nor the greedy nor drunkards nor slanderers nor swindlers will inherit the kingdom of God* (1 Corinthians 6:9-10), wrote Paul. This doesn't mean we'll never stumble or fall, but that we should always get back up and continue to fight against sin.

A Christian man was dying of AIDS as a result of his homosexual sin. His pastor came to see him and referred to him as a homosexual. The man replied, *I am not a homosexual. I am a Christian who struggles with homosexuality. My faith in Christ is deeper than any other part of me.*

That was a good response. God is not against homosexuals, heterosexuals, transexuals, bisexuals, or any other kind of person. God is against sin, and he sent his Son to die on a cross so that *whoever believes in him shall not perish but have eternal life* (John 3:16).

God expects nothing more from homosexuals than from heterosexual singles, namely abstinence. *And God is faithful; he will not let you be tempted beyond what you can bear. But when you are tempted, he will also provide a way out so that you can endure it* (1 Corinthians 10:13), wrote Paul.

For Reflection and Review

- *How did living in Sodom affect Lot's morals?*
- *Why shouldn't Christians look back on what they've left for Christ?*
- *Is God against homosexuals?*

Lesson 13

Genesis 19:30 *Lot and his two daughters left Zoar and settled in the mountains. . . . He and his two daughters lived in a cave.*

At one time they were influential members of a wealthy town, but now they were living apart from civilization. Lot was getting older and, without children of their own, Lot's daughters would have no one to care for them in their old age. So they got their father drunk, slept with him, and bore his children. Sodom's culture had clearly shaped their ways.

One of the most important decisions parents make is how and where to raise their children. Those with every advantage often turn out badly, and those with none can turn out fine. On balance, however, those who are raised well do better than those who aren't. *Start children off on the way they should go, and even when they are old they will not turn from it* (Proverbs 22:6), says Proverbs. And *Bad company corrupts good character* (1 Corinthians 15:33), wrote Paul.

Besides their other mistakes, Lot and his wife raised their daughters in a wicked town. As a result of this, their family became an incestuous mess. Lot's last recorded act, in fact, was drunken sex with his daughters. This also led to future trouble since their offspring became the Moabites and the Ammonites, historic enemies of Israel. The way of sin is always downhill.

*****

Genesis 20:1 *Now Abraham moved on from there into the region of the Negev and lived between Kadesh and Shur. For a while he stayed in Gerar.*

When the king of Gerar wanted Sarah for his harem Abraham feared for his life and said again, *She is my sister* (Genesis 20:2). This is the same lie he told Pharaoh (Genesis 12:1-20), and may've told to others (Genesis 20:13). This was a serious character flaw which made Abraham a repeat offender.

After so many years of following God, we're surprised at Abraham's lack of moral progress. *I am God Almighty; walk before me faithfully and be blameless* (Genesis 17:1), said God. But Abraham was far from blameless. He believed in God (Genesis 15:6), but his life didn't always show it. He had good intentions, but could also be weak.

Other than Jesus Christ, the main characters of the Bible are seldom moral heroes. They have good points, and bad points, and need to be saved like us. God was patient with Abraham and, even though he failed, he was still called *God's friend* (James 2:23). God is also patient with us, and doesn't reject us when we fail.

Genesis 20:3 *God came to Abimelek in a dream one night and said to him, You are as good as dead because of the woman you have taken.*

If not for divine intervention, Abimelek might've made Sarah pregnant and jeopardized God's promise to Abraham: *I will bless her and will surely give you a son by her. I will bless her so that she will be the mother of nations* (Genesis 17:16), said God.

Abimelek told God he was innocent because he didn't know Sarah was married. *Then God said to him in the dream, Yes, I know you did this with a clear conscience, and so I have kept you from sinning against me. That is why I did not let you touch her* (Genesis 20:6), said God.

There may've been times Abimelek planned to sleep with Sarah, but suddenly lost desire. Or there may have been times he had desire, but lacked the opportunity. For however long Sarah was in his harem, God kept Abimelek from sinning against him.

If God did this for Abimelek, how often has he done it for us? There've been times we've had the opportunity to sin but lacked desire, or had the desire but lacked the opportunity. Left to ourselves there's little we wouldn't be guilty of. But God has restrained us and kept us from sinning as often as we would.

Genesis 20:14 *Then Abimelek brought sheep and cattle and male and female slaves and gave them to Abraham, and he returned Sarah his wife to him.*

Once again God treated Abraham better than he deserved. His lack of faith and obedience might've destroyed his future, as well as God's plan to bless the world through him (Genesis 12:3). Thankfully, God's plan to bless the world depends more on God than it does on us. *[I]f we are faithless, he remains faithful* (2 Timothy 2:13), wrote Paul.

Genesis 21:1 *Now the Lord was gracious to Sarah as he had said, and the Lord did for Sarah what he had promised.*

Twenty-five years after the original promise (Genesis 12:2-3), God gave Abraham and Sarah the child they were waiting for. The long wait wasn't easy, but it deepened their faith and heightened their joy.

This was the child through whom the world would be blessed (Genesis 12:3), because through him Messiah would come (Matthew 1:1-2). Abraham and Sarah waited many years for Isaac, and the world would have to wait two thousand more years for Jesus Christ. Isaac came *at the very time God had promised* (Genesis 21:2), and Jesus was born *when the set time had fully come* (Galatians 4:4), wrote Paul. God takes longer than we like, but he's always on time.

Genesis 21:3 *Abraham gave the name Isaac to the son Sarah bore him.*

God had said *you will call him Isaac* (Genesis 17:19), which means *he laughs*. About a year earlier Abraham and Sarah laughed in disbelief at the idea of having a child at such an old age (Genesis 17:17, Genesis 18:12). But when Isaac was born Sarah said, *God has brought me laughter, and everyone who hears about this will laugh with me* (Genesis 20:6).

Abraham and Sarah's laughter of disbelief became the joyful laughter of seeing God's promise fulfilled. Their faith was weak, at times, but God was true to his word, and gave them what he promised. Their laughter makes us think of the joy that will be ours when God fulfills his promises to us in the age to come. We'll laugh at our silly doubts, and be amazed at the greatness of God who does *immeasurably more than all we ask or imagine* (Ephesians 3:20), wrote Paul.

Genesis 21:8 *The child grew and was weaned, and on the day Isaac was weaned Abraham held a great feast.*

Weaning took place around age three and was considered a rite of passage since many children died before then. If children lived until they were weaned, they'd probably make it to adulthood.

Ishmael was Abraham's firstborn son, and heir to the family fortune. But, with all the attention going to Isaac, he may've felt his position slipping away. Instead of celebrating Isaac's weaning, therefore, he began to mock his little brother (Genesis 16:12). And this was noticed by Sarah.

Genesis 21:10 *Get rid of that slave woman and her son, for that woman's son will never share in the inheritance with my son Isaac.*

Abraham was greatly distressed by Sarah's demand, but God told him to listen to her *because it is through Isaac that your offspring will be reckoned* (Genesis 21:12), said God. Then he assured Abraham that Ishmael would also become a nation (Genesis 21:13). So early the next morning, Abraham sent Ishmael and his mother away.

God cares about family, and normally wants to keep it together (Malachi 2:14-16). If we have to choose between family and God, however, we must always choose God. *Anyone who loves their father or mother more than me is not worthy of me; anyone who loves their son or daughter more than me is not worthy of me* (Matthew 10:37), said Jesus. Our commitment to God, through his Son Jesus Christ, must always be our highest commitment.

For Reflection and Review

- *What was Abraham's weakness?*
- *Why did God make Abraham and Sarah wait so long for a child?*
- *Why should we be more committed to God than to our family?*

Lesson 14

Genesis 22:1-2 *Some time later God tested Abraham. . . . Take your son, your only son, whom you love—Isaac—and go to the region of Moriah. Sacrifice him there as a burnt offering on a mountain I will show you.*

Abraham must've wondered what kind of God would give him a child, and then demand the child be killed. The God of the Bible is not who we expect, and Abraham doesn't seem any better. Anyone who kills his son because he thinks God told him to is mentally unstable. This story is off to a terrible start.

Genesis 22:3 *Early the next morning Abraham got up and loaded his donkey. He took with him two of his servants and his son Isaac. When he had cut enough wood for the burnt offering, he set out for the place God had told him about.*

As Abraham cut the wood that morning he probably wondered, *What kind of God would ask me to do this? How can I explain this to my wife? What will people think of me? Should I trust God, or run away from him?*

The Bible hadn't been written yet, but Abraham personified an important truth. *Trust in the Lord with all your heart and lean not on your own understanding; in all your ways submit to him, and he will make your paths straight* (Proverbs 3:5-6), says Proverbs.

Genesis 22:4-5 *On the third day Abraham looked up and saw the place in the distance. He said to his servants, Stay here with the donkey while I and the boy go over there. We will worship and then we will come back to you.*

Over the course of their journey, Abraham worked through the question, *How could a good God tell me to kill my son?* He concluded that God would raise him from the dead. This is why he said, *We will worship and then we will come back to you* (Hebrews 11:19). Abraham was so convinced God was good that, if God told him to sacrifice his son, it would result in a resurrection.

Genesis 22:6 *Abraham took the wood for the burnt offering and placed it on his son Isaac, and he himself carried the fire and the knife.*

But Isaac grew suspicious. *The fire and wood are here . . . but where is the lamb for the burnt offering?* (Genesis 22:7), he asked. *God himself will provide the lamb* (Genesis 22:8), said Abraham. In fact, Abraham spoke better than he knew. God would provide the perfect lamb: *the Lamb of God, who takes away the sin of the world* (John 1:29).

We shouldn't miss the parallel between Isaac carrying the wood to his sacrifice and Jesus carrying the wood to his sacrifice. *These are a shadow of the things that were to come; the reality, however, is found in Christ* (Colossians 2:17), wrote Paul.

If you stand outside on a sunny afternoon, you'll cast a shadow that portrays your likeness. And if you read the Old Testament carefully, you'll find the shadow of Christ in many places. Abraham and Isaac had no idea of the greater significance their story would have. But here we see the shadow of Christ in Isaac and, to some degree, the heavenly Father in Abraham.

This is also a mark of inspiration. The Bible has many human authors, but only one divine author. It has many little stories, but only one big story that binds them all together. If the Bible was a puzzle, there'd be many pieces, but only one picture. And right in the center would be the crucifixion of the Son of God.

Genesis 22:9 *When they reached the place God had told him about, Abraham built an altar there and arranged the wood on it. He bound his son Isaac and laid him on the altar, on top of the wood.*

Isaac was at least an adolescent by this time, since he was able to carry the wood some distance (Genesis 22:6). We might expect a struggle as Abraham tied him up, since most people would fight for their lives. But Isaac trusted his father even in death. Jesus could've also fought for his life, but he also trusted his Father in death. *These are the very Scriptures that testify about me* (John 5:39), he said.

Genesis 22:10 *Then he reached out his hand and took the knife to slay his son.*

Abraham's son was laying on the altar, and the knife was now unsheathed. From Abraham's perspective, his son was good as dead. Nothing is harder than the death of a child, as many parents will testify. Obedience to God isn't always easy, but nothing less will do.

Genesis 22:11-12 *But the angel of the Lord called out to him from heaven, Abraham! Abraham! Here I am, he replied. Do not lay a hand on the boy, he said. Do not do anything to him. Now I know that you fear God, because you have not withheld from me your son, your only son.*

Because he was willing to sacrifice his son, Abraham's loyalty could never again be questioned. And because God was willing to sacrifice his Son, his loyalty can never be questioned either. Some things can only be proven through sacrifice.

Genesis 22:14 *Abraham called that place The Lord Will Provide. And to this day it is said, On the mountain of the Lord it will be provided.*

Abraham looked up and saw a ram in a bush which he sacrificed in place of Isaac. He called that place, *The Lord Will Provide,* and five hundred years later, when Moses wrote this story down, they were still saying: *On the mountain of the Lord it will be provided*—on that particular mountain—in the region of Moriah.

Moriah is only mentioned twice in the Bible. *Take your son . . . to the region of Moriah* (Genesis 22:2) and *the temple of the Lord in Jerusalem [was built] on Mount Moriah* (2 Chronicles 3:1).

It was just a hilltop when Abraham arrived but, centuries later, it's where the temple of God was built. It's where God provided a ram for Isaac, and where thousands of other sheep were sacrificed. Then came Jesus Christ, the *Lamb of God*, who also died in the region of Moriah. So *on the mountain of the Lord*, it really was provided.

The people in the story had no idea they were foreshadowing the crucifixion of Jesus Christ. God telling Abraham to sacrifice his son seemed morally repugnant at first. But when we see that God provided a substitute (first the ram, then his Son) we perceive the glory of God and his purpose for this story.

Notice again the many parallels between the shadow in Isaac, and the reality in Christ. Isaac was the dearly loved son of Abraham, and Jesus is the dearly loved Son of God. Isaac went to the region of Moriah, and Jesus went to the region of Moriah. Isaac went willingly for his father, and Jesus went willingly for his Father.

Isaac carried the wood for his sacrifice, and Jesus carried the wood for his sacrifice. Isaac trusted his father unto death, and Jesus trusted his Father unto death. Isaac rose from the dead figuratively, and Jesus rose from the dead literally. Isaac was the son promised to Abraham, and Jesus was the Son promised to world.

But there's also an important difference: Isaac didn't have to die because God provided a substitute; Jesus did have to die because he was the substitute. *[God] did not spare his own Son, but gave him up for us all* (Romans 8:32), wrote Paul. Jesus died for our sins so that we could live forever. He is our substitute.

For Reflection and Review

- *What's disturbing about this story?*
- *How is the Bible like a puzzle?*
- *How does Isaac remind us of Christ?*

Lesson 15

Genesis 24:1 *Abraham was now very old, and the Lord had blessed him in every way.*

But Isaac was still unmarried, so Abraham sent a trusted servant back to his clan to find a suitable wife. It was a journey of several hundred miles, that would take weeks to complete, with no guarantee of success. But the servant shared his master's faith, so he earnestly prayed for God's help.

Lord, God of my master Abraham, make me successful today, and show kindness to my master Abraham. See, I am standing beside this spring, and the daughters of the townspeople are coming out to draw water. May it be that when I say to a young woman, Please let down your jar that I may have a drink, and she says, Drink, and I'll water your camels too—let her be the one you have chosen for your servant Isaac (Genesis 24:12-14).

Choosing the right wife for someone else was an uncertain task, so the servant asked God to confirm the choice in an obvious way: have the girl offer to water his camels. Camels can drink about twenty-five gallons (and he had ten of them) so this would be a convincing sign. It would also show the woman was kind, and hardworking, which are excellent qualities for a spouse.

Genesis 24:16-19 *The woman was very beautiful, a virgin; no man had ever slept with her. She went down to the spring, filled her jar and came up again. The servant hurried to meet her and said, Please give me a little water from your jar. Drink, my lord, she said, and quickly lowered the jar to her hands and gave him a drink. After she had given him a drink, she said, I'll draw water for your camels too.*

This was precisely the sign he had requested. The servant was convinced she was the one for Isaac, so he gave her some jewelry and asked to meet her family. They were related to Abraham and, to some degree, shared his faith. The servant explained the reason for his visit, and asked for the young lady to return with him to marry Isaac.

Genesis 24:51 *Here is Rebekah; take her and go, and let her become the wife of your master's son, as the Lord has directed.*

The servant gave generous gifts to Rebekah and her family, and began the journey home the following day. Isaac was in the field when he saw the caravan approaching and his heart likely skipped a beat. Had they been successful? Did he have a wife? Would they be compatible? Yes, yes, and yes! *So she became his wife, and he loved her* (Genesis 25:67), wrote Moses.

When Rebekah went to the well that day, she had no idea she'd soon be married to a wealthy young man, and become a leading lady among God's people. This doesn't happen to everyone, but reminds us that God is in control. *And we know that in all things God works for the good of those who love him* (Romans 8:28), wrote Paul. We should even give thanks for unknown blessings already on the way.

Genesis 25:20 *Isaac was forty years old when he married Rebekah.*

They probably wanted to have children soon but, like Sarah, Rebekah was barren. Isaac prayed to God, but the answer didn't come for twenty years. Then at last, *The Lord answered his prayer, and his wife Rebekah became pregnant* (Genesis 20:21).

God enrolls us in the school of prayer by leaving some of our needs unmet. Apart from these, we wouldn't pray as often, and wouldn't know God as well. The needs in our lives are not an oversight, but the means of knowing God better. This is why Jesus taught us to *always pray and not give up* (Luke 18:1).

Genesis 25:22 *The babies jostled each other within her, and she said, Why is this happening to me?*

Rebekah was pregnant with two active boys. *Two nations are in your womb, and two peoples from within you will be separated; one people will be stronger than the other, and the older will serve the younger* (Genesis 25:23), said God.

The first to be born was red and hairy, so they named him *Esau*, which probably means *hairy*. The second was grasping his brother's heel when he came out, so they named him *Jacob*. Jacob literally means *he grasps the heel*, but figuratively means *he deceives*. And he would live up to his name.

They boys were as different as they could be. Esau loved the open country; Jacob preferred to stay at home. Esau thought little of God; Jacob took God seriously. Esau was favored by Isaac; Jacob was favored by Rebekah. From Esau came the Edomites, and from Jacob came the Israelites.

It's surprising how different brothers from the same parents can be—not only physically but emotionally, spiritually, psychologically, relationally, and other ways. The only thing some brothers have in common, it seems, is their sinful nature. This was true for Jacob and Esau, who were frequently at odds.

Genesis 25:29-30 *Once when Jacob was cooking some stew, Esau came in from the open country, famished. He said to Jacob, Quick, let me have some of that red stew! I'm famished!*

Jacob and Esau were now adults, but Jacob never got over the fact that he was born second. Esau had the birthright, which gave him privileges, like being head of the family, and a greater inheritance. He could also expect to receive God's promise to his grandfather Abraham . . . *all peoples on earth will be blessed through you* (Genesis 12:3). This bothered Jacob so much that, short of murder, he'd do whatever he could to get his brother's birthright. He probably nagged Esau for years but, at last, this would be his day. Esau was famished, and Jacob had stew.

Genesis 25:31-34 *First sell me your birthright. Look, I am about to die, Esau said. What good is the birthright to me? But Jacob said, Swear to me first. So he swore an oath to him, selling his birthright to Jacob. Then Jacob gave Esau some bread and some lentil stew. He ate and drank, and then got up and left. So Esau despised his birthright.*

Jacob wanted the birthright more than Esau, so Esau finally gave it up. It simply wasn't that important to him. He wasn't greedy, or ambitious. He didn't care about the inheritance, or being head of the family. But he didn't care about God's promise to Abraham either. He just wanted some food.

In some ways Esau was a better person than Jacob but, according to the Bible, he was *godless* (Hebrews 12:16). God's promise to Abraham mattered less to him than a bowl of stew. Esau could've put off his appetite, and held onto God's promise, but he chose to sell God's promise, and satisfy his appetite.

We too can live for here and now, and lose it all eventually. Or we can live for the age to come, and keep it all forever. *Anyone who loves their life will lose it, while anyone who hates their life in this world will keep it for eternal life* (John 12:25), said Jesus. Esau believed in God to some degree but, in practice, he was godless.

For Reflection and Review

- *How does God get us to pray?*
- *What kind of person was Jacob?*
- *What kind of person was Esau?*

Lesson 16

Genesis 27:1 *When Isaac was old and his eyes were so weak that he could no longer see, he called for Esau.*

Isaac was preparing to die, and wanted to give his fatherly blessing to his firstborn son Esau, rather than to Jacob. This was against God's will, since the Lord had told Rebekah, *the older will serve the younger* (Genesis 25:23). But Isaac favored Esau and sent him away to hunt for game, and then to prepare a meal for him. After dinner, he'd give his blessing to Esau.

The blessing was thought to carry real power, and was a continuation of the blessing God gave to Abraham (Genesis 12:2-3). Esau gave his birthright away but, if possible, he wanted to recover the loss. This was an important moment for him.

But Rebekah overheard the conversation and, since Jacob was her favorite, she took action. *Go out to the flock and bring me two choice young goats, so I can prepare some tasty food for your father, just the way he likes it. Then take it to your father to eat, so that he may give you his blessing before he dies* (Genesis 27:8-10).

The deception grew more complicated but, surprisingly, it worked. *May God give you heaven's dew and earth's richness—an abundance of grain and new wine. May nations serve you and peoples bow down to you. Be lord over your brothers, and may the sons of your mother bow down to you. May those who curse you be cursed and those who bless you be blessed* (Genesis 27:28-29), said Isaac.

Shortly after Jacob received his father's blessing, Esau returned and discovered what happened. He received a secondary blessing, but was furious that his deceptive brother took both his birthright and the primary blessing. He was so angry, in fact, that he planned to kill his brother after his father died. The threat was so real that Jacob had to run for his life, and stayed away for the next twenty years.

Jacob and Esau shared the serious flaw of wanting the blessing of God, without pursuing God himself. God is not a means to an end, but the end for which we are made. The greatest blessing we can receive is more of God in our lives. It's wrong to seek the blessing of God without pursuing God himself. But *he rewards those who earnestly seek him* (Hebrews 11:6), says Hebrews.

Genesis 27:46 *Then Rebekah said to Isaac, I'm disgusted with living because of these Hittite women. If Jacob takes a wife from among the women of this land, from Hittite women like these, my life will not be worth living.*

Esau's choice of wives was a source of grief to Rebekah, and she hoped Jacob would do better while he was away. Few things shape our lives more than whom we marry, but it also affects our larger family. It's often wise, therefore, to consult our parents before we make a final decision.

Isaac and Rebekah struggled with Esau's wives because they were from a different clan. Marriage within a clan was usually preferred due to social customs. We seem to prefer people who are like us, and find them easier to live with. Instead of bringing her joy, Esau's wives brought Rebekah sorrow.

We can think marriage as two overlapping circles. The overlapping part is what we share in common. It may include age, education, personalities, politics, religion, and background. The non-overlapping part is what we don't share in common. It may include all the above, and more. The overlapping part is what makes marriage easy; the non-overlapping part is what makes marriage interesting. Over a lifetime, easy usually matters more.

Genesis 28:10-11 *Jacob left Beersheba and set out for Harran. When he reached a certain place, he stopped for the night because the sun had set. Taking one of the stones there, he put it under his head and lay down to sleep.*

Jacob fled the comfort of home and slept on the ground, surrounded by who knew what. Away from the people he knew, some of whom he loved, he probably felt alone. What Jacob needed most, he thought, was a good night's sleep.

He had a dream in which he saw a stairway resting on the earth, with its top reaching to heaven, and the angels of God were ascending and descending on it. There above it stood the Lord, and he said: I am the Lord, the God of your father Abraham and the God of Isaac. I will give you and your descendants the land on which you are lying. Your descendants will be like the dust of the earth. . . . All peoples on earth will be blessed through you and your offspring (Genesis 28:12-14).

Jacob was at a low point when God appeared in a dream, and affirmed the promise he'd given to Abraham (Genesis 12:2-3), and to Isaac (Genesis 26:2-5), and now to Jacob. Jacob's life wasn't an example to anyone, but his faith in God was not misplaced. God was alive, and would do what he had promised.

The stairway to heaven which Jacob saw in his dream speaks of Jesus Christ. *[Y]ou will see heaven open, and the angels of God ascending and descending on the Son of Man* (John 1:51), said Jesus. Jesus Christ is the only way to God (John 14:6), and the angels go up and down to *serve those who will inherit salvation* (Hebrews 1:14), says Hebrews.

This is also helpful for understanding how Jesus read the Old Testament. *These are the very Scriptures that testify about me* (John 5:39), he said. When Jesus read about the stairway to heaven, he saw himself as the way to God. When he read about sacrificial lambs, he saw himself as *the Lamb of God, who takes away the sin of the world* (John 1:29). When he read about the high priest, he knew that he was the *faithful high priest in service to God* (Hebrews 2:17).

Other examples could be given, but these are enough to show that Jesus saw himself throughout the Old Testament, and we are not wrong to see him there as well. From beginning to end, the Bible points to Jesus Christ. He came to save us from our sins (Matthew 1:21), and restore us to a greater paradise than Adam lost (Genesis 3, Revelation 22).

Genesis 28:16 *When Jacob awoke from his sleep, he thought, Surely the Lord is in this place, and I was not aware of it.*

Jacob thought God was far away, but then he learned that God was near. God didn't seem near when Jacob had only a rock for a pillow, so when God appeared in his dream Jacob was surprised. We too can go through life unaware of God's presence, but if we *Come near to God . . . he will come near to [us]* (James 4:8), wrote James. Worshipping God will make us more aware of his presence, and leave us longing for more.

For Reflection and Review

- *What kind of family did Jacob grow up in?*
- *How does Jacob's dream remind us of Christ?*
- *Why was Jacob surprised that God was in that place?*

Lesson 17

Genesis 29:1 *Then Jacob continued on his journey and came to the land of the eastern peoples.*

That's where his uncle Laban lived, and where Jacob hoped to stay until it was safe to go home (Genesis 27:43-44). Jacob stopped at a well, and was delighted to meet Laban's daughter, Rachel. Uncle Laban was thrilled by Jacob's arrival and received him as part of the family. By God's kindness, Jacob found a home away from home.

Within a month Jacob fell in love with Rachel, and offered to serve Laban seven years if he could marry her. *So Jacob served seven years to get Rachel, but they seemed like only a few days to him because of his love for her* (Genesis 29:20). Seven years is a long time to be engaged but, compared to the treasure of his bride, they seemed like just a few days to Jacob.

This is one of the most romantic statements in the Bible, and reminds us that passionate love is a gift from God (James 1:17). It's wonderful to think that this kind of love is God's idea, and even reflects his love for us. *For this reason a man will leave his father and mother and be united to his wife, and the two will become one flesh. This is a profound mystery—but I am talking about Christ and the church* (Ephesians 5:31-32), wrote Paul. The most passionate love between husband and wife is only a faint reflection of how Christ feels about his church. Human passion fades over time, but we'll delight in the love of Christ forever.

Genesis 29:21 *Then Jacob said to Laban, Give me my wife. My time is completed, and I want to make love to her.*

Laban held a wedding feast and gave his daughter to Jacob. But when Jacob woke up in the morning, the woman lying next to him wasn't Rachel, but Rachel's older sister Leah! Jacob was upset about this, but Laban replied, *It is not our custom here to give the younger daughter in marriage before the older one. Finish this daughter's bridal week; then we will give you the younger one also, in return for another seven years of work* (Genesis 29:26-27).

Jacob deceived his brother Esau, and Laban deceived his nephew Jacob. *A man reaps what he sows* (Galatians 6:7), wrote Paul. The family had problems in the past, and would have problems in the future. But God had chosen them, and wouldn't abandon them. Through all their sin and misbehavior, God would remain faithful. This should comfort us whenever our families are having problems.

Genesis 30:1 *When Rachel saw that she was not bearing Jacob any children, she became jealous of her sister. So she said to Jacob, Give me children, or I'll die!*

Rachel's sister, Leah, had given birth to four sons (Genesis 29:31-35), but Rachel was still childless. In her frustration she turned to Jacob and said, *Give me children, or I'll die!* Not everyone wants to have children but, for some, the desire is nearly as strong as the will to live. God was gracious to Rachel and, soon, she gave birth to Joseph.

Likewise, whenever the gospel is preached, there's potential for new birth. *He chose to give us birth through the word of truth* (James 1:18), wrote James. The preacher who goes to God and says, *Give me children, or I'll die,* will likely receive what he asks for. Every preacher and every church should have the same desire as Rachel.

Genesis 30:25 *After Rachel gave birth to Joseph, Jacob said to Laban, Send me on my way so I can go back to my own homeland.*

After many years of serving Laban, Jacob wanted to go home. He had many children, by this time, and wanted to bring them up in the land that God had promised (Genesis 28:13). Laban didn't want to lose his family, however, so he persuaded Jacob to stay a little longer, in exchange for certain breeding rights. *[Jacob] grew exceedingly prosperous and came to own large flocks, and female and male servants, and camels and donkeys* (Genesis 29:43), wrote Moses.

But as Jacob's fortune increased, Laban's fortune decreased, and this caused tension in the family. It was time for Jacob to go but, instead of saying goodbye, he left without notice. When Laban found out, he was furious, and went with others in pursuit.

Then Laban said to Jacob, What have you done? You've deceived me, and you've carried off my daughters like captives in war. Why did you run off secretly and deceive me? Why didn't you tell me, so I could send you away with joy and singing to the music of timbrels and harps? You didn't even let me kiss my grandchildren and my daughters goodbye. You have done a foolish thing (Genesis 31:26-38), he said.

This was my situation [Jacob replied]: The heat consumed me in the daytime and the cold at night, and sleep fled from my eyes. It was like this for the twenty years I was in your household. I worked for you fourteen years for your two daughters and six years for your flocks, and you changed my wages ten times. If the God of my father, the God of Abraham and the Fear of Isaac, had not been with me, you would surely have sent me away empty-handed (Genesis 31:40-42).

The relationship was severely strained, but they did what they could to separate gracefully. Jacob killed some livestock and they ate a family meal. *Early the next morning Laban kissed his grandchildren and his daughters and blessed them. Then he left and returned home* (Genesis 31:55).

This story is filled with family conflict, and can teach us what not to do. Family's often turn on each other, and inflict emotional pain. This may cause us to separate, but the memories live on.

One lady cried at her father's funeral, and the pastor asked if they were close. *We didn't speak for the last seventeen years*, she replied, *and the last thing I said was, I hope you go to hell*. We should try to be friends with our families because they'll always be a part of us. *If it is possible, as far as it depends on you, live at peace with everyone* (Romans 12:18), wrote Paul.

For Reflection and Review

- *How does romantic love remind us of Christ and the church?*
- *Why are families often so difficult?*
- *Does Jesus make families better or worse?*

Lesson 18

Genesis 32:1-2 *Jacob also went on his way, and the angels of God met him. When Jacob saw them, he said, This is the camp of God! So he named that place Mahanaim.*

Jacob and his family needed protection on their way back to the Promised Land, so God dispatched a camp of angels to watch over them. Jacob's clan was sizable, with plenty of servants, and hundreds of animals, so they were quite a camp in themselves.

When Jacob saw the camp of angels, along with his own camp, he called the place *Mahanaim*, meaning *two camps*. It's a reminder that we're not alone in the world, but that God dispatches angels to watch over us. *Are not all angels ministering spirits sent to serve those who will inherit salvation?* (Hebrews 1:14), says Hebrews.

Genesis 32:3 *Jacob sent messengers ahead of him to his brother Esau in the land of Seir.*

Jacob and Esau hadn't seen each other in twenty years, and they didn't part on the best of terms. Jacob stole his brother's birthright and blessing, and Esau wanted to kill him (Genesis 27:41). So Jacob fled to Harran where he spent the next twenty years working, having a family, and growing rich.

But now he was returning to the Promised Land, and wanted to make peace with his brother, so he sent messengers ahead. When Esau learned his brother was returning, he went out to meet him—with four hundred men! This was not a good sign. When someone who wants you dead comes to meet you with four hundred men, they're not a welcoming committee.

When Jacob learned of this, he had *great fear and distress* (Genesis 32:7). Easu had nursed a grudge for the last twenty years, and this was his chance to get even. The text is not explicit, but he probably planned to kill Jacob, his family, and his servants too.

Then Jacob prayed, O God of my father Abraham, God of my father Isaac . . . I am unworthy of all the kindness and faithfulness you have shown your servant. I had only my staff when I crossed this Jordan, but now I have become two camps. Save me, I pray, from the hand of my brother Esau, for I am afraid he will come and attack me, and also the mothers with their children. But you have said, I will surely make you prosper and will make your descendants like the sand of the sea, which cannot be counted (Genesis 32:9-12).

After Jacob prayed, he sent his brother a series of gifts. He sent two hundred female goats, twenty male goats, two hundred ewes, twenty rams—over five hundred fifty animals in all. He sent them in herds, and spaced them out, so they kept coming one after another (Genesis 32:13-20).

The purpose of the gifts was to appease his brother's wrath. But we can also see that prayer and action are not mutually exclusive. Some people pray without acting; others act without praying. It's best to pray as though everything depends on God, and then to act as though everything depends on us. That's what Jacob did, and hoped for the best.

Genesis 32:24 *So Jacob was left alone, and a man wrestled with him till daybreak.*

Jacob put some space between him and his family, and spent the night alone. He likely wondered if this would be his last night on earth. Would Esau attack in the morning? Would he alone be killed, or would his family also be killed? And what about the servants?

As he thought about these things, Jacob was ambushed by a man who wanted to wrestle. The man didn't have a knife, and didn't want to kill Jacob. He only wanted to wrestle through the night. To make a long explanation short, Jacob's opponent was God (Genesis 32:30). And, as they wrestled, *[God] touched the socket of Jacob's hip so that his hip was wrenched* (Genesis 32:25). God gave Jacob a limp (Genesis 32:31) that may've lasted the rest of his life. But why would God do this?

Jacob was independent by nature because he was strong in himself. He was physically strong, mentally strong, and very strong willed. But suddenly Jacob realized how much he needed God, and God wanted him to remember that. So God gave him a limp. A severe mercy is something that hurts us badly but makes us more dependent on God, as we ought to be. Jacob's limp was his reminder that he needed God wherever he went.

God did something similar for the Apostle Paul. Paul was so gifted he might've become proud, so God gave him a *thorn in [his] flesh*—perhaps a painful eye disease (2 Corinthians 12:7, Galatians 4:15). Three times Paul prayed that God would take it away but God said, *My grace is sufficient for you, for my power is made perfect in weakness* (2 Corinthians 12:8-9).

Almost everyone has some kind of weakness: physical, emotional, mental, financial, relational, or something else. Perhaps you've prayed that God would take your weakness away. If he does you can praise him. But, if not, you should use your weakness to make you more dependent on God. We're always stronger when we lean on God than when we think we can do it alone.

Genesis 32:26 *Then the man said, Let me go, for it is daybreak. But Jacob replied, I will not let you go unless you bless me.*

By this time Jacob knew he was wrestling with God. Even though he was injured, he wouldn't give up until he received a blessing. This can be called *wrestling with God in prayer*. As Paul said to the Colossians, *Epaphras . . . . is always wrestling in prayer for you* (Colossians 4:12).

Like many dads, I used to wrestle with my son when he was just a little guy. I could've easily crushed him, since I was many times his weight. But I wanted to see what he could do, so I matched him strength for strength. I made him work hard until finally, almost miraculously, he'd flip me over and win. God is looking for people who will wrestle him in prayer. And, sometimes, he'll even let us win.

For Reflection and Review

- *Why does God use angels to help us if he could do it himself?*
- *What did Jacob do when he learned Esau was coming with four hundred men?*
- *Why did God make Jacob limp?*

Lesson 19

Genesis 32:28 *Your name will no longer be Jacob, but Israel, because you have struggled with God.*

Israel means *He struggles with God* and is meant in a positive way. God is not an easy person to follow, understand, or even like sometimes. The godless put him out of their minds, but the godly are willing to struggle with him.

In our best moments we love God deeply and, in our worst, we might even hate him. But at least we take God seriously. What God detests is to be taken lightly, as though he's not an important person. The problem isn't that people disbelieve in God, but that he's simply not important to them.

Jacob struggled with God, and God changed his name to Israel. God also changed Abram's name to Abraham (Genesis 17:5), and Sarai's name to Sarah (Genesis 17:15). God shows his authority over us by changing our names whenever he likes. Jesus showed his divine authority over Simon by changing his name to Peter. *You are Simon son of John. You will be called . . . Peter* (John 1:42), he said. Surprisingly, Peter went along with it.

Not everyone in the Bible got a new name, but we learn from the Bible that God knows our names (John 10:3). I went to a large high school and was surprised to discover the principle knew my name, though not for a good reason. But Jesus knows our names because he loves us and, in heaven, he'll give us a new name too. *I will also give that person a white stone with a new name written on it, known only to the one who receives it* (Revelation 2:17), he said.

Some people have pet names for each other that no one else knows. They're not meant to be public names, but private ones that create a bond of closeness. When my daughter was growing up I called her *Bunkerdoodles*. Imagine a God who is so affectionate toward you that he gives you a name known only to you and him.

Genesis 33:1 *Jacob looked up and there was Esau, coming with his four hundred men.*

It was clear to Jacob that he was not in control. He had prayed, of course, but there was Esau marching in his direction with a personal army. Jacob likely trembled since he didn't know if he'd live or die. *But Esau ran to meet Jacob and embraced him; he threw his arms around his neck and kissed him. And they wept* (Genesis 33:4).

Twenty years of estrangement dissolved in a puddle of tears. Jesus drew on this scene to describe what happens whenever a wayward child comes home to God. The father *ran to his son, threw his arms around him and kissed him* (Luke 15:20), wrote Luke. The reconciliation of Jacob and Esau faintly reflects what happens whenever God and sinners are reunited.

Genesis 33:19-20 *[Jacob bought] the plot of ground where he pitched his tent. There he set up an altar and called it El Elohe Israel.*

Esau went back to Seir (Genesis 33:16) and Jacob went to the Promised Land. To commemorate his safe arrival, Jacob built an altar. Altars were places of sacrifice where meals were eaten in fellowship with God. Jacob's altar points forward to the altar at the temple, where sacrificial lambs were offered. That altar points forward to the cross of Christ, where the lamb of God was offered (John 1:29, 19:18).

This is picked up in the book of Hebrews which says, *We have an altar . . .* (Hebrews 13:10). This may be an allusion to the table of the Lord's Supper, which is observed every week in churches around the world. It's not a sacrifice we make, however, but one that God has made for us, when his Son died on a cross for our sins (1 Peter 3:18). We have table fellowship with God as we feast on his Son through faith.

*****

Genesis 34:1 *Now Dinah, the daughter Leah had borne to Jacob, went out to visit the women of the land.*

Jacob and his family were now in the Promised Land. Other than Jacob, everyone was new to the region. With or without her parents' permission, Dinah set out to make some friends. She caught the attention of Shechem, the son of a local ruler.

Shechem was attracted to Dinah but, instead of making polite advances, he raped her. It's not clear if he suffered remorse but he loved Dinah, *spoke tenderly to her* (Genesis 34:3), and wanted to marry her. When Jacob learned his daughter had been raped, he wisely did nothing at first.

That evening, Shechem and his father came by and tried to make amends. *Let me find favor in your eyes, and I will give you whatever you ask. Make the price for the bride and the gift I am to bring as great as you like, and I'll pay whatever you ask me. Only give me the young woman as my wife* (Genesis 34:11-12), said Shechem.

But Jacob's sons wanted revenge. So they agreed to give their sister to Shechem, on the condition that every male in their clan be circumcised. *Three days later, while all of them were still in pain, two of Jacob's sons, Simeon and Levi, Dinah's brothers, took their swords and attacked the unsuspecting city, killing every male. They put Hamor and his son Shechem to the sword and took Dinah from Shechem's house and left.*

The sons of Jacob came upon the dead bodies and looted the city where their sister had been defiled. They seized their flocks and herds and donkeys and everything else of theirs in the city and out in the fields. They carried off all their wealth and all their women and children, taking as plunder everything in the houses (Genesis 34:25-29). When Jacob learned what his sons had done he was very upset. *But they replied, Should he have treated our sister like a prostitute?* (Genesis 34:31).

The revenge of Jacob's sons was worse than the crime by far. To murder innocent men, and carry off their families, was completely unjustified. It may've felt good to release their rage, but now they'd have to live with guilt for the rest of their lives.

Whenever someone we love is hurt, we naturally want revenge. The impulse isn't wrong because *the Lord is a God of justice* (Isaiah 30:18), wrote Isaiah. We don't have to take revenge ourselves, however, because God will do it for us.

The Lord is a jealous and avenging God; the Lord takes vengeance and is filled with wrath. The Lord takes vengeance on his foes and vents his wrath against his enemies (Nahum 1:2), wrote Nahum. *Do not take revenge, my dear friends, but leave room for God's wrath, for it is written: It is mine to avenge; I will repay* (Romans 12:19), wrote Paul.

Since God has promised revenge, we can leave it to him. Then we can obey Christ who said, *love your enemies and pray for those who persecute you* (Matthew 5:44). This is what Jesus did as he hung on the cross (Luke 23:34), and he's the model for us all. His words free us from hate, so we can live in love again.

For Reflection and Review

- *Is it good to struggle with God?*

- *How does Jacob's altar remind us of the Lord's Supper?*
- *How should Dinah's brothers have responded to her rape?*

Lesson 20

Genesis 37:2 *Joseph, a young man of seventeen, was tending the flocks with his brothers.*

The early chapters of Genesis record the creation of the world (Genesis 1-2), our fall into sin (Genesis 3), the story of the flood (Genesis 6-9), the tower of Babel (Genesis 11), and a few other stories about God and the world.

But the world didn't want God, so he turned to Abram saying, *I will make you into a great nation. . . . and all peoples on earth will be blessed through you* (Genesis 12:2-3). God changed Abram's name to Abraham (Genesis 17:5), and gave him a son named Isaac (Genesis 21:1-3), who had a son named Jacob (Genesis 25:26), whose name God changed to Israel (Genesis 32:28).

But if you're going to have a nation, you'll need some people, so Israel had twelve sons (Genesis 35:22-26), who had families of their own. They became the twelve tribes of the nation of Israel (Genesis 49:1-28), and this little nation became the primary setting for the rest of the Bible. Joseph is one of the sons of Israel, but his story is so important it takes up nearly a third of the book of Genesis (Genesis 37-50).

By way of introduction, two things should be noted. First, the story has a U shape. It starts well, turns bad, stays mostly bad, but ends well. This mirrors the life of Christ who came down from heaven, lived a difficult life, but triumphed over sin and death to reign in glory.

Second, it's a story of providence. Behind the scenes of Joseph's life we perceive the hand of God who, in all things, *works for the good of those who love him* (Romans 8:28). God is always at work in this story, even when he seems absent.

Genesis 37:4 *When his brothers saw that their father loved [Joseph] more than any of them, they hated him and could not speak a kind word to him.*

This is one of the first dysfunctional families in the Bible, but there are many more. Cain killed his brother Abel (Genesis 4:8), and Abraham shared his wife with Pharaoh (Genesis 12:19). David's son committed incest (2 Samuel 13:14), and Jesus' own brothers didn't believe in him (John 7:5). Wherever two or more sinners live under the same roof, there's often trouble.

Joseph was actually part of the problem. He had a dream in which the sun, the moon, and eleven stars were bowing down to him (Genesis 37:9). He shared the dream with his family but, if he'd been wiser, he would've kept it to himself. Joseph's family understood the dream to mean that, one day, they'd bow down to Joseph—and they were offended by this. But Joseph didn't know how difficult his life would become before his dream came true.

This is the Christian life in miniature. We know our story ends well, and that God is with us on every page. We're surprised when things go badly but, even then, we know our glorious future will soon be here. So we always have hope.

Genesis 37:19-20 *Here comes that dreamer! they said to each other. Come now, let's kill him and throw him into one of these cisterns and say that a ferocious animal devoured him. Then we will see what comes of his dreams.*

Joseph's brothers were away from home, grazing the family's sheep. Joseph was sent to check on them, and they saw him from a distance. He was wearing a special robe their father had given him, and they were so filled with jealousy they wanted to kill him (Genesis 37:20).

We don't always think of jealousy as a serious sin, but it can be. *Anger is cruel and fury overwhelming, but who can stand before jealousy?* (Proverbs 27:4), says Proverbs. Joseph's brothers were so jealous, in fact, that they decided to kill him (Genesis 37:19-20). But when they saw a band of merchants on their way to Egypt, they decided to sell him into slavery instead (Genesis 37:25-27). Then they dipped his robe in goats' blood, gave it to their father, and let him draw his own conclusion: *Some ferocious animal has devoured him* (Genesis 37:33), he said.

Genesis 37:34-35 *Then Jacob tore his clothes, put on sackcloth and mourned for his son many days. All his sons and daughters came to comfort him, but he refused to be comforted. No, he said, I will continue to mourn until I join my son in the grave. So his father wept for him.*

It must've been hard for the brothers to watch their father suffer for their sin. Children often suffer due to the sins of their parents (Jeremiah 32:18), but parents can also suffer due to the sins of their children. Joseph's brothers got what they wanted, but their father paid the price.

What nobody realized is that God would use their wicked deed to elevate Joseph. God's plan was for Joseph to rule over Egypt, and his brothers helped him get there. *If God is for us, who can be against us?* (Romans 8:31), wrote Paul. The devil is against us. Our family can be against us. The world can be against us. And life itself can seem against us. But if God is for us, there's no power in hell that can prevail against us. Believers always win in the end.

For Reflection and Review

- *How did the nation of Israel begin?*
- *Why is jealousy a serious sin?*
- *How do we know if God is for us?*

Lesson 21

Genesis 37:36 *Meanwhile, the Midianites sold Joseph in Egypt to Potiphar, one of Pharaoh's officials, the captain of the guard.*

Joseph could've been sold to someone obscure but, in the providence of God, he was sold to one of Pharaoh's officials so he could be groomed for higher service. If Joseph was going to be in charge of Egypt he'd have to learn how government works, how leadership behaves, and how to handle responsibility. Joseph learned quickly and handled himself so well, he was soon in charge of Potiphar's entire estate. With Joseph in charge, Potiphar didn't have to worry about a thing, except what to have for dinner (Genesis 39:6).

*****

Genesis 38:1 *At that time, Judah left his brothers and went down to stay with a man of Adullam named Hirah.*

We're not told why Judah left his brothers, at this time, but it may have been due to their sin. Their mutual secret would've weighed on their consciences and poison their relationships. We can't do evil to others without doing it to ourselves. Sin creates disharmony, and Judah wanted to get away.

Genesis 38:2 *Judah met the daughter of a Canaanite man.*

Together they had three sons, and the oldest married a woman named Tamar. He died young, however, so Tamar married Judah's second son. He also died young, so Judah offered Tamar his third son as soon as he grew up. But Judah didn't fulfill his pledge, out of fear that his third son would also die young.

This put Tamar in a difficult position. She was twice a widow, and without any children. Her prospects for marriage were poor, and she'd have no one to take care of her when she was old. In a culture that prized motherhood, her situation was bleak. So Tamar took action.

She veiled her face and went to a place known for prostitution. Judah came by, but he didn't recognize her, and bought her service in exchange for a goat. He didn't have a goat with him, however, so he gave Tamar his seal and staff as a pledge. Tamar became pregnant by her father-in-law on purpose, to secure his financial support.

Genesis 38:24 *About three months later Judah was told, Your daughter-in-law Tamar is guilty of prostitution,* *and as a result she is now pregnant. Judah said, Bring her out and have her burned to death!*

Judah's double standard is regrettable, but many condemn others for the sin they allow in themselves. Judah was ashamed when Tamar produced his seal and staff, proving that he was the one who made her pregnant. She later gave birth to twins, and all four are mentioned in Matthew's genealogy of Jesus Christ (Matthew 1:3).

Here we see the kind of people God sent his Son to save—*not because of righteous things we had done, but because of his mercy* (Titus 3:5), wrote Paul. God used the unseemly union of Judah and Tamar to bring his Son into the world. We should never *do evil that good may result* (Romans 3:8), but nothing is so evil that God can't use it for good (Romans 8:28), even our sin.

*****

Genesis 39:5 *[T]he Lord blessed the household of [Potiphar] because of Joseph.*

It wasn't because Potiphar prayed and obeyed that his household was being blessed, but *because of Joseph*. Joseph may've been the only person in Potiphar's household who believed in God, and it was because of Joseph that God was blessing Potiphar's household.

Likewise, God may bless our employers because of us. Christians ought to serve their employers wholeheartedly, and pray for God's blessing wherever they are. God may bless our places of employment simply because we are there.

Genesis 39:6-7 *Joseph was well-built and handsome, and after a while his master's wife took notice of Joseph and said, Come to bed with me!*

Day after day, Potiphar's wife pursued Joseph. And day after day, he declined her advances. Finally, she grabbed him by the cloak and said, *Come to bed with me*. But Joseph ran out of the house, leaving his cloak behind (Genesis 39:10-12). Potiphar's wife was so angry that she told her husband Joseph had made advances and, when she screamed, Joseph ran out of the house without his cloak. So Potiphar threw Joseph in prison (Genesis 39:11-20).

Life isn't always fair, even for believers. We hope to be rewarded for good behavior, not punished for it. But setbacks are often a setup for God to bring us good. We glorify God by trusting in him, even when things go badly.

Genesis 39:20-21 *But while Joseph was there in the prison, the Lord was with him.*

There he met a couple of Pharaoh's officials whose dreams he was able to interpret. Two years later, when Pharaoh had a dream, one of the officials mentioned Joseph. Pharaoh summoned Joseph to interpret his dream (Genesis 41:14) and, suddenly, Joseph was in the presence of Pharaoh. This wouldn't have happened if Joseph hadn't gone to prison. Sometimes we have to go down before we go up.

When I was in middle school the building had a new section and an old section. If you were on the second floor of the new section, and wanted to go to the third floor of the old section, first you had to go down, then over, then up. That's how it is with God. *Humble yourselves before the Lord, and he will lift you up* (James 4:10), wrote James.

Genesis 41:15 *Pharaoh said to Joseph, I had a dream, and no one can interpret it. But I have heard it said of you that when you hear a dream you can interpret it.*

Pharaoh thought the dream was important, and he was right. Seven skinny cows ate up seven fat cows, and seven skinny grains ate up seven fat grains (Genesis 41:17-24). The meaning was clear to Joseph: there'd be seven years of abundance followed by seven years of famine (Genesis 41:29-30).

Drawing on all he'd learned about Egypt, Joseph advised Pharaoh on how to prepare for the future. Pharaoh was so impressed that he put Joseph in charge of Egypt, second only to himself (Genesis 41:43). In a single day Joseph was taken from the prison to the palace.

It must've seemed like a dream to Joseph, but all who serve God faithfully will also be promoted. To one Jesus will say, *take charge of five cities* (Luke 19:19). And to another he will say, *take charge of ten cities* (Luke 19:17). We might be on the bottom now, but our promotion is coming soon.

For Reflection and Review

- *How did God use Judah and Tamar's sin?*
- *Why did God allow Joseph to be thrown into prison?*
- *What can we learn from Joseph's promotion?*

Lesson 22

Genesis 42:1 *When Jacob learned that there was grain in Egypt, he said to his sons, Why do you just keep looking at each other?*

There was no grain in Canaan, due to the famine, so Joseph sent his sons to Egypt to purchase some. It had been over twenty years since Joseph was sold into slavery, and his brothers considered him dead. So when they went to Egypt they didn't expect to run into Joseph. When they saw him, in fact, they didn't even recognize him.

But Joseph recognized them and, instead of revealing himself, he accused them of being spies, and threw them into prison. There they had time to think and began to reflect on their sin. *Surely we are being punished because of our brother. We saw how distressed he was when he pleaded with us for his life, but we would not listen; that is why this distress has come on us* (Genesis 42:21), they said.

Joseph's brothers saw the desperate look in his eyes, when he pleaded for his life, and they never forgot it. Many nights, perhaps, they woke up in a cold sweat regretting what they had done. Now, at last, they were getting what they deserved. Joseph gave them time to think so they might be properly reconciled.

Genesis 45:4 *Then Joseph said to his brothers . . . I am your brother Joseph, the one you sold into Egypt!*

The brothers were overwhelmed. The dream Joseph had as boy of seventeen was coming true before their eyes. Joseph could've left them in prison but, instead, *he kissed all his brothers and wept over them* (Genesis 45:15). Now they were a family again.

This pleased Pharaoh who promised Joseph's brothers the best land in Egypt (Genesis 45:18). He gave them carts to bring their families down, along with their father Jacob. He gave them *ten donkeys loaded with the best things of Egypt, and ten female donkeys loaded with grain and bread and other provisions for [their] journey* (Genesis 45:23). It seemed like a dream to them. Instead of being punished for their sin, they were being blessed!

Genesis 45:13 *Tell my father about all the honor accorded me in Egypt.*

Joseph had all the honor of Egypt, and all the wealth of the world, but he also wanted his father's approval. He'd done well for himself, and wanted his dad to be proud of him. His father would soon rejoice that Joseph was alive, and Joseph would receive the approval that he longed for.

But many who crave their father's approval never, in fact, receive it. I've sat with men in their sixties who were still deeply pained because of their Father's disapproval. *You'll never amount to a bottle of piss*, one recalled his father saying.

But Christ has promised his approval to all who truly believe in him. *Well done, good and faithful servant* (Matthew 25:21), he will say. We've sinned more times than we can count, but they won't be held against us. Christ *forgave us all our sins* (Colossians 2:13) and will *reward each one for whatever good they do* (Ephesians 6:8), wrote Paul. If Christ forgives all our sins, and remembers all our good deeds, then we'll hear him say, *Well done, good and faithful servant!*

Genesis 48:1 *Some time later Joseph was told, Your father is ill.*

After many years in Egypt, Joseph's father was dying. But, just before he passed, he gave a prophecy that Messiah would come from Judah. *The scepter will not depart from Judah, nor the ruler's staff from between his feet, until he to whom it belongs shall come and the obedience of the nations shall be his* (Genesis 49:10). And Jesus' genealogy shows that he was descended from Judah (Matthew 1:2, 16), not from Joseph.

But Joseph foreshadows Jesus in a number of ways. By looking at Joseph carefully, we can see the reflection of Christ. Joseph was the special son of Jacob, and Jesus is the special Son of God. Joseph was rejected by his brothers, and Jesus was rejected by his brothers (John 7:5). Joseph was about thirty years old when he began his public ministry (Genesis 41:46), and Jesus was about thirty years old when he began his public ministry (Luke 3:23).

Joseph ruled Egypt under Pharaoh, and Jesus rules the world under his Father. Joseph fed the people with grain, and Jesus fed the people with bread (John 6:10-11). Joseph's brothers were saved by coming to him, and we are saved by coming to Christ. These surprising parallels are like fingerprints that reveal the Bible's author.

Genesis 50:15 *When Joseph's brothers saw that their father was dead, they said, What if Joseph holds a grudge against us and pays us back for all the wrongs we did to him?*

So they came to Joseph and said, *we are your slaves* (Genesis 50:18). Joseph had power over his brothers, and could've caused them harm. His many years of suffering might have made him bitter but, due to his theology, they didn't. *You intended to harm me, but God intended it for good* (Genesis 50:20), he said.

This is the climactic verse of the story and makes an important point: God turns evil into good. It didn't seem good to Joseph when he was sold into slavery, or when he was rotting away in prison. But looking back it was clear: if he hadn't been sold into slavery he couldn't have saved Egypt, or his family, or been promoted to such a high position.

Paul likely had this in mind when he wrote . . . *we know that in all things God works for the good of those who love him* (Romans 8:28). It won't appear that way when your house burns down, you get laid off from your job, and they repossess your car. But if you love Jesus Christ, nothing bad can happen to you that God hasn't planned for your good. This is a wonderful comfort through all our ups and downs.

For Reflection and Review

- *Why were Joseph's brothers troubled by their sin?*
- *Why did Joseph want his father's approval?*
- *How did God use the sin of Joseph's brothers?*

Lesson 23

Exodus 1:1-4 *These are the names of the sons of Israel who went to Egypt with Jacob, each with his family: Reuben, Simeon, Levi and Judah; Issachar, Zebulun and Benjamin; Dan and Naphtali; Gad and Asher.*

The book of Exodus was written by Moses for the people of God around 1445 BC. It tells how God delivered his people from Egyptian slavery and made a covenant with them, including laws to govern them.

Exodus 1:7 *[T]he Israelites were exceedingly fruitful; they multiplied greatly, increased in numbers and became so numerous that the land was filled with them.*

When Jacob and his family moved to Egypt there were only about seventy of them (Exodus 1:5). But over the next four hundred thirty years, they grew to more than two million people (Exodus 12:37). Pharaoh was threatened by their numbers, so he turned the Israelites into slaves. Exodus tells the story of their exit from Egypt, and the beginning of their journey to the Promised Land.

Exodus 1:15-16 *The king of Egypt said to the Hebrew midwives, whose names were Shiphrah and Puah, When you are helping the Hebrew women during childbirth on the delivery stool, if you see that the baby is a boy, kill him; but if it is a girl, let her live.*

To reduce the threat of too many Israelites, Pharaoh commanded the Hebrew midwives to kill the boys at birth, so they wouldn't grow up to become an opposing army. Disobeying Pharaoh's command could be fatal, but the midwives *feared God and did not do what the king of Egypt had told them to do* (Exodus 1:17).

Shiphrah and Puah are an example of what Jesus taught many years later. *I tell you, my friends, do not be afraid of those who kill the body and after that can do no more. . . . Fear him who, after your body has been killed, has authority to throw you into hell* (Luke 12:4-5). Disobeying Pharaoh could be deadly, but disobeying God could be even worse. The fear of God delivers us from the fear of anyone else, even the most powerful person on earth.

Notice the midwives are mentioned by name, but Pharaoh is not. Most people would've known Pharaoh's name, but not the midwives' names. Now we know the midwives' names (Shiprah and Puah) but not Pharaoh's name. The wicked will soon be forgotten, but the righteous will be known forever.

Exodus 2:1-2 *Now a man of the tribe of Levi married a Levite woman, and she became pregnant and gave birth to a son.*

This is the beginning of the story of Moses. The midwives refused to kill the boys at birth, but Pharaoh's decree was still in place, and every Israelite boy was at risk. Moses' parents may've prayed for a girl, and been disappointed when they had a boy. They couldn't bring themselves to part with their child at once, however, so they hid him for three months (Exodus 2:2). When he could no longer be concealed, they put him in a box, and placed it in the Nile River. When Pharaoh's daughter came to bathe, she saw the box, and the baby inside. Her maternal instincts were instantly aroused.

Moses' older sister was watching, and said to Pharaoh's daughter, *Shall I go and get one of the Hebrew women to nurse the baby for you?* (Exodus 2:7). Pharaoh's daughter agreed, and actually paid Moses' mother to nurse him. This probably continued for at least a few years until Moses' mother brought him to Pharaoh's daughter, and Moses *became her son* (Exodus 2:10).

Moses was chosen by God, and God was overseeing everything to be sure it went according to plan. The same is true for all who believe in Christ. *In him we were also chosen, having been predestined according to the plan of him who works out everything in conformity with the purpose of his will* (Ephesians 1:11), wrote Paul. Our lives don't always make sense at the time, but one day we'll see that everything went according to God's plan —for our good, and for his glory.

Growing up an Egyptian prince, Moses enjoyed every advantage, including the best education (Acts 7:22). His leadership training equipped him to lead the nation of Israel. His academic training equipped him to write Scripture. And his military training equipped him to fight the Lord's battles (Numbers 21). Moses didn't know it at the time, but God was preparing him for future service.

Then one day, Moses had an awakening. *He regarded disgrace for the sake of Christ as of greater value than the treasures of Egypt* (Hebrews 11:26), says Hebrews. Moses could've enjoyed a wonderful life, if he'd simply been content, but all the treasures of Egypt weren't enough for him. They appeared to be everything a man could want, but they couldn't satisfy his deepest need. God alone could meet that need, and all the treasures of Egypt were nothing in comparison. So Moses gave up Egypt in order to have God.

In the same way, those of you who do not give up everything you have cannot be my disciples (Luke 14:33), said Jesus. This may seem like a steep price, but what is the world, and everything in it, compared to Jesus

Christ? He is the one for whom we were made, and with whom comes everything else. Moses saw the best of Egypt was only temporary, so he threw it away *because he was looking ahead to his reward* (Hebrews 11:26), says Hebrews. The best of everything can't make us happy if it only lasts for a while.

For Reflection and Review

- *Does God want people to be afraid of him?*
- *How did God prepare Moses for his future work?*
- *Why did Moses choose God over Egypt?*

Lesson 24

Exodus 2:11 *One day, after Moses had grown up, he went out to where his own people were and watched them at their hard labor.*

There he saw an Egyptian beating an Israelite and, since no one was around, Moses killed the Egyptian. *Moses thought that his own people would realize that God was using him to rescue them, but they did not* (Acts 7:25), said Stephen.

Moses assumed the Israelites would rally around him, and that he'd lead an insurrection. When things didn't go according to plan, Moses had to run for his life to the land of Midian (Exodus 2:15). He was forty years old (Acts 7:23) and, for the next forty years (Acts 7:30), he'd shepherd another man's sheep in the middle of nowhere.

Moses' life didn't turn out the way he thought it would. He thought he was destined for greatness but, when he took action, things went badly. He spent most of his life as an Egyptian prince, but now he was a lowly shepherd. For the next forty years Moses had time to think. *Should he have believed in God? Should he have killed the Egyptian? Did God still have a plan for his life?* Moses had been so sure of himself, but now he was confused.

What Moses didn't realize is that God was still preparing him. Moses believed in God, but he also believed in Moses. He had to learn that God could work with or without him. God might be happy to use Moses, but God didn't need Moses. Just because you're great doesn't mean you'll be greatly used by God. Moses had to learn the lesson of humility so he might be used by God in the future.

With time, in fact, Moses became a *humble man, more humble than anyone else on the face of the earth* (Numbers 12:3). His youth slipped away along with his self-confidence. He used to be *powerful in speech and action* (Acts 7:22), but now he was *slow of speech and tongue* (Exodus 4:10), it says.

Time is a teacher of humility, and happy are those who learn it soon. *God opposes the proud but shows favor to the humble. Humble yourselves, therefore, under God's mighty hand, that he may lift you up in due time* (1 Peter 5:5-6), wrote Peter. The choice belongs to us: we can humble ourselves, or we can be humbled by God.

Exodus 3:1 *Now Moses was tending the flock of Jethro his father-in-law, the priest of Midian, and he led the flock to the far side of the wilderness and came to Horeb, the mountain of God.*

Horeb means *desert* or *desolation* and may describe Moses' mood as well as the landscape. The first part of his life was filled with promise and potential, but throughout the second part of his life he was painfully underemployed. And since shepherds were detestable to the Egyptians (Genesis 46:34), Moses was doing a job he was conditioned to despise.

If a man succeeds early in life, but not later on, he may carry a sense of shame. Moses had been on top of the world, but was now in a place called *desolate*. There he'd learn that God meets people in desolate places. Whenever our lives become worse than we expect, that's where God is likely to meet us. He is the God of the desert.

Exodus 3:4 *God called to him from within the bush, Moses! Moses! And Moses said, Here I am.*

Moses saw a bush on fire that wouldn't burn up and, when he got closer, he saw that God was in the bush. This seems rather unlikely but the God of heaven and earth is free to reveal himself any way he pleases. God in a bush reminds us that God is humble. What, after all, is more humble than a bush?

We may not always think of God as humble but we should. If I became a worm to save the worms, that would be an act of humility. But I'm much closer to being a worm than God was to being a man. The difference between people and worms is finite, but the difference between God and people is infinite. For God to become one of us required extreme humility.

And being found in appearance as a man, he humbled himself by becoming obedient to death—even death on a cross (Philippians 2:8), wrote Paul. God's humility didn't end with his incarnation but included his crucifixion, death, and burial. The maker of heaven and earth did all this for our salvation. When we understand God's humility, we won't be afraid to humble ourselves in order to know him better.

Exodus 3:5 *Take off your sandals, for the place where you are standing is holy ground.*

This was the same ground where Moses had to watch his step, because his sheep had done their business. The presence of God, however, made it holy. Common ground becomes holy ground whenever God is uniquely present.

This also applies to churches: *For where two or three gather in my name, there am I with them* (Matthew 18:20), said Jesus. If Christians worship in a barn, the place becomes sacred because of the presence of Jesus. But then it becomes a barn again. If Christians worship in a cathedral, it too becomes sacred because of the presence of Jesus. But then it's just a fancy building.

By telling Moses to take off his shoes, God was teaching him to worship with respect. God is not a mild-mannered deity whom we can approach casually. He holds the power of life and death, and must be approached with reverence. This is more important than many people think. The church in Corinth displeased the Lord through careless worship, and some of them died as a result (1 Corinthians 11:31). So let us *worship God acceptably with reverence and awe* (Hebrews 12:28-29), says Hebrews.

Exodus 3:6 *I am the God of your father, the God of Abraham, the God of Isaac and the God of Jacob.*

Abraham, Isaac, and Jacob were the ones to whom God had pledged the Promised Land (Deuteronomy 30:20), where Moses would lead the Israelites. Abraham's son was Isaac, Isaac's son was Jacob, and Jacob's sons became the twelve tribes of Israel.

Abraham, Isaac, and Jacob believed in God, but weren't always perfect. When Pharaoh wanted Abraham's wife, Abraham didn't resist (Genesis 12:10-20). Isaac did something similar with his wife (Genesis 26:7-9). And, while Jacob never gave up his wives, he was often deceitful (Genesis 27:36). Nevertheless, God identified himself as the God of Abraham, Isaac, and Jacob. He's the God of imperfect people who truly believe. It's not perfection that God requires, but genuine faith (Galatians 3:7). This should be a comfort to imperfect believers everywhere.

For Reflection and Review

- *How did God humble Moses?*
- *How do we know that God is humble?*
- *What kind of people were Abraham, Isaac, and Jacob?*

Lesson 25

Exodus 3:10 *I am sending you to Pharaoh to bring my people the Israelites out of Egypt.*

Forty years earlier Moses felt up to the task, but not anymore. Egypt was the last place he wanted to be, and Pharaoh was the last person he wanted to see. But then God said, *I will be with you* (Exodus 3:12), and that was helpful. What Moses couldn't do alone, God was going to do through him.

This is the same promise Jesus gave the church: *Therefore go and make disciples of all nations, baptizing them in the name of the Father and of the Son and of the Holy Spirit, and teaching them to obey everything I have commanded you. And surely I am with you always, to the very end of the age* (Matthew 28:18-20), he said. Moses was called to confront Pharaoh, and the church is called to evangelize the world. Both tasks seem impossible, but nothing is impossible with God (Luke 18:27).

Exodus 3:13-14 *Moses said to God, Suppose I go to the Israelites and say to them, The God of your fathers has sent me to you, and they ask me, What is his name? Then what shall I tell them? God said to Moses, I am who I am. This is what you are to say to the Israelites: I am has sent me to you.*

This name reveals two important things about God. First, he's self-existent. Everything depends on God for existence, but God alone is self-existent. He made the trees, the rocks, and the stars, but no one made him. Everything else began to exist, but God has always existed because he's self-existent.

Second, God is who he is. We can take him or leave him, but we can't change him. There's not a sinner on earth, in fact, who wouldn't change God if they could. We like his promises, but not his threats. We like his love, but not his wrath. We like his forgiveness, but not his commands. We like his blessings, but not his curses. We like his heaven, but not his hell.

Instead of worshipping the God who exists, therefore, many worship the god of their imagination, which is merely an idol. Idols can't save us, and neither can the god of our imagination. If we want God to accept us as we are, we must return the favor. He is who he is.

And God has revealed himself in the person of Jesus Christ. *Very truly I tell you, Jesus answered, before Abraham was born, I am!* (John 8:58). Since Abraham lived two thousand years before Christ, Jesus' listeners correctly understood him to be claiming the sacred name for himself—so they *picked up stones to stone him* (John 8:59). And when they finally did kill him, Jesus rose from the dead because he has existence in himself (John 10:17-18). Jesus Christ is who he is.

Exodus 4:13 *But Moses said, Pardon your servant, Lord. Please send someone else.*

It may surprise us that a man like Moses would try to get out of doing God's will, but he had a few reasons: First, he felt unequal to the task (Exodus 3:11). Second, the people might not believe him (Exodus 4:1). And, third, he didn't speak very well (Exodus 4:10). So he just asked God to send someone else.

Whoever tries to follow God will be reluctant at times, because God often asks us to do what we don't want to do. If we always do what we've always done, we'll never become all we can be for God. We may try to decline the Almighty, but that's not in our best interest.

God rejected Moses' request, but he sent his brother Aaron to help him (Exodus 4:14). For the rest of their lives, these two men fulfilled God's will by working together. Whenever the task seems overwhelming, it may please God to give us a partner.

Exodus 5:1 *Afterward Moses and Aaron went to Pharaoh and said, This is what the Lord, the God of Israel, says: Let my people go.*

But weakness of will didn't bring Pharaoh to the top and, since he didn't want to lose his labor supply, he replied defiantly. *Who is the Lord, that I should obey him and let Israel go? I do not know the Lord and I will not let Israel go* (Exodus 5:2), he said. This is the beginning of a mighty conflict between an earthly king and the heavenly king. Since Pharaoh didn't know the Lord, God introduced himself with a series of plagues (Exodus 7-12).

The first was a plague of blood in the Nile River that killed the fish. The second was a plague of frogs that got into homes and beds. The third was a plague of gnats that infested people and animals. The fourth was a plague of flies that destroyed the land. The fifth was a plague of death on the Egyptians' livestock. The sixth was a plague of boils on men and animals. The seventh was a plague of hail that stripped every tree and ruined the crops. The eighth was a plague of locusts that devoured everything green. The ninth was a plague of darkness that lasted three days. The tenth, and final plague, was the death of firstborn males.

Pharaoh should've softened his heart but, instead, he chose to harden his heart (Exodus 8:15, 8:32, etc.). In response, God hardened Pharaoh's heart even more (Exodus 9:12, 10:20, etc.). This has been called *judicial hardening* and is a fitting response to rebellion. We naturally love either God or self, and harden our hearts against the other. *So, as the Holy Spirit says: Today, if you hear his voice, do not harden your hearts* (Hebrews 3:7-8), says Hebrews.

For Reflection and Review

- *How does the promise of God's presence help us do his will?*
- *What does God's name reveal about him?*
- *Why did Pharaoh harden his heart?*

Lesson 26

Exodus 12:13 *The blood will be a sign for you on the houses where you are, and when I see the blood, I will pass over you.*

The tenth and final plague was the one that broke Pharaoh's will, and allowed God's people to depart from Egypt. Every Israelite family was to slaughter a lamb and apply the blood to the doorframe of their home (Exodus 12:7). When God came to kill every firstborn male, he'd see the blood and pass over them. This became known as *Passover*.

Exodus 12:29-30 *At midnight the Lord struck down all the firstborn in Egypt, from the firstborn of Pharaoh, who sat on the throne, to the firstborn of the prisoner, who was in the dungeon, and the firstborn of all the livestock as well. Pharaoh and all his officials and all the Egyptians got up during the night, and there was loud wailing in Egypt, for there was not a house without someone dead.*

Pharaoh's will was finally broken, and Israel was free to go. Passover has been a Jewish holiday ever since, but this is also important for Christians. *For Christ, our Passover lamb, has been sacrificed* (1 Corinthians 5:7), wrote Paul. Jesus was crucified during the Passover holiday (John 18:39) to fulfill the imagery of the Passover lamb. He does so in other ways as well.

The Passover lamb was to be without defect (Exodus 12:5), and Jesus was without moral defect. The Passover lamb was to be a young male (Exodus 12:5), and Jesus was a young male. Not a bone of the Passover lamb was to be broken (Exodus 12:46), and when the soldiers came to break Jesus' legs, they saw he was already dead, so none of his bones were broken (John 19:32-33).

The blood of the Passover lamb had to be applied to the door frames of their homes (Exodus 12:33) or it wouldn't save them, and the death of Christ must be personally believed in or it will not save us. In this, and many other ways, the Old Testament looks ahead to Jesus Christ who came to fulfill it (Luke 24:44).

Exodus 14:10 *As Pharaoh approached, the Israelites looked up, and there were the Egyptians, marching after them.*

This was a terrifying development for God's people. After the last plague, Pharaoh gave them permission to leave Egypt, and they assumed the battle was over. Egypt was devastated, Pharaoh's will was broken, and God's people were free to begin their journey to the Promised Land.

But as Pharaoh watched his labor supply march out of Egypt, he changed his mind. He marshaled his troops and chariots, and pursued the people of God until they were against the sea. Pharaoh was behind them, the sea was before them, and there was no place to go.

Exodus 14:10 *They were terrified and cried out to the Lord.*

In desperation, God's people cried out to him in prayer. No one had to tell them to pray—they did it instinctively. Trouble drives people to prayer, and prayer is the plea of people in trouble. The trouble may be our own fault, someone else's fault, or no one's fault at all. But it can always be used by God as a way to reveal himself as the one who answers prayer.

God, in fact, has designed our lives to be a series of problems and answered prayers. It's in the tension—between our problems and God's answers—that we experience God most keenly and learn to pray. If not for our problems we'd pray less often, less earnestly, and experience less of God.

Exodus 14:14 *The Lord will fight for you; you need only to be still.*

After crying out to God in prayer, the Lord answered his people through Moses. They wouldn't have to fight the Egyptian army, since God was going to fight for them. All they had to do was wait.

Desperate times call for desperate measures, but not always. Sometimes the proper course of action is to wait for God. *[God] acts on behalf of those who wait for him* (Isaiah 64:4), wrote Isaiah. And, *Wait for your God always* (Hosea 12:6), wrote Hosea. When God's people were desperate, and didn't know what to do, God told them to *be still*.

Exodus 14:21-22 *The waters were divided, and the Israelites went through the sea on dry ground, with a wall of water on their right and on their left.*

Apart from the act of creation, this is the most spectacular miracle in the Bible. Moses held out his staff, and God sent a powerful wind that blew a path right through the Red Sea. There was a wall of water on the right and on the left, and even the bottom became dry ground.

The number of Israelite men who crossed the sea was about six hundred thousand (Exodus 12:37). This means the total number was over two million people. Moms, dads, grandmas, grandpas, teens, and toddlers walked between the walls of water to the other side of the sea. God became their God, and they were his chosen people.

This was a decisive miracle that's still believed by many, since it was recorded by Moses and witnessed by two million people. It's hard to deny a miracle witnessed by that many people, even centuries later. The resurrection of Christ is also supported by the eyewitness testimony of credible witnesses who were willing to suffer and die for what they saw. And none of the Apostles ever changed their story.

In contrast, four swimmers from the United States made up a story that they were robbed at the 2016 Olympics. But they all withdrew their story within a week because their stories wouldn't hold up. The apostles held to their story—not for weeks, but for decades—and many sealed it with their blood. Either they were crazy, or they were just telling the truth that Jesus rose from the dead.

For Reflection and Review
- *How is Jesus like the Passover lamb?*
- *Why is it important to wait for God?*
- *How do we know Jesus rose from the dead?*

Lesson 27

Exodus 14:26 *Then the Lord said to Moses, Stretch out your hand over the sea so that the waters may flow back over the Egyptians and their chariots and horsemen.*

Foolish Pharaoh lead his army into the sea to pursue the people of God. It's hard to know what he was thinking since God's mighty power was all that was holding the water back. After God's people were safely across, God withdrew his power, and the water returned to its place. Pharaoh and his army were buried at sea.

This is a wonderful scene in God's story, and there's a sense in which all history can be seen as *his-story*. We can be the good guys or the bad guys; we can be on God's side or the wrong side. But since we're born into God's world, we all have a part in his story. We may even be part of a miracle more dramatic than the exodus.

Like the exodus, the Lord is coming for his people, and there will be a showdown between good and evil. Someone worse than Pharaoh is coming, and he too will oppose the people of God.

[The antichrist] was given power to wage war against God's holy people and to conquer them. And it was given authority over every tribe, people, language and nation. All inhabitants of the earth will worship the beast—all whose names have not been written in the Lamb's book of life, the Lamb who was slain from the creation of the world (Revelation 13:7-8), wrote John.

But when it seems like the kingdom of God has lost, and the cause of Christ has been defeated, Jesus will return to overthrow the antichrist (Revelation 19:11-21). Then God's people will live happily ever after. Wherever we live, and whenever we live, we all have a part in God's story.

Exodus 15:13 *In your unfailing love you will lead the people you have redeemed. In your strength you will guide them to your holy dwelling*

After God's people got to the other side of the sea, they began to worship in song. Since God had just delivered them from Pharaoh, they could be sure he'd lead them to the Promised Land. *By day the Lord went ahead of them in a pillar of cloud to guide them on their way and by night in a pillar of fire to give them light, so that they could travel by day or night* (Exodus 13:21). When it was time to stop, the pillar would stop. When it was time to go, the pillar would go. All they had to do was follow the pillar, and they would know they were exactly where God wanted them to be.

Thankfully, God is still willing to lead those who are willing to follow. *I am the light of the world. Whoever follows me will never walk in darkness, but will have the light of life* (John 8:12), said Jesus. We are not unlike the Israelites. Through faith in Jesus Christ we've been delivered from the evil one, but we are not home yet. We need God to guide us the rest of the way. *[H]e will be our guide even to the end* (Psalm 48:14), wrote the Psalmist. But how does God lead his people today?

There's a harbor in Italy that, at one time, could only be reached by sailing between dangerous rocks. So many ships were dashed on the rocks, that they set up a navigational system to help guide the captains. Three separate lights were mounted on three separate poles and, when all the lights lined up, the captain could be sure he was safely where he belonged. If the lights didn't line up, the captain had to correct his course.

God has also given us three lights: his word, his Spirit, and his providence. Whenever we have to make a big decision we should ask if it agrees with God's word. If not, God is not leading in that direction. But if it agrees with God's word, we should also ask if it agrees with his indwelling Spirit. If our heart says *No*, that may be an impulse from the Spirit of God (Acts 16:6-10).

But if the decision agrees with God's word, and his Spirit in our heart seems to approve, we can also ask if it agrees with his providence. In other words, is it practical? God's ways are not always practical, but he's unlikely to call a person who's bad at math to be an accountant. God is usually practical, and the most practical thing we can do is carefully follow him.

Exodus 16:31 *The people of Israel called the bread manna. It was white like coriander seed and tasted like wafers made with honey.*

After leading his people out of Egypt, God proceeded to feed them on their way to the Promised Land. Each night, as they slept, bread came down from heaven so they could gather it up in the morning—enough for each of them.

The people called it *manna* which, in Hebrew, sounds like *What is it?* (Exodus 16:15). This is how God fed over two million people, every day, for the next forty years. The Bible contains many stories of God's provision, and this is one the best.

Jesus drew on this story to teach an important lesson about himself. After he fed five thousand people, his popularity went up so dramatically that some wanted to make him king (John 6:15). Instead of being pleased, however, Jesus accused them of wanting another free lunch—which they admitted!

I am the bread of life. Your ancestors ate the manna in the wilderness, yet they died. But here is the bread that comes down from heaven, which anyone may eat and not die. I am the living bread that came down from heaven. Whoever eats this bread will live forever. This bread is my flesh, which I will give for the life of the world (John 6:48-51), he said.

God provides food for temporal life, as well as for eternal life. Whether we have much in this age, matters very little compared to living with Christ forever. Jesus is the bread from heaven who gives eternal life to all who believe in him.

For Reflection and Review

- *Why would Pharaoh lead his army into the sea?*
- *How does God lead his people today?*
- *How is Jesus like manna?*

Lesson 28

Exodus 17:6 *Strike the rock, and water will come out of it for the people to drink.*

As God's people journeyed to the Promised Land they ran out of water. But, instead of praying to God, they complained to Moses. So God told Moses to strike a rock with his rod, and enough water came out for everyone. Even in the desert, God could provide enough water to keep his people alive.

The New Testament provides an interesting commentary on this episode. *[T]hat rock was Christ* (1 Corinthians 10:4), wrote Paul. It's hard to understand how a rock could be Christ, but there's an interesting parallel.

When Moses struck the rock with his rod, water came out. And when the solder thrust his spear into Jesus' side, water came out, mixed with blood (John 19:34). Water from the rock satisfied people's physical thirst, and Jesus satisfies our spiritual thirst. *Let anyone who is thirsty come to me and drink* (John 7:37), he said.

*****

Exodus 17:8 *The Amalekites came and attacked the Israelites at Rephidim.*

On their way to the Promised Land, God's people were opposed. The Amalekites declared war and were a serious threat. Moses told Joshua to lead the Israelites in battle while he went up a hill to watch and pray. *As long as Moses held up his hands, the Israelites were winning, but whenever he lowered his hands, the Amalekites were winning* (Exodus 17:11).

God's people often prayed with their hands lifted up to him (Psalm 141:2). But if you hold your hands up very long, you'll find it's easy at first, but soon becomes difficult. Moses' arms became tired, so a rock was brought for him to sit on, and two other men held up his hands until the Amalekites were defeated.

Important battles are won or lost in prayer. That's why Jesus began his ministry with forty days of prayer and fasting (Matthew 4:1-11). During this time he fought the devil, and was victorious. Three times Satan tempted Jesus, and three times Jesus defeated Satan.

Jesus also cast out demons, but his disciples were less effective. *Why could not we drive it out?* they asked. *This kind can come out only by prayer* (Mark

9:28-29), said Jesus. In the battle between light and darkness, only those who pray have power. Satan wants us to save time by neglecting prayer, because he knows that's where battles are won.

*****

Exodus 19:1-2 *On the first day of the third month after the Israelites left Egypt—on that very day—they came to the Desert of Sinai. . . . and Israel camped there in the desert in front of the mountain.*

About seven weeks after leaving Egypt, God's people arrived at Mount Sinai. There they camped for nearly a year (Numbers 10:11-12), and received God's law. This was a formative time as they learned what it meant to be God's people, and for God to be their God (Exodus 6:7).

Exodus 19:9 *The Lord said to Moses, I am going to come to you in a dense cloud.*

God was about to reveal himself and give his people the Ten Commandments. He wouldn't come on a rainbow, or on a beam of light, but in a *dense cloud*, also called a *thick cloud* (Exodus 19:16). At the very moment God was revealing himself, he'd also be concealing himself.

From this we learn there's always more to God than meets the eye. We can know him truly (John 17:3), but never exhaustively. No matter how much we know about God, there will always be more that we don't know, because God is infinite.

This is why God can never be boring. If you find a piece of music that you really enjoy, you'll want to hear it again. But after you hear it a hundred times, it'll no longer thrill you as at first. This can never happen with God because his perfections are infinite. For all eternity he'll never cease to amaze us.

Exodus 19:16-19 *On the morning of the third day there was thunder and lightning, with a thick cloud over the mountain, and a very loud trumpet blast. Everyone in the camp trembled. Then Moses led the people out of the camp to meet with God, and they stood at the foot of the mountain.*

Mount Sinai was covered with smoke, because the Lord descended on it in fire. The smoke billowed up from it like smoke from a furnace, and the whole mountain trembled violently. As the sound of the trumpet grew louder and louder, Moses spoke and the voice of God answered him.

God revealed himself in power because he was about to give his laws, and he didn't want them taken as suggestions. God is a king whose word is to be obeyed on pain of death (Romans 6:23). Many think of God as an indulgent father, but that image is not found in the Bible. The God of the Bible kills people and sends them to hell. He is to be greatly feared and fully obeyed (Proverbs 10:27).

Exodus 20:1 *And God spoke all these words. . . . You shall have no other gods before me. You shall not make for yourself an image. . . You shall not misuse the name of the Lord your God. . . . Remember the Sabbath. . . . Honor your father and your mother. . . You shall not murder. . . . You shall not commit adultery. . . .You shall not steal. . . .You shall not give false testimony. . . . You shall not covet . . .* (Exodus 20:3-17).

Other laws would be given, but these Ten Commandments were the foundation on which the others rested. They were the only words God spoke to the nation audibly, and were later written in stone by the finger of God (Exodus 31:18). Then they were stored in the ark of the covenant, in the Most Holy Place, inside the tabernacle (Exodus 34:1, 40:20).

It would be hard to overstate the importance of the Ten Commandments to the nation of Israel before the coming of Christ. But a change has taken place. Most of the Ten Commandments are repeated in the New Testament but not all of them. And, surprisingly, we're never told to *Obey the Ten Commandments*.

The Mosaic law is no longer binding in an absolute sense (Hebrews 8:13), but reveals our sin (Romans 3:20), so we might flee to Christ and be *justified by faith* (Galatians 3:24), wrote Paul. Christians are free from the law as a way of salvation (Romans 7:4-6), but are *under Christ's law* (1 Corinthians 9:21) as a way of life. The Ten

Commandments have great historic significance, but are not the way of salvation.

For Reflection and Review

- *What should we learn from Israel's battle with the Amalekites?*
- *Why did God reveal himself in such a frightening way?*
- *Why aren't the Ten Commandments the way to be saved?*

Lesson 29

Exodus 20:18-19 *When the people saw the thunder and lightning and heard the trumpet and saw the mountain in smoke, they trembled with fear. They stayed at a distance and said to Moses, Speak to us yourself and we will listen. But do not have God speak to us or we will die.*

The people of God were terrified by God's voice, and other manifestations, so they begged Moses to mediate. Moses represented the people to God, and God to the people. This was a helpful arrangement because it gave ordinary sinners access to God without fear of being destroyed by his holy wrath.

Priests and prophets were later ordained for a similar purpose, but the ideal mediator came in the person of Jesus Christ. *For there is one God and one mediator between God and mankind, the man Christ Jesus* (1 Timothy 2:5), wrote Paul.

As perfect God, Jesus represents God to people. As perfect human, Jesus represents humans to God. Sinners can never approach a holy God without a mediator and hope to live. But God has provided the perfect mediator in the person of Jesus Christ. *No one comes to the Father except through me* (John 14:6), he said.

*****

Exodus 23:2 *Do not follow the crowd in doing wrong.*

It's easier to follow the crowd than think for ourselves. But that is neither right nor safe. Middle-eastern shepherds were surprised when one of their sheep walked over a cliff. But they were even more surprised when a second one followed, and then a third. Before long the entire flock of four hundred sheep had gone over the cliff to their death. We can follow the crowd, or we can follow the shepherd. *My sheep listen to my voice; I know them, and they follow me* (John 10:27), said Jesus.

*****

Exodus 25:8 *[H]ave them make a sanctuary for me, and I will dwell among them.*

God's presence with his people was seen in a pillar of cloud by day, and a pillar of fire by night (Exodus 13:21). For the additional good of his people, he also ordained a place for them to worship. It was an elaborate tent about fifteen feet wide, fifteen feet high, and forty-five feet long. It wasn't very large, but it was crafted with expensive materials to make it beautiful. God dwelt inside the tabernacle so he could be with his people wherever they went.

The New Testament says something similar about Jesus Christ. *The Word became flesh and made his dwelling among us.* This, in fact, is an allusion to the tabernacle. God lived in a tent so he could be near his people, then he came even nearer in the person of Jesus Christ.

A friend of mine grew up in a family of thirteen children. They all got married, had children of their own, and no one moved out of town. Everyone thought it was great, except Grandma and Grandpa. With everyone stopping by all the time, they were so exhausted that they moved to another state.

But there are other grandparents who follow their children from state to state, because they can't bear to be away from them. That's what God is like. So after Christ returned to heaven, he sent the Spirit to live within us (John 14:17). Notice the progression: God dwelt among his people in the tabernacle, then in Christ, now by the Spirit, and soon in heaven.

I heard a loud voice from the throne saying, Look! God's dwelling place is now among the people, and he will dwell with them. They will be his people, and God himself will be with them and be their God (Revelation 21:3), wrote John. Any separation from God will be a thing of the past, and we'll dwell in his presence forever.

Exodus 29:38 *This is what you are to offer on the altar regularly each day: two lambs a year old.*

Inside the courtyard of the tabernacle was an altar for burning sacrifices. In addition to sacrificial lambs, there were grain offerings, fellowship offerings, sin offerings, and guilt offerings. They were all necessary to stay in a right relationship with God. God was teaching his people that sin is serious, and must be paid for.

All the ceremonies and sacrifices also showed the way to God wasn't completely open yet. God was in the midst of his people, but he wasn't very accessible. If anyone who wasn't a priest got close to God's tent, they were to be killed (Numbers 3:10).

Even most priests could only go in the first room of God's tent, not the back room, where God himself was. Only the High Priest was allowed in there, and only once a year, with sacrificial blood (Leviticus 16). The two rooms were called the *Holy Place* and the *Most Holy Place,* and were separated by an elaborate curtain (Exodus 26:31-33). God was with his people, but he was still hard to get to.

All the animals sacrificed for hundreds of years, in fact, never really atoned for sin, but only pointed forward to the sacrifice of Christ. The moment he died on the cross the curtain in the temple was torn from top to bottom (Matthew 27:51), showing the way to God is now open to everyone who believes in Christ. He is both our great high priest (Hebrews 4:14) and the perfect sacrifice who opened the way to God for us.

*****

Exodus 32:1 *When the people saw that Moses was so long in coming down from the mountain, they gathered around Aaron and said, Come, make us gods who will go before us. As for this fellow Moses who brought us up out of Egypt, we don't know what has happened to him.*

Moses had been on top of Mount Sinai with God for nearly six weeks, and the people were growing restless. In Moses' absence, they turned to his brother Aaron, and asked for gods to lead them. Aaron collected gold from the people, and melted it down to create an idol in the shape of a calf. He also built an altar, and declared a festival the following day. God's people *sat down to eat and drink and got up to indulge in revelry* (Exodus 32:6).

But only weeks earlier, God's people heard him say, *You shall have no other gods before me. You shall not make for yourself an image in the form of anything in heaven above or on the earth* (Exodus 20:3-4). *We will do everything the Lord has said* (Exodus 24:7), they replied.

They had every intention of obeying God but, in Moses' absence, they did the opposite. They planned to obey God. They even pledged to obey God. But then they went astray. Telling sinners not to sin is like telling roaches to stay out of the kitchen.

This is important to understand so we don't despair whenever we fail badly. Even the Apostle Paul struggled with indwelling sin throughout his life. *What a wretched man I am!* (Romans 7:24), he wrote. But then he put his hope in Jesus Christ who saved us from the penalty of sin, is now saving us from the power of sin (Romans 7:25), and will save us from the presence of sin (Revelation 21:27). *[Y]ou are to give him the name Jesus, [said the angel] because he will save his people from their sins* (Matthew 1:21).

For Reflection and Review

- *Why is Jesus a perfect mediator between God and humans?*
- *What does the sanctuary tell us about God?*

- *How does Jesus save us from the penalty, power, and presence of sin?*

Lesson 30

Exodus 32:9-10 *I have seen these people, the Lord said to Moses. . . . Now leave me alone so that my anger may burn against them and that I may destroy them. Then I will make you into a great nation.*

God was so angry at his people for breaking his law, that he wanted to destroy them and start over with Moses. This was an opportunity for Moses to become a great nation. But Moses was more concerned with God's reputation than with his own legacy. He even preferred death to seeing God's people destroyed (Exodus 32:32).

This reminds of Jesus Christ who was willing to die so that we might live forever. *Greater love has no one than this: to lay down one's life for one's friends* (John 15:13), he said. Jesus laid down his life for us, so we could live forever through him (John 6:47).

Exodus 32:14 *Then the Lord relented and did not bring on his people the disaster he had threatened.*

Moses' intercession saved God's people from total destruction, and also reminds us of the intercession of Christ. When we consider how often and badly we sin, it's surprising we didn't perish years ago. This is because Jesus intercedes for us to be sure his salvation is applied for all time. *[H]e is able to save completely those who come to God through him, because he always lives to intercede for them* (Hebrews 7:25), says Hebrews.

Whenever sin threatens to separate us from God, Jesus pleads on our behalf. Because of his death, and constant intercession, God pardons our sins and will never give up on us. *Who then is the one who condemns? No one. Christ Jesus who died—more than that, who was raised to life—is at the right hand of God and is also interceding for us* (Romans 8:34), wrote Paul. We're not only saved by the death of Christ, but also by his intercession.

Exodus 32:15-16 *Moses turned and went down the mountain with the two tablets of the covenant law in his hands. They were inscribed on both sides, front and back. The tablets were the work of God; the writing was the writing of God, engraved on the tablets.*

When Moses approached the camp and saw the calf and the dancing, his anger burned and he threw the tablets out of his hands, breaking them to pieces at the foot of the mountain. And he took the calf the people had made and burned it in the fire; then he ground it to powder, scattered it on the water and made the Israelites drink it (Exodus 32:19-20).

By breaking the tablets in front of God's people Moses was demonstrating how violently the people had broken their covenant with God. It would later be renewed (Exodus 34:10-28), but was presently shattered. This was a recurring problem since God's people broke the covenant often, and had to renew it again and again (Deuteronomy 29, Joshua 8, Joshua 24, 2 Kings 23). This imperfect arrangement showed the need for something better, and was foretold by the prophet Jeremiah.

The days are coming, declares the Lord, when I will make a new covenant with the people of Israel and with the people of Judah. It will not be like the covenant I made with their ancestors when I took them by the hand to lead them out of Egypt, because they broke my covenant, though I was a husband to them, declares the Lord.

This is the covenant I will make with the people of Israel after that time, declares the Lord. I will put my law in their minds and write it on their hearts. I will be their God, and they will be my people. . . . For I will forgive their wickedness and will remember their sins no more (Jeremiah 31:31-34).

This was put into effect by the Lord Jesus Christ the night before his death. *[H]e took the cup, saying, This cup is the new covenant in my blood, which is poured out for you* (Luke 22:20). The new covenant is based on the sacrifice of Christ and is *eternal* (Hebrews 13:20). We show our participation in the new covenant, not by bringing a sacrifice, but by receiving the Lord's Supper (1 Corinthians 11:24-25).

Exodus 32:21 *He said to Aaron, What did these people do to you, that you led them into such great sin?*

Moses' brother was in trouble, and he knew it. So he did what people often do when they're caught in a sin: he lied. *Do not be angry, my lord, Aaron answered. You know how prone these people are to evil. They said to me, Make us gods who will go before us. As for this fellow Moses who brought us up out of Egypt, we don't know what has happened to him. So I told them, Whoever has any gold jewelry, take it off. Then they gave me the gold, and I threw it into the fire, and out came this calf!* (Exodus 32:22-24).

This, of course, was perfect nonsense, but Aaron was desperate. He was the future high priest of God's chosen people, and failed at his calling before he even began. Instead of leading God's people into proper worship, he led them into idolatry.

Aaron's failure reminds us of our need for a perfect high priest—Jesus Christ. *Such a high priest truly meets our need—one who is holy, blameless, pure, set apart from sinners, exalted above the heavens. Unlike the other high priests, he does not need to offer sacrifices day after day, first for his own sins, and then for the sins of the people. He sacrificed for their sins once for all when he offered himself* (Hebrews 7:26-27), says Hebrews.

Exodus 32:25 *Moses saw that the people were running wild and that Aaron had let them get out of control.*

Moses recovered control by having three thousand people put to death (Exodus 32:28). They were probably the worst offenders, and became an example to the others. God also sent a plague to show his disapproval (Exodus 32:35). The penalty was severe, but so was the offense. True religion should never be mixed with false religion . . . *for our God is a consuming fire* (Hebrews 12:29), says Hebrews.

For Reflection and Review

- Why is Jesus' intercession important for our salvation?
- Why did the old covenant need to be replaced by a new covenant?
- Why is Jesus a perfect high priest?

Lesson 31

Leviticus 1:1 *The Lord called to Moses and spoke to him from the tent of meeting.*

The book of Leviticus was written by Moses for the people of God around 1445 BC. The nation was still gathered at the base of Mount Sinai, and was being prepared for their journey to the Promised Land. Through Moses, God gave his people instructions for worship, and regulations for holiness.

Leviticus 9:23 *Moses and Aaron then went into the tent of meeting. When they came out, they blessed the people; and the glory of the Lord appeared to all the people.*

The events of this day were very important because it was the first worship service at the newly constructed tabernacle. Moses brother, Aaron, was high priest, and his four sons were also priests. The nation had just received instructions from God regarding appropriate worship which included the sacred tent, sacrifices, and rituals.

Leviticus 9:24 *Fire came out from the presence of the Lord and consumed the burnt offering and the fat portions on the altar.*

This is the first of five times in which God showed his approval by consuming a sacrifice with fire. It also happened for Gideon (Judges 6:21), David (1 Chronicles 21:26), Solomon (2 Chronicles 7:1), and Elijah (1 Kings 18:38).

Fire and God are connected throughout the Bible. God is called a *consuming fire* (Hebrews 12:29). He led his people with a *pillar of fire* (Numbers 14:14). Before his throne is a *sea of glass glowing with fire* (Revelation 15:2); And his eyes are like a *blazing fire* (Revelation 1:14). Fire is good, but also dangerous. Those who aren't careful end up getting burned.

Leviticus 10:1 *Aaron's sons Nadab and Abihu . . . offered unauthorized fire before the Lord.*

Instead worshipping God the way he prescribed, Aaron's sons worshiped God their own way. *So fire came out from the presence of the Lord and consumed them, and they died before the Lord* (Leviticus 10:2). From this it's clear that we aren't free to worship God any way we please, but only in ways that he has ordained. But how does that apply today?

God is spirit, and his worshipers must worship in the Spirit and in truth (John 4:24), said Jesus. *[E]verything should be done in a fitting and orderly way* (1 Corinthians 14:40), wrote Paul. And we ought to *worship God acceptably with reverence and awe* (Hebrews 12:28), says Hebrews.

Worship in the New Testament is much less regulated, but we must never depart from Scripture, and must always revere the God we are worshipping. Christians in the city of Corinth were disrespectful while receiving the Lord's Supper and, as a result, some became ill, and others even died (1 Corinthians 11:30). Whenever we're part of a public worship service we must be keenly aware of God's presence, and conduct ourselves accordingly.

Leviticus 10:3 *Aaron remained silent.*

Aaron, the high priest, saw his two oldest sons killed by God but didn't say a word. He probably knew that God was right, and feared for his own life. Aaron's sons were carried away, and he was forbidden to mourn (Leviticus 10:4-7).

God still requires a higher commitment to himself than to our own flesh and blood. *Anyone who loves their father or mother more than me is not worthy of me; anyone who loves their son or daughter more than me is not worthy of me* (Matthew 10:37), said Jesus.

This is extremely important because our loved ones can lead us away from Christ if we let them. Parents have led their children away from Christ, and children have led their parents away from Christ. But the best way to help ourselves, and others, is by staying true to our Savior.

A godly man raised his son in the faith, taught him well, and prayed for him daily. But his son refused to live for Christ, and wanted little to do with his earthly father. At his father's funeral, however, it became clear to the son that his father was right after all. He didn't want to die without God, so he gave his life to Christ during his father's funeral. Even after death the father was able to help his son by staying true to Christ.

*****

Leviticus 16:15 *[Aaron] shall then slaughter the goat for the sin offering for the people and take its blood behind the curtain . . . . He shall sprinkle it on the atonement cover . . . .*

The Day of Atonement was the most solemn day of the year, and was to be observed with self-denial (Leviticus 16:29). It was the only day in which the high priest was allowed to enter the Most Holy Place, to offer sacrificial blood for the sins of the nation. After a goat was slain, he'd take some of its blood and sprinkled it on the atonement cover.

The atonement cover was the lid on the ark of the covenant, where the Ten Commandments were stored (Exodus 25:16). On either end were cherubim, made of gold, with wings that overshadowed the cover. (Exodus 25:18, 22). The space between the cherubim was where God himself dwelt. *[H]e sits enthroned between the cherubim* (Psalm 99:1), wrote the Psalmist.

To understand the Day of Atonement we should think of God sitting on a throne of law (contained in the ark of the covenant). Everyone has broken God's law (Romans 3:10), so this could only mean death (Romans 6:23). If blood was sprinkled between God and his law, however, God's people could live in his presence, because the price for sin had been paid.

Likewise, *God presented Christ as a sacrifice of atonement, through the shedding of his blood* (Romans 3:25), wrote Paul. Even though we sin every day, we can live forever with God because Christ has shed his blood for us. He is our atonement.

Leviticus 16:21 *[Aaron] is to lay both hands on the head of the live goat and confess over it all the wickedness and rebellion of the Israelites—all their sins—and put them on the goat's head. He shall send the goat away into the wilderness in the care of someone appointed for the task.* In another ritual on the Day of Atonement, the high priest was to place his hands on the head of a goat and confess the sins of the people. Then a designated person would lead the goat away from the people, into the wilderness. *The goat will carry on itself all their sins to a remote place; and the man shall release it in the wilderness* (Leviticus 16:22), wrote Moses.

God was teaching his people that the way to get rid of their sins was not by ignoring them, or by paying for them, but by transferring them to another. The people must have watched intently as their sins were carried far away. This symbol became so important that, in later times, the scapegoat (Leviticus 16:10) was even pushed off a cliff, to be sure it wouldn't return.

Likewise, *the Lord has laid on [Christ] the iniquity of us all* (Isaiah 53:6), wrote Isaiah. And *as far as the east is from the west, so far has he removed our transgressions from us* (Psalm 103:12), wrote David. All our sins were laid on Christ who not only died for them, but carried them away forever.

For Reflection and Review

- *Why does God require a higher commitment to himself than to family?*
- *What was the ark of the covenant?*
- *What did the scapegoat symbolize?*

Lesson 32

Leviticus 18:17 *Do not have sexual relations with both a woman and her daughter. . . . That is wickedness.*

This chapter contains the most extensive list of sexual prohibitions in the Bible, many of them unmentionable. Sexuality is God's idea, and was pronounced *very good* by him (Genesis 1:31). Sex is God's wedding gift to those who are married, but is often misused by married and single alike. This is why such an extensive list was necessary.

Many applaud themselves for self-control because they've avoided outward misconduct, but Jesus taught that our hearts are also important. *You have heard that it was said, You shall not commit adultery. But I tell you that anyone who looks at a woman lustfully has already committed adultery with her in his heart* (Matthew 5:27-28). Likewise, *there must not be even a hint of sexual immorality* (Ephesians 5:3), wrote Paul.

Sexual immorality is a result of our depravity, but also because the sexual impulse is one of the strongest in human nature. Righteous Job is still a good example to those who want to please God: *I made a covenant with my eyes not to look lustfully at a young woman* (Job 31:1), he said. And God will help everyone who wants to do his will.

*****

Leviticus 24:10 *Now the son of an Israelite mother and an Egyptian father went out among the Israelites, and a fight broke out in the camp between him and an Israelite.*

We don't know what caused the fight, but the young man of mixed descent used the occasion to blaspheme God. This was a violation of the third command, *You shall not misuse the name of the Lord your God, for the Lord will not hold anyone guiltless who misuses his name* (Exodus 20:7). Blasphemy was clearly forbidden, but no penalty had been revealed, so the young man was taken into *custody until the will of the Lord should be made clear* (Leviticus 24:12).

Leviticus 24:13-16 *Then the Lord said to Moses: Take the blasphemer outside the camp. All those who heard him are to lay their hands on his head, and the entire assembly is to stone him. Say to the Israelites: Anyone who curses their God will be held responsible; anyone who blasphemes the name of the Lord is to be put to death.*

To use God's name disrespectfully, is to insult the king of the universe, and risk immediate judgment. Sinful speech is never appropriate

(Ephesians 4:29), but we're not as severely threatened for ordinary profanity as we are for blasphemy. It would be better to use ordinary profanity a hundred times a day than to disrespect the name of God even once.

In light of this fact, it's remarkable how often the name of God is misused around the world, every single day. People seldom misuse the name of Buddha, Muhammad, or Krishna. But the name of God, and his Son Jesus Christ, are misused in the most vulgar ways thinkable, as though Satan himself was speaking the words. *[A]ll day long my name is constantly blasphemed* (Isaiah 52:5), said God. Imagine what it's like to hear your name being used as a curse twenty-four hours a day, seven days a week, three-hundred sixty-five days a year, for centuries.

God may seem to overlook the sin of blasphemy but, actually, he doesn't. *I tell you that everyone will have to give account on the day of judgment for every empty word they have spoken. For by your words you will be acquitted, and by your words you will be condemned* (Matthew 12:36-37), said Jesus.

I had a friend in high school who was as happy and fun as anyone I've ever known. But he spoke of God and Jesus Christ in ways that were straight from hell. Nothing bad ever happened to him until the summer after high school. He was mowing the side of a hill when the tractor tipped over and snuffed out his life. No one heard his final words but, if they were like his ordinary speech, I don't think he died very well.

God is usually patient with us, but we should never put him to the test, because he can call us to account at any time. *It is a dreadful thing to fall into the hands of the living God* (Hebrews 10:31), says Hebrews.

*****

Leviticus 23:1-2 *The Lord said to Moses, Speak to the Israelites and say to them: These are my appointed festivals, the appointed festivals of the Lord, which you are to proclaim as sacred assemblies.*

This chapter outlines Israel's religious calendar, including their many festivals. God wanted his people to rejoice, and gave them occasions to celebrate. The word *rejoice* is found over one hundred times throughout the Old Testament.

Surprisingly, the New Testament has no religious calendar. Christians gathered on the first day of the week (1 Corinthians 16:2), but were not forbidden to work on that day. Even Christmas and Easter are not mentioned, and were not observed until after the apostles died. But God still wants his people to be joyful. *Rejoice in the Lord always. I will say it again: Rejoice!* (Philippians 4:4), wrote Paul.

A large hotel chain interviewed five thousand people for five hundred jobs. The managers were told not to hire anyone who smiled fewer than four times during their interview. Of all the people on earth, Christians have more to smile about than anyone else. *Rejoice in the Lord always. I will say it again: Rejoice!*

Leviticus 25:10 *Consecrate the fiftieth year and proclaim liberty throughout the land to all its inhabitants. It shall be a jubilee for you.*

The Year of Jubilee was God's gift to his people, in which debt was canceled (Leviticus 25:23-28), and slaves were set free (Leviticus 25:39-55). It was to be celebrated every fiftieth year, so most would experience it at least once in their adult life. Those who were being oppressed could always look forward to the time of their release.

Jesus had the Year of Jubilee in mind when he preached at Nazareth: *The Spirit of the Lord is on me, because he has anointed me to proclaim good news to the poor. He has sent me to proclaim freedom for the prisoners . . . to set the oppressed free, to proclaim the year of the Lord's favor* (Luke 4:18-19, Isaiah 61:1-2), he said.

The Year of Jubilee wasn't well observed by Israel, but Jesus fulfills it by setting us free from sin (Acts 13:9) and canceling all our debt. *He forgave us all our sins, having canceled the charge of our legal indebtedness . . . he has taken it away, nailing it to the cross*

(Colossians 2:13-14), wrote Paul. What the Year of Jubilee promised for a year, Christ has given forever.

For Reflection and Review

- *Why does God want to control our sexuality?*
- *What's so bad about blasphemy?*
- *How does Jesus fulfill the Year of Jubilee?*

Lesson 33

Numbers 1:1 *The Lord spoke to Moses in the tent of meeting in the Desert of Sinai on the first day of the second month of the second year after the Israelites came out of Egypt.*

The book of Numbers was written by Moses for the people of God around 1406 BC. It tells the failure of God's people to enter the Promised Land and, as a result, their nearly forty years of wandering in the desert. It contains many stories of sin, punishment, and repentance for our instruction.

Numbers 6:2-3 *If a man or woman wants to make a special vow, a vow of dedication to the Lord as a Nazirite, they must abstain from wine.*

Service at the tabernacle was restricted to the tribe of Levi (Numbers 1:50), so most Israelites never had this privilege. But any Israelite who wanted to be uniquely devoted to God could become a Nazirite. That required avoiding anything from the grapevine, not cutting the hair, and avoiding contact with the dead (Numbers 6:3-8). The vow was normally temporary, but could also last a lifetime.

The Nazirite vow is not for Christians, however, because Christians don't need a special vow to be close to God. We're already close to God through faith in Jesus Christ. *[I]n Christ Jesus you who once were far away have been brought near* (Ephesians 2:3), wrote Paul. And we are *a holy priesthood, offering spiritual sacrifices acceptable to God through Jesus Christ* (1 Peter 2:5), wrote Peter. There are no special vows to be close to God in the New Testament, because we couldn't be any closer than we are in Jesus Christ.

*****

Numbers 11:1 *Now the people complained about their hardships in the hearing of the Lord.*

Life with God wasn't always easy, but he faithfully met the needs of his people. Nevertheless, God's people continued to complain until they finally made him angry. As a result, *fire from God burned among them and consumed some of the outskirts of the camp* (Numbers 11:1b), wrote Moses.

There's a difference between complaining to God and being chronic complainers. God wants to hear our problems (Psalm 142:2), but doesn't want us to complain all the time. What we normally need is to simply adjust our attitude.

The air-conditioning went out at a youth conference where thousands were attending for several days. It was blistering hot, but the leadership came up with a solution. They hung a banner over the stage that read: *You can't make it hot enough for me to complain.* Everyone adjusted their attitude and the conference was a success.

*****

Numbers 12:1-2 *Miriam and Aaron began to talk against Moses . . . . Has the Lord spoken only through Moses? they asked. Hasn't he also spoken through us?*

God's people often complained against Moses, but the complaints of Miriam and Aaron were more serious. Aaron was high priest (Exodus 28:1), and Miriam was a prophet (Exodus 15:20). If they undermined Moses' leadership, the whole nation might die in the desert. Miriam was most at fault, it seems, since God struck her with leprosy. But then Moses prayed for her and, seven days later, she was restored.

Jesus Christ was also opposed by someone very close to him. When he began to speak about his crucifixion, Peter began to rebuke him. *Never, Lord!*

he said. This shall never happen to you (Matthew 16:22). There was simply no room in Peter's thinking for Jesus' crucifixion. Jesus would be the king, and Peter would serve along side him. If Jesus had other ideas, he needed to be corrected.

Thankfully, Peter didn't die, or even get leprosy. But he did receive the strongest rebuke in the Bible. *Get behind me, Satan! You are a stumbling block to me* (Matthew 16:23), said Jesus. Christian leaders might be tempted to think they have better ideas than the Lord. But Jesus is greater than Moses, and should never be opposed.

*****

Numbers 13:1-2 *The Lord said to Moses, Send some men to explore the land of Canaan, which I am giving to the Israelites.*

It was only about a year since Israel came out of Egypt. They camped at Mount Sinai, for almost a year, then marched across the desert until they came to the Promised Land. Then God told Moses to send in a dozen men to explore the land he was giving them. This would help in the conquest, and would assure God's people that it was *a land flowing with milk and honey* (Exodus 3:8). The task would take about forty days, and cover more than four hundred miles. The rest of God's people waited earnestly as they camped outside the land.

Numbers 13:25 *At the end of forty days they returned from exploring the land.*

To show the land was bountiful, the explorers brought back a sample of fruit that was so heavy it took two men and a pole to carry it home (Numbers 13:23). The land was all that God had promised, but there was some concern whether it could be taken (Numbers 13:28-29). Most of the explorers said it could not.

Numbers 13:30 *Then Caleb silenced the people before Moses and said, We should go up and take possession of the land, for we can certainly do it.*

This is one of the most positive statements of faith in the Bible. The land was filled with powerful people, and fortified cities, but they were no match for God. God had promised this land to his people, and was opposed to those who were living there, because of their sin (Genesis 15:16). If God overcame the Egyptians, he could defeat these people as well.

Numbers 13:31-33 *But the men who had gone up with him said, We cannot attack those people; they are stronger than we are. . . . We seemed like grasshoppers in our own eyes, and we looked the same to them.*

The cowardly explorers made the tragic mistake of taking their eyes off God and focusing on their problems. The more they focused on their problems, the bigger they seemed. The less they focused on God, the smaller he seemed. Eventually their problems were bigger than God, and God was no match for their problems.

By contrast, Caleb and Joshua focused on God, rather than on their problems. Some people seem to have faith until they have a problem—then they give way to fear. Joshua and Caleb overcame their fear by focusing on God.

Most of the Israelites didn't share Joshua and Caleb's faith, however, so they chose to rebel against the Lord and Moses. *We should choose [another] leader and go back to Egypt* (Numbers 14:4), they said. After all God had done for them, they were still willing to walk away. This is hard to imagine, but many who are given every spiritual benefit also walk away from God. This was a devastating failure that would have lasting consequences.

For Reflection and Review

- *Why isn't the Nazirite vow for Christians?*
- *What's the right way to complain go God?*
- *Why did Caleb and Joshua think they could conquer the Promised Land?*

Lesson 34

Numbers 14:12 *I will strike them down with a plague and destroy them, but I will make you into a nation greater and stronger than they.*

Once again the Lord was so angry with the Israelites that he was willing to destroy the whole nation and start over with Moses. Given the trouble they'd been to Moses, it's surprising he didn't agree. But Moses was so humble (Numbers 12:3) that he was still less concerned with his legacy than with God's reputation. He thought the Egyptians might hear of it and say, *The Lord was not able to bring these people into the land he promised them on oath, so he slaughtered them in the wilderness* (Numbers 14:16). God listened to Moses, and didn't destroy his people, but there would still be serious consequences.

Numbers 14:29-30 *In this wilderness your bodies will fall—every one of you twenty years old or more . . . except Caleb . . . and Joshua.*

God didn't kill his people at once, but over the next forty years (Numbers 14:34) they'd wander in the desert, until all the adults were dead. They could've conquered the Promised Land, but would have to die in the desert. They could've lived by faith, but would have to wander aimlessly.

The journey of life has forks in the road, at which we must choose to follow Christ, or go another way. Our faithless choices aren't always fatal, but their consequences diminish our lives, and even the lives of others. God's path is seldom easy, but it's the only one that'll take us where we want to go.

Numbers 14:37 *[The] men who were responsible for spreading the bad report about the land were struck down and died of a plague before the Lord.*

Most of God's people lived out the rest of their natural lives, but the ten explorers who incited rebellion were struck down by God and died. This wasn't unfair considering the negative effect their leadership had on others. It also shows that leaders are held to a higher standard. This idea appears in the New Testament as well. *Not many of you should become teachers, my fellow believers, because you know that we who teach will be judged more strictly* (James 3:1), wrote James. People in leadership are held to a higher standard because of the effect they have on others.

Numbers 14:40 *Early the next morning they set out for the highest point in the hill country, saying, Now we are ready to go up to the land the Lord promised.*

Once God's people saw the consequences of their sin, they decided to obey. But now it was too late. Moses told them not to go into battle because the Lord would not be with them (Numbers 14:42). But, rebellious to the end, they went into battle anyway and fell by the sword. Sometimes it really is too late.

A country preacher stood over the casket of a local outlaw. *Too late for Joe*, he said. *He heard the gospel a hundred times but always put it off. Too late for Joe. Too late for Joe.* Some in the church were upset at the preacher's bluntness, but most agreed he was right. Sometimes it really is too late.

This is why the gospel is always urgent. A man crucified next to Jesus said, *remember me when you come into your kingdom* (Luke 23:42). We don't know much about him, except he was a criminal (Luke 23:32). He may've he started out stealing apples, and then went on to bigger things. Perhaps he stole sheep for a while, and then became a bandit. He thought he'd never be caught, but then he was arrested, tried, and crucified—a worst case scenario. With little time left he turned to Christ and wasn't disappointed. *Truly I tell you, today you will be with me in paradise* (Luke 23:43), said Jesus.

A generation of Israelites missed out on the Promised Land of Canaan, but no one who turns to Christ will miss out on the Promised Land of heaven. All our choices have consequences, and choosing Christ has the consequence of eternal life in the best of all possible worlds. *I tell you, now is the time of God's favor, now is the day of salvation* (2 Corinthians 6:2), wrote Paul.

*****

Numbers 15:30 *But anyone who sins defiantly, whether native-born or foreigner, blasphemes the Lord and must be cut off from the people of Israel.*

An example follows of a man who was gathering wood on the Sabbath day. *Then the Lord said to Moses, The man must die. The whole assembly must stone him outside the camp. So the assembly took him outside the camp and stoned him to death, as the Lord commanded Moses* (Numbers 15:35-36).

The Bible makes a distinction between those who sin unintentionally, and those who sin defiantly. Defiant sin is looking God in the face and shaking your fist at him. Such sins are normally premeditated, not followed by repentance, and extremely dangerous.

If we deliberately keep on sinning after we have received the knowledge of the truth, no sacrifice for sins is left, but only a fearful expectation of judgment and of raging fire that will consume the enemies of God. Anyone who rejected the law of Moses died without mercy on the testimony of two or three witnesses. How much more severely do you think someone deserves to be punished who has trampled the Son of God underfoot, who has treated as an unholy thing the blood of the covenant that sanctified them, and who has insulted the Spirit of grace? For we know him who said, It is mine to avenge; I will repay, and again, The Lord will judge his people. It is a dreadful thing to fall into the hands of the living God (Hebrews 10:26-31), says Hebrews.

This is also why Paul required believers who were sinning defiantly to be put out of the church (1 Corinthians 5:2). The goal was not their eternal doom, but repentance and restoration, so their *spirit may be saved on the day of the Lord* (1 Corinthians 5:5), wrote Paul.

Every believer sins unintentionally, every single day (Matthew 5:48). And many believers sin defiantly on occasion. But God is pleased to forgive every sin as long as we trust in Christ, and continue turning back to him (1 John 1:9). *[A] broken and contrite heart you, God, will not despise* (Psalm 51:17), wrote David.

For Reflection and Review

- Why does God hold leaders to a higher standard?
- Is it ever too late to be saved?
- Why is defiant sin so dangerous?

Lesson 35

Numbers 16:1-3 *Korah [and others] became insolent and rose up against Moses. With them were 250 Israelite men, well-known community leaders who had been appointed members of the council. They came as a group to oppose Moses and Aaron and said to them, You have gone too far! The whole community is holy, every one of them, and the Lord is with them. Why then do you set yourselves above the Lord's assembly?*

This was a serious challenge to the authority of Moses and Aaron, who were appointed by God to lead the nation into the Promised Land. After all the miracles God had done through Moses, it's hard to believe such a challenge could be made. Instead of defending himself, however, Moses directed Korah and his supporters to come to the tabernacle the following day.

Then Moses said, This is how you will know that the Lord has sent me to do all these things and that it was not my idea: If these men die a natural death and suffer the fate of all mankind, then the Lord has not sent me.

But if the Lord brings about something totally new, and the earth opens its mouth and swallows them, with everything that belongs to them, and they go down alive into the realm of the dead, then you will know that these men have treated the Lord with contempt.

As soon as he finished saying all this, the ground under them split apart and the earth opened its mouth and swallowed them and their households, and all those associated with Korah, together with their possessions. They went down alive into the realm of the dead, with everything they owned; the earth closed over them, and they perished and were gone from the community (Numbers 16:28-33).

Few things make ministry more miserable than being falsely accused. Some ministers have even wished God would vindicate them as clearly as he did Moses. But this judgment was never repeated, and many good ministers have been forced out.

Even the Apostle Paul had to defend himself against some in the church who undermined his ministry (2 Corinthians 11:5). Every Christian leader should be held accountable, but so should those who accuse them. *Warn a divisive person once, and then warn them a second time. After that, have nothing to do with them* (Titus 3:10), wrote Paul.

Other than Jesus Christ there are no perfect leaders. But any church that allows its leaders to be wrongfully attacked will soon run out of qualified leaders. *Have confidence in your leaders and submit to their authority, because they keep watch over you as those who must give an account. Do this so that their work will be a joy, not a burden, for that would be of no benefit to you* (Hebrews 13:17), says Hebrews.

*****

Numbers 17:1-2 *The Lord said to Moses, Speak to the Israelites and get twelve staffs from them, one from the leader of each of their ancestral tribes.*

God showed his approval of Moses by burying his accusers, and now he'd show his approval of Aaron in a gentler way. A staff was taken from the leader of each ancestral tribe (twelve in all), and each leader's name was written on his staff. Aaron's name was written on the staff of Levi, since he belonged to that tribe.

Then the staffs were placed in the tabernacle. By the following day Aaron's staff had sprouted, budded, blossomed, and produced almonds. This was divine proof that he was, in fact, chosen by God to be the high priest.

Likewise, God has provided proof that we belong to him. *No good tree bears bad fruit, nor does a bad tree bear good fruit* (Luke 6:43-44), said Jesus. And *the fruit of the Spirit is love, joy, peace, forbearance, kindness, goodness, faithfulness, gentleness and self-control* (Galatians 5:22-23), wrote Paul. The more we bear the fruit of the Spirit, the more clearly we belong to Christ.

*****

Numbers 20:2 *Now there was no water for the community, and the people gathered in opposition to Moses and Aaron.*

Nearly forty years earlier Israel also ran out of water, and God told Moses to strike a rock with his staff. Water came out (Exodus 17:1-7) and all the people survived. Now, at the end of their journey, a new generation needed water, and God would meet their need as well. But instead of striking the rod with his staff, God told Moses to speak to the rock (Numbers 20:8).

By now, Moses had led God's people for many years, and he was a little impatient. *Listen, you rebels, must we bring you water out of this rock?* Then *Moses raised his arm and struck the rock twice with his staff. Water gushed out, and the community and their livestock drank* (Numbers 20:10-11).

But God was displeased with Moses because of his disobedience. *Because you did not trust in me enough to honor me as holy in the sight of the Israelites, you will not bring this community into the land I give them* (Numbers 20:12), he said.

Because of his failure, Moses wouldn't be allowed to enter the Promised Land. The punishment was harsh, but Moses had ignored God's instructions and robbed him of his glory. Moses couldn't bring water out of a rock if he tried for a million years. But when he said *must we bring you water out of this rock?* he made it seem that he was at least partly responsible for the miracle. And for that he would die.

From this we learn to give the glory to God for whatever good he does though us. If we have a special talent, we give the glory to God. If we get a promotion, we give the glory to God. If our children turn out well, we give the glory to God. *Not to us, Lord, not to us but to your name be the glory* (Psalm 115:1), wrote the Psalmist.

For Reflection and Review

- *How should churches treat their leaders?*
- *How do we know that we belong to Christ?*
- *Why should believers give the credit to God for anything good they do?*

Lesson 36

Numbers 22:4-5 *Balak son of Zippor, who was king of Moab at that time, sent messengers to summon Balaam son of Beor.*

When Balak saw God's people camping near Moab, he knew he couldn't withstand them, and was alarmed by the apparent threat. So he sent for Balaam, a man known for spiritual power, to curse Israel. *Do not let anything keep you from coming to me, because I will reward you handsomely and do whatever you say. Come and put a curse on these people for me* (Numbers 22:16-17), he said.

Numbers 22:21 *Balaam got up in the morning, saddled his donkey and went with the Moabite officials.*

But God was angry at Balaam, and sent an angel with a sword to oppose him. Balaam didn't see the angel, but his donkey did, and tried to avoid it three times. This made Balaam so angry that he beat his donkey severely.

Then the Lord opened the donkey's mouth, and it said to Balaam, What have I done to you to make you beat me these three times? Balaam answered the donkey, You have made a fool of me! If only I had a sword in my hand, I would kill you right now. The donkey said to Balaam, Am I not your own donkey, which you have always ridden, to this day? Have I been in the habit of doing this to you? No, he said.

Then the Lord opened Balaam's eyes, and he saw the angel of the Lord standing in the road with his sword drawn. So he bowed low and fell facedown. The angel of the Lord asked him, Why have you beaten your donkey these three times? I have come here to oppose you because your path is a reckless one before me. The donkey saw me and turned away from me these three times. If it had not turned away, I would certainly have killed you by now, but I would have spared it.

Balaam said to the angel of the Lord, I have sinned. I did not realize you were standing in the road to oppose me. Now if you are displeased, I will go back. The angel of the Lord said to Balaam, Go with the men, but speak only what I tell you. So Balaam went with Balak's officials (Numbers 22:28-35).

God opposes anyone who'd put a curse on his people. *I will bless those who bless you, and whoever curses you I will curse* (Genesis 12:3), he said. Christians are blessed *with every spiritual blessing in Christ* (Ephesians 1:3), and can never be cursed by anyone.

Numbers 22:36 *When Balak heard that Balaam was coming, he went out to meet him.*

Balak showed Balaam the people he wanted cursed, but Balaam could only bless them. *How can I curse those whom God has not cursed?* (Numbers 23:8), he said. *God is not human, that he should lie, not a human being, that he should change his mind. . . . he has blessed, and I cannot change it* (Numbers 23:19-20), he said again.

When we consider Satan's desire for our harm, we have every reason to be afraid. But when we consider God's desire for our good, our fears are put to flight. *Come, you who are blessed by my Father; take your inheritance, the kingdom prepared for you since the creation of the world* (Matthew 25:34), said Jesus. God's people are blessed by him, and he will bless them forever.

*****

Numbers 25:1 *While Israel was staying in Shittim, the men began to indulge in sexual immorality with Moabite women.*

Some of the Moabite women invited some of the Israelite men to worship Baal and engage in ritual sex. This ignited God's anger and he commanded Moses to execute those who were guilty. Before the sentence was carried out, however, an Israelite man brought a Moabite women into his tent *right before the eyes of Moses and the whole assembly of Israel*

(Numbers 25:6). This wasn't a shameful deed done in secret, but an open act of defiance against Moses and God.

Numbers 25:7-8 *When Phinehas son of Eleazar, the son of Aaron, the priest, saw this, he left the assembly, took a spear in his hand and followed the Israelite into the tent. He drove the spear into both of them, right through the Israelite man and into the woman's stomach.*

The crime was a public violation of the first and seventh commandments: *You shall have no other gods before me* (Exodus 20:3) and *You shall not commit adultery* (Exodus 20:14). The execution carried out by Phinehas was according to the penalty for sins committed defiantly: *anyone who sins defiantly, whether native-born or foreigner, blasphemes the Lord and must be cut off from the people of Israel. Because they have despised the Lord's word and broken his commands, they must surely be cut off* (Numbers 15:30-31), wrote Moses. This no longer applies today (Hebrews 8:13), but Phinehas received God's approval for defending his honor.

As the nation of Israel made its way to the Promised Land, it encountered both opposition and seduction. These are the right and left hands of Satan, which he uses to this day. If the world can't intimidate the church through opposition, it will try to win it back through seduction. *You adulterous people, don't you know that friendship with the world means enmity against God? Therefore, anyone who chooses to be a friend of the world becomes an enemy of God* (James 4:4), wrote James.

For Reflection and Review

- *Can Christians ever be cursed?*
- *How could God speak through a donkey?*
- *What are the two ways Satan tries to harm the church?*

Lesson 37

Deuteronomy 1:1 *These are the words Moses spoke to all Israel in the wilderness east of the Jordan.*

The book of Deuteronomy was written by Moses for the people of God around 1406 BC, while the nation camped in the land of Moab, just outside the Promised Land. In a series of speeches, Moses reviewed the covenant God made with Israel after they came out of Egypt, forty years earlier. The first generation had died, and a new generation needed to hear God's word before entering the land. There's little that's new in Deuteronomy, but it's quoted in the New Testament over forty times. Moses knew that he'd shortly die, and this is his farewell address to the nation.

Deuteronomy 6:4 *Hear, O Israel: The Lord our God, the Lord is one.*

There's only one God, the creator and sustainer of all that exists. This conviction made Israel unique among surrounding nations who worshipped many gods. Whenever Israel turned to other gods, they became weak. But when they trusted the one, true, and living God, they became strong. How awesome to know that this same God has become our heavenly Father, through faith in Jesus Christ (Ephesians 1:5).

Deuteronomy 6:5 *Love the Lord your God with all your heart and with all your soul and with all your strength.*

Jesus identified this as the *first and greatest commandment* (Matthew 22:38), which makes it even more important than feeding our children. The reason God wants us to love him with all our heart, soul, and strength is because that's how he loves us. What God wants most from his people is a deep and loving relationship.

We should express our love for God through prayer, obedience, and service but they are not the same as love. Genuine love for God includes an affectionate yearning for more of him. This means turning away from whatever displeases him, and drawing ever closer. Even if our hearts are dry at times, if we truly desire God, we are on the right track.

Deuteronomy 6:6 *These commandments that I give you today are to be on your hearts.*

It's not enough to have the word of God in our heads. After all, Satan has that. Nor is it enough to believe the word of God, or even obey the word of God. We must have the word of God on our hearts—the place of affection. We should, in fact, have the same affection for the word of God that we have for God himself. A good indication of how we feel about God is how we feel about his word. If we don't love his word, our love for God should be called into question.

Deuteronomy 6:7 *Impress them on your children. Talk about them when you sit at home and when you walk along the road, when you lie down and when you get up.*

The word of God is so important for raising our children that it ought to be a normal part of our daily conversation. Some time ago I was out for a hike. As I walked up the trail, I passed a family that was coming down. As we passed each other I overheard the little girl ask her father this question: *If God is loving, why did he allow so many bad things to happen to Job?* (Job 1:1-2:8).

That's a good question, especially from a child. But what truly impressed me was how naturally it occurred in their conversation. The Bible was so important to them that it wasn't reserved for church alone, or even for family devotions, but was naturally discussed as they were out for a hike.

Deuteronomy 6:12 *[B]e careful that you do not forget the Lord, who brought you out of Egypt, out of the land of slavery.*

When God's people came out of Egyptian slavery, he led them *in a pillar of cloud by day and a pillar of fire by night* (Numbers 14:14). All they had to do was look, and they could see the presence of God made visible. But as they entered the Promised Land, that was about to change. They'd spread out to various regions and no longer see the sign of God's presence. So Moses reminded them not to forget the Lord.

A godly man was suffering from Alzheimer's disease, and wrote down everything on note cards. *Turn off the stove*, *check the mail*, and *flush the toilet* were just a few of the notes he wrote. With the passing of time his condition grew worse, and even the notes weren't enough. So he wrote a note on his hand, and copied it over daily: *Remember God.*

There are many things in our busy lives that compete with God for our attention. But we can remember God each morning through prayer and Bible study. Then, as we go about our daily tasks, God will never be far from our thoughts.

Deuteronomy 6:18 *Do what is right and good in the Lord's sight, so that it may go well with you.*

Since God determines the quality of our lives, it's always wise to obey him. Under the old covenant, God promised to bless his people if they were obedient, and to curse them if they were disobedient (Deuteronomy 28). Since rewards and punishments often came quickly, Moses encouraged God's people to always do the right thing.

Following Christ may involve hardship (John 16:33), but this principle still applies. *[G]odliness has value for all things, holding promise for both the present life and the life to come* (1 Timothy 4:8), wrote Paul. If we do what is right and good in the Lord's eyes, we might be surprised by all the good he does for us.

For Reflection and Review

- *Why does God want us to love him?*
- *Does God ever slip away from your thoughts?*
- *How does serving God improve your life?*

Lesson 38

Deuteronomy 7:6 *The Lord your God has chosen you out of all the peoples on the face of the earth to be his people, his treasured possession.*

Some people are hard to shop for because they have everything they want. God is the owner of everything, so there's nothing we can give him that he doesn't already have—except our hearts. When a sinner gives their heart to God, he's so enriched that the sinner becomes his *treasured possession*.

I was six years old when my dad made a special slingshot just for me. He cut a branch from a tree and whittled it smooth. Then he attached two strips of rubber and leather pouch. It fit my hand perfectly, and made me feel dangerous! I carried my slingshot everywhere and, for a while, it was my treasured possession. Then, one day, I put it in my pocket and, when I got home, it was gone. I traced my steps with tears, but it was never found.

Thankfully, that never happens to God. *I shall lose none of all those he has given me* (John 6:39), said Jesus. All who belong to Jesus Christ will be treasured by him forever. We are his *treasured* possessions.

Deuteronomy 8:3 *[M]an does not live on bread alone but on every word that comes from the mouth of the Lord.*

After fasting forty days, Jesus was hungrier than most people will ever be. But when the devil told him to satisfy his hunger by turning stones into bread, he quoted this verse to him (Matthew 4:4). From this we learn that it's more important to feed our souls than it is to feed our bodies. If we have to choose between breakfast and the Bible, we should always choose the Bible. It's better to have a full soul and an empty stomach, than to have a full stomach and an empty soul.

Getting through the Bible seems like a difficult task, but it's not very hard if we read it daily. By reading a chapter of the Bible, almost every day, we can read the whole Bible in under four years. If we do this repeatedly, we'll probably read the Bible several times before we die.

Deuteronomy 8:4 *Your clothes did not wear out . . . during these forty years.*

Throughout their journey, God fed his people bread from heaven (Exodus 16:4), and gave them water from a rock (Exodus 17:6). These were clear and obvious miracles for everyone to see. What they may've overlooked, however, is that God was doing a more subtle miracle. He was keeping their clothes from wearing out over the course of forty years.

When we get to heaven, we'll likely discover things God did for us that we didn't notice at the time. Some miracles are obvious, others are only seen in hindsight. God is always doing more for us than we know at the time, and we can thank him for it.

Deuteronomy 10:16 *. . . do not be stiff-necked any longer.*

Several times throughout the Bible, God's people are accused of being *stiff-necked*. The problem wasn't medical, but a rebellious attitude. They were like animals that wouldn't be guided by their owners.

Many years ago I rode a horse that was intent on going its own way. When I pulled to the right, it stiffened its neck. When I pulled to the left, it did the same. It even went under a low-hanging branch in order to knock me off. I didn't like that horse at all.

A proper animal responds quickly to a tug on the reigns, and is a joy to its owner. We can't be guided by God if we insist on our own way. Instead of being stiff-necked, we should learn pray like Christ: *not my will, but yours be done* (Luke 22:42).

Deuteronomy 14:1 *You are the children of the Lord your God.*

The Israelites were formerly slaves, and had been living in the desert forty years. In spite of their circumstances, Moses wanted them to know who they really were—dearly loved children of God. This is the highest possible status, and also the happiest. *See what great love the Father has lavished on us, that we should be called children of God!* (1 John 3:1), wrote John.

Few things affect our behavior more than what we think of ourselves. If we think we're unloved, unlovely, and unlovable—that's how we'll act. But if we know that we're dearly loved children of God, then we'll live accordingly.

The king's son behaved badly, and did some things of which he was ashamed. He confided in his father who offered this advice: *No one is surprised when common people misbehave, because that's what common people do. But if you remember that you're royalty, then you'll behave royally. Never forget who and whose you are*, he said. God also wants his children to have a clear identity so he tells us plainly, *You are the children of the Lord your God.*

For Reflection and Review

- *Why are God's people his treasured possession?*
- *Why is it foolish to be stiff-necked?*
- *Why does God tell us that we are his children?*

Lesson 39

Deuteronomy 18:15 *The Lord your God will raise up for you a prophet like me from among you, from your fellow Israelites. You must listen to him.*

This prophecy was fulfilled by Jesus Christ about fifteen hundred years later. Jesus was similar to Moses in the following ways: Moses was laid in a basket (Exodus 2:3), and Jesus was laid in manger (Luke 2:7, 16). Moses spent his early years in Egypt, and Jesus spent his early years in Egypt (Matthew 2:13). Moses gave up the glory of the palace, and Jesus gave up the glory of heaven. Moses was the first person in the Old Testament to do miracles, and Jesus was the first person in the New Testament to do miracles.

Moses fed the people bread from heaven (Exodus 16:14), and Jesus multiplied bread on earth (John 6:11). Moses delivered the people from the tyranny of Pharaoh, and Jesus delivers us from the tyranny of Satan. Moses parted the water, and Jesus walked on the water.

Moses was nearly stoned to death, (Exodus 17:4), and Jesus was nearly stoned to death (John 8:59). Moses sacrificed the blood of animals (Exodus 24:5-8), and Jesus sacrificed his own blood (Matthew 26:28). Moses led people to the Promised Land of Canaan, and Jesus leads people to the Promised Land of heaven. Jesus is the prophet like Moses, to whom we ought to listen.

Deuteronomy 26:11 *[R]ejoice in all the good things the Lord your God has given to you and your household.*

God didn't want his people to take their possessions for granted, but to see them as tokens of love from his fatherly hand. If we see our possessions as things we've have earned, they'll do us no spiritual good, and may even harm us. But if we see them as gifts from our heavenly Father, they'll help us love him more.

Until recently, the wealthiest people in the world lived and died without enjoying many things found in most modern homes. They may have had a palace, but not a refrigerator, television, furnace, or air-conditioner. They may have had servants, but not the internet, hot water, or even indoor plumbing. If we see these things as gifts from our heavenly Father, we'll begin to love him as he deserves.

Deuteronomy 29:29 *The secret things belong to the Lord our God, but the things revealed belong to us and to our children forever.*

The Israelites knew little about God until he delivered them from slavery, and gave them his written word. This answered many of their questions, but likely raised even more. The more God reveals himself, the more questions we seem to have. Who has plumbed the depth of the Trinity? Who has resolved the two natures of Christ? Who has solved the problem of evil? These are just a few of *the secret things that belong to the Lord our God.*

[B]ut the things revealed belong to us and to our children forever, wrote Moses. The Bible is an ocean in which a whale can swim, and a child can wade. Some truths lay on the surface, but we'll never reach the bottom. Little children can learn the basics, but scholars can't exhaust it. God is glorified by the reverent study of his word, and his people are enriched by what they learn.

Deuteronomy 30:20 *[T]he Lord is your life.*

The Lord is not a part of your life, an accessory to your life, or tangential to your life. The Lord *is* your life. No Lord, no life. And, if the Lord is your life, then the more you love the Lord, the more you'll love your life. The surest way to happiness, therefore, is to *Love the Lord your God with all your heart and with all your soul and with all your mind and with all your strength* (Mark 12:30).

Deuteronomy 31:6 *[H]e will never leave you nor forsake you.*

Life was about to change for the people of God as they entered the Promised Land. It flowed with milk and honey (Exodus 3:8), but those who lived there wouldn't give it up without a fight. In all their battles and conflicts, God wanted his people to know that he'd never leave them nor forsake them.

This is important to believe when times are good, but especially when times are bad, because that's when we're likely to feel forsaken. Feelings change with the weather but God is always the same. His word is truer than our feelings, and his commitment is the same on the worst day of our life, as it is on the best day of our life.

The Bible doesn't promise that we'll never be divorced, diseased, or bankrupt. But it does promise that God will never leave us nor forsake us. He's always with us to forgive, strengthen, help, guide, and provide. This is a truth on which we must stand.

For Reflection and Review

- *Why is Jesus' similarity to Moses important?*
- *Why does God want us to rejoice in our possessions?*
- *Why must we believe that God will never leave us nor forsake us?*

Lesson 40

Deuteronomy 31:20 *[W]hen they eat their fill and thrive, they will turn to other gods and worship them.*

This is God's problem. Because he's generous, God wants to bless his people with prosperity. But he knows his people are so perverse that, when he makes them prosperous, they'll turn away from him. Instead of being thankful, and serving him more carefully, they'll feel secure enough to go their own way. Even today, few things are more spiritually lethal than financial prosperity. *[It] is hard for someone who is rich to enter the kingdom of heaven* (Matthew 19:23), said Jesus.

This is why God often leaves some of our needs unmet. The more we need from God, the more likely we are to pray to him. The less we need from God, the more likely we are to ignore him. What seems the best for us is often the worst, and what seems the worst for us is often the best. Instead of complaining about what God has withheld, we ought to praise him for keeping us close to him. What could be worse, after all, than having everything we need and turning away from God?

Deuteronomy 33:27 *The eternal God is your refuge, and underneath are the everlasting arms.*

As Moses prepared to die, he pronounced a blessing on the nation and reminded them of God's *everlasting arms.* He's our heavenly father who carries us close to his heart.

Many years ago I moved to another state and left behind family and friends. I was single at the time and, for about a year, had little social network. This made me feel like I was falling without a safety net. But that's never true for God's people: *underneath are the everlasting arms*. The furthest we can ever fall is into his loving embrace.

*****

Deuteronomy 34:1 *Then Moses climbed Mount Nebo from the plains of Moab to the top of Pisgah, across from Jericho.*

Some time earlier, God told Moses to bring water from a rock by speaking to it. Moses disregarded God's word and struck the rock twice with his staff. Then, instead of giving glory to God, he took credit for the miracle himself. As a result, God informed Moses that he wouldn't enter the Promised Land (Exodus 20:1-13). Now he was going up the mountain to die.

From this we understand that *God does not show favoritism* (Romans 2:11). Even his best servants are not exempt from the consequences of their sins. God could've overlooked Moses' sin, but it was important for the people to see that the justice of God applies to everyone—even Moses.

Deuteronomy 34:4 *Then the Lord said to him, This is the land I promised on oath to Abraham, Isaac and Jacob when I said, I will give it to your descendants. I have let you see it with your eyes, but you will not cross over into it.*

God showed Moses kindness by letting him see the Promised Land before he died. He could've died on the plain below, but God sent him to the top of a mountain (Deuteronomy 32:48-50) where he could have a glimpse. How good it must've been for Moses to see with his own eyes the homeland of God's people. *In wrath*, God also remembered *mercy* (Habakkuk 3:2).

Deuteronomy 34:5-6 *And Moses the servant of the Lord died there in Moab, as the Lord had said. He buried him in Moab, in the valley opposite Beth Peor, but to this day no one knows where his grave is.*

By burying Moses himself, God insured that his grave wouldn't become a shrine. Moses was so greatly used by God, that God's people may've been tempted to worship at his grave, rather than at the tabernacle.

God buries his workers but continues his work. Joshua had already been commissioned to be the new leader of Israel. God also raised up prophets, and later sent his Son, who commissioned the apostles (Matthew 28:18-20). And as the Apostle Paul prepared to die, he wrote to Timothy saying, *the things you have heard me say in the presence of many witnesses entrust to reliable people who will also be qualified to teach others* (2 Timothy 2:2). Ministers come and go, but God continues to work.

Deuteronomy 34:7 *Moses was a hundred and twenty years old when he died, yet his eyes were not weak nor his strength gone.*

Moses didn't die from natural causes, but because God shortened his life. Even at a hundred twenty years old he was still strong, and could've served God much longer. But this isn't the end of Moses' story. About fifteen centuries later he appeared on the mountain of transfiguration to talk with Jesus Christ about his approaching crucifixion (Matthew 17:1-13).

Imagine the honor this was for Moses. He died because of his sin, but spoke to the one who'd die for his salvation. He died outside the Promised Land, but stood inside the Promised Land with Jesus. He led God's people to an earthly Promised Land, but spoke to the one who'd lead us to the Promised Land of heaven. Apart from Jesus Christ, Moses' story didn't end very well. But because of Jesus Christ his story ends in glory.

For Reflection and Review

- *Why does God leave some of our needs unmet?*
- *Should Moses' death be a concern to Christian leaders?*
- *How did God show mercy to Moses, even though he had to die?*

Lesson 41

Joshua 1:1-2 *After the death of Moses the servant of the Lord, the Lord said to Joshua son of Nun, Moses' aide: Moses my servant is dead. Now then, you and all these people, get ready to cross the Jordan River into the land I am about to give to them.*

The book of Joshua was written around 1390 BC and, though anonymous, some of it probably came from Joshua himself. The author recounts how, with God's help, Joshua completed Moses' ministry by leading God's people into the Promised Land.

Joshua was probably a slave in Egypt who saw the plagues and followed Moses through the Red Sea. That generation died in the wilderness but, due to their faith, Joshua and Caleb were allowed to live and enter the Promised Land.

Joshua 1:8 *Keep this Book of the Law always on your lips; meditate on it day and night, so that you may be careful to do everything written in it. Then you will be prosperous and successful.*

It wasn't enough for Joshua to be a military genius, he also had to be a student of God's word. The promise of success was based on obedience, which required daily study and meditation. This was also God's will for the future kings of Israel. *When he takes the throne of his kingdom, he is to write for himself on a scroll a copy of this law.... It is to be with him, and he is to read it all the days of his life* (Deuteronomy 17:18-19), wrote Moses.

When Israel's kings departed from God's law, they lost their right to rule God's kingdom. The reason Jesus is qualified to be king of the world (Revelation 19:16) is because he perfectly kept God's word. *Man shall not live on bread alone, but on every word that comes from the mouth of God* (Deuteronomy 8:3, Matthew 4:4), he said.

Joshua 2:1 *Then Joshua son of Nun secretly sent two spies from Shittim. Go, look over the land, he said, especially Jericho. So they went and entered the house of a prostitute named Rahab and stayed there.*

We're not told why the spies went to the house of a prostitute, but there are at least four possible reasons. First, men going to the house of a prostitute was not likely to raise suspicion. Second, a prostitute might be an excellent source of information due to her various clients. Third, because prostitutes aren't known for integrity, she might've been willing to sell this information. Fourth, since good hotels were scarce, some prostitutes also provided lodging.

Joshua 2:2-3 *The king of Jericho was told, Look, some of the Israelites have come here tonight to spy out the land. So the king of Jericho sent this message to Rahab: Bring out the men who came to you and entered your house, because they have come to spy out the whole land.*

Jericho was a city-state and the king perceived the Israelites to be a serious threat. When he learned that Rahab was harboring two of them, he quickly took action. If a king commands you to turn over a couple spies, you either cooperate or become guilty of treason. You either save your life or lose it.

But sometimes saving your life is losing it, and losing your life is saving it. Rahab could save her life for a little while by turning over the spies, or save it forever by putting her trust in God. That's how it is with Christ. *For whoever wants to save their life will lose it, but whoever loses their life for me and for the gospel will save it* (Mark 8:35), said Jesus.

Joshua 2:4-5 *But the woman had taken the two men and hidden them. She said, Yes, the men came to me, but I did not know where they had come from. At dusk, when it was time to close the city gate, they left. I do not know which way they went. Go after them quickly. You may catch up with them.*

It's a little surprising that the king's men trusted the word of a prostitute, but somehow she convinced them. The spies were actually hiding under stalks of flax on Rahab's roof (Joshua 2:6). Flax was used for making linen and was often dried on rooftops. These are the kind of details that add credibility to the story, and draw the reader in.

Joshua 2:7 *So the men set out in pursuit of the spies on the road that leads to the fords of the Jordan, and as soon as the pursuers had gone out, the gate was shut.*

This gave Rahab the time she needed to talk to the spies at length. She told them that fear had fallen on Jericho because they knew God parted the Red Sea for the Israelites, and defeated other kings for them (Numbers 21:21-35). This would be helpful information for Joshua since few things are more important to the outcome of war than morale. It also fulfilled God's word through Moses: *the people of Canaan will melt away; terror and dread will fall on them* (Exodus 15:15-16).

Rahab also made a profession of faith in God: *for the Lord your God is God in heaven above and on the earth below* (Joshua 2:11), she said. We don't know how she came to this conclusion, but Rahab clearly believed in God since she was now on the side of Israel. When Rahab heard about the God who delivered his people from slavery, she probably longed to be his. She may've even prayed that God would let her change sides. So when the opportunity came, she took it.

Like Rahab, our first allegiance is no longer to the kingdom of this world, but to the kingdom of God. We also foresee the day when *The kingdom of the world [will] become the kingdom of our Lord and of his Messiah* (Revelation 11:15), wrote John. We've also committed treason against the *god of this age* (2 Corinthians 4:4) by giving our allegiance to Christ. In these and other ways, Rahab models the Christian life.

Joshua 2:12 *Now then, please swear to me by the Lord that you will show kindness to my family, because I have shown kindness to you.*

The spies' agreement to spare Rahab and her family is a little surprising in light of an earlier command given by God through Moses. *Make no treaty with them, and show them no mercy* (Deuteronomy 7:2). But, upon her profession of faith, this is precisely what they did.

The division between Israelite and non-Israelite was less about ethnicity than allegiance to God. This is why Paul called the church *the Israel of God* (Galatians 6:16). A true Israelite isn't someone with Abraham's DNA, but with Abraham's faith (Galatians 3:7). Because she believed in the God of Abraham, Rahab was allowed to live.

Joshua 2:21 *So she sent them away, and they departed. And she tied the scarlet cord in the window.*

The scarlet cord was a prearranged sign that would identify Rahab's house to Israel's army. Everyone else in the city would be destroyed, but the soldiers were to spare the house with the scarlet cord in the window.

A scarlet cord was probably used because Rahab had one, and because it could be seen. But, later, it would remind the Israelites of their escape from Egypt. They were saved by the scarlet blood of a Passover lamb, applied to the door frames of their homes (Exodus 12:1-30). And *Christ, our Passover lamb, has been sacrificed* (1 Corinthians 5:7), wrote Paul. Scarlet is the color of blood, and we're saved by the blood of Christ.

Rahab is also mentioned three times in the New Testament: once for her faith (Hebrews 11:31), once for her works (James 2:25), and once in the genealogy of Christ (Matthew 1:5). The woman who started out as Canaanite prostitute became part of God's people and a great, great, grandmother of the Savior of the world. It's truly remarkable what God can do for ordinary people who trust him.

For Reflection and Review

- *Why did God want all the kings of Israel to know his word?*
- *How does Rahab model the Christian life?*
- *Why was Rahab allowed to live?*

Lesson 42

Joshua 3:1 *Early in the morning Joshua and all the Israelites . . . went to the Jordan, where they camped before crossing over.*

Forty years earlier God parted the Red Sea for Moses, so he could lead the people of God out of Egyptian slavery. Now he'd dry up the Jordan River for Joshua, so he could lead them into the Promised Land. Joshua was the new leader of Israel, and this was the moment they'd all been waiting for.

Joshua 3:3 *When you see the ark of the covenant of the Lord your God, and the Levitical priests carrying it, you are to move out from your positions and follow it.*

The ark of the covenant was normally kept in the tabernacle, in the Most Holy Place. But, on a few occasions, it was used to lead the people of God in solemn procession. The ark is so important to this story it's mentioned no fewer than sixteen times.

It's frequently called the *ark of the covenant* because it contained the Ten Commandments (Exodus 25:16), which were the basis of the covenant God made with Israel forty years earlier. The ark symbolized God's throne (Exodus 25:22), so the people were to understand that God, their king, was leading them into the Promised Land.

Joshua 3:4 *But keep a distance of about two thousand cubits between you and the ark; do not go near it.*

Because the ark symbolized God's throne, the people were to keep a respectful distance. Two thousand cubits is over half a mile, which would allow more people to see the ark than if it was being crowded. The ark was so sacred that no one was allowed to touch it on pain of death (2 Samuel 6:7). Even those who carried the ark had to use poles, inserted into rings, that were mounted on its side (Exodus 25:14).

Joshua 3:8 *Tell the priests who carry the ark of the covenant: When you reach the edge of the Jordan's waters, go and stand in the river.*

The Jordan River is neither wide nor deep, but the spring rains (and melting snow from Mount Hermon) caused it swell to about a hundred feet wide and ten feet deep. The strength of the current would also make it difficult to pass. Without any sign of the water's abating, however, the priests were told to *stand in the river*.

This is important because sometimes God requires his people to act on faith before they see his provision. The man with the shriveled hand was healed as he stretched it out (Luke 6:10); the bread and fish were multiplied as they were being distributed (John 6:11); and the Jordan River would cease to flow only after the priests stepped into it.

Joshua 3:15-16 *[A]s soon as the priests who carried the ark reached the Jordan and their feet touched the water's edge, the water from upstream stopped flowing. It piled up in a heap a great distance away, at a town called Adam.*

Perhaps God put his hand in the river at Adam, and stopped the flow himself. But why would he do it so far away? The place where the water stopped flowing is about eighteen miles upstream. Why didn't God put his hand in the water right in front of the Israelites so they could see his mighty power?

God often works directly, but also uses means. More than once the Jordan River has stopped flowing near Adam due to a mudslide. As recently as 1927, in fact, the water stopped flowing for over twenty hours.

The Jordan Valley is on a fault line where earthquakes are known to occur. If an earthquake caused a mudslide to stop the river's flow, just as the priests were stepping in, that would be no less a miracle than if God did it directly. The discovery of a natural cause, in fact, gives additional credibility to the biblical record. We not only know what God did, we may even know how he did it.

Joshua 3:17 *The priests who carried the ark of the covenant of the Lord stopped in the middle of the Jordan* *and stood on dry ground, while all Israel passed by until the whole nation had completed the crossing on dry ground.*

And, *No sooner had they set their feet on the dry ground than the waters of the Jordan returned to their place and ran at flood stage as before* (Joshua 4:18).

By a miracle of timing, God revealed his providential care for his people. If they had arrived an hour sooner the miracle would not have worked. And if they'd taken an hour longer to cross, the miracle would not have worked either. But the moment they stepped into the river, the water stopped flowing. And the moment they stepped out of the river, the water returned to flood stage. The God of Israel is also the Lord of time. We may not always like his timing, but we can always trust it.

*****

Joshua 5:13-15 *Now when Joshua was near Jericho, he looked up and saw a man standing in front of him with a drawn sword in his hand. Joshua went up to him and asked, Are you for us or for our enemies? Neither, he replied, but as commander of the army of the Lord I have now come. Then Joshua fell facedown to the ground in reverence, and asked him, What message does my Lord have for his servant? The commander of the Lord's army replied, Take off your sandals, for the place where you are standing is holy. And Joshua did so.*

As Joshua prepared to fight the battle of Jericho, he met a heavenly figure with a drawn sword. His loyalty wasn't to the Israelites, or to the Canaanites, but to God alone. From this we understand that God is always for himself. Many want God to be on their side, but God is always on his own side. There are only two sides in life, and whoever is on God's side wins in the end.

The heavenly figure in this passage identified himself as the *commander of the army of the Lord* (Joshua 5:14). Israel was God's army on earth, but God also has an army in heaven. *The chariots of God are tens of thousands and thousands of thousands* (Psalm 68:17), wrote the Psalmist. As Joshua fought God's battles on earth, he was encouraged to know that heaven would also be fighting.

The commander revealed his heavenly identity when he said, *Take off your sandals, for the place where you are standing is holy* (Joshua 5:15). Since this is what God said to Moses at the burning bush, we know this figure is divine. And since Jesus said, *These are the very Scriptures that testify about me* (John 5:39), we know this figure is Christ. Not only that, but the fact that his sword is drawn reminds us of Christ's return. *Coming out of his mouth is a sharp sword with which to strike down the nations* (Revelation 19:15), wrote John. The gentle shepherd is also a conquering king.

For Reflection and Review

- Why was the ark of the covenant used to lead God's people?
- How did God stop the Jordan River from flowing?
- How do we know the commander of the army of the Lord was Christ?

Lesson 43

Joshua 6:1 *Now the gates of Jericho were securely barred because of the Israelites.*

The city of Jericho was terrified by Israel's crossing the Jordan River. They knew the God of Israel had parted the Red Sea, and defeated other kings (Joshua 2:10). They also knew that they were next. But instead of surrendering to God, they barred their gates against him. They knew this day was coming, and had probably stored up supplies. They hoped to survive, of course, but would rather die than surrender to Israel's God.

Joshua 6:2 *Then the Lord said to Joshua, See, I have delivered Jericho into your hands, along with its king and its fighting men.*

The conquest of a walled city was a major challenge, but God spoke as though the victory had already been won. Israel would have to fight, but the outcome was assured. They could fight with confidence, not in themselves, but in the God who promised them victory.

The church is also assured of victory as we take the gospel to the world. We don't use the *weapons of the world* (2 Corinthians 10:4), but the gospel of Jesus Christ. And *we are more than conquerers through him who loved us* (Romans 8:37), wrote Paul. The battle has been raging for centuries but, in the end, there will be people *from every nation, tribe, people and language, standing before the throne and before the Lamb* (Revelation 7:9), wrote John. The battle must be fought, but outcome is assured.

Joshua 6:3-5 *March around the city once with all the armed men. Do this for six days. Have seven priests carry trumpets of rams' horns in front of the ark. On the seventh day, march around the city seven times, with the priests blowing the trumpets. When you hear them sound a long blast on the trumpets, have the whole army give a loud shout; then the wall of the city will collapse and the army will go up, everyone straight in.*

This may be the most unusual military strategy ever devised. It was designed by God to be so unlikely that only he would get the credit. The presence of the ark of the covenant also showed that Jericho's defeat was, first and foremost, the work of God.

The soldiers could've complained that the battle plan didn't make sense. But unless they did it God's way they would've been defeated. Children don't always understand why their parents tell them to do something, and often ask *Why?* But parents have authority over their children and, *Because I said so* is still a good reason. That's why we're obligated to obey God, even when his ways don't make sense to us.

But God was also giving the city time to repent. He doesn't want *anyone to perish, but everyone to come to repentance* (2 Peter 3:9), wrote Peter. Jericho was surrounded, and their doom was sure. Why not open the gate and surrender? Some people are so opposed to God that they resist him to the end.

Joshua 6:20 *When the trumpets sounded, the army shouted, and at the sound of the trumpet, when the men gave a loud shout, the wall collapsed; so everyone charged straight in, and they took the city.*

If you go to Jericho today, you'll find the main attraction is the ancient wall that collapsed. It's been thoroughly excavated and the following four items are consistent with the biblical record. First, there's evidence of collapsed walls. Second, there's evidence of a rapid defeat. Third, there's evidence of a fire. And, fourth, there's evidence that it happened around 1400 BC, which is the date of this story. Archaeology can't prove the Bible, but it consistently supports the truthfulness of God's word.

Joshua 6:21 *They devoted the city to the Lord and destroyed with the sword every living thing in it—men and women, young and old, cattle, sheep and donkeys.*

This was consistent with God's command through Moses: *do not leave alive anything that breathes. Completely destroy them . . . as the Lord your God has commanded you. Otherwise, they will teach you to follow all the detestable things they do in worshiping their gods, and you will sin against the Lord your God* (Deuteronomy 20:16-18).

But what kind of God would command the annihilation of an entire region of people? Answer: the God who has a right to. God is the giver of life and has the right to take it away. Every day is a gift from God, and no one deserves tomorrow. *[T]he wages of sin is death* (Romans 6:23), wrote Paul. Because we sin every day, every day should be our last. The fact that anyone lives another day proves that God is gracious.

But like the people of Noah's day (Genesis 6), and the people of Sodom (Genesis 19), those who lived in Canaan were especially wicked. Their rejection of God included worshipping idols, sexual perversion, and killing children. God had been patient for hundreds of years but, finally, their sin had *reached its full measure* (Genesis 15:16). *A faithful God who does no wrong, upright and just is he* (Deuteronomy 32:4), wrote Moses.

The annihilation of Jericho also reminds us of what will happen when Jesus Christ returns. *The armies of heaven were following him, riding on white horses. . . . Coming out of his mouth is a sharp sword with which to strike down the nations. . . . He treads the winepress of the fury of the wrath of God Almighty* (Revelation 19:14-15), wrote John. The return of Jesus Christ to judge the world will make the destruction of Jericho seem like child's play.

Joshua 6:22 *Joshua said to the two men who had spied out the land, Go into the prostitute's house and bring her out and all who belong to her, in accordance with your oath to her.*

Rahab sided with Israel's God by harboring Israel's spies, and by giving them useful information (Joshua 2). She took her life in her hands, and could've been killed for treason. But she sided with God and was saved.

And all who put their faith in Jesus Christ will also be saved. *[T]his is the will of him who sent me, that I shall lose none of all those he has given me* (John 6:39), said Jesus. Not a single man, woman, boy, or girl who truly believes in Jesus Christ will ever be lost. *The Lord knows those who are his* (2 Timothy 2:19), and will not *kill the righteous with the wicked* (Genesis 18:25). He will save each and every person who truly believes in Jesus Christ (John 3:16).

For Reflection and Review

- *Why did God use a battle plan that didn't make sense?*
- *Does archaeology prove the Bible is true?*
- *Why did God command the slaughter of Jericho?*

Lesson 44

Joshua 7:2 *Now Joshua sent men from Jericho to Ai . . . and told them, Go up and spy out the region.*

After the fall of Jericho, Joshua turned his attention to the little town of Ai. If God's army advanced quickly, the whole land could be theirs in a very short time. Like a train gathering speed, they were gathering momentum.

When the spies returned from Ai, they were so confident it could be conquered, that they recommended only two or three thousand soldiers be sent to overthrow it. To everyone's surprise, however, Ai scattered Israel's army, and killed thirty-six of their soldiers. This was a catastrophic disaster because now it was clear to everyone that Israel could be defeated. All their enemies would be emboldened to fight, and all their momentum was lost. It was a devastating setback to the entire military campaign.

Joshua 7:6 *Then Joshua tore his clothes and fell facedown to the ground before the ark of the Lord, remaining there till evening.*

As Joshua lay facedown before the ark of the covenant, God revealed the reason for Israel's defeat: *Israel has sinned . . . . They have taken some of the devoted things [and] put them with their own possessions* (Joshua 7:11), he said.

The previous attack on Jericho came with clear instructions: *All the silver and gold and the articles of bronze and iron are sacred to the Lord and must go into his treasury* (Joshua 6:19). But an Israelite soldier named Achan found some precious things in Jericho, and kept them for himself. God was now withholding his support until Achan be singled out and put to death.

Through a process of elimination God exposed the guilty person. All the tribes of Israel came forward and the tribe of Judah was chosen. That was Achan's tribe. Then the clans of Judah came forward and the Zerahites were chosen. That was Achan's clan. Then the Zerahite families came forward and the family of Zimri was chosen. That was Achan's family. Then the men of Zimri came forward and Achan himself was chosen (Joshua 7:16-18). Now his doom was sure.

At any point in the process, Achan could've confessed and begged for mercy. We can imagine his heart pounding faster and faster as the circle of suspects got smaller and smaller. Should he come clean, or hope to get away with it? He might never outlive the shame, but perhaps he could save his life. The tension nearly killed him, but Achan refused to confess until it was too late.

Joshua 7:19-21 *Then Joshua said to Achan, My son, give glory to the Lord, the God of Israel, and honor him. Tell me what you have done; do not hide it from me. Achan replied, It is true! I have sinned against the Lord, the God of Israel. This is what I have done: When I saw in the plunder a beautiful robe from Babylonia, two hundred shekels of silver and a bar of gold weighing fifty shekels, I coveted them and took them. They are hidden in the ground inside my tent, with the silver underneath.*

We can imagine Achan's temptation when he saw the precious things. It was a life-changing amount of wealth that could have established his family for years. Perhaps he never stole a thing before, but when he saw the opportunity he took it, and hoped for the best. But what he got was the worst.

Joshua 7:24-25 *Then Joshua, together with all Israel, took Achan son of Zerah, the silver, the robe, the gold bar, his sons and daughters, his cattle, donkeys and sheep, his tent and all that he had, to the Valley of Achor. Joshua said, Why have you brought this trouble on us? The Lord will bring trouble on you today. Then all Israel stoned him, and after they had stoned the rest, they burned them.*

From Achan we learn the importance of not concealing our sins. *Whoever conceals their sins does not prosper, but the one who confesses and renounces them finds mercy* (Proverbs 28:13), says Proverbs. When we conceal our sins we put God to the test, and dare him to expose us. But *If we confess our sins, he is faithful and just and will forgive us our sins* (1 John 1:9), wrote John. If Achan could speak from the grave he'd say the best time to confess our sins is before it's too late.

Joshua 8:1 *Then the Lord said to Joshua . . . . go up and attack Ai.*

At God's direction, Israel positioned troops behind the city, to wait in secret. Then Joshua led other troops in front of the city to lure the soldiers out. When Ai's solders saw the troops of Israel, they ran out to fight. Then Joshua gave the signal and the troops behind the city ran in and set it on fire. When Ai's solders saw their city burning, they knew they'd lost the battle. Then Israel's troops turned on them and slaughtered them all. Ai's king was brought to Joshua and his body was hung on a pole as warning to surrounding kings.

In this case, God provided a strategy that made perfect sense and was completely effective. God's ways don't always make sense, but sometimes they do. As the church seeks to spread the gospel, it should consider what strategies God may be pleased to use. Some strategies have worked well in the past, and others are working well today. God works with and through his people to accomplish his mission on earth.

For Reflection and Review

- *Why was the defeat at Ai a catastrophic setback?*
- *Why did God use a process of elimination to identify Achan?*
- *Why are strategies useful for spreading the gospel?*

Lesson 45

Joshua 9:3-4 *[W]hen the people of Gibeon heard what Joshua had done to Jericho and Ai, they resorted to a ruse.*

Gibeon was about nineteen miles from Israel's camp, and they feared for their lives. They knew God had commanded Moses to wipe out everyone who lived in the land (Joshua 9:24, Deuteronomy 7:1-2), so they tricked Israel into making a treaty with them. They put on old clothes, took old bread, and pretended to come from far away. *The Israelites sampled their provisions but did not inquire of the Lord. Then Joshua made a treaty of peace with them to let them live, and the leaders of the assembly ratified it by oath* (Joshua 9:14-15).

When Israel learned that the Gibeonites lived nearby, they were upset with their leaders for being deceived. The Gibeonites were forced into hard labor, but they were allowed to live because of the oath.

We admire the Gibeonites for their fear of God, and the resourceful way they saved their lives. But Israel's leaders, including Joshua, are to be faulted for not seeking God in this matter. Whenever we have to make an important decision we should seek God's will through prayer, his word, and godly advisers (Proverbs 15:22). This is what Joshua failed to do, and he lost credibility because of it.

*****

Joshua 10:5 *Then the five kings of the Amorites—the kings of Jerusalem, Hebron, Jarmuth, Lachish and Eglon—joined forces.*

In a collective effort to stop God's people, five local kings combined armies. But Joshua refused to be stopped and, after an all night march, he surprised the opposing armies with an early morning attack. God helped his people by hurling hail from heaven that killed more enemies than died by the sword.

But Joshua needed more time, so he *said to the Lord in the presence of Israel: Sun, stand still over Gibeon, and you, moon, over the Valley of Aijalon. So the sun stood still, and the moon stopped, till the nation avenged itself on its enemies. . . . There has never been a day like it before or since, a day when the Lord listened to a human being* (Joshua 10:12-14).

Whoever heard Joshua command the sun and the moon to stand still must've wondered what he was thinking. Would a man control the movement of planets? Even Joshua may've been surprised by the words that came out of his mouth.

This kind of faith can only come from above. *Truly I tell you, if anyone says to this mountain, Go, throw yourself into the sea, and does not doubt in their heart but believes that what they say will happen, it will be done for them* (Mark 11:23), said Jesus. If God is going to do an extraordinary miracle, he can give his servants faith, and then do what they ask.

This miracle is so remarkable, in fact, that some have questioned it's truthfulness. But if God can create everything out of nothing (Genesis 1:1), he can certainly lengthen a day. *The God who made the world and everything in it is the Lord of heaven and earth* (Acts 17:24), said Paul. God can do whatever he wants, whenever he wants, wherever he wants. Nothing is too difficult for him (Jeremiah 32:17).

We have further assurance of this account from Jesus Christ himself. *It is easier for heaven and earth to disappear than for the least stroke of a pen to drop out of the Law* (Luke 16:17), he said. Whoever believes in Jesus Christ must believe what Jesus taught, and Jesus taught the Bible is true. Whoever doesn't believe the Bible, doesn't fully believe in Jesus Christ.

*****

Joshua 22:4 *[R]eturn to your homes in the land that Moses the servant of the Lord gave you on the other side of the Jordan.*

It took about seven years for Israel to conquer the Promised Land. Then it was time for the soldiers who settled east of the Jordan to return home. Before they crossed the river, however, they built an altar to the Lord as a reminder to their fellow Israelites that they all served the same God. But those on the west side of the river thought the altar was an act of rebellion against God, and they prepared for war. Thankfully, the confusion was dispelled, and war was avoided.

Zeal for God is good, but Satan can use it against us if we're not careful. Misdirected zeal even led to the crucifixion of Christ. *You have heard the blasphemy. What do you think? They all condemned him as worthy of death* (Mark 14:64), wrote Mark. *[T]hey are zealous for God, but their zeal is not based on knowledge* (Romans 10:2), wrote Paul. This has been true of the church as well.

In the eighteenth century over a dozen women were hanged near Salem Massachusetts, for the crime of witchcraft. Common sense gave way to hysteria as ordinary people tried to do the will of God. Their actions led to wrongful deaths and harmed the cause of Christ. Zeal without knowledge, and knowledge without zeal, are equally harmful to the church. Christians should pray for godly ministers, whose zeal is based on knowledge.

For Reflection and Review

- *What did Joshua do wrong when he negotiated with the Gibeonites?*
- *Why should we believe that God stopped the sun for Joshua?*
- *How can Satan use our zeal for God?*

Lesson 46

Judges 1:1 *After the death of Joshua, the Israelites asked the Lord, Who of us is to go up first to fight against the Canaanites?*

The book of Judges begins where the book of Joshua ends, and covers events from around 1375 to 1100 BC. The author isn't identified, but seems to have written around 1000 BC. Before Israel had a king it was loosely organized, led by various judges, and was often in a state of apostasy. The book of Judges recounts several events from these dark days.

Judges 1:6 *Adoni-Bezek fled, but they chased him and caught him, and cut off his thumbs and big toes.*

After defeating the city of Bezek, Israel captured its king. They should've put him to death (Deuteronomy 20:16-18) but chose, instead, to cut off his thumbs and big toes. This would prevent him from ever wielding a sword effectively, or being sure-footed in battle.

Joshua 1:7 Then Adoni-Bezek said, *Seventy kings with their thumbs and big toes cut off have picked up scraps under my table. Now God has paid me back for what I did to them.*

Adoni-Bezek had cut off the thumbs and big toes of seventy other kings, and fed them scraps under his table. Now that he suffered the same way, he was convinced that God was paying him back. And he was probably right. *Anyone who injures their neighbor is to be injured in the same manner: fracture for fracture, eye for eye, tooth for tooth. The one who has inflicted the injury must suffer the same injury* (Leviticus 24:19-20), said God. From this we understand that God requires nothing less than perfect justice.

This is why Judgment Day should be the dread fear of unrepentant sinners. When we consider the extent of our sins, and the justice of God, we have nothing to look forward to but wrath. *For a fire will be kindled by my wrath, one that burns down to the realm of the dead below* (Deuteronomy 32:22), said God.

But there's more to God than perfect justice; he's also perfect love (1 John 4:8). This is why he sent his Son to die on a cross for our sins (John 3:16). Jesus fulfilled the demands of God's justice by suffering in our place. That's why whoever believes in him *has eternal life and will not be judged* (John 5:24), said Jesus. The God of perfect justice has paid for our sins himself, so that we can receive his perfect love forever.

*****

Judges 3:12 *Again the Israelites did evil in the eyes of the Lord, and because they did this evil the Lord gave Eglon king of Moab power over Israel.*

Israel was subject to the king of Moab for eighteen years. But they cried out to God, and he raised up a leader named *Ehud* to deliver them. Ehud brought tribute to Eglon, king of Moab, but concealed a double-edged sword under his clothing. After he gave Eglon the tribute, Ehud said, *I have a message from God for you* (Judges 3:20).

Eglon was a very fat man and, as he rose from his seat, *Ehud reached with his left hand, drew the sword from his right thigh and plunged it into the king's belly. Even the handle sank in after the blade, and his bowels discharged. Ehud did not pull the sword out, and the fat closed in over it.*

Then Ehud went out to the porch; he shut the doors of the upper room behind him and locked them. After he had gone, the servants came and found the doors of the upper room locked. They said, He must be relieving himself in the inner room of the palace. They waited to the point of embarrassment, but when he did not open the doors of the room, they took a key and unlocked them. There they saw their lord fallen to the floor, dead (Judges 3:21-25).

We're surprised by the graphic details of the story, but they're included for a reason. Kings are often held in awe by ordinary people, but are ordinary too. They have ordinary bodies, and ordinary functions, and are as prone to death as anyone else. They may feel superior, due to their position, but will lie in a grave like everyone else.

Death comes to all, and makes us equal when it comes. The world elevates one above another, but the worms make no distinction. We are what we are in the sight of God, nothing more and nothing less. We should never think that we're successful, therefore, until after Judgment Day. *[M]any who are first will be last, and many who are last will be first* (Matthew 19:30), said Jesus.

Judges 3:26 *While they waited, Ehud got away.*

Then he gathered an army that followed him back to Moab, where they killed about ten thousand soldiers. *That day Moab was made subject to Israel, and the land had peace for eighty years* (Judges 3:30).

Ehud was used by God to deliver his people from foreign oppression. He reminds us that one person with God is greater than an army without him. Our greatest usefulness is not what we can do for God, but what God can do through us. Our first concern should always be to follow God.

*****

Judges 4:1 *Again the Israelites did evil in the eyes of the Lord, now that Ehud was dead.*

Due to their disobedience, God allowed the Israelites to be afflicted by Jabin, the king of Canaan. He had nine hundred chariots and *cruelly oppressed the Israelites for twenty years* (Judges 4:3).

Deborah was Israel's judge, at this time, and was also a prophet. Through her, God commanded an Israelite named *Barak* to gather ten thousand men to defeat Jabin's army, which was being led by a man named *Sisera*.

Barak was reluctant, but agreed to the mission if Deborah would go with him. She agreed but, due to his reluctance, the honor of the battle wouldn't go to him, but to a woman, she predicted (Judges 4:9). *Barak pursued the chariots . . . and all Sisera's troops fell by the sword* (Judges 4:16).

Sisera escaped, however, and fled on foot to a woman's tent. *Jael went out to meet Sisera and said to him, Come, my lord, come right in. Don't be afraid. So he entered her tent, and she covered him with a blanket. I'm thirsty, he said. Please give me some water. She opened a skin of milk, gave him a drink, and covered him up. Stand in the doorway of the tent, he told her. If someone comes by and asks you, Is anyone in there? say No.*

But Jael . . . picked up a tent peg and a hammer and went quietly to him while he lay fast asleep, exhausted. She drove the peg through his temple into the ground, and he died. Just then Barak came by in pursuit of Sisera, and Jael went out to meet him. Come, she said, I will show you the man you're looking for. So he went in with her, and there lay Sisera with the tent peg through his temple—dead (Judges 4:17-22).

With nine hundred chariots Sissera seemed invincible. But he died at the hands of a woman, armed with a hammer and a tent peg. Those with every advantage may lose in the end, but those who trust God will be victorious. *Some trust in chariots and some in horses, but we trust in the name of the Lord our God* (Psalm 20:7), wrote David.

For Reflection and Review

- *What should we learn from Adoni-Bezek?*
- *What should we learn from the graphic details of Eglon's death?*
- *What should we learn from Sissera's defeat?*

Lesson 47

Judges 6:1 *The Israelites did evil in the eyes of the Lord, and for seven years he gave them into the hands of the Midianites.*

The Midianites were so oppressive that Israel was forced to live in caves just to survive. They systematically destroyed Israel's crops, and slaughtered or stole their livestock. Under such distress, Israel remembered God and cried out to him for help.

About that time the angel of the Lord appeared to Gideon, who was threshing wheat in secret to keep it from the Midianites. *The Lord is with you, mighty warrior* (Judges 6:12), said the angel. Gideon didn't look like a mighty warrior, and wasn't behaving like one. But the angel of the Lord saw what Gideon could become, and commissioned him to save the nation. When Gideon objected the Lord answered, *I will be with you* (Judges 6:16).

This is God's response whenever we're given a task that is beyond us. It could be saving a nation, leading a ministry, or raising a difficult child. It could be starting a church, or taking final exams. After he commissioned his disciples to evangelize the world Jesus said, *surely I am with you always, to the very end of the age* (Matthew 28:20). God's presence gives us the courage and strength to do what we couldn't do on our own.

Judges 6:17 *Gideon replied, If now I have found favor in your eyes, give me a sign that it is really you talking to me.*

When Gideon prepared a meal, *the angel of the Lord touched the meat and the unleavened bread with the tip of the staff that was in his hand. Fire flared from the rock, consuming the meat and the bread. And the angel of the Lord disappeared* (Judges 6:21). This was enough for Gideon and now he was ready to do God's will.

Gideon's father had an altar to Baal, and the Lord told Gideon to tear it down. This was a dangerous act, however, so he did it after dark. When the people discovered what Gideon did, they wanted him dead. But his father said, *If Baal really is a god, he can defend himself* (Judges 6:31). Gideon's life was spared, but this event shows how apostate God's people had become. They were willing to kill Gideon for opposing a false religion.

Judges 6:36-37 *Gideon said to God, If you will save Israel by my hand as you have promised—look, I will place a wool fleece on the threshing floor. If there is dew only on the fleece and all the ground is dry, then I will know that you will save Israel by my hand, as you said.*

The weakness of Gideon's faith is surprising. God already gave him a sign, but now he wanted another. He wanted to leave wool on the ground overnight. If the ground was dry in the morning, but the wool was wet, that would be a sign that God would do what he said.

This is precisely what happened but, to be sure it wasn't a coincidence, Gideon asked God to give him the opposite sign the following day. Then the ground was covered with dew, but the wool was completely dry.

Gideon's lack of faith is not commendable, and his method of testing God isn't recommended. But we should remember that Gideon didn't have a Bible, and was about to risk his life. He just wanted some assurance that he was doing the right thing.

Many have followed Gideon's example of testing God's will, but the best way to know God's will is to learn the Bible thoroughly, and then apply it wisely. *Your word is a lamp for my feet, a light on my path* (Psalm 119:105), wrote the Psalmist.

Judges 7:1 *Early in the morning [Gideon] and all his men camped at the spring of Harod.*

Gideon gathered an army of thirty-two thousand men, but God told him to send some away, so Israel wouldn't take credit for the victory. Gideon must've gasped when twenty-two thousand walked away, leaving him with only ten thousand soldiers. But God insisted that was still too many, so Gideon reduced the troops to only three hundred. Now the odds of victory were so remote that all the credit would go to God.

Judges 7:8-9 *Now the camp of Midian lay below him in the valley. During that night the Lord said to Gideon, Get up, go down against the camp, because I am going to give it into your hands.*

Gideon was fearful, so God told him to go and listen to what the Midianites were saying. *Gideon arrived just as a man was telling a friend his dream. . . . A round loaf of barley bread came tumbling into the Midianite camp. It struck the tent with such force that the tent overturned and collapsed. His friend responded, This can be nothing other than the sword of Gideon son of Joash, the Israelite. God has given the Midianites and the whole camp into his hands* (Judges 7:13-14).

Judges 7:15 *When Gideon heard the dream and its interpretation, he bowed down and worshiped. He returned to the camp of Israel and called out, Get up! The Lord has given the Midianite camp into your hands.*

He gave each of his three hundred soldiers a torch, concealed by a clay jar, and also a trumpet. When they surrounded the Midianite camp, they blew their trumpets, revealed their torches, and gave a mighty shout. Three hundred torches and trumpets gave the illusion of thousands of soldiers. The Midianites panicked and, in the darkness, began to kill each other.

God's trumpets and torches are better than the swords of his enemies. It's not the mighty who win in the end, but the weak who trust in Christ. *God chose the weak things of the world to shame the strong. God chose the lowly things of this world and the despised things —and the things that are not—to nullify the things that are, so that no one may boast before him* (1 Corinthians 1:27-29), wrote Paul. God's people win in the end, not because they're mighty, but because their God is mighty.

Judges 8:22 *The Israelites said to Gideon, Rule over us —you, your son and your grandson—because you have saved us from the hand of Midian.*

Gideon declined their request, but asked for gold, from which he made a religious article. This became an idol and *All Israel prostituted themselves by worshiping it* (Judges 8:27). This is a sad conclusion to Gideon's story. The man who won the war against idolatry, led God's people back into it.

We too can become idolators if we're not careful. God wants to be first in our lives, and whatever we put ahead of him is an idol—even if it's something good. Money is good, but it can become an idol if we put it ahead of God. The same is true of health, family, pleasure, and position. Without appropriate caution, today's devoted Christian may be tomorrow's idolater. *Dear children, keep yourselves from idols* (1 John 5:21), wrote John.

For Reflection and Review

- *How did Gideon become courageous?*
- *Should Christians ever ask God for a sign?*
- *What competes with God in your life?*

Lesson 48

Judges 9:5 *[Abimelek] went to his father's home . . . and on one stone murdered his seventy brothers.*

After Gideon died, his son Abimelek wanted to be king. But Gideon had over seventy sons, by several wives, who might be willing to challenge him. So Abimelek killed most of them, and began his ruthless rule.

When the town of Shechem turned against Abimelek, he slaughtered many of them. Those who survived fled to a stronghold which Abimelek set on fire, burning a thousand people to death (Judges 9:49). Then he attacked another town that also had a tower. When he tried to burn it down, however, a woman on the roof dropped a millstone on his head, fatally wounding him (Judges 9:53). As Abimelek was dying, he commanded his servant to kill him with a sword, so it couldn't be said that he died at the hands of a woman. This is how Abimelek died, just three years into his reign.

Some people love power so much they'll do anything to get it, and to keep it. But Abimelek was powerless to keep himself alive, and died a young man. This is very different from Jesus Christ who refused to be made king (John 6:15), and laid down his life for us. Earthly kings often kill their people, but Jesus died for his people. This is the kind of king we need.

*****

Judges 11:1 *Jephthah the Gileadite was a mighty warrior. His father was Gilead; his mother was a prostitute.*

Jephthah's father had other sons by his legal wife and, when they were grown, they rejected Jephthah. So Jephthah went and settled elsewhere. He could've become bitter, or filled with self-pity, but he chose to go on with his life. With time he became such an effective warrior that, when his people needed him, they asked him to be their commander. The one who was an outcast, now become the leader.

Judges 11:29 *[Jephthah] advanced against the Ammonites.*

The battle was so important that Jephthah made a vow to God: *If you give the Ammonites into my hands, whatever comes out of the door of my house to meet me when I return in triumph from the Ammonites will be the Lord's, and I will sacrifice it as a burnt offering* (Judges 11:30-31), he said.

Animals were kept in the house, sometimes, so Jephthah may have had a goat in mind. But when he returned victorious, *who should come out to meet him but his daughter, dancing to the sound of timbrels! She was an only child. Except for her he had neither son nor daughter* (Judges 11:34).

This was a serious problem. *When a man makes a vow to the Lord . . . he must not break his word but must do everything he said* (Numbers 30:2), wrote Moses. And, *If you make a vow to the Lord your God, do not be slow to pay it, for the Lord your God will certainly demand it of you* (Deuteronomy 23:21), wrote Moses again. And, *It is better not to make a vow than to make one and not fulfill it* (Ecclesiastes 5:5), wrote Solomon. As far as Jephthah could tell, there was no way out of his vow.

Judges 11:35 *When he saw her, he tore his clothes and cried, Oh no, my daughter! You have brought me down and I am devastated. I have made a vow to the Lord that I cannot break.*

Jephthah's daughter could hardly believe her ears. Would she really have to die because of her father's ridiculous vow? But, young as she was, she graciously accepted the sentence of death. After two months of grieving, she became a human sacrifice. Sadly, it didn't have to be that way.

Jephthah knew enough of the Bible to take his vows seriously, but not enough to know that child sacrifice was forbidden by God. *Let no one be found among you who sacrifices their son or daughter in the fire* (Deuteronomy 18:10), wrote Moses.

Furthermore, God had made provision for foolish vows. *[I]f anyone thoughtlessly takes an oath to do anything, whether good or evil . . . they must confess in what way they have sinned. As a penalty for the sin they have committed, they must bring to the Lord a female lamb or goat from the flock as a sin offering* (Leviticus 5:4-6), wrote Moses.

Jephthah had good intentions when he made his vow, but he shouldn't have killed his daughter. Breaking his vow would've been a sin, but not so bad as child sacrifice. Whenever we have to choose between two sins, we should choose the lesser. Then we should pray for God's forgiveness, and trust that Jesus' death was sufficient payment for whatever we have done (1 John 1:9).

*****

Judges 13:1 *Again the Israelites did evil in the eyes of the Lord, so the Lord delivered them into the hands of the Philistines for forty years.*

Once again, the nation found itself in trouble due to their sin. And, once again, God raised up a deliverer in the person of Samson. He became an epic warrior capable of killing thirty men with his bare hands (Judges 14:19), and a thousand with the jawbone of a donkey (Judges 15:15).

Judges 13:2 *A certain man of Zorah, named Manoah, from the clan of the Danites, had a wife who was childless, unable to give birth.*

Like Isaac, Jacob, Samuel, and John the Baptist, Samson's parents were childless. They probably prayed for many years that God would give them a baby. Then, one day, the angel of the Lord appeared and told them they'd have a son, whom they were to raise as a Nazarite (Judges 13:3-5). This meant he should never drink wine, cut his hair, or go near a corpse (Numbers 6:1-21). In this way, Samson was to be uniquely devoted to God.

Judges 13:15 *Manoah said to the angel of the Lord, We would like you to stay until we prepare a young goat for you.*

Unaware of the angel's true identity, Manoah and his wife wanted to entertain him by providing a meal. But the angel suggested they present a burnt offering instead. *As the flame blazed up from the altar toward heaven, the angel of the Lord ascended in the flame* (Judges 13:16). Then Manoah and his wife realized the angel of the Lord was God himself (Judges 13:22).

This is most likely a *Christophany*, an appearance of Jesus Christ before his incarnation. Jesus taught the Old Testament was about him (John 5:39, Luke 24:27), so whenever God appears in physical form it's probably Jesus Christ.

Other examples include God walking in the Garden with Adam and Eve (Genesis 3:8), the *commander of the army of the Lord*, who appeared to Joshua (Joshua 5:13-15), and the man who appeared in the furnace with Shadrach, Meshach, and Abednego who looked like a *son of the gods* (Daniel 3:25).

This idea can also be argued from the fact that *there is one God and one mediator between God and mankind, the man Christ Jesus* (1 Timothy 2:5). As the angel *ascended in the flame* (Judges 13:16), never to be seen again, Jesus concluded his earthly ministry by ascending into heaven (Acts 1:9). The Old and New Testaments make up a single book in which Jesus Christ is the central figure.

For Reflection and Review

- *Does power make people corrupt?*
- *What should Christians do when they have to choose between two sins?*
- *Why would Christ appear in the Old Testament?*

Lesson 49

Judges 14:1-2 *Samson went down to Timnah and saw there a young Philistine woman. When he returned, he said to his father and mother, I have seen a Philistine woman in Timnah; now get her for me as my wife.*

Samson was a man of many flaws, and one of his worst was a weakness for Philistine women. Intermarriage was forbidden by God (Deuteronomy 7:3-4), but that didn't bother Samson at all. Even though she was an enemy of God's people, and his parents objected, and God had forbidden it, Samson was determined to marry her. He wanted what he wanted, simply because he wanted it.

God's people can be willful sometimes. An honest believer confessed, *I know the badness of my heart. There are times when I am more than willing to cross the Almighty. Never mind that Jesus bled and died for me, has forgiven my sins, and promised me a home in heaven. There are times when I simply want to do what I want to do, and go ahead and do it.* This kind of behavior is never advisable but underscores the depth of our depravity and need for salvation.

Judges 14:4 *His parents did not know that this was from the Lord.*

This is a troubling statement that can't be fully explained. How could God take responsibility for the evil in Samson's heart, without being the source or cause of that evil? The problem appears in other places as well.

After Joseph's brothers sold him into slavery, God promoted him to second in command over Egypt. Then Joseph said to his brothers, *You intended to harm me, but God intended it for good* (Genesis 50:20).

God intended their wicked act to bring about a greater good, but he still intended their wicked act.

Even more profoundly, God used the wickedest act ever (killing the Messiah) to bring about the greatest good ever (salvation for the world). *This man was handed over to you by God's deliberate plan and foreknowledge; and you, with the help of wicked men, put him to death by nailing him to the cross* (Acts 2:23), said Peter.

We don't know how God can ordain evil, without being the source or cause of evil, or being evil himself. But we do know that God can rule over evil to bring about his perfect will. This is what he'd do through Samson his entire life.

Judges 14:5 *Samson went down to Timnah together with his father and mother.*

Samson and his parents were on their way to meet Samson's future bride, and to make arrangements for the wedding. Along the way they were separated when a young lion came roaring toward Samson. *The Spirit of the Lord came powerfully upon him so that he tore the lion apart with his bare hands as he might have torn a young goat* (Judges 14:6).

This is one of three times *The Spirit of the Lord came powerfully upon [Samson]* (Judges 14:6, 14:19 and 15:14). Some of his exploits are so remarkable they defy human explanation. But when we understand that they were done by the power of the Spirit, they become more plausible because *nothing is too hard* for God (Jeremiah 32:17).

Judges 14:8-9 *Some time later, when he went back to marry her, he turned aside to look at the lion's carcass, and in it he saw a swarm of bees and some honey. He scooped out the honey with his hands and ate as he went along.*

This was Samson's wedding day and, as he went, he found some honey in the carcass of the lion he killed earlier. The wedding feast went on for seven days and, to entertain his new Philistine friends, Samson proposed a riddle: *Out of the eater, something to eat; out of the strong, something sweet* (Judges 14:14).

If they could solve this riddle he'd give them each a new set of clothes. If not, they must each give him a new set of clothes. This may have been amusing for awhile, but not for long. Clothing was expensive, so Samson's friends persuaded his wife to get the answer for them. Samson explained the riddle to her, and she informed his companions.

Suddenly, Samson was deeply in debt. In order to pay his debt, he went to another town, killed thirty Philistine men, and stole their clothes. But he was so angry at his wife that he went back to live with his parents.

Samson is not a good role model for anyone but, in the plan of God, he was disrupting the good relationship between the Philistines and the Israelites. The Israelites were commanded by God to take over the Promised Land, and drive out the inhabitants (Deuteronomy 7:2). Instead, they settled down in the land and were being governed by the inhabitants (Judges 15:11). And this arrangement was so agreeable that God's plan to have a chosen people was in jeopardy.

By committing acts of violence against the Philistines, Samson was keeping Israel from being absorbed. In that case, all the promises God made to his people (Genesis 12:1-3) would've been defeated. God keeps his promises, and was using Samson for that end.

For Reflection and Review

- *Why are God's people willfully disobedient sometimes?*
- *How was Samson able to do acts of amazing strength?*
- *Why was it important for Israel to remain distinct from the Philistines?*

Lesson 50

Judges 15:1 *Later on, at the time of wheat harvest, Samson took a young goat and went to visit his wife. He said, I'm going to my wife's room.*

It's possible that Samson hadn't consummated the marriage, so he went to his wife for that purpose. But in his absence, her father had given her to another. *I was so sure you hated her, he said, that I gave her to your companion* (Judges 15:2).

Samson was so enraged that he caught three hundred foxes and tied their tails in pairs. Then he fastened a torch to each pair of tails and set them lose in the grain fields. The fire consumed not only the grain, but also the vineyards and the olive groves (Judges 15:4-5). This was a massive economic blow to the Philistines.

To retaliate, the Philistines took Samson's former wife, along with her father, and burned them to death. This antagonized Samson even more so *He attacked them viciously and slaughtered many of them* (Judges 15:8).

As a result of Samson's action, the Philistines were willing to wage war on the entire nation of Israel. They'd be satisfied, however, if the Israelites would give them Samson. The Israelites were willing to do this, but the challenge of apprehending Samson was so great, they sent three thousand men to make the arrest.

Samson didn't want to kill his own people, however, so he allowed himself to be bound by two new ropes (Judges 15:13). When the Philistines came for him he broke the ropes, picked up a donkey's jawbone, and killed a thousand of them (Judges 15:14-15). *With a donkey's jawbone I have made donkeys of them. With a donkey's jawbone I have killed a thousand men* (Judges 15:16), he said.

Samson was a warrior of the highest level, and was fighting the Lord's enemies. The kingdom of God and the kingdoms of this world are always at war, and God himself is the ultimate warrior. *The Lord is a warrior; the Lord is his name* (Exodus 15:3), wrote Moses.

The church should never take up arms (Matthew 26:52) because the gospel is a message of peace (Romans 5:1). But when Christ returns he'll come with a vengeance that will make Samson look like a pacifist. *[W]ith fire and with his sword the Lord will execute judgment on all people, and many will be those slain by the Lord* (Isaiah 66:16), wrote Isaiah.

Judges 16:1 *One day Samson went to Gaza, where he saw a prostitute. He went in to spend the night with her.*

This is not the kind of behavior we expect from biblical heroes. Samson was a man of physical strength, combined with moral weakness. There was little he couldn't do physically, and little he wouldn't do morally.

The Philistines learned where Samson was, and planned to kill him in the morning. But in the middle of the night Samson got up, tore out the city gate, and carried it to the top of a hill far away (Judges 16:3-4). This was Samson's greatest display of strength, and reminds us that our strength comes from God. We may never set a world record, but *those who hope in the Lord will renew their strength* (Isaiah 40:31) wrote Isaiah. When our strength is running low, we can look to God.

*****

Judges 16:4 *Some time later, he fell in love with a woman in the Valley of Sorek whose name was Delilah.*

This is the third and final woman in Samson's story, and she leads to his ruin. The Philistine rulers offered her a fortune, if she could discover the secret of Samson's strength, so he could be subdued. With remarkable candor she made her request: *Tell me the secret of your great strength and how you can be tied up and subdued* (Judges 16:6), she said.

This became a lovers game, and Samson misled her three times. But she nagged him *until he was sick to death of it* (Judges 16:16). Then he revealed his secret: *No razor has ever been used on my head, he said, because I have been a Nazirite dedicated to God from my mother's womb. If my head were shaved, my strength would leave me, and I would become as weak as any other man* (Judges 16:17). So when Samson fell asleep, his head was shaved, and his strength departed.

Judges 16:21 *Then the Philistines seized him, gouged out his eyes and took him down to Gaza. Binding him with bronze shackles, they set him to grinding grain in the prison.*

Samson was a remarkably gifted person who had the fatal flaw of unbridled sexuality. First he married a Philistine woman, then he went to a prostitute, then he slept with Delilah. In the end, the eyes with which he lusted were brutally gouged out, and the strongest man in the world became weak.

If Samson had conquered his lust the way he conquered the Philistines, his story would've been different. Most of our misery doesn't come from obeying God, but from disobeying God. We don't break God's laws, so much as we break ourselves upon them.

For Reflection and Review

- *Why shouldn't the church ever use violence?*
- *Will Jesus ever use violence?*
- *Why does sin frequently lead to misery?*

Lesson 51

Judges 16:22 *But the hair on his head began to grow again after it had been shaved.*

In spite of his many mistakes, Samson's life would end triumphantly. As he worked in the prison, day after day, grinding grain for his enemies, Samson's hair began to grow. This was the sign of his Nazarite vow, and the secret of his strength.

Then one day, *the Philistines assembled to offer a great sacrifice to Dagon their god and to celebrate, saying, Our god has delivered Samson, our enemy, into our hands* (Judges 16:23). This was a large gathering with three thousand people on the flat temple roof, and many more inside. Then they brought out Samson for their amusement.

With the help of a servant, Samson made his way to the supporting pillars where he prayed, *Sovereign Lord, remember me. Please, God, strengthen me just once more, and let me with one blow get revenge on the Philistines for my two eyes* (Judges 16:28). *Then he pushed with all his might, and down came the temple on the rulers and all the people in it. Thus he killed many more when he died than while he lived* (Judges 16:30).

Samson is one of the most tragic figures in the Bible, but leaves us with an important point: regardless how badly we fail, God can still use us if we renew our commitment to him. In fact, the New Testament actually applauds Samson because of his faith (Hebrews 11:32). From Samson we learn the most important thing about us is not who we are, or what we've done, but the God in whom we believe.

Judges 16:31 *Then his brothers and his father's whole family went down to get him. They brought him back and buried him between Zorah and Eshtaol in the tomb of Manoah his father. He had led Israel twenty years.*

Samson died in the temple of Dagon, but was buried in the Promised Land. This should be an encouragement to imperfect Christians everywhere. *As it is written: There is no one righteous, not even one* (Romans 3:10). But all who believe in Jesus Christ are kept by him (John 10:29), and will arrive in the Promised Land of heaven.

*****

Judges 17:1-2 *Now a man named Micah from the hill country of Ephraim said to his mother, The eleven hundred shekels of silver that were taken from you and about which I heard you utter a curse—I have that silver with me; I took it.*

The purpose of this story is to show how far away many Israelites had fallen away from God's word. Micah stole some money from his mother, but then he gave it back. In return, she bought an expensive idol and gave it to Micah. He put the idol in a shrine, along with some household gods, and hired a Levite as a priest—all hoping to gain God's favor. But the priest stole Micah's religious items, to became the priest of a larger group.

If you take grape juice, and blend it with apple juice, you could call it *grapple juice*. Syncretism is the blending of religious ideas to come up with something new. Micah took a few ideas from God's word, and blended them with a few ideas from paganism, to come up with a religion that violated God's word at almost every point.

This, in fact, is the natural course of religion unless we're committed to God's word as our final authority in all we think and do. Either God's word is our final authority, or something else is. It could be another person, another book, our culture, or even ourselves. But the further we stray from God's word, the further we stray from God.

*****

Judges 19:1 *Now a Levite who lived in a remote area in the hill country of Ephraim took a concubine from Bethlehem in Judah.*

The Levite was probably already married but took a concubine to have additional children. She didn't have the legal status of a wife, and wasn't happy in the relationship, so she returned home to her parents. Four months later, the Levite traveled to her parents and persuaded her to return to his home. On the way back, they stayed overnight in the town of Gibeah, in the territory of Benjamin. There they received lodging from an old man who let them stay at his house.

Judges 19:22 *While they were enjoying themselves, some of the wicked men of the city surrounded the house. Pounding on the door, they shouted to the old man who owned the house, Bring out the man who came to your house so we can have sex with him.*

This is a shocking development that reminds us of Sodom and Gomorrah, before God destroyed it with fire from heaven (Genesis 19). Morality among God's people had plummeted and, this Levite wasn't any better. In order to save himself, he threw his wife outside, and the men of that town raped her until she was dead (Genesis 19:28).

To get his revenge, the Levite cut her into twelve parts and sent them throughout Israel. The nation was so appalled that it declared war on the town of Gibeah. Victory should've come quickly, but the tribe of Benjamin defended the town of Gibeah, and civil war broke out. There were heavy losses on both sides but, in the end, Benjamin was defeated.

Judges 21:25 *In those days Israel had no king; everyone did as they saw fit.*

This is the final verse in the book of Judges, and is a fitting conclusion to the moral and political chaos of the time. God had parted the Red Sea, and led his people out of slavery. Then he led them through the wilderness to the land he had promised. They didn't conquer the land, however, and were no better morally than the pagans who lived there. What they needed most was a godly king to help them fulfill their destiny.

Kings were later appointed, and things improved a little. But the kings had problems of their own, and often did more harm than good. Finally, a righteous king arrived, and the people *took palm branches and went out to meet him, shouting, Hosanna! Blessed is he who comes in the name of the Lord! Blessed is the king of Israel!* (John 12:13).

That king was Jesus Christ, who died for the sins of the world (1 John 2:2), and will return as *King of kings and Lord of lords* (Revelation 19:16). Then we'll have the king that we need, and the world will be as it ought to be forever. That's where the Bible is going, and that's the movement of history. *Amen. Come, Lord Jesus* (Revelation 22:20), wrote John.

For Reflection and Review

- *How is Samson a positive model for Christians?*
- *What was Micah's biggest mistake?*
- *Why does this world need a great king?*

Lesson 52

Ruth 1:1 *In the days when the judges ruled, there was a famine in the land. So a man from Bethlehem in Judah, together with his wife and two sons, went to live for a while in the country of Moab.*

The book of Ruth was written around 1200 BC, and is considered by some to be the classic love story of the Bible. It begins in the little town of Bethlehem, meaning *house of bread*. But the bread was running out due to a famine. To keep bodies and souls together, a little family of four migrated fifty miles to the land of Moab, where they hoped their situation would improve. Sadly, it would not.

Ruth 1:2 *The man's name was Elimelek, his wife's name was Naomi.*

After they arrived in Moab, Elimelek died, leaving Naomi a widow in a foreign land. Her two sons got married, but also died, about ten years later. Naomi was now a widow in a foreign land with no immediate family. Learning that life had improved in Bethlehem, Naomi decided to return home. Her daughters-in-law planned to go with her but, since there was nothing Naomi could do for them, she encouraged them to remain in Moab and get married again (Ruth 1:9). One of them agreed; the other did not.

Ruth 1:16-17 *Where you go I will go, and where you stay I will stay. Your people will be my people and your God my God. Where you die I will die, and there I will be buried. May the Lord deal with me, be it ever so severely, if even death separates you and me.*

The young lady's name was Ruth, and her words were a pledge to care for Naomi in her old age. The two were apparently close, and Ruth was willing to give up marriage and children in order to care for her aging mother-in-law.

Ruth was also loyal to God. *Your people will be my people and your God my God*, she said. Before she met Naomi, Ruth may have worshipped Chemosh, the god of the Moabites (1 Kings 11:7). He was a local deity who made little difference in her life. But Ruth came to believe in God Almighty, the maker of heaven and earth (Genesis 1:1). Her faith was so firm, in fact, that she was willing to leave family, friends, and homeland to live in the land of Israel, and worship Israel's God.

Ruth 1:19 *When they arrived in Bethlehem, the whole town was stirred because of them, and the women exclaimed, Can this be Naomi?*

Life was hard for Naomi, and she may have aged so much that she was barely recognizable. She went out with a husband and sons, but returned with neither. She went out looking for prosperity, but returned in poverty. *Do not call me Naomi, she told them. Call me Mara, because the Almighty has made my life very bitter* (Ruth 1:20).

Naomi means *pleasant*, and *Mara* means *bitter*. Naomi's life had been so bitter, she wanted to change her name to Mara. It should be frankly admitted that belonging to God is no guarantee against misery. Believing in God, in fact, can make our misery worse. In light of God's promise to answer our prayers (Matthew 7:7-8), when our prayers go unanswered, it can seem like God is mocking us. *I have been disappointed enough times that I simply pray for less and less, in order not to be disappointed more and more*, someone confessed. That's how Naomi felt.

Ruth 1:21 *I went away full, but the Lord has brought me back empty. . . . The Lord has afflicted me; the Almighty has brought misfortune upon me.*

The Bible doesn't whitewash Naomi's speech, or shift the blame away from God. It simply keeps us waiting for God, because that's the essence of faith. Faith believes that, sooner or later, God will act and things will improve.

Ruth 2:1 *Now Naomi had a relative on her husband's side, a man of standing from the clan of Elimelek, whose name was Boaz.*

Boaz features prominently in the rest of the story, but here it's enough to see that he was related to Naomi, and was a man of standing in the community. There's no indication Naomi asked

Boaz for help but, if things got worse, he was someone she could turn to.

Since it was harvest time, Ruth went into the fields to glean. The land didn't belong to her, but Israel had a law that required property owners to leave some produce behind for the poor. *When you are harvesting in your field and you overlook a sheaf, do not go back to get it. Leave it for the foreigner, the fatherless and the widow, so that the Lord your God may bless you in all the work of your hands* (Deuteronomy 24:19), wrote Moses.

Providentially, Ruth found herself in a field that belonged to Boaz. They hadn't met but, when he arrived, Boaz made a good impression. *The Lord be with you*, he said to his workers. *The Lord bless you*, they replied. This little exchanged showed Ruth that Boaz was a man of some godliness, and enjoyed a pleasant rapport with his employees.

Boaz asked about Ruth, and learned she was the Moabite who returned with Naomi. *May the Lord repay you for what you have done. May you be richly rewarded by the Lord* (Ruth 2:12), he said. But he went even further and urged Ruth to continue gleaning in his field, and told his workers to leave her additional grain. He also paid for her lunch. Boaz was so generous to Ruth, in fact, that it's difficult to know if he was just being kind, or if he was being drawn to her. They were both devout in their faith, and apparently single.

Ruth 2:19 *Her mother-in-law asked her, Where did you glean today?*

Ruth informed Naomi that she gleaned in the field of Boaz, and Naomi was delighted. *That man is our close relative; he is one of our guardian-redeemers*, she said. A guardian-redeemer was a close relative who was obligated to help other family members who were in serious trouble. The idea is found in Israel's laws (Leviticus 25:25-55), and appears more prominently in the book of Ruth than anywhere else in the Bible.

Here we see the invisible hand of God beginning to care for Naomi and Ruth. They hadn't imposed on family or friends, but were looking to God for their needs. Now, at last, God was beginning to act.

We find this same idea in the teaching of Jesus: *So do not worry, saying, What shall we eat? or What shall we drink? or What shall we wear? For the pagans run after all these things, and your heavenly Father knows that you need them. But seek first his kingdom and his righteousness, and all these things will be given to you as well* (Matthew 6:31-33).

Jesus didn't say that life will never be hard, or even extremely hard. But he said we have a heavenly Father, who knows exactly what we need. He taught us to put God first in our lives, and then trust God to take care of the rest. Naomi and Ruth were doing exactly that.

For Reflection and Review

- *Have you ever been disappointed with God?*
- *Did Naomi have a right to complain?*
- *How did Naomi and Ruth deal with their poverty?*

Lesson 53

Ruth 3:1 *One day Ruth's mother-in-law Naomi said to her, My daughter, I must find a home for you, where you will be well provided for.*

Ruth had been caring for Naomi, but now Naomi was caring for Ruth. Her intuition told her the kindness of Boaz was more than mere compassion. But Boaz may've been shy since, apparently, he never married. If Naomi and Ruth waited for Boaz to act, they might've waited forever. So Naomi gave her daughter-in-law some bold advice:

Wash, put on perfume, and get dressed in your best clothes. Then go down to the threshing floor, but do not let him know you are there until he has finished eating and drinking. When he lies down, note the place where he is lying. Then go and uncover his feet and lie down. He will tell you what to do (Ruth 3:3-4).

To modern readers this seems extremely forward and, in fact, it was. But there's nothing improper here. Ruth was simply proposing marriage. Boaz was the kind of person who was good at many things, but not love. He may've been turned down in the past, and feared being rejected again. For whatever reason, he didn't seem to have the courage to take the initiative with Ruth. If she didn't make her intentions clear, nothing was going to happen. *So she went down to the threshing floor and did everything her mother-in-law told her to do* (Ruth 3:6).

Ruth 3:7 *Ruth approached quietly, uncovered his feet and lay down.*

Due to cold feet, Boaz soon woke up and was startled. *Who are you? he asked. I am your servant Ruth, she said. Spread the corner of your garment over me, since you are a guardian-redeemer of our family* (Ruth 3:9).

Boaz could hardly believe his ears. He was older than Ruth, and assumed she'd be attracted to younger men (Ruth 1:10). Perhaps he prayed for a wife in the past. Perhaps he even prayed for Ruth to be his wife. Now God was doing all he had hoped for.

By calling Boaz her *guardian-redeemer*, Ruth was also appealing to his obligation to care for her, due to the loss of her first husband. *Her husband's brother shall take her and marry her and fulfill the duty of a brother-in-law* (Deuteronomy 25:5), wrote Moses. Boaz wasn't her brother-in-law, but he was happy to accept the responsibility.

Ruth 3:11 *And now, my daughter, do not be afraid. I will do for you all you ask. All the people of my town know that you are a woman of noble character.*

The Bible never describes Ruth as a beautiful woman, so she may have been rather plain. What mattered most to Boaz was her noble character. *A wife of noble character is her husband's crown* (Proverbs 12:4). *A wife of noble character . . . . is worth far more than rubies* (Proverbs 31:10). *Charm is deceptive, and beauty is fleeting; but a woman who fears the Lord is to be praised* (Proverbs 31:30), says Proverbs.

As Ruth and Boaz looked into heaven that night, we can imagine tears of praise streaming down their faces, for the goodness of God who brought them together. Ruth had found a husband, and Boaz had found wife.

Ruth 3:12 *Although it is true that I am a guardian-redeemer of our family, there is another who is more closely related than I.*

In great romantic stories, there's often a third-person conflict, and this is no exception. There was someone ahead of Boaz who could've cared for Naomi and Ruth if he wanted to. Boaz could've ignored this fact, but he preferred to handle the situation with complete integrity. If God had brought them together, he could work this out as well.

Ruth 4:1 *Boaz went up to the town gate and sat down there just as the guardian-redeemer he had mentioned came along.*

The Bible doesn't tell us the time of day, but it was probably early morning. Boaz went to the town gate, where business was conducted, and there he found the one person ahead of him with the right to care for Naomi and Ruth. *Boaz said, Come over here, my friend, and sit down. So he went over and sat down. Boaz took ten of the elders of the town and said, Sit here, and they did so* (Ruth 4:1b-2).

This was serious business and the presence of elders would insure it was properly conducted and formally witnessed. The gentleman showed some interest, at first, but then he gave the right to Boaz.

We can only imagine the joy and relief Boaz felt when he was given the legal right to care for Naomi and Ruth. *Today you are witnesses [he said]. Then the elders and all the people at the gate said, We are witnesses* (Ruth 4:10-11). And they gave Boaz their blessing.

Ruth 4:13, 17 *So Boaz took Ruth and she became his wife. When he made love to her, the Lord enabled her to conceive, and she gave birth to a son. . . . The women living* *there said, Naomi has a son! And they named him Obed. He was the father of Jesse, the father of David.*

This made Ruth the great-grandmother of the future king David. This story, in fact, may've been told to the little boy David by Grandma Ruth herself. We can imagine how this would've shaped the future king's faith in God.

Because Ruth was the great-grandmother of David, she was also an ancestor of Jesus Christ (Matthew 1:5). By choosing a Moabite woman to be an ancestor of the Messiah, God was showing that participation in the kingdom of God is not determined by birth, but by genuine faith in God. Throughout her story, Ruth is a model of genuine faith.

Boaz is also an ancestor of Jesus Christ, of course, but he is even more. As Ruth's guardian-redeemer, Boaz foreshadows Jesus Christ as our Redeemer (Titus 2:14). As one who took a Gentile wife, Boaz foreshadows Jesus who gladly receives Gentiles (Matthew 28:20). As Boaz brought a reversal of fortune to Naomi and Ruth, Jesus brings a reversal of fortune to all who believe in him (John 5:24). God provided a husband for Ruth, and he provided a Savior for us.

For Reflection and Review

- *What kind of wife does the Bible recommend?*
- *How did Boaz demonstrate his faith?*
- *How does Boaz remind us of Jesus Christ?*

Lesson 54

1 Samuel 1:1 *There was a certain man from Ramathaim, a Zuphite from the hill country of Ephraim, whose name was Elkanah.*

First and Second Samuel were originally one book, and the author is not identified. They tell the history of Israel from around 1105 BC to 970 BC, highlighting the lives of Samuel, Saul, and David. Samuel was an important leader who helped the nation transition from the rule of judges to the rule of kings. The story begins with his birth, which was an answer to prayer.

1 Samuel 1:2 *[Elkanah] had two wives; one was called Hannah and the other Peninnah.*

Not many wives want to share their husbands, so the situation was less than ideal. Elkanah may've married Hannah first, but when she didn't bear children he likely married Peninnah. If Hannah felt jealous or inadequate, it only got worse when Peninnah became pregnant. Instead of showing empathy, she flaunted her fertility, provoking Hannah to tears.

1 Samuel 1:11 *Lord Almighty, if you will only look on your servant's misery and remember me, and not forget your servant but give her a son, then I will give him to the Lord for all the days of his life.*

Hannah prayed at the tabernacle and was observed by Eli the priest. She prayed silently, but her lips were moving, and Eli thought she was drunk. She explained that she wasn't drunk, but was praying out of a broken heart. *Then she went her way and ate something, and her face was no longer downcast* (1 Samuel 1:18).

Before Hannah prayed she was in *deep anguish* (1 Samuel 1:10), but after she prayed *her face was no longer downcast*. From Hannah we learn to give our concerns to God. One of the great benefits of having a heavenly Father is trusting that he'll care for us. *Cast your cares on the Lord and he will sustain you* (Psalm 55:22), wrote David. *Cast all your anxiety on him because he cares for you* (1 Peter 5:7), wrote Peter. God wants us to bring our cares to him, and leave them there. When the burdens of life are too heavy for us, we can give them to God.

1 Samuel 1:20 *So in the course of time Hannah became pregnant and gave birth to a son. She named him Samuel.*

Hannah could've forgotten her vow, as many people do, but she was determined to keep it. Her little boy was around three years old when she brought him to the tabernacle and gave him to Eli the priest. *I prayed for this child, and the Lord has granted me what I asked of him. So now I give him to the Lord. For his whole life he will be given over to the Lord* (1 Samuel 1:27-28), she said.

From that day on, Samuel stayed at the house of God, under the supervision of Eli the priest. It must've been difficult for Hannah to leave her son at the house of God, but she wasn't sad. *My heart rejoices in the Lord* (1 Samuel 2:1), she said.

Somehow Hannah knew that God had a plan for her son, and that was enough for her. Samuel, in fact, would be used by God to anoint the first two kings of Israel. *[God] will give strength to his king and exalt the horn of his anointed*, said Hannah (1 Samuel 2:10).

Anointing was the practice of applying oil to people or things, to show they were set apart for God. Many people and things were anointed in the Old Testament, but kings were especially known as the *Lord's anointed*.

This reminds us of Jesus Christ since *Christ* comes from the Greek word for *anointed*, and *Messiah* comes from the Hebrew word for *anointed*. The words *Christ* and *Messiah* are applied to Jesus hundreds of times in the New Testament because he is God's anointed king.

Jesus wasn't anointed with oil, however, but with the Holy Spirit (John 1:32, Luke 4:18). *The Spirit of the Lord is on me, because he has anointed me to proclaim good news to the poor* (Luke 4:18, Isaiah 61:1), he said. Samuel anointed the first two kings of Israel, but Jesus was anointed by the Spirit of God.

1 Samuel 2:12 *Eli's sons were scoundrels; they had no regard for the Lord.*

Eli's adult sons (Hophni and Phinehas) disregarded God's word, slept with women who served at the tabernacle (1 Samuel 2:22), and were bad examples to Samuel. Nevertheless, their father, Eli, allowed them to continue serving as priests.

For various reasons, people of low moral character sometimes go into the ministry. *They come to you in sheep's clothing, but inwardly they are ferocious wolves* (Matthew 7:15), said Jesus. When ministry positions are held by ungodly leaders, God and his word are neglected, and the people of God suffer.

Eli should've dismissed his sons from the ministry, but he seemed to care more for them than for the Lord. He rebuked his sons (1 Samuel 2:23-25), but let them keep their positions without changing their behavior.

Christian parents may also be tempted to put their children ahead of God. Instead of revolving their lives around God, they revolve their lives around their children. They may even tolerate ungodliness within their own home. But *anyone who loves their son or daughter more than me is not worthy of me* (Matthew 10:37), said Jesus. Putting our children ahead of God is a serious sin, and a disservice to our children.

For Reflection and Review

- *What can we learn about prayer from Hannah?*
- *How can we give our cares to God?*
- *What can we learn about parenting from Eli?*

Lesson 55

1 Samuel 2:27 *Now a man of God came to Eli and said to him, This is what the Lord says:*

. . . . *Those who honor me I will honor, but those who despise me will be disdained* (1 Samuel 2:30). Due to his unfaithfulness, Eli's descendants would die in the prime of life, and his two sons would die on the same day (1 Samuel 2:33-34). God holds leaders to a higher standard (James 3:1), and Eli had failed miserably. As a result, God would replace him with *a faithful priest, who will do according to what is in my heart and mind* (1 Samuel 2:35), said God.

This refers to Zadok, who became the high priest under Solomon. But it reminds us of Jesus Christ, the great high priest of all believers. *Such a high priest truly meets our need—one who is holy, blameless, pure, set apart from sinners, exalted above the heavens. Unlike the other high priests, he does not need to offer sacrifices day after day, first for his own sins, and then for the sins of the people. He sacrificed for their sins once for all when he offered himself* (Hebrews 7:26-27), says Hebrews.

Earthly ministers often fail due to their sinful natures. But we have a priest from heaven who can never fail because he has no sinful nature. And because he's offered a perfect sacrifice, of infinite value, he can bring us to God no matter what we've done. This kind of priest can even save a minister who's failed.

1 Samuel 3:1 *The boy Samuel ministered before the Lord under Eli.*

We don't know Samuel's age at this time, but twelve years old is a reasonable guess. Eli had been his guardian and mentor for several years, and Samuel was familiar with the sacrificial system. He was making steady progress in the work of the ministry.

1 Samuel 3:1b *In those days the word of the Lord was rare; there were not many visions.*

The work of the priests was being carried out, but there weren't many prophets. God was under no obligation to speak, and could even withhold his speech as a form of punishment. *The days are coming, declares the Sovereign Lord, when I will send a famine through the land—not a famine of food or a thirst for water, but a famine of hearing the words of the Lord* (Amos 8:11), wrote Amos. The fact that we can hear God's word proclaimed to us is not a small privilege.

1 Samuel 3:2-7 *One night Eli, whose eyes were becoming so weak that he could barely see, was lying down in his usual place. The lamp of God had not yet gone out, and Samuel was lying down in the house of the Lord, where the ark of God was. Then the Lord called Samuel. Samuel answered, Here I am. And he ran to Eli and said, Here I am; you called me. But Eli said, I did not call; go back and lie down. So he went and lay down. Again the Lord called, Samuel! And Samuel got up and went to Eli and said, Here I am; you called me. My son, Eli said, I did not call; go back and lie down. Now Samuel did not yet know the Lord: The word of the Lord had not yet been revealed to him.*

Samuel knew about God, and was doing God's work, but didn't actually know God. This is more important than many people realize. *Now this is eternal life [said Jesus]: that they know you, the only true God, and Jesus Christ, whom you have sent* (John 17:3). Eternal life doesn't come from knowing about God, but from knowing God personally.

A friend of mine attended seminary and was preparing for pastoral ministry. He studied Greek, Hebrew, systematic theology, and church history. But a lady from church told him that wasn't enough. He had to know God for himself. By repenting of his sin, and turning to Christ with all his heart, he came to know God personally, and was able to tell others about him. Likewise, Samuel was about to meet God for himself.

1 Samuel 3:8 *A third time the Lord called, Samuel! And Samuel got up and went to Eli and said, Here I am; you called me.*

Neither Samuel nor Eli were getting much sleep that night. This was the third time God called Samuel, and the third time Samuel mistook God's voice for Elli's. Finally, Eli understood it was God who was calling Samuel. *So Eli told Samuel, Go and lie down, and if he calls you, say, Speak, Lord, for your servant is listening* (1 Samuel 3:9).

1 Samuel 3:10-11 *The Lord came and stood there, calling as at the other times, Samuel! Samuel! Then Samuel said, Speak, for your servant is listening. And the Lord said to Samuel: See, I am about to do something in Israel that will make the ears of everyone who hears about it tingle.*

God told Samuel that he was about to punish Eli for not restraining his sons. *The guilt of Eli's house will never be atoned for by sacrifice or offering* (1 Samuel 3:14), he said. This was a lot for a boy to bear, and Samuel was afraid to tell Eli. But Eli said, *May God deal with you, be it ever so severely, if you hide from me anything he told you. So Samuel told him everything* (1 Samuel 3:17-18).

Whoever speaks for God must be willing to tell the truth, the whole truth, and nothing but the truth —not just the parts people want to hear. False prophets tell the truth about God's love, but are often silent about his wrath. But the first message God gave Samuel was a message of judgment on his beloved guardian. Even though Samuel was young, he told Eli the cold hard truth.

1 Samuel 3:19 *The Lord was with Samuel as he grew up, and he let none of Samuel's words fall to the ground.*

This probably means that whatever Samuel said came to pass. But it may also reflect the authority with which he spoke. Some preachers' words fall to the ground before they reach the first row, but when Samuel spoke everyone paid attention. This reminds us of Jesus Christ who *taught as one who had authority* (Matthew 7:29). And *all the people hung on his words* (Luke 19:48), wrote Luke.

For Reflection and Review

- *Why is Jesus Christ a perfect high priest?*
- *What is the difference between knowing about God, and knowing God personally?*
- *Why is it often hard to preach the truth?*

Lesson 56

1 Samuel 4:1 *Now the Israelites went out to fight against the Philistines.*

They brought the ark of the covenant into battle hoping it would help them, but it didn't help at all. We read that *Israel lost thirty thousand foot soldiers. The ark of God was captured, and Eli's two sons, Hophni and Phinehas, died* (1 Samuel 4:10-11).

The ark of the covenant was the visible sign of God's power and presence, so for it to be lost was nothing short of disastrous. Eli was ninety-eight years old, and was so overwhelmed that he fell off his chair, broke his neck, and died (1 Samuel 1:18). His daughter-in-law went into labor and also died. But before she passed, *She named the boy Ichabod, saying, The Glory has departed from Israel* (1 Samuel 2:21). Losing the ark of the covenant was like losing God himself.

The judgment of God had been coming for many years, but it came in a single day. Eli, Hophni, and Phinehas had decades to repent but chose not to. They mistook God's patience for his permission, and brought disaster on themselves, and on the people of God. Samuel learned up close that God should be taken seriously. Soon he'd bring the leadership God's people desperately needed.

1 Samuel 5:1 *After the Philistines had captured the ark of God, they took it from Ebenezer to Ashdod.*

The ark of the covenant was a trophy of war, so the Philistines brought it into the temple of Dagon, their national deity. But the following morning, the image of Dagon was lying facedown before the ark of God. They put it back in its place, but the next morning the image was lying before the ark again. This time its hands and head were broken off, and were lying on the threshold of the temple door. God was showing the Philistines that, even though they'd captured the ark, their god was no match for the God of Israel.

Idolatry was common in the ancient world, but we also practice idolatry whenever we trust anything more than God. We can idolize technology, science, medicine, wealth, power, government, or even our own strength if that's where our hope is. Idols fall before the Lord and cannot save us. Our *faith and hope are in God* (1 Peter 1:21), wrote Peter.

1 Samuel 5:6 *The Lord's hand was heavy on the people of Ashdod and its vicinity.*

The Philistines may've hoped the ark of God would bring them blessing, but just the opposite occurred: God afflicted them with tumors. They weren't ready to give up the ark, however, so they sent it to Gath, another Philistine town. But God also afflicted them with tumors, so they sent the ark to Ekron. But for obvious reasons, Ekron didn't want it either.

The power and presence of God were connected to the ark of the covenant (Exodus 25:22), and it could, in fact, be a source of blessing (Joshua 3:15-16). But the power and presence of God are only a blessing to people who are living in obedience. If we disobey, God's power and presence can make us sick, or even kill us (1 Corinthians 11:30). It's only good to be close to God if we're living well before him.

1 Samuel 6:1-2 *When the ark of the Lord had been in Philistine territory seven months, the Philistines called for the priests and the diviners and said, What shall we do with the ark of the Lord? Tell us how we should send it back to its place.*

The Philistines had enough of the ark, and wanted to send it back to Israel. In hope of receiving God's favor, they included an offering of five gold tumors, and five gold rats, which were plaguing the country (1 Samuel 6:5). They put the ark on a cart, pulled by two cows. The cows had never been yoked, and also had calves. Cows that had never been yoked wouldn't know how to pull a cart together and, even if they did, they'd want to return to their calves. But the cows proceeded to the Israelite town of Beth Shemesh. Then the Philistines knew their plagues were from the Lord, not merely a coincidence.

God could've allowed the ark to perish, but oversaw its return. His people didn't deserve the ark, but he graciously gave it back to them. No matter what we've done in the past, God longs to be with us, and moves in our direction.

1 Samuel 6:13 *Now the people of Beth Shemesh were harvesting their wheat in the valley, and when they looked up and saw the ark, they rejoiced at the sight.*

They didn't have to rescue the ark, ransom the ark, or negotiate its return. God simply brought it to them. *The people chopped up the wood of the cart and sacrificed the cows as a burnt offering to the Lord* (1 Samuel 6:14). Then they put the ark on top of a large rock as a memorial. God was back in town!

1 Samuel 6:19 *But God struck down some of the inhabitants of Beth Shemesh, putting seventy of them to death because they looked into the ark of the Lord.*

The ark of God was normally kept in the tabernacle, so most people never caught a glimpse of it. Some of the people of Beth Shemesh used this opportunity to look where they had no business looking. Instead of honoring God, by averting their gaze, they peered into the ark and died. God had previously warned that unauthorized people who *look at the holy things, even for a moment . . . will die* (Numbers 4:20). Once again, we see that God doesn't make idle threats.

We want God on our terms, but God insists on his own terms. God wants us to be close to him, but we're not to become familiar. He's not our buddy, pal, or chum, but *God Almighty* (Genesis 17:1), worthy of respect. Therefore, we must *worship God acceptably with reverence and awe* (Hebrews 12:28), says Hebrews.

For Reflection and Review

- *Why did God allow the ark of the covenant to be captured?*
- *How did God show his power over Dagon?*
- *Is God a safe person to live with?*

Lesson 57

1 Samuel 7:5 *Then Samuel said, Assemble all Israel at Mizpah, and I will intercede with the Lord for you.*

God's people had fallen into idolatry but, under Samuel's leadership, they agreed to throw away their idols and serve the Lord. Samuel gathered the people at Mizpah for a time of spiritual renewal. There they fasted, confessed their sins, and poured out water before the Lord (1 Samuel 7:6).

This ceremony wasn't required by God, but may symbolize pouring out our hearts to him. *[P]our out your heart like water in the presence of the Lord* (Lamentations 2:19), wrote Jeremiah. And, *pour out your hearts to him, for God is our refuge* (Psalm 62:8), wrote David. Prayer is normally calm and quiet but, when the heart is full of emotion, it can be appropriate to pour it out to God.

1 Samuel 7:7 *When the Philistines heard that Israel had assembled at Mizpah, the rulers of the Philistines came up to attack them.*

Satan is never pleased when people are turning to God, so he interrupted the occasion by sending the Philistines to wage war with Israel. God's people were afraid, and asked Samuel to pray while they went out to fight. Samuel offered a sacrifice, and called out to God in prayer. As the Philistines drew near, God sent thunder that was so loud it threw them into a panic, and they were defeated.

This recalls the words of Samuel's mother when she gave him to the Lord. *The Most High will thunder from heaven; the Lord will judge the ends of the earth* (1 Samuel 2:10), she said. Samuel's mother had probably died, but her words were being fulfilled.

1 Samuel 8:1 *When Samuel grew old, he appointed his sons as Israel's leaders.*

This was a bad idea since Samuel's sons were not morally qualified to lead. *They turned aside after dishonest gain and accepted bribes and perverted justice* (2 Samuel 8:3). Samuel should've known not to appoint his corrupt sons, since Eli made the same mistake with terrible results. The desire to see our children succeed can be so strong, it overrides our better judgment.

Samuel's sons were willing to receive whatever advantage their father could provide, but were not willing to serve their father's God. Sadly, this pattern continues even today. *A foolish son brings grief to his father and bitterness to the mother who bore him* (Proverbs 17:25), says Proverbs.

1 Samuel 8:4-5 *So all the elders of Israel gathered together and came to Samuel at Ramah. They said to him, You are old, and your sons do not follow your ways; now appoint a king to lead us, such as all the other nations have.*

It wasn't wrong for the people to ask for a king, since that had been God's plan from the beginning (Deuteronomy 17:14-20). The problem was that they wanted to be like *all the other nations*. Instead of relying on their heavenly king, through prayerful obedience, they wanted an earthly king with a powerful army. God reluctantly agreed, and told Samuel to *give them a king* (1 Samuel 8:21).

The world still longs for someone who'll bring lasting peace and prosperity—and he is coming. *[T]he government will be on his shoulders. And he will be called Wonderful Counselor, Mighty God, Everlasting Father, Prince of Peace* (Isaiah 9:6), wrote Isaiah. The King of kings will rule the world, and happy are those who serve him now.

*****

1 Samuel 9:1 *There was a Benjamite, a man of standing, whose name was Kish. [H]e had a son named Saul, as handsome a young man as could be found anywhere in Israel, and he was a head taller than anyone else.*

Saul enjoyed the benefits of an excellent appearance, and belonging to a prominent family. One day the family's donkeys were missing, and Saul was sent to find them. *Take one of the servants with you and go and look for the donkeys* (1 Samuel 9:3), said his father. After a few days searching, Saul wanted to return home, but the servant suggested seeing the prophet Samuel, who might be able to tell them where the donkeys were.

God told Samuel that Saul was on his way, and to anoint him ruler over Israel. As soon as they arrived, Samuel told Saul the donkeys had been found, and that he was to rule God's people. The following morning Samuel took a flask of olive oil and poured it on Saul's head saying, *Has not the*

Lord anointed you ruler over his inheritance? (1 Samuel 10:1).

It's surprising how little choice Saul seemed to have in the matter. He didn't ask to be king, wasn't trying to be king, and didn't want to be king. But God chose to make him king and, suddenly, everything changed. We never know when God will set a task before us, and we must be ready to obey.

1 Samuel 10:9 *As Saul turned to leave Samuel, God changed Saul's heart.*

We're not told how God changed Saul's heart, but it was likely the work of the Spirit. *I will give you a new heart and put a new spirit in you; I will remove from you your heart of stone and give you a heart of flesh. And I will put my Spirit in you and move you to follow my decrees and be careful to keep my laws* (Ezekiel 36:26-27), wrote Ezekiel. Nothing was more important to Saul's success than a heart that was right with God.

For Reflection and Review

- *Why does God want us to pour out our hearts to him?*
- *Why does the world need a king?*
- *Why did God change Saul's heart?*

Lesson 58

1 Samuel 11:1 *Nahash the Ammonite went up and besieged Jabesh Gilead.*

This was Saul's first test of leadership and it would be decisive. Since his government wasn't established yet, he was plowing his field when he heard about the situation: Nahash the Ammonite was planning to gouge out the right eye of everyone who lived in Jabesh Gilead, even if they surrendered.

Immediately the Spirit of God came on Saul and he marshaled an army. *[T]hey broke into the camp of the Ammonites and slaughtered them until the heat of the day. Those who survived were scattered, so that no two of them were left together* (1 Samuel 11:11).

Saul's reign was off to a very good start. Through this victory he was established as king in the hearts of God's people. He was thirty years old at this time, and would lead Israel for the next forty-two years (1 Samuel 13:1). With God's help, Saul could do great things for the nation.

*****

1 Samuel 13:5 *The Philistines assembled to fight Israel, with three thousand chariots, six thousand charioteers, and soldiers as numerous as the sand on the seashore.*

By this time Saul had been king for many years and was facing a serious challenge. God had given the land to Israel, but the Philistines wouldn't give it up, and often had the advantage. This challenge was so great that Saul's army was *quaking with fear* (1 Samuel 13:7), and many were deserting.

The prophet Samuel had instructed Saul to wait for his arrival, so he could offer a sacrifice before the battle. Since the prophet spoke for God, this was not a suggestion—it was God's command. But Samuel didn't arrive on time and Saul felt compelled to act. Perhaps the prophet was sick, or delayed for some other reason. Saul thought if he waited any longer the battle would be lost. So he offered the sacrifice himself.

1 Samuel 13:10-11 *Just as he finished making the offering, Samuel arrived, and Saul went out to greet him. What have you done? asked Samuel.*

Saul explained his actions but Samuel wasn't pleased. *You have not kept the command the Lord your God gave you; if you had, he would have established your kingdom over Israel for all time. But now your kingdom will not endure* (1 Samuel 13:13-14), he said.

At first reading, the consequences seem disproportionate to Saul's failure. Saul was under pressure to act because the prophet was late. There would've been no problem if Samuel had simply arrived on time. But because of the prophet's delay, Saul took action. And, for this, he wouldn't have a dynasty. He wouldn't be deposed, but he wouldn't have a dynasty either.

This was a test of Saul's faith, and he failed. The word of the prophet was the word of God to Saul, and the word of God was *wait*. If Saul had waited on God, his future would've been different.

Taking action ahead of God is always counterproductive. *[God] acts on behalf of those who wait for him* (Isaiah 64:4), wrote Isaiah. We like to take matters into our own hands but, sometimes, God wants us to wait for him. Whoever waits on God never waits too long.

*****

1 Samuel 14:1 *One day Jonathan son of Saul said to his young armor-bearer, Come, let's go over to the Philistine outpost.*

By this time, Saul's son Jonathan was a grown man and an excellent warrior. He was also a man of faith. Unafraid of battle, he went with his armor-bearer into enemy territory to see what could be done. *Nothing can hinder the Lord from saving, whether by many or by few* (1 Samuel 14:6), he said. Jonathan's confidence wasn't in himself, but in the Lord. Even if they were outnumbered, God could give them victory.

1 Samuel 14:7 *Do all that you have in mind, his armor-bearer said. Go ahead; I am with you heart and soul.*

Jonathan's helper also had faith in God. We are *mutually encouraged by each other's faith* (Romans 1:12), wrote Paul. And *if two of you on earth agree about anything they ask for, it will be done for them by my Father in heaven* (Matthew 18:19), said Jesus. Two people with faith are a mighty force for God.

The odds against them were great, however, so Jonathan and his armor-bearer sought further assurance. They planned to reveal themselves to the Philistines and if they said, *Come up to us*, they'd take it as a sign that God would give them victory. That's what happened, and they defeated twenty enemy soldiers.

1 Samuel 14:15 *Then panic struck the whole army . . . and the ground shook. It was a panic sent by God.*

The Philistine army sensed that God was against them, and they began to flee. Saul saw what was happening, and led his army into battle. With God's help, they thoroughly defeated the Philistines.

None of this would've happened apart from the courageous faith of Jonathan and his armor-bearer. Great works of God often start with one or two. It's not the number of people that matters, but the courage and faith of those involved. One person with God makes a majority.

1 Samuel 14:24 *Now the Israelites were in distress that day.*

They should've been rejoicing because of the victory, but were in distress because Saul had bound them with an oath. *Cursed be anyone who eats food before evening comes, before I have avenged myself on my enemies* (1 Samuel 14:24), he said.

In an effort to get God's support, Saul required his men to fast throughout the day. But God hadn't commanded it, nor was it wise. Fighting is hard work, and even harder on an empty stomach. By commanding a fast, Saul put his soldiers at a serious disadvantage. His lack of good judgment was becoming a liability.

Making matters worse, Jonathan didn't hear his father's command. So when he found some honey in the forest, he ate it. When his father learned of this, he determined to have Jonathan killed because of the oath. Thankfully, the soldiers came to Jonathan's defense and Saul backed down. But his reputation for leadership had been hurt.

For Reflection and Review

- *Are you more inclined to act too quickly, or wait too long?*
- *Who has encouraged your faith the most, and why?*
- *What kind of leader was Saul?*

Lesson 59

1 Samuel 15:1 *Samuel said to Saul, I am the one the Lord sent to anoint you king over his people Israel; so listen now to the message from the Lord.*

Kings of other nations were free to do as they pleased, since they were the highest authority. But among his people, God was the highest authority, and the king was to be his servant. The prophet Samuel had authority over King Saul, because Samuel spoke for God.

1 Samuel 15:3 *Now go, attack the Amalekites and totally destroy all that belongs to them. Do not spare them; put to death men and women, children and infants, cattle and sheep, camels and donkeys.*

The Amalekites were the sworn enemies of God's people, and the time had come for their destruction. This was an excellent opportunity for Saul to recover, since he came under God's disfavor just two chapters earlier. By fully obeying the Lord's command, he could show that he wanted nothing more than to please the Lord. This could be a turning point in the right direction.

1 Samuel 15:7 *Then Saul attacked the Amalekites all the way from Havilah to Shur, near the eastern border of Egypt.*

The attack was very successful but, instead of total destruction, Saul spared the Amalekite king and all the best livestock. *Then the word of the Lord came to Samuel: I regret that I have made Saul king, because he has turned away from me and has not carried out my instructions* (1 Samuel 15:10-11).

Saul was guilty of incomplete obedience. He did some of what God commanded, even most of what God commanded, but not all of what God commanded. This was a serious problem.

Some people think God is pleased with them because they keep a few of his commands. Others think God is pleased with them because they keep most of his commands. But if you're brought into court for stealing, it won't matter if you've never committed murder. *For whoever keeps the whole law and yet stumbles at just one point is guilty of breaking all of it* (James 2:10), wrote James. Incomplete obedience is a violation of God's law, and makes us guilty in his sight.

1 Samuel 15:12 *Early in the morning Samuel got up and went to meet Saul, but he was told, Saul has gone to Carmel. There he has set up a monument in his own honor.*

Instead of giving glory to God, Saul took the glory for himself by setting up a monument in his own honor. This is a key distinction between those who belong to God, and those who don't. *Not to us, Lord, not to us but to your name be the glory* (Psalm 115:1), wrote the Psalmist. By setting up a monument to himself, Saul showed that he was more committed to his own glory than to God's glory.

1 Samuel 15:13-14 *When Samuel reached him, Saul said, The Lord bless you! I have carried out the Lord's instructions. But Samuel said, What then is this bleating of sheep in my ears? What is this lowing of cattle that I hear?*

Saul wanted to convince Samuel that he'd truly obeyed God, and that the livestock were for sacrifice. *But Samuel replied: Does the Lord delight in burnt offerings and sacrifices as much as in obeying the Lord? To obey is better than sacrifice, and to heed is better than the fat of rams. For rebellion is like the sin of divination, and arrogance like the evil of idolatry. Because you have rejected the word of the Lord, he has rejected you as king* (1 Samuel 15:22-23).

These are some of the strongest words in the Bible, and strike at one of our deepest fears—rejection by God. But Saul rejected God before God rejected Saul. By rejecting God's word, Saul was rejecting God himself. How we relate to the word of God, is how we relate to God.

Some people are brazen in their rejection of God's word, while others are more subtle. They remain ignorant of God's word so they won't feel obligated to keep it at every point. But their willing ignorance proves they don't, in fact, love God with all their hearts.

Oh, how I love your law! I meditate on it all day long (Psalm 119:97). *I love your commands more than gold, more than pure gold* (Psalm 119:127). And *I obey your statutes, for I love them greatly* (Psalm 119:167), wrote the Psalmist. Likewise, *Whoever has my commands and keeps them is the one who loves me* (John 14:21), said Jesus. We shouldn't claim to love God unless we love and obey his word.

1 Samuel 15:24 *I was afraid of the men and so I gave in to them.*

To help explain his disobedience, Saul admitted fearing his own men. They fought valiantly, and wanted to keep some of the livestock for themselves. Saul didn't want to seem unreasonable, so he allowed his men to do what God had forbidden. But any leader of God's people must be more afraid of God than of his people. *Fear of man will prove to be a snare, but whoever trusts in the Lord is kept safe* (Proverbs 29:25), says Proverbs. Saul wanted his men's approval more than he wanted God's approval. This made him unqualified to lead the people of God.

1 Samuel 15:30 *Saul replied, I have sinned. But please honor me before the elders of my people and before Israel; come back with me, so that I may worship the Lord your God.*

Since it was no longer possible to deny his guilt, Saul confessed with the hope of regaining Samuel's favor. Everybody sins, and *If we confess our sins, [God] is faithful and just and will forgive us our sins* (1 John 1:9), wrote John. But Saul was less concerned about God's forgiveness than Samuel's approval. If word got out that Samuel didn't approve of Saul, Saul would lose much of his authority. So he begged Samuel to publicly worship God with him. For the good of the nation, Samuel agreed.

1 Samuel 15:31-32 *So Samuel went back with Saul, and Saul worshiped the Lord. Then Samuel said, Bring me Agag king of the Amalekites.*

This was the king Saul was commanded to kill. Since he failed to carry out the Lord's command, Samuel would do it for him. *As your sword has made women childless, so will your mother be childless* (1 Samuel 15:33), he said. Then he killed the Amalekite king in the presence of the Lord.

The Old Testament is filled with blood, much of it spilt at God's command. The New Testament seems better, at first, until we get near the end. There we learn that many will be trampled in the *winepress of God's wrath* until the blood flows *as high as the horses' bridles* (Revelation 14:19-20). This would be bad enough if the blood only ran for a mile, or so, but it'll run for one hundred eighty miles. The God of the Old Testament and the God of the New Testament are the exact same God. And he's not to be taken lightly.

For Reflection and Review

- *Why did Saul set up a monument to himself?*
- *Why do some Christians avoid God's word?*
- *Is Jesus gentle or violent?*

Lesson 60

1 Samuel 16:1 *The Lord said to Samuel, How long will you mourn for Saul, since I have rejected him as king over Israel?*

Samuel was troubled by Saul's failure, and grieved for some time. Then God told him to to go Bethlehem to anoint one of Jesse's sons as the future king of Israel. When Samuel saw Eliab he thought, *Surely the Lord's anointed stands here before the Lord. But the Lord said to Samuel, Do not consider his appearance or his height, for I have rejected him. The Lord does not look at the things people look at. People look at the outward appearance, but the Lord looks at the heart* (1 Samuel 16:6-7).

In a world that prizes beauty, the most attractive are often favored. This is why people diet, exercise, and wear expensive clothing. If we want people's approval, we'll spend time improving our appearance. But if we want God's approval, we'll spend time improving our heart. *People look at the outward appearance, but the Lord looks at the heart.*

And not every heart is equally pure in God's sight. *For it is from within, out of a person's heart, that evil thoughts come—sexual immorality, theft, murder, adultery, greed, malice, deceit, lewdness, envy, slander, arrogance and folly* (Mark 7:21-22), said Jesus.

Some people think their hearts are good by nature, and it's only their bodies that lead them astray. But Jesus taught corruption begins in the heart. If we want to please God, we must banish evil from our hearts and dwell on that which is good. *Blessed are the pure in heart, for they will see God* (Matthew 5:8), said Jesus.

1 Samuel 16:10 *Jesse had seven of his sons pass before Samuel, but Samuel said to him, The Lord has not chosen these.*

Then Jesse called for his youngest son, David, who was tending the sheep. *He was glowing with health and had a fine appearance and handsome features. Then the Lord said, Rise and anoint him; this is the one* (1 Samuel 16:12). Samuel anointed David in the presence of his brothers, and the Holy Spirit came powerfully upon him.

David had a fine appearance but, more importantly, he had a heart for God. Twice the Bible describes him as *a man after [God's] own heart* (1 Samuel 13:14, Acts 13:22). This is not said of anyone else, and distinguished David above others. It could be argued, in fact, that the desire to please God was the most important qualification for being king.

This is just one reason Jesus is qualified to be king of the world forever. David was great, but he wasn't without sin (Psalm 51:5). And *If we claim to be without sin, we deceive ourselves and the truth is not in us* (1 John 1:8), wrote John.

There's only been one person who obeyed God perfectly, every moment of his life. *[F]or I seek not to please myself but him who sent me* (John 5:30). And, *I always do what pleases him* (John 8:29), said Jesus. We should imagine a perfect king ruling the world forever, because that's what the future holds (Luke 1:33).

1 Samuel 16:14 *Now the Spirit of the Lord had departed from Saul, and an evil spirit from the Lord tormented him.*

This is a fascinating insight into the spiritual realm. At one time Saul enjoyed the help of God's Spirit, and was greatly empowered to lead the nation. Due to chronic disobedience, however, the Holy Spirit departed from Saul and was replaced by an evil spirit.

We should be careful about drawing conclusions from this about the Christian life. But we should also be careful *not grieve the Holy Spirit of God, with whom [we] were sealed for the day of redemption* (Ephesians 4:30), wrote Paul. We should, *Instead, be filled with the Spirit* (Ephesians 5:18), and bear the *fruit of the Spirit [which] is love, joy, peace, forbearance, kindness, goodness, faithfulness, gentleness and self-control* (Galatians 5:22-23), wrote Paul again. The spiritual realm is just as real as the physical realm, and we shouldn't *give the devil a foothold* (Ephesians 4:27).

1 Samuel 16:15-16 *Saul's attendants said to him, See, an evil spirit from God is tormenting you. Let our lord command his servants here to search for someone who can play the lyre. He will play when the evil spirit from God comes on you, and you will feel better.*

Saul didn't know that David was anointed the future king of Israel, so when one of Saul's servants recommended David for the job of musician, Saul didn't object. Whenever the evil spirit came on Saul, David played his instrument, and the evil spirit would leave him alone (1 Samuel 16:23).

Everyone is troubled by the devil sometimes (Matthew 4:1-11) and, whenever this happens, we can be helped by listening to godly music, or by singing it. *Sing and make music from your heart to the Lord* (Ephesians 5:19), wrote Paul. Godly music can glorify the Lord, and put the devil to flight.

For Reflection and Review

- *Is the human heart good or evil?*
- *Why did Jesus have a good heart?*
- *Should Christians be concerned about losing the Holy Spirit?*

Lesson 61

1 Samuel 17:1 *Now the Philistines gathered their forces for war and assembled at Sokoh in Judah.*

This begins the account of David and Goliath, one of the most celebrated stories in literature. The Israelites were gathered in the Valley of Elah to fight against the Philistines. They occupied one hill, the Philistines another, and the valley stretched between them. The stakes were high, and the Philistines had an advantage: *A champion named Goliath* (1 Samuel 17:4).

He was over nine and a half feet tall, wore a complete suit of armor, and had a personal shield bearer. From a human point of view, Goliath seemed invincible. For the next forty days, morning and evening, he challenged the Israelite army. *Choose a man and have him come down to me. If he is able to fight and kill me, we will become your subjects; but if I overcome him and kill him, you will become our subjects* (1 Samuel 17:8-9), he said. But there wasn't an Israelite soldier who dared to fight Goliath.

1 Samuel 17:12 *Now David was the son of . . . Jesse, who was from Bethlehem.*

David was watching his father's sheep in Bethlehem, about fifteen miles away from the battle scene. Three of David's brothers were in the Israelite army, and David was sent by his father to bring them supplies. *As he was talking with them, Goliath . . . stepped out from his lines and shouted his usual defiance* (1 Samuel 17:23), and David was appalled.

Who is this uncircumcised Philistine that he should defy the armies of the living God? (1 Samuel 17:26), he asked. David knew that Goliath had every advantage but one: he wasn't circumcised. Circumcision was the mark of the covenant between Israel and God, and included certain promises. *[T]he Lord your God himself will fight for you* (Deuteronomy 3:22). And, *I will be an enemy to your enemies and will oppose those who oppose you* (Exodus 23:22), said God. David believed the promises of God, and wasn't afraid of Goliath.

1 Samuel 17:31 *What David said was overheard and reported to Saul, and Saul sent for him.*

When David stood before Saul he said, *Let no one lose heart on account of this Philistine; your servant will go and fight him.* Saul replied, *You are not able to go out against this Philistine and fight him; you are only a young man, and he has been a warrior from his youth* (1 Samuel 17:32-33). We don't know David's age at the time but, since Israelite men were able to serve in the army at age twenty (Numbers 1:3), he was likely still in his teens.

Nevertheless, David had experience. When a lion went after a sheep from his flock, David killed the lion and rescued the sheep. A bear did the same thing and David killed the bear. *The Lord who rescued me from the paw of the lion and the paw of the bear will rescue me from the hand of this Philistine* (1 Samuel 17:37), he said.

David was courageous in the face of danger because he recalled God's help in the past. If you can remember a time in the past when God took care of you, it can give you courage in the future.

1 Samuel 17:40 *Then he took his staff in his hand, chose five smooth stones from the stream, put them in the pouch of his shepherd's bag and, with his sling in his hand, approached the Philistine.*

No one was more surprised than Goliath to see his opponent. He was expecting a mighty warrior, but encountered a boy not even dressed for battle. *Come here*, he said, *and I'll give your flesh to the birds and the wild animals!* (1 Samuel 17:44).

But David also had words for Goliath. *You come against me with sword and spear and javelin, but I come against you in the name of the Lord Almighty, the God of the armies of Israel, whom you have defied. This day the Lord will deliver you into my hands, and I'll strike you down and cut off your head. This very day I will give the carcasses of the Philistine army to the birds and the wild animals, and the whole world will know that there is a God in Israel. All those gathered here will know that it is not by sword or spear that the Lord saves; for the battle is the Lord's, and he will give all of you into our hands* (1 Samuel 17:45-47).

This is one of the best battle speeches ever recorded, and shows the remarkable faith David had in God. He wasn't merely hoping God would save him; he was absolutely certain God would save him. This is like saving faith in Jesus Christ. *[It] is not from yourselves, it is the gift of God* (Ephesians 2:8), wrote Paul. Sometimes faith is little more than hopefulness. But other times it can be remarkably confident.

1 Samuel 17:48-51 *As the Philistine moved closer to attack him, David ran quickly toward the battle line to meet him. Reaching into his bag and taking out a stone, he slung it and struck the Philistine on the forehead. The stone sank into his forehead, and he fell facedown on the ground.*

So David triumphed over the Philistine with a sling and a stone; without a sword in his hand he struck down the Philistine and killed him. David ran and stood over him. He took hold of the Philistine's sword and drew it from the sheath. After he killed him, he cut off his head with the sword. The Philistine soldiers ran for their lives, and many were cut down. It was a wonderful day for Israel.

It's not unusual for those who read this story to identify with David, but we are not David. We are like the trembling Israelites, defenseless before a powerful enemy. We need someone like David who can rescue us from the power of death. That person is David's great, great, grandson, Jesus Christ (Matthew 1:17). Through his death and resurrection he has conquered death, and given us of eternal life. Through his victory we battle the forces of darkness, knowing their doom is sure.

For Reflection and Review

- Why wasn't David afraid of Goliath?
- How does this story remind us of Christ?
- How does this story increase your faith?

Lesson 62

1 Samuel 18:1 *Jonathan became one in spirit with David, and he loved him as himself.*

Jonathan was the son of Saul, and heir to his father's throne. He could've seen David as a threat, but their mutual respect led to one of the greatest friendships in the Bible. In a private ceremony, Jonathan gave David his sword, implying that he accepted David's right to be king. Unlike his father, Jonathan was willing to accept the role God had for him, instead of grasping for more.

This is a good lesson for everyone. *A person can receive only what is given them from heaven* (John 3:27), said John the Baptist. Many have overreached, and ruined their lives in the process. It's better and wiser to submit to God's will, and do our best within it. It isn't wrong to become all that we can be for God, but God has a limit for everyone. And *godliness with contentment is great gain* (1 Timothy 6:6), wrote Paul.

1 Samuel 18:5 *Whatever mission Saul sent him on, David was so successful that Saul gave him a high rank in the army.*

David was still a young man, but he was rising quickly in Saul's army. He was so successful in battle, in fact, that women were heard singing, *Saul has slain his thousands, and David his tens of thousands* (1 Samuel 18:7). This made Saul so angry that he wanted David dead. He even threw his spear at him, hoping to pin David to the wall (1 Samuel 18:11).

Then Saul offered his daughter in marriage to David, for the price of one hundred Philistine foreskins (1 Samuel 18:25). Saul hoped David would die in battle, but David returned with two hundred Philistine foreskins, and married into the royal family (1 Samuel 18:27). When Saul saw that God was with David, he was even more determined to kill him.

In one of the strangest stories in the Bible, Saul went looking for David and found him with the prophet Samuel. Saul wanted to kill David, but the Spirit of God came on Saul, *and he too prophesied in Samuel's presence. He lay naked all that day and all that night. This is why people say, Is Saul also among the prophets?* (1 Samuel 19:24).

It's difficult to know what's happening here, but it seems Saul was so overcome by God's Spirit, that he couldn't harm David. David was likely amazed to see the one who wanted to kill him, lying on the ground prophesying. From this we understand that there's no limit to what God's Spirit can do.

But Saul's encounter with the Spirit shouldn't be mistaken for saving faith. *Many will say to me on that day, Lord, Lord, did we not prophesy in your name and in your name drive out demons and in your name perform many miracles? Then I will tell them plainly, I never knew you. Away from me, you evildoers!* (Matthew 7:22-23), said Jesus. The best indication of saving faith isn't spiritual experience, but obedience to the one who saves (Matthew 7:21).

1 Samuel 20:4 *Jonathan said to David, Whatever you want me to do, I'll do for you.*

David was still suspicious of Saul, so he went to Jonathan for help. Jonathan agreed to warn David if learned that his father was still hostile. When David was absent from the king's table, and Jonathan made excuses, Saul exploded:

You son of a perverse and rebellious woman! Don't I know that you have sided with [David] to your own shame and to the shame of the mother who bore you? As long as the son of Jesse lives on this earth, neither you nor your kingdom will be established. Now send someone to bring him to me, for he must die! Why should he be put to death? What has he done? Jonathan asked his father. But Saul hurled his spear at him to kill him (1 Samuel 20:30-33).

Saul's opposition to God was affecting his mental health. God is the rational center of the universe, so our best hope for a sound mind is to agree with God about everything. Whenever we disagree with God we're being irrational, which leads to instability and worse. This creates a miserable environment for everyone in the house.

Saul was the most powerful person in Israel, and probably the wealthiest. We might imagine all this power and wealth would make him happy, but such was not the case. *The Lord's curse is on the house of the wicked, but he blesses the home of the righteous* (Proverbs 3:33), says Proverbs.

Many beautiful homes are filled with misery because of God's curse. The people inside might have everything the world has to offer, but they can't find happiness apart from God. Other homes are humble in comparison, but are filled with joy because God is honored there. It's not the size of the house that matters, but the one who's present to bless or curse.

For Reflection and Review

- *Why was Jonathan willing to yield his throne to David?*
- *What can we learn from Saul's encounter with God's Spirit?*
- *Why was Saul becoming mentally unstable?*

Lesson 63

1 Samuel 21:1 *David went to Nob, to Ahimelek the priest.*

David was running from Saul, who wanted him dead. He went to Ahimelek to inquire of the Lord (1 Samuel 22:15), because Ahimelek was the high priest. Ahimelek gave David some bread from the tabernacle, as well as the sword of Goliath. David didn't tell him that he was running from Saul, most likely because he didn't want to make him guilty of helping someone the king opposed.

1 Samuel 21:10 *That day David fled from Saul and went to Achish king of Gath.*

After leaving Ahimelek, David went to the Philistine town of Gath. If he was identified by the Philistines he'd probably be killed, so he tried to blend in as much as possible. But David was recognized in the presence of the king, so he pretended to be insane, letting saliva run down his beard. The king was repulsed, and let David leave on the assumption that he'd lost his mind.

This wasn't David's finest hour, but he thought it was better to lose his dignity than to lose his life. We may never have to make that choice, but in a Christ-rejecting world we may be scorned. *We have become the scum of the earth, the garbage of the world* (1 Corinthians 4:12), wrote Paul. Following Christ will often mean a loss of the world's respect.

1 Samuel 22:1 *David left Gath and escaped to the cave of Adullam.*

This became his home for awhile, and *All those who were in distress or in debt or discontented gathered around him, and he became their commander* (1 Samuel 22:2). David was still on the run, but now had a military base of about four hundred men (1 Samuel 22:2). His kingdom would later become a superpower, but we ought to notice how it began—in a cave with four hundred losers. They were in *distress or in debt or discontented*, but were also the ones God would use to build his glorious kingdom. And the church is not much different.

God chose the foolish things of the world to shame the wise; God chose the weak things of the world to shame the strong. God chose the lowly things of this world and the despised things—and the things that are not—to nullify the things that are (1 Corinthians 1:27-29), wrote Paul.

Those who gather around Jesus Christ are like those who gathered around David, hoping for something better. And, like them, we won't be disappointed. *Do not be afraid, little flock, for your Father has been pleased to give you the kingdom* (Luke 12:32), said Jesus.

1 Samuel 22:3 *From there David went to Mizpah in Moab and said to the king of Moab, Would you let my father and mother come and stay with you until I learn what God will do for me?*

When Samuel anointed David the future king of Israel (1 Samuel 16), his parents may've hoped their lives would soon improve. But such was not the case. When David's life was threatened by King Saul, their lives were also at risk. So David took them to another country where they would be safe.

Mary and Joseph also took Jesus to a foreign country where he would be safe. King Herod wanted to kill him so the family fled to Egypt (Matthew 2:13). The kings of this world often oppose the kingdom of God, but will not overcome it. *The kingdom of the world has become the kingdom of our Lord and of his Messiah, and he will reign for ever and ever* (Revelation 11:15), wrote John. Victory comes to the people of God, but not without resistance.

*****

1 Samuel 22:6 *Saul was seated, spear in hand, under the tamarisk tree on the hill at Gibeah, with all his officials standing at his side.*

Saul and his men were hunting for David, and Saul was becoming increasingly paranoid. When he learned David had been to Nob, he summoned the high priest, Ahimelek, along with all the priests of Nob. Then he accused Ahimelek of conspiracy, and commanded his soldiers to kill all the priests—eighty-five in all.

But his soldiers weren't willing to kill the priests, so Saul commanded Doeg the Edomite to perform the task, which he did singlehandedly. Then Doeg went to the town of Nob, where he killed every man, woman, and child. Like the paranoid king he served, there was no evil he wouldn't do.

With Doeg in mind, David wrote the fifty-second Psalm. *Surely God will bring you down to everlasting ruin: He will snatch you up and pluck you from your tent; he will uproot you from the land of the living* (Psalm

52:5). People get away with terrible crimes in this life, but will face God's judgment in the next.

1 Samuel 22:20 *But one son of Ahimelek son of Ahitub, named Abiathar, escaped and fled to join David.*

This is the first mention of Abiathar, and he would serve as priest during David's reign. The prophet Gad also joined David (1 Samuel 22:5), and would also serve during David's reign. Prophet, priest, and king were brought together by God, to provide appropriate leadership for the kingdom of God.

The offices of prophet, priest, and king were normally kept separate to maintain a balance of power. Kings were not allowed to be priests, and were to obey the word of God given through prophets. But Jesus Christ is prophet, priest, and king all in one person. No balance of power is needed because Jesus is divine, and without a sinful nature.

As the ultimate prophet, Jesus spoke the word of God so clearly that he is called the *Word* (John 1:1). As our great high priest *he entered the Most Holy Place once for all by his own blood, thus obtaining eternal redemption* (Hebrews 9:12). And *On his robe and on his thigh he has this name written: King of kings and Lord of lords* (Revelation 19:16), wrote John. The offices of prophet, priest, and king in the Old Testament look forward to the ultimate prophet, priest, and, king—whose kingdom will never end.

For Reflection and Review

- *What kind of people does God often use to build his glorious kingdom?*
- *What can we learn from Doeg the Edomite?*
- *How does Jesus fulfill the offices of prophet, priest, and king?*

Lesson 64

1 Samuel 24:2 *Saul took three thousand able young men from all Israel and set out to look for David.*

David didn't seem to have a chance. The king of Israel considered him public enemy number one, and was using his army to track him down. David often hid in caves, but God was his ultimate refuge. *The Lord is a refuge for the oppressed* (Psalm 9:9). *Keep me safe, my God, for in you I take refuge* (Psalm 16:1). *[M]y God is my rock, in whom I take refuge* (Psalm 18:2), he wrote. When there are threats on every side, God alone can keep us safe.

More recently a soldier was running for his life, and ducked inside a cave with a very small mouth. Then he watched a spider quickly spin its web across the opening. Minutes later the enemy arrived and was about to enter but, seeing the spider's web, he concluded that no one was in there. Later the soldier wrote, *With God a spider's web is like a wall, and without God a wall is like a spider's web.*

1 Samuel 24:3 *[Saul] came to the sheep pens along the way; a cave was there, and Saul went in to relieve himself.*

What Saul didn't realize is that David and his men were hiding in the back of the cave. It seemed like God had brought this about so David could kill the one who was trying to kill him. But David refused because he respected Saul's authority. *The Lord forbid that I should do such a thing to my master, the Lord's anointed, or lay my hand on him; for he is the anointed of the Lord* (1 Samuel 24:6), he said.

Since God had made Saul the king of Israel, David was determined to submit to his authority until God chose to remove him. This same attitude was taught by the Apostle Paul. *Let everyone be subject to the governing authorities, for there is no authority except that which God has established* (Romans 13:1), he wrote. In a world that disrespects authority, Christians should obey their authorities, as though they were appointed by God.

1 Samuel 24:4 *Then David crept up unnoticed and cut off a corner of Saul's robe.*

After Saul left the cave David called out to him saying, *Why do you listen when men say, David is bent on harming you? This day you have seen with your own eyes how the Lord delivered you into my hands* (1 Samuel 24:9-10). Then he showed him the piece of robe, and Saul realized David could have killed him. He was so overcome with emotion that he wept aloud and said, *You are more righteous than I . . . . You have treated me well, but I have treated you badly . . . . I know that you will surely be king and that the kingdom of Israel will be established in your hands* (1 Samuel 24:17-21).

But tears of remorse and regret are not always tears of repentance. Saul appeared to be repentant, but his future actions would show that he wasn't. Repentance is a change of mind that leads to a change of behavior. If Saul had truly repented he would've given his throne to David, and David would have given Saul a place of honor. That's how it works for those who believe in Jesus Christ. We give him the throne of our hearts, and he gives us a place of honor in his glorious kingdom. Who could wish for anything more?

*****

1 Samuel 25:2 *A certain man in Maon, who had property there at Carmel, was very wealthy. He had a thousand goats and three thousand sheep, which he was shearing in Carmel.*

The man's name was *Nabal* and he's described as *surly* and *mean*. Not everyone is equally nice, but some are truly awful. For whatever reason, they've decided to treat others badly. This is the opposite of Christianity since Jesus commands us to even love our enemies (Matthew 5:44). *And the Lord's servant must not be quarrelsome but must be kind to everyone* (2 Timothy 2:24), wrote Paul. But Nabal was not a servant of God. He was surely and mean.

1 Samuel 25:4 *While David was in the wilderness, he heard that Nabal was shearing sheep.*

Nabal had thousands of sheep, and the wool was worth a fortune. Since David and his men had protected both the sheep and their shepherds, they had a right to share in Nabal's abundance. So David sent some men to ask for a portion but Nabal, of course, treated them badly. *Why should I take my bread and water, and the meat I have slaughtered . . . and give it to men coming from who knows where?* (1 Samuel 25:11), he said.

Nabal was surly and mean because of his love for money—*a root of all kinds of evil* (1 Timothy 6:10), wrote Paul. Those who love money often treat others badly, in order to have more of their money. Nabal was well served by David and his men but, instead of sharing his wealth, he sent them away empty-handed.

For Reflection and Review

- *How is God like a refuge for his people?*
- *How should Christians view those who are in authority?*
- *What is the difference between regret and repentance?*

Lesson 65

1 Samuel 25:12-13 *David's men turned around and went back. When they arrived, they reported every word. David said to his men, Each of you strap on your sword!*

Nabal finally offended the wrong person. David was the future king of Israel, and had an army of six hundred men (1 Samuel 25:13). *He has paid me back evil for good. May God deal with David, be it ever so severely, if by morning I leave alive one male of all who belong to him!* (1 Samuel 25:21-22), he said.

Fearing disaster, one of Nabal's servants informed his wife. *Now think it over and see what you can do, because disaster is hanging over our master and his whole household* (1 Samuel 25:17), he said. So Nabal's wife took an abundance of food, loaded it on donkeys, and went out to meet David.

1 Samuel 25:23-25 *When Abigail saw David, she quickly got off her donkey and bowed down before David with her face to the ground. She fell at his feet and said: Pardon your servant, my lord, and let me speak to you; hear what your servant has to say. Please pay no attention, my lord, to that wicked man Nabal. He is just like his name— his name means Fool, and folly goes with him.*

Nabal was a fool in the eyes of people, but also in the eyes of God. *[F]ools despise wisdom and instruction* (Proverbs 1:7). *[T]he mouth of a fool invites ruin* (Proverbs 10:4). *[F]ools detest turning from evil* (Proverbs 13:19). And *Fools mock at making amends* (Proverbs 14:9), says Proverbs.

But Nabal's wife was just the opposite. *She was an intelligent and beautiful woman* (1 Samuel 25:3). She humbled herself before David, turned away his wrath, and made intercession for her husband. Her timely intervention saved the lives of many.

This reminds of Jesus Christ who *is at the right hand of God and is also interceding for us* (Romans 8:34). Like Nabal, we often play the fool and call down the wrath of God for our sins. Thankfully, we have a Savior who turns away the wrath of God, and intercedes on our behalf. Apart from the intercession of Christ, we'd surely perish for all the foolish things that we've done.

1 Samuel 25:32-33 *David said to Abigail, Praise be to the Lord, the God of Israel, who has sent you today to meet me. May you be blessed for your good judgment and for keeping me from bloodshed this day and from avenging myself with my own hands.*

David was close to making a big mistake. He was rightly offended by Nabal's treatment, but his retaliation would've been worse than Nabal's offense. Abigail was sent by God to keep David from an action that would've brought guilt, regret, and damage to his reputation.

God overruled David's foolish plans and, by his grace, overrules ours sometimes. He might send someone like Abigail, or change our minds himself. God often protects us from the harm we'd do to others, as well as to ourselves.

1 Samuel 25:36 *When Abigail went to Nabal, he was in the house holding a banquet like that of a king. He was in high spirits and very drunk.*

This was not a good time for Abigail to inform Nabal of what just happened, so she waited until morning. When Nabal learned the danger he was in, and the harm he nearly brought on his family, *his heart failed him and he became like a stone.* Nabal probably had a heart attack and, about ten days later, he died.

1 Samuel 25:39 *When David heard that Nabal was dead, he said, Praise be to the Lord, who has upheld my cause against Nabal for treating me with contempt.*

Nabal not only lived as a fool, but also died as one. He lingered ten days without any sign of repentance. He could've turned from his wicked ways, aligned himself with God, and received eternal life. But ten days later, there was no sign of change. Finally, *the Lord struck Nabal and he died* (1 Samuel 25:38), an unrepentant man.

1 Samuel 25:39b *Then David sent word to Abigail, asking her to become his wife.*

By marrying his widow, all Nabal's wealth became David's. Everything Nabal worked for, and everything he acquired, now belonged to someone who cared about God. *[A] sinner's wealth is stored up for the righteous* (Proverbs 13:22), says Proverbs. If we don't manage our money for God, he can give it to someone else.

For Reflection and Review

- *How is the intercession of Abigail like the intercession of Christ?*
- *How does God keep us from making big mistakes?*
- *What was foolish about Nabal?*

Lesson 66

1 Samuel 26:2 *Saul went down to the Desert of Ziph, with his three thousand select Israelite troops, to search there for David.*

Saul still considered David the greatest threat to his throne, even though David had proven his loyalty (1 Samuel 24:3-12). The greatest threat to Saul was actually Saul himself. Since God determined he shouldn't be king (1 Samuel 15:23),

Saul should've arranged a smooth transition to the king of God's choice. By resolving to keep his position, regardless of God's will, Saul became an increasingly tragic figure.

This is true for all who serve in the kingdom of God. The kingdom belongs to Jesus Christ, not to anyone else. Pastors, teachers, musicians, custodians, and ushers serve at the discretion of Jesus Christ and are never promised a permanent position. Opposition doesn't mean a person should resign, but whoever serves in any position should be willing to resign whenever they believe it's God's will for them.

1 Samuel 26:3 *Saul made his camp beside the road on the hill of Hakilah.*

When David learned that Saul and his army were camping nearby, he waited until it was dark, and then went with one of his men into the enemy camp. *So David and Abishai went to the army by night, and there was Saul, lying asleep inside the camp with his spear stuck in the ground near his head. . . . Abishai said to David, Today God has delivered your enemy into your hands. Now let me pin him to the ground with one thrust of the spear; I won't strike him twice* (1 Samuel 26:7-8).

Abishai wanted to kill Saul but, again, David wanted to prove his loyalty. He wanted to show Saul that he could take his life if he wanted to, but that he really didn't want to. *[T]he Lord himself will strike him, or his time will come and he will die, or he will go into battle and perish* (1 Samuel 26:10), said David.

There's a time to act, and a time to wait, and wisdom knows the difference. It'd take over ten years from the time David was anointed king until he actually became king. But David was willing to wait on God no matter how long it took. One of the greatest tests of faith is waiting for God to act. This was a test of David's faith and, unlike Saul, David passed the test.

1 Samuel 26:12 *So David took the spear and water jug near Saul's head, and they left. No one saw or knew about it, nor did anyone wake up. They were all sleeping, because the Lord had put them into a deep sleep.*

Walking into a camp of three thousand enemy soldiers appears to be foolish. But David and Abishai were willing to do this because they believed God was with them. Common sense is a gift from God which he normally wants us to use. But there are also times for taking a risk because we believe God is with us. Taking chances for God (and being willing to fail) are part of the life of faith.

1 Samuel 26:13 *Then David crossed over to the other side and stood on top of the hill some distance away.*

From there David called out to the commander of Saul's army. *Why didn't you guard your lord the king? . . . As surely as the Lord lives, you and your men must die, because you did not guard your master, the Lord's anointed* (1 Samuel 26:15-16), he said.

Then David called attention to the missing spear and water jug, to prove he was there and could've killed Saul if he wanted to. Once again we can imagine Saul's alarm when he learned his life had been spared by the man he was trying to kill.

Wise people learn from their mistakes, and become even wiser. Fools repeat their mistakes, and become more foolish still. The first time David spared his life, Saul should've learned that David was not a threat to him. But the victim of his own paranoia, Saul repeated his mistake and showed himself to be a royal fool. God knows we all make mistakes; may God help us not to repeat them.

1 Samuel 26:17 *Saul recognized David's voice and said, Is that your voice, David my son? David replied, Yes it is, my lord the king.*

This is the final conversation between David and Saul. Saul appeared to repent, and acknowledged David as the future king of Israel (1 Samuel 26:25). But Saul couldn't be trusted, and David knew it. To be in Saul's company was to put David's life, and the lives of his men, at risk. The only wise course, therefore, was to separate—and they never spoke again. Sometimes, we can't just get along.

*****

1 Samuel 27:1 *David thought to himself, One of these days I will be destroyed by the hand of Saul. The best thing I can do is to escape to the land of the Philistines.*

The relentless stress of being hunted by Saul compelled David to form an apparent alliance with Israel's enemy, the Philistines. Achish, king of Gath, gave David and his six hundred soldiers the town of Ziklag. With David on his side, Achish thought he'd have less to fear from the nation of Israel.

1 Samuel 27:8 *Now David and his men went up and raided the Geshurites, the Girzites and the Amalekites.*

These were Israel's enemies, but David led Achish to believe that he was attacking God's people in Judah. To be sure he wasn't found out, David *did not leave a man or woman alive* (1 Samuel 27:9). David was defeating God's enemies, and protecting himself from being discovered.

1 Samuel 27:12 *Achish trusted David and said to himself, He has become so obnoxious to his people, the Israelites, that he will be my servant for life.*

David deceived Achish, and survived in Philistine territory for over a year (1 Samuel 15:7). But then he was made king of God's people, and thoroughly *defeated the Philistines* (1 Chronicles 18:1). David's double-life was over, and he could finally be who he really was.

It's difficult to know if David's double-life met with God's approval. But God's people do, at times, conceal their identity. *Joseph [of Arimathea] was a disciple of Jesus, but secretly because he feared the Jewish leaders* (John 19:38), wrote John. We should pray for Christians who are facing danger, and use the freedom we enjoy to advance the kingdom of God.

For Reflection and Review

- *When and why should God's servants be willing to resign?*
- *Was David being foolish by walking into Saul's camp?*
- *How should Christians evangelize where Christianity is illegal?*

Lesson 67

1 Samuel 28:4 *The Philistines assembled and came and set up camp at Shunem, while Saul gathered all Israel and set up camp at Gilboa.*

Saul was a seasoned warrior, but this battle gave him pause. *When [he] saw the Philistine army, he was afraid; terror filled his heart* (1 Samuel 28:5). The text is not explicit but, apparently, Israel was outnumbered. This didn't mean certain defeat, of course. Saul's son Jonathan proved that *Nothing can hinder the Lord from saving, whether by many or by few* (1 Samuel 14:6). *For the Lord your God is the one who goes with you to fight for you against your enemies to give you victory* (Deuteronomy 20:4), wrote Moses.

But God's help wasn't guaranteed, and Saul wasn't walking with God. Because he rejected the word of the Lord, God had rejected him as king (1 Samuel 15:23). Instead of being filled with faith, therefore, Saul was stricken with fear—*terror filled his heart.*

Obedience isn't always easy, but it allows us to face life fearlessly, knowing that nothing can happen to us apart from the will of our heavenly Father (Luke 12:4-7). Those who refuse to walk with God may seem to prosper temporarily, but are left to themselves when disaster strikes. *I will show them my back and not my face in the day of their disaster* (Jeremiah 18:17), said God.

1 Samuel 28:6 *[Saul] inquired of the Lord, but the Lord did not answer him.*

For many years Saul did as he pleased, but now that he was desperate he inquired of the Lord. He didn't want to live for God; he only wanted God's help. But God isn't obligated to answer the prayers of those who don't want him so, this time, *the Lord did not answer him.*

You will seek me and find me when you seek me with all your heart (Jeremiah 29:23), said God. If Saul would've sought God with all his heart, he would've found the God he was looking for. But that wasn't Saul's way so, instead, he turned to a spiritist.

1 Samuel 28:7 *Find me a woman who is a medium, so I may go and inquire of her.*

Since God wasn't answering Saul, he decided to call on the prophet Samuel instead. But Samuel was dead by now (1 Samuel 25:1), so Saul looked for a medium who might be able to call him up.

Once again Saul revealed his true spiritual condition, since this was clearly forbidden. *Do not turn to mediums or seek out spiritists* (Leviticus 19:31). *I will set my face against anyone who turns to mediums and spiritists* (Leviticus 20:6), said God. In better days, Saul expelled spiritists from the land, but now he was seeking one himself.

1 Samuel 28:7b *There is one in Endor, they said.*

Endor was a two-hour walk, and the day had already passed. But Saul was convinced that if he could just hear from Samuel, he might learn what to do. So he went with two of his men and found the person they were looking for. *Whom shall I bring up for you? Bring up Samuel, he said.*

This is Saul at his lowest. Years earlier God changed his heart and made him a new person (1 Samuel 10:9). *When all those who had formerly known him saw him prophesying . . . they asked each other . . . . Is Saul also among the prophets?* (1 Samuel 10:11). But starting well is no guarantee of finishing well, and Saul was finishing badly. He used to be among the prophets, but now was consulting a medium.

1 Samuel 28:12 *When the woman saw Samuel, she cried out at the top of her voice and said to Saul, Why have you deceived me? You are Saul!*

The woman was afraid because Saul had expelled the spiritists and could've had her killed. But time had changed the king, and the spiritist was now his friend. *Don't be afraid. What do you see? The woman said, I see a ghostly figure coming up out of the earth. What does he look like? he asked. An old man wearing a robe is coming up, she said. Then Saul knew it was Samuel, and he bowed down and prostrated himself with his face to the ground* (1 Samuel 28:13-14).

The Bible condemns calling up the dead, but doesn't deny the possibility. Demons might also impersonate the dead but, in this case, God allowed Samuel to appear. *Why do you consult me, now that the Lord has departed from you and become your enemy? . . . The Lord will deliver both Israel and you into the hands of the Philistines, and tomorrow you and your sons will be with me. The Lord will also give the army of Israel into the hands of the Philistines* (1 Samuel 28:16-19), said Samuel. Saul's greatest fear was confirmed—he was a dead man walking.

1 Samuel 28:24-25 *The woman had a fattened calf at the house, which she butchered at once. She took some flour, kneaded it and baked bread without yeast. Then she set it before Saul and his men, and they ate. That same night they got up and left.*

It must've been a lonely walk back to camp as they thought about the battle. Indeed, the fighting grew fierce, and Saul was critically wounded. Rather than suffering torture at the hands of his enemies, he fell on his sword and died. His sons also died, and the army suffered heavy losses. The Philistines cut off Saul's head, hung his body up, and put his armor in a pagan temple (1 Samuel 31:3-10). Worse than dying in battle, however, Saul died without God. He's one of the most tragic figures in the Bible.

From Saul we learn that there's nothing more important than staying right with God. Every day we're growing closer to God, or drifting further away from him. It's seldom apparent day by day, or even week by week. But over the course of years, a gradual drift can turn into apostasy. Saul had power, fame, and wealth but they couldn't keep him from death—or dying without God. There's only one friend we can't afford to lose, but Saul lost his friendship with God.

For Reflection and Review

- *Why was Saul filled with fear?*
- *Why didn't God answer Saul?*
- *What makes Saul a tragic figure?*

Lesson 68

1 Samuel 30:1 *David and his men reached Ziklag.*

David had a standing army of six hundred men and, together with their families, they adopted Ziklag as their home town. One day, when David and his men returned, they found their town burned to the ground, and all the women and children taken captive. David's soldiers were so distressed that all they could talk about was killing David. By all accounts, it was a very bad day.

After coming to faith in Christ some people think their life will be an unbroken series of blessings. *[W]hatever they do prospers* (Psalm 1:3), wrote the Psalmist. And *you make the way of the righteous smooth* (Isaiah 26:7), wrote Isaiah. This is true, of course, but it's not the whole truth. *We must go through many hardships to enter the kingdom of God* (Acts 14:22), said Paul. And *In this world you will have trouble* (John 16:33), said Jesus. God is pleased to smooth the way for us, but he also allows trouble to help us grow in faith.

1 Samuel 30:4 *So David and his men wept aloud until they had no strength left to weep.*

It's hard to make a grown man cry, especially those who've been hardened by battle. But the loss of their families, and all their possessions, was so great that all six hundred men wept aloud. Imagine six hundred men howling over the loss of everything precious to them. Perhaps they wept for an hour, or two, or even three. They didn't stop weeping *until they had no strength left to weep*, it says.

Weeping is discouraged in many cultures, but not in the Bible. Joseph wept (Genesis 45:14), David wept (2 Samuel 15:30), Job wept (Job 16:16), Jeremiah wept (Lamentations 2:11), Peter wept (Luke 22:62), Paul wept (Acts 20:31), and may others wept. The shortest verse in the Bible, in fact, says *Jesus wept* (John 11:35).

Life hurts, sometimes, and reliable studies show that crying has many benefits such as removing toxins, reducing stress, elevating mood, and releasing negative feelings. *[W]eeping may stay for the night, but rejoicing comes in the morning* (Psalm 30:5), wrote David.

1 Samuel 30:6 *But David found strength in the Lord his God.*

After weeping his heart out, David turned to God and found strength. Human strength comes to an end, but God has an endless supply. *He gives strength to the weary and increases the power of the weak* (Isaiah 40:29), wrote Isaiah.

But how, exactly, did David find strength in God? The Bible doesn't say, but he probably considered the fact that God is mighty, and had helped him in the past. He knew that God was with him, and knew where the women and children were, and could help with their rescue. As David thought this way, his grief gave way to hope, his confusion to clarity, and his weakness to God's strength.

1 Samuel 30:7-8 *Then David said to Abiathar the priest, the son of Ahimelek, Bring me the ephod. Abiathar brought it to him, and David inquired of the Lord.*

Through Abiathar the priest, David inquired of God, and received the guidance he needed. Then he began to give chase. We too are encouraged to seek God whenever we need guidance. *If any of you lacks wisdom, you should ask God, who gives generously to all without finding fault, and it will be given to you* (James 1:5), wrote James. We don't have to navigate life alone. God will guide us if we're willing to follow.

1 Samuel 30:11 *They found an Egyptian in a field and brought him to David.*

David and his army were on the march, searching for their enemies and trusting God to lead them.

As they went, they came across an Egyptian slave who was abandoned by his master because he was sick. It had been three days since he had anything to eat or drink, but as soon as he was nourished he revived. Then he informed David that he was with the Amalekites when they burned Ziklag, and knew where they could be found. On the conditions that his life be spared, and he not be returned to his master, he agreed to lead David and his men to the place.

Whenever we have a problem, God may have a strategic person to help solve it. And whenever someone else has a problem, we may be the strategic person God wants to help solve it. We need each other to help solve our problems, and this is how God likes to use us.

1 Samuel 30:16 *He led David down, and there they were, scattered over the countryside, eating, drinking and reveling because of the great amount of plunder they had taken from the land of the Philistines and from Judah.*

Energized by God, and the desire to save their families, David and his men fought the Amalekites through the night, until the following evening. They recovered all the women and children, plus a great deal of plunder which they divided among themselves. A devastating event was turned into something good.

We should never judge a tragedy at the time it occurs, because we never know how God will use it for good. When David and his men saw the tragedy, they assumed it was the worst day of their lives. By following God and doing his will, however, it became one of the best. *God is able to do immeasurably more than all we ask or imagine* (Ephesians 3:20), wrote Paul.

For Reflection and Review

- *Why does God let bad things happen to his people?*
- *How does God guide his people today?*
- *How does God give us extra strength?*

Lesson 69

2 Samuel 1:1 *After the death of Saul, David returned from striking down the Amalekites and stayed in Ziklag two days.*

David was unaware of Saul's death, but a messenger arrived with an account of the battle. *When [Saul] turned around and saw me . . . he said to me, Stand here by me and kill me! I'm in the throes of death, but I'm still alive. So I stood beside him and killed him, because I knew that after he had fallen he could not survive. And I took the crown that was on his head and the band on his arm and have brought them here to [you]* (2 Samuel 1:7-10).

In fact, however, Saul was wounded in battle and killed himself to avoid being tortured (1 Samuel 31:3-4). This man was probably a scavenger who got to Saul's body before the Philistines. He likely made up this story to gain David's favor and a position in his new administration. He thought he was being smart, but he was playing the fool.

2 Samuel 1:15-16 *Then David called one of his men and said, Go, strike him down! So he struck him down, and he died. For David had said to him, Your blood be on your own head. Your own mouth testified against you when you said, I killed the Lord's anointed.*

Instead of a reward, this man met with death because he didn't understand David's respect for God's king. Saul was chosen by God (1 Samuel 10:1), and only God had the right to remove him. By claiming to kill God's king, this man gave up his life.

Those who want to advance too quickly often turn to schemes. *Whoever plots evil will be known as a schemer* (Proverbs 24:8). *A fool finds pleasure in wicked schemes* (Proverbs 10:23). And *[God] condemns those who devise wicked schemes* (Proverbs 12:2), says Proverbs.

Schemers, in fact, seldom profit for long. An American investor was sentenced to one hundred fifty years in prison for cheating customers out of billions of dollars. He was living high for a while, but then he was brought low. *Better the poor whose walk is blameless than the rich whose ways are perverse* (Proverbs 28:6), says Proverbs.

2 Samuel 2:4 *Then the men of Judah came to Hebron, and there they anointed David king over the tribe of Judah.*

David was thirty years old at this time (2 Samuel 5:4-5), and it would be another seven years before he was king over the whole nation. And the transition wasn't smooth.

Abner (the commander of Saul's army) met with Joab (the commander of David's army) at the town of Gibeon—each with troops. To minimize bloodshed, twelve soldiers were put forward from each side to engage in mortal combat. *Then each man grabbed his opponent by the head and thrust his dagger into his opponent's side, and they fell down together* (2 Samuel 2:16). Since there was no obvious winner, a battle broke out in which Judah lost twenty men, and Israel lost three hundred sixty men (2 Samuel 2:30-31). It could've been worse, but it wasn't pretty.

Some time later Abner agreed to unite Israel under David, but Joab was angry because Abner had killed his brother in the previous battle (2 Samuel 2:23). So *Joab took him aside into an inner chamber, as if to speak with him privately. And there, to avenge the blood of his brother [he] stabbed him in the stomach* (2 Samuel 3:27).

Meanwhile, Saul's son Ish-Bosheth was ruling as king in Israel. He was taking a noonday rest when he was stabbed to death, and his head was removed. His murderers took his head to David, hoping for approval. But David wasn't pleased and had them killed (2 Samuel 4:1-12). Then, at last, the kingdom was united under David.

The church should be united under Christ (John 17:23), but is often at war with itself. Professing Christians have used torture and murder against other professing believers. But it will not always be this way. *[W]hen the times reach their fulfillment [Christ will] bring unity to all things in heaven and on earth* (Ephesians 1:10), wrote Paul. The *Prince of Peace* (Isaiah 9:6) will be the undisputed king. The transition is painful, sometimes, but the end will be glorious.

*****

2 Samuel 5:6 *The king and his men marched to Jerusalem to attack the Jebusites, who lived there.*

Israel had taken Jerusalem before (Judges 1:8, 21), but the Jebusites had taken it back. It'd be worth the fight, however, since it was perfect for David's capital. With valleys on three sides it was easy to defend, but wouldn't be easy to take. David and his men entered through a water shaft, which still exists today. The Jebusites were defeated, and Jerusalem became the *City of David* (1 Samuel 5:9).

Jerusalem had been around for at least a thousand years (Genesis 14:18), and probably even longer. It's also called *Zion*, and is mentioned in the Bible over eight hundred times. It's where the temple was built (1 Kings 6), where Jesus was crucified (John 19:20), and where he'll return (Zechariah 14:4) to rule the world.

And when it's time for a new heaven and a new earth, God will also create a new Jerusalem. *I saw the Holy City, the new Jerusalem, coming down out of heaven from God, prepared as a bride beautifully dressed for her husband. And I heard a loud voice from the throne saying, Look! God's dwelling place is now among the people, and he will dwell with them. They will be his people, and God himself will be with them and be their God. He will wipe every tear from their eyes. There will be no more death or mourning or crying or pain, for the old order of things has passed away* (Revelation 21:2-4), wrote John. Then Jerusalem will be the capital city of the world forever.

For Reflection and Review

- *Why are people tempted by wicked schemes?*
- *Why is the church often divided?*
- *What's significant about Jerusalem?*

Lesson 70

2 Samuel 6:2 *[David] and all his men went to Baalah in Judah to bring up from there the ark of God.*

Having established Jerusalem as the political center of Israel, David proceeded to make it the religious center as well. The ark was more than a religious object, it was God's throne on earth (1 Samuel 4:4). God was uniquely present *between the two cherubim that [were] over the ark* (Exodus 25:22). By bringing the ark to the capital city, David was showing that God was the king of Israel, and that David was merely his servant. *The Lord Almighty—he is the King of glory* (Psalm 24:10), he wrote.

To properly honor God, David arranged a massive celebration. He and thirty thousand young men accompanied the ark of God in a kind of military escort. They put the ark on a new cart and brought it from the house of Abinadab where it had been for many years. The people rejoiced wholeheartedly, with songs and musical instruments. It was a wonderful day for the people of God, but that was about to change.

2 Samuel 6:6 *When they came to the threshing floor of Nakon, Uzzah reached out and took hold of the ark of God, because the oxen stumbled.*

We don't know why the oxen stumbled. Perhaps there was a stone on the road or, perhaps it was uneven. The people likely gasped when they saw ark sliding off the cart. For it to fall to the ground would've been a terrible disgrace.

Thankfully, Uzzah had the presence of mind to reach out his hand and steady the ark. He kept it from falling to the ground and possibly breaking apart. But any sigh of relief was brief. *The Lord's anger burned against Uzzah because of his irreverent act; therefore God struck him down, and he died there beside the ark of God* (2 Samuel 6:7).

It seems like God should've been thankful to Uzzah for keeping the ark from falling to the ground. It also seems like Uzzah should've been rewarded for his prompt behavior—not killed for it. But if anything was worse than God's throne falling to the dirt, it was being touched by sinful hands. Dirt never rebelled against its Maker, but sinners do this all the time. Letting God's throne fall to the ground would've been better by far than touching it with sinful hands.

It's also surprising David planned this event without consulting God's word. God provided clear instructions about how the ark was to be moved. There were rings on the side, through which poles were to be inserted, so the ark could be properly carried (Exodus 25:12-15). It wasn't to be touched by human hands *or they will die* (Numbers 4:15), warned God. And that's what happened.

Some people hope that ignorance will protect them from God's judgment, but that didn't work for Uzzah. He didn't know what God required, but God killed him anyway. *[T]he wages of sin is death* (Romans 6:23), wrote Paul. This is true even if we don't know we're sinning.

It also appears that our worship of God isn't always pleasing to him, even if it's pleasing to us. Thousands of people praising God enthusiastically may seem like a successful worship event. But it's not successful if it is not biblical. *[T]rue worshipers will worship the Father in the Spirit and in truth* (John 4:23), said Jesus. If our worship isn't governed by God's word, then it isn't pleasing to God.

2 Samuel 6:8 *David was angry because the Lord's wrath had broken out against Uzzah.*

David planned a great event, but God ruined the party. The punishment seemed disproportionate to the offense, and this made David angry. It also made him afraid. *David was afraid of the Lord that day and said, How can the ark of the Lord ever come to me?* (2 Samuel 6:9).

David was beginning to understand that God is to be revered. God is good, kind, loving, and gracious, but also holy and just. He often overlooks our sins (Deuteronomy 9:27), but not always. We should *worship God acceptably with reverence and awe, for our God is a consuming fire* (Hebrews 12:28-29), says Hebrews.

2 Samuel 6:10 *[David] was not willing to take the ark of the Lord to be with him in the City of David.*

David didn't know if God was safe, so he sent the ark to the house of Obed-Edom. Three months later he learned that God was blessing the household of Obed-Edom because of the ark. So, once again, David brought the ark to Jerusalem, not on a cart, but properly carried.

2 Samuel 6:14-15 *Wearing a linen ephod, David was dancing before the Lord with all his might, while he and all Israel were bringing up the ark of the Lord with shouts and the sound of trumpets.*

This is one of the most exuberant worship scenes in the Bible. As part of the parade, David was leading God's people in dance. This type of worship isn't found in the New Testament, but is mentioned in the Psalms. *Let them praise his name with dancing and make music to him with timbrel and harp* (Psalm 149:3). *[P]raise him with timbrel and dancing, praise him with the strings and pipe* (Psalm 150:4). God's ancient people could be enthusiastic in their worship.

2 Samuel 6:16 *As the ark of the Lord was entering the City of David, Michal daughter of Saul watched from a window. And when she saw King David leaping and dancing before the Lord, she despised him in her heart.*

Michal was David's first wife, the daughter of King Saul. Since she was raised a princess, she probably had an idea of how royalty should behave—and David wasn't behaving royally. She may also have been embarrassed by David's full-hearted devotion to God. This led to a serious spat, and an unhappy outcome. *Michal daughter of Saul had no children to the day of her death* (2 Samuel 6:23).

This may've been the judgment of God, or the judgment of David. Since David had other wives, he may've stopped sleeping with Michal, thereby depriving her of children. This would be cruel, but underscores how destructive disrespect can be to a marriage, and why Paul said *the wife must respect her husband* (Ephesians 5:33).

If it was the judgment of God, however, it shows that we should not despise those who are more expressive in worship than we are. God's people should be careful not to draw attention away from God by drawing it to themselves. But if someone is more enthusiastic in worship than we are, we should not think less of them. Rather, we should consider whether our own hearts are as full of praise as they ought to be.

For Reflection and Review

- *Why was the ark of God important?*
- *What should we learn from the death of Uzzah?*
- *What should we learn from David's conflict with Michal?*

Lesson 71

2 Samuel 7:1-2 *After the king was settled in his palace and the Lord had given him rest from all his enemies around him, he said to Nathan the prophet, Here I am, living in a house of cedar, while the ark of God remains in a tent.*

David was firmly established as king in Jerusalem, and had built a palace of cedar and stone for himself (2 Samuel 5:11). But the ark of God was still in a tent, as it had been for over four hundred years. It was constructed at the foot of Mount Sinai, shortly after the Israelites were delivered from Egyptian slavery through the Red Sea.

2 Samuel 7:3 *Nathan replied to the king, Whatever you have in mind, go ahead and do it, for the Lord is with you.*

As the prophet Samuel advised King Saul, so various prophets advised King David. This is the first story in which we encounter Nathan, but not the last (2 Samuel 12, 1 Kings 1). He was a faithful servant of the king, and David named one of his sons *Nathan* meaning *gift* (of God).

2 Samuel 7:4-5 *But that night the word of the Lord came to Nathan, saying: Go and tell my servant David, This is what the Lord says: Are you the one to build me a house to dwell in?*

Nathan had advised David to do whatever he had in mind. But this was his advice as David's counselor, not as the mouthpiece of God. That same night God informed Nathan that David was not to build him a temple. *I have not dwelt in a house from the day I brought the Israelites up out of Egypt to this day. . . . did I ever say . . . Why have you not built me a house of cedar?* (2 Samuel 7:6-7).

But God was pleased with David's desire to honor him, and responded with a promise: *The Lord declares to you that the Lord himself will establish a house for you* (2 Samuel 7:11). David wanted to build a house for God, but God would build a house for David. David wanted to build God a physical house, but God would build David an everlasting household. *I will raise up your offspring to succeed you, your own flesh and blood . . . your throne will be established forever* (2 Samuel 7:12-16), said God.

God's promise to David was an everlasting dynasty. One of his sons would rule as king *forever*. Dynasties can last for centuries, or even millennia, but an everlasting dynasty is hard to imagine—humanly speaking.

God's promise to David had roots going back hundreds of years to Abraham's wife, Sarah. *[K]ings of peoples will come from her* (Genesis 17:16), said God. Years later, Abraham's grandson (Jacob) added, *The scepter will not depart from Judah* (Genesis 49:10). Since David was descended from Abraham, Jacob and Judah, God was fulfilling his promises and making them even greater.

But it didn't turn out the way David thought. In 586 BC, the Babylonians destroyed the city of Jerusalem, blinded the king, and took him back to Babylon. To the natural eye this was the end of David's dynasty, and a shock to everyone who believed God's promise.

The eighty-ninth Psalm captures the bewilderment felt by many. God said of David, *I will establish his line forever, his throne as long as the heavens endure. . . . Once for all, I have sworn by my holiness—and I will not lie to David—that his line will continue forever and his throne endure before me like the sun; it will be established forever like the moon, the faithful witness in the sky. . . .*

[But] You have renounced the covenant with your servant and have defiled his crown in the dust. You have broken through all his walls and reduced his strongholds to ruins. All who pass by have plundered him; he has become the scorn of his neighbors. . . . Indeed, you have turned back the edge of his sword and have not supported him in battle. You have put an end to his splendor and cast his throne to the ground (Psalm 89:29-44), wrote the Psalmist.

God's people didn't stop believing in God, even when his promise seemed to fail. But they didn't ignore the problem either. They acknowledged the tension between what God had clearly promised (David's eternal dynasty) and what they had clearly experienced (the collapse of David's dynasty). Many wondered if they could trust God's promises or not.

About six hundred years after Jerusalem fell, we read of the birth of *Jesus the Messiah the son of David, the son of Abraham* (Matthew 1:1). The angel had said to his mother, *You will conceive and give birth to a son, and you are to call him Jesus. The Lord God will give him the throne of his father David . . . his kingdom will never end* (Luke 1:31-33). So when Jesus rode into Jerusalem on a donkey, the people shouted *Hosanna to the Son of David* (Matthew 21:9), and *Blessed is the king of Israel!* (John 12:13).

The prophets also foresaw a future king from David's line. *A shoot will come up from the stump of [David]; from his roots a Branch will bear fruit* (Isaiah 11:1), wrote Isaiah. And, *I will raise up for David a righteous Branch, a King who will reign wisely* (Jeremiah 23:5), said Jeremiah. And, *He will reign on David's throne and over his kingdom . . . forever* (Isaiah 9:7), wrote Isaiah.

What God's people didn't know, and couldn't understand, was that David's messianic Son had been ruling from heaven's throne since before the beginning of time. From a human perspective the collapse of David's dynasty was a theological disaster that couldn't be resolved. But from heaven's perspective there was no problem at all. David's son was king forever—past, present and future. He just hadn't been born yet.

The promises of God find their ultimate fulfillment in Jesus Christ. *For no matter how many promises God has made, they are Yes in Christ* (2 Corinthians 1:20), wrote Paul. And *Remember Jesus Christ . . . descended from David* (2 Timothy 2:8), wrote Paul again. And, *I am the Root and the Offspring of David* (Revelation 22:16), said Jesus Christ himself.

God gave David an everlasting dynasty through his great, great, grandson, Jesus Christ. And, when he returns, Jesus' kingdom will surpass David's in every possible way. God always keeps his promises, even when they seem to fail.

For Reflection and Review

- *Why did it seem that God had broke his promise to David?*
- *How did God fulfill his promise to David?*
- *How do we know that God will keep his word?*

Lesson 72

2 Samuel 9:1 *David asked, Is there anyone still left of the house of Saul to whom I can show kindness for Jonathan's sake?*

Jonathan was the son of King Saul, and David's dear friend. When his life was at risk, David received Jonathan's help, and vowed kindness to his family (1 Samuel 20:15). Since Jonathan had died (1 Samuel 31:2), David looked for a way to keep his promise.

Jonathan's son was *Mephibosheth*, and he was just five years old when his father died in battle. *His nurse picked him up and fled, but as she hurried to leave, he fell and became disabled* (2 Samuel 4:4). With better medical help the injury would've healed correctly but, without it, he became *lame in both feet* (2 Samuel 9:3).

This was a turning point in the young man's life from which he'd never recover. He was born a prince, but lost his position and his health in a single day. He couldn't play games with his friends, and would have trouble earning a living. Not a day passed that he didn't feel the loss.

But this was the kind of person David was looking for. He brought him into his house and said, *Mephibosheth! . . . I will surely show you kindness for the sake of your father Jonathan. I will restore to you all the land that belonged to your grandfather Saul, and you will always eat at my table* (2 Samuel 9:6-7).

This too was a turning point in Mephibosheth's life, but a positive one. In a single day he was adopted into the king's family, and given great wealth. He *bowed down and said, What is your servant, that you should notice a dead dog like me?* (2 Samuel 9:8). But David took care of Mephibosheth, not for his own sake, but for the sake of his friend Jonathan.

This reminds us of what God has done for us because of Jesus Christ. He took us as we were, adopted us into his family, and gave us unexpected wealth. *God raised us up with Christ and seated us with him in the heavenly realms [to] show the incomparable riches of his grace* (Ephesians 2:6-7), wrote Paul. What David did for Mephibosheth, because of Jonathan, is a very faint reflection of what God will do for everyone who believes in Jesus Christ.

*****

2 Samuel 10:1 *In the course of time, the king of the Ammonites died, and his son Hanun succeeded him as king.*

The Ammonite king had been kind to David, perhaps while he was running from Saul. So when the Ammonite king died, David wanted to show kindness to his son, who was reigning in his father's place. This was gracious of David since, at one time, the Ammonites had been Israel's enemies (Judges 11:4, 1 Samuel 11:15).

When David sent a delegation to express his sympathy, however, the new king doubted David's motives and treated the delegation like spies. *[He] shaved off half of each man's beard, cut off their garments at the buttocks, and sent them away* (2 Samuel 10:4).

This was an extreme provocation that revealed the new king's foolishness. By exposing the private parts of David's men, and shaving half their beards, he guaranteed retaliation. Few things are more precious than dignity and, whenever it's violated, it can led to fury. This also reminds us of Jesus Christ.

As David sent a delegation to the Ammonites, God sent his Son into the world. As the Ammonites shaved off half their beards, Jesus' beard was plucked from his face (Isaiah 50:6). As the Ammonites shamefully exposed the delegation, so Jesus was hung on a cross fully exposed. As the Ammonites' behavior incited the wrath of David, so the wrath of God is incited against all who oppose Jesus Christ (John 3:36). *These are the very Scriptures that testify about me* (John 5:39), said Jesus.

2 Samuel 10:6 *When the Ammonites realized that they had become obnoxious to David, they hired twenty thousand Aramean foot soldiers from Beth Rehob and Zobah, as well as the king of Maakah with a thousand men, and also twelve thousand men from Tob.*

The cost of mercenary troops to fight the Israelites was thirty-eight tons of silver (1 Chronicles 19:6). This was a massive amount, and likely depleted the nation's wealth. If the Ammonite king had given this money to David, in order to make amends, the conflict could've been resolved. War could've been avoided and lives could've been spared.

Jesus used this same line of thinking to encourage surrender to him. *[S]uppose a king is about to go to war against another king. Won't he first sit down and consider whether he is able with ten thousand men to oppose the one coming against him with twenty thousand? If he is not able, he will send a delegation while the other is still a long way off and will ask for terms of peace* (Luke 14:31-32), he said.

Like the foolish Ammonite king, we've all provoked the King of kings, and made him very angry (John 3:36). He's coming with the armies of heaven (Revelation 19:14-15), but disaster can still be avoided if we're willing to pay the price: *those of you who do not give up everything you have cannot be my disciples* (Luke 14:33). Jesus requires full surrender of everything we have, and everything we are. In return we're given eternal life in his glorious kingdom. We surrender our rags to receive his riches.

2 Samuel 10:8 *The Ammonites came out and drew up in battle formation.*

Instead of total surrender, the Ammonites decided to go to war. With the support of hired armies they believed their chances were good. The battle was intense, but Israel prevailed. David put to death over forty thousand troops (1 Samuel 10:18). This was a catastrophic loss for the Ammonites, which could've been avoided.

Like the foolish Ammonites, many will oppose Jesus Christ to the very end. Even when Christ returns many will refuse to lay down their arms. *They will wage war against the Lamb, but the Lamb will triumph over them because he is Lord of lords and King of kings* (Revelation 17:14), wrote John. Opposition to Christ is certain defeat, but surrender leads to victory. Our only wisdom is to change sides before it is too late.

2 Samuel 12:30 *David took the crown from their king's head, and it was placed on his own head.*

The crown was made of gold set with precious stones and weighed about seventy-five pounds. By taking the crown for himself, David showed his sovereignty over the Ammonites. If he did this whenever he conquered, he had many crowns. Likewise, it's said of Jesus Christ, *on his head are many crowns* (Revelation 19:12). There's only one king of the universe, and every crown will be his.

For Reflection and Review

- *How does David's kindness to Mephibosheth remind us of God's kindness to us?*
- *How does Jesus compare conversion to a battle between kings?*
- *Why won't the world surrender to Christ when he returns?*

Lesson 73

2 Samuel 11:1 *In the spring, at the time when kings go off to war, David sent Joab out with the king's men and the whole Israelite army.*

Spring was the time for war because the weather was agreeable, and fields provided food for armies on the march. David led many battles in the past, but now that he was a well established king, others could do the task. So David remained at home, a king at his leisure.

2 Samuel 11:2 *One evening David got up from his bed and walked around on the roof of the palace.*

David's palace had a flat roof porch, and may've been the tallest building in Jerusalem. This gave him a view of the region, as well as other people's homes. From there he saw a woman bathing, and noticed she was beautiful. David should have looked away but, instead, he prolonged his gaze. Then he sent for the woman and she became pregnant. Her name was Bathsheba, and she was married to Uriah.

This was a problem since David was a spiritual leader, and the law of God said, *You shall not commit adultery* (Exodus 20:14). Even worse, *If a man commits adultery with another man's wife—with the wife of his neighbor—both the adulterer and the adulteress are to be put to death* (Leviticus 20:10). David and Bathsheba were both in serious trouble.

It would've been better if David had simply looked away. He was a good man who loved God, and served him with all his heart. But goodness is no guarantee against weakness and, in a moment of weakness, David sinned.

2 Samuel 11:6 *David sent this word to Joab: Send me Uriah the Hittite. And Joab sent him to David.*

David's plan was so simple it could hardly fail. He called Bathsheba's husband home from battle to give an account of the war. Having been away for a while, he'd surely want to sleep with his wife. Then, when he learned she was pregnant, he'd assume the child was his.

But Uriah was a man of such character that, as long as his fellow soldiers were sleeping in a field, he refused the comfort of his own bed. So Uriah slept at the entrance of David's palace, along with David's other servants. Then David got him drunk, hoping to weaken his resolve, but this also failed. David was growing desperate so he sent Uriah back to battle with a letter to his commander: *Put Uriah out in front where the fighting is fiercest. Then withdraw from him so he will be struck down and die* (2 Samuel 11:15).

It's hard to imagine what David was thinking when he wrote those terrible words. He believed in God, and in God's law. But desperate people do desperate things, and David was truly desperate. So he set in motion his plan to kill an innocent man.

This is why Jesus taught us to pray, *lead us not into temptation, but deliver us from the evil one* (Matthew 6:13). Under the right circumstances there's nothing of which we're not capable—including adultery and murder. Those who do such things aren't always worse than others, but are truly ensnared by the devil. Their conduct should be condemned, of course, but under similar circumstances we could do similar things.

2 Samuel 11:26-27 *When Uriah's wife heard that her husband was dead, she mourned for him. After the time of mourning was over, David had her brought to his house, and she became his wife and bore him a son.*

As the most powerful man in the nation, David was able to avoid execution for himself and

Bathsheba. Perhaps he married her quickly so the child would seem to come from their marriage. Or maybe he hoped to appear noble by taking the pregnant widow of a worthy soldier. But the trauma of David's sin so hardened his heart that he wasn't relating to God. Instead of confessing and repenting, David seems to have rationalized his sin as the privilege of kings. He already had numerous wives, why not one more? *But the thing David had done displeased the Lord* (1 Samuel 11:27b), it says.

2 Samuel 12:1 *The Lord sent Nathan to David.*

Nathan was the prophet to whom God gave the unhappy task of rebuking the king. It's not clear how Nathan knew of David's sin, but he may have learned it from God. So Nathan went to David with a parable of two men: one rich, the other poor. The rich man had numerous sheep, but the poor man had only one little sheep, which he loved with all his heart. One day the rich man had visitors but, instead of killing one of his own sheep for dinner, he took the poor man's sheep instead.

As surely as the Lord lives, the man who did this must die! (2 Samuel 12:5), said David. *You are the man!* (2 Samuel 12:7), said Nathan. Then he told David about the terrible consequences that would come because of his sin, including the death of his child.

2 Samuel 12:13 *Then David said to Nathan, I have sinned against the Lord.*

God pardoned David's sin, but didn't remove the consequences. The child died, and David never recovered his greatness. The man whom God used to build his kingdom let many people down, especially himself.

The kingdom of God needs a righteous king in order to have God's favor. Jesus is the only king who never sinned (1 Peter 2:22), and his kingdom is coming soon. Then God's people will rejoice forever under the rule of a perfect king.

For Reflection and Review

- *Was David basically good or bad?*
- *What does Uriah teach us about life?*
- *How could David have avoided this catastrophic failure?*

Lesson 74

2 Samuel 13:1 *In the course of time, Amnon son of David fell in love with Tamar, the beautiful sister of Absalom son of David.*

Amnon was the firstborn son of David, and the crown prince of Israel. Regrettably, he allowed himself to fall in love with his half-sister Tamar, to whom marriage was forbidden. *Do not have sexual relations with your sister, either your father's daughter or your mother's daughter, whether she was born in the same home or elsewhere* (Leviticus 18:9), wrote Moses. By setting his affection on what God had forbidden, Amnon became frustrated. There were other young ladies to chose from, but Amnon wanted what God had refused.

2 Samuel 13:2 *Amnon became so obsessed with his sister Tamar that he made himself ill. She was a virgin, and it seemed impossible for him to do anything to her.*

Amnon's love for Tamar could be better described as lust. He wasn't as noble as Job who said, *I made a covenant with my eyes not to look lustfully at a young woman* (Job 31:1). Instead, Amnon fantasized about what it would be like to have her. Jesus' words apply to Amnon perfectly: *anyone who looks at a woman lustfully has already committed adultery with her in his heart* (Matthew 5:28).

2 Samuel 13:3 *Now Amnon had an adviser named Jonadab. . . . [He] was a very shrewd man.*

As advisor to the crown prince, Jonadab wanted to help Amnon get his way, so that he would remain in his favor. Jonadab advised Amnon to fake illness, and arrange for his sister Tamar to come and take care of him. When she arrived, *he grabbed her and said, Come to bed with me, my sister. No, my brother! she said to him. Don't force me! Such a thing should not be done in Israel! Don't do this wicked thing. What about me? Where could I get rid of my disgrace? And what about you? You would be like one of the wicked fools in Israel. Please speak to the king; he will not keep me from being married to you* (2 Samuel 13:11-13), she said.

Tamar was in danger of becoming a victim of rape and incest, which would scar her the rest of her life. For siblings to marry was forbidden in God's law, but it was not without precedent. Abraham, the father of the Israel, was married to his half sister, Sarah (Genesis 20:12). If Amnon spoke to their Father, King David, perhaps he'd allow it.

2 Samuel 13:14 *But [Amnon] refused to listen to her, and since he was stronger than she, he raped her.*

Amnon didn't expect to grow up and become a rapist. Raised in a godly home, he knew this was a terrible sin. But instead of resisting his sinful nature, he repeatedly indulged it until it got the best of him. What had he become?

This is why Jesus reserved some of his strongest language for sexual sin. *If your right eye causes you to stumble, gouge it out and throw it away. It is better for you to lose one part of your body than for your whole body to be thrown into hell. And if your right hand causes you to stumble, cut it off and throw it away. It is better for you to lose one part of your body than for your whole body to go into hell* (Matthew 5:29-30). It would have better for Amnon to pluck out his eye, and cut off his hand, than to do what he had done.

2 Samuel 13:15 *Then Amnon hated her with intense hatred. In fact, he hated her more than he had loved her. Amnon said to her, Get up and get out!*

The Bible doesn't explain the reversal of Amnon's affections, but two explanations are possible. First, whenever we hurt someone deeply we may be tempted to hate them because of the guilt we feel. The more we're able to hate them, the less guilty we'll feel.

Second, instead of accepting his guilt, Amnon may've put the blame on Tamar, convincing himself that she seduced him. Since we're naturally quick to blame others, and slow to blame ourselves, this may be more likely.

2 Samuel 13:16-17 *No! she said to him. Sending me away would be a greater wrong than what you have already done to me. But he refused to listen to her. He called his personal servant and said, Get this woman out of my sight and bolt the door after her.*

Tamar went away weeping, tore the beautiful robe she was wearing, and put ashes on her head as a sign of her grief. She'd never be the same, and never fully recovered.

Sexual crimes are especially bad because the harm can last a lifetime. Emotional damage can leave the victim less responsive sexually, and diminish marital happiness. Or, feeling compromised, the victim may become promiscuous and spiral down morally. This is why the penalty for sexual crimes could even include death (Leviticus 20:10).

For Reflection and Review

- *What kind of friend was Jonadab?*
- *Why did Jesus condemn sexual sin?*
- *Why did Amnon reverse his feelings toward Tamar?*

Lesson 75

2 Samuel 13:20 *Her brother Absalom said to her, Has that Amnon, your brother, been with you? Be quiet for now, my sister; he is your brother. Don't take this thing to heart. And Tamar lived in her brother Absalom's house, a desolate woman.*

Tamar's full brother, Absalom, took his sister into his house and cared for her. Instead of bringing a scandal on the royal family, Absalom advised his sister to keep the matter quiet. His motives aren't clear, but he may've been concerned for his sister's reputation, and her ability to marry in the future.

As a *desolate woman*, however, Tamar seems to have never married or had children. In that culture, there was scarcely anything worse.

2 Samuel 13:21 *When King David heard all this, he was furious.*

But he didn't actually do anything. It wasn't an easy case since, on the one hand, the law required marriage. *If a man happens to meet a virgin who is not pledged to be married and rapes her . . . . He must marry the young woman, for he has violated her. He can never divorce her as long as he lives* (Deuteronomy 22:28-29), wrote Moses.

On the other hand, the law forbad marriage. *If a man marries his sister . . . it is a disgrace. They are to be publicly removed from their people* (Leviticus 20:17), wrote Moses again. And since David also committed sexual sin, he had no moral authority. If he challenged Amnon for his behavior, Amnon could challenge David for his behavior. Even though David was furious, there wasn't much he could do.

2 Samuel 13:22 *Absalom never said a word to Amnon, either good or bad; he hated Amnon because he had disgraced his sister Tamar.*

Absalom waited two full years for his father to take action against Amnon. But when nothing was done, he took matters into his own hands. He invited his brothers to a celebration and, when Amnon had plenty of wine, he commanded his servants to kill him. Then Absalom fled the country.

2 Samuel 13:36 *The king . . . and all his attendants wept very bitterly.*

David mourned the loss of both his sons, Amnon and Absalom. He may've recalled the words of the prophet after he committed adultery with Bathsheba, and had her husband killed: *You struck down Uriah the Hittite . . . and took his wife to be your own. . . . Now, therefore, the sword will never depart from your house* (2 Samuel 12:9-10).

David was guilty of sexual sin and murder—and now his sons were guilty of the same. *Do not be deceived: God cannot be mocked. . . . Whoever sows to please their flesh, from the flesh will reap destruction* (Galatians 6:7-8), wrote Paul. David sowed to please his flesh, and reaped the destruction of his children. If only he controlled himself when he saw Bathsheba bathing! The effect of David's sin spilled over on his family, and our sin will often hurt those who are dearest to us.

But whenever our sin is great, God's grace can be even greater (Romans 5:20). We may have to suffer now, but in the age to come he'll present us *holy in his sight, without blemish and free from accusation* (Colossians 1:22), wrote Paul. And we *will receive a rich welcome into the eternal kingdom of our Lord and Savior Jesus Christ* (2 Peter 1:11), wrote Peter. The good news of God's grace is always greater than the bad news of our sin. Christ died for sinners so that *whoever believes in him shall not perish but have eternal life* (John 3:16), wrote John.

*****

2 Samuel 14:1 *Joab son of Zeruiah knew that the king's heart longed for Absalom.*

After murdering his brother Amnon, for raping their sister Tamar, Absalom fled from the land of Israel to Gesher. This pained his Father David, who grieved the loss of his sons for about three years (2 Samuel 13:38). This was observed by Joab, a high-ranking official, who was concerned for David's happiness.

Communication between David and Absalom was so completely broken down that they needed someone else to bring them together. Joab was acting as a mediator and, in this way, reminds us of Jesus Christ. *For there is one God and one mediator between God and mankind, the man Christ Jesus* (1 Timothy 2:5), wrote Paul.

Jesus could speak to mankind on behalf of God, because he was God in human flesh (John 1:1, 14). And he could speak to God on behalf of mankind, because he's the only human who never sinned (1 Peter 2:22). The rift between God and mankind was so profound that we couldn't come back together without a mediator. But now *we have peace with God through our Lord Jesus Christ* (Romans 5:1), wrote Paul.

2 Samuel 14:21 *The king said to Joab . . . . Go, bring back the young man Absalom.*

Joab went to Geshur and brought back David's son, but David refused to meet with him for about two more years. Then Absalom said to Joab, *I want to see the king's face, and if I am guilty of anything, let him put me to death* (2 Samuel 14:32).

Absalom thought he did nothing wrong by killing his brother for raping their sister. And, if he did, he was willing to die for it. Joab reported this to David who then called for his son. Absalom came into his father's presence and *bowed down with his face to the ground. . . . And the king kissed Absalom* (2 Samuel 14:33).

This sounds like a happy ending to a story of estrangement, but it's not. The kiss was a public sign the crown prince was now in good standing with his father. But the relationship was never fully restored, and there is no happy ending.

God made families for nurture and love, but they can become a living hell. That's why it's important to always get along with our family. It's better to do the hard work of reconciliation than to live with anger the rest of our lives. We can never avoid our families completely (at least mentally) so it's wise to be friends whenever possible.

For Reflection and Review

- *Why did David fail to correct Amnon?*
- *Was Amnon wrong to avenge his sister?*
- *Why is Christ a perfect mediator?*

Lesson 76

2 Samuel 15:1 *In the course of time, Absalom provided himself with a chariot and horses and with fifty men to run ahead of him.*

Absalom was about thirty years old at this time, and had a royal appearance. *In all Israel there was not a man so highly praised for his handsome appearance as Absalom. From the top of his head to the sole of his foot there was no blemish in him. Whenever he cut the hair of his head . . . he would weigh it, and its weight was two hundred shekels by the royal standard* (1 Samuel 14:25-26).

Absalom enhanced his royal appearance with a chariot and a body guard of fifty men. Having murdered his older brother, Amnon, Absalom was next in line for David's throne. He often stood by the road to the city gate, and heard the concerns of the people.

[W]henever anyone approached him to bow down before him, Absalom would reach out his hand, take hold of him and kiss him. Absalom behaved in this way toward all the Israelites who came to the king asking for justice, and so he stole the hearts of the people of Israel (2 Samuel 15:5-6).

Absalom was planning to be king. What's not clear is why David allowed him to act this way. David may've watched Absalom's rise to power with interest, but he underestimated his ambition. Absalom wouldn't wait for David to die of natural causes; he was plotting his father's demise.

2 Samuel 15:7 *At the end of four years, Absalom said to the king, Let me go to Hebron and fulfill a vow I made to the Lord.*

After four years of winning people's hearts, Absalom decided the time had come for him to act. Hebron was about nineteen miles south of Jerusalem, and was a town of some importance. It's where David was anointed king (2 Samuel 2:4), and where Absalom was born (2 Samuel 3:2-3).

To get his father's permission to go to Hebron, Absalom used a religious lie. *While your servant was living at Geshur in Aram, I made this vow: If the Lord takes me back to Jerusalem, I will worship the Lord in Hebron* (2 Samuel 15:8). David may've been pleased with Absalom's apparent commitment to God. Perhaps, at last, he was growing in his faith.

The king said to him, Go in peace (2 Samuel 15:9). But Absalom was planning war.

Absalom's use of a religious lie to conceal his godless plan, shows the bankruptcy of his character. He was an ambitious man in the worst possible sense. Perhaps the murder of his older brother wasn't merely revenge, but a clearing of the way for him to become king. Now that he had the people's support, he was willing to kill his father to make it happen.

Here we see the difference between good ambition and bad ambition. *It has always been my ambition to preach the gospel where Christ was not known* (Romans 15:20), wrote Paul. We ought to be ambitious to do all the good we can, but ambition becomes evil whenever we're willing to hurt others to promote ourselves. *For where you have . . . selfish ambition, there you find disorder and every evil practice* (James 3:16), wrote James. Beware of the person with selfish ambition.

2 Samuel 15:9 *So [Absalom] went to Hebron.*

And while he was there, he declared himself to be king with such success that David and his officials had to flee Jerusalem, lest Absalom come with an army and put the city to the sword (2 Samuel 15:14). This was not a minor challenge, but a total assault on David's reign.

2 Samuel 15:31 *Now David had been told, Ahithophel is among the conspirators with Absalom.*

Ahithophel was one of David's top advisors, and now he was serving the enemy. This gave Absalom a significant advantage since *the advice Ahithophel gave was like that of one who inquires of God* (2 Samuel 16:23). The defection also hurt David personally. *Even my close friend, someone I trusted, one who shared my bread, has turned against me* (Psalm 41:9), he later wrote.

Jesus quoted David's words and applied them to Judas Iscariot (John 13:18). Judas appeared to be Jesus' friend in many ways. He walked with Jesus, talked with Jesus, ate with Jesus, and gave every appearance of being a faithful disciple. But when it became clear that Jesus would be crucified, Judas switched sides (Luke 22:4) to save himself.

Unless we want to be like Judas, we should to be more loyal to Christ than we are to ourselves. *For whoever wants to save their life will lose it, but whoever loses their life for me will save it* (Luke 9:24), said Jesus. Centuries apart from each other, Judas and Ahithophel both committed suicide (Matthew 27:5, 2 Samuel 17:23). If we put ourselves ahead of Christ, we're likely to die despairing.

For Reflection and Review

- *How did Absalom become so evil?*
- *What's the difference between good ambition and bad ambition?*
- *How was Judas like Ahithophel?*

Lesson 77

2 Samuel 15:31 *So David prayed, Lord, turn Ahithophel's counsel into foolishness.*

Soon after David prayed he was met by Hushai the Arkite, a trusted advisor. Hushai was loyal to David, so David sent him back to Jerusalem to pretend to be loyal to Absalom. Hushai would serve as David's spy and, hopefully, undermine Ahithophel.

Then Hushai . . . went to Absalom and said to him, Long live the king! (2 Samuel 16:16). Absalom was a little surprised that Hushai abandoned David so quickly. Hushai explained that Absalom was chosen by God and, therefore, had his support as well. *Just as I served your father, so I will serve you* (2 Samuel 16:19), he said. Absalom then received him, which put Hushai in position to help David.

2 Samuel 16:20-21 *Absalom said to Ahithophel, Give us your advice. What should we do? Ahithophel answered, Sleep with your father's concubines whom he left to take care of the palace. Then all Israel will hear that you have made yourself obnoxious to your father, and the hands of everyone with you will be more resolute.*

True to his reputation, Ahithophel offered brilliant advice. For Absalom to sleep with his father's concubines would completely destroy their relationship, and a possible co-regency. When the people heard of it they'd have to choose between David and Absalom. Since Absalom had the power, more people would quickly align with him. *So they pitched a tent for Absalom on the roof, and he slept with his father's concubines in the sight of all Israel* (2 Samuel 16:22).

This was a literal fulfillment of what God said to David after he committed adultery with Bathsheba. *Before your very eyes I will take your wives and give them to one who is close to you, and he will sleep with your wives in broad daylight. You did it in secret, but I will do this thing in broad daylight before all Israel* (2 Samuel 12:11-12), said God.

The roof on which Absalom did this, in fact, may have been the same roof from which David saw Bathsheba (2 Samuel 11:2). But if David confessed his sin, and God forgave him (2 Samuel 12:13), why did this still happen? The answer isn't provided but the lesson is clear: sin leads to misery.

Before David's spectacular sin his life was triumphant but, afterward, he struggled. Since God is the one who determines the quality of our lives, we should always try to please him. Then, when trouble comes, at least we'll know it wasn't because of our foolish behavior.

2 Samuel 17:1 *Ahithophel said to Absalom, I would choose twelve thousand men and set out tonight in pursuit of David.*

After seizing control of the palace, and taking over the harem, there was only one thing left for Absalom to do: kill his dad. Since David was on the run he'd be weak and vulnerable, so Ahithophel advised Absalom to attack at once. *But Absalom said, Summon also Hushai the Arkite, so we can hear what he has to say as well* (2 Samuel 17:5).

Ahithophel's advice was so good it'd be hard to oppose. But Hushai was loyal to David and had to do his best. *Let all Israel, from Dan to Beersheba . . . be gathered to you, with you yourself leading them into battle. Then we will attack [David] wherever he may be found, and we will fall on him as dew settles on the ground. Neither he nor any of his men will be left alive* (2 Samuel 17:11-12), he said. With these, and other words, Hushai delayed the battle and sent information to David. God was answering David's prayer, *Lord, turn Ahithophel's counsel into foolishness* (2 Samuel 15:31).

2 Samuel 18:1 *David mustered the men who were with him and appointed over them commanders of thousands and commanders of hundreds.*

Even though David was on the run, he still had a sizable army. And even though there'd be a battle, he was still concerned for his son. *Be gentle with the young man Absalom for my sake* (2 Samuel 18:5), he said.

The battle took place in a forest, and Absalom's mule went under a tree. Abaslom's hair got caught in a branch and, when his mule kept going, Absalom was left hanging by his hair. One of David's men took three javelins and plunged them into Absalom's heart (2 Samuel 18:14). He died rather comically, hanging by the hair he loved.

How different things would've been for Absalom if he'd simply served his father, and his father's God. With all the benefits of royalty, and his natural gifts (2 Samuel 14:25-26), Absalom could've been a force for good. But power, privilege, and prestige weren't enough for Absalom. Consumed by selfish ambition he overreached and died a young man.

2 Samuel 18:33 *[David] went up to the room over the gateway and wept. As he went, he said: O my son Absalom! My son, my son Absalom! If only I had died instead of you—O Absalom, my son, my son!*

Only those who've lost a child know the depth of David's grief. The one who brought him sorrow in life, brought him sorrow in death as well. We might expect David to be relieved at the death of his enemy son, but he wished that he had died instead.

This kind of emotion finds it's source in the heart of our heavenly Father. He doesn't want *anyone to perish, but everyone to come to repentance* (2 Peter 3:9), wrote Peter. That's why *there is rejoicing in the presence of the angels of God over one sinner who repents* (Luke 15:10), said Jesus. We've all rebelled against the king, but we need not die like Absalom.

For Reflection and Review

- *Why did Absalom sleep with his father's concubines?*
- *How did Hushai help David?*
- *How does David's grief remind us of God?*

Lesson 78

2 Samuel 20:2 *[A]ll the men of Israel deserted David to follow Sheba son of Bikri.*

Absalom's popularity was so great that, even though he was dead, a man named Sheba continued his revolt. If Sheba wasn't put down, he could divide the nation. This was an emergency that required immediate action. So David sent some troops to eliminate Sheba before he could get organized.

Sheba fled to Abel Beth Maakah, a fortified city in northern Israel. There he was found by David's troops, who began to batter down the city wall (2 Samuel 20:15). But a woman inside spoke with David's general, and offered to give him Sheba's head if he'd agree to withdraw. David's general agreed, and Sheba's head was thrown over the wall. The city was saved, and so was the nation of Israel.

Division is a serious threat to nations, organizations, and churches. There are often those who want to seize control that doesn't belong to them. Unless they're treated firmly, the organization will be hurt. *Drive out the mocker, and out goes strife; quarrels and insults are ended* (Proverbs 22:10), says Proverbs.

*****

2 Samuel 21:15 *David went down with his men to fight against the Philistines, and he became exhausted.*

David was a mighty warrior but he was advancing in age. In a state of exhaustion he was attacked by a massive Philistine who was heavily armed. It appeared that David's life was over when one of his men came to his rescue and struck down the Philistine. *Then David's men swore to him, saying, Never again will you go out with us to battle, so that the lamp of Israel will not be extinguished* (2 Samuel 21:17).

Part of the wisdom of age is knowing our limitations. If we try to do what we could do when we were young, we'll likely meet with injury or even death. Instead of trying to prove ourselves, we ought to accept the limits of our age, and preserve our lives for additional service. David was able to serve God many more years because he stopped going to war.

*****

2 Samuel 24:1 *Again the anger of the Lord burned against Israel, and he incited David against them, saying, Go and take a census of Israel and Judah.*

We're not told why the Lord was angry at Israel, but the nation was often in spiritual decline. Whenever this happened God was known to afflict his people to remind them of their need for him. *Before I was afflicted I went astray, but now I obey your word* (Psalm 119:67), wrote the Psalmist.

It's even less clear why God incited David to take a national census. If God was angry at the nation why not send a plague? Instead, God incited David to take a census, then punished the nation for David's sin. Since taking a census was not forbidden, David's sin seems to be pride. He wanted to know the extent if his military power (2 Samuel 24:2) for the sake of his own glory.

Pride is more serious than many people realize. *When pride comes, then comes disgrace* (Proverbs 11:2). *Pride goes before destruction, a haughty spirit before a fall* (Proverbs 16:18). *Pride brings a person low* (Proverbs 29:23). And, *God opposes the proud but shows favor to the humble* (James 4:6).

But if God doesn't tempt anyone to sin (James 1:13), why did he incite David to sin? A parallel account even blames the devil. *Satan . . . incited David to take a census* (1 Chronicles 21:1), it says. David is clearly sinning but who's to blame—God, David, or Satan?

The same problem occurs elsewhere. *Moses and Aaron performed all these wonders before Pharaoh, but the Lord hardened Pharaoh's heart* (Exodus 11:10). Instead of softening Pharaoh's heart so that he would obey, God hardened Pharaoh's heart so that he would disobey. So who was to blame—God or Pharaoh?

Other examples could also be given (Joshua 11:20, 1 Kings 22:21-23, Ezekiel 14:9), but the clearest is Herod and Pontius Pilate who conspired to crucify Jesus. This was a sin of the highest order, but they only *did what [God's] power and will had decided beforehand should happen* (Acts 4:28), wrote Luke.

If God decided beforehand what would happen, why were Herod and Pilate still to blame? And *why does God still blame us? For who is able to resist his will?* (Romans 9:19), asked Paul.

Along with the Trinity, and the two natures of Christ, this is one of the great mysteries of the Bible. We serve a God who is sovereign over all things, including human sin, but in such a way that he's not the source or cause of sin. Unless this is firmly held, we'll serve a God who's partially evil, or a God who's not in control of the world he created.

For Reflection and Review

- *How should a church manage people who are divisive?*
- *Why do some people ignore the physical limitations of age?*
- *Why is God hard to understand?*

Lesson 79

2 Samuel 24:2 *So the king said to Joab and the army commanders with him, Go throughout the tribes of Israel from Dan to Beersheba and enroll the fighting men, so that I may know how many there are.*

Joab opposed this idea knowing it would inflate David's pride, and cause him to trust in his army instead of God. But David insisted, so Joab obeyed. Nearly ten months later Joab returned with the count: David had well over a million *able-bodied men who could handle a sword* (2 Samuel 24:9).

David should've been thrilled but, instead, he was troubled. *I have sinned greatly in what I have done. Now, Lord, I beg you, take away the guilt of your servant. I have done a very foolish thing* (2 Samuel 24:10), he said.

During the months Joab was gone, it seems that David wrestled with his conscience. In the past, whenever he put his trust in God, he was successful. And whenever he took his eyes off God, he failed. So why was David taking his eyes off God, and putting them on his army? When the numbers came back, David realized how faithful God had been to him, and how faithless he had been toward God. *I have sinned*, he said.

We also sin whenever we put our trust anywhere but God. Family, friends, and doctors ought to be trustworthy—but our trust shouldn't be in them. Nor should it be in our savings, skills, or the military. *Some trust in chariots and some in horses, but we trust in the name of the Lord our God* (Psalm 20:7), wrote David. Whenever our highest trust isn't in God, we sin like David.

2 Samuel 24:11-12 *Before David got up the next morning, the word of the Lord had come to Gad the prophet, David's seer: Go and tell David, This is what the Lord says: I am giving you three options.*

God let David choose between three years of famine, three months of fleeing from his enemies, or three days of plague. Again we see that sin has consequences repentance may not remove. None of the options David faced would be easy and, as a result, he was in *deep distress* (2 Samuel 24:14).

This is what happens whenever we have to face the consequences of our sin. Whoever steals from his employer, and is found out, goes through deep distress. Whoever cheats on their taxes, and is found out, goes through deep distress. And whoever has an affair, and is found out, goes through deep distress. Almost every day there's someone in the news who's going through deep distress because of what they've done.

The best time to think about this isn't after we sin, but before we sin. There's not much we can do after we sin but, if we think about the deep distress before we sin, we might find the presence of mind to avoid it. God sees everything we do, and *through the fear of the Lord evil is avoided* (Proverbs 16:6), says Proverbs.

David chose three days of plague, not only because it was brief, but because of God's mercy. *Let us fall into the hands of the Lord, for his mercy is great* (2 Samuel 24:14), he said. When we consider the great evil that we've done, and the little justice we've received, we'll agree with David that God is merciful. The consequences may be severe, but they're always less than we deserve.

2 Samuel 24:15 *So the Lord sent a plague on Israel from that morning until the end of the time designated, and seventy thousand of the people from Dan to Beersheba died.*

This wasn't only due to David's sin, but also to the people's sin. God was angry at the nation (2 Samuel 24:1), and this would get their attention. God is easy to ignore when things are going well. We might pray a little less, give a little less, serve a little less, and sin a little more. But when tragedy strikes, we come back to the importance of knowing and serving God. It's not the way it ought to be, but often the way it is.

2 Samuel 24:16-17 *When the angel stretched out his hand to destroy Jerusalem, the Lord relented concerning the disaster and said to the angel who was afflicting the people, Enough! Withdraw your hand. The angel of the Lord was then at the threshing floor of Araunah the Jebusite. When David saw the angel who was striking down the people, he said to the Lord, I have sinned.*

The plague was due, in part, to David's sin, and he took responsibility. *I, the shepherd, have done wrong,* he said. David was a good shepherd, most of the time. But in this case he was a bad shepherd, and the people suffered because of him.

This contrasts with Jesus Christ who is the good shepherd all the time. *I am the good shepherd . . . and I lay down my life for the sheep* (John 10:14-15) he said. Many of David's sheep died because of his sin, but those who belong to Christ will live because of his righteousness.

2 Samuel 24:18 *On that day Gad went to David and said to him, Go up and build an altar to the Lord on the threshing floor of Araunah the Jebusite.*

When David arrived, Arunah was there with oxen and wood for the sacrifice. He offered them to David, free of charge, but David insisted on paying. *I will not sacrifice to the Lord my God burnt offerings that cost me nothing* (1 Samuel 24:14), he said. *So David paid Araunah six hundred shekels of gold for the site* (1 Chronicles 21:25). This was a great amount, even for David, and the Lord accepted his sacrifice. He even sent fire from heaven to consume it (1 Chronicles 21:26).

Sacrifice reveals our commitment to God, but also God's commitment to us. *God presented Christ as a sacrifice of atonement* (Romans 3:25), wrote Paul. *For by one sacrifice he has made perfect forever those who are being made holy* (Hebrews 10:14), says Hebrews. And, *This is love: not that we loved God, but that he loved us and sent his Son as an atoning sacrifice* (1 John 4:10), wrote John. Whatever we sacrifice for God is nothing, compared to the sacrifice he has made for us.

For Reflection and Review

- *How did David sin by taking a census?*
- *Why does sin cause deep distress?*
- *What's unique about the sacrifice of Christ?*

Lesson 80

1 Kings 1:1-4 *When King David was very old, he could not keep warm even when they put covers over him. So his attendants said to him, Let us look for a young virgin to serve the king and take care of him. She can lie beside him so that our lord the king may keep warm. Then they searched throughout Israel for a beautiful young woman and found Abishag, a Shunammite, and brought her to the king. The woman was very beautiful; she took care of the king and waited on him, but the king had no sexual relations with her.*

The author of First and Second Kings isn't known, but they were written for the people of God, around 550 BC. The first four verses are an honest account of David's frailty at the end of his life. He could no longer keep himself warm, and lacked the virility to have sex with a beautiful young woman. This was a different stage of David's life than when he was slaying Goliath (1 Samuel 17), or adding to his harem (2 Samuel 5:13).

David was only about seventy years old at this time (2 Samuel 5:4), but his life had been hard and worn him out. He wouldn't live much longer, but hadn't appointed a successor. This became a problem when one of his sons took matters into his own hands.

1 Kings 1:5 *Adonijah . . . put himself forward and said, I will be king.*

Adonijah was the oldest of David's remaining sons, and a likely successor to his father's throne. His chariots, entourage, and natural good looks gave him a kingly appearance. But, like his brother Absalom, Adonijah was overly ambitious.

Since David was frail, Adonijah appointed himself king without expecting much resistance. He had the support of many officials including Joab (David's general), and Abiathar (David's priest). So Adonijah held a celebration where his kingship was made official. Once again, David's throne was being challenged by one of his sons.

Even the best parents can have rebellious children, but some of David's children were awful. Amnon raped his sister Tamar (2 Samuel 13:14), Absalom led a revolt (2 Samuel 15-17), and Adonijah was trying to steal his father's throne. Where did David go wrong?

Because he was busy, David probably delegated most parental duties to the mothers of his children. Mothers are well equipped for this, but religious training is the duty of fathers. Fathers should raise their children *in the training and instruction of the Lord* (Ephesians 6:4), wrote Paul. Mothers can be helpful and, with God's help, successful (2 Timothy 1:5). But there is no substitute for a good and godly father.

1 Kings 1:11 *Then Nathan asked Bathsheba, Solomon's mother, Have you not heard that Adonijah, the son of Haggith, has become king, and our lord David knows nothing about it?*

Solomon was the second son born to David and Bathsheba, after the child of their adultery died (2 Samuel 12:15-24). David promised Bathsheba that Solomon would be king (1 Kings 1:13) but, unless David acted quickly, this wouldn't be the case. Even worse, if Adonijah came to power he might have Solomon and Bathsheba put to death, to eliminate any challenge to his leadership.

1 Kings 1:12 *Now then, let me advise you how you can save your own life and the life of your son Solomon.*

Nathan the prophet advised Bathsheba to tell David what was happening and, while she was there, he'd arrive to confirm it. When David learned of the situation, he quickly arranged a ceremony for Solomon to be installed as king. *Then they sounded the trumpet and all the people shouted, Long live King Solomon!* (2 Kings 1:39). When Adonijah's party learned that David had made Solomon king, they quickly dispersed so they wouldn't be killed for their rebellion.

1 Kings 1:51 *Then Solomon was told, Adonijah is afraid of King Solomon and is clinging to the horns of the altar.*

Afraid for his life, Adonijah ran to the place of sacrifice and grabbed hold of the altar. This didn't guarantee his safety but, since the place was sacred, Adonijah hoped for mercy. *If he shows himself to be worthy, not a hair of his head will fall to the ground*, said Solomon. So *Adonijah came and bowed down* (1 Kings 52-53).

Solomon was now the undisputed king of Israel. He'd rule the nation forty years (1 Kings 11:42) and bring it to its height. *The Lord loved him* (2 Samuel 12:24) and he was greatly used by God.

Again we see that God is able to bring good out of evil. God was displeased when David committed adultery with Bathsheba (2 Samuel 12:18), and had her husband killed (2 Samuel 11:16-17). But God used their second son to lead the nation to greatness.

Sexual sin isn't uncommon among God's people, and murder isn't unheard of. But they're not in a separate category of sin, nor are they handled differently. *If we confess our sins, he is faithful and just and will forgive us our sins and purify us from all unrighteousness* (1 John 1:9), wrote John. The consequences of sin may last a lifetime, but we don't live under a cloud of God's wrath. God completely forgives, and can even bring a blessing out of our rebellion.

For Reflection and Review

- *Why do children of godly parents often become ungodly.*
- *Why was David slow to transfer his throne to Solomon?*
- *How did God bring a blessing out of David's sin with Bathsheba?*

Lesson 81

1 Kings 2:13 *Adonijah . . . went to Bathsheba, Solomon's mother.*

Having lost his bid for the throne, Adonijah wanted to marry Abishag. Even though she was a member of David's harem, it may've been allowable since she was still a virgin. Instead of making the request himself, Adonijah improved his odds by persuading Bathsheba to ask her son. *Solomon answered his mother . . . . You might as well request the kingdom for him—after all, he is my older brother* (1 Kings 2:22).

In the minds of many, Adonijah had a claim to the throne since he was David's oldest remaining son. If he married David's companion, that would only strengthen his claim. While pretending to support Solomon, Adonijah was really supporting himself. So Solomon struck him down and he died (1 Kings 2:25).

Adonijah thought he could hide his motives from Solomon, but he was fatally wrong. And so it is with Christ. *He will bring to light what is hidden in darkness and will expose the motives of the heart* (1 Corinthians 4:5), wrote Paul. It's not enough to appear Christian; we must be Christians from the heart.

*****

1 Kings 3:4 *The king went to Gibeon to offer sacrifices, for that was the most important high place, and Solomon offered a thousand burnt offerings on that altar.*

Solomon was just a young man when he began to reign, and felt unequal to the task. But after he honored God with a sacrifice, God appeared to him in a dream and said, *Ask for whatever you want me to give you* (1 Kings 3:5).

Solomon could've asked for bottomless wealth, military might, long life, or whatever his heart desired. But, more than anything else, he wanted *wisdom and knowledge* (2 Chronicles 1:10) to govern God's people well. The Lord was so pleased with his request that he gave Solomon what he asked for, plus so much *wealth and honor* that he had *no equal among kings* (1 Kings 3:13).

Think about this: if we ask God for what he wants to give us, he might give us even more. Many ask for health, wealth, and happiness when they should be asking for holiness or usefulness. *When you ask, you do not receive, because you ask with wrong motives, that you may spend what you get on your pleasures* (James 4:3), wrote James. But if we ask God for what he wants to give, we might be surprised at what else he gives.

1 Kings 3:16 *Now two prostitutes came to the king and stood before him.*

The wisdom God gave Solomon was quickly put to the test. Two prostitutes lived together, and each gave birth to a son. During the night, one of them accidentally laid on her son and he died. So she took her dead son, and put him in bed with her roommate, and took her roommate's son as her own. But the following morning, when her roommate awoke, she knew the dead baby wasn't her own.

Apparently the lower courts weren't able to solve the dispute, so it was taken to Solomon. Since there were no other witnesses, it was impossible to determine who the real mother was by ordinary means. With the wisdom of God, however, Solomon called for a sword to divide the baby in half.

The real mother dropped the case at once in order to save her baby's life. She'd much rather lose her baby than have her child cut in half. Her strong reaction made it clear that she was the real mother, and the case was solved. Then Solomon was held in awe by all the people *because they saw that he had wisdom from God to administer justice* (1 Kings 3:28).

*****

1 Kings 6:1 *In the four hundred and eightieth year after the Israelites came out of Egypt, in the fourth year of Solomon's reign over Israel . . . [Solomon] began to build the temple of the Lord.*

On their way to the Promised Land God's people worshiped at a special tent, commonly called *the tabernacle*. It worked well for many years, because God's people were on the move, and it was portable. But the tabernacle was centuries old, by now, and God's people were in the Promised Land. It was time for something better.

My father David had it in his heart to build a temple for the Name of the Lord, the God of Israel. But the Lord said to my father David, You did well to have it in your heart to build a temple for my Name. Nevertheless, you are not the one to build the temple, but your son, your own flesh and blood—he is the one who will build the temple for my Name (1 Kings 8:17-19), said Solomon.

With the help of God's Spirit, David made plans for the temple (1 Chronicles 28:19), and gathered materials including wood, stone, iron, bronze, silver, gold, and precious stones—all in large quantities (1 Chronicles 29:2). Since David was still alive at this time, he commissioned Solomon to carry out the work (1 Chronicles 28:20).

The temple itself wasn't very big: about ninety feet long, thirty feet wide, and forty-five feet high (1 Kings 6:2). But other structures were added, along with courtyards, that made it very impressive. It took thousands of workers (1 Kings 5:13-16) seven years to finish the work (1 Kings 6:38). And it was one of the greatest buildings of the ancient world.

Upon its completion God showed his approval in two important ways. First, *When the priests withdrew from the Holy Place, the cloud filled the temple of the Lord. And the priests could not perform their service because of the cloud, for the glory of the Lord filled his temple* (1 Kings 8:10-11).

This also happened at the tabernacle many years earlier: *Then the cloud covered the tent of meeting, and the glory of the Lord filled the tabernacle. Moses could not enter the tent of meeting because the cloud had settled on it, and the glory of the Lord filled the tabernacle* (Exodus 40:34-35). This was clear and convincing proof of God's approval.

Second, God showed his approval by sending fire to consume Solomon's sacrifice (2 Chronicles 7:1), as he also did for Moses at the tabernacle (Leviticus 9:24). It was important for God's people to know that the temple was pleasing to God, and that he wanted to be approached in this way.

The temple stood for many years, but was later replaced by Jesus Christ. *Destroy this temple, and I will raise it again in three days* (John 2:19), he said of himself. The temple of his body was destroyed on the cross, and his resurrection proved that God accepted his sacrifice. We no longer need a building to worship God, but come to him through faith in Jesus Christ.

And because the church is united to Christ, it's his temple on earth. As the glory of God filled the temple in the Old Testament, so Jesus gave his Spirit to the church on the day of Pentecost (Acts 2:1-4). God is no longer found in a temple of stone, but among his gathered children. *Don't you know that you yourselves are God's temple and that God's Spirit dwells in your midst?* (1 Corinthians 3:16), wrote Paul. And *where two or three gather in my name, there am I with them* (Matthew 18:20), said Jesus. Every Christian has the Holy Spirit (1 Corinthians 6:19), but God's Spirit is especially present whenever we gather for worship.

For Reflection and Review

- *Why are motives important to God?*
- *Is it wrong to pray for what we want?*
- *How is Jesus like a temple?*

Lesson 82

1 Kings 10:1 *When the queen of Sheba heard about the fame of Solomon and his relationship to the Lord, she came to test Solomon with hard questions.*

If Sheba was in modern day Yemen, the trip was over twelve hundred miles. The queen came with her questions, but also with a caravan of merchandize. When she heard Solomon's wisdom, and saw his wealth, she was overwhelmed.

The report I heard in my own country about your achievements and your wisdom is true. But I did not believe these things until I came and saw with my own eyes. Indeed, not even half was told me; in wisdom and wealth you have far exceeded the report I heard. How happy your people must be! (1 Kings 10:6-8), she said. Then she gave the king her treasure, but Solomon gave her more in return (1 Kings 10:10, 2 Chronicles 9:12).

The Queen of Sheba recognized Solomon's wisdom, but many overlook the wisdom of Christ. *The Queen of the South will rise at the judgment with this generation and condemn it; for she came from the ends of the earth to listen to Solomon's wisdom, and now something greater than Solomon is here* (Matthew 12:42), said Jesus.

Solomon had wisdom from God, but Jesus is wisdom from God. Christ has *become for us wisdom from God* (1 Corinthians 1:30), wrote Paul. Jesus makes us wise about the most important things. Even those who are naturally dull can become eternally wise by obeying Jesus Christ.

*****

1 Kings 11:1 *King Solomon, however, loved many foreign women.*

Even though Solomon had wisdom, he didn't always apply it to himself. Instead of following the pattern for marriage established by God at creation (Genesis 1:27), he chose to take many wives. This was often practiced by kings to stabilize relationships with surrounding nations. When a king's daughter was given to a foreign king, the two kingdoms were less likely to go to war.

1 Kings 11:2 *They were from nations about which the Lord had told the Israelites, You must not intermarry with them, because they will surely turn your hearts after their gods.*

One of the greatest threats to God's people was losing their distinction through intermarriage. Even before they reached the Promised Land some Israelite men were having sex with foreign women, and worshipping their gods (Numbers 25). The anger of God burned so fiercely that twenty-four thousand perished.

Solomon may've thought the command against intermarriage didn't apply to him because, as king, his situation was unique. This is a common way of thinking whenever we face temptation. Because our situation is unique we think God will overlook our behavior, or make an exception for us. But God knows our situation is never unique.

No temptation has overtaken you except what is common to mankind. And God is faithful; he will not let you be tempted beyond what you can bear. But when you are tempted, he will also provide a way out (1 Corinthians 10:13), said Paul. God is willing to help us, and would've helped Solomon too, if he was willing to obey.

1 Kings 11:2b *Nevertheless, Solomon held fast to them in love.*

Solomon took many wives not only for political reasons, but also for sexual pleasure. This was so important to him that he had *seven hundred wives of royal birth and three hundred concubines* (1 Kings 11:3). If Solomon slept with a different woman every night, it'd take about three years to see each one again. By taking so many partners he may've pleased himself, but he denied most of them any hope of a meaningful relationship. It was a very selfish practice.

1 Kings 11:4 *As Solomon grew old, his wives turned his heart after other gods.*

Solomon's heart didn't turn to other gods all at once, but by degrees. At first he probably found the worship of foreign gods to be repulsive. But for the sake of his wives, he was willing to put up with it. After many years, however, Solomon grew accustomed to the worship of foreign gods, and the situation seemed normal to him. With the passing of even more time the worship of foreign gods not only seemed normal but desirable. After all, shouldn't everyone be allowed to worship according to their conscience?

Finally, the worship of foreign gods was not only good for others, but also good for Solomon. If the God of Israel had richly blessed him, perhaps the other gods would bless him even more. The human heart seldom turns away from God all at once, but usually by degrees.

1 Kings 11:5-8 *He followed Ashtoreth the goddess of the Sidonians, and Molek the detestable god of the Ammonites. . . . Solomon built a high place for Chemosh the detestable god of Moab, and for Molek the detestable god of the Ammonites. He did the same for all his foreign wives, who burned incense and offered sacrifices to their gods.*

Solomon didn't abandon God completely, but added other gods to his religion. When different religions come into contact they're often blended in a process called *syncretism*.

Christians in Corinth were invited to eat at pagan temples and some accepted the invitation. But *You cannot drink the cup of the Lord and the cup of demons too; you cannot have a part in both the Lord's table and the table of demons* (1 Corinthians 10:21), wrote Paul.

Many Christians read the Bible, but also read their horoscope. They believe in heaven and hell, but also in reincarnation. I met a girl at a bookstore who called herself a Christian Buddhist. This may be fashionable but it's not Christianity.

No one comes to the Father except through me (John 14:6), said Jesus. And *there is no other name under heaven given to mankind by which we must be saved* (Acts 4:12), said Peter. If we don't limit our religion to the Bible, it will contradict the Bible. Believers should always be on guard against syncretism.

1 Kings 11:9 *The Lord became angry with Solomon because his heart had turned away from the Lord, the God of Israel, who had appeared to him twice.*

Not only was Solomon raised with the knowledge of God, but encountered God on two separate occasions (1 Kings 3:5, 9:2). This is a privilege given to few, and made Solomon's apostasy even worse.

Encountering God is a gift, but is no guarantee against turning away from him. Many who've experienced God deeply in the past aren't living for him now. It's not enough to rely on the past; we must *seek his face always* (Psalm 105:4), wrote the Psalmist.

Solomon's departure from God is also alarming because of his great wisdom. But what good is wisdom if we don't follow our own advice? We recommend the high road, but often take the low road.

When we consider Solomon's wisdom, and his encounters with God, we should be shocked by his apostasy and fear for our souls. If Solomon turned away from God, what might happen to us? *[W]ork out your salvation with fear and trembling* (Philippians 2:12), wrote Paul. The Bible gives us enough assurance to be secure, but never enough to be careless.

1 Kings 11:13 *I will not tear the whole kingdom from him, but will give him one tribe for the sake of David my servant and for the sake of Jerusalem, which I have chosen.*

Solomon led the nation to its peak, but only for a while. Whenever God's word contradicted his common sense, Solomon rejected God's word and followed his common sense (Deuteronomy 17:14-20). This made him successful for a while, but not for very long. God split the kingdom after he died and all his gains were lost. God's work must be done God's way in order to have lasting results.

For Reflection and Review

- *Why did Solomon turn away from God?*
- *Why is Solomon's apostasy alarming?*
- *Why was Solomon's success so brief?*

Lesson 83

1 Kings 12:1 *Rehoboam went to Shechem, for all Israel had gone there to make him king.*

After Solomon died, his son Rehoboam ruled in his place. But his father's success was financed through heavy taxation, and the people were feeling oppressed. They hoped the installation of a new king would be an opportunity to negotiate something more agreeable.

1 Kings 12:2 *When Jeroboam son of Nebat heard this . . . he returned from Egypt.*

Jeroboam was an important leader in Solomon's labor force (1 Kings 11:28). He received word from the prophet Ahijah that he'd rule over most of Israel (1 Kings 11:29-39). Solomon didn't like this prophecy so he *tried to kill Jeroboam, but Jeroboam fled to Egypt* (1 Kings 11:40). When Solomon died, Jeroboam returned to fulfill his God-given destiny. He was a serious threat to Rehoboam.

1 Kings 12:4 *[The people said to Rehoboam] Your father put a heavy yoke on us, but now lighten [it] and we will serve you.*

Rehoboam promised to respond within three days, which would give him time to consult his advisors. Those who had served his father encouraged the new king to answer the people favorably. *If today you will be a servant to these people and serve them and give them a favorable answer, they will always be your servants* (1 Kings 12:7), they said.

These men understood that the purpose of power is to serve, not to be served. *[W]hoever wants to become great among you must be your servant, and whoever wants to be first must be your slave* (Matthew 20:26-27), said Jesus. To be successful, Rehoboam needed to serve the people. But that's not what he had in mind.

1 Kings 12:8 *Rehoboam rejected the advice the elders gave him and consulted the young men who had grown up with him and were serving him.*

These young men weren't familiar with the daily pain and misery of ordinary Israelites. They were children of privilege who wanted to live in the manner to which they had grown accustomed. Solomon was the greatest king they'd ever known, and his authority was absolute. If Rehoboam appeared weak, he might never recover. Instead of giving into the people, he should be stronger than his father.

1 Kings 12:13 *The king answered the people harshly. . . . My father made your yoke heavy; I will make it even heavier. My father scourged you with whips; I will scourge you with scorpions.*

Scorpions may've referred to a brutal kind of lash. In other words, Rehoboam's policies would be harsher than his father's, and the punishment for breaking them would also be worse. He wasn't the kind of king who was willing to negotiate.

1 Kings 12:16 *When all Israel saw that the king refused to listen to them, they answered the king: What share do we have in David, what part in Jesse's son? . . . So the Israelites went home.*

This was nothing short of catastrophic for Rehoboam and the nation. The glorious kingdom was now divided, north and south, never to be united again. Instead of a single powerful nation, they became two weaker nations, less able to defend themselves. It was a breach that would never be healed.

Rehoboam was an inexperienced leader, and apparently insecure. He viewed the challenge to his leadership as a threat, which caused him to overreact. If he had listened to the people, and made a few concessions, the nation would've been saved. Instead of a weakness, his loving concern for his people would've been a strength.

1 Kings 12:20 *When all the Israelites heard that Jeroboam had returned, they sent and called him to the assembly and made him king over all Israel. Only the tribe of Judah remained loyal to the house of David.*

The prophecy given to Jeroboam (1 Kings 11:29-39) was coming true. But God's word to Jeroboam also had conditions: *If you do whatever I command you and walk in obedience to me and do what is right in my eyes by obeying my decrees and commands, as David my servant did, I will be with you. I will build you a dynasty as enduring as the one I built for David and will give Israel to you* (1 Kings 11:38). But Jeroboam wouldn't be faithful to God, and things would turn out badly.

1 Kings 12:26 *Jeroboam thought to himself, The kingdom will now likely revert to the house of David.*

The southern kingdom (Judah) and the northern kingdom (Israel) were politically distinct, but shared a common religion. Since the temple was in Judah, faithful Israelites would travel there at least three times a year, as the law of God required (Exodus 23:17).

This shouldn't have been a problem, but Jeroboam was convinced that a common religion would cause the Israelites to give their allegiance back to Judah, and he'd be killed for treason. So instead of trusting God, he changed the nation's religion.

1 Kings 12:28-29 *[Jeroboam] made two golden calves. He said to the people, It is too much for you to go up to Jerusalem. Here are your gods, Israel, who brought you up out of Egypt. One he set up in Bethel, and the other in Dan.*

Bethel and Dan were at the southern and northern ends of Israel, so the people wouldn't have to go even further south to worship God in Jerusalem. Jeroboam also appointed a priesthood and planned a yearly religious festival. His religion was similar to the Jewish religion, except it wasn't in the Bible. It was nothing short of idolatry.

Most of the northern kingdom followed Jeroboam, but not all. Some abandoned their property, and went to live in Judah, so they could worship God according to his word (2 Chronicles 11:13-16). They're like Christians who leave a church because the church has left the word of God. We are not free to worship God any way we choose, but only according to his word. The further we stray from the word of God, the further we stray from Christ.

For Reflection and Review

- *How did Rehoboam misunderstand the purpose of leadership?*
- *Why did so many people reject Rehoboam's leadership?*
- *Why did Jeroboam set up golden calves?*

Lesson 84

1 Kings 13:1 *By the word of the Lord a man of God came from Judah to Bethel, as Jeroboam was standing by the altar to make an offering.*

Because the northern kingdom departed from God's pattern for worship, he could've turned his back on them. Instead, God reached out to his people through a series of prophets. The first one isn't named, but is simply called *a man of God*.

As Jeroboam stood by the altar, the man of God (from the southern kingdom) began to speak: *Altar, altar! This is what the Lord says: A son named Josiah will be born to the house of David. On you he will sacrifice the priests of the high places who make offerings here, and human bones will be burned on you* (1 Kings 13:2).

This man risked his life by interrupting a worship service led by King Jeroboam. He mentioned a future king (Josiah) who would later demolished the altar that Jeroboam built (2 Kings 23:15). Josiah ruled about three hundred years after Jeroboam, and did what the man of God foretold. Telling the future is easy for God because he knows the end from the beginning (Isaiah 46:10).

1 Kings 13:3 *That same day the man of God gave a sign: This is the sign the Lord has declared: The altar will be split apart and the ashes on it will be poured out.*

To show that his distant prophecy would be fulfilled, the man of God foretold something that would happen that very day. The altar would split apart, and the ashes would spill out. But the man of God was being a nuisance, so Jeroboam *stretched out his hand from the altar and said, Seize him!* Immediately the hand he stretched out shriveled up, the altar split apart, and the ashes poured out —just as the prophet foretold.

The prophet was clearly speaking for God, so the king asked for his hand to be restored. And, as soon as the prophet prayed, the king's hand was healed. After all this, we expect the king to abandon his false religion and lead God's people in true religion. Instead, he tried to bribe the man of God with a gift. If he could win the prophet's support, it would add credibility to the king's new religion.

To his many other sins, Jeroboam added stubbornness. He determined his course of action and resolved to follow through no matter what. Even when God made his will clear, Jeroboam wouldn't change.

If we condemn Jeroboam, however, we must also condemn ourselves, because there's an obstinate streak in all of us. Even when God's will is clear to us, we often go against it. *All day long I have held out my hands to an obstinate people* (Isaiah 65:2), said God. Jeroboam was wrong to be stubborn, and so are we sometimes.

1 Kings 13:11 *Now there was a certain old prophet living in Bethel, whose sons came and told him all that the man of God had done there that day.*

The old prophet's sons seem to have been at the sacrifice and witnessed the events. They knew their father would be interested so they quickly brought him the news. The old prophet wanted to meet the younger man of God, so he mounted his donkey and went after him. Then he invited him home to eat.

The younger man of God was hungry and would've gone home with the old prophet but, earlier, God told him not to eat or drink in that place. *The old prophet answered, I too am a prophet, as you are. And an angel said to me by the word of the Lord: Bring him back with you to your house so that he may eat bread and drink water* (1 Kings 13:18).

But the old prophet was lying. He probably wanted to spend time with the younger man of God and hear everything God was saying to him. Since everyone lies a little, what could possibly happen? The younger man of God believed the older prophet and went back to his house. But while they were sitting at table, the word of the Lord came to the old prophet.

This is what the Lord says: You have defied the word of the Lord and have not kept the command the Lord your God gave you. You came back and ate bread and drank water in the place where he told you not to eat or drink. Therefore your body will not be buried in the tomb of your ancestors (1 Kings 13:21-22).

Many families owned a burial place, but those who died away from home were usually buried where they died. The old prophet was telling the younger man of God that he wouldn't make it home that day.

This is a very strange story, but it reveals the low level of godliness even among the religious leaders. The king was leading a false religion, the old prophet was a liar, and the younger man of God allowed himself to be deceived to satisfy his appetite—all on the same day!

One of God's best gifts to his people are religious leaders who are faithful to what God says. But even good religious leaders fail privately, and even publicly. Since the beginning, in fact, there's only been one religious leader with a perfect record. *I always do what pleases [my Father]* (John 8:29), said Jesus. He's the only religious leader who's absolutely trustworthy.

1 Kings 13:23 *When the man of God had finished eating and drinking, the prophet who had brought him back saddled his donkey for him.*

It must've been a strange parting. They both knew God, and were able to hear his voice. The older prophet would've felt terribly, and the younger man of God would've felt foolish. He began the journey home, but didn't get very far before he was killed by a lion. The older prophet buried him, and asked to be buried in the same place (1 Kings 13:31).

Perhaps the reason neither man is named is because they both fell short of what God required. *[A]ll have sinned and fall short of the glory of God* (Romans 3:23), wrote Paul. This is why we need to be saved. If even the prophets fell short, how much more do we? Whoever hopes to get to heaven on their own will be very disappointed. But *everyone who calls on the name of the Lord will be saved* (Acts 2:21), said Peter.

For Reflection and Review

- *What can we learn about God from this story?*
- *If Jeroboam knew he was wrong, why didn't he change?*
- *What do the man of God and the old prophet teach us about religious leaders?*

Lesson 85

1 Kings 14:1 *At that time Abijah son of Jeroboam became ill.*

If Abijah was Jeroboam's firstborn son, he was also the crown prince. Jeroboam was so concerned for his son that he sent his wife to the prophet Ahijah, hoping for a good word from God. Ajijah was old and blind, but God told him Jeroboam's wife was on her way, and what he should say to her:

Go, tell Jeroboam that this is what the Lord, the God of Israel, says: I raised you up from among the people and appointed you ruler over my people Israel. I tore the kingdom away from the house of David and gave it to you, but you have not been like my servant David, who kept my commands and followed me with all his heart, doing only what was right in my eyes. You have done more evil than all who lived before you. You have made for yourself other gods, idols made of metal; you have aroused my anger and turned your back on me (1 Kings 14:7-9).

Because of this, I am going to bring disaster on the house of Jeroboam. I will cut off from Jeroboam every last male in Israel—slave or free. I will burn up the house of Jeroboam as one burns dung, until it is all gone. Dogs will eat those belonging to Jeroboam who die in the city, and the birds will feed on those who die in the country. . . . As for you, go back home. When you set foot in your city, the boy will die (1 Kings 14:10-12).

[Furthermore] the Lord will strike Israel, so that it will be like a reed swaying in the water. He will uproot Israel from this good land that he gave to their ancestors and scatter them beyond the Euphrates River, because they aroused the Lord's anger by making Asherah poles. And he will give Israel up because of the sins Jeroboam has committed and has caused Israel to commit (1 Kings 14:15-16).

From Jeroboam we learn that one person can lead millions into sin. Jeroboam's son died, and all the prophet's other words were fulfilled in due time (1 Kings 15:25-30), including the nation's exile. If God holds us responsible not only for our own sin, but also for the sins we lead others to commit, our guilt is beyond measure. We ought to keep in mind the affect our sin will have on others, as well as ourselves therefore.

Notice also that leadership matters. Jeroboam led millions into sin, but Christ has led even more into righteousness. Jeroboam's kingdom was sent into exile, but Christ's kingdom is being gathered from all over the world. Jeroboam's kingdom was filled with shame, but Christ's kingdom will be filled with glory. And no matter what we've done in the past, we can be part of Christ's kingdom if we'll simply receive him as our Lord (Colossians 2:6). As goes the king, so goes the kingdom.

*****

1 Kings 14:25 *In the fifth year of King Rehoboam, Shishak king of Egypt attacked Jerusalem.*

Rehoboam allowed evil to flourish in Judah (1 Kings 14:23-24), so God sent the king of Egypt to attack them. *This is what the Lord says, You have abandoned me; therefore, I now abandon you to Shishak* (2 Chronicles 12:5). God is under no obligation to protect those who abandon him.

When Rehoboam heard this, he humbled himself and said, *The Lord is just* (2 Chronicles 12:6). Then God softened the punishment and said, *My wrath will not be poured out on Jerusalem through Shishak. They will, however, become subject to him, so that they may learn the difference between serving me and serving the kings of other lands* (2 Chronicles 12:7-8).

Rehoboam loved freedom so much that he wanted to be free from God. But when he was free from God, there was no one to protect him from Shishak. So instead of serving the King of heaven, he had to serve an evil king.

That's how it is with us as well. If we serve God, he'll protect us from the evil one (Matthew 6:13). But if we won't serve God, there's no one to protect us from the one who hates us most. Perfect freedom is serving the God who loved us enough to die for us. *So if the Son sets you free, you will be free indeed* (John 8:36), said Jesus.

*****

1 Kings 16:15 *Zimri reigned in Tirzah seven days.*

Zimri had the shortest reign of all the kings of Israel. He began by killing the previous king, and taking the throne for himself. To reduce the odds of retaliation, he also killed the previous king's extended family. But when General Omri heard what Zimri had done, he marched on the capital city. Sensing certain defeat, Zimri went into the royal palace, set it on fire, and perished in the flames.

Zimri thought it better to die by fire than fall into the hands of Omri. He may've been right, but he wasn't mindful of the flames of hell, a place where *the fire is not quenched* (Mark 9:48), said Jesus. Zimri thought his suffering would be brief, only to find that it will never end.

This is what gave Polycarp, the second century bishop of Smyrna, courage to be burned at the stake. *You threaten me with fire which burns for an hour, and is then extinguished, but you know nothing of the fire of the coming judgment*, he said. Few people like the idea of hell, but it's so important to Christianity that Jesus taught about it frequently. Christ didn't die to save us from mild discomfort, but from the worst conceivable agony.

*****

1 Kings 16:23 *Omri became king of Israel, and he reigned twelve years.*

One of his greatest achievements was the purchase of a hill called *Samaria* which became the capital city of Israel. It was centrally located, and rose three hundred feet above the surrounding area. This made it difficult to attack, and helped stabilize the nation. Omri was so successful militarily that, many years later, Assyrian records still referred to Israel as the *house of Omri*.

But in spite of his achievements the Bible gives little space to Omri, and concludes that he *did evil in the eyes of the Lord* (1 Kings 16:25). From him we should learn that the judgment of history is nothing compared to the judgment of God. Omri was applauded by many in his day, but is only known by a few today. *The world and its desires pass away, but whoever does the will of God lives forever* (1 John 2:17), wrote John.

*****

1 Kings 16:29-30 *Ahab son of Omri became king of Israel, and he reigned in Samaria over Israel twenty-two years. Ahab son of Omri did more evil in the eyes of the Lord than any of those before him.*

Ahab's worst offense was leading the nation to worship Baal instead of God. He even built a temple to Baal in the capital city of Samaria. So Ahab *did more to arouse the anger of the Lord, the God of Israel, than did all the kings of Israel before him* (1 Kings 16:33).

Remarkably, God didn't abandon Israel, or even Ahab, but sent his prophets to warn them. This is because God is patient with us, *not wanting anyone to perish, but everyone to come to repentance* (2 Peter 3:9), wrote Peter. We ought to be amazed by Gods patience, but never put it to the test. *Will you try the patience of my God?* (Isaiah 7:13), asked Isaiah. But most of us do, at one time or another.

For Reflection and Review

- *Why was Jeroboam's sin so bad?*
- *What can we learn from Rehoboam?*
- *What can we learn from Omri?*

Lesson 86

1 Kings 17:1 *Now Elijah the Tishbite, from Tishbe in Gilead, said to Ahab, As the Lord, the God of Israel, lives, whom I serve, there will be neither dew nor rain in the next few years except at my word.*

Ahab and his wife Jezebel were making Baal worship the official religion of Israel. Rather than turn away from his people, God sent the prophet Elijah to turn them back to him. Elijah's name means *the Lord is my God*, and that was the heart of his message.

To show his people the foolishness of serving Baal (the god of crops and fertility) God sent a drought that would last three and a half years (James 5:17). Most people can live a few weeks without food, but only a few days without water. God can get our attention anytime by turning off the water. Whenever we take a drink of God's water, we should thank him for the rain.

1 Kings 17:2-4 *Then the word of the Lord came to Elijah: Leave here, turn eastward and hide in the Kerith Ravine, east of the Jordan. You will drink from the brook, and I have directed the ravens to supply you with food there.*

Because of the king's wrath, Elijah would have to hide for the next few years. God sent him to a brook that would flow for some time, and commanded the ravens to feed him. Twice a day they brought Elijah bread and meat, and he drank water from the brook (1 Kings 17:6). God can provide for his people even in difficult times. Regardless of economic conditions, we should always look to God.

1 Kings 17:8-9 *Then the word of the Lord came to him: Go at once to Zarephath in the region of Sidon and* *stay there. I have directed a widow there to supply you with food.*

After the brook dried up, God sent Elijah to a town outside Israel. There he saw a widow gathering sticks and asked for some bread and water. But she was so poor that she was preparing her final meal, so she and her son could eat it and die. *Elijah said to her, Do not be afraid. Go home and do as you have said. But first make a small loaf of bread for me from what you have and bring it to me, and then make something for yourself and your son* (1 Kings 17:13).

The prophet's request seems selfish at first. Would he really deny a poor widow and her son part of their final meal in order to feed himself? Not actually. *For this is what the Lord, the God of Israel, says: The jar of flour will not be used up and the jug of oil will not run dry until the day the Lord sends rain on the land* (1 Kings 17:14), he said.

All the widow had was a little flour and oil, but Elijah assured her that God would replenish it until the drought was over. She obeyed the prophet's word, and God kept his promise. Her food supply never ran out (1 Kings 17:15).

We too should give what we have to God, while hoping to receive from him. *Honor the Lord with your wealth, with the firstfruits of all your crops; then your barns will be filled to overflowing, and your vats will brim over with new wine* (Proverbs 3:9-10), says Proverbs.

God is generous with us, and wants us to be generous with him. By giving back to God we acknowledge that he's the source of all we have, and that we trust him for the future. Regardless how little we have, we can always give some away.

1 Kings 17:17 *Some time later the son of the woman who owned the house became ill.*

This would be a concern to any parent but, since the boy was her only child, the situation was even worse. And, since she was a widow, her son was her only hope of support in old age. But the child's condition grew worse, and he died. *She said to Elijah, What do you have against me, man of God? Did you come to remind me of my sin and kill my son?* (1 Kings 17:18).

The woman's reply is interesting for two reasons. First, she blamed Elijah for the death of her son. Since God is over everything, and Elijah represented God, the death of her son was Elijah's fault. Her logic wasn't fair to Elijah, but when people are angry at God they sometimes lash out at his ministers.

The woman's reply is also interesting because she was reminded of her sin. We don't know what her sin was, but it must've been serious if she thought it was related to the death of her son. David's sin with Bathsheba caused the death of their son (2 Samuel 12:14), so she might've been right. But probably not.

For God so loved the world that he gave his one and only Son, that whoever believes in him shall not perish but have eternal life (John 3:16), wrote John. God punished Jesus for our sins, so that he could look on us with favor. *For I will forgive their wickedness and will remember their sins no more* (Jeremiah 31:34), said God. Since we never know infallibly what God is doing, it's seldom wise to connect particular suffering with any particular sin. It's better to confess all our sins (1 John 1:9), and focus on God's love for us in Christ Jesus.

1 Kings 17:19 *Give me your son, Elijah replied.*

Elijah took the boy into a room, where he could earnestly pray for him, and the boy's life returned. What a joy for his mother to receive her son alive again. This miracle anticipates the raising of the widow's son by Jesus (Luke 7:11-17), and the general resurrection at the end of the age. *[F]or a time is coming when all who are in their graves will hear his voice and come out—those who have done what is good will rise to live, and those who have done what is evil will rise to be condemned* (John 5:28-29), said Jesus.

It's not enough to think that our souls will go to heaven or hell when we die. That is true, but the day is coming when all who've died will be reunited with their bodies forever. The lost will suffer in their bodies forever, and the righteous will flourish in their bodies forever. The pleasure and pain we experience now reminds us of the pleasure or pain we'll experience then. This is terrible news for the lost, but wonderful news for the righteous. *[Y]ou will fill me with joy in your presence, with eternal pleasures at your right hand* (Psalm 16:11), wrote David.

For Reflection and Review

- *What can we learn from the widow about giving to God?*
- *Why did the loss of her son remind the widow of her sins?*
- *Why is the resurrection important to the age to come?*

Lesson 87

1 Kings 18:1 *After a long time, in the third year, the word of the Lord came to Elijah: Go and present yourself to Ahab, and I will send rain on the land.*

The land was parched because of the draught, but the nation hadn't returned to God. God was about to make it rain again, but he wanted the people to know it was from him, not from Baal. So Elijah challenged the king to meet him on Mount Carmel with hundreds of false prophets and many others. We should think of thousands of people who followed a false religion, and Elijah as the only one speaking for God.

Here we see that truth is not determined by majority opinion. Most people have no reason for their beliefs except that others believe them too. They go along with the majority, believing the majority is usually right. But God alone is always right. If everyone in the world disagrees with God, then everyone in the world is wrong. It's not easy to stand with God against the majority, but Elijah was a man of character.

1 Kings 18:21 *Elijah went before the people and said, How long will you waver between two opinions? If the Lord is God, follow him; but if Baal is God, follow him.*

The Israelites had a long history of believing in God, but also believing in other gods. But the other gods weren't helping very much, and now God's people were wondering what to do. Elijah told them to stop wavering and make up their minds.

Christians also waver between serving God and other possibilities. We accept Jesus Christ as Lord and Savior, but we also accept the values of our culture, even when they contradict the Bible. Instead of following the Lord wholeheartedly, we might follow him halfheartedly—or even less. We're like someone with a foot in two boats: unless we make up our minds, we'll end up in the water.

1 Kings 18:22-23 *Then Elijah said to them, I am the only one of the Lord's prophets left, but Baal has four hundred and fifty prophets. Get two bulls for us.*

To demonstrate who was the real God, Elijah proposed a sacrifice. He and the prophets of Baal would each prepare a bull, put it on wood, but not start a fire. Then they'd pray, and whatever deity answered by fire was God.

The prophets of Baal went first. They called on Baal and danced around the altar from morning until noon. When there was no response, *Elijah began to taunt them. Shout louder! he said. Surely he is a god! Perhaps he is deep in thought, or busy, or traveling. Maybe he is sleeping and must be awakened. So they shouted louder and slashed themselves with swords and spears, as was their custom, until their blood flowed. . . . But there was no response, no one answered, no one paid attention* (1 Kings 18:27-29).

Then Elijah built an altar with stones, and dug a trench around it. He cut up the bull, laid it on the wood, and had water poured on the sacrifice until the trench was full. Then he offered a simple prayer, and *the fire of the Lord fell and burned up the sacrifice, the wood, the stones and the soil, and also licked up the water in the trench. When all the people saw this, they fell prostrate and cried, The Lord—he is God! The Lord—he is God!* (1 Kings 18:38-39).

This was an awesome display of God's power that seemed to carry the day. God revealed himself so clearly that it was hard not to believe. We might wish that God would do this more often, but it's not his normal way of bringing people to faith.

Ordinarily, God calls us to believe in him due to his revelation in nature, Scripture, conscience, and Christ. The evidence is conclusive, so there's no excuse for not believing in God (Romans 1:20). Ordinarily, God doesn't overwhelm us with dramatic displays of his power—though he has in the past and will in the future (Matthew 24:27).

1 Kings 18:40 *Then Elijah commanded them, Seize the prophets of Baal. Do not let anyone get away! They seized them, and Elijah had them brought down to the Kishon Valley and slaughtered there.*

This may seem a little harsh, but it was actually less than the law of God required. The full penalty would've required the destruction of entire towns (Deuteronomy 13:12-18). It's a serious thing to teach a false religion, and God hates it. To lead anyone away from the truth of God is no longer a capital crime, but it's still a serious sin. *If anyone causes one of these little ones—those who believe in me—to stumble, it would be better for them to have a large millstone hung around their neck and to be drowned in the depths of the sea* (Matthew 18:6), said Jesus.

1 Kings 18:41 *Elijah climbed to the top of Carmel, bent down to the ground and put his face between his knees.*

God had promised rain (1 Kings 18:1), and Elijah knew it was coming (1 Kings 18:41), so he began to pray. *Go and look toward the sea, he told his servant. And he went up and looked. There is nothing there, he said* (1 Kings 18:43). Seven times Elijah told him to go back and look again, and on the seventh time he saw *a cloud as small as a man's hand* rising out of the sea. The sky grew black with clouds, the wind picked up, and a heavy rain began to fall.

Here we learn the importance of prayer for bringing about the will of God. God doesn't need our prayers, but he likes to use them to bring about what he has promised. God's will is to bring about his kingdom, so Jesus taught us to pray *your kingdom come* (Matthew 6:10). God could bring his kingdom without our prayers, but wants to use our prayers to bring his will to pass. Whenever we understand the will of God, we should pray for God to do it.

1 Kings 18:46 *The power of the Lord came on Elijah and, tucking his cloak into his belt, he ran ahead of Ahab all the way to Jezreel.*

Jezreel was about sixteen miles away but, empowered by God, Elijah ran ahead of Ahab's chariot. He must've been thrilled over the defeat of Baal in the presence of the king and thousands of others. Now God was sending the blessing of rain to show his approval. In Elijah's mind, God mightily used him to turn the nation back to God. It was the finest moment of his life so far.

For Reflection and Review

- *Why is it hard to stand for God against the majority?*
- *How does God reveal himself ordinarily?*
- *Why did Elijah pray for rain if he knew it was on the way?*

Lesson 88

1 Kings 19:1 *Now Ahab told Jezebel everything Elijah had done and how he had killed all the prophets with the sword.*

Since a triumph like this could only come from God, Elijah must've thought Queen Jezebel would surely come over to God's side. The King and Queen would lead the nation in a revival, and the worship of God would be restored. It might even spread to the ends of he earth. Elijah was amazed at what God was doing through him.

1 Kings 19:2 *So Jezebel sent a messenger to Elijah to say, May the gods deal with me, be it ever so severely, if by this time tomorrow I do not make your life like that of one of them.*

This was the opposite of what Elijah was expecting. The demonstration of God's power and blessing were so obvious they couldn't be denied. Elijah should've become an advisor to Ahab and Jezebel as they reformed the nation. Instead, the queen was determined to kill him, just as she had killed other prophets of God (1 Kings 18:4).

We naturally assume that people want the truth, and all we have to do is reveal it. The heart is so corrupt, however, that people don't want the truth about God. We'd rather *suppress the truth by [our] wickedness* (Romans 1:18) than believe in the God of the Bible. That's what Jezebel did, and that's what we do by nature.

1 Kings 19:3 *Elijah was afraid and ran for his life.*

Sadly, there wasn't much else he could do. When you fight with all you have, but it's not enough, all you can do is run. Instead of being the winner, Elijah became the loser. The ecstasy of victory, became the agony of defeat.

The battle against evil is never won in this age, but only fought. *For our struggle is not against flesh and blood, but against . . . the spiritual forces of evil in the heavenly realms* (Ephesians 6:12), wrote Paul. The devil *is filled with fury, because he knows that his time is short* (Revelation 20:10), wrote John. We know who wins in the end, but we may have to run for our lives sometimes.

1 Kings 19:4 *[Elijah] came to a broom bush, sat down under it and prayed that he might die.*

This is the prophet at his lowest. He just a hundred twenty miles to escape the wrath of Jezebel, and was exhausted. The trauma of his struggle was so great that it took away his will to live. *I have had enough, Lord . . . Take my life*, he said.

Godly leaders aren't exempt from feelings of despair. Moses (Numbers 11:15), Job (Job 6:8-9), and Jonah (Jonah 4:3) also prayed for death, but God had a future for each of them. As long as he keeps us alive, God has a reason for us to live.

1 Kings 19:5-6 *Then he lay down under the bush and fell asleep. All at once an angel touched him and said, Get up and eat. He looked around, and there by his head was some bread baked over hot coals, and a jar of water. He ate and drank and then lay down again.*

This happened a second time and, strengthened by the food, Elijah traveled another forty days until he reached Mount Sinai. That's where God met with Moses and established his covenant with Israel (Exodus 19-20). Elijah was hoping to find God there as well.

1 Kings 19:9 *There he went into a cave and spent the night. And the word of the Lord came to him: What are you doing here, Elijah?*

Elijah poured out his complaint to God, and the Lord displayed his power. *[A] great and powerful wind tore the mountains apart and shattered the rocks before the Lord, but the Lord was not in the wind. After the wind there was an earthquake, but the Lord was not in the earthquake. After the earthquake came a fire, but the Lord was not in the fire. And after the fire came a gentle whisper* (1 Kings 19:11-12).

God wasn't working in the dramatic way Elijah longed for, but he was still speaking. And if Elijah would pay attention, he could still be used by God. This is not an invitation to listen to the voices in our heads, but a reminder to listen to what God has said in his word. We might wish for mighty acts, but God's word is always mighty. *Is not my word like fire, declares the Lord, and like a hammer that breaks a rock in pieces?* (Jeremiah 23:29). As long we are listening, we can still be used by God.

For Reflection and Review

- *Why did Jezebel reject God?*
- *Why do God's people pray to die sometimes?*
- *How does God speak to us today?*

Lesson 89

1 Kings 21:1 *Some time later there was an incident involving a vineyard belonging to Naboth the Jezreelite.*

Naboth lived in Jezreel, and owned a vineyard that was close to Ahab's palace. Ahab wanted to buy Naboth's vineyard to use as a vegetable garden, and was willing to pay whatever Naboth asked, or give him a better vineyard. But Naboth wanted to keep the vineyard in his family since that's what God required. *The land must not be sold permanently, because the land is mine and you reside in my land as foreigners and strangers* (Leviticus 25:23), said God.

God gave the land to Israel by tribes (Joshua 13-21), and family property was to be passed down from generation to generation. Naboth could obey God or sell his vineyard but he couldn't do both. It took a measure of courage, but he said *Yes* to God and *No* to the king.

1 Kings 21:4 *So Ahab went home, sullen and angry because Naboth the Jezreelite had said, I will not give you the inheritance of my ancestors. He lay on his bed sulking and refused to eat.*

It's inappropriate for grown men to pout, especially kings, but that's what Ahab did. He couldn't have what he wanted, so he lay on his bed and sulked. When his wicked wife, Jezebel, discovered the reason for his mood she said, *Cheer up. I'll get you the vineyard* (1 Kings 21:7).

Jezebel was the daughter of Ethbaal, king of the Sidonians (1 Kings 16:31), so she had an idea how kings should rule. Pagan kings often took whatever land they wanted because, theoretically, it all belonged to them. Jezebel had no concern for God, or Naboth, but only for what she wanted. *So she wrote letters in Ahab's name, placed his seal on them, and sent them to the elders and nobles who lived in Naboth's city with him* (1 Kings 21:8).

Jezebel wrote that Naboth should be accused of cursing both God and the king, and then be stoned to death. The sentence was carried out, and Naboth's sons were also killed (2 Kings 9:26) to eliminate their claim on the land.

1 Kings 21:15 *As soon as Jezebel heard that Naboth had been stoned to death, she said to Ahab, Get up and take possession of the vineyard.*

That very day God sent the prophet Elijah to meet Ahab at his newly acquired vineyard. And Elijah had a word from God: *I will wipe out your descendants and cut off from Ahab every last male in Israel . . . . [and] dogs will devour Jezebel* (1 Kings 21:21-23), he said.

Ahab killed Naboth and his sons, so God would kill Ahab and his sons—and dogs would eat his wife. Sometime later Ahab's sons were slaughtered, and their heads were put in baskets (2 Kings 10:7). Jezebel was thrown from an upper room and trampled by horses. *[W]hen they went out to bury her, they found nothing except her skull, her feet and her hands* (2 Kings 9:35). The rest was eaten by dogs (2 Kings 9:36), just as the prophet foretold.

Naboth suffered injustice but his story isn't over yet. *Blessed are those who are persecuted because of righteousness, for theirs is the kingdom of heaven* (Matthew 5:10), said Jesus. Naboth's place in the kingdom probably has a better vineyard than he ever had before. He'll show us around and tell us even more about Ahab and Jezebel—but they won't be there to talk about him. We may suffer injustice now, but Christ will make it right in the end.

*****

1 Kings 22:3 *The king of Israel had said to his officials, Don't you know that Ramoth Gilead belongs to us and yet we are doing nothing to retake it from the king of Aram?*

Ramoth Gilead was about twenty-eight miles east of the Jordan River, and rightly belonged to the nation of Israel. It was taken over by the Arameans, but Ahab wanted to take it back. He requested help from Jehoshaphat, the king of Judah, who agreed to help. But Jehoshaphat wanted to consult the Lord, so Ahab gathered four hundred prophets who all agreed that God would give them victory. Zedekiah, son of Kenaanah, even made iron horns declaring, *This is what the Lord says: With these you will gore the Arameans until they are destroyed* (1 Kings 22:11).

But Jehoshaphat wasn't convinced. He thought these prophets were only telling the king what he wanted to hear, so he asked for a more reliable prophet. Then Ahab called for Micaiah, son of Imlah, who was encouraged to agree with what the other prophets had said. But Micaiah was a man of conviction who only cared what God said. *I saw all Israel scattered on the hills like sheep without a shepherd* (1 Kings 22:17), he said. In other words, the king would be killed, and his army would be scattered.

1 Kings 22:24 *Then Zedekiah son of Kenaanah went up and slapped Micaiah in the face.*

Micaiah's words flatly contradicted the other prophets, and they forcefully objected. To be publicly slapped in the face is very insulting, and Micaiah may have blushed. Then King Ahab had Micaiah thrown in prison until he returned from battle. *If you ever return safely, the Lord has not spoken through me*, said Micaiah. *Then he added, Mark my words, all you people!*

1 Kings 22:29 *So the king of Israel and Jehoshaphat king of Judah went up to Ramoth Gilead.*

Jehoshaphat wanted to hear from a true prophet but, when he did, he disregarded his words. The prophet told him the word of God, but Jehoshaphat went to battle anyway. This is how many people listen to sermons. They want to know what God says, not to obey him, but to see what he thinks about what they plan to do.

1 Kings 22:30 *The king of Israel said to Jehoshaphat, I will enter the battle in disguise, but you wear your royal robes.*

Ahab was concerned Micaiah's prophecy might come true so, instead of wearing his royal robes, he went into battle in disguise. Jehoshaphat agreed to wear the royal robes, and nearly died as a result.

Meanwhile, *someone drew his bow at random and hit the king of Israel between the sections of his armor* (1 Kings 22:34). Ahab told his chariot driver to get him out of battle, but remained propped up in his chariot so his soldiers wouldn't lose heart. The battle raged all day long, but the king's bleeding wouldn't stop. That evening Ahab died, just as Micaiah foretold.

Here we see that the random shot of an arrow wasn't random to God. An inch to the left or right, and the arrow would've struck the king's armor. But God directed the arrow to its mark so the king would die as he decreed. No amount of protection can save a man whom God has decided to kill.

Ahab was one of the wickedest kings Israel ever had. Along with wicked Jezebel, he led God's people to worship Baal. He partly believed in God, but never truly turned to him. The purpose of God's patience is to lead us to repentance (Romans 2:4). But if we don't repent, all that is left is judgment.

For Reflection and Review

- *What can we learn from Naboth?*
- *Why was Jezebel evil?*
- *Why didn't Jehoshaphat listen to Micaiah?*

Lesson 90

2 Kings 1:2 *Now Ahaziah had fallen through the lattice of his upper room in Samaria and injured himself.*

Ahaziah, son of Ahab and Jezebel, ruled the northern kingdom of Israel from 853 to 852 BC, and *did evil in the eyes of the Lord* (1 Kings 22:52). He fell from an upper room and was injured so severely that it wasn't clear if he'd live or die. But instead of turning to God, he sent messengers to consult with the god of Ekron, to see if he'd recover.

Some people respond to hardship by turning to God, others by turning away from him, and others by ignoring him. On one floor of a hospital there may be someone who's praising God, another who's cursing God, and another who's ignoring God. Suffering doesn't change our view of God, so much as it reveals it. Ahaziah thought the God of Israel was irrelevant, so he didn't bother to consult him.

2 Kings 1:3 *But the angel of the Lord said to Elijah the Tishbite, Go up and meet the messengers of the king of Samaria and ask them, Is it because there is no God in Israel that you are going off to consult Baal-Zebub, the god of Ekron?*

The king's messengers didn't make it the few days journey to Ekron, because God sent the prophet Elijah with the answer to Ahaziah's question. It seemed that God was reaching out to Ahaziah, even when Ahaziah wasn't reaching out to God.

2 Kings 1:5 *When the messengers returned to the king, he asked them, Why have you come back?*

The messengers weren't expected for several days, so the king was surprised to see them. They explained their meeting with Elijah and gave the king his answer: *You will certainly die!* (2 Kings 1:6). It wasn't the answer Ahaziah wanted, since he was still in his early twenties. But long life isn't promised to anyone—only certain death. *[P]eople are destined to die once, and after that to face judgment* (Hebrews 9:27), says Hebrews.

At least Ahaziah could use his remaining time to prepare to meet God. *[I]f someone who is wicked repents, that person's former wickedness will not bring condemnation* (Ezekiel 33:12), said God. This was an opportunity that could lead to eternal life. But the wicked often reject repentance, even on their death bed. So instead of turning to God, Ahaziah sent fifty men to arrest Elijah.

2 Kings 1:9-10 *The captain went up to Elijah, who was sitting on the top of a hill, and said to him, Man of God, the king says, Come down! Elijah answered the captain, If I am a man of God, may fire come down from heaven and consume you and your fifty men! Then fire fell from heaven and consumed the captain and his men.*

Word got back to Ahaziah, but he was unfazed. He just sent another fifty men and got the same results. Then he sent another fifty men, but the captain approached the prophet differently. He fell on his knees and begged Elijah for his life, and for the lives of his soldiers. So Elijah spared their lives, and went to see the king. Then the king died, just as Elijah said.

It's unfortunate that a hundred soldiers had to die because the king was stubborn, but people often suffer because of their leaders. This is true for nations, organizations, and even families. *[God] punishes the children and their children for the sin of the parents* (Exodus 34:7), recorded Moses.

Ahaziah was the wicked son of the wicked king Ahab. If Ahab had followed God, and taught his children well, his son's future would've been different. But since Ahab rejected God, and worshipped a false god, that's what his son did too. Everything we do, for good or evil, ripples out to those around us.

*****

2 Kings 2:1 *When the Lord was about to take Elijah up to heaven in a whirlwind, Elijah and Elisha were on their way from Gilgal.*

Some time earlier God told Elijah to anoint Elisha to succeed him as a prophet (1 Kings 19:16). When Elijah found him, Elisha was plowing with twelve yoke of oxen (twenty-four in all) which shows he was a person of wealth.

Elijah threw his cloak around Elisha to show his prophetic ministry was being passed to him. Elisha kissed his parents goodbye, and prepared a feast by slaughtering his oxen, and cooking them on his plowing equipment. He then became Elijah's servant.

This reminds us that the call of God is more important than anything else in life. When Jesus called Matthew from his tax collecting business, Matthew *got up, left everything and followed him* (Luke

5:28). Whoever follows Christ can serve him by preaching his word, raising children, waiting tables, or any legitimate occupation. Thinking of our job as a way to serve God, elevates it to the highest possible level.

For Reflection and Review

- *How does suffering affect our view of God?*
- *How does God punish children for the sins of their parents?*
- *Why is it helpful to see our jobs as a way of serving Christ?*

Lesson 91

2 Kings 2:2 *Elijah said to Elisha, Stay here; the Lord has sent me to Bethel. But Elisha said, As surely as the Lord lives and as you live, I will not leave you.*

Elisha was aware that Elijah would soon be taken away, and was determined to stay by his side. Elijah may've wanted to be alone with God, but Elisha was determined to be a witness. So they went together to see the company of the prophets at Bethel and Jericho. These were probably religious communities that looked to Elijah for leadership during this time of apostasy. Elijah was stopping by to say farewell.

2 Kings 2:6 *Then Elijah said to him, Stay here; the Lord has sent me to the Jordan.*

Again Elisha refused, and they walked together to the Jordan River, followed by fifty men from the company of the prophets. When they got to the river, *Elijah took his cloak, rolled it up and struck the water with it. The water divided to the right and to the left, and the two of them crossed over on dry ground* (2 Kings 2:8).

This was an important miracle for Elijah's disciples to see because it put Elijah in the same category as Joshua who also parted the Jordan River (Joshua 3:9-17). It also identified him with Moses who parted the Red Sea (Exodus 14:15-22). They could be confident, therefore, the instruction they received from Elijah was truly from God.

The religion of the Bible is not only theological, but also historical. More than mere assertions, it tells of real events with real witnesses. The fifty men who observed Elijah's final miracle would be sufficient to overcome any unbelief the religious community had.

The ministry of Jesus Christ was also authenticated by miracles done before many witnesses. Some people are willing to die for what they believe is true, but few are willing to die for what they know is false. The disciples were in a position to know if Jesus was a fake, and none of them believed that. They saw his miracles, and were willing to die for the truth of Jesus Christ.

2 Kings 2:9-10 *When they had crossed, Elijah said to Elisha, Tell me, what can I do for you before I am taken from you? Let me inherit a double portion of your spirit, Elisha replied. You have asked a difficult thing, Elijah said, yet if you see me when I am taken from you, it will be yours —otherwise, it will not.*

Elisha wanted twice the spiritual power that Elijah had, in order to carry out his ministry. Elijah established the condition that Elisha would have to see his departure in order to receive his request. But he didn't rebuke Elisha for wanting such a thing.

Likewise, *your Father [will] give the Holy Spirit to those who ask him* (Luke 11:13), said Jesus. By paying attention to Christ, and asking for more of his Spirit, we too can do the work of our Master. *[B]e filled with the Spirit* (Ephesians 5:18), said Paul. And, *apart from me you can do nothing* (John 15:5), said Jesus. Effective ministry can only take place with the help of the Holy Spirit.

2 Kings 2:11 *As they were walking along and talking together, suddenly a chariot of fire and horses of fire appeared and separated the two of them, and Elijah went up to heaven in a whirlwind.*

In one of the most dramatic scenes in the Bible, the prophet was taken into heaven by a chariot of fire drawn by horses of fire. Elijah was one of only two people in the Old Testament who were taken into heaven without dying. The other was Enoch, who *walked faithfully with God; then he was no more, because God took him away* (Genesis 5:24).

Elijah and Enoch remind us of what will happen to Christians who are alive when Jesus returns. *[We] will be caught up together with them in the clouds to meet the Lord in the air* (1 Thessalonians 4:17), wrote Paul.

And he will send his angels with a loud trumpet call, and they will gather his elect from the four winds, from one end of the heavens to the other (Matthew 24:31), said Jesus. Christians should live like birds on a branch, ready to fly at any moment (John Calvin).

2 Kings 2:13 *Elisha then picked up Elijah's cloak that had fallen from him and went back and stood on the bank of the Jordan.*

This was the same cloak that Elijah had put on Elisha when he was first called to the prophetic ministry (1 Kings 19:19). It was also the cloak that Elijah just used to part the Jordan River (2 Kings 2:8). As he was going up to heaven, Elijah either dropped the cloak by accident, or let it fall on purpose for Elisha to use. After seeing his master go into heaven, and recovering his cloak, Elisha decided use it.

2 Kings 2:14 *He took the cloak that had fallen from Elijah and struck the water with it. Where now is the Lord, the God of Elijah? he asked. When he struck the water, it divided to the right and to the left, and he crossed over.*

This was Elisha's first miracle and assured him, and others, that *The spirit of Elijah [was] resting on Elisha* (2 Kings 2:15). The passing of Elijah's cloak symbolized the succession of ministry. Elisha was now the lead prophet of Israel, and would do even more miracles than Elijah did.

2 Kings 2:23 *From there Elisha went up to Bethel. As he was walking along the road, some boys came out of the town and jeered at him.*

The boys were probably in their teens, and there were at least forty-two of them (2 Kings 2:24). They were a physical threat to Elisha and were clearly disrespectful. *Get out of here, baldy! they said. Get out of here, baldy!* (2 Kings 2:23b).

Elisha was either going bald or had shaved his head. Either way, the boys were insulting a man of God and, therefore, God himself. So Elisha *called down a curse on them in the name of the Lord. Then two bears came out of the woods and mauled forty-two of the boys* (2 Kings 2:24).

It's not clear if they died, but youthfulness is no excuse for wickedness. God knows that *every inclination of the human heart is evil from childhood* (Genesis 8:21), and he called these youth to account. Not all young people are equally wicked, but there are no innocent youth. Even the most vile adults began as beautiful babies.

A church was having a special service for parents to dedicate their children to God. Someone asked if they could pin white roses on the children to symbolize their purity. The pastor said they could use any color rose they liked, as long as it was black. Children need to repent and follow Jesus Christ as soon as they are able, or they too will come under his wrath (John 3:36).

For Reflection and Review

- *Are miracles still important for faith?*
- *How does the Holy Spirit empower us for ministry?*
- *Are children good or evil by nature?*

Lesson 92

2 Kings 3:5 *[T]he king of Moab rebelled against the king of Israel.*

For some time the Moabites were forced to pay a yearly tax to Israel of *a hundred thousand lambs and the wool of a hundred thousand rams* (2 Kings 3:4). When Israel's king died, however, the king of Moab asserted his independence by refusing to pay the tax.

Joram, the new king of Israel, set out at once to subdue the Moabites. He recruited the kings of Judah and Edom to go with him but, on their way across the desert, these three armies ran out of water. They were in serious danger when they consulted the prophet Elisha, who assured them of God's help.

For this is what the Lord says: You will see neither wind nor rain, yet this valley will be filled with water, and you, your cattle and your other animals will drink (2 Kings 3:17). The following morning the water flowed until all the land was filled. But God was doing even more.

When the Moabites saw the water on the reddish soil, in the light of the morning sun, it looked like blood to them. They thought the armies had turned on each other, and filled the land with their blood. So they rushed to the plunder, only to be slaughtered by the Israelites who were very much alive. Israel then advanced to conquerer many towns.

2 Kings 3:26-28 *When the king of Moab saw that the battle had gone against him . . . . he took his firstborn son, who was to succeed him as king, and offered him as a sacrifice on the city wall. The fury against Israel was great; they withdrew and returned to their own land.*

The conclusion to this story is entirely unexpected. The Israelites were victorious until the king of Moab sacrificed his son to a pagan god. Then his army rallied, and Israel was forced to retreat. Moab's god seemed to defeat the God of Israel, and Moab remained independent.

This was not the desired outcome, but it gives credibility to the whole account. If the story was fictitious it would have a different ending. By including the embarrassing facts, however, the writer gives us reason to believe the whole story, including God's supply of water in the desert.

This story is also supported by a source outside the Bible known as the *Mesha Stele*. It's an engraved stone about four feet high, two feet wide, and two inches thick. It has a curved top and is housed in the Louvre Museum in Paris. The inscription includes an account of this battle including Moab's victory. It mentions other people and places in the Bible, and belongs to this exact period of time. It's widely received as corroborating documentation of the biblical record from the king of Moab himself.

The Bible authenticates this story by including the embarrassing facts, and the king of Moab authenticated this story by writing it in stone. The Bible is reliable in all its parts because it is the word of God (2 Timothy 3:16).

*****

2 Kings 4:1 *The wife of a man from the company of the prophets cried out to Elisha, Your servant my husband is dead, and you know that he revered the Lord. But now his creditor is coming to take my two boys as his slaves.*

This dear woman was in a difficult situation. In spite of her husband's commitment to God, he hadn't prospered financially. His devotion, in fact, may've kept him from earning as much as could. Or he may've been so generous that he became poor. Then he found himself in debt, and died prematurely, leaving his family in financial distress.

All this woman had in her house was a little jar of olive oil, so Elisha told her to borrow as many empty jars as she could. Then she was to go in her house and pour the oil from her little jar into all the other jars until they were all full.

2 Kings 4:6-7 *When all the jars were full, she said to her son, Bring me another one. But he replied, There is not a jar left. Then the oil stopped flowing. She went and told the man of God, and he said, Go, sell the oil and pay your debts. You and your sons can live on what is left.*

God knows the burden of crushing debt, and is able to deliver us. The fault may belong to us, or to someone else, or it may be circumstantial. In any case, we should pray for God's help, and do all that we can to pay our debts.

But there's another debt we can never repay, and that's our debt of sin. *Be perfect, therefore, as your heavenly Father is perfect* (Matthew 5:48), said Jesus. *If anyone, then, knows the good they ought to do and doesn't do it, it is sin for them* (James 4:17), wrote James. Every bad thing we do, and every good thing we fail to do, puts us further into God's debt.

This is the problem the gospel is meant to solve. What we couldn't do for ourselves, Jesus did for us. We owed a debt we couldn't pay; he paid a debt he didn't owe. As the oil was poured out to pay the widow's debt, so the blood of Christ was poured out for us (Ephesians 1:7). Instead of being in debt forever, Christ has made us eternally rich (2 Corinthians 8:9).

*****

2 Kings 4:8 *One day Elisha went to Shunem. And a well-to-do woman was there, who urged him to stay for a meal. So whenever he came by, he stopped there to eat.*

The woman and her husband put on a guest room for Elisha, but they also had a problem: she was childless, and he was old. It was only a matter of time before the wealthy woman became a lonely widow. Elisha informed the woman that she'd give birth and, within a year, she was holding a baby. But a few years later tragedy struck: the boy developed a headache and died. So Elisha went to his room to raise him from the dead.

2 Kings 4:34-35 *Then he got on the bed and lay on the boy, mouth to mouth, eyes to eyes, hands to hands. As he stretched himself out on him, the boy's body grew warm. Elisha turned away and walked back and forth in the room and then got on the bed and stretched out on him once more. The boy sneezed seven times and opened his eyes.*

Resurrections aren't very common in the Bible, but they're important because they anticipate the general resurrection at the end of the age (John 5:28-29). Jesus raised three people from the dead, and even raised himself (John 10:18). *The one who believes in me will live, even though they die* (John 11:25), he said.

At the moment of death, all who believe in Jesus Christ go to be with him in heaven. *[We] prefer to be away from the body and at home with the Lord* (2 Corinthians 5:8), wrote Paul. But this is an in-between stage before we are raised physically. At that moment, *he will transform our lowly bodies so that they will be like his glorious body* (Philippians 3:21), wrote Paul again.

This is a wonderful promise for anyone who's ever wanted a glorious body. How strong do you want to be? How smart do you want to be? How attractive do you want to be? How well do you want to sing or dance? *We believe in the resurrection of the body and everlasting life in the age to come* (Apostles Creed, paraphrased).

For Reflection and Review

- *How do we know the Bible is true?*
- *How can we pay our debt of sin?*
- *Should believers look forward to a glorious body?*

Lesson 93

2 Kings 5:1 *Now Naaman was commander of the army of the king of Aram.*

In the political, order Naaman was probably second only to the king. He was a valiant man and highly regarded because of his many victories. But even the strongest are frail and, one day, Naaman noticed a patch of skin that was different from the rest. He may've treated it with balm, and hoped it would go away. But it didn't. The condition worsened, in fact, and began to spread. So Naaman went to an expert who confirmed his deepest concern: it was leprosy. This meant the end of Naaman's military career, and even his family life, since he'd likely live in isolation until he died.

2 Kings 5:2 *Now bands of raiders from Aram had gone out and had taken captive a young girl from Israel, and she served Naaman's wife.*

It was a terrible day when this little girl was snatched from her home, and she must've wondered why God allowed it to happen. But nothing happens by accident, and she had important work to do. When she learned of Naaman's condition, she told his wife that the prophet Elisha could heal him. Her child-like faith appears simplistic, but God was using her for something big. Whenever bad things happen to us, we should be alert to how God may want to use us.

2 Kings 5:4 *Naaman went to his master and told him what the girl from Israel had said.*

The words of a little girl from Israel were now the subject of conversation between a king and his commander. Naaman's situation was desperate and, since there was no hope for him in Aram, the king encouraged Naaman to go to Israel. He also gave him a letter to Israel's king.

Some people only seek God when they're desperate, but seeking God is never a bad idea. *You will seek me and find me when you seek me with all your heart* (Jeremiah 29:13), said God. Our prayers won't always be answered the way we want, but God will always do what is best. And nothing in the world compares to having God himself.

2 Kings 5:6 *The letter that he took to the king of Israel read: With this letter I am sending my servant Naaman to you so that you may cure him of his leprosy.*

Israel's king was alarmed. Miracles aren't available on demand so, by expecting a miracle, the king of Aram seemed to be starting a fight. But Elisha wasn't concerned at all. *Have the man come to me and he will know that there is a prophet in Israel* (2 Kings 5:8), he said. *So Naaman went with his horses and chariots and stopped at the door of Elisha's house* (2 Kings 5:9).

This was a very important moment for Naaman. He'd come a long way and his hopes were high. He even imagined what would happen next. Elisha would wave his hand over the spot, call on God, and cure him of the leprosy (2 Kings 5:11). But that didn't happen.

Elisha, in fact, didn't even come to the door. His messenger told Naaman to wash in the Jordan seven times. Naaman was so insulted that he left in a rage. But his servants calmed him down and he went to the Jordan and dipped seven times. When he came out, his skin was completely restored.

God opposes the proud but shows favor to the humble (James 4:6), wrote James. If Naaman remained proud he would not have received a thing. But when he humbled himself, and obeyed Elisha, God gave him what he wanted. Whoever wants to receive from God will be helped by a little humility.

2 Kings 5:15 *Then Naaman and all his attendants went back to the man of God. He stood before him and said, Now I know that there is no God in all the world except in Israel.*

Naaman was a changed man. He wasn't only healed, but converted. He confessed that Israel's God existed, and that all other gods did not. This was a bold profession of faith but Naaman went even further. *[P]lease accept a gift*, he said. He had 750 pounds of silver, 150 pounds of gold and ten sets of clothing (2 Kings 5:5). This was an extreme amount of wealth, but seemed like very little compared to his life.

2 Kings 5:16 *The prophet answered, As surely as the Lord lives, whom I serve, I will not accept a thing. And even though Naaman urged him, he refused.*

Elisha could've built a school, a house, or any number of things with the money from Naaman. But he refused to accept it because he didn't earn it. God did the miracle, not Elisha. And he didn't want Naaman to think his motives were mixed. *You cannot serve both God and money* (Matthew 6:24), said Jesus. Success in ministry isn't determined by income, but by faithfulness. Christian ministries should be careful to handle financial matters with complete integrity.

2 Kings 5:17 *[I] will never again make burnt offerings and sacrifices to any other god but the Lord.*

As Naaman thought about his future, he resolved never to sacrifice to pagan gods again. But he had a problem: part of his royal duty was to escort the king of Aram to a pagan temple and bow down. For this he wanted forgiveness. *Go in peace*, Elisha said (1 Kings 5:19).

This was quite a concession in light of the second commandment: *You shall not make for yourself an image in the form of anything . . . . You shall not bow down to them* (Exodus 20:4-5). But Elisha's consent seems to imply God's consent as well. If so, it shows God's understanding toward those who want to follow him, even if they do so imperfectly.

He will not always accuse, nor will he harbor his anger forever; he does not treat us as our sins deserve or repay us according to our iniquities. For as high as the heavens are above the earth, so great is his love for those who fear him; as far as the east is from the west, so far has he removed our transgressions from us. As a father has compassion on his children, so the Lord has compassion on those who fear him; for he knows how we are formed, he remembers that we are dust (Psalm 103:9-14), wrote David.

2 Kings 5:19-20 *After Naaman had traveled some distance, Gehazi, the servant of Elisha the man of God, said to himself, My master was too easy on Naaman, this Aramean, by not accepting from him what he brought. As surely as the Lord lives, I will run after him and get something from him.*

Gehazi was astonished that Elisha declined a fortune without a second thought. Surely it was meant to be a blessing from God for their many years of faithful service! So Ghazi went after Naaman and requested a gift, which Naaman was happy to give. But when he returned Elisha said to him: *Naaman's leprosy will cling to you and to your descendants forever* (1 Kings 5:17). This was severe, but Gehazi had done a bad thing. He pursued money ahead of God, and it cost him everything.

Some people, eager for money, have wandered from the faith and pierced themselves with many griefs (1 Timothy 6:10), wrote Paul. One man stole a bag of coins and put it into his backpack. To avoid police he jumped in a river and tried to swim to the other side. But the coins weighed more than he thought, and he sunk to the bottom and died. First he got the money, then the money got him.

For Reflection and Review

- Why did Elisha allow Naaman to participate in paganism?
- Is it wrong for Christian ministries to ask for money?
- Is it wrong for Christians to pursue wealth?

Lesson 94

2 Kings 6:2 *Let us go to the Jordan, where each of us can get a pole; and let us build a place there for us to meet.*

Elisha's disciples wanted to build a meeting place near the Jordan River. *As one of them was cutting down a tree, the iron axhead fell into the water. Oh no, my lord! he cried out. It was borrowed!* (2 Kings 6:5). Elisha threw a stick near where the axhead fell, and it floated to the surface.

This miracle violates the laws of nature, but that's what miracles do. It was no more difficult for God to make the axhead float, than for Christ to walk on the water (John 6:16-24). Violating the laws of nature is not a challenge for God, since he created the laws of nature, and can pause them whenever he likes.

*****

2 Kings 6:8 *Now the king of Aram was at war with Israel. After conferring with his officers, he said, I will set up my camp in such and such a place.*

But every time he set up his camp, the prophet Elisha informed the king of Israel where the king of Aram was staying. The king of Aram thought one of his officers had become an enemy spy, but then he learned the problem was Elisha. So, one night, the king of Aram sent his soldiers to surround the town where Elisha was staying. The next morning Elisha's servant saw the town surrounded, and feared for his life.

2 Kings 6:16 *Don't be afraid, the prophet answered. Those who are with us are more than those who are with them.*

Then Elisha prayed that his servant's eyes would be opened and, when they were, he *saw the hills full of horses and chariots of fire all around Elisha* (2 Kings 6:17). Elisha wasn't afraid of the enemy soldiers because he saw the heavenly soldiers. There's always more to life than meets the eye!

Angelic armies gave confidence to Elisha, and also to Jesus at the time of his arrest. *Do you think I cannot call on my Father, and he will at once put at my disposal more than twelve legions of angels?* (Matthew 26:53), he asked. A Roman legion could be as many as six thousand soldiers, so Jesus was claiming access to over seventy-two thousand angels.

Not only that, but angels watch over believers as well. *Are not all angels ministering spirits sent to serve those who will inherit salvation?* (Hebrews 1:14), asks Hebrews. God can protect us himself, of course, but he also likes to use angels.

2 Kings 6:18 *As the enemy came down toward him, Elisha prayed to the Lord, Strike this army with blindness. So he struck them with blindness, as Elisha had asked.*

Then Elisha led them to the King of Israel, who suggested killing them. But Elisha told the king to give them food instead. *So he prepared a great feast for them, and after they had finished eating and drinking, he sent them away, and they returned to their master. So the bands from Aram stopped raiding Israel's territory* (2 Kings 6:23).

This was a strange way to settle a war, but it worked. *If your enemy is hungry, feed him; if he is thirsty, give him something to drink* (Romans 12:20), wrote Paul. *Love your enemies, do good to those who hate you* (Luke 6:27), said Jesus. If you show your enemies kindness, they'll find it harder to oppose you.

*****

2 Kings 6:24 *Some time later, Ben-Hadad king of Aram mobilized his entire army and marched up and laid siege to Samaria.*

The situation was bleak. The capital city of Israel was under siege, and a famine was causing such hunger that people were eating their children. So the king of Israel lashed out at Elisha: *May God deal with me, be it ever so severely, if the head of Elisha . . . remains on his shoulders today!* (2 Kings 6:31), he said.

Widespread hunger was making the king angry at God. But since God was out of reach, he directed his anger at God's representative. This is irrational, but not uncommon. The prophets were treated badly, and when Christ came into the world they hung him on a cross (Luke 23:33). So far from being neutral, *The mind governed by the flesh is hostile to God* (Romans 8:7), wrote Paul.

2 Kings 6:32 *Now Elisha was sitting in his house, and the elders were sitting with him.*

Israel's king arrived with an officer, ready to remove Elisha's head. But his life was spared because Elisha predicted relief the following day. When the officer doubted the prophet's word, Elisha said: *You will see it with your own eyes . . . but you will not eat any of it!* (2 Kings 7:2).

The following morning four Israelite men decided to surrender, but when they got to the enemy's camp they found it abandoned. The previous night God caused the Arameans to hear the sound of horses and chariots. They thought Israel hired foreign armies, so they ran for their lives and left their supplies behind. When word got back to the city, the people ran out and found more than enough for everyone. The king's officer saw it with his eyes, but was trampled to death by the people.

The prophet's word to the officer was fulfilled, despite his unbelief.

Christians can also be prone to unbelief if we're not careful. *How foolish you are, and how slow to believe all that the prophets have spoken!* (Luke 24:25), said Jesus. No one ever had greater confidence in the Bible than Jesus Christ (Luke 16:17), and this should be true of us.

Christians believe the Bible, in all its parts, because that's what Jesus believed. Whoever doesn't believe the Bible in all its parts thinks they know better than Jesus. Anyone who leads us away from the Bible leads us away from Christ. Doubting the Bible is never wise; according to Christ it is *foolish*.

*****

2 Kings 9:6 *This is what the Lord, the God of Israel, says: I anoint you king over the Lord's people Israel.*

Elisha sent a young prophet to anoint Jehu as the new king of Israel. Almost at once, Jehu sought to eliminate Baal worship from the nation. He pretended to host a sacrifice, and summoned every prophet, priest, and servant of Baal to attend. When they crowded into Baal's temple, Jehu commanded his guards to kill them, and not one escaped. The temple was then torn down, and became a public toilet. *The Lord said to Jehu . . . you have done well in accomplishing what is right in my eyes* (2 Kings 10:30).

God's approval of this event reveals his hatred of idolatry. Since God is our maker (Psalm 100:3), and sustainer (Acts 17:25), he alone is to be worshipped. This is made clear in the first commandment: *You shall have no other gods before me* (Exodus 20:3). If we love anything more than God, we are guilty of idolatry.

A church was having a rummage sale, and a man donated his classic motorcycle. When someone asked *why*, he said: *I loved that motorcycle, but wanted God to know that I love him even more.*

For Reflection and Review

- *If God can take care of us himself, why does he also use angels?*
- *Are some people neutral toward God?*
- *Why is it foolish not to believe the Bible?*

Lesson 95

2 Kings 11:1 *When Athaliah the mother of Ahaziah saw that her son was dead, she proceeded to destroy the whole royal family.*

Athaliah led the southern kingdom of Judah from 841 to 835 BC. She was one of the wickedest rulers to ever take the throne. Her father and grandfather had ruled the northern kingdom of Israel, and were worshippers of Baal. Athaliah also worshipped Baal, and married Jehoram (king of Judah) to strengthen ties between the northern and southern kingdoms.

Athaliah's husband died when he was forty years old, and was succeeded by their son Ahaziah, who ruled for just a year before he was captured and put to death (2 Chronicles 22:1-9). This was Athaliah's opportunity to seize power, which she did by killing her grandchildren, so they couldn't challenge her claim to the throne. This was more than raw ambition; it was a demonic assault on God's plan for Messiah to come from David (2 Samuel 7:16, Matthew 1:1). Athaliah's attack on the royal family was an attack on God's plan of salvation.

2 Kings 11:2 *But Jehosheba, the daughter of King Jehoram and sister of Ahaziah, took Joash son of Ahaziah and stole him away from among the royal princes, who were about to be murdered.*

Joash was an important child because he was the son of Ahaziah (the previous king) and, therefore, a descendent of David. Jehosheba acted courageously and was probably encouraged by her husband, Jehoiada, an influential priest who knew the importance of having a descendent of David on the throne.

Athaliah's massacre of heirs to David's throne reminds us of Herod's massacre of Bethlehem's children in order to eliminate Christ (Matthew 2:16). In both cases God intervened to preserve his future king. *There is no . . . plan that can succeed against the Lord* (Proverbs 21:30), says Proverbs. Many have tried but all have failed.

2 Kings 11:3 *[Joash] remained hidden with his nurse at the temple of the Lord for six years while Athaliah ruled the land.*

Athaliah was queen of Judah for six years while little Joash grew. Then, at just the right time, Jehoiada arranged for the young boy to be crowned king. Joash was surrounded by guards and brought in front of the temple. In the presence of many witnesses, Jehoiada put a crown on the young man's head. *[T]he people clapped their hands and shouted, Long live the king!* (2 Kings 11:12).

When Athaliah heard the commotion she went to investigate. *Then Athaliah tore her robes and called out, Treason! Treason!* (2 Kings 11:14). Jehoiada ordered her execution, and she was removed from the temple grounds and put to death.

2 Kings 11:17-18 *Jehoiada then made a covenant between the Lord and the king and people that they would be the Lord's people. . . . All the people of the land went to the temple of Baal and tore it down. They smashed the altars and idols to pieces and killed Mattan the priest of Baal in front of the altars.*

Jehoiada's faithfulness kept the nation from turning away from God completely. Through his courageous work, the worship of God was reestablished and idolatry was restrained. Jehoiada's contribution was so great, in fact, that *He was buried with the kings in the City of David, because of the good he had done in Israel for God and his temple* (2 Chronicles 24:16).

Sadly, King Joash was faithful to God only as long as Jehoiada lived. When his godly uncle died, Joash turned to idols. This proved disastrous for Joash, and also for the nation. Every religious advantage is no guarantee of faithfulness.

The apostasy of Joash got the attention of Zechariah, Jehoiada's son, who preached to the people saying, *This is what God says: Why do you disobey the Lord's commands? You will not prosper. Because you have forsaken the Lord, he has forsaken you* (2 Chronicles 24:20).

This kind of preaching was not acceptable to Joash, so he ordered the execution of Zechariah, the son of Jehoiada, who saved his life as a baby and made him king. As Zechariah lay dying he said to Joash, *May the Lord see this and call you to account* (2 Chronicles 24:22). Within a year, Joash was murdered (2 Chronicles 24:25).

This story has many twists and turns, heroes, villains, and lessons. The battle against evil is never won in this age, only fought. But the day is coming when Christ will *put all his enemies under his feet* (1 Corinthians 15:25) and rule the world forever. Even so, *Come, Lord Jesus* (Revelation 22:20).

For Reflection and Review

- *Are men or women better leaders?*
- *Why did Joash finish badly?*
- *How do believers fight evil today?*

Lesson 96

2 Kings 14:1 *In the second year of Jehoash son of Jehoahaz king of Israel, Amaziah son of Joash king of Judah began to reign.*

Amaziah ruled the southern kingdom of Judah from around 796 to 767 BC. He had some good qualities, but his reign was marred by an act of idolatry. *When Amaziah returned from slaughtering the Edomites, he brought back the gods of the people of Seir. He set them up as his own gods, bowed down to them and burned sacrifices to them. The anger of the Lord burned against Amaziah, and he sent a prophet to him, who said, Why do you consult this people's gods, which could not save their own people from your hand?* (2 Chronicles 25:14-15).

The prophet's logic is clear: If the local gods couldn't save their own people, why would a victorious king bow down them? Amaziah probably thought he was victorious because the local gods changed sides, and bowed down to them in order to give thanks. Nevertheless, *The anger of the Lord burned against Amaziah*, and he was later put to death (2 Kings 14:19).

God is a real person, with real emotions, one of which is jealousy. *Do not worship any other god, for the Lord, whose name is Jealous, is a jealous God* (Exodus 34:1), wrote Moses. And *The Lord is a jealous and avenging God; the Lord takes vengeance and is filled with wrath* (Nahum 1:2), wrote Nahum. Amaziah thought he received additional help from other gods, but he only inflamed God's jealous wrath.

Tragically, whole segments of Christianity do the same thing. Instead of praying to God alone, they encourage believers to bow down to various statues or images. Many think they're receiving additional help, but all they're really doing is inflaming God's wrath. It's a dangerous thing to be loved by a God whose name is *Jealous*. We must pray to him alone.

*****

2 Kings 15:1 *In the twenty-seventh year of Jeroboam king of Israel, Azariah son of Amaziah king of Judah began to reign.*

Azariah is more famously known as King Uzziah (2 Chronicles 26:1). *Azariah* was likely his personal name, and *Uzziah* was likely his throne name. Uzziah ruled the southern kingdom of Judah for fifty-two years, from around 791 to 739 BC. He ruled alongside his father at first, and alongside his son near the end.

2 Kings 15:3 *He did what was right in the eyes of the Lord.*

And *As long as he sought the Lord, God gave him success* (2 Chronicles 26:5). Uzziah was financially successful, militarily successful, and had many successful building projects. *[H]is fame spread as far as the border of Egypt, because he had become very powerful* (2 Chronicles 26:8), it says.

The Bible makes a clear connection between righteousness and success. *He holds success in store for the upright* (Proverbs 2:7), says Proverbs. This is a good incentive to be righteous, but we shouldn't to press the idea too far. Success can be a sign of God's favor, but it's not a sure sign of God's favor. The wicked may also prosper (Psalm 73:3), and many false religions have prospered.

The best indication of success isn't the size of our house, or the extent of our reputation, but what God says to us on Judgment Day. If we live to hear him say, *Well done, good and faithful servant!* (Matthew 25:21), we're on the road to success. If we live for anything else, we're on the road to misery. We should never consider ourselves successful until after Judgment Day.

(2 Chronicles 26:16) *But after Uzziah became powerful, his pride led to his downfall.*

The problem with too much earthly success is that it can lead to pride, which often leads to a fall. *Pride goes before destruction, a haughty spirit before a fall* (Proverbs 16:18), says Proverbs. *You save the humble, but your eyes are on the haughty to bring them low* (2 Samuel 22:28), said David.

Not content with political power, Uzziah wanted religious power too. He went into God's temple to burn incense, which was something only priests were allowed to do (Numbers 3:10). Risking their lives, some of the priests followed the king into the temple and opposed him to his face. But he refused to back down, so God struck with him with leprosy. Uzziah lived in isolation the rest of his life and was banned from the temple of God (2 Chronicles 26:21).

From Uzziah we learn that starting well is no guarantee of finishing well. When he lived righteously, God gave him success. But when he was filled with pride, he had a tragic fall. It's better to struggle throughout our lives than succeed at the cost of our souls. *Better a little with the fear of the Lord than great wealth with turmoil* (Proverbs 15:16), says Proverbs.

For Reflection and Review

- *Why is it wrong to bow down to images?*
- *What does it mean to be successful?*
- *Why is pride so dangerous?*

Lesson 97

2 Kings 18:1 *In the third year of Hoshea son of Elah king of Israel, Hezekiah son of Ahaz king of Judah began to reign.*

Hezekiah began to rule as king when he was twenty-five years old. He led the southern kingdom of Judah from about 715 to 686 BC, twenty-nine years in all. *He did what was right in the eyes of the Lord* (2 Kings 18:3) by getting rid of idolatry and reestablishing the worship of God. *Hezekiah trusted in the Lord, the God of Israel. There was no one like him among all the kings of Judah, either before him or after him* (2 Kings 18:5).

Hezekiah's greatest strength was his simple trust in God. It was severely tested, but served him well throughout his life. *Trust in the Lord with all your heart and lean not on your own understanding; in all your ways submit to him, and he will make your paths straight* (Proverbs 3:5-6), says Proverbs.

2 Kings 18:10 *Samaria was captured in Hezekiah's sixth year, which was the ninth year of Hoshea king of Israel.*

This event was catastrophic, and probably reinforced Hezekiah's reliance on God. Samaria was the capital city of Israel, and it's capture by the Assyrians in 722 BC was the end of the northern kingdom.

The northern kingdom of Israel split from the southern kingdom of Judah in 931 BC. Over the next two hundred years, or so, the northern kingdom of Israel had twenty kings, none of them good. So God allowed them to be destroyed by the Assyrians, just as Moses foretold: *The Lord will drive you and the king you set over you to a nation unknown to you or your ancestors. There you will worship other gods, gods of wood and stone* (Deuteronomy 28:36), he wrote.

This proved to Hezekiah that God doesn't make idle threats. If the southern kingdom of Judah obeyed God, they'd enjoy his blessing. If not, they'd be exiled too. In fact, now that the northern kingdom was destroyed, there was no geographical buffer between Assyria and Judah.

2 Kings 18:13 *In the fourteenth year of King Hezekiah's reign, Sennacherib king of Assyria attacked all the fortified cities of Judah and captured them.*

In spite of Hezekiah's obedience to God, the king of Assyria invaded Judah and captured many towns. Hezekiah gave him a fortune to withdraw, but it wasn't enough. The king of Assyria wanted to capture Jerusalem too. So Hezekiah prayed: *Now, Lord our God, deliver us from his hand, so that all the kingdoms of the earth may know that you alone, Lord, are God* (2 Kings 19:19).

Isaiah the prophet was aware of Hezekiah's prayer and sent a reply: *[T]his is what the Lord says concerning the king of Assyria: He will not enter this city or shoot an arrow here. He will not come before it with shield or build a siege ramp against it. By the way that he came he will return; he will not enter this city, declares the Lord* (2 Kings 19:33-34). This was a wonderful promise, but how could it be fulfilled?

2 Kings 19:35-36 *That night the angel of the Lord went out and put to death a hundred and eighty-five thousand in the Assyrian camp. When the people got up the next morning—there were all the dead bodies! So Sennacherib king of Assyria broke camp and withdrew.*

This event is so important the Bible records it three separate times (2 Chronicles 32:20-21, Isaiah 37:36). It was also recorded by the Greek historian Herodotus (fifth century BC), who attributed it to an outbreak of the bubonic plague.

We even have corroboration from the king of Assyria himself.

The Sennacherib prism is on display in the British museum and, while it doesn't mention the loss of soldiers, it claims to have captured forty-six towns in Judah, taken a fortune in silver and gold, and shut up Hezekiah *like a caged bird*. This is all consistent with the biblical account, including the fact that he didn't conquer Jerusalem.

2 Kings 19:37 *One day, while [Sennacherib] was worshiping in the temple of his god Nisrok, his sons Adrammelek and Sharezer killed him with the sword.*

The one who put so many people to the sword, died by the sword of his sons. Pagan gods are of little help at the time of death, and Nisrok was no exception. But Jesus gives eternal life to all who truly believe. *Very truly I tell you, the one who believes has eternal life* (John 6:37), he said.

2 Kings 20:1 *In those days Hezekiah became ill and was at the point of death. The prophet Isaiah son of Amoz went to him and said, This is what the Lord says: Put your house in order, because you are going to die; you will not recover.*

Hezekiah was still a young man and didn't want to die, so he prayed earnestly and *wept bitterly* (2 Kings 20:3). God spoke to the prophet again saying, *Go back and tell Hezekiah, the ruler of my people, This is what the Lord, the God of your father David, says: I have heard your prayer and seen your tears; I will heal you* (2 Kings 20:5), he said.

This is very interesting because we don't expect God to change his mind. *God is not human . . . that he should change his mind* (Numbers 23:19), said Balaam. And *all the days ordained for me were written in your book before one of them came to be* (Psalm 139:16), wrote David. And *[We're] predestined according to the plan of him who works out everything in conformity with the purpose of his will* (Ephesians 1:11), wrote Paul.

These verses might suggest that human choice and behavior have little influence with God, since everything has been determined. But other verses should also be considered. *If I tell a righteous person that they will surely live, but then they trust in their righteousness and do evil, none of the righteous things that person has done will be remembered; they will die for the evil they have done. And if I say to a wicked person, You will surely die, but they then turn away from their sin and do what is just and right. . . that person will surely live* (Ezekiel 33:13-15), said God.

A good example is the response of Nineveh to the preaching of Jonah: *Forty more days and Nineveh will be overthrown* (Jonah 3:4), he said. But the city of Nineveh turned from their sin and called on God. *When God saw what they did and how they turned from their evil ways, he relented and did not bring on them the destruction he had threatened* (Jonah 3:10), wrote Jonah.

It's difficult to reconcile the unchanging plan of God with his willingness to change based on our response to him. But this only shows that we're dealing with a personal God, not impersonal fate. God and his plan are both unchanging, but he changes his plans based on our response to him. Hmmm. Since this is beyond our comprehension we're tempted to accept one set of verses against the other. It's better to hold both together, and admit there are some things we won't understand until the age to come.

2 Kings 20:7 *Then Isaiah said, Prepare a poultice of figs. They did so and applied it to the boil, and he recovered.*

God told the prophet Isaiah that King Hezekiah would be healed (1 Kings 20:5), so we might expect a miracle. But Isaiah called for a poultice of figs to be applied to the boil, and Hezekiah recovered within a few days (2 Kings 20:8). We don't have to choose between God and other remedies, since God often uses other remedies to heal. There's nothing inconsistent about taking medicine and asking God to heal.

For Reflection and Review

- *What extra-biblical records confirm Assyria's withdrawal from Jerusalem?*

- *If Hezekiah was so godly, why was he tested so severely?*
- *Why is God so hard to understand?*

Lesson 98

2 Kings 21:1 *Manasseh was twelve years old when he became king, and he reigned in Jerusalem fifty-five years.*

Manasseh was the king of Judah from 696 to 642 BC. His reign of fifty-five years likely included several years of co-regency with his godly father Hezekiah. Unlike his father, however, Manasseh *did evil in the eyes of the Lord* (2 Kings 21:2). This included worshipping false gods, desecrating the temple, killing innocent people, sacrificing his children, practicing witchcraft, consulting mediums, and leading the nation astray (2 Kings 21:1-9, 2 Chronicles 33:1-9). He was a very bad man.

Children of godly parents often grow up to be godly adults (Proverbs 22:6), but the opposite may also occur. Instead of following God, some do everything he forbids. By pursuing freedom from God, however, they become Satan's slaves. That's what happened to Manasseh. The *commanders of the king of Assyria . . . took Manasseh prisoner, put a hook in his nose, bound him with bronze shackles and took him to Babylon* (2 Chronicles 33:11).

He deserved nothing less, of course, but the long walk to Babylon gave Manasseh time to think about his ways. He'd rejected the God of his father to do whatever he liked. Now he had a hook in his nose, and was being led to a foreign land. Once he sat on a throne, now he was a beast. Once he ruled, now he was enslaved. Perhaps his dad was right about God after all.

(2 Chronicles 33:12) *In his distress [Manasseh] sought the favor of the Lord his God and humbled himself greatly before the God of his ancestors.*

Manasseh's road of rebellion became a dead end, but there he turned to God. *And when he prayed to him, the Lord was moved by his entreaty and listened to his plea; so he brought him back to Jerusalem and to his kingdom. Then Manasseh knew that the Lord is God* (2 Chronicles 33:13).

Children raised in godly homes may reject their parents' faith because they aren't sure it's true. Many put it to the test by breaking God's commands, and living for themselves. As long as things go well, they may never change. But if things go badly, they often reconsider, and turn back to the God of their parents. It's better to start badly and finish well, than to start well and finish badly.

Manasseh is one of the best examples of God's grace in the Bible. He not only ruined his own life, but the lives of many others. There was little he wasn't guilty of, and God was under no obligation to save him. But God heard his prayer, and made him a trophy of grace. *For it is by grace you have been saved . . . not by works, so that no one can boast* (Ephesians 2:8-9), wrote Paul. Manasseh proves that no one is to bad to be saved, if they're willing to repent.

(2 Chronicles 33:15-16) *He got rid of the foreign gods and removed the image from the temple of the Lord, as well as all the altars he had built on the temple hill and in Jerusalem; and he threw them out of the city. Then he restored the altar of the Lord and sacrificed fellowship offerings and thank offerings on it, and told Judah to serve the Lord, the God of Israel.*

Manasseh had clearly changed. We don't become good in order to be saved, but once we're saved we'll want to be good. *I will show you my faith by my deeds* (James 2:18), wrote James. Having served the devil for many years, Manasseh spent the rest of his life serving God.

Godly parents ought to be encouraged by this story, and trust the long arm of God's grace for their own wayward children. At his worst, Manasseh seemed out of God's reach. But he never forgot his father's faith, and found his way back to his father's God. Others have done the same.

The story is told of a Spanish father, and his teenage son, whose relationship was strained. The son ran away from home, and his father went searching far and wide. Then he put an ad in the paper that read: *Dear Paco, meet me in front of the newspaper office at noon. All is forgiven. I love you.* At noon, the following day, eight hundred Pacos showed up (Ernest Hemingway, paraphrased). The world is filled with wayward children who want to return to their heavenly Father. And God is so gracious that he longs to receive them back.

For Reflection and Review

- *What are some advantages to being raised in a godly home?*
- *Are there any disadvantages to be being raised in a godly home?*
- *How can godly parents help their wayward children?*

Lesson 99

2 Kings 22:1 *Josiah was eight years old when he became king, and he reigned in Jerusalem thirty-one years.*

Josiah led God's people from 640 to 609 BC, and implemented greater reform than any king before or since. Because the previous king had been wicked, the nation was apostate. The temple was used for male prostitution (2 Kings 23:7), and children were being sacrificed (2 Kings 23:10). The days were extremely dark, and it was time for godly leadership.

2 Kings 22:8 *Hilkiah the high priest said to Shaphan the secretary, I have found the Book of the Law in the temple of the Lord.*

For many years the temple was standing, and the priesthood was active, but the word of God was completely lost. And no one seemed to notice! While the temple was being repaired, however, God's word was rediscovered.

This would be hard to imagine if it wasn't so common today. Many churches have busy pastors who do everything but teach the Bible. As a result, people don't know the Bible, and do much that it forbids. But when the apostles were asked to turn their attention elsewhere they said, *. . . we will give our attention to prayer and the ministry of the word* (Acts 6:4). This is the first duty of Christian ministers.

2 Kings 22:11 *When the king heard the words of the Book of the Law, he tore his robes.*

Josiah was alarmed by the terrible threats of punishment for turning away from God. *The Lord will send on you curses, confusion and rebuke in everything you put your hand to, until you are destroyed and come to sudden ruin because of the evil you have done in forsaking him. . . . Because of the suffering your enemy will inflict on you during the siege, you will eat the fruit of the womb, the flesh of the sons and daughters the Lord your God has given you. . . . You will live in constant suspense, filled with dread both night and day, never sure of your life. In the morning you will say, If only it were evening! and in the evening, If only it were morning!* (Deuteronomy 28:20-67). Since much of this had already happened to the northern kingdom of Israel, Josiah knew it could happen to them.

Jesus Christ could also be very threatening. *Every tree that does not bear good fruit is cut down and thrown into the fire* (Matthew 7:19), he said. And *Depart from me, you who are cursed, into the eternal fire prepared for the devil and his angels* (Matthew 25:41), many will hear him say.

An important idea that led to my conversion was the possibility of waking up in hell, and never getting out. Jesus is the most credible person who ever lived, and he threatened me with eternal fire. I could either force the idea out of my mind, or repent of my sins and follow him. The severity of his threat helped me to make the right decision.

2 Kings 22:13 *Go and inquire of the Lord for me and for the people and for all Judah about what is written in this book that has been found. Great is the Lord's anger that burns against us because those who have gone before us have not obeyed the words of this book; they have not acted in accordance with all that is written there concerning us.*

Josiah sent representatives to the prophet Huldah, to see if there was any hope, but her answer wasn't encouraging: *This is what the Lord says: I am going to bring disaster on this place and its people, according to everything written in the book. . . . Because they have forsaken me and burned incense to other gods and aroused my anger by all the idols their hands have made, my anger will burn against this place and will not be quenched* (2 Kings 23:16-17), she said.

No matter what we've done individually, we can turn to Christ and be saved. *For I will forgive their wickedness and will remember their sins no more* (Hebrews 8:12), said God. But the collective sins of the nation had reached a point where God's wrath wouldn't be turned away. They could be saved individually, but the nation would suffer disaster.

God deals with people individually, but also with every nation. *God reigns over the nations; God is seated on his holy throne* (Psalm 47:8), wrote the Psalmist. When a nation becomes too corrupt, God is free to pour out his wrath (Genesis 15:16). He did this to Egypt, Assyria, Babylon, and to many others throughout the Old Testament. We ought to be concerned for our own righteousness, but also for the righteousness of our nation.

2 Kings 23:1 *Then the king called together all the elders of Judah and Jerusalem.*

Josiah wasn't inclined to keep God's word to himself, so he gathered the leaders and read it to them. After hearing God's word, they also agreed to serve him. *For the word of God is alive and active. Sharper than any double-edged sword, it penetrates even to dividing soul and spirit, joints and marrow; it judges the thoughts and attitudes of the heart* (Hebrews 4:12), says Hebrews. God's word is powerful and he wants it spread around.

This is what happened in the days of the early church: *the word of God spread* (Acts 6:7). . . . *the word of God continued to spread* (Acts 12:24). . . . *The word of the Lord spread through the whole region* (Acts 13:49) . . . . *[and] the word of the Lord spread widely* (Acts 19:20), wrote Luke. The work of the church isn't to keep God's word to itself, but to spread it around to the world until everyone knows that Jesus Christ is Lord.

2 Kings 23:29 *Pharaoh Necho king of Egypt went up to the Euphrates River to help the king of Assyria. King Josiah marched out to meet him in battle, but Necho faced him and killed him at Megiddo.*

Josiah's death seemed premature since he was under forty years old. Why didn't God preserve him to continue reforming the nation? God's ways don't always make sense to us, but Josiah is remembered as one of the finest kings to lead the nation, and he died a servant of God. Who could ask for anything more?

For Reflection and Review

- *Why was Josiah alarmed when the Bible was read to him?*
- *How do we know that God will fulfill his threats?*
- *Why should we care about the sins of our nation?*

Lesson 100

2 Kings 23:31 *Jehoahaz was twenty-three years old when he became king, and he reigned in Jerusalem three months.*

The book of Second Kings concludes with the account of four kings who ruled in quick succession, each of them evil. Jehoahaz was the son of King Josiah, and ruled for just three months after his father's death in 609 BC. After doing evil in the eyes of the Lord (2 Kings 23:32), he was dethroned by Pharaoh Necho, and taken to Egypt.

Jehoahaz may've dreamed of a long and glorious reign in which he'd build up his kingdom. But all his dreams were suddenly dashed by circumstances beyond his control. He reminds us how easily our dreams can be destroyed, and that the only wise course is to *seek first* the kingdom of

God (Matthew 6:33). Then we'll flourish forever regardless what happens in this life.

*****

2 Kings 23:36 *Jehoiakim was twenty-five years old when he became king, and he reigned in Jerusalem eleven years.*

Jehoiakim also did evil in the eyes of the Lord (2 Kings 23:7), and disregarded the words of Jeremiah. When the prophet's words were read to him, he took the scroll and threw it into a fire (Jeremiah 36:23). But the prophet's words came true when the king of Babylon attacked Jerusalem, raided the temple, and carried Jehoiakim into exile (Jeremiah 36:29, 2 Chronicles 36:6).

The Bible is the most hated book ever written, but also the most loved and widely read. Haters of God reject the Bible but can't stop it from coming true. *The grass withers and the flowers fall, but the word of our God endures forever* (Isaiah 40:8), wrote Isaiah.

*****

2 Kings 24:8 *Jehoiachin was eighteen years old when he became king, and he reigned in Jerusalem three months.*

Not long after he came to the throne, Jehoiachin surrendered to King Nebuchadnezzar (2 Kings 24:12). He too was taken to Babylon, with ten thousand others, leaving only the poorest behind (2 Kings 24:14). *He did evil in the eyes of the Lord, just as his father had done* (2 Kings 24:9).

There was little Jehoiachin could've done politically, since he was only eighteen years old, but he surely could've prayed. Some people only turn to God when life is hard, but Jehoiachin wouldn't even do that. Like many before and since he wanted nothing to do with God.

Under King David the nation of Israel became a dominant force, and Solomon took it to its greatest height. But when Solomon died in 931 BC, the nation split and never reunited. The northern kingdom of Israel fell to the Assyrians in 722 BC and never recovered. The southern kingdom of Judah was now greatly reduced, and would be destroyed by the Babylonians in 586 BC. As long as God's people followed God they prospered. But when they turned away from him, they suffered for their sins.

*****

2 Kings 24:18 *Zedekiah was twenty-one years old when he became king, and he reigned in Jerusalem eleven years.*

Zedekiah was the last king to rule the people of God before the southern kingdom of Judah was completely destroyed. He did evil in the eyes of God (2 Kings 24:19), and also in the eyes of Nebuchadnezzar by rebelling against him.

Nebuchadnezzar, king of Babylon, responded to Zedekiah's revolt by surrounding the city of Jerusalem and cutting off the food supply. Then he broke through the city walls and captured Zedekiah. Then he killed Zedekiah's sons in front of him, and put out his eyes, making the death of his sons the last thing he saw (2 Kings 25:7).

The Babylonians burned down the temple, and most other buildings in Jerusalem. They also destroyed the city walls and carried most of the remaining people into exile. Only a few of the poorest were left behind to work the fields (2 Kings 25:12). *So Judah went into captivity, away from her land* (2 Kings 25:21).

The Promised Land was God's gift to his people on the condition of obedience. So when they turned their backs on God, he kicked them out of his land. Knowing this would happen, God gave his people a promise through Moses centuries earlier. *Even if you have been banished to the most distant land under the heavens, from there the Lord your God will gather you and bring you back* (Deuteronomy 30:4), he said. This happened decades later, around 537 BC.

Some of the kings who led God's people were better than others, but most were terrible. Instead of leading God's people to worship him, they led God's people astray. The results were catastrophic, but the point is clear: *As goes the king, so goes the kingdom.*

All the kings' failures remind us of our need for a better king—a perfect one. If only God's people had a king who was perfectly righteous and mighty, the kingdom of God would flourish forever.

This is our greatest need, and what God has provided in the person of Jesus Christ. By dying on the cross, he proved his loyalty to God, as well as to God's people. Soon he'll return, and *his kingdom will never end* (Luke 1:33). *Now to the King eternal, immortal, invisible, the only God, be honor and glory for ever and ever* (1 Timothy 1:17), wrote Paul.

For Reflection and Review

- *Do you ever hope everything in the Bible won't come true?*
- *What kind of leaders does the world need today?*
- *Why is Jesus Christ a perfect king?*

Lesson 101

1 Chronicles 1:1-4 *Adam, Seth, Enosh, Kenan, Mahalalel, Jared, Enoch, Methuselah, Lamech, Noah. The sons of Noah: Shem, Ham and Japheth.*

First and Second Chronicles were originally one book. The author isn't identified but may've been Ezra the priest, writing around 450 BC, for those who returned from Babylonian exile. It was a difficult time, for many reasons, and the Chronicler wanted to assure God's people that he was still with them.

Much of the material in First and Second Chronicles is also found in First and Second Kings, so is not repeated here. What follows is unique to Chronicles, and a great encouragement whenever we're feeling threatened.

2 Chronicles 20:1 *After this, the Moabites and Ammonites with some of the Meunites came to wage war against Jehoshaphat.*

It was an ordinary day when Jehoshaphat awoke, but soon he learned that a vast army was marching toward Jerusalem, and they were only one day away. Most kings would've used that time to get their army ready, but Jehoshaphat thought of something even more important: he proclaimed a fast, and turned to God in prayer.

Lord, the God of our ancestors, are you not the God who is in heaven? . . . Power and might are in your hand, and no one can withstand you. Our God, will you not judge them? For we have no power to face this vast army that is attacking us. We do not know what to do, but our eyes are on you (2 Chronicles 20:6-13).

This isn't the first time Jehoshaphat prayed. The depth, sincerity, and spontaneity of his words show he was familiar with prayer, and with the God who saves. Jehoshaphat didn't wait for disaster to strike before he learned how to pray; he knew how to pray when disaster arrived.

2 Chronicles 20:14-17 *Then the Spirit of the Lord came on Jahaziel son of Zechariah . . . . This is what the Lord says to you: Do not be afraid or discouraged because of this vast army. . . . You will not have to fight this battle. Take up your positions; stand firm and see the deliverance the Lord will give you.*

These were hopeful words, but would they come true? Jehoshaphat may've slept lightly that night, but the following morning he set out with his army and a choir. He put the choir in front of the army and, as they marched, they sang: *Give thanks to the Lord, for his love endures forever* (2 Chronicles 20:21). If the whole army joined in, it was an amazing time of worship.

2 Chronicles 20:22 *As they began to sing and praise, the Lord set ambushes against the men of Ammon and Moab and Mount Seir.*

We don't know who was ambushing, but we know the result. All three armies turned on each other and completely destroyed each other. By the time the choir arrived, not a man was left standing. And the plunder was so great it took three days to pick it all up.

From this we learn that praise is a powerful weapon. They praised God on their way to the battle, and didn't have to lift a sword. As they gave praise to God, God worked on their behalf. We can choose to fight our battles alone, or to enlist God's help through prayer and praise.

*****

2 Chronicles 36:23 *This is what Cyrus king of Persia says: The Lord, the God of heaven, has given me all the kingdoms of the earth and he has appointed me to build a temple for him at Jerusalem in Judah. Any of his people among you may go up, and may the Lord their God be with them.*

Jerusalem fell to the Babylonians in 586 BC, and the Jews were taken into exile because of their sin. But God had promised, through Jeremiah, that they'd return after seventy years. *When seventy years are completed for Babylon, I will come to you and fulfill my good promise to bring you back* (Jeremiah 29:10), he said. In 539 BC Cyrus, king of Persia, defeated the Babylonians, and allowed God's people to go back home. The God who brought his people out of Egypt, and gave them the Promised Land, now brought them out of Babylon, and gave it back to them. On this positive note the Chronicler ends. But how does it apply to us?

God preserved his people in a foreign land until it was time to go home, and that's what he's doing for the church. The world opposes the church, and even hates the church (John 15:19), but hasn't overcome the church. God is the one who saves, God is the one who keeps, and God is the one who brings us home.

For Reflection and Review

- *How can we learn how to pray?*
- *How did Jehoshaphat's choir help his army?*
- *How has God kept you in the faith?*

Lesson 102

Ezra 1:1 *In the first year of Cyrus king of Persia, in order to fulfill the word of the Lord spoken by Jeremiah, the Lord moved the heart of Cyrus king of Persia to make a proclamation throughout his realm and also to put it in writing.*

The book of Ezra was likely written by *Ezra the priest, [and] teacher of the Law* (Ezra 7:11) around 430 BC. It tells how God's people returned from Babylonian exile, rebuilt the temple, and struggled to live God's way. It a story of starting over that covers nearly a hundred years, from 538 to 433 BC.

Ezra 1:5 *Then the family heads of Judah and Benjamin, and the priests and Levites—everyone whose heart God had moved—prepared to go up and build the house of the Lord in Jerusalem.*

Cyrus, king of Persia, had defeated the Babylonians, and allowed the Jews to go home (Ezra 1:2-4). The generation that went into exile had mostly died, and a new generation had taken its place. They were born in Babylon, and were comfortable there, so those who returned to the Promised Land were only about fifty thousand (Ezra 2:64-65). The reason they returned was because God *moved* their hearts.

This is why many people do what they do for God. It's why some become missionaries, or serve an important cause, or give financial support. God moved the heart of Cyrus to allow the Jews to go home (Ezra 1:1), and he moved the hearts of his people to make the journey back. When God wants to do something great, he often begins by moving our hearts.

Ezra 3:6 *On the first day of the seventh month they began to offer burnt offerings to the Lord.*

Shortly after God's people arrived back in the Promised Land, they gathered in Jerusalem, built an altar, and began to sacrifice daily. This was important because *without the shedding of blood there is no forgiveness* (Hebrews 9:22), says Hebrews. No sacrifice had been offered for nearly seventy years because they were living in Babylon. Now, at last, sacrificial blood was being spilt again.

This was a relief to their collective conscience, but is only a little comfort compared to what Christians enjoy. All the animals ever sacrificed merely pointed ahead to Jesus Christ, *the Lamb of God, who takes away the sin of the world* (John 1:29). And, *we have been made holy through the sacrifice of the body of Jesus Christ once for all* (Hebrews 10:10), says Hebrews. Christians no longer sacrifice animals (Hebrews 10:18), but only confess our sins (1 John 1:9), and remember what Christ has done for us.

Ezra 3:10-11 *When the builders laid the foundation of the temple of the Lord . . . . all the people gave a great shout of praise to the Lord, because the foundation of the house of the Lord was laid.*

After building the altar, God's people started to work on the temple itself. When the foundation was laid they gave a great shout, but those who had seen the earlier temple began to weep. They wept so loudly, in fact, that no one could distinguish between the shouts of joy and the sound of weeping (Ezra 3:12-13).

The new generation was excited about the temple, but the old generation was discouraged by how badly it compared to the previous temple. They were wrong to be discouraged, however, since this temple would also bring glory to God. They should've been thankful for the honor of serving God, but were discouraged by comparing their work to an earlier generation's.

Churches can also be discouraged by comparing themselves with other churches. The church of Jesus Christ is always growing, declining, and being rebuilt. The important thing is not the size of the church, but its faithfulness to God. It's always an honor to serve the Lord of the church.

Ezra 4:4 *Then the peoples around them set out to discourage the people of Judah and make them afraid to go on building.*

Whenever God's people try to do something great for God, they'll be opposed. But God is greater than the opposition and, in this case, actually made them pay for it. *Their expenses are to be fully paid . . . so that the work will not stop* (Ezra 6:8), decreed the king of Persia. *Furthermore, I decree that if anyone defies this edict, a beam is to be pulled from their house and they are to be impaled on it* (Ezra 6:11-12), he said.

God's people must've been amazed. When there was little they could do themselves, God made their enemies pay for the temple or die. The temple was being rebuilt, not because God's people were great, but because their God was great. *Nothing is too hard for you* (Jeremiah 32:17), wrote Jeremiah.

Ezra 6:15 *The temple was completed on the third day of the month Adar, in the sixth year of the reign of King Darius.*

This was about twenty years after the project began, and was a milestone for the people of God. There was a great celebration *because the Lord had filled them with joy by changing the attitude of the king . . . so that he assisted them in the work on the house of God* (Ezra 6:22).

Great things are often accomplished by people working together for years. Some of the workers were masons, others were engineers, and others were simply helpers. The prophets Haggai and Zechariah also helped (Ezra 5:1) through their preaching. The important thing in any work of God is for everyone to do what they can.

A little girl sat on the steps of a new church building, and a gentleman paused to admire it. She explained that she was involved in the project because her dad was a worker and she brought his lunch. It takes many people to do God's work, and everyone is important.

For Reflection and Review

- *Has God ever moved your heart to do something for him?*
- *Why did God require sacrifice for sin?*

- *How has God called you to serve him?*

Lesson 103

Ezra 7:6 *[Ezra] was a teacher well versed in the Law of Moses, which the Lord, the God of Israel, had given.*

About eighty years after the Jews returned from Babylonian exile, Ezra returned with a few thousand more of his countrymen. He was a priest, and a capable teacher of God's word. The temple had been rebuilt for some time, but the word of God wasn't being carefully followed. Ezra received permission from the king of Persia to return to Israel and strengthen the people of God in their faith. Ezra wanted God's people to conform their lives to the word of God, so they'd enjoy the blessing of God.

Ezra 7:10 *For Ezra had devoted himself to the study and observance of the Law of the Lord, and to teaching its decrees and laws in Israel.*

Ezra was an effective minister of God's word for three reasons: First, he was a devoted student. We should think of him getting up early, staying up late, and pouring over Scripture until he knew it forward and backward. Second, he applied the Bible to himself. He didn't read it for knowledge alone, but to conform his life to the will of God. Third, he taught God's word to others. He wanted all God's people to receive the riches of the Bible. This kind of minister can be a great blessing to God's people in any generation.

Ezra 7:15 *Moreover, you are to take with you the silver and gold that the king and his advisers have freely given to the God of Israel, whose dwelling is in Jerusalem.*

The king of Persia not only gave Ezra permission to return to Jerusalem, but sent him back with a fortune. While the temple was being rebuilt Haggai prophesied, *I will shake all nations, and what is desired by all nations will come, and I will fill this house with glory, says the Lord Almighty. The silver is mine and the gold is mine, declares the Lord Almighty* (Haggai 2:7-8). God's people had little money themselves, but God provided for his work in other ways. The God of heaven and earth is never short of cash.

Ezra 7:27 *Praise be to the Lord, the God of our ancestors, who has put it into the king's heart to bring honor to the house of the Lord in Jerusalem in this way.*

It seemed strange that a foreign king would finance God's work in Jerusalem, but Ezra saw it as a sign of God's power. God is sovereign over the hearts of kings, and can make them sympathetic to his will. *In the Lord's hand the king's heart is a stream of water that he channels toward all who please him* (Proverbs 21:1), wrote Solomon.

Ezra 9:1-2 *After these things had been done, the leaders came to me and said, The people of Israel, including the priests and the Levites, have not kept themselves separate from the neighboring peoples with their detestable practices. . . . They have taken some of their daughters as wives for themselves and their sons, and have mingled the holy race with the peoples around them.*

About four months after Ezra returned to Jerusalem, a serious problem was brought to his attention: some of God's people had intermarried with pagans. This was a direct violation of the word of God through Moses. *Do not intermarry with them. Do not give your daughters to their sons or take their daughters for your sons, for they will turn your children away from following me to serve other gods, and the Lord's anger will burn against you and will quickly destroy you* (Deuteronomy 7:3-4), he wrote.

Knowing the seriousness of the situation, Ezra tore his clothes, pulled out his hair, and prayed (Ezra 9:3). A crowd gathered, joined him in prayer, and agreed to put away their wives. Women and children were sent away from their homes, husbands, and fathers so the purity of God's people would be preserved. It was a drastic and painful solution to a very serious problem.

Like the ancient people of God, Christians are only allowed to marry in the faith (1 Corinthians 7:39). *Do not be yoked together with unbelievers. For what do righteousness and wickedness have in common? Or what fellowship can light have with darkness? What harmony is there between Christ and Belial? Or what does a believer have in common with an unbeliever?* (2 Corinthians 6:14-15), wrote Paul.

But unlike the ancient people of God, Christians who are married to an unbeliever shouldn't seek a divorce. *If any brother has a wife who is not a believer and she is willing to live with him, he must not divorce her. And if a woman has a husband who is not a believer and he is willing to live with her, she must not divorce him* (1 Corinthians 7:12-13), wrote Paul. Getting married is easy; staying married is difficult; staying happily married is the challenge of a lifetime.

For Reflection and Review

- *Why was Ezra an effective minister?*
- *How did God provide for the temple?*
- *Why did God forbid intermarriage with pagans?*

Lesson 104

Nehemiah 1:1 *The words of Nehemiah son of Hakaliah.*

The book of Nehemiah begins around 445 BC, about ten years after the close of the book of Ezra, and was likely written by Ezra the priest around 430 BC. Many of the Jews had returned from exile, and were living in and around Jerusalem. The temple had been rebuilt, but the city walls were still in ruins, exposing the people to constant danger. Nehemiah was the cupbearer for the king of Persia when he received news about the poor condition of Jerusalem.

Nehemiah 1:2 *Hanani, one of my brothers, came from Judah with some other men, and I questioned them about the Jewish remnant that had survived the exile, and also about Jerusalem.*

When Nehemiah learned the city was still in disrepair, he mourned and fasted several days. Then he prayed that God would give him favor with the king of Persia, so he could return to Jerusalem and help his people. *If it pleases the king and if your servant has found favor in his sight, let him send me to the city in Judah where my ancestors are buried so that I can rebuild it* (Nehemiah 2:5), he said. The king granted his request and even provided materials for the project. Nehemiah attributed this to the gracious hand of God being upon him (Nehemiah 2:8).

Nehemiah 2:11-12 *I went to Jerusalem, and after staying there three days I set out during the night with a few others. I had not told anyone what my God had put in my heart to do for Jerusalem.*

Nehemiah didn't want his plans to be known too early, because he didn't want to alarm Jerusalem's enemies before the rebuilding began. So he examined the walls at night, to avoid detection, and then brought his plan to God's people. *Let us start rebuilding* (Nehemiah 2:18), they said. But starting well is no guarantee of finishing well and, soon, they encountered problems.

Nehemiah 4:7-8 *But when Sanballat, Tobiah, the Arabs, the Ammonites and the people of Ashdod heard that the repairs to Jerusalem's walls had gone ahead and that the gaps were being closed, they were very angry. They all plotted together to come and fight against Jerusalem and stir up trouble against it.*

Israel's enemies weren't inclined to sit and watch as the city was being rebuilt. And because they had an army, (Nehemiah 4:2) they were a serious threat. Just because God is involved in a project doesn't mean there won't be problems. But Nehemiah was a man of faith, and knew how to respond.

Nehemiah 4:9 *[W]e prayed to our God and posted a guard day and night to meet this threat.*

They didn't just pray to God, or just post a guard, but prayed to God *and* posted a guard. They also armed the laborers, who worked even harder than before. They prayed as though everything depended on God, and worked as though everything depended on them. This is the surest way to success.

Some people are willing to pray like everything depends on God, but aren't willing to work very hard. Others are willing to work like everything depends on them, but aren't willing to pray very hard. But when God's people are willing to pray like everything depends on God, and work like everything depends on them, success can't be far away.

Nehemiah 5:1 *Now the men and their wives raised a great outcry against their fellow Jews.*

Some of God's people were going into debt because working on the wall gave them less time to work at their jobs. And some of the rich were growing richer, by making loans to them, and charging interest. But this was forbidden by God. *Do not charge a fellow Israelite interest* (Deuteronomy 23:19), wrote Moses. Nehemiah was angry at those who oppressed their fellow Jews, and they agreed to restore what had been wrongly taken. *For the love of money is a root of all kinds of evil* (1 Timothy 6:10), wrote Paul.

The building project was threatened from within and without, but Nehemiah provided good and godly leadership to see it completed in just fifty-two days (Nehemiah 6:15). It must've seemed like a miracle, but the work wasn't over. Now that the city was secure, it was time to build up God's people.

Nehemiah 8:1 *They told Ezra the teacher of the Law to bring out the Book of the Law of Moses, which the Lord had commanded for Israel.*

They built a platform for the occasion, and Ezra read from God's word for several hours, while the people listened attentively. And, as they listened, they understood how badly they had sinned, and began to weep. They agreed with God against themselves, and were starting to be renewed.

Ezra is a good example to those who teach and preach God's word. The preacher's job isn't to entertain the people, or tell them something new, but to clearly proclaim God's word to them. He's to keep the people of God and the word of God together. It's the people's job to listen attentively, and conform their lives to what the Bible says. This is how the church of God is constantly renewed.

Nehemiah 8:10 *Nehemiah said, Go and enjoy choice food and sweet drinks, and send some to those who have nothing prepared. This day is holy to our Lord. Do not grieve, for the joy of the Lord is your strength.*

It was good for the people to grieve their sins, but Nehemiah didn't want them to be overcome with grief. God had done great things for them, and they were turning back to him. This was reason to rejoice. *Rejoice in the Lord always. I will say it again: Rejoice!* (Philippians 4:4), wrote Paul.

We ought to rejoice in the Lord because he gives or withholds the ability to enjoy everything else. All other joys are derivative; God alone is the source. The more we rejoice in the Lord, the more we'll enjoy everything else he gives.

Nehemiah 13:6-7 *[I]n the thirty-second year of Artaxerxes king of Babylon I had returned to the king. Some time later I asked his permission and came back to Jerusalem.*

After leading God's people for twelve years, Nehemiah went back to Babylon for some time. We're don't know how long he was gone but, when he returned, the situation had declined. The temple was being misused, the Sabbath was being broken, and God's people were marrying pagans again.

Nehemiah was so angry about the mixed marriages that he *rebuked them and called curses down on them. [He] beat some of the men and pulled out their hair.* Nehemiah was a forceful leader, and wasn't afraid to hurt people's feelings.

There's no place for physical punishment in the church, of course, but when Titus was dealing with unruly Christians, Paul wrote that he should *rebuke them sharply, so that they will be sound in the faith* (Titus 1:13). Ordinarily, *the Lord's servant . . . must be kind to everyone* (2 Timothy 2:24). But he must also be willing to rebuke if necessary.

Nehemiah reminds us of the value of powerful leadership. When he was gone, the city fell into sin. When he returned, things were set right again. Good and godly leaders are a gift to the church, and ought to be highly regarded. *Have confidence in your leaders and submit to their authority, because they keep watch over you as those who must give an account* (Hebrews 13:17), says Hebrews.

For Reflection and Review

- *Why do prayer and work lead to success?*
- *Why is it important to rejoice in God?*
- *Why should good and godly leaders be highly regarded?*

Lesson 105

Esther 1:1 *This is what happened during the time of Xerxes, the Xerxes who ruled over 127 provinces stretching from India to Cush.*

The book of Esther is named after a Jewish girl who became the queen of Persia, and delivered her people from a plot to destroy them. The author isn't named but probably wrote from Persia around 460 BC to explain the origin of the festival of Purim, which commemorates this event. Esther is a unique book because it doesn't mention God by name, but highlights his providential care in a series of remarkable coincidences. Even when God is silent, he's caring for his people.

Esther 1:10-12 *On the seventh day, when King Xerxes was in high spirits from wine, he commanded . . . to bring before him Queen Vashti, wearing her royal crown, in order to display her beauty to the people and nobles, for she was lovely to look at. But when the attendants delivered the king's command, Queen Vashti refused to come. Then the king became furious and burned with anger.*

The King and Queen were hosting separate banquets when Xerxes decided to parade his beautiful wife before his many guests. By refusing to comply, Vashti disrespected her husband and publicly embarrassed him. The king consulted with his advisors, and they recommended Vashti be removed as queen so that women everywhere wouldn't disrespect their husbands. This opened the way for someone else to become queen.

High position comes with responsibility, and a single misstep can cause a fall. We might imagine life is better near the top, but many have found this isn't always so. Instead of envying people above us we ought to cultivate contentment, for *godliness with contentment is great gain* (1 Timothy 6:6), wrote Paul.

Esther 2:2 *Then the king's personal attendants proposed, Let a search be made for beautiful young virgins for the king.*

These were added to his harem so that he might have his choice among many. Esther *had a lovely figure and was beautiful* (Esther 2:7), so she was also added to the king's harem. After a year of beauty treatments she slept with the king (Esther 2:14), and he preferred her over the others. *So he set a royal crown on her head and made her queen instead of Vashti* (Esther 2:17).

Esther appears to have gained her royal position through moral compromise. The Bible doesn't condemn or condone her behavior, but simply states the facts. It's never right to disobey God, of course, but God is so great that he's able to bring good out of evil—even the evil of our sin. This is not a reason to sin, of course, but a reason to glorify God who always works for the good of those who love him (Romans 8:28).

Esther 3:1 *After these events, King Xerxes honored Haman son of Hammedatha, the Agagite, elevating him and giving him a seat of honor higher than that of all the other nobles.*

Haman was a descendent of Agag, king of the Amalekites, an ancient enemy of Israel. By the order of King Xerxes, people were to honor Haman by kneeling in his presence. But Esther's cousin (Mordecai) refused to kneel because of the ancient hostility, or because he thought such honor was due to God alone. Mordecai was also Esther's guardian because, after her parents died, he raise her (Esther 2:7).

Honor was important to Haman and, when he learned that Mordecai was a Jew, he determined to kill all the Jews in the kingdom (Esther 3:6), not just Mordecai. Since Esther hadn't revealed her Jewish ethnicity, Haman unknowingly set in motion a plan that, if carried out, would kill the king's wife.

Esther may've planned to hide her ethnicity, but Mordecai urged her to go directly to the king. This was complicated since, on pain of death, no one was allowed into the king's presence without an invitation, even the king's wife (Esther 4:11). Exceptions were made but it was risky.

Mordecai said to her: *Do not think that because you are in the king's house you alone of all the Jews will escape. For if you remain silent at this time, relief and deliverance for the Jews will arise from another place, but you and your father's family will perish. And who knows but that you have come to your royal position for such a time as this?* (Esther 4:13-14).

Esther could do the right thing, and possibly die, or she could do the wrong thing and possibly die. Neither option was agreeable but, perhaps, God made her queen for this very occasion. She was entrusted by God with high position, and dare not fail now. *From everyone who has been given much, much will be demanded; and from the one who has been entrusted with much, much more will be asked* (Luke 12:48), said Jesus.

For Reflection and Review

- *What can we learn from Vashti?*
- *Was it wrong for Esther to sleep with the king?*
- *Why is the world so dangerous?*

Lesson 106

Esther 5:1-2 *Esther put on her royal robes and stood in the inner court of the palace, in front of the king's hall. The king was sitting on his royal throne in the hall, facing the entrance. When he saw Queen Esther standing in the court, he was pleased with her and held out to her the gold scepter that was in his hand. So Esther approached and touched the tip of the scepter.*

Instead of making her request at once, Esther invited both the king and Haman to a banquet. Haman felt honored to be included but, afterward, he encountered Mordecai who disrespected him again. Not content to wait for the killing of all the Jews, Haman planed to execute Mordecai early. He even set up a pole on which to impale him (Esther 5:14).

Esther 6:1-2 *That night the king could not sleep; so he ordered the book of the chronicles, the record of his reign, to be brought in and read to him. It was found recorded there that Mordecai had exposed . . . two of the king's officers who guarded the doorway, who had conspired to assassinate King Xerxes.*

This episode occurred years earlier, but was never brought to the king's attention. Xerxes didn't know that Mordecai was Jewish, and he commanded Haman to honor Mordecai by leading him throughout the city on horseback while proclaiming, *This is what is done for the man the king delights to honor!* (Esther 6:11). Haman was embarrassed and alarmed as things began turning against him.

Here we see the invisible hand of God working on behalf of his people. God is the one who kept the king awake, so he'd request the record of his reign be read to him, so he'd discover what Mordecai had done for him.

God takes center stage, sometimes, but normally works behind the scenes. Either way, he's in control of everything that happens. *Are not two sparrows sold for a penny? Yet not one of them will fall to the ground outside your Father's care. And even the very hairs of your head are all numbered* (Matthew

10:29-30), said Jesus. Our heavenly Father is always in control so we needn't be afraid.

Esther 7:1-2 *So the king and Haman went to Queen Esther's banquet, and as they were drinking wine on the second day, the king again asked, Queen Esther, what is your petition? It will be given you. What is your request? Even up to half the kingdom, it will be granted.*

When the King learned that Esther was Jewish, he became so angry at Haman for his plan to kill the Jews that he left the room to think. Haman fell on the couch, where Esther was reclining, and begged for his life. When the king returned it appeared that Haman was molesting Esther, and Haman's fate was sealed. He was impaled on the pole on which he planned to impale Mordecai.

Then Mordecai was given Haman's position and began to defend the Jews. Since the first decree couldn't be repealed, Mordecai and Xerxes wrote a new decree permitting the Jews to defend themselves (Esther 8:11). Some attacks were made, but God's people were victorious. Then Mordecai made the next two days a holiday to be celebrated every year with feasting and gifts (Esther 9:20-22).

Notice the many coincidences that made this outcome possible. *Coincidentally*, Esther became queen. *Coincidentally*, Mordecai discovered a plan to assassinate the king. *Coincidentally*, the king was sleepless shortly before Haman planned to have Mordecai killed. *Coincidentally*, the account read to the king was the record of Mordecai saving his life. Sometimes God reveals himself through miracles, but also through the obvious care of his people. This can be called a *conspicuous providence*.

Esther 10:3 *Mordecai the Jew was second in rank to King Xerxes, preeminent among the Jews, and held in high esteem by his many fellow Jews, because he worked for the good of his people and spoke up for the welfare of all the Jews.*

Mordecai was faithful to God, faithful to God's people, and faithful to the king. As a result, he was promoted to the highest position under King Xerxes. It must've seemed like a dream to him, but it was real.

And those who serve Christ will also be promoted. Imagine hearing him say to you, *Well done, good and faithful servant! You have been faithful with a few things; I will put you in charge of many things. Come and share your master's happiness!* (Matthew 25:21). It may seem like a dream at the time, but it will never end. A lifetime of service will be nothing by comparison.

For Reflection and Review

- *Have you ever received a conspicuous providence?*
- *Is every coincidence important?*
- *How can we be more faithful to Christ?*

Lesson 107

Job 1:1 *In the land of Uz there lived a man whose name was Job.*

Job may've lived around 2100 BC, but his story was written down many years later, perhaps around 500 BC. It takes place in the land of Uz, which was just outside the land of Israel. If God is fair, why do the righteous suffer? That's the concern of this book. The problem is not entirely solved, but insights are provided.

Job 1:6 *One day the angels came to present themselves before the Lord, and Satan also came with them.*

We seldom think of Satan in heaven, but here he appears with angels in the presence of God. Satan will be thrown into hell *for ever and ever* (Revelation 20:10), but currently roams the earth (Job 1:7), and even appears before God. God and Satan even talk.

Job 1:8 *Then the Lord said to Satan, Have you considered my servant Job?*

At the time of this conversation, Job's life was going well. He had seven sons, three daughters, and enough livestock to make him the wealthiest person around (Job 1:3-4). He wasn't only rich, however, but also righteous. The Lord said to Satan, *There is no one on earth like him; he is blameless and upright, a man who fears God and shuns evil* (Job 1:8b). Job was rich, righteous, and greatly blessed by God.

Job 1:9-11 *Does Job fear God for nothing? Satan replied. Have you not put a hedge around him and his household and everything he has? You have blessed the work of his hands, so that his flocks and herds are spread throughout the land. But now stretch out your hand and strike everything he has, and he will surely curse you to your face.*

There are five important things we should learn from this conversation. First, we have an enemy. We expect to be punished for our sins and rewarded for our righteousness, but it's not that simple. There's a powerful evil being who delights to see the righteous suffer.

Second, God is our protector. He put a hedge around Job and everything he had (Job 1:10). A proper hedge can be an effective means to keep outside what doesn't belong inside. God can surround us with a hedge, and protect us from all harm.

Third, our lives are not private. Job's ordeal is played out in the presence God, Satan, and angels. To this the New Testament adds *a great cloud of witnesses* (Hebrews 12:1), those who've gone to heaven before us. Privacy is an illusion. God and many witnesses see everything we do.

Fourth, hardship reveals our loyalty. Satan thought Job's first loyalty wasn't to God, but to Job. He thought Job was serving God because of what he got from God, not because he was loyal to God. If God took away Job's prosperity, Job would turn away from God. This is the heart of the issue.

Fifth, Satan wants us to curse God. *[S]tretch out your hand and strike everything he has, and he will surely curse you to your face* (Job 1:11), said Satan. God is the object of more and greater cursing every day than any other being in the universe. Some people even curse God for the pleasure it brings them. Even the righteous are tempted to curse God sometimes. This was Satan's goal for Job, and also for us.

Job 1:12 *The Lord said to Satan, Very well, then, everything he has is in your power, but on the man himself do not lay a finger.*

Satan is the enemy of God, of course, but also of God's people, and everyone made in God's image. Since he can't attack God directly, he attacks the people God loves. Every disease, sorrow, pain, murder, torture, war, and death can be traced, directly or indirectly, back to Satan.

But Satan is under God's control. He was free to destroy all that Job had, but he wasn't free to attack Job's person. *[O]n the man himself do not lay a finger*, said God. Satan's power is greater than any human power, but is nothing compared to the power of God. Satan is a awesomely powerful, but he's on a leash—God's leash.

Job 1:13-19 *One day when Job's sons and daughters were feasting and drinking wine at the oldest brother's house, a messenger came to Job and said, The oxen were plowing and the donkeys were grazing nearby, and the Sabeans attacked and made off with them. They put the servants to the sword, and I am the only one who has escaped to tell you!*

While he was still speaking, another messenger came and said, The fire of God fell from the heavens and burned up the sheep and the servants, and I am the only one who has escaped to tell you!

While he was still speaking, another messenger came and said, The Chaldeans formed three raiding parties and swept down on your camels and made off with them. They put the servants to the sword, and I am the only one who has escaped to tell you!

While he was still speaking, yet another messenger came and said, Your sons and daughters were feasting and drinking wine at the oldest brother's house, when suddenly a mighty wind swept in from the desert and struck the four corners of the house. It collapsed on them and they are dead, and I am the only one who has escaped to tell you!

The day began like any other day. Job probably got out of bed and thanked God for all the blessings he enjoyed. Perhaps he had eggs for breakfast, and planned to join the celebration at his son's house later that day. It was nice to have the family together, enjoying the abundance God had provided.

But in just a few minutes Job went from riches to rags. One after another the messengers came with news of catastrophic loss: oxen, donkeys, servants, sheep, and camels were suddenly gone. Then, worst of all, the loss of his children. Seven sons and three daughters died when the house collapsed on them. How does a man of God respond to such a disaster?

For Reflection and Review

- *Why does God allow bad things to happen to his people?*
- *Why does Satan want to hurt people?*
- *How would you respond if you were Job?*

Lesson 108

Job 1:20-21 *At this, Job got up and tore his robe and shaved his head. Then he fell to the ground in worship and said: Naked I came from my mother's womb, and naked I will depart. The Lord gave and the Lord has taken away; may the name of the Lord be praised.*

Job, of course, was devastated but he chose to worship God instead of cursing him. Praising God in heaven is easier than praising God on earth. And praising God when things go right is easier than praising him when things go wrong. By worshipping God in the midst of loss, Job brought more glory to God than angels above.

Job was able to respond this way because he understood two important things: First, everything he had on earth was only temporary. *Naked I came from my mother's womb, and naked I will depart*, he said. He came into the world with nothing, and would leave with nothing. The important thing was that he still had God.

Second, Job understood that God was in control of his loss. *The Lord gave and the Lord has taken away*, he said. Job wasn't in the hands of fate, chance, or the devil. He was in the hands of a good and loving God who is always worthy of praise. So even in the midst of loss, Job gave praise to God.

Job 1:22 *In all this, Job did not sin by charging God with wrongdoing.*

Whenever evil strikes it seems like God isn't doing his job, or is doing it badly. If the disaster is bad enough, we might even think that God is evil. But no matter how things appear, we must trust that God is good, and is doing something good for us.

A child begged his father not to take him into surgery, but the father did anyway because it was best for the child. He wasn't trying to hurt the child, but to help the child. God may have to hurt us in order to help us, but he will never harm us. No matter how great the affliction, we can never charge God with wrongdoing. We should praise him, in fact, for the good he's doing, even if we can't understand it.

Job 2:1-6 *On another day the angels came to present themselves before the Lord, and Satan also came with them to present himself before him. And the Lord said to Satan, Where have you come from? Satan answered the Lord, From roaming throughout the earth, going back and forth on it.*

Then the Lord said to Satan, Have you considered my servant Job? There is no one on earth like him; he is blameless and upright, a man who fears God and shuns evil. And he still maintains his integrity, though you incited me against him to ruin him without any reason.

Skin for skin! Satan replied. A man will give all he has for his own life. But now stretch out your hand and strike his flesh and bones, and he will surely curse you to your face. The Lord said to Satan, Very well, then, he is in your hands; but you must spare his life.

Job did so well in his first round of testing that God honored him with a second. In the first round, Satan was allowed to destroy all that belonged to Job, but not his health. Now he was free to destroy even that. This was a staggering test because, apart from health, there's little in the world that can even be enjoyed.

Job 2:7-9 *So Satan went out from the presence of the Lord and afflicted Job with painful sores from the soles of his feet to the crown of his head. Then Job took a piece of broken pottery and scraped himself with it as he sat among the ashes. His wife said to him, Are you still maintaining your integrity? Curse God and die!*

Perhaps the only reason Satan didn't take Job's wife, along with his children, is because he wanted to speak to Job through her. This is the only time she's quoted in the Bible, and it doesn't reflect well on her. But she lost everything too. And as the mother of ten dead children, her pain may've been worse than Job's.

Job's wife told him to *Curse God and die*, but Job wouldn't do either. Some are willing to curse God, and some are willing to kill themselves, but Satan's joy is most complete when people curse God and kill themselves. We don't know how often this happens, but this was Satan's will for Job. Here we see the evilness of Satan, and his will for each of us.

Job 2:10 *Shall we accept good from God, and not trouble?*

Job was the kind of person who did what was right because it was right, not because it worked. He was loyal to his Maker because it's always right to be loyal to your Maker.

A middle-aged man was taken to the hospital with neck pain. Soon he was paralyzed and unable to speak. Over many years he recovered his speech, but always needed a wheel chair. His son was angry at God and asked his father why he wasn't angry too. *Why should I accept good from God and not trouble?* he said. God is to be honored for who he is, not only for what he gives.

Job 2:11-13 *When Job's three friends, Eliphaz the Temanite, Bildad the Shuhite and Zophar the Naamathite, heard about all the troubles that had come upon him, they set out from their homes and met together by agreement to go and sympathize with him and comfort him.*

When they saw him from a distance, they could hardly recognize him; they began to weep aloud, and they tore their robes and sprinkled dust on their heads. Then they sat on the ground with him for seven days and seven nights. No one said a word to him, because they saw how great his suffering was.

The presence of friends must've been a comfort to Job, at least for awhile. They showed sensitivity by sitting with him in silence, which isn't always easy. We're uncomfortable with people in pain, and want to say something helpful. We're tempted to say, *I know what you're going through, I know how you feel* or something theological. But most of the time we don't know what they're going through, how they feel, or how it relates to God. It's wiser to show our concern by simply showing up and saying very little.

For Reflection and Review

- *Why did Job give praise to God?*
- *Why does Satan want us to curse God and die?*
- *What should we do for friends who are suffering deeply?*

Lesson 109

Job 3:1 *After this, Job opened his mouth and cursed the day of his birth.*

He was, after all, human. Job wasn't cursing God, as the devil intended, but only the day of his birth. The loss of health, wealth, and family were so overwhelming that he wished he'd never been born. Life can be so miserable that we regret the day of our birth.

The best remedy for this is a vivid view of the age to come. The Apostle Paul was no stranger to suffering, or to heaven (2 Corinthians 12:2-4). And when he compared the two he was greatly encouraged: *I consider that our present sufferings are not worth comparing with the glory that will be revealed in us* (Romans 8:18), he said. The worst possible life on earth is nothing compared to the glory that will be ours forever. That is a great encouragement to all who suffer in faith.

Job 3:25 *What I feared has come upon me; what I dreaded has happened to me.*

Believing in God is no guarantee against losing everything. If we think nothing bad can happen to us, because we believe in God, then we'll stop believing in God when something bad happens to us. Faith knows that God is in control (Matthew 10:29-31), and won't allow anything to happen to us, that's not for our ultimate good (Romans 8:28). This kind of faith enjoys the best, endures the worst, and glorifies God in everything.

Job 10:3 *Does it please you to oppress me, to spurn the work of your hands?*

Job didn't have the benefit of the Bible, so it's no surprise he drew some wrong conclusions. His suffering made him think of God as an oppressor who enjoyed watching his servant suffer. Suffering can deepen our knowledge of God, but it can also distort our theology. We might conclude that God is all good but not entirely powerful, or that he's all powerful but not entirely good. But the Bible insists that God is all good, and all powerful, and allows suffering to make us like Christ (Romans 8:28-29).

Job 19:25-27 *I know that my redeemer lives, and that in the end he will stand on the earth. And after my skin has been destroyed, yet in my flesh I will see God; I myself will see him with my own eyes—I, and not another. How my heart yearns within me!*

Throughout his suffering Job's faith went up and down, but this was a high point. He looked ahead to a time after death, when he'd see his redeemer on earth. Without understanding fully, Job looked forward to the redemption Christ would provide, to his second coming, and to the resurrection of believers (John 5:28-29). This is our comfort in times of loss.

A young lady earned a doctorate in literature and became a university professor. She was a brilliant wordsmith until a brain tumor eroded her ability to think and speak. Toward the end of her life she only quoted Scripture, and her last words were, *I know that my redeemer lives.*

Job 23:10 *[W]hen he has tested me, I will come forth as gold.*

Job was starting to see his hardship as a form of purification. Gold must go through fire for dross to be removed, and Christians must go through suffering for their faith to be purified. *The crucible for silver and the furnace for gold, but the Lord tests the heart* (Proverbs 17:3), says Proverbs.

Job 38:1 *Then the Lord spoke to Job out of the storm.*

After thirty-five chapters of speeches from Job and his friends, we finally hear from God. But God didn't provide the answer Job or his friends were looking for. Instead of explaining why a good and powerful God would allow the righteous to suffer, God reminded them that his wisdom is beyond our comprehension. Children can't understand everything their parents do, so we shouldn't expect to understand everything God does. What we know of his goodness, power, and wisdom is enough for us to trust him.

Job 42:5-6 *My ears had heard of you but now my eyes have seen you. Therefore I despise myself and repent in dust and ashes.*

Throughout the story, Job insisted he was a pretty good person. And, compared to everyone else, he was. But even though he was the most righteous person around (Job 1:8), Job was still a sinner who fell short of the glory of God (Romans 3:23). It wasn't until he saw himself in the light of God's glory that he could say, *I despise myself and repent in dust and ashes.*

This is why it's never wise to compare ourselves to other sinners. *When they measure themselves by themselves and compare themselves with themselves, they are not wise* (2 Corinthians 10:12), wrote Paul. Most people think they're better than average, but God's standard is perfection (Matthew 5:48). When we compare ourselves to other sinners, we think too much of ourselves. It's only when we see ourselves in the light of God's holiness that we can say with Job, *I despise myself and repent in dust and ashes.*

Job 42:12 *The Lord blessed the latter part of Job's life more than the former part.*

God gave Job twice as much as he had before, and many more years to enjoy it. Whenever we go through difficult times, we might think they'll never end—but they usually do. *We went through fire and water, but you brought us to a place of abundance* (Psalm 66:12), wrote the Psalmist.

Life is hard for everyone, and God tests the faith of his servants. But God also delights in blessing his children, and will bring us to a place where there are no more tears (Revelation 21:4). *Tough times never last but tough people do.*

For Reflection and Review

- *How does suffering affect our faith?*
- *What comfort is there for Christians who are suffering?*
- *Why did Job despise himself and repent?*

Lesson 110

Psalm 1:1 *Blessed is the one who does not walk in step with the wicked.*

The book of Psalms is a collection of prayers and praise that were set to music and used for worship by the people of God. King David authored many of them but Asaph, Solomon, and Moses were also authors, along with a few others.

Various Psalms date from between 1500 and 500 BC, and the book was put into its final form in the fourth century BC. The book of Psalms expresses the full range of religious emotions, from breathtaking highs to suffocating lows. It reflects the religious feelings of believers in all circumstances, throughout the ages.

The first word of the first verse of the first Psalm is the word *blessed*. The Hebrew word can also be translated *happy*, so the point of the first psalm is to direct our feet into the way of happiness. *All men seek happiness. There are no exceptions. However different the means they may employ, they all strive towards this goal* (Blaise Pascal).

The reason some people go to church is to be happy, and the reason some people stay home is to be happy. The reason some people get married is to be happy, and the reason some people get divorced is to be happy. I've been on several diets, over the years, and I always start because I think that being thinner will make me happy. But when I get hungry enough, I think that eating will make me happy. Whether I eat or starve, I do both for the same reason. Psalm one tells us how to be happy in God.

Psalm 1:1b *[He] does not walk in step with the wicked or stand in the way that sinners take or sit in the company of mockers.*

Few things will influence our lives for good or evil more than those around us. This is why parents are concerned about what kind of friends their children make. I was thirteen years old when I began to run with the wrong crowd, and my mother expressed her concern. I said, *The reason I run with them is to be a good influence.* But I was lying through my teeth and she knew it. She shook her head and said, *Tell me who you run with, and I'll tell you who you are.*

A young lady was also going out with the wrong crowd, and told her parents the same lie. They said, *If you're going out with unbelievers make the ratio three to one: three friends who are on the right track for every one who is not.* That's good advice. The sinful nature is so powerful that it's easier to be influenced toward evil, than to influence others toward good. Your best friends are the ones who bring out the best in you.

Psalm 1:2 *. . . but whose delight is in the law of the Lord, and who meditates on his law day and night.*

We don't know the author of Psalm One, but he clearly loved the Bible. He didn't merely read the Bible, he made it his meditation. A good way to meditate on God's word is by committing it to memory. *I have hidden your word in my heart that I might not sin against you* (Psalm 119:11), wrote the Psalmist. As we memorize the word of God, it sinks into our soul, and helps us throughout the day.

Psalm 1:3 *That person is like a tree planted by streams of water, which yields its fruit in season and whose leaf does not wither.*

Israel's climate is mostly hot and dry, so it's not always easy to make things grow. But along the Jordan River everything grows nicely because of the constant water supply. The writer is saying the closer you are to God, the more you'll flourish.

A young missionary who'd later die for his faith these words: *I walked out on the hill just now and it is exalting. It is delicious to stand and be embraced by the shadow of a friendly tree with the wind tugging at your coattail and the heavens tugging at your heart. To gaze and glory and give oneself again to God. What more could a man ask. The fullness, pleasure, and sheer excitement of knowing God on earth* (Jim Elliot).

Psalm 1:3b *. . . whatever they do prospers.*

Prosperity doesn't come easily in a fallen world. Some people prosper financially, but their relationships are a mess. Others prosper relationally, but their finances are a mess. Others prosper outwardly, but inwardly they're a mess. And some people are just a mess. But here we learn that prosperity often comes from knowing God's word and being among his people—*whatever they do prospers.*

Whenever you buy something that requires assembly, it's wise to read the instructions. Otherwise you may assemble it incorrectly, and it won't work the way it should. God knows how life is supposed to work, and has revealed it in his word. It's the only way to true prosperity.

Psalm 1:4 *Not so the wicked! They are like chaff that the wind blows away.*

In many places wheat and chaff are still separated the way they were in the Bible. Both are tossed into the air and, because the chaff is lighter, it's blown off to the side. The wheat is stored in a barn, and the chaff is burned in a fire.

John the Baptist used this image to describe how Christ will separate the righteous from the wicked. *[H]e will clear his threshing floor, gathering his wheat into the barn and burning up the chaff with unquenchable fire* (Matthew 3:12), he said. They are mingled now, but will be sorted out in the end.

Psalm 1:5-6 *Therefore the wicked will not stand in the judgment, nor sinners in the assembly of the righteous. For the Lord watches over the way of the righteous, but the way of the wicked leads to destruction.*

The first word in this Psalm is *blessed*, and the last word is *destruction*. Those who belong to Jesus Christ will enjoy eternal blessedness, and those who die apart from Christ will endure eternal destruction. This Psalm teaches us how to be happy in this life, and in the one to come.

For Reflection and Review

- *Why is it important to be happy in God?*
- *How is the Bible like an owner's manual?*
- *Do God's people always prosper in this age?*

Lesson 111

Psalm 2:11 *Serve the Lord with fear and celebrate his rule with trembling.*

We don't normally celebrate God's rule with trembling, but that's the response called for by this text. David is speaking to kings, before whom ordinary people trembled. Since kings held the power of life and death, it could be a dreadful thing to stand in their presence. How much more the king of all the earth?

A proper response to God includes both celebration and trembling. *[T]remble before him, all the earth* (Psalm 96:9). *My flesh trembles in fear of you;* (Psalm 119:20). *Do not be arrogant, but tremble* (Romans 11:20). And *work out your salvation with fear and trembling* (Philippians 2:12), wrote Paul.

The Bible gives us enough assurance to be secure, but never enough to be careless. Excessive assurance will cause a person to be spiritually lax, and insufficient assurance will cause a person to be spiritually tense. Sufficient assurance allows us to celebrate the rule of God with trembling.

Psalm 4:8 *In peace I will lie down and sleep, for you alone, Lord, make me dwell in safety.*

David had powerful enemies, and had to run for his life sometimes. He needed God's protection when he was awake, but even more while he slept. Instead of sleeping lightly, he committed himself to God's care, knowing that God alone could make him dwell in safety.

For those who live in fear nothing is more precious than feeling secure, and none are safer than those who trust in God. Being a Christian doesn't mean you won't be murdered at midnight, but that you won't be murdered by chance, because God will preserve your life until he calls you home.

Psalm 8:3-4 *When I consider your heavens, the work of your fingers, the moon and the stars, which you have set in place, what is mankind that you are mindful of them, human beings that you care for them?*

When we consider the expanse of the universe, it's easy to feel insignificant by comparison. Even our planet is tiny compared to many others. But earth is the place of God's special work. This is the place to which he came, lived, and taught. These are the people for whom he died. And this is where he'll live in the future. The vastness of the universe shouldn't make us feel insignificant, but compel us to worship the God who made it all, and numbers the hairs of our heads (Matthew 10:30).

Psalm 10:1 *Why, Lord, do you stand far off? Why do you hide yourself in times of trouble?*

There are times in life when God seems remarkably close. *With him at my right hand, I will not be shaken* (Psalm 16:8). *But as for me, it is good to be near God* (Psalm 73:28). And, *The Lord is near to all who call on him* (Psalm 145:18), wrote the Psalmists.

But there are other times when God seems painfully absent. *Lord, do not forsake me; do not be far from me* (Psalm 38:21). *Why do you hide your face and forget our misery?* (Psalm 44:24). *Why, Lord, do you reject me and hide your face from me?* (Psalm 88:14), wrote the Psalmists also.

The felt presence of God, and the felt absence of God, are both legitimate feelings expressed in God's word. They're powerful, and often undeniable, but are not our most reliable guide. Regardless of what we're going through, we should always trust in the promise of Christ: *I am with you always, to the very end of the age* (Matthew 28:20), he said. God wants us to *live by faith* (2 Corinthians 5:7), more than by our feelings.

Psalm 14:1 *The fool says in his heart, There is no God.*

God is self-evident from the world he created (Romans 1:20), and anyone who disagrees is a fool. This also applies to those who believe God may exist, but is so irrelevant that he may as well not exist. The conviction may be philosophical, or merely practical, but it's the prevailing view of many. And yet, God refuses to go away.

A young atheist was going through a difficult time and found himself angry at God. He had to remind himself that it didn't make sense to be angry at God because he didn't believe in God. But pain makes us think about God whether we believe in him or not. Many who hit their thumb with a hammer speak of God instinctively. So why doesn't everyone simply admit that they believe in God?

The answer is that God is inconvenient. Saying *yes* to him often means saying *no* to ourselves. The good news of atheism is that there is no Judgment Day, so we can live as we please now. This is very appealing, even if it isn't true.

But those who've come to God through faith in Jesus Christ are normally happier than atheists for several reasons: First, they've resolved their guilt through faith, repentance, and forgiveness. Second, they're not afraid of death, because they have eternal life. Third, they're more optimistic because they believe that God is good. Fourth, they have better relationships because they've learned to love and forgive. And fifth, they're less worried about this life because they're looking forward to the next.

Those who argue against God argue against the very one who gives them the ability to argue at all. They're like a little girl who's able to slap her father's face, only because he holds her up (Cornelius Van Til). Apart from sin, everyone would believe in God immediately and without any argument.

Psalm 16:11 *[Y]ou will fill me with joy in your presence, with eternal pleasures at your right hand.*

King David understood pleasure, and saw it as a gift from God. This helped him look forward to the age to come when he he'd enjoy *eternal pleasures* at God's right hand. The greatest pleasures on earth are only a foretaste of what the righteous will enjoy forever.

The devil wants us think that God is against pleasure, but this is contrary to Scripture and reason. When God created Adam and Eve, he put them in the Garden of Eden, a place of sensual bliss. He also gave them physical senses to enjoy all that he made: the beauty of nature, the taste of food, the sound of birds, the sense of touch, and the smell of lilacs in bloom. To this he added the joy of his presence to make us glad (Psalm 21:6). It can even be argued that we were made for pleasure—the pleasure of God and all he's created.

But pleasure is so powerful it can destroy us if we're not careful. Many who were once rich have died penniless due to an excessive pursuit of pleasure. Others have lost their health, or their reputations, by pursuing pleasure without restraint. The proper use of pleasure is to enjoy it within the limits God has set. God himself should be our highest pleasure, and his commandments our first concern. Then we'll enjoy pleasure as he intends, and look forward to *eternal pleasures* at his right hand.

Psalm 19:7 *The statutes of the Lord are trustworthy, making wise the simple.*

David found God's word to be his most reliable guide. It was more trustworthy than the counsel of his friends, or even of his own thoughts and feelings. Even today, the Bible should be trusted above all else.

A military aircraft was returning from a mission and, due to a tailwind, arrived home sooner than expected. Their instruments showed the airbase was right below them, but their instincts told them otherwise. Instead of trusting their instruments, they relied on their instincts, and never made it back. On our journey to heaven, the Bible is our most reliable guide.

For Reflection and Review

- *Why should everyone tremble before God?*
- *Why doesn't everyone believe in God?*
- *What's the danger of too much pleasure?*

Lesson 112

Psalm 22:1 *My God, my God, why have you forsaken me?*

These are haunting words to pray, but David was in desperate need and felt abandoned by God. He was being attacked by ruthless men, and God seemed strangely absent. David trusted God, served God, and worshipped God. But where was God when David needed him most?

Some people think life with God is uniformly joyful, but nothing could be further from the truth. There are moments of both joy and despair. Jesus himself quoted this verse while he hung on the cross: *My God, my God, why have you forsaken me?* (Matthew 27:46).

Jesus' fellowship with the Father had never been interrupted, because Jesus never sinned (Hebrews 4:15). But when he bore the penalty for our sins on the cross, God apparently withdrew all sense of his favor. By quoting the first verse of this Psalm, Jesus drew attention to the whole Psalm, which parallels his crucifixion in many ways.

Psalm 22:7 *All who see me mock me; they hurl insults, shaking their heads.*

And as Jesus hung on the cross, *the chief priests and the teachers of the law mocked him* (Mark 15:31). *Those who passed by hurled insults at him, shaking their heads* (Matthew 27:39). The parallel is undeniable. David and Jesus both experienced public ridicule and mocking.

Psalm 22:13 *Roaring lions that tear their prey open their mouths wide against me.*

David's opponents reminded him of a lion tearing its prey. Likewise, before Jesus was crucified, his flesh was torn from the lashing he received (John 19:1).

Psalm 22:14 *I am poured out like water, and all my bones are out of joint.*

Crucifixion could lead to the dislocation of bones, as victims hung on the cross for hours before they died. The gospels don't mention this explicitly, but it's at least possible that some of Jesus' bones came out of their joints as he hung on the cross.

Psalm 22:15 *My mouth is dried up like a potsherd, and my tongue sticks to the roof of my mouth.*

If you've ever been extremely thirsty you know what this is like. The tongue naturally sticks to the roof of the mouth as if it's seeking moisture. And as Jesus hung on the cross he became parched and said, *I am thirsty* (John 19:28).

Psalm 22:16 *Dogs surround me, a pack of villains encircles me; they pierce my hands and my feet.*

David's enemies were like dogs biting his hands and feet. But the word *pierce* reminds us of the piercing of Jesus' hands and feet when he was nailed to the cross. Even after he rose from the dead Jesus' hands had holes in them (John 20:27). *But he was pierced for our transgressions* (Isaiah 53:5), said Isaiah. And *They will look on me, the one they have pierced* (Zechariah 12:10), predicted Zechariah.

Psalm 22:17 *All my bones are on display; people stare and gloat over me.*

Crucifixion was meant to humiliate, so the victims were normally naked. All Jesus' bones were on display and, as he looked down from the cross, he saw his enemies gloating in triumph. We can imagine his shame and humiliation as his enemies stared at his naked, bony, crucified body.

Psalm 22:18 *They divide my clothes among them and cast lots for my garment.*

The parallel here is extraordinary. *When the soldiers crucified Jesus, they took his clothes, dividing them into four shares, one for each of them, with the undergarment remaining. This garment was seamless, woven in one piece from top to bottom. Let's not tear it, they said to one another. Let's decide by lot who will get it* (John 19:23-24). So they divided Jesus' clothes, and cast lots for his garment, just as David described.

Psalm 22:26 *The poor will eat and be satisfied.*

The Psalm begins somberly, but ends triumphantly. A meal for the poor is provided that will leave them completely satisfied. This reminds us of the meal Jesus gave us the night before his death (Luke 22:17-19). *For whenever you eat this bread and drink this cup, you proclaim the Lord's death* (1 Corinthians 11:26), he said. Jesus gave his body and blood, so we could feast on him through faith.

Psalm 22:27 *All the ends of the earth will remember and turn to the Lord.*

After Jesus rose from the dead, he told his followers to *make disciples of all nations* (Matthew 28:19). They didn't stay in Jerusalem, but spread out far and wide, preaching the gospel. Two thousand years later, people around the world gather each week to remember Christ, and turn to him in faith.

Psalm 22:31 *They will proclaim his righteousness, declaring to a people yet unborn: He has done it!*

This is the last verse of the Psalm and reminds us of Jesus' last words from the cross: *It is finished* (John 19:30). This is a close parallel to *He has done it!* When Jesus died on the cross, his work of redemption was complete.

Psalm 22 sounds like an eyewitness account of the crucifixion of Jesus Christ, so we have to remind ourselves that David wrote this Psalm about a thousand years before Christ was born. By quoting the first verse of this Psalm, Jesus gave us a glimpse of what he was going through on the cross. But, because the Psalm ends well, he was also pointing to the good that would come as a result. This kind of prediction and fulfillment are a clear indication of divine authorship.

For Reflection and Review

- *How did this Psalm help Jesus prepare for his crucifixion?*
- *What can we learn about God from this Psalm?*
- *Why did Christ have to suffer so much?*

Lesson 113

Psalm 23:1 *The Lord is my shepherd, I lack nothing.*

The twenty-third Psalm was written by David about three thousand years ago, and may be the most loved poem in the world. He spent his youth as a shepherd, so he had a good idea of what sheep are like: stubborn, nearsighted, no sense of direction, mostly defenseless, and not very smart. In a flash of insight David realized that people are a lot like sheep, and that even he needed someone to watch over him.

This is surprising because David was one of the most capable people to ever walk the planet. He was a gifted poet and musician, a lethal warrior, and a remarkable leader. If anyone had reason to feel self-sufficient, it should've been David. But David felt dependent on God, and became one of the greatest people who ever lived.

Psalm 23:2-3 *He makes me lie down in green pastures, he leads me beside quiet waters, he refreshes my soul.*

This is the life most people long for: an everyday stroll down to the riverside for a picnic and relaxation. It's a life of leisure, the purpose of which is to know and love our shepherd.

The patriarch Jacob was also a shepherd, and was moving his flocks to another town. The journey was long, but he was patient, and refused to drive the sheep too hard. *If they are driven hard just one day, all the animals will die* (Genesis 33:13), he said. God is a gentle shepherd who knows how to care for his sheep. *Come with me by yourselves to a quiet place and get some rest* (Mark 6:31), said Jesus.

Psalm 23:3 *He guides me along the right paths for his name's sake.*

A good shepherd cared for his sheep by keeping them on the right path. The only way for a sheep to get into serious trouble, in fact, was to get off the path and go his own way. This was a bad idea because, in the eyes of a wolf, sheep are lamb chops waiting to happen.

Years ago I was walking along a path when I was surprised by a large dog. He was tied up to a tree and, when he saw me coming, he actually hid behind it. Then, the moment I was within striking distance, he lunged at me and nearly got my throat. Thankfully his leash ran out, and he fell in a heap. But it's not hard to imagine what might've happened if I was off the path.

Psalm 23:4 *Even though I walk through the darkest valley, I will fear no evil, for you are with me.*

We can imagine David passing through a valley where bandits were known to attack, especially after sunset. David wondered how he'd defend himself, and began to feel afraid. Then he remembered that God was with him, and that nothing bad could happen except what God allowed for his good (Genesis 50:20, Romans 8:28-29). This brought him comfort, courage, and confidence.

On our journey to heaven we may walk through valleys of fear, depression, rejection, guilt, addiction, unemployment, confusion, sickness, poverty, pain, and other effects of living in a sin-cursed world. But God is with us in every valley, and is leading us to a place where there'll be no more *death or mourning or crying or pain* (Revelation 21:4). *Never will I leave you; never will I forsake you* (Hebrews 13:5).

Psalm 23:4b *. . . your rod and your staff, they comfort me.*

David was familiar with the rod and staff, which he used to coral his sheep and comfort them. They were an extension of his touch, to remind the sheep of his presence.

A shepherd was watching his flock in a place that was torn by war. Whenever a shot rang out the sheep would tremble uncontrollably. Then he'd reach out his staff and touch each one as if to say, *It's okay. Don't be afraid. I am here for you.* Likewise, we can comfort others in distress by saying, *It's okay. Don't be afraid. God is here for you.*

Psalm 23:5 *You prepare a table before me in the presence of my enemies. You anoint my head with oil; my cup overflows.*

Notice the wonderful change of imagery. David's no longer a wandering sheep, but a guest of honor at a heavenly banquet. In that culture, a good host would welcome his guests by filling their cups and anointing their foreheads with oil.

Likewise, the Bible speaks of a banquet at the end of the age, where God himself will be the host, and we'll be his guests (Isaiah 25:6). He will fill our cups, anoint our heads and say, *Welcome home my child.*

But as someone capable of both adultery and murder, David seems optimistic about his reception at the heavenly banquet. I'd be happy to slip in quietly and take a place near the back. And, if there was a place for the most unworthy, I'd be happy to sit there. But that's not what the Bible teaches.

[Y]ou will receive a rich welcome into the eternal kingdom of our Lord and Savior Jesus Christ (2 Peter 1:11), wrote Peter. When you walk through heaven's door there'll be shouts of praise to God for his amazing grace, and for the blood of Christ which makes the foulest clean. God himself will be your host, filling your cup, anointing your head, and rejoicing at your arrival.

Psalm 23:6 *Surely your goodness and love will follow me all the days of my life, and I will dwell in the house of the Lord forever.*

David lived in a palace, but was looking forward God's house. My wife and I used to look at new home magazines and discovered we have very similar taste. We both like anything over two million dollars. But can you imagine God's house?

My Father's house has many rooms; if that were not so, would I have told you that I am going there to prepare a place for you? And if I go and prepare a place for you, I will come back and take you to be with me that you also may be where I am (John 14:2-3), said Jesus.

Shepherd's who take their sheep into the high country for the summer say the sheep anticipate going home in the fall. As they go back down the mountain, their excitement grows the closer they get to their home. Our excitement should also grow the closer we get to our Father's house.

A young lady was hospitalized for depression. She never took her eyes off ground and rarely spoke word. Then, one day, she was assigned a new doctor with an unusual last name. He introduced himself as *Dr. Heaven*. That was his real name, and it made her think of the age to come. She began taking her eyes off her problems, and putting them on God. Within five weeks she was released from the hospital and went on to become a successful teacher. Regardless what happens on earth, we'll dwell in the house of the Lord forever.

For Reflection and Review

- *What are some ways that people like sheep?*
- *How can the dark valleys of life strengthen our faith?*
- *What should we expect when we arrive in heaven?*

Lesson 114

Psalm 25:11 *For the sake of your name, Lord, forgive my iniquity, though it is great.*

David didn't request forgiveness because God is forgiving, loving, or merciful but *For the sake of [his] name*. This idea appears more than once in the Bible: *forgive our sins for your name's sake* (Psalm 79:9), and, *your sins have been forgiven on account of his name* (1 John 2:12), wrote John.

God's name is glorified by forgiving our sins because it enhances his reputation as the God who forgives. The greater our sins, in fact, the more God is glorified by forgiving them. It's one thing to forgive the sins of gossip and unkindness, but quite another to forgive the sins of murder, rape, and blasphemy.

But you are a forgiving God, gracious and compassionate, slow to anger and abounding in love (Nehemiah 9:17), said the Levites. *The Lord our God is merciful and forgiving, even though we have rebelled against him* (Daniel 9:9), wrote Daniel. God wants a reputation for forgiveness, so he's willing to forgive anyone for anything, if they come to him through faith in Jesus Christ (1 John 1:9).

If God only forgave little sins, or few sins, he couldn't be known as exceptionally forgiving. Everyone on earth forgives sins that are little or few. But if God forgives the worst possible repeat offenders, who believe in Jesus Christ, then he deserves a reputation as the God who forgives sinners. Once we've done our worst, and there's no other reason for God to forgive, we should pray like David: *For the sake of your name, Lord, forgive my iniquity, though it is great.*

Psalm 27:8 *My heart says of you, Seek his face! Your face, Lord, I will seek.*

David wasn't content to go through religious motions; he wanted to encounter God. He wanted to be so close to God that it was like seeing his face. Think of your mother's face, or your father's face, or your spouse's face. We seldom look at a person's face for long unless we're committed to them.

Here's a game you can play with children: Put some pennies in your hand and make a fist. Let them pry your fingers open, one by one, so they can take the pennies and run away. It's a wonderful game for children, but that's how some people pray. They don't seek God for himself, but for what he has in his hand. It's not wrong to pray for our needs, but we should also seek his face. Our heart's real desire isn't what we can get from God, but for more of God himself.

Psalm 29:11 *[T]he Lord blesses his people with peace.*

The biblical idea of peace is broader than the absence of conflict. It's more like *things as they're supposed to be*. Imagine things as they're supposed to be in your body. Then imagine things as they're supposed to be in your heart. Then imagine things as they're supposed to be in your mind, at home, at work, and at church. Then imagine things as they're supposed to be throughout the whole world because, one day, the peace of God will permeate every molecule of his creation. Sin has made a mess of things, but Christ is making it right again. Even now, he *blesses his people with peace*.

Psalm 31:19 *How abundant are the good things that you have stored up for those who fear you.*

For many years David lived with little, but later he received an abundance of things that God had stored up for him: power, privilege, health, wealth, friends, family, and more. David wasn't unique in this way. God is storing up things for everyone who fears him, and he wants us to be aware of it.

When my children were small their grandmother stored up things under her bed for them. Some were for their birthdays, some were for Christmas, and some were just for fun. They weren't allowed to look under the bed, but I think they used to dream of all that was being stored up for them—and so should we. Some of our hearts' desires have been planted by God because he plans to fulfill them eventually. It may happen suddenly, gradually, or not until eternity. But the gifts of God will come, and they will be abundant.

Psalm 32:5 *Then I acknowledged my sin to you and did not cover up my iniquity. I said, I will confess my transgressions to the Lord. And you forgave the guilt of my sin.*

David didn't identify the sin he committed, but he acknowledged the difficulty of coming to repentance. Instead of confessing his sin, and requesting forgiveness, he wanted to ignore the fact that he did something wrong. He may've justified his sin, or put it out of his mind, but he couldn't go forward with God until he owned up to it. Then he confessed his sin and God forgave him.

A woman took part in a bank robbery in which an officer was shot and killed. She changed her identity and avoided arrest for twenty-three years. But her first thought every morning, and her last at night, was of the man who was killed. She took a class on depression but found no relief. So, after twenty-three years, she turned herself in to authorities. *I have had to examine my conscience and accept any responsibility I have*, she said.

If our conscience is working properly we'll have feelings of guilt whenever we break God's law. These aren't to make us miserable the rest of our lives, but to help us to turn ourselves in to God. As soon as we confess, God will forgive. Then our feelings of guilt will gradually subside. There's no other way to go forward with God.

Psalm 34:3 *Glorify the Lord with me; let us exalt his name together.*

David wasn't content to be a solitary worshipper, but wanted others to join him. He was so in love with God, and so concerned for God's glory, that he wanted to enlarge the circle of praise as far as he could. This should be the attitude of every church, and every true believer in Jesus Christ. Christianity isn't a solitary religion, but one that gathers corporately and invites others to glorify the Lord with us.

A nobleman built a church for his village but didn't include any lights. Instead, he gave each family lamp and reminded them that, whenever they missed church, it would be a little darker. Have you noticed when someone you know isn't in church, it seems a little darker? We ought to invite others to worship God, and we ought to go ourselves.

Psalm 34:8 *Taste and see that the Lord is good.*

David's relationship with God was so delicious, he wanted others to taste for themselves. As the tongue tastes food, we can experience God by drawing near to him. One of my favorite foods is watermelon, and I believe it's proof that God is good, because only a good God would invent something that delicious! But God and watermelon also have this in common: the closer you get to the heart, the better they are. *Taste and see that the Lord is good.*

Psalm 36:8 *. . . you give [us] drink from your river of delights.*

A college I attended had a river nearby, where we liked to swim in the spring. There was a tree near the bank, with a rope-swing attached. So we'd swing over the river, flip in the air, and splash down in the water. It was, to us, a river of pure delight.

But this is only a foretaste of what's ahead. In the last chapter of God's word we read of *the river of the water of life, as clear as crystal, flowing from the throne of God* (Revelation 22:1). In glorified bodies we'll swing and flip and swim and laugh to our hearts content. Whatever is delightful in this age, is only a foretaste of what's to come.

For Reflection and Review

- *Why does God like to forgive?*
- *What does it mean to seek God's face?*
- *Why is hard to confess our sins?*

Lesson 115

Psalm 51:1 *Have mercy on me, O God, according to your unfailing love; according to your great compassion blot out my transgressions.*

After committing adultery with Bathsheba, and having her husband killed, David's initial impulse was not to ask for mercy, but to run away from God. So God sent the prophet Nathan to restore him. Then David wrote this remarkable Psalm of repentance, which begins with a plea for mercy. David didn't shift the blame for his behavior, like Adam and Eve. Nor did he blame God for making him a sexual being, or Bathsheba for bathing in plain sight. He simply begged for mercy.

We do not make requests of you because we are righteous, but because of your great mercy (Daniel 9:18) wrote Daniel. *You do not stay angry forever but delight to show mercy* (Micah 7:18), wrote Micah. And *The Lord is full of compassion and mercy* (James 5:11), wrote James. Serious sinners need to know that God is the most merciful being in the universe, even to the worst of us.

Psalm 51:2 *Wash away all my iniquity and cleanse me from my sin.*

Sin is so unnatural that, if our conscience is working properly, we'll feel dirty whenever we do wrong. We can bathe ourselves in water, and use the strongest soap, but the sense of being defiled won't go away until we're cleansed by God.

Banks that are robbed may include permanent dye with the money, so when the crooks reach for the cash their hands are instantly marked. They can use every kind of detergent, and scrub until they're raw, but the dye won't come off. Their guilt is clear for everyone to see.

Apart from the cleansing work of Christ, every sin we ever commit leaves a permanent stain on our soul. They can't be removed by time, regret, remorse, sacrifice, service, or anything other than the blood of Christ. But *the blood of Jesus . . . purifies us from all sin* (1 John 1:7), wrote John.

Psalm 51:3 *I know my transgressions, and my sin is always before me.*

Whenever David looked in the mirror, he saw an adulterous murderer looking back at him. He was a very important person, lived in a beautiful home, and had accomplished many things—but he didn't like himself. And people can't be happy unless they're happy with themselves.

Many have done such terrible things, they wish they'd never been born. Some have even killed themselves due to the pain of their guilt. But the purpose of guilt isn't to make us hate ourselves forever; it's to lead us to the one who can wash and forgive us, and give us a glorious future.

Psalm 51:4 *Against you, you only, have I sinned and done what is evil in your sight.*

David sinned against Bathsheba in the act of adultery, and against her husband by arranging his death. But he claimed to sin primarily against God. Some people think sin is okay, if no one gets hurt, but that never happens. God is always hurt. This is why forgiveness is never complete until we're forgiven by God. We should ask forgiveness from those we've offended but, even if the whole world forgives us, we're never completely forgiven until we're forgiven by God.

Psalm 51:5 *Surely I was sinful at birth, sinful from the time my mother conceived me.*

As David reflected on his life, he couldn't recall a time when he wasn't a sinner. He concluded that his sinfulness began the moment he was conceived. This is true for everyone because we're all descendants of Adam and Eve—the first human sinners. Their righteous natures were corrupted by sin, and passed down to their children. Now, *The heart is deceitful above all things and beyond cure* (Jeremiah 17:9), wrote Jeremiah.

It's so bad, in fact, that we're not only sinners by nature, but also by choice. Not everyone is inclined toward music, or athletics, but we're all inclined toward sin. It's such a part of our nature that we not only enjoy it, but do it with skill. In this regard, we have more in common with the devil than we do with Jesus Christ. But our Savior took our penalty so we could be forgiven.

Psalm 51:7 *Cleanse me with hyssop, and I will be clean; wash me, and I will be whiter than snow.*

Hyssop is a small plant that could be dipped in water, and used in a cleansing ceremony (Numbers 19:17-19). David was convinced that if God would cleanse him, he'd be whiter than snow. The words *Cleanse me*, in fact, can also be translated *Un-sin me* (NIV Study Bible). God's forgiveness is so complete, it's like we never even sinned.

David learned that murder is a difficult thing to get over, and those who abort their babies often struggle terribly. But God is so good that he not only wants to forgive us, but longs to help us recover. That is why he offers to un-sin us.

Psalm 51:13 *Then I will teach transgressors your ways, so that sinners will turn back to you.*

After asking God to forgive him, David wondered if anything good could come from his sin. Then he recalled that other people also struggle with sin and, if he could find his way back to God, he could help others do the same. By writing this Psalm, David has helped countless sinners come back to God.

David's sin strangely comforts us because if God can forgive David, then he can forgive us. God used David's sin to demonstrate the extent of his forgiveness, so that other sinners wouldn't lose heart. God is willing to forgive our sin, and even to use it for good somehow.

For Reflection and Review

- *Why do we feel dirty when we sin?*
- *Why does sin hurt God?*
- *How did God use David's sin for good?*

Lesson 116

Psalm 55:22 *Cast your cares on the Lord and he will sustain you.*

Life isn't carefree, for most people, very long. We're concerned about our money, our marriage, our health, our kids, our jobs, our parents, the economy, aging, war, death and more. Too many cares weigh us down, and will break us, if we're not careful.

A man was buying plywood, at a home improvement store, and stacking it on the roof of his car. There was no problem, at first, and the car seemed to handle it fine. But fifty sheets later his roof caved in, and his car was completely destroyed. One at a time, our problems seem quite manageable. But, stacked high enough, they'll crush us. Casting our cares on the Lord isn't just good advice, it may be the only way to survive.

Psalm 56:3 *When I am afraid, I put my trust in you.*

David's life was in serious danger as he fled from his enemies. If they had their way, his life would soon be over. David was naturally afraid, but refused to let his fear overwhelm him. Instead, he put his trust in God.

Trusting God is easy when the bills are paid, the job is secure, and your health is holding up. But we know from Scripture, and experience, that terrible things happen to God's holy people sometimes. Trusting God isn't believing nothing bad will ever happen, but that God is always in control, and is up to something good (Romans 8:28).

Imagine a veterinarian who wants to free a bear caught in a trap. First he has to shoot it with a tranquilizer, which the bear perceives as an attack. But by thrashing around, the bear only makes things worse. If the bear understood the veterinarian was trying to do it good, it could relax (Peter Kreeft, slightly revised). That's what David did whenever he was afraid. That's what it means to trust.

Psalm 65:3 *When we were overwhelmed by sins, you forgave our transgressions.*

Everyone sins every day, but some days are worth than others. If the world, the flesh, and the devil conspire, we can find ourselves doing things we never thought we'd do.

I swam in the ocean, years ago, and tried to body surf. But instead of riding on top of the wave, it dragged me along the bottom. I was absolutely powerless, and came up a bloody mess.

Overwhelming sin is like that. It'll drag us down and bloody our lives severely. But God's answer to overwhelming sin is overwhelming forgiveness. *When we were overwhelmed by sins, you forgave our transgressions.* What a wonderful God he is!

Psalm 69:14 *Rescue me from the mire, do not let me sink.*

As David faced the pressures of life, he felt like he was in quicksand. If God didn't rescue him, he would surely die. It's a situation many have faced before and since.

Two men were walking an Alaskan shoreline, when one stepped into quicksand. A helicopter was sent to lift him out, but the pain was so intense they had to stop. Soon he was up to his armpits, and the tide was coming in, so they tried again and, this time, it worked. Whether our quicksand is real, or metaphorical, we can call to God for help. *Our God is a God who saves; from the Sovereign Lord comes escape from death* (Psalm 68:20), wrote David.

Psalm 73:25 *Whom have I in heaven but you? And earth has nothing I desire besides you.*

The Psalmist was disappointed when he saw the prosperity of the wicked, compared to the little that was given to him (Psalm 73:3). But when he thought about God, he felt so rich there was nothing on earth that he even desired. God became his greatest treasure and, therefore, his greatest pleasure.

A minister was having lunch with a wealthy man who described himself as the most miserable person on earth. *I have everything I need to be happy but I'm miserable as hell*, he said. Later he spoke to an elderly Christian man who lost his wife and was caring for his ailing sister. *I don't have two nickels to rub together, but I'm the happiest person I know*, he said. No one in the Bible was happy all the time, but if there's a secret to happiness it could be this: *Delight yourself in God, for he gives or withholds the ability to enjoy everything else.*

Psalm 73:26 *My flesh and my heart may fail, but God is the strength of my heart and my portion forever.*

Heaven's greatest joy isn't what it contains, but the one to whom it belongs. We'll delight ourselves in everything else, but our greatest joy will be God.

A prince disguised himself, and went on a journey, to find a bride who'd love him for who he was. But his disguise was so convincing that most of the young ladies wanted nothing to do with him. Then, at last, he found a bride who loved him deeply and sincerely. When they returned to his kingdom, she was amazed by his power, privilege, and possessions—which now belonged to her as well. Whoever loves Christ for his own sake, will have everything else thrown in. But Christ himself is our *portion forever*.

For Reflection and Review

- *How does God help us with our fears?*
- *Why are many believers miserable?*
- *How can we strengthen our view of heaven?*

Lesson 117

Psalm 78:4 *[We] will tell the next generation the praiseworthy deeds of the Lord.*

The person who wrote this had no idea how many generations he'd influence with his advice. Three thousand years later, God is stilling using his words to inspire parents to pass down their faith to the next generation.

This is what God had in mind when he chose Abraham to be the father of Israel. *For I have chosen him so that he will direct his children and his household after him to keep the way of the Lord* (Genesis 18:19), said God. Abraham taught Isaac, Isaac taught Jacob, Jacob taught his children, and so forth. Over time, a nation of believers was formed.

Likewise, Moses taught the Israelites to pass down the words of God to their children. *[Talk] about them when you sit at home and when you walk along the road, when you lie down and when you get up* (Deuteronomy 11:19), he said. *Start children off on the way they should go, and even when they are old they will not turn from it* (Proverbs 22:6), says Proverbs.

My dear wife is a third generation believer. Her Grandparents came to Christ shortly after they were married, and raised their children in the faith. Then my wife's parents raised their children in the faith, and we raised our children in the faith. Today there are four generations of Christians who trace their heritage to one set of godly grandparents who've gone to be with the Lord.

When our children were small, we simply read a chapter of the Bible together almost every day. Most of the time they didn't know what it meant, but we finished the whole Bible in about four years. Then we started over. When they were in their teens I allowed them to read on their own, but we got together once a week to discuss what they had learned.

The reason I did this was not only to teach my children, but to teach them how to teach their children. By God's grace there could be several generations who arrive in heaven because we told *the next generation the praiseworthy deeds of the Lord*.

Psalm 90:12 *Teach us to number our days, that we may gain a heart of wisdom.*

Most tombstones have a date-of-birth and a date-of-death, separated by a little dash. A million years from now, all that will matter is what we did with our dash. If you live to be ninety years old, you'll spend over thirty-two thousand days doing something. You can spend those days on yourself, or on the Lord, but how you spend your days is how you spend your life.

No one knows when their life will end (Ecclesiastes 9:12), but if you want a hopeful estimate, subtract your age from ninety and multiply that by three hundred sixty-five. Then purchase that many marbles and put them into a container. Removing a marble a day will help you keep track of how many days you might have left. But there are no guarantees.

When I was a kid, I jumped belly first into an large inner tube and got wedged in the middle. My face was against the rubber and I couldn't move or breathe. My friends were swimming nearby, and I could hear them playing, but they didn't know I was dying. I still remember thinking, *I didn't expect to die today; I'm only nine years old!* Somehow I wiggled free, but I learned the end is always near. *Only this life will soon be past; only what's done for Christ will last.*

Psalm 100:3 *Know that the Lord is God. It is he who made us, and we are his.*

The first duty of creatures is to find their Maker and obey him. We didn't make ourselves, and don't belong to ourselves. We were made by God and, therefore, *we are his*. Turning away from God is nothing short of criminal.

Imagine building the house of your dreams, on a perfect piece of property. Imagine a brick exterior, hardwood floors, a finished garage, and more. But the day you planned to move in, you found the door was locked, and someone else was living there. That's how God feels when we take the life he made for himself and lock him out. Repentance is giving our lives back to God and letting him live within us, not as a visitor but as the rightful owner (1 Corinthians 6:19-20). Our life doesn't belong to us; it belongs to our Maker.

For Reflection and Review

- *How can we pass down faith to our children.*
- *How can we make every day count for God?*
- *Why does God have the right to govern our lives?*

Lesson 118

Psalm 103:10 *[H]e he does not treat us as our sins deserve or repay us according to our iniquities.*

A nomadic youth got into a fight with his friend, and hit him so hard that he killed him. The law of the land was *life for a life*, so the boy was in serious trouble. But instead of running away, he ran a day and a half back to the tribal chief. He admitted his crime, and begged the chief to protect him. After some consideration, the chief agreed.

But when boys' accusers arrived, they told the chief something he didn't know: the boy who was killed was the chief's only son. The chief was visibly shaken, but after a moment to think he said, *Then the one who killed my son will become my son, and all I have will be his.*

This, of course, is nothing less than gospel. God sent his Son into the world and we killed him. But if we return to God, he'll forgive our sins, and all he has will be ours.

Psalm 103:11 *For as high as the heavens are above the earth, so great is his love for those who fear him.*

We can imagine David lying under a starry sky, amazed at the expanse above him. He may've been in awe at the power of God, but that's not what gripped his heart. What moved him deeply was the truth that God's love for him was greater than the expanse above him.

This is rather surprising because David did many things to make himself unlovely to God. He was a sinner, like everyone else, and there was nothing of which he wasn't capable. Yet, somehow, he came into a special relationship with God, and knew he was the object of infinite love.

If you had a spaceship that could travel the speed of light, you'd pass the moon in just over a second. About eight and a half minutes later you'd pass the sun. To get to the next galaxy would take twenty-five thousand years, and to get to the edge of the universe would take ninety-three billion years. Imagine God stretching out his hands from one end of the universe to the other. That's how much he loves us.

Psalm 103:12 *[A]s far as the east is from the west, so far has he removed our transgressions from us.*

Whenever David thought about God he was reminded of his sin, because God is against sin. But many years later Christ would go to the cross, so we could be saved through him (John 3:16). His work was so effective that David could say in advance, *as far as the east is from the west, so far has he removed our transgressions from us.*

The distance from the North Pole to the South Pole is over twelve thousand miles, but the distance from east to west is harder to measure because there aren't any poles. David was saying that God has removed our sins completely and forever—*as far as the east is from the west.*

Psalm 104:5 *He set the earth on its foundations; it can never be moved.*

For many years this verse was used to support the idea that the sun revolves around the earth. If the earth *can never be moved*, then it can't revolve around the sun. When science showed the earth does, in fact, revolve around the sun some people lost their confidence in the Bible.

But the Psalmist wasn't making a scientific argument for an earth-centered universe. He was saying poetically that God made the world a stable place in which to live. By overstating what the Bible teaches, the church embarrassed itself and gave the world a reason to doubt God's word.

If God is the author of nature and Scripture, they cannot contradict each other. When they appear to contradict, we are misunderstanding nature, Scripture, or both. Contradictory opinions don't need to be settled at once, but can be held in tension until more information is becomes available.

We can think of nature and Scripture as two books from the same author, both requiring interpretation. With time our knowledge of each continues to improve. Christians must be careful not to make the Bible say what it doesn't, or yield to scientific theories that oppose it. Scientific theories come and go, *but the word of our God endures forever* (Isaiah 40:8), wrote Isaiah.

Psalm 106:1 *Give thanks to the Lord, for he is good; his love endures forever.*

Whenever you feel depressed, make a list of one hundred things for which you can be thankful. If you slept inside, on a bed, with a pillow and a blanket, that's four. If you used a toothbrush, toothpaste, soap, and shampoo, that's eight. If you had coffee with sugar and cream in your favorite mug, that's twelve. The more we're thankful for what we have, the less we'll be bothered by what we don't have.

A pastor went to a leper colony where he led a worship service and took song requests. One lady raised a fingerless hand and said, *Let's sing Count your many blessings. Count them one by one. Count your many blessings and see what God has done.* Even with a fingerless hand we can *Give thanks to the Lord, for he is good; his love endures forever.*

For Reflection and Review

- *Why is it important to know God loves us?*
- *Why is it important to know we're forgiven?*
- *Why do the Bible and science seem to disagree sometimes?*

Lesson 119

Psalm 116:14 *I will fulfill my vows to the Lord in the presence of all his people.*

Making and fulfilling vows was an important expression of faith in the Old Testament. Jacob said, *If God will be with me and will watch over me on this journey I am taking and will give me food to eat and clothes to wear so that I return safely to my father's household, then the Lord will be my God . . . and of all that you give me I will give you a tenth* (Genesis 28:20-22).

And when Hannah wanted a baby she said, *Lord Almighty, if you will only look on your servant's misery and remember me, and not forget your servant but give her a son, then I will give him to the Lord for all the days of his life* (1 Samuel 1:11).

But most people are better at making vows than keeping them. Imagine a man lost in the woods who prayed, *Lord, if you save me, I'll give you my life.* Then he heard children playing and, by walking in their direction, found his way out. Later he wondered if God really answered his prayer, or if it was just a coincidence. Since he wasn't sure, he decided the vow wasn't binding, and went on living as before.

It is better not to make a vow than to make one and not fulfill it (Ecclesiastes 5:5), wrote Solomon. Oaths and vows were so abused, in fact, that they're never taught in the New Testament as an expression of Christian faith. They're not forbidden, but they're not encouraged either.

Shortly after I believed, a minister encouraged me to vow that I'd read four chapters of the Bible a day. I wanted to please my heavenly Father, so I made the vow and kept it—for about a week. If I hadn't made the vow I wouldn't have been guilty of sin, but since I made the vow I was.

Breaking a vow is a serious sin, but it's handled like every other sin. *If we confess our sins, he is faithful and just and will forgive us our sins and purify us from all unrighteousness* (1 John 1:9), wrote John. It's not wrong to tell God what you'd like to do for him but, because of human weakness, it's better not to vow.

*****

Psalm 119:1 *Blessed are those whose ways are blameless, who walk according to the law of the Lord.*

This is the first verse of the longest chapter of the Bible, which is a celebration of God's word. It begins with the word *blessed*, which occurs over two hundred times in the Bible, and refers to the happiness of those who belong to God and follow his ways. The ways of God aren't always easy, but they're always best for us, and result in our greatest happiness. Human sorrow is the result of disobeying God, not the result of obeying him.

Psalm 119:11 *I have hidden your word in my heart that I might not sin against you.*

Few things are more helpful to combating sin than committing God's word to memory. Satan wanted Jesus to turn stones into bread but Jesus replied, *It is written: Man shall not live on bread alone, but on every word that comes from the mouth of God* (Matthew 4:4). Then Satan urged him to throw himself off the temple but Jesus replied, *It is also written: Do not put the Lord your God to the test* (Matthew 4:7). Then Satan urged Jesus to worship him, but Jesus replied, *Away from me, Satan! For it is written: Worship the Lord your God, and serve him only* (Matthew 4:10).

Three times Jesus was tempted by the Devil, and three times Jesus quoted God's word. By committing God's word to memory, we're able to use it against Satan whenever we're tempted to sin.

Psalm 119:14 *I rejoice in following your statutes as one rejoices in great riches.*

The Bible is a treasure to those who know its worth. It's like a pile of money that can never be exhausted. The better we understand the Bible, the wealthier we'll feel.

An archaeologist uncovered five million dollars worth of jewelry from the fifteenth century, eighteen inches beneath a cottage floor. The owners never worried about the economy, medical bills, or having enough to eat because they were so rich.

Eventually they died, and the cottage was occupied by others for hundreds of years. Many couples sat at the kitchen table, wondering how to pay their bills, while a fortune lay just beneath their feet. Whoever has a Bible but doesn't read it is sitting on buried treasure. Whoever reads it often will rejoice in all it contains.

Psalm 119:16 *I will not neglect your word.*

Like everyone else, the writer had commitments that competed with his desire to study God's word. Instead of rising early, and staying up late, he was probably tempted to get extra sleep. But he resolved not to neglect God's word, regardless of other commitments.

If a pastor stood up in church and started tearing out pages of the Bible many people would be upset. But unless we study every page of the Bible we may as well tear it out. Everyone who believes the Bible should be able to say with conviction, *I will not neglect your word.*

For Reflection and Review

- *What are some benefits of memorizing Scripture?*
- *How does the Bible enrich our lives?*
- *Why do we often neglect God's word?*

Lesson 120

Psalm 119:18 *Open my eyes that I may see wonderful things in your law.*

It's impossible to understand the teaching of the Bible adequately without divine assistance. When Jesus spoke of his approaching death and resurrection, for example, *The disciples did not understand any of this. Its meaning was hidden from them, and they did not know what he was talking about* (Luke 18:34). But after he rose from the dead, Jesus *opened their minds so they could understand the Scriptures* (Luke 24:45).

My family and I studied a drawing, years ago, that left me unsettled. To me it looked like a random assortment of dots, colors, and lines. But they saw something more. There was a clear and distinct image which they all assured me was there. But even though I studied the drawing carefully, for another twenty minutes, I couldn't see what they saw. Likewise, we can study the Bible for hours, and get very little out of it. But with the help of the Spirit we may be surprised how much there is to see. *Open my eyes that I may see wonderful things in your law.*

Psalm 119:20 *My soul is consumed with longing for your laws at all times.*

The writer had a consuming appetite for God's word. No matter how much he read or studied, he always wanted more. This is a sign of spiritual health. *Like newborn babies, crave pure spiritual milk, so that by it you may grow up in your salvation* (1 Peter 2:2), wrote Peter. A baby who doesn't crave milk isn't healthy. And a Christian who doesn't crave God's word isn't healthy either. The moment we lose our appetite for God's word, we become spiritually weak.

Psalm 119:24 *Your statutes are my delight; they are my counselors.*

Whenever we don't know what to do, we need someone to counsel us. Friends are often helpful, but there may be times we need a professional. Legal counselors can help with a lawsuit; financial counselors can help with our money; and family counselors can help us get along. Many pay hundreds of dollars to speak with a counselor. How much would you pay for an hour with God?

Your Maker understands you better than you understand yourself, and his counsel is free. Rejecting his word often leads to problems, and obeying his word often leads to peace. Many who read and follow the Bible find it more helpful than many counselors. A Bible that's coming apart, usually belongs to someone who isn't.

Psalm 119:34 *Give me understanding, so that I may keep your law and obey it with all my heart.*

The writer is familiar with God's word, but finds himself in need of more understanding. This is true for every student of the Bible—even the Apostle Peter. Speaking of Paul he said, *His letters contain some things that are hard to understand* (2 Peter 3:16). With God's help, however, the Bible can be understood.

Those who practice an instrument fifteen minutes a day will eventually learn the instrument. They won't become masters, but they'll learn how to play. And those who read a chapter of the Bible almost every day will eventually learn the Bible. If done repeatedly, they'll read it more than a dozen times in the course of an average life. The most important things aren't always easy, but they're always worth the effort.

Psalm 119:60 *I will hasten and not delay to obey your commands.*

People can deceive themselves into thinking they're obedient, because they plan to obey God eventually. They plan to quit lying and cheating in the future, so they think they're obedient now. But delayed obedience is nothing more than disobedience. If you tell your child to do something, and they wait ten minutes to do it, they've been disobedient for ten minutes. The writer understood this so he resolved to *hasten and not delay* to obey God's commands.

Psalm 119:67 *Before I was afflicted I went astray, but now I obey your word.*

The writer didn't identify his affliction, but it may've been a sickness. Before his affliction he was confident enough to stray from God. But his suffering taught him the importance of obeying God at all times. Not all suffering is the direct result of disobedience, but it should remind us of our frailty and dependence on God. When suffering brings us closer to God we'll see it as a blessing. That's why the Psalmist said elsewhere, *in faithfulness you have afflicted me* (Psalm 119:75).

Psalm 119:102 *I have not departed from your laws, for you yourself have taught me.*

One lady started reading a new book but didn't finish because she found it boring. Then she met the author and fell in love with him. When she started reading his book again, she found it full of things that taught her more about the one she loved. That's how it is with the Bible.

For Reflection and Review

- *Has God ever helped you understand his word?*
- *How can we understand God's word better?*
- *Have you ever delayed obeying God?*

Lesson 121

Psalm 119:105 *Your word is a lamp for my feet, a light on my path.*

Electric lights didn't exist when the Bible was written, so darkness was taken seriously. If you were out on a cloudless night, and didn't have an oil lamp, you could be lost until morning. Oil lamps weren't very bright, but provided enough light to take the next step. That's what the Bible does for us, until we're safely home. It's a lamp for our feet, and a light for our path.

Psalm 119:164 *Seven times a day I praise you for your righteous laws.*

The writer was so in love with God's word that he wanted to praise him seven times a day for it. Perhaps he praised God when he got up, on his way to work, during lunch, on his way home, at dinner, before he went to bed, and whenever he woke up at night.

Praising God is a wonderful way to overcome sorrow and make us thankful. Nothing is more effective at banishing gloom than habitual praise. The more we learn to praise the Lord, the more we'll enjoy him. And, the more we enjoy him, the more we'll enjoy our lives.

Psalm 119:176 *I have strayed like a lost sheep. Seek your servant, for I have not forgotten your commands.*

This is a shocking conclusion to the longest chapter in the Bible, especially from someone who loved God and was spiritually mature. As much as the writer studied the Bible, and tried to follow it, he found himself wandering away from God. This side of heaven there will always be a part of us that wants to stray. *What a wretched man I am!* (Romans 7:24), wrote Paul.

Thankfully, the good shepherd will not forsake us even when we wander. He'll come looking for us, and bring us back to his fold (Matthew 18:12-14). He's the one who saves us, and also the one who keeps us (John 10:28).

*****

Psalm 130:5 *I wait for the Lord, my whole being waits.*

Wait for the Lord; be strong and take heart and wait for the Lord (Psalm 27:14), wrote David. *I wait for the Lord more than watchmen wait for the morning* (Psalm 130:6), wrote the Psalmist. And, *Blessed are all who wait for him!* (Isaiah 30:18), wrote Isaiah.

One of the scariest moments in a trapeze act is when the flyer lets go of his trapeze, and waits for the catcher to catch him. Both agree the flyer must never try to catch the catcher, but must wait for the catcher to catch the flyer. That's how it is with God sometimes. Waiting isn't easy, but it's how we show our faith. *Blessed are all who wait for him!*

Psalm 131:2 *I am like a weaned child with its mother; like a weaned child I am content.*

Weaning occurred around age three, and was a rite of passage from infancy to childhood. It also marked a change in relationship between a child and their mother. Before they're weaned, children love their mother for who she is, but also for what they receive from her. After weaning, children love their mother without receiving her breast.

This is how David saw himself with God. He was less concerned with what he received from God than simply to be with him. This is a mark of spiritual growth. David continued to make requests, but was also content to simply be in God's presence. He was like a weaned child sitting with their mother.

Psalm 138:7 *Though I walk in the midst of trouble, you preserve my life.*

David avoided sword and spear countless times over the course of his life. He must've been surprised, on occasion, to find he was still alive. As he thought about this, he gave credit to God. *Our God is a God who saves; from the Sovereign Lord comes escape from death* (Psalm 68:20), he wrote.

A lady was cleaning the balcony of her ninth floor apartment when she toppled over the railing. She fell a hundred feet, but landed in a canopy above the entry. A young man wasn't wearing his seatbelt when his car flipped over. He was catapulted into the air, and landed in some power lines. But they were insulated, so he wasn't electrocuted, and he was later rescued without injury. God is the giver of life, and the one who preserves it. Every day we should give him a reason for keeping us alive.

Psalm 139:20 *They speak of you with evil intent; your adversaries misuse your name.*

Throughout the Psalms, God's people sing praises to his name (Psalm 7:17), declare his name (Psalm 22:22), trust in his name (Psalm 33:21), exalt his name (Psalm 34:3), hope in his name (Psalm 52:9), fear his name (Psalm 61:5), love his name (Psalm 69:36), call on his name (Psalm 80:18), glorify his name (Psalm 86:12), rejoice in his name (Psalm 89:16) and extol his name (Psalm 145:2). It's characteristic of the wicked, however, to *misuse* God's name.

You shall not misuse the name of the Lord your God, for the Lord will not hold anyone guiltless who misuses his name (Exodus 20:7), said God. Ordinary profanity is a terrible sin (Ephesians 4:19), but it's immeasurably worse to misuse God's name. And *anyone who blasphemes the name of the Lord is to be put to death* (Leviticus 24:16), said God. This should no longer be enforced (Hebrews 8:13), but it reveals the seriousness of misusing God's name.

God's name should never be used as an exclamation, a casual expression, and certainly not as a curse. God's name should only be used with the highest reverence, as when we are speaking directly to him. To misuse God's name in anyway puts us in league with his enemies—*your adversaries misuse your name.*

For Reflection and Review

- *Why should believers praise God often?*
- *Why do even good Christians wander from God sometimes?*
- *Why is misusing God's name such a serious sin?*

Lesson 122

Proverbs 1:1 *The proverbs of Solomon son of David, king of Israel.*

Solomon was the king of Israel in the tenth century BC, and led the nation to the height of its glory. His intellect was nothing short of remarkable. *God gave Solomon wisdom and very great insight, and a breadth of understanding as measureless as the sand on the seashore. . . . He spoke three thousand proverbs and his songs numbered a thousand and five.*

He spoke about plant life, from the cedar of Lebanon to the hyssop that grows out of walls. He also spoke about animals and birds, reptiles and fish. From all nations people came to listen to Solomon's wisdom (1 Kings 4:29-34). And we also have the privilege of learning from him.

The book of Proverbs is a collection of wisdom sayings gathered from the school of life. They're general principles of how the world works, and may be the fastest route to practical wisdom anywhere. Others also contributed to the book of Proverbs such as Agur (Proverbs 30:1) and Lemuel (Proverbs 31:1), but the largest contributor seems to be Solomon.

Proverbs 1:7 *The fear of the Lord is the beginning of knowledge.*

Epistemology is the branch of philosophy that asks, *how do we know what we know?* Do we know things are true by induction, deduction, abduction, intuition, or some other way? It's an important question because, unless we understand how we know something, how can we be sure that we actually know it? According to this verse, true knowledge begins with the fear of God—the basic intuition that God exists, and is to be obeyed.

To deny this truth leads to irrationalism because *without an ultimate mind the logic system of every mind is equally valid, and there's no basis for a common rationality.* Without belief in God there can be no categories of right and wrong, only preferences. There can be no absolute truth, only your truth and my truth. The rejection of God, therefore, is the loss of reason. This explains why the world is such a conflicted place.

When I was a child I learned the alphabet. Then I learned to read words. Then I learned to read sentences. Now I read books. In a way, the alphabet became for me the beginning of knowledge. But, according to this verse, there's something even more basic to knowledge than the alphabet, and that is the fear of God. A child who fears God knows more about ultimate reality than a university professor who doesn't fear God.

Proverbs 2:14 *[Wicked Men] delight in doing wrong and rejoice in the perverseness of evil.*

One of the most shocking things I've ever read is a quote from a wicked man who said, *I thank God, in whom I do not believe, that I'm able to do all the evil in my heart.* There is something in the unconverted heart that rejoices not only in the pleasure of sin, but also in the perverseness of sin.

A classic example comes from Saint Augustine who recounts an episode from his youth. *There was a pear tree close to our own vineyard, heavily laden with fruit, which was not tempting either for its color or for its flavor. Late one night . . . a group of young scoundrels, and I among them, went to shake and rob this tree.*

We carried off a huge load of pears, not to eat ourselves, but to dump out to the hogs . . . . Doing this pleased us all the more because it was forbidden. . . . [I had] no inducement to evil but the evil itself. It was foul, and I loved it. I loved my own undoing. I loved my error—not that for which I erred but the error itself. . . . seeking nothing from the shameful deed but shame itself (Confessions, book two, chapter four.)

Augustine was stealing pears, not because he needed pears, but because he delighted in stealing. This is evil for its own sake. Before knowing Christ, wickedness brings us joy, but now it brings us grief. The righteous still sin, of course, but do so almost unwillingly, and loathe themselves while they're doing it. This is different from the wicked who, *delight in doing wrong and rejoice in the perverseness of evil.*

Proverbs 3:5-6 *Trust in the Lord with all your heart and lean not on your own understanding; in all your ways submit to him, and he will make your paths straight.*

The highest court of appeal for many people is what makes sense to their minds. One of the greatest challenges of faith, therefore, is submitting our minds to God, especially when he doesn't make sense to us. This is the essence of faith, and is not unreasonable. It's simply acknowledging that God knows better than we do.

When I was twelve years old, I went deer hunting with my Dad, and followed him into the woods. On our way out he turned right, but my instincts told me to go left. And when he turned left, I was sure we should go right. There were times I wanted to abandon my dad and go my own way. But I'm glad I didn't, because we came out in precisely the right place. That's how is with God. If we trust him more than we trust ourselves, he will make our paths straight, and keep us from going in circles.

For Reflection and Review

- *Why is the fear of the Lord the beginning of knowledge?*
- *Why do people rejoice in the perverseness of evil?*
- *Why should we trust God more than we trust ourselves?*

Lesson 123

Proverbs 3:9-10 *Honor the Lord with your wealth, with the firstfruits of all your crops; then your barns will be filled to overflowing, and your vats will brim over with new wine.*

This is one of the great promises of God regarding our money. The language is agrarian but the principle clear: *if we are generous with God, he'll be generous with us.* But, sadly, many preachers shamefully distort the Bible's teaching to raise money for themselves, and their ministries.

A famous example is Johann Tetzel, a preacher from the sixteenth century, who became famous for raising money to build a cathedral. He promised people that if they'd put their money into the coffer (a chest with a hole in the top) their deceased loved ones would be released from purgatory (a mythical place of punishment). His most famous saying was this: *As soon as a coin in the coffer rings, the soul from purgatory springs.* With this little rhyme he raised a fortune. But it annoyed Martin Luther, who made it part of his ninety-five theses, which led to the Protestant Reformation.

More recently I saw a man on television asking people to use their credit cards to give a thousand dollars to his ministry. In return he promised that God would bless them financially, especially those who were in debt. *Your credit card got you into debt, and your credit card can get you out of debt*, he said.

But even those awful examples don't negate the biblical truth that if we are generous with God, he will be generous with us. The best financial advice I know is to save ten percent, give ten percent, and live on the rest. How much we give us up to us, but *God loves a cheerful giver* (2 Corinthians 9:7), wrote Paul.

Proverbs 3:33 *The Lord's curse is on the house of the wicked, but he blesses the home of the righteous.*

Some homes are filled with happiness, harmony, and joy. Others are filled with hatred, rage, and despair. Some homes are unusually happy, and others are so miserable no one wants to be there.

Our misery or happiness may have various causes but, on balance, righteousness brings a blessing, and wickedness brings a curse.

This is why it's so important for the righteous to guard their hearts and homes from wickedness. If your home is not as happy as it could be, start by cleansing your heart of everything impure. Then remove from your house anything that belongs to you, but doesn't bring glory to God. Then be careful what comes into your home electronically. If Jesus feels at home in your house, he will bring a blessing. If not, all that is left is a curse.

Proverbs 4:18 *The path of the righteous is like the morning sun, shining ever brighter till the full light of day.*

The elderly are sometimes described as living in their *sunset years*. This is a pleasant way to describe life's end, since few things are more beautiful than a painted sky at the day's close. If you complete the analogy, childhood is morning, adulthood is afternoon, and retirement is evening. But that's not the image we find here. For those who belong to God, all of life is morning, and the day of death is high noon. We don't ride off into the sunset, but step into an even brighter light.

The city does not need the sun or the moon to shine on it, for the glory of God gives it light, and the Lamb is its lamp. The nations will walk by its light, and the kings of the earth will bring their splendor into it. On no day will its gates ever be shut, for there will be no night there (Revelation 21:23-25), wrote John. Christianity a faith of radical optimism, not because there are no hardships, but because our story ends well and then goes on forever.

Proverbs 4:23 *Above all else, guard your heart, for everything you do flows from it.*

Whatever you allow into your heart affects every part of your life. This is true of love, joy, and peace as well as hatred, bitterness, and wrath. That's why guarding your heart must always be a priority.

An American soldier on foreign soil didn't know he was in danger, but a professional sniper had his heart in the crosshairs. The sniper gently squeezed the trigger and the bullet hit its mark. The soldier went down, but was able to get back up again, because was wearing protective armor. Since we're always in the devil's crosshairs, guarding our heart is life or death.

Proverbs 4:27 *Do not turn to the right or the left; keep your foot from evil.*

Our sinful nature is like a dog on a leash, trying to pull us off the path. He's a big dog, curious about everything, and pulls hard right and left. Our job is to control the dog and make it obey. If we don't control our sinful nature, it'll control us, and take us where we don't want to go. That's about as silly as a dog walking it's owner.

Proverbs 6:32 *[A] man who commits adultery has no sense; whoever does so destroys himself.*

There are a number of proverbs that deal with the subject of adultery, perhaps because it ran in Solomon's family. King David was Solomon's father, and started out as a humble shepherd boy who followed the Lord with all his heart. God blessed him and gave him success in leading the nation.

But one of the turning points in David's life was an act of adultery with a woman named Bathsheba (2 Samuel 11:2-4). Prior to the event, David's life was characterized by victory and success, but afterwards by hardship and failure. Solomon knew from his father's experience that few things are more destructive than adultery and, by extension, all sexual sin.

The sexual impulse is one of the strongest in human nature, however, and isn't always subject to reason. Many who know the risks are sexually reckless, and believe that sex is worth dying for. There are also those who never commit adultery with their bodies, but do it in their minds on a regular basis.

This is why so many wives are hurt to find their husbands looking at pornography, and why so many husbands are hurt to learn their wives are drawn to someone else. The sexual ideal is an exclusive union between husband and wife, in a covenant of marriage, committed for life. That ideal hasn't been improved since the beginning, and is worth a little self-control.

Proverbs 9:10 *The fear of the Lord is the beginning of wisdom.*

Wisdom always thinks about the future. The farmer who puts off caring for his crops until the day before the harvest isn't wise. The student who puts off studying until the night before exams isn't wise. And the athlete who puts off training until the day before the event isn't wise. But the person who doesn't get ready for Judgment Day is the biggest fool of all. Wisdom uses every day to get ready for the future. *The fear of the Lord is the beginning of wisdom.*

For Reflection and Review

- *How much money should we give to God?*
- *How can we make our homes a joyful place to live?*
- *How can we prepare for Judgment Day?*

Lesson 124

Proverbs 10:9 *Whoever walks in integrity walks securely, but whoever takes crooked paths will be found out.*

The idea of integrity includes honesty, truthfulness, decency, righteousness, and trustworthiness. For most people, it's when the inside matches the outside. Hanani is given little space in the Bible, but his character is summarized nicely: *he was a man of integrity and feared God more than most people do* (Nehemiah 7:2). If God summarized your character in a sentence, what would he say?

A professor said to his students, *I'm giving two tests today: one is trigonometry and the other is integrity. I hope you pass them both. But if you have to fail one, fail trigonometry. There are many good people who can't pass trigonometry. But there are no good people who can't pass integrity.* This agrees with David who prayed, *I know, my God, that you test the heart and are pleased with integrity* (1 Chronicles 29:17).

Proverbs 10:22 *The blessing of the Lord brings wealth.*

Getting money from God isn't the point of the Bible, but neither is God against people acquiring wealth. Solomon's wealth was legendary, and he saw it as a blessing from God. We too should be thankful for whatever God has given to us.

I don't have Solomon's bank account, but I sleep on a better mattress every night. I don't have a personal orchestra, but I have access to better music at the touch of a button. I don't have a personal chef, but I have a refrigerator, a microwave, and a grocery close to my home. I don't have a stable of horses, but I have a little truck that tops sixty miles an hour. I don't have a palace, but I have climate control, indoor plumbing, and hot running water. God is the source of our wealth, and he should be praised for all that he's given.

Proverbs 10:24 *What the wicked dread will overtake them; what the righteous desire will be granted.*

A common dream we have as children, and even as adults, is to be chased by a beast from which we can't escape. We're running against the wind, up a hill, or are falling down as the beast gets closer and closer. Thankfully, we tend to wake up in time, and are glad it was just a dream. But the nightmare of waking up in hell will never end. And who knows how demons will torment the lost forever?

Heaven is just the opposite: *what the righteous desire will be granted.* There are at least four universal desires: physical beauty, financial freedom, loving relationships, and a reason to live. Imagine the best possible you, in the best possible place, with the best possible people, and the best possible God to praise. God's answer to every request in heaven is *yes*, and his answer to every request in hell is *no*.

Proverbs 13:9 *The light of the righteous shines brightly.*

The more righteous we are, in fact, the more brightly we'll shine. My friend bought a lamp to help him work on his car, but it kept falling to the ground. When he picked it up for the third time he said, *I bought you to shine for me.* Likewise, we've been purchased by Christ to shine for him. *[L]et your light shine before others, that they may see your good deeds and glorify your Father in heaven* (Matthew 5:16), he said.

Proverbs 14:15 *The simple believe anything.*

Part of the fun of raising kids is telling them that chocolate milk comes from brown cows, and that the moon is made of cheese. But even adults tend to believe much of what they're told. When I was in college someone told me the word *gullible* wasn't in the dictionary—to which I replied, *Really?* Gullibility is normal in children, but if we never grow out of it we become superstitious. Then we give people money to tell us our fortunes.

Many react against gullibility by becoming so skeptical they refuse to believe almost anything. A good example are those who refuse to believe the earth is round because it appears to be flat. Regardless of the evidence, they refuse to believe in a round earth, because they don't want to be wrong. But skepticism leads to wrong conclusions just as often as gullibility, since both are ways to avoid thinking.

The biblical approach to wisdom takes the middle way of discernment. It reviews the evidence, and carefully draws conclusions. The gullible require no evidence at all, and no amount of evidence will ever convince the skeptics. But Christianity is a reasonable faith based on sufficient evidence. It invites us to check the facts, and make our decision in light of them.

Proverbs 14:26 *Whoever fears the Lord has a secure fortress.*

This verse speaks to our need for security and protection from all who would harm us. Life can be threatening, and we need a place of safety where we can flee for refuge. Herod the Great built Masada for this very purpose. Imagine twenty acres on top of a high rock, with luxurious accommodations, and seemingly impregnable. It was, no doubt, one of the most secure places on earth.

So when the Romans destroyed Jerusalem, in AD 70, about a thousand Israelites made their way to Masada. But the Romans built a battering ram and, after several months, were able to breach the wall. Most of the people committed suicide, so when the Romans marched in they found a thousand dead bodies. Tragically, the fortress was not as secure as they hoped. Only God is a secure fortress in whom we can live and never die. He alone is our refuge.

For Reflection and Review

- *What are the benefits of integrity?*
- *How should Christians use discernment?*
- *How does God keep us safe?*

Lesson 125

Proverbs 14:31 *[W]hoever is kind to the needy honors God.*

My mother was a God fearing woman, which is why I was surprised the first time I heard her cuss. With six kids, and a part-time job, she had little time to spare. Saturdays were precious because that's when she did the housework.

One Saturday morning she was catching up on laundry, when a needy person pulled into the driveway. This dear lady was going through a difficult time and, even though they weren't close friends, she found my mom to be supportive. But when my mother saw her car, I heard her quietly say, *oh spit* (slightly revised).

What she did next, however, made an even bigger impression. She put down the laundry, got out some refreshments, and gave this dear lady a couple hours of time and attention. It was one of the most beautiful things I've ever seen, and I'll never forget it. *[W]hoever is kind to the needy honors God.*

Proverbs 15:3 *The eyes of the Lord are everywhere, keeping watch on the wicked and the good.*

This is a comfort to us when we're being good, but not so much when we're being bad. *Nothing in all creation is hidden from God's sight. Everything is uncovered and laid bare before the eyes of him to whom we must give account* (Hebrews 4:13), says Hebrews.

When I was growing up we had a picture above the fireplace of a lady whose eyes followed you everywhere. If you were standing by the door, her eyes were on you. If you were sitting on the couch, her eyes were on you. And if you looked at her from the stairway, her eyes were still on you. I didn't like that picture very much and, if we're honest, there are times we'd rather avoid the relentless gaze of God.

God's relentless gaze is the result of his omnipresence and omniscience. There is nowhere God is not, and nothing he doesn't see. *He sees you when you are sleeping; he knows when you are awake; he knows if you've been bad or good so be good for goodness' sake.*

When my daughter was in middle school she played the clarinet and, in the band room, was an enormous drum she always wanted to try. So she stayed after school one day and, assuming the teacher had left, pounded the drum with all her might. You can imagine her surprise when the teacher stepped out of her office and said, *Sarah, what are you doing?* And wouldn't you be surprised, the next time you misbehaved, if a voice from heaven said, *What are you doing?*

Proverbs 17:3 *The crucible for silver and the furnace for gold, but the Lord tests the heart.*

When silver and gold are melted, impurities rise to the surface. Then they're removed to make the metal purer. Silver melts at 1763 degrees Fahrenheit, and gold melts around 1948 degrees Fahrenheit. God may turn up the heat in our lives, to purify our hearts. When the impurities rise to the surface, we should let God remove them, so we'll become more like Christ. God wants our hearts to be so pure that, when he looks at them, he sees his own reflection. That's the purpose of our trials.

Proverbs 17:25 *A foolish son brings grief to his father and bitterness to the mother who bore him.*

Almost nothing is more important to Christian parents than seeing their children live for God. And nothing weighs more heavily on them than seeing their children serve the devil. But even with excellent training, children make their own choices: some turn out beautifully and others go astray.

A disappointed mom wrote the following: *How does a parent, who has prayed daily, deal with the rebellion of a child? How does a loving parent accept the rejection of her offspring? How does a parent keep from giving up hope? Why do children see loving parents as their enemies? Why are these children choosing the wrong path? Why are they so selfish?*

These are excellent questions that don't have easy answers. But if earthly parents feel this way, how much more our heavenly Father? How he must rejoice whenever we do well, and grieve whenever we go astray. We should pray for our children, but not forget that we are children too. Every day we have the opportunity to make our Father proud, or break his heart.

Proverbs 18:9 *One who is slack in his work is brother to one who destroys.*

Vandalism costs the United States hundreds of millions of dollars per year. Windows are broken, buildings are burned, and property is defaced. But those who are lazy cost the public even more. By withholding their contribution to society, they're robbing the government of taxes, and stealing from their neighbors. Everyone on earth owes it to God, country, and neighbor to be as productive as they can. To the degree we're not doing our best, we're in league with one who destroys.

Proverbs 18:21 *The tongue has the power of life and death.*

With our tongues we kill and make alive, we resurrect and send to the grave. A few good words can give us hope, and a few bad words can fatally wound. Nothing we do, perhaps, will have a greater impact on those around us than the words we say to them.

A young lady took her life own and left an unfinished note with just two words: *He said.* We don't know what he said, but it was painful enough to put her over the edge. Our deepest suffering often comes, not from what others do to us, but from what other people say to us—or say about us.

Thankfully, words can also give life. I was going through a difficult time, many years ago, when I made a new friend named Dave. He was smart and outgoing, and did me a greater favor than he'll ever know. Whenever he saw me he'd shake my hand, look me in the eye, and say, *You're great.* I have no idea why he said it, or why he said it so often. But those words were life to me. And when I meet him in heaven I'm going to shake his hand, look him in the eye and say, *Hello Dave, you're great!*

For Reflection and Review

- *How do you feel about the needy?*
- *How do you respond to trials?*
- *Why do people say hurtful things?*

Lesson 126

Proverbs 22:24 *Do not make friends with a hot-tempered person, do not associate with one easily angered.*

Anger management is an important theme in Proverbs because it's so important to life. Everyone becomes angry at times, and anger itself is not a sin. But uncontrolled anger can ruin everything.

After King Saul drifted away from God, the Spirit of God departed from him and *an evil spirit . . . tormented him* (1 Samuel 16:14). In order to get relief Saul had the young man David play the lyre. But while David played his instrument the evil spirit troubled Saul again and, filled with rage, he hurled his spear across the room trying to pin David to the wall (1 Samuel 18:10-11, 19:9-10). Notice that Saul's rage was literally demonic. *[Satan] is filled with fury* (Revelation 12:12), and whenever a sinner becomes furious, the situation may actually be satanic.

Venting our rage may feel good, but it's not a sign of wisdom. *Fools give full vent to their rage* (Proverbs 29:11), says Proverbs. A young man wasn't happy with his golf shot so he swung his club at a nearby bench. The club snapped, ricocheted back, pierced his heart, and he died.

Another man was having trouble at his bank, trying to cash a check at the drive-through window. He was told he'd have to come inside but, since the lobby was closed, he'd have to come back the following day. But he wanted to settle it then, so he drove his truck into the lobby and asked to close his account.

Anger manages everything badly. It's a brief insanity that's obvious to everyone except the person who's angry. It makes people feel powerful but has the opposite effect. It destroys reputations as well as relationships. Anger is so destructive, in fact, that we shouldn't even associate with those who have anger issues. *Do not make friends with a hot-tempered person, do not associate with one easily angered.*

Proverbs 22:29 *Do you see someone skilled in their work? They will serve before kings.*

Solomon had many employees, and whenever he needed to fill a position he'd search the land for the best cook, gardener, builder, or whatever he needed. The most skillful workers were promoted to serve the king, and may've been paid very well.

A good strategy for work is to find something you're good at, and never stop improving. One lady was passed over for a promotion and complained that she had twenty-six years of experience. But her supervisor explained that she had one year of experience, twenty-six times. It's not enough to do the same thing over and over; there must be a strategy for improvement.

My wife is a dental hygienist who truly loves her job. She's been cleaning teeth for over thirty years, and still comes home excited about how much plaque she removed. If that's not strange enough, in her spare time she reads dental hygiene magazines, takes dental hygiene courses, watches dental hygiene videos, and keeps up on the latest products. She's adored by her employer and is paid very well.

Proverbs 23:19 *Set your heart on the right path.*

The text doesn't say *Set your feet on the right path* but *Set your heart on the right path.* Wherever the heart goes, the feet will eventually follow. It may take a week, a month, a year, or longer. But eventually the feet will follow the heart.

Solomon's rule as king started out extremely well. God appeared to him twice (1 Kings 11:9) and gave him wonderful promises. But Solomon's preoccupation with worldly success led to the neglect of his soul, and a pattern of compromise. By the end of his life he was building temples to foreign gods. There's something in the best of us that wants to leave the God we love. Unless we keep our heart on the right path, it'll lead us to regret.

Proverbs 26:4-5 *Do not answer a fool according to his folly, or you yourself will be just like him. Answer a fool according to his folly, or he will be wise in his own eyes.*

These two sayings are helpful for understanding how proverbs work. They're not promises that always come true, or commands to be obeyed in every situation. Proverbs are short sayings that often apply, but not always. There is a time to answer a fool, so he doesn't think he's wise. But there's also a time not to answer a fool, so you don't become like him. Proverbs are a fast path to wisdom, but it takes wisdom to know which proverb to apply in any situation.

For Reflection and Review

- *How do you control your anger?*
- *What are some ways to succeed at work?*
- *How is a proverb different from a promise?*

Lesson 127

Proverbs 27:17 *As iron sharpens iron, so one person sharpens another.*

I watched my dad sharpen steak knives at the table when I was just a child. He'd run the blade across the sharpening rod, back and forth, until the dull knife became sharp again. As steel sharpens steel, good friends can have a sharpening effect on each other.

One of God's best gifts to me was a roommate who was totally committed to Jesus Christ. We were both in our early twenties and his example of commitment and sacrifice raised my standards considerably. His greatest strength was prayer, and mine was Bible study. We truly sharpened each other in our devotion to Christ.

Likewise, one of the best gifts you can give yourself is a friend who helps you grow in your faith. You can both commit to reading a chapter of the Bible, almost every day, and underlining whatever you find interesting. Then get together, once a week, and discuss what you've learned. You'll be surprised how much you sharpen each other's devotion to Christ.

Proverbs 28:13 *Whoever conceals their sins does not prosper, but the one who confesses and renounces them finds mercy.*

No one wants to appear as bad as they are, so nothing comes more naturally than concealing our sins. We don't have to reveal everything to everyone, but we should be honest with God at all times. This will mean agreeing with God against ourselves so we can receive his mercy.

One dear lady had a seven-year affair with a married man that ended when he left her for a younger woman. She was so depressed that she went to a psychiatrist for counseling and medication, but only spiraled downward. She blamed the world for her misery, and despised any sense of guilt or responsibility. As a result, her life became a bottomless pit. But if we confess our sins, and renounce them, God will smile on us and help us live a new life.

Proverbs 28:26 *Those who trust in themselves are fools.*

Self-assurance can be a strength, but also a terrible weakness. I was getting my hair cut, some time ago, and the subject of religion came up. I asked the lady if she trusted Christ and she said, *No. I only trust myself.* Her answer sounded good, but I wondered if it was true. Did she trust herself enough to cut her own hair? Probably not.

If I have a medical problem, I need a trustworthy doctor. If I have a legal problem, I need a trustworthy attorney. If I have a sin problem, I need a trustworthy Savior. Jesus Christ is the most trustworthy person who ever lived, and he died to save his people from their sins (Matthew 1:21). Those who trust in him will be saved. But *Those who trust in themselves are fools.*

Proverbs 29:23 *Pride brings a person low, but the lowly in spirit gain honor.*

Proud people think the way to attain honor is by promoting themselves. They boast of their achievements, and seek the approval of others. This works for a while but usually not for long, because *God opposes the proud* (James 4:6), wrote James.

King Herod put on his royal robes and gave a public address. The speech was so well received that the people shouted, *This is the voice of a god, not of a man* (Acts 12:22). Herod enjoyed the people's praise so much that, instead of giving glory to God, he kept the glory for himself. As a result, *an angel of the Lord struck him down, and he was eaten by worms and died* (Acts 12:23).

Herod was eaten by worms before he died, and most are eaten by worms after they die. We can step on the worms, but the worms win. That's why pride is such a foolish thing. It's the only disease that makes everyone sick except the one who has it. But if we humble ourselves under the hand of God, he will lift us up in due time (1 Peter 5:6). The proud prefer their honor now, but the humble wait to be honored by God.

Proverbs 29:27 *The righteous detest the dishonest; the wicked detest the upright.*

The deepest divide in the world isn't between the races, or the sexes, but between the righteous and the wicked. *If the world hates you, keep in mind that it hated me first. If you belonged to the world, it would love you as its own. As it is, you do not belong to the world, but I have chosen you out of the world. That is why the world hates you* (John 15:18-19), said Jesus.

The divide between the righteous and the wicked is often reflected in culture wars. Believers want the world to honor God, and the wicked want the world to be free from God. Conflicts break out in politics, the media, the academy, at work, and even in homes. As a result, the gospel is often marginalized.

Believers should always keep in mind that the goal of Christianity isn't to take over governments, or even cultures, but to preach the gospel everywhere, for the salvation of those who believe. *Many will be purified, made spotless and refined, but the wicked will continue to be wicked* (Daniel 12:10), wrote Daniel.

Proverbs 30:8 *[G]ive me neither poverty nor riches, but give me only my daily bread.*

Until recently, the human diet has been fairly simple. Many have lived on bread and fish, fruits and vegetables, and whatever else could be gathered. Food for the day wasn't assumed or taken for granted. But in recent times this has changed. No one in the Bible could've imagined today's grocery store, or the abundance we enjoy. Second only to church, going to the grocery store should be an act of worship.

Thank you God for coffee and bagels—the best breakfast ever! Thank you also for hamburger, ketchup, pickles, onions, lettuce, tomatoes, and cheese. Thank you also for milk: one percent, two percent, fat-free, or whole. Thank you also for orange juice, grape juice, and even cranberry juice. Thank you for cookies, and chips, and candy in small amounts. And finally, Lord, thanks for my daily bread—with peanut butter and jelly, of course.

For Reflection and Review

- *How can godly friends help us grow in our faith?*
- *When is it wrong to trust in yourself?*
- *Why is it foolish to be proud?*

Lesson 128

Ecclesiastes 1:1 *The words of the Teacher, son of David, king in Jerusalem.*

The author of Ecclesiastes doesn't identify himself by name, but King Solomon is the most likely candidate. He probably wrote around 950 BC to help God's people understand some of life's frustrations. Ecclesiastes is written from the perspective of someone who believes in God, but doesn't seem to love God. The tone is bleak, but numerous insights can be gleaned.

Ecclesiastes 1:2 *Meaningless! Meaningless! says the Teacher. Utterly meaningless! Everything is meaningless.*

An important difference between people and beasts is that people can't be happy without meaning. Cows don't ask the meaning of life, or why they were born, but people often do. And sometimes they find the answer illusive. A wealthy person was asked what he learned from his success that he wished he knew when he was younger. He said, *When you get to the top, nothing is there.*

But if he'd gone all the way to the top, he would've found God. Apart from him, everything else is pointless. The meaning of life is that there is a life-giver, to whom we owe our lives. It's only through loving and serving God that we find ultimate meaning and purpose.

Ecclesiastes 1:14 *I have seen all the things that are done under the sun; all of them are meaningless, a chasing after the wind.*

The little phrase *under the sun* occurs over two dozen times throughout Ecclesiastes, and contrasts with what's above the sun, namely God. Apart from God, our earthly activities are meaningless, like *chasing after the wind*.

Imagine a little boy blowing bubbles and chasing after them. It's fun, of course, but they quickly pop and he must chase another. That's how many people live. They chase money, pleasure, romance, and success but none of them bring lasting satisfaction. That only comes from pursuing God.

Ecclesiastes 3:11 *He has also set eternity in the human heart.*

Because we're made in the image of God (Genesis 1:27), and because God is eternal (Genesis 21:33), people know in their hearts that they will live forever. That, of course, is a very long time.

If God told a little bird to gather every grain of sand on Earth and carry it to the Moon, then take both to Venus, then all three to Saturn, and so forth, by the time that little bird gathered up the entire universe, it would be 9:35 in the morning, on the first day of eternity.

That's why the most important thing we can do is secure the salvation of our souls. *What good is it for someone to gain the whole world, yet forfeit their soul?* (Mark 8:36), said Jesus. And, *[some] will go away to eternal punishment, but the righteous to eternal life* (Matthew 25:46), he said. We ought to be the most concerned about where we'll spend the longest, not just the next few years.

Ecclesiastes 5:10 *Whoever loves money never has enough; whoever loves wealth is never satisfied with their income.*

Few things on earth are more helpful than money, but there's a limit to what money can buy. A wealthy banker lived in a mansion and pursued wealth above everything else. Among other things, he wanted to buy the property around his home, as far as he could see. But the people living there hated him, and refused to sell their land. Years past, and the man became so miserable that he took his own life.

The desire for wealth isn't evil in itself, but reflects the fact that we were made for more. This is why heaven is described as a place of inconceivable wealth, where even the street is made of gold (Revelation 21:21). God is the source of infinite wealth, and whoever has him will have everything else (Revelation 21:7).

Ecclesiastes 7:2 *It is better to go to a house of mourning than to go to a house of feasting, for death is the destiny of everyone; the living should take this to heart.*

We don't look forward to funerals, but we can certainly learn from them. There we see that all our earthly dreams will come to an end some day. Sooner or later, we'll take our place in the coffin and people will talk about us. Perhaps they'll say nice things, but we won't be there to enjoy it. We're all *destined to die once, and after that to face judgment* (Hebrews 9:27), says Hebrews. Funerals help us keep the end in view.

As part of his medical training a doctor watched many people die, and knew the symptoms well. He was checking a patient who barely had a pulse, and whose blood pressure was dropping steadily. His eyes were as blank as billiard balls and he thought he'd check the retinas—but he was shocked by what he saw. As he looked into the eyes of a man who was almost dead, he saw a clear reflection of himself. *Who can live and not see death, or who can escape the power of the grave?* (Psalm 89:48), wrote the Psalmist. Those who are wise live each day preparing for their last.

Ecclesiastes 7:10 *Do not say, Why were the old days better than these? For it is not wise to ask such questions.*

The old days are often better than our declining years, but the future is best of all. *Forgetting what is behind . . . God has called me heavenward in Christ Jesus* (Philippians 3:13-14), wrote Paul. Regardless how great the past, the future is better by far for those who follow Christ.

A young man went to hear an old, but legendary, preacher. Afterward, he shook hands at the door and repeated the same phrase to almost everyone. *Just keep going. Just keep going*, he said. There are better things in the future than anything in the past.

For Reflection and Review

- *Why do people care about meaning?*
- *Why is it good to go to funerals?*
- *Do you ever think about the good old days?*

Lesson 129

Ecclesiastes 7:20 *Indeed, there is no one on earth who is righteous, no one who does what is right and never sins.*

This idea is so important it's repeated several times throughout the Bible. *Who can say, I have kept my heart pure; I am clean and without sin?* (Proverbs 20:9). *[A]ll have sinned and fall short of the glory of God* (Romans 3:23). And *If we claim to be without sin, we deceive ourselves and the truth is not in us* (1 John 1:8), wrote John. We aren't sinners because we sin, we sin because we're sinners.

But this wasn't always the case. Our first parents were without sin until they ate the forbidden fruit (Genesis 3:6). At that point, human nature became so corrupt that *every inclination of the human heart is evil from childhood* (Genesis 8:21), wrote Moses. Now we're sinners by nature, and by choice. It's who we are, and what we do.

Thankfully, Jesus Christ is changing us. We've been saved from the penalty of sin (John 5:24); we're being saved from the power of sin (2 Peter 1:5-8); and we will be saved from the presence of sin (Revelation 21:27). *[Y]ou are to give him the name Jesus, because he will save his people from their sins* (Matthew 1:21), said the angel.

Ecclesiastes 8:8 *[N]o one has power over the time of their death.*

A normal life-span, according to the Bible, is between seventy and eighty years (Psalm 90:10). But these aren't guaranteed, of course. Some are cut down by war, others by disease, and others in surprising ways.

One man thought he was safe in bed when an airplane crashed through his roof. Another was driving his car when a deer jumped through his window and punctured his neck with an antler. Another was standing in his own front yard when he was struck by lightning. Instead of trying to live longer, we should prepare to meet our Maker. *[N]o one has power over the time of their death.*

Ecclesiastes 9:10 *Whatever your hand finds to do, do it with all your might.*

Life is a gift, and God doesn't want us to live it half-heartedly. He sets a task before each one, and wants us to do it with vigor. God is honored when we live to the fullest, serving him with all our might.

If a man is called to be a street sweeper, he should sweep streets even as a Michelangelo painted, or Beethoven composed music or Shakespeare wrote poetry. He should sweep streets so well that all the hosts of heaven and earth will pause to say, Here lived a great street sweeper who did his job well (Martin Luther King Jr.).

An athlete suffered an injury that forced him into retirement. His only regret was not knowing that his previous game would be his last—or he would've been untouchable. *Whatever you do, work at it with all your heart, as working for the Lord* (Colossians 3:23), wrote Paul.

Ecclesiastes 9:11 *The race is not to the swift or the battle to the strong, nor does food come to the wise or wealth to the brilliant or favor to the learned; but time and chance happen to them all.*

This is important for understanding how the world works. We naturally think the fastest person is the one who wins the race, the strongest person is the one who wins the battle, and the most intelligent are those who become rich. But this isn't always true.

The fastest person on earth might live in a remote village, unknown to the rest of the world. The best soldier might die from a sniper's bullet, and the most brilliant might be poor if the world isn't ready for their ideas. Only when God matches our gifts with the right opportunities will we encounter success. When we understand that gifts and opportunities are both from God, we'll give him all the glory and keep none for ourselves.

Ecclesiastes 10:18 *Through laziness, the rafters sag; because of idle hands, the house leaks.*

More than once, the Bible condemns laziness. *Sluggards do not plow in season; so at harvest time they look but find nothing* (Proverbs 20:4). *A little sleep, a little slumber . . . and poverty will come on you like a thief* (Proverbs 24:33-34), says Proverbs.

The greatest condemnation of laziness actually came from Christ: *You wicked, lazy servant! . . . throw that worthless servant outside, into the darkness, where there will be weeping and gnashing of teeth* (Matthew 25:30), he said.

An old farmer died, and willed all that he owned to the devil. The town agreed to honor his wish by doing nothing with his possessions. Years later the house was broken down, the tractor was rusted through, and the field was covered with weeds. If you want to give your life to the devil, just do nothing for God.

Ecclesiastes 12:13-14 *Now all has been heard; here is the conclusion of the matter: Fear God and keep his commandments, for this is the duty of all mankind. For God will bring every deed into judgment, including every hidden thing, whether it is good or evil.*

Some sins are open for everyone to see; others wait for Judgment Day. *There is nothing concealed that will not be disclosed, or hidden that will not be made known* (Luke 12:2), said Jesus. Time doesn't erase what was done in the past.

One lady stole some cigarettes when she was eighteen years old, and failed to pay the court. Twenty-two years later she was getting off a cruise ship when she was arrested and thrown in jail. Officials were looking for terrorists but, when they saw the warrant for her arrest, they simply did their job. Whoever believes in Jesus Christ won't be condemned (Romans 8:1), but *Nothing in all creation is hidden from God's sight* (Hebrews 4:13), says Hebrews.

For Reflection and Review

- *How is Jesus saving us from our sin?*
- *What's wrong with being lazy?*
- *Why should believers care about Judgment Day?*

Lesson 130

Song of Songs 1:1 *Solomon's Song of Songs.*

This book celebrates romantic love as one of God's best gifts to us. It was probably written by King Solomon around 950 BC. The title means it's the best of songs, which is appropriate given the rapturous experience it describes. The language is surprisingly sensuous, but its inclusion in the Bible shows God's approval of sexual expression in marriage. It's never quoted in the New Testament, or even alluded to, but marital love does reflect the love of Christ for his church (Ephesians 5:32).

Song of Songs 1:2 *Let him kiss me with the kisses of his mouth—for your love is more delightful than wine.*

Most of the song is written from the perspective of the woman, and here she expresses her powerful longing for the affection of her husband. She's not passive or shy, but surprisingly forward and clear.

This reminds us of Adam and Eve, in the Garden of Eden, shortly after they were created. *Adam and his wife were both naked, and they felt no shame* (Genesis 2:25), wrote Moses. God designed them for physical union, and they were happy being naked. They covered themselves with fig leaves after they sinned (Genesis 3:7). But, at first, they enjoyed uninhibited sexual expression. Within the context of marriage, this remains a gift from God.

Song of Songs 2:15 *Catch for us the foxes, the little foxes that ruin the vineyards.*

Foxes are pests that destroy entire vineyards, if they're not stopped. Loving relationships are also destroyed by little problems, if they're not resolved. Relationships aren't only ruined by big problems, but by many little problems if they are not settled in a timely way.

Husbands and wives should be open with each other about the little ways they annoy each other. Neither should assume the other knows what's troubling them, for that isn't fair or reasonable. Little annoyances must be expressed without nagging (Proverbs 21:19), and then resolved. By eliminating little problems quickly, good relationships can become even better.

Song of Songs 4:1 *How beautiful you are, my darling! Oh, how beautiful! Your eyes behind your veil are doves. Your hair is like a flock of goats descending from the hills of Gilead.*

Several times the husband extols the beauty of his wife with images that don't translate well into other cultures. But both apparently beautiful, and he gladly gives her the approval she desires. Relationships need frequent reinforcement in order to flourish.

One study showed it takes nine compliments to offset every criticism. This is why few things are more important to being happily married than expressing appreciation. Find the best qualities in your spouse and reinforce them constantly.

Song of Songs 4:16 *Let my beloved come into his garden and taste its choice fruits.*

Again the woman is surprisingly forward in her request for sex. *The husband should fulfill his marital duty to his wife, and likewise the wife to her husband. The wife does not have authority over her own body but yields it to her husband. In the same way, the husband does not have authority over his own body but yields it to his wife* (1 Corinthians 7:3-4), wrote Paul. Sexual attentiveness often leads to happiness.

Song of Songs 7:10 *I belong to my beloved, and his desire is for me.*

The exclusive nature of this couple's relationship gave them reason to rejoice. She belonged to him alone, and he belonged to her alone. *That is why a man leaves his father and mother and is united to his wife, and they become one flesh* (Genesis 2:24), wrote Moses.

Many find happiness in marriage they couldn't find anywhere else. It's the most binding of all human relationships, and provides the security necessary for love to flourish. That's why marriage often begins with vows to love, honor, and cherish until death.

A Christian man married a delightful young lady who was struck by lightning on their honeymoon. She was paralyzed but, due to their vows, the marriage was secure and they remained together until she died, thirty-nine years later (BB Warfield and Annie Kinkaid). Marriage is a commitment for life, and should never be entered into without this kind of resolve.

Song of Songs 8:7 *Many waters cannot quench love; rivers cannot sweep it away.*
If one were to give all the wealth of one's house for love, it would be utterly scorned.

Love is so strong it can't be quenched, and is better than wealth by far. It's why Jesus left his throne in heaven to die on a cross for our sins. *This is how we know what love is: Jesus Christ laid down his life for us* (1 John 3:16), wrote John.

Even the best marriage is a only a faint reflection of the love Christ has for his bride. There'll be no marriage in the age to come (Matthew 22:30), because the church will be married to Christ. *[A]s a bridegroom rejoices over his bride, so will your God rejoice over you* (Isaiah 62:5), wrote Isaiah. The deepest longing of our hearts will be fulfilled, and his passionate love for us will never end.

For Reflection and Review

- *Why is marriage the best context for romantic love?*
- *Why should little problems be settled quickly?*
- *Why is it important to compliment your spouse?*

Lesson 131

Isaiah 1:1 *The vision concerning Judah and Jerusalem that Isaiah son of Amoz saw during the reigns of Uzziah, Jotham, Ahaz and Hezekiah, kings of Judah.*

The prophet Isaiah wrote the book that bears his name from about 740 to 680 BC. He seems to have spent most his life in Jerusalem, and is considered by many to be the greatest of the writing prophets because of the depth, breath, and beauty of his work. He's also been called the *fifth evangelist* (after Matthew, Mark, Luke and John) for his depiction and explanation of the Messiah's death (Isaiah 52:13-53:12). He may also have died a martyr by being sawed in two (Hebrews 11:37).

The Dead Sea Scrolls (discovered in 1947) include a nearly complete scroll of Isaiah from before 100 BC. Before the discovery of the Dead Sea Scrolls, the earliest copy of Isaiah was from around AD 935—over a thousand years later.

Since Isaiah wrote around seven hundred years before Christ, and since our earliest copy of Isaiah was from around nine hundred years after Christ, critics assumed the biblical text was corrupt due to so many years of copying. But scholars found the earlier and later copies of Isaiah to be almost identical. Most differences were due to spelling, and no differences affected the meaning of the text. This is because the biblical texts were copied by professionals who believed they were preserving the very words of God. The text of Scripture we have today is extremely reliable.

*****

Isaiah 6:1 *In the year that King Uzziah died, I saw the Lord, high and exalted, seated on a throne; and the train of his robe filled the temple.*

The death of a king was an anxious moment for God's people, since other nations might view it as a good time to attack. But after the death of godly King Uzziah, the prophet had a vision of the eternal king sitting on his throne. Whenever life is uncertain, we should think of the one who sits on heaven's throne, ruling over all.

The king Isaiah saw was so majestic that *the train of his robe filled the temple*. We don't have much experience with royal trains today, but we are familiar with bridal trains. Some are longer than others, but the longest bridal train on record is over a mile in length. Isaiah doesn't tell us the exact length of God's train, but it was so long that it filled his temple. In other words, God's majesty is unsurpassed by any earthly king.

Isaiah 6:2 *Above him were seraphim, each with six wings: With two wings they covered their faces, with two they covered their feet, and with two they were flying.*

The seraphim are heavenly beings not mentioned by name outside this passage. But may correspond to the *living creatures* mentioned elsewhere (Revelation 4:8). Their name probably means *burning ones*, and may be due to their closeness to God, who's a *consuming fire* (Hebrews 12:29).

They probably covered their faces because they couldn't withstand the brightness of God. And they may've covered their feet because they were dirty. The seraphim remind us that heavenly creatures exist, about whom we know very little. There's more to the spiritual realm than we can imagine.

Isaiah 6:3 *And they were calling to one another: Holy, holy, holy is the Lord Almighty.*

Holiness includes the ideas morality and separation, but is fuller than both ideas combined. Holiness is so closely identified with God, in fact, that to say *holy, holy, holy* is nearly the same as saying *God, God, God*. God is never called three-times anything in the Bible other than *Holy, holy, holy*. This is terrible news for sinners, because God's holiness and human sinfulness are completely incompatible.

Isaiah 6:4-5 *At the sound of their voices the doorposts and thresholds shook and the temple was filled with smoke. Woe to me! I cried. I am ruined! For I am a man of unclean lips, and I live among a people of unclean lips, and my eyes have seen the King, the Lord Almighty.*

In the previous chapter Isaiah pronounced a series woes on the wicked. *Woe to those who call evil good and good evil* (Isaiah 5:20). *Woe to those who are wise in their own eyes* (Isaiah 5:21). *Woe to those who are heroes at drinking wine and champions at mixing drinks* (Isaiah 5:22), he said. But after coming into the presence of God the prophet cried out, *Woe to me! . . . I am ruined!*

Isaiah was a pretty good person, compared to many others, but in the presence of God he saw himself for who he really was—a sinner exposed to wrath. The closer we are to God, the more we'll feel our sin. And the further we are from God, the more we'll feel righteous. The righteous know they are wicked, and the wicked think they are righteous.

Job had a similar experience when he encountered God. *My ears had heard of you but now my eyes have seen you. Therefore I despise myself and repent in dust and ashes* (Job 42:5-6), he said. And Peter said to Jesus, *Go away from me, Lord; I am a sinful man!* (Luke 5:8). Sin is so common it doesn't normally bother us, but in the presence of a holy God, it becomes our greatest concern.

There may've been several areas in which Isaiah fell short, but the sin that troubled him most was his speech. *For I am a man of unclean lips*, he said. We don't think of inappropriate speech as a terrible sin, but Jesus did. *Everyone will have to give account on the day of judgment for every empty word they have spoken. For by your words you will be acquitted, and by your words you will be condemned* (Matthew 12:36-37), he said. And since Isaiah spoke for God, he was even more accountable (James 3:1). If a surgeon wouldn't mix clean and unclean instruments, a prophet shouldn't mix clean and unclean words.

Isaiah 6:6-7 *Then one of the seraphim flew to me with a live coal in his hand, which he had taken with tongs from the altar. With it he touched my mouth and said, See, this has touched your lips; your guilt is taken away and your sin atoned for.*

Sinners can't approach a holy God apart from sacrifice but, thankfully, there was an altar in God's presence. The sacrifice isn't mentioned, but the purpose of the sacrificial system was to point ahead to the sacrifice of Christ. *God presented Christ as a sacrifice of atonement, through the shedding of his blood* (Romans 3:25), wrote Paul.

By taking a coal from the altar, and applying it to the prophet's lips, the angel was showing that God's provision was sufficient for the prophet's wicked speech. And, happily, the sacrifice of Christ is sufficient for the wickedest things we've ever done.

Isaiah 6:8 *Then I heard the voice of the Lord saying, Whom shall I send? And who will go for us? And I said, Here am I. Send me!*

With his sin atoned for, the prophet was in a position to speak for God to others. He'd spend the rest of his life proclaiming the terrible problem of sin, and the coming remedy of Jesus Christ. The church has a similar task, but enjoys the distinct advantage preaching after the death and resurrection of Christ. What a glorious privilege this is.

For Reflection and Review

- *Why are the Dead Sea Scrolls important?*
- *Why was Isaiah concerned about his sin?*
- *Why did Isaiah want to tell others about God?*

Lesson 132

Isaiah 13:19-20 *Babylon, the jewel of kingdoms, the pride and glory of the Babylonians, will be overthrown by God like Sodom and Gomorrah. She will never be inhabited or lived in through all generations.*

Babylon was one of the greatest cities of the ancient world, and for it to destroyed was almost unthinkable. But, in 539 BC, Babylon was overthrown by Cyrus the Great, and eventually ceased to exist as anything like a glorious city.

But if you go to Babylon today, you'll find it's not completely abandoned. There's some restoration going on, and a few tourists to be seen. This has caused some to wonder if this prophecy has been fulfilled, or if we should still be waiting. The answer is found in Isaiah's use of prophetic hyperbole.

Hyperbole is intentional exaggeration in order to make a point. If we say *Joe is older than dirt*, or *Mary never stops talking*, we don't mean to be taken literally. Isaiah was simply predicting that Babylon would never rise again. That has been the case for thousands of years, and is a stunning fulfillment of prophecy.

*****

Isaiah 20:2 *[God said to Isaiah] Take off the sackcloth from your body and the sandals from your feet. And he did so, going around stripped and barefoot.*

This is one of the most bizarre episodes in the Bible. God told Isaiah to walk naked through

Jerusalem for a period of three years. *Just as my servant Isaiah has gone stripped and barefoot for three years . . . so the king of Assyria will lead away stripped and barefoot the Egyptian captives . . . with buttocks bared* (Isaiah 20:3-4), said God.

The purpose of this prophetic action was to warn the Jews to look to God for protection, not to Egypt, since Assyria would defeat the Egyptians. But we also see how embarrassing the prophetic ministry could be. Speaking for God was an honor, of course, but when God wanted to make his point graphically, the prophet was not allowed to decline. We can only imagine his embarrassment, and that of his wife and children.

This also reminds us of the humiliation of Jesus Christ as he hung on the cross. We know that he was naked because the soldiers gambled for his clothing, including his undergarment (John 19:23-24). Since crucifixion was meant to degrade, it's unlikely he was left with even a stitch to cover himself. Imagine hanging fully exposed before friends, family, and foes. To God's wonderful qualities of power, love, and justice, we must also add humility.

*****

Isaiah 23:1 *A prophecy against Tyre: . . . Tyre is destroyed and left without house or harbor.*

Tyre was an important seaport on the Mediterranean, which included an island about a half mile offshore. If the mainland was attacked, residents could flee to the island for protection. This made Tyre feel invincible, and for many years it was. Nebuchadnezzar took the mainland in 572 BC, but couldn't take the island even though he tried for another fifteen years. Then the people on the island went back to the mainland.

But many years later, Alexander the Great conquered the mainland, and used the ruins to build a road to the island. The prophet Ezekiel caught a glimpse of this and wrote: *they will break down your walls and demolish your fine houses and throw your stones, timber and rubble into the sea* (Ezekiel 26:12). After taking the island-city in 332 BC, Alexander crucified two thousand people, and sold thirty thousand others into slavery. Tyre was destroyed and left without house or harbor.

*****

Isaiah 29:13 *These people come near to me with their mouth and honor me with their lips, but their hearts are far from me.*

There was plenty of religion, but it wasn't very heartfelt. The temple was open, prayers were offered, and songs were sung, but few were drawing near to God with their hearts. This is so often the case, that Jesus applied this verse to the people of his day (Matthew 15:8).

It's easier to worship God outwardly than it is to worship him inwardly. Many churches have excellent attendance, but little devotion. *You have forsaken the love you had at first* (Revelation 2:4), said Jesus. And, *You are always on their lips but far from their hearts* (Jeremiah 12:2), said Jeremiah.

Christian hearts won't be filled with love on Sundays unless it's cultivated throughout the week. When we gather for worship, we must lift our hearts to God as he desires. It takes more energy to get a plane in the air than to keep it there, so we must make the effort to worship God from our hearts until it comes naturally.

*****

Isaiah 32:8 *But the noble make noble plans, and by noble deeds they stand.*

The culture of Isaiah's day was so corrupt, it was tempting for some to do little or nothing for God. Many were growing old without any godly accomplishments. This, of course, is never acceptable for those who are noble. Noble people *make noble pans, and by noble deeds they stand*.

For many years I had noble deeds, but didn't have noble plans. I was twenty-five years old, and nearly broke, when I was gripped by the fear that life was passing me by. So I drew a line on a piece of paper with the my age at one end and the number seventy at the other.

Then I wrote down what I wanted to accomplish, when I wanted to accomplish it, and what I'd have to do to see it happen. I was seeking first the kingdom of God (Matthew 6:33) so all my plans were noble. Then I began to work my plan.

I've revised it several times, since then, but it's always served me well. Many things have come to pass, and others are coming to pass. Some people plan without doing, others do without planning. But those who are *noble make noble plans, and by noble deeds they stand.*

For Reflection and Review

- *What is prophetic hyperbole?*
- *How do we know that God is humble?*
- *Why is it important to make noble plans?*

Lesson 133

Isaiah 34:4 *All the stars in the sky will be dissolved and the heavens rolled up like a scroll; all the starry host will fall like withered leaves from the vine, like shriveled figs from the fig tree.*

Isaiah foresaw the destruction of the universe as a result of our sin. Sin brought a curse on the earth (Genesis 3:17-20) that spread like a virus, and God's judgment will be so severe that it will reach the furthest star. *The heavens will disappear with a roar; the elements will be destroyed by fire, and the earth and everything done in it will be laid bare* (2 Peter 3:10), wrote Peter.

Aristotle (384-322 BC) taught that the universe is eternal in both directions and, for many years, that was the accepted theory. But now it's thought the universe had a beginning (the big bang) and that it will have an end (the big crunch). This is more consistent with the Biblical view: *In the beginning God created the heavens and the earth* (Genesis 1:1). And in the end, *all the starry host will fall.*

But that is not the end of the story. *[W]e are looking forward to a new heaven and a new earth, where righteousness dwells* (2 Peter 3:13), wrote Peter. God will create a whole new world, perhaps with the same materials. Then the curse will be reversed, and the new creation will endure forever (Isaiah 66:22). This is the biblical view of the future.

*****

Isaiah 35:10 *Everlasting joy will crown their heads.*

God's people would go through difficult times, but, through it all, they could look forward to everlasting joy. Everlasting happiness is all that we hope for, but God has promised joy. Joy surpasses happiness as far as happiness surpasses sorrow. And a million years of joy wouldn't be as joyful, if we knew it would ever end. But it will go on forever.

My Grandpa was riding in my uncle's speed boat when he smiled so widely that his false teeth flew into the lake. His joy went away with his teeth, but in the age to come our joy will never end. Think of the happiest moment of your life, and double it twice. If that's what you have to look forward to, you can enjoy it now. *Everlasting joy will crown [our] heads.*

*****

Isaiah 41:13 *For I am the Lord your God who takes hold of your right hand and says to you, Do not fear; I will help you.*

On your first day of school your mother probably held your hand as she brought you into class. She helped you meet the teacher, and find your desk, but then she had to go. God never does that. From cradle to grave he holds your hand and helps you along the way. He doesn't want you to be afraid, but to hold on tightly through every stage of life.

*****

Isaiah 42:3 *A bruised reed he will not break, and a smoldering wick he will not snuff out.*

Here Isaiah describes the gentleness that Jesus would show to those who were bruised by sin, and whose flame of faith was about to go out. He wouldn't rebuke or reject them, but nurture and assure them.

A sinful woman came to Jesus and washed his feet with her tears, dried them with her hair, kissed them, and poured perfume on them. Some were repulsed by her behavior, but Jesus said, *Your sins are forgiven. . . . Your faith has saved you; go in peace* (Luke 7:48-50).

That's what Jesus says to every broken person who looks to him in faith—no matter how badly they've failed in the past, are failing in the present, or will fail in the future. Instead of breaking those who are bruised by sin, Jesus heals them. Instead of snuffing out the smoldering wick of faith, he fans it into flame. This is the kind of ministry Jesus had in the past, and continues to have today.

*****

Isaiah 44:28 *[The Lord] says of Cyrus, He is my shepherd and will accomplish all that I please; he will say of Jerusalem, Let it be rebuilt, and of the temple, Let its foundations be laid.*

About a hundred fifty years before Cyrus became the king of Persia, the prophet Isaiah identified him by name, making this one of the most remarkable prophecies in the Bible. God can foretell the future because he planned it long ago. *[We've] been predestined according to the plan of him who works out everything in conformity with the purpose of his will* (Ephesians 1:11), wrote Paul. Nothing happens by chance, including the rule of kings.

Josephus (the early Jewish historian) claimed that Cyrus was informed about the prophecies concerning him (Antiquities of the Jews, XI.1.2). The prophet Daniel was a high ranking official living in Babylon at this time, and may've had a scroll of Isaiah which he showed to Cyrus. Whether or not this happened, Cyrus took action.

This is what Cyrus king of Persia says: The Lord, the God of heaven, has given me all the kingdoms of the earth and he has appointed me to build a temple for him at Jerusalem in Judah. Any of his people among you may go up to Jerusalem in Judah and build the temple of the Lord, the God of Israel (Ezra 1:2-3).

Cyrus' decree is corroborated by an artifact known as the *Cyrus Cylinder*, which was found in AD 1879, and is housed in the British Museum. It doesn't mention the Jews by name, but states Cyrus' policy of allowing displaced peoples to return home, and restore their temples. So God's people were allowed to return to their homeland, just as Isaiah foretold.

Isaiah 48:17 *I am the Lord your God, who teaches you what is best for you, who directs you in the way you should go.*

One of the things that persuaded me to follow Christ was the idea that he was more qualified to run my life I was. Since he had made the universe, and kept it running for years, perhaps he could run my life as well. This seems obvious to some, but not to everyone.

When a young man asked Jesus, *what must I do to inherit eternal life?* Jesus said, *Sell everything you have . . . . Then come, follow me.* He should've been delighted, but went away sad, because he was very wealthy (Luke 18:18-23). But what's everything you have compared to eternal life? Faith is believing Jesus knows best, and will lead us in the way that's best for us.

For Reflection and Review

- *What's the biblical view of the universe?*
- *How should the church treat sinners?*
- *Why was Cyrus important?*

Lesson 134

Isaiah 52:13 *See, my servant will act wisely; he will be raised and lifted up and highly exalted.*

This begins a passage which describes the suffering, death, burial, and resurrection of Jesus

Christ, and what it means for his people. It's so vivid that it's often been called *the fifth gospel*, and was so important to the writers of the New Testament that they quote or refer to it over thirty times. It's so precise that it's difficult to believe it was written over seven hundred years before the event it describes. But this simply proves what God said elsewhere: *I make known the end from the beginning, from ancient times, what is still to come* (Isaiah 46:10).

Isaiah 52:14 *[H]is appearance was so disfigured beyond that of any human being and his form marred beyond human likeness.*

This is a description of Jesus Christ after he was flogged, in preparation for his crucifixion. Jewish floggings were limited to forty lashes (Deuteronomy 25:3), but the Romans could lash without limit. The whips were made of leather, with metal and bone attached, for the purpose of tearing off flesh. Floggings were so severe that many didn't survive.

The gospel writers show remarkable restraint when describing the suffering and death of Jesus Christ. They simply say he was *flogged* and *crucified* (Matthew 27:26, Mark 15:15). Since the original readers were familiar with flogging and crucifixion, no more description was needed. But what the gospel writers left out, Isaiah included. Jesus was so *marred* and *disfigured* that he barely seemed human. This is how he appeared as he hung on the cross.

Isaiah 52:15 *[H]e will sprinkle many nations, and kings will shut their mouths because of him.*

The covenant between God and Israel was ratified when Moses took animal blood, sprinkled it on the people, and said, *This is the blood of the covenant that the Lord has made with you* (Exodus 24:8). But Isaiah spoke of the blood of the new covenant (1 Corinthians 11:25), shed by Christ for all nations (Matthew 28:19). *[W]ith your blood you purchased for God persons from every tribe and language and people and nation* (Revelation 5:9), wrote John.

This even included kings, wrote Isaiah. Kings have great authority, and speak with great authority, until they meet a greater king. Then they shut their mouths out of respect. Countless kings and powerful leaders have acknowledged Christ as *King of kings* (Revelation 17:14), and shut their mouths before him.

Isaiah 53:1 *Who has believed our message . . . ?*

The gospel has spread around the world, but is strangely rejected by most. The apostles John and Paul referred to this verse to explain this surprising reaction. *Even after Jesus had performed so many signs in their presence, they still would not believe in him. This was to fulfill the word of Isaiah the prophet: Lord, who has believed our message* (John 12:37-38), wrote John.

But not all the Israelites accepted the good news. For Isaiah says, Lord, who has believed our message? (Romans 10:16), wrote Paul. Since Jesus died for the sins of the whole world (1 John 2:2) we might expect the whole world to believe in Jesus Christ. But this has never been the case, and God is not surprised. Christianity is a global religion but, compared to the whole, only a few truly believe (Matthew 7:14).

Isaiah 53:2 *He had no beauty or majesty to attract us to him, nothing in his appearance that we should desire him.*

Whenever the Bible speaks of a person's appearance, it's usually positive. *Sarai was a very beautiful woman* (Genesis 12:14). *Rachel had a lovely figure and was beautiful* (Genesis 29:17). *Joseph was well-built and handsome* (Genesis 39:6); David *had a fine appearance and handsome features* (1 Samuel 16:12). And, *there was not a man so highly praised for his handsome appearance as Absalom* (2 Samuel 14:25).

But the Bible tells us nothing of Jesus' appearance except that *he had no beauty or majesty to attract us to him, nothing in his appearance that we should desire him*. This may be the politest way Isaiah could say that Jesus was homely. He had *no beauty*. There was *nothing in his appearance that we should desire him*. This contradicts most depictions of Christ in art and film.

Since Jesus was homely, he wouldn't be singled out as a natural leader, or receive the special attention given to those with a good appearance. Whenever he opened his mouth he'd have to overcome a bias against him. This would make him less inclined to seek the approval of anyone other than his heavenly Father.

For Reflection and Review

- *What was Christ's condition as he hung on the cross?*
- *Since Christianity is true, why don't more people believe?*
- *Why is Jesus most often portrayed as handsome?*

Lesson 135

Isaiah 53:3 *He was despised and rejected by mankind, a man of suffering, and familiar with pain. Like one from whom people hide their faces he was despised.*

Some people stare at those who are suffering to satisfy their curiosity; others turn away to avoid the pain. As Jesus hung on the cross some people stared, and others turned away.

But since he was *a man of suffering,* Jesus can relate to us whenever we suffer. He doesn't turn away from us, or stare out of curiosity. He looks on us with compassion, and enters into our pain. The reason he can do this is because he knows what it is to suffer.

Isaiah 53:4 *Surely he took up our pain and bore our suffering, yet we considered him punished by God, stricken by him, and afflicted.*

The fact that Jesus died on a cross was proof, for some, that he wasn't the Messiah: *anyone who is hung on a pole is under God's curse* (Deuteronomy 21:23), wrote Moses. The fact that Jesus was hung on a pole proved that he wasn't blessed by God, but cursed by him. But he became *a curse for us* (Galatians 3:13), wrote Paul. The pain and suffering Jesus endured wasn't for sins he committed, but for sins we committed. Jesus was under God's curse, but he was there for us.

Isaiah 53:5 *[H]e was pierced for our transgressions, he was crushed for our iniquities.*

The piercing of his hands and feet was visible to all, but the crushing he received was only seen by God. *Our offenses and sins weigh us down* (Ezekiel 33:10), wrote Ezekiel. The terrible weight of all our sins were laid on Christ so that *he was crushed for our iniquities.*

An earthquake caused a home to collapse and, beneath the rubble, a baby's cry was heard. The child was found beneath her mom, cradled in her arms. The mom allowed herself to be crushed to save her baby's life. And Jesus was *crushed for our iniquities* that we might live forever.

Isaiah 53:6 *We all, like sheep, have gone astray, each of us has turned to our own way.*

Even after we come to Christ, there's part of us that wants to wander. *Prone to wander, Lord I feel it, prone to leave the God I love* (Robert Robinson). A little girl wandered away from her parents, and found herself deep in a swamp, surrounded by snakes and alligators. There she spent a horrible night but, against all odds, was rescued the following day.

Jesus is the good shepherd who seeks the lost (Matthew 18:12), but he often uses his people to do it. *[I]f one of you should wander from the truth and someone should bring that person back, remember this: Whoever turns a sinner from the error of their way will save them from death and cover over a multitude of sins* (James 5:19-20), wrote James.

Isaiah 53:7 *[H]e was led like a lamb to the slaughter [and] did not open his mouth.*

Jesus knew this passage well, so when he stood trial before the high priest he *remained silent* (Matthew 26:63). And when he was examined by Pontius Pilate, he *gave him no answer* (John 19:9). Pilate knew that Jesus was innocent (John 19:4), and thought he'd fight for his life. But Jesus came to die for our sins, so he had no need to fight for his life. He's the *Lamb of God, who takes away the sin of the world* (John 1:29).

Isaiah 53:9 *He was assigned a grave with the wicked, and with the rich in his death.*

The wicked and the rich were linked in people's thinking because some of the rich got their money by oppressing the poor. Not all the rich were wicked, of course, but a burial site for the wealthy would likely include the graves of some who were wicked.

Joseph of Arimathea was rich, but he wasn't wicked. He was a member of the Jewish high court, but didn't consent to the crucifixion of Jesus (Luke 23:50-51). He was *a disciple of Jesus, but secretly because he feared the Jewish leaders* (John 19:38), wrote John. But after Jesus died, Joseph went to Pilate and requested Jesus' body.

Joseph took the body, wrapped it in a clean linen cloth, and placed it in his own new tomb that he had cut out of the rock (Matthew 27:59-60). So Jesus *was assigned a grave with the wicked, and with the rich in his death.* The odds of this happening by chance are extremely remote.

Isaiah 53:10 *Yet it was the Lord's will to crush him and cause him to suffer.*

How could the heavenly Father love his Son (Luke 3:22) and also want him to suffer? The answer is twofold. First, ever since our first parents were banished from the Garden of Eden (Genesis 3:23), it's been God's purpose to bring us back (Genesis 3:15). Because he's a *God of justice* (Psalm 50:6), sin had to be punished; and because he is a God of mercy (Deuteronomy 4:31), he was willing to bear it himself.

Second, through the cross Jesus would gain a people for himself, to be part of his glorious kingdom. He will say to his own, *Come, you who are blessed by my Father; take your inheritance, the kingdom prepared for you since the creation of the world* (Matthew 25:34). God created the world to prepare a kingdom for his Son, and we'll be his joyful subjects forever.

For Reflection and Review

- *How was Jesus crushed on the cross?*
- *Why do people wander away from God?*
- *What did Jesus gain from the cross?*

Lesson 136

Isaiah 53:11 *After he has suffered, he will see the light of life and be satisfied.*

Jesus knew his death and burial would not be the end of his life. *On the third day [I] will be raised* (Matthew 20:19), he said. The disciples didn't expect the crucifixion, or the resurrection, but Jesus expected both. And when it was over, he was *satisfied*. His mission was accomplished, and he's enjoyed the love of his people ever since.

Isaiah 53:12 *For he bore the sin of many, and made intercession for the transgressors.*

One of our greatest needs is for someone who is close to God to pray for us. No one is closer to God the Father, than Jesus Christ his Son. And even though we sin, God will not reject us, because Jesus intercedes for us. He makes sure that his saving work will always be applied. *[H]e is able to save completely those who come to God through him, because he always lives to intercede for them* (Hebrews 7:25), says Hebrews.

The night of his arrest Jesus prayed for Peter that his faith would *not fail* (Luke 22:32). Peter stumbled badly by denying Jesus three times with a curse (Matthew 26:69-75). But his faith didn't fail because Jesus prayed for him.

Likewise, *Christ Jesus . . . is at the right hand of God and is also interceding for us* (Romans 8:34), wrote Paul. The reason God doesn't turn away from us, and that we don't turn away from God, is because

Jesus lives to intercede for us. The prophet Isaiah saw this hundreds of years in advance.

*****

Isaiah 61:1-2 *The Spirit of the Sovereign Lord is on me, because the Lord has anointed me to proclaim good news to the poor. He has sent me to bind up the brokenhearted, to proclaim freedom for the captives and release from darkness for the prisoners, to proclaim the year of the Lord's favor and the day of vengeance of our God.*

Jesus applied these words to himself when he preached at Nazareth (Luke 4:16-20). But he didn't mention *the day of vengeance of our God* because that applies to his second coming, not his first coming. Biblical prophecies are often compressed to include more than one fulfillment. Prophetic compression is characteristic of many biblical prophecies.

A mountain range appears to be one from a distance. But sometimes there are two, with a great valley between them. The prophets often describe future events as one, when there are actually two fulfillments, with a valley of time between them. This is the case with the first and second coming of Christ.

*****

Isaiah 62:5 *[A]s a bridegroom rejoices over his bride, so will your God rejoice over you.*

Marriage is so important to the story of the Bible that it opens and closes with a wedding. The first was in the Garden of Eden, where God took a rib from Adam's side and made him a wife (Genesis 2:21-22). Adam was so delighted that he burst into poetry: *This is now bone of my bones and flesh of my flesh; she shall be called woman, for she was taken out of man* (Genesis 2:21-23), he said.

But the honeymoon didn't last forever. When sin entered the picture, Adam blamed his wife. *The woman you put here with me—she gave me some fruit from the tree, and I ate it* (Genesis 3:12), he said.

The New Testament refers to the church as the bride of Christ (Ephesians 5:25, Revelation 19:7), and to Jesus as the *last Adam* (1 Corinthians 15:45).

He's not the first Adam who blamed his bride, but the last Adam who died for his bride—and whose wedding day is coming. *For the wedding of the Lamb has come, and his bride has made herself ready* (Revelation 19:7), wrote John.

We become Christians, in fact, the same way we get married—by saying *yes. Yes, Lord, I believe you died on the cross for my sins, and I accept your invitation to live happily forever with you.* When we say *yes* to Christ, he becomes our Lord and Savior, and heaven becomes our eternal home.

Isaiah 66:13 *As a mother comforts her child, so will I comfort you.*

God's people go through hardship, like everyone else, but have the benefit of his tender comfort. God is so tender, in fact, that he compares himself to an affectionate mother. A mother's hug and kiss has made everything better for children throughout the ages.

But children aren't the only ones who need to be comforted. Life can be rough, and the wounds so deep, that only God is sufficient for the pain. He's *the God of all comfort, who comforts us in all our troubles* (2 Corinthians 1:3-4), wrote Paul.

A preacher was thrown in a cell beneath a slaughter house, where blood and guts dripped all around. Shrieks of death filled the air, mingled with the foulest smells. But the presence of God was so dear to him that it seemed like the Garden of Eden. However bleak our situation, God is our companion. *As a mother comforts her child, so will I comfort you.*

For Reflection and Review

- *Why do we need Jesus to pray for us?*
- *What is prophetic compression?*
- *What are the first and last weddings of the Bible?*

Lesson 137

Jeremiah 1:1 *The words of Jeremiah son of Hilkiah, one of the priests at Anathoth in the territory of Benjamin.*

Jeremiah ministered to the people of Judah over the course of forty years, from 626 BC until Jerusalem fell to the Babylonians in 586 BC. His primary message was that God's people would be exiled to Babylon because of their many sins. This made Jeremiah a prophet of doom, and extremely unpopular. Jeremiah wrote the longest book of the Bible, and is sometimes called the *weeping prophet* because of his spiritual anguish.

Jeremiah 1:4 *The word of the Lord came to me.*

Jeremiah was living an ordinary life when the word of the Lord came to him. He wasn't expecting God to speak, or planning to be a prophet. He may've thought God was making a mistake, but God assured him otherwise. *Before I formed you in the womb I knew you, before you were born I set you apart; I appointed you as a prophet to the nations* (Jeremiah 1:5), he said.

God didn't see the need for a prophet, and pick the best man for the job. He created Jeremiah to do the job for which he was made. When the word of the Lord came to Jeremiah, he found the purpose for which he was born.

Not many receive a call to ministry as clear as Jeremiah's, but we're all called to serve God with the gifts that he has given us. A good way to discern our calling is to find where our gifts meet the needs of the world. This could be as a teacher, poet, plumber, or mechanic. Our jobs are more than a way to make money; they're a way to serve God in the world.

Jeremiah 1:6 *Alas, Sovereign Lord, I said, I do not know how to speak; I am too young.*

The text does not say how old Jeremiah was, but he felt too young for the task, so he may've been in his teens. The prophetic office would be difficult and, at least once, Jeremiah considered quitting (Jeremiah 20:9). God uses people with strong personalities, like King David and the Apostle Paul. But he also uses people who are less sure of themselves, like Jeremiah and Timothy (2 Timothy 1:7). Whether we're bold or timid by nature, God wants us to *be strong in the Lord and in his mighty power* (Ephesians 6:10), wrote Paul.

Jeremiah 1:7 *But the Lord said to me, Do not say, I am too young. You must go to everyone I send you to and say whatever I command you.*

Jeremiah was given the honor of speaking for God, but it wouldn't be easy. God's message is often opposed, and Jeremiah's life would be at risk. He wasn't to hold back, however, or change the message in any way. He was to say whatever God wanted him to say, to whomever God told him to say it. This would take courage, but was also his greatest honor.

Jeremiah 1:9 *Then the Lord reached out his hand and touched my mouth and said to me, I have put my words in your mouth.*

God put his words in Jeremiah's mouth, and Jeremiah spoke for God. It's hard to imagine such authority, but all Christians speak for God whenever they share his word. This includes condemnation for sin, but also the hope of the gospel.

One preacher was robbed at gunpoint and quoted Scripture to the robber. *[T]he blood of Jesus . . . purifies us from all sin* (1 John 1:7), he said. Years later a man approached him after a sermon and confessed to being the man who robbed him. He said that verse of Scripture so lodged in his heart that it brought him to conversion.

Jeremiah 1:11-12 *The word of the Lord came to me: What do you see, Jeremiah? I see the branch of an almond tree, I replied. The Lord said to me, You have seen correctly, for I am watching to see that my word is fulfilled.*

The Hebrew word for *watching* sounds like the Hebrew word for *almond tree*. Because the almond tree was the first to bloom, it was said to be *watching* for spring. And God was watching to be sure that his word was fulfilled.

If the God of the Bible can predict the future, and no other religion can do so, then we should believe in the God of the Bible. The Bible has dozens of prophecies that have already been fulfilled, so we can be sure the others will be fulfilled in their time. God is always watching to see that his word is fulfilled.

For Reflection and Review

- *How can we discover our calling?*
- *How do you feel about sharing God's word?*
- *How do we know God's word will be fulfilled?*

Lesson 138

Jeremiah 1:13-14 *The word of the Lord came to me again: What do you see? I see a pot that is boiling, I answered. It is tilting toward us from the north. The Lord said to me, From the north disaster will be poured out on all who live in the land.*

God was going to pour out his scalding judgment on Judah from the north. We should imagine a massive cauldron of boiling water that, when poured out, would destroy everything in its path. The agent of God's judgment is identified elsewhere as the Babylonians (Jeremiah 32:24), and they would completely destroy Judah in Jeremiah's lifetime.

The Bible is filled with images that are meant to terrify so that people will respond to them. They're not always meant to be taken literally, but are always meant to be taken seriously. Time and again we learn that God doesn't make idle threats. The only appropriate response is to believe what God says, and take refuge in him.

Jeremiah 5:25 *[Y]our sins have deprived you of good.*

When the people of God were about to enter the Promised Land, God promised blessing for obedience, and cursing for disobedience (Deuteronomy 28:1-68). Tragically, they chose to disobey and were deprived of the blessing they might've enjoyed. Their sins had deprived them of good.

This is like a father who bought his son a car for his sixteenth birthday. But the night before, his son came home drunk, and the father realized he wasn't mature enough to have his own car. His sin deprived him of the good his father had planned for him.

We can also deprive ourselves of good if we're not careful. *[N]o good thing does he withhold from those whose walk is blameless* (Psalm 84:11), wrote the Psalmist. And, *godliness has value for all things, holding promise for both the present life and the life to come* (1 Timothy 4:8), wrote Paul.

There's a price attached to every sin, and it's usually higher than we think. At the very least we deprive ourselves of the purity of heart that leads to a deeper relationship with God. Who knows what other blessings we might forfeit? If we saw the real price attached to sin, we'd be less inclined to buy. Thankfully, we can take God's word for it.

Jeremiah 9:23-24 *Let not the wise boast of their wisdom or the strong boast of their strength or the rich boast of their riches, but let the one who boasts boast about this: that they have the understanding to know me.*

Judah would soon be destroyed, and all the wisdom of the wise couldn't save it. Neither could the strong, or those who had wealth. But even as captives in Babylon, the godly would still have something to boast about: at least they had the good understanding to know God.

The Apostle Paul also had a difficult life, but referred to this idea more than once: *[We] boast in God through our Lord Jesus Christ* (Romans 5:11); *Let the one who boasts boast in the Lord* (1 Corinthians 1:31); And, *May I never boast except in the cross of our Lord Jesus Christ* (Galatians 6:14).

This is all that matters in the end. What good is a college degree if you don't know the way of salvation? What good is a gold medal on your deathbed? What good is a million dollars if you can't take it with you? But even the most miserable believer in Jesus Christ will have the best of everything in the age to come (Luke 23:43). And that's something to boast about!

Jeremiah 16:1-2 *Then the word of the Lord came to me: You must not marry and have sons or daughters in this place.*

God called Jeremiah to remain single in order to keep him from needless sorrow. The future was so bleak that many would die prematurely. *They will not be mourned or buried but will be like dung lying on the ground. They will perish by sword and famine, and their dead bodies will become food for the birds and the wild animals* (Jeremiah 16:4), said God. To spare Jeremiah this hardship, God told him not to marry.

Getting married and raising children are God's plan for most (Genesis 1:28), but not for everyone. Jesus and Paul were single, and recommended it to others (Matthew 19:12, 1 Corinthians 7:7). Life is often hard, but marriage and children can make it even harder. To keep us from unforeseen misery, God may call us to be single.

Jeremiah 17:17 *[Y]ou are my refuge in the day of disaster.*

Many prepare for disaster by building a place of refuge. Most are rather simple, but one of the most remarkable cost over a billion dollars. It's an underground mansion, carved out of rock, that's able to survive earthquakes and flooding, as well as biological and chemical attacks. It can even withstand a nuclear explosion. But if your heart stops beating, it won't start it again. And if your lungs collapse, it won't fill them with air. Every earthly refuge has its limitations.

Jeremiah had an unpopular message and was often in danger. He could've run for his life but, instead, he took refuge in God. His enemies made him suffer but, when his life was over, he found it had just begun. *[T]he one who believes has eternal life* (John 6:47), said Jesus. And *Blessed are all who take refuge in him* (Psalm 2:12), wrote the Psalmist.

For Reflection and Review

- *Should God's word be taken literally?*
- *Should Christians be proud of knowing God?*
- *Do you recommend being single for God?*

Lesson 139

Jeremiah 18:1-2 *This is the word that came to Jeremiah from the Lord: Go down to the potter's house, and there I will give you my message.*

So Jeremiah went to the potter's house and found him working at his wheel. But the pot between his hands was marred, so he started over and shaped it as he pleased. *Can I not do with you, Israel, as this potter does? . . . Like clay in the hand of the potter, so are you in my hand* (Jeremiah 18:6), said God.

I took a pottery class in high school where I learned to knead the clay to make it soft, and throw it down to make it pliable. Then I spun it on the wheel, removed a stone, and started over more than once. Then it was glazed and fired in a kiln and, in the end, I had a piece of art.

It's not easy for clay to become fine china, or for us to become like Christ. But if we yield to our Maker, he'll shape us into something good. It is amazing, in fact, what God can do with a lump of clay. *We are the clay, you are the potter; we are all the work of your hand,* (Isaiah 64:8), wrote Isaiah.

Jeremiah 23:24 *Do not I fill heaven and earth? declares the Lord.*

To go from one end of the universe to the other takes billions of years. But if the universe was ten times larger, it still couldn't contain God. The God of our imagination is always smaller than the God who exists, and our greatest thought of God is nothing compared to reality. *Do not I fill heaven and earth? declares the Lord.*

Jeremiah 26:2 *Tell them everything I command you; do not omit a word.*

Jeremiah may've been tempted to leave out the hardest parts of God's message. Preachers are human too, and want to please their listeners. But the desire to please must never overrule the command to preach the truth, the whole truth, and nothing but the truth—so help us God.

The word of God includes law and gospel, threats and promises, blessings and curses. There are words of grace, mercy, and prosperity as well as wrath, judgment, and hardship. Preachers miss the mark whenever they focus on the positive at the expense of the negative, or on the negative at the expense of the positive.

People need the whole word of God, not just the parts that please them, or displease them. When Paul finished his work in Ephesus he could say with a clear conscience, *I have not hesitated to proclaim to you the whole will of God* (Acts 20:27). God's word to Jeremiah applies to preachers everywhere. *Tell them everything I command you; do not omit a word.*

*****

Jeremiah 28:10-11 *Then the prophet Hananiah took the yoke off the neck of the prophet Jeremiah and broke it, and he said before all the people, This is what the Lord says: In the same way I will break the yoke of Nebuchadnezzar king of Babylon off the neck of all the nations within two years.*

Jeremiah wore a yoke to show it was time for God's people to serve the king of Babylon (Jeremiah 27:1-7). The false prophet Hananiah embarrassed Jeremiah by removing the yoke and breaking it in front of everyone. Then he boldly predicted that Babylon's power would be broken within two years. It was an impressive confrontation, and Hananiah seemed to win.

Jeremiah 28:15 *Then the prophet Jeremiah said to Hananiah the prophet, Listen, Hananiah! The Lord has not sent you, yet you have persuaded this nation to trust in lies. Therefore this is what the Lord says: I am about to remove you from the face of the earth. This very year you are going to die, because you have preached rebellion against the Lord. In the seventh month of that same year, Hananiah the prophet died.*

Not all religious disputes are settled this clearly, but this event raises the issue of false religious claims. Other religions disagree with Christianity, and many who claim to be Christians preach another gospel (Galatians 1:8). With so much confusion, it's tempting to say nothing.

This can be wise, sometimes, but we're also encouraged to *contend for the faith that was once for all entrusted to God's holy people* (Jude 1:3), wrote Jude. We should study God's word and speak it faithfully whenever it's appropriate.

God told the prophet Jeremiah not to back down from the false prophets who only spoke their dreams. *Let the prophet who has a dream recount the dream, but let the one who has my word speak it faithfully. For what has straw to do with grain? declares the Lord* (Jeremiah 23:28). False religious claims won't be defeated until the Lord returns. Until then, God's people should know and speak the truth, even if the whole world disagrees.

For Reflection and Review

- *How does God shape his people?*
- *Why are preachers tempted to compromise God's message?*
- *Is it always appropriate to share God's word?*

Lesson 140

Jeremiah 30:11 *Though I completely destroy all the nations among which I scatter you, I will not completely destroy you.*

Many ancient people groups no longer exist, but the nation of Israel has survived. This is remarkable since, for many years, they lived outside their homeland: first in Egypt, then in Babylon, then around the world. They should've been absorbed through intermarriage, but God preserved his ancient people and brought them back to their homeland in 1948.

This is rather significant because the Apostle Paul predicted a time when all Israel will turn to Christ and be saved (Romans 11:26). Their preservation through the ages is a remarkable sign of God's faithfulness, and a fulfillment of prophecy. *Though I completely destroy all the nations among which I scatter you, I will not completely destroy you.*

Jeremiah 31:33-34 *This is the covenant I will make with the people of Israel after that time, declares the Lord. I will put my law in their minds and write it on their hearts. I will be their God, and they will be my people. No longer will they teach their neighbor, or say to one another, Know the Lord, because they will all know me, from the least of them to the greatest, declares the Lord. For I will forgive their wickedness and will remember their sins no more.*

God's people violated the covenant he made with them at Sinai (Exodus 20) but, instead of turning away from them, God promised to make a new covenant in which he'd forgive and forget their sins. If God rejected us after a thousand sins, few would last very long. But since he's willing to forgive and forget, we can live with him now and forever.

This new covenant can never fail because it's based on the sacrifice of God's own Son. After his last meal, Jesus *took the cup, saying, This cup is the new covenant in my blood, which is poured out for you* (Luke 22:20). Then he allowed himself to be arrested, and was crucified the following day. We no longer relate to God on the basis of our obedience, but on the basis of Christ who lived and died for us. It's because of him that God can forgive and forget.

*****

Jeremiah 38:4 *Then the officials said to the king, This man should be put to death. He is discouraging the soldiers who are left in this city, as well as all the people, by the things he is saying to them.*

Jeremiah was telling the people it was God's will for them to surrender to the Babylonians. This discouraged the soldiers, who were defending the city, so the officials wanted Jeremiah dead. They didn't want to kill him themselves, however, so they put him in a cistern. *[I]t had no water in it, only mud, and Jeremiah sank down into the mud* (Jeremiah 38:6).

Jeremiah wasn't a young man anymore. His life had been hard, and this was his lowest point. As he sank in the mud, he may've quoted David: *I sink in the miry depths, where there is no foothold. . . . Rescue me from the mire, do not let me sink; deliver me from those who hate me* (Psalm 69:2, 14).

Ministry isn't always easy, and ministers are often abused. But the Lord heard Jeremiah's prayer and sent some people to help. *Put these old rags and worn-out clothes under your arms to pad the ropes. Jeremiah did so, and they pulled him up with the ropes and lifted him out of the cistern* (Jeremiah 28:12-13).

Whenever we are sinking down we should pray to God for help. There are people he can send to pull us out. And if we're not sinking down, we should look for those who are. The men who helped Jeremiah are remembered for their kindness. And *whatever you did for one of the least of these brothers and sisters of mine, you did for me* (Matthew 25:40), said Jesus.

*****

Jeremiah 40:6 *Jeremiah went to Gedaliah . . . and stayed with him among the people who were left behind in the land.*

After destroying Jerusalem, and deporting most of the Jews, the Babylonians appointed Gedaliah to govern the few that remained. But Gedaliah was murdered and, fearing retaliation, the remaining Jews fled to Egypt, taking Jeremiah with them.

But Jeremiah was against going to Egypt, and had warned against it (Jeremiah 42:7-22). While they were there, he prophesied the king of Babylon would *. . . come and attack Egypt, bringing death to those destined for death, captivity to those destined for captivity, and the sword to those destined for the sword. He will set fire to the temples of the gods of Egypt; he will burn their temples and take their gods captive. As a shepherd picks his garment clean of lice, so he will pick Egypt clean and depart* (Jeremiah 43:11-12). This occurred around 568 BC, as stated in an ancient text housed by the British Museum.

God's people had a long history of rebellion, and got what they deserved. *[R]ebels and sinners will both be broken, and those who forsake the Lord will perish* (Isaiah 1:28), wrote Isaiah. Those who oppose the Almighty should never expect to prosper long, certainly not forever.

For Reflection and Review

- *Why is the survival of the Jews surprising?*
- *What's so good about the new covenant?*
- *Have you ever been helped when you were sinking down?*

Lesson 141

Lamentations 1:1 *How deserted lies the city, once so full of people! How like a widow is she, who once was great among the nations! She who was queen among the provinces has now become a slave.*

The book of Lamentations is anonymous but was probably written by the prophet Jeremiah shortly after the fall of Jerusalem (586 BC), to comfort those who were carried off to Babylon. Losing their homeland was catastrophic, and this little book of poems provided comfort by expressing their feelings and giving them hope.

Lamentations 1:5 *Her foes have become her masters; her enemies are at ease. The Lord has brought her grief because of her many sins.*

Wherever there is suffering people want to know, *Why is this happening?* The answer is seldom clear, but in this case it was. God's people were suffering because of their *many sins*.

About a thousand years earlier God promised his people wonderful blessings if they would obey (Deuteronomy 28:1-14). But he also threatened terrible curses if they wouldn't obey (Deuteronomy 28:15-68). Since God's people wouldn't obey, the curses he threatened finally came upon them.

Because you did not serve the Lord your God joyfully and gladly in the time of prosperity, therefore in hunger and thirst, in nakedness and dire poverty, you will serve the enemies the Lord sends against you. He will put an iron yoke on your neck until he has destroyed you (Deuteronomy 28:47-48), warned Moses.

It's clear from the Bible and history that whatever God says comes to pass eventually. All his promises will come to pass, and all his threats will come to pass. *Does he speak and then not act? Does he promise and not fulfill?* (Numbers 23:19).

Many want to dwell on the promises of God without concern for his threats, but this is never wise. We must pay equal attention to the parts of the Bible we like and to the parts we don't. Otherwise, we'll be taken by surprise.

Lamentations 1:9 *Look, Lord, on my affliction, for the enemy has triumphed.*

The story of the Bible is one of continuous conflict. Pharaoh's armies pursued the people of God, but were drowned in the sea (Exodus 14:23-28). Before they entered the Promised Land, the Israelites had to battle Sihon and Og (Numbers 21:21-35). After they entered the Promised Land, they had to fight for every inch of it. (Joshua 1-24). Now, to their dismay, everything seemed lost. The enemy had finally triumphed.

The kingdom of God suffers defeat, but defeat is never final. Jesus was crucified, but he rose from the dead. The early church was persecuted, but also grew in numbers. Missionaries are martyred, but leave converts behind.

The goal of the church is not to win the world for Christ, once and for all, but to stay in the battle by preaching the gospel. *For our struggle is not against flesh and blood, but against . . . the spiritual forces of evil in the heavenly realms* (Ephesians 6:12), wrote Paul.

Lamentations 1:14 *My sins have been bound into a yoke; by his hands they were woven together. They have been hung on my neck, and the Lord has sapped my strength. He has given me into the hands of those I cannot withstand.*

A yoke is a harness placed around an animal's neck, so it can pull a plow. Yokes were usually made out of wood but, in this case, it was made out of sin. God had woven the sin of his people into a yoke so they could plow for the king of Babylon. Sin masquerades as freedom, but always leads to bondage.

Jesus invites us to trade our yoke of sin for his yoke of discipleship. *Take my yoke upon you and learn from me. . . . For my yoke is easy and my burden is light* (Matthew 11:29-30), he said. Our greatest freedom doesn't come from serving sin, but from serving Jesus Christ.

Lamentations 2:12 *They say to their mothers, Where is bread and wine? as they faint like the wounded in the streets of the city, as their lives ebb away in their mothers' arms.*

This is one of the saddest scenes in the Bible. The king of Babylon surrounded the city of Jerusalem and cut off the food supply for over a year. The famine was so severe that mothers watched their children faint from hunger and die in their arms. But their own hunger was so intense that, instead of burying their children, they ate them. *With their own hands compassionate women have cooked their own children, who became their food when my people were destroyed* (Lamentations 4:10), wrote Jeremiah.

This is also what Moses threatened about a thousand years before: *The most gentle and sensitive woman among you . . . will begrudge the husband she loves and her own son or daughter the afterbirth from her womb and the children she bears. For in her dire need she intends to eat them secretly because of the suffering your enemy will inflict on you during the siege of your cities* (Deuteronomy 28:56-57).

People accused of a terrible crime often say emphatically, *I'm not capable of doing such a thing.* But under the right circumstances, there's nothing of which we're not capable. This is why Jesus taught us to pray, *lead us not into temptation, but deliver us from the evil one* (Matthew 6:13).

Lamentations 2:14 *The visions of your prophets were false and worthless; they did not expose your sin to ward off your captivity. The prophecies they gave you were false and misleading.*

The duty of the prophets was to protect God's people from divine wrath, by pointing out their sin, so they'd repent. But God's people didn't want to repent, so they surrounded themselves with prophets who told them what they wanted to hear.

The Bible has much to say about God's love, patience, kindness, and forgiveness. But it also speaks of sin, judgment, wrath, and hell. Any preacher who only tells the people what they want to hear isn't speaking for God. *Woe to you when everyone speaks well of you, for that is how their ancestors treated the false prophets* (Luke 6:26), said Jesus. Faithful preachers must proclaim the love of God, as well as his terrible threats.

For Reflection and Review

- *Why was the book of Lamentations written?*
- *Why does sin lead to grief?*
- *Why isn't biblical preaching more popular?*

Lesson 142

Lamentations 3:21-23 *Yet this I call to mind and therefore I have hope: Because of the Lord's great love we are not consumed, for his compassions never fail. They are new every morning; great is your faithfulness.*

As the prophet considered the terrible things that happened, he realized that he and a few others were still alive. He attributed this to the love, compassion, and faithfulness of God. This is one of the finest statements of faith in the Bible. It's easy to praise God when things are at their best, but praising God when things are at their worst is a mark of genuine faith.

And things were truly at their worst. The city was in ruins, many had died, others were in exile, and the prophet himself was now an old man. But Jeremiah still had God, so his future was bright.

Whom have I in heaven but you? And earth has nothing I desire besides you. My flesh and my heart may fail, but God is the strength of my heart and my portion forever (Psalm 73:25-26), wrote Asaph. Whoever has God has all they need for the future.

Lamentations 3:32 *Though he brings grief, he will show compassion, so great is his unfailing love.*

We can never experience the comfort of God's compassion until we to through suffering. Through sickness we learn the value of health. Through cold we learn the value of warmth. And through suffering we learn the value of God's compassion. He is *the Father of compassion and the God of all comfort, who comforts us in all our troubles, so that we can comfort those in any trouble with the comfort we ourselves receive from God* (2 Corinthians 1:3-4), wrote Paul. And that comfort is real.

A godly mom and dad raised their children through hard financial times. They were so poor, in fact, they feared their children might lose faith, because God didn't seem to provide for them. But their children grew up to love the Lord, and one began a ministry to the poor. When all they had was God, he said, God made all the difference. God is compassionate to those who suffer and, through suffering, we learn to be compassionate too.

Lamentations 3:38 *Is it not from the mouth of the Most High that both calamities and good things come?*

The disaster that overtook God's people was so extreme they may've wondered how God could allow it. If God was good, how could he allow the Babylonians to inflict such misery on his chosen people? The problem is theological, but can be deeply personal when suffering comes our way.

Some people try to resolve the problem by thinking that everything pleasant comes from from God, and everything painful comes from Satan. But that's not what the Bible teaches. *Shall we accept good from God, and not trouble?* (Job 2:10), asked Job. *When disaster comes to a city, has not the Lord caused it?* (Amos 3:6), asked Amos. *I bring prosperity and create disaster* (Isaiah 45:7), said God.

The Christian solution to the problem of evil is that God allows terrible things to happen for a good reason. This is seen most clearly in crucifixion of Jesus Christ. *This man was handed over to you by God's deliberate plan and foreknowledge* (Acts 2:23), said Peter. *They did what your power and will had decided beforehand should happen* (Acts 4:28), said the church.

God used the greatest evil ever (the crucifixion of Christ) to bring about the greatest good ever (salvation for the world). God's sovereignty over evil is a comfort to Christians because it means we're never in the hands of fate, chance, or the devil, but always in the hands of our heavenly Father who loves us.

The Christian heart, since it has been thoroughly persuaded that all things happen by God's plan, and that nothing takes place by chance, will ever look to him as the principal causes of things, yet will give attention to the secondary causes in their proper place (John Calvin).

Lamentations 3:39 *Why should the living complain when punished for their sins?*

God's people had lost everything, and their lives were worse than ever, so they probably felt like complaining. But any punishment in this life is always less than we deserve. The greatness of our sin isn't only in the deed, but in the greatness of the one we've offended. There are no little sins because there is no little God to sin against. The fact that we aren't always punished immediately is a sign of God's patience and grace.

The badness of our sin is also revealed in the biblical teaching of hell (Matthew 18:8). The punishment of eternal fire seems disproportionate to even a lifetime of sin, but reveals that our sin is worse than we commonly think. Sin is treason against the Most High God to whom we owe everything, and hell is perfect justice.

But Christ has died for our sin so that, instead of justice, we can receive eternal life (John 3:16). The better we understand the bad news, the more we'll appreciate the good news. *To him belongs eternal praise* (Psalm 111:10), wrote the Psalmist.

Lamentations 3:40 *Let us examine our ways and test them, and let us return to the Lord.*

In light of their devastation, Jeremiah called the people of God to examine their ways. If they had lived uprightly, things would've been different. But this was an opportunity for them to change, so they could enjoy God's favor once again.

Search me, God, and know my heart. . . . See if there is any offensive way in me, and lead me in the way everlasting (Psalm 139:23-24), wrote David. David was so concerned about his relationship with God that he not only examined himself, but asked God to examine him as well. We can't avoid sin completely, but at the end of every day we can confess our sins and ask God to reveal those we've overlooked. Through careful examination we can stay close to God and please him.

Lamentations 5:21-22 *Restore us to yourself, Lord, that we may return; renew our days as of old unless you have utterly rejected us and are angry with us beyond measure.*

The book of Lamentations ends on an uncertain note. In light of their disaster, Jeremiah was concerned that God had rejected his people forever. Perhaps they had sinned to the point of no return. Thankfully, this was not the case. About seventy years later God allowed his people to return from exile and rebuild the city of Jerusalem. Sin is always more serious than we think, and the consequences can be extreme. But those who turn to the Lord should be assured of his mercy. *[W]hoever comes to me I will never drive away* (John 6:37), said Jesus.

For Reflection and Review

- *Has suffering made you compassionate?*
- *Why does God allow terrible things to happen?*
- *Why shouldn't people complain about their suffering?*

Lesson 143

Ezekiel 1:1 *In my thirtieth year, in the fourth month on the fifth day, while I was among the exiles by the Kebar River, the heavens were opened and I saw visions of God.*

The prophet Ezekiel wrote from around 593 to 571 BC, to the exiled Jews in Babylon. He wanted to assure them of God's plan to bring them back to Jerusalem, and to restore the temple. Some Jews were still in Jerusalem, since the city hadn't fallen yet, but Ezekiel predicted its doom. In his thirtieth year (the fifth year of his exile) he received an elaborate vision from God.

Ezekiel 1:4 *I looked, and I saw a windstorm coming out of the north—an immense cloud with flashing lightning and surrounded by brilliant light.*

He also saw living creatures with wings and four faces: one of a human being, one of a lion, one of an ox, and one of an eagle. Beside each creature was a wheel full of eyes. *When the living creatures moved, the wheels beside them moved; and when the living creatures rose from the ground, the wheels also rose* (Ezekiel 1:19). Overhead was a throne on which a man was seated who had the radiance of a rainbow (Ezekiel 1:26-28).

This seems to be a vision of God riding in a strange and glorious chariot. This was important to the exiled Jews in Babylon, because they were accustomed to worshipping God at the temple in Jerusalem. Since that was no longer possible, they may've felt cut off from God. But through this vision God revealed his mobility. He wasn't tied to a temple, but could go wherever his people were.

King David expressed a similar idea many years earlier: *Where can I go from your Spirit? Where can I flee from your presence? If I go up to the heavens, you are there; if I make my bed in the depths, you are there* (Psalm 139:7-8). No matter how far away from God we feel, he's always closer than we think.

*****

Ezekiel 3:1 *And he said to me, Son of man . . . eat this scroll; then go and speak to the people of Israel.*

In his vision, the prophet was given a scroll containing words of *lament and mourning and woe* (Ezekiel 2:10). These were words he'd bring to God's people in Babylon. He was to eat the scroll, meaning he should inwardly digest it. He wasn't to deliver God's words until they were a part of him.

Like the prophet Ezekiel, Christian preachers aren't free to say whatever they want, however they want. They should immerse themselves in God's word until it becomes part of their inner being. Then they should deliver God's word with the earnestness of someone speaking for God. *If anyone speaks, they should do so as one who speaks the very words of God* (1 Peter 4:11), wrote Peter. Speaking God's words should never be done lightly.

Ezekiel 3:17 *Son of man, I have made you a watchman for the people of Israel; so hear the word I speak and give them warning from me.*

Watchmen were positioned on the walls of a city to warn of approaching danger. If they failed at their jobs they were held accountable, and could be put to death. In this case, the approaching enemy was God. If Ezekiel failed to warn the people, he'd be held accountable, and possibly put to death.

Ezekiel 3:18-19 *When I say to a wicked person, You will surely die, and you do not warn them or speak out to dissuade them from their evil ways in order to save their life, that wicked person will die for their sin, and I will hold you accountable for their blood. But if you do warn the wicked person and they do not turn from their wickedness or from their evil ways, they will die for their sin; but you will have saved yourself.*

This command was given to the prophet Ezekiel, but some application can be made to those who preach the gospel. In order to be more agreeable, and to reach more people, some preachers avoid the subject of sin, or only speak of it generally. But, apart from sin, there is no need for salvation. Without the bad news of future judgment, the good news of salvation becomes no news at all. Preachers must never fail to warn sinners of their need to be saved (Acts 4:12).

Ezekiel 3:26-27 *I will make your tongue stick to the roof of your mouth so that you will be silent and unable to rebuke them, for they are a rebellious people. But when I speak to you, I will open your mouth and you shall say to them, This is what the Sovereign Lord says.*

Ezekiel couldn't speak for several years, unless he had a message from God. He didn't talk about sports, the whether, the economy, his health, or any other small talk. The only time he opened his mouth was to speak God's word. The effect, of course, was that his words had greater authority because they weren't diluted by chatter.

Likewise, Paul instructed Timothy to *Avoid godless chatter, because those who indulge in it will become more and more ungodly* (2 Timothy 2:16). Likewise, Solomon observed that *many words mark the speech of a fool* (Ecclesiastes 5:3). For several years I served on the governing board of a church with a gentleman who said very little. But whenever he opened his mouth, everyone else shut theirs. Whoever wants to be taken seriously can learn from the prophet Ezekiel.

Ezekiel 4:1 *Now, son of man, take a block of clay, put it in front of you and draw the city of Jerusalem on it.*

God commanded the prophet to make a model of Jerusalem under siege, with battering rams around it. This symbolized the Babylonians cutting off their food supply.

Ezekiel 4:3 *Then take an iron pan, place it as an iron wall between you and the city and turn your face toward it.*

This symbolized God hiding his face. *I will hide my face from them, and they will be destroyed . . . . I will certainly hide my face in that day because of all their wickedness* (Deuteronomy 31:17-18), said God.

Ezekiel 4:4 *Then lie on your left side and put the sin of the people of Israel upon yourself.*

God told the prophet to lie on his left side for three hundred ninety days, and on his right side for forty days, each day representing a year. The meaning isn't clear, but it may represent the number of years of punishment for Israel and Judah respectively.

Ezekiel 4:10 *Weigh out twenty shekels of food to eat each day and eat it at set times.*

This symbolized the scarcity of food while Jerusalem was under siege. Even more dramatically, God told the prophet to cook his food using human excrement to show the scarcity of wood. When the prophet objected, God allowed him to use cow dung instead (Ezekiel 4:15).

Ezekiel 5:1 *Now, son of man, take a sharp sword and use it as a barber's razor to shave your head and your beard.*

The prophet was commanded to shave his head and beard even though this was normally forbidden. *Do not cut the hair at the sides of your head or clip off the edges of your beard* (Leviticus 19:27), said God. The baldness of the prophet would show that his message was out of the ordinary.

The prophet was then told to divide his hair into three equal parts, representing the people in Jerusalem. The first was to be burned, the second was to be chopped, and the third was to be scattered (Ezekiel 5:2). This was how God planned to punish his people.

These five prophetic actions were symbolic ways of showing how God would punish his people. Ezekiel's ministry was unique, and shows how far God will go to communicate his message.

For Reflection and Review

- *Why did the Jews in Babylon need to know that God was still with them?*
- *Why did God tell Ezekiel to eat a scroll?*
- *Why did God make Ezekiel's tongue stick to the roof of his mouth?*

Lesson 144

Ezekiel 18:24 *But if a righteous person turns from their righteousness and commits sin and does the same detestable things the wicked person does, will they live? None of the righteous things that person has done will be remembered. Because of the unfaithfulness they are guilty of and because of the sins they have committed, they will die.*

As the prophet preached God's word, he saw people respond in at least three ways. Some rejected God's word and remained wicked. Others received God's word and became righteous. Others became righteous for a while, but then returned to their wickedness.

The Apostle Peter was also concerned for those who received God's word but later turned away. *If they have escaped the corruption of the world by knowing our Lord and Savior Jesus Christ and are again entangled in it and are overcome, they are worse off at the end than they were at the beginning. It would have been better for them not to have known the way of righteousness, than to have known it and then to turn their backs on the sacred command that was passed on to them* (1 Peter 2:20-21), he wrote.

We can understand why people turn away from wickedness to become righteous. But why would anyone turn away from righteousness to become wicked? One answer is *fatigue*. It's not hard to be good for a while, but being good all the time can be exhausting. Denying our sinful natures day after day requires moral stamina. A man who was in prison for committing serious crimes admitted this freely. *I know what it is to be good, and I know what it is to be bad, and being bad is easier*, he said.

Even youths grow tired and weary, and young men stumble and fall; but those who hope in the Lord will renew their strength. They will soar on wings like eagles; they will run and not grow weary, they will walk and not be faint (Isaiah 40:30-31), wrote Isaiah. Followers of Jesus Christ need supernatural strength to follow him, and he will supply it if we keep on asking (Matthew 7:7).

Ezekiel 18:32 *I take no pleasure in the death of anyone, declares the Sovereign Lord. Repent and live!*

Many of God's people were living in exile, others had died of starvation, and others were put to the sword. Given the severity of their punishment, some may've wondered if God enjoyed afflicting his people. To this we can add the biblical teaching of eternal punishment (Matthew 25:41). If God is good, why does he let people suffer and die, only to send them to hell? What kind of God would do this?

Against the problem of suffering, the biblical writers insisted that God is good, and wants everyone to be saved. *[God is] not wanting anyone to perish, but everyone to come to repentance* (2 Peter 3:9), wrote Peter. And *[God] wants all people to be saved and to come to a knowledge of the truth* (1 Timothy 2:4), wrote Paul. *For he does not willingly bring affliction or grief to anyone* (Lamentations 3:33), wrote Jeremiah.

But the greatest proof that God is good doesn't come from what he's said, but from what he's done. *For God so loved the world that he gave his one and only Son, that whoever believes in him shall not perish but have eternal life* (John 3:16), wrote John.

Human suffering is real, and so is eternal punishment. But when we see what God has done for our salvation, we can never question his goodness or love again. He took the suffering we deserve, and put it on himself, so we cold live forever. Whenever we question the goodness of God we must think about the cross.

Ezekiel 20:43 *There you will remember your conduct and all the actions by which you have defiled yourselves, and you will loathe yourselves for all the evil you have done.*

God's people sinned by turning from God to idols, and were largely unrepentant. But God promised a time when they would loathe themselves for what they had done. *Then you will remember your evil ways and wicked deeds, and you will loathe yourselves for your sins and detestable practices* (Ezekiel 36:31), said God.

The Apostle Paul is a good example of this. Before he knew Christ, he considered himself to be *faultless* (Philippians 3:6). But after he knew Christ, he considered himself to be *wretched*. We tend to think we're pretty good people until we see ourselves in the light of God's presence. Then we understand we're not. This can be helpful in making spiritual progress, because in order to become what we are not, we must be unhappy with what we are.

Thankfully, there will be no self loathing in heaven, because there will be no more sin. *[H]e who began a good work in you will carry it on to completion until the day of Christ Jesus* (Philippians 1:6), wrote Paul. A billion years from now it'll be almost a billon years since the last time we sinned. This is the longing of every redeemed heart.

*****

Ezekiel 21:21 *For the king of Babylon will stop at the fork in the road, at the junction of the two roads, to seek an omen: He will cast lots with arrows, he will consult his idols, he will examine the liver.*

As Nebuchadnezzar marched out to war, he came to a fork in the road and sought direction from his gods. Arrows were apparently marked and tossed to the ground, to discern which way to go. Idol's were also consulted, and livers of sacrificed animals were studied, to get direction from gods that didn't exist.

Here we see the darkness of the world before the coming of Christ. Even kings were making important decisions based on superstition. But all that changed when Jesus came. *The people walking in darkness have seen a great light; on those living in the land of deep darkness a light has dawned* (Isaiah 9:2), wrote Isaiah.

I am the light of the world. Whoever follows me will never walk in darkness (John 8:12), said Jesus. The remarkable thing about Christianity is that it not only makes sense in itself, but makes sense of everything else. *I believe in Christianity as I believe that the sun has risen, not only because I see it but because by it I see everything else* (CS Lewis).

For Reflection and Review

- *Why do some people quit God?*
- *If God is good, why does he let people suffer?*
- *How should Christians feel about themselves?*

Lesson 145

Ezekiel 23:25 *I will direct my jealous anger against you, and they will deal with you in fury. They will cut off your noses and your ears, and those of you who are left will fall by the sword.*

Mutilation was common in ancient warfare, but could also be used to punish adultery. If a man's wife had an affair he could have her nose cut off, and have her lover castrated. God's people committed spiritual adultery by abandoning him for other gods. God's jealous anger was so intense that he planned to send foreign armies to mutilate their faces.

Again we see the intensity of God's jealous anger against those who commit spiritual adultery. Paul may've had this in mind when he warned believers in Corinth not to attend idol feasts: *Are we trying to arouse the Lord's jealousy? Are we stronger than he?* (1 Corinthians 10:22), he asked. God's love for his people is like the love of a jealous husband, and it's wise for us to be faithful.

*****

Ezekiel 24:16 *Son of man, with one blow I am about to take away from you the delight of your eyes. Yet do not lament or weep or shed any tears.*

Suddenly, the prophet's wife was dead. We're not told how she died except that it happened quickly —*with one blow*. In spite of his terrible loss, the prophet wasn't allowed to grieve. The people of God were puzzled by this, and asked what it meant. The prophet explained that they too would suffer loss. The temple they loved, and the family they left behind in Jerusalem, would soon be destroyed by the Babylonians. They weren't to grieve either because this was the judgment of God due to their sins (Ezekiel 24:21-23).

The death of Ezekiel's wife was traumatic for him, but a blessing for her. *Blessed are the dead who die in the Lord* (Revelation 14:13), wrote John. And *[we] prefer to be away from the body and at home with the Lord* (2 Corinthians 5:8), wrote Paul. Whether times are good or bad, death is always a blessing for those who belong to Christ. This must've been a comfort to the prophet whenever he missed his wife.

*****

Ezekiel 33:11 *I take no pleasure in the death of the wicked, but rather that they turn from their ways and live. Turn! Turn from your evil ways!*

The prophet explained that if a righteous person turned from their righteousness they'd die, but if a wicked person turned from their wickedness they'd live (Ezekiel 33:12). This is quite different from the popular idea that God's favor is won or lost, based on the whether our good deeds outweigh our bad deeds. In fact, God's eternal favor is won or lost based on our relationship with Christ. If we die in faith we'll be saved (John 3:16), if not we'll be lost (John 3:36).

This means a person who's lived wickedly can turn to Christ with their dying breath and be saved (Luke 23:43). But the person who's followed Christ for years dare not turn away from him (2 Peter 2:21). God's eternal favor isn't determined by how many good or bad deeds we've done, but by trusting Christ to the end.

Ezekiel 33:31-32 *My people come to you, as they usually do, and sit before you to hear your words, but they do not put them into practice. . . . Indeed, to them you are nothing more than one who sings love songs with a beautiful voice and plays an instrument well, for they hear your words but do not put them into practice.*

The prophet was such a popular speaker that he had no problem getting a crowd. But those who gathered saw him as little more than entertainment—like someone who could sing and play the guitar. They had no intention of putting his words into practice.

Jesus shared the same frustration and gave the people a warning: *everyone who hears these words of mine and does not put them into practice is like a foolish man who built his house on sand. The rain came down, the streams rose, and the winds blew and beat against that house, and it fell with a great crash* (Matthew 7:26-27). Hearing God's word is a blessing, but we turn it into a curse if we don't do what God says.

*****

Ezekiel 36:26 *I will give you a new heart and put a new spirit in you; I will remove from you your heart of stone and give you a heart of flesh.*

The peoples' hearts were so calloused by sin that they'd never respond to God with the loving obedience he desired. So God a planned radical surgery. *I will remove from them their heart of stone and give them a heart of flesh* (Ezekiel 11:19), he said.

A middle-aged man had heart disease, and little time to live. But another man died, about that time, and his heart became available. The surgery was successful and, sometime later, the man was married. His new wife was a widow, and together they learned that the heart inside his chest belonged to her former husband. It's a strange story, but it actually strengthened the love they share.

In order to get a new heart, someone with a good heart has to die. The only person with a perfectly good heart was Jesus Christ, and he died to give us his heart. This is another way of describing what happens when the Spirit of Christ comes into us (Acts 2:38). The Spirit within us is the Spirit of Jesus Christ (Romans 8:9). This is the source of our love for him.

For Reflection and Review

- *How is God like a jealous husband?*
- *What hope is there for the wicked?*
- *How has God changed your heart?*

Lesson 146

Ezekiel 37:1-2 *The hand of the Lord was on me, and he brought me out by the Spirit of the Lord and set me in the middle of a valley; it was full of bones. He led me back and forth among them, and I saw a great many bones on the floor of the valley, bones that were very dry.*

In what seems to be a vision, Ezekiel was transported by the Spirit to a valley full of bones, *a great many bones*. It may've been a battle scene in which everyone died, and no one was left to bury the dead. The prophet didn't view the scene from a distance, but was escorted throughout the valley by God himself. The fact that the bones were *very dry* shows they had been dead for some time.

Ezekiel's valley of death is a place of despair. All the dreams and aspirations of the deceased had come to nothing. Once young, and full of potential, they were now a bony shadow of their former selves. Their tender flesh was eaten by birds until nothing was left but bones. Here we see ourselves as well. Not today, perhaps, but eventually. Life as we know it comes to an end.

Ezekiel 37:3 *He asked me, Son of man, can these bones live? I said, Sovereign Lord, you alone know.*

The prophet may've considered a few accounts where someone came back from the dead. The prophet Elijah raised the son of a widow (1 Kings 17:21-22). The prophet Elisha raised the son of a Shunammite woman (2 Kings 4:34-35). And when a man was placed in Elisha's tomb, he . . . *stood up on his feet* (2 Kings 13:21). But these had only died recently, and their bodies were still in tact. Did God have the power to raise a valley of bones that were completely dry?

Ezekiel 37:4-6 *Then he said to me, Prophesy to these bones and say to them, Dry bones, hear the word of the Lord! This is what the Sovereign Lord says to these bones: I will make breath enter you, and you will come to life. I will attach tendons to you and make flesh come upon you and cover you with skin; I will put breath in you, and you will come to life.*

The word translated *breath* can also be translated *wind* or *spirit*, and occurs several times in this passage. The same idea also occurs in the creation of man. *Then the Lord God formed a man from the dust of the ground and breathed into his nostrils the breath of life, and the man became a living being* (Genesis 2:7). Likewise, *[God] gives everyone life and breath and everything else* (Acts 17:25), said Paul. Since God is the source of life, he's able to create it, and create it again. This is good news for the believing dead.

Ezekiel 37:7-8 *So I prophesied as I was commanded. And as I was prophesying, there was a noise, a rattling sound, and the bones came together, bone to bone. I looked, and tendons and flesh appeared on them and skin covered them, but there was no breath in them.*

As the prophet spoke God's word, the bones began to assemble before his very eyes. Other parts were added until a vast number of bodies were completely in tact. But they weren't breathing.

Ezekiel 37:9 *Then he said to me, Prophesy to the breath; prophesy, son of man, and say to it, This is what the Sovereign Lord says: Come, breath, from the four winds and breathe into these slain, that they may live.*

Then the breath of God came into the bodies and *they came to life and stood on their feet—a vast army* (Ezekiel 37:10). God's army was raised from the dead, never to die again. Likewise, *the trumpet will sound, [and] the dead will be raised* (1 Corinthians 15:52), wrote Paul.

This idea is not very developed in the Old Testament, but does appear occasionally. *[A]fter my skin has been destroyed . . . in my flesh I will see God* (Job 19:26), said Job. *Multitudes who sleep in the dust of the earth will awake* (Daniel 12:2), wrote Daniel. *[Y]our dead will live, Lord; their bodies will rise* (Isaiah 26:19), wrote Isaiah. *I will deliver this people from the power of the grave; I will redeem them from death* (Hosea 13:14), said God. As hard as it is to imagine, God is planning a resurrection.

Ezekiel 37:11-12 *Then he said to me: Son of man, these bones are the people of Israel. They say, Our bones are dried up and our hope is gone; we are cut off. Therefore prophesy and say to them: This is what the Sovereign Lord says: My people, I am going to open your graves and bring you up from them; I will bring you back to the land of Israel.*

God's people were in exile, far away from the Promised Land. The northern kingdom fell to the Assyrians, and the southern kingdom fell to the Babylonians. The temple was destroyed, and the city was in ruins. God's people were dying outside the Promised Land, without any hope for the future. But through Ezekiel, God declared that he'd not only raise his people from the dead, but bring them back to the Promised Land. We too will be raised, not to live on a cloud, but on a renewed earth (2 Peter 3:13).

After God made the world, he paused to admire his work, and declared it *very good* (Genesis 1:31). This included Adam and Eve, and the soil from which they came (Genesis 2:7). Sin has made a mess of things, but won't have the last word—God is reversing the curse.

Blessed are the meek, for they will inherit the earth (Matthew 5:5), said Jesus. *The righteous will inherit the land and dwell in it forever* (Psalm 37:29), wrote David. *Then I saw a new heaven and a new earth* (Revelation 21:1), wrote John. God will raise his people from the dead to live forever on a new earth.

Ezekiel 37:13-14 *Then you, my people, will know that I am the Lord, when I open your graves and bring you up from them. I will put my Spirit in you and you will live, and I will settle you in your own land. Then you will know that I the Lord have spoken, and I have done it, declares the Lord.*

God has given proof that he will do this through the resurrection of Jesus Christ. Paul called Christ *the firstfruits of those who have fallen asleep* (1 Corinthians 15:20). Firstfruits were harvested early, and were a sign of the greater harvest to come. By raising Jesus from the dead, God has assured us that we'll be raised as well. *[I]f the Spirit of him who raised Jesus from the dead is living in you, he who raised Christ from the dead will also give life to your mortal bodies* (Romans 8:11), wrote Paul.

Most of us struggle with our mortal bodies for years. In the beginning, perhaps, our bodies are strong, healthy, and even graceful. But with the passing of time they decline. And with the passing of more time, they begin to fail. Good health, as we know it, is only dying slowly.

But in the age to come our bodies will be raised with a glory we can't imagine. Jesus *will transform our lowly bodies so that they will be like his glorious body* (Philippians 3:21), wrote Paul. Most people never have a glorious body in this age, but in the age to come all God's people will have a glorious body that will never die. This is the the resurrection which Ezekiel saw so many years ago.

For Reflection and Review

- *What does the resurrection tell us about the age to come?*
- *How do we know that God will raise the dead?*
- *How will our bodies be different in the age to come?*

Lesson 147

Daniel 1:1 *In the third year of the reign of Jehoiakim king of Judah, Nebuchadnezzar king of Babylon came to Jerusalem and besieged it.*

The prophet Daniel wrote around 530 BC to Jews who were exiled in Babylon. He wanted them to know that God was in control, and had a future for them. He was also a model of how to live faithfully in a pagan culture.

The Babylonian exile began in 605 BC, when God sent the king of Babylon to take some of the Jews into captivity as a result of their unfaithfulness. This happened again in 597 BC, and again in 586 BC, when Jerusalem was destroyed, and the temple was burned (2 Chronicles 36:5-23). This fulfilled what God threatened through Moses many years before: *I will scatter you among the nations and will draw out my sword and pursue you. Your land will be laid waste, and your cities will lie in ruins* (Leviticus 26:33).

Daniel 1:3-4 *Then the king ordered Ashpenaz, chief of his court officials, to bring into the king's service some of the Israelites from the royal family and the nobility—young men without any physical defect, handsome, showing aptitude for every kind of learning, well informed, quick to understand, and qualified to serve in the king's palace.*

Nebuchadnezzar saw the wisdom of bringing the most promising young people into his government, even if they were captives. Daniel, Hananiah, Mishael, and Azariah were likely about fifteen years old when they were enrolled in the king's academy. They were exiles in a foreign land, with no rights or privileges when, suddenly, they were singled out for government service. This was the opportunity of a lifetime.

Daniel 1:5 *The king assigned them a daily amount of food and wine from the king's table.*

Their academic training would be rigorous, and would last for the next three years. During that time they were to be well fed, and assimilated into the Babylonian culture. To that end, their God-honoring names were replaced with names that honored the gods of Babylon: *to Daniel, the name Belteshazzar; to Hananiah, Shadrach; to Mishael, Meshach; and to Azariah, Abednego.* This would've been a jolt to the godly young men who worshipped the God of Israel.

Being drafted into the king's service became a mixed blessing, and raised an important question: How do God's people live when they find themselves in a culture opposed to God? Do they revolt, or go along with it? Or do they find a middle way? Sometimes the devil attacks, other times he seduces. Both have the same goal: to persuade God's people to abandon their faith.

Daniel 1:8 *Daniel resolved not to defile himself with the royal food and wine.*

This was not an easy decision. The king's food and wine were probably dedicated to idols, and this troubled Daniel's conscience. We can imagine his struggle as he considered how far he'd go to accommodate the pagan culture in which he found himself. He believed in the God of Abraham, but was no longer in the Promised Land. Since the Babylonians were treating him well, perhaps he should abandon his former faith, and go with the flow of his new situation. To go against it could mean expulsion from the king's academy, or even worse.

Daniel's struggle is not unique. The ways of God are holy, and the ways of the world are not. As long as God's people live in an unholy world, they have to consider how far they'll go to get along. It's not an easy tension and the stakes are often high. *But Daniel resolved not to defile himself with the royal food and wine.*

Daniel 1:8b *[Daniel] asked the chief official for permission not to defile himself this way.*

Daniel displayed maturity beyond his teenage years. The zeal of his youth may've urged him to defy the king's orders but, instead, he asked permission. He was determined not to eat the royal food and wine no matter what, but he knew it was foolish to make demands when he could ask a favor. So that's what he did.

Daniel 1:10 *[T]he official told Daniel, I am afraid of my lord the king, who has assigned your food and drink. Why should he see you looking worse than the other young men your age? The king would then have my head because of you.*

The official was sympathetic toward Daniel but didn't want to lose his head—a reasonable concern. So Daniel proposed a ten-day diet for himself and his three friends. Afterward, their appearance could be compared to the other students, and the official could do as he pleased. Daniel may've reasoned that if they were doing the will of God, God could give them better health, with less nutrition. And he was right.

Daniel 1:15-16 *At the end of the ten days they looked healthier and better nourished than any of the young men who ate the royal food. So the guard took away their choice food and the wine they were to drink and gave them vegetables instead.*

We shouldn't assume what God will do in any situation but, in this case, God honored the noble desire of these young men by giving them excellent health in spite of their meager diet.

We should also notice the power of positive peer pressure. It's less likely Daniel's friends would've had the courage of their convictions apart from Daniel. But when one person is willing to follow God, others will often go along. It's important to walk with God, not only for ourselves, but for others who want to do the same.

We should also notice the power of faith in young people. Knowledge and wisdom are often lacking in youth, but faith in God provides insight many never attain. It also provides the strength of character that avoids foolish mistakes. God often works deeply in the lives of young people, and can distinguish them above their peers.

Daniel 1:17 *To these four young men God gave knowledge and understanding of all kinds of literature and learning.*

Much of what they learned in the king's academy was contrary to the Bible. But, like good missionaries, they mastered the culture's knowledge to better represent God. They didn't suspend what they knew about God in order to learn new things. They used what they knew about God to distinguish truth from error.

This is important to Christians in academic settings because, in any field of study, there will be perspectives that challenge the Christian faith. But Christianity enjoys the distinct advantage of being true. Christians should be humble because they're often wrong. But God is never wrong, and he's a Christian. To the degree that Christians remain in God's truth they'll be right, even if others disagree.

Daniel 1:18 *At the end of the time set by the king to bring them into his service, the chief official presented them to Nebuchadnezzar.*

This was a graduation event that included an oral examination by the king himself. Nebuchadnezzar talked with the students and *found none equal to Daniel, Hananiah, Mishael and Azariah*. This was a relief to them, and they quickly went to work for the Babylonian government.

This was the same government that attacked the southern kingdom of Judah, so some of God's people may've thought they were traitors. But their actions agreed with the God's word through the prophet Jeremiah. *[S]eek the peace and prosperity of the city to which I have carried you into exile. Pray to the Lord for it, because if it prospers, you too will prosper* (Jeremiah 29:7).

Christians don't serve God in the world by turning their backs on the world, but by using their gifts to make the world a better place. We don't forsake the world into which God has called us, but serve the world with whatever skills we have, to the best of our ability. This is implied in God's command to *Love your neighbor as yourself* (Leviticus 19:18, Matthew 22:39).

For Reflection and Review

- *Did Daniel and his friends compromise their faith by accepting pagan names?*
- *Why is it usually better to ask a favor than to make a demand?*
- *How should Christians serve God in the world?*

Lesson 148

Daniel 2:1 *In the second year of his reign, Nebuchadnezzar had dreams; his mind was troubled and he could not sleep.*

Kings in the ancient world paid attention to their dreams because they were thought to foreshadow future events. Pharaoh dreamed of seven skinny cows eating seven fat cows, and it foreshadowed seven years of abundance followed by seven years of famine (Genesis 41:1-40). God also spoke to the king of Gerar in a dream (Genesis 20:6).

Nebuchadnezzar employed professional interpreters, but wasn't always sure they were helpful. This time, to be sure they were telling the truth, he required they tell him the dream itself. Then he could be sure of their interpretation.

This is what I have firmly decided: If you do not tell me what my dream was and interpret it, I will have you cut into pieces and your houses turned into piles of rubble. But if you tell me the dream and explain it, you will receive from me gifts and rewards and great honor. So tell me the dream and interpret it for me (Daniel 2:5-6), he said. When the interpreters objected, the king became so angry that he ordered the execution of all his interpreters (Daniel 2:12), also known as *wise men*.

Daniel 2:14 *When Arioch, the commander of the king's guard, had gone out to put to death the wise men of Babylon, Daniel spoke to him with wisdom and tact.*

Daniel and his friends were still quite young, but were counted among the king's wise men. When the executioner came to see him, Daniel didn't overreact. He simply asked the king for time, and was granted his request. Then he explained the situation to his friends and they began to pray. That same night the dream was revealed to Daniel in a vision (Daniel 2:19). *Praise be to the name of God for ever and ever. . . . He reveals deep and hidden things; he knows what lies in darkness, and light dwells with him* (Daniel 2:20-22), he said.

Nothing is unknown to God, and sometimes he reveals things to his people. Whenever we have a problem, to which we don't know the answer, we can ask God to reveal it. *If any of you lacks wisdom, you should ask God* (James 1:5), wrote James. If you need to solve a problem, God can help you think it through. If you lose your car keys, he can remind you where you left them. But if we fail to pray, we may forfeit the help that God wants to give us.

Daniel 2:26 *The king asked Daniel . . . Are you able to tell me what I saw in my dream and interpret it?*

[T]here is a God in heaven who reveals mysteries (Daniel 2:28), said Daniel. Then he explained the dream

and gave the interpretation. The king dreamed of large dazzling statue. The head was made of gold; the chest and arms were made of silver; the belly and thighs were made of bronze; the legs were made of iron; and the feet were made of iron and clay. But a rock struck the statue on the feet and broke it to bits. Then the rock became a mountain and filled the whole earth (Daniel 2:31-35).

The interpretation was straightforward. Nebuchadnezzar was the head of gold. After him would come three other kingdoms (Daniel 2:36-43). These weren't specified but are commonly identified as the empires of Medo-Persia, Greece, and Rome.

The rock that crushed the statue and grew into a mountain is the kingdom of God. *[T]he God of heaven will set up a kingdom that will never be destroyed . . . . It will crush all those kingdoms and bring them to an end, but it will itself endure forever* (Daniel 2:44), Daniel explained.

Time has shown Daniel's prophecy to be accurate. The kingdoms he described came and went. But at the time of the Roman Empire, Christ came into the world, and established the kingdom of God. For two thousand years that kingdom has been spreading throughout the earth, and it will endure forever. *The kingdom of the world has become the kingdom of our Lord and of his Messiah, and he will reign for ever and ever* (Revelation 11:15), wrote John.

This passage also reminds us that God is in charge of history. The world may seem chaotic, at times, but it isn't random. God created the world to prepare a kingdom for his Son, and is preparing us to live in it forever. The world is moving toward a predetermined goal, and will arrive at the proper time. The only way to be on the right side of history is to be in the kingdom of God. This is the greatest possible destiny.

For Reflection and Review

- *Why should we pray when we're confused?*
- *How is the kingdom of God filling the earth?*
- *What's the benefit of knowing the future?*

Lesson 149

Daniel 3:1 *King Nebuchadnezzar made an image of gold, sixty cubits high and six cubits wide, and set it up on the plain of Dura in the province of Babylon.*

The Babylonians were highly diverse, and Nebuchadnezzar wanted to unify them through common worship. So he put up a statue of gold, about a hundred feet tall, and summoned his officials to the dedication ceremony.

The statue's image is not described but it may've represented the Babylonian god, Nabu, since that was part of Nebuchadnezzar's name. Nebuchadnezzar needed loyalty from his officials, and worshipping the statue likely implied a pledge of allegiance to him, or at least to his agenda.

Daniel 3:3 *So the satraps, prefects, governors, advisers, treasurers, judges, magistrates and all the other provincial officials assembled for the dedication of the image that King Nebuchadnezzar had set up, and they stood before it.*

Nebuchadnezzar had assembled an orchestra and, at the sound of the first note, everyone was to bow down and worship. To ensure compliance, anyone who refused to bow down would be thrown into a blazing furnace.

Most bowed down, of course, but there were three exceptions: Shadrach, Meshach, and Abednego. From childhood they were taught not to worship idols. *You shall not bow down to them or worship them* (Exodus 20:5), said God. That settled the matter, as far as they were concerned, but Nebuchadnezzar wasn't pleased.

Daniel 3:13 *Furious with rage, Nebuchadnezzar summoned Shadrach, Meshach and Abednego.*

Nebuchadnezzar went to great lengths to prepare this event, and wanted a show of unity. The noncompliance of these three men was a fracture that filled the king with rage. They weren't surprised, of course, since they knew this day was coming, and knew what to expect. They may've had some sleepless nights, but considered it better to cross the king of Babylon, than to cross the Lord Almighty.

Daniel 3:16-17 *King Nebuchadnezzar, we do not need to defend ourselves before you in this matter. If we are thrown into the blazing furnace, the God we serve is able to deliver us from it, and he will deliver us from Your Majesty's hand.*

Shadrach, Meshach, and Abednego seem to have known what God was going to do for them. God doesn't always deliver his people but, somehow, they sensed that God would deliver them. Perhaps God had spoken to them through the prophet Daniel, or maybe they simply felt in their hearts that God was going to save them.

They weren't obeying God because he was going to save them, however, but because God is to be obeyed. *[E]ven if he does not [deliver us], we want you to know, Your Majesty, that we will not serve your gods or worship the image of gold you have set up* (Daniel 3:18), they said. This is the kind of faithful resolve that glorifies God.

Daniel 3:19-20 *Nebuchadnezzar was furious [and] ordered the furnace heated seven times hotter than usual and commanded some of the strongest soldiers in his army to tie up Shadrach, Meshach and Abednego and throw them into the blazing furnace.*

The nearby furnace may've been used to prepare the gold for the statue. It was probably built into the side of a hill with openings at the top and front, and was big enough for people to stand inside. At the king's command the furnace was made so hot that it actually killed the soldiers who threw in the servants of God.

Daniel 3:24-25 *Then King Nebuchadnezzar leaped to his feet in amazement and asked his advisers, Weren't there three men that we tied up and threw into the fire? They replied, Certainly, Your Majesty. He said, Look! I see four men walking around in the fire, unbound and unharmed, and the fourth looks like a son of the gods.*

The fourth person was probably a pre-incarnate appearance of Jesus Christ. *These are the very Scriptures that testify about me* (John 5:39), said Jesus. We can't be emphatic, but it's not wrong to see Jesus caring for his own in their time of need. This is good to remember when everything around us seems to be on fire.

Daniel 3:27 *They saw that the fire had not harmed their bodies, nor was a hair of their heads singed; their robes were not scorched, and there was no smell of fire on them.*

The only effect of the fire, in fact, was to burn away the ropes that bound them. *When you walk through the fire, you will not be burned; the flames will not set you ablaze* (Isaiah 43:2), said God. Sometimes, when we go through fiery trials, all we lose are the ropes that bind us.

Daniel 3:28-29 *Praise be to the God of Shadrach, Meshach and Abednego, who has sent his angel and rescued his servants! . . . Therefore I decree that the people of any nation or language who say anything against the God of Shadrach, Meshach and Abednego be cut into pieces and their houses be turned into piles of rubble, for no other god can save in this way.*

This was a wonderful outcome not only for Shadrach, Meshach, and Abednego but for all the Jews in Babylon. If these three men had bowed down, others would've followed them, resulting in widespread apostasy. Not only that, but whoever refused to bow down would've been killed. These three men were saved by standing firm, and so were many others. We never know how God may use our faithfulness for the good of those around us.

But Shadrach, Meshach, and Abednego are exceptions to many believers who've gone up in flames. Emperor Nero had Christians tarred and set on fire as human torches, and many others have been burned at the stake.

The tyrants of this world may threaten us with fire but Jesus threatens them with worse. *Then he will say to those on his left, Depart from me, you who are cursed, into the eternal fire prepared for the devil and his angels* (Matthew 25:41). The promise of Christ is not that we'll never be burned, but that we'll *never perish* (John 10:28). *Be faithful [unto] death, and I will give you life* (Revelation 2:10), he said.

For Reflection and Review

- *Why is it better to cross a king than God Almighty?*
- *How can fiery trials set us free?*
- *How did God use the faithfulness of Shadrach, Meshach, and Abednego?*

Lesson 150

Daniel 4:1 *King Nebuchadnezzar, To the nations and peoples of every language, who live in all the earth: May you prosper greatly!*

Nebuchadnezzar was the most powerful man on earth, and an unlikely candidate for conversion. But this is the account of how he came to know God for himself, given in his own words.

Daniel 4:2-3 *It is my pleasure to tell you about the miraculous signs and wonders that the Most High God has performed for me. How great are his signs, how mighty his wonders! His kingdom is an eternal kingdom; his dominion endures from generation to generation.*

Nebuchadnezzar was so excited about his conversion that he wrote a letter to the whole world: *To the nations and peoples of every language, who live in all the earth* (Daniel 4:1), he began. When people come to know God they naturally want to share it with others. This is usually just a few, but since Nebuchadnezzar was in a position to share what he learned with the whole world, that's what he did.

Daniel 4:4-5 *I, Nebuchadnezzar, was at home in my palace, contented and prosperous. I had a dream that made me afraid.*

Humanly speaking, Nebuchadnezzar had no reason to be afraid. His enemies were subdued, his storehouses were full, and he was enjoying life at its best. Then, one night, he dreamed of an immense tree with abundant fruit, *visible to the ends of the earth*. Then a messenger from heaven called for the glorious tree to be cut down.

Then the messenger said, *Let him be drenched with the dew of heaven, and let him live with the animals among the plants of the earth. Let his mind be changed from that of a man and let him be given the mind of an animal, till seven times pass by for him* (Daniel 4:15-16).

Since no one else could interpret the dream, Nebuchadnezzar called for Daniel who made the meaning clear: The tree stood for Nebuchadnezzar, who would lose his position due to insanity. *[Y]ou will eat grass like the ox and be drenched with the dew of heaven* (Daniel 4:25), Daniel explained.

The affliction would be severe but not permanent. *Seven times will pass by for you until you acknowledge that the Most High is sovereign over all kingdoms on earth and gives them to anyone he wishes* (Daniel 4:25b), said Daniel.

The *seven times* aren't specified but may refer to seven years. If so, Nebuchadnezzar would live outside, and eat grass, for an extended period of time. The condition is bizarre but not unheard of. Boanthropy is a psychological disorder in which a person thinks they're a cow, or an ox, and behaves accordingly.

Nebuchadnezzar needed to learn a lesson. He thought he was a great king because he had earned it. He defeated his enemies and transformed Babylon into a superpower. But he failed to realize that God *is sovereign over all kingdoms on earth and gives them to anyone he wishes*.

Many think they're successful because of their own abilities, but those abilities come from God, along with the opportunities to use them. *For who makes you different from anyone else? What do you have that you did not receive? And if you did receive it, why do you boast as though you did not?* (1 Corinthians 4:7), wrote Paul. No matter how great our success, all the credit goes to God.

Daniel 4:27 *Therefore, Your Majesty, be pleased to accept my advice: Renounce your sins by doing what is right, and your wickedness by being kind to the oppressed. It may be that then your prosperity will continue.*

Daniel knew it was possible for God's judgment to be avoided through repentance. When Jonah declared to Nineveh the impending judgment of God, they repented deeply. *When God saw what they did and how they turned from their evil ways, he relented and did not bring on them the destruction he had threatened* (Jonah 3:10). If Nebuchadnezzar repented, he might also be spared.

Daniel 4:29-30 *Twelve months later, as the king was walking on the roof of the royal palace of Babylon, he said, Is not this the great Babylon I have built as the royal residence, by my mighty power and for the glory of my majesty?*

Instead of taking Daniel's advice, Nebuchadnezzar continued to walk in pride. This went on day after day, week after week, and month after month. It appeared God's judgment would never come, but it was on the way.

God often gives us time to repent because he's patient. *[H]e is patient with you, not wanting anyone to perish, but everyone to come to repentance* (2 Peter 3:9), wrote Peter. The passing of time doesn't mean God has forgotten his threats, but that he's waiting for us to respond. *I have given her time to repent of her immorality, but she is unwilling. So I will cast her on a bed of suffering* (Revelation 2:21-22), said God elsewhere. God often gives us time to repent, but will suddenly bring his judgment if we refuse.

Daniel 4:33 *Immediately what had been said about Nebuchadnezzar was fulfilled. He was driven away from people and ate grass like the ox. His body was drenched with the dew of heaven until his hair grew like the feathers of an eagle and his nails like the claws of a bird.*

Nebuchadnezzar could've learned the easy way, but chose to learn the hard way. He could've listened to Daniel, but chose to wait and see. In a moment, he went from being a powerful king to thinking he was a beast. Once treated with lotion, his skin became like hyde. Once carefully groomed, his hair became like feathers. Once properly trimmed, his nails became like claws. Instead of humbling himself before the Lord, Nebuchadnezzar was humbled by the Lord.

Daniel 4:34 *At the end of that time, I, Nebuchadnezzar, raised my eyes toward heaven, and my sanity was restored.*

Sanity comes from seeing things as they are, not as we want them to be. When we focus on ourselves, as though they were ultimate, we become a little insane. But when we focus on God, and see everything else in his light, our sanity is restored. Whenever we feel crazy, we should raise our eyes toward heaven.

Daniel 4:34 *Then I praised the Most High; I honored and glorified him who lives forever.*

After he found God, Nebuchadnezzar was restored to his throne, and became even greater than before. He reminds us that salvation is a gift from God, to the most unlikely people. *For it is by grace you have been saved, through faith—and this is not from yourselves, it is the gift of God* (Ephesians 2:8), wrote Paul.

If God can save an arrogant pagan king, he can save anyone. *[So pray] for kings and all those in authority, that we may live peaceful and quiet lives* (1 Timothy 2:2), wrote Paul. Imagine what would happen if some of the wickedest rulers in the world suddenly turned to Christ? This should give us hope, and keep us on our knees.

For Reflection and Review

- *Why did Nebuchadnezzar want to tell the world about his conversion?*
- *Why is pride a fantasy?*
- *How does raising our eyes toward heaven help restore our sanity?*

Lesson 151

Daniel 5:1 *King Belshazzar gave a great banquet for a thousand of his nobles and drank wine with them.*

The reason for the banquet isn't stated, but Daniel wasn't invited. He was about eighty years old at this time, and not as well known as before. Nebuchadnezzar had died, and Babylon was at war. But King Belshazzar wanted a party, so he invited a thousand guests. He didn't know his city would fall that night, and that he'd be dead by morning.

Daniel 5:2 *While Belshazzar was drinking his wine, he gave orders to bring in the gold and silver goblets that Nebuchadnezzar his father had taken from the temple in Jerusalem, so that the king and his nobles, his wives and his concubines might drink from them.*

This was an act of defiance against the God of Israel. The gold and silver goblets were to be used in God's temple, but were taken to Babylon when Jerusalem fell. In his drunken pride Belshazzar used them for his party, and as they drank from the sacred vessels, they praised their pagan gods. This turned out to be a fatal mistake.

I am the Lord; that is my name! I will not yield my glory to another or my praise to idols (Isaiah 42:8), said God. *Suddenly the fingers of a human hand appeared and wrote on the plaster of the wall* (Daniel 5:5). The hand appeared to be human, but represented the hand of God. It wasn't a vision, seen by one, but a holy manifestation, seen by all.

Details aren't provided, but we can imagine large letters everyone could read. There may've been a crackling sound as the plaster crumbled beneath the press. Since the hand appeared at a moment of high blasphemy, the message wouldn't be good.

Daniel 5:5b-6 *The king watched the hand as it wrote. His face turned pale and he was so frightened that his legs became weak and his knees were knocking.*

The king had reason to be afraid. He was bold in his blasphemy, but was about to meet the one whom he had blasphemed. Whoever blasphemes God without fear, should expect to be afraid at the hour of death.

Daniel 5:7 *The king summoned the enchanters, astrologers and diviners. Then he said to these wise men of Babylon, Whoever reads this writing and tells me what it means will be clothed in purple and have a gold chain placed around his neck, and he will be made the third highest ruler in the kingdom.*

Belshazzar was co-ruler with his father, so the highest position he could offer was *third highest ruler in the kingdom*. Despite the incentives, however, none of the wise men could understand the message. Then Daniel was brought before the king and, after being offered the same incentives replied, *You may keep your gifts for yourself and give your rewards to someone else. Nevertheless, I will read the writing for the king and tell him what it means* (Daniel 5:17).

Then Daniel rehearsed Nebuchadnezzar's conversion story and rebuked the king: *But you, Belshazzar . . . have not humbled yourself, though you knew all this. Instead, you have set yourself up against the Lord of heaven. You had the goblets from his temple brought to you, and you and your nobles, your wives and your concubines drank wine from them. You praised the gods of silver and gold, of bronze, iron, wood and stone, which cannot see or hear or understand. But you did not honor the God who holds in his hand your life and all your ways* (Daniel 5:22-23), he said.

Belshazzar's knew about God from his grandfather, Nebuchadnezzar, so his guilt was even more serious. Like many before and since, he dismissed the knowledge of God and had to face the consequences: *mene, mene, tekel, parsin* (Daniel 5:25), was the writing on the wall.

Daniel explained the words: *Mene: God has numbered the days of your reign and brought it to an end. Tekel: You have been weighed on the scales and found wanting. Peres: Your kingdom is divided and given to the Medes and Persians* (Daniel 5:26-28). Before the night was over Belshazzar was slain, and Babylon fell to the Medo-Persians.

Belshazzar should've kept the faith of his grandfather, but chose the way of his peers. When the writing on the wall appeared, the party was over and the end had come. *It is a dreadful thing to fall into the hands of the living God* (Hebrews 10:31), says Hebrews.

Belshazzar is a tragic figure because he threw away the knowledge of God. The testimony of his grandfather, the light of nature, his own conscience, and the witness of the Spirit (1 John 5:6) should've brought him to God and kept him there. But Belshazzar preferred the pleasure of sin, and the approval of his peers. *What good will it be for someone to gain the whole world, yet forfeit their soul?* (Matthew 16:26), said Jesus.

For Reflection and Review

- *Why do some children reject their parents' faith in Christ?*
- *Why is Belshazzar a tragic figure?*
- *Why is it better to have God than the world?*

Lesson 152

Daniel 6:1-2 *It pleased Darius to appoint 120 satraps to rule throughout the kingdom, with three administrators over them, one of whom was Daniel.*

Darius the Mede took over Babylon (Daniel 5:31) and was setting up his administration. By this time Daniel was old, but he had a good reputation, and many years of government experience. This made him a natural choice for high office.

Daniel 6:3 *Daniel so distinguished himself among the administrators . . . that the king planned to set him over the whole kingdom.*

This was the high point of Daniel's career and he was likely pleased. Politics can be rough, however, and some of Daniel's colleagues wanted to bring him down. They examined his years of public service, with the hope of finding corruption or incompetence, but they found nothing at all (Daniel 6:4).

Then they knew the only way to ensnare Daniel was with regard to his faith. So they conspired to have a law passed that would make it illegal to pray to anyone but the king, for thirty days, on pain of death (Daniel 6:5-7). This flattered the king, and reinforced his authority over his newly acquired region. In Daniel's absence, the king issued the decree and made it the law of the land (Daniel 6:9).

Daniel 6:10 *Now when Daniel learned that the decree had been published, he went home to his upstairs room where the windows opened toward Jerusalem. Three times a day he got down on his knees and prayed, giving thanks to his God, just as he had done before.*

All Daniel had to do to save his life was to not be seen praying for a month. His pattern of prayer wasn't required by Scripture, so he could've set it aside, perhaps with a clear conscience. But Daniel was less concerned to save his life than to honor God. Failure to pray as he had in the past would imply Daniel was willing to honor his earthly king above his heavenly king. This he wouldn't do. So Daniel went to his room and prayed three times daily, just like before.

Daniel 6:12-13 *So they went to the king and spoke to him about his royal decree: Did you not publish a decree that during the next thirty days anyone who prays to any god or human being except to you, Your Majesty, would be thrown into the lions' den?*

The king answered, The decree stands—in accordance with the law of the Medes and Persians, which cannot be repealed. Then they said to the king, Daniel, who is one of the exiles from Judah, pays no attention to you, Your Majesty, or to the decree you put in writing. He still prays three times a day.

Daniel's opponents made him appear disrespectful, but the king saw through their hypocrisy. Now he understood the real purpose for the law they proposed was to get rid of Daniel. The king wasn't upset with Daniel, but with himself, and with those who misled him.

But once a law was passed it couldn't be repealed, or it would undermine the public's confidence in the wisdom of the king. The king wanted to save Daniel but there was nothing he could do to change the law. Daniel's opponents seemed to have won.

Daniel 6:16-17 *So the king gave the order, and they brought Daniel and threw him into the lions' den. The king said to Daniel, May your God, whom you serve continually, rescue you! A stone was brought and placed over the mouth of the den, and the king sealed it with his own signet ring and with the rings of his nobles, so that Daniel's situation might not be changed.*

It'd be a long night for both Daniel and the king. The king returned to his palace and spent the night without food, entertainment, or sleep (Daniel 6:18). Daniel spent the night in a pit with hungry lions, waiting to be devoured. But there was an angel in the pit that shut the lions' mouths (Daniel 6:22), and Daniel survived the night. Early the next morning, the king went to the pit, and was overjoyed to find Daniel alive. Not even a scratch was found on him because Daniel had trusted in God (Daniel 6:23).

The story seems fantastic but this sort of thing has been known to happen. A family went on vacation in Africa, and enjoyed lunch under a tree, while the tour guide took their picture. Sometime later, when they looked at the picture, they saw a lion in the tree looking down on them. The whole time they were under the tree eating lunch, there was a lion in the tree that could've eaten them for lunch. Many times we're in danger and don't even know it. It'll be interesting to learn, one day, how often we were saved by angels.

But we must also acknowledge that many Christians have been thrown to lions and died. The Bible contains accounts of miraculous preservations, and heroic martyrdoms, because life or death are equally welcome when heaven is our home. *If we live, we live for the Lord; and if we die, we die for the Lord. So, whether we live or die, we belong to the Lord* (Romans 14:8), wrote Paul.

Daniel 6:24 *At the king's command, the men who had falsely accused Daniel were brought in and thrown into the lions' den, along with their wives and children. And before they reached the floor of the den, the lions overpowered them and crushed all their bones.*

The legal principle was that anyone who made a false accusation was to receive the same penalty they sought for their victim. This idea is also found in the law of Moses. *[I]f the witness proves to be a liar, giving false testimony against a fellow Israelite, then do to the false witness as that witness intended to do to the other party* (Deuteronomy 19:18-19). The execution of the accusers' families may seem to be unfair, but guilt was often seen as a collective responsibility, and children often suffer for the sins of their parents.

Daniel 6:25-27 *Then King Darius wrote to all the nations and peoples of every language in all the earth: May you prosper greatly! I issue a decree that in every part of my kingdom people must fear and reverence the God of Daniel. For he is the living God and he endures forever; his kingdom will not be destroyed, his dominion will never end. He rescues and he saves; he performs signs and wonders in the heavens and on the earth. He has rescued Daniel from the power of the lions.*

Daniel's faithfulness brought glory to God throughout the earth. And even though our faithfulness to Christ may never capture the world's attention, it always captures his. That's reason enough to be faithful.

For Reflection and Review

- *Why was Daniel more concerned to honor God than save his life?*
- *Should Christians pray three times daily?*
- *Does God always honor faithfulness?*

Lesson 153

Daniel 7:1 *In the first year of Belshazzar king of Babylon, Daniel had a dream, and visions passed through his mind as he was lying in bed.*

Daniels's dream took place around 552 BC, when he was old. In his dream he saw four beasts which likely represent the Babylonian empire (625-539 BC), the Medo-Persian empire (539-331 BC), the Greek empire (331-63 BC), and the Roman empire (63 BC-AD 476). These were important to the Jewish people because they'd be governed by each of them. Difficult times were ahead, but God wanted his people to know that he was in control, and that his kingdom would be established.

Daniel 7:9 *As I looked, thrones were set in place, and the Ancient of Days took his seat. His clothing was as white as snow; the hair of his head was white like wool. His throne was flaming with fire, and its wheels were all ablaze.*

The eternal God is the Ancient of Days, without beginning or end. The day is coming when he'll hold court, and judge his opponents. Their kingdoms will come to an end, but *His dominion is an everlasting dominion that will not pass away, and his kingdom is one that will never be destroyed* (Daniel 7:14), wrote Daniel.

Empires rise and fall as kings compete for dominance in a world that doesn't belong to them. But the day is coming when God will take back his world and give it to his people. Then, *the holy people of the Most High will receive the kingdom and will possess it forever—yes, for ever and ever* (Daniel 7:18), wrote Daniel.

Daniel 7:13-14 *In my vision at night I looked, and there before me was one like a son of man, coming with the clouds of heaven. He approached the Ancient of Days and was led into his presence. He was given authority, glory and sovereign power; all nations and peoples of every language worshiped him.*

This is an important passage for understanding Jesus Christ, since his favorite title for himself was *Son of Man*. It's a confusing title because there are two ways to understand it. Ezekiel was called the *son of man* to emphasize his humanity. But Daniel's *son of man* is clearly divine, since he rightly received worship. Jesus' listeners would have to decide whether Jesus was merely human, or also divine.

When he was on trial for his life, Jesus was clear about which son of man he was. *Again the high priest asked him, Are you the Messiah, the Son of the Blessed One? I am, said Jesus. And you will see the Son of Man sitting at the right hand of the Mighty One and coming on the clouds of heaven* (Mark 14:61-62), he said.

Since Jesus identified himself as Daniel's *son of man*, he was claiming to be divine. Since the religious leaders didn't believe Jesus was divine, they considered his words to be blasphemy. *You have heard the blasphemy. What do you think? They all condemned him as worthy of death* (Mark 14:64).

*****

Daniel 7:21—22 *As I watched, this horn was waging war against the holy people and defeating them, until the Ancient of Days came and pronounced judgment in favor of the holy people of the Most High, and the time came when they possessed the kingdom.*

Some interpreters think this horn represents the antichrist who'll appear at the end of the age. *He will speak against the Most High and oppress his holy people* (Daniel 7:25), wrote Daniel. *He will oppose and will exalt himself over everything that is called God or is worshiped, so that he sets himself up in God's temple, proclaiming himself to be God . . . . whom the Lord Jesus will overthrow with the breath of his mouth and destroy by the splendor of his coming* (2 Thessalonians 4, 9), wrote Paul.

The kingdoms of this world are in revolt against the kingdom of God, and will oppress God's people until the end. We shouldn't be surprised by persecution, nor should we try to establish the kingdom of God here and now. We should faithfully witness to our king, and wait for his appearing to establish his kingdom forever.

Daniel 7:27 *Then the sovereignty, power and greatness of all the kingdoms under heaven will be handed over to the holy people of the Most High.*

The kingdom of God won't be completely different from the kingdoms of this age. There will be similarities, but without any *death or mourning or crying or pain* (Revelation 21:4), wrote John. *Everyone will sit under their own vine and under their own fig tree, and no one will make them afraid,* (Micah 4:4), wrote Micah. *The wolf and the lamb will feed together, and the lion will eat straw like the ox* (Isaiah 65:25), wrote Isaiah.

The kingdom of God will be a world of love for God and neighbor, without any curse (Revelation 22:3). The potential for human and social development will be unhindered, and we'll enjoy the world as it was meant to be forever—*yes, forever and ever* (Daniel 7:18), wrote Daniel. This is the Bible's view of the future, and it's nothing short of glorious.

For Reflection and Review

- *Why is God called the Ancient of Days?*
- *How is Jesus like Daniel's son of man?*
- *What should we expect in the age to come?*

Lesson 154

Hosea 1:1 *The word of the Lord that came to Hosea son of Beeri during the reigns of Uzziah, Jotham, Ahaz and Hezekiah, kings of Judah, and during the reign of Jeroboam son of Jehoash king of Israel.*

The prophet Hosea served the northern kingdom of Israel for at least thirty-eight years, until it was destroyed by the Assyrians in 722 BC. Israel abandoned God for idols, and was characterized by materialism, immorality, and injustice. God was offended, and related to Israel like a brokenhearted lover.

Hosea 1:2 *When the Lord began to speak through Hosea, the Lord said to him, Go, marry a promiscuous woman and have children with her, for like an adulterous wife this land is guilty of unfaithfulness to the Lord.*

Under most circumstances a prophet would want to marry a godly woman and, together, bear godly offspring. But Hosea was living in a time of national apostasy, and God wanted to illustrate what it was like to be married to Israel. So God gave Hosea the unusual command to marry a promiscuous woman.

Hosea 1:3 *So he married Gomer daughter of Diblaim, and she conceived and bore him a son.*

Hosea was likely delighted to have a son, and certainly wanted the best for him. Perhaps he thought of names like Elijah (meaning *The Lord is my God*), or Elisha (meaning *God is salvation*). Then the Lord said to Hosea, Call him *Jezreel* (Hosea 1:4), which means *God scatters*. In this way the prophet's son would reinforce the prophet's message: the nation of Israel would soon be scattered.

Hosea 1:6 *Gomer conceived again and gave birth to a daughter. Then the Lord said to Hosea, Call her Lo-Ruhamah (which means not loved), for I will no longer show love to Israel, that I should at all forgive them.*

It was probably difficult for Hosea and Gomer to name their little girl *not loved*. But Israel had sinned against God so profoundly, and for so long, that he was threatening to remove his love from them. God is loving by nature but, if we reject his love to the end, we'll become unloved. This is something to think about.

Hosea 1:8-9 *After she had weaned Lo-Ruhamah, Gomer had another son. Then the Lord said, Call him Lo-Ammi (which means not my people), for you are not my people, and I am not your God.*

Israel strained their relationship with God to the breaking point by turning their backs on him. Some people think we can never lose our relationship with God, but that's not true. *If we deliberately keep on sinning after we have received the knowledge of the truth, no sacrifice for sins is left, but only a fearful expectation of judgment and of raging fire that will consume the enemies of God* (Hebrews 10:26-27), says Hebrews. God is a real person, and our relationship with him must be cultivated in order for it to flourish.

Hosea 3:1-2 *The Lord said to me, Go, show your love to your wife again, though she is loved by another man and is an adulteress. . . . So I bought her for fifteen shekels of silver and about a homer and a lethek of barley.*

Gomer had moved out of the house, and left her family behind. Desperate for money, she apparently sold herself to another man as a sexual slave. At God's command, however, Hosea paid the price to get her back. The biblical word for this is *redemption*, and reminds us of what Christ did for us. *In him we have redemption through his blood* (Ephesians 1:7), wrote Paul.

God's love for sinners is so great that he redeemed us at the highest possible price. That's why no amount of sin can keep us away from him, if we're willing to return. Like the prophet Hosea, God comes looking for us in order to bring us home. This is good news for Christians who've wandered away.

*****

Hosea 4:6 *[M]y people are destroyed from lack of knowledge.*

The greatest contributing factor to Israel's apostasy was the people's lack of interest in God's word. Their collective memory was short and, because the priests were no longer teaching the Bible, true religion had nearly vanished. *Because you have rejected knowledge, I also reject you as my priests* (Hosea 4:6b), said God.

Like the nation of Israel, churches are seldom stronger than their knowledge of the Bible. That's why Paul told Timothy to *Preach the word . . . . For the time will come when people will not put up with sound doctrine. Instead, to suit their own desires, they will gather around them a great number of teachers to say what their itching ears want to hear. They will turn their ears away from the truth and turn aside to myths* (2 Timothy 4:2-4).

The tendency of sinners is to turn away from God's word, never toward it. The minister's job is not to win people's approval, by telling them what they want to hear, but to faithfully proclaim God's word, even when they don't want to hear it. The further a church strays from God's word, the further it strays from Christ.

For Reflection and Review

- *Why did God tell Hosea to marry a promiscuous woman?*
- *How is God like a frustrated lover?*
- *What does God do for people who've wandered away from him?*

Lesson 155

Hosea 5:14-15 *For I will be like a lion to Ephraim, like a great lion to Judah. I will tear them to pieces and go away; I will carry them off, with no one to rescue them. Then I will return to my lair until they have borne their guilt and seek my face—in their misery they will earnestly seek me.*

God compared himself to a ferocious lion that would tear his people to pieces. His purpose wasn't only to punish, however, but also to restore. *[I]n their misery they will earnestly seek me*, he said.

A survey was given to hundreds of Christians to help discover the most effective means of spiritual growth. Prayer, Bible study, and church were the expected answers. But the most effective means of spiritual growth for those who were surveyed was pain. God wants his people to grow through prayer, Bible study, and church, but he also uses suffering. Whenever God allows us to suffer, we should use it to turn more fully to him.

Hosea 6:4 *Your love is like the morning mist, like the early dew that disappears.*

God complained that the love of his people was fleeting. They'd make an occasional effort, but it never seemed to last. They'd make promises, but not keep them. They'd have good intentions, but not follow through. Their devotion to God was inconsistent, and their love was unreliable.

I had a friend who was put on trial for a serious crime. I went to court with him and heard him pray as never before. By the grace of God he received a minimal sentence, for which he was extremely thankful. But as soon as his life became stable again he drifted away from the Lord. Our love can be *like the morning mist, like the early dew that disappears*.

Hosea 7:2 *[T]hey do not realize that I remember all their evil deeds.*

People who've committed terrible sins may see their need to be saved more clearly than those who've only committed little sins (Luke 18:13). Whoever commits murder will probably feel more guilt than someone who's only been rude. But what if all our little sins add up to more than our big sins?

If we only sin three times a day, that's over a thousand sins a year. Imagine standing before God with over fifty thousand sins. We forget our little sins, but God remembers every one. Even the best need to be forgiven, every single day.

Hosea 9:9 *They have sunk deep into corruption.*

The nation of Israel was guilty of idolatry, immorality, materialism, injustice, and many other sins. They should've been a light to the world, but became a source of darkness. Like falling into quicksand, they sank into corruption.

Children get a taste of corruption and develop an appetite for more. Puberty accelerates the process and, by adulthood, we're proficient. The tendency of sinners is not toward ever-increasing righteousness, but *ever-increasing wickedness* (Romans 6:19), wrote Paul. Unless the process is reversed, we'll become moral monsters over time. Hell, of course, is full of horrible monsters who used to be beautiful children.

Hosea 13:14 *I will deliver this people from the power of the grave; I will redeem them from death. Where, O death, are your plagues? Where, O grave, is your destruction?*

The tragedy of sin is that it always leads to death (Romans 6:23). This seems final, but isn't the last word for those who belong to Christ. Paul quoted this verse and applied it to the resurrection of believers (1 Corinthians 15:55). Since Christ died for our sins, and rose from the dead, those who trust in Christ will also rise to live forever.

A seventy-three year old farmer in Kenya was tending his bean crop when he was attacked by a hungry leopard. This would signal the end for most people, but the farmer fought back. He thrust his hand into the leopard's mouth, ripped out its tongue, and watched it die in its own blood. Christ also went into the jaws of death and killed it by his resurrection. *I am the resurrection and the life. The one who believes in me will live* (John 11:25), he said.

Hosea 13:6 *When I fed them, they were satisfied; when they were satisfied, they became proud; then they forgot me.*

Prosperity should result in gratitude, and bring us closer to God, but often has the opposite effect. *[W]hen they eat their fill and thrive, they will turn to other gods* (Deuteronomy 31:20), wrote Moses. And, *the deceitfulness of wealth choke[s] the word, making it unfruitful* (Matthew 13:22), said Jesus. Everyone wants more money, but it's seldom very good for us.

Missionaries have noticed that wherever the gospel is received, life seems to improve. Children are clothed, roofs are fixed, and people go to work. This can be called *redemptive lift* and comes from obeying God's word. Obeying God's word normally leads to greater prosperity than disobeying God's word.

But missionaries have also noticed that, after growing prosperous, some of God's people turn away from him. Their newfound wealth makes them less dependent on God, and more inclined to what money can buy. *Godliness gives birth to prosperity, and the daughter eats the mother.* This is what happened to Israel, and can happen to us as well.

For Reflection and Review

- *How does suffering help us turn to God?*
- *Why do people sink into corruption?*
- *What is redemptive lift?*

Lesson 156

Joel 1:1 *The word of the Lord that came to Joel son of Pethuel.*

The prophet Joel probably wrote from Jerusalem around 500 BC, after many Jews returned from Babylonian exile. He foresaw a locust invasion that would devastate the land, and called God's people to repent. He also foresaw physical and spiritual blessing for God's people, and judgment on their enemies. The prophet's name means *the Lord is God*, which suggests he came from a godly home.

Joel 1:4 *What the locust swarm has left the great locusts have eaten; what the great locusts have left the young locusts have eaten; what the young locusts have left other locusts have eaten.*

A plague of locusts would strip the nation of everything green, leaving little for God's people to eat. Making matters worse, they'd also suffer fire (Joel 1:19) and drought (Joel 1:20). It's hard to imagine a more thorough devastation.

This wasn't an act of nature, however, but an act of God—punishment for his peoples' disobedience. God had given his people warning: *You will sow much seed in the field but you will harvest little, because locusts will devour it. . . . Swarms of locusts will take over all your trees and the crops of your land* (Deuteronomy 28:38, 42), wrote Moses.

Joel 2:1-2 *Blow the trumpet in Zion; sound the alarm on my holy hill. Let all who live in the land tremble, for the day of the Lord is coming. It is close at hand—a day of darkness and gloom, a day of clouds and blackness. Like dawn spreading across the mountains a large and mighty army comes, such as never was in ancient times nor ever will be in ages to come.*

The locusts were seen as the army of God, and the event was seen as *the day of the Lord*. That day was important to Joel, but also to other prophets. *Wail, for the day of the Lord is near; it will come like destruction from the Almighty* (Isaiah 13:6), wrote Isaiah. *See, the day of the Lord is coming—a cruel day, with wrath and fierce anger—to make the land desolate and destroy the sinners within it* (Isaiah 13:9), wrote Isaiah again. *For the day is near, the day of the Lord is near—a day of clouds, a time of doom for the nations* (Ezekiel 30:3), wrote Ezekiel. *The day of the Lord is great; it is dreadful. Who can endure it?* (Joel 2:11), wrote Joel.

Will not the day of the Lord be darkness, not light—pitch-dark, without a ray of brightness? (Amos 5:20), asked Amos. *Neither their silver nor their gold will be able to save them on the day of the Lord's wrath* (Zephaniah 1:18), wrote Zephaniah. *Seek righteousness, seek humility; perhaps you will be sheltered on the day of the Lord's anger* (Zephaniah 2:3), wrote Zephaniah again.

In short, *the day of the Lord* is any catastrophic judgment which points ahead to the ultimate catastrophic judgment. The Apostle Peter referred to this when he said, *the day of the Lord will come like a thief. The heavens will disappear with a roar; the elements will be destroyed by fire, and the earth and everything done in it will be laid bare* (2 Peter 3:10). According to God's word, the worst is yet to come.

Joel 2:12 *Even now, declares the Lord, return to me with all your heart, with fasting and weeping and mourning.*

The spiritual purpose behind every disaster is to turn us more fully to God. *[U]nless you repent, you too will all perish* (Luke 13:3), said Jesus. My friend asked if he could live a sinful life, turn to God on his deathbed, and still be saved. I admitted there was some evidence in the Bible to support that idea (Luke 23:43). *Then that's what I will do,* he said. But many who plan to repent at the eleventh hour die at ten-thirty. We can never repent too soon, because we never know when it'll be too late.

Joel 2:13 *Return to the Lord your God, for he is gracious and compassionate, slow to anger and abounding in love, and he relents from sending calamity.*

With all the calamity in the Bible, we might imagine God enjoys it—but he doesn't. *[He] doesn't willingly bring affliction or grief to anyone* (Lamentations 3:33), wrote Jeremiah. *I take no pleasure in the death of the wicked, but rather that they turn from their ways and live* (Ezekiel 33:11), wrote Ezekiel. *[He is] not wanting anyone to perish, but everyone to come to repentance* (2 Peter 3:9), wrote Peter.

Unfortunately, sin has such a grip on us that, apart from pain, many will never turn in God's direction. *God whispers to us in our pleasures, speaks in our conscience, but shouts in our pains: it is his megaphone to rouse a deaf world* (CS Lewis).

For Reflection and Review

- *Should Christians fear the future?*
- *When is the best time to turn to God?*
- *Why does pain awaken us to God?*

Lesson 157

Joel 2:23 *Be glad, people of Zion, rejoice in the Lord your God, for he has given you the autumn rains because he is faithful. He sends you abundant showers, both autumn and spring rains, as before.*

Not only had the locusts eaten everything green, but a drought threatened the following year's harvest (Joel 1:17). Without a word of hope, God's people might've despaired, so the prophet assured them of a glorious future. *The threshing floors will be filled with grain; the vats will overflow with new wine and oil* (Joel 2:24), he said.

Those who experience terrible loss often think their lives will never improve. One dear lady was asked if she was doing okay. She burst into tears and said, *I will never be okay for the rest of my life.* That is how it often seems, but God can turn things around. After losing health, wealth, and family, Job said *my eyes will never see happiness again* (Job 4:7). But over time his situation changed, and the Lord *gave him twice as much as he had before* (Job 42:10).

I went through a season of pain that lasted many years. It wasn't apparent to everyone, but I suffered deeply within. Over the course of time, however, things slowly improved until, one day, I realized the pain was gone. *[Y]our days of sorrow will end* (Isaiah 60:20), wrote Isaiah.

And if they never end in this life, they'll certainly end in the one to come, for all who belong to Christ. *He who did not spare his own Son, but gave him up for us all—how will he not also, along with him, graciously give us all things?* (Romans 8:32), wrote Paul. Nothing needed for our happiness will ever be lacking in the age to come.

Joel 2:25 *I will repay you for the years the locusts have eaten.*

God's people would suffer loss, but were assured by the prophet that God would repay them in the future. This is a wonderful way to think about the age to come. Imagine being repaid for everything you've ever lost: possessions, relationships, health, wealth, innocence, respect, youth, years, pets, memories, love. The pain of loss can be devastating, but whatever we lose in this age will be more than repaid in the age to come. *I will repay you for the years the locusts have eaten.*

Joel 2:28 *And afterward, I will pour out my Spirit on all people.*

The power of the Spirit was restricted to just a few in the Old Testament (Numbers 11:16-17). But after Jesus rose from the dead the Spirit came so mightily that Peter said, *this is what was spoken by the prophet Joel* (Acts 2:16). Ever since that day, whoever believes in Jesus Christ receives the Holy Spirit (Romans 8:9).

We believe in many things on the authority of others such as atoms, radiation, and galaxies. We've never seen them, but are willing to trust the experts. Eternal life is so important, however, that we need to know ourselves. *Now this is eternal life: that they know you, the only true God, and Jesus Christ, whom you have sent* (John 17:3), said Jesus. When we put our trust in Christ, his Spirit comes to live in us, and we know God for ourselves. And if we know God for ourselves, then we have eternal life. This is the work of the Spirit promised by the prophet Joel.

Joel 3:2 *I will gather all nations and bring them down to the Valley of Jehoshaphat. There I will put them on trial for what they did to my inheritance.*

Proper trials are solemn events for those who stand accused. Even those who are normally self-assured are gripped by the fact that their future is in the hands of another. The Judge's determination can even be a matter of life or death. And, if the judge is Jesus Christ, it can be a matter of heaven or hell.

When the Son of Man comes in his glory, and all the angels with him, he will sit on his glorious throne. All the nations will be gathered before him, and he will separate the people one from another as a shepherd separates the sheep from the goats. He will put the sheep on his right and the goats on his left.

Then the King will say to those on his right, Come, you who are blessed by my Father; take your inheritance, the kingdom prepared for you since the creation of the world (Matthew 25:31-34). *But to those on his left he will say, Depart from me, you who are cursed, into the eternal fire prepared for the devil and his angels* (Matthew 25:41).

This will be the most decisive event in history. Evil abounds in the present age but will be dealt with, once and for all, on Judgment Day. The wicked will be thrown into hell, and the righteous will inherit the kingdom of God forever.

Joel 3:18 *In that day the mountains will drip new wine, and the hills will flow with milk; all the ravines of Judah will run with water. A fountain will flow out of the Lord's house and will water the valley of acacias.*

The prophet foresaw a time when the Garden of Eden will be restored, the curse will be reversed, and the people of God will dwell with him forever (Joel 3:20). What a comfort these words must have been to those who suffered so much.

When my daughter was a little girl she liked to read before going to sleep. Once she had a book of some length, and I caught her reading the end of the story first. When I asked her why she did that, she explained that if she knew the story ended well, she could enjoy the whole book, no matter what happened. Since we know our story ends well, we can enjoy the journey.

For Reflection and Review

- *Do difficult times always pass?*
- *How do we know that we have eternal life?*
- *Why is it important to know our story ends well?*

Lesson 158

Amos 1:1 *The words of Amos, one of the shepherds of Tekoa—the vision he saw concerning Israel two years before the earthquake, when Uzziah was king of Judah and Jeroboam son of Jehoash was king of Israel.*

Amos lived in the small town of Tekoa, about six miles south of Bethlehem, where he was a shepherd and also cared for sycamore-fig trees (Amos 7:14). But around 755 BC he was sent by God to prophesy to the northern kingdom of Israel (Amos 7:14-15).

Israel was enjoying a time of prosperity but had fallen into idolatry and moral corruption. Amos announced that God would send them into exile (Amos 5:27) and, within a few decades, Israel fell to the Assyrians (722 BC). Most of the people were deported and never returned home.

Amos 2:7 *Father and son use the same girl and so profane my holy name.*

Having a family prostitute was apparently somewhat common. There was no specific command against it, but there was a command not to *have sexual relations with your father's wife* (Leviticus 18:18). God's people were to live by strict sexual guidelines, or the land would vomit them out, as it had the nations before them (Leviticus 18:28).

Likewise, a professing Christian in the city of Corinth was sleeping with his father's wife, and refused to give her up (1 Corinthians 5:1). *Expel the wicked person from among you* (1 Corinthians 5:13), wrote Paul. *Neither the sexually immoral nor idolaters nor adulterers nor men who have sex with men nor thieves nor the greedy nor drunkards nor slanderers nor swindlers will inherit the kingdom of God* (1 Corinthians 6:9-10), he wrote. We're not saved by being good, but we won't be saved without it. *[W]ithout holiness no one will see the Lord* (Hebrews 12:14), says Hebrews.

Amos 2:11-12 *I also raised up prophets from among your children and Nazirites from among your youths. . . . But you made the Nazirites drink wine and commanded the prophets not to prophesy.*

Not only had God given the nation his law, but he raised up prophets to proclaim it, and Nazarites to model holiness. But God's people broke his law, told the prophets to be quiet, and encouraged the Nazirites to break their vow by drinking wine (Numbers 6:3).

Godly people aren't surprised when the world tries to lead them astray, but they are surprised when fellow believers want them to live like the world. Worldly Christians dislike talk about the Bible, and turn the conversation elsewhere. They're less concerned about prayer than worldly entertainment. They encourage their godly friends to relax and be less devoted to Christ. In effect, they command the prophets not to prophesy, and the Nazirites to drink a little wine.

Amos 3:2 *You only have I chosen of all the families of the earth; therefore I will punish you for all your sins.*

Israel felt secure because they were chosen by God, but failed to understand that they were held to a higher standard precisely because they were chosen. Parents don't usually care if the neighbor's children break the law, but if their own children break the law, there will be serious consequences.

The people of God were also held to a higher standard because they knew what was expected. *The servant who knows the master's will and does not . . . do what the master wants will be beaten with many blows* (Luke 12:47), said Jesus. *From everyone who has been given much, much will be demanded* (Luke 12:48), he said. The most blameworthy people aren't those who know the least about God, but those who know the most, and disobey him anyway. With privilege comes responsibility.

Amos 4:12 *[P]repare to meet your God.*

Because they refused to serve him in life, many of the Israelites were about to meet God in death. Since this was the most important meeting of their lives, perhaps they'd want to prepare.

A man in his fifties was diagnosed with terminal cancer. He never paid much attention to God previously, but wanted to prepare for meeting him personally. So he repented of his sins and *received Christ Jesus as Lord* (Colossians 2:6). He was so transformed that the last three days of his life were the happiest he ever knew. The time was filled with singing, laughing, and reading the Bible. He was finally prepared to meet his God.

Amos 5:21-23 *I hate, I despise your religious festivals; your assemblies are a stench to me. Even though you bring me burnt offerings and grain offerings, I will not accept them. Though you bring choice fellowship offerings, I will have no regard for them. Away with the noise of your songs! I will not listen to the music of your harps.*

The Israelites worshipped God with festivals, sacrificial offerings, and loud singing. They were having a wonderful time worshipping God, but

God was not having a wonderful time being worshipped. They were giving him lip-service, without giving him life-service.

Not every worship service is pleasing to God. Many consider God important enough to worship, but not important enough to serve. But apart from obedient service, our worship is worth little to God, and can even be offensive.

We should prepare ourselves for worship by living for God throughout the week, and by confessing our failures with the assurance of his forgiveness (1 John 1:9). We can also go to bed early the night before so we'll be alert in the morning. We can also get up early to prepare our hearts for public worship by worshipping God privately.

We can also arrive at church early, to greet others, and then be seated early to focus our hearts and minds. When the music is played we can sing with all our hearts, and when the sermon is preached we can hang on every word. Then, when the service is over, we can go out and apply all that we have learned. This is how we can *worship God acceptably with reverence and awe* (Hebrews 12:28-29).

For Reflection and Review

- *Why is God against sexual immorality?*
- *How should we prepare to meet God in death?*
- *How should we prepare for public worship?*

Lesson 159

Amos 5:24 *But let justice roll on like a river, righteousness like a never-failing stream!*

As God looked upon his people he wanted to see both justice and righteousness. Justice demands fairness in court, fairness in business, and protection of the weak. Righteousness demands integrity in relating to God and others. Both are essential to a healthy society.

But when it comes to their personal rights, Christians should be willing to suffer some justice, and overlook some unrighteousness. *If someone slaps you on one cheek, turn to them the other also* (Luke 6:29), said Jesus. Jesus was treated unfairly and we should expect the same. We should stand up for the rights of others, but lay down our own rights in service to Christ.

Amos 6:1 *Woe to you who are complacent in Zion, and to you who feel secure on Mount Samaria.*

The problem with spiritual complacency is that it always leads to spiritual decline. If we're not growing closer to God, we'll soon be falling away from him. No one stays in the same place for long, and if we're not moving in the right direction, we'll soon be moving in the wrong direction.

This was the problem with the Ephesian church. *Consider how far you have fallen! Repent and do the things you did at first* (Revelation 2:5), said Jesus. If they didn't repent, in fact, Jesus threatened to take away their church. There are places in the world where the church used to flourish, but is no more, because it grew complacent.

Satan doesn't care if he turns believers away from Christ all at once, or gradually. If we turn away from Christ just one degree a month, in fifteen years we'll be diametrically opposed to him. If we're not growing in holiness we're growing in sinfulness, and it all begins with complacency.

Amos 7:7-8 *The Lord was standing by a wall that had been built true to plumb, with a plumb line in his hand. And the Lord asked me, What do you see, Amos? A plumb line, I replied. Then the Lord said, Look, I am setting a plumb line among my people Israel; I will spare them no longer.*

A plumb line is a string with a weight at the end, that's hung next to a wall to see if it's straight. Israel was leaning badly and would have to be torn down. This is precisely what happened when it fell to the Assyrians. If Israel had built according to God's word, it would've remained standing. But since it leaned toward sin, it had to come down.

The same idea can be applied to Christians, but with the hope of repair. If our lives are leaning toward sin, they can be rebuilt according to God's word. But for this to happen we must read the Bible almost daily. This will make us aware of our faults, so we can make repairs, before a collapse occurs. There are many degrees at which we can lean, but only one at which we can stand straight. The Bible is God's plumb line for our lives.

Amos 8:9 *In that day, declares the Sovereign Lord, I will make the sun go down at noon and darken the earth in broad daylight.*

Amos foresaw a cosmic disturbance on the day of God's judgment, which came to pass when Jesus was crucified. This was recorded in three of the four gospels: *From noon until three in the afternoon darkness came over all the land* (Matthew 27:45). *At noon, darkness came over the whole land until three in the afternoon* (Mark 15:33). *It was now about noon, and darkness came over the whole land until three in the afternoon, for the sun stopped shining* (Luke 23:44-45). With the death of Jesus Christ the light of the world (John 8:12) went out.

But, three days later, Jesus rose from the dead (Matthew 28:1-10), and the light of his resurrection has been spreading ever since. Jesus bore God's wrath on our behalf so we could have *every spiritual blessing in Christ* (Ephesians 1:3), wrote Paul. The darkness has passed, for those who believe, and the light of God's grace is shining upon us (Proverbs 4:18).

Amos 9:11 *In that day I will restore David's fallen shelter.*

After David built the nation of Israel into a regional superpower, God promised his throne would be *established forever* (2 Samuel 7:16). But, some time after his death, David's kingdom was split in two, and greatly weakened (933 BC). The northern kingdom would fall to the Assyrians (722 BC) and the southern kingdom would fall to the Babylonians (586 BC). It would appear that God's promise to David had failed.

The promises of God may seem to fail for a while, but never fail completely. God would *restore David's fallen shelter* through the return of the exiles (537 BC), but ultimately through Jesus Christ. *The Lord God will give him the throne of his father David, and . . . his kingdom will never end* (Luke 1:32-33), said the angel to Mary.

After Jesus rose from the dead he ascended into heaven (Acts 1:9), and will soon return as *King of kings* (Revelation 19:16). At that time God's promise to David, and to Israel, will be fulfilled beyond all expectation. *For no matter how many promises God has made, they are Yes in Christ* (2 Corinthians 1:20), wrote Paul.

For Reflection and Review

- Why shouldn't Christians insist on their rights?
- How can believers fight against complacency?
- How do we know that God will keep his promises?

Lesson 160

Obadiah 1:1 *The vision of Obadiah.*

Obadiah is the shortest book in the Old Testament. It was probably written after the fall of Jerusalem, in 586 BC, by an otherwise unknown prophet whose name means, *servant of the Lord*. It's a prophecy against the nation of Edom, which was located in the mountainous region southeast of the Dead Sea.

When Judah was attacked and destroyed by the Babylonians, instead of coming to their aid, the Edomites assisted the Babylonians. By attacking God's people they were attacking God himself, and came under his judgment.

Edomites and Israelites were ancient enemies, whose feud began in their mother's womb. When Rebekah was pregnant with twins, *The babies jostled each other within her, and she said, Why is this happening to me?* (Genesis 25:22). *The Lord said to her, Two nations are in your womb, and two peoples from within you will be separated; one people will be stronger than the other, and the older will serve the younger* (Genesis 25:23).

The firstborn child was Esau, who became the father of the Edomites. The second born child was Jacob, who became the father of the Israelites. God gave his opinion of the two nations when he said, *I have loved Jacob, but Esau I have hated, and I have turned his hill country into a wasteland and left his inheritance to the desert jackals* (Malachi 1:2-3).

When Israel journeyed to the Promised Land, they asked the Edomites for safe passage through their territory. *But Edom answered: You may not pass through here; if you try, we will march out and attack you with the sword. The Israelites replied: We will go along the main road, and if we or our livestock drink any of your water, we will pay for it. We only want to pass through on foot—nothing else. Again they answered: You may not pass through. Then Edom came out against them with a large and powerful army. Since Edom refused to let them go through their territory, Israel turned away from them* (Numbers 20:18-21).

Even though they were brother nations, the Edomites opposed Israel before and after after they possessed the Promised Land. They represent all the enemies of God who will be defeated eventually, even if they flourish for a while.

Obadiah 1:3 *The pride of your heart has deceived you, you who live in the clefts of the rocks and make your home on the heights, you who say to yourself, Who can bring me down to the ground?*

Edom was known for its high and secure lodging in mountain caves, thousands of feet above the ground. It was an inconvenient place to live, but the Edomites considered it worth their trouble because it made them feel secure.

Security is one of our greatest needs and we'll go to great lengths to achieve it. We'll store up money to protect us from poverty. We'll buy alarm systems to protect us from intruders. And we'll buy insurance to protect us from calamity. But security apart from God is pure illusion because disaster can strike at any moment.

This is why the Bible tells us to find our security in God. *Let the beloved of the Lord rest secure in him* (Deuteronomy 33:12), wrote Moses. *Blessed are all who take refuge in him* (Psalm 2:12), wrote the Psalmist. *I give them eternal life, and they shall never perish* (John 10:28), said Jesus. Jesus is the only one who can provide the eternal security everyone longs for.

Obadiah 1:13-14 *You should not march through the gates of my people in the day of their disaster, nor gloat over them in their calamity in the day of their disaster, nor seize their wealth in the day of their disaster. You should not wait at the crossroads to cut down their fugitives, nor hand over their survivors in the day of their trouble.*

God was using the Babylonians to punish his people for apostasy. But instead of supporting their brother nation, the Edomites gloated over them, seized their wealth, killed some, and handed others over to the Babylonians. *Remember, Lord, what the Edomites did on the day Jerusalem fell. Tear it down, they cried, tear it down to its foundations!* (Psalm 137:7), recalled the Psalmist.

God finally had enough, so he decided the Edomites would be *destroyed forever* (Obadiah 1:10). They began to suffer defeat, almost immediately, and were gradually displaced by the Nabateans. By the end of the first century the Edomites were no more.

It's never appropriate to gloat or take advantage of others in the day of their disaster. *Love your enemies, do good to those who hate you, bless those who curse you, pray for those who mistreat you* (Luke 6:27-28), said Jesus.

A terrorist group was attacking American soldiers on foreign soil. One of the terrorists was captured, but was in danger of dying due to loss of blood. The medical unit requested volunteers to donate blood and, immediately, ten American soldiers lined up to save their enemy's life. That is how Christians should respond to their enemies on the day of their disaster.

Obadiah 1:17 *But on Mount Zion will be deliverance; it will be holy, and Jacob will possess his inheritance.*

The Babylonians defeated God's people and carried them into exile. But there they found hope in an ancient promise. *[W]hen you and your children return to the Lord your God and obey him with all your heart and with all your soul according to everything I command you today, then the Lord your God will restore your fortunes and have compassion on you and gather you again from all the nations where he scattered you* (Deuteronomy 30:2-3), wrote Moses.

And that's precisely what happened. Seventy years after they were exiled to Babylon, God's people returned to the Promised Land. This was also what God promised through Obadiah: *Jacob will possess his inheritance.*

Obadiah 1:21 *And the kingdom will be the Lord's.*

Repossessing the Promised Land was a small example of what will happen at the end of the age, when Christ returns. *The kingdom of the world has become the kingdom of our Lord* (Revelation 11:15), wrote John. The Promised Land of the Old Testament will be enlarged to cover the whole world, and Jesus Christ will rule forever. This world belongs to God, and he's taking it back—*the kingdom will be the Lord's.*

For Reflection and Review

- *Why is there so much war in the world?*
- *How does Jesus Christ meet our need for security?*
- *Why should Christians treat their enemies well?*

Lesson 161

Jonah 1:1 *The word of the Lord came to Jonah son of Amittai.*

Jonah was a prophet to the northern kingdom of Israel in the eighth century BC (2 Kings 14:25). The book doesn't identify its author but may've been written by Jonah himself around 750 BC. It's the story of God's concern for Assyria, and Jonah's reluctance to preach to them. God wanted Israel to know about his love for others so they'd become a greater witness to the world.

Jonah 1:2 *Go to the great city of Nineveh and preach against it, because its wickedness has come up before me.*

Nineveh was an important city in Assyria with a population of over a hundred twenty thousand (Jonah 4:11). Jonah mentioned violence as one of her sins (Jonah 3:8), and the prophet Amos identified others including witchcraft (Nahum 3:4) and cruelty (Nahum 3:19). Assyria's military acts included ripping open pregnant women, and skinning their captives alive.

A monument from the ninth century BC has this inscription from an Assyrian king: *I built a pillar over against his gate, and I flayed all the chief men . . . and I covered the pillar with their skins . . . Many captives . . . I burned with fire . . . From some I cut off their hands and their fingers, and from others I cut off their noses, their ears . . . of many I put out the eyes.* Because Assyria was a major threat to Israel, it was probably the last place on earth Jonah wanted to go.

Jonah 1:3 *Jonah ran away from the Lord and headed for Tarshish. He went down to Joppa, where he found a ship bound for that port. After paying the fare, he went aboard and sailed for Tarshish to flee from the Lord.*

The prophet should've known that he couldn't run from God but, apparently, he was desperate. He was willing to leave family, friends, and country just to flee God's presence. He probably enjoyed serving God most of the time, but now God was asking too much.

Obeying God is usually easy, but sometimes it's not. Jesus said, *my yoke is easy and my burden is light* (Matthew 11:30). But he also said, *whoever does not carry their cross and follow me cannot be my disciple* (Luke 14:27). Sometimes following Christ is an easy yoke, other times it' a heavy cross. When Christianity becomes difficult, some people run away by closing their Bibles and avoiding church. But God's long arm is always able to reach us.

Jonah 1:4 *Then the Lord sent a great wind on the sea, and such a violent storm arose that the ship threatened to break up.*

Jonah's mistake was thinking that by running away from God he'd be safe. But there's no where in the world that we can hide from God. *Though they hide from my eyes at the bottom of the sea, there I will command the serpent to bite them* (Amos 9:3), wrote Amos. Since God is unavoidable, it's foolish to ignore him.

Jonah 1:5 *All the sailors were afraid and each cried out to his own god. And they threw the cargo into the sea to lighten the ship.*

To keep the ship from being submerged, the cargo was thrown overboard. It was worth a fortune, but was wasted because of Jonah's sin. If Jonah hadn't run from God, he wouldn't have sent the storm, and the cargo wouldn't have been lost. But, because of Jonah's sin, a vast fortune was thrown away.

Sin is always more expensive than we think. How many careers have been lost to sin? How many families have been lost to sin? How many children have been lost to sin? How many fortunes have been lost to sin? Sin will take us further than we want to go, keep us longer than we want to stay, and cost us more than we want to pay. Sadly, the price of our sin is often paid by those around us.

Jonah 1:5b-6 *But Jonah had gone below deck, where he lay down and fell into a deep sleep. The captain went to him and said, How can you sleep? Get up and call on your god! Maybe he will take notice of us so that we will not perish.*

Everyone on the boat was praying except the only one who knew God. Prayer is awkward when you're living in sin, because God only wants to talk about one thing. You might want to talk about your hopes, dreams, or fears, but God only wants to talk about your sin. *If I had cherished sin in my heart, the Lord would not have listened* (Psalm 66:18), wrote David.

Jonah 1:7 *Then the sailors said to each other, Come, let us cast lots to find out who is responsible for this calamity.*

Under God's providence, the lot fell to Jonah. Jonah knew he was guilty, of course, but now his guilt was revealed to others. The sea was growing rougher, and the sailors asked Jonah what they should do. *Pick me up and throw me into the sea, he replied, and it will become calm* (Jonah 1:12).

But the sailors didn't want to kill Jonah, so they tried to row to shore. When the sea grew even rougher, they reluctantly tossed him overboard, and the sea became calm. *At this the men greatly feared the Lord, and they offered a sacrifice to the Lord and made vows to him* (Jonah 1:16). Jonah should've been a good example, but he became a terrible warning.

For Reflection and Review

- *Is following God easy or hard?*
- *How do people run from God today?*
- *Why does sin make it hard to pray?*

Lesson 162

Jonah 2:1 *From inside the fish Jonah prayed to the Lord his God.*

God provided a fish to preserve the prophet, but Jonah didn't know if he'd live or die, so he prayed to the Lord his God. It'd been a while since Jonah prayed, but now he was praying earnestly. *In my distress I called to the Lord* (Jonah 2:2), he said. God was actually causing the prophet's distress to help him repent. Some people respond to hardship by hardening their hearts, but the purpose of hardship is to soften our hearts so we'll pray. Sometimes we pray best when life is at its worst.

Jonah 2:3 *You hurled me into the depths, into the very heart of the seas.*

Jonah could've blamed the sailors for his trouble since they were the ones who threw him into the sea. But Jonah knew they were God's instruments to bring about the discipline he deserved. *[T]he Lord disciplines those he loves, as a father the son he delights in* (Proverbs 3:12), says Proverbs. It's tempting to blame others when life gets hard, but we ought to examine ourselves and consider whether God is teaching us obedience. God doesn't want spoiled children, and will enroll us in the school of suffering to help us improve.

Jonah 2:4 *I said, I have been banished from your sight; yet I will look again toward your holy temple.*

Banishment has always been the dread fear of God's people, and rightly so. After their rebellion, Adam and Eve were banished from the Garden of Eden (Gen.3:23). God's people were later banished from the Promised Land. And Christ will say to his enemies, *Depart from me, you who are cursed* (Matthew 25:41). Jonah was trying to get away from God and feared he may've succeeded. God is good, and close to him is where we want to be. *Come near to God and he will come near to you* (James 4:8), wrote James.

Jonah 2:7 *When my life was ebbing away, I remembered you, Lord.*

When Jonah got on the boat, he was trying to forget about God. But when his life was ebbing away, Jonah remembered God. *If you attempt to talk with a dying man about sports or business, he is no longer interested. He now sees other things as more important. People who are dying recognize what we often forget, that we are standing on the brink of another world* (William Law).

One dear lady followed Christ in her youth, but turned away during college. Years later she was in a boating accident and nearly drowned. As she struggled to keep her head above water, she had a vivid recollection of her Sunday school teachers, and the lessons they taught her when she was young. In light of her approaching death, she recognized her foolishness, and recommitted her life to Christ.

Jonah 2:8 *Those who cling to worthless idols turn away from God's love for them.*

Israel was prone to idolatry, and Jonah saw how foolish that was. But he wasn't any better. He put self-will, self-interest, and self-determination ahead of God. In this way Jonah became his own idol, and turned away from God's love for him. This is the opposite of Jesus who prayed . . . *not my will, but yours be done* (Luke 22:42).

Jonah 2:9 *What I have vowed I will make good. I will say, Salvation comes from the Lord.*

Jonah's vow isn't stated, but likely had something to do with obedience. Perhaps he prayed that if God would save him, he'd do whatever God wanted. Making vows to God is seldom wise because we often fail in our commitments. *It is better not to make a vow than to make one and not fulfill it* (Ecclesiastes 5:5), wrote Solomon.

Instead of making a vow to God, and hoping he'll answer our prayer, we ought to simply obey God, which often leads to answered prayer. *We receive from him anything we ask, because we keep his commands* (1 John 3:22), wrote John. Instead of getting in trouble and making vows, we should walk in obedience and trust God to do what's best.

Jonah 2:10 *And the Lord commanded the fish, and it vomited Jonah onto dry land.*

Jonah spent about three days in the fish, which Jesus found significant. *For as Jonah was three days and three nights in the belly of a huge fish, so the Son of Man will be three days and three nights in the heart of the earth* (Matthew 12:40), he said.

Jonah's ministry paralleled Jesus' ministry in other ways as well. Jonah was disciplined for his sin, and Jesus was punished for our sins. Jonah recovered from a near death experience, and Jesus was raised from a real death experience. Jonah preached to the Ninevites, and Jesus is preached to the world. We don't want to follow Jonah, but we truly want to follow Christ.

For Reflection and Review

- *How did being in a fish help Jonah pray?*
- *How do Christians practice idolatry?*
- *How does Jonah remind us of Jesus?*

Lesson 163

Jonah 3:1 *Then the word of the Lord came to Jonah a second time.*

The first time the word of the Lord came to Jonah he wasn't receptive. By running away from God, he brought many into danger, and caused massive financial loss. Jonah may've thought God would never use him again. But God still had big plans for Jonah, so *the word of the Lord came to Jonah a second time.*

God doesn't dwell on our failures, and neither should we. If Moses dwelt on his failure after murdering the Egyptian, who would've delivered the Israelites from slavery? If Peter dwelt on his failure after disowning Jesus, who would've preached on Pentecost when three thousand were saved? And if Paul dwelt on his failure after approving the stoning of Stephen, who would've evangelized the Gentiles, and written so much of the New Testament?

Forgetting what is behind and straining toward what is ahead, I press on toward the goal to win the prize for which God has called me heavenward (Philippians 3:13-14), wrote Paul. Two things are necessary to succeed as a Christian: *Forgetting what is behind and straining toward what is ahead.*

An electrician flipped the wrong switch at a power plant and caused a million dollars worth of damage. To no one's surprise, he was promptly fired. But a similar thing happened at another company, and when the worker turned in his resignation his boss said, *I just spent a million dollars training you. Why would I let you go now?* That's God's method of management. He doesn't fire us when we make a mistake; he uses our mistake to make us better.

Jonah 3:2-4 *Go to the great city of Nineveh and proclaim to it the message I give you. . . . Forty more days and Nineveh will be overthrown.*

Jonah wasn't free to embellish the message, or change it in any way. The message was from God, and Jonah was the messenger. And the message was brief: *Forty more days and Nineveh will be overthrown.*

It's not the number of words that matters, but the power of the words. *Is not my word like fire, declares the Lord, and like a hammer that breaks a rock in pieces?* (Jeremiah 23:29). A single sentence can change a life if it's sent by God and believed in the heart.

Many years ago I heard a teacher say, *True information is always your friend.* I was in the habit of rejecting true information, that I didn't want to hear, only to suffer later on. Then I began to welcome true information, even if I didn't want to hear it, because it helped me make wiser decisions. A single sentence changed my life.

Jonah 3:5 *The Ninevites believed God.*

This was so completely unexpected it's hard to imagine why it happened. Some think Jonah's fish story got to Nineveh before him, so they were ready for his message. And if his skin was bleached by gastric juices, it would've reinforced the story. There was also an eclipse of the sun at this time, that would've been considered ominous, and made the people of Nineveh open to a word from God.

But, ultimately, turning people to God is the work of the Holy Spirit. So when Jesus sent the Spirit on the day of Pentecost, three thousand believed (Acts 2:41). Similar things have also happened at other times.

In 1859, one hundred thousand people were gathered into the churches of Ireland, in what became known as the Ulster Revival. A year later there was so little crime that police were laid off, jails were empty, and judges had little to do. Taverns were also empty, churches were full, and families were strong. The Holy Spirit empowered the message of the gospel, and lives were transformed.

Jonah 3:5b *A fast was proclaimed, and all of them, from the greatest to the least, put on sackcloth.*

Sackcloth was made from goat's hair, and was normally worn by slaves, prisoners, and the destitute. When combined with fasting, wearing sackcloth was an expression of grief for sins, also known as *contrition*. *My sacrifice, O God, is a broken spirit; a broken and contrite heart you, God, will not despise* (Psalm 51:17), wrote David. If our hearts are broken by sin, we know that God accepts our repentance, through faith in in Jesus Christ.

Jonah 3:6 *When Jonah's warning reached the king of Nineveh, he rose from his throne, took off his royal robes, covered himself with sackcloth and sat down in the dust.*

The king got off his throne in order to be saved. Perhaps he understood that God alone is king, and only God has the right to rule. The king could've stayed on his throne if he chose, but he would've lost it forty days later. Instead, he gave up his throne, submitted to God, and received it back as a gift.

Something even better happens when we surrender the throne of our lives to Jesus Christ. He shares his throne with us in the age to come. *To the one who is victorious, I will give the right to sit with me on my throne* (Revelation 3:21), said Jesus. If we surrender the throne of our lives to Jesus now, we'll share his throne forever. When fighting God, surrender is victory.

Jonah 3:7-8 *By the decree of the king and his nobles: Do not let people or animals, herds or flocks, taste anything; do not let them eat or drink. But let people and animals be covered with sackcloth. Let everyone call urgently on God.*

The king took Jonah's message so seriously that he decreed a fast of food and water for both people and their animals. Everyone was to show their repentance by wearing sackcloth and calling *urgently* on God. This was only appropriate since the need to get right with God is always urgent.

We can imagine Satan and his demons plotting to keep people out of heaven. One demon suggests telling people there is no God, and many others agree. Another suggests telling people there is no hell, and others agree with that as well. Another suggests telling people there is no hurry, and they all begin to cheer! Those who wait too long, will discover it's too late.

Jonah 3:8-9 *Let them give up their evil ways and their violence. Who knows? God may yet relent and with compassion turn from his fierce anger so that we will not perish.*

In addition to fasting and prayer, the king commanded his people to *give up their evil ways*. This is also what God said through the prophet Isaiah: *Let the wicked forsake their ways and the unrighteous their thoughts. Let them turn to the Lord, and he will have mercy on them, and to our God, for he will freely pardon* (Isaiah 55:7).

In a single day Nineveh went from being wicked to being righteous. Instead of lying, they told the truth. Instead of cheating, they were honest. Instead of being violent, they were gentle. Instead of being selfish, they were generous. It became like heaven on earth. A family, city, or nation can never be better than the people who live there. The more people are living for God, the better that place will be.

Jonah 3:10 *When God saw what they did and how they turned from their evil ways, he had compassion and did not bring upon them the destruction he had threatened.*

God makes threats and promises, and wants us to believe both. He threatens us with judgment, to turn us from our sins. Then he promises salvation through faith in Jesus Christ. The Bible and history show that God doesn't make idle threats, or break his promises. This is dreadful news for the wicked, and the best possible news for the righteous.

For Reflection and Review

- Why does God give people more than one chance?
- Why did Nineveh repent when they heard Jonah's message?
- How does repentance make the world a better place?

Lesson 164

Jonah 4:1 *But to Jonah this seemed very wrong, and he became angry.*

It seems strange that God's prophet didn't want these people to turn to God. But the Ninevites were still a threat and, within a few decades, they'd attack and destroy the northern kingdom of Israel. Jonah was likely afraid of this, so he wanted God to kill the Ninevites, not save them.

A psychology magazine asked its readers to respond to this question: *If you could secretly push a button and thereby eliminate any person, with no repercussions to yourself, would you push the button?* More than half the readers said *Yes*. Enemies make us angry, and our anger varies from irritation to blind rage. Jonah was beyond irritation; he was becoming enraged.

Jonah 4:2 *I knew that you are a gracious and compassionate God, slow to anger and abounding in love, a God who relents from sending calamity.*

This is one of the best summary descriptions of God's character in the Bible, and occurs repeatedly. *The Lord, the Lord, the compassionate and gracious God, slow to anger, abounding in love and faithfulness* (Exodus 34:6). *But you are a forgiving God, gracious and compassionate, slow to anger and abounding in love* (Nehemiah 9:17).

But you, Lord, are a compassionate and gracious God, slow to anger, abounding in love and faithfulness (Psalm 86:15). *The Lord is compassionate and gracious, slow to anger, abounding in love* (Psalm 103:8). Jonah's problem was that he wanted God's love for himself, but wanted God's wrath for his enemies.

Jonah 4:3 *Now, Lord, take away my life, for it is better for me to die than to live.*

Jonah had at least two reasons to be depressed. When the Israelites learned that he aided the enemy, he might be considered a traitor. And if they discovered his prediction didn't come true (*Forty more days and Nineveh will be overthrown*), he might be considered a false prophet (Deuteronomy 18:22). Jonah's obedience to God was costing him professionally, socially, emotionally, and spiritually. Serving God isn't always sweetness and light.

Jonah 4:5 *Jonah had gone out and sat down at a place east of the city. There he made himself a shelter, sat in its shade and waited to see what would happen to the city.*

Jonah was still hoping Nineveh would be destroyed, like Sodom and Gomorrah (Genesis 19). That day is coming for the whole world (2 Peter 3:10), but this was a day of grace.

Jonah 4:6 *Then the Lord God provided a leafy plant and made it grow up over Jonah to give shade for his head to ease his discomfort, and Jonah was very happy about the plant.*

The temperature there can soar above a hundred degrees, so God provided a plant for shade, to ease Jonah's discomfort. It may seem like a little thing, but it was a token of kindness that made a difference to Jonah. God was caring for the prophet's needs, and Jonah was thankful.

Jonah 4:7-8 *But at dawn the next day God provided a worm, which chewed the plant so that it withered. When the sun rose, God provided a scorching east wind, and the sun blazed on Jonah's head so that he grew faint. He wanted to die, and said, It would be better for me to die than to live.*

God can be exasperating. First he gave Jonah a blessing, then he took it away. But God wasn't toying with the prophet; he was teaching him maturity. God wants us to honor him in good times and in bad. This is not an easy lesson to learn.

Many years ago I was driving home from my minimum wage job, praising God for an unexpected bonus. I only had one pair of pants that I could wear to church, and now I could replace them. But as I was praising God, I saw flashing blue lights in my mirror, and was given a ticket for the exact amount of the bonus. Just like Jonah, my praising turned to complaining.

But after losing family and fortune, Job replied, *The Lord gave and the Lord has taken away; may the name of the Lord be praised* (Job 1:21). God is less concerned with our comfort than he is with our character. He gives and takes away to help us mature. This is why the Bible says to *give thanks in all circumstances; for this is God's will for you in Christ Jesus* (1 Thessalonians 5:18), wrote Paul.

Notice also that God used the big fish and the little worm to help the prophet grow up. God is sovereign over big things, little things, and everything in-between. In fact, he uses *all things . . . for the good of those who love him* (Romans 8:28), wrote Paul. God's ways don't always agree with us, but he's always working for our good.

Jonah 4:9 *God said to Jonah, Is it right for you to be angry about the plant? It is, he said. And I'm so angry I wish I were dead.*

Unresolved anger leads to depression, and Jonah's lack of anger management was making him depressed. It's not a perfect life that makes us happy, but the ability to forgive and forget.

An attorney was resentful toward some of his clients, who didn't pay their bills, and his anger was making things worse. So he wrote them each a letter saying, *Your bill is forgiven. In exchange, please forgive at least one person who owes you money or has offended you.* He got over his resentment, and experienced so much joy that he did the same thing every year. A good way to manage anger is to receive God's forgiveness, and forgive those who've hurt you.

Jonah 4:10-11 *But the Lord said, You have been concerned about this plant, though you did not tend it or make it grow. It sprang up overnight and died overnight. And should I not have concern for the great city of Nineveh, in which there are more than a hundred and twenty thousand people who cannot tell their right hand from their left—and also many animals?*

Jonah was more concerned for his comfort than for the lost souls of Nineveh. But Paul said, *I could wish that I myself were cursed and cut off from Christ for the sake of my people* (Romans 9:2-3). To go to hell for another person is beyond what God asks of us, but to care lost souls is not.

A Christian man was thrown into prison and tortured for his faith, but he shared the gospel with those who tortured him. The closer he came to death, in fact, the more burdened he was for their souls. He knew that if he died, their chances of being saved would diminish. He died eventually, but not until one of the guards was converted. As God's prophet, it was time for Jonah to get over himself, and start caring for the people God sent him to reach.

For Reflection and Review

- *Why was Jonah angry that Nineveh repented?*
- *Why does God give and take away?*
- *Do you really want God to love your enemies?*

Lesson 165

Micah 1:1 *The word of the Lord that came to Micah of Moresheth.*

The prophet Micah lived in the little town of Moresheth, about twenty-two miles southwest of Jerusalem. Approximate dates for his ministry are 735 to 700 BC, with his book being written near the latter. Micah reminded God's people of the *kindness and sternness of God* (Romans 11:22), with messages of both doom and hope.

Micah 2:11 *If a liar and deceiver comes and says, I will prophesy for you plenty of wine and beer, that would be just the prophet for this people!*

True prophets were often opposed by false prophets, who preached a message of prosperity. False prophets got an audience by telling people what they wanted to hear, and little has changed over time. The most popular preachers are often those who preach health, wealth, and happiness through faith in Jesus Christ.

But, *In this world you will have trouble* (John 16:33), said Jesus. And the early church experienced plenty of it. *You suffered along with those in prison and joyfully accepted the confiscation of your property, because you knew that you yourselves had better and lasting possessions* (Hebrews 10:34), says Hebrews. The gospel of Jesus Christ isn't always good news for the present age, but is the best possible news for the age to come.

If believers are taught to expect too much in the present age, they'll soon be disappointed, and may conclude that God's word isn't true. But if they're taught to expect hardship, they won't be surprised when it comes, and will trust God all the way to glory. Life in a fallen world isn't easy for anyone, even Christians. But *God is our God for ever and ever [and] he will be our guide even to the end* (Psalm 48:14), wrote the Psalmist.

Micah 3:8 *But as for me, I am filled with power, with the Spirit of the Lord, and with justice and might, to declare to Jacob his transgression.*

Contrary to the false prophets, Micah was empowered by the Spirit to confront God's people with their sins. He accused the judges of bribery, the priests of serving for money, and the prophets of telling fortunes (Micah 3:11). The indictments were so many and severe, that few could avoid their sting.

The prophet didn't attribute his courageous preaching to the strength of his personality, but to the *Spirit of the Lord*. We see this again in the Apostle Peter, who preached with the Spirit's power to those who crucified Jesus. *God has made this Jesus, whom you crucified, both Lord and Messiah* (Acts 2:36), he said. Spirit empowered preachers aren't afraid to confront people with their sin, in order to bring them to repentance.

Micah 4:1-2 *In the last days the mountain of the Lord's temple will be established as the highest of the mountains... Many nations will come and say, Come, let us go up to the mountain of the Lord, to the temple of the God of Jacob. He will teach us his ways, so that we may walk in his paths.*

The prophet saw a time, after God's judgment, when Jerusalem will be exalted above all other cities, and the mountain of the Lord above all other mountains. He spoke of a glorious age of prosperity when Messiah will rule the world (Micah 4:3).

Prophecy is best understood after it comes to pass, but many believe the Bible teaches a golden age of a thousand years, that'll occur after the return of Christ, before the eternal age. This idea is made explicit in the last book of the Bible.

He seized the dragon, that ancient serpent, who is the devil, or Satan, and bound him for a thousand years. He threw him into the Abyss, and locked and sealed it over him, to keep him from deceiving the nations anymore until the thousand years were ended (Revelation 20:2-3). This make sense of passages that speak of a glorious age in the future, that's not entirely perfect.

Never again will there be... an old man who does not live out his years; the one who dies at a hundred will be thought a mere child (Isaiah 65:20), wrote Isaiah. This doesn't describe the present age, since people die young sometimes. And it doesn't describe the eternal age, since people still die. But it may describe the time after Jesus returns, before the eternal age begins. When the eternal age begins, *There will be no more death or mourning or crying or pain, for the old order of things has passed away* (Revelation 21:4), wrote John.

Micah 4:3 *He will judge between many peoples and will settle disputes for strong nations far and wide. They will beat their swords into plowshares and their spears into* *pruning hooks. Nation will not take up sword against nation, nor will they train for war anymore.*

When Christ returns to rule, there will still be many nations, but not any war. Nations will still disagree, but they'll take their concerns to Jerusalem, where their disputes will be settled by Christ. There will be no more need for weapons of war, which will be converted into equipment for farming.

War is so normal it's hard to imagine a world without it. But under the rule of Christ, there won't even be the fear of war, since nations won't have armies. This will result in national savings, lower taxes, and greater wealth for everyone. Instead of working long hours to pay the rent, *Everyone will sit under their own vine and under their own fig tree, and no one will make them afraid* (Micah 4:4), wrote Micah.

For Reflection and Review

- *How was Micah different from the false prophets?*
- *How will the world change when Christ returns?*
- *How will the eternal age be even better?*

Lesson 166

Micah 5:2 *But you, Bethlehem Ephrathah, though you are small among the clans of Judah, out of you will come for me one who will be ruler over Israel, whose origins are from of old, from ancient times.*

This is one of the most remarkable prophecies in the Bible. Not only did the prophet foresee the place of Messiah's birth, but also his preexistence as one who was *from ancient times*.

Jesus also spoke of his preexistence in several places: *For I have come down from heaven not to do my will but to do the will of him who sent me* (John 6:38). *[W]hat if you see the Son of Man ascend to where he was before!* (John 6:62). *[B]efore Abraham was born, I am!* (John 8:58). *I came from the Father and entered the world; now I am leaving the world and going back to the Father* (John 16:28). *And now, Father, glorify me in your presence with the glory I had with you before the world began* (John 17:5), he said.

It may've been through the prophet Micah, in fact, that Jesus first became aware of his eternality. We can imagine him as a youth sitting in the synagogue as this passage was read. Knowing he was born in Bethlehem, and that the Bible was about him (John 5:39), Jesus heard the reader say *whose origins are from of old, from ancient times*—and began to grasp his eternality. If that's how it happened, then Jesus got a lot out of the service that day!

Micah 6:6-7 *With what shall I come before the Lord and bow down before the exalted God? Shall I come before him with burnt offerings, with calves a year old? Will the Lord be pleased with thousands of rams, with ten thousand rivers of olive oil? Shall I offer my firstborn for my transgression, the fruit of my body for the sin of my soul?*

God's people may've thought that God was hard to please, or even impossible to please. In light his many commands, and their many failures, this is understandable. Countless Christians, in fact, have come to the same conclusion. But Micah wanted God's people to know that he isn't hard to please.

Micah 6:8 *He has shown you, O mortal, what is good. And what does the Lord require of you? To act justly and to love mercy and to walk humbly with your God.*

Micah condensed the many commands of the Old Testament into just three: *To act justly and to love mercy and to walk humbly with your God.* That's all God wanted from his people. If we think that God is hard to please, we insult his character. And sooner or later, we'll stop trying to please him.

But Jesus can also seem hard to please. *Be perfect, therefore, as your heavenly Father is perfect* (Matthew 5:48), he said. Since we can't live up to that, we might think we're always living under God's frown. But God isn't an ogre, and doesn't want us to think he's always frowning at us.

It's better to think of God as a heavenly Father who's pleased with every good thing we do: every good thought, every good word, and every good deed. God is easy to please, but difficult to satisfy. Like a good parent, he's always looking for some improvement. We can think of him saying, *Well done! And I know you can do even better tomorrow!* This allows us to serve God with joy, because he's always bringing out the best in us.

Micah 7:18-19 *Who is a God like you, who pardons sin and forgives the transgression of the remnant of his inheritance? You do not stay angry forever but delight to show mercy. You will again have compassion on us; you will tread our sins underfoot and hurl all our iniquities into the depths of the sea.*

Sin is so destructive it can separate us from God forever (Matthew 25:46). Sin is so evil that it required nothing less than the death of Christ to pay for it (1 Peter 1:18-19). But having paid for our sin in full, God will *hurl all our iniquities into the depths of the sea.*

Imagine God forging your sins into a steel ball, winding up like a major league pitcher, and hurling them into the middle of the sea. With a splash they hit the water and sink to the bottom, never to be recovered. God makes no offer of partial forgiveness. *I will forgive their wickedness and will remember their sins no more* (Hebrews 8:12), says Hebrews.

For Reflection and Review

- *How did Jesus exist before he was born?*
- *Why can God seem hard to please?*
- *Why does God want us to know that we're completely forgiven?*

Lesson 167

Nahum 1:1 *A prophecy concerning Nineveh. The book of the vision of Nahum the Elkoshite.*

Nahum wrote around 650 BC, and foretold the destruction of Nineveh, which happened in 612 BC. Jonah announced the destruction of Nineveh about a hundred years earlier, but that judgment was delayed due to their repentance (Jonah 3:5). Nineveh returned to her evil ways, however, and sealed her own doom.

The city of Nineveh stands for the whole Assyrian empire, of which it was the capital. The Assyrians destroyed the northern kingdom of Israel in 722 BC, and were a threat to the southern kingdom of Judah, which they had already plundered (2 Kings 18:13-16). The Assyrians inflicted terrible suffering on their enemies, and struck fear in the hearts of many. The prophet's name means *comfort*, and his prophecy was a comfort to the people of Judah for whom he wrote.

Nahum 1:2 *The Lord is a jealous and avenging God; the Lord takes vengeance and is filled with wrath. The Lord takes vengeance on his foes and vents his wrath against his enemies.*

The Assyrians didn't understand that by attacking God's people, they were attacking God himself. *[W]hoever touches you touches the apple of his eye* (Zechariah 2:8), wrote Zechariah. Likewise, when Saul was persecuting Christians, the Lord appeared to him and said, *Saul, Saul, why do you persecute me?* (Acts 9:4). Whoever attacks a child of God, attacks God himself, and may incur the wrath of God.

One man attacked his pastor's reputation and was destroying his ministry. Because the town was small, most people knew about the attack, and knew it was wrong. But while the man was waging war, he went up in his airplane, and died when it crashed. Reading providence is seldom wise, but the people of the town drew their own conclusions. *The Lord takes vengeance on his foes and vents his wrath against his enemies.*

Nahum 1:3 *[T]he Lord will not leave the guilty unpunished.*

Any judge who pardoned criminals, just because he was merciful, wouldn't be qualified for the job.

If the criminal was a murdering rapist, in fact, the judge would be considered evil for not imposing justice. This is why there has to be a Judgment Day. *[T]he Lord will not leave the guilty unpunished.*

And since we're all guilty of something, we have reason to be concerned. We might be better than other sinners, but that doesn't make us righteous. If God gives us what we deserve, we'll all be in hell forever (Matthew 25:41).

But, wanting to be merciful, God sent his Son to bear the punishment we deserve. *[H]e was pierced for our transgressions, he was crushed for our iniquities; the punishment that brought us peace was on him* (Isaiah 53:5), wrote Isaiah.

Since God himself bore the penalty for our sins, he can now *be just and the one who justifies those who have faith in Jesus* (Romans 3:26), wrote Paul. God can be a righteous judge, and still be merciful to those who believe in Jesus Christ, because justice was fulfilled when Jesus died on a cross for our sins. It would, in fact, be wrong for God to punish believers for their sins, because their sins have already been paid for on the cross. To require a double payment for sin wouldn't be just.

Nahum 1:6 *Who can withstand his indignation? Who can endure his fierce anger? His wrath is poured out like fire; the rocks are shattered before him.*

Think of lightning striking the top of a mountain, splitting rocks, and causing them to fall. God's wrath is even worse. *They called to the mountains and the rocks, Fall on us and hide us from the face of him who sits on the throne and from the wrath of the Lamb! For the great day of their wrath has come, and who can withstand it?* (Revelation 6:16-17), wrote John. It's better to have a mountain fall on your head, than face the wrath of God.

Nahum 2:6 *The river gates are thrown open and the palace collapses.*

This probably describes the fall of Nineveh. A river flowed through the city, and outside were dams which likely had gates to regulate the flow. These gates could've been closed until a massive amount of water was backed up. When released, the mighty flow breached the city walls and provided access for the opposing army. No one is safe from God's judgment, no matter how strong their defense.

Nahum 3:19 *Nothing can heal you; your wound is fatal. All who hear the news about you clap their hands at your fall, for who has not felt your endless cruelty?*

This final verse assures the reader that Nineveh will never rise again. The destruction was so complete that Nineveh was covered with sand, and lost to the world, until it was rediscovered by archaeologists in 1845. God's people will live forever, but the memory of his enemies will be buried in the sand.

For Reflection and Review

- *Why is it dangerous to attack God's people?*
- *Why can't God pardon our sins apart from Jesus Christ?*
- *What is the wrath of God like?*

Lesson 168

Habakkuk 1:1 *The prophecy that Habakkuk the prophet received.*

Habakkuk wrote from Judah around 605 BC, during a time of moral decline. Jerusalem fell within a couple decades, and Habakkuk probably lived to see it. He couldn't understand God's ways, but he learned to trust and rejoice in him.

Habakkuk 1:2 *How long, Lord, must I call for help, but you do not listen?*

Habakkuk was bothered by the moral decline of his day, and called on God to do something. He likely prayed for years, without results, and was bewildered at God's apparent indifference. King David also felt this way at times: *How long, Lord? Will you forget me forever? How long will you hide your face from me? How long must I wrestle with my thoughts and day after day have sorrow in my heart?* (Psalm 13:1-2), he wrote.

God's failure to act is a recurring problem for his people, and a serious test of faith. By one estimate, sixty percent of believers struggle with a problem, for which they have no foreseeable solution. As a result, some even stop believing. Such a response is sad, however, since the only thing worse than suffering with God, is suffering without him. At least with God there's hope; without him is only despair.

Habakkuk 1:3 *Why do you make me look at injustice? Why do you tolerate wrongdoing?*

Like many before and since, the prophet thought he could do a better job running the world than God. The world is so full of evil that it could be much improved by simply removing the worst ten percent. If God is good and powerful, why does he allow so much evil?

We can't answer that question completely, but it's helpful to understand that God overcomes evil with good. Jesus overcame the crucifixion through his resurrection, and has promised a glorious future to all who believe (John 14:2). If God overcomes evil with good, then evil won't have the last word.

One dear lady was raped and, as a result, conceived a child. Her pain could've been crippling, but she believes God is in control, and has a future for both her and her child. She's not bound by the past, therefore, but lives by faith in the goodness and power of God. The more we believe God overcomes evil with good, the better we can handle evil when it comes.

Habakkuk 1:5 *I am going to do something in your days that you would not believe, even if you were told.*

God's answer to the prophet's problem turned out to be worse than the problem itself. Habakkuk's problem was that God was allowing evil to go unchecked among his people. God's answer was that he'd use the Babylonians to punish his people (Habakkuk 1:6). But the Babylonians were even worse than the people of God! How could God use a nation that was worse than the Jews to punish the Jews?

The unbelievability of this event foreshadows the unbelievability of what Jesus did on the cross for us. So when Paul preached Christ to a gathering of Jews he quoted Habakkuk: *I am going to do something in your days that you would never believe, even if someone told you* (Acts 13:41), he said. The gospel is hard to believe, but that doesn't mean it isn't true. It's also hard to believe in microwaves but, somehow, they heat our food.

Habakkuk 1:8-11 *Their horses are swifter than leopards, fiercer than wolves at dusk. Their cavalry gallops headlong; their horsemen come from afar. They fly like an eagle swooping to devour; they all come intent on violence. Their hordes advance like a desert wind and gather prisoners like sand. . . . Then they sweep past like the wind and go on—guilty people, whose own strength is their god.*

With poetic flair the prophet described the coming invasion of the Babylonians. But notice his conclusion: their *own strength is their god*. The Babylonians were a mighty force, but were later defeated by Cyrus, king of Persia. That's what happens to those whose strength is their god—they're defeated by someone stronger.

An important part of biblical faith is relying on God, not on ourselves. We depend on him for breath, sight, memory, pulse, and everything else. And whenever our bodies fail, we understand even better how dependent on God we are. That's why the Bible never condones self-reliance, but only reliance on God.

Habakkuk 2:4 *[T]he righteous person will live by his faithfulness.*

The word translated *faithfulness* can also be translated *faith*. The ideas are closely related since those who have faith will also be faithful (James 2:26). The Apostle Paul referred to this verse twice to support the idea that people are saved by faith (Romans 1:17, Galatians 3:11).

The prophet didn't understand what God was doing, but continued to believe in him anyway. And those who believe in Jesus Christ won't give up, even when they're confused. God is always God, and the righteous will live by faith in him.

Habakkuk 2:14 *For the earth will be filled with the knowledge of the glory of the Lord as the waters cover the sea.*

Habakkuk quoted the Prophet Isaiah (Isaiah 11:19), who wrote about a century earlier. Both were familiar with Solomon's prayer: *may the whole earth be filled with his glory* (Psalm 72:19). After Solomon built the temple, *the glory of the Lord filled the temple* (2 Chronicles 5:14). And the day is coming when the glory of the Lord will fill the whole earth.

The glory of God is that which makes him praiseworthy. We're attracted to the glory of art, the glory of sports, the glory of music, the glory of nature, the glory science, and many other things. The glory of God includes every other glory and exceeds them all by far. Now the world is blinded by sin, but it will see the glory of God. *For the earth will be filled with the knowledge of the glory of the Lord as the waters cover the sea.*

Habakkuk 3:17-18 *Though the fig tree does not bud and there are no grapes on the vines, though the olive crop fails and the fields produce no food, though there are no sheep in the pen and no cattle in the stalls, yet I will rejoice in the Lord, I will be joyful in God my Savior.*

The prophet knew better than others that difficult times were ahead. But he also knew that, even in the worst of times, he could rejoice in the Lord. That's why Paul and Silas could give praise to God at midnight, after being beaten and thrown into prison (Acts 16:22-25). *Rejoice in the Lord always. I will say it again: Rejoice!* (Philippians 4:4), wrote Paul.

If we wait until our problems are solved before we're happy, we'll never be happy this side of heaven. Problems are a fact of life, but so is God. *It is the duty of every Christian, by faith in the goodness, power, and love of God, to cultivate a cheerful frame of mind, even though this may be difficult by reason of afflictions* (J.G. Vos).

For Reflection and Review

- *How would you change the world if you were in charge?*
- *What's the difference between having faith and being faithful?*
- *Why can believers rejoice in the Lord, even when times are bad?*

Lesson 169

Zephaniah 1:1 *The word of the Lord that came to Zephaniah son of Cushi, the son of Gedaliah, the son of Amariah, the son of Hezekiah, during the reign of Josiah son of Amon king of Judah.*

Zephaniah began his book with his ancestry to show he was a fourth-generation descendent of King Hezekiah and, therefore, a person of status in Judah. His main theme is *the day of the Lord*, which will bring judgment on the wicked and blessing to the righteous. Zephaniah preached to the people of Judah during the reign of Josiah, perhaps around 625 BC. He seems familiar with the writings of Isaiah and Amos, and probably knew the young Jeremiah personally.

Zephaniah 1:2-3 *I will sweep away everything from the face of the earth, declares the Lord. I will sweep away both man and beast; I will sweep away the birds in the sky and the fish in the sea—and the idols that cause the wicked to stumble.*

The severity of this judgment is difficult to overstate. It's worse than the flood in Noah's day (Genesis 6-8) because then, at least, the fish survived. This prophecy was echoed by the Apostle Peter who wrote, *The heavens will disappear with a roar; the elements will be destroyed by fire, and the earth and everything done in it will be laid bare* (2 Peter

3:10). In his passion for holiness, God will purge evil from the world by consuming it with fire.

This is why the world isn't a good place to settle down. It'd be foolish to build a house next to an active volcano, and it would be equally foolish to be at home in this world. Like Abraham, believers are *looking forward to the city with foundations, whose architect and builder is God* (Hebrews 11:10). We confess that we are *foreigners and strangers on earth* (Hebrews 11:13), passing through to a place of our own.

What the prophet foresaw, however, is not the end of the world. *I will create new heavens and a new earth* (Isaiah 65:17), wrote Isaiah. *Then I saw a new heaven and a new earth, for the first heaven and the first earth had passed away* (Revelation 21:1), wrote John. The present world will be destroyed because of sin, but God will create something new and improved, where his people will live with him forever. Once and for all, we'll be delivered from sin and its terrible curse.

Zephaniah 1:12 *At that time I will search Jerusalem with lamps and punish those who are complacent, who are like wine left on its dregs, who think, The Lord will do nothing, either good or bad.*

Like settled wine, the people of God were settled in their complacency, convinced that God would neither bless nor curse, reward nor punish. They hadn't ceased to believe in God, but considered him irrelevant. They had a do-nothing attitude toward God, and believed that he would do nothing for or against them. But the God of the Bible is always acting, and requires his people to act as well. *Woe to you who are complacent* (Amos 6:1) said Amos.

Some who've fallen away from Christ have written books about their de-conversion, and there is a pattern to the process. It begins with spiritual complacency evidenced by a decline in prayer, Bible-reading, and going to church. With a declining interest in God, there's an increased interest in sin, making God seem even less desirable. Then they fall away. The way to avoid this is to always be growing in Christ.

Zephaniah 2:3 *Seek the Lord, all you humble of the land, you who do what he commands. Seek righteousness, seek humility; perhaps you will be sheltered on the day of the Lord's anger.*

In light of the coming judgment, the prophet urged God's people to seek the Lord. The only way to flee from God's wrath is to run toward him. Seeking God means pursuing an ever deepening relationship with him, which is something the Bible often commands.

Now devote your heart and soul to seeking the Lord your God (1 Chronicles 22:19), said David. *If you seek him, he will be found by you; but if you forsake him, he will reject you forever* (1 Chronicles 28:9), said David again. *Look to the Lord and his strength; seek his face always* (Psalm 105:4), wrote the Psalmist. *Seek the Lord while he may be found; call on him while he is near* (Isaiah 55:6), wrote Isaiah.

Imagine a little girl who lived next door to Abraham Lincoln, sat on his porch, and even played games with him. Then imagine a scholar who knew everything about Lincoln, but didn't know him personally. We could debate which one knew him better, but if the scholar became Lincoln's friend, he'd know him best of all. Seeking the Lord requires head knowledge and heart knowledge, Bible-study and prayer.

Zephaniah 3:17 *He will take great delight in you; in his love he will no longer rebuke you, but will rejoice over you with singing.*

It's easier to imagine God speaking to us, than singing to us. But the feeling of love is so powerful it's often expressed through music. That is why there are so many love songs, and why we sing to God in church. But here it's God who's doing the singing. *[He] will rejoice over you with singing.* In heaven, we'll sing to God, and he will sing over us. Then we will sing to him some more, and he will sing over us some more. And this will go on forever, because we were made for an eternal love relationship with God, through his Son Jesus Christ.

For Reflection and Review

- *What is the future of the world?*
- *What is the pattern of de-conversion?*
- *What will singing be like in heaven?*

Lesson 170

Haggai 1:1 *In the second year of King Darius, on the first day of the sixth month, the word of the Lord came through the prophet Haggai to Zerubbabel son of Shealtiel, governor of Judah, and to Joshua son of Jozadak, the high priest.*

Cyrus king of Persia conquered Babylon, in 539 BC, and decreed that the Jews could go back to their homeland. About fifty thousand returned, and promptly laid the foundation for a new temple. Due to opposition, however, the work ceased until 520 BC, when Darius reigned over Persia. Then the prophet Haggai began to preach that it was God's will to finish the temple, and it was completed in the next five years.

Haggai 1:2 *This is what the Lord Almighty says: These people say, The time has not yet come to rebuild the Lord's house.*

God's people planned to finish the temple eventually, but not at the moment. They may've been waiting for a better economy, better leadership, or for others to go first. Instead of doing God's work, they were making excuses. Instead of making the most of their sacred opportunity, they were wasting their lives.

One man came to Christ near the end of his life but, instead of being joyful, he was filled with grief. His pastor assured him of God's forgiveness, but that didn't help. *I could've spent my whole life for God but I spent it on myself. . . . I have completely wasted my life*, he said. The time is always right for serving God, and it should never be delayed.

Haggai 1:4 *Is it a time for you yourselves to be living in your paneled houses, while this house remains a ruin?*

The primary building material at the time was stone, but the wealthy could afford paneling. They built and finished their own homes, but neglected the house of God. They dared to live in costly homes, while the house of God remained in ruins. Instead of putting God ahead of themselves, they put themselves ahead of God. This is the opposite of what Jesus taught: *seek first his kingdom and his righteousness, and all these things will be given to you as well* (Matthew 6:33), he said.

A college athlete loved God and football, and dreamed of being drafted by a professional team. But instead of putting God ahead of football, he started putting football ahead of God. Then football took the place of God. Then he injured his knee, and his football career was over. With a little time for thought, he concluded the only thing that lasts forever is the kingdom of God. It's not unusual for God's people get their priorities confused. This is what Haggai was preaching against.

Haggai 1:5-6 *Now this is what the Lord Almighty says: Give careful thought to your ways. You have planted much, but harvested little. You eat, but never have enough. You drink, but never have your fill. You put on clothes, but are not warm. You earn wages, only to put them in a purse with holes in it.*

Because God's people were putting themselves ahead of God, God wasn't blessing their finances. In fact, he was actually draining them. *You expected much, but see, it turned out to be little. What you brought home, I blew away* (Haggai 1:9). *I called for a drought on the fields and the mountains, on the grain, the new wine, the olive oil and everything else the ground produces* (Haggai 1:11), said God.

God's people neglected him financially, so he neglected them financially. We shouldn't expect God to be generous toward us, if we're not generous toward him. If we're not doing well financially, we ought to evaluate how much we're giving to God. Sometimes there's a correlation.

But there's not always a correlation. The wicked often prosper (Psalm 73:3), and the righteous often suffer (Job 1-2). Jesus was rich in heaven, but so poor on earth that he had *no place to lay his head* (Matthew 8:20). We shouldn't assume financial distress is always the result of neglecting God financially. We ought to give what we can, and trust God to provide for our needs.

Haggai 1:12 *Then Zerubbabel son of Shealtiel, Joshua son of Jozadak, the high priest, and the whole remnant of the people obeyed the voice of the Lord their God and the message of the prophet Haggai, because the Lord their God had sent him.*

God's people responded to God's word, and began to do God's work. For many years the temple lay in ruins, but now it was being rebuilt. This was due, in part, to the regular preaching of Haggai. Satan knows that if he can separate the people of God from the word of God, the work of God will suffer.

Haggai 1:13 *Then Haggai, the Lord's messenger, gave this message of the Lord to the people: I am with you, declares the Lord.*

This is always the promise of God to his people, especially when the task is great. *Moses said to God, Who am I that I should go to Pharaoh and bring the Israelites out of Egypt? And God said, I will be with you* (Exodus 3:11-12). God said to Joshua, *As I was with Moses, so I will be with you* (Joshua 1:5). God said to Israel, *Do not be afraid, for I am with you* (Isaiah 43:5). And Jesus said to the disciples, *surely I am with you always, to the very end of the age* (Matthew 28:20).

David Livingstone was a pioneer medical missionary and explorer in Africa. His achievements were extraordinary, and he gave the credit to God: *Would you like me to tell you what supported me through all the years of exile among a people whose language I could not understand and whose attitude to me was always uncertain and often hostile? It was this, I am with you always . . . . On these words I staked everything, and they never failed* (slightly revised).

Haggai 2:3 *Who of you is left who saw this house in its former glory? How does it look to you now? Does it not seem to you like nothing?*

Solomon's temple was destroyed by the Babylonians, sixty-six years earlier, and some of the people remembered it. It was so grand (1 Kings 6:2-36) that it's still considered a wonder of the ancient world. When the people compared the temple they were building, with the one Solomon built, they were discouraged.

Haggai 2:9 *The glory of this present house will be greater than the glory of the former house, says the Lord Almighty.*

Solomon's temple was glorious by human standards, but the temple they were building would be even more glorious due to the presence of Christ. There he was presented as a baby (Luke 2:25-27) and there, as a boy, he discussed theology (Luke 2:41-50). There he was tempted by the devil (Luke 4:9) and there he also taught (Luke 20:1). There he healed many (Matthew 21:14) and there he drove out merchants (Luke 19:45). The temple was a place to worship God, But Jesus was God in the midst of the temple.

It's hard to imagine the ministry of Jesus Christ apart from the temple in Jerusalem. His presence made that place more glorious than Solomon's temple, even though the builders couldn't understand it. We should never be discouraged by the smallness of our work, but encouraged by the way God may plan to use it.

For Reflection and Review

- *Why is serving God our greatest opportunity?*
- *Why should we give money to God?*
- *How does God's presence give us courage?*

Lesson 171

Zechariah 1:1 *In the eighth month of the second year of Darius, the word of the Lord came to the prophet Zechariah son of Berekiah, the son of Iddo.*

Zechariah began his ministry to God's people in Judah, in the year 520 BC. He was born in Babylon, but returned with others about eighteen years earlier. Work on the temple had stalled so Zechariah brought a message of rebuke. He also spoke words of encouragement based on God's faithfulness. Several New Testament books quote or allude to the book of Zechariah, especially Revelation.

Zechariah 1:5-6 *Where are your ancestors now? And the prophets, do they live forever? But did not my words . . . overtake your ancestors?*

God's people ignored the prophets and, for many years, seemed to get away with it. But the words of the prophets caught up with them, and they were taken into exile. The prophets eventually died, but God's word came to pass. *It will not return to me empty, but will accomplish what I desire and achieve the purpose for which I sent it* (Isaiah 55:11), recorded Isaiah. This is why Jesus said, *the Scriptures must be fulfilled* (Mark 14:49). Whatever God decrees will come to pass eventually.

Since everything the Bible predicted about the past has been fulfilled, we can be sure that everything the Bible predicts about the future will also be fulfilled. This includes the return of Christ (Revelation 19:11-21), the defeat of Satan (Revelation 20:1-10), the punishment of the wicked (Revelation 20:15), and the eternal happiness of God's people (Revelation 21:1-27). *The grass withers and the flowers fall, but the word of our God endures forever* (Isaiah 40:8), wrote Isaiah.

Zechariah 1:16-17 *Therefore this is what the Lord says: I will return to Jerusalem with mercy, and there my house will be rebuilt. . . . My towns will again overflow with prosperity, and the Lord will again comfort Zion and choose Jerusalem.*

God's discouraged people needed to know that God was on their side, and had a preferred future for them. With this information they could work with confidence, knowing their labor would not be in vain. *Always give yourselves fully to the work of the Lord, because you know that your labor in the Lord is not in vain* (1 Corinthians 15:58), wrote Paul.

My friend was given an old car for his sixteenth birthday. It was in bad condition, but he spent countless hours, and thousands of dollars, making it like new again. Then he was in an accident, and all his work was lost. But our work for Christ can never be lost. *[I] will reward each person according to what they have done* (Matthew 16:27), said Jesus. The only loss for Christians is what we could've done for Christ, but didn't.

Zechariah 3:1 *Then he showed me Joshua the high priest standing before the angel of the Lord, and Satan standing at his right side to accuse him.*

This is a heavenly courtroom scene in which Satan accuses Israel's high priest of not being worthy of his office. The priest is dressed in filthy clothes, which represent his moral failures. But without a high priest Israel has no access to God, and is no different than other nations. The situation is bleak.

Zechariah 3:2 *The Lord said to Satan, The Lord rebuke you, Satan!*

Satan's charges were legitimate, but he was rebuked by God, because God had chosen Joshua. *Is not this man a burning stick snatched from the fire?* (Zechariah 3:2b), said God. Joshua was pulled from the fire of Babylonian exile to serve God as high priest. He wasn't disqualified by his sin, because God was going to remove his sin. God had chosen him, and would make him fit for service.

When Satan accused Joshua before God, he was doing what he loves to do. His name means *adversary*, and he's the enemy of God's people. First he tempts us to sin, then he condemns us for our sin, then he accuses us to God of being sinners. Then he tells us to abandon God because we're so unworthy.

Satan is *the accuser of our brothers and sisters, who accuses them before our God day and night* (Revelation 12:10), wrote John. But like Joshua, those who believe in Jesus Christ won't be rejected. Nor will the one who died for our sins put up with the devil forever. Satan will *thrown into the lake of burning sulfur [to be] tormented day and night for ever* (Revelation 20:10), wrote John.

Zechariah 3:4 *The angel said to those who were standing before him, Take off his filthy clothes. Then he said to Joshua, See, I have taken away your sin, and I will put fine garments on you.*

The removal of Joshua's filthy clothes symbolizes the removal of his sin. Like Adam and Eve before the Fall, he was naked and unashamed (Genesis 2:25). But this was not as good as being clothed so God said, *I will put fine garments on you.* Now his salvation was complete.

After their fall into sin, God clothed Adam and Eve with *garments of skin* (Genesis 3:21), possibly lamb's skin to prefigure *the Lamb of God, who takes away the sin of the world* (John 1:29). When we come to Christ, he not only takes away our sin, but clothes us with himself. *[H]e has clothed me with garments of salvation and arrayed me in a robe of his righteousness* (Isaiah 61:10), wrote Isaiah. And, *all of you who were baptized into Christ have clothed yourselves with Christ* (Galatians 3:27), wrote Paul. We're no longer naked, or wearing filthy clothes, but are beautifully clothed with Christ.

For Reflection and Review

- *Why is it helpful to know that our work for Christ is never a waste of time?*
- *How does Satan oppose God's people?*
- *What is illustrated by the reclothing of the high priest?*

Lesson 172

Zechariah 4:6 *This is the word of the Lord to Zerubbabel: Not by might nor by power, but by my Spirit, says the Lord Almighty.*

Zerubbabel was governor of Judah at this time, and was given the task of rebuilding God's temple with limited resources. He may've felt overwhelmed, but God assured him that it wouldn't happen by human might or power, but by the Spirit of God.

This is why Jesus told the disciples not to start their mission until they received the Holy Spirit (Acts 1:4-5). *[Y]ou will receive power when the Holy Spirit comes on you; and you will be my witnesses . . . to the ends of the earth* (Acts 1:8), he said. So they waited and prayed until the Spirit came on Pentecost, and then they preached to the ends of the earth (Acts 2-28). Our job isn't to build the church ourselves, but to *keep in step with the Spirit* (Galatians 5:25), wrote Paul.

Zechariah 9:9 *Rejoice greatly, Daughter Zion! Shout, Daughter Jerusalem! See, your king comes to you, righteous and victorious, lowly and riding on a donkey, on a colt, the foal of a donkey.*

Centuries later, when Jesus rode into Jerusalem, he mounted a colt in fulfillment of this prophecy. *They took palm branches and went out to meet him, shouting, Hosanna! Blessed is he who comes in the name of the Lord!* (John 12:13), wrote John.

The colt was a suitable beast for Christ to ride in his humility, but it won't be what he rides when he returns. *[T]here before me was a white horse, whose rider is called Faithful and True. . . . He treads the winepress of the fury of the wrath of God Almighty. On his robe and on his thigh he has this name written: king of kings and lord of lords* (Revelation 19:11-16), wrote John.

Jesus came on a mule, but will come back on a horse. He came as a humble king, but will return as a conquering king. He came to shed his own blood, but is coming back to shed the blood of others. We can receive him as our Lord (Colossians 2:6), or face him as our judge. *I tell you, now is the time of God's favor, now is the day of salvation* (2 Corinthians 6:2), wrote Paul.

Zechariah 11:12-13 *So they paid me thirty pieces of silver. And the Lord said to me, Throw it to the potter—the handsome price at which they valued me! So I took the thirty pieces of silver and threw them to the potter at the house of the Lord.*

The prophet's payment appears to be his last, and showed how little the people valued God. So God told Zechariah to throw his meager wages to the potter at temple.

In a curious parallel, Judas sold Jesus for thirty pieces of silver (Matthew 26:15), but was so overwhelmed by guilt that he *threw the money into the temple . . . and hanged himself* (Matthew 27:5). Then the religious leaders used that money to buy a *potter's field as a burial place for foreigners* (Matthew 27:7).

When Zechariah threw his thirty pieces of silver to the potter in the temple, he foreshadowed Judas throwing his thirty pieces of silver in the temple for the purchase of a potter's field. The role of Judas Iscariot was a definite part of God's plan, and those who undervalue God will sell him to their own destruction.

Zechariah 12:10 *They will look on me, the one they have pierced, and they will mourn for him as one mourns for an only child.*

These remarkable words refer to the crucifixion of Christ, and to the response of many when he returns. *[E]very eye will see him, even those who pierced him; and all peoples on earth will mourn because of him* (Revelation 1:7), wrote John. This could be a sign of repentance, but is probably the grief of losing everything, due to rejecting Jesus Christ.

When King Zedekiah was captured by the Babylonians they killed his sons, blinded his eyes, and put him in chains (2 Kings 25:7). In a single day he lost his throne, his sons, and his sight (2 Kings 25:7). But what is that compared to losing heaven, and waking up in hell? That loss will be so great the mourning will never end. We can grieve over sin and be saved, or we can grieve our loss forever.

Zechariah 13:1 *On that day a fountain will be opened to the house of David and the inhabitants of Jerusalem, to cleanse them from sin and impurity.*

There are many fountains where dirt can be washed away, but only one where sin can be washed away. Any stream can wash away physical dirt, but only one can wash away spiritual dirt. To be sure that Christ was dead, *one of the soldiers pierced Jesus' side with a spear, bringing a sudden flow of blood and water* (John 19:34), wrote John. John was surprised by this (John 19:35), but later wrote *the blood of Jesus . . . purifies us from all sin* (1 John 1:7).

There is a fountain filled with blood drawn from Immanuel's veins; and sinners, plunged beneath that flood, lose all their guilty stains. The dying thief rejoiced to see that fountain in his day, and there may I, though vile as he, wash all my sins away. Ever since by faith I saw the stream your flowing wounds supply, redeeming love has been my theme, and shall be till I die (William Cowper).

For Reflection and Review

- *How can believers keep in step with the Spirit?*
- *How will Christ's second coming be different from his first coming?*
- *Why is Christ's death described as a fountain that washes away sin?*

Lesson 173

Malachi 1:1 *A prophecy: The word of the Lord to Israel through Malachi.*

The prophet Malachi spoke to the people of God in the Promised Land around 430 BC. This was about a hundred years after their parents returned from the Babylonian exile. The temple had been rebuilt, and worship was being offered, but it was formalistic with little vitality. Malachi wanted to awaken God's people to the importance of living for God. His name means *My Messenger* and he may've been the last prophet of the Old Testament.

Malachi 1:2 *I have loved you, says the Lord. But you ask, How have you loved us?*

The economy was poor, and morale was low, so some of God's people wondered if God really loved them. There was little in their experience to make them believe in God's love, so how could they be sure? This is still an important question because we can never love God more than we believe he loves us. And if we look to our circumstances as proof of God's love, we may be disappointed. But God has given us better proof than that.

Greater love has no one than this: to lay down one's life for one's friends (John 15:13), said Jesus. Whenever we doubt God's love, all we have to do is remember the crucifixion of Christ. Love is proven through sacrifice, and God has proven his love for us through the sacrifice of his Son. Now that God has sacrificed for our salvation, we should never doubt his love again.

Since the prophet lived before Christ, however, he spoke of God's special love for the Israelites compared to the Edomites. The Israelites were descended from Jacob, and the Edomites were descended from Esau. *I have loved Jacob, but Esau I have hated* (Malachi 1:2-3), said God. The Edomites had already been destroyed, but God's people were back in their land as proof of God's love for them.

But if God loves everyone, how could he hate the Edomites? God hated the Edomites, compared to the Israelites, in the same way that Jesus taught us to hate our families compared to loving him (Luke 14:26). We love them both, of course, but have chosen to love Jesus Christ supremely.

And, whoever loves Jesus Christ supremely, is uniquely loved by God the Father. *[T]he Father himself loves you because you have loved me and have believed that I came from God* (John 16:27), said Jesus. God loves everyone, but has a special love for all who believe in his Son.

Malachi 2:11 *Judah has been unfaithful . . . . by marrying women who worship a foreign god.*

This was a serious threat to the future of God's people. *Do not give your daughters to their sons or take their daughters for your sons, for they will turn your children away from following me to serve other gods, and the Lord's anger will burn against you and will quickly destroy you* (Deuteronomy 7:3-4), wrote Moses.

The crisis was so severe, in fact, that Nehemiah said, *I rebuked them and called curses down on them. I beat some of the men and pulled out their hair. I made them take an oath in God's name and said: You are not to give your daughters in marriage to their sons, nor are you to take their daughters in marriage for your sons or for yourselves* (Nehemiah 13:25).

This principle also applies to Christians. *Do not be yoked together with unbelievers. For what do righteousness and wickedness have in common? Or what fellowship can light have with darkness?* (2 Corinthians 6:14), wrote Paul. Few things are more dangerous to the faith of future generations than marriages between Christians and unbelievers.

Malachi 2:16 *The man who hates and divorces his wife . . . does violence to the one he should protect, says the Lord Almighty.*

Marriage is a sacred bond between a man and a woman, that should never be violated by either party. *Therefore what God has joined together, let no one separate* (Matthew 19:6), said Jesus. And, *Anyone who divorces his wife and marries another woman commits adultery, and the man who marries a divorced woman commits adultery* (Luke 16:18), said Jesus again.

In most cases, divorce should be seen as a terrible sin which is made even worse by the sin remarriage. But neither divorce nor remarriage are unforgivable sins, or in a separate category from other sins. They are forgiven the same way as murder, theft, or gossip.

If we confess our sins, he is faithful and just and will forgive us our sins and purify us from all unrighteousness (1 John 1:9), wrote John. A marriage that begins as an act of adultery can, by God's grace, become pure and holy in his sight. This is not an excuse to divorce and remarry, but is proof of God's amazing grace.

For Reflection and Review

- *How do we know God loves us regardless of our circumstances?*
- *Why is it wrong for Christians to marry an unbeliever?*
- *Is God displeased with people who divorce and remarry?*

Lesson 174

Malachi 3:6 *I the Lord do not change. So you, the descendants of Jacob, are not destroyed.*

Considering all they'd been through, it was surprising God's people were back in the Promised Land. According to Malachi, this was because God doesn't change. He had chosen them, and hadn't changed his mind. For a perfect God to change, in fact, would make him less than perfect. So God can never change. And because he'll never change, he'll always keep his word.

Men promise to be faithful to their wives, but then commit adultery. Gamblers promise to quit gambling, but then go back to the casino. Sinners promise to walk with God, but then they turn away from him. People are hard to trust, but we can always trust God. *I the Lord do not change.* And *Jesus Christ is the same yesterday and today and forever* (Hebrews 3:8), says Hebrews.

Malachi 3:7 *Return to me, and I will return to you, says the Lord Almighty.*

This is a wonderful promise to all who've wandered from Christ. No matter how far we've strayed, or badly we've sinned, we can always be sure that God will take us back, if we return to him. *[W]hoever comes to me I will never drive away* (John 6:37), said Jesus. *Come near to God and he will come near to you* (James 4:8), wrote James.

This is like a marriage where the husband and wife have drifted apart. If neither wants a closer relationship, it'll never happen. If one of them wants a closer relationship, it might happen. But if both of them want a closer relationship, they could grow closer than ever. The wonderful news about God is that he always wants to be closer to us, and wants us to be closer to him. *Return to me, and I will return to you, says the Lord Almighty.*

Malachi 3:8 *Will a mere mortal rob God? Yet you rob me. But you ask, How are we robbing you? In tithes and offerings.*

God's people were suffering financially, and were giving less to the temple in order to support themselves. This was a violation of God's law which said, *A tithe of everything . . . belongs to the Lord* (Leviticus 27:30). The word *tithe* means *tenth* and ten percent of a person's income was the standard for giving to God. Malachi warned God's people that anyone who gave less than ten percent was actually robbing God.

An usher was in charge of collecting the offering, but always went to the restroom before taking the offering to the church office. The treasurer noticed that whenever this usher was in charge of the offering, there was an absence of twenty dollar bills. The usher was put under surveillance and was caught in the act of robbing God. Few would ever think of taking money out of the offering, but some were robbing God by putting little in.

Malachi 3:10 *Bring the whole tithe into the storehouse, that there may be food in my house. Test me in this, says the Lord Almighty, and see if I will not throw open the floodgates of heaven and pour out so much blessing that there will not be room enough to store it.*

God's people withheld their money because they didn't seem to have enough. But God was saying if they'd be generous toward him, he'd be generous toward them. The Apostle Paul said something similar to believers in Corinth. *Whoever sows sparingly will also reap sparingly, and whoever sows generously will also reap generously. Each of you should give what you have decided in your heart to give . . . for God loves a cheerful giver* (2 Corinthians 9:6-7).

Giving to God is in our best interest because God likes to give back. But giving ten percent was never taught by Jesus or the apostles. They emphasized generosity along with sacrifice.

As Jesus looked up, he saw the rich putting their gifts into the temple treasury. He also saw a poor widow put in two very small copper coins. Truly I tell you, he said, this poor widow has put in more than all the others. All these people gave their gifts out of their wealth; but she out of her poverty put in all she had to live on (Luke 21:1-4).

Those who can give more than ten percent should certainly do so. But those who give less than ten percent are not disapproved by God, as long as they give sacrificially. God proved his love through sacrifice, and we should do the same.

Malachi 4:5-6 *See, I will send the prophet Elijah to you before that great and dreadful day of the Lord comes. He will turn the hearts of the parents to their children, and the hearts of the children to their parents; or else I will come and strike the land with total destruction.*

These verses are remarkable for at least two reasons. First, they are the last words in the Old Testament, and show the story is incomplete. The New Testament ends with paradise restored (Revelation 21-22), which is a perfect conclusion to the whole Bible. The Old Testament is an unfinished book, which is finished perfectly by the New Testament.

Second, these verses are remarkable because they predict the coming of Elijah *before that great and dreadful day of the Lord*. John the Baptist came in the *spirit and power of Elijah* (Luke 1:17), and Jesus recognized him as the one predicted by Malachi (Matthew 11:10, Malachi 3:1). For the Bible to predict the coming of Messiah is amazing, but to also predict his forerunner is even more amazing.

It's also amazing that the Old Testament ends by looking ahead to Messiah's forerunner, and the New Testament begins with the arrival of Messiah's forerunner (Matthew 3, Luke 1). This is simply another way of God signing his book (2 Timothy 3:16).

For Reflection and Review

- *Why is it impossible for God to change?*
- *What is the standard of giving in the New Testament?*
- *What's unusual about how the Old Testament ends?*

Lesson 175

Matthew 1:1 *This is the genealogy of Jesus the Messiah.*

Although anonymous, the gospel of Matthew was almost certainly written by the tax collector whom Jesus called to be an apostle (Matthew 9:9). It was likely written around AD 60, and includes more references to the Old Testament than any other book in the New Testament.

Genealogies were important in Bible days because property rights could be determined by what family you were from. Also, you could only be involved in temple service if you were descended from Levi, and you could only be a priest if you were descended from Aaron. Furthermore, the Old Testament contains genealogical clues about who the Messiah would be. This is why God's people kept careful genealogical records, which Matthew and Luke include in their gospels.

Luke traced Jesus' lineage to the first man Adam (Luke 3:38), demonstrating Jesus' true humanity, as well as our common ancestry. Luke may've also been thinking of Adam's sin, after which God promised to send someone who'd crush the devil's head (Genesis 3:15).

Having died on the cross for our sins, Jesus crushed Satan's power to separate us from God, thus beginning God's promise to defeat the devil. One of the great themes of the Bible is that God keeps his promises (2 Corinthians 1:20), and this is reflected in the genealogies of Jesus Christ.

Matthew 1:2 *Abraham was the father of Isaac.*

Matthew traced Jesus' lineage through Abraham, to whom God had said, *all peoples on earth will be blessed through you* (Genesis 12:3). Jesus told the apostles to *make disciples of all nations* (Matthew 28:19), bringing the blessing of salvation to the whole world, thereby fulfilling God's promise to Abraham.

Matthew 1:3 *Judah the father of Perez.*

Matthew traced Jesus' lineage through Judah, which is important because of a promise given centuries before. *The scepter will not depart from Judah, nor the ruler's staff from between his feet, until he to whom it belongs shall come and the obedience of the nations shall be his* (Genesis 49:10). Out of the twelve tribes of Israel, Jesus came from Judah, and is winning obedience from the nations.

Matthew 1:5 *Salmon the father of Boaz, whose mother was Rahab.*

Matthew included a number of disreputable people in his genealogy, including Rahab the prostitute. Jesus' family history includes incest, adultery, prostitution, murder, and other sins, so that no matter who we are, or what we've done, we might have hope.

It is as though God intended for people to hear this genealogy and say to themselves: Oh, Christ is the kind of person who is not ashamed of sinners. See, he even puts them in his family tree (Martin Luther). *Both the one who makes people holy and those who are made holy are of the same family. So Jesus is not ashamed to call [us] brothers and sisters* (Hebrews 2:11), says Hebrews.

Matthew 1:6 *David was the father of Solomon.*

Matthew traced Jesus' lineage through David to whom God promised, *your throne will be established forever* (2 Samuel 7:16). That's why the angel said to Jesus' mother, *The Lord God will give him the throne of his father David* (Luke 1:32). Jesus currently rules from heaven (Hebrews 1:8, 1 Peter 3:22), but will eventually rule on earth, fulfilling God's promise to David that his throne will be established forever.

Matthew 1:12 *Jeconiah was the father of Shealtiel.*

Matthew identified Shealtiel's father as Jeconiah, but Luke identified Shealtiel's father as Neri (Luke 3:27). The genealogies in Matthew and Luke have differences that are difficult to reconcile, but not impossible.

If your natural father died when you were young, and your mother remarried, you'd have two fathers—one biological and the other adopted. Legitimate genealogies could be traced either way. The differences between Matthew's genealogy and Luke's genealogy don't cast doubt on either, but show they were not copying from each other to keep their records straight.

Three observations are in order: First, the rootedness of Jesus in genealogical records underscores the fact that he lived in history, and is not the invention of someone's imagination. The historicity of Jesus is so evident, that almost every professional historian accepts it as a settled fact.

Second, the number of first century males who were genealogically qualified to be the Messiah (descended from Abraham, Judah, David, etc.) was less than one tenth of one percent, making Jesus' lineage a remarkable fulfillment of prophecy.

Third, since Jesus never had children, it's impossible to be his biological descendent. But *Whoever does God's will is my brother and sister . . .* (Mark 3:35), he said. If you do God's will by following Jesus Christ, you're truly a part of his family, and closer to him than his natural relatives. *So Jesus is not ashamed to call [us] brothers and sisters* (Hebrews 2:11), says Hebrews.

For Reflection and Review

- *Why are so many sinners mentioned in Jesus genealogy?*
- *Why is it important that Jesus came from David?*
- *Is there any benefit to having Jesus as your brother?*

Lesson 176

Matthew 1:18 *This is how the birth of Jesus the Messiah came about: His mother Mary was pledged to be married to Joseph, but before they came together, she was found to be pregnant through the Holy Spirit.*

No one knows how old Mary was at this time, but it wasn't uncommon for young women to marry around age thirteen, and for young men to marry around age eighteen. The families would make an arrangement, and the children would become engaged. The engagement was legally binding, and to break it required a divorce. Sexual union was strictly forbidden until after the wedding, and adultery was punishable by death (Deuteronomy 22:22-24).

It was during their engagement, before they came together, that the angel Gabriel was sent to inform Mary that she would bear the Messiah. When she inquired how this would be, the Angel said, *The Holy Spirit will come on you, and the power of the Most High will overshadow you. So the holy one to be born will be called the Son of God* (Luke 1:35). Jesus came into the world fully God and fully human, to bring humans back to God.

But Joseph had a problem. Since Mary was pregnant, and he wasn't the father, it seemed she had been unfaithful. The Old Testament called for her execution, but the Romans wouldn't allow it, so Mary's life was spared. Joseph planned to divorce her quietly (Matthew 1:19).

Matthew 1:20 *But after he had considered this, an angel of the Lord appeared to him in a dream and said, Joseph son of David, do not be afraid to take Mary home as your wife, because what is conceived in her is from the Holy Spirit.*

The good news was that Mary hadn't been unfaithful, and God had done a miracle. The bad news was that few would understand it, and Joseph's life was about to become complicated. All he wanted was to settle down, marry a nice girl, and have a normal family. But, instead, he was given the honor of being Messiah's step-father, and the embarrassment of being thought a fornicator who was married to a tramp.

This would plague Mary, Joseph, and Jesus for many years, and may be one of the reasons Jesus preached against judging (Matthew 7:1). Even though his mother became pregnant out of wedlock, everyone who judged her was wrong. And if it's possible to be wrong about that, what else could we be wrong about? The next time you're tempted to judge someone, remember that Mary was also judged, and everyone who judged her was wrong.

Matthew 1:21 *She will give birth to a son, and you are to give him the name Jesus, because he will save his people from their sins.*

Jesus is the Greek form of the name *Joshua*, meaning *the Lord saves*. Salvation is the main theme of the Bible, and isn't only personal but global. Early in the Bible's story, humans are expelled from paradise, and earth comes under a curse (Genesis 3:1-24). At the end of the Bible's story, heaven comes down to earth, and paradise is restored (Revelation 20-22). Somewhere in the middle we learn what made this possible.

Imagine this: God came into the world to save sinners, by dying on a cross for our sins. *The most perfect being in the universe was slaughtered for the very people who would slaughter such a being* (John Piper). The Bible's story moves from paradise lost, to paradise regained, with the God/man crucified somewhere near the middle. *Give him the name Jesus,* said the angel, *because he will save his people from their sins.*

Matthew 1:22-23 *All this took place to fulfill what the Lord had said through the prophet: The virgin will conceive and give birth to a son, and they will call him Immanuel (which means God with us).*

Jesus' divinity wasn't obvious to everyone but, on occasion, he revealed himself to those who were paying attention. Once they wanted to kill him *because you, a mere man, claim to be God* (John 10:33), they said. And when he forgave a man's sins they thought, *Who can forgive sins but God alone?* (Mark

2:7). And when he walked on water *those who were in the boat worshiped him* (Matthew 14:33). And after the resurrection *Thomas said to him, My Lord and my God!* (John 20:28). Jesus is the greatest human who's ever lived, but he's more than that. He's *Immanuel (which means God with us)*.

For Reflection and Review

- *Why was it important for Christ to be conceived by the Holy Spirit?*
- *How did Jesus save us from our sins?*
- *How do we know that Jesus is divine?*

Lesson 177

Matthew 2:1 *After Jesus was born in Bethlehem in Judea, during the time of King Herod, Magi from the east came to Jerusalem.*

The events of this chapter probably took place several months after Jesus was born (Luke 2:1-21). The Magi were likely Babylonian astrologers with some knowledge of the Scriptures. They would've received this from Jews who were exiled to Babylon in the sixth century BC. If, in fact, the Magi came from Babylon, their trip was hundreds of miles, and took several weeks, assuming they traveled by camel. This is a rebuke to those who won't go across town to worship the Lord on Sundays.

Matthew 2:2 *Where is the one who has been born king of the Jews? We saw his star when it rose and have come to worship him.*

It's difficult to know if this was an ordinary star, or something else, but it seems related to the prophecy of Balaam: *A star will come out of Jacob; a scepter will rise out of Israel* (Numbers 24:17). The scepter refers to a king, and here it's related to a star. The Magi followed the star, and it led them to the king. In fact, he was the king who made the stars, and *calls them each by name* (Psalm 147:4).

Matthew 2:3 *When King Herod heard this he was disturbed, and all Jerusalem with him.*

Herod was disturbed because this little king was a threat to his throne. Jesus was born king, and Herod knew it. But Herod liked being king, and would defend his throne at any cost. He'd already killed a wife and two sons, so if he had to murder Jesus Christ he was certainly willing to do it.

But if Jesus was a threat to Herod, he's also a threat to us. We must surrender the rule of our lives (Luke 14:33), or hear him say *Depart from me, you who are cursed, into the eternal fire prepared for the devil and his angels* (Matthew 25:41).

Jesus taught more about hell than anyone else in the Bible, for good reason. I heard about God's love since I was a child, but it never led me to surrender my life to Christ. It wasn't until I heard about God's wrath that I understood the importance of total surrender. Herod refused to to give his life to Christ, and it was the worst decision he ever made.

Matthew 2:6 *But you, Bethlehem, in the land of Judah, are by no means least among the rulers of Judah; for out of you will come a ruler who will shepherd my people Israel.*

When Herod asked the experts where Messiah would be born, they all agreed on Bethlehem since the prophet Micah foretold it centuries earlier (Micah 5:2). This is one of the most remarkable prophecies fulfilled by Jesus Christ, but there are many more. The phenomenon of biblical prophecy is unique among the world's religions, and is sufficient to establish Christianity as true. *I make known the end from the beginning, from ancient times, what is still to come* (Isaiah 46:9-10), said God.

Other religions are less convincing. The oracle at Delphi was famous in her day, but her prophecies were always shrouded in mystery. A general asked about the outcome of an approaching battle, and she predicted a day of great victory. The general was defeated but the oracle wasn't embarrassed because she hadn't identified who the victor would be.

There's mystery in biblical prophecy too, but there's also much that is plain, such as identifying the little town of Bethlehem as the place of Messiah's birth. Since Jesus fulfilled all the prophecies regarding his first coming, we can be sure he'll fulfill the rest when he returns.

Matthew 2:11 *On coming to the house, they saw the child with his mother Mary, and they bowed down and worshiped him.*

Mary must've been amazed. The prophet Simeon called Jesus a *revelation to the Gentiles* (Luke 2:32). Now these Gentiles were bowing down and worshipping Jesus Christ. And this isn't the last time Jesus would be worshipped.

On a dark and stormy night, Jesus came to his disciples, walking on the water. He climbed into their boat and *those who were in the boat worshiped him* (Matthew 14:33). Likewise, a man who was healed from blindness said *Lord, I believe, and he worshiped him* (John 9:38). And after Jesus rose from the dead some women *clasped his feet and worshiped him* (Matthew 28:9). And the prophet Daniel foresaw a time when *peoples of every language will worship him* (Daniel 7:14). This happens every Sunday as people around the world gather in churches to worship Jesus Christ. This, too, is a remarkable fulfillment of prophecy.

Matthew 2:13 *When they had gone, an angel of the Lord appeared to Joseph in a dream. Get up, he said, take the child and his mother and escape to Egypt.*

Mary and Joseph didn't know they were in danger, but God knew Herod was plotting to kill Jesus, so he told Joseph in a dream to flee to Egypt. It must've been a vivid dream since they began the journey that night. Egypt was only about eighty miles away, but they may've gone all the way to Alexandria, which was about four hundred miles away. That city had a population of about a million Jews, and they would've felt more at home there.

But travel wasn't cheap, and it would take time for Joseph to find work. So God provided for their needs through the Magi's gifts: *gold, frankincense and myrrh* (Matthew 2:11). These were expensive gifts that Mary and Joseph probably used to pay for their time away. Maybe Jesus was thinking of this when he said, *your Father knows what you need before you ask him* (Matthew 6:8).

Matthew 2:16 *When Herod realized that he had been outwitted by the Magi, he was furious, and he gave orders to kill all the boys in Bethlehem and its vicinity who were two years old and under.*

The Magi didn't return to Herod, as he had requested, because God warned them in a dream not to go back to him (Matthew 2:12). But, not to be outsmarted, Herod killed all the little boys in and around Bethlehem, assuming Jesus would be among them. The number of boys killed was probably around twenty, and this would scar the community for years.

This gives us a glimpse into the badness of Herod's heart. He was about seventy years old, and would be dead within a year. But even at this late age, Herod was more concerned about himself than he was about meeting God. When he was dying, in fact, Herod feared no one would grieve his passing, so he commanded a group of men to be killed. That way at least there'd grieving at the time of his death, even if it wasn't for him (Josephus). Thankfully, the order wasn't carried out, but Herod still went down on the wrong side of history. Worse, by far, he went down on the wrong side of God.

But there's a problem here: If God was able to protect Jesus from being massacred, why didn't he protect the other children too? It's not a little problem since the primary argument against the existence of God is the existence of evil. If God is good and powerful, why doesn't he prevent more evil. Many books have been written on the subject, and there are no easy answers. But those little ones who died for the sake of Christ will be known in heaven as the first Christian martyrs. And they'll praise God forever, for the honor of that distinction.

For Reflection and Review

- *Why did Herod refuse to honor Christ?*
- *Why was Jesus willing to receive worship?*
- *What can we learn about God from the slaughter at Bethlehem?*

Lesson 178

Matthew 2:23 *[Mary, Joseph and Jesus] went and lived in a town called Nazareth. So was fulfilled what was said through the prophets, that he would be called a Nazarene.*

After Herod died, the family moved back to Nazareth where Jesus grew up. The word *Nazarene* doesn't appear in the Old Testament, nor is the town of Nazareth ever mentioned. So why did Matthew say that the prophets foretold that Jesus would be called a *Nazarene*?

Years ago I lived in a city with a suburb that people like to joke about. It's a factory town without a reputation for wealth or refinement. People like to make fun of it, and imitate the accent of people who live there. And if you happen to be from there, people will chuckle behind your back. Nazareth wasn't much different.

To be from Nazareth meant that you were despised, which is what the prophets foretold about Messiah. He would be *despised by the people* (Psalm 22:6), *despised and abhorred* (Isaiah 49:7), *despised and rejected* (Isaiah 53:3). So when Nathanael heard about *Jesus of Nazareth* he said, *Can anything good come from there?* (John 1:46). Being despised and being from Nazareth were essentially the same. *[H]e would be called a Nazarene.*

*****

Matthew 4:12 *When Jesus heard that John had been put in prison, he withdrew to Galilee.*

When John the Baptist was imprisoned for criticizing King Herod Antipas (Matthew 14:3-4), Jesus moved about eighty miles north of Jerusalem, to Galilee, where he carried out much of his ministry. This was according to God's plan as foretold by the prophet Isaiah: *Galilee of the nations. . . . The people walking in darkness have seen a great light; on those living in the land of deep darkness a light has dawned* (Matthew 4:15-16, Isaiah 9:1-2), he wrote.

The prophets not only foretold that Christ would be born in Bethlehem (Micah 5:2), but that he'd spend time in Egypt (Matthew 2:15, Hosea 11:1), and minister in Galilee, as well as in Jerusalem (Malachi 3:1). This prophetic foresight is nothing short of remarkable, and assures us that the ultimate author of Scripture is God.

Galilee was called a place of *darkness* because it was far away from Jerusalem, and home to both Jews and Gentiles. It wasn't known for godliness, but was where the light of Christ could be clearly seen by many who were in need. As always, the gospel came as a gift to people who didn't deserve it (Ephesians 2:8-9).

Matthew 4:17 *From that time on Jesus began to preach, Repent, for the kingdom of heaven has come near.*

Jesus began his preaching ministry with a call to repentance. This has been misunderstood to mean punishing yourself, or feeling badly about your behavior. But repentance is simply a change of mind, that leads to a change in direction. *I preached that they should repent and turn to God and demonstrate their repentance by their deeds* (Acts 26:20), said Paul.

A group of mountain climbers made it to the top of Mount Everest and then began their descent. A storm came in and reduced their visibility to almost zero, so they decided to camp through the night. The sky was clear in the morning and, when they they looked to the south, they discovered they were one step away from a thousand foot drop. Repentance is waking up to the danger we face, and going another direction.

*****

Matthew 5:3 *Blessed are the poor in spirit, for theirs is the kingdom of heaven.*

When Jesus looked at a crowd of his followers, he saw many who were trampled down by life, whom he described as *poor in spirit*. The phrase occurs only here in the Bible and means dispirited, discouraged, and defeated. Jesus isn't teaching that sorrow is a virtue but that, even in misery, Christians are blessed because the kingdom of heaven is theirs.

Those who describe the Christian life as uniformly joyful represent it badly. The night of his arrest Jesus said, *My soul is overwhelmed with sorrow to the point of death* (Matthew 26:38). If not God's kingdom, we might despair at the burdens of life, and many people do. But if the kingdom of heaven is real to us, then our burdens won't destroy us. In every situation believers are blessed, *for theirs is the kingdom of heaven*.

Matthew 5:4 *Blessed are those who mourn, for they will be comforted.*

The world mourns over things that are lost, and there is no shortage: lost family, lost friends, lost love, lost health, lost fortunes, lost youth, lost jobs, lost innocence, lost reputations, lost pets, and anything else that can be lost. The mourning is so deep, sometimes, that we look for comfort wherever we can find it: the liquor store, the pharmacy, the internet, or elsewhere. But Jesus wants us to know that we can look to God for comfort.

For the Lord comforts his people (Isaiah 49:13). *As a mother comforts her child, so will I comfort you* (Isaiah 66:13). *I will give them comfort and joy instead of sorrow* (Jeremiah 31:13). And, *the God of all comfort . . . comforts us in all our troubles* (2 Corinthians 1:3-4), wrote Paul. Our deepest knowledge of God doesn't come from happiness alone, but also from the comfort he provides in our grief.

Matthew 5:5 *Blessed are the meek, for they will inherit the earth.*

One of the Bible's best promises to earthlings, is that we'll *inherit the earth*. The earth was made for people, and people were made from the earth (Genesis 2:7), so earth is our natural habitat. That's why many people want little more from life, than a small plot of land they can call their own. But others want it too, and nations go to war for it.

One of the saddest chapters in Israel's history was their defeat by the Babylonians. Families were forced to leave their homes and live in a foreign land. And many are forced to leave their homes today because they can't afford the payments. But that won't always be the case. *A little while, and the wicked will be no more; though you look for them, they will not be found. But the meek will inherit the land* (Psalm 37:10-11), wrote David.

A nice couple in their sixties was building their dream home and looking forward to their retirement. Their children were grown and now it was time for them. Hours of dreaming and choosing went into the project but, half way through, she died. And just before it was finished, he also died.

That's the problem with living in a fallen world. Even if you get a little piece of paradise, you can't hold onto it. But the time is coming when *The righteous will inherit the land and dwell in it forever* (Psalm 37:29), wrote David. We won't have to fight for it, work for it, or even pay for it. And we'll never be able to lose it. *Blessed are the meek, for they will inherit the earth*.

For Reflection and Review

- *Why is repentance important?*
- *How does Christ comfort us?*
- *What and where is your dream house?*

Lesson 179

Matthew 5:6 *Blessed are those who hunger and thirst for righteousness, for they will be filled.*

Some people hunger and thirst for success. Others hunger and thirst for approval, security, love, or pleasure. Christians are unique because they hunger and thirst for righteousness, and won't be disappointed.

W]hen Christ appears, we shall be like him, for we shall see him as he is (1 John 3:2), wrote John. He'll not only perfect us physically and mentally, but also morally. We'll never have to feel guilty, repent, or ask forgiveness because we'll never sin. Then, at last, we'll love God with all our hearts, and our neighbors as ourselves (Luke 10:27). This is God's will for us, and he will bring it to pass.

Matthew 5:8 *Blessed are the pure in heart, for they will see God.*

God doesn't have to be proven to those who are pure in heart because they already see him. No one was more convinced of God than Jesus Christ, because he had the purest heart of all. Like bugs on a windshield, sin obscures our vision of God. But when our hearts are purified through prayer and confession of sin, we see God once again.

Matthew 5:9 *Blessed are the peacemakers, for they will be called children of God.*

These are surprising words from the most divisive person who ever lived. *Do not suppose that I have come to bring peace to the earth. I did not come to bring peace, but a sword. For I have come to turn a man against his father, a daughter against her mother, a daughter-in-law against her mother-in-law—a man's enemies will be the members of his own household* (Matthew 10:34-36), he said.

Jesus's first concern wasn't to reconcile the world to itself, but sinners to God. *[W]e have peace with God through our Lord Jesus Christ* (Romans 5:1), wrote Paul. It's better to be at peace with God, and at war with the world, than to be at peace with the world, and at war with God.

Once we have peace with God, however, believers should *Make every effort to live in peace with everyone* (Hebrews 12:14) says Hebrews. And, *as far as it depends on you, live at peace with everyone* (Romans 12:18), wrote Paul. If we do something wrong, we may even have to apologize.

A friend of mine was a schoolyard bully who came to Christ as a young adult. In prayer, one day, he thought of a person in middle-school whom he used to pick on. He hadn't seen him in years, and couldn't remember his name, but he asked God to make their paths cross so he could ask forgiveness.

To my friend's surprise he saw that person, two weeks later, at a shopping center. He explained what Christ had done for him, and asked the man's forgiveness. The man treated it lightly saying *kids will be kids*, but my friend explained it wasn't about being a kid. With tears he said, *I was wrong, and I ask your forgiveness*—which the man was happy to give. *Blessed are the peacemakers, for they will be called children of God.*

Matthew 5:10 *Blessed are those who are persecuted because of righteousness, for theirs is the kingdom of heaven.*

The devil is such a wicked being that he's against everything good, even if it's not specifically Christian. Anyone who does good, therefore, is likely to be persecuted simply *because of righteousness*. This occurs so often that it's even said, *No good deed will go unpunished.*

If you are kind, people may accuse you of ulterior motives. Be kind anyway. If you are honest, people may cheat you. Be honest anyway. If you find happiness, people may be jealous. Be happy anyway. The good you do today may be forgotten tomorrow. Do good anyway. Give the world the best you have and it may never be enough. Give your best anyway. For you see, in the end, it is between you and God. It was never between you and them anyway (Mother Teresa).

Matthew 5:17-18 *Do not think that I have come to abolish the Law or the Prophets; I have not come to abolish them but to fulfill them. For truly I tell you, until heaven and earth disappear, not the smallest letter, not the least stroke of a pen, will by any means disappear from the Law until everything is accomplished.*

The radical nature of Jesus' teaching caused some to wonder about his view of the Old Testament. So Jesus stated clearly that none of God's words would disappear until everything was fulfilled. Through his sinless life, death, and resurrection, Jesus fulfilled everything God's word required for him and his people. The Old Testament will always be God's word but, since it was fulfilled by Christ, it has now become *obsolete* (Hebrews 8:13), says Hebrews.

Matthew 5:48 *Be perfect, therefore, as your heavenly Father is perfect.*

This answers the highly important question, *What does God require of me?* God is a perfect being who'd be less than perfect if lowered his standard for sinners. God requires absolute perfection, and commands nothing less.

A young pastor was invited to the home of a prominent family for Sunday lunch. As they were eating, Grandma asked this question: *How good do you have to be to go to heaven?* It got rather quiet as everyone put down their forks and looked at the pastor. *That's easy*, he replied. *Be perfect . . . as your heavenly Father is perfect* (Matthew 5:48).

This isn't easy, even for serious Christians. *Indeed, there is no one on earth . . . who does what is right and never sins* (Ecclesiastes 7:20), wrote Solomon. And *all have sinned and fall short of the glory of God* (Romans 3:23), wrote Paul. And *If we claim to be without sin, we deceive ourselves* (1 John 1:8), wrote John.

It's also why we can't be saved apart from Jesus Christ. He lived the perfect life God requires, then died on the cross for our sins. The only way to be perfect, as our heavenly Father is perfect, is to be found in his perfect Son (Philippians 3:9). God requires perfection, and received it from Jesus Christ, who lived and died for his people. He will *present you holy in his sight, without blemish and free from accusation* (Colossians 1:22), wrote Paul.

Matthew 6:6 *But when you pray, go into your room, close the door and pray to your Father, who is unseen. Then your Father, who sees what is done in secret, will reward you.*

Some people don't spend time alone with God because they don't think it's worth the effort. Life is busy and there are many things to accomplish. Why spend time in prayer when we could do something productive? We might not say it publicly, but we've probably thought it privately.

But according to Jesus, prayer pays. Our heavenly Father rewards those who pray to him. If you had a wealthy uncle who gave you a thousand dollars every time you came to visit, how often would you visit? God is richer than your uncle, and has promised to *reward* you for praying.

Until we believe prayer is in our best interest, we'll never pray much or well. But when we believe God rewards us for praying, we'll become remarkably prayerful. We can even remind God of his promise to reward us, and then ask him to reward us by answering our prayers.

For Reflection and Review

- *Was Jesus Christ a peacemaker?*
- *How can Christians be perfect?*
- *Why is prayer so difficult?*

Lesson 180

Matthew 6:9 *Our Father in heaven.*

Jesus had just finished praying when one of his disciples said, *Lord, teach us to pray* (Luke 11:1). He probably noticed Jesus had unusual power in prayer, and wanted to know his secret. Jesus began by teaching us to call God *Our Father*.

To call God *Father* is to believe in him as the one who gives life, love, provision, protection, and even his nature. This idea appears vaguely in the Old Testament, but was developed by Jesus Christ, and then by his apostles. The implications are profound.

[T]he Father himself loves you (John 16:27). *[Y]our Father has been pleased to give you the kingdom* (Luke 12:32). *[Y]our Father in heaven [will] give the Holy Spirit to those who ask him* (Luke 11:13). *[T]he righteous will shine like the sun in the kingdom of their Father* (Matthew 13:43). *See what great love the Father has lavished on us, that we should be called children of God!* (1 John 3:1).

The most moving portrait of the heavenly father was given to us by Jesus, in his story of the Lost Son. *[W]hile he was still a long way off, his father saw him and was filled with compassion for him; he ran to his son, threw his arms around him and kissed him* (Luke 15:20). Who would've thought that God was so affectionately in love with sinners that he'd run to, embrace, and kiss them?

Through faith in Jesus Christ we come into a warm, loving, and affectionate relationship with our heavenly Father. The devil will tell us differently; our emotions will tell is differently; and our circumstances will tell us differently. But God's word is more reliable than any of these, and tells us that we're dearly loved children of God, through faith in Jesus Christ.

A Christian scholar traveled the world teaching and preaching. After several weeks away he returned home to see his baby girl, but wasn't sure that she'd recognize him. They got into a staring match, for about a minute, when she suddenly realized who he was. Her face lit up, her arms shot out, and she nestled in his neck for the longest time.

In those few minutes I learned more about the meaning of life than in all the philosophy books I have ever read. The meaning of life is relationships (Ravi Zacharias), he said. *This, then, is how you should pray: Our Father in heaven.*

Matthew 6:9b *[H]allowed be your name.*

Donald Trump, Justin Bieber, Judas Iscariot, Albert Einstein, Oprah Winfrey—they each have a name, and a reputation. God also has a name, and he cares about his reputation. And since God is our Father, we should care about his reputation too.

I grew up in a small town where there weren't many big buildings. But on the way to the city, one day, I saw a large building with a man's name at the top. I hadn't heard of the man, but he must've been important since his name was at the top of a building. In my little boy dreams I imagined becoming so successful, one day, that my name would be at the top of a building too.

But an interesting thing happened when I began to read the Bible. I found a verse that said, *not to us but to your name be the glory* (Psalm 115:1), and another that said, *your name and renown are the desire of our hearts* (Isaiah 26:8), and another that said, *your name alone do we honor* (Isaiah 26:13).

This idea was so important to the apostles, in fact, that we can barely remember their names. Peter, Andrew, James, and John come to mind but whatever happened to Bartholomew, or Thaddeus, or those other guys?

They were so concerned about the name of Jesus Christ that they didn't even care about their own names. Self promotion never even crossed their minds. If you want to examine your values, ask which matters more to you—your Father's reputation or your own.

And if you care about your Father's reputation you'll be careful not to tarnish it. Hallowed be your name in my thinking. Hallowed be your name in my speaking. Hallowed be your name in my driving. Hallowed be your name in my parking. Hallowed be your name in my working. Hallowed be your name in my playing. Hallowed be your name in my saving. Hallowed be your name in my spending. In everything I am, and in everything I do, *hallowed be your name*.

Matthew 6:10 *[Y]our kingdom come.*

The kingdom of God is like a little seed that grows into a large plant (Matthew 13:31-32, paraphrased), said Jesus. What started out as a little group of believers, on the other side of the world, now has over two billion people who call themselves Christians. And whenever someone believes in Jesus Christ, the kingdom grows a little bit more.

But the kingdom won't come in its fulness until the king returns in glory. *At that time people will see the Son of Man coming in clouds with great power and glory* (Mark 13:26), said Jesus.

I read of a school for the mentally challenged where they teach the children that Jesus will split the skies when he returns for them. The children are simple enough to believe it and, every day, they smudge up the windows looking for Jesus' return. The custodians don't like it very much because, every day, they have to clean the windows. But who has more spiritual sense: those dear little ones, or smart people like us? *You also must be ready, because the Son of Man will come at an hour when you do not expect him* (Luke 12:40), said Jesus.

In the mean time, Jesus taught us to not only pray *your kingdom come*, but to *seek first his kingdom* (Matthew 6:33). It's been observed that we only succeed in life by identifying a single overriding objective, and making everything else yield to that objective. If your objective is to win a gold medal, then your diet must yield to that objective; your leisure must yield to that objective; your bed time must yield to that objective; and your friendships must yield to that objective. God is looking for people who'll not only pray *your kingdom come*, but who'll make it their first priority.

For Reflection and Review

- *What does it mean to call God, Father?*
- *How can we bring honor to God's reputation?*
- *Why should God's kingdom be our first priority?*

Lesson 181

Matthew 6:10b *[Y]our will be done, on earth as it is in heaven.*

The night before he was crucified Jesus asked his heavenly Father that his life be spared (Matthew 26:39). Knowing Judas was on his way with a band of soldiers, Jesus could've run away. But instead he prayed, *not my will, but yours be done* (Luke 22:42). Whenever God's will contradicts our own will it takes the form of a cross. Part of us wants to run away, but instead we pray: *your will be done, on earth as it is in heaven.*

It's our belief in heaven, in fact, that helps us do this. If this world is all there is, then we're compelled to grab all the pleasure we can, and shun all the pain we can. But if there really is a place where there's *no more death or mourning or crying or pain* (Revelation 21:4), where every day is better than before, where thoughts are clearer and bodies are stronger, and there's no possibility of sin, sorrow, or sickness—then the will of God becomes a joy, and every crucifixion comes with a little resurrection.

Matthew 6:11 *Give us today our daily bread.*

This is what God did for the Israelites as they traveled to the Promised Land. There weren't any shopping centers in the desert so every day God gave them manna from heaven. *It was white like coriander seed and tasted like wafers made with honey* (Exodus 16:31), wrote Moses. All they had to do was go outside and pick it up. And every day there was enough.

But how much is enough? Daily bread is fine but I really want a big screen TV, a three car garage, and a million dollars in the bank. But Jesus never had a lot of money. He was born in a borrowed stable (Luke 2:7), and was buried in a borrowed tomb (Matthew 27:57-60). He made the world, but had no place to lay his head (Matthew 8:20).

And when it was time to pay the temple tax, he and Peter were short of cash. So he told Peter to go catch a fish, and in the fish's mouth was a four-drachma coin—just enough for the two of them (Matthew 17:24-27). But why not a six-drachma coin so they could all go out for ice cream?

According to Luther's Small Catechism, *Daily bread includes everything needed for this life, such as food, drink, clothing, shoes, house, home and the like.* I agree with this but we're never taught to pray for excess. *[G]ive me neither poverty nor riches, but give me only my daily bread. Otherwise, I may have too much and disown you and say, Who is the Lord? Or I may become poor and steal, and so dishonor the name of my God* (Proverbs 30:8-9), says Proverbs. This agrees with the old English prayer: *Give us Lord a bit of sun, a bit of work, a bit o fun. Give us all in the struggle and sputter, our daily bread and a bit of butter.*

Matthew 6:12 *And forgive us our debts, as we also have forgiven our debtors.*

The reason Christians are so forgiving is because we've been so forgiven. *When we were overwhelmed by sins, you forgave our transgressions* (Psalm 65:3). *[A]s far as the east is from the west, so far has he removed our transgressions from us* (Psalm 103:12). *Though your sins are like scarlet, they shall be as white as snow* (Isaiah 1:18).

[Y]ou have put all my sins behind your back (Isaiah 38:17). *I . . . am he who blots out your transgressions . . . and remembers your sins no more* (Isaiah 43:25). *I have swept away your offenses like a cloud, your sins like the morning mist* (Isaiah 44:22). *[I] will forgive all their sins of rebellion against me* (Jeremiah 33:8). *[Y]ou will tread our sins underfoot and hurl all our iniquities into the depths of the sea* (Micah 7:19).

[E]veryone who believes in [Jesus] receives forgiveness of sins (Acts 10:43). *[T]hrough Jesus the forgiveness of sins is proclaimed to you* (Acts 13:38). *Blessed is the one whose sin the Lord will never count against them* (Romans 4:8). *[He will] present you holy in his sight, without blemish and free from accusation* (Colossians 1:22). *He forgave us all our sins* (Colossians 2:13). When we begin to understand the extent of God's forgiveness, it becomes easier to forgive others.

I read of a Christian family with a beautiful home, and wonderful children, but the mother has a gambling problem. It's so bad, in fact, that she steals from her family to support her addiction. She's been to doctors, counselors, and pastors but nothing seems to help. And, yet, her husband keeps forgiving her.

She's a good mom most of the time and my children need her. But more than that they need to know the love of their God. How can they know of a Father in heaven who forgives them if their own father will not even forgive their own mother? I'm not sure this is the best strategy but it makes the point. *Forgive us our debts as we also have forgiven our debtors.*

Matthew 6:13 *And lead us not into temptation, but deliver us from the evil one.*

Temptation isn't the same as sin, but it brings us very close to sin. Sometimes that agrees with us because we enjoy the pleasure of being tempted. You might be on a diet but decide to bake cookies because you enjoy the aroma of freshly baked cookies. The aroma doesn't have any calories, so there's no harm in baking cookies as long as you don't eat them. The argument makes sense but, is it wise?

An American student in Ecuador attended a bullfight one afternoon. At one point the fans were invited to enter the arena, and get as close to the bull as they dared. The student approached the bull from behind and wanted to touch it in order to have bragging rights. Unfortunately, the bull turned around and thrashed him so severely that he had to be hospitalized. *I thought I could get close and run away—but I was wrong*, he said. The best way to avoid the devil is to keep a little distance. *Lead us not into temptation but deliver us from the evil one.*

For Reflection and Review

- *How much stuff do you want in this life?*
- *Why does God want you to know that you're forgiven?*
- *Why does God allow temptation?*

Lesson 182

Matthew 6:20-21 *But store up for yourselves treasures in heaven, where moths and vermin do not destroy, and where thieves do not break in and steal. For where your treasure is, there your heart will be also.*

Our bank account in heaven is just as real as the one we have on earth. Many have a fortune on earth, but very little in heaven. Jesus wants us to put our money in heaven, not only because it's wise, but because *where your treasure is, there your heart will be also.*

If you had a million dollars tucked inside your mattress, you'd think about your mattress all the time. One lady actually did this and, while she was away, her daughter bought her a new mattress and threw the old one away. They went to three different garbage dumps, but it was never recovered. If she'd only put her money in heaven, it would still be there.

Likewise, if a country is changing currency, the residents have until a certain date to exchange their old currency. Once that date has passed their money is worthless, so they must trade it or lose it. Our present currency will have no value in eternity, so we must trade it now or lose it forever.

Matthew 6:31-32 *So do not worry, saying, What shall we eat? or What shall we drink? or What shall we wear? For the pagans run after all these things, and your heavenly Father knows that you need them.*

As Jesus preached God's word to the people, he saw that some had worry in their eyes. Their clothes were wearing out, and they had no money for food. Their little ones were hungry, and the rent was coming due. Many had a list of problems that would never go away. But to all their valid concerns Jesus said, *do not worry.*

Jesus knew, better than others, that most of our anxiety comes from making too much of this life, and not enough of the one to come. If we could see the glory that awaits us, and that'll be ours forever, all our fears would vaporize. The troubles of this life will soon be over, and perfect joy will take their place. If we can live in the light of this, then most of our fears will go away.

But Jesus also wants us to know that we have a *heavenly Father,* and whatever comes into our lives is Father-filtered. Children don't always understand the actions of their parents, and we can't always understand the ways of God. But Jesus knew that his Father could be trusted.

A little girl was diagnosed with an inoperable brain tumor, and her parents were overwhelmed by the idea of losing her. They held her tightly and wept together for several minutes. But then she looked into her parents' eyes and said, *God tells us not to worry.* We can only imagine the comfort this brought.

Christians have the same problems as everyone else, but we also have a heavenly Father. He's honored by our trust, and will always do what is best. *Cast all your anxiety on him because he cares for you* (1 Peter 5:7), wrote Peter.

Matthew 6:33 *[S]eek first his kingdom and his righteousness, and all these things will be given to you as well.*

If we pursue our own kingdom, it'll be very small, and death will take it away. But if we pursue God's kingdom, he'll meet our present needs, and give us eternal life. Several years ago I was having a Bible study with my son and we came to this passage. I looked at him with surprise and said, *This is all I've ever done. I didn't seek a house, family, car, or anything else. All I've ever done is to seek first the kingdom of God, and God has taken care of the rest.*

One of God's best provisions was the girl of my dreams. Until my middle twenties I had almost no dating experience. But when I met Julene we were able to talk for a couple hours, without interruption, and it was magic.

She found out I was studying for ministry, and I found out she was doing ministry. She found out I was taking a class in theology, and I found out she was conversant in theology. She found out I was seeking the kingdom of God, and I found out she was seeking the kingdom of God. After two hours it was clear to me that I was speaking to the future Mrs. Houle. Seven months later we were married, and thirty years later I'd choose her all over again. If we seek first the kingdom of God, God will take care of the rest.

For Reflection and Review

- *Why should we put treasure in heaven?*
- *Is it realistic not to worry?*
- *Why is it wise to seek first God's kingdom?*

Lesson 183

Matthew 7:1 *Do not judge, or you too will be judged.*

This was a serious problem in first century Judaism, when so many people were trying to live according to the Bible. In addition to the six hundred thirteen commands in the Old Testament, many others were added by way of tradition. Those who kept them best felt good about themselves, and enjoyed looking down on others. To this Jesus said, *Do not judge, or you too will be judged.*

This doesn't mean we shouldn't talk about sin, or distinguish right from wrong. Jesus did this all the time. But, like Jesus, we must uphold God's word without becoming judgmental. It isn't very difficult once you know how.

Whenever you see rudeness in others, repent of the same in yourself. Whenever you see immodesty in others, repent of the same in yourself. Whenever you see arrogance in others, repent of the same in yourself. *Why do you look at the speck of sawdust in your brother's eye and pay no attention to the plank in your own eye?* (Matthew 7:3), said Jesus.

God may even be bringing these people across your path to remind you of your own faults. If you had the same DNA and background, in fact, you'd likely behave the same way. We should apply God's word to ourselves before applying it to others. This will help us not to be judgmental.

Matthew 7:7-8 *Ask and it will be given to you; seek and you will find; knock and the door will be opened to you. For everyone who asks receives; the one who seeks finds; and to the one who knocks, the door will be opened.*

It's no surprise that Jesus was in favor of prayer since, whenever Jesus prayed, amazing things happened. The blind saw, the deaf heard, and hungry people were fed. With those results it's no wonder Jesus believed in prayer. But most of us have less success than Jesus, and unanswered prayer can even make us doubt.

A thirteen year old boy had a friend with leukemia so he prayed earnestly and it went into remission. But three months later the sickness came back and she died. Many children have prayed for their parents to get along, only to watch them separate, and then divorce. And countless parents have prayed for their children, only to watch them walk away from God.

Is prayer a waste of time? Is Jesus getting our hopes up only to let us down? Many Christians think so, even if they wouldn't say so. But, like financial investing, prayer requires a longer view. Those who take a short view of prayer will underestimate its value, while those who take a longer view will see their reward eventually.

I know a lady whose son who was born with a disability that would limit him severely. She was determined to get a miracle so she prayed, fasted, and took him to every prayer meeting in town. But the miracle never came. He struggled to walk, struggled in school, and struggled socially.

But, along the way, he picked up his mother's faith. He also went to college and earned a Master's degree. Then he married a Christian woman and became successful in every way, except that he does his work from a wheel chair. His mother is so amazed that she calls it a miracle. Prayer is never a waste of time; it only requires a longer view.

Matthew 7:11 *If you, then, though you are evil, know how to give good gifts to your children, how much more will your Father in heaven give good gifts to those who ask him!*

God's generosity often goes unnoticed because of our dullness. Pigs are fond of eating acorns, but never look up to the branches from which they fall. God pours out his blessings from above, but we seldom acknowledge their source.

This is why the Bible reminds us that *Every good and perfect gift is from above* (James 1:17). A well-cooked meal, a kind embrace, and a joyful heart are gifts from God. Our heavenly Father loves to give, simply because he's generous.

One of my greatest joys as a parent was taking my children to the dollar store, and giving them one dollar each. There were so many toys to choose from, they could hardly decide. Once I felt so generous that I gave them five dollars each. They thought they won the lottery! And I was willing to do this even though I'm evil. *If you, then, though you are evil . . .* said Jesus.

The world is still confused about whether people are basically good or basically evil. Most admit they're evil, but also believe they're basically good. Clarity on this point is important because if we assume people are basically good, then all we will need to perfect society is more education, more opportunity, and more government. But if we assume people are basically evil, then we need salvation, because the problem is a part us that we can't change on our own.

Thankfully, the Bible is clear about this. *[E]very inclination of the human heart is evil from childhood* (Genesis 8:21), wrote Moses. *Surely I was sinful at birth, sinful from the time my mother conceived me* (Psalm 51:5), wrote David. *There is no one righteous . . . . no one who does good* (Romans 3:10-12), wrote Paul.

This doesn't mean we're all equally bad, or couldn't be any worse. But, like a bent arrow, we can't fly straight, and will never hit the mark on our own. God gives us the Spirit to help us fight against sin, and in the age to come he'll take away our sinful nature. Then our salvation will be complete, and we'll live in harmony with God others forever.

For Reflection and Review

- *How can we believe in right and wrong without being judgmental?*
- *Does prayer always work?*
- *Are most people good or evil?*

Lesson 184

Matthew 7:12 *So in everything, do to others what you would have them do to you, for this sums up the Law and the Prophets.*

This is often called the *Golden Rule* and is found, in various forms, in Judaism, Hinduism, Buddhism, Confucianism, and Greco-Roman ethics. These, however, state it negatively: *Do not do to others what you do not want them to do to you.* By stating it positively, Jesus taught us to be proactive in caring for those around us.

A young man was on his way to a job interview when he saw a lady with a flat tire. He was wearing his best suit, and didn't have time, but he felt compelled to help her anyway. This made him late for the interview, but the interviewer was also late. When she arrived, he was happy to see that she was the lady with the flat tire. And, yes, he got the job.

This verse is also helpful for maintaining good relationships. If I need to correct my children, I want to do it in a way that I'd like to be corrected if the roles were reversed. And, if someone needs money, I try to give it anonymously since that's how I'd like to receive it. And, if someone offends me, I try to make excuses for them since that's what I'd like others to do for me. The Golden Rule is nothing less than relational genius.

Matthew 7:13-14 *Enter through the narrow gate. For wide is the gate and broad is the road that leads to* *destruction, and many enter through it. But small is the gate and narrow the road that leads to life, and only a few find it.*

In a single verse, Jesus contradicts the overwhelming consensus of popular theology. Among those who believe in heaven and hell, the vast majority believe that most people go to heaven, and only a few go to hell. Hell is a place for axe murderers and child molesters. Everyone else goes to heaven by default. I've never been to a funeral, in fact, where the dead person wasn't assumed to be in heaven, no matter how they lived, or what they believed.

But, if Jesus is right, almost everyone goes to hell, and only a few go to heaven. When God destroyed the world with a flood (Genesis 7:1-23), everyone died except Noah and his family. Only eight were saved; everyone else perished. Likewise, when God destroyed Sodom and Gomorrah with fire (Genesis 19:1-29), everyone died except Lot and his daughters. Only three people were saved, and everyone else perished. Majority opinion is not a reliable guide to how God will judge the world.

When Jesus spoke of the *narrow gate*, he was referring to himself. *I am the gate; whoever enters through me will be saved* (John 10:9), he said. And, *No one comes to the Father except through me* (John 14:6), he said. And, *Salvation is found in no one else, for there is no other name under heaven given to mankind by which we must be saved* (Acts 4:12), said Peter.

When Jesus spoke of the narrow road, he meant the way of obedience. Antinomianism is the idea that, since we're saved by grace (Ephesians 2:8), we can do as we please and still go to heaven. You probably don't believe that, but you may've been tempted by it.

A friend of mine was invited to spend the night with a young lady, but declined on the grounds that he was a Christian. She explained that she was a Christian too and, if they asked forgiveness in the morning, all would be well. But this attitude suggests she wasn't a Christian at all.

Matthew 7:21 *Not everyone who says to me, Lord, Lord, will enter the kingdom of heaven, but only the one who does the will of my Father who is in heaven.*

When Jesus returns many will greet him with *Lord, Lord*, as though they were friends. But Jesus won't be fooled. He knows that many who claim to be his friends aren't really his friends. Perhaps they were acquaintances, but were never true disciples. To them he'll say, *I never knew you. Away from me, you evildoers!* (Matthew 7:23). Since the word *Lord* means *master*, we shouldn't call Jesus our *Lord*, if he isn't our master.

Or do you not know that wrongdoers will not inherit the kingdom of God? Do not be deceived: Neither the sexually immoral nor idolaters nor adulterers nor men who have sex with men nor thieves nor the greedy nor drunkards nor slanderers nor swindlers will inherit the kingdom of God (1 Corinthians 6:8-10), wrote Paul. The best indication of what people believe isn't what they say, but what they do. You can't get to heaven by being good, but you won't get there without it.

Matthew 7:24-27 *Therefore everyone who hears these words of mine and puts them into practice is like a wise man who built his house on the rock. The rain came down, the streams rose, and the winds blew and beat against that house; yet it did not fall, because it had its foundation on the rock.*

But everyone who hears these words of mine and does not put them into practice is like a foolish man who built his house on sand. The rain came down, the streams rose, and the winds blew and beat against that house, and it fell with a great crash.

The test of a house isn't how it looks when the weather is fine, but how holds up when the weather is fierce. Many years ago, after a devastating hurricane, countless homes were off their foundations. One, however, was standing strong. The owner explained that his house was built according to the highest recommended standards, and was bolted to its foundation. Likewise, whoever bolts their life to Christ, and builds according to his word, will survive every storm.

For Reflection and Review

- *Why does the golden rule improve relationships?*
- *Why is it important to obey God?*
- *How can we build our lives on the words of Jesus Christ?*

Lesson 185

Matthew 8:5 *When Jesus had entered Capernaum, a centurion came to him, asking for help.*

Centurions were the backbone of the Roman military, and were highly respected by all. Each was responsible for about a hundred soldiers, and for maintaining discipline within the rank. They were so highly valued that their pay could be five times more than a common soldier's. This man was sympathetic to Judaism, and even helped pay for a synagogue (Luke 7:5). He was also a man of compassion.

Lord, he said, my servant lies at home paralyzed, suffering terribly (Matthew 8:6). He wasn't interceding for his wife, or child, but for his servant. With all the battle and bloodshed he'd known, we might expect him to be a little more calloused. But when he saw his servant's misery, he was compelled to do what he could.

Some have argued that God must not exist, because a good God wouldn't allow pain. But God knows without pain there can be no compassion, and we'd never know that part of him. *As a father has compassion on his children, so the Lord has compassion on those who fear him* (Psalm 103:3), wrote David.

An American soldier was wounded in battle and, when the nurse washed the dirt from his face, she saw he was still a boy. She began to weep, and the tears rolled off her face onto his lips. Startled, he opened his eyes and was so deeply moved that he called it the *most tender moment* of his life. Through giving and receiving compassion we experience the compassion of God.

Matthew 8:7 *Jesus said to him, Shall I come and heal him?*

Gentile homes were considered unclean by Jews, so Jesus' offer probably shocked those around him, including the centurion. For a rising Rabbi to tarnish his reputation by going to a Gentile's home was unheard of. But Jesus cared about the needs of others more than his reputation. And, above all, he wanted to please his heavenly Father.

This is also what it takes to follow Jesus Christ. *How can you believe since you accept glory from one another but do not seek the glory that comes from the only God?* (John 5:44), he said. If we care what others think, more than what God thinks, we'll never follow Jesus Christ.

Matthew 8:8 *The centurion replied, Lord, I do not deserve to have you come under my roof. But just say the word, and my servant will be healed.*

The centurion was familiar with how authority works. If he needed something done, twenty miles away, he could give the command and it would be done. All authority belonged to the emperor and, because he was under the emperor's authority, distance made no difference. Since Jesus was under God's authority, the centurion knew he could give the command and it would happen.

We don't understand authority very well because our culture is democratic, and we prefer to vote. And if we don't get our way, we simply bend the rules, or break them. We even do this with God.

But Jesus was perfectly submitted to God so he had great authority. *[H]e taught as one who had authority* (Matthew 7:29). He had *authority on earth to forgive sins* (Mark 2:10). He had *authority to judge* (John 5:27). He had *authority over all people* (John 17:2). And *All authority in heaven and on earth has been given to me* (Matthew 28:18), he said. The centurion knew that Jesus had the authority to make things happen.

Matthew 8:10 *When Jesus heard this, he was amazed and said to those following him, Truly I tell you, I have not found anyone in Israel with such great faith.*

This was a strong rebuke since most of the people present were Israelites. They had the Bible, the temple, and other spiritual benefits, but were lacking faith. *And without faith it is impossible to please God, because anyone who comes to him must believe that he exists and that he rewards those who earnestly seek him* (Hebrews 11:6), says Hebrews. All the religion in the world won't please God if we don't have genuine faith.

Matthew 8:11-12 *[M]any will come from the east and the west, and will take their places at the feast with Abraham, Isaac and Jacob in the kingdom of heaven. But the subjects of the kingdom will be thrown outside, into the darkness, where there will be weeping and gnashing of teeth.*

The Jews were *subjects of the kingdom* in the sense that they believed the Bible, went to synagogue, and considered themselves to be God's people. But unless they believed in God's Messiah they'd be thrown outside in the age to come. You can't be part of God's eternal kingdom if you don't believe in his eternal king.

Matthew 8:13 *Then Jesus said to the centurion, Go! Let it be done just as you believed it would. And his servant was healed at that moment.*

We don't know how many people Jesus healed, since most of his miracles weren't recorded (John 21:25). But an important purpose of his miracles was to show that he was the Promised One. *Then will the eyes of the blind be opened and the ears of the deaf unstopped. Then will the lame leap like a deer, and the mute tongue shout for joy* (Isaiah 35:5-6), wrote Isaiah. But if Jesus healed so many people back then, why doesn't he heal more today?

It's not an easy question, but we seem to be living *between the times.* Jesus healed everyone when he came the first time, and will heal everyone when he comes the second time. But we're currently living between the times. The kingdom of God has come in Jesus Christ, but it won't come in fullness until he returns. That's why some of our prayers are answered, and others are not.

For Reflection and Review

- *How does suffering help us to experience God's compassion?*
- *Why was Jesus able to heal from a distance?*
- *Why doesn't Jesus heal more people today?*

Lesson 186

Matthew 10:2-4 *These are the names of the twelve apostles: first, Simon (who is called Peter) and his brother Andrew; James son of Zebedee, and his brother John; Philip and Bartholomew; Thomas and Matthew the tax collector; James son of Alphaeus, and Thaddaeus; Simon the Zealot and Judas Iscariot, who betrayed him.*

The remarkable thing about the apostles was how unremarkable they were. They were just ordinary people, from ordinary walks of life, and weren't even great role models. James and John were volatile (Luke 9:54), Thomas struggled with doubt (John 20:27), and Peter denied Jesus three times with a curse (Matthew 26:69-75). The success of Christianity wasn't due to the greatness of the apostles, but to the greatness of Jesus Christ. But why twelve?

Truly I tell you, at the renewal of all things, when the Son of Man sits on his glorious throne, you who have followed me will also sit on twelve thrones, judging the twelve tribes of Israel (Matthew 19:28).

The nation of Israel consisted of twelve tribes (Genesis 49:28), and the apostles will rule over them when Jesus Christ returns. Israel was the geographical center of God's kingdom, and will be again. This reveals a rich continuity between the Old Testament and the New Testament.

Matthew 10:5-6 *These twelve Jesus sent out with the following instructions: Do not go among the Gentiles or enter any town of the Samaritans. Go rather to the lost sheep of Israel.*

After Jesus rose from the dead, he told his apostles to *make disciples of all nations* (Matthew 28:19). But, at this point, he restricted their mission to the nation of Israel. Christianity began within Judaism, and Jews should always be included in the outreach of the church. Wherever Paul evangelized, he took the gospel *first to the Jew, then to the Gentile* (Romans 1:16).

The Jews have been mostly unresponsive to the gospel, but this won't always be the case. *Israel has experienced a hardening in part until the full number of the Gentiles has come in, and in this way all Israel will be saved. As it is written: The deliverer will come from Zion; he will turn godlessness away from Jacob* (Romans 11:25-26), wrote Paul. This seems to mean there'll be a great turning of Jews to Christ near the end of this age.

This and other passages assume the continued existence of Israel, which is surprising in itself. They were deported to Babylon in the sixth century BC, and regathered in their homeland decades later. They were exiled again in AD 70, and regathered in their homeland centuries later.

Most people lose their national identity within a few generations of leaving their homeland, due to intermarriage. For the Jews to maintain their identity, and return to their homeland centuries later, is truly remarkable. If God preserved the Jews, and brought them back to their homeland twice, he can turn them to the Messiah in due time. What Jesus said to the apostles, he says to the church today: *Go . . . to the lost sheep of Israel.*

Matthew 10:8 *Freely you have received; freely give.*

Giving and receiving are both important to following Jesus Christ. The disciples freely received from him, and were to freely give to others. Some want to give without receiving; others want to receive without giving. But spiritual vitality requires both.

The Sea of Galilee has been teeming with life for thousands of years. Water flows in from the north, out at the south, and life continues to flourish. The Dead Sea also receives water from the north, but it has no outlet at the south. And it's been dead for thousands of years.

If we receive from Christ, but don't give, we'll never flourish spiritually. If we give, but don't receive, we'll soon become depleted. Vital spirituality requires giving and receiving. *Freely you have received; freely give.*

Matthew 10:16 *I am sending you out like sheep among wolves.*

Where Christianity is well established the message often becomes harmless: Jesus was a very nice teacher who taught his disciples to be very nice people. But that isn't true. Jesus is a king who demands absolute allegiance (Luke 14:33), and threatens sinners with the fire of hell (Matthew 18:9).

The gospel is a dangerous message that creates opposition whenever it's understood. This is clear from the book of Acts where the disciples were often imprisoned and beaten for their faith. Some were even killed. But going out with the gospel was never optional.

Likewise, a member of the coast guard was being sent out to save a boat in a terrible storm. *I don't know if I'll make it back*, he said. *You don't have to make it back*, replied his captain, *but you do have to go out.* This was the attitude of Christ to his apostles. They did their job courageously, and so have many since.

For Reflection and Review

- *Why is the existence of Israel surprising?*
- *Why are giving and receiving both important to spiritual vitality?*
- *Why were the disciples willing to live like sheep among wolves?*

Lesson 187

Matthew 10:22 *You will be hated by everyone because of me, but the one who stands firm to the end will be saved.*

An American tourist in Turkey asked his Muslim guide if he'd like to believe in Jesus Christ. The tour guide seemed on the verge of faith but then explained, *You do not know what you are asking . . . [M]y wife would leave me. My family would disown me. My boss would fire me. . . . the government would not give me an exit visa. . . . I would starve to death in my own culture.*

This is why many who begin to follow Christ later fall away. It's perfectly understandable, but a terrible mistake since the Bible doesn't promise anything good to those who turn away. *If we deliberately keep on sinning after we have received the knowledge of the truth, no sacrifice for sins is left, but only a fearful expectation of judgment and of raging fire that will consume the enemies of God* (Hebrews 10:26-27), says Hebrews.

And, *If they have escaped the corruption of the world by knowing our Lord and Savior Jesus Christ and are again entangled in it and are overcome, they are worse off at the end than they were at the beginning. It would have been better for them not to have known the way of righteousness, than to have known it and then to turn their backs on the sacred command that was passed on to them* (1 Peter 2:20-21), wrote Peter.

God will forgive murder, adultery, incest, and anything else for those who follow Christ. But those who turn away from him add to all their other sins the worst sin of all—rejecting the Savior of the world. There's no prize for beginning the Christian life, but the *one who stands firm to the end will be saved.*

Matthew 10:29-31 *Are not two sparrows sold for a penny? Yet not one of them will fall to the ground outside your Father's care. And even the very hairs of your head are all numbered. So do not be afraid; you are worth more than many sparrows.*

Given the trouble the apostles would face, it was important for them to know that God was in control. This isn't hard when the bills are paid, the family is getting along, and everyone's healthy. But when you're sitting in a cold dark cell, with starving rats gnawing at your feet, it can be hard to believe that God is in control.

This is why Jesus assured us that God has numbered the hairs on our head, and that even a sparrow can't fall to the ground apart from his loving care. This is not a promise that nothing bad will ever happen, but that nothing bad will ever happen apart from our Father's will, for his glory, and for our ultimate good (Romans 8:28).

It's helpful to understand that God governs the little things, just as much as the big things, since both are interrelated. This has been illustrated by a nail that fell out of a horse's shoe: *For lack of a nail, the shoe was lost. For lack of a shoe, the horse was lost. For lack of a horse, the rider was lost. For lack of a rider, the battle was lost. For lack of a battle, the war was lost—all for lack of a nail.*

If God isn't in control of everything, he's not in control of anything, because everything depends on everything else. In all their hardships, the apostles could be sure they'd never lose a hair, apart from their Father's good and perfect will.

Matthew 10:32-33 *Whoever acknowledges me before others, I will also acknowledge before my Father in heaven. But whoever disowns me before others, I will disown before my Father in heaven.*

Due to the gospel's radical nature, and to opposition, it wasn't always easy for the apostles to acknowledge Jesus publicly. Sometimes they were bold, but sometimes they were afraid, not knowing how things would turn out. *I came to you in weakness with great fear and trembling* (1 Corinthians 2:3), wrote Paul. In spite of their fear, however, they spent the rest of their lives acknowledging Jesus Christ, and calling others to do the same. It often began with baptism.

In the early days of his ministry, Jesus preached while his disciples baptized (John 4:1-2). As long the crowds stayed out of the water, they were merely being entertained. But when a person stepped into the water they were identifying with Jesus Christ, and acknowledging him before others. Even today, we acknowledge Jesus publicly when we choose to be baptized.

Another way to acknowledge Christ is by going to church. A man in his nineties went to church every week, even though his voice was too weak to sing, his ears were too weak to hear, and his eyes were too weak to read the Bible. Every Sunday he got up early, put on a suit, and walked several blocks to church. His daughter said, *Dad, you can't sing anymore, you can't hear anymore, and you can't read anymore. Why do you go to church?* The old man replied, *I want everyone to know whose side I'm on.*

*****

Matthew 13:44 *The kingdom of heaven is like treasure hidden in a field. When a man found it, he hid it again, and then in his joy went and sold all he had and bought that field.*

Imagine a man in Jesus' time who made his living plowing fields. The days were long and hot, the work was dirty, and the pay was barely enough. Worst of all, there were so many rocks that it was hard to complete a row without hitting one or two of them.

Again the man's plow jerked to a stop and he wanted to cuss. He stooped to remove the stone but, to his surprise, it wasn't a stone, but a box. With interest, he dug around the box and carefully opened the lid. There, inside, were diamonds, rubies, and pearls worth more than he could spend.

Cautiously, he looked around to see if there were any witnesses and, thankfully, there weren't. So he covered the box, marked the spot, and went back to plowing the field. But now his heart was racing as he considered what to do.

If he stole the treasure, he'd surely be caught, and lose everything. But if he could somehow buy the field, the treasure would be legally his, and his life would never be the same. With barely concealed joy, he sold his home, his ox, his plow—everything he had—and bought the field. That's what the kingdom of God is like. It will cost you everything, but make you unspeakably rich (source unknown).

For Reflection and Review

- *Is there any hope for those who fall away from Christ?*
- *How can we acknowledge Christ before others?*
- *How is God's kingdom like a treasure hidden in a field?*

Lesson 188

Matthew 14:22-23 *Jesus made the disciples get into the boat and go on ahead of him to the other side . . . . [Then] he went up on a mountainside by himself to pray.*

When the moon is full you can see across the Sea of Galilee at night. If Jesus watched his disciples rowing to the other side, he saw they were having a difficult time. The wind was against them, and their boat was being pounded by the waves (Matthew 14:24).

If we're in the middle of God's will, we might think that life will be smooth sailing. And if things aren't going well, perhaps we've done something wrong. But the disciples were doing exactly what Jesus told them to do and, yet, the wind was against them. That's just how it is sometimes.

Botanists speak of a natural phenomenon which they call the *adversity principle*. A tree that's given plenty of water may never put down roots, but a tree in the desert may have roots over a hundred feet deep. Both can appear strong but, when the wind blows hard, one remains standing and the other falls down. The sturdiest Christians are often those who've weathered the most adversity. Sometimes the wind will be against us.

Matthew 14:25 *Shortly before dawn Jesus went out to them, walking on the lake.*

There are about thirty-five miracles of Christ recorded in the gospels. These can be divided into twenty-three healing miracles, three resurrections, and nine miracles of nature. These include turning water into wine (John 2), feeding multitudes (Matthew 15, John 6), and walking on water. By walking on water Jesus showed his lordship over nature, and fulfilled something Job said about God: *He alone . . . treads on the waves of the sea* (Job 9:8).

Matthew 14:26 *It's a ghost, they said, and cried out in fear.*

The Bible doesn't have a lot of humor but this is funny: a dozen men in a fishing boat, screaming like little girls, because they think they've seen a ghost. A mark of the Bible's authenticity is that it never portrays the disciples as better than they were. They were real people, with real fears and failures, who needed a real Savior. And that's what they found in Jesus Christ.

This also gives us permission to be ourselves. We want to be our best, of course, but we don't want to seem better than we are. We're not mannequin Christians, but flesh and blood believers in Jesus Christ. Mannequin Christians are so uptight about their image that they appear to be plastic, and aren't very convincing. Jesus saves ordinary people, who remain rather ordinary, even after they are saved.

Matthew 14:27 *Take courage! It is I. Do not be afraid.*

The words, *It is I* can also be translated, *I am*. As God said to Moses, *I am who I am* (Exodus 3:14). This may've calmed their fears as when God said, *do not fear, for I am with you; do not be dismayed, for I am your God. I will strengthen you and help you; I will uphold you with my righteous right hand* (Isaiah 41:10).

During the Gulf War of 1991, Iraq launched a number of missiles against Israel, and many people died. But after the war they discovered that most of the dead hadn't died from missiles, but from heart attacks brought on by fear. Without God's help we can be so afraid of tomorrow that we don't enjoy today.

Matthew 14:28-29 *Lord, if it is you, Peter replied, tell me to come to you on the water. Come, he said. Then Peter got down out of the boat, walked on the water and came toward Jesus.*

I think the other disciples rolled their eyes. It wasn't enough for Jesus to walk on the water; Peter had to join him. Why not stay in the boat? Why not play it safe? Why do people do such crazy things sometimes?

When I was a freshman in college, a few of the guys were going skydiving, and asked if I wanted to join them. I weighed the risks and benefits, and decided to give it a try. After all, what go wrong?

We were thousands of feet in the air when the instructor opened the door. One at a time, we climbed out of the plane, onto a little platform, where we held onto the wing-support, and waited for the signal to jump. I was outside the airplane, waiting for the signal, when a thought came into my head: *Why would anyone get out of a perfectly good airplane and hope that a bed sheet will get them safely to the ground?*

When the signal came, I let go of the wing-support, and plummeted several feet until my parachute opened automatically. Then I floated gently down. I never did it again, but I think I stepped out of the airplane for the same reason Peter stepped out of the boat: everyone needs adventure. Some need more than others, but everyone needs a little.

So if your faith has become boring, do something risky for God. There's no guarantee you won't die, much less that you'll succeed. But if you're never scared, you'll never know what you and God can do together. And your faith will become what it was never meant to be—boring.

Matthew 14:30-31 *But when he saw the wind, he was afraid and, beginning to sink, cried out, Lord, save me! Immediately Jesus reached out his hand and caught him. You of little faith, he said, why did you doubt?*

Peter deserved a trophy, it seems, but what he got was correction: *why did you doubt?* How couldn't he doubt? Wasn't it enough that he tried? It's easy to think of Jesus walking on water because Jesus is divine. He's able to do things that we can't do in ourselves, like rise from the dead (Matthew 28:7), and ascend into heaven (Acts 1:9). But we should never forget that Jesus is also human. *Very truly I tell you, the Son can do nothing by himself; he can do only what he sees his Father doing* (John 5:19), he said.

So when Jesus took those first few steps on the water, he was looking to his Father. And as he walked, mile after mile, he was looking to his Father. And when the waves were crashing all around him, he never stopped looking to his Father. So when Peter got out of the boat, and was immediately distracted by the wind and waves, Jesus got impatient. *Why did you doubt?* he said.

The reason Peter doubted, of course, is that he took his eyes off Christ. The Christian life isn't terribly complicated. As long as we focus on Jesus, we're fine. But the moment we focus anywhere else, we sink. The devil would have us focus on our fears, failures, and circumstances. But the Bible tells us to focus on Christ. He is *the perfecter of our faith* (Hebrews 12:2), says Hebrews.

Matthew 14:32-33 *And when they climbed into the boat, the wind died down. Then those who were in the boat worshiped him, saying, Truly you are the Son of God.*

The emperor had no idea what just happened. Neither did the surrounding towns, or even the media. But those in the boat knew what happened, and they worshipped Jesus Christ. *Truly you are the Son of God*, they said.

This is like the church. Every church is a little boat with Jesus in our midst. We encounter him, worship him, and bow our hearts before him. The world takes little notice, but we know that we have touched reality. And, like the disciples, we take our faith into the world, and spread the good news that Jesus is the Son of God.

There's a final detail in John's gospel that's not included in Matthew's account: *immediately the boat reached the shore where they were heading* (John 6:21). One minute they were worshipping Jesus, and the next they reached their destination. We too could arrive at any moment.

For Reflection and Review

- *Do you ever worry about your image?*
- *How can we keep our faith from being boring?*
- *Why do we take our eyes off Christ?*

Lesson 189

Matthew 16:13 *When Jesus came to the region of Caesarea Philippi, he asked his disciples, Who do people say the Son of Man is?*

Caesarea Philippi was about twenty-five miles north of the Sea of Galilee, and was a center of paganism. They worshipped Caesar, Baal, and the Greek god Pan. Among the false gods, Jesus led a conversation about his true identity.

Matthew 16:14 *Some say [you're] John the Baptist; others say Elijah; and still others, Jeremiah or one of the prophets.*

Jesus' real concern wasn't what others thought of him however. He wanted to know what his disciples thought. *But what about you? he asked. Who do you say I am?* (Matthew 16:15). It was an important question for them, but it's important for us too. Who do we think Jesus is regarding creation, salvation, forgiveness, prayer, and Judgment Day? These are among the most important questions we can ever ask, and Jesus wants to know our answer.

Matthew 16:16-17 *Simon Peter answered, You are the Messiah, the Son of the living God. Jesus replied, Blessed are you, Simon son of Jonah, for this was not revealed to you by flesh and blood, but by my Father in heaven.*

Peter wasn't smart enough to figure this out on his own, or even to learn it from others. He may've thought he did, but Jesus informed Peter that his correct understanding was a revelation from God.

There are some things we can know about God apart from special revelation. We can know that he exists, because someone made the world. And we know that he has laws, because we're pretty sure we've broken them. But we can't know that God is forgiving, or that he has a Son, or what it's like to know him personally, apart from special revelation. These are things God reveals to some, but not to others.

I praise you, Father, Lord of heaven and earth, because you have hidden these things from the wise and learned, and revealed them to little children (Matthew 11:25), said Jesus. *[N]o one knows the Father except the Son and those to whom the Son chooses to reveal him* (Matthew 11:27), said Jesus again.

If you believe in Jesus Christ it's not because you're smarter than others, but because God has revealed himself to you through the gospel. And if you don't believe in Jesus Christ it's because you've closed your heart to God. Light received brings more light; light refused brings darkness. *Whoever has will be given more; whoever does not have, even what they think they have will be taken from them* (Luke 8:18), said Jesus.

That's what happened to Judas Iscariot. First he listened carefully, then he listened selectively, then he turned away. We depend on God for revelation; we have a duty to receive it.

Matthew 16:18 *I tell you that you are Peter, and on this rock I will build my church, and the gates of Hades will not overcome it.*

Peter and *rock* are similar in Greek, so Jesus was making a play on words. Peter was foundational to the church, as seen in the the book of Acts (Acts 2:14-41). Paul taught that the church is built on the *foundation of the apostles* (Ephesians 2:20). And, in John's vision of the New Jerusalem, *The wall of the city had twelve foundations, and on them were the names of the twelve apostles* (Revelation 21:14).

The apostles are foundational, but Jesus Christ is the builder: *I will build my church*, he said. This has been going on for two thousand years, and is our best opportunity for real significance. If Jesus Christ is building his church, and we partner with him, then we'll spend our lives on what's important. All we have to do is join a church and make it better.

But there are many who join a church and actually make it worse. That's what I did before I was truly converted. I was apathetic toward Christ, and a bad example to my peers. I went to church on Sundays, but lived for myself the rest of the week. Thankfully, all that changed after I truly believed. Suddenly, the church was important to me.

The first Sunday I arrived early, and sat in the front row. It felt a little strange but I didn't want to miss a thing. When the music played I sang with all my heart, and when the offering came I gave what I could. And, when the service was over, I stayed for a while because I wanted to connect with God's people. Anyone can make their life count forever, by joining a church and make it better.

Matthew 16:19 *I will give you the keys of the kingdom of heaven; whatever you bind on earth will be bound in heaven, and whatever you loose on earth will be loosed in heaven.*

Whoever has the gospel of Jesus Christ can open the door to the kingdom of heaven. Peter used these keys on the day of Pentecost, and thousands entered through faith in Christ (Acts 2:14-41). Whenever the gospel is preached, the door is open to all who believe. But what about *binding* and *loosing*?

In some rabbinic literature the words mean *forbidding* and *permitting*. The church isn't bound by the words of Moses, but by the words of the apostles . . . not by the Old Testament, but by the New Testament. This is stated clearly in the letter to the Hebrews. *By calling this covenant new, he has made the first one obsolete* (Hebrews 8:13).

For many years I had a typewriter in the basement on which the children played. But when it was time to write their papers, they wanted nothing to do with it. It didn't have spell-check, grammar-check, or even a delete key. At one time it was useful but, due to the computer, it became obsolete.

There's much in the Old Testament that's useful to us, but when it comes to the dietary laws, and many other laws, we're no longer bound—we have been loosed. This is a wonderful freedom, and reason to rejoice. Now we live for God in the simplicity of the gospel, not through countless commands.

For Reflection and Review

- *Why does God hide certain things from unbelievers?*
- *What's an easy way to make our life count?*
- *Are there any laws in the New Testament?*

Lesson 190

Matthew 16:21 *Jesus began to explain to his disciples that he must go to Jerusalem and suffer many things at the hands of the elders, the chief priests and the teachers of the law, and that he must be killed and on the third day be raised to life.*

This was not what the disciples wanted to hear. They didn't understand it because it didn't fit their concept of the Messiah. *Of the greatness of his government and peace there will be no end. He will reign on David's throne . . . forever* (Isaiah 9:7). *[T]he earth will be filled with the knowledge of the Lord as the waters cover the sea* (Isaiah 11:9), wrote Isaiah. This is what the disciples had in mind, and this is what will happen when Christ returns. But like many others, they understood the Bible selectively.

[H]e was led like a lamb to the slaughter. . . . By oppression and judgment he was taken away. . . . For he was cut off from the land of the living; for the transgression of my people he was punished. He was assigned a grave with the wicked, and with the rich in his death (Isaiah 53:7-9), wrote Isaiah also. These make it clear that before Messiah's glorious reign he had to be killed. But when Jesus tried to explain this, Peter got upset. *Peter took him aside and began to rebuke him. Never, Lord! he said. This shall never happen to you!* (Matthew 16:22).

But rebuking Jesus is seldom wise, and he responded sharply. *Get behind me, Satan! You are a stumbling block to me; you do not have in mind the concerns of God, but merely human concerns* (Matthew 16:23), he said. Within just a few verses Peter plummeted from the divine to the demonic. First he spoke for God, then he spoke for Satan—literally.

When Jesus was tempted by the devil, Satan offered him *all the kingdoms of the world* without going to the cross (Matthew 4:8-9). Peter was doing the same thing. He was telling Jesus to usher in the Messianic golden age without dying for the sins of the world. *Get behind me, Satan!* was not an overreaction, but a measured response to someone who was speaking for Satan. Like Peter, we can say words that are divine, and others that are demonic.

Matthew 16:24 *Whoever wants to be my disciple must deny themselves and take up their cross and follow me.*

This is the opposite of what the disciples expected. They planned to be part of Jesus' glorious kingdom, but now he was talking crucifixion—not just his own, but theirs! Jesus was committed to dying for his disciples, and he expected the same from them.

On any given day, in fact, there are many who pay the ultimate price for their faith in Jesus Christ. In an atheist country a twenty-two year old evangelist was beaten to death by police. In a Muslim country a twelve year old boy was sentenced to death for telling others about Jesus. In some places rewards are given for information leading to the arrest and execution of believers. *[T]he time is coming when anyone who kills you will think they are offering a service to God* (John 16:2), said Jesus.

There's not much persecution in the United States, but there is still a cross for each of us—the cross of discipleship. Following Jesus means denying ourselves for the sake of the gospel.

But crosses are uncomfortable so we tend to whittle them down: a little less believing, a little less obeying, a little less praying, a little less reading, a little less gathering, a little less giving, a little less serving, and a little less telling. Over time we whittle down our crosses until they're just the right size to fit into our pockets.

Pocket-sized Christianity is the religion of choice for many. But this is the devil's counterfeit for real Christianity, which is following Jesus Christ. *Whoever wants to be my disciple must deny themselves and take up their cross daily and follow me* (Luke 9:23), said Jesus.

Matthew 16:26 *What good will it be for someone to gain the whole world, yet forfeit their soul?*

There's little advantage to gaining the whole world, since we can't hold on to it. Alexander the Great nearly conquered the world by the time he was thirty-two years old, but then he died of an unknown cause. By the time of Christ he'd been dead for over three hundred years. Gaining the world for a little while, and losing your soul forever, is not a good trade.

In spite of the time they spent with Jesus, the disciples still had worldly ambitions. They may've been kingdom-minded, but they hadn't become eternity-minded. In light of his approaching death, Jesus turned the conversation to the value of their eternal souls.

A good definition of wisdom is *preparing for the future*. Parents are glad when their children do their homework, chose good friends, and make wise choices because that's the way to happiness. If they despise education, choose bad friends, and make poor choices their future is probably bleak. *A wise son brings joy to his father, but a foolish son brings grief to his mother* (Proverbs 10:1), says Proverbs.

Jesus takes wisdom even further by making us think about eternity. It's better to lose your life now, and save your soul forever, than to save your life now, and lose your soul forever. The purpose of time is to prepare for eternity. That's biblical wisdom.

It's also excellent news for both winners and losers. If you're a loser now, you can be a winner then. And if you are a winner now, you can be a winner then too. A wealthy business man called his partner at two in the morning and said, *I just made the greatest deal of my life. I just traded here for the hereafter; I just traded time for eternity.* That's the offer Jesus makes to each of us. *What good will it be for someone to gain the whole world, yet forfeit their soul?*

For Reflection and Review

- *Why was Peter upset with Jesus?*
- *What does it mean to carry a cross?*
- *How are you preparing for eternity?*

Lesson 191

Matthew 18:8 *If your hand or your foot causes you to stumble, cut it off and throw it away. It is better for you to enter life maimed or crippled than to have two hands or two feet and be thrown into eternal fire.*

No one ever spoke more radically about the serious danger of sin. A young man was scaling the side of a cliff and put his hand into a crevice. A boulder suddenly shifted and he was unable to free himself. Three days later, when no help arrived, he cut off his hand to save his life. No one wants to cut off their hand, of course, but most prefer it to death.

Jesus isn't teaching self-mutilation, since sin comes from the heart (Matthew 15:19). But he does want us to cut off our sin in order to follow him. We should never allow anything to come between us and our Savior, or be willing to imperil our souls.

*****

Matthew 18:21 *Then Peter came to Jesus and asked, Lord, how many times shall I forgive my brother or sister who sins against me? Up to seven times?*

We live in a world of sinners, and will be sinned against occasionally, even by those who are close to us. Friends, family, and coworkers all have sinful natures, and are prone to offend us routinely. Since Jesus preached a message of forgiveness

(Luke 6:37), Peter wanted to know if there were any limits.

Matthew 18:22 *Jesus answered, I tell you, not seven times, but seventy-seven times.*

Peter was likely stunned. Who could forgive seventy-seven times, especially if the offense was serious. In fact, Jesus isn't saying we can retaliate on the seventy-eighth time, but that we must forgive indefinitely.

This seems like a dreadful command, but there's a hidden blessing. Everyone in the world has a favorite sin which they're prone to repeat. It could be lying, lust, gossip, greed, or something unmentionable. Those who belong to Christ should promptly confess their sins (1 John 1:9), but we might wonder if God has a limit to how many times he'll forgive. Here's the good news: if God requires us to forgive others an indefinite number of times, he'll never turn us away for sinning one too many times—unless, of course, we don't forgive others.

Jesus illustrated this by telling the story of a man who owed the king *ten thousand bags of gold* (Matthew 18:24). Since the man couldn't repay, the king had pity on him and canceled his debt. But on the way out, the man encountered a fellow servant who was slightly in debt to him. Since the fellow servant couldn't repay at once, the man had him thrown into prison. When the king heard of this, he revoked his forgiveness and had the man turned over to be tortured. *This is how my heavenly Father will treat each of you unless you forgive your brother or sister from your heart* (Matthew 18:35), said Jesus.

I like to pray as Jesus taught, and when I come to the line, *forgive us our debts, as we also have forgiven our debtors* (Matthew 6:12), I'm reminded what a gracious arrangement this is. God will forgive me for whatever I've done, and simply requires that I forgive others. When I consider how often and badly I've sinned, this seems like a bargain. *For if you forgive other people when they sin against you, your heavenly Father will also forgive you. But if you do not forgive others their sins, your Father will not forgive your sins* (Matthew 6:14-15), said Jesus. This is a wonderful promise, and a very solemn warning.

*****

Matthew 20:1-2 *For the kingdom of heaven is like a landowner who went out early in the morning to hire workers for his vineyard. He agreed to pay them a denarius for the day.*

The landowner needed more workers, however, so he hired others at nine, noon, three, and five. Naturally, those who were hired late would expect less pay, but the landowner paid them all the same. When those who were hired first complained, he said, *Don't I have the right to do what I want with my own money?* (Matthew 20:15).

There are two things we should learn from this unusual parable. First, those who serve Christ for many years, will be in heaven with those who serve him briefly (Luke 23:43). In that sense, we're all paid the same. Second, we shouldn't expect more from Jesus Christ than what he gives to us. *[W]hen you have done everything you were told to do, [you] should say, We are unworthy servants; we have only done our duty* (Luke 17:10), said Jesus. Serving the Lord of glory is the highest honor there is, and he'll never owe us anything. Whatever we receive from him is a gift, for which we should be eternally thankful. This is the proper attitude for servants of Jesus Christ.

*****

Matthew 22:15-17 *Then the Pharisees went out and laid plans to trap him in his words. . . . Is it right to pay the imperial tax to Caesar or not?*

A more explosive question could not have been asked. The Jews were taxed by the Romans to the point of oppression, and many thought paying taxes to Caesar was morally wrong, since God alone was their king. If Jesus condoned paying taxes to Rome, he'd alienate everyone. But if he opposed paying taxes to Rome, he could be arrested for insurrection. There was nothing Jesus could do, it seemed. He was trapped.

Matthew 22:18-19 *But Jesus, knowing their evil intent, said, You hypocrites, why are you trying to trap me? Show me the coin used for paying the tax.*

They brought Jesus a Roman coin stamped with the image of Caesar. The suspense was overwhelming, but Jesus wasn't even nervous. *Whose image is this? And whose inscription? [he asked]. Caesar's, they replied. Then he said to them, So give back to Caesar what is Caesar's, and to God what is God's* (Matthew 22:20-21).

This amazed everyone. *[A]stonished by his answer, they became silent* (Luke 20:26), wrote Luke. *And they were amazed at him* (Mark 12:17), wrote Mark. *So they left him and went away* (Matthew 22:22), wrote Matthew. They wanted to silence Jesus, but Jesus silenced them.

Whenever I'm confronted, I can usually think of a witty reply about thirty minutes later. But Jesus was so close to his Father that he never lacked an answer. *For I did not speak on my own, but the Father who sent me commanded me to say all that I have spoken* (John 12:49), he said.

But Jesus' reply was more than witty: it was theologically and politically correct. Since everyone bears the image of God (Genesis 1:27), they rightly belong to God, and should give themselves back to God. But God has also given Caesar the right to govern within certain limits. *Let everyone be subject to the governing authorities* (Romans 13:1), wrote Paul.

The purpose of the church is not to run the government, and the purpose of the government is not to run the church. There's a proper role for each, which ought to be maintained until Jesus Christ returns. *[Give] to Caesar what is Caesar's, and to God what is God's.*

For Reflection and Review

- *Why is it hard to forgive sometimes?*
- *How does God help us forgive?*
- *Should the church try to control the world?*

Lesson 192

Matthew 23:1-3 *Then Jesus said to the crowds and to his disciples: The teachers of the law and the Pharisees sit in Moses' seat. So you must be careful to do everything they tell you. But do not do what they do, for they do not practice what they preach.*

This is the beginning of the most excoriating chapter in the Bible. Jesus Christ is enraged. Since the religious leaders would soon have him crucified, Jesus warned the people of their deceitfulness. He called them *blind guides* (Matthew 23:24), *snakes* and *vipers* (Matthew 23:33), and launched seven accusations against them, each beginning with the phrase, *Woe to you*. If Jesus wanted to avoid the cross he could've changed his tone. But since they were determined to kill him (and he was determined to die) he censured them so severely that the outcome was set: Jesus would be crucified.

The recurring charge that Jesus brought against the religious leaders was hypocrisy. *Woe to you, teachers of the law and Pharisees, you hypocrites!* he said. This little phrase occurs no fewer than six times in this brief discourse. No one likes to be called a hypocrite, but for the religious leaders it was especially condemning. We expect more from our leaders than we do from each other, and rightly so. All people in authority should be held to a higher standard.

A police officer was arrested for selling drugs which he obtained in the course of his work. Whenever he made an arrest, he kept some of the drugs to sell, and turned in the rest for evidence. The sentence for this kind of offense can be very severe because the public trust has been violated. The religious leaders pretended to stand for God, but rejected God's Messiah. They were hypocrites of the highest possible order.

Matthew 23:5 *Everything they do is done for people to see. They make their phylacteries wide and the tassels on their garments long.*

A phylactery is a small leather box, containing Bible verses, and was worn as a visual aid. *Tie them as symbols on your hands and bind them on your foreheads* (Deuteronomy 6:8), wrote Moses. Tassels were also a visual aid. *You will have these tassels to look at and so you will remember all the commands of the Lord* (Numbers 15:39), wrote Moses. There was nothing wrong with phylacteries or tassels. But instead of an aid to holiness, they became a badge of honor. The religious leaders were more concerned with people's approval, than they were with knowing God. Their religion was external, but not internal.

True religion has always been both external and internal. Jesus said, *let your light shine before others* (Matthew 5:16). *But when you pray, go into your room [and] close the door* (Matthew 6:6). If we pray and read the Bible, but never go to church, we've kept some of the internal, but not the external. If we often go to church, but never pray or read the Bible, we've kept some of the external, but not the internal. True devotion to Christ begins in the heart, and works itself out in what we do.

*****

Matthew 23:8-11 *But you are not to be called Rabbi, for you have one Teacher, and you are all brothers. And do not call anyone on earth father, for you have one Father, and he is in heaven. Nor are you to be called instructors, for you have one Instructor, the Messiah. The greatest among you will be your servant.*

First century Judaism was structured around a politico-religious hierarchy with the Sanhedrin at the top, the riffraff at the bottom, and everyone else in-between. Those at the top wanted everyone to know it, so titles became important. Becoming a Rabbi wasn't easy, and whoever earned the distinction wanted the recognition that came with it.

But Jesus had another idea: *you are all brothers*, he said. This was a radical concept, and still is. Our Father is in heaven, and all who believe are brothers and sisters. There's no spiritual hierarchy in the church. Greatness doesn't come from title or position, but from serving. *The greatest among you will be your servant*, said Jesus.

So the night before his death, he got up from dinner, took off his outer clothing, and wrapped himself in a towel. Then he poured water in a basin and began to wash the disciples' feet. Peter, Andrew, James, John, Philip, Bartholomew, Thomas, Matthew, James, Thaddaeus, Simon and Judas—even Judas Iscariot.

And he probably did a thorough job, running his fingers between their toes and carefully drying each of them. *I have set you an example that you should do as I have done for you. . . . Now that you know these things, you will be blessed if you do them* (John 13:15-17), he said. Here's the point: if Jesus was willing to do the humblest task, there's nothing too lowly for one of his followers.

The service was about to begin at church, when I decided to use the restroom. Someone had an accident in one of the stalls, and it was a terrible mess. I couldn't clean it myself because I had to start the service, but a respected elder walked in and willingly volunteered. No act of service is beneath a servant of Christ.

For Reflection and Review

- *Why did Jesus choose to offend the religious leaders?*
- *Is true religion primarily internal or external?*
- *Why is humility good for community?*

Lesson 193

Matthew 23:23 *Woe to you, teachers of the law and Pharisees, you hypocrites! You give a tenth of your spices—mint, dill and cumin. But you have neglected the more important matters of the law—justice, mercy and faithfulness. You should have practiced the latter, without neglecting the former.*

The religious leaders paid attention to little things (like tithing from their garden) but missed the most important things (like justice, mercy, and faithfulness). Everything in the Bible is equally inspired (2 Timothy 3:16), but not everything is equally important. *He was delivered over to death for our sins and was raised to life for our justification* (Romans 4:25) is more important than *Do not cook a young goat in its mother's milk* (Exodus 23:19).

Whenever we give too much attention to a less important passage, we make the same mistake the religious leaders did. A proper reading of God's word will give the right amount of emphasis to any given passage. We should do everything God requires, of course, but give the most attention to the most important things.

Matthew 23:27-28 *You are like whitewashed tombs, which look beautiful on the outside but on the inside are full of the bones of the dead and everything unclean. In the same way, on the outside you appear to people as righteous but on the inside you are full of hypocrisy and wickedness.*

Tombs in Jesus' day were often painted white in order to honor the dead, but also to guard against contamination. *[A]nyone who touches a human bone or a grave, will be unclean for seven days* (Numbers 19:16), wrote Moses. Tombs were made beautiful outwardly, but were smelly and rotten inside. That was Jesus' assessment of the Pharisees: outwardly beautiful, inwardly corrupt.

This is Jesus at his most judgmental. He's not merely judging actions, but also motives. This seems to contradict his earlier teaching: *Do not judge, or you too will be judged* (Matthew 7:1).

But it's not wrong for Jesus to judge, because Jesus is the judge. Some will hear him say, *Well done, good and faithful servant!* (Matthew 25:21). Others will hear him say, *throw that worthless servant outside, into the darkness, where there will be weeping and gnashing of teeth* (Matthew 25:30). But everyone will give an account to Jesus Christ, because Jesus is the judge.

Matthew 23:33 *You brood of vipers! How will you escape being condemned to hell?*

The word translated *hell* in this verse is *Gehenna*. This was a valley outside Jerusalem which may've served as a garbage dump. During the reigns of Ahaz and Manasseh it was used as a place to burn children as human sacrifices to idols (2 Chronicles 28:3; 33:6).

When Jesus wanted a metaphor for hell, Gehenna was an obvious choice. *It is better for you to lose one part of your body than for your whole body to go into [Gehenna]* (Matthew 5:30). *Do not be afraid of those who kill the body but cannot kill the soul. Rather, be afraid of the One who can destroy both soul and body in [Gehenna]* (Matthew 10:28), he said.

These are some of the hardest words in the Bible, but are meant to awaken us to the fact of eternal suffering, and lead us to Christ for salvation. Jesus taught more about hell than anyone else in the Bible because he didn't want people to go there.

A book came out several years ago titled, *The Worst Case Scenario Survival Handbook*. Chapter titles include: *How to Escape From a Giant Octopus. How to Survive if Your Parachute Doesn't Open. How to Stop a Car With No Brakes. How to Survive a Plummeting Elevator. How to Survive Being Buried Alive. How to Survive an Airplane Crash.* And, *How to Survive if Lost in the Jungle*.

The only chapter missing is *What to do if You Wake Up in Hell*, because there is nothing you can do if you wake up in hell. It's the ultimate, eternal, everlasting, never-ending, worst case scenario. That's why the Apostle Paul said *now is the time of God's favor, now is the day of salvation* (2 Corinthians 6:2).

Matthew 23:37 *Jerusalem, Jerusalem, you who kill the prophets and stone those sent to you, how often I have longed to gather your children together, as a hen gathers her chicks under her wings, and you were not willing.*

Jesus was using imagery from the book of Psalms. *[H]ide me in the shadow of your wings* (Psalm 17:8). *[U]nder his wings you will find refuge* (Psalm 91:4). And, *I will take refuge in the shadow of your wings* (Psalm 57:1). Jesus longs to gather sinners under the protection of his wings, to shelter us *from the coming wrath* (1 Thessalonians 1:10). But how does this work?

A farmer's field caught fire and, when he surveyed the damage, he noticed one of his hens perished in the flames. He turned it over with his foot, and three little chicks scurried out from beneath her charred body. If you think of Jesus bearing God's wrath on the cross, you can imagine taking shelter beneath his outstretched arms, like chicks beneath the wing. *For God so loved the world that he gave his one and only Son, that whoever believes in him shall not perish but have eternal life* (John 3:16), wrote John.

For Reflection and Review

- *How do we know which parts of the Bible are most important?*
- *What kind of judge is Jesus Christ?*
- *What do you think about hell?*

Lesson 194

Matthew 24:2 *Truly I tell you, not one stone here will be left on another; every one will be thrown down.*

The temple was one of the most beautiful buildings in the world, and had been under construction for decades. Many of the stones were massive, and some weighed almost a million pounds. But within forty years, the Romans captured Jerusalem, and set fire to the temple. The gold leaf on the roof melted between the stones, and the Romans pried them apart to recover it. No two stones were left together, just as Jesus foretold.

Biblical prophecy not only proves the Bible is God's word, but that Jesus is God's Messiah. Christ would be born in Bethlehem (Micah 5:2), would be descended from David (Jeremiah 23:5), would perform miracles (Isaiah 34:5-6), would ride a donkey into Jerusalem while receiving praise (Zechariah 9:9), would be rejected (Isaiah 53:3), would die for our sins (Isaiah 53:5), and would rise from the dead (Psalm 16:10).

Imagine a meeting between a spy and a government employee, in which the spy was to identify himself by seven pre-arranged signs. First, he was to write a letter to the government employee saying he was in town. Second, he was to wait until a certain date. Third, he was to go to a certain statue. Fourth, he was to wear red socks. Fifth, he was to stand with his middle finger in a book. Sixth, when approached, he was to comment on the statue. Seventh, he was to say he was from Oklahoma. The prearranged signs would guarantee that he was the proper contact. Likewise, the prophecies that Jesus fulfilled guarantee he's God's Messiah (source unknown).

Matthew 24:10 *[M]any will turn away from the faith and will betray and hate each other.*

Instead of the world becoming increasingly Christian, we can expect much of the world to become post-Christian. There was a time when most of Europe was at least culturally Christian, but today church attendance there is extremely low. Many can remember a time when the United States was at least culturally Christian, but today it has become post-Christian as well.

I know I'm getting old, but I can still remember when chastity was a virtue, and premarital sex was sin. Living together apart from marriage was called *living in sin*, and homosexuality was *an abomination*. Today the highest civic virtue is tolerance, and we tolerate everything except calling sin by name. We live in an age of national apostasy.

But apostasy is personal before it's national, and often comes with a sense of impending doom. A college professor was raised in a Christian home and studied for the ministry. But then he rejected Christianity and now has frightening thoughts.

When I fell away from my faith—not just in the Bible as God's inspired word, but in Christ as the only way of salvation, and eventually from the view that Christ was himself divine, and beyond that from the view that there is an all-powerful God in charge of this world—I still wondered, deep down inside: could I have been right after all? What if I was right then but wrong now? Will I burn in hell forever? The fear of death gripped me for years, and there are still moments when I wake up at night in a cold sweat.

Whenever we're tempted to walk away from Christ we ought to reconsider. The Christian life isn't easy, but it's not as hard as eternal misery. And if you know someone who's fallen away from Christ, don't forget about them. *Whoever turns a sinner from the error of their way will save them from death and cover over a multitude of sins* (James 5:20), wrote James.

Matthew 24:14 *And this gospel of the kingdom will be preached in the whole world as a testimony to all nations, and then the end will come.*

In spite of a great apostasy, Jesus also predicted a great advance of his kingdom. This must have seemed optimistic in light of how small the movement was at the time of Jesus' death. The core group was just a hundred twenty people (Acts 1:15). But it expanded dramatically on the day of Pentecost and, today, is the largest religion in the world.

And with the help of technology, Bible translation is happening faster than ever. Some estimates say by the year 2025 every known people-group will have part of the Bible in their own language. This may signal the end of the age since Jesus said, *this gospel of the kingdom will be preached in the whole world . . . and then the end will come.*

It's remarkable that Jesus predicted the globalization of Christianity, and a great apostasy, since they seem to be contradictory. Globalization suggests progress, and apostasy suggests regress. One speaks of gaining ground, the other of losing ground. But over the course of history that's precisely what we find. Christianity is always growing somewhere, and dying somewhere else. This would be difficult to predict apart from the mind of God.

For Reflection and Review

- *How does biblical prophecy prove that Jesus is the Messiah?*
- *Have you ever been tempted to turn away from Christ?*
- *Do you think Christ will return before you die?*

Lesson 195

Matthew 24:24 *For false messiahs and false prophets will appear and perform great signs and wonders to deceive, if possible, even the elect.*

Anyone who claims to speak for God, but contradicts the gospel, is either a false teacher, a false prophet, or a false messiah. *[E]ven if we or an angel from heaven should preach a gospel other than the one we preached to you, let them be under God's curse!* (Galatians 1:8), wrote Paul. Nevertheless, history has produced a long line of false teachers, false prophets, and false messiahs—some even doing miracles.

For example, Pharaoh's magicians turned their staffs into snakes, and water into blood (Exodus 7:12, 7:22). And the Bible speaks of a false prophet at the end of the age who'll do *great signs, even causing fire to come down from heaven to the earth in full view of the people. Because of the signs . . . it deceived the inhabitants of the earth. It ordered them to set up an image in honor of the beast. . . . It also forced all people . . . to receive a mark on their right hands or on their foreheads, so that they could not buy or sell unless they had the mark* (Revelation 13:13-17), wrote John.

But if someone does greater miracles than Jesus Christ, how do we know whom to believe? What if someone else comes back from the dead? What if they're attended by glorious angels? What if their miracles are more compelling than Jesus' miracles? How do we know who speaks for God?

Thankfully, we're not in the dark. *Anyone who chooses to do the will of God will find out whether my teaching comes from God* (John 7:17), said Jesus. If you want to do God's will, no matter what, God will lead you straight to Jesus Christ and keep you there. But if you're not resolved to do God's will, you're on your own. You are, in fact, already deceived.

Furthermore, those who belong to Christ have the Spirit of Christ to guide them. *[H]is sheep follow him because they know his voice. But they will never follow a stranger; in fact, they will run away from him because they do not recognize a stranger's voice* (John 10:4-5). *My sheep listen to my voice; I know them, and they follow me* (John 10:27), said Jesus. Christians aren't persuaded primarily by miracles, logic, or majority opinion. We're persuaded by the Spirit of Christ himself.

Matthew 24:35 *Heaven and earth will pass away, but my words will never pass away.*

Two thousand years later, Jesus is the most quoted person in the history of the world—and he never wrote a book! If you want to be quoted, you should at least write a book. But Jesus never wrote a sentence that we know of, and yet he's the most quoted person to ever live. Who else could pull this off?

*****

Matthew 25:14-15 *Again, it will be like a man going on a journey, who called his servants and entrusted his wealth to them. To one he gave five bags of gold, to another two bags, and to another one bag, each according to his ability.*

Jesus didn't want his followers to be idle while he was away, so he gave this parable about investing our lives in God's kingdom. We don't all have the same abilities, but we all have the ability to do something. And we'll give an account to Christ, when he returns, for how we invested our lives.

The first and second servant did well, and earned their master's approval. *Well done, good and faithful servant! You have been faithful with a few things; I will put you in charge of many things. Come and share your master's happiness* (Matthew 25:23), said Jesus.

Friends may've thought these servants were foolish by investing so heavily in the kingdom of God, instead of pleasing themselves. But the servants turned out to be wise, and gained eternal happiness. They denied themselves for a while, but their investment paid off wonderfully.

The third servant didn't do as well. His ability was less than the others, so he thought it wasn't worth investing. Instead of doing what he could, he simply did nothing at all. But when he gave an account *His master replied, You wicked, lazy servant* (Matthew 25:26). These are words that'll ring in people's ears forever.

Years ago I worked at a busy factory where the employees could be almost anywhere. This made them hard to track, and one was found asleep in the back of a closet. He thought he could get away with being lazy, but he was discovered and had to face the consequences.

And there will be consequences for those who fail to serve Christ: *throw that worthless servant outside, into the darkness, where there will be weeping and gnashing of teeth* (Matthew 25:30), said Jesus. His lack of initiative showed the worthless servant wasn't a servant of Christ at all. And he was eternally condemned.

Each of us will give an account to Christ for how we spend our lives. We can spend them on ourselves, and be eternally condemned. Or we can invest them in his kingdom, and gain an eternal reward. *Be very careful, then, how you live—not as unwise but as wise, making the most of every opportunity* (Ephesians 5:15-16), wrote Paul.

For Reflection and Review

- *Why are Christians persuaded to follow Christ instead of someone else?*
- *Why is Jesus the most quoted person to ever live?*
- *Why should we invest our lives in God's kingdom?*

Lesson 196

Matthew 25:31-33 *When the Son of Man comes in his glory, and all the angels with him, he will sit on his glorious throne. All the nations will be gathered before him, and he will separate the people one from another as a shepherd separates the sheep from the goats. He will put the sheep on his right and the goats on his left.*

In this remarkable parable (the last in Matthew's gospel) Jesus provided a vivid account of the final judgment. The only two categories are sheep and goats: true believers and unbelievers. Everyone is present, in one group or the other. You may see someone you love in the other group, but there's no crossing over. The time for that is past. The tension is overwhelming as both groups wait for the King's pronouncement.

Then the King will say to those on his right, Come, you who are blessed by my Father; take your inheritance, the kingdom prepared for you since the creation of the world. For I was hungry and you gave me something to eat, I was thirsty and you gave me something to drink, I was a stranger and you invited me in, I needed clothes and you clothed me, I was sick and you looked after me, I was in prison and you came to visit me (Matthew 25:34-35).

These are wonderful words, but the righteous fear there's been a mistake, since they don't recall caring for Christ in this way. Then *The King will reply, Truly I tell you, whatever you did for one of the least of these brothers and sisters of mine, you did for me* (Matthew 25:40).

Jesus' *brothers and sisters* are those who put their faith in him. *Jesus is not ashamed to call [us] brothers and sisters* (Hebrews 2:11), says Hebrews. Our brother is the king, and we are part of his royal family. Whenever we're kind to other believers, we're being kind to him. This has important implications for the church.

A friend of mine was pastoring a new church, and told me about a problem he was having. A man was attending who didn't fit in very well due to a mental illness. He didn't bathe, smelled badly, and wasn't well received. My friend wondered what to do, and I told him to be careful because the man was probably Jesus in disguise. Whatever we do for the least of his brothers and sisters, we do for him.

Matthew 25:41-43 *Then he will say to those on his left, Depart from me, you who are cursed, into the eternal fire prepared for the devil and his angels. For I was hungry and you gave me nothing to eat, I was thirsty and you gave me nothing to drink, I was a stranger and you did not invite me in, I needed clothes and you did not clothe me, I was sick and in prison and you did not look after me.*

The wicked are also surprised by Jesus' pronouncement since they don't remember neglecting him. But even if they went to church, they never cared enough for God's people to lend a helping hand. By neglecting Jesus' brothers and sisters, they also neglected Christ.

This is not to say that Christians shouldn't care for those outside the faith. Jesus taught us to love our neighbors (Matthew 19:19) regardless of their religion. But needy believers ought to be our first concern. *[L]et us do good to all people, especially to those who belong to the family of believers* (Galatians 6:10), wrote Paul.

Matthew 25:46 *Then they will go away to eternal punishment, but the righteous to eternal life.*

The wicked and the righteous have this in common: both will live forever. Since everyone is made in the image of God, and God is eternal, we'll never cease to exist. There was a time when we were not, but will never be a time when we are not. This is why it's so important to know where we are going.

A man was stranded on a barren planet, and all he had were two small pills. One would bring him instant death, and the other would make him live forever. His life was so bleak that he decided to end it all by eating the pill of death. But, several minutes later, he discovered he ate the wrong pill. One of the best words in heaven, and worst in hell, is *eternal*. The purpose of *here and now* is to get ready for *there and then*.

For Reflection and Review

- *Why should we give careful attention to how we treat believers?*
- *Why do most people think they'll live forever?*
- *How should our knowledge of eternity affect our daily lives?*

Lesson 197

Matthew 26:17 *[T]he disciples came to Jesus and asked, Where do you want us to make preparations for you to eat the Passover?*

Passover recalled the important event that convinced Pharaoh to let God's people go from Egyptian slavery. Israelite families slaughtered a lamb, and applied the blood to the door frames of their homes (Exodus 12:7). When God struck down the firstborn males in Egypt, he saw the blood and *passed over* them.

Jesus had to die during Passover because he was *the Lamb of God, who takes away the sin of the world!* (John 1:29). The Passover lamb saved the Israelites from Egyptian slavery, and the Lamb of God saves us from the slavery of sin. Jesus was getting ready to eat this final meal with his disciples.

Matthew 26:20-21 *When evening came, Jesus was reclining at the table with the Twelve. And while they were eating, he said, Truly I tell you, one of you will betray me.*

We might imagine every eye turned toward Judas Iscariot, since he didn't truly believe (John 6:64). But, knowing the badness of their own hearts, the disciples doubted themselves. *They were very sad and began to say to him one after the other, Surely you don't mean me, Lord?*

Like the disciples, we should never be too confident of our own moral ability. *[I]f you think you are standing firm, be careful that you don't fall* (1 Corinthians 10:12), wrote Paul. When we consider the evil in our own hearts (Jeremiah 17:9), and how often we've betrayed the Lord in little ways, we'll put no confidence in ourselves, but only in Christ to keep us *firm to the end* (1 Corinthians 1:8).

Matthew 26:25 *Then Judas, the one who would betray him, said, Surely you don't mean me, Rabbi? Jesus answered, You have said so.*

Judas had already made an arrangement with the religious leaders to betray the Lord (Matthew 26:14-16). They feared a riot, however, so they didn't want it to happen during Passover (Matthew 26:5), when so many people were in Jerusalem. But the religious leaders weren't in charge of Jesus' death, even though they thought they were. *No one takes it from me, but I lay it down of my own accord* (John 10:18), said Jesus. Jesus would die during Passover, just as he determined.

Matthew 26:26-28 *While they were eating, Jesus took bread, and when he had given thanks, he broke it and gave it to his disciples, saying, Take and eat; this is my body. Then he took a cup, and when he had given thanks, he gave it to them, saying, Drink from it, all of you. This is my blood of the covenant, which is poured out for many for the forgiveness of sins.*

This was Jesus' final meal, and he used it to introduce the *Lord's Supper* (1 Corinthians 11:20), which the church has observed ever since. The bread represents Jesus' body, and the cup represents his blood. They both remind us of his death for our salvation. Jesus bore the punishment for our sins so that we could be forgiven (Isaiah 53:5).

But who should receive the Lord's Supper? Anyone who wants to? Only those who are good enough? What about children? The question is answered nicely by a reliable catechism. *Who are to come to the table of the Lord? Those who are truly displeased with themselves because of their sins and yet trust that these are forgiven them and that their remaining weakness is covered by the suffering and death of Christ, and who also desire more and more to strengthen their faith and amend their life. . . .* (Heidelberg Catechism, Question 81. See also 1 Corinthians 10-11). The Lord's Supper should never be taken thoughtlessly, or carelessly, but may be received by anyone who truly believes in Jesus Christ, and is trying to follow him.

*****

Matthew 26:36 *Then Jesus went with his disciples to a place called Gethsemane.*

This was a garden, outside Jerusalem, where Jesus often went with his disciples (John 18:1-2). Judas was no longer with them, but he knew where he could find them. *Gethsemane* means *oil press*, and olives were probably pressed there to extract their oil.

Here Jesus prayed until *his sweat was like drops of blood* (Lk.22:44). He may've developed *hematidrosis*, a medical condition caused by stress, in which capillaries in the sweat glands rupture, causing blood and sweat to mix. Like olives being crushed *it was the Lord's will to crush him* (Isaiah 53:10), wrote Isaiah. And he was *in anguish* (Luke 22:44), wrote Luke.

Matthew 26:38 *My soul is overwhelmed with sorrow to the point of death.*

Jesus wasn't exaggerating. The depth of his sorrow was so overwhelming it nearly killed him before he went to the cross. It wasn't the physical pain he dreaded so much as bearing the Father's wrath against our sin. This was his greatest source of agony, and something we'll never have to experience.

Matthew 26:39 *My Father, if it is possible, may this cup be taken from me.*

Jesus referred to the cup of God's wrath mentioned by the prophets (Isaiah 51:17, Jeremiah 25:15). Nothing was more important to Jesus than pleasing his heavenly Father (John 8:29), so nothing was worse for him than bearing his Father's furious wrath. He could barely bring himself to do it.

If there was any other way for the world to be saved, Jesus wanted to avoid the cross. But there was no other way for the world to be saved. The death of a million angels couldn't atone for our sin—only the death of God's Son could do that. If there was any other way for the world to be saved, the Father would've answered Jesus' prayer.

Matthew 26:39b *Yet not as I will, but as you will.*

The one who always did his Father's will would do it to the end. *Not your will but mine be done,* is what we say to God whenever we sin. In effect, this is what Adam and Eve said when they ate the forbidden fruit (Genesis 3:6). And, clearly, we are their offspring. By putting our will ahead of God's will, paradise was lost. But by putting his Father's will ahead of his own will, Jesus won it back for us. As soon as he prayed, therefore, Jesus went out and surrendered to the guards.

For Reflection and Review

- *What is the meaning of the Lord's Supper?*
- *Why was Gethsemane an appropriate name for the garden where Jesus prayed?*
- *Why was Jesus afraid of the cross?*

Lesson 198

Matthew 27:46 *About three in the afternoon Jesus cried out in a loud voice, Eli, Eli, lema sabachthani? (which means My God, my God, why have you forsaken me?).*

As the time of his death drew near, Jesus nearly screamed the saddest sentence in the Bible: *My God, my God, why have you forsaken me?* We'll never grasp the agony of the one who walked so perfectly with God as he bore the sins of the world. The intimate fellowship Jesus enjoyed with his heavenly Father, every day of his life, was apparently broken. Darkness filled his soul.

Jesus felt these words more deeply than anyone ever could, but he wasn't the first to say them. *My God, my God, why have you forsaken me?* is a quotation from King David (Psalm 22:1). It's the first sentence from the twenty-second Psalm which parallels Jesus' death in many other ways.

All who see me mock me; they hurl insults, shaking their heads. He trusts in the Lord, they say, let the Lord rescue him. Let him deliver him, since he delights in him. Yet you brought me out of the womb; you made me trust in you, even at my mother's breast. From birth I was cast on you; from my mother's womb you have been my God (Psalm 22:7-10).

I am poured out like water, and all my bones are out of joint. My heart has turned to wax; it has melted within me. My mouth is dried up like a potsherd, and my tongue sticks to the roof of my mouth; you lay me in the dust of death. Dogs surround me, a pack of villains encircles me; they pierce my hands and my feet. All my bones are on display; people stare and gloat over me. They divide my clothes among them and cast lots for my garment (Psalm 22:14-18).

To fully appreciate these words we must recall that they were written about a thousand years before the crucifixion. And, yet, Jesus fulfilled them perfectly. Furthermore, the Psalm ends on a positive note, describing the good effect of Jesus' death: *Posterity will serve him; future generations will be told about the Lord. They will proclaim his righteousness, declaring to a people yet unborn: He has done it!* (Psalm 22: 30-31). Since Jesus knew the end of the Psalm, his cry of despair was also a cry of hope. In his darkest hour Jesus looked ahead to what his death would accomplish.

*****

Matthew 28:1 *After the Sabbath, at dawn on the first day of the week, Mary Magdalene and the other Mary went to look at the tomb.*

Jesus was crucified Friday morning, and died that afternoon. With Pilate's permission he was promptly entombed by Nicodemus and Joseph of Arimathea. They had to be done before sunset (since that's when the Sabbath began) so the burial was done rather hastily (John 19:38-42).

To better honor Jesus' body, some women prepared additional spices for his burial, and came to the tomb early Sunday morning, after the Sabbath had passed (Luke 24:1). Jesus had predicted his resurrection several times, but the disciples didn't know what he meant (Luke 18:31-34). The fact that these women brought spices for Jesus' body shows they had no expectation of his resurrection.

Matthew 28:2 *There was a violent earthquake, for an angel of the Lord came down from heaven and, going to the tomb, rolled back the stone and sat on it.*

The angel rolled back the stone, not to let Jesus out, but to let the witnesses in. According to Luke's gospel, there were actually two angels (Luke 24:4). This not a contradiction, but simply a fuller account. *In their fright the women bowed down with their faces to the ground, but the men said to them, Why do you look for the living among the dead? He is not here; he has risen!* (Luke 24:5-6).

It was early in the morning and the sun was beginning to rise. The light of understanding was beginning to rise on these women as well. Jesus' crucifixion was a tragedy to them, and all their hope was buried with him. But the God of hope raised Jesus from the dead, and now their hope was rising too.

It's important to note that the first witnesses were women, because the testimony of women was considered less reliable than the testimony of men. If the gospel writers invented this story, the apostles would've arrived first to provide a unified and credible witness of the empty tomb. The fact that all four gospels report the first witnesses were women shows they only cared about presenting the facts. This is simply another way that the gospels reveal their authenticity.

Matthew 28:8-9 *So the women hurried away from the tomb, afraid yet filled with joy, and ran to tell his disciples. Suddenly Jesus met them. Greetings, he said. They came to him, clasped his feet and worshiped him.*

Because they were able to clasp his feet, the women understood that Jesus had risen physically, not just spiritually. The empty tomb was compelling evidence for the resurrection of Jesus Christ, but it wasn't the only evidence. *[Jesus] appeared to [his disciples] over a period of forty days and spoke about the kingdom of God* (Acts 1:3), wrote Luke.

If Jesus' body was missing from the tomb, but he didn't make appearances, then another explanation might be possible. (Perhaps the body was stolen). Or, if Jesus made appearances, but his body was still in the tomb, then his appearances would've been ghostly, and not very credible. But since Jesus' body was not in the tomb, and he appeared in the flesh many times, the disciples could be absolutely certain that Jesus had conquered death.

The resurrection of Jesus Christ is as verifiably certain as any event in history can be. It's the one miracle that's sufficient to justify our faith, and is completely open to investigation. The reason more people don't believe in the resurrection of Jesus Christ is because it requires a change of life. Since most people don't want to change their life, they choose not to believe in the resurrection. It has little to do with evidence, and much to do with change.

For Reflection and Review

- *Why did Jesus cry out, My God, my God, why have you forsaken me?*
- *How do the female witnesses add credibility to the gospel accounts of Jesus' resurrection?*
- *Why don't more people believe in Jesus Christ?*

Lesson 199

Matthew 28:11 *While the women were on their way, some of the guards went into the city and reported to the chief priests everything that had happened.*

After Jesus was buried, the religious leaders went to Pilate and requested a guard for the tomb, because they knew that Jesus predicted his resurrection (Matthew 27:64). Pilate wanted this ordeal to be over so he said, *Take a guard . . . Go, make the tomb as secure as you know how* (Matthew 27:65).

We don't know how many guards were at the tomb, but it was probably more than a few. Jesus had many disciples in town, and it would've been foolish for the guards to be outnumbered. We should probably think of at least dozens of guards standing outside the tomb of Jesus Christ. But when the angels appeared, *The guards were so afraid . . . they shook and became like dead men* (Matthew 28:4). When their strength returned, they went and told the religious leaders everything that happened.

At this point we expect the guards and religious leaders to all become Christians. *[They] killed the author of life, but God raised him from the dead* (Acts 3:15). This was a perfect time to repent and believe. But instead, they engaged in a coverup. The religious leaders gave the soldiers money to say, *His disciples came during the night and stole him away while we were asleep* (Matthew 28:13).

But were they all asleep? And if they were all asleep, how did they know what happened to the body? And if they weren't all asleep, why didn't those who were awake also wakeup the others? This is just another example of people refusing to believe in Jesus Christ regardless of the evidence.

But this is precisely what Jesus predicted. *[T]hey will not be convinced even if someone rises from the dead* (Luke 16:31), he said. And, since many still refuse to believe in the resurrection of Jesus Christ, they've had to come up with alternate theories.

The *swoon theory* argues that Jesus didn't really die on the cross, but only fainted. He recovered in the tomb and the disciples mistook it for a resurrection. The *hallucination theory* argues that the disciples only hallucinated Jesus' resurrection appearances. The *identical twin theory* argues that Jesus had a twin who convinced the disciples that he was Jesus, raised from the dead. The *unknown tomb* theory argues that the disciples mistook an empty tomb for the one Jesus was buried in, and jumped to the wrong conclusion. A final theory argues that Jesus really did rise from the dead, but that doesn't prove he's the Messiah.

In spite of alternate theories, however, the disciples preached the gospel throughout the Roman empire, and many believed. This created a great commotion and, eventually, disturbing a grave was made a capital offense. This is documented on a slab of marble called the *Nazareth Inscription* which is currently housed in the Louvre Museum. Whether the decree was a response to the resurrection of Jesus Christ, or just a coincidence, is ours to decide.

Matthew 28:16-17 *Then the eleven disciples went to Galilee, to the mountain where Jesus had told them to go. When they saw him, they worshiped him; but some doubted.*

Even after Jesus rose from the dead, and appeared to his disciples, some struggled with doubt. The evidence was clear, but that didn't make it easy to believe. Who could believe that God became a man and lived among us? Who could believe that he died on a cross for our sins? Who could believe that he rose from the dead to give eternal life to all who receive him? (John 1:12). These are all true, of course, but that doesn't make them easy to believe.

We can also be slow to believe because we don't want to be disappointed. If someone tells me that I've won a million dollars, I'll believe it when the money is in my bank account. Likewise, when Jesus appeared another time it says, *they still did not believe it because of joy and amazement* (Luke 24:41). If Jesus rose from the dead then all our sins are forgiven, and we'll spend forever with him in the best of all possible worlds. This is the best news there could ever be, and it just happens to be true.

Matthew 28:18 *Then Jesus came to them and said, All authority in heaven and on earth has been given to me.*

Jesus wanted the disciples to know who was in charge. He didn't say, *Some authority in heaven and on earth has been given to me;* or, *Most authority in heaven and on earth has been given to me;* but *All authority in heaven and earth has been given to me.*

Jesus has authority over the entire universe, including planet earth. He has authority over the world's economies, governments, and militaries. He has authority over our lives, the lives of our children, and even our grandchildren. Jesus Christ is Lord of all.

Matthew 28:19-20 *Therefore go and make disciples of all nations, baptizing them in the name of the Father and of the Son and of the Holy Spirit, and teaching them to obey everything I have commanded you.*

The apostles did this by going out and starting churches. Those who believed were baptized, and given further instruction on what to believe and obey. This is the mission of the church, and is often called *the Great Commission*.

If you want a mission for your life, this is a good place to start. I've personalized the Great Commission this way: *My mission is to make more and better disciples of Jesus Christ, beginning with myself, my family, and others as God enables me.* I begin with myself because I can't lead others where I will not go. I proceed to my family because they are nearest and dearest to me. Then I proceed to others because God *wants all people to be saved and to come to a knowledge of the truth* (1 Timothy 2:4), wrote Paul. Imagine what would happen if all God's people embraced the Great Commission!

Matthew 28:20b *And surely I am with you always, to the very end of the age.*

As the disciples went out to preach the gospel, they could be assured that Christ was with them. He'll never leave us or forsake us (Hebrews 13:5), but is uniquely with us whenever we share his message.

A friend of mine was having lunch with a coworker at Chinese restaurant, and used the opportunity to explain the way of salvation. For thirty minutes he explained how sin separates us from God, how Christ paid for our sins on the cross, and how we need to believe in Christ to be saved. Just before they left, his coworker opened a fortune cookie that said: *Advice just heard should be followed.*

For Reflection and Review

- *What are some alternate theories to the resurrection of Christ?*
- *Why was it hard for some of Jesus' disciples to believe that he rose from the dead?*
- *How does it help us to share the gospel if we know that Christ is with us?*

Lesson 200

Mark 1:1 *The beginning of the good news about Jesus the Messiah.*

Although anonymous, the gospel according to Mark was most likely written by John Mark (Acts 12:12), who was associated with the Apostle Peter (1 Peter 5:13), and from whom he received his information. It was probably written around AD 50, primarily to Gentile readers. Nearly all of Mark's material is also found in Matthew or Luke, so little is covered here.

Mark 4:26-27 *This is what the kingdom of God is like. A man scatters seed on the ground. Night and day, whether he sleeps or gets up, the seed sprouts and grows, though he does not know how.*

This parable is found only in Mark's gospel, and teaches that God's kingdom comes from spreading God's word, (Luke 8:11), just as a harvest comes from scattering seed. Three things should be noticed:

Notice first, unless the seed is planted, there can be no harvest. This is why the most important work of the church is to preach God's word. If the church doesn't start hospitals, someone else will. If the church doesn't build orphanages, someone else will. If the church doesn't feed the poor, someone else will. But if the church doesn't preach God's word, no one else will. The word of God must be planted into the hearts of people everywhere.

Notice second, the seed has power in itself. *Night and day, whether he sleeps or gets up, the seed sprouts and grows, though he does not know how.* The farmer can stay awake if he wants to, but it won't help the seed grow. He can wring his hands if he wants to, but that won't help the seed grow either. He can shout at the seed, or sing to it, but that won't help it grow either. The seed has the power to grow in itself, and doesn't need the farmer's help once it has been planted. God's word has power, and is able to grow on its own.

Notice third, the harvest can't be rushed. *All by itself the soil produces grain—first the stalk, then the head, then the full kernel in the head* (Mark 4:28). Many were hoping the kingdom of God would appear at once, but Jesus taught it would take some time (Luke 19:11-27). The return of Christ could happen at any moment (Luke 12:40), but it could also be a thousand years from now. Christians should be ready to greet the Lord today, but be willing to wait as long as necessary.

Mark 4:29 *As soon as the grain is ripe, he puts the sickle to it, because the harvest has come.*

The harvest is an image of the consummation of God's kingdom. Here it refers to the righteous, but elsewhere to the wicked. *The angel swung his sickle on the earth, gathered its grapes and threw them into the great winepress of God's wrath. They were trampled in the winepress outside the city, and blood flowed out of the press, rising as high as the horses' bridles* (Revelation 14:19-20), wrote John. God's sickle is coming to earth. The righteous will be harvested for heaven, and the wicked will be harvested for hell.

*****

Mark 7:21-22 *For it is from within, out of a person's heart, that evil thoughts come—sexual immorality, theft, murder, adultery, greed, malice, deceit, lewdness, envy, slander, arrogance and folly.*

Many to whom Christ preached were concerned about what they ate, for fear it would make them unclean before God. But Jesus taught it wasn't what went into their mouths that made them unclean, but what came out of their hearts.

Many believe their hearts are good, no matter what their hands have done. They imagine that deep inside every sinner, there's a part that's pure, and that's the part God sees. He knows the wicked things we've done, but also knows that, deep inside, there's goodness and love. Unfortunately, that's never taught in the Bible.

According to Christ, the heart is the source of all our sins: *sexual immorality, theft, murder, adultery, greed, malice, deceit, lewdness, envy, slander, arrogance and folly*. The heart isn't a holy place, but a sin-factory that never shuts down. Day and night it manufactures every abomination under heaven. The persuasion that our hearts are good only shows that our hearts have deceived us. *The heart is deceitful above all things and beyond cure* (Jeremiah 17:9), wrote Jeremiah.

During the second world war, Nazi doctors conducted experiments on Jewish prisoners. Identical twins were sown together to see if they could be conjoined. Muscles and nerves were removed from others without the use of anesthesia. Head trauma was studied by bludgeoning a man's skull with a hammer until he went insane. After the war, some of these doctors were brought to trial and appeared to be normal, decent, educated people who loved their families. They weren't better or worse than other people—just ordinary.

This is the human condition, and the reason we need to be saved. Since our hearts are wicked and deceitful, what we really need is a new heart. *I will give you a new heart and put a new spirit in you; I will remove from you your heart of stone and give you a heart of flesh* (Ezekiel 36:26), said God.

Jesus died on the cross to take away our sins, and gives us the Holy Spirit when we believe. And *he who began a good work in you will carry it on to completion until the day of Christ Jesus* (Philippians 1:6), wrote Paul. Then we'll be cured of heart disease, and our hearts will be pure forever.

For Reflection and Review

- *How can God's people spread his word?*
- *Are unbelievers able to do good things?*
- *How is God changing your heart?*

Lesson 201

Mark 7:32 *[S]ome people brought to him a man who was deaf and could hardly talk, and they begged Jesus to place his hand on him.*

Since the man could hardly talk, he'd probably been deaf most of his life, or maybe all of it. Since hearing and speaking are the primary means of human communication, he'd truly missed out on much. But *Jesus put his fingers into the man's ears. Then he spit and touched the man's tongue. He looked up to heaven and with a deep sigh said to him, Ephphatha! (which means Be opened!). At this, the man's ears were opened, his tongue was loosened and he began to speak plainly* (Mark 7:33-35).

For the rest of his life this man enjoyed hearing words from others, and sharing words with them. After Jesus died and rose, in fact, he may've heard the gospel and passed it on. This is the highest use of hearing and speaking, and a privilege we take for granted. The best use of our ears and mouth, is to hear God's word and share it.

*****

Mark 8:22-23 *They came to Bethsaida, and some people brought a blind man and begged Jesus to touch him. He took the blind man by the hand and led him outside the village.*

To receive his sight would mean everything to this man, so his hopes were very high. Jesus could've healed him publicly but, to avoid creating a scene, took him by the hand and led him outside the village.

Notice that Jesus didn't take him by the arm or elbow, but by the hand. The hand is more personal than the arm or elbow, and they walked this way for some time. Whenever we lose our way, Jesus takes us by the hand, not the arm or elbow. Our highest joy, in fact, is to put our hand in his, and walk with him through life.

Mark 8:23b-24 *When he had spit on the man's eyes and put his hands on him, Jesus asked, Do you see anything? He looked up and said, I see people; they look like trees walking around.*

The man was able to see, but only vaguely. It was better than blindness, but wasn't perfect. So, once again, Jesus put his hands on the man's eyes, and this time *his sight was restored, and he saw everything clearly* (Mark 8:25).

This story is unique because it's the only time Jesus healed in two stages. We aren't told why he used spittle, or why it wasn't perfect the first time. But, if there is a parallel, it's that most people don't see clearly all at once. Our eyes are opened the moment we believe in Jesus Christ, but the more we learn of him, the better our vision becomes.

*****

Mark 9:17-18 *Teacher, I brought you my son, who is possessed by a spirit that has robbed him of speech. Whenever it seizes him, it throws him to the ground. He foams at the mouth, gnashes his teeth and becomes rigid.*

The boy's condition was so severe that his life was often in danger. The father was hopeful that Jesus could help, but wasn't entirely sure. *[I]f you can do anything, take pity on us and help us [he said]. If you can? said Jesus. Everything is possible for one who believes. . . . I do believe; help me overcome my unbelief* (Mark 9:22-24), he replied.

Overcoming unbelief is the challenge of a lifetime, even for true believers. Miracles are rare, of course, but even our modest prayers may seem to go unanswered. That's why the Bible calls us to *persevere* (Hebrews 10:36), and to *Be merciful to those who doubt* (Jude 1:22), wrote Jude.

A pastor called on a man who lost his business due to a partner who ran off with the money. Then he lost his wife due to the stress of losing his business. Then he got cancer. The pastor offered to read him the Bible, but the man said he didn't believe in God anymore.

So the pastor reminded him that God didn't promise health, wealth, and happiness, but something even better: forgiveness for all our sins, an eternal home in heaven, and never to leave us or forsake us (Hebrews 13:5). Whenever hardship threatens our faith we can pray, *I do believe; help me overcome my unbelief.*

Mark 9:25-26 *You deaf and mute spirit, he said, I command you, come out of him and never enter him again. The spirit shrieked, convulsed him violently and came out.*

In this case, the boy's condition was caused by the devil. We shouldn't imagine that every illness is the result of demonic affliction, but some apparently are. *Resist the devil, and he will flee from you. Come near to God and he will come near to you* (James 4:7-8), wrote James. God's prescription for overcoming evil is to always *Resist the devil* and *Come near to God*. The help of a trustworthy doctor can also be an answer to prayer.

For Reflection and Review

- *How has Jesus improved your hearing and speaking?*
- *How has Jesus clarified your vision?*
- *Do you ever struggle with unbelief?*

Lesson 202

Luke 1:1-2 *Many have undertaken to draw up an account of the things that have been fulfilled among us, just as they were handed down to us by those who from the first were eyewitnesses and servants of the word.*

Although anonymous, the gospel according to Luke was likely written by the missionary companion of the Apostle Paul (2 Timothy 4:11), perhaps around AD 60. Luke was not an eyewitness of Jesus' ministry, but gathered his material from those who were, such as the apostles. Luke wrote his gospel so that we *may know the certainty of the things [we] have been taught* (Luke 1:4). Christianity isn't a blind faith. It's a faith with eyes wide open, based on historical fact, which should lead to certainty.

Luke 1:5 *In the time of Herod king of Judea there was a priest named Zechariah.*

Zechariah was married to Elizabeth and, together, they had served God for decades (Luke 1:7). Having walked with God for so many years, they could speak of his goodness and faithfulness. If they only had one complaint, it's probably that they were childless.

Infertility has been a concern for many but, in Bible times, it could be disastrous. There was no social security system, so children were the means of support in old age. And since children were considered a blessing from God (Psalm 127:3), if you didn't have children, some would think you weren't being blessed. And who wants a priest who isn't blessed by God?

Zechariah and Elizabeth could've become bitter, but chose to serve God in spite of their problems. We prefer to serve God without any problems but, this side of heaven, we're called to serve God alongside our problems. That's part of being faithful.

Luke 1:9 *[Zechariah] was chosen by lot, according to the custom of the priesthood, to go into the temple of the Lord and burn incense.*

This was an important event for Zechariah, since many priests lived and died without ever having the privilege of going inside the temple. Zechariah had probably never been inside the temple before, so this would be the high point of his ministry. The honor of serving in the temple was so great, in fact, that it had to be decided by lot.

The lot was used out of fairness, but also to rely on the sovereignty of God. *The lot is cast into the lap, but its every decision is from the Lord* (Proverbs 16:33), says Proverbs. God's sovereignty over the lots was clearly seen in the case of Zechariah since, out of the many priests available, the lot fell to him. This was precisely as God intended for this event to occur.

The apostles also cast lots to replace Judas Iscariot. They narrowed it down to two men who were equally qualified, and then they prayed: *Show us which of these two you have chosen to take over this apostolic ministry, which Judas left to go where he belongs. Then they cast lots, and the lot fell to Matthias; so he was added to the eleven apostles* (Acts 1:24-26). There's no record of lots being used after Pentecost, however, since guidance was sought from the Holy Spirit.

Luke 1:10 *And when the time for the burning of incense came, all the assembled worshipers were praying outside.*

The worshippers were praying outside the temple, not inside the temple. Most religious buildings are for worshippers to go inside, but the temple was like God's own house (Exodus 23:19), and wasn't open to the public. By divine command, in fact, any unauthorized person who tried to go inside the temple was to be killed (Numbers 3:10). The temple was for God to be close to his people—but not too close, since the full payment for sin hadn't been made.

We can imagine Zechariah's anxiousness as he passed from outside the temple, to inside the temple to burn incense. The altar of incense was in a room called the *Holy Place* and right behind it was a room called the *Most Holy Place*, where God himself was dwelling (Exodus 25:22). These two rooms were separated by a curtain, and only the High Priest was allowed into the Most Holy Place, once a year, to offer blood for the sins of the people (Leviticus 23).

But something amazing happened the moment Jesus died. *At that moment the curtain of the temple was torn in two from top to bottom* (Matthew 27:51), by the invisible hand of God. This showed the way to

God was now open to everyone through the shed blood of Jesus Christ. We're no longer at arm's length from God, but are invited into his holy presence through the atoning death of Jesus Christ.

Luke 1:13 *But the angel said to him: Do not be afraid, Zechariah; your prayer has been heard.*

Zechariah was inside the temple, serving nervously, when an angel appeared with the message: *Your prayer has been heard.* The angel didn't say, *Your prayers have been heard,* but rather, *Your prayer has been heard*—as though Zechariah only had one prayer his entire adult life. *Your wife Elizabeth will bear you a son, and you are to call him John* (Luke 1:13), said the angel.

This was quite a surprise. Since they were both very old (Luke 1:7), Zechariah and Elizabeth probably hadn't asked for a son for years. They likely assumed it wasn't God's will, and simply accepted it. But God didn't forget their prayer; he answered in his time.

When prayer isn't answered quickly, it's easy to become discouraged. *[D]o not turn a deaf ear to me* (Psalm 28:1); and *do not be deaf to my weeping* (Psalm 39:12), wrote the Psalmist. But God isn't deaf, and he doesn't forget our prayers. Zechariah and Elizabeth would have a son.

For Reflection and Review

- *Why isn't Christianity blind faith?*
- *Why wasn't God's house open to everyone?*
- *Why doesn't God answer all our prayers right away?*

Lesson 203

Luke 1:15 *[H]e will be filled with the Holy Spirit even before he is born.*

John the Baptist would never know a time when he wasn't filled with the Holy Spirit. This is truly remarkable, but shouldn't be confused with the virginal conception of Jesus Christ. Jesus was conceived by the Holy Spirit (Luke 1:35), in the womb of the virgin Mary, without a biological father. John the Baptist had two biological parents, but was filled with the Spirit sometime before he was born.

The Bible doesn't tell us when this happened, but a reasonable guess is when Mary (who was pregnant with Jesus) visited Elizabeth (who was pregnant with John). *When Elizabeth heard Mary's greeting, the baby leaped in her womb, and Elizabeth was filled with the Holy Spirit. In a loud voice she exclaimed: Blessed are you among women, and blessed is the child you will bear! But why am I so favored, that the mother of my Lord should come to me? As soon as the sound of your greeting reached my ears, the baby in my womb leaped for joy. Blessed is she who has believed that the Lord would fulfill his promises to her!* (Luke 1:41-44).

We can't be sure, but this may be the moment John was filled with the Holy Spirit. For an infant to be filled with the Spirit is unusual, but we have similar testimony from King David. *[Y]ou made me trust in you, even at my mother's breast. From birth I was cast on you; from my mother's womb you have been my God* (Psalm 22:9-10). Apparently, God is even able to work in the hearts of infants.

This is important because many who believe in Jesus Christ can't remember a time when they didn't believe. They're truly converted, and filled with the Spirit, but can't identify the time and place they received Christ. God is able to give the Spirit to whom he chooses, at any age he chooses. The critical thing isn't knowing precisely when you believed, but that you currently believe.

Luke 1:17 *And he will go on before the Lord, in the spirit and power of Elijah.*

The last two verses of the Old Testament (Malachi 4:5-6) promise that God will send the prophet Elijah. The Old Testament is a book without an ending, similar to a television show that concludes with the words, *to be continued.* Then, at the beginning of the New Testament, we have the promise and birth of John the Baptist, whom the angel compared to Elijah.

In this way the New Testament picks up where the Old Testament leaves off. It should also be noted that, unlike the Old Testament, the New Testament comes to a perfect conclusion. In the final chapter (Revelation 22) paradise is restored to God's people, just as it was lost in the beginning (Genesis 3).

The storyline of the Bible is paradise lost through sin, and paradise regained through Jesus Christ. It's remarkable that a book written over centuries, through so many writers, really tells one story.

It was important for John the Baptist to resemble Elijah in order to fulfill the last prophecy of the Old Testament, but also to be the connecting link between the Old and New Testaments. John modeled himself after Elijah, and they had many things in common. Both were confrontational; both lived in the Judean wilderness; both wore a garment of hair and a leather belt (2 Kings 1:8, Matthew 3:4); both denounced a king; both were opposed by queens; both became discouraged; and both were followed by someone even greater. John truly came in the *spirit and power of Elijah.*

Luke 1:18 *Zechariah asked the angel, How can I be sure of this?*

The visitation of an angel wasn't enough to convince Zechariah that his prayer would be answered. At this point the angel appears offended and says, *I am Gabriel. I stand in the presence of God, and I have been sent to speak to you and to tell you this good news. And now you will be silent and not able to speak until the day this happens, because you did not believe my words, which will come true at their appointed time* (Luke 1:19-20).

From this moment Zechariah was unable to speak and, perhaps, unable to hear—since others communicated with him using sign language (Luke 1:62). It's ironic that a person of faith also struggled with doubt, but it's not unusual. We also believe wholeheartedly, even if we doubt sometimes.

For Reflection and Review

- *Why doesn't everyone know when they came to faith?*
- *How does John connect the Old and New Testaments?*
- *Why did Zechariah doubt the angel Gabriel?*

Lesson 204

Luke 1:26-27 *In the sixth month of Elizabeth's pregnancy, God sent the angel Gabriel to Nazareth, a town in Galilee, to a virgin pledged to be married to a man named Joseph, a descendant of David. The virgin's name was Mary.*

One of the most remarkable things about Mary is how unremarkable she appears in the Bible. Compared to many others, there's little that's even said about her. She was from Nazareth, a place so small and out-of-the-way that it's not even mentioned in the Old Testament. Since girls were often married within a year of puberty, she may've only been twelve at the time of this story. And apart from some knowledge of the Bible (Luke 1:46-55), there's no indication that she was unusually godly.

Mary was a good mom, no doubt, but she wasn't perfect. When Jesus was twelve years old she accidentally left him alone in Jerusalem for three full days (Luke 2:41-50). During Jesus' ministry, she tried to take control of him because she thought he was out of his mind (Mark 3:20-35). And, although she truly believed in her Son, not all her children were convinced (John 7:5).

Nevertheless, this ordinary girl from Nazareth was given the extraordinary honor of being chosen by God—not because of anything in her, but because of God's choice. For the rest of her life she must have said, *I don't know why you chose me, God, but I'm so glad that you did.*

This, in fact, is the right attitude for all who belong to Christ. *For he chose us in him before the creation of the world* (Ephesians 1:4), wrote Paul. *[N]ot because of anything we have done but because of his own purpose and grace* (2 Timothy 1:9), wrote Paul again. Every Christian ought to say, every day of their lives, *I don't know why you chose me, God, but I'm so glad that you did.*

Luke 1:31 *You will conceive and give birth to a son, and you are to call him Jesus.*

This was an appropriate name for Messiah since it means, *The Lord Saves*. The angel said to Joseph, *you are to give him the name Jesus, because he will save his people from their sins* (Matthew 1:21). The world's greatest problem isn't ignorance, poverty, or disease, but sin. From Genesis to Revelation the problem is always sin; the answer is always salvation; and the only Savior is Jesus Christ.

Luke 1:32 *The Lord God will give him the throne of his father David.*

To Mary, this could only mean that Jesus would grow up to be king, and she would be queen mother. If that ignited her youthful imagination, we can only imagine her bewilderment when Jesus was crucified. When Jesus died on the cross, it seemed like every promise of God died with him.

There's an important lesson here for anyone who's ever been disappointed with God. Sometimes it seems like God over promises and under delivers. He promised Mary that Jesus would sit on David's throne (ruling over Israel) but, instead, he died and went to heaven. But when Jesus returns he'll rule the whole world forever and ever. This is more than Mary would've imagined.

In the short-term God may seem to over-promise and under-deliver. But in the long-term it's the opposite. The age to come will surpass every expectation, because our God is *able to do immeasurably more than all we ask or imagine* (Ephesians 3:20), wrote Paul.

Luke 1:34 *How will this be, Mary asked the angel, since I am a virgin?*

Mary understood how babies were made, and wanted to understand how a virgin could give birth. It's no surprise that the virginal birth of Jesus Christ has been one of the most attacked teachings of Christianity, because of what it implies. If Jesus is the offspring of God and Mary, he can rightly be called the God-man. If Jesus Christ is God in human flesh, then he must be taken seriously.

Luke 1:35 *The Holy Spirit will come on you, and the power of the Most High will overshadow you. So the holy one to be born will be called the Son of God.*

The prophet Isaiah also spoke of this event hundreds of years before: *The virgin will conceive and give birth to a son, and will call him Immanuel* (Isaiah 7:14), meaning *God with us*. This is more than wonderful, but how could it possible? How can one person be both human and divine at the same time? God is all-powerful; humans are not. God is all-knowing; humans are not. God is everywhere; humans are not. So how can Jesus Christ be truly God and truly human? Here is the answer: *We don't know.*

Theologians call it a *mystery*. They're not saying it's illogical, irrational, or contradictory, but that it's beyond our understanding. If we understood everything about God, it wouldn't be the true God, but one of our own making. The God of the Bible isn't the God we would invent, or one that can be fully understood. We just have to live with that.

Luke 1:38 *I am the Lord's servant, Mary answered. May your word to me be fulfilled.*

The angel's word would be fulfilled, but not without cost to Mary. First, to get pregnant outside marriage was an offense punishable by death (Deuteronomy 22:21). Second, Joseph might not believe the Holy Spirit made Mary pregnant, so he might break off the engagement (Matthew 1:19). Third, even if Mary convinced Joseph, she wouldn't convince most people, and would bear the stigma the rest of her life (John 8:41). Fourth, even though she didn't know it, the only crown Jesus would wear in her lifetime would be a crown of thorns (Matthew 27:29).

So when Mary said, *I am the Lord's servant*, she had no idea what she had agreed to. But she knew the one with whom she had agreed. The honor of being called by God, and identified with Jesus Christ, outweighs any earthly cost. Jesus seldom makes our lives easier or simpler, but always makes them deeper and more significant. He may cost us everything, but will make us unspeakably rich.

For Reflection and Review

- *Why did God choose Mary to be the mother of Christ?*
- *Why was it important for Jesus to be conceived by the Holy Spirit?*
- *Did Jesus make Mary's life better or worse?*

Lesson 205

Luke 1:57 *When it was time for Elizabeth to have her baby, she gave birth to a son.*

This was the child the angel Gabriel promised to Zechariah, when he was serving in the temple nine months earlier. Everyone gathered to celebrate, and wanted to name the baby after his father. But Zechariah and Elizabeth insisted his name was John, since that's what the angel commanded (Luke 1:13). *John* means *the Lord is gracious*. But John's preaching wouldn't seem very gracious.

You brood of vipers! Who warned you to flee from the coming wrath? . . . The ax is already at the root of the trees, and every tree that does not produce good fruit will be cut down and thrown into the fire (Matthew 3:7-10), he'd say.

John's preaching was nothing less than ferocious, and didn't seem gracious at all. But John's preaching was gracious because it helped people get right with God. Upon hearing his threats many turned from their sins and began to live for the Lord. Comforting people who are still in their sins may appear to be gracious, but is ungracious if they die and go to hell. Threatening people with the wrath of God may appear to be ungracious, but is very gracious if it leads to repentance and faith in Jesus Christ.

Luke 1:68 *Praise be to the Lord, the God of Israel, because he has come to his people and redeemed them.*

Zechariah was unable to speak for several months because he didn't believe the angel Gabriel. But the moment he recovered his speech, he began praising God. Sometimes we don't appreciate what we have until God takes it away. If God took away everything we have and struck us blind—but gave us back our sight tomorrow—we'd be extremely thankful. We should be thankful every day for what we normally take for granted.

Luke 1:72-73 *. . . to remember his holy covenant, the oath he swore to our father Abraham.*

Zechariah referred to God's promise to Abraham, to make him into a great nation, and bless the world through him (Genesis 12:2-3). God also promised our first parents that he'd send someone to crush the devil's head (Genesis 3:15). And God promised David that his throne would be established forever (2 Samuel 7:16). These and other promises were fulfilled by Jesus Christ who defeated Satan through his cross, is blessing the world through his gospel, and is sitting heaven's throne. *For no matter how many promises God has made, they are Yes in Christ* (2 Corinthians 1:20), wrote Paul.

Promise and fulfillment are what keep God's story moving forward. Since Christ fulfilled so many promises the first time he came, we know he'll fulfill the rest when he returns. This gives us something to look forward to every day of our lives.

A Christian lady was in the hospital dying of cancer. A nurse came by to see how she was doing, scribbled a note on her chart, and left the room. The note said, *inappropriately joyful*. The only way to be joyful at the time of death is to know the one who conquered death. The best is always yet to come for those who know the Lord.

Luke 1:76-77 *And you, my child, will be called a prophet of the Most High; for you will go on before the Lord to prepare the way for him, to give his people the knowledge of salvation through the forgiveness of their sins.*

Salvation and forgiveness are closely related in the Bible. In its broadest sense, salvation is from everything wrong in the world—from hurricanes to bad neighbors. But since everything wrong in the world is due to sin, salvation is most concerned with forgiveness. That's why John pointed to Jesus and said, *Look, the Lamb of God, who takes away the sin of the world!* (John 1:29). The way to be saved from our sins is by looking to Jesus Christ.

Luke 1:78-79 *[T]he rising sun will come to us from heaven to shine on those living in darkness and in the shadow of death.*

This is a wonderful image for all who like the sun. When I was sixteen years old, I went hiking in the mountains of Utah early one morning. It was cold and dark, and I was in a valley. But as the sun came up in the east, the light made its way down the western slope with a very sharp dividing line between the darkness and the light.

I waited for the moment the light would get to me, and wasn't disappointed when it did. Warmth, beauty, and joy were instantly mine. My location had barely changed at all, but the difference between walking in darkness and walking in light was so distinct, I'll never forget it.

That's how it is when we come to faith in Christ. *The people walking in darkness have seen a great light; on those living in the land of deep darkness a light has dawned* (Isaiah 9:2), wrote Isaiah. Truly, *the rising sun [has] come to us from heaven.*

Luke 1:80 *[John] lived in the wilderness until he appeared publicly to Israel.*

Zechariah and Elizabeth were old when John was born (Luke 1:7), and may have died while he was young. This would've been hard for John, and probably made him even more dependent on God. With no one else to care for, John was able to focus on God without distraction. After many years of solitude, he was ready to be used by God in a brief but powerful way.

For Reflection and Review

- *What is salvation?*
- *How is Jesus like the rising sun?*
- *How does solitude help us know God better?*

Lesson 206

Luke 2:1 *In those days Caesar Augustus issued a decree that a census should be taken of the entire Roman world.*

Caesar Augustus was the first and, arguably, the greatest of all the Roman emperors. For the purpose of taxation he decreed a census that reached all the way to Nazareth, where Mary and Joseph lived. The timing wasn't great since Mary was nine months pregnant. She'd have to make the three day, seventy-five mile, journey from Nazareth to Bethlehem to register for the tax. Doubtless, she preferred to be at home, in a safe and secure environment, surrounded by family and friends. But she found herself on the back of a mule, praying she wouldn't have the baby until she returned.

Life doesn't always go the way we think it should. If God was really in control, things would move in a smooth and orderly way. And, because they seldom do, we wonder who's in charge.

This story is helpful because, behind the decree of Caesar Augustus, we discover the decree of God. God determined long before that his Son would be born in Bethlehem, not Nazareth. *But you, Bethlehem . . . though you are small among the clans of Judah, out of you will come for me one who will be ruler over Israel, whose origins are from of old, from ancient times* (Micah 5:2). The prophet Micah wrote these words several hundred years before Christ was born.

The population of the world back then was about two hundred fifty million, and there may've been about a million towns. We can calculate the odds of identifying the exact town where Messiah would be born to be about one in a million. If there were only a hundred towns this would still be an impressive prophecy. And if there were a thousand towns it would be even more impressive. But to identify the exact town, out of a million possible towns, is nothing less than divine.

But this prophecy tells us even more about Jesus. His *origins are from of old, from ancient times*. Bethlehem would be the place of his birth but, since he was from heaven, his origins were ancient. Jesus Christ is the eternal Son of God.

God made his plans in eternity past, and carried them out in time, through the decree of Caesar Augustus. God was in control even when it didn't seem like God was in control. The world is never out of control, and our lives are never out of control, because our God is in control.

Luke 2:6-7 *[T]he time came for the baby to be born, and she gave birth to her firstborn, a son.*

Mary found herself in labor, and then her water broke. She writhed in pain and pushed with all her might. Joseph watched as Jesus crowned, and then came out. He placed the baby in his mother's arms and she gave Jesus the breast. Mary's little Messiah began to nurse, and the love she felt for him can hardly be imagined.

Can a mother forget the baby at her breast and have no compassion on the child she has borne? Though she may forget, I will not forget you! (Isaiah 49:15), said God.

It would've been easier for Mary not to love her nursing baby than for God not to love us. The amazing thing about the Savior's birth is not that Mary loved Jesus, but that *God so loved the world that he gave his one and only Son, that whoever believes in him shall not perish but have eternal life* (John 3:16).

Some theologians speak of Mary as the mother of God. This sounds wrong at first but, in fact, it's not. They're not saying Mary existed before God, or that God has his source in Mary, but that the one to whom Mary gave birth was truly divine. Since Mary gave birth to Christ, who is truly divine, she's called the mother of God in that sense. The one who came through Mary's birth canal was God in human flesh—born to save us from our sins.

Luke 2:7b *She wrapped him in cloths and placed him in a manger, because there was no guest room available for them.*

A manger is a feeding trough for animals, and this is the only place the Bible suggests that Jesus was born in a stable. If so, the animals did what animals do, and the stable smelled badly. But Jesus came into the stench of a stable because he loves us, and the stench of our lives will not drive him away.

For Reflection and Review

- *How do we know that God is in control?*
- *How does God's love for us compare to a mother's love for her child?*
- *Why should Mary be called the mother of God?*

Lesson 207

Luke 2:8 *And there were shepherds living out in the fields nearby, keeping watch over their flocks at night.*

Sheep were kept in the fields of Bethlehem because it was about five miles away from the temple in Jerusalem. Jerusalem needed sheep for sacrifice, and never more than at the yearly Passover festival, when every family was required to offer a sacrificial lamb (Exodus 12:3, 14). John the Baptist would identify Jesus as the *Lamb of God, who takes away the sin of the world* (John 1:29). So Jesus was born in Bethlehem, to be sacrificed in Jerusalem, during Passover, a few decades later.

Luke 2:9 *An angel of the Lord appeared to them, and the glory of the Lord shone around them, and they were terrified.*

The appearance of an angel can be frightening, but these shepherds had other reasons to be afraid, since they were likely thieves. Shepherds were often on the move, and many used their mobility to steal other people's sheep. These shepherds may've stolen some sheep that day, in fact, and now were confronted by an angel of God.

The angels will come and separate the wicked from the righteous and throw them into the blazing furnace, where there will be weeping and gnashing of teeth (Matthew 13:49-50), said Jesus. Angels aren't always friendly toward sinners . . . but this time they were.

Luke 2:10 *Do not be afraid. I bring you good news that will cause great joy for all the people.*

The good news wasn't for some of the people, or most of the people, but for *all the people*. No matter who you are, where you've been, or what you've done, Jesus Christ is for everyone who believes in him. Whether you're a prodigal, priest, or prostitute (or even all three) God *wants all people to be saved and to come to a knowledge of the truth* (1 Timothy 2:4), wrote Paul. The offer of salvation is to everyone.

Luke 2:11 *Today in the town of David a Savior has been born to you.*

The words Savior, save, saved, and salvation occur over five hundred times in the Bible. *Salvation is found in no one else, for there is no other name under heaven . . . by which we must be saved* (Acts 4:12). *Believe in the Lord Jesus, and you will be saved* (Acts 16:31). *[God] wants all people to be saved* (1 Timothy 2:4). *[A]nd you are to give him the name Jesus, because he will save his people from their sins* (Matthew 1:21).

This is different from other religions in which people are able to save themselves. In Hinduism the problem isn't sin, but ignorance. What we need is to be enlightened. In Buddhism the problem isn't sin, but desire. Nirvana is getting rid of desire. In Islam if our good deeds outweigh our bad deeds we go up; if not, we go down.

But, according to the Bible, even our best deeds are infected with sin (Isaiah 64:6), so we're all going down. That was our situation apart from Christ. We were *without hope and without God in the world* (Ephesians 2:12), wrote Paul.

In the year 2010, thirty-three miners were trapped beneath two thousand feet of rock when their tunnel collapsed. Their only hope of getting out was to be rescued from above. Rescue teams worked around the clock trying to reach them in time. First, they built a capsule in which the miners could rise. Then they began to drill. Two months later the miners were reached. And, by climbing into the capsule, they were saved. They couldn't save themselves, of course, but they couldn't ignore the capsule either.

And *how shall we escape if we ignore so great a salvation?* (Hebrews 2:3), says Hebrews. All we have to do to go to heaven is believe in Jesus Christ. But all we have to do to go to hell is nothing. Just ignore the fact that Jesus died for you and commands you to believe in him. Believing in Jesus Christ is like getting married. If we take him, he'll take us. But if we say *no*, we're on our own.

Luke 2:14 *Glory to God in the highest heaven, and on earth peace to those on whom his favor rests.*

Suddenly a great assembly of angels appeared with the first angel and they began praising God together. The Bible doesn't tell us that they sang but, if they did, it must've been quite a performance. First they gave *Glory to God in the highest heaven*, and then announced *peace to those on whom his favor rests*.

Peace with God through Jesus Christ is not primarily a feeling, but an objective reality that was accomplished by Christ, and is received by faith in him. Our feelings of peace can change with the weather, but the fact of peace remains forever.

A missionary was working with warring tribes known for cannibalism, and was finding it difficult to explain the gospel in a way they could understand. Then, one day, he saw a peace ceremony in which a man from one tribe gave his son to an enemy tribe in order to prove sincerity. The missionary began to speak of Jesus Christ as God's *peace child* whom he gave to the world (Don Richardson).

The analogy works in a way but, like other analogies, breaks down eventually. The enemy tribe was expected to treat the son well, or there'd be war again. But God sent his Son into the world knowing that he'd be crucified. And the Son was willing to die for a world that hated his Father. And they were willing to do this because there was no other way to establish peace between sinful people and a holy God. Jesus Christ is God's peace child. *[W]e have peace with God through our Lord Jesus Christ* (Romans 5:1), wrote Paul.

Luke 2:15-18 *When the angels had left them and gone into heaven, the shepherds said to one another, Let's go to Bethlehem and see this thing that has happened, which the Lord has told us about. So they hurried off and found Mary and Joseph, and the baby, who was lying in the manger. When they had seen him, they spread the word concerning what had been told them about this child, and all who heard it were amazed at what the shepherds said to them.*

The shepherds were amazed at the birth of Jesus Christ, and they must've been amazed, years later, if they heard him preach. And they must've been amazed if they saw him heal the sick or raise the dead. And they must've been amazed if they saw him feed the multitudes or calm the storm. And they must've been amazed if they saw him crucified. And they must've been amazed if they saw him risen from the dead. Jesus Christ is the most amazing person who ever lived.

I sat in a restaurant, shortly after believing in Christ, and was amazed at what I had discovered. I sat around with Christian friends in absolute astonishment saying, *I can't believe it's actually true. I can't believe it's actually true.* Forty years later I'm still saying the most amazing thing about Christianity is that it is, in fact, actually true.

For Reflection and Review

- *Are angels safe?*
- *Why do we need to be saved?*
- *What does it mean to have peace with God?*

Lesson 208

Luke 2:25 *Now there was a man in Jerusalem called Simeon, who was righteous and devout. He was waiting for the consolation of Israel.*

The consolation of Israel is a wonderful and often overlooked description of Jesus Christ. He's the one who comforts those who are suffering. God's people had suffered much throughout their history, but Messiah would bring them comfort. The day is coming, in fact, when *He will wipe every tear from [our] eyes* (Revelation 21:4), wrote John. Even now we can give him our sorrow, and receive the comfort that only he can provide.

Luke 2:26 *It had been revealed to [Simeon] by the Holy Spirit that he would not die before he had seen the Lord's Messiah.*

Jesus was a few weeks old when Mary and Joseph brought him to the Temple. Moved by the Spirit, Simeon went into the temple courts and took the baby in his arms saying, *Sovereign Lord, as you have promised, you may now dismiss your servant in peace. For my eyes have seen your salvation* (Luke 2:29-30). Simeon was old and, now that he'd seen the Savior, he could die in peace.

One of the most remarkable things about Jesus Christ is how he changes death. We normally cling to life, but when it's time for us to go, we're ready. *I desire to depart and be with Christ, which is better by far* (Philippians 1:23), wrote Paul. Some even catch a glimpse of glory before they slip away.

In his final moments a man looked at his wife and said, *I love you.* Then he closed his eyes and said—*amazing.* A lady on her deathbed called for a pastor and said in the tiniest voice, *It's all true. Tell them it's all true.* Death is the ultimate enemy for some, but for many it leads to life in the presence of God.

Luke 2:34 *Then Simeon blessed them and said to Mary, his mother: This child is destined to cause the falling and rising of many in Israel.*

Jesus will make us better or worse, but will never leave us the same. Depending on our response to him, we'll either rise or fall. Peter, for example, wasn't the kind of person who'd be known today, apart from Jesus Christ. But he preached the first sermon of the church, and three thousand people believed (Acts 2:41). Then he wrote a couple letters that were included in the New Testament so, even today, he's read and quoted by millions. Peter was not exceptional apart from Jesus Christ. But, because of Christ, he became greater than he ever imagined.

Judas is another story. He pretended to belong to Christ, but betrayed him for thirty pieces of silver (Matthew 26:15). Then he was so overcome with guilt that he returned the money and hanged himself (Matthew 27:5). He apparently hung himself over a cliff since *he fell headlong, his body burst open and all his intestines spilled out* (Acts 1:18). *It would be better for him if he had not been born* (Matthew 26:24), said Jesus.

Whether we go up or down, become glorious or hideous, depends entirely on our relationship with Jesus Christ. Peter and Judas are good examples, but we can also think of Pilate, Paul, Matthew, and Herod. Jesus will do us good or harm, depending on our response to him.

Luke 2:35 *And a sword will pierce your own soul too.*

These are the last words Simeon spoke to Mary, and it would take over thirty years before she knew what they meant. As he hung on the cross, the soldiers thrust a spear into Jesus' side (John 19:34), to be sure he was dead. This was the final act of violence to his body and, as Mary watched, she felt a stabbing in her soul. Simeon foretold the child's death, as well as his mother's pain. *A sword will pierce your own soul too.*

Luke 2:36 *There was also a prophet, Anna, the daughter of Penuel, of the tribe of Asher.*

After the story of Simeon we have the account of Anna, another elderly person. She was eighty-four years old, and her life didn't go the way she planned. After seven years of marriage her husband died, and there's no mention of any children.

The normal path for Anna would've been to remarry but, instead, she devoted her life to prayer. *She never left the temple but worshiped night and day, fasting and praying* (Luke 2:37), wrote Luke. Many would consider this a sheltered life, but Anna probably saw more in prayer than if she had traveled the world.

Many years ago I was at the Louvre Museum in Paris, and saw the Mona Lisa. It's the most famous painting in the world, and is valued at hundreds of millions of dollars. I took a brief look and checked it off my list. Of another painting, Vincent VanGoth said, *I would give ten years of my life to sit fourteen days before that painting with barely a crust to eat.* That's how it is with God. Some people see; most do not.

But here's a promise for all of us: *You will seek me and find me when you seek me with all your heart* (Jeremiah 29:13), wrote Jeremiah. Anna sought God for decades, and found him in the flesh. While Simeon was still holding the baby she came up, *gave thanks to God and spoke about the child to all who were looking forward to the redemption of Jerusalem* (Luke 2:38).

Our usefulness to God may seem to diminish with age, but Anna and Simeon were both very old when God used them as never before. Our usefulness to God is never done until we die, and then we'll serve him forever. Our final years on earth can even be our best, if we devote ourselves to seeking God.

For Reflection and Review

- *How does Jesus change our view of death?*
- *How did Jesus elevate Peter?*
- *What are the benefits of growing old?*

Lesson 209

Luke 2:41 *Every year Jesus' parents went to Jerusalem for the Festival of the Passover.*

This was a major religious event, drawing thousands of people from all around. Jesus was twelve years old at the time, and traveled with his parents to the capital city. But, on the way home, he was accidentally left behind.

Worshippers often traveled in groups and, with so many people, Mary and Joseph probably assumed Jesus was with the other parent. Their attention would've been divided since they likely had other children by then (Matthew 13:55). Since Jesus was the oldest, they would've been more concerned about their little ones.

When Jesus found himself left behind, he went to the temple and waited for his parents to return. While he was there, he spoke with the religious teachers, and made quite an impression. *Everyone who heard him was amazed at his understanding and his answers* (Luke 2:47), wrote Luke. This was a sign of things to come. As an adult they'd say, *How did this man get such learning?* (John 7:15). *No one ever spoke the way this man does* (John 7:46). And, *all the people hung on his words* (Luke 19:48). Jesus knew his stuff.

Luke 2:48 *His mother said to him, Son, why have you treated us like this? Your father and I have been anxiously searching for you.*

We can imagine the look on Mary's face when she finally found her twelve-year-old son. They traveled a day's journey before they knew he was missing. Then they traveled another day back. Then they spent a third day searching frantically before they found him in the temple. Mary was not happy with Jesus.

Why were you searching for me? he asked. Didn't you know I had to be in my Father's house? (Luke 2:49). This sounds rather adolescent, but Jesus was truly surprised they wouldn't know where to find him. He loved his heavenly Father and wanted to be in his Father's house.

The only other time Jesus spoke of his Father's house was the night before he was crucified. *My Father's house has many rooms; if that were not so, would I have told you that I am going there to prepare a place for you? And if I go and prepare a place for you, I will come back and take you to be with me* (John 14:2-3).

To stay in a world class hotel can cost thousands of dollars a night. The rooms are fabulous, with spectacular views, and come with every amenity. Heaven will be better than any hotel, and we'll never have to leave. We'll be with our heavenly Father, Jesus Christ, the Holy Spirit, and all our brothers and sisters. It'll be the ultimate family reunion, and will never end. Our Father's house has many rooms.

Luke 2:51 *Then he went down to Nazareth with them and was obedient to them.*

Jesus didn't obey his parents because they were always right, but because God said to *Honor your father and your mother* (Exodus 20:12). Christian children should obey their father and mother for the exact same reason. In fact, God likes authority and submission in every sphere of life. *Submit yourselves for the Lord's sake to every human authority* (1 Peter 2:13), wrote Peter. This will please our heavenly Father, make us more like Jesus Christ, and make us unique to the world.

*****

Luke 3:2 *[T]he word of God came to John son of Zechariah.*

It was time for John to introduce the Messiah. The Old Testament often foretold the coming of Jesus Christ, but also foretold the coming of John the Baptist to announce Jesus' arrival: *I will send my messenger, who will prepare the way before me. Then suddenly the Lord you are seeking will come to his temple* (Malachi 3:1), wrote Malachi. So the word of God came to John the Baptist, who introduced Jesus Christ, who later taught at the temple (John 7).

Malachi foretold this event about four hundred years before it took place, and was the last prophet to speak for God in the Old Testament. If you want to say something important, it may be helpful to pause for dramatic effect. The longer you pause, sometimes, the more dramatic the effect. After four hundred years of prophetic silence, God had something important to say through John: *Look, the Lamb of God, who takes away the sin of the world!* (John 1:29).

Luke 3:3 *[John preached] a baptism of repentance for the forgiveness of sins.*

John didn't preach baptism alone for the forgiveness of sins, but a *baptism of repentance* for the forgiveness of sins. Baptism doesn't work automatically. It requires turning away from sin, and turning to God. Since most people don't take sin very seriously, John stood in the water and preached about God's wrath. Those who believed repented of their sin, stepped into the water, and were baptized.

Standing in the crowd and listening to John preach was easy—even entertaining. But stepping out of the crowd, and being baptized, was a public admission of guilt, and a public pledge to live for God. *Repent, for the kingdom of heaven has come near* (Matthew 3:2), he said.

Luke 3:4-5 *A voice of one calling in the wilderness, Prepare the way for the Lord, make straight paths for him. Every valley shall be filled in, every mountain and hill made low. The crooked roads shall become straight, the rough ways smooth.*

John found his job description in these words from the prophet Isaiah (Isaiah 40:3-4). If a king was coming to town, back then, messengers were sent to the town ahead of the king, so the town could make preparations, such as road repair. This king was so great that whole mountains were to be leveled, and valleys were to be filled. This wasn't a physical road, but a highway into people's hearts, which John would build through his preaching.

For Reflection and Review

- *Have you ever been homesick for heaven?*
- *Why should Christians respect authority?*
- *Is faith enough to be saved, or must we also repent?*

Lesson 210

Luke 3:7 *You brood of vipers! Who warned you to flee from the coming wrath?*

John was less concerned with winning people's approval than confronting them with their sin. By calling them a *brood of vipers* he alluded to the Garden of Eden where Satan took the form of a serpent (Genesis 3:1). By living in opposition to God, they proved they were the devil's offspring (Genesis 3:15). And, without a serious change, they should expect God's wrath.

Luke 3:9 *The ax is already at the root of the trees, and every tree that does not produce good fruit will be cut down and thrown into the fire.*

John was thinking of an orchard owner who was checking his trees for fruit. Whenever he found a tree that didn't bear fruit, he put his ax to the root and prepared to swing. Once the tree was down, it was thrown into the fire.

John wasn't thinking of trees, of course, but of people who should be living for God. Those who aren't should feel the ax at their feet, and the heat of the fire nearby. God is doing nothing inappropriate since he owns the orchard, and has a right to expect fruit—the character and lifestyle that come from knowing him.

Some of John's listeners would've found this objectionable, and many still do. God with an axe is not a popular image, but John wasn't afraid to use it, and neither was Jesus. *Every tree that does not bear good fruit is cut down and thrown into the fire* (Matthew 7:19), he said.

Luke 3:16 *I baptize you with water. But one who is more powerful than I will come, the straps of whose sandals I am not worthy to untie.*

Removing a master's sandals was such a humble task that Jewish masters didn't require it of Jewish servants. John had such a high view of Jesus, however, that he felt unworthy to even remove his sandals. No matter how humble the task, serving Jesus Christ is our highest possible honor.

Luke 3:17 *His winnowing fork is in his hand to clear his threshing floor and to gather the wheat into his barn, but he will burn up the chaff with unquenchable fire.*

After the grain was harvested, it was brought to a threshing floor, to be winnowed with a wooden pitchfork. When it was tossed into the air, the grain would fall to the ground, and the lighter chaff would blow off to the side. Then it was burned in a fire. But, unlike literal chaff, the ungodly will suffer *unquenchable fire*.

A friend of mine was badly burned at work, hospitalized for weeks, and required multiple skin grafts. It was the most horrible suffering I've ever seen, so the idea of fire as punishment is troubling to me. I'd rather do away with the idea, but this is the second time John used fire to describe the punishment of the wicked. It appears, in fact, throughout the Bible.

In the fire of his jealousy the whole earth will be consumed (Zephaniah 1:18). *Depart from me, you who are cursed, into the eternal fire prepared for the devil and his angels* (Matthew 25:41). *Sodom and Gomorrah. . . . serve as an example of those who suffer the punishment of eternal fire* (Jude 7). *Anyone whose name was not found written in the book of life was thrown into the lake of fire* (Revelation 20:15).

Preachers who talk this way are sometimes mocked as *fire and brimstone* preachers. But any preacher who never talks this way is being unfaithful to God, unfaithful to the Bible, and unfaithful to those who hear.

Luke 3:21 *When all the people were being baptized, Jesus was baptized too.*

This took John by surprise and, at first, he resisted (Matthew 3:14-15). We can understand his reluctance because John was merely a prophet, and Jesus was the Messiah. It didn't seem right for a mere prophet to baptize God's Messiah. Furthermore, John preached a baptism of repentance, but Jesus never sinned. So why would a sinless Messiah want to be baptized?

There are at least three answers to this question. First, by being baptized, Jesus was endorsing John's ministry. Second, Jesus was modeling the right thing for others to do. Third, and primarily, he was identifying with those he came to save.

Imagine a party at which everyone was wearing a name tag that also identified their most terrible sin. There was Mark the Murderer, Bonnie the Blasphemer, Ron the Rapist, Sally the Slanderer, Larry the Luster, Lynn the Liar, Erica the Embezzler, Paul the Pornographer, Amy the Adulteress, Charlie the Cheat, and Alyssa the Addict. Everyone was wearing a name tag, but no one was having a good time, because everyone felt ashamed.

Then Jesus arrived but they wouldn't give him a name tag because he never sinned. So Jesus took everyone else's name tags and put them on himself. Then he stepped into the pool and went under water. When he came out the names were still on the tags but the sins were washed away (source unknown).

The church is a party of redeemed sinners, whose sins have been washed away by Jesus Christ. It's illustrated in baptism, and was fulfilled at the cross. Jesus was baptized, not for himself, but for those who would believe in him. He washed all our sins away (1 John 1:7).

Luke 3:21b-22 *And as he was praying, heaven was opened and the Holy Spirit descended on him in bodily form like a dove.*

This reminds us of the dove that was released from Noah's ark (Genesis 8:12). As the dove went out to the renewed earth, so the whole world will be renewed by Christ and his gospel, through the Holy Spirit. This is why the Spirit took the form of a dove.

We should also notice that all three members of the Trinity were apparent at Jesus' baptism. The Father spoke from heaven, the Spirit descended like a dove, and the Son was on earth. The idea of the Trinity isn't easily grasped, but the Bible teaches that one God eternally exists in three persons. *Therefore go and make disciples of all nations, baptizing them in the name of the Father and of the Son and of the Holy Spirit* (Matthew 28:20), said Jesus. The Father is God, the Son is God, and the Spirit is God—but there's only one God. That's the biblical concept of the Trinity: one God in three persons.

For Reflection and Review

- *Why did people respond to John's preaching?*
- *Should preachers imitate John today?*
- *How does Jesus' baptism remind us of the Trinity?*

Lesson 211

Luke 4:1-2 *Jesus, full of the Holy Spirit, left the Jordan and was led by the Spirit into the wilderness, where for forty days he was tempted by the devil.*

There was more at stake in this event than may appear. Adam and Eve were tempted by the devil and, by failing, plunged the human race into death and destruction. Because Jesus came to lead us out of death and destruction, he had to succeed where Adam and Eve failed. Like the rest of us, Jesus was tempted throughout his life. But, unlike the rest of us, Jesus never gave in. So at the starting point of his ministry, Satan did his best to disqualify Jesus from becoming the Savior of the world.

Luke 4:3 *The devil said to him, If you are the Son of God, tell this stone to become bread.*

Jesus hadn't eaten anything for forty days, which is about as long as a person can go without permanent injury. Satan is a master of timing, and waited until Jesus was at his weakest before he began his assault.

The soil in that region is rocky, and some of the stones resemble loaves of bread. Since Jesus would later multiply bread to feed thousands (Matthew 14:19-20), he could've turned a stone into bread if he wanted to. But the fast was God's idea (Luke 4:1), so to break it prematurely would've been a sin. This would've disqualified Jesus from his mission to save us from our sins (Matthew 1:21).

Luke 4:4 *Jesus answered, It is written: Man shall not live on bread alone.*

This is the first of three quotations from the Old Testament which Jesus used to combat the devil's temptations. Jesus' first line of defense was to quote God's word. The Bible is the *sword of the Spirit* (Ephesians 6:17), with which we can battle Satan. Christians who know the Bible well are in a better position to overcome temptation than those who don't. Jesus knew the Bible well enough to quote it, and he is our example.

Luke 4:5-8 *The devil led him up to a high place and showed him in an instant all the kingdoms of the world. And he said to him, I will give you all their authority and splendor; it has been given to me, and I can give it to anyone I want to. If you worship me, it will all be yours. Jesus answered, It is written: Worship the Lord your God and serve him only.*

This is one of the most fascinating conversations in the Bible. In exchange for a moment of worship, Satan offered Jesus all the kingdoms of the world, because *it has been given to me* [he said] *and I can give it to anyone I want to.* The only thing more shocking than Satan's claim is that Jesus didn't refute it.

Satan's claim can even be supported by additional Scripture. Three times Jesus called Satan the *prince of this world* (John 12:31, 14:30, 16:11). The Apostle Paul called him *the god of this age* (2 Corinthians 4:4), and *the ruler of the kingdom of the air* (Ephesians 2:2). And the Apostle John was very clear when he wrote, *the whole world is under the control of the evil one* (1 John 5:19). This may be shocking, but it does explain a few things.

First, if Satan controlled the world we'd expect the world to be completely confused about God. And, after thousands of years, the world has come to no consensus on the two most important questions: *Is there a God and what is he like?*

Second, if Satan controlled the world we'd expect the world to be filled with pain, sorrow, and death. And every person born into the world goes through pain, sorrow, and death.

Third, if Satan controlled the world we'd expect to hear stories of rape, murder, and war. And all we have to do is turn on the news to hear stories of rape, murder, and war.

Fourth, if Satan controlled the world, and God came into the world, we'd expect the world to crucify God. So God came into the world, in the person of Jesus Christ, and it was only a matter of time before he was crucified. It seems like *the whole world is under the control of the evil one*. But how did this happen?

The explanation is found in the first few chapters of the Bible. God created the world, and put Adam and Eve in charge. As long as they obeyed, every day was paradise, and Satan couldn't harm them. But when they ate the forbidden fruit, they stepped out from under God's authority, and found themselves under Satan's authority. That was the end of paradise, and the beginning of Satan's rule (Genesis 1-3). Ever since that day our greatest need has been for someone to save us from the tyranny of Satan.

Luke 4:9-12 *The devil led him to Jerusalem and had him stand on the highest point of the temple. If you are the Son of God, he said, throw yourself down from here. For it is written: He will command his angels concerning you to guard you carefully; they will lift you up in their hands, so that you will not strike your foot against a stone. Jesus answered, It is said: Do not put the Lord your God to the test.*

This temptation was unique because Satan used the Bible to make his argument. He quoted from the ninety-first Psalm, and argued that if Jesus threw himself off the temple, God would send angels to catch him. If the Bible is true, and Jesus believed it, he should prove his faith by taking a leap. But Jesus didn't leap.

The purpose of the ninety-first Psalm, isn't to encourage rash behavior, but simple trust in God. So Jesus rebuffed the devil by quoting another verse. *Do not put the Lord your God to the test* (Deuteronomy 6:16).

This is how we should treat all the promises of God. Jesus said, *If you believe, you will receive whatever you ask for in prayer* (Matthew 21:22). We ought to pray in faith, therefore, and believe that God will answer. But we should never use such promises as a way of forcing God to act, since God will not be forced to do anything.

This may seem obvious but, in the name of faith, some parents have withheld medicine from their children with tragic results. Satan is able to quote Scripture for his own purpose, as he did with Jesus. The broad counsel of Scripture, however, is to pray in faith without putting God to the test. As Jesus prayed elsewhere, *not my will, but yours be done* (Luke 22:42).

Luke 4:13 *When the devil had finished all this tempting, he left him until an opportune time.*

We're not told when the opportune time was, but one of the last temptations Jesus faced was to come down from the cross. *Come down from the cross, if you are the Son of God!* (Matthew 27:40), said his opponents. Perhaps the devil was speaking through them, and perhaps Jesus was mightily tempted to take his revenge (Deuteronomy 32:41). But like his other temptations, Jesus didn't give in.

Adam and Eve enjoyed a perfect environment, and were only forbidden the fruit of one tree, to show their loyalty to God (Genesis 2:17). But they failed. Jesus endured hardship in life and death, but never failed once. Everything Adam lost was recovered by Christ, who has reopened paradise for all who believe. *For as in Adam all die, so in Christ all will be made alive* (1 Corinthians 15:22), wrote Paul.

For Reflection and Review

- *Why is the world under Satan's control?*
- *How does Satan misuse the Bible?*
- *How does the Bible help us defeat Satan?*

Lesson 212

Luke 4:16 *[Jesus] went to Nazareth, where he had been brought up, and on the Sabbath day he went into the synagogue, as was his custom.*

Shortly after he began his ministry, Jesus went to his home town to preach. Many people love their home town, but Jesus probably had mixed feelings about Nazareth. By most standards it wasn't a great town. It's not mentioned in the Old Testament and didn't enjoy a good reputation. *Can anything good come from there?* (John 1:46), asked Nathaniel.

And Jesus knew Nazareth better than most. As a child he played games with the other children so he knew who the bullies and cheaters were. As a carpenter (Mark 6:3) he probably did work for people who refused to pay even when they could. At synagogue he knew those who made a good appearance but didn't really believe.

But Nazareth also knew Jesus. They knew he was conceived out of wedlock, which probably tainted their view of him. They knew he never married, which probably tainted their view of him too. And because he was fully devoted to God, he didn't laugh at their off-colored jokes, or fit in as they preferred. Jesus wasn't their favorite son.

Luke 4:16-17 *He stood up to read, and the scroll of the prophet Isaiah was handed to him.*

People didn't have Bibles back then, but the sacred scrolls were kept in the synagogue for public worship. The attendant gave Jesus the scroll of Isaiah, and Jesus began to read.

The Spirit of the Lord is on me, because he has anointed me to proclaim good news to the poor. He has sent me to proclaim freedom for the prisoners and recovery of sight for the blind, to set the oppressed free, to proclaim the year of the Lord's favor (Luke 4:18-19, Isaiah 61:1-2). The people heard it many times before but, this time, you could hear a pin drop. *The eyes of everyone in the synagogue were fastened on him* (Luke 4:20).

Luke 4:21 *Today this scripture is fulfilled in your hearing.*

His audience didn't understand him perfectly, but Jesus was saying he came to fulfill what the prophet had written. For the rest of his ministry he preached the good news, gave sight to the blind, set people free, and announced the time of God's favor.

But what Jesus didn't say is just as important as what he did say. The very next line of Isaiah's prophecy says, *and the day of vengeance of our God* (Isaiah 61:2). Jesus concluded with *the year of the Lord's favor*, and left out *the day of vengeance of our God*.

He didn't do this because he was the kind of preacher who only preached positive messages. He did it because *the year of the Lord's favor* applied to his first coming, and *the day of vengeance of our God* applies to his second coming.

This will happen when the Lord Jesus is revealed from heaven in blazing fire with his powerful angels. He will punish those who do not know God and do not obey the gospel of our Lord Jesus. They will be punished with everlasting destruction and shut out from the presence of the Lord and from the glory of his might (2 Thessalonians 1:7-9), wrote Paul.

Jesus' sermon had gone fairly well so far. *All spoke well of him and were amazed at the gracious words that came from his lips* (Luke 4:22). But then he did something that became almost typical. He deeply offended his listeners to reveal the badness of their hearts.

Luke 4:23 *Surely you will quote this proverb to me: Physician, heal yourself! And you will tell me, Do here in your hometown what we have heard that you did in Capernaum.*

Jesus had a reputation for miracles, and the people of Nazareth weren't unclear about their expectations. If Jesus healed in other towns, he'd surely heal in his own town. Backaches, headaches, toothaches, blindness, deafness, and other disorders were all represented. The time for preaching was over; now it was time for healing.

But instead of doing what the people expected, Jesus told a couple stories in which God's prophets did miracles for outsiders, but not for Israel. By implication, Jesus would bypass the town of Nazareth and take his ministry elsewhere. He flatly refused to heal anyone who came to service that day.

Luke 4:28-30 *All the people in the synagogue were furious when they heard this. They got up, drove him out of the town, and took him to the brow of the hill on which the town was built, in order to throw him off the cliff. But he walked right through the crowd and went on his way.*

There are two important things we ought to learn from this. First, Jesus doesn't owe anything to anyone. Due to our sin, we all deserve wrath (Ephesians 5:6). The fact that Jesus does anything for anyone is a matter of pure grace. He freely gives whatever he wants, whenever he wants, to whomever he wants—or not.

The second thing to learn flows out of the first: we don't approach Jesus with our demands. Ordinarily, whoever came to Jesus with humility received what they came for. But if we make demands of Christ we've misunderstood the master/servant relationship. We are not the master.

Nazareth knew more about Jesus than any other town, but rejected him most emphatically. The Bible says little more about them until the time of Jesus' death. Pilate put a sign on the cross that said, JESUS OF NAZARETH, THE KING OF THE JEWS (John 19:19). The rejection of Christ at Nazareth anticipated his future rejection by the world.

For Reflection and Review

- *How do you like your hometown?*
- *How will Jesus act differently when he returns?*
- *Why did Jesus refuse to heal in Nazareth?*

Lesson 213

Luke 4:31-32 *Then he went down to Capernaum.... They were amazed at his teaching, because his words had authority.*

Capernaum is situated on the northern shore of the Sea of Galilee, and is about a day and a half's journey from Nazareth by foot. It's where Peter lived and ran his fishing business. The people there were amazed at Jesus' teaching, and took note of his authority.

[T]he Son of Man has authority on earth to forgive sins (Matthew 9:6). *All authority in heaven and on earth has been given to me* (Matthew 28:18). And, *I have authority to lay [my life] down and authority to take it up again* (John 10:18).

Jesus proved his authority by casting out demons (Matthew 8:32), stopping a storm (Mark 4:39), raising the dead (John 11:43-44), and in many other ways. He had more authority than anyone else on earth, not because he was head of an empire, but because he was God in human flesh.

Luke 4:34 *What do you want with us, Jesus of Nazareth? Have you come to destroy us? I know who you are—the Holy One of God!*

As Jesus preached in the synagogue, a man possessed by a demon began acting up. The demon recognized Jesus as the *Holy One of God*, and feared being destroyed. Demons are fallen angels (Jude 1:6) that'll be thrown into the lake of burning sulfur (Revelation 20:10). They're more afraid of Jesus than many people are because they understand who he is.

Luke 4:35 *Be quiet! Jesus said sternly. Come out of him!*

The demon threw the man down and came out. We don't know how the man came to be possessed, only that Jesus delivered him. He couldn't set himself free, but was freed by Jesus Christ.

Even God's people are troubled by demons, sometimes, but Jesus can set us free. *Submit yourselves, then, to God. Resist the devil, and he will flee from you. Come near to God and he will come near to you* (James 4:7-8), wrote James. Demons are like rats that that feed on the garbage of sin. If we get rid of the garbage, the rats will go too.

Luke 4:38 *Jesus left the synagogue and went to the home of Simon.*

Simon Peter's home was nearby and, since the synagogue service was over, it was probably time for lunch. When they arrived, Peter's mother-in-law was suffering from a high fever. This may've been life-threatening, so they brought the matter to Jesus, and he rebuked the fever. *She got up at once and began to wait on them* (Luke 4:39). She didn't wait on them so Jesus would heal her; Jesus healed her and she began to wait on them. Grateful service was her response to the grace of Jesus Christ.

My friend Jerry was eighteen years old when he came to faith in Christ. A few years later he moved to Mexico where he and his wife reached out to abandoned children. God blessed their work and an orphanage now exists that serves hundreds of kids who used to be homeless.

This may be the last thing Jerry would've done apart from Jesus Christ. But when he learned what Jesus did for him, a lifetime of service seemed natural. Not everyone will start an orphanage, but everyone who believes in Jesus Christ should respond with grateful service.

Luke 4:42 *At daybreak, Jesus went out to a solitary place. The people were looking for him and when they came to where he was, they tried to keep him from leaving them.*

Jesus' ministry in Capernaum was so effective that the people didn't want him to leave. But Jesus wouldn't be detained. *I must proclaim the good news of the kingdom of God to the other towns also, because that is why I was sent* (Luke 4:43), he said.

It would've been easier for Jesus to stay in Capernaum and let everyone come to him. But Jesus was compelled by his heavenly Father to take the good news far and wide. In doing so, Jesus anticipated the church's work of taking the gospel to the whole world. *[Y]ou will be my witnesses in Jerusalem, and in all Judea and Samaria, and to the ends of the earth* (Acts 1:8), he said.

The church is often tempted to settle down and forget its mission. But whenever this happens, we not only lose our focus, but also our effectiveness. Like Christ himself, the church *must proclaim the good news of the kingdom of God to the other towns also, because that is [where we're] sent.*

*****

Luke 5:1 *One day as Jesus was standing by the Lake of Gennesaret, the people were crowding around him and listening to the word of God.*

As Jesus was preaching by the lake, the crowds were pressing in, so he got into Peter's boat and preached from off shore. Then he told Peter and the boys to let down their nets. They hadn't caught a fish all night, but did what Jesus said, and caught so many fish their nets began to break.

Peter fell at Jesus knees and said, *Go away from me, Lord; I am a sinful man!* (Luke 5:8).

We might expect Peter to say, *Let's go into business Lord; together we'll make a fortune.* But as Jesus taught from the boat, that day, Peter listened to the pure word of God, and felt a sense of unworthiness. He was a common fisherman sitting in the same boat as the holiest person who ever lived. When Jesus showed his power, in the remarkable catch of fish, Peter felt undeserving of his presence.

A shaft of light reveals dust in the air that we normally don't see. And a glimpse of God reveals sin in the soul of which we're normally unaware. The further we are from God, the more we'll feel righteous; and the closer we are to God, the more we'll sense our sin. Sinners think they are righteous, and the righteous know they are sinful.

Luke 5:10 *Do not be afraid; from now on you will fish for people.*

For many years, Peter's occupation was to catch fish for people. Now his occupation was to catch people for Christ. Peter preached on the day of Pentecost, and three thousand believed (Acts 2:41). A short time later he preached again, and two thousand more believed (Acts 4:4). The fisherman from Galilee became a man who fished for people.

More recently, a man was fishing off a riverbank, and was startled to see a human corpse floating downstream. He cast a line and reeled it in, only to find the corpse wasn't completely dead. But he would've been dead soon, if he hadn't been caught by the fisherman. The task of the church is to catch people for Christ, so they will *not perish but have eternal life* (John 3:16).

For Reflection and Review

- *How should Christians resist the devil?*
- *Why did Peter feel unworthy of Christ?*
- *How does the church catch people for Christ?*

Lesson 214

Luke 5:12-13 *While Jesus was in one of the towns, a man came along who was covered with leprosy. When he saw Jesus, he fell with his face to the ground and begged him, Lord, if you are willing, you can make me clean. Jesus reached out his hand and touched the man. I am willing, he said. Be clean! And immediately the leprosy left him.*

Several conditions were called leprosy, back then, but this man's case was advanced—he was *covered* with it. *Anyone with such a defiling disease must wear torn clothes, let their hair be unkempt, cover the lower part of their face and cry out, Unclean! Unclean! . . . They must live alone; they must live outside the camp* (Leviticus 13:45-46), wrote Moses.

No cure was in sight for this man, so he seemed destined to to a life of sorrow, misery, and loneliness. But then he learned of Jesus Christ. Perhaps he heard him preach from a distance, and learned about his miracles. He likely sought him out and, eventually, found him. *When he saw Jesus, he fell with his face to the ground and begged him . . . .*

The man's desperation left no room for dignity. He bowed as before a king, and pleaded for his life. *[I]f you are willing, you can make me clean,* he said. There may've been a moment when he wasn't sure what Jesus would do. Perhaps he'd be turned away because of his sin. Or maybe Jesus would send him to the Jordan to wash (2 Kings 5:10). But then Jesus did the unthinkable. He *reached out his hand and touched the man.*

Fear of catching the disease kept anyone else from touching him. It may've been years since he felt the loving touch of his wife, children, or anyone else. Jesus could've healed him with a word (Matthew 8:8), but *reached out his hand and touched the man.* Everyone else considered him untouchable, but Jesus will touch anyone. *I am willing, he said. Be clean!*

The disease of sin is infinitely worse than than any case of leprosy. No matter what we've done, however, or how many times we've done it, Jesus will take away our sin if we're willing to ask. *I am willing, he said. Be clean!*

*****

Luke 5:17 *One day Jesus was teaching, and Pharisees and teachers of the law were sitting there.*

They weren't there to support Jesus, but to scrutinize and oppose him. Most preachers would be intimidated by this, but Jesus was the most confident person who ever lived. He often clashed with religious leaders, and was never put to shame. But they were often put to shame.

Luke 5:18 *Some men came carrying a paralyzed man on a mat and tried to take him into the house to lay him before Jesus.*

These men heard that Jesus could heal, so they brought their paralyzed friend to the place where Jesus was teaching. The crowd was so dense, however, that they couldn't get through. So they went up on the flat roof porch and started tearing it off. The people inside heard the noise, and suddenly saw the light of day. Then they saw a man on a cot being lowered by ropes until he was right in front of Jesus. This was not a boring meeting.

The homeowner isn't mentioned, but he was remarkably gracious, even while his house was being destroyed. Most people would say, *Get off my roof!* But he was willing to let his roof be destroyed for the sake of the gospel. He must've been an honorable man, and it'll be a joy to talk about this event with him in heaven.

Luke 5:20 *When Jesus saw their faith, he said, Friend, your sins are forgiven.*

This is a little unusual. Jesus responded to *their faith*, not just the paralytic's faith. They may've had more faith than their friend, since they were the ones who brought him to Jesus. Those who are strong in faith should be a friend to those who aren't.

A godly man's faith began to spiral down when he lost his wife of many years. Months later, he told his friends that he no longer believed in God. They said, *That's okay, we're going to believe for you.* Every week they gathered for prayer and encouragement, until the dark night of this man's soul began to pass. He was able to believe again, with a little help from his friends.

We should also notice that Jesus ignored the man's paralysis, and addressed his greater need, which was forgiveness. It wasn't the response the paralytic was hoping for, but God knows that being forgiven is more important than being healed.

A friend of mine was a model of fitness before an accident left him a quadriplegic. I only knew him after the accident but, at his house, I saw a poster of a water skier putting up an enormous wall of water. It was the kind of poster you'd buy at a store, but it was my friend before his accident. He said, *I thank God every day for my accident because that's what he used to bring me to Christ.*

It's also interesting that Jesus was unnecessarily controversial. He could've simply healed the man, as he did many others, but instead he made the extraordinary claim of pardoning his sin. If Jesus wanted to upset the religious leaders, he couldn't have done it any better.

Luke 5:21 *Who is this fellow who speaks blasphemy?*

Blasphemy was a serious charge since, according to the Old Testament, *anyone who blasphemes the name of the Lord is to be put to death* (Leviticus 24:16). It was the charge of blasphemy, in fact, for which Jesus was put to death. *[T]he high priest tore his clothes and said, He has spoken blasphemy! . . . What do you think? He is worthy of death, they answered* (Matthew 26:65-66). And they were right. If Jesus wasn't God in human flesh, then much of what he said was blasphemy, and he was worthy of death for impersonating God.

Who can forgive sins but God alone? (Luke 5:21b), they asked. This, of course, was Jesus' point. Only God can forgive sins; Jesus forgave sins; therefore Jesus is God. Great claims require great proof, however, so Jesus would also provide the proof.

Luke 5:23 *Which is easier: to say, Your sins are forgiven, or to say, Get up and walk?*

Anyone can say *Your sins are forgiven* because it can't be disproven. But to say *Get up and walk* required a miracle. If Jesus could heal the paralytic, he could also claim to forgive sins. *So he said to the paralyzed man, I tell you, get up, take your mat and go home. Immediately he stood up in front of them, took what he had been lying on and went home praising God* (Luke 5:24-25).

This was an undeniable miracle, in front of many witnesses, which established Jesus' authority to forgive sins. Imagine the man's delight as feeling and strength spread throughout his body, making him completely whole. It also reminds us of what Jesus will do for us when he returns. *[He] will transform our lowly bodies so that they will be like his glorious body* (Philippians 3:21), wrote Paul.

One dear lady wrote the following: *I still can hardly believe it. I, with shriveled, bent fingers, atrophied muscles, gnarled knees, and no feeling from the shoulders down, will one day have a new body, light, bright, and clothed in righteousness – powerful and dazzling.*

Can you imagine the hope this gives someone spinal-cord injured like me? Or someone who is cerebral palsied, brain-injured, or who has multiple sclerosis? Imagine the hope this gives someone who is manic-depressive. No other religion, no other philosophy promises new bodies, hearts, and minds. Only in the Gospel of Christ do hurting people find such incredible hope (Joni Eareckson Tada).

For Reflection and Review

- *How is being forgiven like being healed from leprosy?*
- *How can friends strengthen each other's faith?*
- *Why is being forgiven more important than being healed?*

Lesson 215

Luke 6:1 *One Sabbath Jesus was going through the grainfields, and his disciples began to pick some heads of grain, rub them in their hands and eat the kernels.*

Some might consider this stealing, but there was a provision in the law of Moses that allowed people to eat their neighbor's produce, so long as they weren't harvesting. *If you enter your neighbor's grainfield, you may pick kernels with your hands, but you must not put a sickle to their standing grain* (Deuteronomy 23:25), wrote Moses.

When the Pharisees caught the disciples picking grain, their objection wasn't that they were stealing, but that they were working on the Sabbath. *On it you shall not do any work* (Exodus 20:10), said God. The Pharisees thought picking grain was a form of work, which shouldn't be done on the Sabbath.

Jesus' defense of his disciples' behavior is interesting. He referred to an Old Testament episode in which David was given bread from the Tabernacle, which only priests were allowed to eat (1 Samuel 21:1-6, Leviticus 24:8-9). In desperation, David broke the law of God without being punished or corrected. Jesus was making the point that human need takes priority over legal minutia. Picking grain on the Sabbath to satisfy hunger was perfectly acceptable.

The Pharisees seem extreme, at points, but wanted to protect the Sabbath because it was an important part of biblical religion. *Anyone who desecrates [the Sabbath] is to be put to death; those who do any work on that day must be cut off from their people* (Exodus 31:14), said God.

On one occasion a man was caught gathering wood on the Sabbath, and was placed under arrest until a determination could be made. *Then the Lord said to Moses, The man must die. The whole assembly must stone him outside the camp. So the assembly took him outside the camp and stoned him to death, as the Lord commanded Moses* (Numbers 15:35-36). Honoring the Sabbath was very serious business.

Luke 6:5 *Then Jesus said to them, The Son of Man is Lord of the Sabbath.*

This probably made the religious leaders crosseyed. The Sabbath was ordained by God, so Jesus' claim to be *Lord of the Sabbath* was nothing less than a claim to be God. Why did Jesus say such things? Did he want to be crucified?

Sabbath controversies are one of the ways Jesus turned the religious leaders against him. He did this to bring about his crucifixion for the sins of the world. Crucifixion wasn't something that happened to Jesus; he intentionally brought about his execution by contradicting the religious leaders. One of the most effective ways he did this was by often opposing their view of the Sabbath (John 9:16).

*****

Luke 6:6 *On another Sabbath he went into the synagogue and was teaching, and a man was there whose right hand was shriveled.*

We can only imagine how much this man hated his shriveled hand, and prayed for healing as a boy. Every night, perhaps, he'd stretch out his hand and say, *Dear God, please heal me. I'm willing to do whatever you want. If you'll just heal me I will be your servant for the rest of my life.* This may've gone on for years, until he finally accepted the fact that he wouldn't be healed. He didn't abandon his faith in God, but sadly accepted his condition.

Then, one Sabbath, he went to a synagogue service where Jesus was teaching. Maybe it was his regular synagogue, or maybe he traveled to get there. Maybe Jesus saw him when he came in, or maybe their eyes met during the service. But the moment came when Jesus told him to stand in front of everyone. *Stretch out your hand*, he said. So one more time the man stretched out his hand. But this time it began to open. Tendons stretched, muscles formed and, suddenly, it was a perfect match to the other. What an amazing answer to prayer, so many years later!

Luke 6:11 *But the Pharisees and the teachers of the law were furious and began to discuss with one another what they might do to Jesus.*

Most of the religious leaders thought sick people shouldn't be cared for on the Sabbath, unless they might die before sunset. By healing a man on the Sabbath, Jesus publicly refuted this teaching, and undermined the authority of the religious leaders. This made them so furious they began to plot *how they might kill Jesus* (Mark 3:6).

This, of course, was Jesus' plan all along. Since the religious leaders weren't willing to believe in him, Jesus used their wicked hearts to bring about his death, for the salvation of all who would believe. Even those who oppose Jesus will serve his purpose in some other way.

For Reflection and Review

- *Why were the religious leaders so concerned about the Sabbath?*
- *How did Jesus use the Sabbath to bring about his crucifixion?*
- *How should Christians view the Sabbath?*

Lesson 216

Luke 6:22-23 *Blessed are you when people hate you, when they exclude you and insult you and reject your name as evil, because of the Son of Man. Rejoice in that day and leap for joy, because great is your reward in heaven. For that is how their ancestors treated the prophets.*

As Jesus' popularity increased, so did his opposition. Knowing the hatred toward him would spill over on his followers, Jesus prepared them for insult and rejection. They'd be considered evil because they followed Jesus Christ.

This is because there are *spiritual forces of evil in the heavenly realms* (Ephesians 6:12), wrote Paul. These demonic forces oppose everything right by confusing good and evil. *Woe to those who call evil good and good evil, who put darkness for light and light for darkness, who put bitter for sweet and sweet for bitter* (Isaiah 5:20), wrote Isaiah.

As Christianity spread throughout the empire, Christians were accused of being atheists who practiced incest and cannibalism. They were atheists because they didn't worship the Roman gods; they were incestuous because they married their brothers and sisters; and they were cannibals because they ate the body and blood of Jesus.

Each of these rumors was essentially false, but true in a sense. The early Christians weren't atheists, but refused to worship the Roman gods. They weren't incestuous, but married fellow believers whom they called *brothers* and *sisters*. They weren't cannibals, but partook of bread and wine which they called the body and blood of Christ. The world will never understand Christianity, and will often mistreat believers. But we are in good company. *For that is how [they] treated the prophets,* said Jesus.

Luke 6:27-28 *Love your enemies, do good to those who hate you, bless those who curse you, pray for those who mistreat you.*

This was contrary to the practice in Jesus' day, which was to *hate your enemies* (Matthew 5:43). Hating our enemies feels good, but hurts us more than if we choose to love. Hatred is an infection that will kill us from a simple wound.

Two brothers had a nasty argument over their inheritance. A genie appeared to one, and offered him anything, on the condition that his brother got twice as much. He thought for a moment and said, *Okay, make me blind in one eye.* Hatred harms the hater more than the one who's hated.

Jesus preached the opposite, and practiced what he preached. When they crucified him he prayed, *Father, forgive them, for they do not know what they are doing* (Luke 23:34). It's one thing to pray for your enemies after they stop hurting you, but Jesus prayed for his killers while they were still killing him.

Following Jesus' example, Stephen also prayed for his killers: *Lord, do not hold this sin against them* (Acts 7:60), he said. Christians can forgive others because we've been forgiven, and because we have eternal life in the best of all possible worlds. Everything doesn't have to be perfect for us right now, because it will be in the age to come.

*****

Luke 6:38 *Give, and it will be given to you. A good measure, pressed down, shaken together and running over, will be poured into your lap.*

This is the image of a grain merchant giving his customer a very good deal. He filled the container, pressed it down, shook it together and poured in even more. Our sinful nature wants to keep as much as possible, but Jesus taught *It is more blessed to give than to receive* (Acts 20:35). Could he be right?

One of the greatest joys of my youth was giving my little brother a bicycle for his sixth birthday. I couldn't afford a new one, but I found some parts in the garage that made a good start. I repainted the frame, cleaned the wheels and made several other improvements. The project took a few weeks, and I replaced so many parts, that it completely drained my savings.

What kept me going was the joy that it would bring my little brother. Every hour was a labor of love, and every new part was a gift of love. I was so excited that I woke him up slightly after midnight, on the day of his birthday, to give him the gift I built for him. He was thrilled, of course, but I had even greater joy from giving. That little labor of love enriched my life more than his. This is the culture of heaven, and what Jesus wants on earth. *Give, and it will be given to you.*

*****

Luke 6:39 *Can the blind lead the blind? Will they not both fall into a pit?*

If you were in the middle of a large city, and suddenly lost your sight, you'd reach out for someone to lead you. But if you grabbed onto someone who was also blind, you could both step into traffic and be killed.

That's what it's like to follow anyone other than Jesus Christ. Everyone else is a blind guide who will lead us into the pit of hell. Jesus is the only one who sees with perfect clarity. Since we're all incurable followers, our only wisdom is to follow the best.

Whoever leads us away from Christ, wants us to follow them instead. This is true of our peers, professors, and cultural elites. Before we follow anyone else we should ask, *Who's more reliable than Jesus Christ?* Would you rather follow a blind guide, or the only one who sees?

*****

Luke 6:45 *A good man brings good things out of the good stored up in his heart, and an evil man brings evil things out of the evil stored up in his heart. For the mouth speaks what the heart is full of.*

People may've guarded their speech in front of Rabbi Jesus, but we can imagine the adolescent Jesus overhearing the speech of ordinary people. He must've been surprised by what came out of their mouths. Jesus concluded that how people talk is a good indication of what's in their heart.

I was waiting for an elevator at a hospital when a man came walking down the hall. He was around the corner, so I couldn't see him, but I heard his approaching steps. Then, before he turned the corner, he let out a single word—an expletive. I'd never met the man, or even seen his face, but immediately I knew something about him: his vocabulary wasn't entirely Christian.

Many people would say, *It just came out.* But, according to Jesus, nothing comes out that's not already in. One of the most certain indicators of what's in our hearts, therefore, is what comes out our mouths. And *everyone will have to give account on the day of judgment for every empty word they have spoken. For by your words you will be acquitted, and by your words you will be condemned* (Matthew 12:36-37), said Jesus.

For Reflection and Review

- *Why should believers love their enemies?*
- *Why is it hard to be generous?*
- *Why is what we say important?*

Lesson 217

Luke 7:11 *Soon afterward, Jesus went to a town called Nain, and his disciples and a large crowd went along with him.*

Nain was a little village a few miles south of Nazareth. It's only mentioned here, and was considered a place of little significance. But Jesus' was passing by, and would grace them with his presence.

Luke 7:12 *As he approached the town gate, a dead person was being carried out—the only son of his mother, and she was a widow.*

To beat the smell of decomposition, funerals were carried out quickly, so the boy probably died that day. We don't know if he died of an illness, or if it was an accident, but the funeral was especially sad because his mother was a widow. First she lost her husband, then she lost her only son. There were few paying jobs for women, back then, so she'd also become poor. This was likely the saddest day of her life.

Luke 7:13 *When the Lord saw her, his heart went out to her and he said, Don't cry.*

This is something you should never say to a woman who's lost her only son, and her only source of income. This dear woman suffered a terrible loss, and needed to grieve more than ever. But Jesus would turn her grief into joy, and he will do the same for us (Revelation 21:4). Even if we grieve for years, we won't have to grieve forever.

Luke 7:14 *Then he went up and touched the bier they were carrying him on, and the bearers stood still.*

They may've known who Jesus was, and heard about his miracles. But Jesus hadn't raised anyone from the dead before, so they weren't sure what to expect. Then he said, *Young man, I say to you, get up! The dead man sat up and began to talk, and Jesus gave him back to his mother* (Luke 7:15).

Instead of going to the cemetery, they went back to their village, to enjoy the rest of their lives. If they had planned a funeral meal, it became a party. The conversation went on for hours, as they talked about Jesus' power over death.

This reminds us of our own resurrection, and eternal life in the kingdom of God. *There will be no more death or mourning or crying or pain, for the old order of things has passed away* (Revelation 21:4b), wrote John. What Jesus did for this young man he'll do for all who believe in him, and will give us eternal joy. *I am the resurrection and the life. The one who believes in me will live, even though they die* (John 11:25), he said.

*****

Luke 7:19 *Are you the one who is to come, or should we expect someone else?*

John the Baptist was in prison for preaching against King Herod, who married his own brother's wife (Mark 6:17-18). She probably came for a visit, when Herod convinced her to leave his brother, and marry him instead. John couldn't leave this alone and, as a result, found himself in prison where he'd shortly die (Mark 6:27-28). During this time his faith in Christ began to weaken, so he sent a couple of his own disciples to ask Jesus, *Are you the one who is to come, or should we expect someone else?*

These are the last recorded words of John the Baptist, and we're surprised by them. John was the last person we'd expect to doubt Jesus Christ. When he baptized Jesus, John saw the Spirit descend on him like a dove, and heard a voice from heaven saying, *You are my Son, whom I love; with you I am well pleased* (Luke 3:22). John had visible and audible proof that Jesus was the Messiah.

But in the dungeon of despair, John began to doubt what he once believed so firmly. Deep in his soul he wondered if he'd been wrong. If Jesus was the Messiah, why didn't he help John?

For many, doubt is a matter of convenience. It's easier to doubt than to follow Jesus Christ, so many remain in a state of doubt, to avoid the cost of discipleship. But those who doubt most earnestly, are those with a serious faith, that has been seriously challenged. Like the young mother whose baby was born with a birth defect, that rang up medical bills, impoverished the family, and caused her husband to leave. As life crumbled around her she began to doubt what she once believed about a loving God (source unknown).

In such cases the Bible says, *Be merciful to those who doubt* (Jude 1:22). Faith and doubt of this kind aren't opposites, but alternate rungs on the ladder of spiritual growth. In order to reach the next level of faith, we have to climb over doubt.

A complete absence of doubt can even be a sign we haven't truly believed. *Those who believe they believe in God but without passion in the heart, without anguish of mind, without uncertainty, without doubt, and even at times without despair, believe only in the idea of God, and not in God himself* (Madeleine L'Engle).

Luke 7:22 *Go back and report to John what you have seen and heard: The blind receive sight, the lame walk, those who have leprosy are cleansed, the deaf hear, the dead are raised, and the good news is proclaimed to the poor.*

When the disciples of John arrived, Jesus was healing the sick, just as the prophet foretold. *Then will the eyes of the blind be opened and the ears of the deaf unstopped. Then will the lame leap like a deer, and the mute tongue shout for joy* (Isaiah 35:5-6), wrote Isaiah.

This was compelling evidence but, somehow, John was hoping for more. He expected Jesus to set up the kingdom of God (Matthew 3:2) and rule the world. The healing miracles were fine, but they fell short of the kingdom John was expecting.

He probably also expected great things for himself. If Jesus was king of the world, John would have an important role. Instead, he was languishing in prison, while the wicked King Herod was still on his throne. The difference between what John was hoping for, and what he received, was causing him to wonder about Jesus. Like millions after him, John was trying to *pick up the pieces of a once unshakeable faith* (Philip Yancey).

Luke 7:23 *Blessed is anyone who does not stumble on account of me.*

Jesus sent a promise of blessing to John that applies to anyone who refuses to stumble on account of Jesus Christ. John was close to stumbling, and this is what he needed to hear. Perhaps he got down on his knees and prayed something like this: *Dear God, this is not what I expected. I thought Jesus would set up his kingdom, and I would help him rule. I thought kings would bow down to Jesus, but King Herod has thrown me in prison. I don't understand what's going on, God, but I'm going to trust you, and your Son Jesus Christ to the end.*

Not much later, some of the Herod's men stopped by with a sword. John put his head on a block (Matthew 14:6-12) and the next thing he knew, he was in a better place by far. John fulfilled his mission on earth, and received his reward in heaven.

One of the things we learn from John is the importance of taking the long view. If we expect too much in this life we'll be disappointed. But if we expect great things in the age to come, our disappointments won't derail our faith. The message of the Bible is never *our best life now*, but always *our best life then*.

For Reflection and Review

- *What will it be like to be raised from the dead?*
- *Why did John the Baptist doubt?*
- *How can we overcome our doubts?*

Lesson 218

Luke 7:36 *[Jesus] went to the Pharisee's house and reclined at the table.*

This was not a friendly meal, so much as a formal interview with a rising rabbi. Invited guests probably included the Pharisee's friends and Jesus' disciples. Such events could be semi-public, with uninvited guests staying away from the table, and paying quiet attention to the conversation.

Luke 7:37-38 *A woman in that town who lived a sinful life learned that Jesus was eating at the Pharisee's house, so she came there with an alabaster jar of perfume. As she stood behind him at his feet weeping, she began to wet his feet with her tears. Then she wiped them with her hair, kissed them and poured perfume on them.*

To imagine this scene correctly, it helps to understand the dining arrangement. They weren't sitting on chairs around a high table, but lying on mats around a low table, just a few inches off the ground. This explains how the woman had access to Jesus' feet without going under the table.

The Bible doesn't tell us the woman's name, but reveals quite a bit about her. First, she lived a *sinful life*, which probably means she was a prostitute. This wasn't something women aspired to, but was often a matter of survival. Her issues would've included guilt, shame, and social rejection.

Second, she knew something of Jesus Christ, or she wouldn't have come to this event. Perhaps she heard him preach, and saw the radical difference he made in the lives of others. Her sin contrasted with his holiness but, somehow, she felt drawn to him.

Third, she was extremely courageous, since she invited herself to the most self-righteous party in town. If you've ever been to a party where you felt out of place, you know how awkward it can be. Double that feeling, or triple it, and you know what she was going through.

Fourth, she understood worship. She washed Jesus' feet with her tears, dried them with her hair, kissed them, and poured perfume on them. This is the most lavish display of worship found in the gospels. It made everyone feel uncomfortable except Jesus, who actually enjoyed her lavish display of love.

Jesus was always happy to receive worship, not only for the glory it brought him, but for the good it brought to others. By adoring Jesus Christ we see him at the center, and find our rightful place in the world he created.

Luke 7:39 *When the Pharisee who had invited him saw this, he said to himself, If this man were a prophet, he would know who is touching him and what kind of woman she is—that she is a sinner.*

Pharisees were repulsed by physical contact with sinners because they feared religious contamination. But Jesus knew he wasn't being contaminated by this woman; she was being purified by him. She was being transformed from a woman of vice to a woman of virtue, from a woman of the night to a woman of the light.

Several years ago I met a woman who used to be a prostitute, and ran a business of prostitution. Then she was arrested and sent to prison. While she was there, she came to faith in Jesus Christ, and her life was wonderfully changed. By the time I met her, she was one of the godliest people I've ever known, and it was almost impossible to think of her as anything else. The power of Christ to change lives is one of the most remarkable things about him.

Luke 7:44-46 *Then he turned toward the woman and said to Simon, Do you see this woman? I came into your house. You did not give me any water for my feet, but she wet my feet with her tears and wiped them with her hair. You did not give me a kiss, but this woman, from the time I entered, has not stopped kissing my feet. You did not put oil on my head, but she has poured perfume on my feet.*

This little dinner party had started badly. Not only was Simon a terrible host, but he was shockingly rude to his guest of honor. Foot washing was a minimal hospitality, and a common courtesy in every home. Not offering it to Jesus wasn't an accident, but a deliberate snub.

A kiss on the cheek is still practiced in Eastern culture, and corresponds to our handshake. But Jesus wasn't welcomed in this way either. Perfumed oil was sometimes applied to the head, but this hospitality was also forgone. The sinful woman did everything Simon the Pharisee had not. She washed Jesus' feet with her tears, kissed them, and poured perfume on them.

Luke 7:47 *Therefore, I tell you, her many sins have been forgiven—as her great love has shown. But whoever has been forgiven little loves little.*

The woman's gratitude didn't earn her forgiveness, but showed she was forgiven. Forgiveness always evokes gratitude. Simon had religion but not forgiveness. That's why he had no affection for Jesus Christ. Whoever is thankful to Jesus Christ is probably forgiven, and whoever is not thankful to Jesus Christ is probably not forgiven. It's almost inconceivable that a person would be forgiven, and not want to worship Jesus.

Luke 7:48-50 *Then Jesus said to her, Your sins are forgiven. . . . Your faith has saved you; go in peace.*

These are the most comforting words in the world to those who've felt the weight of their sins. We need to hear them the first time we come to Christ, and many times thereafter.

A young lady and her fiancé were youth leaders in their church, and led many of the young people to faith in Jesus Christ. They taught about sexual purity, but failed themselves, and she became pregnant. In order to save their reputations, they had an abortion, and were later married in the church.

My wedding day was the worst day of my life, she said. *As I was marching up the aisle in my lily white dress with all the people smiling and congratulating me, a voice within me was screaming—you are a murderer.*

Years later she couldn't get over her sin, because she couldn't believe that God would forgive her.

So she went to a Christian counselor who explained that she had underestimated two important things: her own sinfulness, and the grace of Jesus Christ. *For if, while we were God's enemies, we were reconciled to him through the death of his Son, how much more, having been reconciled, shall we be saved through his life!* (Romans 5:10), wrote Paul.

Jesus has always been a friend of sinners—even Christian sinners. One of the great ironies of Christianity is that our sin can bring us closer to Christ if we believe in his forgiveness. He died for our sins, so we can be forgiven, and love him forever. *Your sins are forgiven. . . . Your faith has saved you; go in peace.*

For Reflection and Review

- *How does worshipping Jesus help the worshipper?*
- *Why is gratitude a good indication that we are forgiven?*
- *How can sin bring us closer to Christ?*

Lesson 219

Luke 8:4 *While a large crowd was gathering and people were coming to Jesus from town after town, he told this parable.*

Jesus loved parables, and about twenty-five of them are found throughout the gospels. They are short comparison stories, from everyday life, that make a spiritual point. This parable is dear to me because of the way God used it, early in my Christian life.

I was eighteen years old, and had only been a believer for a few months. I shared my faith with friends, but most of them thought I was crazy. As my popularity declined, I wondered if I could back away from Jesus, and recover my reputation. I knew little of the Bible, but opened it up at random, and came to this parable. Here I saw myself so vividly that I got down on my knees, and recommitted my life to Christ.

Luke 8:5 *A farmer went out to sow his seed. As he was scattering the seed, some fell along the path; it was trampled on, and the birds ate it up.*

Most of Jesus' audience recognized this scene because it was so common. When it was time to plant, farmers would take a bag of seed into their field, and scatter it on the ground. Every field had a path, where some of the seed would fall, and birds would come and eat it up.

This is one of the few parables for which Jesus provided the interpretation, so we know exactly what he meant. *The seed is the word of God. Those along the path are the ones who hear, and then the devil comes and takes away the word from their hearts, so that they may not believe and be saved* (Luke 8:11-12), he said.

Like seed on a path, the word of God rests lightly on these people. To them, it has little more significance than children's stories. If you want to know where the devil is on Sunday mornings, he's in the parking lot of many churches, waiting to steal God's word from people's hearts.

Luke 8:6 *Some fell on rocky ground, and when it came up, the plants withered because they had no moisture.*

[These] are the ones who receive the word with joy when they hear it, but they have no root. They believe for a while, but in the time of testing they fall away (Luke 8:13), said Jesus.

If there's rock beneath an inch of soil, plants will shoot up quickly because all the growth is above ground. The plant appears to be healthy, but it will not last, because the roots are very shallow. Under the scorching sun, the plant withers and dies.

This is where I saw myself in the story. I believed for a little while, but in the time of testing I wanted to reconsider. There are many unbelievers, in fact, who once claimed to be Christians. They made a profession of faith, but didn't put down roots, so it was only a matter of time before their faith withered and died.

Many years ago I led a young man to Christ, and his eyes lit up with faith. I encouraged him to read a chapter of the Bible almost every day, to spend time in prayer, and join a good church. I said, *If you do this your faith will grow. If you don't, it'll wither and die.* He stayed with it for a while, but his church attendance declined, and then he fell away. I wish I could say this was unusual, but it's been a pattern for two thousand years.

Luke 8:7 *Other seed fell among thorns, which grew up with it and choked the plants.*

Weeds are nasty things that want to take over the world. They compete for sunlight and soil, so good plants can't reach their potential. Many years ago, we owned a house with a steep hill. To avoid mowing, we let it go wild, but the weeds grew over ten feet tall. The town even gave us a fine for not controlling our weeds!

The seed that fell among thorns stands for those who hear, but as they go on their way they are choked by life's worries, riches and pleasures, and they do not mature (Luke 8:14), said Jesus.

Perhaps you know someone who hasn't matured as a Christian. They make a profession of faith, but there hasn't been any growth for years. Instead of bearing fruit for God, they remain fruitless due to the weeds in their life. All we have to do for this to happen to us is nothing. The weeds will grow all by themselves. The only way to grow in faith is to pull out the weeds whenever we see them.

Luke 8:8 *Still other seed fell on good soil. It came up and yielded a crop, a hundred times more than was sown.*

Jesus said *the seed on good soil stands for those with a noble and good heart, who hear the word, retain it, and by persevering produce a crop* (Luke 8:15). This is how we make the most of our lives. It's not a matter of wealth or fame, but of hearing God's word, retaining God's word, and living God's word to the end.

My mother-in-law is in her eighties but continues to visit women in prison, to share God's word with them. It's not always easy, but she's done this faithfully for decades. Through her service many have believed, and will thank her in heaven. Serving the Lord is more than a duty; it's our best opportunity for a life well spent.

For Reflection and Review

- *Why does God's word rest lightly on some?*
- *What things keep God's word from being most effective?*
- *Why did Jesus stress the importance of remaining in his word?*

Lesson 220

Luke 8:22 *One day Jesus said to his disciples, Let us go over to the other side of the lake.*

The Sea of Galilee is only eight miles wide, but the disciples may've never been to the other side. It was Gentile territory and was normally avoided. But Jesus wanted to go there and, as they went, he fell asleep. Then they encountered a storm, and were in danger of losing their lives. So they woke up Jesus and said, *don't you care if we drown?* (Mark 4:38).

This has been asked by Christians throughout the ages. As long as the waters are calm, we believe God is taking care of us. But the moment we enter a storm, our hearts begin to accuse. *Don't you care that I'm unemployed? Don't you care that I'm losing my house? Don't you care that my child is sick?* But storms are also an opportunity for Jesus to reveal his power. So *He got up and rebuked the wind and the raging waters; the storm subsided, and all was calm* (Luke 8:24).

I got on the freeway, years ago, and hit a patch of ice. Suddenly I was going sideways. Then I was going backward. Then I was going sideways again. Then I was going forward. I did a complete circle, in regular traffic, at fifty miles an hour—and ended up going in the same direction. It was like nothing even happened, except that my heart was beating a little faster. It's surprising how quickly we can find ourselves in trouble, and how quickly the Lord can turn things around. He *rebuked the wind and the raging waters; the storm subsided, and all was calm.*

Luke 8:25 *In fear and amazement they asked one another, Who is this?*

This little question occurs throughout the gospels, to help us think more deeply about who Jesus is. Here we see he's Lord over nature. Elsewhere we see that he's Lord over Satan, Lord over sickness, Lord over death, and Lord over all. This is the Bible's conclusion, but we must come to it ourselves. The better we understand the lordship of Christ, the more we'll be in awe of him.

Luke 8:27 *When Jesus stepped ashore, he was met by a demon-possessed man from the town.*

From the various gospel accounts, we know this man was chained, but had broken free, and couldn't be subdued. He lived in the tombs, and refused to wear clothes. Night and day he cried out, and cut himself with stones. He was so frightening, in fact, no one would go near him.

This is the most extreme case of demonic possession in the Bible. The moment they saw this man, the disciples probably wanted to get back in their boat and go home. But this was the one for whom Jesus came. He didn't come by accident, but for the purpose of saving this troubled soul.

Luke 8:28 *When he saw Jesus, he cried out and fell at his feet, shouting at the top of his voice, What do you want with me, Jesus, Son of the Most High God? I beg you, do not torture me!*

Here it's clear that demons can speak through people. Through the man's vocal apparatus, the demons begged Jesus not to torture them. This is surprising enough, but Satan can also speak through Christians. When Peter tried to convince Jesus not to go to the cross, Jesus replied, *Get behind me, Satan!* (Matthew 16:23). If Satan can speak through Christians, then we ought to be careful he doesn't speak through us.

It's also interesting that the demons recognized Jesus. *What do you want with me, Jesus, Son of the Most High God?* they said. To the natural eye, Jesus looked like a regular person. But from the gospel accounts of demon possession, it's clear the demons knew who Jesus was. *I know who you are—the Holy One of God* (Mark 1:24), they said. *Whenever the impure spirits saw him, they fell down before him and cried out, You are the Son of God* (Mark 3:11). The gospels contain more demonic conflicts than other parts of the Bible because Jesus was the center of their attention.

Luke 8:30 *Jesus asked him, What is your name? Legion, he replied, because many demons had gone into him.*

A legion was a Roman military unit of six thousand men, so this man was host to many demons. Evil is not an impersonal force, and neither is good. Angels, demons, people, and God are all caught up in a cosmic conflict between good and evil. The outcome is certain, but the battle's not over.

Luke 8:31 *And they begged Jesus repeatedly not to order them to go into the Abyss.*

Hell is such a dreadful place that even demons fear to go there. Many inhabit the earth, but some are in hell even now. *[T]he angels who did not keep their positions of authority but abandoned their proper dwelling—these he has kept in darkness, bound with everlasting chains for judgment on the great Day* (Jude 1:6), wrote Jude. The demons in this story knew their day was coming, and trembled before the one who'd be their judge.

Luke 8:32 *A large herd of pigs was feeding there on the hillside. The demons begged Jesus to let them go into the pigs, and he gave them permission.*

But when the demons entered the pigs, they ran into the lake and were drowned. The number of pigs was about two thousand (Mark 5:13), which was a great financial loss. Jesus might've been surprised by this but, more likely, he was showing that a human being is worth more than two thousand pigs. Jesus would also show the value of human beings by shedding his blood on the cross for us. The least valued members of society are precious to God, and worth more than we can imagine.

Luke 8:35 *When they came to Jesus, they found the man from whom the demons had gone out, sitting at Jesus' feet, dressed and in his right mind.*

Jesus has power to heal the mind as well as the body. Since he's the center of reality, staying close to him is staying close to reality. Jesus gave the man his sanity, and the man sat at Jesus' feet. Our mental health is best maintained by sitting Jesus' feet.

Luke 8:38-39 *The man from whom the demons had gone out begged to go with him, but Jesus sent him away, saying, Return home and tell how much God has done for you. So the man went away and told all over town how much Jesus had done for him.*

His story was remarkable. He was so possessed by the powers of darkness that he couldn't function socially. Then one day, Jesus showed up, and gave him back his life. Perhaps the people said, *Tell us more*, so he went into greater detail.

After the resurrection, some of Jesus' disciples probably went back to this town, and explained that Jesus died for our sins, and rose to give us eternal life. If so, they had a ready audience due to this man's story. He didn't own a Bible, or go to seminary, but knew Jesus Christ, and had been changed by him.

Whoever knows Jesus Christ can talk about the difference he's made in their lives. The easiest way to do this is to think of your life in three parts: your life before Christ, how you came to Christ, and how Christ changed your life.

Before I came to Christ I was insecure and lacking direction. But the summer after high school a friend helped me find God through faith in Jesus Christ. Ever since then I've known God personally, and found great joy in living for him.

A testimony doesn't have to be long or impressive. It should briefly tell your story, and point people to Christ. The purpose of your testimony isn't to talk about yourself, but to tell others about your Savior.

For Reflection and Review

- *Has Jesus ever calmed a storm for you?*
- *How does Jesus restore our mental health?*
- *How has Jesus Christ changed your life?*

Lesson 221

Luke 8:41-42 *Then a man named Jairus, a synagogue leader, came and fell at Jesus' feet, pleading with him to come to his house because his only daughter, a girl of about twelve, was dying.*

Most religious leaders weren't favorable toward Jesus, but the urgency of his need compelled Jairus to seek the Lord's help, regardless what others might think. By throwing himself at Jesus' feet, he honored him as one might honor a king. Then he begged a favor.

Desperation can awaken us to our need for Jesus Christ. When life is going well, we might feel free to do as we please, without concern for God. But in a crisis, we turn to God instinctively, and even reform our lives. After the crisis has passed, some return to their old ways. But this is never wise, because our need for God is always the same. Desperation simply makes it clear to us.

Luke 8:42-43 *As Jesus was on his way, the crowds almost crushed him. And a woman was there who had been subject to bleeding for twelve years, but no one could heal her.*

We don't know her condition exactly, but it appears to be menstrual. It kept her from a normal lifestyle, and may've kept her from marriage. *She had suffered a great deal under the care of many doctors and had spent all she had, yet instead of getting better she grew worse* (Mark 5:26), wrote Mark.

This dear lady was so miserable, she was willing to spend her last penny trying to get better. She likely traveled from town to town, seeking the best physicians, and taking their medications. But all the doctors, and all their advice, only made her worse. And now she was broke.

Luke 8:44 *She came up behind [Jesus] and touched the edge of his cloak, and immediately her bleeding stopped.*

Instead of approaching Jesus directly, she snuck up behind him. The explanation is found in an Old Testament passage she probably knew well. *When a woman has a discharge of blood for many days at a time other than her monthly period or has a discharge that continues beyond her period, she will be unclean* (Leviticus 15:25), wrote Moses.

Not only that, but anyone who touched her would also be unclean (Leviticus 15:27). Since Jesus was a holy man, he might try to avoid her, so she decided to get her healing secretly. *If I only touch his cloak, I will be healed* (Matthew 9:21), she said to herself.

Luke 8:45 *Who touched me? Jesus asked.*

Having received the healing she came for, the woman wanted to slip away unnoticed. But Jesus called her out. Her condition was publicly known, and he wanted her healing to be publicly known, so she'd be received by others. *Then the woman, seeing that she could not go unnoticed, came trembling and fell at his feet. In the presence of all the people, she told why she had touched him and how she had been instantly healed. Then he said to her, Daughter, your faith has healed you. Go in peace* (Luke 8:47-48).

The woman's physical, emotional, and spiritual suffering came to an end because of Jesus Christ. This reminds us of what Christ will do for everyone in the age to come. Sin brought misery into the world (Genesis 3:16-19), but Christ is reversing the curse. We may have to wait for a while, but we won't be disappointed.

Luke 8:49 *While Jesus was still speaking, someone came from the house of Jairus, the synagogue leader. Your daughter is dead, he said. Do not bother the teacher anymore.*

Time was of the essence for Jairus, and any delay caused by the woman's healing certainly made him nervous. Then came the dreadful news: *Your daughter is dead*. The hope went out of his eyes, the blood drained from his face, and he went weak in the knees. What could be worse than the death of a child?

Luke 8:50 *Hearing this, Jesus said to Jairus, Do not be afraid; just believe.*

This wouldn't be easy, of course, since faith and fear often compete within us. We can allow fear to overcome our faith, or we can allow faith to overcome our fear. *So do not fear, for I am with you; do not be dismayed, for I am your God. I will strengthen you and help you; I will uphold you with my righteous right hand* (Isaiah 41:10), said God. So instead of giving into fear, Jairus put his faith in God's Son.

Luke 8:51 *When he arrived at the house of Jairus, he did not let anyone go in with him except Peter, John and James, and the child's father and mother.*

Peter, John, and James were Jesus' closest disciples. They were given the honor of being with him, not only here, but also at his transfiguration (Matthew 17:1-13), and while he prayed in the garden of Gethsemane (Mark 14:32-34). The closer we are to Jesus Christ, the more we'll see of him, and the more we'll be amazed by him.

Luke 8:52 *Meanwhile, all the people were wailing and mourning for [Jairus' daughter].*

Funerals often took place the day someone died, and professional mourners were occasionally used to help with the grieving process. If you go to a funeral where everyone is weeping, something inside you will want to weep, even if you normally wouldn't. The ministry of mourners was to help people weep so they could heal emotionally. But Jesus thought this was premature.

Luke 8:52 *Stop wailing, [he] said. She is not dead but asleep.*

The death of God's people is sometimes described as sleep because we wake up in a better place. But, in this case, Jesus was about to turn her death into a nap. So, *he took her by the hand and said, My child, get up! Her spirit returned, and at once she stood up* (Luke 8:54-55).

We can imagine her parent's delight as they received their little girl back to life. What a party must've followed! *You turned my wailing into dancing; you removed my sackcloth and clothed me with joy* (Psalm 30:11), wrote David. *I will turn their mourning into gladness; I will give them comfort and joy instead of sorrow* (Jeremiah 31:13), said God.

A young man developed cancer and found himself afraid of dying. Then it dawned on him that, even if he survived, it was only a matter of time before he'd die anyway. Through it all he came to faith in Jesus Christ and said, *I finally found the answer to the six foot hole* (Paul Azinger). Life's ultimate concern isn't how to live long, but how to live forever. The answer is found in Jesus Christ.

For Reflection and Review

- *Why does desperation awaken us to our need for God?*
- *How does faith overcome fear?*
- *Why are some people afraid of dying?*

Lesson 222

Luke 9:28 *[Jesus] took Peter, John and James with him and went up onto a mountain to pray.*

Mountains are significant in the Bible because they are where heaven and earth connect. *I lift up my eyes to the mountains—where does my help come from? My help comes from the Lord, the Maker of heaven and earth* (Psalm 121:1-2), wrote the Psalmist. When God talked to Moses, they met on top of a mountain (Exodus 19:3). And some Christians who've encountered God profoundly have called it a *mountaintop experience*. So when Jesus wanted to reveal his glory, he took Peter, John, and James up a mountain.

Luke 9:29 *As he was praying, the appearance of his face changed, and his clothes became as bright as a flash of lightning.*

This event is called the *Transfiguration* since Matthew's account says, *he was transfigured before them. His face shone like the sun, and his clothes became white as the light* (Matthew 17:2). Mark's account says, *His clothes became dazzling white, whiter than anyone in the world could bleach them* (Mark 9:3). This is the greatest revelation of the glory of Jesus Christ before his resurrection, and is a preview of his future glory.

The Apostle John saw the risen Christ in the revelation which he received on the island of Patmos. *His face was like the sun shining in all its brilliance* (Revelation 1:6), he wrote. Jesus is the most glorious being in the universe, and something similar is promised to us. *[T]he righteous will shine like the sun in the kingdom of their Father* (Matthew 13:43), said Jesus.

The desire to shine is natural but, in this life, few ever do for long. Olympic medal winners enjoy a brief ceremony during which the world applauds, and then forgets their names. But the children of God will shine like the sun, and their glory will never end.

Luke 9:30 *Two men, Moses and Elijah, appeared in glorious splendor, talking with Jesus.*

Moses and Elijah are towering figures in the Old Testament, and represent the Law and the Prophets. Moses gave Israel the Law, and Elijah was a noteworthy prophet. *Do not think that I have come to abolish the Law or the Prophets; I have not come to abolish them but to fulfill them* (Matthew 5:17), said Jesus.

Moses and Elijah came to support Jesus, who would fulfill the Law and the Prophets when he died on the cross. Jesus fulfilled the Law by obeying it perfectly, and by paying the penalty for those who don't. He fulfilled the prophets by doing what they foretold.

Luke 9:31 *They spoke about his departure, which he was about to bring to fulfillment at Jerusalem.*

This was a positive way of talking about Jesus' death. Moses and Elijah understood what the disciples couldn't grasp: Jesus would die on a cross for their sins. The Bible doesn't record their conversation, but perhaps they talked about heaven. That's where Moses and Elijah came from, and that's what Jesus would think about during his crucifixion. *For the joy set before him he endured the cross* (Hebrews 12:2), says Hebrews.

Luke 9:32 *Peter and his companions were very sleepy, but when they became fully awake, they saw his glory and the two men standing with him.*

After a day of mountain climbing, the disciples were exhausted, and seem to have gone to sleep. If Jesus' transfiguration took place after dark, his glory was even more dramatic. But the disciples didn't see it until they were *fully awake*. Like the disciples, we can become drowsy when we should be paying attention. An important part of the spiritual life is staying awake to God.

I went for a morning walk, several years ago, and my thoughts were foggy and dull. But as my body moved I gradually awoke, and discovered a spectacular day in which all creation seemed to celebrate the greatness of God. The more awake we are to God, the more we'll see his glory. *Wake up, sleeper, rise from the dead, and Christ will shine on you* (Ephesians 5:14), wrote Paul.

Luke 9:33 *As the men were leaving Jesus, Peter said to him, Master, it is good for us to be here. Let us put up three shelters—one for you, one for Moses and one for Elijah. (He did not know what he was saying.)*

Scholars have no idea what Peter was thinking, or where he'd get the tools and materials to build the shelters. He was simply so amazed that he opened his mouth and said something ridiculous. The disciples must've laughed about it later, and we can imagine Luke chuckling as he put this in his gospel. The disciples were ordinary people, involved with an extraordinary Savior.

Luke 9:34 *While he was speaking, a cloud appeared and covered them, and they were afraid as they entered the cloud.*

Clouds suggest a number of things in the Bible: *I have swept away your offenses like a cloud* (Isaiah 44:22). *You have covered yourself with a cloud so that no prayer can get through* (Lamentations 3:44). And *He makes the clouds his chariot* (Psalm 104:3). That's what is happening here. God came to them in a cloud, and they were feeling afraid.

Luke 9:35 *A voice came from the cloud, saying, This is my Son, whom I have chosen; listen to him.*

Peter may've been so excited by Moses and Elijah that he wanted to hear what they had to say. Moses was held in such high regard by the Jews that, even today, he's preferred by most of them over Jesus Christ. But speaking from the cloud God said, *This is my Son, whom I have chosen; listen to him.*

A young man climbed to the top of Mount Everest, even though he was blind. He did it by listening to a bell that was attached to the person ahead of him, and by listening to warnings such as, *death-fall two feet to your right*. And if we hope to arrive in heaven, we must never stop listening to Jesus Christ.

Luke 9:36 *When the voice had spoken, they found that Jesus was alone.*

This event made such an impression on Peter that he wrote about it many years later. *He received honor and glory from God the Father when the voice came to him from the Majestic Glory, saying, This is my Son, whom I love; with him I am well pleased. We ourselves heard this voice that came from heaven when we were with him on the sacred mountain* (2 Peter 1:17-18), he wrote.

Their mountain-top experience came to an end, however, and the disciples made their way down. They'd enjoy the Lord's ministry a little while longer, and then he'd go to the cross. If the transfiguration was their highest spiritual experience, the cross would be their lowest. That's what it's like to follow Jesus Christ. There is triumph and defeat, jubilation and despair. The mountaintop doesn't last forever, but neither does the valley.

If the Bible was a hoax, it would emphasize the positive and minimize the negative. But it never does that. *[Y]our love is better than life* (Psalm 63:3), and the *darkness is my closest friend* (Psalm 88:18), wrote the Psalmists. Ecstasy and agony are both part of the Christian life, for now, but not forever. Everything unhappy will soon be fading away.

For Reflection and Review

- *Have you ever had a mountain top experience?*
- *Why doesn't God reveal himself equally to everyone?*
- *Why is it often hard to listen to Jesus Christ?*

Lesson 223

Luke 9:62 *No one who puts a hand to the plow and looks back is fit for service in the kingdom of God.*

The only way to plow a straight row, back then, was to focus on an object across the field. As long as you kept your focus, your row would be straight. If you looked anywhere else, it would bend. Jesus wants us to focus on him, and not look back on the world we've left behind. As long as he's our focus, our life will be spiritually straight.

A father was teaching his son to plow, and told him to gaze at a post at the other end of the field. Half way there the son wanted to see how he was doing, so he looked back and saw that his row was straight. But then he wondered if it was still straight, so he looked back again and saw that it was crooked where he looked back before. Then he wondered if he did it again, so he looked back a third time. By the time he finished the row there were several bends from each time he looked back. The only way to live a straight life is to keep our eyes on Jesus Christ, and never look back even once.

*****

Luke 10:1-2 *After this the Lord appointed seventy-two others and sent them two by two ahead of him to every town and place where he was about to go. He told them, The harvest is plentiful, but the workers are few.*

The harvest metaphor compares the world to a field of grain, in which every person is a stalk. It was a powerful metaphor in Jesus' day because many people were farmers, and few things were more important than bringing in the harvest.

More recently, a farmer called his pastor with a frantic prayer request because he needed to bring in the harvest before it rained. The grain was cut and, if it got wet, it'd rot. Then the farmer would lose everything. The farmer was going to town to find additional workers who usually stood at the corner until noon. But it was past noon, and the farmer begged his pastor to pray that he'd find enough workers to bring in the harvest. This is the kind of urgency the church should have about harvesting souls for Christ.

Luke 10:2b *Ask the Lord of the harvest, therefore, to send out workers into his harvest field.*

The kingdom of God has always been understaffed. The need is so great that we must always pray for additional workers. On most days about two people die every second. That's about one hundred twenty people a minute, or seventy-two hundred people an hour. On any given day about a hundred seventy two thousand souls slip into eternity, many of them unbelievers. If it's tragic to lose a harvest of grain, how much worse to lose a harvest of souls?

Luke 10:3 *Go! I am sending you out like lambs among wolves.*

To be a lamb in a pack of wolves is not something most sheep would sign up for. Jesus was telling his disciples that they should expect to die. The number of Christian martyrs is higher than most people realize. About three believers are killed every day, just for believing in Jesus. More Christians were martyred in the last century than all other centuries combined.

A young man was recently shot to death because of his newfound faith in Christ. When his old friends couldn't win him back to his previous lifestyle, they put a bullet through his heart. The young man could've lived by walking away from Jesus, but he wasn't afraid to die because he had eternal life. That's how Christianity works. Jesus gives us eternal life, and we give him our earthly life.

Luke 10:9 *Heal the sick who are there and tell them, The kingdom of God has come near to you.*

Jesus gave his disciples power to heal the sick in order to give credibility to their message. This still happens today, sometimes, especially where the gospel is little known.

A woman from India was in chronic pain for about three years. She could barely sleep at night and, because of her crying, no one else in the house could sleep either. Then a missionary arrived and prayed for the woman in pain. He also shared the gospel with her and her family. That night, for the first time in three years, she slept peacefully. The next morning, she and her family became believers. By the end of the day, seventeen others were also believers, and a church was born.

Luke 10:10-11 *But when you enter a town and are not welcomed, go into its streets and say, Even the dust of your town we wipe from our feet as a warning to you.*

Wiping dust from the feet was a way of saying, *We have absolutely nothing in common.* The disciples were responsible for delivering the message, but not for the people's response. It wasn't their job to convince people, or beg them to receive the message. The gospel needs to be proclaimed, but the response is up to those who hear.

When a certain man wanted eternal life, Jesus told him to give away his wealth and follow him. The man should've been delighted, but went away sad because he was so rich (Mark 10:21-22). Jesus didn't lower his price, run after the man, or ask him to reconsider. God wants everyone to be saved, and invites everyone to be saved, but doesn't beg anyone to be saved. The response is up to those who hear.

Luke 10:12 *I tell you, it will be more bearable on that day for Sodom than for that town.*

Sodom was so wicked that God destroyed it by raining down burning sulfur (Genesis 19:24). But those who reject the gospel will be punished even more severely on the day of God's judgment. *That day will be darkness, not light* (Amos 5:18). *That day will be a day of wrath—a day of distress and anguish* (Zephaniah 1:15). *[T]hat day will close on you suddenly like a trap* (Luke 21:34). *That day will bring about the destruction of the heavens by fire* (2 Peter 3:12).

Many will say to me on that day, Lord, Lord, did we not prophesy in your name and in your name drive out demons and in your name perform many miracles? Then I will tell them plainly, I never knew you. Away from me, you evildoers! (Matthew 7:22-23), said Jesus.

Throughout the Bible the two days that matter most are *this day* and *that day*. If you don't spend *this day* getting ready for *that day*, then *this day* will be held against you on *that day*. But if you spend *this day* getting ready for *that day*, then *that day* will be a day to rejoice.

For Reflection and Review

- *Why is evangelism urgent?*
- *Why is evangelism dangerous?*
- *How can we use this day to get ready for that day?*

Lesson 224

Luke 10:19 *I have given you authority to trample on snakes and scorpions and to overcome all the power of the enemy.*

As the disciples proclaimed the gospel, they'd encounter demonic resistance, so they needed to know that they had authority over Satan. Satan has more power than the strongest Christian, but less authority than the weakest Christian.

Imagine a traffic cop in the middle of an intersection, and a garbage truck barreling toward him. The traffic cop puts up his hand, and the garbage truck comes to a stop. This happens not because the traffic cop has more power than the garbage truck, but because he has more authority. *I have given you authority . . . to overcome all the power of the enemy*, said Jesus.

Luke 10:20 *However, do not rejoice that the spirits submit to you, but rejoice that your names are written in heaven.*

Most places on earth keep a record of the people who live there. When a person dies, or moves away, their name is removed from the record book. But if our names are written in heaven, we'll never die or move away. We should rejoice every day that our names are written in heaven.

Luke 10:21 *At that time Jesus, full of joy through the Holy Spirit, said, I praise you, Father, Lord of heaven and earth, because you have hidden these things from the wise and learned, and revealed them to little children.*

Most of the religious leaders were highly educated, and were nearly unanimous in their rejection of Jesus Christ. Many of those who believed were simple by comparison. Faith is not a matter of intelligence, or education, but revelation. God hid it from the wise, and revealed it to little children.

For it is written: I will destroy the wisdom of the wise; the intelligence of the intelligent I will frustrate. Where is the wise person? Where is the teacher of the law? Where is the philosopher of this age? Has not God made foolish the wisdom of the world? For since in the wisdom of God the world through its wisdom did not know him, God was pleased through the foolishness of what was preached to save those who believe (1 Corinthians 1:18-21), wrote Paul.

Shortly after receiving Christ as Lord (Colossians 2:6), a young friend of mine shared the gospel with an uncle who had advanced degrees in philosophy and religion. Predictably, his educated uncle dismissed him with a scoff. But my newly converted friend knew more about the grace of God than his educated uncle did. The reason we believe in Jesus Christ isn't because we're smart, but because God has made himself known to us through the gospel.

Luke 10:22 *No one knows who the Son is except the Father, and no one knows who the Father is except the Son and those to whom the Son chooses to reveal him.*

Jesus should get an award for being the only person who was never boring. In one of the most religious places on earth he said in effect, *No one knows God but me, and those to whom I reveal him*. We don't know God by induction, deduction, or abduction, but by introduction. And only Jesus Christ can introduce us. Jesus was accused of many things, but never of being boring.

*****

Luke 10:29 *And who is my neighbor?*

Jesus was talking to a religious leader about the command, *Love your neighbor as yourself* (Luke 10:27). To help narrow the list, the man wanted to know who, exactly, were his neighbors. Jesus replied with an unexpected story.

He told of a man who was robbed, beaten, and left for dead on a road. A couple religious leaders passed by, but didn't bother to help. Then came someone who bandaged the man's wounds, took him to an inn, and paid for his room. *Which of these three do you think was a neighbor to the man? [asked Jesus]. The one who had mercy on him. Jesus told him, Go and do likewise* (Luke 10:36-37). According to Jesus Christ, love has no boundaries, and every needy person is our neighbor. Perhaps our needy neighbors are the reason we're still here.

*****

Luke 10:38 *As Jesus and his disciples were on their way, he came to a village where a woman named Martha opened her home to him.*

This was not a small favor since Jesus and his disciples totaled more than a dozen men. To receive that many guests, without notice, was a real act of kindness. Jesus was friends with Martha, and her sister Mary, and their brother Lazarus (John 11-12). Since they all lived near Jerusalem, Jesus may've come by often.

[Martha] had a sister called Mary, who sat at the Lord's feet listening to what he said. But Martha was distracted by all the preparations that had to be made. She came to him and asked, Lord, don't you care that my sister has left me to do the work by myself? Tell her to help me! Martha, Martha, the Lord answered, you are worried and upset about many things, but few things are needed—or indeed only one. Mary has chosen what is better, and it will not be taken away from her (Luke 10:39-42).

It's a little surprising dinner was served that night, or that Jesus was ever invited back. Mary sat at Jesus' feet, while Martha did all the work, and Jesus corrected Martha! But Jesus made his point: it's more important to listen to him than anything else we do. *This is my Son, whom I love. Listen to him!* (Mark 9:7), said God.

Mary knew that sitting at Jesus' feet was the greatest honor of her life. Paul was *educated at the feet of Gamaliel* (Acts 22:3, ESV), but Mary was sitting at the feet of Jesus. Rabbis rarely took women as students, so Mary felt highly honored.

We too have the honor of sitting at Jesus' feet every day. With an open Bible, we have the privilege of learning from the greatest teacher who ever lived—tuition free! Like Mary, we can sit in his presence, take in his word, and give him our attention. And if we rise to serve him, we'll live out the virtues of Mary and Martha—two of Jesus' dearest friends.

For Reflection and Review

- *Why does Jesus hide the truth from some, and reveal it to others?*
- *With so much need in the world, how do we know who to help?*
- *What does it mean to be a disciple?*

Lesson 225

Luke 11:1 *One day Jesus was praying in a certain place. When he finished, one of his disciples said to him, Lord, teach us to pray, just as John taught his disciples.*

We commonly ask others the best that they can give to us. We ask a trainer, *Teach us to exercise*. We ask a chef, *Teach us to cook*. We ask a golfer, *Teach us to putt*. When the disciples saw Jesus praying, and realized how much they could learn from him, they said *Lord, teach us to pray* (Haddon Robinson). Nothing is more basic to our relationship with God, and nothing is more productive.

Many years ago a young man submitted an idea for time management to a large company. If the owner liked the idea, he could send a check for whatever amount he thought the idea was worth. A few weeks later the young man received a check for two hundred fifty thousand dollars.

The plan had three parts: First, at the beginning of each day, make a list of everything that has to be done. Second, put the list in order from the most important things to the least important things. Third, do the most important things first. Since we'll never get to the bottom of our list, we ought to begin with whatever is most important. What could be more important than talking to God?

Luke 11:2-4 *He said to them, When you pray, say: Father, hallowed be your name, your kingdom come. Give us each day our daily bread. Forgive us our sins, for we also forgive everyone who sins against us. And lead us not into temptation.*

Prayer doesn't need to be long or complicated, but it does need to be frequent. There's no way to have a meaningful relationship with your heavenly Father apart from regular prayer. The more we talk to God, the more natural it will seem; the less we talk to him, the more distant we'll become.

The Lord's prayer is complete in itself, but can also serve as an outline for extended prayer. I often pray like this: *Dear Father, thank you that you really are my Father. Help me to honor your name in all my words, thoughts, and deeds. May your kingdom come in glory, but also in my heart today. Thank you for the food you provide, and for everything else I often take for granted. My sins are too many to count, but I renounce them all, and thank you for sending Christ to bear the punishment I deserve. I freely forgive all who've sinned against me, and ask you to bless them richly. Keep me from temptation, and where it wants to lead me. Help me, instead, to follow you all the way to eternal glory. I pray in Jesus' name. Amen.*

*****

Luke 11:23 *Whoever is not with me is against me, and whoever does not gather with me scatters.*

Jesus Christ is so controversial that neutrality is impossible. We are either friend or foe, for him or against him. And the way we show our loyalty is by helping him gather the lost: *whoever does not gather with me scatters*. This is not the duty of a few, but of all who belong to Jesus Christ.

If a great preacher won a thousand people to Christ every day, he'd only win a tiny fraction of the people alive over the course of his life. But if I win someone to Christ this year, and the two of us each win someone to Christ next year, and the four of us each win someone to Christ the following year, and so forth, the whole world would be won in thirty-three years.

This won't happen, of course, since Jesus taught that only a few will be saved (Matthew 7:14). But whoever belongs to Christ should try to gather as many as they can. One of the easiest ways to do this is with the *Seven Minute Bible Study*. Find a small Bible you can carry in your pocket, and highlight the following verses:

Yet to all who did receive him, to those who believed in his name, he gave the right to become children of God (John 1:12).

Whoever believes in the Son has eternal life, but whoever rejects the Son will not see life, for God's wrath remains on them (John 3:36).

Jesus answered, I am the way and the truth and the life. No one comes to the Father except through me (John 14:6).

But God demonstrates his own love for us in this: While we were still sinners, Christ died for us (Romans 5:8).

If you declare with your mouth, Jesus is Lord, and believe in your heart that God raised him from the dead, you will be saved (Romans 10:9).

And he died for all, that those who live should no longer live for themselves but for him who died for them and was raised again (2 Corinthians 5:15).

Here I am! I stand at the door and knock. If anyone hears my voice and opens the door, I will come in . . . . (Revelation 3:20).

Then find a friend or a stranger who'll give you seven minutes of their time. Turn to each verse, let them read it aloud, and ask what they think it means. It's probably best not to instruct or correct at all, but to simply let the word of God speak for itself. *For the word of God is alive and active* (Hebrews 4:12), says Hebrews.

After the final verse, you might ask them to read a prayer you've written in the back of your Bible: *Dear Lord Jesus, I know I'm a sinner. I believe you died for my sins, and I want to live for you. I turn away from my sins, and ask for your forgiveness. Please lead me in the way of eternal life.*

Different verses can be used depending on culture and context. The strength of this study is that it doesn't rely on the knowledge of the person presenting, but only on God's word. The presenter doesn't need to control the outcome, but only to give others the privilege of reading God's word for themselves. This is a simple way to gather others to the Savior.

*****

Luke 11:52 *Woe to you experts in the law, because you have taken away the key to knowledge.*

Jesus is the key to knowledge which the religious experts had taken away. He's the key that unlocks the meaning of the Bible and, therefore, the meaning of life.

When I was growing up I thought adults had all the answers, and it was only a matter of time before I'd have all the answers too. But when I became an adult I discovered they don't have all the answers, and stopped asking the most important questions: *Who am I? Where did I come from? Where am I going? How should I live? What's the meaning of life?*

People stop asking these questions because, humanly speaking, they're unknowable. The answers from philosophy aren't compelling, because philosophy can argue in any direction. But if God has spoken from heaven, and even come to earth, then it's possible to make sense out of life.

This is why Christianity explains the human experience so compellingly. Created in the image of God, we have dignity and worth. Fallen into sin, there's no evil of which we are not capable. Redeemed by Christ, we are promised a glorious future. Jesus is the key to knowledge that unlocks the meaning of life.

For Reflection and Review

- *How do you normally pray?*
- *Why is evangelism difficult?*
- *How is Jesus the key to knowledge?*

Lesson 226

Luke 12:1 *Be on your guard against the yeast of the Pharisees, which is hypocrisy.*

The Pharisees found it difficult to live up to their religion, so they chose hypocrisy instead. They appeared to be devoted to God, but were really devoted to themselves.

Most people have a public self, which is open for everyone to see. We also have a personal self, which only our friends and family see. We also have a private self, which no one sees but ourselves. The greater the distinction between these three selves, the greater our sin of hypocrisy.

But it's also hard to be a hypocrite, so most give it up over time. When our lifestyle doesn't fit our beliefs, we become uncomfortable. Then we change our lifestyle, or our beliefs. Most people don't change their beliefs because of new information, but because God is hard to live for. Rather than change their lifestyle to fit their beliefs, they change their beliefs to fit their lifestyle. They trade hypocrisy for apostasy.

Luke 12:2 *There is nothing concealed that will not be disclosed, or hidden that will not be made known.*

Few things are more precious to us than privacy, but here we learn that privacy is an illusion. Everything we've ever done will become public information. *What you have said in the dark will be heard in the daylight, and what you have whispered in the ear in the inner rooms will be proclaimed from the roofs* (Luke 12:3), said Jesus.

This is so unnerving that some have argued it only applies to unbelievers, not to Christians. Consider the following texts: *I, even I, am he who blots out your transgressions, for my own sake, and remembers your sins no more* (Isaiah 43:25). *I will forgive their wickedness and will remember their sins no more* (Jeremiah 31:34). *[A]s far as the east is from the west, so far has he removed our transgressions from us* (Psalm 103:12). *[Y]ou will tread our sins underfoot and hurl all our iniquities into the depths of the sea* (Micah 7:19).

All these texts are true, and assure us of complete forgiveness through faith in Jesus Christ. Never again for all eternity will our sins be held against us. Christ has paid the price for them, and they are forgiven in full. But does that mean they won't be revealed on Judgment Day? Unfortunately, there are a few other texts to consider as well.

For God will bring every deed into judgment, including every hidden thing, whether it is good or evil (Ecclesiastes 12:14). *Nothing in all creation is hidden from God's sight. Everything is uncovered and laid bare before the eyes of him to whom we must give account* (Hebrews 4:13). *He will bring to light what is hidden in darkness and will expose the motives of the heart* (1 Corinthians 4:5). *This will take place on the day when God judges people's secrets through Jesus Christ* (Romans 2:16).

Furthermore, the Bible reveals some of the most embarrassing episodes of God's people. These include Noah's drunkenness, Lot's incest, and David's adultery. If God revealed the worst episodes of his people in the Bible, why wouldn't he make all things public in the age to come, even if we're forgiven?

But here's a radical thought: *Sin will be no shame, but honor* (Julian of Norwich). If God reveals our sins to the world, they will appear as sins that are forgiven, to the glory of God. All heaven will rejoice in the mercy of God, who pardons notorious sinners. And we'll rejoice in the blood of Jesus Christ that *purifies us from all sin* (1 John 1:7), wrote John. Our sins will never be held against us, or even embarrass us, but will bring glory and honor to God for his amazing grace. We'll praise the Lord forever, not only for his pardon, but for changing our natures so that we'll never sin again.

Luke 12:4 *I tell you, my friends, do not be afraid of those who kill the body and after that can do no more.*

Martyrdom is easy when it happens quickly, and without much pain. It's not death believers fear, so much as dying painfully. That's why Satan has developed some horrifying methods of martyrdom, such as being slowly cooked, or eaten to death by rats. But, even through torture, many have found the courage to die bravely.

In the sixteen hundreds, French Protestants often sang Psalms on their way to be burned at the stake. And as they were being burned, they often preached so bravely that it annoyed their persecutors. As a result, it became the practice to cut out their tongues before they were set on fire. Still, they refused to fear those who killed the body, and after that could do no more.

Luke 12:5 *But I will show you whom you should fear: Fear him who, after your body has been killed, has authority to throw you into hell. Yes, I tell you, fear him.*

Popular views of God minimize his severity, but the God of the Bible kills people and sends them to hell. We ought to obey God out of love but, when our love is weak, we ought to obey him out of fear.

Some believers who were living under atheistic communism were forced to march naked onto a frozen lake, and freeze to death for their faith. But a warm bath was prepared on shore for any who'd turn away from Christ. Most died for their faith, that day, but one man walked to shore, trading his faith for a warm bath. After his bath, however, he was put to death, so he died as a Christ-rejecting apostate. *Fear him who, after your body has been killed, has authority to throw you into hell.*

Luke 12:6 *Are not five sparrows sold for two pennies? Yet not one of them is forgotten by God.*

It's easy to believe that God cares for us when things are going well, but here we're assured that God cares for us even when things are going badly. If God watches over the sparrows, how much more does he watch over us?

I was at the home of a friend, when a bird flew into a large window, and broke its neck. We went outside to investigate and, beneath the window, were several birds that died the same way. How many other birds have fallen prey to their natural enemies?

Jesus wasn't talking about sparrows chirping nicely in a tree, but about those that had been captured and were being sold for lunch. They were so common that you could buy two for a penny (Matthew 10:29), and for two pennies you'd get an extra one free. Yet even the extra sparrow wasn't forgotten by God. *Do not be afraid; you are worth more than many sparrows* (Luke 12:7), said Jesus.

For Reflection and Review

- *Why is it difficult to be a hypocrite?*
- *Why does God reveal the sins of his people?*
- *How does Jesus give us courage to live and die for him?*

Lesson 227

Luke 12:7 *Indeed, the very hairs of your head are all numbered.*

No one ever loved himself so much that he counted the hairs of own his head. A new mom might count the first few hairs on her baby's head, but even she would stop after a hundred or so. The average human head has a hundred thousand hairs, but God's love for us is so great they're not only counted, but numbered. Not one of them will be lost apart from his loving consent.

Luke 12:8-9 *I tell you, whoever publicly acknowledges me before others, the Son of Man will also acknowledge before the angels of God. But whoever disowns me before others will be disowned before the angels of God.*

Believing in Jesus Christ could be expensive for his disciples. It could lead to family conflict, being barred from the synagogue, and financial hardship as people took their business elsewhere. It's no wonder some of Jesus' followers were tempted to keep their faith a secret.

Joseph of Arimathea was a member of the Jewish high court. *[He] was a disciple of Jesus, but secretly because he feared the Jewish leaders* (John 19:38), wrote John. But after Jesus was crucified, Joseph threw caution to the wind. He *went boldly to Pilate and asked for Jesus' body* (Mark 15:43) and *placed it in his own new tomb* (Matthew 27:60). Having acknowledged Jesus on earth, he could be assured that Jesus would acknowledge him before the angels of God in heaven.

More recently, a high school student was sitting in the library when a crazed student put a gun to her head and asked if she believed in God. As a Christian, there was only one way she could answer. The next thing she knew, Jesus was introducing her to the angels of God in heaven (Cassie Bernall). Whoever acknowledges Jesus Christ will face disapproval on earth. But this will be more than offset by the approval of Christ and his angels in heaven.

Luke 12:10 *And everyone who speaks a word against the Son of Man will be forgiven, but anyone who blasphemes against the Holy Spirit will not be forgiven.*

And so I tell you, every kind of sin and slander can be forgiven, but blasphemy against the Spirit will not be forgiven (Matthew 12:31).

And, *Truly I tell you, people can be forgiven all their sins and every slander they utter, but whoever blasphemes against the Holy Spirit will never be forgiven; they are guilty of an eternal sin* (Mark 3:28-29), said Jesus.

Blaspheming the Holy Spirit is the most serious sin, and is probably more common than we think. If you commit adultery every day, and commit just as many murders, you can still be forgiven. But if you blaspheme the Holy Spirit you can never be forgiven since no one can come to Christ apart from the Holy Spirit. *[N]o one can say, Jesus is Lord, except by the Holy Spirit* (1 Corinthians 12:3), wrote Paul.

The religious leaders accused Jesus of casting out demons by the power of Satan (Matthew 12:24, Mark 3:22), and were so settled in their conviction that they refused to believe in Jesus no matter what. Because of their stubborn rejection of Christ, the Spirit no longer drew them to Christ. They committed *an eternal sin* by becoming eternal rejectors of Jesus Christ.

The blasphemy of the Holy Spirit is evidenced by a settled refusal to come to Christ under any circumstance. Those who commit this sin are not distressed by their situation, but simply have no concern about coming to Christ.

Whoever wants to come to Christ has not blasphemed the Spirit, since the desire to come to Christ is proof that God is drawing them. *No one can come to me unless the Father who sent me draws them* (John 6:44), said Jesus. If God is drawing a person to Christ, they haven't blasphemed the Holy Spirit.

The desire to come to Christ doesn't mean a person is saved, of course. It simply means they can be saved if they'll come to Jesus Christ. The desire to come to Christ should never be resisted, or postponed, but acted on at once. There's too much at risk to put it off a single day.

*****

Luke 12:16-19 *And he told them this parable: The ground of a certain rich man yielded an abundant harvest. He thought to himself, What shall I do? I have no place to store my crops. Then he said, This is what I'll do. I will tear down my barns and build bigger ones, and there I will store my surplus grain. And I'll say to myself, You have plenty of grain laid up for many years. Take life easy; eat, drink and be merry.*

This gentleman farmer was so successful that he ran out of room to store his grain. The only sensible thing was for him to tear down his old barns and build bigger barns. He was so successful, in fact, that he needed multiple barns to store up all his wealth.

This man was smart, hard working, and employed a number of people. He was admired, respected, and consulted frequently. His wife and children had many good things that money could buy, and status in the community. Now, at last, this gentleman farmer could retire and enjoy the fruit of his labor—a very successful man.

Many of God's servants have also been financially prosperous. Abraham had 318 trained men in his household (Genesis 14:14). Job was the wealthiest man in the East (Job 1:3). King David amassed a fortune (1 Chronicles 29:1-5). And, because of his position under Pharaoh (Genesis 41:41-43), Joseph was also very rich. *The blessing of the Lord brings wealth* (Proverbs 10:22), says Proverbs. But being wealthy is no guarantee that God is pleased with you.

Luke 12:20 *God said to him, You fool! This very night your life will be demanded from you. Then who will get what you have prepared for yourself?*

The farmer's problem was not his success, but his near-sightedness. He prepared for retirement, but not for eternity. He was wise for a moment, but a fool forever. In all his planning there's no mention of prayer, worship, faith, or God. He may, in fact, be the most self-centered person in the Bible. *What shall I do? I have no place to store my crops. . . . This is what I'll do. I will tear down my barns . . . I will store my surplus grain. . . . I'll say to myself, . . . Take life easy; eat, drink and be merry. But God said to him, You fool!*

If look up *fool* in the dictionary you'll find synonyms like: *idiot, imbecile, schmuck, buffoon, sap, blockhead, dimwit, dope, dumbbell, nitwit, numskull* and *birdbrain*. To everyone else this man appeared wise, but to God he was a fool. So no one would miss the point, Jesus said, *This is how it will be with whoever stores up things for themselves but is not rich toward God* (Luke 12:21).

My daughter was six years old when she heard a commercial on the radio explaining that thirty dollars would feed a hungry child for a month. She went to her savings jar, and discovered that she had sixty dollars, so she asked if she could feed two children for a month. I agreed in the hope that it would become a pattern with her. *For where your treasure is, there your heart will be also* (Matthew 6:21), said Jesus. And at the hour of death it'll be better to hear, *Well done* (Luke 19:17) than to hear, *You fool!*

For Reflection and Review

- *Why do some people want to keep their faith a secret?*
- *What does it mean to blaspheme the Holy Spirit?*
- *Why should we be generous toward God?*

Lesson 228

Luke 12:22 *Therefore I tell you, do not worry about your life, what you will eat; or about your body, what you will wear.*

Jesus often spoke as though money wasn't important, but terrible things can happen when people run out of money. Families have been broken up, and children sold as prostitutes. Some have gone to debtor's prison, and others have been sold as slaves. Even in places that are wealthy, some people live in sewers because they can't afford a place to stay. And the line between prosperity and poverty is surprisingly thin.

A friend of mine bought a new home before the old one was sold, and was paying two mortgages. Then he lost his high-paying job and, since the economy was down, he couldn't find a similar job. His savings was soon depleted, and he started missing payments, which ruined his credit. What assurance could he give his wife and children that God would take care of them?

First, we have a heavenly Father who's able to provide whatever we need. We may be astonished at his generosity, or bewildered by his apparent indifference. But he's always there, and has our best interests at heart. Even in the worst times, this should give us hope.

Second, a billion years from now it'll be nearly a billion years since the last time we had any lack. Apart from Jesus Christ every setback is a tragedy, because this life is all there is. But because of Jesus Christ even the worst life can be taken in stride, since it leads to eternal glory. If we keep these things in mind, we'll be less afraid when the money runs out.

Luke 12:32 *Do not be afraid, little flock, for your Father has been pleased to give you the kingdom.*

Many think of God's kingdom as a place on the far side of the galaxy but, in Jesus' day, the idea was more earthly. God told Abraham that he'd become a great nation (Genesis 12:1) and, under king David, that's what happened. Israel was the kingdom of God, but God promised even more.

The wolf will live with the lamb, the leopard will lie down with the goat, the calf and the lion and the yearling together; and a little child will lead them (Isaiah 11:6). *Everyone will sit under their own vine and under their own fig tree, and no one will make them afraid* (Micah 4:4). So when Jesus talked about the kingdom of God, the people thought of a king, a people, a place, and God—all together on earth!

The idea of an eternal worship service in the sky doesn't excite children or adults. The Bible looks forward to a glorified earth, with glorified people, and Jesus Christ as our glorious king (Revelation 21:1-5). Truest heaven is earth made perfect.

When my daughter was ten years old, we went for a walk on a hiking trail that went through a meadow, down to a river, along some rolling hills. It was a beautiful day and the landscape was so delicious that I had to make a point: *You know, Sarah, the world can be so beautiful that I would fight for it if I had to. But we don't have to fight because God has said, The righteous will inherit the land and dwell in it forever* (Psalm 37:29). The kingdom of God is a gift, which we receive through faith in Jesus Christ.

Luke 12:33 *Sell your possessions and give to the poor. Provide purses for yourselves that will not wear out, a treasure in heaven that will never fail, where no thief comes near and no moth destroys.*

One of the biggest problems for people with money is holding on to it. The banking system in Jesus' day wasn't guaranteed, so many kept their money at home. But, even there, thieves could come and steal it. So Jesus taught the safest place to put our money is in heaven, where there are no thieves (1 Corinthians 6:9-10).

More recently, thieves broke into a bank and stole the contents of several safe deposit boxes. One lady lost half a million dollars worth of Jewelry and nearly collapsed. She said, *My whole life was in that box.* Another person won the lottery but was later murdered for his money. The more you have, it seems, the harder it is to hold on to.

The Apostle Paul wrote to the church in Philippi to thank them for their financial support. *[W]hat I desire is that more be credited to your account* (Philippians 4:17), he wrote. God keeps track of whatever we give, and credits it to our heavenly bank account. It's good to have a bank account on earth, but better to have one in heaven. And, if God pays interest, there's no telling what could happen over billions of years.

Luke 12:40 *You also must be ready, because the Son of Man will come at an hour when you do not expect him.*

The more we believe in the soon return of Jesus Christ, the more we'll live for him. The less we believe in the soon return of Jesus Christ, the more we'll live for ourselves. Jesus taught us to be ready because he's going to come when we don't expect him. So if you don't expect Jesus to come tonight, that would be a perfect time for his return. *For as lightning that comes from the east is visible even in the west, so will be the coming of the Son of Man* (Matthew 24:27), he said.

Many years ago, on a hot summer night, I went to bed with my window open. In the middle of the night there was a bolt of lighting and a clap of thunder like I had never seen or heard. Without even thinking I sat up straight and said: *He's Back!* It turned out he wasn't actually back but that's how it'll be when he does come back. *[B]e ready*, said Jesus, *because the Son of Man will come at an hour when you do not expect him.*

For Reflection and Review

- *What is our comfort when the money runs out?*
- *What will the kingdom of God be like when Christ returns?*
- *How can we be ready for Christ's return?*

Lesson 229

Luke 13:1 *Now there were some present at that time who told Jesus about the Galileans whose blood Pilate had mixed with their sacrifices.*

The Bible doesn't tell us any more about this episode but, apparently, the same Pilate who'd later sentence Jesus to crucifixion, slaughtered some Galileans while they were at the temple offering their sacrifices. We don't know why Pilate did this, but he had a reputation for cruelty.

Luke 13:2-3 *Do you think that these Galileans were worse sinners than all the other Galileans because they suffered this way? I tell you, no! But unless you repent, you too will all perish.*

A popular idea among Jews, back then, was that most people got what they deserved. If they were good people God would take care of them; if they were bad people something terrible might happen.

Nadab and Abihu worshipped God contrary to the way he prescribed, *So fire came out from the presence of the Lord and consumed them* (Leviticus 10:2). Korah led a rebellion against Moses, *and the earth opened its mouth and swallowed [him]* (Numbers 16:32). Since God has the power to execute his wrath when and where he pleases, many people reasoned from disaster back to sin.

Luke 13:4-5 *Or those eighteen who died when the tower in Siloam fell on them—do you think they were more guilty than all the others living in Jerusalem? I tell you, no! But unless you repent, you too will all perish.*

This is another event of which we have no more information. Perhaps they were building a tower in the section of Jerusalem's wall near the pool of Siloam. Something went terribly wrong and eighteen people died. Some thought it was the judgment of God, but Jesus disagreed.

Two mistakes need to be avoided when trying to understand the relationship between God and disaster. The first is to assume that, whenever someone comes to a violent end, they did something wrong. That might be true, but there's no way to know for sure. Instead of judging others in light of their disaster, Jesus taught us to view disaster as a warning to ourselves. *[U]nless you repent, you too will all perish*, he said.

The second mistake is to assume God no longer pours out his wrath, as he did in the Old Testament. *God is a righteous judge, a God who displays his wrath every day* (Psalm 7:11), wrote David. When Ananias and Sapphira lied about how much money they gave to the church, they both fell over dead (Acts 5:1-10). This New Testament story shows that God is free to kill even after the coming of Christ.

Since *the wages of sin is death* (Romans 6:23), God has a right to strike every time we sin. Thankfully, he often delays his judgment. *[H]e is patient with you, not wanting anyone to perish, but everyone to come to repentance* (2 Peter 3:9), wrote Peter. We ought to be thankful for God's patience, and never put it to the test.

*****

Luke 13:10-11 *On a Sabbath Jesus was teaching in one of the synagogues, and a woman was there who had been crippled by a spirit for eighteen years. She was bent over and could not straighten up at all.*

The ability to stand up straight is often taken for granted, especially by those who are young. With age, however, many curve forward, and some can't straighten up at all. We don't know this woman's age, but she'd been in that condition for eighteen years. She saw little but the ground, seldom looked at faces, and only saw the sun with effort.

Luke 13:12-13 *When Jesus saw her, he called her forward and said to her, Woman, you are set free from your infirmity. Then he put his hands on her, and immediately she straightened up and praised God.*

She probably praised God every time she stood up straight for the rest of her life. Likewise, those who were healed of blindness probably praised God every time they opened their eyes. And those who were healed of deafness probably praised God every time they heard a sound. From these we learn to praise God for the many things we take for granted.

If your arms bend at the elbows you ought to praise God for that. And if your legs bend at the knees you ought to praise God for that too. Our bodies have countless parts, any of which can fail at any time. When we consider all the things that can go wrong, it's a wonder we're ever healthy.

And even though we're not all healed in this life, all who believe in Jesus will be healed eventually. *[He] will transform our lowly bodies so that they will be like his glorious body* (Philippians 3:21), wrote Paul. We may have to suffer eighteen years, or more, but this will make us want to praise the Lord forever, in a glorious body that will never disappoint.

*****

Luke 13:25 *Once the owner of the house gets up and closes the door, you will stand outside knocking and pleading, Sir, open the door for us. But he will answer, I don't know you or where you come from.*

This applies to people who want to sin a little longer before coming to Christ. They know there's much at stake, but assume there will always be time to make their peace with God.

Years ago I went to a store and pulled into the parking lot at 8:59 in the evening. I didn't know what time they closed, so I parked the car and ran to the door. But the moment I got to the door a lady inside turned the key. I looked at her with pleading eyes but she said, *We're closed*. With a look of dismay I threw up my hands and begged, but she shook her head decisively and said, *We're closed*. If I had arrived a few seconds earlier I could've been in. But now it was too late. That's how it'll be on the last day. *What . . . . he shuts no one can open* (Revelation 3:7), wrote John.

For Reflection and Review

- *How does God punish people today?*
- *Why do our bodies give us so much grief?*

- *What do you want to be doing when Jesus returns?*

Lesson 230

Luke 14:12-14 *Then Jesus said to his host, When you give a luncheon or dinner, do not invite your friends, your brothers or sisters, your relatives, or your rich neighbors; if you do, they may invite you back and so you will be repaid. But when you give a banquet, invite the poor, the crippled, the lame, the blind, and you will be blessed. Although they cannot repay you, you will be repaid at the resurrection of the righteous.*

Jesus could be the rudest guest you ever had in your home. He was being entertained, along with many others, by a prominent Pharisee—a leader in the community. This could be an excellent opportunity for Jesus to win friends in high places. But, always the teacher, Jesus chose to instruct his host on how to entertain. Instead of inviting all the right people, he should invite the wrong people, and be repaid in the age to come. Jesus calls us to lower our social status to care for the needs of the poor.

I knew a high school student who was quite above average academically, athletically, and socially. He could've sat at any table, but recruited his friends to spend their lunch eating with students who have special needs. They talked with them, carried their trays, and built relationships over lunch. This idea would've never crossed their minds if it wasn't for the radical teaching of Jesus Christ. By following Jesus' teaching they made some friends, found some joy, and changed the culture of their school.

Luke 14:15 *When one of those at the table with him heard this, he said to Jesus, Blessed is the one who will eat at the feast in the kingdom of God.*

This man had social intelligence. Jesus had offended everyone, and he was trying to get the party back on track by saying something agreeable. What could be more agreeable than *Blessed is the one who will eat at the feast in the kingdom of God?* But Jesus will talk about this in a way that will offend everyone again.

As godly Jews, they all assumed they'd be at this feast. But Jesus would tell them, *probably not.* He proceeded to tell a story about a man who prepared a great banquet and invited many guests. But they all began to make excuses like *I just bought a field,* or *I just bought some oxen* or *I just got married.*

So the master sent his servant into the streets to gather the poor and the lame. But there was still room. So he sent him out again saying, *compel them to come in, so that my house will be full* (Luke 14:23). God is trying to have a party but no one wants to come. This is just like church.

People have time for everything else but are often too busy to gather with God and his people. They have to go to work, buy a car, mow the lawn, or feed the cat—anything but church. But if people won't gather for worship on earth, why would they hope to be gathered in heaven?

A young lady was celebrating her sixteenth birthday, and her parents wanted to give her a party. They rented a roller rink and bought enough food for a hundred people. They decorated lavishly, and invited everyone from her class. But they all began to make excuses, and only two people came to the party. It's the birthday she'll never forget.

Parties are risky. But God has taken the risk and wants his house to be full. We've received our invitation, and he wants us to spread the word. Thinking of those who declined Jesus said, *I tell you, not one of those who were invited will get a taste of my banquet* (Luke 14:24).

*****

Luke 14:25 *Large crowds were traveling with Jesus.*

Jesus didn't need a praise band, a microphone, or even a building to get a crowd. There were no hot dogs, beer tents, or special prizes—just thousands of people hanging on his words. Most preachers never see more than a couple hundred and, whenever the crowd swells, they like to gather contact information to invite them to another event.

But whenever Jesus got a crowd he might say something radical to make them go away (John 6:53, John 6:66). This is because he wanted to make disciples, not just gather a crowd. His radical sayings had the power to separate curiosity seekers from those who truly believed. But what Jesus said next was radical even for him.

Luke 14:26 *If anyone comes to me and does not hate father and mother, wife and children, brothers and sisters—yes, even their own life—such a person cannot be my disciple.*

Most people assume that God is pro-family, and there's much in the Bible to support that idea. God created marriage (Genesis 2:21-22), is against divorce (Matthew 19:8), commands us to honor our parents (Exodus 20:12), and provided a family for Jesus to grow up in (Matthew 1:18).

But if God is pro-family, he's pro-Jesus even more. We're commanded to follow Jesus Christ even at the cost of losing our family. Many Christian wives have been rejected by their husbands, and many Christian husbands have been rejected by their wives. Many Christian children have been rejected by their parents, and many Christian parents have been rejected by their children.

Do not suppose that I have come to bring peace to the earth. I did not come to bring peace, but a sword. For I have come to turn a man against his father, a daughter against her mother, a daughter-in-law against her mother-in-law—a man's enemies will be the members of his own household (Matthew 10:34-36), said Jesus.

But when Jesus said we are to *hate father and mother, wife and children, brothers and sisters . . .* he didn't mean we are to wish them harm. He meant our love for him is to be so great that it makes all other loves seem like hatred in comparison.

Perpetua lived in a time and a place when following Jesus was a capital offense. She was a nursing mother, just twenty-two years old, when she was arrested and sentenced to death. All she had to do was renounce Christ and she could return to her family. And, for the sake of her child, they begged her to do so. But out of love for Jesus Christ she committed her family to God, and was thrown to lions.

Under normal circumstances Christians should be the best family members possible. But if there's a conflict between obedience to Christ and obedience to family, our first loyalty must always to Christ.

For Reflection and Review

- *What does Jesus think about status?*
- *What did Jesus think about crowds?*
- *How important are families to God?*

Lesson 231

Luke 14:27 *And whoever does not carry their cross and follow me cannot be my disciple.*

Likewise, *Whoever wants to be my disciple must deny themselves and take up their cross and follow me* (Matthew 16:24). And again, *Whoever wants to be my disciple must deny themselves and take up their cross daily and follow me* (Luke 9:23).

Following Jesus was fun and exciting most of the time. There were miracles, parties, and speeches—you never knew what would happen next. It seemed like things would keep getting better as Jesus' influence grew. But then he'd talk about the cross—not only for him, but for his followers' too.

Spartacus led a failed revolt around 71 BC, leading to the crucifixion of six thousand of his followers. Jesus' disciples knew about this, so when he started talking about the cross, it made them nervous. We don't know the thoughts of Judas Iscariot, but he had no intention of dying with Christ. Any talk of the cross wasn't for him.

Many believers have been crucified literally, but crucifixion is also a metaphor for the Christian life. *I have been crucified with Christ and I no longer live, but Christ lives in me* (Galatians 2:20), wrote Paul. Paul identified with Christ's death and resurrection so thoroughly, that he felt dead to the world and alive to God. This should also be true for us.

Once we take up our cross and follow Jesus Christ, we'll be less concerned for the present world, since we're on our way to a better one. We'll care less about the stock market, the super bowl, or even a nuclear war. The present world is fading away, and the eternal one is almost here.

Luke 14:28-30 *Suppose one of you wants to build a tower. Won't you first sit down and estimate the cost to see if you have enough money to complete it? For if you lay the foundation and are not able to finish it, everyone who sees it will ridicule you, saying, This person began to build and was not able to finish.*

There's a large building in the town where I live that has never been completed. Construction stopped, due to a recession, and a great deal of money was lost. The uncompleted building is a disgrace to the community, and an embarrassment to whoever started it. Jesus is saying it's better not to start the Christian life, than to start and not finish. Like getting married, we shouldn't come to Christ unless we're prepared to stay with him.

Luke 14:31-32 *Or suppose a king is about to go to war against another king. Won't he first sit down and consider whether he is able with ten thousand men to oppose the one coming against him with twenty thousand? If he is not able, he will send a delegation while the other is still a long way off and will ask for terms of peace.*

After advising people to think carefully about their decision to follow him, Jesus encouraged the right decision. A little king with ten thousand troops was being challenged by a big king with twenty thousand troops. The outcome was certain death for the little king, so he sent for terms of peace. Unfortunately, this could be expensive.

Luke 14:33 *In the same way, those of you who do not give up everything you have cannot be my disciples.*

Jesus is the big king, and we are all little kings, defending our little kingdoms. Opposing Jesus is certain death, and peace will cost us everything. All we have, and all we are, must become his. This seems rather drastic until we understand that surrender makes us part of his glorious kingdom. Surrendering to Jesus Christ is like Cinderella saying *yes* to Prince Charming. We give up our rags to receive his riches.

*****

Luke 15:8 *Or suppose a woman has ten silver coins and loses one.*

The ten silver coins were probably about ten days wages. They may've been her life's savings, and were needed for something important. She probably counted them often but then, one day, discovered one of them was missing. To her alarm she counted them again, but there were only nine.

Archaeology has turned up many silver coins, showing it wasn't uncommon for them to be lost. Wasting no time, this dear woman lit a lamp and swept her house. Many homes were windowless, with only dirt floors, so her search wouldn't be easy. We can imagine her joy when she saw a glint of silver, picked it up, and recovered what was lost. This made her so happy that she rejoiced with her friends and neighbors! (Luke 15:9).

Luke 15:10 *In the same way, I tell you, there is rejoicing in the presence of the angels of God over one sinner who repents.*

The world doesn't rejoice when a sinner repents because it means very little to them. Demons cringe when a sinner repents because they've lost one of their own. The church is happy when a sinner repents because their fellowship is enlarged. But angels rejoice when a sinner repents because they see a change of destiny. There's a party in heaven whenever a sinner repents, and the celebration will never end.

*****

Luke 15:11 *There was a man who had two sons.*

One was lost in a distant land; the other was lost in his own back yard.

The younger son asked for an early inheritance, so he could get away from his father. He went to a distant land and spent his fortune on wild living (Luke 15:13). When it was gone, and life became unbearable, he returned to his father with a speech: *Father, I have sinned against heaven and against you. I am no longer worthy to be called your son* (Luke 15:18-19).

But as he came up the road, his father saw him, and ran out to meet him. He *threw his arms around him and kissed him* (Luke 15:20). The son tried to make his speech, but his father called for a party instead. *For this son of mine was dead and is alive again; he was lost and is found* (Luke 15:24), he said.

The older son began to complain: *All these years I've been slaving for you and never disobeyed your orders. Yet you never gave me even a young goat so I could celebrate with my friends. But when this son of yours who has squandered your property with prostitutes comes home, you kill the fattened calf for him!* (Luke 15:29-30).

The older brother's attitude shows he was just as lost as his younger brother. There was no love in his heart, only bitterness, pride, and self-righteousness. His sins weren't as obvious, but they were just as deadly. Whether we are near to God, or far away from him, we all need to come home.

For Reflection and Review

- *How is following Christ like carrying a cross?*
- *Why is surrendering to Christ a good choice?*
- *How can self-righteousness keep us away from God?*

Lesson 232

Luke 16:19-21 *There was a rich man who was dressed in purple and fine linen and lived in luxury every day. At his gate was laid a beggar named Lazarus, covered with sores and longing to eat what fell from the rich man's table. Even the dogs came and licked his sores.*

Both men eventually died and went to separate places. Lazarus went to be with Abraham, and the rich man went to hell. *Father Abraham, have pity on me and send Lazarus to dip the tip of his finger in water and cool my tongue, because I am in agony in this fire* (Luke 16:24). But Abraham replied, *those who want to go from here to you cannot, nor can anyone cross over from there to us* (Luke 16:26).

Luke 16:27-31 *Then I beg you, father, send Lazarus to my family, for I have five brothers. Let him warn them, so that they will not also come to this place of torment. Abraham replied, They have Moses and the Prophets; let them listen to them. No, father Abraham, he said, but if someone from the dead goes to them, they will repent. He said to him, If they do not listen to Moses and the Prophets, they will not be convinced even if someone rises from the dead.*

There's much that we can learn from this remarkable story. First, those who appear to be forgotten by God, may actually be his children. Lazarus was so far down the social ladder that he was barely above the dogs that licked his sores. Health, wealth, and circumstances are no indication of a person's standing with God. This was a challenge to the religious leaders, who thought wealth was a sign of God's favor.

Second, death may bring a great reversal. Lazarus went to heaven and the rich man went to hell. Heaven is open to all who believe in Jesus Christ (John 3:16), but the poor are often more receptive than the rich. *Has not God chosen those who are poor in the eyes of the world to be rich in faith and to inherit the kingdom he promised those who love him?* (James 2:5), wrote James.

Third, hell is a place of torment. *I am in agony in this fire,* said the rich man. Elsewhere, Jesus described hell a place of *weeping and gnashing of teeth*

(Matthew 13:50). Some people can't believe God would create a place of eternal misery. But if God allows misery on earth, there's no reason to think there won't be misery in the age to come.

Fourth, there is no second chance. *[T]hose who want to go from here to you cannot, nor can anyone cross over from there to us,* said Abraham. Many people hope that if they don't go to heaven at first, they might get there eventually. But that idea is not in the Bible. At the moment of death, everyone goes to heaven or hell forever.

Fifth, those in hell feel sorry for their loved one's who follow them. The rich man wanted Lazarus to warn his brothers not to *come to this place of torment.* We can imagine the sorrow for each of his siblings who dropped into hell after him. If he was the oldest child, he set a terrible example for them to follow.

We can also imagine the sorrow of parents who fail to teach their children the gospel, and to model the Christian life for them. Their everlasting sorrow will be intensified when they see their children drop into hell, followed by their grandchildren, for countless generations.

Sixth, God's word is warning enough. The rich man thought if Lazarus warned his brothers they'd certainly repent. But Abraham replied, *If they do not listen to Moses and the Prophets, they will not be convinced even if someone rises from the dead.*

This became obvious when Jesus himself rose from the dead. The guards saw an angel but they *were so afraid of him that they shook and became like dead men* (Matthew 28:4). Instead of repenting, however, they accepted a bribe and said *His disciples came during the night and stole him away* (Matthew 28:13).

The guards knew perfectly well what happened, but refused to repent and believe in Christ, even though he rose from the dead. Stubborn unbelief is not an intellectual problem, but a moral problem. People won't repent and believe because they don't want to change their lives. This story is a warning to everyone.

*****

Luke 17:12-14 *As [Jesus] was going into a village, ten men who had leprosy met him. They stood at a distance and called out in a loud voice, Jesus, Master, have pity on us! When he saw them, he said, Go, show yourselves to the priests. And as they went, they were cleansed.*

And yet, only one returned to give thanks. *Were not all ten cleansed? Where are the other nine?* (Luke 17:17), asked Jesus. The apparent ingratitude of those who didn't return to give thanks truly surprised the Lord. We can surprise him too, if we're not as thankful as we ought to be.

Every good and perfect gift is from above (James 1:17), wrote James. And God *richly provides us with everything for our enjoyment* (1 Timothy 6:17), wrote Paul. While the rest of the world complains, believers should excel at giving thanks. This, in turn, will lead to further happiness.

All happy people are grateful, and ungrateful people cannot be happy. We tend to think that it is being unhappy that leads people to complain, but it is truer to say that it is complaining that leads to people becoming unhappy. Become grateful and you will become a much happier person (Dennis Prager).

A Christian man was robbed one evening and later wrote the following: *I thank you first, because I was never robbed before. I thank you second, because although they took my money they didn't take my life. I thank you third, because although they took my all, it wasn't much. And I thank you fourth, because it was I who was robbed and not I who robbed* (Matthew Henry).

*****

Luke 17:21 *[T]he kingdom of God is in your midst.*

The kingdom of God was in their midst because the king was in their midst. Wherever Christ is present, the kingdom of God is present. Before the coming of Christ, the world was characterized by sin, sorrow, and death. When Christ returns the world will be characterized holiness, happiness, and life. For now, Christ is in the midst of his people (Matthew 28:20) bringing their future into the present.

Imagine two overlapping circles: one dark and the other light. Christians live in the overlapping part. Christ has given us holiness, happiness, and life. But we still experience sin, sorrow, and death. When the *present evil age* (Galatians 1:4) gives way to the *age to come* (Luke 20:35) whatever is dark will give way to the light.

Understanding this will keep us from expecting too little, or too much, from the Christian life. Those who expect too little underestimate the holiness, happiness, and life that Jesus came to give. Those who expect too much will either doubt or despair, whenever they suffer or sin.

This also explains why some of our prayers are answered, and others are not. The kingdom of God has come in Christ, but it hasn't come in fullness. The king is in our midst, but hasn't appeared in glory. Christians live in the overlap between the present evil age, and the glorious age to come. The present is good, but the future is better by far.

For Reflection and Review

- *What can we learn from Lazarus and the rich man?*
- *Why does gratitude make us happy?*
- *How is the Christian life like two overlapping circles?*

Lesson 233

Luke 18:9 *To some who were confident of their own righteousness and looked down on everyone else, Jesus told this parable*:

Jesus lived in a culture where those who were most religious received approval from others, and approved of themselves as well. But they looked down on those who were less religious, and felt superior to them. This is not uncommon, but it's not the way of Christ. So Jesus told a story that would shock the religious establishment.

Luke 18:10 *Two men went up to the temple to pray, one a Pharisee and the other a tax collector.*

These men were at opposite ends of the religious spectrum. Pharisees were devoted to God and the Bible; tax collectors were devoted to themselves and to money. They gathered taxes for Rome, and enriched themselves by over-charging honest people. They were hated for betraying their nation, but felt the money was worth it.

Luke 18:11-12 *The Pharisee stood by himself and prayed: God, I thank you that I am not like other people—robbers, evildoers, adulterers—or even like this tax collector. I fast twice a week and give a tenth of all I get.*

The Pharisee was entirely sincere. Who fasts twice a week, and gives ten percent of their money to God? He didn't even take the credit, but thanked God that he wasn't like other sinners. His religious devotion surpassed many of Jesus' followers.

Luke 18:13 *But the tax collector stood at a distance. He would not even look up to heaven, but beat his breast and said, God, have mercy on me, a sinner.*

This man knew that he was sinful. He'd broken many of God's commands, and deserved to be condemned. He wasn't proud of himself, and could only plead for mercy. But he would get it. *I tell you that this man, rather than the other, went home justified before God* (Luke 18:14a), said Jesus.

This gets at the heart of Christianity. *Jesus came into the world to save sinners* (1 Timothy 1:15), wrote Paul. And those who think they're pretty good people can't repent of their sins. That's why tax collectors and prostitutes enter the kingdom of God ahead of many others (Matthew 21:31). The more dreadful our sins, the more clearly we need to be saved. But what about those who really are better than average people?

The secret of repentance is knowing what God requires. *Be perfect, therefore, as your heavenly Father is perfect* (Matthew 5:48). Since no one other than Jesus ever lived up to this, we're all in need of forgiveness every single day. The more we try to be perfect, the more we'll be aware of our failures.

When we realize what God requires, and how miserably we fail, we'll beg for his mercy, and cast off any self-righteousness.

*****

Luke 19:1-6 *Jesus entered Jericho and was passing through. A man was there by the name of Zacchaeus; he was a chief tax collector and was wealthy. He wanted to see who Jesus was, but because he was short he could not see over the crowd. So he ran ahead and climbed a sycamore-fig tree to see him, since Jesus was coming that way. When Jesus reached the spot, he looked up and said to him, Zacchaeus, come down immediately. I must stay at your house today. So he came down at once and welcomed him gladly.*

As a professional tax collector, Zacchaeus became rich by overcharging people, and keeping the difference for himself. He was hated by most, and many resented the fact that Jesus stayed at his house. *He has gone to be the guest of a sinner* (Luke 19:7), they said.

But Zacchaeus responded with joy, and gave half his wealth the poor. He also promised to pay back everyone he cheated, four times the amount (Luke 19:8). This probably left him without a dime, but in his heart he was richer than ever. How happy he must've been to hear Jesus say, *Today salvation has come to this house . . . . For the Son of Man came to seek and to save the lost* (Luke 19:9-10).

Seeking and saving the lost was Jesus' mission, and should be ours as well. People who lose a pet will stop everything until they find it. We do the same whenever we lose our keys, wallet, or phone. If the loss of these things matters to us, how much more do lost people matter to God?

A celebration was held at a city pool, and several lifeguards were invited. When the party was over, a fully clothed body was found at the bottom of the pool. The lifeguards were so busy socializing that they didn't notice someone was drowning. It's not enough to celebrate the gospel, we must bring it to those who are perishing.

For Reflection and Review

- *What is the cure for self-righteousness?*
- *Why was Zacchaeus filled with joy, even though he was broke?*
- *How can we seek and save the lost?*

Lesson 234

Luke 19:30-31 *Go to the village ahead of you, and as you enter it, you will find a colt tied there, which no one has ever ridden. Untie it and bring it here. If anyone asks you, Why are you untying it? say, The Lord needs it.*

As Jesus approached Jerusalem, where he'd soon be crucified, he called for a colt in order to fulfill an ancient prophecy: *Rejoice greatly, Daughter Zion! Shout, Daughter Jerusalem! See, your king comes to you, righteous and victorious, lowly and riding on a donkey, on a colt, the foal of a donkey* (Zechariah 9:9), wrote Zechariah.

Jesus' fame had spread because of his many miracles (Luke 19:37), especially the raising of Lazarus (John 11:43-44). As a result, many from the city came out to greet him with messianic praise. *Hosanna to the Son of David! Blessed is he who comes in the name of the Lord! Hosanna in the highest heaven!* (Matthew 21:9), they said. They also spread their cloaks on the road, along with palm branches, to create a royal path (Matthew 21:8). At last, it seemed, the people were receiving their Messiah.

But Jesus knew their faith was superficial, and that some would soon be calling for his crucifixion (Luke 23:21). So as he approached Jerusalem he *wept over it* (Luke 19:41), and also foretold its doom. *The days will come upon you when your enemies will build an embankment against you and encircle you and hem you in on every side. They will dash you to the ground, you and the children within your walls. They will not leave one stone on another, because you did not recognize the time of God's coming to you* (Luke 19:43-44).

This prophecy was fulfilled about forty years later. In AD 66 the Jews revolted against Rome, and soon found their city surrounded by Romans soldiers. It took a few years, but the city fell in AD 70. Hundreds of thousands were killed, the temple was burned, and Jerusalem was destroyed —just as Jesus foretold.

The explanation Jesus gave for this disaster is that the Jews rejected their Messiah (Luke 19:44). Many appeared to receive him, but the nation as a whole rejected him. Likewise, much of the world appears to receive Jesus Christ but, as a whole, it rejects him. And when he returns, the world will meet a similar fate (Revelation 14:19-20).

From this we learn that excitement for Jesus Christ is not a clear indication of salvation. Saving faith is marked by faithful obedience (Matthew 7:21) until the time of death. The excitement of many fades, *but the one who stands firm to the end will be saved* (Matthew 24:13), said Jesus. It's good to be excited for Christ, but excitement means nothing apart from faithful obedience.

*****

Luke 23:26 *As the soldiers led him away, they seized Simon from Cyrene, who was on his way in from the country, and put the cross on him and made him carry it behind Jesus.*

Soon after his triumphal entry, Jesus was arrested, tried, and condemned to crucifixion. He was forced to carry his cross (John 19:17), but was so weakened by the beating he received (John 19:1-3) that he couldn't carry it all the way. So a man named *Simon*, from the city of *Cyrene*, was forced to carry it for him.

Humanly speaking, Simon was in the wrong place at the wrong time. To be forced to carry a cross in a parade of execution seemed a terrible misfortune. If there was confusion, Simon could've been crucified, since he was carrying the cross.

We know little more about Simon, except that he had a family. His sons, *Alexander and Rufus* (Mark 15:21), became known to the church in Rome, and his wife is mentioned by the Apostle Paul (Romans 16:13). Putting the evidence together, it seems that Simon and his family were converted due, in part, to this encounter. They may've returned for Pentecost, heard Peter preach, and been baptized (Acts 2:14-41).

Simon didn't want to carry Jesus' cross, but it turned out to be the honor of his life. We shouldn't judge misfortune on the day it occurs, because we never know what good it'll bring. And if you're ever tempted to panic, wait three days. That's how long it took for Jesus to rise from the dead.

*****

Luke 23:34 *Father, forgive them, for they do not know what they are doing.*

This is how Jesus prayed for his executioners. He didn't quote Jeremiah: *Bring on them the day of disaster; destroy them with double destruction* (Jeremiah 17:18). Or even King David: *Pour out your wrath on them; let your fierce anger overtake them* (Psalm 69:24). Instead, Jesus followed his own teaching: *Love your enemies, do good to those who hate you, bless those who curse you, pray for those who mistreat you* (Luke 6:27-28).

Jesus wants the best for everyone, including his enemies. God is *not wanting anyone to perish, but everyone to come to repentance* (2 Peter 3:9), wrote Peter. God *wants all people to be saved and to come to a knowledge of the truth* (1 Timothy 2:4), wrote Paul.

A young butcher had a troubling experience while slaughtering his first lamb. After slitting its throat, the lamb got away and staggered around the pen. Just before it died, it staggered back to the butcher and licked his hand. Likewise, Jesus loved his killers while they were still killing him. *God demonstrates his own love for us in this: While we were still sinners, Christ died for us* (Romans 5:8), wrote Paul.

For Reflection and Review

- *Why was Jesus sad as he rode into Jerusalem?*
- *What can we learn from Simon of Cyrene?*

- *Why did Jesus want his enemies to be forgiven?*

Lesson 235

Luke 24:13 *Now that same day two of them were going to a village called Emmaus, about seven miles from Jerusalem.*

These were disciples of Christ, but weren't his apostles. One was named *Cleopas* (Luke 24:18) and the other may've been his wife, but we're not told her name. They were disheartened and confused, since they didn't expect Jesus to be crucified. But they also heard a rumor that he had risen from the dead. What did this mean?

As they talked and discussed these things with each other, Jesus himself came up and walked along with them; but they were kept from recognizing him (Luke 24:15-16). Jesus looked normal enough that they would've recognized him if they weren't *kept from recognizing him*. First he wanted to talk about the Bible.

Luke 24:27 *And beginning with Moses and all the Prophets, he explained to them what was said in all the Scriptures concerning himself.*

We can imagine their amazement as this stranger turned their attention to what the Bible said about Messiah. From passage after passage Jesus explained what the Scriptures said about himself. He'd been reading the Bible this way most of his life, and was able to make it clear.

Perhaps they began with God's promise to crush the devil's head, and die in the process (Genesis 3:15). Surely they discussed the words of Isaiah: *But he was pierced for our transgressions, he was crushed for our iniquities* (Isaiah 53:5). And also Zechariah: *They will look on me, the one they have pierced* (Zechriah 12:10). Perhaps they finished with the words of a Psalm: *you will not abandon me to the realm of the dead, nor will you let your faithful one see decay* (Psalm 16:10). This was the most exciting Bible study they ever had!

To understand the Bible well, we must ask what any given passage teaches about Christ. We won't find him in every verse but, if we zoom out far enough, we'll see that he's the main message of the whole Bible.

In the country of Peru, there are a series of strange lines covering several miles. For many years they were thought to be ancient irrigation ditches. But in 1939 they were seen from the window of an airplane, and it was clear they were enormous drawings of animals. In a similar way, when we get an overview of the Bible, we see it's all about Jesus Christ. *These are the very Scriptures that testify about me* (John 5:39), he said.

Luke 24:28-29 *As they approached the village to which they were going, Jesus continued on as if he were going farther. But they urged him strongly, Stay with us, for it is nearly evening; the day is almost over. So he went in to stay with them.*

It's not clear why Jesus *continued on as if he were going farther* except that, like us, he prefers to stay where he's wanted. We ought to be mindful of his presence, therefore, and always treat him like an honored guest.

Luke 24:30-35 *When he was at the table with them, he took bread, gave thanks, broke it and began to give it to them. Then their eyes were opened and they recognized him, and he disappeared from their sight. . . . They got up and returned at once to Jerusalem. There they found the Eleven and those with them, assembled together and saying, It is true! The Lord has risen and has appeared to Simon. Then the two told what had happened on the way, and how Jesus was recognized by them when he broke the bread.*

If this wasn't exciting enough, suddenly Jesus appeared and said *Peace be with you* (Luke 24:36). They needed a little peace, since they were hiding behind locked doors, afraid of the Jewish leaders (John 20:19). And now they thought they were seeing a ghost! (Luke 24:37). So Jesus showed them his hands and feet, and ate some fish in their presence (Luke 24:39-43). He wanted them to know that he was truly alive, and that his body was the same one that hung on the cross.

Jesus' resurrection body had some improvements, but it was still the same body. There was continuity as well as discontinuity, and we should expect the same. Our resurrection bodies won't be entirely different than the ones we have now, but will be much improved.

Luke 24:46-47 *He told them, This is what is written: The Messiah will suffer and rise from the dead on the third day, and repentance for the forgiveness of sins will be preached in his name to all nations, beginning at Jerusalem.*

So Peter preached on the day of Pentecost saying, *Repent and be baptized, every one of you, in the name of Jesus Christ for the forgiveness of your sins* (Acts 2:38). And God *commands all people everywhere to repent* (Acts 17:30), said Paul. And, *I have declared to both Jews and Greeks that they must turn to God in repentance* (Acts 20:21), said Paul again. Likewise, God is *not wanting anyone to perish, but everyone to come to repentance* (2 Peter 3:9), wrote Peter.

In each case, the apostles were speaking of initial repentance, leading to salvation. We continue repenting the rest of our lives (Matthew 6:12), but the Christian life begins with initial repentance.

A man asked his pastor when the best time to repent was, and his pastor said, *the last day of your life.* The man said he didn't know when that would be, so his pastor urged him to repent at once. The call to repentance is always urgent because it leads to eternal salvation.

For Reflection and Review

- *What's the main purpose of the Bible?*
- *How was Jesus' body the same after his resurrection?*
- *How often should Christians repent?*

Lesson 236

John 1:1 *In the beginning was the Word, and the Word was with God, and the Word was God.*

The gospel according to John was written by the apostle John around AD 90. He includes much that isn't found in the other gospels, and stated his purpose clearly: *these are written that you may believe that Jesus is the Messiah, the Son of God, and that by believing you may have life in his name* (John 20:31).

John began his gospel with an echo from the first verse of the Bible: *In the beginning God . . .* (Genesis 1:1). The same God who spoke the world into being, spoke through his Son, whom John called *the Word.*

In the Old Testament *the word of the Lord came to Abram* (Genesis 15:1), *the word of the Lord came to Samuel* (1 Samuel 15:10), *the word of the Lord came to Nathan* (2 Samuel 7:4), *the word of the Lord came to Solomon* (1 Kings 6:11), and to many others.

In fact, that little phrase occurs well over two hundred times. The word of the Lord came most fully, however, in the person of Jesus Christ. He's the personification of God's word, the clearest expression of God there is.

Some people say that if we received a single word from outer space, it'd prove that alien life exists. Jesus is the *Word* from heaven that proves that God exists. If you ever want to hear from God, all you have to do is listen to Jesus Christ.

John 1:3 *Through him all things were made; without him nothing was made that has been made.*

Heaven and earth, fish and fowl, atoms and galaxies, owe their existence to Jesus Christ. A carpenter from Nazareth, one who made tables and chairs, also made the world and everything in it. To know Jesus Christ is to know your Maker. This can be compared to a perfect marriage.

To find a compatible spouse is like finding the one for whom you were made. It brings a completion and fulfillment that surpasses other human relationships. A great spouse will bring out the best in you, and help you reach your potential. Marriage isn't easy, of course, but it will teach us more about ourselves than if we remain single.

That's that's how it is with Jesus Christ. He's the one for whom we were made, who brings out the best in us, who helps us reach our potential, and teaches us more about ourselves than we'd ever known apart from him. It really helps to know your Maker.

John 1:11 *He came to that which was his own, but his own did not receive him.*

This is one of the strangest facts of history. God came into the world, but the world rejected God. The world can't even exist apart from God but, when God came into the world he created, the world rejected its Creator.

We'd be even more surprised, but God's chosen people also had a history of not knowing God. *The ox knows its master, the donkey its owner's manger, but Israel does not know, my people do not understand* (Isaiah 1:3), said God. When it comes to knowing their Master, people are dumber than beasts.

John 1:12 *Yet to all who did receive him, to those who believed in his name, he gave the right to become children of God.*

This is one of the clearest verses in the Bible about how to become a child of God. If Jesus knocks on your door, but you don't open it, you haven't received him. If you open the door a crack, you haven't received him either. But if you open the door wide, and invite him to come inside, then you have received him. That's how we become children of God. We open the door of our hearts to Christ, and invite him in forever.

*****

John 1:29 *The next day John saw Jesus coming toward him and said, Look, the Lamb of God, who takes away the sin of the world!*

The purpose of John the Baptist's ministry was to point people to Christ. And he was never more clear than when he identified Jesus as *the Lamb of God, who takes away the sin of the world*.

Lambs were an important part of the sacrificial system, but not any lamb would do. About two dozen times God stated the lamb must be *without defect* (Numbers 28:3, etc.). The worshipper didn't have to be without defect, but the lamb had to be without defect, because it pointed ahead to the Lamb of God, *a lamb without blemish or defect* (1 Peter 1:19), wrote Peter. We aren't accepted by God because we are perfect, but because we have a perfect lamb.

For Reflection and Review

- *Why is Jesus called the Word?*
- *How do we become God's children?*
- *Why did sacrificial lambs have to be without defect?*

Lesson 237

John 2:1-2 *[A] wedding took place at Cana in Galilee. Jesus' mother was there, and Jesus and his disciples had also been invited to the wedding.*

Little is known about weddings in Jesus' day, except the celebration could last a week. It's surprising that Jesus took time out of his messianic mission to be at a wedding. If anyone had places to go, people to see, and limited time for small talk, it had to be Jesus Christ. But there he was at a wedding, eating finger food, and chatting with aunt Rebecca.

At the very least we can say that Jesus liked people. He went to so many parties, in fact, that he got a reputation as *a glutton and a drunkard, a friend of tax collectors and sinners* (Matthew 11:19). He even said, *where two or three gather in my name, there am I with them* (Matthew 18:20). Jesus is a social person who enjoys being with people.

John 2:3 *When the wine was gone, Jesus' mother said to him, They have no more wine.*

The cost of a wedding could produce a financial strain, just as it does today. The families in charge probably had a limited budget, and may've hoped their guests wouldn't be very thirsty. But the guests had taken off work, put on their best clothes, and wanted to celebrate. For the party to end early would've been a disgrace to the families, and a lasting embarrassment to the bride and groom.

Mary's husband, Joseph, was probably dead, since he's never mentioned during Jesus' adult life. As the first born son, Jesus would've picked up many of Joseph's responsibilities so, naturally, Mary turned to him. It's hard to know what she expected since Jesus hadn't done a miracle yet (John 2:11). But she seemed to have a mother's intuition that, somehow, Jesus could help.

John 2:4 *Woman, why do you involve me? Jesus replied. My hour has not yet come.*

Jesus' reply was abrupt because he refused do anything apart from his heavenly Father (John 5:19). But Mary wouldn't be denied. She apparently had some authority at the wedding, since she turned to the servants and said, *Do whatever he tells you* (John 2:5). From Mary we learn that Jesus' reluctance can be overcome at times.

Jesus also made this point in a story he told. A man needed bread in the middle of the night, so he went to his friend's house and knocked on the door. His friend refused to get out of bed, so he kept on knocking until he finally got up and gave him some bread—not because they were friends, but because of the man's persistence (Luke 11:5-8, paraphrased). Jesus may seem reluctant, at times, but we can often get what we want if we persist.

John 2:7 *Jesus said to the servants, Fill the jars with water; so they filled them to the brim.*

There were six stone jars nearby which, together, could hold about one hundred fifty gallons (John 2:6). Jesus could've used one or two of them, which would've been enough, but he used all six to produce an extraordinary amount of wine.

This may seem excessive, but it was a sign of messianic abundance, just as the prophets foretold. *In that day the mountains will drip new wine* (Joel 3:18), wrote Joel. And, *New wine will drip from the mountains and flow from all the hills* (Amos 9:13), wrote Amos.

John 2:8 *Now draw some out and take it to the master of the banquet.*

This was a quiet miracle. Jesus didn't wave his hands, or even pray out loud. Most were unaware that a miracle even occurred. Even the master of the banquet didn't know, because the miracle was done so quietly.

This is how Jesus usually works. An illness quietly goes away. A marriage is quietly healed. A sinner is quietly forgiven. Even when Jesus rose from the dead, there were no trumpets or flags. He just got up and left behind an empty tomb. Unless we're paying attention, we'll miss out on what Jesus has done, and much of what he's doing today.

John 2:10 *Everyone brings out the choice wine first and then the cheaper wine after the guests have had too much to drink; but you have saved the best till now.*

People drank too much at weddings even back then. To save a little money, hosts would serve the best wine first, and the cheaper wine when no one could tell the difference. But Jesus saved the best for last, and often does.

My mother had a difficult life but, when she was fifty years old she said, *This is the best part of my life so far.* She said it again when she was sixty, and again when she was seventy, and again when she was eighty. Perhaps the Christian life is meant to get better with age. The longer we walk with God, the more we should enjoy him.

*****

John 2:13 *When it was almost time for the Jewish Passover, Jesus went up to Jerusalem.*

Every family was required to offer a sacrificial lamb during Passover (Exodus 12:3-6). It was inconvenient for people to bring their animals with them, so they were made available to purchase. And since everyone had to use the proper currency, money changers were also made available.

But there were a couple problems with how business was conducted. First, it was done in the temple courts, which should've been a place of prayer . . . *for my house will be called a house of prayer for all nations* (Isaiah 56:7), said God. Second, the animal sellers and money changers took advantage of people by making too much profit. This made Jesus angry.

John 2:15-16 *So [Jesus] made a whip out of cords, and drove all from the temple courts, both sheep and cattle; he scattered the coins of the money changers and overturned their tables. To those who sold doves he said, Get these out of here! Stop turning my Father's house into a market!*

It's hard to imagine Jesus with a whip, but he cracked it so effectively that everyone fled. *His disciples remembered that it is written: Zeal for your house will consume me* (John 2:17, Psalm 69:9). Like the temple, the church has become so commercialized we barely see anything wrong with it. But Jesus was more concerned with prayer than profit—and we should be as well.

John 2:18 *The Jews then responded to him, What sign can you show us to prove your authority to do all this? Jesus answered them, Destroy this temple, and I will raise it again in three days.*

The temple was the pride of the Jews. It'd been under reconstruction for forty-six years (John 2:20), and would be for many more. It was one of the grandest buildings on earth, so for Jesus to even mention its destruction became a controversy that wouldn't go away.

When he was on trial some even testified: *We heard him say, I will destroy this temple made with human hands and in three days will build another, not made with hands* (Mark 14:58). And when he was crucified some were *shaking their heads and saying, So! You who are going to destroy the temple and build it in three days, come down from the cross and save yourself!* (Mark 15:29-30).

Even later, when Stephen was put on trial for preaching, his accusers made a similar charge: *This fellow never stops speaking against this holy place . . . . For we have heard him say that this Jesus of Nazareth will destroy this place* (Acts 6:13-14). *But the temple he had spoken of was his body* (John 2:21), wrote John.

The Jews destroyed his body by nailing it to a cross, but three days later Jesus raised it up. The earthly temple was destroyed in AD 70, and has never been rebuilt. We no longer come to God through an earthly temple, but through his Son Jesus Christ (John 14:6).

For Reflection and Review

- Why did Jesus make so much wine?
- Is it wrong for the church to sell things?
- How is Jesus like the temple?

Lesson 238

John 3:1 *Now there was a Pharisee, a man named Nicodemus who was a member of the Jewish ruling council.*

Nicodemus was one of the most prominent people in the nation of Israel. He was a member of the highest political body, and a leading Bible teacher. He was well known and highly regarded. He was also aware of Jesus and his miracles, and may've head him preach more than once. He was so impressed with Jesus that he arranged a meeting at the end of the day for an unhurried theological conversation. And he was very respectful.

John 3:2 *Rabbi, we know that you are a teacher who has come from God.*

This was quite an endorsement from a renowned teacher at the top of the socio-religious hierarchy. Jesus was many years younger than Nicodemus, and hadn't received rabbinical training in any formal sense (John 7:15). Yet Nicodemus addressed him as *Rabbi*, and *a teacher who has come from God*. If Jesus would be even slightly diplomatic, Nicodemus could connect him to some of the most influential people in the nation. But, as usual, Jesus wasn't diplomatic.

John 3:3 *Very truly I tell you, no one can see the kingdom of God unless they are born again.*

Given the deference Nicodemus showed Jesus, we might expect a little more small talk. (*Thank you, Nicodemus, I've heard good things about your ministry too.*) But with a total disregard for pleasantries Jesus made his point: *no one can see the kingdom of God unless they are born again.*

This was all the more troubling since Nicodemus was a respected teacher of the Bible. He'd given his life to the study and teaching of Scripture, and was famous for it. In the public's mind, if anyone was in the kingdom of God, it was Nicodemus. But Jesus had the temerity to tell him otherwise. Jesus could be rude.

But Jesus was never rude in order to be mean. Sometimes Jesus shocks us in order to awaken us. Sometimes he condemns us in order to convert us. Sometimes he wounds us in order to heal us. Like a good doctor, first he tells us what we need to hear, then he provides an effective cure.

John 3:7 *You should not be surprised at my saying, You must be born again.*

And yet we are surprised. When I was growing up my mother took me to church every week. And, because I was in church, I assumed I was in the kingdom of God. But then a friend brought this passage to my attention. He opened his Bible, in fact, and read it out loud to me. When I heard the words, *You must be born again* (and realized I wasn't) I knew I had a problem.

Christianity is a supernatural religion from beginning to end. We have a supernatural Savior who died on the cross for our sins, and rose from the dead to prove it. And when we believe, something supernatural happens to us: the Spirit of Christ comes into us and we're born again. *And if anyone does not have the Spirit of Christ, they do not belong to Christ* (Romans 8:9), wrote Paul. The indwelling Spirit is the mark of a true Christian.

John 3:8 *The wind blows wherever it pleases. You hear its sound, but you cannot tell where it comes from or where it is going. So it is with everyone born of the Spirit.*

We can imagine this conversation taking place on a flat roof porch, wherever Jesus was staying. Perhaps a gust of wind came up which Jesus used to illustrate the work of the Spirit. The Greek word for *wind* and *spirit* is exactly the same, as also in Hebrew. The Spirit is like the wind because he is powerful, unpredictable, and beyond human control.

Sometimes wind is a hurricane, and other times a gentle breeze. For some the new birth is dramatic and, for others, it's barely perceptible. The crucial thing isn't the force of the experience, but believing in Jesus Christ. Real faith comes from the Spirit (Ephesians 2:8), and produces deep confidence in the person and work of Jesus Christ.

John 3:10 *You are Israel's teacher, said Jesus, and do you not understand these things?*

Jesus chided Nicodemus because he should've known about the new birth from the prophet Ezekiel. *I will give you a new heart and put a new spirit in you; I will remove from you your heart of stone and give you a heart of flesh* (Ezekiel 36:26). Being born again is like getting a new heart from God.

Suppose you went to the doctor and he said, *Congratulations, you are my ten thousandth patient and you just won a free heart transplant.* You might not think that was very good news at first. But if you learned that your heart was bad, and without a new heart you'd die, it would be very good news indeed.

Christianity is only good news to people who understand the bad news—the badness of their heart. Everyone's heart is infected with sin, the most deadly form of heart disease. But everyone who believes in Jesus Christ receives a new heart, and will live forever. This is another way of talking about the new birth.

John 3:14-15 *Just as Moses lifted up the snake in the wilderness, so the Son of Man must be lifted up, that everyone who believes may have eternal life in him.*

Jesus ended the conversation by comparing his crucifixion to a strange event in Israel's history. Many were dying from snake bite, so God commanded Moses to put a snake on a pole, and lift it up for everyone to see. Whenever they were bitten, all they had to do was look at the snake on the pole, and they would live (Numbers 21:4-9).

Likewise, Jesus was lifted up on a cross, so all who look to him will live forever. The snake on a pole is a suitable image of the Savior on the cross, bearing our sins. *God made him who had no sin to be sin for us* (2 Corinthians 5:21), wrote Paul. Jesus is the cure for the snake-bite of sin.

John 3:16 *For God so loved the world that he gave his one and only Son, that whoever believes in him shall not perish but have eternal life.*

This is the clearest summary of the gospel in Scripture and presents us with two important facts. First, God's love is extreme. To send his Son to die on a cross for sinners is the greatest act of sacrificial love ever performed. God proved his love, once and for all, by paying the ultimate price for our salvation.

Second, anyone can be saved by believing in Jesus Christ. No matter what we've done in the past, how often we've done it, or even if we do it in the future—all we need to be saved is faith in Jesus Christ. His perfect life and sacrificial death are sufficient payment for all our sins.

But these important facts bring us to a choice: we can believe in Jesus Christ and live forever, or not believe and perish forever. What we can't do is remain undecided, since that is the same as not believing.

If your car stalls on the railroad tracks, and a train is coming, you have to decide to abandon your car or die. The train of God's judgment is coming, so we must chose to believe in Christ or not. The stakes couldn't be higher, and happy are those who choose well.

For Reflection and Review

- *What does it mean to be born again?*
- *How is the Spirit like the wind?*
- *What is the gospel?*

Lesson 239

John 3:3-4 *[Jesus] left Judea and went back once more to Galilee. Now he had to go through Samaria.*

The Samaritans were Jews who intermarried with Assyrians, and altered the Jewish religion. This made the tension between Jews and Samaritans even worse than between Jews and Gentiles. When traveling between Galilee and Jerusalem, stricter Jews often went around Samaria to avoid religious contamination. But Jesus had to go through Samaria because there were people there he wanted to reach.

John 4:7 *When a Samaritan woman came to draw water, Jesus said to her, Will you give me a drink?*

In the previous chapter Jesus spoke to Nicodemus, a man at the top of the social pyramid. He was a member of the high court, and a renowned Bible teacher, but spiritually lost. In this chapter Jesus speaks to a woman at the bottom of the social pyramid, who was also spiritually lost. Jesus cares about lost people from every possible background.

The woman was surprised that Jesus asked her for water, since he wasn't only Jewish but male. Women were considered culturally inferior, but that didn't bother Jesus at all. Cultural barriers were no concern to him when it came to winning souls. That was the business of Jesus Christ, and the business of those who follow him.

I was about twenty years old when I stopped by a convenience store, and saw a young lady from church. On the way out, we encountered a homeless man whom she began to evangelize. She told him of God's love for sinners, and that he could live forever through faith in Jesus Christ. I wasn't very interested in the homeless man, but I was somewhat interested in her, so I waited patiently. When she was done she said something I never forgot. *You know, Shane, everyone has a soul.*

When we look at people not as rich or poor, wise or foolish, godly or godless—but as eternal souls who need to be saved—then we'll begin to see them through the eyes of Jesus Christ.

John 4:10 *If you knew the gift of God and who it is that asks you for a drink, you would have asked him and he would have given you living water.*

Most people didn't have running water back then. Instead, they'd go to the community well, let down a bucket, and carry it home. The idea of a river in her own back yard would have been appealing. But Jesus was speaking of the Holy Spirit because, deep inside, she was thirsting for God. *My soul thirsts for God, for the living God* (Psalm 42:2), wrote the Psalmist.

It can even be argued that spiritual thirst is a sign of God's existence. We desire water, and it'd be strange if the world had no water. We desire food, and it'd be strange if the world had no food. We desire companionship, and it'd be strange if the world had no companions. For everything we desire, it seems, there is a corresponding something to meet that desire. The universal desire for God is a good indication that he exists (CS Lewis, slightly revised).

John 4:16 *Go, call your husband and come back.*

This poor woman had the worst sexual history in town. She'd gone through five husbands, and was now living with a man to whom she wasn't married. As a little girl she may've dreamed of a knight in shining armor, but her first husband didn't work out that way. Neither did her second, third, fourth, or fifth. By this time her options were few, so she settled for a man who wouldn't even marry her. In a religious community, this put her on the same level as a prostitute. She was likely shunned by many, but not by Jesus Christ. He not only loved her, but even seemed to like her.

And if Jesus liked sinners, while they were still sinning, how much more his own, even when we fail? Don't believe the devil's lie that even though God loves you, he doesn't like you very much. If that's what you believe, then you'll never feel close to God, which is what the devil wants. If Jesus didn't like people with sin in their lives, he wouldn't have a friend on earth. But he's the kind of Savior who not only loves people, but likes them, in spite of their sin.

John 4:20 *Our ancestors worshiped on this mountain, but you Jews claim that the place where we must worship is in Jerusalem.*

The Samaritan woman didn't want to talk about her sin, so she changed the subject to religion, and Jesus went along with it. *[He] replied, believe me, a time is coming when you will worship the Father neither on this mountain nor in Jerusalem. . . . true worshipers will worship the Father in the Spirit and in truth, for they are the kind of worshipers the Father seeks* (John 4:21-23).

Before the coming of Christ, God was to be worshipped at the temple in Jerusalem. Depending on where you lived, you might have to cross land and sea to get there. On the day of Pentecost there were people from Egypt, Libya, Rome, and many other places (Acts 2:9-11). But the prophet Zephaniah foresaw a time when that would change. *Distant nations will bow down to him, all of them in their own lands* (Zephaniah 2:11), he wrote.

Worship at the temple is no longer required because Jesus is the temple. *Destroy this temple, and I will raise it again in three days* (John 2:19), he said of himself. God's people used to go to the temple to worship, but now the temple has come to us. *For where two or three gather in my name, there am I with them* (Matthew 18:20), said Jesus.

John 4:23 *Yet a time is coming and has now come when the true worshipers will worship the Father in the Spirit and in truth, for they are the kind of worshipers the Father seeks.*

Dictators often have a policy of compulsory adoration. Whenever they appear in public, people are required to praise them or be punished. God is just the opposite. He's looking for true worshippers, who'll worship *in the Spirit and in truth*. Our day is never complete until we've taken time to adore him, and given our hearts to him anew.

John 4:25-26 *The woman said, I know that Messiah (called Christ) is coming. When he comes, he will explain everything to us. Then Jesus declared, I, the one speaking to you—I am he.*

Jesus seldom revealed his messianic identity, but revealed it here to a very unlikely person. She wasn't a virtuous woman, who deserved to meet the Messiah. She was a sinful woman, trapped in a bad relationship. Yet Jesus revealed himself more fully to her than to almost anyone else.

And that's what he's done for us . . . *not because of anything we have done but because of his own purpose and grace* (2 Timothy 1:9), wrote Paul. When there was nothing in us but sin, Jesus revealed himself to us through the gospel.

For Reflection and Review

- *How can we see people through the eyes of Jesus Christ?*
- *Why is spiritual thirst a sign that God exists?*
- *Why did Jesus reveal himself to a Samaritan woman?*

Lesson 240

John 5:1 *Jesus went up to Jerusalem for one of the Jewish festivals.*

He'd use the occasion to pick a fight with the religious authorities, because he wanted to expose their hypocrisy, and set in motion his crucifixion. *No one takes [my life] from me, but I lay it down of my own accord* (John 10:18), he said. So Jesus went to the pool of Bethesda, to heal a man on the Sabbath, knowing this would infuriate the religious leaders.

There were many candidates around the pool that day (John 5:3), and Jesus chose a difficult case. The man struggled with a disability for thirty-eight years, perhaps a form of paralysis. *Do you want to get well?* (John 5:6), asked Jesus.

Most people want to be well, of course, but there are a few who prefer to be sick, in order to avoid the expectations that come from being healthy. If Jesus healed this man, he'd be expected to get a job, take care of himself, and contribute to society. This is more than some people are willing to do.

Shortly after a man got out of prison, he threw a rock through a jewelry store window. Then he went inside, and waited for police. He'd been in prison for years, and didn't want the responsibility of living in society. Not everyone wants to get well.

John 5:8-9 *Then Jesus said to him, Get up! Pick up your mat and walk. At once the man was cured; he picked up his mat and walked.*

Jesus often worked in response to people's faith. *Take heart, daughter, . . . your faith has healed you* (Matthew 9:22). *According to your faith let it be done to you* (Matthew 9:29). And, *Woman, you have great faith! Your request is granted* (Matthew 15:28). But in this case, Jesus healed a man without any appearance of faith. We ought to pray with faith, of course, but Jesus doesn't need our faith in order to work.

John 5:14 *Later Jesus found him at the temple and said to him, See, you are well again. Stop sinning or something worse may happen to you.*

It's hard to imagine anything worse than what this man had been through. But even though his body was well, all was not well with his soul. So Jesus warned the man about his sin, which isn't identified, but must've been serious.

Perhaps he struggled with bitterness since he'd been in that condition for thirty-eight years. Since he couldn't support a family, he probably never married or had children. Now he was past the prime of life, so he'd never reach his potential, or recover the lost years. In spite of being healed, the man might've spent the rest of his life complaining. So Jesus warned him, *Stop sinning or something worse may happen to you.*

Fanny Crosby was the author of over eight thousand hymns, including some that are sung today. When she was six weeks old she developed an eye condition and was taken to the doctor. Tragically (it seemed) the doctor put the wrong medicine in her eyes, and she was permanently blinded.

She might've become bitter, but she thought of her blindness as a gift to help her focus on God. She said *If I could meet [the doctor] now, I would say thank you, over and over again for making me blind.* The most important thing about our hardships is how we respond to them. They can make us bitter or sweet.

John 5:22 *[T]he Father judges no one, but has entrusted all judgment to the Son.*

Jesus healed this man on the Sabbath to offend the religious leaders. Here he defends himself, but intentionally made things worse. They were already concerned that he was making himself equal to God (John 5:18), so Jesus confirmed their fear by claiming that he would judge the world.

The Bible supports this claim in many places. *[H]e is the one whom God appointed as judge of the living and the dead* (Acts 10:42), said Peter. *For he has set a day when he will judge the world with justice by the man he has appointed* (Acts 17:31), said Paul. *For we must all appear before the judgment seat of Christ* (2 Corinthians 5:10), said Paul again. Since Jesus is both God and man, he is uniquely qualified to be our judge.

This is a great encouragement for believers, because our judge is the one who died for our sins. *Therefore, there is now no condemnation for those who are in Christ Jesus* (Romans 8:1), wrote Paul. We don't have to wait until Judgment Day to see how it will go for us, because the Bible tells us how it will go for us. *[God will] present you before his glorious presence without fault and with great joy* [Jude 1:24], wrote Jude. The dread fear of Judgment Day has been replaced with joyful expectation.

John 5:24 *Very truly I tell you, whoever hears my word and believes him who sent me has eternal life and will not be judged but has crossed over from death to life.*

This may be the clearest statement in the Bible that sinners have eternal life the moment they believe in Jesus Christ. We can imagine a line in the sand, with Jesus on one side, and everyone else on the other. The moment of faith is like taking the Savior's hand, and crossing over to his side. At that precise moment we are assured of eternal life.

Some people think they're right with God because they're moving toward the line. With age, perhaps, they're becoming more kind, caring, and compassionate. But moving toward the line isn't the same as crossing over the line. You can move toward the line your entire life, and still die on the wrong side of it.

Others think they're right with God because they're very close to the line. Perhaps they go to church, give their money, and sing in the choir. But being close to the line isn't the same as crossing over the line. You could be close to the line your entire life, and still die on the wrong side of it.

Crossing over the line is taking the hand of Jesus Christ and saying, *I believe in you, Lord, and I'm coming over to your side today.* It doesn't matter who you are, where you've been, what you've done, how many times you've done it, or how many times you do it in the future. The moment you believe in Jesus Christ you have eternal life. You will not be judged. You have *crossed over from death to life*.

For Reflection and Review

- *Why did Jesus heal on the Sabbath?*
- *Why don't some people want to get well?*
- *How is coming to Jesus like crossing over a line?*

Lesson 241

John 6:5 *When Jesus looked up and saw a great crowd coming toward him, he said to Philip, Where shall we buy bread for these people to eat?*

Since Philip was from the nearby town of Bethsaida (John 1:44), Jesus asked him where they could buy some bread. Including women and children, however, the crowd numbered around fifteen thousand. Even if they found a bakery with that much bread, they wouldn't have enough money to pay for it.

John 6:9 *[Andrew said] Here is a boy with five small barley loaves and two small fish, but how far will they go among so many?*

Under the leadership of Moses, God fed his people bread from heaven (Exodus 16). Jesus could've done the same, but accepted the lunch of an unnamed boy (John 6:9), and multiplied it until everyone had enough. This miracle is so important that it's the only one recorded in all four gospels, other than the resurrection.

John 6:11 *Jesus then took the loaves, gave thanks, and distributed to those who were seated.*

By giving thanks before eating, Jesus left an example for us to follow. The custom in my parents' house was to pray before every meal. *Bless us, Oh Lord, and these your gifts, which we are about to receive, from your generosity, through Christ our Lord. Amen.* This is the first prayer I learned as a child, and I prayed it many times without a thought. But, as an adult, I found the words to be a true expression of my heart, and a wonderful way to give thanks.

John 6:11 *[They all had] as much as they wanted.*

Not a single person there went away hungry. The disciples kept serving bread and fish until everyone was full. *They all ate and were satisfied* (Mark 6:42), wrote Mark.

But we have other appetites too. In addition to food we want pleasure, possessions, companions, adventure, and entertainment. We're so insatiable, in fact, that we can never be satisfied with anything less than God. *You have made us for yourself, O Lord, and our hearts are restless until they rest in you* (Augustine).

When every other need is met, what we really need is more of Jesus Christ. To have everything else in the world, except him, is to be hungry and not know why. *For the bread of God . . . comes down from heaven and gives life to the world* (John 6:33), said Jesus. He alone can satisfy our deepest need.

John 6:12 *Gather the pieces that are left over. Let nothing be wasted.*

Jesus fed thousands with a few loaves of bread and some fish, but made his disciples pick up the scraps. The only person with unlimited resources wasn't willing to waste a bite. Since Jesus was frugal, frugality is a Christian virtue.

I have a friend who's the cheapest person I've ever known. For some time he wouldn't use the toilet before work, because he wanted to save money on the flush. We were talking before church, one day, when a man came in with panic in his eyes. He'd lost an envelope containing a thousand dollars, and his rent was due that day. My friend said, *I have a thousand dollars—it's a gift, not a loan.*

The reason my friend was cheap, I learned, was to save money for people in need. And *though he was rich, yet for your sake [Christ] became poor, so that you through his poverty might become rich* (2 Corinthians 8:9), wrote Paul. Frugality is a virtue, if we're saving money to help people in need.

John 6:15 *Jesus, knowing that they intended to come and make him king by force, withdrew again to a mountain by himself.*

People were so excited about their free lunch that some wanted to make Jesus king. The disciples may've agreed, but there were a few problems with this idea: First, no one makes Jesus king; Jesus is the king. Second, Jesus didn't come to sit on a throne, but to die on a cross. Third, what they really wanted was another free lunch.

But if people come to Jesus for the wrong reason, they'll leave him just as quickly. The reason we should come to Christ is to be forgiven for our sins. That's what we need the most, and that's why Jesus came. He's often pleased to meet our other needs, but his first concern is for our salvation.

John 6:28-29 *Then they asked him, What must we do to do the works God requires? Jesus answered, The work of God is this: to believe in the one he has sent.*

The people asked the right question, and Jesus gave the right answer, but they didn't like his answer. They wanted to do something to earn eternal life, but the only way to heaven is through faith in Jesus Christ (John 14:6).

John 6:30 *What sign then will you give that we may see it and believe you?* (John 6:30).

Jesus just fed thousands of people with someone's lunch, and this was witnessed by more people than all his other miracles combined. It was a little insincere for them to ask for yet another miracle before they'd believe in Jesus. The problem wasn't the miracles, of course, but their determination not to believe no matter what. *Even after Jesus had performed so many signs in their presence, they still would not believe in him* (John 12:37), wrote John.

Jesus never met a disease he could not cure, a birth defect he could not reverse, a demon he could not exorcise. But he did meet skeptics he could not convince and sinners he could not convert (Philip Yancey). Jesus Christ has provided enough evidence for anyone who's willing to believe. But for those who aren't willing to believe, no amount of evidence will ever be enough.

John 6:35 *Then Jesus declared, I am the bread of life.*

Scholars identify this as the first of seven *I am* statements in the Gospel of John. *I am the bread of life* (John 6:35); *I am the light of the world* (John 8:12); *I am the gate for the sheep* (John 10:7); *I am the good shepherd* (John 10:11); *I am the resurrection and the life* (John 11:25); *I am the way and the truth and the life* (John 14:6). And, *I am the vine* (John 15:5), he said.

The central message of Jesus Christ was himself. In many ways he was selfless, but his message was completely self-centered. And yet it's right for Christ to be self-centered, because he really is the center.

What if the sun decided not to be the center of the solar system? And what if the earth decided not to revolve around the sun? It's good for the sun to be the center, and for the earth to revolve around it. And it's good for Jesus to be the center, and for us to revolve around him. The only reason things went bad in the first place, is because we decided to be the center, and have the world revolve around us. But that hasn't worked very well for most of human history.

For Reflection and Review

- *How does Jesus satisfy our deepest need?*
- *Why do some people refuse to believe in Christ no matter what?*
- *Why should our lives revolve around Christ?*

Lesson 242

John 6:37 *All those the Father gives me will come to me.*

People who come to Christ for salvation are a gift from the Father to the Son. *[I] give eternal life to all those you have given [me]* (John 17:2). *I am not praying for the world, but for those you have given me* (John 17:9). *Father, I want those you have given me to be with me* (John 17:24), he said.

In Jesus' day, marriages were often arranged by parents, and those who believe in Jesus Christ are the Father's gift to his one and only Son. The reason we believe in Jesus Christ isn't primarily because we chose him, but because the Father chose us for him (Ephesians 1:4). This shows our value to the Father, and makes us want to be faithful to his one and only Son.

John 6:38 *I have come down from heaven not to do my will but to do the will of him who sent me.*

Whenever Jesus felt like over-eating, over-drinking, over-sleeping (or any other overindulgence) he put aside his own will, and did the will of his Father. This he did over the course of his childhood, adolescence, and adulthood—every minute until he died.

This is important because the death of Jesus Christ would have no saving value if Jesus ever sinned. But *He committed no sin, and no deceit was found in his mouth* (1 Peter 2:22), wrote Peter. *[He was] obedient to death—even death on a cross* (Philippians 2:8), wrote Paul. And *[He was] tempted in every way, just as we are—yet he did not sin* (Hebrews 4:15), says Hebrews.

This is also important because we aren't only right with God through the death of Jesus Christ, but through his perfect righteousness. *For he has clothed me with garments of salvation and arrayed me in a robe of his righteousness* (Isaiah 61:10), wrote Isaiah. And *This righteousness is given through faith in Jesus Christ to all who believe* (Romans 3:22), wrote Paul.

This is summed up nicely in the Heidelberg Catechism, Question 60: *How are you right with God?* Answer: *Only by true faith in Jesus Christ.*

Although my conscience accuses me that I have grievously sinned against all God's commandments, have never kept any of them, and am still inclined to all evil, yet God, without any merit of my own, out of mere grace, imputes to me the perfect satisfaction, righteousness, and holiness of Christ. He grants these to me as if I had never had nor committed any sin, and as if I myself had accomplished all the obedience which Christ has rendered for me, if only I accept this gift with a believing heart. Now that's something to think about!

John 6:54 *Whoever eats my flesh and drinks my blood has eternal life, and I will raise them up at the last day.*

This is one of the least popular things Jesus ever said, and the results were predictable. *From this time many of his disciples turned back and no longer followed him* (John 6:66). No wonder! Eating bloody meat, and drinking blood itself, were both forbidden by God in the Old Testament (Leviticus 19:26, Deuteronomy 12:23). And the idea of cannibalism is simply appalling.

But the concept was so important to Jesus that he used similar language regarding the Lord's Supper. *The Lord Jesus, on the night he was betrayed, took bread, and when he had given thanks, he broke it and said, This is my body, which is for you; do this in remembrance of me. In the same way, after supper he took the cup, saying, This cup is the new covenant in my blood; do this, whenever you drink it, in remembrance of me* (1 Corinthians 11:23-25). We're so accustomed to these words that they've lost their impact, but the imagery is edgy.

Years ago a plane went down in the mountains of Uruguay and most of the passengers died. The food on the plane was soon depleted, and the survivors discovered they only had two options: they could die of starvation, or eat their friends. By choosing to eat their friends, the survivors stayed alive until they were finally rescued. According to Jesus, the human situation isn't much different. We survived the wreckage of sin, but it's only a matter of time before we die anyway. So he laid down his life for us, that we might feast on him and live forever.

This is how we should think about the Lord's Supper. His body was shredded on the cross so we could tear off a piece and put it in our mouth. His blood was poured out so we could fill our cup and drink it down. Receiving the Lord's Supper doesn't save us, but it graphically portrays what Jesus did to save us. Receiving the Lord's Supper doesn't save anyone, but whoever receives Jesus Christ will be saved. *[T]o all who did receive him, to those who believed in his name, he gave the right to become children of God* (John 1:12), wrote John.

For Reflection and Review

- *Why is it important to know that you're the Father's gift to his one and only Son?*
- *Why was the obedience of Christ important for our salvation?*
- *What do the bread and cup of the Lord's Supper represent?*

Lesson 243

John 7:4 *No one who wants to become a public figure acts in secret. Since you are doing these things, show yourself to the world.*

The Festival of Tabernacles was approaching, and many were going to Jerusalem for a week long celebration of Israel's journey from Egypt to the Promised Land. The religious leaders wanted to kill Jesus, so he was keeping a low profile by living and preaching in Galilee, a few days north. But his brothers were mocking him for not taking his ministry to the big city.

John 7:5 *For even his own brothers did not believe in him.*

Jesus' mother believed in him, and Joseph had believed in him, but his own brothers didn't believe in him. Jesus was the oldest of at least seven children including James, Joseph, Simon, Judas, and two or more sisters (Matthew 13:55). After the resurrection, James and Jude came to believe in Jesus, and wrote the books that bear their names. But we don't know if his other siblings ever believed or not.

It's worth noticing that John wasn't embarrassed to include the fact that Jesus' brothers didn't believe in him. If John's account was fictional, he would've said it was obvious to those who knew Jesus best that he was the Messiah. The gospel writers included many embarrassing facts which prove they had nothing to hide, but were only concerned to report the truth.

It's also clear that Jesus' divinity wasn't at all obvious. He got hungry, thirsty, and tired like everyone else. He didn't have a halo, didn't glow in the dark, and didn't walk above the ground. Jesus was fully God, but also fully human. He was one person with two natures, and these weren't blended to produce a hybrid. Jesus seemed remarkably similar to everyone else.

We should also notice it was possible to be very close to Jesus and not believe in him. Many grow up in church, and learn the Bible thoroughly, but never truly believe. Some even stay in church, and gain a Christian reputation, without ever coming to faith. Some even go into occupational ministry.

Familiarity with Jesus can even result in contempt for him, as it did with his brothers. Many who grow up in church later despise Christianity as unworthy of their time, talent, or treasure. Imagine being so close to Jesus Christ and still missing out on his salvation. The thought should make us shudder.

John 7:17 *Anyone who chooses to do the will of God will find out whether my teaching comes from God.*

When Jesus got to the festival he discovered the crowds were whispering about him. Some thought he was a good man, others thought he was a deceiver. But how could they know for sure? Jesus could do another miracle, but that wouldn't change anyone's mind. Instead, he gave a universal way. *Anyone who chooses to do the will of God will find out whether my teaching comes from God.*

This is revolutionary. Even a child can know that Christianity is true, simply by choosing to do God's will. The truth of Christianity isn't rationally discerned, so much as morally discerned. If we choose to do God's will, God will persuade us that Christianity is true.

This was important in Jesus' day because believing in Christ often came with a price. You could be excluded from the synagogue, and shunned by family and friends. Employers wouldn't want to hire you, and you'd have to live on the margins of society. Becoming a Christian could even cost your life, so it was important to be sure that Christianity was true.

Thankfully, God is willing to guide anyone who chooses to do his will. If someone prays, *God I want to do your will no matter what*—then God will lead them to Christ. But God is under no obligation to those who reject his will. Intellectual objections are often just an excuse for rebelling against God.

Several years ago I spoke with a young man who claimed to be an atheist. He was quite above average, intellectually, but his lifestyle could only be sustained if God did not exist. So I asked if he'd be willing to follow Christ if he could be certain that Christianity was true. To my surprise, he said he would not. Then I understood his first concern wasn't for the truth, but for his lifestyle. That's how it usually works. We change our lives to fit the truth, or distort the truth to fit our lives.

John 7:27 *But we know where this man is from; when the Messiah comes, no one will know where he is from.*

At this point the crowd was completely confused. They were surprised Jesus hadn't been arrested, and were wondering if the religious leaders had changed their minds about him. Jesus couldn't be the Messiah, of course, since they knew where he was from—and no one would know where the Messiah was from. Right?

Actually, the prophet identified Bethlehem as the place of Messiah's birth. *But you, Bethlehem . . . out of you will come for me one who will be ruler over Israel* (Micah 5:2), wrote Micah. We understand ignorance at the popular level, but even the experts were confused. *Look into it, and you will find that a prophet does not come out of Galilee* (John 7:52), they said. Never mind that Jonah was from Galilee (2 Kings 14:25), and possibly others.

And never mind that Isaiah clearly identified Galilee with the Messiah. *[I]n the future he will honor Galilee. . . . The people walking in darkness have seen a great light; on those living in the land of deep darkness a light has dawned. . . . For to us a child is born, to us a son is given, and the government will be on his shoulders. And he will be called Wonderful Counselor, Mighty God, Everlasting Father, Prince of Peace* (Isaiah 9:1-6), he wrote.

The religious leaders didn't reject Jesus because of their knowledge of the Bible, but because of their ignorance of the Bible. They assumed from various texts that Messiah would rule the world—which he will in the future. But they missed the texts about his crucifixion (Psalm 22:16, Isaiah 53:5, Zechariah 12:10). Some think ignorance is bliss, but ignorance of what we ought to know can be fatal.

Consider what God said to the Old Testament clergy: *Because you have rejected knowledge, I also reject you as my priests; because you have ignored the law of your God, I also will ignore your children* (Hosea 4:6). If Bible reading isn't part of your daily schedule, you need to adjust your schedule. Ignorance of Scripture is ignorance of Christ, and ignorance of Christ is sin—a very dangerous sin.

For Reflection and Review

- *Why didn't Jesus' brothers believe in him?*
- *How can we know that Christianity is true?*
- *Why did the religious leaders reject Christ?*

Lesson 244

John 8:12 *When Jesus spoke again to the people, he said, I am the light of the world. Whoever follows me will never walk in darkness, but will have the light of life.*

No one ever believed in himself more than Jesus Christ, or had a higher opinion of himself than Jesus Christ. Jesus knew that he was God in human flesh, and wasn't afraid to speak of himself in ways that were normally reserved for God.

Jesus was at the Festival of Tabernacles, which recalled the nation's journey from Egypt to the Promised Land. *By day the Lord went ahead of them in a pillar of cloud to guide them on their way and by night in a pillar of fire to give them light, so that they could travel by day or night* (Exodus 13:21). Even in the darkest hours they never got lost, because God was with them to light their way. Jesus drew on this to say that he's the light of the world, who lights our way to the Promised Land of heaven.

The Bible makes many connections between God and light. *God said, Let there be light,* (Genesis 1:3). *God turns my darkness into light* (Psalm 18:28). *God . . . made his light shine in our hearts* (2 Corinthians 4:6). *The Lord is my light and my salvation* (Psalm 27:1). *Let us walk in the light of the Lord* (Isaiah 2:5). And, *The Lord will be your everlasting light* (Isaiah 60:19). By calling himself *the light of the world*, Jesus was clearly proclaiming his divinity.

Years ago my wife and I drove from Milwaukee to Saint Paul and, on the way back, it began to snow. Three lanes of traffic became two, then one—then it got dark. Mile after mile the ditches were filled with cars, and we were trying not to become one of them. Eventually we got behind a semi-truck and, for the next several hours, I focused on its taillights. Our six hour journey became twelve, but those two little lights led us all the way home. *Whoever follows [Christ] will never walk in darkness, but will have the light of life.*

John 8:29 *The one who sent me is with me; he has not left me alone, for I always do what pleases him.*

Here we should notice the relationship between courage and a clear conscience. Jesus was speaking to people who wanted to kill him, but was fearless because he knew that God was with him, because he always did what pleased him. This allowed Jesus to face his opponents fearlessly.

And the courage of Christ is contagious. After the resurrection, Peter and John were arrested and brought before the same leaders who crucified Jesus. *Salvation is found in no one else, for there is no other name under heaven given to mankind by which we must be saved [said Peter]. When they saw the courage of Peter and John and realized that they were unschooled, ordinary men, they were astonished and they took note that these men had been with Jesus* (Acts 4:12-13).

The Apostle Paul was equally courageous when he was on trial before governor Felix. *As Paul talked about righteousness, self-control and the judgment to come, Felix was afraid and said, That is enough for now!* (Acts 24:25). Paul was on trial before the governor-judge, but he put the governor-judge on trial before God. The prisoner was self-assured, but the governor-judge became afraid. *The wicked flee though no one pursues, but the righteous are as bold as a lion* (Proverbs 28:1), says Proverbs.

John 8:31 *To the Jews who had believed him, Jesus said, If you hold to my teaching, you are really my disciples.*

At first, the early church was almost entirely Jewish. Jesus was Jewish, the apostles were Jewish, and almost every book of the New Testament was written by a Jewish author. But it wasn't easy being a Jewish Christian because, within Judaism, Christianity remained a minority movement. Most Christians were Jewish, but the majority of Jewish people rejected Christianity.

If you're raised in a religious community, and decide to change religions, they can be hard on you. So when persecution came, some who claimed to be Christians turned away from Jesus Christ. Jesus saw this coming and gave his followers this warning: *If you hold to my teaching, you are really my disciples.* The test of true discipleship isn't becoming a Christian, but remaining a Christian.

The most difficult part of the Christian life is the beginning, middle, and end. The moment we believe in Christ, Satan starts trying to lead us away from him, and never gives up until we die. We should be aware of this so we're not surprised when we're tempted to quit the faith.

It's also why one of the most repeated commands in the Bible is to hold on. *By this gospel you are saved, if you hold firmly to the word I preached to you* (1 Corinthians 15:2). *[H]old firmly to the word of life* (Philippians 2:16). *[H]old fast to the teachings* (2 Thessalonians 2:15). *[H]old firmly to the trustworthy message* (Titus 1:9). *[H]old firmly to the faith* (Hebrews 4:14). If the Bible says something once it's important. But if it repeats it many times, it might be even more important.

For Reflection and Review

- *Why do some people avoid the light?*
- *Why does obedience lead to courage?*
- *Have you ever been tempted to turn away from Christ?*

Lesson 245

John 8:36 *So if the Son sets you free, you will be free indeed.*

The Jewish people wanted to be free from the Romans, and their thoughts of Messiah were mostly political. They weren't completely wrong because Messiah will, in fact, rule the world one day. Jesus Christ will overthrow the antichrist (2 Thessalonians 2:8) and put an end to oppression everywhere. In the mean time, Jesus sets us free from the oppression of the evil one.

The classic case is the man who was possessed by a legion of demons (Mark 5:1-20). People were afraid of him because he couldn't function socially, and preferred to go without clothing. *Night and day among the tombs and in the hills he would cry out and cut himself with stones* (Mark 5:5), wrote Mark.

Self-cutting can be a distraction from the emotional pain of self-hatred. The work of Satan is to make us lonely, disturbed, and haunted. First he draws us away from God, then he binds us with chains of despair. But after Jesus set him free, this same man sat at Jesus' feet, *fully clothed and in his right mind* (Mark 5:15). He found his freedom at the feet of Jesus Christ, and so do we.

Some people stay away from Jesus because he's so demanding, but his demands are good for us. I've never met a converted person who said, *I wish I was still a blasphemer. I wish I still took drugs. I wish I was still a thief. I wish I was still a hater. I wish I was still a liar. I wish I was still far away from God.* Jesus rules over us to set us free from the sins that would destroy us.

In fact, the Bible is *the perfect law that gives freedom* (James 1:25), wrote James. We don't think of laws as producing freedom, but they do. If you take away the traffic laws, it wont' be safe to drive. And if you take away all the laws, it won't be safe to go outside. Laws produce the freedom that we need to live without fear.

Children at a city school huddled in the middle of the playground because they didn't feel safe. When the school put a fence around the playground, the children felt free to run and play. The freest people on earth are those who live in the safety of God's revealed will.

*****

John 8:44 *You belong to your father, the devil.*

Jesus was speaking to religious people who thought they were children of God. To call them children of the devil was one of the most provocative things Jesus ever said. But if the Jews who didn't believe in Christ were children of the devil, what about people of other religions? What about everyone who's not a Christian? Are they all children of the devil? Is everyone who doesn't believe in Jesus Christ a child of Satan? Is that what the Bible teaches?

Do we not all have one Father? Did not one God create us? (Malachi 2:1), asked Malachi. According to the prophet, there's only one God, the Creator and Father of everyone. Everyone in the world is designed, created, and loved by their heavenly Father. This is what the Bible teaches, but it's not all the Bible teaches. There is always more to the story.

In the Garden of Eden our first parents had a choice to follow God or Satan. God had given them everything, with only one restriction: not to eat of a certain tree. But the devil came by and implied that God was being unreasonable, so Adam and Eve flipped (Genesis 3). Because they sided with Satan, human nature was corrupted. God is still our Maker, but we can also resemble the devil sometimes.

A man and a woman had an affair, and she became pregnant. They were both married, and wanted to stay married, so the woman pretended the child was her husbands. He was happy about it, but things became complicated because both families went to the same church. And, as the child grew, he began to resemble his biological father more and more, until everyone at church could see whose child he really was.

At the time of our birth we appear to be children of God. But, as we grow, it becomes clear that someone else was involved. According to Jesus the only solution is to be *born again* (John 3:3). Then we become children of God, not only by creation, but also by regeneration, and eventually by glorification. Christianity isn't about good manners, but about who and whose we really are.

John 8:47 *Whoever belongs to God hears what God says. The reason you do not hear is that you do not belong to God.*

Jesus didn't say, *The reason you do not belong to God is because you do not hear;* but *The reason you do not hear is that you do not belong to God.* Likewise, *Why is my language not clear to you? Because you are unable to hear what I say* (John 8:43).

One of the most offensive teachings of Christianity is that, in and of ourselves, we're unable to hear God's word. Our ears pick up the sound, and our brains sort out the meaning, but we cannot accept, receive, and embrace the teachings of Jesus Christ without divine assistance. We're all born spiritually deaf but, thankfully, Jesus Christ can heal us.

On one occasion Jesus put his fingers into a deaf man's ears, looked toward heaven and said, *be opened*. Immediately the deaf man was able to hear (Mark 7:32-35). Whether we know it or not, that's what Jesus did for us when we finally heard the word of God.

When I was growing up, I went to church every week, but the words didn't seem to register. I could make sense of them, but they rested so lightly on me that I completely missed their significance. This changed dramatically after my conversion. I was hearing the exact same words, but now they had ultimate significance. I was stunned by how often I heard them, without ever really hearing them.

A sadder example was an outspoken atheist who said, *Whenever I hear talk about God, the gospel or the Holy Spirit it is like white noise.* This brilliant man was hearing the words of eternal life but, to him, they were nothing more than white noise. *Though seeing, they do not see; though hearing, they do not hear or understand* (Matthew 13:13), said Jesus.

John 8:51 *Very truly I tell you, whoever obeys my word will never see death.*

Since everyone dies eventually, we tend to think of death as natural, and sometimes even desirable. But those who have health, wealth, and happiness usually want to keep on living. The eternal life that Jesus gives is more than mere existence. It's a higher quality of life than we can imagine, in a better place than we can imagine, with better people than we can imagine, in better bodies than we can imagine. And, best of all, it will never end.

That's the life Jesus offers to everyone who follows him.

For Reflection and Review

- Why does obeying Christ lead to freedom?
- Are unbelievers children of God or Satan?
- Why is it hard for some people to hear God's word?

Lesson 246

John 9:1 *As [Jesus] went along, he saw a man blind from birth.*

When his parents were asked if they wanted a boy or a girl, they probably said it didn't matter, as long as the baby was healthy. So when he was born, they counted his fingers and toes, and everything seemed to be normal. With the passing of time, however, they noticed his eyes were dull and didn't seem to focus. They didn't want to accept the obvious, but soon it was undeniable their little boy was blind. He'd never earn a living, never get married, never have children, and never see the light of day.

John 9:2 *His disciples asked him, Rabbi, who sinned, this man or his parents, that he was born blind?*

Some of the rabbi's taught that babies could sin in the womb, so maybe that's why he was born blind. The Bible says God punishes *children for the sin of the parents* (Exodus 20:5), so maybe that's why he was born blind. Reincarnation says he did something bad in a previous life, so maybe that's why he was born blind. Atheism says suffering is random, so maybe that's why he was born blind.

The Christian answer begins with the fall of mankind in the garden of Eden. *Cursed is the ground because of you . . . dust you are and to dust you will return* (Genesis 3:17-19). Adam and Eve brought a curse on the earth that makes life hard for everyone. It's not the way it was meant to be, which is why suffering seems unnatural. Instead of a picnic in paradise, life is a struggle for survival, which we lose in the end. The universal curse is the source of all our problems. But our problems are never random.

Who gave human beings their mouths? Who makes them deaf or mute? Who gives them sight or makes them blind? Is it not I, the Lord? (Exodus 4:11). We're not in the hands of fate, chance, or the devil. We're in the hands of a sovereign God who loves us.

John 9:3 *Neither this man nor his parents sinned, said Jesus, but this happened so that the works of God might be displayed in him.*

God uses hardship to display his work in our lives. This may include a miracle, but his first concern is to make us like Christ. *For those God foreknew he also predestined to be conformed to the image of his Son* (Romans 8:29), wrote Paul. This is the reason for everything that happens to us, whether good or evil.

If you lose your health, it's to make you like Christ. If you win the lottery, it's to make you like Christ. If you lose your job, it's to make you like Christ. If you get a job, it's to make you like Christ. Wise people cooperate with God by using every situation to become more like Jesus Christ. We never have to wonder why something happens to us, because it's always to make us like him.

A man opened a package that exploded in his face and blew off both his hands. He also lost an eye, his hearing, and his sense of smell. Thankfully, he didn't lose his mind. He knew if he became filled with hatred, or self-pity, his life was over. So he turned to God and became a minister to victims of violence. *If a man has experience, and doesn't use it, he has failed. If he only uses part of it, he has partly failed. But if he uses all of it, all of his life, he has gloriously succeeded and won a satisfaction few will ever know.*

John 9:6-7 *[Jesus] spit on the ground, made some mud with the saliva, and put it on the man's eyes. Go, he told him, wash in the Pool of Siloam . . . . So the man went and washed, and came home seeing.*

There are some wonderful healing miracles in the Old Testament, but no one was ever healed of blindness. Nevertheless, the prophet Isaiah spoke of a time when blind eyes would be opened. *[T]he eyes of the blind will see* (Isaiah 29:18). And, *the eyes of the blind [will] be opened* (Isaiah 35:5), he wrote. Throughout the gospels no fewer than seven people were healed of blindness by Jesus Christ.

Jesus opened the eyes of the blind, but others preferred darkness. This was a first class miracle followed up by an investigation. First they interviewed the man, then they interviewed his parents, then they interviewed the man again. Since there was no denying the miracle, they concluded Jesus was a sinner (John 9:24). Elsewhere they concluded he did his miracles by the power of Satan (Matthew 12:24). *Light [came] into the world, but people loved darkness instead of light because their deeds were evil* (John 3:19), wrote John.

John 9:31-33 *God does not listen to sinners. He listens to the godly person who does his will. . . . If this man were not from God, he could do nothing.*

The man who never read a book was giving the religious leaders a lecture in theology. He probably heard the Bible read in synagogue, and paid attention. *God does not listen to sinners. He listens to the godly person who does his will.*

There are at least three places he may've picked this up. *If I had cherished sin in my heart, the Lord would not have listened* (Psalm 66:18). *The eyes of the Lord are on the righteous, and his ears are attentive to their cry* (Psalm 34:15). And, *The Lord is far from the wicked, but he hears the prayer of the righteous* (Proverbs 15:29). We have further corroboration from the New Testament. *The prayer of a righteous person is powerful and effective* (James 5:16), wrote James.

This is why the prayers of Jesus Christ were so effective. It seemed like he could pray for anything and get an immediate answer. But even Jesus didn't have all his prayers answered. Before he went to the cross he prayed: *Father, if you are willing, take this cup from me* (Luke 22:42). But the prayer of the most righteous person who ever lived was denied, because there was no other way for sinners to be saved, or for the wrath of God to be appeased, or for the world to be redeemed, except through the shed blood of Jesus Christ.

John 9:34 *You were steeped in sin at birth; how dare you lecture us! And they threw him out.*

The religious leaders didn't like being lectured by someone who couldn't read, so they threw him out of the synagogue. If this was a formal excommunication the implications were serious. Synagogues were the center of religious and social life, so to be excommunicated meant you were cut off from friends, family, and employment.

It can be difficult for people from other religions to come to Jesus Christ because the social structures are often against it. A seventeen year-old girl in Tanzania was sentenced to two years in prison for her faith. She'd been a Christian for about three years, and her family had disowned her. She was pressured to renounce her faith and, when she refused, she was accused of urinating on the Quran. She was brought before a judge, convicted without evidence, and given two years in prison. *If they persecuted me, they will persecute you* (John 15:20), said Jesus.

John 9:35-38 *Jesus heard that they had thrown him out, and when he found him, he said, Do you believe in the Son of Man? . . . Then the man said, Lord, I believe, and he worshiped him.*

What a day it had been. First he was blind, then he was healed, then he was kicked out of the synagogue, then he met the Lord. When he put his head on the pillow, that night, he found it hard to close his eyes. He not only received his physical sight, but also his spiritual sight. He met the man who was from God, and he worshipped him.

For Reflection and Review

- *Why is life filled with pain?*
- *How can pain make us like Christ?*
- *Why does wickedness hinder prayer?*

Lesson 247

John 10:11 *I am the good shepherd. The good shepherd lays down his life for the sheep.*

The relationship between Christ and his people is like a shepherd and his flock. Good shepherds guide and protect their flock with love and compassion. When a sheep wanders off he goes after it, and brings it home again (Luke 15:4-5). The sheep can't care for themselves very well, so they look to their shepherd to meet their daily needs.

Jesus went beyond the normal duties of shepherding, however, and laid down his life for the sheep. This seems noble, at first, but then it seems absurd. If I owned a ranch, and my son was a shepherd, I'd tell him to take good care of the sheep, but never to risk his life for them. It'd be foolish to get between a sheep and a lion, for example, since a person is worth far more than a sheep.

But if this is true for people and sheep, how much more for God and people. If it's foolish for a person to die for a sheep, what can be said of God on a cross? The difference between people and sheep is great, but the difference between people and God is infinite. For the infinite God to lay down his life for people like us defies comprehension.

And yet, the good shepherd's death was foretold by the prophet Zechariah. *Awake, sword, against my shepherd, against the man who is close to me! declares the Lord Almighty* (Zechariah 7:3). When Jesus read these words, he understood that part of his mission was to lay down his life for his sheep.

John 10:14-15 *I know my sheep and my sheep know me—just as the Father knows me and I know the Father.*

By spending time with his sheep, day after day, the shepherd got to know them well. The shepherd loved his sheep and, in a small way, the sheep loved him back. But love between people and animals should never be compared to love between human beings. A child is a child, and a dog is still a dog.

And yet, Jesus compared his relationship with us to the highest relationship anywhere—that between him and his heavenly Father. *I know my sheep and my sheep know me—just as the Father knows me and I know the Father.*

Once again, this sounds ridiculous, but it's also the experience of all who belong to Christ. Muslims don't know Muhammad. Confucians don't know Confucius. Buddhists don't know the Buddha. But we know Jesus Christ because he not only died for us, but sent his Spirit to live in our hearts. *God's love has been poured out into our hearts through the Holy Spirit, who has been given to us* (Romans 5:5), wrote Paul. Christianity is more than knowing about Jesus Christ; it's knowing Christ himself.

John 10:20 *Many of them said, He is demon-possessed and raving mad. Why listen to him?*

It was hard to listen to Jesus for long without believing in him, or rejecting him. If he wasn't God in human flesh, then he was *demon-possessed* or *raving mad*—the greatest deceiver who ever lived, or completely insane.

And just to be clear Jesus said, *I and the Father are one* (John 10:30). *Again his Jewish opponents picked up stones to stone him. . . . We are not stoning you for any good work [but] because you, a mere man, claim to be God* (John 10:31-33), they said.

Even today, whoever listens to Jesus Christ must decide if he was demon-possessed, raving mad, or divine. Some want to say that he was a great human teacher, but a great human teacher wouldn't teach that he was God if it wasn't true. So let's avoid *any patronizing nonsense about his being a great human teacher. He hasn't left that open to us. He didn't intend to* (CS Lewis).

John 10:28-29 *I give them eternal life, and they shall never perish; no one will snatch them out of my hand. My Father, who has given them to me, is greater than all; no one can snatch them out of my Father's hand.*

No words in the Bible describe the believer's security better than these. Our security doesn't depend on our strength or resolve, but on Jesus Christ who said, *I shall lose none of all those he has given me* (John 6:39).

Furthermore, we're not only in the hand of Christ, but also in the Father's hand. And *no one can snatch them out of my Father's hand*, said Jesus. Believers in heaven are happier than believers on earth, but they're no more secure. We couldn't be more secure if we were in heaven already.

For Reflection and Review

- *How does Christ shepherd his flock?*
- *How do believers know Jesus Christ?*
- *Why can't Jesus be just a good religious teacher?*

Lesson 248

John 11:1 *Now a man named Lazarus was sick.*

This wasn't normally a problem if you were friends with Jesus Christ. The Bible records about thirty times when Jesus healed individuals, and several other times when he healed many more (Matthew 4:23-25, Matthew 8:16, etc.). Mary, Martha, and Lazarus had good reason to think Jesus would come to their aid. They were, after all, his friends.

But whenever you think you know what Jesus is going to do next, you're probably wrong. *So when [Jesus] heard that Lazarus was sick, he stayed where he was two more days* (John 11:6). This must've been confusing. *Why, Lord, do you stand far off? Why do you hide yourself in times of trouble?* (Psalm 10:1), wrote the Psalmist.

This is one of the most frustrating parts of being a Christian. We have an urgent request, and need Jesus to move swiftly. Instead, he does nothing at all. We assume, therefore, that he doesn't care, that he's unaware, or that he's not who he claimed to be. But according to this story, the reason Jesus waited is because he loved Mary, Martha, and Lazarus (John 11:5-6). Jesus was involving them in one of his greatest miracles, through which they'd come to know him even better.

In dramatic stories it's not uncommon for the hero to arrive at the last possible moment. Sometimes, in fact, the hero doesn't arrive until it's too late, and everything has been lost. But because of his mighty power, the hero is able to save the day anyway. That's the kind of story this is, and that's the kind of story the Bible is.

It's also why waiting is such an important part of the Christian life. *Wait for the Lord; be strong and take heart and wait for the Lord* (Psalm 27:14). *Be still before the Lord and wait patiently for him* (Psalm 37:7). *[W]ait for your God always* (Hosea 12:6). And *God . . . acts on behalf of those who wait for him* (Isaiah 64:4). We tend to think of waiting as a waste of time, but whoever waits for God never waits too long.

John 11:21 *Lord, Martha said to Jesus, if you had been here, my brother would not have died.*

Martha had opened her home to Jesus, and given him hospitality time and again. When he arrived with his disciples, without notice, she fed the whole group at her own expense. Jesus was willing to receive her kindness, but where was Jesus when she needed him most?

There's little of this in the Bible, but the forty-fourth Psalm is a good example of a godly person who's angry at God. The people were destroyed in battle because God hadn't protected them, so the writer took issue.

You gave us up to be devoured like sheep and have scattered us among the nations. You sold your people for a pittance, gaining nothing from their sale. You have made us a reproach to our neighbors, the scorn and derision of those around us. You have made us a byword among the nations; the peoples shake their heads at us. I live in disgrace all day long, and my face is covered with shame at the taunts of those who reproach and revile me . . . .

All this came upon us, though we had not forgotten you; we had not been false to your covenant. Our hearts had not turned back; our feet had not strayed from your path. But you crushed us and made us a haunt for jackals; you covered us over with deep darkness (Psalm 44:11-19). In other words, God, you make me mad.

God knows our anger is a natural response to the unfairness we feel, and allows us to express our anger as long as we do it respectfully. Remember who you're talking to!

The only way to get beyond anger, however, is to trust that God is good, even when life is not. So in the last verse the Psalmist said, *[R]escue us because of your unfailing love* (Psalm 44:26). The Psalmist chose to believe in God's unfailing love even when the love of God appeared to fail. And Martha would learn that Jesus could be trusted, even when he appeared to fail.

John 11:23-24 *Jesus said to her, Your brother will rise again. Martha answered, I know he will rise again in the resurrection at the last day.*

Martha took the same comfort in the resurrection that we do because it was taught in the Old Testament. *And after my skin has been destroyed, yet in my flesh I will see God* (Job 19:26), said Job. *But your dead will live, Lord; their bodies will rise* (Isaiah 26:19), wrote Isaiah. And, *Multitudes who sleep in the dust of the earth will awake: some to everlasting life, others to shame and everlasting contempt* (Daniel 12:2), wrote Daniel.

The age to come is not an eternal worship service in the sky, but the resurrection of a physical body on a physical earth. There's an intermediate stage, when our souls go to be with Christ in heaven (2 Corinthians 5:8), but that's not the end of the story. The end of the story is *a new heaven and a new earth, where righteousness dwells* (2 Peter 3:13), wrote Peter. There is continuity between this age and the one to come. When we think of the age to come, we should think of the present age but without sin, sorrow, suffering, or death.

When my son was ten years old I took him to a motorcycle store and bought him a dirt-bike. I told him we were only looking, so he wouldn't get his hopes up. But we found a little Honda just his size. When he sat on it, I could see his imagination soaring. Finally I said, *should we buy it?*

He was so excited that he started to hyperventilate. But he managed to reply, *Can you get one too Dad?* We had so much fun together that he wanted to know if there'd be dirt bikes in the age to come. I told him that I think so, because I believe in the resurrection of the body, and eternal life on a new earth.

For Reflection and Review

- *Why didn't Jesus go to heal Lazarus?*
- *Have you ever been angry at God?*
- *What does the resurrection tell us about the age to come?*

Lesson 249

John 11:25 *I am the resurrection and the life. The one who believes in me will live, even though they die.*

Jesus wanted to increase Martha's faith, so he asked her if she believed. *Yes, Lord, she replied, I believe that you are the Messiah, the Son of God* (John 11:27). Martha had no idea what would happen next, but she believed in Jesus Christ, and in the resurrection. This would allow her to face the future, no matter what happened. *Therefore we will not fear, though the earth give way and the mountains fall into the heart of the sea* (Psalm 46:2), wrote the Psalmist.

A young lady was voted employee of the year but asked to leave a meeting due to a headache. Two hours later she was completely paralyzed due to a brain tumor. What do you say to a person who will spend the rest of her life entombed in a body that won't respond? The world has little comfort for those who suffer most, but we believe in the resurrection of the body, and eternal life in the best of all possible worlds.

John 11:35 *Jesus wept.*

By this time Martha's sister, Mary, had made her way out to see Jesus. *When Jesus saw her weeping, and the Jews who had come along with her also weeping, he was deeply moved in spirit and troubled* (John 11:33).

Jesus was never easily troubled, but the death of his friend apparently got to him. He knew what was going to happen next, but he wept because that's what you do when you go to a funeral. You enter into the family's sorrow and suffer with them.

The word *compassion* literally means *to suffer with*, and *our God is full of compassion* (Psalm 116:5), wrote the Psalmist. He's not the kind of God who sits in heaven and says, *I know what you're going through*. He's the kind of God who comes down to suffer with us. There's no sorrow we go through, that he doesn't go through too.

Perhaps the death of Lazarus reminded Jesus of Joseph's death. Or maybe he thought of the slaughter of the babes in Bethlehem, so many years earlier (Matthew 2:16). Or maybe he thought of all the stillborn babies, and all the young people who've died in battle. Or maybe he thought of the orphans left behind by parents who died too soon. Or maybe he thought about the rest of us who grow old slowly, lose our powers gradually, but die just the same. Death is the ultimate trauma.

Or maybe Jesus thought of his own death. It was only days away, and he would weep again. *[H]e offered up prayers and petitions with fervent cries and tears to the one who could save him from death* (Hebrews 5:7), says Hebrews.

As Jesus waited for his arrest in the Garden of Gethsemane, he didn't think his prayers, or whisper them, but cried them loudly with tears. We can imagine Jesus howling into the darkness, *Abba, Father . . . Take this cup from me* (Mark 14:36).

This much we know for sure: *Jesus wept*. The shortest verse in the Bible speaks volumes.

John 11:43 *Jesus called in a loud voice, Lazarus, come out!*

The man who was four days dead emerged like someone waking up from a deep sleep. *Take off the grave clothes and let him go* (John 11:44), said Jesus. Suddenly the resurrection wasn't just a religious doctrine—it was reality. Jesus raised Lazarus from the dead and, a short time later, he'd also raise himself (John 10:17-18). What Jesus did for Lazarus, and for himself, he'll certainly do for us.

There was a pile of dirt in the cemetery where a fresh grave had been dug. A little boy was concerned and said, *Look, Dad, one of them got out!* The day is coming, in fact, when all God's people will get out, but with a glory we can't imagine. *[T]hanks be to God! He gives us the victory through our Lord Jesus Christ* (1 Corinthians 15:57), wrote Paul.

*****

John 12:1-2 *Six days before the Passover, Jesus came to Bethany, where Lazarus lived, whom Jesus had raised from the dead. Here a dinner was given in Jesus' honor.*

Jesus would be dead in less than a week, and must've relished this time with friends. Dinner was served by Martha, who was probably helped by her sister Mary. The evening proceeded nicely until Mary did the unexpected. *[She] took about a pint of pure nard, an expensive perfume; she poured it on Jesus' feet and wiped his feet with her hair. And the house was filled with the fragrance of the perfume* (John 12:3), wrote John.

By almost any measure, Mary's action was extravagant. Feet were normally washed by servants, but not perfumed. For a woman to let down her hair in public was considered inappropriate. But worst of all was the waste of money.

John 12:5 *Why wasn't this perfume sold and the money given to the poor? It was worth a year's wages [said Judas].*

Judas was less concerned for the poor than he was for himself, since he was a thief and keeper of the money bag (John 12:6). But he wasn't alone in his conviction. *When the disciples saw this, they were indignant. Why this waste? they asked* (Matthew 26:8). *And they rebuked her harshly* (Mark 14:5).

We can see their point. To spend a year's wages on a single act of devotion seemed highly irresponsible. But Mary wasn't thinking about the cost. She was just so taken with Jesus Christ that she wanted to give him her best. So she poured her perfume on his feet, and wiped them with her hair.

John 12:7 *Leave her alone, Jesus replied. It was intended that she should save this perfume for the day of my burial.*

Perfume was poured on bodies at death to hide the smell of decay. Since Jesus would soon be dead, he saw Mary's act as preparing him for burial. *Truly I tell you, wherever this gospel is preached throughout the world, what she has done will also be told, in memory of her* (Matthew 26:13), said Jesus.

By including these words in his gospel, Matthew insured they'd be fulfilled. Throughout the years, and around the world, people have heard this story and been inspired to worship Jesus Christ. What the disciples thought was a waste of money, turned out to be the best use of it.

For Reflection and Review

- *How can the resurrection comfort those who suffer physically?*
- *Why do you think Jesus wept?*
- *Why were the disciples angry at Mary?*

Lesson 250

John 13:1 *Jesus knew that the hour had come for him to leave this world and go to the Father.*

Jesus' popularity rose dramatically after he raised Lazarus from the dead. When he entered Jerusalem multitudes shouted, *Blessed is the king of Israel!* (John 12:13). This was precisely what the disciples had in mind. Jesus would be king, and they would be his team.

They were so convinced that this was about to happen, they even began to quarrel *which of them was considered to be greatest* (Luke 22:24). Would Peter and Andrew have rank over James and John? Or would James and John have rank over everyone else? What they didn't understand (although Jesus told them often) was that their king would soon be crucified. The meal they were about to enjoy together, would be their last before his death.

Jesus was concerned about his disciples' quarreling because the team he spent three years developing, was coming apart at the worst possible time. So Jesus gave them another lesson in humility. *[H]e got up from the meal, took off his outer clothing, and wrapped a towel around his waist. After that, he poured water into a basin and began to wash his disciples' feet, drying them with the towel that was wrapped around him* (John 13:4-5).

This was truly radical. There's not a single example in ancient Greek, Roman, or Jewish literature of a master washing his servant's feet. The task was so menial that, in Jewish homes, it was reserved for Gentile servants, not Jewish servants. It was also the opposite of the disciples' ambition for power, position, and prestige.

Jesus knew that *he had come from God and was returning to God* (John 13:3). His sense of identity was so secure that he could do slave-work without concern for what others thought. And because he's made us *children of God* (1 John 3:1), we're secure as well. We don't have to pull others down to get to the top. We're at the top already, and are glad to help others up. We do this by serving them.

John 13:6-7 *He came to Simon Peter, who said to him, Lord, are you going to wash my feet? Jesus replied, You do* *not realize now what I am doing, but later you will understand.*

Peter was deeply bothered. For Messiah to wash his feet seemed absolutely wrong to him. So Jesus assured Peter that, even though he didn't understand it at the time, he would understand in the future.

I was walking around the neighborhood, years ago, and overheard a lady on her phone. She was about thirty years old, and was sitting on her front porch, with two beautiful children. Everything looked wonderful, but then I heard her say, *I don't understand.* Then she raised her voice and said it again. *I don't understand.* Then she began to sob and said, *I don't understand.*

My heart went out to her because life can be confusing when it doesn't go the way we think it should. That's when we must hear the words of Christ to Peter. *You do not realize now what I am doing, but later you will understand.*

John 13:8-9 *No, said Peter, you shall never wash my feet. Jesus answered, Unless I wash you, you have no part with me. Then, Lord, Simon Peter replied, not just my feet but my hands and my head as well!*

Peter's response is a strange combination of humility and pride. He was so humble that he couldn't bear to have Jesus wash his feet. But he was so proud that he thought he had a better idea —*not just my feet but my hands and my head as well!* Nobody ever had to wonder what Peter was thinking.

John 13:10 *Those who have had a bath need only to wash their feet; their whole body is clean.*

If you were going to a party, back then, you'd probably take a bath before you left home. But as you walked the dusty roads, your feet would get dirty. When you arrived at the party you didn't need another bath, you just needed to wash your feet.

Coming to Jesus is like taking a bath, symbolized by baptism. *Get up, be baptized and wash your sins away* (Acts 22:16), said Ananias. If you were baptized in the Jordan River, you could imagine all your sins being washed downstream, never to return. You were absolutely clean, and never had to be re-baptized. But the moment your feet hit the shore they'd be dirty again. They'd need to be washed, not for salvation, but for continued fellowship with Jesus Christ.

An ancient theologian prayed these words: *Jesus, my feet are dirty. Come even as a slave to me. Pour water in your bowl, come and wash my feet. In asking such a thing I know I am overbold. But I dread what was threatened when you said: If I do not wash your feet you have no fellowship with me. Wash my feet then, because I long for your companionship* (Origen).

Foot-washing is not an ordinance (like baptism or the Lord's Supper) but an illustration of God's promise to forgive and restore us throughout our Christian life. *If we confess our sins, he is faithful and just and will forgive us our sins and purify us from all unrighteousness* (1 John 1:9), wrote John. Jesus still cleans dirty feet.

*****

John 13:21 *Very truly I tell you, one of you is going to betray me.*

Judas Iscariot didn't believe in Jesus the same way the others did (John 6:64). He believed enough to preach, and even did some miracles in Jesus' name (Matthew 10:1). As long as things were going in his direction, Judas was willing to follow Christ.

But then Jesus started talking about his death. *[T]he Son of Man will be delivered over to the chief priests and the teachers of the law. They will condemn him to death and will hand him over to the Gentiles, who will mock him and spit on him, flog him and kill him* (Mark 10:33-34).

The other disciples didn't understand what Jesus was saying, but Judas apparently got the message. He could see that Jesus was determined to die and, if they crucified him, the disciples could be next. Why not seek immunity before it was too late? Why be part of a losing cause when it wasn't too late to survive?

Here we see an important difference between true-believers and make-believers. True believers make mistakes, but have no upper limit. They'll never say, *I will follow Jesus unless or until it becomes too expensive.*

A make-believer will go to church, pray, give, and even become a preacher—but will always have an upper limit. *I will follow Jesus unless or until it costs my career; unless or until it costs my reputation; unless or until it costs my family; unless or until it costs my life.* When Jesus started talking about the cross, Judas reached his upper limit. *It would be better for him if he had not been born* (Matthew 26:24), said Jesus.

This is why Jesus preached against the upper limit. *Whoever wants to be my disciple must deny themselves and take up their cross and follow me. For whoever wants to save their life will lose it, but whoever loses their life for me will find it. What good will it be for someone to gain the whole world, yet forfeit their soul? Or what can anyone give in exchange for their soul?* (Matthew 16:24-26). There's no upper limit for those who truly believe in Jesus Christ.

For Reflection and Review

- *Why does every church need humility?*
- *How does Jesus wash our feet today?*
- *Why do some people have an upper limit?*

Lesson 251

John 13:31 *When he was gone, Jesus said, Now the Son of Man is glorified and God is glorified in him.*

By dismissing Judas from the table, Jesus set in motion the events that would lead to his crucifixion. Soon he'd take his disciples to the Garden of Gethsemane, where they often slept. That way Judas would know where to take the guards in order to make the arrest. Jesus was in control of his crucifixion every step of the way.

We tend to think of the crucifixion as the most inglorious thing that ever happened to Jesus—nails, blood, misery, and shame. But Jesus saw his crucifixion as an act of radical obedience that brought glory to the Father and to himself. It glorified the Father to see his Son laying down his life for the world, and it glorified the Son to do his Father's will. It can be argued, convincingly, that the crucifixion of Jesus Christ was the most glorious event that has ever occurred.

John 13:35 *By this everyone will know that you are my disciples, if you love one another.*

Purest hate would nail Jesus to the cross, and purest love would keep him there. The world can be a hateful place, but God's people should be known for their love. The Father loves the Son and the Spirit; the Son loves the Father and the Spirit; and the Spirit loves the Father and the Son. Love is such a part of God's nature that twice the Bible says *God is love* (1 John 4:8, 16). And because *God is love*, it's impossible for him to love some people ten, twenty, or even ninety percent. He can only love one hundred percent, because *God is love.*

So God determined to love the world by giving his one and only Son (John 3:16). And the Son determined to love the world by laying down his life (John 15:13). And the Spirit determined to love the world by living within our hearts (Romans 5:5).

And because *God is love*, Jesus said the two most important commands are to *Love the Lord your God with all your heart and with all your soul and with all your mind* (Matthew 22:37), and to *Love your neighbor as yourself* (Matthew 22:39). That's why it only makes sense for the distinguishing mark of the church to be love.

A study revealed seven emotional needs most people have that the church is able to meet. The seventh is to be accepted; the sixth is to be respected; the fifth is to be secure; the fourth is to be recognized; the third is to be appreciated; the second is to be needed; and the first is to be loved. Every baby comes into the world with a need to be loved, and never outgrows it.

I went through a difficult time, many years ago, and had to find a new church. I walked into the service and, to my surprise, the question in my heart was not, *Will I like the preaching?* Or, *Will I like the music?* Or, *Will I like the programs?* But, rather, *Will these people love me?* It took a while, but eventually they did, and it became my church for many years.

John 14:2-3 *My Father's house has many rooms; if that were not so, would I have told you that I am going there to prepare a place for you? And if I go and prepare a place for you, I will come back and take you to be with me that you also may be where I am.*

When a young man became engaged, back then, he and his father would add a room to the family home. When the room was complete, the young man would go get his bride, and bring her home. This is what Jesus had in mind, and it should stir our hearts. He's preparing a room for us, and will soon return to take us home.

John 14:5-6 *Thomas said to him, Lord, we don't know where you are going, so how can we know the way? Jesus answered, I am the way and the truth and the life. No one comes to the Father except through me.*

The religion of Jesus Christ and the religion of the world are opposite in many ways. The world's religion says people are basically good, no one is really lost, and we don't need Christ to be saved. But Christ's religion says that people are basically bad (Mark 7:21-22), everyone is lost (Luke 19:10) and only Jesus saves (John 14:6).

The world's religion is broad and easy, but Christ's religion is narrow and hard. *Enter through the narrow gate. For wide is the gate and broad is the road that leads to destruction, and many enter through it. But small is the gate and narrow the road that leads to life, and only a few find it* (Matthew 7:13-14), said Jesus.

A missionary was being guided through the jungle by a native guide wielding a machete. There was no path so the missionary asked the guide if he was sure he knew the way. The native guide smiled and said, *I am the way.* If you don't know where you're going, any path will get you there. But if you want to go to heaven you must know the one who is the way.

John 14:26 *[T]he Holy Spirit, whom the Father will send in my name, will teach you all things and will remind you of everything I have said to you.*

The same Holy Spirit who oversaw the writing of the Old Testament would oversee the writing of the New Testament. Since Jesus taught the Old Testament was inspired down to the spelling (Matthew 5:18), we should have the same view of the New Testament. Peter recognized Paul's writing as Scripture (2 Peter 3:16); Paul recognized Luke's gospel as Scripture (1 Timothy 5:18, Luke 10:7); and *All Scripture is God-breathed* (2 Timothy 3:16), wrote Paul.

Since the Spirit oversaw the writing of Scripture, he can help us understand it. *Open my eyes that I may see wonderful things in your law* (Psalm 119:18), wrote the Psalmist. This is what Jesus did for the disciples on the Road to Emmaus: *he opened their minds so they could understand the Scriptures* (Luke 24:45), wrote Luke. The same God who wrote the Bible will help us understand it if we'll ask him.

For Reflection and Review

- *How did the crucifixion bring glory to the Father and the Son?*
- *How do we know God is love?*
- *How does the Spirit help us understand God's word?*

Lesson 252

John 15:18-20 *If the world hates you, keep in mind that it hated me first. If you belonged to the world, it would love you as its own. As it is, you do not belong to the world, but I have chosen you out of the world. That is why the* *world hates you. . . . If they persecuted me, they will persecute you also.*

Persecution takes many forms, but *everyone who wants to live a godly life in Christ Jesus will be persecuted* (2 Timothy 3:12), wrote Paul. It may take the form of shunning, divorce, demotion, or something unexpected.

I know a theology student who didn't receive a doctorate because his professors didn't believe the Bible. He was a brilliant student, who did all his work, but they wouldn't give him what he deserved. He later earned a doctorate from another school, but his unbelieving professors cost him thousands of dollars and years of his life. The emotional scar remains.

Others bear physical scars. A girl on her way to school had her face cut in half by a man with a machete, while three of her friends lost their heads. Others are disfigured by acid, or doused with gasoline and burned. No one welcomes this kind of treatment, but many count it an honor to suffer for their faith. *If they persecuted me, they will persecute you also.*

John 16:8 *When [the Holy Spirit] comes, he will prove the world to be in the wrong about sin and righteousness and judgment.*

The world seldom thinks about sin, righteousness, or the coming judgment. Prisons are filled with people who've done terrible things and either deny them, or dismiss them with a shrug. Others add to their sins every day, and don't even pray when they're dying. But all this changes when the Holy Spirit awakens us to sin, righteousness, and the coming judgment.

I know a man whose vocabulary was so wicked it likely made the devil blush. Then he heard a preacher say that he'd give an account to God for every word he'd ever spoken (Matthew 12:37). He was so shaken that he got down on his knees to pray, and found his way to Jesus Christ. This is the work of the Spirit.

Sinners naturally love their sin, and want to remain in it, but true believers hate their sin and want to turn away from it. Judgment Day is often in our thoughts, and we want to be found righteous. This isn't because we're better than others, but because the Holy Spirit is working in our lives.

John 17:3 *Now this is eternal life: that they know you, the only true God, and Jesus Christ, whom you have sent.*

Eternal life doesn't come from knowing about God, but from knowing God personally. This is part of the New Covenant foretold by the prophet Jeremiah: *they will all know me, from the least of them to the greatest, declares the Lord* (Jeremiah 31:34).

When my son was three years old, he was playing in the back yard with some older kids from a Christian home. Afterward he said to his mom, *Those kids are nice!* She replied, *That's because they know the Lord.* He said, *I want to know the Lord too.* She said, *You're too young.* But he persisted, so she explained the gospel (John 3:16) and led him to Christ in prayer. To our surprise, we saw a genuine change that's never gone away.

His little sister also came to know the Lord, and later asked her mom this question: *Is it okay that I love God even more than I love you?* This was her mom's delight, of course, and is exactly what God foretold: *they will all know me, from the least of them to the greatest.*

John 17:18 *As you sent me into the world, I have sent them into the world.*

Perhaps the disciples thought of forming a little community, apart from the world, where they could live out their faith in peace. That idea appeals to many, but it's not what Jesus had in mind. He sends his disciples into the world to make even more disciples of Jesus Christ. We can never be fully Christian apart from the church and the world.

My friend was surprised by the question of a coworker as they sat down to eat their lunch. *Everyday we get out of bed, come to work, do our jobs, go home and do it again the following day—what's the point?* My friend explained that the point of life is to know Christ and to make him known. That's what gives life direction, meaning, and purpose. It's why we get out of bed, everyday, and go into the world.

John 17:23 *[May] they may be brought to complete unity.*

The disciples weren't always united, even while Christ was with them (Luke 22:24). How would they stay united after he went to heaven? There are no easy answers, but since Jesus prayed for unity, we should do the same. One hundred pianos tuned to the same fork will also be tuned to each other. If the members of a church are tuned to Christ, they'll be tuned to each other too.

One Sunday morning, two men argued over politics, on their way into church. Their voices were raised enough for others to hear, and they nearly came to blows. But as they received the Lord's Supper, both understood that what united them was greater than what divided them. After the service they embraced, and put their differences aside.

There are other times when unity must be preserved through strength. *[S]avage wolves will come in among you and will not spare the flock* (Acts 29:29), said Paul. Any church that's not prepared to handle wolves should expect to suffer badly. Thankfully, God has given authority to church leaders to maintain unity, so the flock won't be destroyed.

Warn a divisive person once, and then warn them a second time. After that, have nothing to do with them (Titus 3:10), wrote Paul. For this to be effective there must be unity among the most influential leaders of any church. If a wolf can turn them against each other he's already won. But if the leaders are united, they can put down trouble whenever it arises.

There was a lady in a church I served who was constantly causing problems. She was insubordinate to her director, and spoke disrespectfully to others. I went to her with an open Bible and read the words: *Warn a divisive person once, and then warn them a second time. After that, have nothing to do with them.* Then I explained her behavior was wrong, and wouldn't be tolerated. Not surprisingly, she left and never returned. Keeping peace isn't always pleasant, but it's what leaders do.

For Reflection and Review

- *How does the Holy Spirit turn us away from our sins?*
- *Why do Christians need both the church and the world?*
- *Why does Jesus care about unity?*

Lesson 253

John 18:6 *When Jesus said, I am he, they drew back and fell to the ground.*

Earlier that evening, Jesus dismissed Judas Iscariot to do what was in his heart. Possessed by the devil (John 13:27), Judas went to the religious leaders and obtained a detachment of soldiers to arrest Jesus. The evening provided a cloak of darkness that would minimize any commotion.

First, perhaps, Judas led them to the upper room where they had eaten the Last Supper (Luke 22:12). Finding it empty, he took them to the Garden of Gethsemane because Jesus often went there with his disciples (John 18:2). When they arrived Jesus said to them, *Who is it you want? Jesus of Nazareth*, they replied. *I am he*, said Jesus. Immediately the soldiers *drew back and fell to the ground* (John 18:4-6).

This is interesting for at least three reasons. First, falling to the ground is a common reaction to dcity. The Prophet Ezekiel had a vision of God and he *fell facedown* (Ezekiel 1:28). When the risen Christ appeared to Saul he *fell to the ground* (Acts 22:7). And when John encountered the risen Christ he *fell at his feet as though dead* (Revelation

1:17). The authority of Jesus Christ is so overwhelming that even professional soldiers couldn't remain standing.

Second, the word *detachment* (John 18:3) refers to a tenth of a legion, which could be as many as six hundred men. This seems like a lot of man-power, just to make an arrest. But when the Apostle Paul was escorted to Caesarea, he was taken by over four hundred soldiers (Acts 23:23). Since Jesus had disciples who might be willing to fight, it's not unreasonable to think of hundreds of soldiers assigned to make the arrest.

Third, when Jesus said *I am he,* what he literally said (in Greek) was, *I am.* This is the meaning of God's name, which occurs over six thousand times in the Old Testament. Even in apparent weakness, Jesus was in control, because he was God in human flesh.

Another explanation may also be helpful. These were Jewish soldiers who were familiar with the stories of the Old Testament. When the king of Israel sent fifty men to arrest the prophet Elijah, he called fire out of heaven that consumed them. When the king sent another fifty men, the same thing happened to them (2 Kings 1:1-12). Jesus did many miracles, and had a reputation as a powerful prophet. The men who came to arrest him probably feared for their lives and were terrified by his presence. So *When Jesus said, I am he, they drew back and fell to the ground.*

John 18:10-11 *Then Simon Peter, who had a sword, drew it and struck the high priest's servant, cutting off his right ear. . . . Jesus commanded Peter, Put your sword away!*

Then Jesus *touched the man's ear and healed him* (Luke 22:51). This was good for the man, but also for Peter, and for the church. Peter would've been arrested for cutting off a man's ear, and the church would have lost a leader. But Jesus overruled Peter's mistake, and has probably done the same for us at times. If we consider all the foolish things we've done, we'll be amazed how often God has kept us out of trouble.

John 18:11b *Shall I not drink the cup the Father has given me?*

This is an allusion to the cup of God's wrath mentioned elsewhere in the Bible. *Take from my hand this cup filled with the wine of my wrath* (Jeremiah 25:15). *[D]rink the cup of the wrath of the Almighty* (Job 21:20). *[T]hey, too, will drink the wine of God's fury, which has been poured full strength into the cup of his wrath* (Revelation 14:10). And, *[God] gave her the cup filled with the wine of the fury of his wrath* (Revelation 16:19). The cup that Jesus would drink on the cross was the cup of God's wrath against our sin.

It's important to understand that, until we believe in Christ, the wrath of God is upon us. *[W]hoever rejects the Son will not see life, for God's wrath remains on them* (John 3:36), said John the Baptist. Jesus bore God's wrath on our behalf, so we wouldn't have to bear it ourselves. *[T]he punishment that brought us peace was on him* (Isaiah 53:5), wrote Isaiah. And *[We're] saved from God's wrath through him* (Romans 5:9), wrote Paul. When we believe in Jesus Christ, God is no longer angry at us.

The story is told of a child king who had a thousand servants at his command. His brother asked, *What happens when you do something bad?* The child king replied, *Someone else is punished for me.* To demonstrate, he broke an expensive vase, and one of his servants was given a beating. But Jesus reversed the order by taking a beating in the place of his servants. He bore the wrath of God so that we could have peace with God (Romans 5:1).

John 18:26-27 *Didn't I see you with him in the garden? Again Peter denied it, and at that moment a rooster began to crow.*

Earlier that night Jesus told the disciples they'd all fall away from him (Matthew 26:31), and that Peter would deny him three times before the rooster crowed (John 13:38). Peter denied this emphatically: *Even if all fall away on account of you, I never will* (Matthew 26:33). *Even if I have to die with you, I will never disown you* (Matthew 26:35). *I am ready to go with you to prison and to death* (Luke 22:33). *I will lay down my life for you* (John 13:37), he said.

So when Jesus was arrested, and the other disciples ran for their lives (John 18:8), Peter and John followed him into the courtyard of the High Priest (Matthew 26:58). It's hard to know what Peter was thinking, unless he was hoping to rescue Jesus. He'd have to avoid being identified, of course, so he denied that he even knew Jesus (Matthew 26:69-75). He wasn't really denying Jesus, it only appeared that way—once, twice, and then again.

Suddenly the rooster crowed, and Peter remembered what Jesus said earlier. *[B]efore the rooster crows, you will disown me three times* (John 13:38). In spite of himself, somehow, somewhere, Peter crossed a line.

Maybe you've promised God that you'd never do something, or never do it again. You were perfectly sincere, but then it happened, or happened again. It doesn't mean you were lying, but that sin is bigger than all of us. If Peter failed so can anyone, provided it's the right temptation, in the right place, at the right time.

If there's a clue to Peter's failure, it could be the confidence he had in himself. *[I]f you think you are standing firm, be careful that you do not fall!* (1 Corinthians 10:12), wrote Paul. A friend of mine was getting the mail when he slipped on a patch of ice. The next thing he knew he was flat on his back wondering what happened. We don't depend on moral resolve for our stability, but on Jesus Christ who taught us to pray, *lead us not into temptation, but deliver us from the evil one* (Matthew 6:13).

For Reflection and Review

- *Why did the guards fall to the ground?*
- *Has Jesus ever kept you out of trouble?*
- *Should Christians make promises to God?*

Lesson 254

John 18:28 *Then the Jewish leaders took Jesus from Caiaphas to the palace of the Roman governor.*

The Jewish leaders condemned Jesus, but didn't have the authority to kill him, so they took him to Pontius Pilate. They wouldn't enter his palace, however, because they believed going into a Gentile's home could disqualify them from celebrating the Passover. Ironically, the religious leaders kept their religion while pleading for the death of God's Son. Being religious is no guarantee we're right with God.

John 18:32 *This took place to fulfill what Jesus had said about the kind of death he was going to die.*

Jesus predicted he'd die by crucifixion (John 12:32-33), even though the Jews preferred death by stoning. At least twice during his ministry they picked up stones to stone him (John 8:59, 10:31). And when Stephen gave testimony to Christ, they actually did stone him (Acts 7:54-60). But the Jews were under Roman rule, and weren't supposed to kill anyone. So they took Jesus to the Roman governor to have him killed the Roman way—by crucifixion. This was also important for theological reasons.

[A]nyone who is hung on a pole is under God's curse (Deuteronomy 21:23), wrote Moses. If you lived in Moses' day, and committed a capitol offense, your body might be hung on a pole, after your execution, as a deterrent to others. And because you committed a capital offense, you apparently died under God's curse. Jesus had to be hung on a pole to show he was bearing God's curse for us, so we could have *every spiritual blessing in Christ* (Ephesians 1:3), wrote Paul.

But, for many, the crucifixion of Jesus was proof that he wasn't the Messiah, since it was inconceivable that Messiah would ever be under God's curse. This may have emboldened Rabbi Saul to go on his rampage against Christianity. *I put many of the Lord's people in prison, and when they were put to death, I cast my vote against them* (Acts 26:10), he said. But, after he met the risen Lord,

Rabbi Saul learned that Jesus was hung on a pole for us (Galatians 3:13), and Rabbi Saul became the Apostle Paul.

John 18:37 *Everyone on the side of truth listens to me.*

Pilate's job was to get at the truth about Jesus but, in a world full of lies, that wouldn't be easy. Pilate's gut was telling him one thing and Jesus' enemies were telling him another. So Jesus gave Pilate a clue: *Everyone on the side of truth listens to me.* In other words, Pilate, if you want to know the truth, you have to be on the side of truth, and be willing to follow the truth wherever it leads.

A friend of mine shared the gospel with a co-worker and warned about the awfulness of hell. The co-worker said, *I don't believe in hell.* My friend replied, *That's like not believing in gravity. You can jump off a building but it's still going to hurt when you hit the ground.* After time to reflect the man confessed, *I've been praying for someone to tell me the truth.*

John 18:38 *What is truth?* retorted Pilate.

If you were on trial for your life and the judge said, *What is truth?* that wouldn't be a good sign. But Jesus came into a world of lies, so he wasn't surprised when the person in charge of his trial wasn't concerned about truth.

When I was nine years old we were having dinner at my aunt's house and she had just cleaned all the windows. I was on my way out to the patio when I slammed into the sliding glass door and almost knocked myself out. Truth is that which doesn't go away, even when we ignore it. God exists and so do his commands. We have broken them and, apart from Christ, there will be hell to pay. Pilate said, *What is truth?* But he was looking at the truth when he said it.

And truth has a way of winning. *Crucified under Pontius Pilate* is part of a creed recited by countless Christians around the world, every week. Jesus is known as the greatest person who ever lived, and Pilate is known as the one who killed him. Truth matters more in the long run, than often appears at first.

John 19:12 *Pilate tried to set Jesus free, but the Jewish leaders kept shouting, If you let this man go, you are no friend of Caesar. Anyone who claims to be a king opposes Caesar.*

Pilate knew Jesus was innocent, and that the religious leaders were acting out of self-interest (Mark 15:10). But if he set Jesus free, the high priest could report him to Rome, for not putting down a rival king. Tiberius Caesar could put an end to Pilate's career, or even his life. Pilate had to choose: he could do the right thing, or sacrifice Jesus to save himself.

If the tension wasn't high enough, it seemed like God himself was reaching out to Pilate. His wife sent him a message saying, *Do not have anything to do with that innocent man, for I have suffered a great deal today in a dream because of him* (Matthew 27:19). If she dreamed of Judgment Day, she may have seen the roles reversed. As Jesus stood trial before Pilate, the day was coming when Pilate would stand trial before Jesus. Whatever Pilate decided about Christ would have very serious consequences.

Adam and Eve ate the forbidden fruit and that had serious consequences (Genesis 3). Achan kept some of gold for himself and that had serious consequences too (Joshua 7). David took another man's wife and that had serous consequences too (2 Samuel 11). But nothing has more serious consequences than what we do with Christ.

We don't know what happened to Pilate later in life. Some say he was converted; others say he killed himself. We only know for sure that he crucified the Son of God. But even that wouldn't keep Pilate out of heaven if he chose to repent and believe. First we make our choices, then our choices make us.

For Reflection and Review

- *Why did Jesus have to die by crucifixion?*
- *Why didn't Pilate care about truth?*
- *Was Pilate evil?*

Lesson 255

John 19:17 *Carrying his own cross, [Jesus] went out to the place of the Skull (which in Aramaic is called Golgotha).*

We don't know the exact location of the crucifixion, or even why it was called *the place of the Skull*. Perhaps it was an expression for the place of death, where people were normally crucified. What's really important is that it was outside the city. Jesus *suffered outside the city gate* (Hebrews 13:12), says Hebrews.

Under the law of Moses a young man who was guilty of blasphemy was taken *outside the camp* and put to death (Leviticus 24:14). A man who broke the Sabbath was also taken *outside the camp* and put to death (Numbers 15:35). As the one who'd bear the sins of the world, Jesus was taken *outside the city gate* (Hebrews 13:12) and put to death.

Jesus is the ultimate outsider, and everyone who follows Jesus will be an outsider too. But it's better to be outside the camp with Jesus, than to be inside the camp without him. It's better to be rejected by the world and received by Christ, than to be received by the world and rejected by Christ. *Let us, then, go to him outside the camp, bearing the disgrace he bore* (Hebrews 13:13), says Hebrews.

John 19:18 *There they crucified him, and with him two others—one on each side and Jesus in the middle.*

Luke records a conversation that took place between the three of them. *One of the criminals who hung there hurled insults at him: Aren't you the Messiah? Save yourself and us! But the other criminal rebuked him. Don't you fear God, he said, since you are under the same sentence? We are punished justly, for we are getting what our deeds deserve. But this man has done nothing wrong. Then he said, Jesus, remember me when you come into your kingdom. Jesus answered him, Truly I tell you, today you will be with me in paradise* (Luke 23:39-43).

Both criminals were getting what they deserved, but had the good fortune of being crucified next to the one who could save them. The damned fool mocked Christ, died in his sin, and went to hell. The other man turned to Christ and was saved. He wasn't saved by being a good person, but by believing in the only good person who ever lived.

Salvation is easy for us, but it wasn't easy for Christ. *We have laws against cruel and unusual punishment, but crucifixion was designed to be cruel and unusual punishment. It was a method of slow and painful execution in which the victim was nailed to a large wooden cross and left to hang until dead.*

The horizontal beam was placed on the ground and the victim was attached to it by nails through his hands. It was then attached to the vertical beam and the victim was attached to it by nails through his feet. Pain in the feet intensified as the victim lifted himself repeatedly in order to draw breath. Strain on the arms sometimes caused the dislocation of elbow and shoulder joints.

The agony of tearing nerves, flesh, and muscle, along with difficulty breathing, made for a miserable way of dying. The formal cause of death was often suffocation, but it could also come from heart failure, brain damage, or shock (gathered from multiple sources.)

You who think of sin but lightly, Nor suppose the evil great, Here may view its nature rightly, Here its guilt may estimate (Thomas Kelly).

John 19:24 *Let's not tear it, they said to one another. Let's decide by lot who will get it. This happened that the scripture might be fulfilled that said, They divided my clothes among them and cast lots for my garment.*

After Jesus was crucified the soldiers divided up his clothing, and thus fulfilled an ancient prophecy. The prophecy is so remarkable we ought to ask, *What are the odds?* How often do people divide up another person's clothing *and gamble for it? They divided my clothes among them and cast lots for my garment* (Psalm 22:18), wrote David. We can imagine dividing up another person's clothing *or* gambling for it. But it must be extremely rare to divide up another person's clothing *and* gamble for it at the same time.

The traditional clothing for an adult male Jew in Jesus' day consisted of five pieces: headdress, robe, sash, sandals, and undergarment. Since there were four soldiers (John 19:23), and five pieces of clothing, they each took one piece and gambled for the fifth. *They divided [his] clothes among them and cast lots for [his] garment*—just as the Bible foretold.

Even more amazing are the many other prophecies fulfilled at Jesus' death. *Strike the shepherd, and the sheep will be scattered* (Zechariah 13:7). *I offered my back to those who beat me, my cheeks to those who pulled out my beard; I did not hide my face from mocking and spitting* (Isaiah 50:6). *He was assigned a grave with the wicked, and with the rich in his death* (Isaiah 53:9). *They will look on me, the one they have pierced* (Zechariah 12:10). *[N]ot one of [his bones] will be broken* (Psalm 34:20). *I am poured out like water, and all my bones are out of joint. . . . they pierce my hands and my feet. All my bones are on display; people stare and gloat over me* (Psalm 22:14-17).

These sound like eye-witness accounts, but were written hundreds of years before the event. It may be hard to believe in Jesus Christ, but it's harder not to believe, when all the evidence is honestly considered.

John 19:30 *When he had received the drink, Jesus said, It is finished. With that, he bowed his head and gave up his spirit.*

Jesus took the drink just before dying in order to shout the words, *It is finished*. As Mark wrote, *With a loud cry, Jesus breathed his last* (Mark 15:37). We should think of Jesus hanging on the cross and asking for a drink of water, so with his dying breath he could shout, *It is finished*. It wasn't a cry of defeat, but a shout of victory. We were all defeated by sin but God *gives us the victory through our Lord Jesus Christ* (1 Corinthians 15:57), wrote Paul.

For Reflection and Review

- *Do Christians have to be outsiders?*
- *What can we learn from the two thieves?*
- *How does fulfilled prophecy help our faith?*

Lesson 256

John 20:1 *Early on the first day of the week, while it was still dark, Mary Magdalene went to the tomb and saw that the stone had been removed from the entrance.*

Jesus' body was prepared for burial quickly (John 19:38-42), so Mary came with spices to complete the task more thoroughly (Mark 16:1). Seeing the stone removed from the entrance of the tomb, she assumed Jesus' body had been taken away or stolen. She reported this to Peter and John, who came to the tomb to investigate. They found it empty, except for the strips of cloth in which Jesus' body had been wrapped (John 20:6-7).

This is very interesting. If Jesus' body was taken away by Roman officials, or grave robbers, they wouldn't have taken the time to unwrap the grave clothes. Either Jesus removed them himself, or his body passed through them. This was enough to convince John that Jesus rose from the dead (John 20:8). He didn't understand it fully, but he became the first to believe in the resurrection of Christ.

John 20:11 *Now Mary stood outside the tomb crying.*

She wasn't weeping because of Jesus' death, but because his body was missing. The death of a loved one is traumatic enough, but a stolen body makes it even worse. Mary was likely sobbing when she looked into the tomb *and saw two angels in white, seated where Jesus' body had been, one at the head and the other at the foot* (John 20:12). This reminds us of the two angelic images over the ark of the covenant, where God was uniquely present (Exodus 25:22). But God had now come out to make himself known.

John 20:16 *Jesus said to her, Mary. She turned toward him and cried out in Aramaic, Rabboni! (which means Teacher).*

At first, Mary mistook Jesus for the gardener, but when she heard him pronounce her name she recognized him. This is a mark of authenticity because loved ones often pronounce our names in a recognizable way. Anyone can pronounce my wife's name, but no one says it exactly the way I do. By the loving way he said her name, Mary recognized her teacher.

John 20:17 *Jesus said, Do not hold on to me, for I have not yet ascended to the Father.*

Mary probably fell at Jesus' feet in worship (Matthew 28:9). Having lost him once, she likely held on as though she'd never let him go. Jesus' ascension was several weeks away so he assured her that he wouldn't be leaving quickly. There were more appearances to come.

John 20:19 *On the evening of that first day of the week . . . the disciples were together, with the doors locked for fear of the Jewish leaders.*

Jesus had risen from the dead, but the Jewish leaders might accuse the disciples of stealing his body (Matthew 28:13). And, since they crucified Jesus, the disciples could be next. So they met behind locked doors, and may've discussed leaving town. Jerusalem was a dangerous place to be.

John 20:19b *Jesus came and stood among them and said, Peace be with you!*

The disciples were so overwhelmed, they thought they were seeing a ghost. So Jesus asked for something to eat, to prove he was still human. After all he'd been through, in fact, he was probably hungry. So the disciples gave him some fish, which he ate in their presence (Luke 24:37-39).

Jesus' resurrection body was similar to the one he had before, but not exactly the same. He was able to eat, but could also pass through doors and disappear (Luke 24:31). And, later, he appeared to John in transcendent glory (Revelation 1:12-16).

Perhaps from this we can catch a glimpse of our future bodies. *[He] will transform our lowly bodies so that they will be like his glorious body* (Philippians 3:21), wrote Paul. And *We know that when Christ appears, we shall be like him* (1 John 3:2), wrote John. Our resurrection bodies will be similar to the ones we have now, but better by far.

John 20:22 *And with that he breathed on them and said, Receive the Holy Spirit.*

This is difficult to understand until we recall what God did for Adam. *[T]he Lord God formed a man from the dust of the ground and breathed into his nostrils the breath of life, and the man became a living being* (Genesis 2:7). Adam could've lived forever, but went the way of sin and death. So after Jesus conquered death, he gave the Spirit of life to his disciples. God breathed life into Adam, and Jesus breathed the Spirit into his own. He came to those who were dying, and gave us the Spirit of life.

John 20:24-25 *Now Thomas . . . was not with the disciples when Jesus came. So the other disciples told him, We have seen the Lord!*

The death of Messiah was such an emotional blow to Thomas that he refused to believe in his resurrection with anything less than absolute proof. *Unless I see the nail marks in his hands and put my finger where the nails were, and put my hand into his side, I will not believe,* he said.

A week later his disciples were in the house again, and Thomas was with them. (John 20:26). It had been a long week for Thomas. If Jesus revealed himself to others, why not to him? Had he fallen out of favor? Had he been rejected? Had Jesus turned away from him? Why didn't Jesus reveal himself?

John 20:26b *Though the doors were locked, Jesus came and stood among them and said, Peace be with you! Then he said to Thomas, Put your finger here; see my hands. Reach out your hand and put it into my side. Stop doubting and believe.*

Jesus seemed absent when Thomas spoke his words of doubt, so Jesus repeated them plainly. That way Thomas would know that Jesus heard him, even when he couldn't be seen. This should comfort us whenever Jesus seems absent, and challenge us whenever we doubt. Jesus knows what we're going through, because he's always with us (Matthew 28:20), even when he seems painfully absent.

John 20:28 *Thomas said to him, My Lord and my God!*

This may be the clearest assertion of Jesus' divinity anywhere in the Bible, and is the climax of John's gospel. It's also why Jesus appeared to the others when Thomas was absent. Few of Thomas' words are recorded in Scripture, but *My Lord and my God* weigh more than a thousand pounds. Jesus put Thomas through a season of doubt to draw out his statement of faith. This was a blessing to Thomas, as well as to all who believe.

John 20:30-31 *Jesus performed many other signs in the presence of his disciples, which are not recorded in this book. But these are written that you may believe that Jesus is the Messiah, the Son of God, and that by believing you may have life in his name.*

John repeatedly emphasized the importance of believing in Jesus Christ for eternal life. In fact the word *believe*, occurs over seventy times in various forms. *Whoever believes in him is not condemned, but whoever does not believe stands condemned already* (John 3:18). *Whoever believes in the Son has eternal life, but whoever rejects the Son will not see life, for God's wrath remains on them* (John 3:36). And *if you do not believe that I am he, you will indeed die in your sins* (John 8:24), said Jesus.

An argument was developed years ago to show the wisdom of believing in Jesus Christ: If you believe in Jesus Christ and are right, you'll gain everything when you die. If you believe in Jesus Christ and are wrong, you'll lose nothing when you die. Since everyone is going to die, the only reasonable thing is to believe in Jesus Christ (Pascal's Wager, revised).

For Reflection and Review

- *Why did Jesus' grave clothes convince John that Christ had risen?*
- *Why didn't Jesus appear to Thomas at first?*
- *Why is it wise to believe in Jesus Christ?*

Lesson 257

John 21:3 *I'm going out to fish, Simon Peter told them, and they said, We will go with you.*

As long as Peter was following Jesus, Jesus took care of Peter's needs. It wasn't always first class, but there was always enough. But after the resurrection, Jesus was harder to follow, and Peter was low on cash. So he went back to fishing and the others said, *We will go with you.*

They fished all night, without any luck, until a stranger on the shore gave them some advice. *Throw your net on the right side of the boat* (John 21:6), he said. Then they caught so many fish, they could hardly get them back to shore. Jesus was teaching his disciples that he could still provide for their needs.

John 21:9 *When they landed, they saw a fire of burning coals there with fish on it, and some bread.*

Ever since our fall into sin, God has been bringing us back to his table. Moses, Aaron, and others went up a mountain where *they saw God, and they ate and drank* (Exodus 24:11). The Israelites ate in the presence of the Lord (Deuteronomy 12:7) at the temple. And now the disciples were having breakfast on the shore, with Jesus as their cook. Eating with God is a sign of our intimate fellowship with him.

Likewise, the night before his death, Jesus sat at table with his disciples. They broke bread, drank wine, and Jesus said, *do this in remembrance of me* (1 Corinthians 11:24). Whenever we receive the Lord's Supper we're having table fellowship with God.

And when Christ returns, *he will dress himself to serve, will have [us] recline at the table and will come and wait on [us]* (Luke 12:37), said Jesus. Imagine sitting down for dinner in the kingdom of God, with Jesus as your waiter. He cooked for the disciples on the shore, and will be our waiter in the age to come. He's made us children of God, and we'll eat at his table forever.

John 21:17 *Simon son of John, do you love me? . . . He said, Lord, you know all things; you know that I love you. Jesus said, Feed my sheep.*

Shortly before the crucifixion Peter denied Jesus three times with a curse (John 18:15-27, Matthew 26:69-75), and Jesus wanted to clear that up. He had big plans for Peter and, in the eyes of the others, he may've lost some credibility. So Jesus used the opportunity to re-commission Peter, in front of the other apostles, so they'd know he was still in good standing.

A pastor fell behind in his work and, instead of preparing a sermon, he stole one from the internet. Unfortunately, it was by a pastor who was famous, and someone in the congregation recognized the sermon. Since the Bible is against stealing, there was some question whether this man was fit to be the pastor. In fact, they decided to let him go. But was this the right decision?

Every situation is unique, but there are examples in the Bible of spiritual leaders who fell. Aaron would become the high priest of Israel, but he made a golden calf and led the nation into idolatry (Exodus 32:1-4). You'd expect God to get someone else, but Aaron served as high priest for the rest of his life.

King David stumbled badly when he committed adultery with Bathsheba and had her husband killed (2 Samuel 11). You'd expect God to get someone else, but David was also allowed to continue as king for rest of his life.

This is not to say Christian leaders should get away murder, adultery, idolatry, or disavowing Jesus Christ. But God's handling of Peter, Aaron, and David suggest a gentle approach. Church discipline isn't for everyone who sins, but for those who won't repent—in order to help them repent. *Brothers and sisters, if someone is caught in a sin, you who live by the Spirit should restore that person gently* (Galatians 6:1), wrote Paul.

John 21:18 *Very truly I tell you, when you were younger you dressed yourself and went where you wanted; but when you are old you will stretch out your hands, and someone else will dress you and lead you where you do not want to go.*

To *stretch out your hands* was a euphemism for crucifixion, and there's reason to believe that Peter was crucified under Caesar Nero, around AD 65. Whether we die a martyrs death, or something less dramatic, Jesus taught that the purpose of death is to *glorify* God (John 21:19). That's what Jesus did when he prayed, *Father, into your hands I commit my spirit* (Luke 23:46). And while Stephen was being stoned he also prayed, *Lord Jesus, receive my spirit* (Acts 7:59). These are good words to rehearse, so we'll know what to say when death comes for us.

John 21:22 *If I want him to remain alive until I return, what is that to you? You must follow me.*

Jesus and Peter were walking, and John was following behind. *When Peter saw him, he asked, Lord, what about him?* (John 21:21). Jesus told Peter to mind his own business, and to simply follow him. Since Jesus is the only way to heaven it's no surprise the words *follow me* are found on his lips no fewer than twenty times throughout the gospels. The most important thing we can ever do is to follow Jesus Christ.

For Reflection and Review

- *Why will Jesus serve us dinner in the age to come?*
- *What is the purpose of church discipline?*
- *How can we glorify Christ in our death?*

Lesson 258

Acts 1:1 *In my former book, Theophilus, I wrote about all that Jesus began to do and to teach.*

The book of Acts is part two, of a two volume work, commonly called Luke/Acts. Together, Luke and Acts comprise about twenty-seven percent of the New Testament, and were likely paid for by Theophilus (Luke 1:3, Acts 1:1), whose name means *lover of God*. The book of Acts was probably completed around AD 62.

Three important questions are answered by this book. First, *How did the church begin?* Jesus said *I will build my church* (Matthew 16:18), and Acts covers the first thirty-two years of church history. Second, *What is the role of the Holy Spirit?* Jesus promised to send the Spirit (John 16:7-15), and Acts shows how the Spirit builds the church. Third, *Who was the Apostle Paul?* Paul wrote thirteen letters of the New Testament, but is never mentioned in the gospels. His story is told in the book of Acts, which serves as bridge between the gospels and the letters of Paul.

Acts 1:8 *[Y]ou will be my witnesses in Jerusalem, and in all Judea and Samaria, and to the ends of the earth.*

The apostles had many responsibilities but, first and foremost, they were to be Christ's *witnesses*. This is a legal term for someone who gives testimony of what they've seen or heard. Since the apostles were with Jesus after he rose from the dead, they could testify that he really was alive. *God has raised this Jesus to life, and we are all witnesses* (Acts 2:32), said Peter.

We believe Jesus rose from the dead because we have eyewitness testimony from credible witnesses, who were willing to suffer and die for what they saw. It's hard to imagine more compelling evidence in any court of law. We believe in Jesus Christ because we believe his witnesses.

Acts 1:9 *[Jesus] was taken up before their very eyes, and a cloud hid him from their sight.*

After his resurrection, Jesus met with his disciples over the course of forty days, and spoke about the kingdom of God (Acts 1:3). The disciples were so traumatized by the crucifixion, they needed time to adjust to the fact that Jesus had truly risen from the dead. Then, after forty days of teaching, Jesus' earthly ministry officially closed with his ascension into heaven. This was the conclusion of his earthly ministry, and the beginning of his heavenly ministry.

*****

Acts 2:1 *When the day of Pentecost came, they were all together in one place.*

Jesus had told the apostles: *Do not leave Jerusalem, but wait for the gift my Father promised* (Acts 1:4). So they waited in Jerusalem until the Spirit came from heaven. The sound of a violent wind filled the house, and what seemed to be tongues of fire came to rest on each of them (Acts 2:2-3).

The text is not explicit, but the wind may speak of power (as in a hurricane) and the tongues of fire may stand for God's speech. *Is not my word like fire, declares the Lord* (Jeremiah 23:29). When you add wind to fire it begins to spread, and the fire of God's word was about to spread among the people.

One of the first things we learn about God in the Bible is that he speaks. *God said Let there be light* (Genesis 1:3), *God said Let the land produce* (Genesis 1:24) and *God said Let us make mankind* (Genesis 1:26). God also spoke to the prophets, who said to the people, *this is what the Lord says* (Isaiah 8:11).

And since God only had one Son, he made him a preacher (Matthew 4:17). Jesus appointed apostles to preach (Mark 3:14), and they appointed pastors to preach. So Paul told Timothy to *Preach the word* (2 Timothy 4:2). Martin Luther called the church a *mouth house*, because that's where God's word is preached. With his word God made the world, and with his word he makes the church.

Acts 2:14 *Then Peter stood up with the Eleven, raised his voice and addressed the crowd.*

Peter was accustomed to crowds, from being with Jesus, and this was a crowd of many thousands. It's hard to imagine speaking to that many people without a microphone, but it's been done before. In the eighteenth century George Whitfield often preached to over ten thousand people outside. He spoke so loudly that, after a sermon, he was known to spit up blood.

Peter also raised his voice and began to preach as never before. First he preached from the prophet Joel (Joel 2:28-32), who foretold the coming of the Holy Spirit, which they were experiencing. Then he preached from a Psalm of David (Psalm 16:9-11), which foretold the resurrection of Christ. Then he said, *God has made this Jesus, whom you crucified, both Lord and Messiah* (Acts 2:36).

Something had clearly happened to Peter. Several weeks earlier he denied Jesus three times with a curse (Matthew 26:69-75). But now he was preaching Christ so fearlessly that he didn't care what happened to him. How can this be explained?

Peter saw Jesus crucified, and then he saw him raised. Then he understood that Jesus died for our sins, and was raised for our salvation. Then he was filled with the Spirit of Christ. What else could Peter possibly do but preach? *God has made this Jesus, whom you crucified, both Lord and Messiah,* (Acts 2:36), he said.

Acts 2:37 *When the people heard this, they were cut to the heart and said to Peter and the other apostles, Brothers, what shall we do?*

That's a good question. What do you do after you've killed the Messiah? They thought they were pretty good people. They read the Bible, said their prayers, went to synagogue, and tried to keep the commandments. But the word of God preached in the power of the Spirit revealed the true nature of their little black hearts—and ours.

Notice Peter's use of the second person pronoun (you), which he used throughout his sermon. *[Y]ou, with the help of wicked men, put him to death by nailing him to the cross* (Acts 2:23), he said. I prefer to say *we* since everyone sins, it's theologically correct, and much more polite. But Peter pointed his finger as though it were loaded and said, *you put him to death.*

The word of God is most powerful when the application is most personal. No one gets to heaven by saying, *we have sinned*. But when we say, *I have sinned, by my fault, by my own fault, by my own most miserable fault*—then we're in a position to receive salvation through faith in Jesus Christ.

For Reflection and Review

- *Why is the book of Acts important?*
- *Why was Peter so bold in his preaching?*
- *Why should preachers emphasize sin?*

Lesson 259

Acts 2:38 *Repent and be baptized, every one of you, in the name of Jesus Christ for the forgiveness of your sins.*

Peter didn't say, *Repent or be baptized*, but *Repent and be baptized*. Some people repent but are never baptized, others are baptized but never repent. But entrance into the Christian life has always been marked by repentance and baptism.

Repentance is simply a change of mind that leads to a change in direction. If you're on the highway to hell, and you want to go to heaven, you have to turn around. Baptism makes repentance public.

John the Baptist was a fearless preacher of repentance (Matthew 3:2), but as long as people remained on the shore they weren't committed. Only when they stepped out of the crowd, in front of family and friends, were they saying their life was going to change.

[Baptism is] not the removal of dirt from the body but the pledge of a clear conscience toward God (1 Peter 3:21), wrote Peter. It isn't a pledge that we'll never sin again, but that we'll keep our conscience clear. If we're not living with a clear conscience, we're not fulfilling our baptismal pledge. Everyone sins, of course, but believers confess their sin (1 John 1:9), and go on following Christ.

Acts 2:38b *And you will receive the gift of the Holy Spirit.*

When we commit ourselves to living for Christ, he commits himself to living in us. Before we come to Christ we don't have the Spirit, but the moment we come to Christ we receive the Spirit. And *The Spirit himself testifies with our spirit that we are God's children* (Romans 8:16), wrote Paul.

A friend of mine has several brothers and sisters who all resemble each other. Some take after their father, and some take after their mother, but they all bear a family resemblance. The people of God don't need a medical test to prove who our heavenly Father is. The indwelling Spirit is proof that we are his.

Acts 2:41 *Those who accepted his message were baptized, and about three thousand were added to their number that day.*

The church of Jesus Christ didn't begin gradually, but popped into existence after Peter's sermon. If the disciples wanted to start a false religion, they would've gone far away from the people who knew the facts. They would've made a few converts, and the church would have grown gradually. But that's not what happened.

The disciples stood in the same city where Jesus was crucified and proclaimed his resurrection without any fear of contradiction. They knew for a fact that Jesus rose from the dead, and that it couldn't be disproven. Jesus' enemies could've stopped the Christian movement in a minute by simply producing a body. They had enough manpower to turn every stone in Jerusalem, but there wasn't even a search because the rulers knew there was no body (Matthew 28:1-15). So Christianity exploded.

The religion of the Bible is unique because it's based on acts of God in history, that could be verified or falsified. The main act of God in the Old Testament is the parting of the Red Sea (Exodus 14:10-31). The Israelites were on one side when the waters parted, and they walked to the other side before the waters closed. Whoever wasn't there could ask those who were, and they'd confirm it actually happened.

The main act of God in the New Testament is the resurrection of Jesus Christ. First he was dead, then he was alive. Whoever wasn't there could ask those who were, and they'd confirm it actually happened. The disciples' testimony was convincing because they were willing to die for what they saw, and even go to hell if they were lying. They were devout Jews and, if they were lying about God, they could expect nothing but wrath in the age to come. Good Jewish boys don't lie about God.

It's easy to sit down and come up with a new religion, and many people have. It's harder to proclaim an act of God in history, unless it actually happened. *For he has set a day when he will judge the world with justice by the man he has appointed. He has given proof of this to everyone by raising him from the dead* (Acts 17:31), said Paul.

Acts 2:46 *Every day they continued to meet together in the temple courts.*

The church began as a community of believers that met together frequently. The biblical word *church*, actually means *assembly, gathering,* or *congregation.* Everyone who believes in Jesus Christ belongs to his church, but we're uniquely the church whenever we come together. Strictly speaking, there are no solitary Christians.

This is also important for spiritual growth. California Redwoods grow as high as three hundred feet because their root systems interlock with each other. If they try to grow alone, they're often blown over by a strong wind. Christians also grow better together, so we're not to give *up meeting together, as some are in the habit of doing* (Hebrews 10:25), says Hebrews.

Acts 2:47 *And the Lord added to their number daily those who were being saved.*

The early church experienced dramatic growth as people came to Christ every day. Many shared their faith, and many others believed. Two thousand years later the church continues to grow, but not always consistently. Like a rising tide, a wave comes in and a wave goes out. But the waves are coming in further and, one day, *the earth will be filled with the knowledge of the Lord as the waters cover the sea* (Isaiah 11:9), wrote Isaiah.

For Reflection and Review

- *Why is baptism important?*
- *How does the birth of the church help prove the gospel?*
- *How does gathering together help believers grow?*

Lesson 260

Acts 3:1 *One day Peter and John were going up to the temple at the time of prayer—at three in the afternoon.*

Peter and John were leading a large church, but they still took time for prayer. They could've been planning events, feeding the poor, or doing outreach. But, instead, they went to a prayer meeting at three in the afternoon. This may've been due to something Jesus said the night before his death. *I am the vine; you are the branches. If you remain in me and I in you, you will bear much fruit; apart from me you can do nothing* (John 15:5).

The apostles understood that the most important thing they did each day, was to strengthen their relationship with Christ through prayer. The effectiveness of their ministry wasn't determined by the strength of their personality, but by their relationship with Jesus Christ. Likewise, the better we know him, the more others will see him in us, and take him seriously. Without Jesus Christ, we can do nothing of spiritual value.

Acts 3:2 *Now a man who was lame from birth was being carried to the temple gate called Beautiful, where he was put every day to beg from those going into the temple courts.*

We don't know the man's name, but we know he was *lame from birth*, and was *over forty years old* (Acts 4:22). He was put at the temple gate because people are more inclined to be generous when they're on their way to worship. There he sat, year after year, a nameless beggar on the lowest rung of the social ladder.

But there was another benefit to sitting near the temple. Since Jesus and the apostles were often there, he may've heard their sermons. Perhaps his faith was stirred, and he hoped that God would do something for him. When Peter and John approached the man, he asked for money (Acts 3:3). Peter replied, *Silver or gold I do not have, but what I do have I give you. In the name of Jesus Christ of Nazareth, walk* (Acts 3:6). Taking him by the hand, Peter helped him up, and his feet and ankles became strong. He began walking, jumping, and praising God (Acts 3:7-9). It was a miracle.

There are about a hundred miracles in the Bible (depending on how you count) and they tend to cluster around a few specific people such as Moses, Elijah, Elisha, Jesus, Peter, and Paul—with Jesus doing the most by far.

Miracles point ahead to a time when prayer will be answered immediately. *Before they call I will answer; while they are still speaking I will hear* (Isaiah 65:24), said God. In the age to come, prayer will be answered before it's even offered. But what about today?

God can do miracles anywhere and anytime he pleases. *You are the God who performs miracles* (Psalm 77:14), wrote the Psalmist. But God also works through ordinary means such as doctors, friends, and family. The things God does providentially are just as much from him as when he acts directly. We ought to pray for a miracle, whenever one is needed, but we should also thank God for his ordinary providence since that's how he normally works in this age.

Acts 3:11 *While the man held on to Peter and John, all the people were astonished and came running to them.*

Since Peter had a crowd, he began to preach to thousands, like on the day of Pentecost. *You disowned the Holy and Righteous One and asked that a murderer be released to you* (Acts 3:14), he said. We should think about this.

Pilate wanted to let Jesus go, because he was clearly innocent, but the Jewish leaders wanted Jesus dead. Since it was the custom to let a prisoner go free at Passover, Pilate offered the people a choice: they could have the *Holy and Righteous One* or they could have a murdering insurrectionist by the name of *Barabbas*.

Which of the two do you want me to release to you? asked the governor. Barabbas, they answered. What shall I do, then, with Jesus who is called the Messiah? Pilate asked. They all answered, Crucify him! (Matthew 27:21-22).

Three things should be noticed: First, some people prefer murderers over the Messiah. Sinners love sinners more than the Savior, as long as they're living in sin. As long as we think little of sin, we'll never think highly of Christ.

Second, the crucifixion of Jesus allowed Barabbas to go free. He was on death row, without any hope, but because of Jesus Christ he was set free from the punishment he deserved. Likewise, Jesus took the punishment we deserve, so we could be set free.

Third, *Barabbas* means *son of the father*. And the reason Jesus died was to make us sons and daughters of the Father. *See what great love the Father has lavished on us, that we should be called children of God* (1 John 3:1), wrote John. Jesus gives hope to people like Barabbas.

Acts 3:19 *Repent, then, and turn to God, so that your sins may be wiped out.*

Imagine you're in court on Judgment Day, and there's a massive whiteboard listing all your sins. The smaller sins are written small, and the bigger sins are written big. God is out of the room but, when he comes back and sees what you've done, there'll be hell to pay. So you go to the whiteboard and try to erase your worst sins, only to discover they've been written in permanent ink. No matter how hard you try to erase them, they won't come off.

Then Jesus comes into the room and pulls out an eraser dipped in his own blood. One by one he erases your sins until the white board is absolutely glistening (1John 1:7). *Repent, then, and turn to God, so that your sins may be wiped out*, said Peter. With an offer like that, the number of believers grew to five thousand men (Acts 4:4), plus women and children.

For Reflection and Review

- *Why is it important to spend time in prayer?*
- *What can we learn from Barabbas?*
- *How thoroughly does Jesus forgive?*

Lesson 261

Acts 4:1 *The priests and the captain of the temple guard and the Sadducees came up to Peter and John while they were speaking to the people.*

Peter and John weren't approved preachers, and weren't preaching an approved message. So they were arrested and brought out the following day to appear before the Jewish high court. This was the same court that condemned Jesus Christ not long before. The odds of getting a fair trial weren't very good, but Peter was fearless.

Acts 4:11 *[Jesus is] the stone you builders rejected, which has become the cornerstone.*

With this sentence, Peter turned the accusers into the accused. If the entire court was present, there may've been over seventy of the most powerful people in the nation, whom Peter was accusing. They were the religious builders who rejected God's Messiah—the *cornerstone* of their religion.

Peter was a Galilean fisherman with an unrefined accent who hadn't been to college. But he had been with Jesus, who applied this verse to himself. *The stone the builders rejected has become the cornerstone* (Matthew 21:42), he said. This is a direct quotation from the Old Testament (Psalm 118:22), which the religious leaders knew well.

Think of builders going to a quarry and passing over a stone they considered unworthy of their project. But, in the providence of God, the stone the builders rejected became the most important one in the building. Peter quoted this verse to say, in effect, *The Bible said you would do this.* With a single verse of Scripture Peter condemned the entire high court, and they knew it.

Acts 4:12 *Salvation is found in no one else, for there is no other name under heaven given to mankind by which we must be saved.*

Peter was giving the high court an ultimatum. There was no other way for them to be saved except to believe in the one they had killed. This was offensive to them, and remains offensive today. What about Moses, Muhammad, Buddha, and Krishna?

Peter should've known, to get along in the world, the first thing you must do is give up the exclusiveness of Christianity. Instead of saying Jesus is the only way to God, you must say he's a good way to God, an excellent way to God, or even the best way to God.

But then, of course, you'd have to give up Jesus Christ who said, *No one comes to the Father except through me* (John 14:6). The offensive thing about Christianity is that there is no other way to be saved. The amazing thing about Christianity is that there is a way to be saved.

On 9/11, six hundred people died on the floors above where the plane collided with the South Tower of World Trade Center. Most of them were unaware of a stairway leading down to the street by which only eighteen people made their escape. Of those eighteen people, not one of them complained there was no other way to be saved. They were just glad there was a way.

Those who are offended by the exclusiveness of Christianity may also want to consider the inclusiveness of Jesus. *[W]hoever comes to me I will never drive away* (John 6:37), he said. This includes thieves, addicts, murderers, blasphemers, liars, gossips, and cheats. Jesus will take anyone who's willing to take him. Christianity is an exclusive religion, but Jesus Christ is an inclusive Savior.

Acts 4:13 *When they saw the courage of Peter and John and realized that they were unschooled, ordinary men, they were astonished and they took note that these men had been with Jesus.*

A couple fisherman empowered by the Spirit put the court to silence. *[T]here was nothing they could say* (Acts 4:14), recorded Luke. When is the last time seventy politicians had nothing to say? But this is precisely what Jesus Christ had taught his apostles. *[W]hen they arrest you, do not worry about what to say or how to say it. At that time you will be given what to say, for it will not be you speaking, but the Spirit of your Father speaking through you* (Matthew 10:19-20).

God was speaking to the leaders, through the apostles, and telling them how to be saved. They killed God's Son, but God was inviting them to repent. God also speaks to us through the apostles, and we too must decide how to respond. We can die in our sin, or repent and be saved.

Acts 4:16 *What are we going to do with these men? they asked. Everyone living in Jerusalem knows they have performed a notable sign, and we cannot deny it.*

The court had a problem. If they did nothing at all they'd appear weak. But if they overreacted they could make the situation worse. So they warned the apostles not to teach in Jesus' name, and let them go. An option they didn't consider was to admit they were wrong and believe in Jesus Christ. That would've cost them everything but gained them even more. Given the choice between time and eternity, it's surprising how many people choose time.

A rancher took his childhood friend to the middle of his property. He said, *Look north, south, east, and west.* With the excitement of a little child he said, *As far as the eye can see in any direction it's all mine.* Then he clutched his chest and fell over dead. *What good will it be for someone to gain the whole world, yet forfeit their soul?* (Matthew 16:26), said Jesus. The choice between time and eternity is obvious, but many make the wrong choice anyway.

Acts 4:33 *With great power the apostles continued to testify to the resurrection of the Lord Jesus.*

The main theme of the apostles' preaching was the resurrection of Jesus Christ. If Jesus rose from the dead, then everything he taught is true. Everything he taught about God, life, heaven, hell, salvation, and the Bible is certainly true if, in fact, he rose from the dead. We know that Jesus rose from the dead because we have eyewitness testimony in the gospels, but also because we can know him for ourselves.

Imagine a hero you wanted to meet, but wondered if he was alive. Your research said he was, but you wanted to know for sure. So you went to his house and saw that his name was still on the mailbox. Then you knocked on the door, and his housekeeper said he was in. Then you heard him talking on the phone in another room.

The name on the mailbox, the word of the housekeeper, and the voice in the other room were all good evidence that your hero was alive. But when he came to the door, and shook your hand, all the other evidence became less important. That's how it is with Jesus Christ.

When we come to faith in Christ, the Spirit of Christ comes into us, and we know him personally. Then we can say with Paul, *I know whom I have believed* (2 Timothy 1:12), not just *what* I have believed, but *whom* I have believed. Knowing Christ personally gives boldness to our Christian witness.

For Reflection and Review

- *Why were the apostles bold?*
- *Is Christianity inclusive or exclusive?*
- *How do we know Jesus is alive?*

Lesson 262

Acts 5:1 *Now a man named Ananias, together with his wife Sapphira, also sold a piece of property.*

A spontaneous movement of generosity occurred in the early church. People of wealth were selling their property to provide for the needs of the poor. Those who did so were appreciated, and recognized for their kindness.

Ananias and Sapphira were aware of this, and wanted to enhance their own reputations. So they also sold a piece of property and gave some of the money to the apostles. They wanted to appear more generous than they were, however, so they claimed to give all the proceeds, but kept back some for themselves. All things considered, this doesn't seem like a terrible crime.

Acts 5:3 *Then Peter said, Ananias, how is it that Satan has so filled your heart that you have lied to the Holy Spirit?*

Imagine making a generous donation only to be confronted by an apostle. Once again, Peter seemed to be overreacting. Everyone wants to appear better than they are, and no one has perfect motives. If the church had more people like Ananias and Sapphira, in fact, it could do even more for the poor. The church needs generous people, even if their motives aren't always perfect.

Acts 5:4 *What made you think of doing such a thing? You have not lied just to human beings but to God.*

Ananias and Sapphira were guilty of hypocrisy, but who isn't? Those who try to appear righteous are at least a little bit better than those who don't even try. The world would be better by far if everyone tried to appear righteous, even if they weren't as righteous as they appeared.

But Peter saw hypocrisy as a threat to the church, and Jesus reserved some of his strongest language for hypocrites. *He will cut him to pieces and assign him a place with the hypocrites, where there will be weeping and gnashing of teeth* (Matthew 24:51), he said.

Acts 5:5-6 *When Ananias heard this, he fell down and died. And great fear seized all who heard what had happened. Then some young men came forward, wrapped up his body, and carried him out and buried him.*

This was the first church funeral and, to be honest, it was a little bit spare. There was no liturgy, flowers, music, eulogy, or even a sermon—just a quick burial. Ananias died for the sin of hypocrisy, and this falls into the category of judgment miracles.

We generally think of miracles as something good, like healing the sick, or calming a storm. But the Bible contains a number of judgment miracles including the plagues on Egypt: locusts, frogs, boils and gnats (Exodus 7-11). Others were infected with leprosy (2 Chronicles 26:19), mauled by bears (2 Kings 2:24), eaten by worms (Acts 12:23), driven insane (Daniel 4:33), and struck blind (2 Kings 6:18). For Korah's sin of rebellion, the earth opened up and swallowed many (Numbers 16).

We'd be wrong to think this can only happen to unbelievers. Christians in the city of Corinth died for receiving the Lord's Supper without sufficient reverence (1 Corinthians 11:29-30). Judgment miracles teach us that if we can't be a good example, we might become a terrible warning.

Acts 5:7-8 *About three hours later his wife came in, not knowing what had happened. Peter asked her, Tell me, is this the price you and Ananias got for the land? Yes, she said, that is the price.*

This was Sapphira's opportunity to come clean. Her heart was probably pounding while her conscience pleaded with her to confess. All she had to do was tell the truth, but she was loyal to her husband, who probably led her in this sin of deception.

It's not unusual for a husband to drag his wife into sin, or vice versa. We all have a spiritual influence on those around us, and should be careful not to lead them in the wrong direction. *Things that cause people to stumble are bound to come, but woe to anyone through whom they come. It would be better for them to be thrown into the sea with a millstone tied around their neck than to cause one of these little ones to stumble* (Luke 17:1-2), said Jesus. It's a terrible thing to sin, but even worse to lead others astray.

Acts 5:9 *Peter said to her, How could you conspire to test the Spirit of the Lord?*

Children test their parents by pushing the limit, to see how much they can get away with, and Adults do the same with God. But patience isn't the same as permission, and one day brings the wrath a thousand days deserve. Sapphira fell over dead, and they took her out and buried her (Acts 5:10).

Acts 5:11 *Great fear seized the whole church.*

We might expect the church to rapidly decline, but the opposite occurred. It grew numerically and also in purity (Acts 5:13-14). Some may've left because they found out God is dangerous, but others joined and took God seriously.

The fear of God is a comfort to the righteous because it keeps us close to him. The more we fear God in a positive sense, the less we fear him in a negative sense. The more we fear God properly, the less we'll be afraid of him. The fear of God is not like being followed by the police when you're learning how to drive. It's more like having a parent in the car to help you get safely home.

For Reflection and Review

- *Have you ever been a hypocrite?*
- *Why didn't Sapphira confess her sin?*
- *What's the right way to fear God?*

Lesson 263

Acts 5:17 *Then the high priest and all his associates, who were members of the party of the Sadducees, were filled with jealousy.*

The religious leaders were used to being honored by the people, but the apostles were doing so many miracles (Acts 5:12), it was clear that God was with them. The loss of prestige made the religious leaders jealous, so they had the apostles arrested and thrown in jail.

But during the night an angel of the Lord opened the doors of the jail and brought them out. Go, stand in the temple courts, he said, and tell the people all about this new life (Acts 5:19-20).

The apostles had lives before they met Jesus: they worked, they got married, they had children—it was life. But after they met Jesus their lives were dramatically changed. Sometimes it was harder, but it was also much fuller. *I have come that they may have life, and have it to the full* (John 10:10), said Jesus.

A friend of mine went through cancer and was surprisingly changed by it. Before the cancer he said, *I was caught up in the normal things of life: family, friends, and career. But during the cancer I discovered that life is all about God—beginning, middle, and end.* This is the life the apostles preached through faith in Jesus Christ. Christianity is life with Jesus at the center.

Acts 5:31 *God exalted [Jesus] to his own right hand as Prince and Savior that he might bring Israel to repentance and forgive their sins.*

The apostles were brought before the court to give an account of their preaching. Along with the message of forgiveness, they insisted on repentance from both the nation and the court. They killed the Son of God, and you can't have a relationship with God if you're not sorry for killing his Son. All God wanted was for them to repent.

Imagine some godly parents who struggled with a son who didn't turn out very well. They raised him in a godly home, took him to church, and modeled the Christian life for him. But when he came of age he chose to live like the devil. Then he went to prison which made him even worse. After prison he wanted to move back with his parents, but without changing his lifestyle. Even though he was their son, their feelings were conflicted.

This is different than the prodigal son, who took his father's wealth, and wasted it in on wild living. It was fun for a while, but when the money ran out he found himself in squalor. Then, it says, *he came to his senses* (Luke 15:17). This is the beginning of repentance.

Repentance isn't feeling bad about yourself, although it may include that. It's not a promise of perfection, since we'll never be perfect in this life. It's not even a promise never to do something again, since that's the most broken promise on earth.

Repentance is agreeing with God against ourselves, and turning back in his direction. When the prodigal son *came to his senses* he went back with the following words: *Father, I have sinned against heaven and against you* (Luke 15:18). His father was so thrilled that he ran to him, embraced him, and kissed him (Luke 15:20). That's how God treats us whenever we come back to him through faith in Jesus Christ.

Acts 5:33 *When they heard this, they were furious and wanted to put them to death.*

The high court was clearly wrong, and knew that they were wrong, but wouldn't admit they were wrong. As a result they became so furious they wanted to kill the apostles. When people are wrong, and won't admit it, they often become angry.

I went out for coffee with a Christian gentleman who was guilty of sin, but wouldn't admit it. He had many explanations, none of which were valid, so I continued to press him. First I watched him become angry, then hostile, then so furious I thought he would strike me. I was glad we were in public or I might've been hurt. The high court was furious and wanted to hurt the apostles.

Acts 5:34 *But a Pharisee named Gamaliel, a teacher of the law, who was honored by all the people, stood up in the Sanhedrin.*

Gamaliel was a leading scholar, and the Apostle Paul's teacher before Paul was converted. Gamaliel spoke sense to the court, and was able to calm them down. They decided not to kill the apostles, but only to have them flogged, in order to teach them a lesson.

Flogging was more than a slap on the hand. *If the guilty person deserves to be beaten, the judge shall make them lie down and have them flogged in his presence with the number of lashes the crime deserves, but the judge must not impose more than forty lashes* (Deuteronomy 25:2-3), wrote Moses. So the Jews limited the number of lashes to thirty-nine, to allow for miscounting.

We should imagine the apostles before a professional flogger, who was expected to flog with all his might. They may've used rods or leather, but they usually gave two blows to the back, and one to the chest, repeated thirteen times. We'd expect the apostles to be discouraged but, surprisingly, they weren't.

Acts 5:41 *The apostles left the Sanhedrin, rejoicing because they had been counted worthy of suffering disgrace for the Name.*

While they were being flogged, the apostles may've been thinking of the flogging Jesus received, before his crucifixion. Unlike the Jews, the Romans weren't bound to thirty-nine lashes, but went as long as they liked. The whips were made of leather, embedded with chunks of lead and bone, designed to tear the flesh away. Many of those who were flogged by the Romans died as a result.

When the apostles thought of the flogging Jesus received, compared to the flogging they received, they were happy to share in the sufferings of Christ. Most of our sufferings are not related to the fact that we are Christians, but they can remind us of the suffering Jesus received on our behalf. If we allow our sufferings to remind us of his sufferings, they'll serve a good purpose and keep us close to him.

For Reflection and Review

- *Why is Christianity like a new life?*
- *Why does God demand repentance?*
- *Why did the apostles rejoice at being flogged?*

Lesson 264

Acts 6:1 *In those days when the number of disciples was increasing, the Hellenistic Jews among them complained against the Hebraic Jews because their widows were being overlooked in the daily distribution of food.*

The church was still essentially Jewish, but there were two distinct groups: Hellenistic and Hebraic. The Hellenistic Jews were born outside Judea, spoke Greek, and were more Greek in culture. The Hebraic Jews spoke Aramaic, and were more Jewish in culture.

As the church grew, tension developed between the two groups because one felt their widows were being slighted in the distribution of food. The church looked to the apostles for direction, but the apostles wouldn't get involved. *It would not be right for us to neglect the ministry of the word of God in order to wait on tables* (Acts 6:2), they said.

Instead, they instructed the church to choose seven men who were full of the Spirit and wisdom to oversee the food ministry. That way the apostles could continue giving their *attention to prayer and the ministry of the word* (Acts 6:4). This pleased everyone, and the word of God spread (Acts 8:7).

If the apostles turned from prayer and preaching, to other things, the word of God would not have spread. But if the food ministry wasn't working properly, the church might have divided. The solution was a division of labor between the various ministries. Every ministry in the church is important, but the most important ministry of the church is the prayer-empowered proclamation of God's word. That's what Jesus did, it's what the apostles did, and it's how the word of God spreads.

*****

Acts 6:8 *Now Stephen, a man full of God's grace and power, performed great wonders and signs among the people.*

Stephen was not an apostle, but God used him to preach the gospel, and confirmed his message with miracles. He was opposed by men who accused him of blasphemy, and was brought before the court to give a defense.

Acts 7:1 *Then the high priest asked Stephen, Are these charges true?*

Stephen responded with a lengthy speech about Israel's history that ended with this charge: *Was there ever a prophet your ancestors did not persecute? They even killed those who predicted the coming of the Righteous One. And now you have betrayed and murdered him* (Acts 7:52).

Acts 7:54-60 *When the members of the Sanhedrin heard this, they were furious and gnashed their teeth at him. But Stephen, full of the Holy Spirit, looked up to heaven and saw the glory of God, and Jesus standing at the right hand of God.*

Look, he said, I see heaven open and the Son of Man standing at the right hand of God. At this they covered their ears and, yelling at the top of their voices, they all rushed at him, dragged him out of the city and began to stone him.

Meanwhile, the witnesses laid their coats at the feet of a young man named Saul. While they were stoning him, Stephen prayed, Lord Jesus, receive my spirit. Then he fell on his knees and cried out, Lord, do not hold this sin against them. When he had said this, he fell asleep.

Stephen has the noble distinction of being the first Christian martyr. He refused to compromise his message, and prayed that God would pardon those who killed him. An important beneficiary of that prayer was Rabbi Saul, who later became the Apostle Paul. Praying for those who harm us may lead to their conversion.

Acts 8:1 *On that day a great persecution broke out against the church in Jerusalem, and all except the apostles were scattered throughout Judea and Samaria.*

The apostolic church enjoyed about a year of favor (Acts 2:46) after it first began. But when Stephen was martyred (Acts 7:54-60), a persecution broke out, and most believers had to run for their lives. *Those who had been scattered preached the word wherever they went* (Acts 8:4), wrote Luke. They may've thought the end of the world was near, so their words were especially urgent. And since Christ is the only way to be saved (John 14:6), they preached this message wherever they went.

Persecution isn't to be desired, and has destroyed the church in many places. But God can also use persecution to purify his church and advance the gospel. It's even been said that, *The blood of the martyrs is the seed of the church* (Tertullian). This was certainly true in the case of Stephen.

*****

Acts 8:5 *Philip went down to a city in Samaria and proclaimed the Messiah there.*

Like the apostles, Philip was able to do miracles to authenticate his message. Crowds paid attention, and many who were paralyzed found healing. This caught the attention of Simon, a man who practiced sorcery, and was known as the *Great Power of God* (Acts 8:10). He was so amazed by Philip's miracles that he also believed and was baptized (Acts 8:13).

When the apostles heard about all that was happening, they sent Peter and John to investigate. When they arrived, they prayed for the new believers to receive the Holy Spirit. The text is not explicit but, elsewhere, this was accompanied by praise, prophecy, and speaking in tongues (Acts 2:4, 10:46, 19:6). Simon was so impressed that he offered Peter and John money: *Give me also this ability so that everyone on whom I lay my hands may receive the Holy Spirit* (Acts 8:19), he said.

May your money perish with you, because you thought you could buy the gift of God with money! You have no part or share in this ministry, because your heart is not right before God. Repent of this wickedness and pray to the Lord in the hope that he may forgive you for having such a thought in your heart. For I see that you are full of bitterness and captive to sin (Acts 8:20-23), said Peter.

This makes us wonder if Simon was truly converted, even though he was baptized. Many who think they are Christians are only deceiving themselves (Matthew 7:21-23). They're like Judas Iscariot who appeared to believe, but didn't truly believe (John 6:64). Genuine faith and counterfeit faith can be very similar, so we shouldn't make assumptions. *Examine yourselves to see whether you are in the faith* (2 Corinthians 13:5), wrote Paul.

Acts 8:26 *Now an angel of the Lord said to Philip, Go south to the road—the desert road—that goes down from Jerusalem to Gaza.*

As Philip went, he encountered a high ranking official from Ethiopia, sitting in his chariot, reading the Book of Isaiah. *Do you understand what you are reading? Philip asked. How can I, he said, unless someone explains it to me? So he invited Philip to come up and sit with him* (Acts 8:30-31).

The man just happened to be reading a passage that describes the death of Jesus Christ. *He was led like a sheep to the slaughter, and as a lamb before its shearer is silent, so he did not open his mouth. In his humiliation he was deprived of justice. Who can speak of his descendants? For his life was taken from the earth* (Acts 8:31-33, Isaiah 53:7-8). Philip explained that this was about Jesus Christ and, at once, the man believed and was baptized (Acts 8:38).

Notice that God was at work in the man's life before Philip arrived. He'd been to Jerusalem, where he probably bought the scroll, and happened to be reading of Christ when Philip arrived. Philip explained the gospel, God gave him faith to believe (Ephesians 2:8), and he was promptly baptized. God is active in the work of evangelism, but we also play a vital role, as we share what Christ has done for us.

For Reflection and Review

- *How did persecution help advance the gospel?*
- *What can we learn from Simon about conversion?*
- *What can we learn from Philip about evangelism?*

Lesson 265

Acts 9:1 *Meanwhile, Saul was still breathing out murderous threats against the Lord's disciples.*

This is the account of the most famous conversion in the history of the church. It's how Rabbi Saul became the Apostle Paul. Paul saw Christianity as a radical threat to Judaism, and thought the best way for him to serve God was by opposing Christianity. His murderous threats were more than talk, since he was present at the stoning of Stephen (Acts 7:58).

Acts 9:3 *As he neared Damascus on his journey, suddenly a light from heaven flashed around him.*

The light was *brighter than the sun* (Acts 26:13) and caused Paul to go temporarily blind. *I have appeared to you to appoint you as a servant and as a witness of what you have seen and will see of me* (Acts 26:16), said Jesus.

Notice the sovereignty of Christ in Paul's conversion. No one else persuaded him, preached to him, or prayed with him. Jesus simply appeared to Paul, and converted him, as though Paul had little to say in the matter. This should keep us from thinking that Jesus lacks the power to convert whomever he wants, whenever he wants, wherever he wants, however he wants.

The normal way for Christ to convert someone is through hearing the gospel. *Faith comes from hearing the message* (Romans 10:17), wrote Paul. Most people are listening to a sermon, as they often have before. But during that particular sermon Jesus gives them faith to believe (Ephesians 2:8-9). Saul is an exception that shows Jesus can convert anyone, anywhere, anyway he pleases. We should cooperate with Christ by sharing the gospel, but he's the one who converts.

Acts 9:4 *He fell to the ground and heard a voice say to him, Saul, Saul, why do you persecute me?*

Jesus didn't say, *why do you persecute my people*, but *why do you persecute me?* Any assault on a believer is an assault on Jesus Christ. The church is the body of Christ (Colossians 1:18), so whatever happens to the church, happens to Christ. He not only knows what we're going through, but feels what we're going through. Whenever we're treated badly, or treat other believers badly, Jesus takes it personally.

Acts 9:7 *The men traveling with Saul stood there speechless; they heard the sound but did not see anyone.*

Jesus revealed himself to Paul, but not to those around him. Paul was having a life-changing encounter with Christ, but those around him were oblivious to what was happening. If Jesus revealed himself to Paul, why not to the others?

Paul later explained that *God has mercy on whom he wants to have mercy, and he hardens whom he wants to harden* (Romans 9:18). We may not like this explanation, or fully understand it, but it's the one Paul provided, and it agrees his conversion.

Likewise, whenever a person comes to faith in Jesus Christ, there are often others nearby who don't understand. The conversion might be explained as getting religion, joining a cult, or any number of things. *[T]he message of the cross is foolishness to those who are perishing, but to us who are being saved it is the power of God* (1 Corinthians 1:18), wrote Paul.

Years later Paul testified before a government official named Festus. *You are out of your mind, Paul! he shouted. Your great learning is driving you insane. I am not insane, most excellent Festus, Paul replied. What I am saying is true and reasonable* (Acts 26:24-25). This type of exchange has been repeated countless times, as Christians try to explain their faith to an unbelieving world.

Acts 9:9 *For three days he was blind, and did not eat or drink anything.*

Paul was so shaken by his encounter with Christ that he couldn't eat or drink, or chose not to. For three full days he sat bewildered trying to understand what happened to him. He was blinded by a light, but his spiritual eyes were opened. If you asked him which was more important, physical sight or spiritual sight, he would've said spiritual sight by far.

Acts 9:10-12 *In Damascus there was a disciple named Ananias. The Lord called to him in a vision, Ananias! . . . Go to the house of Judas on Straight Street and ask for a man from Tarsus named Saul, for he is praying. In a vision he has seen a man named Ananias come and place his hands on him to restore his sight.*

About the same time Ananias was having a vision about going to pray for Paul, Paul was having a vision about Ananias coming to pray for him. This is the only double-vision in the Bible, and would've assured Paul that he wasn't losing his mind. Insane people may have visions, but they seldom have the same vision as someone else. This would verify Paul's experience.

Acts 9:15 *This man is my chosen instrument to proclaim my name.*

Paul was uniquely chosen by Jesus Christ to spread the gospel. Even today, we can hardly imagine Christianity apart from Paul, and the letters he wrote. Because of his service to Christ, Paul became one of the most influential people in history.

Paul not only carried the gospel, but also proves the gospel, since you can't explain Paul apart from the gospel. Paul was a rising rabbi, with a promising career, until he was converted. Then he suffered as a missionary, the rest of his life, until he was put to death. Why would he do that if the gospel wasn't true? There's no explanation for Paul apart from Jesus Christ. He was God's *chosen instrument* to spread the gospel, and does so to this day.

Acts 9:16 *I will show him how much he must suffer for my name.*

The man who inflicted so much suffering on the church, would now begin to suffer for the church he once afflicted. *[I have] been in prison more frequently, been flogged more severely, and been exposed to death again and again. Five times I received from the Jews the forty lashes minus one. Three times I was beaten with rods, once I was pelted with stones, three times I was shipwrecked, I spent a night and a day in the open sea, I have been constantly on the move. . . . I have labored and toiled and have often gone without sleep; I have known hunger and thirst and have often gone without food* (2 Corinthians 11:23-27), he wrote.

It was a difficult life for Paul, but he rarely complained, because he saw his misery in light of eternal glory. *For our light and momentary troubles are achieving for us an eternal glory that far outweighs them all* (2 Corinthians 4:17), he wrote.

If this life is all there is, then every hardship is a disaster, and death is the ultimate tragedy. But if we'll live forever, in the best of all possible worlds, then every step brings us closer to eternal glory. This was the secret of Paul's endurance, and should be ours as well.

Acts 9:17 *Then Ananias went to the house and entered it. Placing his hands on Saul, he said, Brother Saul, the Lord—Jesus, who appeared to you on the road as you were coming here—has sent me so that you may see again and be filled with the Holy Spirit.*

Paul was happy to receive his sight, and to be filled with the Spirit. The Spirit became so important to Paul that he's mentioned over one hundred times in his thirteen letters. As Paul proclaimed the gospel, he discovered that everyone who believes in Christ receives the Holy Spirit (Ephesians 1:13).

Paul described the Spirit as *a deposit, guaranteeing what is to come* (2 Corinthians 5:5). If you're selling your car and someone gives you a deposit, that guarantees they'll return with the rest. The indwelling Spirit is Christ's deposit, guaranteeing he'll return with the rest of our salvation. We don't have to take his word for it: the Spirit is a *guarantee* of what's to come.

For Reflection and Review

- *Why didn't Jesus save Paul's companions?*
- *How does Paul prove the gospel?*
- *How does the Spirit guarantee what's to come?*

Lesson 266

Acts 10:1 *At Caesarea there was a man named Cornelius, a centurion in what was known as the Italian Regiment.*

Cornelius was a high-ranking soldier, who worshipped the God of the Bible, but was neither Jewish nor Christian. One afternoon he had a vision of an angel telling him to send for Peter, who was staying in the city of Joppa, about thirty miles away. So he sent some men to get him.

Acts 10:9 *About noon the following day as they were on their journey and approaching the city, Peter went up on the roof to pray.*

Peter was staying at the home of Simon the tanner (Acts 10:6) and went up on his flat roof porch to pray. There he fell into a trance and *saw heaven opened and something like a large sheet being let down to earth by its four corners. It contained all kinds of four-footed animals, as well as reptiles and birds.*

Then a voice told him, Get up, Peter. Kill and eat. Surely not, Lord! Peter replied. I have never eaten anything impure or unclean. The voice spoke to him a second time, Do not call anything impure that God has made clean. This happened three times, and immediately the sheet was taken back to heaven (Acts 10:11-16).

Some of the creatures in the sheet were forbidden to eat in the Old Testament (Leviticus 11). *You must distinguish between the unclean and the clean, between living creatures that may be eaten and those that may not be eaten* (Leviticus 11:47), wrote Moses. Peter may've thought his faith was being tested so, at first, he resisted. But shortly after the vision, the men from Cornelius arrived, and the Spirit told Peter to go with them. He did so, along with some other believers.

When he arrived at the home of Cornelius, Peter found a large gathering of people. He said to them: *You are well aware that it is against our law for a Jew to associate with or visit a Gentile. But God has shown me that I should not call anyone impure or unclean* (Acts 10:28). Peter's vision convinced him the food laws were no longer binding, and that Gentiles were not to be called unclean. This was a departure from the Old Testament which had become *obsolete* (Hebrews 8:13) because it was replaced by the new covenant under Jesus Christ (Jeremiah 31:31, Luke 22:20).

Acts 10:34 *Then Peter began to speak.*

Peter rehearsed the life, death, and resurrection of Christ for the forgiveness of our sins. While he was speaking, the Spirit came on those who were listening, and they spoke in tongues. Then they were baptized in the name of Jesus Christ. This was similar to when the Spirit came on the Jews on the day of Pentecost. They also spoke in tongues, Peter preached, and many were baptized (Acts 2:1-41). God used Peter to reach the Jews, and then to reach the Gentiles.

An important point of this story is that God was taking the initiative to get his gospel out. Peter didn't plan the day of Pentecost—God did. And Peter didn't plan to take the gospel to the Gentiles—God did. Throughout the book of Acts, it's God who takes the initiative. He uses people, of course, but he's the primary worker.

The book of Acts records some extraordinary ways God spread his word in the first few decades of the church. He continues to spread his word in extraordinary ways, but also has an ordinary way: through the faithful ministry of local churches.

It's through the ordinary ministry of teaching and preaching that most people come to faith, and have their faith nurtured throughout their lives. We should thank God for his extraordinary ways of working, but never despise his ordinary way, since that's how he normally cares for us.

*****

Acts 12:1 *It was about this time that King Herod arrested some who belonged to the church, intending to persecute them.*

King Herod Agrippa the First reigned for a period of seven years over Palestine, from AD 37 to AD 44. He was a powerful king who could administer the death sentence without a trial. He was the grandson of Herod the Great who slaughtered the babies of Bethlehem (Matthew 2:13-18). He was also related to Herod Antipas who beheaded John the Baptist. Wickedness and righteousness often run in families, because children learn from their parents. Herod is a negative example, but there are good examples.

Jonathan Edwards was an American preacher from the seventeen hundreds who was a model of godliness. His descendants include thirteen college presidents, sixty-five professors, one hundred lawyers, one hundred missionaries, thirty judges, sixty-six physicians, three senators, three governors, and one vice-president of the United States. *Start children off on the way they should go, and even when they are old they will not turn from it* (Proverbs 22:6), says Proverbs.

Acts 12:2 *[Herod] had James, the brother of John, put to death with the sword.*

James was the brother of the Apostle John, and the first apostle to be martyred. This was a serious development for at least two reasons: First, Herod may've planned to stop Christianity by killing all the apostles. Some would be martyred eventually, but if they had all died before the New Testament was written, the results would've been disastrous. Second, persecution had previously come from within Judaism, but was now coming from the Roman government. Whenever a government becomes involved in persecution, the devastation can be extreme.

At certain times and places Christians have been declared enemies of the state, and forced to sign documents renouncing their faith. Their homes have been confiscated, they've been thrown into prison, brutally tortured, and killed. This is why we should *[pray] for kings and all those in authority,* that *we may live peaceful and quiet lives* (1 Timothy 2:2), wrote Paul. The devil hates the church and will turn the world against it whenever he can.

Acts 12:3 *When [Herod] saw that this met with approval among the Jews, he proceeded to seize Peter also.*

Peter was placed in a high security prison and the church began to pray for him (Acts 12:4-5). *Peter was sleeping between two soldiers, bound with two chains, and sentries stood guard at the entrance* (Acts 12:6). He might be executed in the morning, but he slept like a baby that night. *In peace I will lie down and sleep, for you alone, Lord, make me dwell in safety* (Psalm 4:8), wrote David. Peter knew his life wasn't in the hands of an earthly tyrant, but in the hands of his heavenly king.

This conviction is also stated in the first question of the Heidelberg catechism. *What is your only comfort in life and in death?* Answer: *That I am not my own, but belong body and soul, in life and in death, to my faithful Savior Jesus Christ. He has fully paid for all my sins with his precious blood, and has set me free from the tyranny of the devil. He also watches over me in such a way that not a hair can fall from my head without the will of my Father in heaven: in fact, all things must work together for my salvation.*

Acts 12:7 *Suddenly an angel of the Lord appeared and a light shone in the cell. He struck Peter on the side and woke him up. Quick, get up! he said, and the chains fell off Peter's wrists.*

Peter followed the angel out of prison, past two sets of guards, and through an iron gate which opened by itself (Acts 12:10). *Are not all angels ministering spirits sent to serve those who will inherit salvation?* (Hebrews 1:14), says Hebrews. The Bible doesn't teach that all God's people have a personal angel, but the idea isn't ruled out (Acts 12:14, Matthew 18:10). The ministry of angels is real, and should be a comfort to all who believe.

For Reflection and Review

- *Why is the ordinary work of faithful churches important?*
- *Why should we pray for political leaders?*
- *Why was Peter able to sleep peacefully while he was in danger?*

Lesson 267

Acts 12:12 *[Peter] went to the house of Mary the mother of John, also called Mark, where many people had gathered and were praying.*

When Peter knocked on the door, a servant named Rhoda answered, and was so overjoyed that she ran back and exclaimed, *Peter is at the door!* (Acts 12:14). They thought she was *out of her mind* (Acts 12:15), but Peter continued knocking until they let him in. When they saw him, *they were astonished* (Acts 12:16).

The church was praying for Peter but had little expectation their prayers would be answered so dramatically. When our prayers are a blend of faith and unbelief we can say to God, *I do believe; help me overcome my unbelief!* (Mark 9:24). God is so gracious that he even answers prayers that are mingled with doubt.

Acts 12:17 *Peter motioned with his hand for them to be quiet and described how the Lord had brought him out of prison.*

The prayer meeting became a share meeting as Peter shared how God had answered their prayers. The more time we spend in prayer, the more we'll have to share. But while Peter was delivered from Herod's sword, James was not (Acts 12:2). It's hard to know why, but the Psalmist provides some help. *[A]ll the days ordained for me were written in your book before one of them came to be* (Psalm 139:16). God ordains the day of our birth, the day of our death, and every day in-between.

Why some people live to old age, and others die in youth, is a mystery. But we know that God is in control, and never makes a mistake. We've *been predestined according to the plan of him who works out everything in conformity with the purpose of his will* (Ephesians 1:11), wrote Paul. God wants us to rest in his goodness, wisdom, and sovereign control over all things.

Acts 12:18 *In the morning, there was no small commotion among the soldiers as to what had become of Peter.*

The penalty for allowing a prisoner to escape was whatever the prisoner's penalty would be. Since Peter would've likely been killed, the guards were forced to pay with their lives (Acts 12:19). The previous night they may've felt sorry for Peter, but now they felt sorry for themselves. The greatest joy is to be a Christian, and the greatest sorrow is to be anything else.

*****

Acts 12:21 *On the appointed day Herod, wearing his royal robes, sat on his throne and delivered a public address.*

The historian Josephus reports that Herod was fifty-four years old at this time, and wore a silver robe designed to reflect the sun. The people shouted: *This is the voice of a god, not of a man* (Acts 12:22). But their words were only flattery since they depended on the king for their food (Acts 12:20). Herod probably knew this, but was willing to receive their praise as though he were a god.

The wicked aren't content to minimize God, but will deify themselves if possible. Like Herod, the antichrist *will oppose and will exalt himself over everything that is called God or is worshiped, so that he sets himself up in God's temple, proclaiming himself to be God* (2 Thessalonians 2:4). The pattern of the wicked seems to be this: first oppose God, then eliminate god, then deify themselves.

Acts 12:23 *Immediately, because Herod did not give praise to God, an angel of the Lord struck him down, and he was eaten by worms and died.*

What Herod considered his finest hour was the beginning of his end. Josephus reports that Herod lingered five days before dying, and that his misery was extreme. Intestinal ringworms grow between ten and sixteen inches long, and eat their victims alive from the inside out. During this time, the body violently expels some of the worms from both ends.

When someone dies a horrible and lingering death, we comfort ourselves with the idea that at least their suffering is over. But Jesus described hell as a place where *the worms that eat them do not die* (Mark 9:48). If God allows hell on earth, there's no reason to think there won't be hell in the age to come. Jesus didn't die on a cross to save us from nothing, but from the everlasting torment we all deserve.

*****

Acts 13:7 *The proconsul, an intelligent man, sent for Barnabas and Saul because he wanted to hear the word of God.*

Around AD 48, about fourteen years after his conversion, Paul began his life's work as a missionary. With Barnabas and Mark, he went to the island of Cyprus. There he was invited to share the gospel with a high ranking official named Sergius Paulus. Sergius was a religious man who employed a Jewish sorcerer known as Elymas. Sorcery was forbidden by God (Deuteronomy 18:10), but some Jews practiced a demonic blend of Judaism and paganism.

As Paul explained the gospel to Sergius, Elymas tried to convince him it wasn't true. Paul became so angry he said to Elymas: *You are a child of the devil and an enemy of everything that is right! You are full of all kinds of deceit and trickery. Will you never stop perverting the right ways of the Lord? Now the hand of the Lord is against you. You are going to be blind for a time, not even able to see the light of the sun* (Acts 13:10-11). At that very moment Elymas went blind, and Sergius believed in Jesus Christ.

Whenever people hear the gospel, there are often others nearby who want to convince them it isn't true. They are agents of the devil who are spiritually blind. Elymas went blind for a while, but whoever rejects the gospel will live in darkness forever.

For Reflection and Review

- *Why did God save Peter but not James?*
- *What can we learn from Herod*
- *What kind of person was Elymas?*

Lesson 268

Acts 14:8 *In Lystra there sat a man who was lame. He had been that way from birth and had never walked.*

The man's situation was bleak, but as he heard Paul preach he began to think that he might be healed. Then Paul looked at him and said, *Stand up on your feet!* (Acts 14:10). At once the man got up and began to walk. Instead of believing Paul's message, however, the people concluded that Paul and Barnabas were gods. Bulls were brought, and Paul and Barnabas barely restrained the people from offering them a sacrifice.

This may seem illogical, but people from different religions often find the gospel difficult to grasp. I was raised with biblically clear ideas about God and the devil, heaven and hell, sin and salvation, Christ and forgiveness. So when the gospel was rightly explained to me, I understood it easily. But those who are raised outside the faith often find the gospel hard to understand and require extra patience.

Acts 14:19 *Then some Jews came from Antioch and Iconium and won the crowd over.*

Paul's opponents traveled for several days, over a hundred miles, in order to cause him trouble. Paul understood their motivation since he too had traveled to persecute the church (Acts 9:1-2). How happy he must've been to be on the right side of Christ, even if it meant hostile opposition.

The people of Lystra wanted to worship Paul, but then they turned against him. Christians can also be fickle by giving their leaders semi-divine status, and then rejecting them when they turn out to be merely human. True Christianity exalts Christ alone, and isn't surprised by the humanness of its leaders.

Acts 14:19b *They stoned Paul and dragged him outside the city, thinking he was dead.*

Paul's few disciples gathered around to grieve when, suddenly, he opened his eyes and got up. We're not told if this was a miracle, or if Paul was only unconscious. Either way, he was willing to take his knocks and keep going for Christ. *We must go through many hardships to enter the kingdom of God* (Acts 14:22), he said.

Paul may've been surprised that healing a man who was lame from birth didn't lead to more conversions. What starts big doesn't always end big, and what starts small doesn't always stay small. What mattered to Paul was that a few believed, and a little church was born.

*****

Acts 15:1 *Certain people came down from Judea to Antioch and were teaching the believers: Unless you are circumcised, according to the custom taught by Moses, you cannot be saved.*

One of the most serious threats to the early church was the false idea that people had to keep the Old Testament laws to be accepted by God. The early church had many Jews with a high regard for their Scriptures, so it's not surprising this idea emerged. The discussion was important because it concerned the way of salvation. One view would base salvation on faith in Christ alone (Ephesians 2:8-9), the other would base salvation on faith in Christ plus obedience to the law of Moses. To help answer the question, a conference was held in Jerusalem around AD 48.

Acts 15:5 *Then some of the believers who belonged to the party of the Pharisees stood up and said, The Gentiles must be circumcised and required to keep the law of Moses.*

These people considered the Jewish religion to be the foundation of the church. To become a Christian, therefore, people first had to become Jewish. Paul would insist that Christ alone is the foundation of the church. *For no one can lay any foundation other than the one already laid, which is Jesus Christ* (1 Corinthians 3:11), he wrote.

Acts 15:7-8 *After much discussion, Peter got up and addressed them: Brothers, you know that some time ago God made a choice among you that the Gentiles might hear from my lips the message of the gospel and believe. God, who knows the heart, showed that he accepted them by giving the Holy Spirit to them, just as he did to us.*

Peter preached to the Jews (Acts 2) as well as to the Gentiles (Acts 8). In both cases, God showed his acceptance by giving them the Spirit. The indwelling Spirit was also the sign of acceptance for Paul. *And if anyone does not have the Spirit of Christ, they do not belong to Christ* (Romans 8:9), he wrote. Whoever has the Spirit has Christ; whoever does not have the Spirit does not have Christ.

Acts 15:12-13 *The whole assembly became silent as they listened to Barnabas and Paul telling about the signs and wonders God had done among the Gentiles through them. When they finished, James spoke up.*

James was the half brother of Jesus (Matthew 13:55), and an influential member of the church in Jerusalem. He argued from Scripture that Gentiles were an important part of God's plan. *It is my judgment, therefore, that we should not make it difficult for the Gentiles who are turning to God. Instead we should write to them, telling them to abstain from food polluted by idols, from sexual immorality, from the meat of strangled animals and from blood* (Acts 15:19-20).

The purpose of these stipulations wasn't for salvation, but to make it easier for Jewish and Gentile believers to have fellowship together. Paul would later insist that Christian living requires sexual purity (1 Corinthians 6:18-20), but the concern of the council was to keep the gospel clear (John 3:16), and make it easier for Jewish and Gentile Christians to worship and eat together.

The council helped preserve the gospel, and unify the church. The leaders didn't make up their minds independently, but gathered for discussion and debate, as they reasoned from the Scriptures. This doesn't guarantee a proper outcome, but is a pattern the church has followed, often with good results.

For Reflection and Review

- *Why do people misunderstand the gospel?*
- *Do all Christians have the Holy Spirit?*
- *How should the church determine what is true?*

Lesson 269

Acts 16:12 *[W]e traveled to Philippi, a Roman colony and the leading city of that district.*

There was no synagogue there so Paul and his companions went to the river where they met some women who had gathered for prayer. Paul explained the gospel and one of them believed. She was promptly baptized (along with her household) and invited Paul and his coworkers to stay at her home. This is how the church in Philippi began.

The woman's name was Lydia, and she was apparently wealthy. As Paul explained the gospel, *The Lord opened her heart to respond to Paul's message* (Acts 16:14). It's not said that she opened her own heart, or that Paul opened her heart, but that God opened her heart. Others were present, but we're not told that God opened their hearts, only Lydia's heart.

The human heart is so perverse that, apart from God, it won't receive the gospel. *The heart is deceitful above all things and beyond cure* (Jeremiah 17:9), wrote Jeremiah. *This is why I told you that no one can come to me unless the Father has enabled them* (John 6:65), said Jesus. *It does not, therefore, depend on human desire or effort, but on God's mercy* (Romans 9:16), wrote Paul. God alone receives the credit for opening hearts to the gospel.

*****

Acts 16:16-17 *Once when we were going to the place of prayer, we were met by a female slave who had a spirit by* *which she predicted the future. . . . She followed Paul and the rest of us, shouting, These men are servants of the Most High God, who are telling you the way to be saved.*

This seems like good publicity, but Paul became annoyed. *[H]e turned around and said to the spirit, In the name of Jesus Christ I command you to come out of her!* (Acts 16:18). At once the spirit departed, but her owners were upset because she was no longer able to make them money by predicting the future. From this we learn that those who make money by predicting the future may be assisted by demons. But only God knows the future perfectly, and only God is to be trusted.

Acts 16:19 *When her owners realized that their hope of making money was gone, they seized Paul and Silas and dragged them into the marketplace to face the authorities.*

Without due process, Paul and Silas were stripped of their clothes and beaten with rods. They weren't given a trial, or even allowed to defend themselves. The beating was meant to be a deterrent, so we can only imagine the pain that was inflicted.

Acts 16:23 *After they had been severely flogged, they were thrown into prison, and the jailer was commanded to guard them carefully.*

The jailer put Paul and Silas in the inner cell, and fastened their feet in the stocks. This would make it hard for them to move, and would increase their pain substantially. We might expect Paul and Silas to despair but, surprisingly, they sang hymns to God (Acts 16:25).

Blessed are you when people insult you, persecute you and falsely say all kinds of evil against you because of me. Rejoice and be glad, because great is your reward in heaven (Matthew 5:11-12), said Jesus. Christianity offers so much hope that we can rejoice even in the worst of times.

Acts 16:26 *Suddenly there was such a violent earthquake that the foundations of the prison were shaken. At once all the prison doors flew open, and everyone's chains came loose.*

The punishment for losing prisoners was death, so when the jailer saw the prison doors were open, he drew his sword to kill himself. *Don't harm yourself! We are all here!* (Acts 16:28), said Paul. Trembling, he fell before Paul and Silas saying, *Sirs, what must I do to be saved?* (Acts 16:30).

We don't know why he asked this question, but perhaps he heard the woman shouting, *These men are servants of the Most High God, who are telling you the way to be saved.* Or perhaps he knew he wasn't right with God. Or perhaps he heard Paul and Silas singing about sin and salvation. Regardless, he knew the right question: *what must I do to be saved?*

Acts 16:31 *Believe in the Lord Jesus, and you will be saved.*

This is truly amazing. He didn't have to go to church, read the Bible, or pass an exam. The only requirement Paul set forth was believing in Jesus Christ. The gospel has implications for how we live, of course, but we're saved the moment we first believe.

Ministers ought to be careful about what they add to the gospel. We're saved by believing in Jesus Christ, and we stay saved by believing in Jesus Christ. *I write these things to you who believe in the name of the Son of God so that you may know that you have eternal life* (1 John 5:13), wrote John.

Acts 16:34 *The jailer brought them into his house and set a meal before them; he was filled with joy because he had come to believe in God.*

The jailer was ready to kill himself, but then he was filled with joy. He received forgiveness, eternal life, the Holy Spirit, adoption into God's family (Romans 8:15), and a wonderful inheritance (Romans 8:17). This is enough to make us happy the rest of our lives. *Rejoice in the Lord always. I will say it again: Rejoice!* (Philippians 4:4), wrote Paul.

For Reflection and Review

- *Why must God open our hearts to believe the gospel?*

- *Why did Paul and Silas sing in prison?*
- *Why was the jailer filled with joy?*

Lesson 270

Acts 17:16 *While Paul was waiting for them in Athens, he was greatly distressed to see that the city was full of idols.*

Paul arrived in Athens, ahead of Silas and Timothy, and was immediately struck by the city's sin of idolatry. *You shall not make for yourself an image in the form of anything in heaven above or on the earth beneath or in the waters below* (Exodus 20:4), said God.

Athens was home to Socrates, Plato, and Aristotle many years before. The city was past its philosophical prime, but considered itself to be a source of enlightenment. Their idolatry showed they were in darkness, however, and needed to be enlightened themselves. The Athenians would be a difficult audience, but Paul was there to bring them the gospel.

Acts 17:18 *A group of Epicurean and Stoic philosophers began to debate with him. Some of them asked, What is this babbler trying to say?*

Philosophy and Christianity are both concerned with ultimate truth. Philosophy is people seeking truth from below; Christianity is God revealing truth from above. Philosophical arguments come and go, *but the word of our God endures forever* (Isaiah 40:8), wrote Isaiah.

Acts 17:22-23 *Paul then stood up in the meeting of the Areopagus and said: People of Athens! I see that in every way you are very religious. For as I walked around and looked carefully at your objects of worship, I even found an altar with this inscription: to an unknown god. So you are ignorant of the very thing you worship—and this is what I am going to proclaim to you.*

The Athenians prided themselves on knowledge, but admitted their knowledge had limits. Their altar to *an unknown god* was an admission of their spiritual ignorance which Paul would use to proclaim the truth of Christ to them. Paul was alert to the culture of Athens and, starting where they were, sought to bring them to Christ. *I have become all things to all people so that by all possible means I might save some* (1 Corinthians 9:22), he said. In the case of Athens, this meant engaging them philosophically.

In order to reach a culture, a church will need to engage the culture, but without compromising biblical truth. This isn't easy, and those who try are often misunderstood. Even Jesus was accused of being *a glutton and a drunkard, a friend of tax collectors and sinners* (Matthew 11:19). *For the Son of Man came to seek and to save the lost* (Luke 19:10), he said.

Acts 17:24 *The God who made the world and everything in it is the Lord of heaven and earth.*

To help the Athenians understand God, Paul echoed the first verse of the Bible: *In the beginning God created the heavens and the earth* (Genesis 1:1). The Bible never attempts to prove the existence of God, but simply proclaims the obvious. He's the one who made all the stuff. This is why a group has never been found without a word for the Creator.

A missionary visited a tribe that hadn't heard the gospel, but had a clear idea of the God who made the world. The missionary asked how they knew about the Creator, and they looked at him like he was confused. *No rain, no mushrooms; no God, no world,* they said. This is the logic of the Bible, and the best explanation for all that exists.

Acts 17:25 *[H]e is not served by human hands, as if he needed anything. Rather, he himself gives everyone life and breath and everything else.*

In polytheism the gods want people to provide for them, but Paul argued that God is the one who provides for us—not only food, but *life and breath and everything else.*

When I was a boy I fell out of a tree and lost my wind. I couldn't inhale no matter how hard I tried. Something I'd done since I was born, I was no longer able to do. I lay on the ground not knowing if I would live or die when, suddenly, my breath returned. I had a fresh awareness that God is the giver of *life and breath and everything else*. Therefore, *Let everything that has breath praise the Lord* (Psalm 150:6), wrote the Psalmist.

Acts 17:27-28 *[H]e is not far from any one of us. For in him we live and move and have our being.*

Paul wanted the Athenians to know that God is not so far away that he can't be found, but couldn't be any closer. God is closer to us than we are to ourselves, and there's nowhere that he is not. *Do not I fill heaven and earth? declares the Lord* (Jeremiah 23:24).

A person who doesn't believe in God is like a fish that doesn't believe in water. The problem isn't the absence of water, but that water is all the fish has ever known. But once we understand how close God is, we can *reach out for him and find him* (Acts 17:27), said Paul. *For in him we live and move and have our being.*

Acts 17:29-30 *[W]e should not think that the divine being is like gold or silver or stone—an image made by human design and skill. In the past God overlooked such ignorance, but now he commands all people everywhere to repent.*

Before the coming of Christ, God dealt primarily with the nation of Israel. But since the coming of Christ, *he commands all people everywhere to repent*. This is not a suggestion, but an order from God, because of his love for us.

When a parent sees their child running into traffic, they don't suggest the child stop, turn around, and come back. Because the parent loves the child, they command obedience to save the child's life. The command to repent is one of most common in Scripture, and is Gods' way of saying, *Don't hurt yourself*. As Jesus warned, *unless you repent, you too will all perish* (Luke 13:3).

Acts 17:31 *For he has set a day when he will judge the world with justice by the man he has appointed. He has given proof of this to everyone by raising him from the dead.*

God has given proof of Christianity by raising Jesus from the dead. If Jesus rose from the dead, then everything he taught is true. The apostles were in a position to know if Jesus rose from the dead or not, and wouldn't have suffered and died for something they knew wasn't true. Many will suffer and die for something they believe is true, even if they're wrong. But few are willing to suffer and die for something they know is false, because there's no advantage to that.

People conspire to make up stories, but if one changes their mind, the truth comes out. This happens every day in police investigations. But none of the apostles ever changed their minds about Jesus Christ, even under threat of death. The resurrection of Jesus Christ is as verifiably certain as any historical event can be.

Acts 17:34 *Some of the people became followers of Paul and believed. Among them was Dionysius, a member of the Areopagus, also a woman named Damaris, and a number of others.*

Intellectual centers can be difficult places to evangelize, but even there the gospel can prevail. Dionysius, Damaris, and a number of others believed, and became the first church of Athens. There's no place too educated for Christianity, since Christianity alone has the advantage of being true. Paul's ministry in Athens was not spectacular, but he laid the foundation for a church that remains to this day.

For Reflection and Review

- *What is the difference between Christianity and Philosophy?*
- *How can everyone be sure that God exists?*
- *How do we know Jesus rose from the dead?*

Lesson 271

Acts 19:13 *Some Jews who went around driving out evil spirits tried to invoke the name of the Lord Jesus over those who were demon-possessed.*

No one ever exercised greater power over demons than Jesus, and those who were delivered experienced great relief (Luke 8:35). Jesus gave this power to his representatives who also cast out demons (Luke 10:17). Paul exercised such power over Satan that even handkerchiefs he touched were *taken to the sick, and their illnesses were cured and the evil spirits left them* (Acts 19:12).

Paul's success at driving out demons led seven imposters to imitate him. *In the name of the Jesus whom Paul preaches, I command you to come out* (Acts 19:13), they said. But the evil spirit replied, *Jesus I know, and Paul I know about, but who are you?* (Acts 19:15). Then the demonized man gave them such a beating that they ran away naked and bleeding (Acts 19:16).

Demons are real, and can even target believers. *Our struggle is not against flesh and blood, but against . . . the spiritual forces of evil in the heavenly realms* (Ephesians 6:12), wrote Paul. This has led some Christians to wonder if they could be helped by having a demon cast out.

The Apostles never taught believers to cast out demons, or to seek deliverance. Once we receive Christ as Lord (Colossians 2:6), we have all the power we need to resist Satan. *[T]ake up the shield of faith, with which you can extinguish all the flaming arrows of the evil one* (Ephesians 6:16), wrote Paul.

James, the brother of Christ, is equally helpful. *Submit yourselves, then, to God. Resist the devil, and he will flee from you. Come near to God and he will come near to you* (James 4:7-8), he wrote. Satan won't be completely defeated until he's thrown into the lake of fire (Revelation 20:10). Until then, we must oppose him daily by saying *yes* to Christ and *no* to sin.

*****

Acts 19:23 *About that time there arose a great disturbance about the Way.*

Paul's ministry in Ephesus lasted a couple years, and was so successful *that all the Jews and Greeks who lived in the province of Asia heard the word of the Lord* (Ephesians 19:10). But this was bad for the idol making industry, and those involved began to push back.

Acts 19:24-27 *A silversmith named Demetrius, who made silver shrines of Artemis, brought in a lot of business for the craftsmen there. He called them together, along with the workers in related trades, and said: You know, my friends, that we receive a good income from this business. And you see and hear how this fellow Paul has convinced and led astray large numbers of people here in Ephesus and in practically the whole province of Asia.*

He says that gods made by human hands are no gods at all. There is danger not only that our trade will lose its good name, but also that the temple of the great goddess Artemis will be discredited; and the goddess herself, who is worshiped throughout the province of Asia and the world, will be robbed of her divine majesty.

Ephesus was home to the temple of Artemis, one of the seven wonders of the ancient world. It was over four hundred feet long, two hundred feet wide, sixty feet high, and had over one hundred white marble columns. People came from all over the world to see it, and to buy images of Artemis.

Paul stepped into this world of idolatry and taught that it was false. Artemis was not divine, and idolatry was a sin (Exodus 34:17). Paul's preaching undermined the city's religious foundation, and hurt it financially. He was causing a severe social, religious, and economic problem.

The purpose of Christianity is not to improve people's lives. That's often the effect, but it's not the point. The point of Christianity is to reconcile people to God, through faith in Jesus Christ, so they can avoid eternal punishment, and live with him forever. The only thing that matters is whether or not it's true.

Acts 19:29 *Soon the whole city was in an uproar.*

They went to the amphitheater (which could seat around twelve thousand people) and *shouted in unison for about two hours: Great is Artemis of the Ephesians!* (Acts 19:34). But all their shouting didn't prove a thing. Their devotion to Artemis was based on an image they thought *fell from heaven* (Acts 19:35). But did anyone see it fall? And were they reliable witnesses? This was a weak foundation on which to build a religion, and few follow Artemis today. All that's left of her temple is a single column built from fragments recovered at the site.

Christianity is not a frenzied religion, with little or no proof. It's a thoughtful religion based on *many convincing proofs* (Acts 1:3). The most compelling, besides the resurrection, is knowing Christ for ourselves. *Now this is eternal life: that they know you, the only true God, and Jesus Christ, whom you have sent* (John 17:3), said Jesus.

*****

Acts 20:7 *On the first day of the week we came together to break bread.*

Paul was in the city of Troas, but was leaving the following day. Since he was only there for a week, he wanted to impart as much teaching as possible. So he talked *on and on* (Acts 20:9) until midnight. Most of those gathered probably enjoyed it, but a young man named Eutychus drifted off to sleep. He may be the first person to fall asleep in church, but not the last. Sometimes preachers go on too long! But preachers everywhere should be encouraged that even the Apostle Paul put people to sleep.

Acts 20:9b *When he was sound asleep, he fell to the ground from the third story and was picked up dead.*

Imagine the alarm this brought to the little congregation. They had a wonderful time with Paul, but this was a terrible way to end. It'd take years for this memory to fade, and his parents might never recover. And Paul would likely blame himself.

Paul had done many miracles (Acts 19:11-12), but never raised anyone from the dead. Perhaps he thought of the prophet Elijah who raised a child from the dead by laying on him (1 Kings 17:21). A few years later, in fact, the prophet Elisha did the same thing (2 Kings 4:35). So *Paul went down, threw himself on the young man and put his arms around him. Don't be alarmed, he said. He's alive!* (Acts 20:10). This was no time to go home, of course, so they went back upstairs and Paul talked until morning. Some preachers never learn.

For Reflection and Review

- *Should Christians cast out demons?*
- *What is the purpose of Christianity?*
- *Is Christianity boring?*

Lesson 272

Acts 23:12 *The next morning some Jews formed a conspiracy and bound themselves with an oath not to eat or drink until they had killed Paul.*

Paul was facing opposition in Jerusalem, and was taken into custody. During that time, more than forty men plotted to take his life. They sought help from the religious leaders saying, *We have taken a solemn oath not to eat anything until we have killed Paul* (Acts 23:14).

In the providence of God, however, Paul's nephew learned about the plot. We're not told his age, but he seems to have been around twelve (Acts 23:19). First he told Paul, then he told an officer, then the officer transferred Paul to another city where he'd be safe. This is how God preserved the life of his servant.

God didn't use an angel to save Paul, or a miracle, but chose to work providentially. Providence may seem like coincidence, but is actually God, *who works out everything in conformity with the purpose of his will* (Ephesians 1:11), wrote Paul. We don't live in a world of chance, but in a world that's governed by God down to every detail (Luke 12:7). That's why we can trust him.

This was also the view of king David. *[A]ll the days ordained for me were written in your book before one of them came to be* (Psalm 139:16), he wrote. We won't die before our time, and won't be shot if we're supposed to be hung. Our lives are not in the hands of fate, chance, or the devil but in the hands of our heavenly Father who loves us.

*****

Acts 27:20 *When neither sun nor stars appeared for many days and the storm continued raging, we finally gave up all hope of being saved.*

Paul was under arrest for preaching the gospel, and was on his way to stand trial in Rome. The ship encountered a storm that was so severe, however, that no one even hoped to survive. The passengers, the sailors, and even Paul had given up *all hope of being saved.*

God doesn't spare his people the troubles of life. The storm wasn't a judgment from God, as in the case of Jonah (Jonah 1:4), nor was it from Satan. It was simply a natural storm which Paul encountered on his way to Rome. Everyone has to die eventually, and Paul assumed this was his time. Thankfully, he was wrong.

If Paul had died on his way to Rome we wouldn't have his letters to the Ephesians, Philippians, Colossians, or Philemon. God still had work for Paul, and God was preserving his life. As long as God preserves our lives, he has something for us to do.

Acts 27:22 *But now I urge you to keep up your courage, because not one of you will be lost; only the ship will be destroyed.*

An angel assured Paul that, even though the ship would be lost, everyone on board would be saved. The loss of a ship was bad enough, but not so bad as the loss lives. Loss is never easy, but we can always be thankful we didn't lose more.

If we lose our wealth, we can be thankful we didn't lose our health. If we lose our health, we can be thankful we didn't lose our family. If we lose our family, we can be thankful we didn't lose our faith. As long as we have faith in Christ, we're assured of all good things in the age to come. This should give us courage through all the storms of life.

Acts 27:40 *Then they hoisted the foresail to the wind and made for the beach.*

Land was spotted the following morning, and they wasted no time in getting there. But, as they approached, the ship got stuck in a sandbar and was broken apart by the crashing waves. Those who could swim jumped overboard and made it to land first. The rest got there on pieces of the ship. And, *In this way everyone reached land safely* (Acts 27:44), wrote Luke.

If God preserved the lives of all on board that ship, how much more will he preserve his own until we get to heaven's shore. *I give them eternal life, and they shall never perish; no one will snatch them out of my hand My Father, who has given them to me, is greater than all; no one can snatch them out of my Father's hand* (John 10:28-29), said Jesus.

Life has many adventures, but none that are fatal for the children of God. *Through many dangers, toils and snares we have already come. God's grace has brought us safe this far, and grace will lead us home* (John Newton, slightly revised).

Acts 28:1 *Once safely on shore, we found out that the island was called Malta.*

It was rainy and cold, but the islanders were gracious, and built a fire to welcome their guests. Paul gathered some brushwood, but when he put it on the fire, a viper bit his hand. The islanders thought he must be a murderer since, though he survived the shipwreck, justice wouldn't let him live. But when Paul suffered no bad effects *they changed their minds and said he was a god* (Acts 28:6).

Apart from God's word, there's no reliable way to understand the world in which we live. Left to our imaginations we'll conclude there is no God, there are many gods, or everything is God. We can imagine a spirit behind every tree, and a demon under every bed. That's why God gave us his word. After thousands of years the Bible remains the best explanation of reality, because the Bible is true. *The unfolding of your words gives light; it gives understanding to the simple* (Psalm 119:130), wrote the Psalmist.

Acts 28:11 *After three months we put out to sea in a ship that had wintered in the island.*

Paul finally made it to Rome, and was placed under house arrest until he stood trial before Caesar. *For two whole years Paul stayed there in his own rented house and welcomed all who came to see him. He proclaimed the kingdom of God and taught about the Lord Jesus Christ—with all boldness and without hindrance!* (Acts 28:30-31), wrote Luke.

This is how the book of Acts ends. It was about AD 62, and Paul was around the same age. We have no record of his trial before Caesar (Acts 27:24), but he was probably released for a few more years, before he was imprisoned again, and put to death around AD 67.

Apart from Jesus Christ, Paul would likely be lost to history. But because of Jesus Christ, he's known and read by millions. Paul was so gripped by the gospel that he had to proclaim it. *Woe to me if I do not preach the gospel!* (1 Corinthians 9:16), he wrote. We should thank God for the gospel, and for sending Paul to preach it.

For Reflection and Review

- *Why is it important to know that God is in control?*
- *Has God ever preserved your life through danger?*
- *How does the Bible help us understand the world?*

Lesson 273

Romans 1:1 *Paul, a servant of Christ Jesus, called to be an apostle and set apart for the gospel of God.*

The book of Romans was written by the Apostle Paul, to the church in Rome, around AD 57. Paul wrote to introduce himself, and to prepare the church for an apostolic visit (Romans 15:28). He arrived a couple years later, and came back a few years after that. He was likely martyred in Rome, after a cold and lonely imprisonment (2 Timothy 4:13).

The major theme of Romans is the gospel of Jesus Christ, but it includes related themes such as the righteousness of God, the law of God, guilt, salvation, sanctification, and assurance. Romans is the most comprehensive outline of Christian doctrine in the New Testament, and became a model for the later development of systematic theology.

Jews from Rome were in Jerusalem on the day of Pentecost (Acts 2:10), and probably took the Christian faith back to Rome when they returned. Rome was the capital of the empire, and home to about a million people, so we might expect a fairly large church. But the final chapter of Romans suggests a fairly small church, where most people knew each other.

Romans 1:5 *[We] call all the Gentiles to the obedience that comes from faith.*

The Bible makes a close connection between obedience and faith. They're not the same, but are so closely related that there is no faith without obedience, and no obedience without faith. If you don't believe, you haven't begun to obey. And if you don't obey, you haven't really believed.

This was made clear by James, the brother of Jesus. *As the body without the spirit is dead, so faith without deeds is dead* (James 2:26), he wrote. God commands us to believe (Mark 1:15) on the basis of sufficient revelation in nature, Scripture, and Christ. Then he commands us to obey as a demonstration of our faith. Faith and obedience go together like two sides of a coin. If you have a coin with heads, but not tails, it's a fake. We are called *to the obedience that comes from faith.*

Romans 1:12 *[We are] mutually encouraged by each other's faith.*

Paul was a great encouragement to other believers, and they were a great encouragement to him. Whenever we spend time with others who believe in Jesus Christ, our own faith is encouraged. The Spirit of Christ in us, recognizes the Spirit of Christ in them, and this mutual recognition builds our confidence that God's promises are true.

If we're encouraged by each other's faith, however, we're also discouraged by each other's unbelief. If the godliest people you know fall away from Jesus Christ, you might be tempted to do the same. We ought to be the best Christians we can be, since there are others who need us, or may be watching from a distance. Believers should also gather frequently since a fire of many coals burns hot, but a coal that's left alone goes out.

Romans 1:16 *For I am not ashamed of the gospel, because it is the power of God that brings salvation to everyone who believes.*

Paul wasn't ashamed of the gospel, but he may've been embarrassed at times. If you've never been embarrassed by the gospel, in fact, you may've never believed the gospel, because the gospel is embarrassing.

To believe the gospel is true, you must believe that a Jewish carpenter, one who made tables and chairs, also made the world. You must also believe that he died on a cross for your sins, and rose to give you eternal life. You must also believe he's coming back to judge the world, and those who are his will live happily ever after, and those who are not will burn in hell forever.

If you try to say this to most educated people, they will laugh at you, and make you feel embarrassed. That's what it was like to be a Christian in Rome during the first century, and that's what it is like to be a Christian today.

But Paul wasn't ashamed of the gospel, *because it is the power of God that brings salvation to everyone who believes*. As Paul preached this hard-to-believe gospel, something unusual happened. Those who believed were demonstrably saved. The Holy Spirit empowered them to believe, and then to live as citizens of heaven.

None of this happened because Paul was persuasive, but because God works through the gospel to save those who believe—good and bad, rich and poor, smart and not-so-smart. Telling the gospel without embarrassment isn't easy, but the fact that God works through the gospel makes it a little easier.

Romans 1:18 *The wrath of God is being revealed from heaven against all the godlessness and wickedness.*

The wrath of God is not our favorite thing about him, but the God of the Bible is angry at sin. Every time we sin, we call down the wrath of God —or at least his fatherly displeasure. But why is God so angry at sin?

Two boys were playing in the back yard when a fight broke out, and the bigger boy began to pummel the smaller boy. This was witnessed by the mother of the smaller boy, who was so enraged that she jumped into the fight and beat up the bigger boy, who then went home in tears. The reason the mother was so angry at the bully was because she loved her son. In a similar way, the wrath of God the Father is a result of the love he has for his Son, and for the Holy Spirit.

From eternity past, the Father has loved the Son and the Spirit; the Son has loved the Father and the Spirit; and the Spirit has loved the Father and the Son. Whenever we sin against any member of the Trinity, each divine person is enraged at the offense done to the others.

But God can also be angry at us because of the love he has for us. If the boy next door gets hooked on drugs, I may feel sorry for him, but I won't be angry at him because I don't love him like my own. But if my own son gets hooked on drugs, I will be filled with anger because I love him deeply, and it pains me to see him destroy himself. Whenever God sees us harm our character (and our relationship with him) it pains him deeply. God's wrath is real, but it's the righteous response of his love for us, and for himself.

Romans 1:18b *[People] suppress the truth by their wickedness.*

By nature we are truth suppressors. Our greatest problem isn't that we don't know the truth, but that we don't want the truth. The truth of the gospel is so firmly established that everyone would believe, if it wasn't so demanding. Our sinful nature wants a lifestyle that can only be sustained if God doesn't exist, so we suppress the truth in order to live the way we want. The gospel is the best possible news that no one wants to hear.

When I was a child, we played with a volleyball in the swimming pool and tried to hold it under water. Sometimes we'd sit on it, other times we'd stand on it, but whenever we let it go, the volleyball resurfaced. Likewise, after they buried Jesus, he also resurfaced. And all the unbelievers in the world can't put Jesus back in the tomb. The gospel is fiercely opposed, but it's just as irrepressible as Jesus Christ himself. The wicked try to suppress the truth but, sooner or later, it pops up.

For Reflection and Review

- *Why is the gospel embarrassing?*
- *Why is God angry at sin?*
- *Why do we suppress the truth?*

Lesson 274

Romans 1:20 *For since the creation of the world God's invisible qualities—his eternal power and divine nature—have been clearly seen, being understood from what has been made, so that people are without excuse.*

There's no excuse for not believing in God, because creation proves that he exists. Something cannot come from nothing, since out of nothing, nothing comes. For the world to exist, therefore, it had to be created. This is the default position according to the Bible. The burden of proof isn't on people who believe in God, but on those who don't.

Creation also has marks of design—the signature of a great designer. These are apparent in every plant and animal in the world. The closer we look at anything, the more remarkable it appears. *The visible marks of extraordinary wisdom and power appear so plainly in all the works of creation that a rational creature who will but seriously reflect on them, cannot miss the discovery of a deity* (John Locke).

The fact that some refuse to acknowledge God doesn't bring his existence into question. It only proves that people are dishonest which, of course, we already know. The Bible is clear: there's no excuse for not believing in God.

Romans 1:21 *For although they knew God, they neither glorified him as God nor gave thanks to him.*

This is one of the saddest verses in the Bible. The response of sinners to the revelation of God is to give him neither glory nor thanks. By refusing to honor their Creator, they forfeit the purpose for which they were made. The first question of the Westminster Confession makes this clear: *What is the chief end of man?* Answer: *Man's chief end is to glorify God, and enjoy him forever.*

If you write beautiful music, but don't glorify God, you've missed the point of your life. If you find a cure for cancer, but don't glorify God, you've also missed the point of your life. You're a phone that never made a call, a Porsche that never saw the open road, a plane that never left the ground. *Man's chief end is to glorify God, and enjoy him forever.*

Romans 1:24 *Therefore God gave them over in the sinful desires of their hearts to sexual impurity for the degrading of their bodies with one another.*

God's fitting response to those who reject his ways is to give them over to their sin. This idea was so important to Paul that he repeated it three times in five verses. *God gave them over . . . to sexual impurity*

(Romans 1:24), *God gave them over to shameful lusts* (Romans 1:26), and *God gave them over to a depraved mind* (Romans 1:28), he wrote.

God is the one who restrains us from sin, so if we turn our backs on God, there's no one to restrain us. Paul called attention to sexual sin because that's where human fallenness is so apparent. Whoever deviates from God's idea of perfect sexuality has become a sexual deviant to some degree. But every kind of sin is rebellion against God and, taken far enough, will destroy us. Habits are cobwebs before they are cables, and many find themselves bound by sins they planned to quit eventually.

But there's always hope for those who turn to God through faith in Jesus Christ. *[H]e will not let you be tempted beyond what you can bear. But when you are tempted, he will also provide a way out so that you can endure it* (1 Corinthians 10:13), wrote Paul. God isn't against believers because of our sins, so much as he's with us against our sins. We're never alone in the battle, as long as we stay in the fight.

Romans 1:25 *They exchanged the truth about God for a lie, and worshiped and served created things rather than the Creator.*

The worship of idols has been around for ages, and was a temptation to the people of Israel. *[T]hey cut a tree out of the forest, and a craftsman shapes it with his chisel. They adorn it with silver and gold; they fasten it with hammer and nails so it will not totter. Like a scarecrow in a cucumber field, their idols cannot speak; they must be carried because they cannot walk* (Jeremiah 10:3-5), wrote Jeremiah.

But idolatry can also be more subtle. Imagine a young man who bought his fiancé the most beautiful ring he could afford. Perhaps he worked overtime, and sold his favorite possessions to buy a truly amazing ring. He wanted to show his love for her, and hoped she would love him even more. But what if she loved the ring more than she loved her fiancé, and loved him a little less because of his generosity.

That's what happens whenever we love created things more than our Creator. This could include music, money, pleasure, possessions, people, or anything other than God. *Every good and perfect gift is from above* (James 1:17), wrote James. If we love the gifts more than the giver, we've become idolaters. *Therefore, my dear friends, flee from idolatry* (1 Corinthians 10:14), wrote Paul.

Romans 1:28 *[T]hey did not think it worthwhile to retain the knowledge of God, so God gave them over to a depraved mind.*

The fact that God exists, and has a right to govern his world, is obvious from creation. And yet, the knowledge of God has nearly disappeared in many cultures. As punishment for not retaining this important knowledge, God abandons people to their own depravity, so they become increasingly corrupt.

Likewise, many who learn the Bible in their youth, forget it with age, because they watch television instead of reading the Bible. Instead of becoming more like Jesus Christ, they become more like the devil, as God gives them over to a depraved mind. It's not enough to obtain the knowledge of God; we must retain the knowledge of God by frequently reading his word.

Love for Jesus Christ and love for the Bible are closely related, because the Bible is all about Jesus Christ. If we don't love the Bible, our love for Christ should be called into question. Having obtained the knowledge of God, we must retain the knowledge of God, and then grow in the knowledge of God. Otherwise we'll become depraved.

Romans 2:1 *You, therefore, have no excuse, you who pass judgment on someone else, for at whatever point you judge another, you are condemning yourself, because you who pass judgment do the same things.*

Paul was trying to convince self-righteous people that they too were sinners who needed to be saved. This is not an easy task because some people really are morally superior. But everyone has standards to which they don't measure up. We not only fall short of God's standards, we even fall short of our own standards—which are always lower than God's. So whenever we judge another person, we also condemn ourselves, because we too fall short on a regular basis.

I consider myself to be an honest person, but that same honesty forces me to admit that I haven't been completely honest. When I was eight years old, my bicycle was missing a valve cap, and I didn't know where to buy one. So I rode my bike to a car dealer, stooped down between two cars, and transferred a valve cap from one of the cars to my bicycle. The valve cap had a value of about two cents, and I doubt it was ever missed, but I didn't ask permission. I stole it. I am a thief.

This seems insignificant compared to what other thieves have done, but puts me in the same category. If I condemn theft in any form, I stand under the same judgment. I don't need to hear it from a judge. Like everyone else, I'm self-condemned. *[A]t whatever point you judge another, you are condemning yourself, because you who pass judgment do the same things.*

For Reflection and Review

- *What is the main purpose of our lives?*
- *What is idolatry?*
- *Why is it important to grow in the knowledge of God?*

Lesson 275

Romans 2:4 *Or do you show contempt for the riches of his kindness, forbearance and patience, not realizing that God's kindness is intended to lead you to repentance?*

Some to whom Paul wrote misunderstood the kindness of God to be a sign of his favor. Since God had been kind to them in the past, they had no reason to think he wouldn't be kind to them in the future, even on Judgment Day. But the purpose of God's kindness wasn't to give them false assurance, but to lead them to repentance.

Two months after my conversion, I went away to college, and found myself living in temptation city. By the second semester there was little outward difference between me and most other people on campus. But at the end of the year I went to church, and God met with me.

I should've been listening to the sermon, but allowed my mind to wander, and was surprised by thoughts of God's unusual kindness to me. I lived in a prosperous country, had loving parents, enjoyed good health, and had some friends. What struck me most, however, was that God would send his Son to die on a cross for my sins.

Then I began to think of the way that I had treated God. I'd given up on prayer, stopped reading his word, and avoided church. I spurned his commands, rejected his will, and did as I pleased. When I compared the way God had treated me, to the way I had treated God, I found myself in tears. I agreed with God that he was good and I was bad. I told him I wanted to change and, if he'd take me back, I'd never walk away again. That was over thirty years ago, and he's kept me ever since. The kindness of God led me to repentance.

Romans 2:8-9 *But for those who are self-seeking and who reject the truth and follow evil, there will be wrath and anger. There will be trouble and distress for every human being who does evil.*

Trouble and distress come from getting caught doing something we shouldn't be doing. This is common in the lives of unbelievers, but even Christians can fall into trouble. A friend of mine was an excellent business man, with a beautiful family, and a good reputation at church. Then he went to a club and got involved with a young lady who blackmailed him for money. He quickly went through his savings, then his retirement fund, then he stole from his company. Then he went to prison, and lost his family, along with everything else.

Others have a similar story, and we can imagine their trouble and distress as everything slipped away. But can we imagine the trouble and distress of standing before God and seeing heaven slip away? Christians aren't above temptation, or a world of sorrow.

Romans 2:15 *[T]he requirements of the law are written on their hearts, their consciences also bearing witness, and their thoughts sometimes accusing them and at other times even defending them.*

Paul argued from conscience that all people have an inward knowledge of right and wrong. It accuses them of violating God's law, even if they've never read the Bible. Because we're made in the image of God, we all know right from wrong, even without being taught.

This is a powerful argument for God's existence, because a moral law requires a moral law giver. There can be no right or wrong apart from God, because there's no one with sufficient authority to say what's right or wrong. If an ultimate authority doesn't exist, everyone gets to choose right and wrong for themselves. This sounds good, at first, but it doesn't agree with our best judgment.

Torturing children for pleasure is always wrong. It's not enough to say *torturing children for pleasure is wrong for you but not for me*. We know instinctively that torturing children for pleasure is objectively wrong, for all people, all the time.

For this to be true, however, there must be an ultimate authority to say so. The best explanation for right and wrong is God, because you can't have a moral law without a moral law giver. And God has written his law on our hearts, so it can't be avoided.

Romans 2:24 *God's name is blasphemed among the Gentiles because of you.*

Because the ancient Israelites failed to keep God's law, God allowed them to be defeated by the Babylonians. Since the Babylonians were victorious, they assumed the God of Israel was not to be taken seriously. So they blasphemed the one true God.

Likewise, whenever a Christian leader falls into sin, people will use the occasion to mock Christianity. To some degree, this is true for all believers. That's why Paul insists that *Everyone who confesses the name of the Lord must turn away from wickedness* (2 Timothy 2:19).

Our behavior should never give people a reason to disrespect the gospel of Jesus Christ. *Live such good lives among the pagans that, though they accuse you of doing wrong, they may see your good deeds and glorify God on the day he visits us* (1 Peter 2:12), wrote Peter.

Romans 3:10-12 *As it is written: There is no one righteous, not even one; there is no one who understands; there is no one who seeks God. All have turned away, they have together become worthless; there is no one who does good, not even one.*

Here and elsewhere, Paul drew on the Old Testament to show the depth and breadth of human depravity. By comparing ourselves to other sinners, we might imagine we're pretty good people. But God's standard of goodness is absolute perfection. *Be perfect, therefore, as your heavenly Father is perfect* (Matthew 5:48), said Jesus. When we stop comparing ourselves to others, and compare ourselves to what God requires, we see that everyone in the world is bad, including ourselves. No one's very good at being very good.

Romans 3:20 *Therefore no one will be declared righteous in God's sight by the works of the law; rather, through the law we become conscious of our sin.*

The purpose of the commandments aren't to show us how to be good enough for heaven, but to show us that we're not good enough for heaven, and need to be saved through faith in Jesus Christ. He's the only one who's good enough for heaven, and we only get in through him.

When I present the gospel I like to begin with a few questions to help people see their need for Christ. First, I ask if they've ever told a lie and, if so, what that makes them—a liar. Then I ask if they've ever stolen anything and, if so, what that makes them—a thief. Then I ask if they've ever lusted after someone to whom they weren't married and, if so, what that makes them—a luster. Then I ask if they've ever misused God's name and, if so, what that makes them—a blasphemer (Ray Comfort, revised). By their own admission most people are lying, thieving, lusting, blasphemers. Then I explain that, apart from Christ, there will be hell to pay.

For Reflection and Review

- *How does the goodness of God lead us to repentance?*
- *How does sin cause trouble and distress?*
- *How does God's law prepare us for his gospel?*

Lesson 276

Romans 3:25 *God presented Christ as a sacrifice of atonement, through the shedding of his blood.*

This is one of the most important things the Bible has to say to us. When Jesus was crucified, he bore the wrath of God against our sins, so God and people could be *at one* again. That's the idea behind the word *atonement*. It's the payment for our sins, that satisfies the righteous anger of God.

Imagine you were in the back yard with God, and he was indignant because you'd been sinning for a very long time. God reviewed your sins, from beginning to end, and became increasingly angry. Then he picked up a steel rod and walked to a nearby tree. For the next six hours he beat that tree so severely that, when he was done, it barely resembled a tree anymore (Isaiah 52:14). But now God's anger was completely spent and, instead of being the object of his wrath, you become the object of his grace. Don't miss the point: Jesus Christ was on that tree. He bore the wrath of God so we can be at one with him. He's the *sacrifice of atonement*.

Romans 3:28 *For we maintain that a person is justified by faith apart from the works of the law.*

Paul continued to emphasize the importance of faith in Christ, and changed the image to the courtroom by using the word *justified*. This is an important word for Paul which he used over thirty times throughout his letters.

When we hear the word *justified* we should think of a courtroom, bench, gavel, and judge. It's Judgment Day, and after your trial the judge will open up the gate to glory, or cast you into the lake of fire (Revelation 20:15). After reviewing your life from beginning to end, the gavel will drop, and the judge will say *guilty*, or *not guilty*. If he says *guilty*, you'll drop into hell and howl with the damned for all eternity. But if he says *not guilty*, the gate to heaven will open wide and you'll be welcomed into eternal glory. This will happen because you've been justified by faith in Christ, apart from any good works.

A pastor was leading a Bible study for men, and was concerned about one who didn't seem to know Christ. After the study, one week, the pastor asked him privately, *Bob, are you a Christian?* Bob said he was, so the pastor asked for more information. He said, *It happened this week. I looked in the mirror and said, Bob why should God let you into heaven? I thought to myself, Because I am betting my soul on Jesus Christ*. Faith is putting all our chips on Christ, and none on ourselves. That's what it means to be *justified by faith* in Christ, *apart from the works of the law*.

Romans 4:3 *What does Scripture say? Abraham believed God, and it was credited to him as righteousness.*

Paul used the example of Abraham to prove from the Old Testament that we're made right with God by faith, not works. Abraham is a good example because he was the Father of the Jewish nation, and also God's friend (Isaiah 41:8). If Abraham was right with God through faith, then that's the way for us.

To make his point Paul quoted a verse that some of his readers knew well. *Abraham believed God, and it was credited to him as righteousness* (Genesis 15:6). He didn't work his way into God's favor, or obey his way into God's favor, but simply *believed God*.

Many in Paul's day thought the way to be right with God was by being a pretty good person. But other than Jesus Christ, there are no pretty good people. We're all pretty good compared to the devil, of course, but the devil isn't the standard of goodness. Like the devil, in fact, we all sin every day. It's impossible to get right with God by being a pretty good person because we have more in common with the devil (at least morally) than we do with Jesus Christ. Thankfully, there's another way.

Since Jesus never sinned, and paid the penalty for our sins, we can be right with God through faith in Jesus Christ. *Very truly I tell you, the one who believes has eternal life* (John 6:47), said Jesus. Like Abraham, we're made right with God through faith, not works (Ephesians 2:8-9).

Romans 4:5 *However, to the one who does not work but trusts God who justifies the ungodly, their faith is credited as righteousness.*

The idea that God *justifies the ungodly* is shocking, and seems entirely wrong at first. Imagine a judge who let murdering rapists go free. That might be popular with murdering rapists, but what about justice? Thankfully, God took care of justice when Jesus died on the cross for our sins. He took the punishment we deserve, so even the worst can be forgiven.

This should even comfort us whenever we misbehave. Even Christians sin sometimes and, whenever that happens, we can wonder about our status with God. Then we should recall that God *justifies the ungodly*. God is in the business of saving sinners, so he isn't surprised that we still sin. The important thing (the really crucial thing) is to keep on trusting God who *justifies the ungodly*.

Romans 4:8 *Blessed is the one whose sin the Lord will never count against them.*

Paul was making a difficult argument to very religious people. He wanted to convince them that God justifies the ungodly, not counting their sins against them. The first example was Abraham, the father of the Jewish nation, and God's friend. The second example is King David, a man after God's heart (Acts 13:22). To help make his argument, Paul quoted a line from one of David's Psalms: *Blessed is the one whose sin the Lord will never count against them.*

We're not sure if David wrote this verse before or after he committed adultery with Bathsheba, and arranged for her husband's death. Either way, David is happy to be among those *whose sin the Lord will never count against them.*

The level of assurance here is breathtaking. Even though there was nothing of which he wasn't capable, and plenty of which he was already guilty, David was sure God would never hold his sin against him. And whoever believes in Jesus Christ can have this same assurance. This is not ordinary good news; it's the best good news that's ever been told.

Romans 5:1 *Therefore, since we have been justified through faith, we have peace with God through our Lord Jesus Christ.*

Jesus established peace between us and God by paying the penalty for our sins. God is no longer angry at us because his anger was spent on Christ. We may incur his fatherly displeasure, and even his discipline (Proverbs 3:12), but that's quite a different thing than his righteous wrath.

Apart from Jesus Christ, of course, there is no real peace. Even if our bills are paid, and our health is good, we'll always have a sense of guilt and impending doom. But since Christ has established peace objectively, we can enjoy peace within. Even if our health is failing, and our bills are overdue, we're assured of eternal happiness and therefore we have peace.

For Reflection and Review

- *What's the meaning of atonement?*
- *What kind of people does God accept?*
- *Why do Christians want to be good?*

Lesson 277

Romans 5:3-4 *Not only so, but we also glory in our sufferings, because we know that suffering produces perseverance; perseverance, character; and character, hope.*

God uses suffering to improve our character, and this caused Paul to rejoice. Christians who've suffer deeply always have more depth than those who've suffered little. Many who've suffered deeply are even thankful (after it's over) for how it shaped their lives.

There are at least four other reasons Christians can rejoice in their suffering. First, our suffering is always less than we deserve. If we consider how many times we've sinned, we'll be amazed our suffering isn't any worse. Second, our suffering will shortly end. Even if we have to suffer a hundred years or more, what is that compared to eternity with Christ? Third, suffering can deepen our faith. Many Christians have gone from a shallow relationship with Christ, to a deep relationship with Christ, due to their suffering. Fourth, suffering can increase our longing for heaven.

A missionary couple lost three small children in a car accident. They could've become resentful, and quit the ministry, but they believe God does everything well. They also believe in heaven. The thought of seeing their children, along with their Savior, has made heaven much more real to them. Suffering seems pointless apart from God, but God uses suffering for the good of his own.

Romans 5:8 *God demonstrates his own love for us in this: While we were still sinners, Christ died for us.*

God didn't wait for us to repent before he made the way of salvation. The world was in revolt when God sent his Son to die for our sins. Paul saw this as proof of God's love.

If you were a millionaire, and your child was kidnapped, you'd probably give your millions to get him back. And if you were a billionaire, and your child was kidnapped, you'd probably give your billions to get him back. But what if your child was evil? What if your child hated you, ran away from you, did everything you forbad, and even cursed your name? Would you still be willing to give everything you had to get your wicked child back? Maybe not. *But God demonstrates his own love for us in this: While we were still sinners, Christ died for us.*

Romans 5:10 *For if, while we were God's enemies, we were reconciled to him through the death of his Son, how much more, having been reconciled, shall we be saved through his life!*

We're not only saved by the death of Jesus Christ, but also by his resurrection. It's like a rich man who left many in his will, and came back from the dead to be sure they received their inheritance. Jesus purchased our salvation when he died on the cross, then rose from the dead to be sure we receive the eternal life he provided.

And all this happened while we were *God's enemies*. It doesn't say he was *our enemy* but that we were *God's enemies*. We were involved in a one-sided war against God. Our hostility was so great, in fact, that when he sent his Son into the world we killed him. I can't think of a single friend for whom I'd give my son. But while we were *God's enemies* he gave his Son for us.

Romans 5:19 *For just as through the disobedience of the one man the many were made sinners, so also through the obedience of the one man the many will be made righteous.*

As head of the human race, Adam's sin was imputed to each of us. As head of the new human race, Christ's righteousness is imputed to all who believe. We became sinners because of Adam's sin, and we become righteous because of Christ's righteousness.

The obedience of Christ took him to the cross, but began at his incarnation. The moment he came into the world Jesus began winning our salvation through his obedient life. *For I have come down from heaven not to do my will but to do the will of him who sent me* (John 6:38). And, *I always do what pleases him* (John 8:29), he said.

This is important for at least two reasons. First, if Jesus ever sinned, he couldn't have died for sinners. Second, salvation isn't only being forgiven, but also being righteous. Since none of us is righteous in ourselves, *This righteousness is given through faith in Jesus Christ* (Romans 3:22), wrote Paul. Adam's sin was imputed to everyone, and Christ's righteousness is imputed to all who believe.

This is why Jesus had to live to adulthood to die for our salvation. He couldn't have died when he was five years old, because he hadn't been righteous long enough. Only after thirty-some years of perfect obedience was the Father willing to apply the righteousness of Christ to all who believe. This helps us appreciate the perfect life of Christ for our salvation, not only his death.

As he lay dying an American theologian sent a telegram to his friend saying, *I'm so thankful for the active obedience of Christ. No hope without it* (J. Gresham Machen). As he thought about meeting God, he enjoyed the double comfort of knowing Jesus died for his sins, and also lived for his righteousness. *For he has clothed me with garments of salvation and arrayed me in a robe of his righteousness* (Isaiah 61:10), wrote Isaiah.

Romans 6:4 *We were therefore buried with him through baptism into death in order that, just as Christ was raised from the dead through the glory of the Father, we too may live a new life.*

With so much talk about grace and forgiveness, the church in Rome may've thought Christianity was a license to sin. If God is glorified by forgiving our sin, the more we sin, the more he's glorified. There's a certain logic to this argument, but it comes to the wrong conclusion. Paul used baptism to illustrate why Christians shouldn't sin.

When a Christian goes under the water in baptism, it's an image of union with Christ in his death. As Jesus died *for* sin, the Christian dies *to* sin. When a Christian comes up from the water, it's an image of union with Christ in his resurrection. Coming to faith in Christ is like dying to sin, so we can live a new life. The wonderful thing about baptism is that it's more than an illustration. It's the inward experience of all who believe.

Before I came to Christ, sin was a source of pleasure, and obedience was a burden. But after I came to Christ, sin became a source of grief, and obedience became a joy. This is because the Holy Spirit troubles us whenever we sin, and gives us joy whenever we obey. Something truly happens when we come to faith in Jesus Christ. We die to sin, and come alive to God.

Romans 6:12 *Therefore do not let sin reign in your mortal body so that you obey its evil desires.*

Paul wanted believers in Rome to understand they had a new master. Before they came to Christ, sin ruled over them. But since they came to Christ, sin was no longer their master, and had no right to tell them what to do.

I'm the second of six children, and my big sister is several years older. For many years she bossed me around like a second mom. Because it'd always been that way, I assumed she had the right. But in a moment of clarity, I stood up to her. I said, *You're not the boss of me. Mom and Dad are the boss of me and I have to obey them, but you're not the boss of me and I don't have to obey you.* To my surprise, she backed down, and that was the end of it.

If we belong to Jesus Christ, sin is not the boss of us. Jesus Christ is the boss of us and we must obey him. But sin is not the boss of us and we don't have to obey it anymore.

For Reflection and Review

- *How is our relationship to Christ like our relationship to Adam?*
- *Why was Jesus' righteous life important?*
- *How does baptism illustrate conversion?*

Lesson 278

Romans 6:19 *Just as you used to offer yourselves as slaves to impurity and to ever-increasing wickedness, so now offer yourselves as slaves to righteousness leading to holiness.*

Some of the Roman Christians were slaves, who'd been bought and sold more than once. If they were owned by an evil master, then were bought by a good master, their lives could improve dramatically. Likewise, we used to be slaves to impurity, but then became slaves to righteousness.

The problem with impurity is that it leads to *ever-increasing wickedness*. We might imagine that with age comes wisdom, and with wisdom comes virtue. But, according to this verse, that isn't true. Apart from divine intervention wickedness tends to be *ever-increasing*. If wickedness is a bang, then every one wants a bigger bang.

Adolf Hitler and others like him were once beautiful children. But thought by thought, word by word, and deed by deed, they became moral monsters over time. Likewise, it's not uncommon for one spouse to say to the other, *You're not the same person I married twenty years ago.*

Thankfully, the Holy Spirit is able to change our moral trajectory. Instead of the downward path that leads to the world below, we travel the upward path that leads to the presence of God. *Just as you used to offer yourselves as slaves to impurity and to ever-increasing wickedness, so now offer yourselves as slaves to righteousness leading to holiness.*

Romans 6:22 *[Y]ou have been set free from sin and have become slaves of God.*

When God's people were slaves in Egypt, Pharaoh was their master and he cruelly oppressed them. He forced them to make bricks, make more bricks, and make bricks without straw (Exodus 5:18). When God delivered his people, he became their master. Unlike Pharaoh, God took care of his people, and loved them as his own. God was a much better master than Pharaoh.

In the Roman world, slavery could be good or bad, depending on who your master was. If your master was evil, it could be terrible. But if your master was wealthy and kind, you could be well paid, and treated like family. And if he was important, you could even have status. Being Satan's slave is miserable and degrading, but being God's slave is the highest honor there is. We have been *set free from sin and have become slaves of God*.

Romans 6:23 *For the wages of sin is death, but the gift of God is eternal life in Christ Jesus our Lord.*

Jesus had to be killed because *the wages of sin is death*. It wasn't enough for him to live a perfect life, teach the word of God, and heal the sick. It wasn't enough for him to be mocked, spat on, and have the beard pulled from his face. It wasn't enough for him to be lashed and crucified. Jesus had to die, because the *wages of sin is death*. Jesus never sinned, of course, but he bore the punishment for our sins so that we could live forever.

Since the fall of humankind (Genesis 3:6) the two greatest problems in the world have been sin and death. They seem normal to us, but we should imagine the world without them. If not for sin, the earth would cooperate with all our efforts and we'd never die (Genesis 3:16-19). With God's help, we could create a perfect society with enough wealth for the wants and needs of every single person. It would quickly become heaven on earth. That's what Jesus came to accomplish. By solving the problems of sin and death, he solved every other problem as well.

Romans 7:5 *[T]he sinful passions aroused by the law were at work in us.*

Whenever people want to be good, they look around for a code of ethics. The Bible has many commands in the Old Testament, as well as the New. Even Paul wasn't afraid to lay down some rules, if he thought they would be helpful.

But he also knew that *sinful passions* can be *aroused by the law*. If you tell your children not to look under the couch, for example, they'll have no rest until they look under the couch. And when God says *You shall not*, part of us says *We'll see about that*.

When I was sixteen years old I spent the summer in Utah, and met some nice Mormon youth. One of their rules was against drinking caffeine, so I was surprised to be invited to an unsupervised party where they'd all be drinking Coca-Cola. Some of the kids were even known to drink a six-pack. Most people have no desire to drink that much soda but, since it was forbidden, it had a secret charm. Rules can be helpful up to a point, but they can also backfire due to our sinful nature.

Romans 7:7 *For I would not have known what coveting really was if the law had not said, You shall not covet.*

Paul apparently thought he was a pretty good person, except for coveting. As he reviewed the ten commandments (Exodus 20:1-17) his conscience was clear regarding (1) having no other gods; (2) having no idols; (3) not misusing God's name; (4) keeping the Sabbath; (5) honoring parents; (6) not murdering; (7) not committing adultery (8) not stealing; and (9) not lying.

But when he came to the tenth commandment, *You shall not covet your neighbor's house. You shall not covet your neighbor's wife, or his male or female servant, his ox or donkey, or anything that belongs to your neighbor* (Exodus 20:17), Paul knew he had a problem.

Perhaps his neighbor was rich, had a beautiful home, a beautiful wife, and a rolex watch. Perhaps he had everything Paul ever wanted, and he wanted it badly. This may've seemed fine to Paul until he read the tenth commandment: *You shall not covet*. That's where Paul discovered he had a problem. He, too, was a sinner.

An important function of the law is to reveal our sin, and need for God's forgiveness. If the law hadn't said, *You shall not covet*, Paul would've thought too much of himself. But when he discovered he couldn't keep all the rules, no matter how hard he tried, Paul knew he was in trouble. *For whoever keeps the whole law and yet stumbles at just one point is guilty of breaking all of it* (James 2:10), wrote James.

Romans 7:15 *For what I want to do I do not do, but what I hate I do.*

Even after he came to Christ, Paul wasn't perfect, and those he led to Christ weren't perfect either. *For the flesh desires what is contrary to the Spirit, and the Spirit what is contrary to the flesh* (Galatians 5:17), he wrote. The battle against sin won't be over until we die, and we won't be perfect until we're in heaven.

God is always against our sin, but he also knows that we are weak. *As a father has compassion on his children, so the Lord has compassion on those who fear him; for he knows how we are formed, he remembers that we are dust* (Psalm 103:13-14), wrote David. If we think of God as overly stern, we'll come to resent him. But if we think of him as our heavenly Father, filled with love and compassion, we'll want to please him the rest of our lives.

For Reflection and Review

- *Why do many become increasingly wicked?*
- *Why are sin and death our greatest problems?*
- *What's wrong with having too many rules?*

Lesson 279

Romans 7:20 *Now if I do what I do not want to do, it is no longer I who do it, but it is sin living in me that does it.*

This verse is so unusual it hardly seems to belong in the Bible. If you stole something from your employer, and tried to explain that it wasn't you who stole it, but sin living in you—you'd probably still be fired. But Paul is saying when Christians sin, they're so out of character it's not the real them. It's leftover sin living in them.

Nebuchadnezzar was a powerful king who lost his mind, and ate grass like an ox for seven years (Daniel 4). Then his sanity returned, and he began to rule again. None of those who knew him would've said the man who ate grass like an ox was the real Nebuchadnezzar. God knows who we are, who we are becoming, and who we'll be forever. Sin is not the real us, but a brief insanity left over from our sinful nature.

Romans 7:24 *What a wretched man I am! Who will rescue me from this body that is subject to death?*

Paul didn't say *What a wretched man I was*, but *What a wretched man I am*. He didn't say that he used to be bad, but then he was saved. He openly confessed that, even after believing in Christ, he still had remaining sin, which was a source of grief to him. *Christ Jesus came into the world to save sinners—of whom I am the worst* (1 Timothy 1:15), he wrote.

Only those who want to be good understand how bad they are. *If you, Lord, kept a record of sins, Lord, who could stand?* (Psalm 130:3), wrote the Psalmist. And *Do not bring your servant into judgment, for no one living is righteous before you* (Psalm 143:2), wrote David. We should always try to please our heavenly Father, but also understand that no one is perfect in this life (1 John 1:8).

Romans 8:1 *Therefore, there is now no condemnation for those who are in Christ Jesus.*

Christians don't have to wait until Judgment Day to see how it will go for them. The moment we believe in Jesus Christ, we're assured that we'll never be condemned. *Whoever believes in him is not condemned* (John 3:18), wrote John.

After his arrest, Jesus was dragged into court and cross examined. *The high priest said to him, I charge you under oath by the living God: Tell us if you are the Messiah, the Son of God. You have said so, Jesus replied. . . . Then the high priest tore his clothes and said, He has spoken blasphemy! . . . What do you think? He is worthy of death, they answered* (Matthew 23:63-66).

This is how the only person who never sinned was condemned to death for those who'd believe. We can never be condemned because Jesus was condemned for us. Jesus heard the words of condemnation so we'll never have to.

Shortly after I started driving, I passed a cop who was parked by the side of the road in a police van. He gave me a ticket for running a stop sign which I didn't see. After he left, I went back and discovered the officer's van had blocked my view of the sign. I went to court, explained what happened, and the judge gave his ruling—*not guilty*. There was a moment, however, when I didn't know what his verdict would be. That's a moment we'll never experience on judgment day because *there is now no condemnation for those who are in Christ Jesus.*

Romans 8:9 *[I]f anyone does not have the Spirit of Christ, they do not belong to Christ.*

The mark of a true Christian isn't prayer, going to church, reading the Bible, or even becoming a missionary. We can do all those things, and still not be true Christians. The indispensable mark of a true Christian is the indwelling Spirit, which people receive the moment they believe in Christ. It's not a matter of being religious, but having the Spirit within.

If you give a fifty dollar bill to a cashier, they'll hold it up to the light and look for certain characteristics, like a vertical strip that says *USA*. If it doesn't have the strip, it's not genuine currency, no matter how much it looks like a fifty dollar bill. The indwelling Spirit is the authenticating mark of a true believer.

Romans 8:16 *The Spirit himself testifies with our spirit that we are God's children.*

Many years ago I went to a Christian meeting with a friend and, on the way there, a question popped into my head: *Are you sure you're going to heaven when you die?* I didn't think it was possible to be sure, so I dismissed the question as quickly as it came. But at the meeting I gave my life to Christ, and something unexpected happened—he sent the Spirit to live inside me.

On the way home the same question returned: *Are you sure you're going to heaven when you die?* To my surprise I had to answer *yes* because I could feel the Spirit of Christ giving me assurance that I was a child of God. Christianity is more than knowing about God, it's knowing God personally. *The Spirit himself testifies with our spirit that we are God's children.*

Romans 8:17 *Now if we are children, then we are heirs—heirs of God and co-heirs with Christ.*

Jesus is the *heir of all things* (Hebrews 1:2), and shares all things with his brothers and sisters. *Come, you who are blessed by my Father; take your inheritance, the kingdom prepared for you* (Matthew 25:34), he'll say. Few people have much in life, and whatever we have we must give up eventually. But those who belong to Christ will have everything they want, and forever to enjoy it. Our inheritance isn't pie in the sky, but genuine wealth secured for us by Jesus Christ.

For you know the grace of our Lord Jesus Christ, that though he was rich, yet for your sake he became poor, so that you through his poverty might become rich (2 Corinthians 8:9), wrote Paul. Whoever has Christ gets everything else for free.

Romans 8:18 *I consider that our present sufferings are not worth comparing with the glory that will be revealed in us.*

Christianity wasn't easy for Paul. He was hated, imprisoned, impoverished, and eventually killed. What kept him going was *the glory that will be revealed in us*. His vision of the future carried him through the present.

If you want to imagine the age to come, take a sheet of paper and draw a line down the middle. On one side put everything you want to be there, like strawberry ice-cream and music you can dance to. On the other side put everything you don't want to be there, like tooth decay and overdue bills. Make the list as long as you like, because whatever you can think of won't even compare to what God has prepared for us.

Romans 8:23 *[W]e wait eagerly for our adoption to sonship, the redemption of our bodies.*

Few things are nearer and dearer to us than our bodies. We admire those who are healthy and attractive, and do our best to be like them. We diet and exercise, and even have plastic surgery. One lady had her legs lengthened about two inches to make her that much taller. But even the best grow old, gradually lose their powers, and die.

My mother was stunning when she was young. But after having so many kids, her beauty slipped away. Her only consolation was that it didn't happen all at once. But God has given us real consolation—not just the redemption of our souls, but *the redemption of our bodies*. Imagine loving every part of your body forever. Our bodies are God's idea, and he's going to make them new and improved.

For Reflection and Review

- *How do we know we have the Spirit of Christ?*
- *Is it good to receive an inheritance when we're young?*
- *What would you like to receive in the age to come?*

Lesson 280

Romans 8:26 *We do not know what we ought to pray for, but the Spirit himself intercedes for us through wordless groans.*

We can imagine Paul groaning under the burden of his ministry, as he sought to proclaim Christ to a world that didn't want him. He may've also groaned from bodily pains, and the burden of his remaining sin (Romans 7:24). But in all his wordless groans, Paul discerned the pleading of the Holy Spirit on his behalf. The Spirit took his wordless groans and turned them into prayers that God could hear and understand.

This is like a young man who had a stroke that left him unable to speak. He tried to express his needs by groaning, but only his wife could understand. Whenever he groaned in a certain way, she could lovingly meet his need. Likewise, the Spirit groans for our holiness, wisdom, strength, and perseverance. He expresses our deepest needs to the Father, who meets them at just the right time.

Romans 8:28 *And we know that in all things God works for the good of those who love him.*

What if Jesus appeared to you and promised that nothing bad would ever happen to you for the rest of your life? That's the point of this verse. God has promised that whatever happens to us will be for our ultimate good. *Lord, you are perfect love, and only want the best for me. You are perfect wisdom, and know what is best for me. And you are perfect power, and able to make it happen. Therefore, I will trust in you.*

Romans 8:29 *For those God foreknew he also predestined to be conformed to the image of his Son.*

Imagine a person of perfect wisdom, beauty, strength, love, and everything good. Then imagine God resolving to make you like that person. This is what God is doing for everyone who believes in Jesus Christ. It's the reason for all our circumstances, whether we just won the lottery, just got cancer, or both. Since everything that happens is to make us more like Christ, the best way to optimize our lives is to use all our circumstances to become like him.

An artist created a magnificent horse out of a single piece of marble. The finished product was flawless, and someone asked how he was able to do it. *I just chipped away everything that wasn't a horse,* he said. Every day God is chipping away from our lives whatever doesn't resemble his Son.

Romans 8:30 *And those he predestined, he also called; those he called, he also justified; those he justified, he also glorified.*

Nothing regarding our salvation is left to chance. What God decreed in eternity past, will be fulfilled eventually. It's so certain, in fact, that Paul speaks of our glorification as though it has already taken place.

If I had to choose a symbol for my life it'd be a caterpillar. They're creepy little things, with no indication they'll ever be anything else. But after some time creeping around, the caterpillar forms a cocoon that resembles a coffin. After some time in the coffin, it comes out a beautiful creature with wings. If God does that for caterpillars, what will he do for those who love him?

Romans 8:38-39 *For I am convinced that neither death nor life, neither angels nor demons, neither the present nor the future, nor any powers, neither height nor depth, nor anything else in all creation, will be able to separate us from the love of God that is in Christ Jesus our Lord.*

Nothing is more important to those who've trusted Christ than being with him forever. We'll be attacked by mighty forces, but nothing will ever separate us from our beloved. This chapter begins with *no condemnation* and ends with *no separation*. This agrees with what God said elsewhere: *my salvation will last forever* (Isaiah 51:6).

A Christian man was dying and asked for a Bible. He could no longer see but asked that his finger be put on the words, *neither death nor life . . . will be able to separate us from the love of God.* Believing this promise, he breathed his last.

I give them eternal life, and they shall never perish; no one will snatch them out of my hand. My Father, who has given them to me, is greater than all; no one can snatch them out of my Father's hand. I and the Father are one (John 10:28-30). Whoever is saved by Jesus Christ will be kept by him forever.

Romans 9:3-4 *For I could wish that I myself were cursed and cut off from Christ for the sake of my people, those of my own race, the people of Israel.*

When we consider how much Paul loved Jesus Christ, and looked forward to heaven, we can hardly believe these words. Paul's concern for his fellow Israelites was so profound that he was willing to go to hell on their behalf, if that would result in their salvation.

To go to hell for another person is more than what God asks of us, but to care for lost souls is not. Once we understand the gospel of Jesus Christ, and all that's at stake, our first concern should be the salvation of those who are lost.

David Brainard was a missionary to Native Americans in the eighteenth century. He died at the age of twenty-nine but left a remarkable legacy. *I care not where I go, how I live, or what I endure—only that I may save souls. When I sleep, I dream of them; when I awake, they are my first thoughts.*

A friend of mine was driving through a neighborhood where there was little gospel witness. He was so concerned that he pulled over on the side of the road and wept. He asked God to start a church in that area, so God used him to help start a church that's flourishing to this day. Until we care deeply for souls, God is unlikely to use us to bring others to Christ. We don't have to go to hell for them, but we ought to be concerned.

Romans 9:18 *Therefore God has mercy on whom he wants to have mercy, and he hardens whom he wants to harden.*

This is one of the least popular verses in the Bible because it clearly states that God is the one who determines who will be saved, and who will be lost. It's difficult to understand how this relates to God's love, or human responsibility. But it's a recurring theme throughout the New Testament, so it shouldn't be disregarded.

Paul used Pharaoh as an example of one whose heart was hardened by God. He referred to the story of the Exodus in which, no fewer than nine times, God is said to have hardened Pharaoh's heart (Exodus 4:21, 7:3, 9:12, 10:1, 10:20, 10:27, 11:10, 14:4: 14:8). But a few times Pharaoh is said to have hardened his own heart (Exodus 8:15, 8:32, 9:34). Since Pharaoh hardened his own heart, before God hardened his heart, God's hardening can be understood as *judicial hardening*.

The punishment for hardening our heart is that God will harden our heart even more. Since we've all hardened our heart, the fact that any respond to God is due to his mercy and grace.

At the tender age of six I flew into a rage and said, *Damn God to hell*. There was no one around to hear me, and the words tasted so good, that I said them over and over, with all my heart, a hundred times or more. The memory is so vivid I could take you to the exact place I was standing when I uttered such terrible blasphemy.

By nature and by choice we are sinners from our youth and, unless we repent, there will be hell to pay. That anyone ever repents, however, is due to God's mercy. *God has mercy on whom he wants to have mercy, and he hardens whom he wants to harden.*

For Reflection and Review

- *What part of life makes you groan?*
- *How does God make us like Christ?*
- *Do you care about lost people?*

Lesson 281

Romans 9:20 *But who are you, a human being, to talk back to God?*

Having raised the idea of predestination, Paul anticipated his readers' reaction and told them, in effect, to shut up. This is seldom a good argument but, in this case, it is. If a squirrel can't understand calculus, we shouldn't be surprised if we can't understand God perfectly. If everything the Bible taught about God was easy to understand, it wouldn't be about the true God, but one of our own making. We should be thankful for what we understand, and trust God with what we don't.

Let us also keep in mind something Jesus said: *whoever comes to me I will never drive away* (John 6:37). Our first concern isn't what God has decreed, but whether we've come to Christ for salvation. Whoever comes to him will never be turned away.

Romans 10:3 *Since they did not know the righteousness of God and sought to establish their own, they did not submit to God's righteousness.*

Some people refuse to come to Christ because they won't let go of their sins. Others refuse to come to Christ because they won't let go of their righteousness. Many to whom Paul preached were religious and, compared to others, were very good people. But religious people often resist the gospel because they don't think they need it. They may've spent a lifetime being good, and believe that heaven's gate will open wide for them.

What they fail to see is that even our best deeds are contaminated by sin. This is like a mechanic who cleans his house while his hands are covered with grease—everything he touches becomes dirty. No matter how good his intention, the outcome is unacceptable.

That's why the Bible says *all our righteous acts are like filthy rags* (Isaiah 64:6). If God asks why he should let you into heaven, and you list a hundred of the best things you ever did, it'll be like waving a hundred filthy rags in the face of God and saying, *This is why you should let me into heaven*. The very things you thought would get you into heaven, will be enough to keep you out.

Jesus died for our sins and lived for our righteousness. In fact, he is *our righteousness* (1 Corinthians 1:30), wrote Paul. When we put our faith in Christ, he not only takes away our sins, but gives us his record of perfect obedience. We don't get into heaven based on our own righteousness, but on the righteousness of Jesus Christ.

Romans 10:9 *If you declare with your mouth, Jesus is Lord, and believe in your heart that God raised him from the dead, you will be saved.*

Paul wanted his readers to know that salvation is available to anyone, at any stage of life, no matter what they've done. The gospel is unlike anything else, and even applies to those who are at death's door.

A hospital chaplain called on an older woman and asked how it was with her soul. She replied, *Not good. I know that God cannot forgive me because I can't forgive myself for the sin of my youth. I got drunk one night and committed incest with my brother; now I'm dying and going to hell.*

The chaplain explained that Jesus didn't come to save the righteous, but sinners, and doesn't want anyone to perish. Then he read this verse to her, and promised to come back the following day. The lady died that night, but not before leaving a note: *Tell the chaplain everything is okay because I made my peace with God.*

When sin is dragging us down to hell, and time is almost gone, we can still be saved. *If you declare with your mouth, Jesus is Lord, and believe in your heart that God raised him from the dead, you will be saved.*

Romans 10:15 *As it is written: How beautiful are the feet of those who bring good news!*

When a distant battle was fought, a runner was sent to inform his people of the outcome. If the battle was lost the runner might shout, *run for your lives!* But if the battle was won, he'd proclaim the victory. Although his feet were dirty and smelly, they'd be considered beautiful because of the good news he carried.

As Paul went around preaching the gospel, he thought of himself as this kind of messenger. The battle against sin, death, and the devil was won by Jesus Christ; and all who believe share in his victory. We don't need to run for our lives; our king has won the battle.

The gospel isn't a way of life, or something we could figure out. It's the clear announcement that God came down from heaven, to bear our sins on a cross, and rose from the dead victoriously. Those who proclaim it are like messengers with dirty feet that are beautiful, because of the message they carry.

The church's obligation to take the gospel to the *ends of the earth* (Acts 1:8) didn't die with the apostles. Many have left the comforts of home to carry this message elsewhere. Some became slaves in order reach slaves; others lived in garbage dumps in order to reach the poor. They follow the one who left his home in heaven, to bring the gospel down to earth. Their feet are dirty and smelly but, to those who believe, they're beautiful.

Romans 11:22 *Consider therefore the kindness and sternness of God.*

We prefer the kindness of God to the sternness of God, but the Bible insists we consider both. Christian ministers are ordinary people who want to please their congregation, and are tempted to emphasize God's kindness at the expense of his sternness. If they do this well enough, they'll enjoy a growing church and the approval of their listeners. But Paul was more concerned about truth than popularity, so he emphasized God's kindness to those who were living for him, and his sternness to those who weren't.

Paul taught that Israelites who rejected the Messiah were not God's people, while Gentiles who received the Messiah were God's people. Then he warned believers that they too would be cut off if they didn't keep the faith. The proper response to this kind of God is not only love but fear.

A Woman told her pastor she was leaving her husband to move in with her boyfriend. *Don't you fear God?* asked her pastor. *Not at all*, she replied. *I'm a Christian and that means God will forgive whatever I do.* But that kind of attitude is never taught in the Bible, and reveals an unbelieving heart.

Fear him who, after your body has been killed, has authority to throw you into hell (Luke 12:5). *Then he will say to those on his left, Depart from me, you who are cursed, into the eternal fire prepared for the devil and his angels* (Matthew 25:41). *It is a dreadful thing to fall into the hands of the living God* (Hebrews 10:31), says Hebrews.

The healthiest Christians aren't those who dwell on the kindness of God alone, or the sternness of God alone. Nor do they allow the two to blend, or cancel each other out. The healthiest Christians are overwhelmed by God's amazing kindness toward those who belong to Christ, and awestruck by his dreadful wrath toward those who don't belong to Christ. *Consider therefore the kindness and sternness of God.*

For Reflection and Review

- *Is God hard to understand?*
- *Why do some people think they're good enough for heaven?*
- *Would you rather hear about God's kindness or sternness?*

Lesson 282

Romans 12:1 *[O]ffer your bodies as a living sacrifice, holy and pleasing to God.*

Sacrifice was an important part of Old Testament worship, and a constant reminder of sin. But animal sacrifice came to an end with the death of Jesus Christ, because *by one sacrifice he has made perfect forever those who are being made holy* (Hebrews 10:14), says Hebrews. Instead of offering animals, we offer ourselves in service to Christ. We don't do this to be saved, but out of thankfulness for being saved.

An old Roman coin had an image of an ox that was facing an altar and a plow. The inscription said, *Ready for Either*. Comfortable Christians need to be reminded that Christianity is a sacrificial religion. God sacrificed his Son for our salvation, and we sacrifice our lives in loving service to him.

Romans 12:2 *Do not conform to the pattern of this world, but be transformed by the renewing of your mind.*

If Paul could teach believes to think differently, he knew it would transform their lives from the inside out. Instead of thinking about whatever comes into our minds, we can tell our minds what to think about: *whatever is true, whatever is noble, whatever is right, whatever is pure, whatever is lovely, whatever is admirable—if anything is excellent or praiseworthy—think about such things* (Philippians 2:8), wrote Paul.

By one estimate, most people have about five thousand separate and distinct thoughts every day. One of the easiest ways to improve our lives, therefore, is to improve the quality of our thoughts.

When I came to Christ I began to read the Bible with a stack of note cards on my desk. Whenever I came to a verse that made a strong impression, I wrote it down and added it to my collection. I reviewed them often, and they started coming to mind throughout the day. My thinking became more godly and I grew in my love for Christ. We can be transformed by the renewing of our minds.

Romans 12:3 *Do not think of yourself more highly than you ought, but rather think of yourself with sober judgment.*

Studies show that most people rate themselves more highly than they're rated by their peers. If you give yourself a seven in terms of your personality, looks, or intelligence, your peers probably give you a six. But some think too poorly of themselves, and suffer from self-loathing. The Bible gives us the right perspective. It helps us think well of ourselves, without thinking too well of ourselves.

An art museum received a painting they assumed had little value, so they put it into storage. Years later they discovered it was an original work by a famous painter, and the value went up dramatically. As creatures made in the image of God (Genesis 1:27) we are his self-portraits. Everyone has extraordinary value, and should be treated accordingly.

Our value to God was also proven by the death of Jesus Christ. The real value of a person isn't what others think of them, but what Christ was willing to pay for them. Whenever we look in the mirror we should see someone of tremendous value and significance.

But this should never result in pride. We've sinned more times than we can count, and have reason to be ashamed. If others knew everything about us, in fact, we couldn't lift our heads. And if we have some talent or ability, it has come from God as a gift. *For who makes you different from anyone else? What do you have that you did not receive? And if you did receive it, why do you boast as though you did not?* (1 Corinthians 4:7), wrote Paul.

If we have beauty, brains, or other gifts, they are from the Lord. We did nothing to earn them, and God could take them away tomorrow. Knowing our value to God, and that all we have is a gift from God, gives us proper self-esteem as well as proper humility.

Romans 12:10 *Honor one another above yourselves.*

Two men came to a parking spot at the same time and neither was willing to yield. They got out of their cars and exchanged words, then blows. One went back to his car, pulled out an ax, and began to chop the other person's car. That's where the conflict stopped, but we can imagine even worse.

The best way to handle conflict isn't by force, but by honoring others above ourselves. It dignifies the one who yields, and transforms relationships. It's the culture of heaven which God is bringing to earth. If it's practiced in the home, it'll transform the home. If it's practiced in the workplace, it'll transform the workplace. If it's practiced in the world, it'll transform the world. Honoring others above ourselves is nothing less than relational genius.

Romans 12:11 *Never be lacking in zeal, but keep your spiritual fervor, serving the Lord.*

Even in the early church it wasn't uncommon for spiritual fervor to wane. Many began the Christian life with zeal, but over the years grew cold. Paul saw this pattern emerging and warned believers against it.

Top performing professionals were studied to discover what made them successful. They came from various backgrounds, had different personalities, and various levels of intelligence. But one thing they all had in common was passion. Paul knew the impact we have as Christians may be linked to passion more than anything else.

The ancient Greeks had an athletic event called the torch race, in which the runners carried a torch as they ran. The winner wasn't the first to cross the finish line, but the first to cross the finish line with his torch still lit. The goal of the Christian life isn't to merely finish the race, but to keep the flame alive.

For Reflection and Review

- *Why does God care about our thoughts?*
- *Would you rather think too highly of yourself, or too lowly of yourself?*
- *How can we honor others above ourselves?*

Lesson 283

Romans 12:12 *Be . . . faithful in prayer.*

Paul was a prayerful person and wanted the church to be prayerful as well. Even then busy schedules, and other priorities, could crowd out prayer. So Paul called the believers to be *faithful in prayer*. This means having a regular time and place for seeking God. I've found it helpful to underline verses in my Bible and pray them back to God.

In the beginning God created the heavens and the earth (Genesis 1:1). Thank you, Father, that you're God of heaven and earth, not just the Milky Way galaxy. Thank you for calling the stars by name and numbering the hairs of my head. Thank you for making the grass green, the sky blue, the birds sing, and the crickets chirp. Help me live in your world as someone who's fully alive, and to give you glory as I enjoy what you have made.

If we confess our sins, he is faithful and just and will forgive us our sins and purify us from all unrighteousness (1 John 1:9). Father, I confess my sins to you, not only in general, but also in particular. Forgive me for being rude to my wife and impatient with my children. Forgive me for watching television when I should've been reading your word. Forgive me for spending too much money on comfort, and not enough on your kingdom. Thank you for the privilege of coming clean before you, and receiving your forgiveness.

Romans 12:16 *Do not be proud, but be willing to associate with people of low position.*

One of the first things Paul noticed as he preached the gospel is that not many wise, noble, or influential people responded (1 Corinthians 1:26). *Has not God chosen those who are poor in the eyes of the world to be rich in faith* (James 2:5), wrote James. Belonging to a church often means being part of a group we wouldn't normally join. And that's a good thing.

Years ago I was part of a singles group that could be a little exclusive. But one of my friends went out of his way to invite a young man who didn't fit in very well. He was mentally and socially challenged, with an underdeveloped sense of hygiene. But every week my friend invited him to be part of our group, and to join us for every outing.

Perhaps he was thinking of something Jesus said: *[W]hatever you did for one of the least of these brothers and sisters of mine, you did for me* (Matthew 25:40). God wants us to be willing to associate with people of low position because that's what he does for us.

Romans 12:21 *Do not be overcome by evil, but overcome evil with good.*

Whenever people hurt us, we naturally want to hurt them back. And to be sure they get the point, we want to hurt them a little bit more. In return for a slap we want to throw a punch. A better way, says Paul, is to overcome evil with good.

One lady told her attorney that she wanted a divorce and, because her husband was evil, she wanted to hurt him deeply. The attorney advised her to go home and treat her husband like the most wonderful man on earth. Then, when he was happier than ever, she should serve him divorce papers. That way he'd know what he was losing, and it would break his heart.

About a month later the attorney called to ask if she was ready to file for divorce. *Why would I want to divorce the most wonderful man on earth?* she said. By treating her husband wonderfully, he became wonderful, and they became happily married.

Romans 13:1 *Let everyone be subject to the governing authorities, for there is no authority except that which God has established. The authorities that exist have been established by God.*

When they came under the authority of Jesus Christ, it was natural for Christians to wonder about their relationship to ungodly governments like Rome. If Jesus Christ is King of kings, and the governments don't acknowledge him, are Christians obligated to obey their ungodly government? The short answer is, *yes*. Paul saw government as established by God.

This is a little surprising since the emperor at the time Paul wrote was Nero. He was an evil man who killed his mother, and probably set fire to a poor part of Rome to make space for new buildings. When the rumor that Nero started the blaze wouldn't go away, he blamed the Christians. Then he began a persecution in which Christians were burned, crucified, and thrown to wild animals.

Paul wrote to the Christians in Rome before this event, but if he required them to support a government led by Nero, then Christians should support their government whenever possible. When government breaks down completely, chaos erupts, and murder and rape go unpunished. This is why Christians should think of government as a gift from God to be valued, obeyed, and appreciated.

The only time Christians should disobey the government is when it commands something God forbids. *We must obey God rather than human beings* (Acts 5:29), said the apostles. Otherwise, we should *Be subject to the governing authorities, for there is no authority except that which God has established.*

Romans 13:3 *Do you want to be free from fear of the one in authority? Then do what is right and you will be commended.*

Christians should obey the law out of principle, but also out of fear, since whoever breaks the law must live in fear punishment. *[Rulers] are God's servants, agents of wrath to bring punishment on the wrongdoer* (Romans 13:4), wrote Paul. If you break the law, God may send the police to punish you.

I received a speeding ticket for exceeding the limit by twenty miles an hour. I was upset at the time, but thanked the officer for doing his job. I don't like to be punished for breaking the law, but I like to live in a place where the roads are kept safe from people like me. Because of the punishment, I'm a safer driver today.

For Reflection and Review

- *How do you benefit from prayer?*
- *Why does God want us to associate with people of low position?*
- *What is your attitude toward the law?*

Lesson 284

Romans 13:7 *If you owe taxes, pay taxes.*

Governments provide many things worth paying for like roads, water, and defense. But they can also be corrupt, wasteful, and unfair. That's why many people resent paying taxes, and under-report their income. But the Bible is clear: *If you owe taxes, pay taxes.*

It was even worse for many Jews at this time, since they not only sent their taxes to Jerusalem, but also to Rome. It seemed wrong for God's people to support a pagan government, so they asked Jesus what to do. In one of his most quotable statements Jesus said, *give back to Caesar what is Caesar's, and to God what is God's* (Matthew 22:21).

Romans 13:11 *[O]ur salvation is nearer now than when we first believed.*

Many begin the Christian life with great enthusiasm. Their heads are high, their pace is fast, and their eyes are on the sky. But, after a while, many slow down and forget that heaven is near. We need to be reminded, more than once, that heaven is closer than we think.

When I was fifteen, my cousin and I rode our bicycles to his cabin, which was about sixty miles away. I didn't understand how far that was and, after twenty miles, I started getting tired. My cousin kept saying, *We're almost there . . . just a little further . . . I think it's around the corner.* It was quite a bit further, actually, but every time he said it I found a little strength. The preacher's job is to keep on saying, *We're almost there.* He may seem redundant, but he's not mistaken. It may take a lifetime, but *our salvation is nearer now than when we first believed.*

Romans 14:12 *So then, each of us will give an account of ourselves to God.*

Thankfully, we'll stand before God completely forgiven—*holy in his sight, without blemish and free from accusation* (Colossians 1:22), wrote Paul. *For by one sacrifice he has made perfect forever those who are being made holy* (Hebrews 10:14), says Hebrews. But if our sins are forgiven, why should we still be concerned about Judgment Day?

First, many who thought they were Christians will discover they weren't true Christians. *Many will say to me on that day, Lord, Lord, did we not prophesy in your name and in your name drive out demons and in your name perform many miracles? Then I will tell them plainly, I never knew you. Away from me, you evildoers!* (Matthew 7:22-23).

Second, Christians will still be judged. *I tell you that everyone will have to give account on the day of judgment for every empty word they have spoken* (Matthew 12:36-37). *For there is nothing hidden that will not be disclosed, and nothing concealed that will not be known or brought out into the open* (Luke 8:17), said Jesus. *He will bring to light what is hidden in darkness and will expose the motives of the heart* (1 Corinthians 4:5), wrote Paul.

Third, Christians will be rewarded for the good they've done. *[T]he Lord will reward each one for whatever good they do* (Ephesians 6:8), wrote Paul. *For the Son of Man is going to come in his Father's glory . . . and then he will reward each person according to what they have done.* (Matthew 16:27), said Jesus. *Look, I am coming soon! My reward is with me, and I will give to each person according to what they have done* (Revelation 22:12), said Jesus again.

A professional football player was asked about the secret of his success. He said, *Every game is filmed and I have to give an account to the coach for every move I make, or fail to make. What inspires me most is that my coach sees every single move.* This is also why believers should live each day in the light of Judgment Day.

Romans 14:13 *Therefore let us stop passing judgment on one another.*

The church in Rome was made up of Jews and Gentiles who came from very different backgrounds. Jewish Christians observed a religious diet, and were careful about the Sabbath. Gentile Christians seemed to eat anything, and cared very little about the Sabbath. The Jewish Christians were looking down on the Gentile Christians, and the Gentile Christians were becoming impatient with the Jewish Christians—and the church was being divided. Paul was never afraid of taking sides but, in this case, he simply encouraged both sides to be less judgmental.

Whenever I see another believer acting badly I try to put myself in their shoes. If I had their DNA, family background, and personal experiences, I'd probably act the same way. Sometimes evil has to be confronted (1 Corinthians 5:1-2), but it's usually best not to judge.

Romans 15:13 *May the God of hope fill you with all joy and peace as you trust in him.*

The Assyrians, Babylonians, Greeks, and Romans all had numerous deities. They had gods of war, gods of weather, gods of crops, and many other gods. In the pantheon of pagan gods, however, there was never a god of hope. The only God of hope is the God and Father of our Lord Jesus Christ, to whom nothing is impossible. Paul wanted the Christians in Rome to know they could always have hope no matter how difficult their situation.

Scientists placed a rat into a tub of water and, after forty-five minutes, it drowned. Another rat was placed into a tub of water but, after thirty minutes, it was rescued. The next day it was placed in the water again, and was able to swim for hours because it had the hope of being rescued. No matter our situation, we can always have hope. *[My] hope is in you all day long* (Psalm 25:5), wrote David.

For Reflection and Review

- *What does God provide through governments?*
- *What would you change if you thought that Christ would return in a year?*
- *Why should Christians be concerned about Judgment Day?*

Lesson 285

1 Corinthians 1:1-2 *Paul, called to be an apostle of Christ Jesus by the will of God . . . To the church of God in Corinth.*

Paul wrote to believers in Corinth around AD 55, while he was staying in Ephesus. Corinth was an important city in Greece that was flourishing commercially, politically, and intellectually. It was also a religious city, boasting numerous temples to various gods. But the culture was so immoral that *to Corinthianize* meant *to practice sexual immorality.*

While he was in Ephesus, Paul received reports that the church in Corinth was struggling with problems of division, immorality, false teaching, and other issues. He wrote to provide correction, but also to encourage the church, which was only a few years old at the time. Paul had spent a year and a half in Corinth and loved them very much.

1 Corinthians 1:8 *He will also keep you firm to the end, so that you will be blameless on the day of our Lord Jesus Christ.*

The problems Paul wrote to correct show the Corinthian Christians were anything but firm or blameless. They appear, in fact, to be the most sinful church Paul ever started. Because they were Christians, however, their status before God was *blameless*, and God would keep *firm to the end*.

When we consider the enticements of the world, our sinful nature, and the work of Satan, it's amazing anyone remains a Christian very long. But God is the one who saves, and he is the one who keeps. *[H]e who began a good work in you will carry it on to completion until the day of Christ Jesus* (Philippians 1:6), wrote Paul. We don't save ourselves, and we don't keep ourselves. Salvation is the work of God.

Several years ago my niece came to faith in Jesus Christ. She was right out of high school, without Christian friends, and without any knowledge of the Bible. She bounced around from church to church, and eventually moved out of state. Once in a while we'd cross paths and I was always surprised to see that she was still a believer. She eventually found a wonderful church and, over years, became a strong, mature woman of God. God is the one who begins the work, and carries it on to completion.

1 Corinthians 1:10 *I appeal to you, brothers and sisters, in the name of our Lord Jesus Christ, that all of you agree with one another in what you say and that there be no divisions among you, but that you be perfectly united in mind and thought.*

The Corinthian church had good and godly ministers, to whom they were loyal. But some preferred one, while some preferred another, and this was dividing the church. The ministers weren't divided among themselves, but the people were dividing over their ministers. To this Paul said, *agree with one another*.

Agreeability is a virtue to be taught, learned, and practiced by the church. Some people are so contrary by nature that if you say right they'll say left; if you say up they'll say down; and if you say east they'll say west.

Being agreeable doesn't mean having no opinion, but hearing people in the best possible way. Even if they say something with which you disagree, you can try to understand their point of view, and agree wherever you can. *If a house is divided against itself, that house cannot stand* (Mark 3:25), said Jesus. *Divide and conquer* is one of Satan's oldest strategies against the church.

1 Corinthians 1:18 *For the message of the cross is foolishness to those who are perishing.*

A woman from an atheist state was brought to trial for believing in Jesus Christ. Instead of sending her to prison, the judge had her committed to an insane asylum because he thought she must be crazy. To be fair, what's less likely than a crucified Jew being the only way to God? I've heard Christians describe other religions as foolish, and maybe they're right. But humanly speaking, Christianity is absurd, and the Bible frankly admits this. Being misunderstood is the price of seeing what others cannot see.

1 Corinthians 1:18b *. . . but to us who are being saved it is the power of God.*

The gospel appears foolish at first, but powerfully brings salvation to those who believe. Paul was radically changed by Jesus Christ (Acts 9) and, when he told others about Christ, many of them were changed as well.

Missionaries were visiting homes in India when they saw a woman's body hanging from the rafters. They kicked open the door, discovered she was alive, and called a doctor. They discovered her husband was an alcoholic who beat her. Through the witness of the missionaries, the woman and her husband came to Christ, and their lives were wonderfully changed. They began holding a prayer meeting and many others came to faith. The gospel has the power to change lives. *[I]t is the power of God that brings salvation to everyone who believes* (Romans 1:16), wrote Paul.

1 Corinthians 1:26-29 *Brothers and sisters, think of what you were when you were called. Not many of you were wise by human standards; not many were influential; not many were of noble birth. But God chose the foolish things of the world to shame the wise; God chose the weak things of the world to shame the strong. God chose the lowly things of this world and the despised things—and the things that are not—to nullify the things that are, so that no one may boast before him.*

When the believers in Corinth looked around their church, it was clear they weren't from the upper levels of society. There were a few exceptions, but most of them were unremarkable in any way. God took the weak, lowly, and despised and made them part of his glorious kingdom.

Before he was Israel's king, David was an outcast living in caves. Some who were distressed, or in debt (1 Samuel 22:2), decided to join him and, together, they dreamed of the kingdom of God. They were the ones God used to turn the nation of Israel into a regional super-power. The kingdom of God doesn't depend on the greatness of the ones he chooses, but on the greatness of the Father, the Son, and the Holy Spirit.

For Reflection and Review

- *Do you try to be agreeable?*
- *Why is the gospel hard to believe?*
- *Why is the gospel powerful?*

Lesson 286

1 Corinthians 2:14 *The person without the Spirit does not accept the things that come from the Spirit of God but considers them foolishness, and cannot understand them because they are discerned only through the Spirit.*

As Paul preached the gospel, he depended on the Holy Spirit to work in the hearts of his listeners, so they'd believe and be saved. Without the Holy Spirit, unconverted people will always remain unconverted. That's why the guards at Jesus' tomb didn't become Christians after he rose from the dead (Matthew 28:11-15). All the proof in the world won't make a Christian, apart from the work of the Spirit.

1 Corinthians 3:16 *Don't you know that you yourselves are God's temple and that God's Spirit dwells in your midst?*

For many years God dwelt in a temple of stone, in the city of Jerusalem. But with the coming of the Spirit on the day of Pentecost (Acts 2), the local church became God's temple. And *If anyone destroys God's temple, God will destroy that person; for God's temple is sacred, and you together are that temple* (1 Corinthians 3:17), wrote Paul. The Bible doesn't threaten us for leaving a church, and joining another. But to remain in a church and cause division, disruption, or any other harm exposes a person to destruction from God.

A church in a small town flourished for many years until two of the men began to quarrel. They spoke against each other at every opportunity and refused to reconcile. People took sides and the church became divided. Members sought fellowship elsewhere until, eventually, nothing was left of the church. Then both men died of unrelated causes, well before their time. *If anyone destroys God's temple, God will destroy that person.*

1 Corinthians 4:7 *For who makes you different from anyone else? What do you have that you did not receive? And if you did receive it, why do you boast as though you did not?*

Pride was a source of problems in the church, so Paul pointed out an obvious fact: whatever they had was a gift from God. If they had wisdom, it was a gift. If they had the Spirit, it was a gift. If they had eloquence, it was a gift. If they had knowledge, it was a gift. Instead of making us proud, our gifts should make us humble since we did nothing to earn them. Comparing ourselves to others will always make us jealous or proud, until we understand that God is the giver of gifts, and that he can take them away whenever he likes.

1 Corinthians 5:1 *It is actually reported that there is sexual immorality among you, and of a kind that even pagans do not tolerate: A man is sleeping with his father's wife.*

This would've been a scandal in most churches, but the Corinthian culture was so depraved that the church took it in stride. Even Paul wouldn't have been alarmed if the man had simply repented. But this was an ongoing relationship for which the man refused to repent, nor would he leave the church. He wanted to maintain his inappropriate relationship, and remain in good standing with the church. But Paul wouldn't have it.

1 Corinthians 5:13 *Expel the wicked person from among you.*

Paul outlined a ceremony of excommunication to remove the unrepentant man. *So when you are assembled and I am with you in spirit, and the power of our Lord Jesus is present, hand this man over to Satan for the destruction of the flesh, so that his spirit may be saved on the day of the Lord* (1 Corinthians 5:4-5), he wrote.

The purpose of the excommunication wasn't to harm the man, but to help him repent. Perhaps he'd see the error of his way, turn from his sin, and *be saved on the day of the Lord.* Excommunication isn't for Christians who are struggling with sin, repenting, and trying to do better. Nor is it for those who are visiting church, but haven't become Christians. It's for people who claim to be Christians, but want to bring their sin into the church, as though there was nothing wrong with it.

Not everyone who says to me, Lord, Lord, will enter the kingdom of heaven, but only the one who does the will of my Father (Matthew 7:21), said Jesus. And *without holiness no one will see the Lord* (Hebrews 12:14), says Hebrews. The church doesn't help people by allowing them to remain in church, along with their open sins, only to go to hell when they die. Excommunication is tough love to help people repent and be saved.

1 Corinthians 6:1 *If any of you has a dispute with another, do you dare to take it before the ungodly for judgment instead of before the Lord's people?*

Legal disputes between Christians in Corinth were hurting the church and its reputation. Instead of using worldly courts, Paul wanted matters to be settled by believers who were *wise enough to judge* (1 Corinthians 6:5). Then he proposed something even more radical: *Why not rather be wronged? Why not rather be cheated?* (1 Corinthians 6:7), he asked.

If you pay a person from church to fix your roof, but the roof still leaks, they should make it right. If they refuse, you can bring your complaint to the church (Matthew 18:15-19). But you can also choose to let it go. *If someone slaps you on one cheek, turn to them the other also. If someone takes your coat, do not withhold your shirt* (Luke 6:29), said Jesus. Sometimes the best way to handle injustice is to allow yourself to be wronged.

For Reflection and Review

- *Why does God like to use ordinary people?*
- *Why do we need the Holy Spirit to believe?*
- *Why should a church excommunicate those who refuse to repent?*

Lesson 287

1 Corinthians 6:19 *Do you not know that your bodies are temples of the Holy Spirit, who is in you, whom you have received from God?*

Some in the church didn't believe their bodies had much to do with their relationship with God, so it didn't matter what they did with their bodies, including sex outside of marriage. But Paul insisted the bodies of Christians are temples of the Holy Spirit and, therefore, should be treated honorably. Pleasure is a gift from God (Psalm 16:11), including sexual pleasure, but it should only be expressed between a husband and wife as God designed (Genesis 2:23-25).

1 Corinthians 6:19b-20 *You are not your own; you were bought at a price. Therefore honor God with your bodies.*

We ought to honor God with our bodies, not only because of the indwelling Spirit, but also because of our redemption. We used to be slaves to sin, but Christ bought us for himself at the cross. Now we belong to him.

When I was sixteen years old I said to my mom, quite emphatically, *It's my life and I'll do what I want with it*. This is a common idea, but reveals a stunning immaturity and lack of understanding. We don't belong to ourselves, but to the God who made us, redeemed us, and put us here for others.

God made us for himself, but also for our family, friends, neighbors, country, and world. First he created us, then he bought us with his blood, then he commanded us to love and serve others (Matthew 22:37-39). When we understand who and whose we are, we'll live differently than if we think we belong to ourselves.

1 Corinthians 7:3-5 *The husband should fulfill his marital duty to his wife, and likewise the wife to her husband. . . . Do not deprive each other.*

The Corinthian believers had questions about sex, which Paul was happy to answer. God created sex not only for procreation, but also for pleasure in marriage. But the sexual needs of husband and wife are seldom the same, so one can feel deprived if the other is unresponsive. Paul instructed married Christians not to deprive each other, but to attend to each other's needs.

Sex in the marriage relationship is just as important as it is to the one to whom it's most important. If it's not important to either, it's not important at all. But if it's important to one, it's precisely that important to the marriage. Attending to each other's needs is a proper thing to do, and a safeguard against immorality.

1 Corinthians 7:35 *[L]ive in a right way in undivided devotion to the Lord.*

The best way for Paul to live in *undivided devotion to the Lord* was by remaining single. Other apostles were married (1 Corinthians 9:5) but, by choosing not to marry, Paul was able to serve God without concern for a family. Paul enjoyed being single and recommended it to others, not as the ideal, but as an excellent way for those who were able. Whether married or single, however, we should always try to live in *undivided devotion to the Lord.*

1 Corinthians 9:14 *In the same way, the Lord has commanded that those who preach the gospel should receive their living from the gospel.*

Paul refused to be paid for his ministry in Corinth, because some people thought he was preaching for profit. To prove this wasn't true, Paul refused to accept a salary. But, ordinarily, preachers ought to be paid. *Who serves as a soldier at his own expense? Who plants a vineyard and does not eat its grapes? Who tends a flock and does not drink the milk?* (1 Corinthians 9:7), he asked.

Every Christian ought to feel some responsibility to help pay the salaries of those who serve their church. Those who serve should not be overpaid, or under paid, but fairly paid—*for the worker deserves his wages* (Luke 10:7), said Jesus. The Lord wants his gospel preached around the world (Mark 13:10), and it's the duty of every Christian to assist. If Christians won't pay to have the gospel preached, no one else will.

1 Corinthians 9:24 *Do you not know that in a race all the runners run, but only one gets the prize? Run in such a way as to get the prize.*

Athletic games were common in Corinth, and Paul saw them as an illustration for the Christian life. If Paul was going to run a race, he didn't want to come in second. Like a professional athlete, Paul was willing to do whatever he could to come in first.

Sometimes Christians wonder, *What's the least I need to do to go to heaven?* I've wondered that myself because following Christ can be difficult, and no one wants a harder life than necessary. But the Bible never answers that question; it only tells us how to be our best. Paul wanted to be the best Christian who ever lived, and he may've achieved his goal.

1 Corinthians 10:12 *So, if you think you are standing firm, be careful that you do not fall!*

The church in Corinth had an appearance of strength that was making them careless. They were a large church (Acts 18:10), with enthusiastic worship, and many spiritual gifts (1 Corinthians 12-14). But they also had some problems such as disorder (1 Corinthians 11:17-34), immorality, (1 Corinthians 5), and doctrinal confusion (1 Corinthians 15). If these issues weren't resolved, they could lead to a fall (Proverbs 16:18).

A Redwood tree in California stood tall and strong for hundreds of years. It survived earthquakes, storms, floods, and other natural disasters. Suddenly, it came down with a crash. The problem wasn't lighting, or wind, but tiny beetles that ate the tree from the inside out. It appeared to be strong, but had become hollow. Churches can also become hollow if important issues aren't resolved. *So, if you think you are standing firm, be careful that you do not fall!*

1 Corinthians 10:13 *No temptation has overtaken you except what is common to mankind. And God is faithful; he will not let you be tempted beyond what you can bear. But when you are tempted, he will also provide a way out so that you can endure it.*

Corinth was so immoral that some believers may've thought the only way to survive was to compromise with sin. On the contrary, Paul wanted them to know their temptations were *common* and that God would *provide a way out* for them.

This is one of the most helpful verses in the Bible for overcoming sin. Temptation can be wickedly forceful, but our temptation is not unique, and we are not alone. *So do not fear, for I am with you; do not be dismayed, for I am your God. I will strengthen you and help you; I will uphold you with my righteous right hand* (Isaiah 41:10), said God.

For Reflection and Review

- *How should Christians settle disputes?*
- *Why don't we belong to ourselves?*
- *Why should Christians help pay for ministry?*

Lesson 288

1 Corinthians 11:17 *In the following directives I have no praise for you, for your meetings do more harm than good.*

This is part of a scathing rebuke for the state of corporate worship in Corinth. Some weren't getting along, and others getting drunk at the Lord's Supper (1 Corinthians 11:18-21). Many Christians assume that, whenever we gather for worship, some good will come as a result. But here we learn that church services can do more harm than good.

Churches can honor Jesus Christ through heartfelt worship, or insult him through heartless worship. They can build each other up with Christian love, or tear each other down through disrespect. They can give careful attention to God's word, or disregard it entirely. Corporate worship can glorify God, or do more harm than good. Gathering to worship God should be the most important event of the week, and should never taken lightly.

1 Corinthians 11:23-25 *For I received from the Lord what I also passed on to you: The Lord Jesus, on the night he was betrayed, took bread, and when he had given thanks, he broke it and said, This is my body, which is for you; do this in remembrance of me. In the same way, after supper he took the cup, saying, This cup is the new covenant in my blood; do this, whenever you drink it, in remembrance of me.*

The central act of Christian worship is a meal in which believers eat and drink in remembrance of Jesus Christ. This is more than recalling his death, but focusing intensely on his body given, and blood shed, for our salvation.

Whenever we receive the Lord's Supper we should force other thoughts out our minds and focus on his crucifixion. We should see his body shredded by the lashing he received, and the blood flowing from his wounds. As we prepare to take the emblems, we should recall that Jesus died for us specifically—for our sins, and for our salvation. In doing so we observe the Lord's Supper properly, and receive the benefit Christ intended when he ordained it.

1 Corinthians 12:27 *Now you are the body of Christ, and each one of you is a part of it.*

Some within the Corinthian church were highly gifted, and this led others to think of themselves as unimportant, or even unnecessary. But this way of thinking would weaken the church, so Paul instructed them on the true nature of the body of Christ.

Christ is the head of the church (Ephesians 4:15), and every believer is a hand, foot, eye, or some other part. The inconspicuous parts may seem less important, but they serve a vital role. You probably don't think about your elbows very often, but if they stopped working you'd think about them constantly. It'd be hard to comb your hair, brush your teeth, button your shirt, or do other things you normally take for granted. When Christians understand how important they are to the body of Christ, they'll participate fully and not be merely spectators.

1 Corinthians 13:13 *And now these three remain: faith, hope and love. But the greatest of these is love.*

In addition to their other problems, the Corinthian Church wasn't very loving. This was so important that Paul wrote an entire chapter on love, and how it should look in the local church.

A lady with several children was asked which one she loved the most. She claimed to love them all the same but, when pressed, admitted that wasn't true. *When one is sick I love that one the most. When one is hurt I love that one the most. When one is confused I love that one the most. When one is struggling I love that one the most.* These are also the ones we should love in the church.

Jesus emphasized the importance of love when he said the two greatest commandments are to love God and neighbor (Matthew 22:37-39). And, *By this everyone will know that you are my disciples, if you love one another* (John 13:35), he said. Love is not a secondary concern for the people of God—it's their first concern.

1 Corinthians 14:40 *But everything should be done in a fitting and orderly way.*

Worship services in Corinth could be chaotic. Some were prophesying and others were speaking in tongues. Paul didn't condemn these practices as long as order was maintained, and the church was being *built up* (1 Corinthians 14:26).

Paul wanted the worship service to accomplish three things. First, God was to be rightly worshipped. Second, believers were to be rightly instructed. Third, unbelievers were to be rightly exposed to true and orderly worship (1 Corinthians 14:23-25).

These priorities ought to be maintained in their proper order. If God isn't rightly worshipped, he won't be pleased. If believers aren't rightly instructed, they won't grow as they should. And if unbelievers aren't exposed to true and orderly worship, they'll be confused.

The continuing validity of prophesying and speaking in tongues is a matter of discussion, because there's little evidence of them from the time of the apostles, until they reemerged in the early twentieth century. But now, as then, *everything should be done in a fitting and orderly way.*

1 Corinthians 15:6 *After that, he appeared to more than five hundred of the brothers and sisters at the same time, most of whom are still living.*

Since Paul wrote to the Corinthians about twenty-five years after the resurrection of Christ, some of the witnesses had died, but most were still alive. This is a powerful argument for the resurrection of Christ because, if it wasn't true, it could've been disproven. Travel between Israel and Corinth was common, and Paul was inviting the Corinthians to investigate his claim as thoroughly as they liked.

If the church in Corinth didn't believe Paul, they could've sent a delegation to Judea, to interview the eyewitnesses. If Paul's claim proved to be false, there'd be no reason for them to remain Christians. The boldness of Paul's claim is strong evidence of the resurrection of Christ, even today.

For Reflection and Review

- *How can Christian gatherings do more harm than good?*
- *How should we take the Lord's Supper?*
- *What three things should a worship service accomplish?*

Lesson 289

1 Corinthians 15:17 *And if Christ has not been raised, your faith is futile; you are still in your sins.*

Paul's proof of Christianity was the resurrection of Christ. If Jesus didn't rise from the dead, he wasn't the person he claimed to be, and cannot save us from our sins. But if he did rise from the dead, then we can be sure that everything he taught is true.

This is why we believe the Bible. *For truly I tell you, until heaven and earth disappear, not the smallest letter, not the least stroke of a pen, will by any means disappear from the Law until everything is accomplished* (Matthew 5:18), said Jesus.

Belief in the resurrection of Christ doesn't depend on belief in the gospels as Scripture, only as honest reports of what actually happened. Careful examination shows the gospels to be extremely honest accounts of the life, death, and resurrection of Christ, based on eye-witness testimony from reliable witnesses.

We believe in the resurrection of Christ based on the credibility of the gospels, and the testimony of Paul. Then we believe in the inerrancy of the Bible because that's what Jesus taught. If we don't believe in the inerrancy of the Bible, we aren't disciples of Christ.

From the perspective of the New Testament, Christianity stands or falls with the resurrection of Christ. The apostles weren't afraid to base everything on the resurrection because they knew for themselves that it actually happened. It's the Father's *Amen* to the Son's *It is finished* (John 19:30).

1 Corinthians 15:19 *If only for this life we have hope in Christ, we are of all people most to be pitied.*

Some say they'd like to believe in Christianity, even if it wasn't true, because Christianity is a good way to live. Paul considered that to be nonsense. Christianity requires self-denial and sacrifice. If it's not true, Christians are the most pitiful people on earth. How sad it would be to give away time, talent, and treasure for a religion that isn't true! But Christianity is true, and worth any cost.

1 Corinthians 15:52 *For the trumpet will sound, the dead will be raised imperishable, and we will be changed.*

Many in the early church wondered what our resurrection bodies will look like, but no clear answer is given. *[W]hat we will be has not yet been made known* (1 John 3:2), wrote John. But Paul provided a few things for us to think about. Our resurrection bodies will be *glorious*, *powerful* and *imperishable* (1 Corinthians 15:42-44), he wrote.

We should imagine living forever in a glorious, powerful, body with a mind to match. Imagine eyes so powerful they can function as microscopes and telescopes. Instead of five senses, why not more? (Randy Alcorn). Since God is the source of beauty, how beautiful will his glorified children be? *What no eye has seen, what no ear has heard, and what no human mind has conceived—the things God has prepared for those who love him* (1 Corinthians 2:9), wrote Paul.

1 Corinthians 15:55 *Where, O death, is your victory? Where, O death, is your sting?*

Ever since our first parents sinned (Genesis 3:6), life has been a journey to the grave. We start off well enough, but after adolescence signs of aging begin to appear. Our bodies struggle and our minds decline, slowly at first, then more rapidly until we return to the ground from which we came. The killer bee of sin stung our first parents, and the venom was so powerful it kills all their children.

It was a warm summer day and the car windows were open as a family drove home from church. A bee flew inside the car, and the little girl in the back seat began to scream. Her father turned around just enough to grab the bee, and was stung by it. When he opened his hand the bee began to fly again, but it could no longer sting because the stinger was left in the father's hand.

Christ was also stung in the hand when they nailed him to the cross. He took away the sting of death when he rose from the dead. *Where, O death, is your victory? Where, O death, is your sting?*

1 Corinthians 15:57 *But thanks be to God! He gives us the victory through our Lord Jesus Christ.*

The most brutal form of athletics in Corinth were the gladiatorial games, in which contestants fought to the death. Combatants were normally slaves, but free men were also known to compete, since the victors earned a large sum of money. The stakes were high and there was no prize for second place.

We too were in line to fight, and our opponent was death itself. He was undefeated and our chances were slim to none. Then Christ stepped in and took our place in line. Nailed to a cross he appeared to lose at first. But then he triumphed over death by his resurrection, and shares his victory with all who believe. So we can say with Paul, *thanks be to God! He gives us the victory through our Lord Jesus Christ.*

1 Corinthians 15:58 *Always give yourselves fully to the work of the Lord, because you know that your labor in the Lord is not in vain.*

The church's job is to announce the victory Jesus won for all who believe in him. This means starting new churches until the whole world is reached. The work is seldom easy, and often appears to fail. So the Apostle Paul assured us that our *labor in the Lord is not in vain.*

A good man built his own company from the ground up. He was always honest, worked long hours, and eventually had success. But in a single year he lost everything due to circumstances beyond his control. Through no fault of his own the business disappeared, and never recovered. Many have a similar story of loss, but our *labor in the Lord is not in vain.* Even if we never seem to succeed, he will reward our labor in the age to come (Revelation 22:12). The important thing is to keep on serving.

1 Corinthians 16:22 *If anyone does not love the Lord, let that person be cursed!*

This verse would've come as a shock to everyone who heard it. How could the same apostle who wrote an entire chapter on love (1 Corinthians 13) conclude his letter with a curse on anyone who doesn't love the Lord?

Having just considered the death of Christ for his people, and his gift of eternal life, Paul's heart was aflame for Christ. It was clear to him that not to love Christ, after all he's done, is the height of ingratitude, and worthy of a curse. It could even be a call for eternal punishment!

This agrees with John the Baptist who said, *Whoever believes in the Son has eternal life, but whoever rejects the Son will not see life, for God's wrath remains on them* (John 3:36). Every good thing we have is a gift from Jesus Christ, and not to return his love puts us in league with the devil. *If anyone does not love the Lord, let that person be cursed!*

For Reflection and Review

- *Why do we believe in the inerrancy of Scripture?*
- *Why do we need to know that working for Christ is never a waste of time?*
- *Why does Paul pronounce a curse on anyone who doesn't love Christ?*

Lesson 290

2 Corinthians 1:1 *Paul, an apostle of Christ Jesus by the will of God . . . To the church of God in Corinth.*

Paul's second letter to the church in Corinth was probably written in AD 55, just several months after his first letter. In addition to what we know as First and Second Corinthians, there appears to be other correspondence and possibly a visit. False teachers had come to Corinth and challenged Paul's apostleship, so an important purpose of this letter was to confront that opposition.

2 Corinthians 1:3-4 *Praise be to the God and Father of our Lord Jesus Christ, the Father of compassion and the God of all comfort, who comforts us in all our troubles, so that we can comfort those in any trouble with the comfort we ourselves receive from God.*

Paul suffered a great deal throughout his ministry, and some of it was due to Christians in Corinth. Paul loved them deeply but, like rebellious children, they often went astray and questioned his authority. The relational strain caused pain on both sides, but also allowed them to experience the *God of all comfort, who comforts us in all our troubles*.

The remarkable thing about the spiritual comfort God provides is that it's real. It's hard to describe but often expressed when Christians say, *I don't know how people get through this without the Lord.* In times of terrible distress we can come to our heavenly Father and receive the consolation we need and the strength to go on.

2 Corinthians 1:11 *. . . you help us by your prayers.*

Some of the Christians in Corinth opposed the Apostle Paul, but others were loyal to him, and prayed for him. Their prayers didn't produce miraculous results, but provided a measure of help. *. . . you help us by your prayers*, he said.

Since most of our prayers aren't answered dramatically, we might wonder if prayer is a waste of time. But if we could see the collective value of our prayers, especially when joined with the prayers of others, it'd be clear that prayer is the greatest power on earth. God can use a single prayer to cast a mountain into the sea (Matthew 21:21), but often uses the prayers of many to move things in the right direction.

A good example is found in the prayer that Jesus taught: *your kingdom come, your will be done, on earth as it is in heaven* (Matthew 6:10). This has been prayed by billions of people, over thousands of years, but hasn't been fully answered. Nevertheless, God is using this prayer to advance his kingdom one day at a time. Prayer isn't always answered at once, but faithful prayer moves things along in the right direction.

2 Corinthians 1:20 *For no matter how many promises God has made, they are Yes in Christ.*

Jesus is the present and future fulfillment of everything God has promised. God promised someone who'd crush the devil's head (Genesis 3:15), and Christ defeated Satan through his death and resurrection. But that's just the beginning. *He who did not spare his own Son, but gave him up for us all—how will he not also, along with him, graciously give us all things?* (Romans 8:32), wrote Paul.

You may die of sickness, but you'll wake up to health. You may die of poverty, but you'll wake up to wealth. You may die of sorrow, but you'll wake up to joy. You may die of conflict, but you'll wake up to peace. You may die alone, but you'll wake up to friends. You may die in weakness, but you'll wake up to strength. You may die disgraced, but you'll wake up to honor. You may die in pain, but you'll wake up to pleasure. *For no matter how many promises God has made, they are Yes in Christ.*

2 Corinthians 1:21 *Now it is God who makes both us and you stand firm in Christ.*

The world, the flesh, and the devil conspire to knock Christians off their feet, and often succeed. But God makes us *stand firm* in Christ. This was a great encouragement to Paul as he led many to faith, and saw the battles they had to fight.

The idea of standing firm is so important it's found throughout the Bible, along with threats and promises. *[S]tand firm and see the deliverance the Lord will give you* (2 Chronicles 20:17). *If you do not stand firm in your faith, you will not stand at all* (Isaiah 7:9). *[T]he one who stands firm to the end will be saved* (Matthew 10:22). *Stand firm, and you will win life* (Luke 21:19).

Sumo wrestling is a contact sport in which the main goal is to knock your opponent outside a ring that's less than fifteen feet in diameter. The opponent has the same goal and the contest can be fierce. Winning and losing depend on the wrestler's ability to stand firm against his opponent. When the world, the flesh and the devil conspire to knock you out of the ring, *Stand firm, and you will win life.*

2 Corinthians 2:14 *But thanks be to God, who always leads us as captives in Christ's triumphal procession.*

Triumphant generals were given parades to celebrate their victories. Multitudes lined the streets and cheered as the general led the parade in his chariot, with his troops marching behind. At the end of the parade were captives who had now become slaves.

Paul viewed himself as a captive of Christ but, instead of despairing, he delighted in his new king and country. He used to serve an evil king, but was captured by a heavenly king, who shares the blessings of victory with all his captives. Paul wasn't being led to a place of sorrow, but to a better place than he ever dreamed of.

This is what it's like for many who come to Christ. At first they oppose him, and don't want to serve him. But, after being captured, they are joyful and want to serve him forever. The greatest victory is to be captured by Christ.

For Reflection and Review

- *Have you ever felt God's comfort when you suffered?*
- *Why is it important to stand firm in Christ?*
- *Did you oppose Christ before you were captured?*

Lesson 291

2 Corinthians 2:15-16 *For we are to God the pleasing aroma of Christ among those who are being saved and those who are perishing. To the one we are an aroma that brings death; to the other, an aroma that brings life.*

As people lined the streets, to watch the victory parade, they spread a sweet aroma by burning spices. To some it was the smell of victory, and to others the smell of death. The aroma of Christ is sweet to believers because it reminds us of eternal life. But that same aroma is hated by others because it reminds them of their doom.

2 Corinthians 3:18 *And we all, who with unveiled faces contemplate the Lord's glory, are being transformed into his image with ever-increasing glory.*

Paul compared the believer's glory to the glory of Moses when he received the Ten Commandments at the top of Mount Sinai. *[H]e was not aware that his face was radiant because he had spoken with the Lord* (Exodus 34:29). Moses' glory faded, but Christians enjoy an *ever-increasing glory* as they contemplate the glory of Christ.

Paul isn't just speaking theoretically, but experientially. Prayer and worship are communing with Christ who is the *radiance of God's glory* (Hebrews 1:3), says Hebrews. Looking at the sun tans the face, and communing with Christ transforms the believer.

A college freshman drifted from Christ and was trying to be an atheist. But on a cold winter night he walked past a church that was having a service, so he went inside and sat in the back. He was unmoved by the service until a time of prayer in which he didn't participate. But as he looked around he saw his physics professor, and saw in his face an aura of divine fellowship that was so convincing the student put his trust in Christ again, and went on to become a missionary. We should want to know Christ so well that others can see it in our face.

2 Corinthians 4:1 *Therefore, since through God's mercy we have this ministry, we do not lose heart.*

Paul knew from experience that Christian ministry can be disheartening. The long hours, opposition, lack of results, and apparent lack of divine assistance can all be discouraging. This is why so many who enter occupational ministry leave it for something else.

But, in spite of his troubles, Paul saw his ministry as the gift of *God's mercy*. Having received the mercy of God, Paul could imagine no better life than sharing God's mercy with others. He came to accept hardship as a way of life, and to be joyful *because he was looking ahead to his reward* (Hebrews 11:26).

2 Corinthians 4:4 *The god of this age has blinded the minds of unbelievers, so that they cannot see the light of the gospel.*

Ever since our fall into sin (Genesis 3:6), the influence of Satan on earth has been so pervasive that Scripture calls him *the god of this age*. Similar titles include *prince of this world* (John 12:31) and *ruler of the kingdom of the air* (Ephesians 2:2). Satan has more power than anyone else in the universe other than God. And he uses his power to *[blind] the minds of unbelievers, so that they cannot see the light of the gospel*.

A little boy in a developing country was taken to the hospital for stomach cramps. The next day his mother came to see him, and was surprised to find a bandage on his head, that also covered his eyes. She took him to another hospital and learned that her son was the victim of an ICR—illegal cornea removal. A doctor had stolen his corneas to sell them for profit, and left the boy forever blind. We can hardly imagine such cruelty, but Satan is worse by far. He *has blinded the minds of unbelievers, so that they cannot see the light of the gospel.*

2 Corinthians 4:7 *But we have this treasure in jars of clay.*

Paul compared the knowledge of the gospel in a Christian's heart to a fistful of diamonds in a flowerpot. There's nothing special about the flowerpot, but the treasure inside is priceless. Most Christians aren't impressive outwardly, but what they possess is invaluable. We must constantly guard this treasure through church, prayer, and Bible study.

2 Corinthians 4:16 *Though outwardly we are wasting away, yet inwardly we are being renewed day by day.*

Once we reach the age of fifty it becomes apparent to everyone that we're *wasting away*. Normal signs include thinning hair, sagging skin, increased weight, loss of memory, reduced energy, and many other things. In spite of aging, however, Paul could rejoice that he was being inwardly renewed.

My wife has a friend whom she rarely sees, but whenever they get together the conversation moves to what God is doing in their lives. They share how they've grown in Christ, how God has kept them, and how he's working through them. Whatever physical problems they have are nothing compared to the joy they share in Christ. They both continue to age, but are also *being renewed*. This makes life worth living.

2 Corinthians 4:17 *For our light and momentary troubles are achieving for us an eternal glory that far outweighs them all.*

Paul was no stranger to hardship, and went through more than most. But, compared to the coming glory, he considered all his troubles to be *light and momentary*. This is how we should think of our troubles as well. *They are light compared to the sufferings of Christ; they are light compared to what we deserve; and they are light compared to eternal glory. They are momentary because this life is momentary and will quickly pass away* (A.W. Pink, paraphrased).

Troubles can take us by surprise, as though God isn't doing his job. But suffering is part of God's perfect plan. *Did not the Messiah have to suffer these things and then enter his glory?* (Luke 24:26), said Jesus. *[We] share in his sufferings in order that we may also share in his glory* (Romans 8:17), wrote Paul. And, *I consider that our present sufferings are not worth comparing with the glory that will be revealed in us* (Romans 8:18), wrote Paul again. Suffering isn't an accident, but the way to eternal glory. Ten minutes in heaven will make a lifetime of suffering seem insignificant by comparison.

For Reflection and Review

- *Have you ever sensed the presence of Christ?*
- *Have you ever been disheartened by ministry?*
- *Why doesn't everyone believe in Christ?*

Lesson 292

2 Corinthians 5:1 *For we know that if the earthly tent we live in is destroyed, we have a building from God, an eternal house in heaven.*

Paul was a tentmaker by trade (Acts 18:3), and saw that our physical bodies are like an *earthly tent*. The Apostle Peter also used this image. *I live in the tent of this body [and] will soon put it aside* (2 Peter 1:13-14), he wrote. Tents aren't always comfortable, and wear out rather quickly. Our earthly tents are wearing out, but our *eternal house in heaven* will last forever. The difference between your present body and future body is like a tent compared to a mansion.

2 Corinthians 5:2 *Meanwhile we groan, longing to be clothed instead with our heavenly dwelling.*

Paul was about fifty-five years old when he wrote these words, and would live another twelve years. Due to his age, and difficult life, he found himself groaning. He probably groaned in the morning, throughout the day, and when he lay down at night. The more he aged, the more he groaned. But as a person of the future, Paul understood each groan as a wish for the resurrection. He longed to be clothed with his *heavenly dwelling*.

Physical pains are God's way of weaning us from this age, and helping us long for the age to come. Then our temporal pains will give way to everlasting joy and pleasure. *[Y]ou will fill me with joy in your presence, with eternal pleasures at your right hand* (Psalm 16:11), wrote David. Our best days are always yet to come.

2 Corinthians 5:5 *Now the one who has fashioned us for this very purpose is God, who has given us the Spirit as a deposit, guaranteeing what is to come.*

The hope of heaven is so wonderful that we might be tempted to think it's only make-believe. But God has given us the Spirit as proof he'll give us everything else. If you want to buy a home, you'll likely be required to make a deposit that guarantees you'll be back with the rest. The indwelling Spirit is Christ's guarantee that he'll be back with all that he's promised. The discernible sense of the indwelling Spirit is the believer's assurance of eternal life with Christ in the best of all possible worlds. So *do not grieve the Holy Spirit of God* (Ephesians 4:30), wrote Paul.

2 Corinthians 5:9 *[W]e make it our goal to please him.*

Goals are like magnets that pull us into the future. Some people's goal is to have a large family. Others want to start their own business. Others want to write a book. Paul's highest goal was to please God. To succeed at every other goal, and fail at that one, would be tragic. But to fail at every other goal, and succeed at that one, would be ultimate success. Whenever you face a challenging situation, make it your goal to please the Lord.

2 Corinthians 5:15 *[H]e died for all, that those who live should no longer live for themselves but for him who died for them and was raised again.*

Paul's logic isn't fuzzy: if Christ died for us, we should live for him. *If Jesus Christ be God and died for me, then no sacrifice can be too great for me to make for him* (CT Studd). *I live by faith in the Son of God, who loved me and gave himself for me* (Galatians 2:20), wrote Paul. When we understand that Jesus died for us, we naturally want to live for him.

Suppose you had a million dollars and gave it all to God. Then he gave it back to you in quarters. Your job is to give them all away, one at a time, before you die. *And if anyone gives even a cup of cold water to one of these little ones who is my disciple, truly I tell you, that person will certainly not lose their reward* (Matthew 10:42), said Jesus. Love's secret is to always be doing little things for God.

2 Corinthians 5:17 *Therefore, if anyone is in Christ, the new creation has come: The old has gone, the new is here!*

The old creation was spoiled when we fell into sin (Genesis 3:17-20), but God didn't walk away. He promised to make *a new heaven and a new earth, where righteousness dwells* (2 Peter 3:13), wrote Peter. Christ transforms his people so they'll fit into his new creation.

A man worked for a company before he was a Christian, and was one of the wickedest people there. Then he worked somewhere else and, during that time, was dramatically converted to Christ. Then he was rehired at his old company, and was excited to return so everyone could see the change Christ had made in his life. God is making a new creation, beginning with those who believe.

2 Corinthians 5:21 *God made him who had no sin to be sin for us, so that in him we might become the righteousness of God.*

This is one of the most important verses in the Bible for understanding how the gospel works. All our words, thoughts, and deeds equal sin. All Christ's words, thoughts, and deeds equal righteousness. God put all our sin on Christ, and all Christ's righteousness on us.

This can be called *double-imputation* and is reflected in the following short prayer: *Lord Jesus you are my righteousness, I am your sin. . . . You became what you were not that I might become what I was not* (Martin Luther).

A little lamb was orphaned, and given a new mother to nurse it. But the new mother could sense the orphaned sheep wasn't her own, so she rejected it. One of her own sheep died, however, so they skinned it, and covered the orphaned sheep with the skin of the dead sheep. Then the mother accepted the orphaned sheep because she thought it was her own.

Likewise, the lamb of God was slain on our behalf, so we could be clothed with his righteousness, and be accepted by God. *For he has clothed me with garments of salvation and arrayed me in a robe of his righteousness* (Isaiah 61:10), wrote Isaiah. When God sees us in Christ, he loves us just as much as Christ (John 17:23), and is equally pleased with us.

For Reflection and Review

- *How does the Spirit guarantee our future happiness?*
- *What are your goals for this life?*
- *What is double-imputation?*

Lesson 293

2 Corinthians 6:2 *I tell you, now is the time of God's favor, now is the day of salvation.*

The gospel isn't just a matter of life and death, but heaven and hell. Since tomorrow isn't guaranteed (or even the next half hour) the call to believe is always urgent.

A lady invited her neighbor to church and, at the end of his sermon, the minister gave an invitation to receive Jesus Christ (John 1:12). Many responded, but this dear lady declined because she was seventy-eight years old, and it's hard to change at that age. But she couldn't sleep that night, so she called her neighbor and they talked until midnight. Finally, she *received Christ Jesus as Lord* (Colossians 2:6), went back to bed, and died in her sleep. *I tell you, now is the time of God's favor, now is the day of salvation.*

2 Corinthians 6:12 *We are not withholding our affection from you, but you are withholding yours from us.*

Paul was trying to reconcile with those who turned against him, and was feeling the pain of rejection. Christian ministers are often rejected by the very ones they serve. Instead of gratitude, they often receive abuse. They might be tempted to respond in kind but, like Paul, should not withhold their affection. To be rejected by those we serve is to share in the sufferings of Christ (Philippians 3:10). This is never easy, but can make us more like the Savior.

2 Corinthians 6:14 *Do not be yoked together with unbelievers.*

Animals were used for plowing and, for extra power, two animals could be yoked together. If a farmer didn't have two oxen, he might try to yoke an ox with a donkey. This wasn't pleasant for either, and made it hard to plow a straight row. *Do not plow with an ox and a donkey yoked together* (Deuteronomy 22:10), wrote Moses.

Paul applied this to Christians and their relationships with unbelievers. He was probably thinking of false teachers in the church (2 Corinthians 11:13-15). And, today, Christians shouldn't belong to a church where the pastor doesn't teach and believe the Bible (2 Timothy 3:16). But there are other applications.

Any relationship that leads a believer to adopt views and values contrary to the Bible is a problem. The most common example is marriage. Many Christians have married an unbeliever, hoping to convert them. Often, however, believers get converted back to the world. Christian marriage should be like a triangle with husband and wife at the bottom, and God at the top. They closer each draws to God, the closer they'll draw to each other.

2 Corinthians 7:4 *I am greatly encouraged; in all our troubles my joy knows no bounds.*

In spite of the grief the Corinthians had caused Paul, he was greatly encouraged and filled with joy. Trouble and joy were not mutually exclusive for Paul, and shouldn't be for us. If we wait until all our problems are solved before we have joy, we'll never be joyful this side of heaven.

A missionary was thrown into prison with one of his converts, who lost everything for Jesus Christ. His house, wife, children, and reputation were all gone as he sat in a cold dark cell with the missionary. The missionary felt so sorry for the man, that he apologized for leading him to the Savior. But the man replied, *Having Jesus is more precious to me than any other happiness*. All the trouble in the world can't take away our joy, if we understand what we have in Christ.

2 Corinthians 7:10 *Godly sorrow brings repentance that leads to salvation . . . but worldly sorrow brings death.*

The night of Jesus' arrest, Peter denied him three times with a curse. He was so filled with remorse that he went out and wept bitterly (Luke 22:62). But soon, Peter was restored. That same evening, Judas betrayed Jesus for thirty pieces of silver (Matthew 26:14-16). He too was filled with remorse, but went out and hanged himself (Matthew 27:3-5).

Everyone who tries to follow Christ will fail at times. We can grieve to the point of death, or trust in God's forgiveness. Satan wants us to think that we're so bad, there's no hope for us. But Jesus came to *save sinners* (1 Timothy 1:15), and *justifies the ungodly* (Romans 4:5). Sorrow for sin is good, if it leads us back to the Savior.

2 Corinthians 8:9 *For you know the grace of our Lord Jesus Christ, that though he was rich, yet for your sake he became poor, so that you through his poverty might become rich.*

Jesus gave up the riches of heaven to enrich his people forever. He proved his love through sacrifice, and we can do the same. You can tell how much people love God, sometimes, by how much they're willing to spend on him. Paul called the Corinthians' generosity the *proof of [their] love* (2 Corinthians 8:24).

A middle-school boy mowed lawns all summer, and earned a good amount of money. He could've bought any number of things for himself, but he took the bundle of cash and put it in the hands of a missionary, so the gospel could be spread. Love delights to spend itself on the beloved.

2 Corinthians 9:7 *Each of you should give what you have decided in your heart to give, not reluctantly or under compulsion, for God loves a cheerful giver.*

When Christians discover how rich they are in Christ, they often become surprisingly generous. When Jesus went to the home of a tax-collector the man was so overjoyed he said, *Look, Lord! Here and now I give half of my possessions to the poor*. To which Jesus replied, *Today salvation has come to this house* (Luke 19:8-9). A generous heart is one indication that we truly belong to Christ.

Feelings of generosity are seldom constant, however, so Paul provided a more stable rule: *Each of you should give what you have decided in your heart to give.* Instead of waiting for a generous impulse, Christians should consider what they'd like to give, and then do it. Some will give more, and some will give less, but each should decide on their own and then follow through. They can adjust their giving whenever they like, but should do so conscientiously.

The minimal standard for giving in the Old Testament was ten percent. *Bring the whole tithe into the storehouse* (Malachi 3:10), said God. But with the coming of Christ, the Old Testament Law became *obsolete* (Hebrews 8:13), says Hebrews. And we're no longer *under the law, but under grace* (Romans 6:14), wrote Paul. The New Testament doesn't require Christians to give ten percent of their income, but it does require them to be generous (Luke 6:38). Believers are free to tithe if they like, but it shouldn't be done *reluctantly or under compulsion*.

For Reflection and Review

- *Why shouldn't Christians marry unbelievers?*
- *What is the difference between godly sorrow and worldly sorrow?*
- *How much should believers give?*

Lesson 294

2 Corinthians 10:5 *We demolish arguments and every pretension that sets itself up against the knowledge of God, and we take captive every thought to make it obedient to Christ.*

Paul's powerful mind was saturated with Gods word, and he was ready to demolish every false idea. Satan has filled the world with false doctrines, false religions, and false philosophies to keep people away from God. But Christianity has the advantage being true, and Paul was ready to defend it intellectually. *[For] the wisdom of the wise will perish, [and] the intelligence of the intelligent will vanish* (Isaiah 29:14), wrote Isaiah.

Since Christianity is true, and everything opposed to it is false, it's no surprise that many of the greatest thinkers have been Christians. Christian thinkers shouldn't withdraw from the intellectual arena, but challenge and refute the false ideas of their time. The more false ideas are refuted, the more room there is for truth.

The battle for truth is also fought in the mind of every believer. Our thoughts are the first and final frontier of our discipleship, so we ought to apply Paul's words to ourselves: *take captive every thought to make it obedient to Christ.*

2 Corinthians 12:9 *My grace is sufficient for you, for my power is made perfect in weakness.*

Fourteen years earlier, Paul was taken into heaven, perhaps even physically. There he heard *inexpressible things, things that no one is permitted to tell* (2 Corinthians 12:4). He might've become proud, but to keep him humble he was given a *thorn in the flesh* (2 Corinthians 12:7) that tormented him. Three times he prayed for Christ to take it away, but the Lord replied, *My grace is sufficient for you, for my power is made perfect in weakness* (2 Corinthians 12:8-9).

Paul said little about his affliction, except that it was physical. It was probably known to the Corinthians, which is why he wasn't more specific. They may've even used it against Paul, by suggesting that if he was really an apostle, the Lord would've healed him. But Paul understood his weakness to be an opportunity for Christ to work through him more powerfully. *For when I am weak, then I am strong* (2 Corinthians 12:10), he wrote.

The principle of strength through weakness is difficult to understand, but can be compared to a baseball glove. When a glove is new, it doesn't work very well, because it's too stiff. It has to be broken in through twisting, turning, and bending until it becomes pliable. When it's new and strong, it's weak. When it's old and pliable, it's strong.

Some Christians are so strong-willed that Christ isn't able to use them very much. When they're made pliable through hardship, however, Christ can be strong through their weakness.

2 Corinthians 12:20 *I fear that there may be discord, jealousy, fits of rage, selfish ambition, slander, gossip, arrogance and disorder.*

The church in Corinth was almost certainly the worst church Paul ever started. They were guilty of many sins, and some of them were slow to repent (2 Corinthians 12:21). Nevertheless, they were a real church, *sanctified in Christ Jesus and called to be his holy people* (1 Corinthians 1:2), wrote Paul.

The church in Corinth reminds us not to expect too much from our own church. The church isn't a gathering of good people, but of believing sinners who often behave sinfully. They should be better than they were, but are never as good as they should be.

If you've been disappointed by the people in your church, make a list of what they did wrong, and then do the opposite. If they've been unkind, be extra kind. If they've been gossipy, speak all the good you know. *If someone slaps you on one cheek, turn to them the other also* (Luke 6:29), said Jesus. Their bad example can make you a better Christian, and you can make your church a better place.

2 Corinthians 13:5 *Examine yourselves to see whether you are in the faith; test yourselves.*

The Corinthians' behavior was so deplorable that Paul had reason to question their faith. And many who thought they were true Christians will find out on Judgment Day that they weren't (Matthew 7:22). Paul didn't want this to happen to the Corinthians so he told them to *examine* themselves.

We can examine ourselves by asking the following questions: (1) Do I believe that Jesus Christ is God in human flesh, crucified for my sins and raised from the dead, so that I can live with him forever? (2) Since Jesus is Lord of all, do I allow him to govern my words, thoughts, and deeds? (3) Do I have a discernible sense of the Spirit of Christ dwelling within me? (4) Do I feel more at home with Christians than with unbelievers? (5) Am I looking forward to the return of Jesus Christ? (6) Do I spend my leisure for Christ? (7) Do I spend my money for Christ?

Since nothing is more important than eternal salvation, the Apostle Peter also taught believers to *make every effort to confirm your calling and election* (2 Peter 1:10). Our right standing before God should never be assumed, or taken for granted. *Examine yourselves to see whether you are in the faith.*

2 Corinthians 13:14 *May the grace of the Lord Jesus Christ, and the love of God, and the fellowship of the Holy Spirit be with you all.*

Paul's final words to the Corinthians are a Trinitarian blessing. The word Trinity doesn't occur in the Bible, but represents what the Bible teaches: The Father is God, the Son is God, and the Spirit is God—but there's only one God.

The Father, Son, and Spirit are three separate persons, but not three separate Gods, because they share the same divinity. This is why Jesus told his disciples to baptize *in the name of the Father and of the Son and of the Holy Spirit* (Matthew 28:19). We don't have to understand this, but we do have to believe it, because it's what the Bible teaches.

For Reflection and Review

- *How can we become better thinkers?*
- *How can you improve your church?*
- *How can we know we are true Christians?*

Lesson 295

Galatians 1:1 *Paul, an apostle—sent not from men nor by a man, but by Jesus Christ and God the Father, who raised him from the dead.*

Paul began his letter to the Galatians with a strong assertion of his authority, in order to combat the heresy of legalism, which the churches in that region were beginning to embrace. Legalistic teachers were telling the Galatians they had to be circumcised, and keep the law of Moses, in order to be saved. This was an attack on the gospel itself, and brought a fierce response from the Apostle Paul. The letter was likely written around AD 48, from Paul's home church in Antioch, Syria.

Galatians 1:8-9 *But even if we or an angel from heaven should preach a gospel other than the one we preached to you, let them be under God's curse! As we have already said, so now I say again: If anybody is preaching to you a gospel other than what you accepted, let them be under God's curse!*

Everyone who preaches something other than the true gospel of Jesus Christ is under this curse. Some people think all religions are equal, but Paul insisted there's only one religion that saves, and that it must be guarded against all who oppose it. Since the gospel is a matter of heaven and hell, it's crucial to get it right.

Galatians 1:10 *Am I now trying to win the approval of human beings, or of God? Or am I trying to please people? If I were still trying to please people, I would not be a servant of Christ.*

The false teachers accused Paul of trying to be popular by preaching an easy religion, free from the law of Moses. But Paul insisted he wasn't trying to win the approval of people, but of God. He wasn't free to adjust the truth to fit what people wanted; he could only proclaim the truth as God had revealed it.

Some people want their preacher to make Christianity easier. Others want him to make it more demanding. But the preacher's job is to proclaim the gospel as it's found in the Bible. *For the time will come when people will not put up with sound doctrine. Instead, to suit their own desires, they will gather around them a great number of teachers to say what their itching ears want to hear* (2 Timothy 4:3), wrote Paul.

Preachers must resist the desire for popularity, and communicate God's truth unflinchingly. Preachers will give an account to Christ, and *we who teach will be judged more strictly* (James 3:1), wrote James. Christians should even pray for their preacher to contradict them, whenever necessary, since this will lead to a healthier church.

Galatians 2:16 *[A] a person is not justified by the works of the law, but by faith in Jesus Christ.*

Jesus Christ is the toughest teacher who ever lived. *[T]hose of you who do not give up everything you have cannot be my disciples* (Luke 14:33). *Be perfect, therefore, as your heavenly Father is perfect* (Matthew 5:48). *Whoever wants to be my disciple must deny themselves and take up their cross daily* (Luke 9:23), he said.

There are at least three reasons Jesus spoke this way. First, he always told the truth, no matter what people wanted to hear. Second, he wanted to separate the sheep from the goats, since most goats won't put up with this kind of talk. Third, he wanted to destroy all confidence in ourselves, so we'd look only to him for our salvation. This is known as the law/gospel distinction.

The law is any verse in the Bible that commands us to obey. When Jesus said the greatest command is to *Love the Lord your God with all your heart and with all your soul and with all your mind* (Matthew 22:37), he wasn't making a suggestion. If we only love God with ninety-nine percent of our being, we fall one percent short. And, to that degree, we're under the just condemnation of God.

When Jesus said the second greatest command is to *Love your neighbor as yourself* (Matthew 22:39), he was equally serious. If we're even slightly less concerned with our neighbor's health, wealth, and happiness than our own, we also fall under the just condemnation of God. This is the bad news of the law, which makes us receptive to the gospel.

For God so loved the world that he gave his one and only Son, that whoever believes in him shall not perish but have eternal life (John 3:16). Jesus Christ is the only person who fulfilled the law perfectly, including the law's penalty for sin, which is death. His perfect life and sacrificial death were for our sins and our salvation. The purpose of the law is to reveal our need, so that we'll flee to Christ to be saved by faith.

It must be stated plainly that we're saved by faith (not works), and that we stay saved by faith (not works). *For it is by grace you have been saved, through faith. . . not by works* (Ephesians 2:8-9), wrote Paul.

God doesn't give with one hand and take away with the other. He gives us the law, to reveal our sin, so we'll depend on Christ, not on ourselves. God's standard is perfection, and Jesus Christ is the only perfect person who ever lived. We're not saved by being good, but by believing in the one who was perfectly good for us.

Due to a stroke, a man lost most of the feeling on his left side—which should've made him sad. But he also lost the part of his brain that normally feels sadness—so he was very happy. The law tells us we have a serious problem—which ought to make us sad. But the gospel tells us we have a Savior—which makes us very happy.

For Reflection and Review

- *How is Christianity different from other religions?*
- *Do you prefer sermons that are easy or demanding?*
- *What's the difference between the law and the gospel?*

Lesson 296

Galatians 2:20 *The life I now live in the body, I live by faith in the Son of God, who loved me and gave himself for me.*

Paul didn't say, *I live by faith in the Son of God, who loved the world and gave himself for the world*, or . . . *who loved us and gave himself for us*, but . . . *who loved me and gave himself for me*. Paul was passionate about Christ because he believed Christ loved him enough to die on a cross for him. Until we understand that Christ loves us enough to die for us personally, we'll never feel about Christ the way he feels about us.

Galatians 2:21 *I do not set aside the grace of God, for if righteousness could be gained through the law, Christ died for nothing!*

If we think we're going to heaven because we're pretty good people, we're saying *Christ died for nothing*. If we think we're going to heaven because our good deeds outweigh our bad deeds, we're saying Christ died for nothing. If we think we're going to heaven because of the best thing we've ever done, we're saying *Christ died for nothing*. If there was anything we could do to get ourselves into heaven, then it wasn't necessary for Christ to die on a cross for us.

A man escaped from prison and went on to become a model husband, father, citizen, and employee. He lived a perfect life, in every way, except that he was a fugitive. Years later, he was brought to court, and argued that his good deeds should make up for his bad deeds. But the judge said that was no defense, and that justice had to be served.

Muslims believe if their good deeds outweigh their bad deeds they're going to heaven—which they aren't. Hindus believe if their good karma outweighs their bad karma they'll have a better reincarnation—which they won't. Others believe they're going to heaven because they keep the Ten Commandments—which they don't. Others believe they're going to heaven because they're pretty good people—which they aren't.

The one thing all these beliefs have in common, is that they make the death of Christ unnecessary. If you try to get to heaven by being a pretty good person, or any other way, you're saying the death of Christ on the cross was unnecessary. You're saying the eternal plan of redemption was unnecessary. You're saying the greatest price ever paid for anything was unnecessary. And you will go to hell—unnecessarily.

Galatians 3:1 *You foolish Galatians! Who has bewitched you? Before your very eyes Jesus Christ was clearly portrayed as crucified.*

The center of Paul's preaching was Jesus Christ crucified, for the salvation of all who believe. The crucifixion of Jesus Christ wasn't something Paul mentioned in passing, or stated without detail, but *clearly portrayed* through words.

With the help of the Holy Spirit, Paul portrayed the crucifixion so vividly that the Galatians could see it in their minds. They could see his body bloodied from the beating. They could see his nail-pierced hands and feet. They could see the pain in his eyes, and hear it in his voice, as he cried out, *My God, my God, why have you forsaken me?* (Matthew 27:46).

They also saw the wickedness of their sin, and the love of God who atoned for it. As they heard this remarkable message, they found themselves believing, and trusting Christ for their salvation. That's why Paul said elsewhere, *we preach Christ crucified* (1 Corinthians 1:23).

This must also be the central message of the church. The preacher's job is to remind God's people of what they already know. God Almighty came into the world to die on a cross for our sins. He bore the lash for us. He took the nails for the evil that we've done, and bore the shame for the good that we haven't done. His love can never be doubted because he loved us unto death. Therefore *we have peace with God* (Romans 5:1), and everlasting life with him (John 5:24). That's the gospel of Jesus Christ, and the message of the church.

Galatians 3:10 *For all who rely on the works of the law are under a curse, as it is written: Cursed is everyone who does not continue to do everything written in the Book of the Law.*

Paul wanted to show the foolishness of trying to be saved by being good, so he paraphrased Moses who received God's law from God himself: *Cursed is anyone who does not uphold the words of this law by carrying them out* (Deuteronomy 27:26), he wrote.

But even Moses couldn't keep the law of God. God told him to get water for his people by speaking to a rock. Instead, Moses struck the rock twice with his staff. Water came out, but Moses had to die for his sin (Numbers 20:1-12). Moses was better than most people, but *the wages of sin is death* (Romans 6:23), wrote Paul.

If you get pulled over for speeding, the cop won't care if you've never stolen, lied, or had an impure thought. You broke the law and are going to get a ticket. That's how the law of God works: *Cursed is everyone who does not continue to do everything written in the Book of the Law.*

But has anyone ever kept the law of God perfectly? Indeed! *Do not think that I have come to abolish the Law or the Prophets; I have not come to abolish them but to fulfill them* (Matthew 5:17), said Jesus. Jesus did the will of God perfectly, every day of his life, so he could be a perfect sacrifice for our sins. So we *have put our faith in Christ Jesus that we may be justified by faith in Christ and not by the works of the law, because by the works of the law no one will be justified* (Galatians 2:16b), wrote Paul.

For Reflection and Review

- *Why do so many people think they're going to heaven by being good?*
- *Why can't our good deeds make up for our bad deeds?*
- *How long can you go without sinning?*

Lesson 297

Galatians 3:13 *Christ redeemed us from the curse of the law by becoming a curse for us, for it is written: Cursed is everyone who is hung on a pole.*

This may be the reason Paul rejected Christianity at first. The fact that Jesus was *hung on a pole* seemed to be proof that he died under God's curse. *[A]nyone who is hung on a pole is under God's curse* (Deuteronomy 21:23), wrote Moses. Imagine Paul's surprise when he learned that Christ was hung on a pole to bear the curse for Paul! We're all born under God's curse because of our sin (Genesis 3:17), but *Christ redeemed us from the curse of the law by becoming a curse for us.* Jesus bore the curse of God so we could be blessed by God. *[God] has blessed us . . . with every spiritual blessing in Christ* (Ephesians 1:3), wrote Paul.

Galatians 3:26-27 *So in Christ Jesus you are all children of God through faith, for all of you who were baptized into Christ have clothed yourselves with Christ.*

Jesus told the story of a wedding banquet for the king's son, at which someone arrived underdressed. The king asked, *How did you get in here without wedding clothes, friend? The man was speechless. Then the king told the attendants, Tie him hand and foot, and throw him outside, into the darkness, where there will be weeping and gnashing of teeth* (Matthew 22:12-13).

No one gets into heaven without being properly dressed, and the dress code for heaven is Christ. You might be a very nice person, who supported all the right causes, but if you're not clothed with Christ, you'll be turned away. You might have gone to church every week, and sung in the choir, but if you're not clothed with Christ, you'll be turned away. You might have done a good deed every day of your life, and been greatly loved by all, but if you're not clothed with Christ, you'll be turned away. The dress code for heaven is Christ, and we're clothed with him through faith.

Galatians 4:6 *Because you are his sons, God sent the Spirit of his Son into our hearts, the Spirit who calls out, Abba, Father.*

The Aramaic word for *father* is *Abba*. Because of its easy pronunciation it was one of the first words a child learned: *Mama, Papa, Abba*. It's a term of tender familiarity, and seldom appears in the Bible. But the night before he was crucified Jesus prayed, *Abba, Father* (Mark 14:36).

It's remarkable that God wants all believers to enjoy the same relational closeness to him that Jesus enjoyed. That's why he *sent the Spirit of his Son into our hearts* so that we too would call him *Abba, Father*. The Spirit of Christ is always drawing us into a closer relationship with our heavenly Father.

Galatians 4:7 *[S]ince you are his child, God has made you also an heir.*

Many of the early Christians were financially poor, with no chance of receiving an earthly inheritance. They were born poor, lived poor, and died poor. But through faith in Jesus Christ they became heirs to the greatest fortune ever known. *[Y]ou will receive an inheritance from the Lord as a reward* (Colossians 3:24), wrote Paul. And, *This inheritance is kept in heaven for you* (1 Peter 1:4), wrote Peter.

Heaven is the best place to receive an inheritance for at least three reasons. First, many who hope for an earthly inheritance die before they receive it. Second, many watch their inheritance dwindle before they receive it. And, third, many receive an inheritance only to watch it disappear through carelessness, or circumstances beyond their control.

But this will never happen to children of God, because we'll receive an *eternal inheritance* (Hebrews 9:15). This is better than any inheritance ever received in this life. Faith in Jesus Christ not only brings spiritual blessings, but lasting material blessings in the age to come.

Galatians 4:10-11 *You are observing special days and months and seasons and years! I fear for you, that somehow I have wasted my efforts on you.*

Under the influence of false teachers, believers in Galatia were taught to observe certain times on the calendar as having special religious significance. They probably corresponded to the religious calendar of the Old Testament, but were never required in the New Testament. Paul was so concerned about this that he feared his ministry to the Galatians might've been a waste. To the degree they trusted in religious holidays to make them right with God, they weren't trusting in Christ.

Therefore do not let anyone judge you by what you eat or drink, or with regard to a religious festival, a New Moon celebration or a Sabbath day. These are a shadow of the things that were to come; the reality, however, is found in Christ (Colossians 2:16-17), he wrote.

When Jewish Christians stopped observing Jewish holidays, they were looked down on by their fellow Jews. Paul didn't want them to be concerned, because the reality was found in Christ. Jewish families were expected to sacrifice a lamb on Passover. But *Christ, our Passover lamb, has been sacrificed* (1 Corinthians 5:7), wrote Paul. So how does this apply to us?

Many churches follow a religious calendar in which they celebrate certain days like Christmas and Easter. If they think observing those days earns them favor with God, they are absolutely wrong. The only way to find favor with God is through faith in Jesus Christ. Observing certain days doesn't make us pleasing to God.

But it would also be wrong to emphasize this too strongly. *One person considers one day more sacred than another; another considers every day alike. Each of them should be fully convinced in their own mind* (Romans 14:5), wrote Paul. Every day is equally sacred, but Christians who know this should be patient with those who don't, and not create a fuss.

For Reflection and Review

- *What does it mean to call God Abba?*
- *Why should believers think about their inheritance?*
- *Are Christmas and Easter more sacred than other days?*

Lesson 298

Galatians 5:4 *You who are trying to be justified by the law have been alienated from Christ; you have fallen away from grace.*

Many of the early Christians struggled with the heresy of Antinomianism. It's the idea that we can sin without restraint and still be saved. Jesus refuted this idea when he said, *Not everyone who says to me, Lord, Lord, will enter the kingdom of heaven, but only the one who does the will of my Father who is in heaven* (Matthew 7:21).

The heresy in Galatia was just the opposite. Instead of trusting in Christ alone for their salvation, they wanted to be saved by trusting Christ, and keeping the law of Moses. But to the degree that we rely on anything other than Christ, we're not relying on Christ alone. And, to that degree, we imperil our souls.

Whoever believes in Christ alone will be careful to obey him, but obedience is not the basis of our salvation. We're saved by faith alone, but not by faith that is alone. *[F]aith without deeds is dead* (James 2:26), wrote James. True belief behaves, and real faith works. Faith in Christ is the root of our salvation; obedience to Christ is the fruit of our salvation.

Galatians 5:5 *For through the Spirit we eagerly await by faith the righteousness for which we hope.*

Even though we're *children of God through faith* (Galatians 3:26), we're not perfectly righteous. We make a little progress now, but wait for the age to come before we'll be completely righteous. At that point, our human natures will be so transformed, that sin will be as repugnant to us as maggots on a corpse.

The desire to be perfectly righteous makes little sense to the unconverted, because sin is a source of pleasure (Hebrews 11:25). But the indwelling Spirit makes the sin we love a source of sorrow. So *through the Spirit we eagerly await . . . the righteousness for which we hope*. We'll never again be sorry for our moral failures. And a billion years from now it'll be nearly a billion years since the last time we sinned.

Galatians 5:9 *A little yeast works through the whole batch of dough.*

Yeast is a fermenting agent used to raise bread, and doesn't stop working until it has permeated the whole batch of dough. Paul quoted this proverb to show how the negative effect of false teaching can permeate a whole church. Jesus also used yeast to describe the spread of hypocrisy (Luke 12:1). Since we all have an influence beyond ourselves, we should all be the best Christians we can possibly be.

If one person in church grows cold, they'll have a cooling effect on others. If one person in church grows hot, they'll have a warming effect on others. Everyone ought to join a church and make it better, but some join a church and make it worse by their terrible example. Every church member is a little bit of yeast that has an effect on all the others.

Galatians 5:12 *As for those agitators, I wish they would go the whole way and emasculate themselves!*

Paul was again referring to the false teachers who wanted Christians to submit to the law of Moses, including circumcision. But blending the law of Moses with Christianity would've created a radically different religion. Paul was so alarmed by this that he wished the agitators *would go the whole way and emasculate themselves!* Castration is the removal of the testicles. Emasculation is the removal of the entire sexual organ, including the testicles.

This shows what a serious error legalism is. Anytime we make salvation depend on anything other than faith in Christ, we are guilty of legalism. Anytime we make salvation depend on faith and works, we are guilty of legalism. Whoever believes in Jesus Christ will sincerely try to follow him, but salvation depends on Christ alone, not on anything else.

Even the multiplication of rules for Christian living isn't wise, because it can lead to legalism. It also creates a culture that's harmful to people and churches. Those who accept and keep the rules tend to become judgmental. Those who fail to keep the rules tend to become discouraged. And those who are in authority tend to become controlling. No wonder Paul wanted the circumcisers to *go the whole way and emasculate themselves!*

Galatians 5:15 *If you bite and devour each other, watch out or you will be destroyed by each other.*

Legalism was already having a negative effect on the Christian community. Instead of loving and accepting each other, they were biting and devouring each other, and would soon be *destroyed by each other*. Satan took their desire to please God, and used it to turn them against each other.

A zookeeper threw a hotdog into a snake pit and, immediately, two snakes began to devour the piece of meat—one at either end. When the two snakes met at the middle, the bigger snake kept going and consumed the smaller snake. When Christians bite and devour each other, with unkind words, they're acting like snakes that are willing to kill each other.

For Reflection and Review

- *What is Antinomianism?*
- *What is legalism?*
- *How are Christians like yeast?*

Lesson 299

Galatians 6:1 *Brothers and sisters, if someone is caught in a sin, you who live by the Spirit should restore that person gently.*

The Bible contains many examples of godly people who did ungodly things. Noah got drunk (Genesis 9:1), Abraham lied (Genesis 12:19), Jacob cheated (Genesis 27), Moses murdered (Exodus 12:2), David committed adultery (2 Samuel 11), and Peter denied Christ (Matthew 26:74).

Good people aren't always strong, and God's people don't always act like godly people. *We all stumble in many ways* (James 3:2), wrote James. The best we can hope for is to stumble in the right direction. If we get back up every time we fall, we'll arrive in heaven along with all the other sinners who've been saved by God's grace. So when someone you know is caught in a sin, *restore that person gently*. Try to handle the situation the way you'd like if the roles were reversed.

Galatians 6:1b *But watch yourselves, or you also may be tempted.*

Paul wanted the Galatians to know that even the most mature believers are never out of temptation's reach. And the more we indulge temptation, the greater danger we face. That's why Jesus taught us to pray, *lead us not into temptation* (Matthew 6:13).

The family dog saw a duck paddling by the shore, and chased it further out. The duck could've swam away, but stayed close enough for the dog to nearly catch it. They got to the middle of the lake when the dog discovered it was exhausted, and finally turned around. But land was far away, and its head got lower and lower in the water until all you could see were two little nostrils. Somehow the dog made it to shore and passed out for several minutes. But when it opened its eyes, there was that stupid duck. Sin is a pleasure many chase, but not everyone survives. *[L]ead us not into temptation, but deliver us from the evil one.*

Galatians 6:5 *[E]ach one should carry their own load.*

The early church in Jerusalem established a daily distribution of food to care for its widows (Acts 6:1). This was an important program because Jesus taught that whatever we do for the least, we do for him (Matthew 25:40). Every church should be a loving community that cares for the needs of its own. *Carry each other's burdens, and in this way you will fulfill the law of Christ* (Galatians 6:2), wrote Paul.

But there have always been some who take advantage of those who are generous, even when they can care for themselves. A man by the side of the road was holding a sign that said, *Will work for food.* My friend was willing to give him a job, but the man said he didn't really want a job—he just wanted donations.

Sadly, there are also some in church who try to appear needy because they're hoping for a handout. The truly needy should be willing to receive, without shame, but it should always be with a view to giving back when they're able. This is how we can carry each other's burdens, and our own load too.

Galatians 6:9 *Let us not become weary in doing good, for at the proper time we will reap a harvest if we do not give up.*

Worshipping God, serving others, and obeying Christ can be exhausting. It's not hard to be good for a while, but being good all the time is harder than it looks. Like the farmer who plows, plants, and weeds, however, we too will reap a harvest if we don't give up. The harvest will be so abundant, in fact, that it'll make a lifetime of effort seem like nothing in comparison. When following Christ seems wearisome, we should look ahead to the harvest.

Galatians 6:14 *May I never boast except in the cross of our Lord Jesus Christ, through which the world has been crucified to me, and I to the world.*

Paul so identified with Jesus Christ that he thought of himself as crucified to the world. This delivered Paul from the sin of worldliness, because it's hard to love the world after you've been crucified. Instead of looking to the world for joy, we'll look to the world to come for joy. Instead of looking to the world for acceptance, we'll look to Christ for acceptance. The best way to combat the sin of worldliness, is through the cross of Christ.

Galatians 6:17 *From now on, let no one cause me trouble, for I bear on my body the marks of Jesus.*

Slaves were often branded to prove who their owners were. Because of his many beatings, Paul's body was covered with scars. Instead of being resentful, Paul viewed his scars with pride, because they proved who his owner was.

Not very many have been scarred for Jesus physically, but many have been scarred for him emotionally. Wounds to the soul often come from those who are close to us, and may even last a lifetime. They shouldn't be despised, but cherished, because they're visible to Christ and mark us as his own. Suffering is never pleasant but, when we suffer in faith, we have reason to rejoice.

Galatians 6:18 *The grace of our Lord Jesus Christ be with your spirit.*

Since the Christian life is based on God's undeserved favor, from beginning to end, Paul concluded this letter with a word of God's grace. We're saved by grace (Ephesians 2:8), kept by grace (1 Corinthians 1:8), and need it every day.

A boy was caught in a sin and warned by his father: if he ever did it again, he'd receive a punishment he would never forget. To the boy's alarm, his father caught him again. The father walked his son into a field, too far away for anyone to hear. The further they went, the more the boy feared for his life.

Then the father plucked a grain of wheat and gently stroked the boy's face with it. *That' a punishment you'll never forget*, he said. This helped the boy hate his sin, and love his father even more. That's how grace works. When we compare how we've treated God, with how he's treated us, we're amazed at his wonderful grace.

For Reflection and Review

- *Why should we be gentle toward those who are caught in sin?*
- *Why is it hard to be good all the time?*
- *Does anyone ever deserve grace?*

Lesson 300

Ephesians 1:1 *Paul, an apostle of Christ Jesus by the will of God, To God's holy people in Ephesus, the faithful in Christ Jesus.*

Paul wrote to the believers in Ephesus around AD 62, while he was under house arrest in Rome (Acts 28). Ephesus was a leading city in the region of Asia Minor (modern Turkey), and Paul ministered there for over two years (Acts 19). He wrote this letter a few years later to summarize the gospel of God's grace, and to explain the nature of the church.

Ephesians 1:4 *For he chose us in him before the creation of the world to be holy and blameless in his sight.*

The reason people come to faith in Jesus Christ is not because they're good, wise, or better than other sinners. They come to Christ because they were *chosen before the creation of the world*. The Biblical word for this is *election* (Romans 9:11), and those who believe are called *the elect* (2 Timothy 2:10).

The Bible never places the cause of election in the elect themselves, but in the sovereign will of God. *[H]e saved us, not because of righteous things we had done, but because of his mercy* (Titus 3:5), wrote Paul. The cause of our election is not in anything God foresaw in us, but in his sovereign choice. God chooses whom he chooses because he chooses to do so. He owes salvation to none, but graciously gives it to some.

Ephesians 1:5 *[H]e predestined us for adoption to sonship through Jesus Christ, in accordance with his pleasure and will.*

Believers in Jesus Christ are adopted into the family of God. Some people adopt beautiful babies. Fewer adopt older children. And very few adopt an older child with disabilities. But God adopts notorious sinners, and makes us his children forever.

[A] slave has no permanent place in the family, but a son belongs to it forever (John 8:35), said Jesus. Slaves belonged to a family as long as they were useful. If they became sick, or injured, they could be discarded (1 Samuel 30:13). But whoever is a child of God, will always be a child of God. When God becomes our Father, he's our Father forever.

A little boy from an abusive background was adopted into a loving Christian home, but had some personal issues. He'd never experienced love before, so he was very insecure and afraid of being punished. One day he used his adopted father's comb, and put it into his pocket. When his father asked if he took the comb he said *no*, but couldn't explain how it got into his pocket.

So he ran into his room and hid under the bed, afraid he'd be forced to leave. But his new mom squeezed herself under the bed and held him close saying, *Nothing you did got you into this family, and nothing you ever do will get you out*. That's how our heavenly Father treats his adopted children as well.

Ephesians 1:10 *[God will] bring unity to all things in heaven and on earth under Christ.*

Heaven is the place where Jesus dwells at the right hand of God (Acts 2:33). It's the place of angels, glory, and joy. Because earth has fallen under a curse (Genesis 3:17), it has some problems, but isn't completely desolate. There are mountains, rivers, meadows and loving relationships. We shouldn't imagine the age to come as heaven only, nor merely a glorified earth, but as heaven and earth together under Christ (Revelation 21:2). This will be the best of all possible worlds.

Ephesians 1:11 *In him we were also chosen, having been predestined according to the plan of him who works out everything in conformity with the purpose of his will.*

God isn't making up the future as he goes along, but has planned out everything from the beginning. *I make known the end from the beginning, from ancient times, what is still to come. I say, My purpose will stand, and I will do all that I please* (Isaiah 46:10). The world is never out of control, because God is in control. There are no maverick molecules in God's universe, and he never says *oops*. This is a wonderful comfort when things go wrong.

A young man died in a mountain climbing accident, and his father was devastated by the loss. But believing God was in control saved him from a debilitating case of the *if onlys*. *If only* his son had been safer; *if only* he'd gone somewhere else; *if only* he hadn't gone at all. Since the father believed that God was in control, he could also believe *that in all things God works for the good of those who love him* (Romans 8:28), even if we can't understand it.

God's perfect control is a comfort to many, but others oppose the idea because it seems to make God the cause of evil. If God is in control of everything, and evil exists, then he must be the cause of evil. Or worse, if God created hell, and predestined some to go there, he must be the cause of people going to hell (1 Peter 2:8).

This is a serious problem and qualifies as one of the great mysteries of the Bible, along with the doctrines of the Trinity (how can God be three and one?), and the two natures of Christ (how can Jesus be both God and man, finite and infinite?). The solution to the problem of God's sovereignty and human responsibility for sin, is not to deny either since the Bible teaches both. Like the Bible, we must hold both ideas together, even though we can't understand how they can both be true. A theological mystery is not a contradiction, but something beyond our understanding. God ordains all things that come to pass, but in such a way that he's not the source or cause of evil.

Ephesians 1:13 *When you believed, you were marked in him with a seal, the promised Holy Spirit.*

Kings often owned a ring that was uniquely engraved, and served as their seal of ownership. Whatever was marked with the king's seal was identified as belonging to him. Whenever someone comes to faith in Christ, they receive the seal of the Great King, *the promised Holy Spirit*. The indwelling Spirit is the mark of God's ownership.

Many years ago my dad got an engraver for Christmas, and fell in love with it. He went to the garage and put his name on everything: the lawnmower, the snowblower, the chainsaw, all his tools, and anything else he could find. There could be no mistake about ownership, because he put his name on everything. The Holy Spirit is God's signature, proving that we belong to him.

For Reflection and Review

- *Is it wrong for God to choose some but not others?*
- *What is a theological mystery?*
- *What do you think of God's perfect control of all things?*

Lesson 301

Ephesians 1:17 *I keep asking that the God of our Lord Jesus Christ, the glorious Father, may give you the Spirit of wisdom and revelation, so that you may know him better.*

When the Ephesians came to Christ, they entered into a personal relationship with God. More than knowing about God, they came to know God personally. *Now this is eternal life: that they know you, the only true God, and Jesus Christ, whom you have sent* (John 17:3), said Jesus. One of the great truths of Christianity is that we can know God for ourselves.

Before I met my wife I had a roommate who told me about a young lady who was BBU: bright, beautiful, and unattached. He told me she came from a wonderful family, was active in ministry, and had a heart for God. He told me so many things about her, in fact, I almost felt like I knew her. We were finally introduced, and spoke for a couple hours. Then I wanted to marry her. There's a world of difference between knowing about someone, and knowing them personally.

But even though the Ephesian believers had come to know God personally, Paul wanted them to know him even better. This is accomplished through prayer, Bible study, obedience, and in many other ways. Many come to a point in their relationship with God where they wonder, *Is this all there is?* God's answer to that question is always *No*. As long as we're getting to know God better, the relationship will always be fresh and new.

Ephesians 2:1-5 *As for you, you were dead in your transgressions and sins . . . . But because of his great love for us, God, who is rich in mercy, made us alive.*

All the descendants of Adam and Eve arrive in the world spiritually dead. We may be alive physically, mentally, and emotionally but, apart from Christ, we're spiritually dead. The only solution is for Jesus Christ to give us life.

On his way to the city of Nain, Jesus encountered a funeral procession in which a young man was being carried out for burial. It was especially sad because he was the only son of his mother, and she was a widow. Jesus interrupted the funeral and spoke to the corpse: *Young man, I say to you, get up!* To everyone's surprise, the dead man came alive (Luke 7:11-15). Likewise, we were dead in sin, but when Jesus spoke the word to us, we came alive to God.

Ephesians 2:6 *And God raised us up with Christ and seated us with him in the heavenly realms.*

Because Jesus is seated at the right hand of God, those who belong to Christ are also seated at the right hand of God. From God's perspective, those who belong to Christ are just as secure as if they were already in heaven.

This can be compared to a helicopter rescue, in which a person is attached to a cable, and pulled into the helicopter. The person is saved, not when they reach the helicopter, but the moment they're attached to the cable. The Spirit of Christ is stronger than any cable, and unites us to Christ the moment we believe. At that very moment we are just as secure as if we were already in heaven.

Ephesians 2:7 *. . . in the coming ages he [will] show the incomparable riches of his grace.*

If you owed someone a million dollars, and were suddenly forgiven, you'd be very thankful, but you'd still be poor. The good news of Jesus Christ is that God has not only forgiven our debt, but has made us extremely rich.

Incomparable riches are those riches to which no other riches can be compared. If you gathered all the riches of the world, and doubled them twice, you wouldn't even be close to the incomparable riches that'll be ours in the age to come.

God is like a billionaire father who doesn't want his children to be spoiled by wealth. He plans to make the rich eventually, but first he wants us to mature through hard work and discipline. We may struggle for a lifetime, but will inherit eternal glory.

Ephesians 2:8-9 *For it is by grace you have been saved, through faith—and this is not from yourselves, it is the gift of God—not by works, so that no one can boast.*

Salvation is the gift of God to those who believe in Jesus Christ. But even the faith to believe has been given to us by God, so that no one can boast about earning their salvation. This is the meaning of grace.

A little boy was so impressed with the Washington Monument that he wanted to buy it. So he went to a security guard and offered everything in his pocket, which was thirty-five cents. The security guard said, *Let me tell you about the Washington Monument. First, it's not for sale. Second, if it was for sale, you couldn't afford it. Third, if you're an American, it's already yours.*

The same can be said about salvation. First, it's not for sale. Second, if it was for sale, we couldn't afford it. Third, if we believe in Jesus Christ it's already ours. This is what it means to be saved by grace.

Ephesians 2:10 *For we are God's handiwork, created in Christ Jesus to do good works, which God prepared in advance for us to do.*

Christianity can be thought of in terms of guilt, grace, and gratitude. We are guilty before God and deserve nothing but wrath. But God sent his Son to die for our sins, so he could give us salvation. This makes us so thankful we want to do good works to please him. God has even prepared good works in advance for us to do.

My wife came out of a store, and saw a lady in a wheel chair, struggling in the parking lot. The woman lived a mile away, and my wife decided to push her all the way home. This gave them time to talk about the Lord and, when my wife returned, she was filled joy. She had done a good work which God prepared in advance for her to do.

For Reflection and Review

- *Is knowing God easy?*
- *How does Jesus make us alive spiritually?*
- *Has serving God ever made you joyful?*

Lesson 302

Ephesians 2:13 *But now in Christ Jesus you who once were far away have been brought near by the blood of Christ.*

Our emotions aren't the best indicator of our relationship with God. They might tell us we are near to God when, in fact, we are far away from him. Or, they might tell us we are far from God when, in fact, we are near to him. Paul wanted his readers to know that whoever believes in Jesus Christ has *been brought near by the blood of Christ*, no matter how far away they feel. When we understand how close we are to God, because of Jesus Christ, we are more likely to feel that way as well.

Ephesians 3:8 *Although I am less than the least of all the Lord's people, this grace was given me: to preach to the Gentiles the boundless riches of Christ.*

Paul wrote these words while he was under house arrest in Rome (Acts 28). It wasn't as bad as prison, but he spent much of his time in chains (Ephesians 6:20). In spite of his situation, however, Paul continued to preach the *boundless riches of Christ*. He appeared to be poor, but felt richer than a king.

An old prospector died and his relatives came by for his possessions. All they found was a table, a cot, and a lantern. As they were leaving, his friend arrived and asked if he could have whatever was left. Of course they agreed, so he went inside, pulled up a floorboard, and found more gold than he could spend in a lifetime. As the relatives drove away he thought, *Too bad they didn't know him better.* The better we know Christ, the richer we will feel.

Ephesians 3:12 *In him and through faith in him we may approach God with freedom and confidence.*

This is a privilege that shouldn't be taken lightly. To approach a king without permission could result in death (Esther 4:11). If an unauthorized person approached God's sanctuary, they too would be put to death (Numbers 3:38). God is the greatest being in the universe, so access to him is a wonderful privilege.

A former president boarded a plane with his bodyguards and, after being seated, was approached by a total stranger. The bodyguards intervened, but the stranger said, *Mr. President, I know your son from college.* At once the man was warmly received. The only way to the Father is through his Son. This is why we pray in Jesus' name (John 14:13).

Ephesians 3:17-18 *And I pray that you, being rooted and established in love, may have power, together with all the Lord's holy people, to grasp how wide and long and high and deep is the love of Christ.*

The need to be loved is both universal and powerful. It's so compelling, in fact, that it may cause us to do things against our better judgment. But human love will never meet our deepest emotional need, which is to be deeply loved by God.

During the Spanish Inquisition, many godly Christians were put to the cruelest tortures hell could devise. A skeleton was found in one of the prisons chained to the wall. The man apparently starved to death but, before he died, he scratched four words into the wall: *wide, long, high, deep.* Even in the worst situations, God wants us to know *how wide and long and high and deep is the love of Christ.*

Ephesians 3:20 *[God] is able to do immeasurably more than all we ask or imagine.*

The remarkable thing about this verse is that it actually proves what it says. Paul wanted this letter to encourage the Ephesians, but he never imagined it would encourage billions of Christians around the world for centuries. God was doing immeasurably more than anything Paul asked or imagined even while he wrote those very words. This is something we should keep in mind whenever we pray. Instead of expecting God to do less than we ask or imagine, we should expect God to do even more than we ask or imagine.

A Saudi king was so impressed by an American golf professional that he offered him a gift. The American requested a golf club to commemorate the round they played together. The next day he was given a key to a golf club, complete with eighteen holes and a beautiful clubhouse. *You are coming to a King, large petitions with you bring. For his grace and power are such, none can ever ask too much.*

Ephesians 4:2 *Be completely humble and gentle; be patient, bearing with one another in love.*

Paul didn't tell the Ephesian believers to correct each other, rebuke each other, or fix each other. He simply said, *be patient, bearing with one another in love.* When we consider how difficult it is to change ourselves, we can figure the odds of changing others. There's a place for correction, of course, but there's a much bigger place for simply putting up with each other. In the age to come we'll all be perfect but, for now, we must be patient with each other—and even with ourselves.

Ephesians 4:7 *But to each one of us grace has been given as Christ apportioned it.*

Paul isn't speaking of *saving grace* (Ephesians 2:8-9), but *serving grace.* This is an important subject because whoever receives saving grace also receives serving grace. *Each of you should use whatever gift you have received to serve others, as faithful stewards of God's grace in its various forms* (1 Peter 4:10), wrote Peter.

The gifts we have from Christ aren't for ourselves, but for building up his church. *So Christ himself gave the apostles, the prophets, the evangelists, the pastors and teachers, to equip his people for works of service* (Ephesians 4:11-12), wrote Paul.

Gifts of service aren't given equally to all, but have been *apportioned* by Christ. John the Baptist was a mighty servant of God, but when his ministry began to decline he lamented, *A person can receive only what is given them from heaven* (John 3:27). It's normal to desire greater gifts, but God determines their measure.

Again, it will be like a man going on a journey, who called his servants and entrusted his wealth to them. To one he gave five bags of gold, to another two bags, and to another one bag, each according to his ability (Matthew 25:14-15), said Jesus. The money wasn't for them to spend, but to invest for their master. He didn't give each person the same, but apportioned his wealth as he pleased. The important thing isn't who receives the most to work with, but doing our best with what we've been given. This will keep us from viewing others with jealousy or pride.

For Reflection and Review

- *How important are your feelings to your relationship with Christ?*
- *What is the advantage of praying in Jesus' name?*
- *How are you investing your life for Christ?*

Lesson 303

Ephesians 4:15 . . . *speaking the truth in love.*

Truth is such a precious thing that it must be spoken in love. The more lovingly it's said, sometimes, the easier it is to receive. Many years ago I used a sermon illustration that wasn't quite appropriate and, after the service, a man corrected me so harshly I nearly collapsed. I even wondered if I could preach the next service. Then another man said something similar, but in a very different way. *That was one of the best sermons I've ever heard you preach, and I think it can be even better if you refine that illustration.*

Both men said the same thing, but in very different ways. It doesn't take a great deal of thoughtfulness to say what you think, but it takes a little thoughtfulness to say it in a way that will be helpful. Christians should always speak the truth, and always do it in love.

Ephesians 4:16 *From him the whole body, joined and held together by every supporting ligament, grows and builds itself up in love, as each part does its work.*

One of Paul's favorite images for the church is the body of Christ. Every part of a body has an important function, and everyone in the body of Christ has an important role to play. A fingernail doesn't seem important until you lose one, and you seldom think of your pancreas until it stops working. Likewise, the body of Christ *grows and builds itself up in love, as each part does it is work.*

A couple began attending a church I served, and often stayed after the service to ask questions. They were deciding whether to become members and wanted more information. *We're not trying to be difficult [they said] but this is very important to us. We don't just want to attend a church; we want to build the church we attend.* I was so amazed that I went back to my office and wrote down what they said. But this should be the attitude of all God's people. The body of Christ *grows and builds itself up in love, as each part does its work.*

Ephesians 4:18 *They are darkened in their understanding and separated from the life of God because of the ignorance that is in them due to the hardening of their hearts.*

Alienation from God is largely due to hardness of heart. *While sitting on the bank of a river one day, I picked up a solid round stone from the water and broke it open. It was perfectly dry [inside] in spite of the fact that it had been immersed in water for centuries. The same is true of many people in the western world.*

For centuries they have been surrounded by Christianity; they live immersed in the waters of its benefits. And yet it has not penetrated their hearts; they do not love it. The fault is not in Christianity, but in people's hearts, which have been hardened by materialism and intellectualism (Sadhu

Sundar Singh, slightly revised). *Today, if you hear his voice, do not harden your hearts* (Hebrews 3:15), says Hebrews.

Ephesians 4:26 *In your anger do not sin: Do not let the sun go down while you are still angry.*

Anger is an appropriate response to injustice, and is not sinful in itself. But anger brings us close to sin because it's difficult for sinners to manage their anger well. *Anyone can become angry, that is easy. But to be angry with the right person, to the right degree, at the right time, for the right purpose, in the right way—that is not always easy* (Aristotle, slightly revised).

Several years ago a lady had a can of soup sticking out of her wall and I inquired how it got there. She explained that she and her husband disagreed the previous night, and she threw it at her husband's head. Thankfully he ducked, and the can stuck in the wall instead of his head.

Another woman I know used a kitchen plate as a frisbee aimed at her husband's head. Thankfully she also missed, and the plate flew out the window. Unfortunately the window was closed at the time. I've noticed in myself that when anger goes up, intelligence goes down. Anger is a brief insanity, and the best remedy is a little time to think.

Ephesians 4:29 *Do not let any unwholesome talk come out of your mouths.*

Some people have one vocabulary for Sundays, and another one for the rest of the week. Paul wanted Christians to be consistent in their speech, and to guard against anything inappropriate ever coming out their mouths.

A friend of mine was raised in a Christian home and never heard his father curse. But he was surprised by what came out his father's mouth when he slammed his thumb in drawer. He said, *Owie—that really hurt*. The Apostle Paul would have been pleased.

Ephesians 4:30 *And do not grieve the Holy Spirit of God.*

The Holy Spirit is not a force, but a person with real emotions. The indwelling Spirit helps us become like Christ, and is disappointed whenever we fail. God's response to our sin isn't always anger but sorrow, sadness, and grief.

Imagine you saw your son or grandson taking a spelling test, and could see he was stuck on a word. You could also see the smart child next to him wasn't covering his paper. You wanted your child to do the right thing but, instead, he took a long steady gaze and stole the answer. The disappointment in your heart is how God feels whenever you disobey him. Whenever we do the right thing we bring our Father joy, and whenever we do the wrong thing we bring him grief.

For Reflection and Review

- *Have you ever been corrected harshly?*
- *Why do some people harden their hearts?*
- *What do you think about profanity?*

Lesson 304

Ephesians 5:1 *Follow God's example, therefore, as dearly loved children.*

Not all children are equally loved by their parents. Those who are bright, beautiful, and talented are often favored above their siblings. Similar personalities may also cause parents to prefer one child over another. And, of course, some children alienate their parents through rebellion.

But there's something more important than what your earthly parents think of you, and that's what your heavenly Father thinks of you. Paul assured the Ephesian Christians that they were God's dearly loved children—not just the best of them, but all of them. The core identity of all who believe in Jesus Christ is that we are dearly loved children of God.

At the start of his ministry Jesus was baptized. When he came out of the water a voice from heaven said: *This is my Son, whom I love; with him I am well pleased* (Matthew 3:17). And before his crucifixion, the voice came a second time: *This is my Son, whom I love; with him I am well pleased* (Matthew 17:5).

Jesus was emotionally secure because he knew he was dearly loved by his heavenly Father. God loves everyone, of course, but Christians have the added assurance that we are dearly loved because we are *in Christ* (Ephesians 1:1).

This is why Jesus could pray for his disciples saying, *[You] have loved them even as you have loved me* (John 17:23). This is the same as saying, *You have loved them as much as you have loved me*. We're dearly loved children of God, not because we're bright, beautiful, and talented (or even good) but because we are *in Christ*.

Ephesians 5:3 *But among you there must not be even a hint of sexual immorality.*

The reason some people don't come to Christ is because they want to be in charge of their own sexuality. Contrary to the permissive culture of their time, Paul directed the Ephesian Christians to be sexually pure.

Several years ago I married a beautiful young couple in their twenties, and could tell they were very much in love. Before the wedding I was standing back stage with the groom, and gave him some last minute advice. I suggested when it was time to kiss the bride he make it brief, so as not to embarrass her. He said he'd do his best, but was a little nervous since this would be their very kiss. Even in a promiscuous culture, they were sexually pure.

Ephesians 5:5 *For of this you can be sure: No immoral, impure or greedy person—such a person is an idolater—has any inheritance in the kingdom of Christ and of God.*

We might think of greed as a little sin, but Paul considered it idolatry—the worship of another god. We can test ourselves for idolatry by asking: *what do I love more than anything else? Whatever a man loves, that is his god for he carries it in his heart. He goes about with it night and day; he sleeps and wakes with it whatever it is—wealth or self, pleasure or renown* (Martin Luther, slightly revised). If we love anything more than God, we are guilty of idolatry and are outside the kingdom of God.

Ephesians 5:8 *For you were once darkness, but now you are light in the Lord.*

Paul didn't say the Ephesian Christians were *in* darkness but, at one time, they actually *were* darkness. They were like black holes that swallowed up the light around them. You may even know someone who brightens up a room just by leaving.

We are no longer darkness, however, but are *light in the Lord*. We have no light of our own but, like the moon, we reflect a greater light. *You are the light of the world* (Matthew 5:14), said Jesus. And *let your light shine before others* (Matthew 5:16), he said. This is something to keep in mind whenever we enter a room.

Ephesians 5:18 *Do not get drunk on wine, which leads to debauchery. Instead, be filled with the Spirit.*

The Bible doesn't condemn drinking wine in moderation, but strongly condemns drunkenness. Some Ephesian believers may've been heavy drinkers, and Paul didn't want this to be part of their Christian life. Instead of being drunk, he wanted them to be *filled with the Spirit*. Both produce a kind of joy (Zechariah 10:7, Galatians 5:22), but one leads to debauchery, and the other leads to holiness.

The way to be filled with the Spirit is mentioned next: *Sing and make music from your heart to the Lord, always giving thanks to God the Father for everything, in the name of our Lord Jesus Christ* (Ephesians 5:19-20).

A friend of mine received a voicemail message, but the caller forgot to hang up. After the message there were several minutes of loud singing to the glory of God. This good man wasn't drunk on wine; he was filled with the Holy Spirit. This is what Paul wanted for the Ephesians, and what God wants for us.

Ephesians 6:10 *Finally, be strong in the Lord and in his mighty power.*

Christianity wasn't easy for the apostles, or for the early Christians. They struggled against their opponents, against their sinful natures, and against demonic forces. Left to themselves they couldn't win, but with the help of Christ they wouldn't lose.

A Christian man was imprisoned for his faith and severely tortured for many years. The guards told him to give up his stupid Christianity, in favor of atheism, so he could be released. He said, *The test of a bridge is not when a cat walks over it, but when a train rolls over it* (Richard Wurmbrand). He explained that many atheists became Christians on their deathbeds, but no Christians became atheists on their deathbeds. God kept him strong to the end, and will do the same for us.

Ephesians 6:11 *Put on the full armor of God, so that you can take your stand against the devil's schemes.*

Roman soldiers didn't go to war without proper equipment: sword, shield, breastplate, helmet, and footgear were basic. Likewise, Paul wanted Christians to be dressed for spiritual battle. Prayer, faith, truth, righteousness, and salvation is what we ought to wear. Soldiers aren't prepared for war unless they're completely dressed, and neither are believers.

God's people were defeated in the Old Testament, sometimes, because they didn't have the proper gear. At one point, *Not a blacksmith could be found in the whole land of Israel, because the Philistines had said, Otherwise the Hebrews will make swords or spears!* (1 Samuel 13:19). By keeping God's people disarmed, the Philistines made them powerless.

The devil wants to disempower the church by taking away its gear, and the church disempowers itself by not getting dressed for battle. Prayer, faith, truth, righteousness, and salvation belong to every believer. We should never leave home without being fully dressed.

For Reflection and Review

- *Why should we think of ourselves as God's dearly loved children?*
- *What are the dangers of sex outside of marriage?*
- *Why is the church often weak?*

Lesson 305

Philippians 1:1 *Paul and Timothy, servants of Christ Jesus, To all God's holy people in Christ Jesus at Philippi, together with the overseers and deacons.*

The Apostle Paul started the church in Philippi during his second missionary journey around AD 51. Ten years later he was under house arrest in Rome, and wrote to thank them for their recent financial support. Paul described the Philippian believers as *God's holy people in Christ Jesus.* He wasn't referring to the spiritual leaders only, but to all believers, including those who were struggling.

Consciously or not, Paul was making the point that all God's people are holy in Christ Jesus. In and of ourselves we are filled with sin. But, in Christ Jesus, we are *God's holy people.* Christianity is a gift of radical forgiveness which makes us holy and acceptable to God.

Philippians 1:4-5 *In all my prayers for all of you, I always pray with joy because of your partnership in the gospel from the first day until now.*

The gospel ministry has always been a joint effort between God and his people. Jesus put together a team of twelve, and received financial support from generous donors (Luke 8:3). Likewise, Paul received financial support from the Philippians. When Paul was in Thessalonica, in fact, the Philippians sent him aid more than once (Philippians 4:16). Now that he was in Rome, they sent him help again. Paul brought the gospel to the Philippians, and the Philippians helped Paul bring the gospel to others.

Partnering in the gospel is an important mark of spiritual maturity. I was raised in a church that other people built, and received the gospel because others brought it to me. When I grew up, I understood my duty was to do the same for others.

Partnering in the gospel is also a good investment. When the Philippians sent a gift to Paul they never imagined his thank-you letter would become part of the Bible, read by millions of people for thousands of years. If they hadn't partnered with Paul, our New Testament would be a little lighter because it wouldn't contain this wonderful letter. It'll be a joy to meet the Philippian Christians in heaven, and to thank them for supporting the Apostle Paul.

Philippians 1:6 *[H]e who began a good work in you will carry it on to completion until the day of Christ Jesus.*

Paul was amazed, not only by the saving power of Jesus, but also by the keeping power of Jesus. After starting the church in Philippi, Paul moved on rather quickly. How would they survive without him? But, ten years later, the church was still going strong. God is the one who brought them to faith, and he would *carry it on to completion*. Many people start projects without finishing, but this can never be said of God.

Philippians 1:8 *God can testify how I long for all of you with the affection of Christ Jesus.*

Before he was a Christian Paul hated believers, and wanted them dead (Acts 7:54-58). But after he came to Christ he loved them with the *affection of Christ Jesus*. Here we see that Christ not only loves us, but loves us with affection. This is important to know, because can never love Christ more than we believe he loves us. And we can never love him affectionately, unless we're convinced that he loves us affectionately.

This is why the story of the Prodigal Son is so emotionally powerful. When the father saw the son coming home he didn't wait for an explanation. *[H]e ran to his son, threw his arms around him and kissed him* (Luke 15:20). The greatest emotional need we have is to be hugged and kissed by God. This is the God we meet in the Bible.

Philippians 1:15-17 *It is true that some preach Christ out of envy and rivalry, but others out of goodwill. The latter do so out of love, knowing that I am put here for the defense of the gospel. The former preach Christ out of selfish ambition, not sincerely, supposing that they can stir up trouble for me while I am in chains.*

Some preachers were using Paul's imprisonment as an opportunity to grow their own ministries. With Paul out of the way, they were able to attract a larger audience. We might expect Paul to be upset but he replied, *[W]hat does it matter? The important thing is that in every way, whether from false motives or true, Christ is preached* (Philippians 1:18).

Paul had this attitude because he wasn't concerned to make a name for himself, but to make the name of Jesus known. *[Y]our name and renown are the desire of our hearts* (Isaiah 26:8), wrote Isaiah. This should be the attitude of every Christian minister.

Philippians 1:21 *For to me, to live is Christ and to die is gain.*

As Paul waited for his trial in Rome, he knew he could be facing death. He had mixed feelings about this because he'd no longer be able to preach the gospel, but he'd be in the presence of Christ. Either outcome was agreeable to Paul, because *to live is Christ and to die is gain*.

Another preacher lay dying and said, *I am not discouraged. I want to live as long as I am useful, but when my work is done I want to be up and off*. The next day he said, *Earth recedes, Heaven opens . . . . If this is death, it is sweet. . . . God is calling me, and I must go* (DL Moody).

Death is only gain, however, if we live for Jesus Christ. If we live for money or pleasure, death is not gain. If we live for popularity or success, death is not gain. If we live for excitement or leisure, death is not gain. But if we live for Jesus Christ then, earth will receded, heaven will open, and death will be our gain.

For Reflection and Review

- *What are your favorite ways to partner in the gospel?*
- *Are you amazed that God has kept you in the faith?*
- *What do you think of God's affection?*

Lesson 306

Philippians 1:25 *Convinced of this, I know that I will remain, and I will continue with all of you for your progress and joy in the faith.*

There's a relationship between progress and joy in many things. If you're making progress at a sport, you'll enjoy it a little more. If you're making progress at work, you'll enjoy it a little more too. A ninety year old cello player practiced his instrument several hours a day. When his niece asked *why?* he said, *I think I'm making a little progress.*

Christianity is a happy religion as long as we're making progress. Show me a Christian who's making progress and I'll show you a happy Christian. Show me a Christian who's not making progress and I'll show you someone to pray for.

Philippians 2:2 *. . . make my joy complete by being like-minded, having the same love, being one in spirit and of one mind.*

Church unity was never far from the apostle's mind. *[B]e perfectly united in mind and thought* (1 Corinthians (1:10). *Make every effort to keep the unity of the Spirit* (Ephesians 4:3). And be *united in love* (Colossians 2:2), he wrote. Persecution from outside the church was no less serious than disunity within. Many churches stop growing the moment there's conflict, because no one wants to invite others into an unhealthy situation.

If children are raised in a healthy home, they'll invite their friends to share the joy. But if there's conflict in the home, they'll stop inviting their friends, because they don't want to be embarrassed. That's why Jesus prayed for the church to be united. *Then the world will know that you sent me* (John 17:23), he said. If Jesus prayed for unity, and Paul pled for unity, it may be more important than we think.

Philippians 2:5-8 *In your relationships with one another, have the same mindset as Christ Jesus: Who, being in very nature God, did not consider equality with God something to be used to his own advantage; rather, he made himself nothing by taking the very nature of a servant, being made in human likeness. And being found in appearance as a man, he humbled himself by becoming obedient to death—even death on a cross!*

Theologians divide the humiliation of Christ into various stages. He left his throne in glory, to be born in a manger, and began sucking and drooling. Years later he was mocked, spat on, whipped, and crucified. He said, *It is finished* and *gave up his spirit* (John 19:30). Finally, he was laid in a cold, dark, tomb and began to decompose. Incarnation, suffering, death, and burial are various stages of Christ's humiliation.

Philippians 2:9 *Therefore God exalted him to the highest place and gave him the name that is above every name.*

Theologians also divide the exaltation of Christ into various stages. First he rose from the dead, then he ascended into heaven, now he rules the world, and he will return in glory. First he was crowned with thorns, then he was crowned with honor. First he was humiliated, then he was exalted. First he suffered, then he was glorified.

This is also the pattern for those who follow Christ. *[W]e share in his sufferings in order that we may also share in his glory* (Romans 8:17), wrote Paul. And, *our present sufferings are not worth comparing with the glory that will be [ours]* (Romans 8:18), wrote Paul again. And, *you participate in the sufferings of Christ, so that you may be overjoyed when his glory is revealed* (1 Peter 4:13), wrote Peter.

When we understand the pattern God has established for the Christian life, we aren't surprised by suffering. We simply look ahead to future glory. The only thing that could make the best of all possible worlds better, is to get there through suffering. The way of tears is the way to eternal happiness.

Philippians 2:12 *Therefore, my dear friends, as you have always obeyed—not only in my presence, but now much more in my absence—continue to work out your salvation with fear and trembling.*

The good news of our salvation, and God's affectionate love for us, might've led some to think God wasn't dangerous. But that idea is flatly wrong, so Paul commanded the Philippians to work out their salvation with *fear and trembling*.

[H]e is the one you are to fear, he is the one you are to dread (Isaiah 8:13), wrote Isaiah. Many want to soften the fear of God to a mild reverence or respect. But the word *dread* should clear that up. As long as we're living for God we don't need to be afraid of him. But if we're turning away from God we should be filled with dread.

When I was sixteen years old my family went on a ski vacation, and I rode a lift to the top of a mountain. I'd never been there before and, when I reached the top, I was gripped by fear because the mountain had two sides. To my alarm, there was nothing to keep me from going down the wrong side. If I went down the right side of the mountain I'd be fine. But if I went down the wrong side of the mountain I could possibly die. It was fear that helped me choose the right side. There's a right side of God and wrong side of God, so *work out your salvation with fear and trembling*.

For Reflection and Review

- Have you ever watched a church fight?
- How does Christ's humiliation and exaltation apply to us?
- Should Christians be afraid of God?

Lesson 307

Philippians 2:13 . . . *for it is God who works in you to will and to act in order to fulfill his good purpose.*

The desire to do God's will doesn't come from ourselves, but from God. We choose to respond, not because we're noble, but because God is working in us. Some people imagine they can ignore the Spirit of God, without danger, but God's ancient people serve as a warning. *Israel would not submit to me. So I gave them over to their stubborn hearts to follow their own devices* (Psalm 81:11-12), said God. The desire to do God's will is a gift of grace, that shows he's working in our lives.

Philippians 3:7 *But whatever were gains to me I now consider loss for the sake of Christ.*

Before his conversion, Paul kept a plus and minus column in his mind. On the plus side was everything religiously good; on the minus side was everything religiously bad. Since he had more good than bad, Paul thought he was right with God.

But this idea has more in common with Islam than with Christianity. *Those whose good deeds weigh heavy in the scales shall triumph, but those whose deeds are light shall forfeit their souls and abide in Hell forever* (Koran, sura twenty-three), wrote Muhammad.

The last judgment, according to Islam, is determined by a scale. If our good deeds outweigh our bad deeds we go up; if not, we go down. But Jesus taught the opposite: only bad people go to heaven.

A Pharisee and a tax collector went to the temple to pray. The Pharisee was thankful he was so good, and the tax collector was ashamed he was so bad. He wouldn't even raise his eyes, but beat his breast saying, *God, have mercy on me, a sinner*. To everyone's surprise, Jesus said, *this man, rather than the other, went home justified before God,* (Luke 18:9-14). Good people don't go to heaven because there are no good people. Christianity isn't about the scales, but about the mercy of God through faith in Jesus Christ.

Philippians 3:8 *What is more, I consider everything a loss because of the surpassing worth of knowing Christ Jesus my Lord, for whose sake I have lost all things.*

Paul renounced all confidence in his good deeds, so that he might trust in Christ alone. This isn't hard for ordinary sinners, but for those who've spent a lifetime trying to earn their way to heaven, it can be difficult. Paul came to see that even his best deeds were nothing more than *garbage* (Philippians 3:8b), because they came from sinful hands. *[A]ll our righteous acts are like filthy rags* (Isaiah 64:6), wrote Isaiah. Trusting in our good deeds to get us to heaven is nothing more than trusting in our sins to get us to heaven.

Philippians 3:9 *. . . not having a righteousness of my own that comes from the law, but that which is through faith in Christ—the righteousness that comes from God on the basis of faith.*

Even though Paul was better than other sinners, he knew he wasn't good enough for God. So he traded his imperfect righteousness, for the righteousness of Christ, which God freely gives to those who believe. Jesus obeyed his heavenly Father in word, thought, and deed, every day of his life. *I always do what pleases him* (John 8:29), he said. We've never had a sinless moment, but Christ never had a moment of sin.

But when he was on the cross, *God made him who had no sin to be sin for us, so that in him we might become the righteousness of God* (2 Corinthians 5:21), wrote Paul. If you were a million dollars in debt, and married a billionaire, all your debt would go away, and you'd be very rich. That's what Jesus does for us. He takes away our sin, and gives to us his righteousness. He takes away our our rags, and gives us his riches.

When my daughter was in fourth grade, she was paired with another girl for an assignment. My daughter did all the work, and her partner did absolutely nothing, but they both got an A. That's how it is with Christ. He did all the work for our salvation, and we get the same grade, by putting our trust in him.

Philippians 3:10 *I want to know Christ.*

One of the reasons for Paul's effectiveness in ministry is that he didn't rely on past experience, but wanted to know Christ better every day. He was able to do this though prayer, obedience, service, Bible study, and many other ways. The more and better he knew Christ, the more and better he loved Christ, and the more effective he was in ministry.

My wife and I graduated from seminary many years ago, but I still recall the school's motto: *To know Christ and to make him known*. Some people want to know Christ without making him known. Others want to make him known without knowing him deeply. Paul's practice was to know Christ deeply, then to make him known to others.

Philippians 3:10b *. . . to know the power of his resurrection and participation in his sufferings.*

Adoniram Judson was a missionary to Burma, in the nineteenth century, when there wasn't a single Christian there. He labored six years, with no results, and was thrown into prison where he was shackled with thirty-two pounds of chain. Unable to swat the mosquitoes, they nearly ate him alive.

When he was finally released, his wife and daughter died, and he was so depressed that he dug a grave for himself as well. But he continued to labor for decades and, today, there are over a million Christians there who trace their spiritual lineage to Adoniram Judson. It's not enough to know Christ in *the power of his resurrection*; we must know him by *participation in his sufferings*. There can be no resurrection power without a little dying.

For Reflection and Review

- *Why shouldn't Christians trust their good works to earn favor with God?*
- *Is knowing Christ easy or difficult?*
- *Why did Paul want to share in Christ's suffering?*

Lesson 308

Philippians 3:13-14 *Forgetting what is behind and straining toward what is ahead, I press on toward the goal to win the prize for which God has called me heavenward in Christ Jesus.*

Paul thought of the Christian life as a race toward heaven and, as he ran, he did two things: he forgot about the past and strained toward the future. He didn't dwell on former achievements, or failures. He kept his eyes on the finish line, and pressed on with all his might.

If you've ever done something good for God, you might be tempted to rest, as though you'd done enough. And if you've ever done something terrible, you might be tempted to dwell on it. Both must be forgotten in order to press on.

God remembers our good deeds so we don't have to, and he forgets our sins so we can forget them too. *Their sins and lawless acts I will remember no more* (Hebrews 10:17), says Hebrews. Like Paul, we can forget about the past, and strain toward the future, as we approach the finish line.

Philippians 3:16 *Only let us live up to what we have already attained.*

Due to the downward pull of sin, nothing is more common in the Christian life than spiritual slippage. We ought to make progress daily, but if that seems out of reach, we should at least live up to what we've already attained.

Years ago I could do a double back flip, but I haven't lived up to that. I could lift one hundred sixty pounds, but I haven't lived up to that either. I could ride my bike a hundred miles, but I haven't lived up to that either. By God's grace, however, I know the Bible better, and have constantly grown in my faith. I wish I could do the other things, but I've done the most important thing.

Philippians 3:20 *. . . our citizenship is in heaven.*

Philippi was a Roman colony and the people were proud of their citizenship. Most had never been to Rome, but they belonged to the world's greatest empire, and enjoyed their status. Paul was also a Roman citizen, which gave him certain legal rights that probably saved his life (Acts 23:27).

If being a Roman citizen was good, however, being a citizen of heaven is even better. Roman citizens eventually died, but citizens of heaven never die. Roman citizenship could be lost, but heavenly citizenship can never be lost (John 10:28). The Roman empire faded away, but the kingdom of heaven will never fade away.

A young lady immigrated to the United States and stayed the rest of her life. She became a model citizen, who loved her country, and never went anywhere else. When she died, her children went to the bank, and opened her safe-deposit box. Inside they found another box, securely locked, and without a key. They drilled through the box and found an envelope inside containing a legal document: her United States citizenship. Nothing in the world was more precious to her, and nothing is more precious to us than our citizenship in heaven.

Philippians 3:20b *And we eagerly await a Savior from there, the Lord Jesus Christ.*

Paul wanted believers to eagerly await the return of Jesus Christ. He didn't want them to passively wait, or to be indifferent, but to watch and wait expectantly, hopefully, and joyfully.

I had a flash of inspiration, when I was a teen, and rallied my siblings to clean the house while our mother was away for half a day. Because there were six of us, the house was seldom spotless, so we worked together for several hours to make it as clean as we could. It even became a race to see how much we could accomplish before our mother returned. When she finally arrived she was delighted, and we were as happy as she. That's how it is with Christ. The better we serve him now, the more excited we'll be for his return.

Philippians 4:1 *Therefore, my brothers and sisters . . . stand firm in the Lord.*

Since Philippi was a Roman colony, with a military presence, Paul's instruction to stand firm may recall the duty of a soldier to stand firm in battle. Soldiers could be punished for not fighting well, and an untimely retreat could result in the death penalty. If we think of Christianity as a battlefield, we won't be surprised by hardship, and won't quickly retreat.

Philippians 4:4 *Rejoice in the Lord always. I will say it again: Rejoice!*

One of the most attractive things about Paul was his ability to rejoice, even in the midst of hardship. He didn't write to the Philippians while vacationing on a Mediterranean beach; he was chained to a guard while under house arrest. It wasn't a dungeon, but neither was it pleasant.

The Philippians may've also recalled that when Paul and Silas were in Philippi, they were flogged, thrown in prison, and fastened to the stocks. Their bodies were wracked with pain but, around midnight, they sang hymns to God (Acts 16:23-25). From this we learn that whoever has God, has all they need to be happy.

Though the fig tree does not bud and there are no grapes on the vines, though the olive crop fails and the fields produce no food, though there are no sheep in the pen and no cattle in the stalls, yet I will rejoice in the Lord, I will be joyful in God my Savior (Habakkuk 3:17-18), wrote the prophet Habakkuk.

For Reflection and Review

- *Why shouldn't Christians dwell on the past?*
- *Why aren't more believers eager for the Lord's return?*
- *Why can we be joyful even when life is hard?*

Lesson 309

Philippians 4:5 *Let your gentleness be evident to all.*

Gentleness is such an important virtue that Paul wanted it to be seen in all God's people. Gentleness shouldn't to be a hidden virtue, like prayer or generosity, but an open virtue for everyone to see.

I am gentle and humble in heart (Matthew 11:29), said Jesus. *[Y]our king comes to you, gentle and riding on a donkey* (Matthew 21:5), wrote Matthew. *By the humility and gentleness of Christ, I appeal to you* (2 Corinthians 10:1), wrote Paul. And *if someone is caught in a sin . . . restore that person gently* (Galatians 6:1), wrote Paul again.

The gentleness of Christians should be evident to Republicans and Democrats, to Jews and Muslims, to heterosexuals and homosexuals, to the righteous and the wicked. *Let your gentleness be evident to all*, wrote Paul.

Philippians 4:6-7 *Do not be anxious about anything, but in every situation, by prayer and petition, with thanksgiving, present your requests to God. And the peace of God, which transcends all understanding, will guard your hearts and your minds in Christ Jesus.*

High level stress can lead to headaches, upset stomach, high blood pressure, heart problems, skin problems, asthma, arthritis, depression, chest pain, insomnia and more. By one estimate, seventy-five percent of adult doctor visits are for stress related ailments. Paul had a stressful life, but he learned to receive God's peace.

What if there was a God who loved you like a son or daughter, and secured an eternal home for you, in the best of all possible worlds? (John 14:2). And what if there was a God who numbered all your hairs, and promised not one would be lost apart from his perfect plan? (Matthew 10:30). And what if there was a God who promised to watch over you so carefully that nothing bad would happen to you that wasn't for your ultimate good? (Romans 8:28-29). Since all these things are true, *Do not be anxious about anything.* Instead, *Cast all your anxiety on him because he cares for you* (1 Peter 5:7), wrote Peter.

Philippians 4:8 *[W]hatever is true, whatever is noble, whatever is right, whatever is pure, whatever is lovely, whatever is admirable—if anything is excellent or praiseworthy—think about such things.*

Most people think about whatever pops into their head, but God wants us to control our thoughts. Lucius Seneca (the Roman statesman and philosopher) lived at the same time as Paul, and may've been in Rome when Paul wrote this letter.

Seneca wasn't a Christian, but he was highly regarded by the early church for his noble thoughts and character. *I will govern my life and thoughts as if the whole world were to see the one and read the other, for what [good is it] to make anything a secret to my neighbor, when to God . . . all our privacies are open,* he wrote.

Governing our thoughts is also the way to mental health. One study showed that most people have about two hundred negative thoughts a day, and depressed people have about six hundred negative thoughts a day. It also showed the average person is in a bad mood about a hundred days a year. If we exchange one hundred negative thoughts for one hundred positive thoughts, every day, we'll improve our lives substantially.

Philippians 4:11 *I am not saying this because I am in need, for I have learned to be content whatever the circumstances.*

Roman prisoners depended on friends and family to provide for their needs (Philippians 2:25). This is why the Bible says to *remember those in prison as if you were together with them in prison* (Hebrews 13:3). The reference is to Christians who were imprisoned for their faith. The church was to *remember* them by providing for their needs.

While Paul was in prison, he *learned the secret of being content in any and every situation, whether well fed or hungry* (Philippians 4:12). With Job he cold say, *Naked I came from my mother's womb, and naked I will depart. The Lord gave and the Lord has taken away; may the name of the Lord be praised* (Job 1:21).

A professional athlete didn't have much growing up, but eventually earned over ten million dollars a year. He had a yacht, and several cars, but considered himself poor because he wasn't a billionaire. But even billionaires should feel poor if they don't have God. What's a billion dollars, when you only have a few short years to spend it? But if you'll soon inherit bottomless wealth, and have all eternity to spend it, then you're truly rich. Believers can be content with what they have because, soon, they'll have all they could ever want.

Philippians 4:19 *And my God will meet all your needs according to the riches of his glory in Christ Jesus.*

Paul was happy to receive financial support from the Philippians, and believed God would take care of them as well. Paul didn't promise there'd never be lean times, but that God would take care of them at all times.

Only once in my life was I out of money and food at the same time. I was in my early twenties, and it was the night before payday. I was ready to go to bed hungry but, when I knelt to pray, I remembered a stack of returnable bottles in the basement. I took them to the store and had just enough for a loaf of bread, a carton of milk, some peanut butter, and some jelly. I went to bed that night giving thanks to God who met all my needs *according to the riches of his glory in Christ Jesus.*

For Reflection and Review

- *How do you handle stress?*
- *How do you handle negative thoughts?*
- *Would you rather be content or rich?*

Lesson 310

Colossians 1:1 *Paul, an apostle of Christ Jesus by the will of God.*

The book of Colossians was written by the Apostle Paul around AD 60, while he was under house arrest in Rome. He wrote to a correct a false teaching which is now called the *Colossian heresy*. It had several characteristics including an emphasis on ceremonies, angels, philosophy, harsh treatment of the body, and secret knowledge. Worst of all, it minimized the importance of Jesus Christ.

The greatest external threat to the church is often persecution, and the greatest internal threat is often heresy. Heresies are something all Christians must guard against by immersing themselves in God's word. The more we know the truth, the less vulnerable we'll be to error.

Colossians 1:2 *To God's holy people in Colossae, the faithful brothers and sisters in Christ.*

The idea of being *in Christ* was so important to Paul, that he used the phrase over seventy-five times, to describe the closest possible relationship. Being *in Christ* is like an unborn child being inside their mother. The child is inside the mother and, genetically, the mother is inside the child. Likewise, we are *in Christ* and the Spirit of Christ is in us (Romans 8:9). In this sense, we can't be any closer to Christ than we are right now.

Colossians 1:2 *Grace and peace to you from God our Father.*

Paul was so excited about grace and peace that he used these words to begin every one of his thirteen letters in the New Testament. When we're overwhelmed by sin, God speaks grace to us. And when we're overwhelmed by trouble, God speaks peace to us. The gospel is grace and peace from God our Father, through his Son Jesus Christ.

Colossians 1:3 *We always thank God, the Father of our Lord Jesus Christ.*

The only God who exists is the *Father of our Lord Jesus Christ*. Some people say, *My God would never do this*, or *My God would never do that*. But unless your God is the *Father of our Lord Jesus Christ*, as revealed in Scripture, he's only the product of your imagination.

Colossians 1:5 *. . . the hope stored up for you in heaven.*

The Christian's hope in heaven isn't like someone who hopes to win the lottery. It's more like a high school senior, with perfect grades, who hopes to graduate in spring. It's certainly going to happen; it just hasn't happened yet.

Colossians 1:6 *[T]he gospel is bearing fruit and growing throughout the whole world.*

Christianity spread so dramatically in the first century that Paul could say it was *growing throughout the whole world*. Two thousand years later, Christianity is the largest movement the world has ever known. More people come to Christ every day, in fact, than on the day of Pentecost when three thousand were baptized (Acts 2:41). Jesus said *I will build my church* (Matthew 16:18) and that's what he's doing.

Colossians 1:7 *You learned [the gospel] from Epaphras, our dear fellow servant, who is a faithful minister of Christ.*

The church in Colossae was started by Epaphras, a missionary church planter associated with Paul. Epaphras probably went to Paul to report on the church in Colossae, and this letter is probably Paul's response to what he learned from Epaphras.

Epaphras was a *faithful minister of Christ*, which is one of God's gifts to his church (Ephesians 4:11). A faithful minister's job is to keep the people of God and the word of God together, by faithfully teaching God's word to his people. Just before his sermon a faithful pastor prayed, *Thank you, God, for your holy word. Take our riches, take our homes, take our health, take our families. Take everything, Lord, but never take away your word.* We ought to say amen to this, with all our heart.

Colossians 1:12 *[God] has qualified you to share in the inheritance of his holy people in the kingdom of light.*

Like an athlete cut from the team for using drugs, we've all been cut from God's team because of our sin. We were disqualified when our first parents sinned, and became even more disqualified because of our own sin. The only person qualified for heaven, in fact, is Jesus Christ. He lived a perfect life without ever sinning once. He also paid for our sins on the cross in order to qualify us for heaven. No one gets into heaven without being qualified, but we've been qualified by the life, death, and resurrection of Jesus Christ.

Colossians 1:13 *For he has rescued us from the dominion of darkness.*

The people of God spent many years under Egyptian slavery, before they were dramatically rescued (Exodus 14:26-31). Likewise, believers in Jesus Christ have been dramatically rescued from the dominion of darkness. Imagine a place where lies are more common than truth, where people take what doesn't belong to them, and where everyone dies eventually. Then imagine the people who live there think it's normal, because it's all they've ever known.

[T]he whole world is under the control of the evil one (1 John 5:19), wrote John. Jesus came to rescue us from this place of death, and bring us into his glorious kingdom. We've been rescued from the dreadful rule of Satan, and brought into the glorious rule of God. Christianity is not about self-improvement, but about a heavenly rescue.

For Reflection and Review

- *How does heresy destroy the church?*
- *Why is the gospel growing throughout the world?*
- *What minister or ministry has helped you the most?*

Lesson 311

Colossians 1:14 *. . . in whom we have redemption, the forgiveness of sins.*

If your son was sold into slavery, and you wanted him back, you could purchase his *redemption*. Depending on the market, the cost could be high or low. But the cost of our redemption was so great that all the money in the world wasn't enough. It took nothing less than the blood of God's Son to buy us back.

If someone pays ten thousand dollars for a car that's only worth one thousand dollars, they've made a foolish mistake. God isn't a fool who overpays for anything. He wasn't obligated to redeem us but, by doing so, showed how much he values us. Whenever you want to know how much you're worth to God, think of Jesus Christ hanging on the cross. That's what he paid to get you back.

Colossians 1:15 *The Son is the image of the invisible God.*

It'd be easier to believe in God if he wasn't so invisible. We identify with Philip who said, *Lord, show us the Father and that will be enough for us* (John 14:8). Jesus replied, *Anyone who has seen me has seen the Father* (John 14:9). Philip must've been a little disappointed. He wanted to see God, but all he got was Jesus Christ.

If God gave us a statue of himself, it'd be so big that we wouldn't be able to recognize him. But if that statue was somehow miniaturized, to exactly the right size for us, it'd look precisely like Jesus Christ (Origen). If you want to know what God is like, look at Christ. He's *the image of the invisible God.*

Colossians 1:16 *[A]ll things have been created through him and for him.*

Jesus is the maker of everything, and everything was made for him. This answers the question, *What am I here for?* Those who are highly talented may think they were made for athletics, music, academics, business, or whatever they excel at.

This is a wonderful experience, but can be misleading.

What will it matter, a million years from now, how good you were at something, if you didn't do it for Christ? Everything you accomplished will be completely forgotten. But when you know that you were made for Christ, everything you do becomes significant. It might include a famous career, or simply staying married. This is why we get out of bed every day, and do whatever we do. We were made for Christ, and live to do his will.

Colossians 1:17 *He is before all things, and in him all things hold together.*

Jesus created the world and continues to hold it together. The world doesn't exist on its own, but depends on Christ to keep it from flying apart. If Jesus stopped holding the world together, it would cease to exist. This is true for the world as a whole, but also for its parts. If God forgot about your ears, they would cease to exist. If God forgot about the roof on your house, it would cease to exist too.

This idea isn't found on every page of the Bible, but is found in at least one other place. *[He is] sustaining all things by his powerful word* (Hebrews 1:3), says Hebrews. This helps us understand how much we depend on God to keep us from going back to nothing. We only started existing because of him, and we only continue existing because of him.

Colossians 1:22 *[H]e has reconciled you by Christ's physical body through death.*

God punished Jesus for our sins, so that he wouldn't have to punish us. In the past, prominent families have used whipping boys to bear the punishment their children deserved. When a privileged child behaved badly, the whipping boy was brought in and given the punishment the privileged child deserved. Justice was served, and the privileged child was spared. The logic of the gospel is similar, but even more appalling. God sent his own Son to be the whipping boy so that we could become his privileged children.

Colossians 1:22b *. . . to present you holy in his sight, without blemish and free from accusation.*

This may be the best verse in the Bible for people with a guilty conscience. And we should all have a guilty conscience, if not for previous sins, at least for remaining sin. What makes this verse so helpful is that it repeats the promise of forgiveness through faith in Jesus Christ, in three different ways.

First, we are *holy in his sight*. I might be able to convince others that I'm holy, but God knows what I'm really like. Yet he declares me *holy in his sight* because of Jesus Christ. My wife can't say that I'm holy in her sight, but God says that I'm *holy in his sight*.

Second, we are *without blemish*. After examining every moral fiber in our being, God finds nothing reprehensible in us. There is no blemish of sin in our hearts, minds, or anywhere else. He thoroughly examines us, with perfect vision, and finds no blemish at all.

Third, because we are *holy in his sight*, and *without blemish*, it follows that we are *free from accusation*. Our forgiveness is so complete that there's nothing we can even be accused of. We have perfect peace with God because of Jesus Christ (Romans 5:1).

For Reflection and Review

- *Why do we need to be rescued?*
- *How do we know that we matter to God?*
- *How should we respond to God's absolute forgiveness?*

Lesson 312

Colossians 1:23 *. . . if you continue in your faith, established and firm, and do not move from the hope held out in the gospel.*

The promise of complete forgiveness is only given to those remain in the faith. *[T]he one who stands firm to the end will be saved* (Matthew 10:22), said Jesus. And *By this gospel you are saved, if you hold firmly to the word I preached to you. Otherwise, you have believed in vain* (1 Corinthians 15:2), wrote Paul.

A crucial test of faith is believing in Jesus Christ to the very end of life. This is essential because there is no salvation apart from him (John 14:6). Many who've fallen away from Christ hope to be saved in the end, but this is never promised. We must continue in the faith, *established and firm*, never moving from the hope held out in the gospel.

Colossians 1:24 *I fill up in my flesh what is still lacking in regard to Christ's afflictions, for the sake of his body, which is the church.*

Paul isn't claiming to be a co-redeemer with Christ, as though he had to suffer for our salvation too. But just as the gospel was purchased through suffering, so it's also promoted through suffering. Paul was beaten, imprisoned, slandered, and impoverished, as he worked to spread the gospel.

But this is also proof of the gospel. If Paul became rich through his missionary work, that could explain his motive. But to continue his ministry through, suffering and martyrdom, only makes sense if the gospel is true. Why else would he do it? Paul would've known if the gospel was false, but his suffering proves it is true.

Colossians 1:28 *He is the one we proclaim, admonishing and teaching everyone with all wisdom, so that we may present everyone fully mature in Christ.*

After people came to Christ, Paul wanted them to mature. This isn't automatic since Jesus taught that many who receive the word *do not mature* (Luke 8:14). After believing in Christ, we should spend the rest of our lives maturing in our faith.

It may be helpful to think of spiritual maturity as having four levels, at which we often operate. Level one: *I'm going to do what I want regardless of any thought for God*. Level two: *If God gives me what I want then I will give him what he wants*. Level three: *I will give God what he wants with faith that he will give me what I want*. Level four: *I will give God what he wants regardless of any thought for myself* (John Maxwell, slightly revised). This is the level of maturity that God is seeking in all his children.

Colossians 2:2 *. . . the full riches of complete understanding.*

Many have lived and died without ever knowing why they were here. Imagine the confusion of going through life without a clue about the most important things? The gospel of Jesus Christ not only brings salvation, but *complete understanding* of the world in which we live: created by God, ruined by sin, and redeemed by Jesus Christ. The light of understanding isn't something that we should take for granted.

An aviation missionary landed near a secluded village that knew nothing of the outside world. But when he tried to leave, he found a native strapped to the side of his plane. The native explained that, no matter what happened, he had to find out where the plane came from. Thankfully we don't have to go to heaven to get our answers. Christ came down from heaven to give us *the full riches of complete understanding*.

Colossians 2:3 *[In Christ] are hidden all the treasures of wisdom and knowledge.*

False teachers in Colossae apparently claimed to have secret treasures of wisdom and knowledge. Paul replied that *all the treasures of wisdom and knowledge* are found in Jesus Christ. He answers all the big questions like: *Who are we? How did we get here? Where are we going? What's the meaning of life? How should I live? What really matters?* These are called *world view questions* and are religious in nature.

There are about a dozen major religions, with thousands of variations, but there are only about five possible world views. Theism claims there is one God. Polytheism claims there are many gods. Pantheism claims everything is God. Deism claims God is outside creation. Atheism claims God does not exist. Agnosticism isn't a world view but claims you can't know if God exists, or what he's like if he does exist.

After thousands of years, the world is still divided on life's most important questions. But a child who understands the gospel knows more about ultimate reality than a scientist or philosopher who doesn't believe in Christ. *[In Christ] are hidden all the treasures of wisdom and knowledge.*

Colossians 2:4 *I tell you this so that no one may deceive you by fine-sounding arguments.*

The devil has many fine-sounding arguments like: *there is no absolute truth; the Bible is a matter of interpretation; a loving God wouldn't send people to hell;* and *it can't be wrong if it feels so right.* These arguments sound reasonable, and even self-evident. But they're meant by the devil to lead us away from the truth.

The devil knows that if he tells a lie long enough, loud enough, and often enough, people will believe it. If you're wearing a red shirt, but a million people say your shirt is yellow, you'll begin to wonder what color your shirt really is. If we can be deceived about things that are obvious, what about spiritual things? This is why it's crucial to immerse ourselves in the Bible almost every day. *[B]e transformed by the renewing of your mind* (Romans 12:2), wrote Paul.

Colossians 2:6 *So then, just as you received Christ Jesus as Lord, continue to live your lives in him.*

The way to begin the Christian life is by receiving *Christ Jesus as Lord.* We don't receive him as advisor, friend, or peer—but as Lord. This means he has access to every part of our life. If you're the head of your house, and one of your children puts a lock on their closet, that's a challenge to your authority. You'll insist the lock be removed because, as head of the house, there's nowhere you're not allowed to go.

When we receive Christ Jesus as Lord, we're saying there's no part of our lives in which he's not allowed. He's Lord of our thoughts, Lord of our language, Lord of our money, Lord of all. We'll never be perfect in this life, but we should always be trying.

For Reflection and Review

- *How does Paul's suffering prove the gospel?*
- *Why do some Christians never mature?*
- *What does it mean to receive Jesus Christ as Lord?*

Lesson 313

Colossians 2:8 *See to it that no one takes you captive through hollow and deceptive philosophy.*

Philosophy and Christianity are both concerned with matters of truth, so they often overlap. But for many philosophical arguments, there's an equal and opposite philosophical argument, so one person's truth is another person's fallacy. This makes philosophy an uncertain way of arriving at truth. What we really need is a word from God.

If you saw a picture of a man breaking into a house in the middle of the night, you might assume he was a burglar. But if you saw the picture from a wider angle, you'd see flames coming out of the roof, and a firetruck parked on the street. Then you'd understand the man was not a burglar, but a fireman.

Notice that the big picture determines the meaning of the little picture. Only God has the big picture of reality, so only God is in a position to say what is actually true. Don't be taken *captive through hollow and deceptive philosophy.* Just believe what God has said in his word. That's what Jesus did.

Colossians 2:9 *For in Christ all the fullness of the Deity lives in bodily form.*

The biblical understanding of Christ is not someone who's only human, or only divine, or partially human and partially divine, but fully human and fully divine. If Jesus wasn't fully human, he couldn't have died for the sins humankind. And if he wasn't fully God, his death wouldn't have been sufficient for the sins of humankind.

I do not think of Christ as God alone, or man alone, but both together. For I know He was hungry, and I know that with five loaves he fed five thousand. I know he was thirsty, and I know that he turned the water into wine. I know he was carried in a boat, and I know that he walked on the sea. I know that he died, and I know that he raised the dead. I know that he was set before Pilate, and I know that he sits on a heavenly throne. I know that he was worshipped by angels, and I know that he was [nearly] stoned by men. . . . For by reason of this he is said to have been both God and man (John Chrysostom, slightly revised).

Colossians 2:10 *[I]n Christ you have been brought to fullness.*

There's no such thing as a fulfilled person apart from Jesus Christ. All our possessions, pleasures, achievements, and relationships are not enough to fill us up. *There is a God shaped vacuum in the heart of every man which cannot be filled by any created thing, but only by God, the Creator, made known through Jesus Christ* (Blaise Pascal, paraphrased).

A young man found a trombone case but didn't know what it was for. He used it as a lunch box, but that didn't work very well. Then he used it as a tackle box, but that didn't work very well either. Then he used it as a tool box, but that didn't work very well either. One day he went to a garage sale, where he saw a trombone, and he bought it on a hunch. He put it in the case and, to his delight, it filled every crevice. Until people find God, they'll put all kinds of things into their souls, but none will fill them up.

But even Christians aren't fulfilled all the time, or as much as we'd like to be. False teachers in Colossae took advantage of this by offering Christians something more. But whenever we feel empty, what we really need is more of Christ. In Christ we are *brought to fullness.*

Colossians 2:11 *In him you were also circumcised with a circumcision not performed by human hands.*

Abraham was ninety-nine years old when God required him, and his posterity, to be circumcised (Genesis 17:1, 10-14). This symbolized the covenant between Abraham and God, like a wedding band symbolizes the covenant between husband and wife.

The problem with symbols is that they can become a substitute for what they were meant to symbolize. It's easier to wear a wedding band than to be a faithful spouse. It's easier to wear a cross than to follow Jesus Christ. And it was easier to be circumcised than to live in a covenant relationship with God. That's why Moses said, *The Lord your God will circumcise your hearts . . . so that you may love him with all your heart* (Deuteronomy 30:6).

Physical circumcision has now been replaced by circumcision of the heart—the indwelling Spirit who marks us as God's children. Physical circumcision is no longer required since, in Christ, we are *circumcised with a circumcision not performed by human hands.*

Colossians 2:13 *He forgave us all our sins.*

Sin is so common that we underestimate its criminality, and its consequences. We think of sin as a minor lapse from our normally good behavior, but it's nothing less than treason against the Most High God to whom we owe everything. Our greatest need at every moment isn't oxygen, but forgiveness.

The penalty for sin is death, (Romans 6:23) followed by eternal fire (Matthew 18:8), so the best news we can ever receive is that we've been forgiven. The gospel of Jesus Christ isn't that God has forgiven some of our sins, or most of our sins, but that *He forgave us all our sins.*

When my daughter was in the fourth grade, she came home from school distraught, because she failed a math quiz. She was a conscientious child, and feared she might not make it to the next grade. The following day she talked to her teacher, and learned that her policy was to throw out the lowest quiz before calculating the final grade. With great excitement she exclaimed, *It's deleted, Dad! It's completely deleted!* Likewise, *He forgave us all our sins.*

For Reflection and Review

- *How are philosophy and Christianity similar?*
- *How are philosophy and Christianity different?*
- *Is it important to feel fulfilled?*

Lesson 314

Colossians 2:15 *And having disarmed the powers and authorities, he made a public spectacle of them, triumphing over them by the cross.*

There's a three-fold effect that Christ's death had on the Devil and his demons. First, they were *disarmed*. Satan can no longer threaten Christians with condemnation for breaking the law of God, because Jesus fulfilled the law of God on our behalf, and paid the penalty for every sin.

Second, through his death, Jesus *made a public spectacle* of the devil and his demons. In Paul's day, a victorious general was often honored with a parade. Behind his chariot were his enemies, now defeated and publicly disgraced. Paul envisioned a parade in heaven with Jesus as the conquering general, and the devil and his demons a mere spectacle.

Third, through his death and resurrection, Jesus *triumphed over* the devil and his demons. At first it appeared that Satan triumphed over Jesus. He was stripped, beaten, spat on, crucified, and buried. But three days later there was a great reversal, and Jesus emerged victorious over sin, death, and the devil. Satan tried to use the cross to overcome Jesus, but Jesus used the cross to overcome Satan.

Colossians 2:16 *Therefore do not let anyone judge you by what you eat or drink, or with regard to a religious festival, a New Moon celebration or a Sabbath day.*

The New Testament clearly states that the Old Testament Law is *obsolete* (Hebrews 8:13), including the command to observe the Sabbath (Exodus 20:8-9). Observing the Sabbath was one of the Ten Commandments written in stone by the finger of God (Exodus 31:8). But nowhere in the New Testament does it ever say, *obey the Ten Commandments*. This is more than a little surprising.

Paul never suggested that Christians were allowed to be morally lax. Many of the Old Testament commands are repeated in the New Testament and must be obeyed. But they're never to serve as the foundation of our relationship with God, which is Jesus Christ (1 Corinthians 3:11).

Another surprising difference between the Old and New Testaments is the observance of religious holidays. The early church met together on the first day of the week (1 Corinthians 16:2), but the church didn't celebrate Christmas or Easter until many years after the apostles died. Jesus' birth and resurrection should be a cause of rejoicing every day, not just on special days.

Colossians 2:17 *These are a shadow of the things that were to come; the reality, however, is found in Christ.*

Paul used the idea of a shadow to describe the way the Old Testament relates to Jesus Christ. As the shadow of a tree provides an image of the tree, much of the Old Testament provides an image of Christ. The New Testament identifies several examples, of which we'll consider five.

First, a plague of snakes was afflicting the nation of Israel, and many were dying as a result. So God instructed Moses to make a snake, and put it on a pole, so anyone who looked at it would live (Numbers 21:8). *Just as Moses lifted up the snake in the wilderness, so the Son of Man must be lifted up, that everyone who believes may have eternal life* (John 3:14-15), said Jesus. The snake on a pole was a shadow of Christ on the cross. Jesus is the cure for the snakebite of sin.

Second, over the span of forty years, God gave his people bread from heaven as they wandered in the desert (Exodus 16:4, Joshua 5:12). *I am the living bread that came down from heaven. Whoever eats this bread will live forever* (John 6:51), said Jesus. The bread from heaven was a shadow of Christ, the bread of life.

Third, the Patriarch Jacob dreamed of a ladder between heaven and earth, with angels going up and down (Genesis 28:12). *[Y]ou will see heaven open, and the angels of God ascending and descending on the Son of Man* (John 1:51), said Jesus. Jacob's ladder was a shadow of Christ, the stairway to heaven.

Fourth, Jonah spent three days and nights in the belly of a huge fish before he was vomited out on shore (Jonah 1-4). *[A]s Jonah was three days and three nights in the belly of a huge fish, so the Son of Man will be three days and three nights in the heart of the earth* (Matthew 12:40), said Jesus. Jonah was a shadow of Christ in his death and resurrection.

Fifth, the final plague on the Egyptians was the death of their firstborn sons (Exodus 12). To save their own sons, God told his people to kill a spotless lamb and apply the blood to the door frames of their homes. When the death angel came, he saw the blood and *passed over* them. Likewise, *Christ, our Passover lamb, has been sacrificed* (1 Corinthians 5:7), wrote Paul. The Passover lamb was a shadow of Christ, the Lamb of God.

Colossians 2:23 *Such regulations indeed have an appearance of wisdom, with their . . . harsh treatment of the body, but they lack any value in restraining sensual indulgence.*

False teachers in Colossae thought Paul's Christianity was too easy, and that serious Christians should treat their bodies harshly, as a means of self-control. But Paul knew this had no *value in restraining sensual indulgence.*

Consider this confession from a fourth century man, who tried to escape his lust by living in the desert. *How often, when I was living in the desert . . . parched by a burning sun, how often did I fancy myself among the pleasures of Rome! . . . Sackcloth disfigured my unshapely limbs and my skin from long neglect had become as black as [night]. . . .*

[A]lthough in my fear of hell I had consigned myself to this prison, where I had no companions but scorpions and wild beasts, I often found myself [thinking] of girls. My face was pale and my frame chilled with fasting; yet my mind was burning with desire, and the fires of lust kept bubbling up before me when my flesh was as good as dead (Saint Jerome, slightly revised).

Christianity is a demanding religion, but it doesn't require harsh treatment of the body, since that has no value for restraining sensual indulgence.

For Reflection and Review

- *If Satan is defeated, why is he still at work?*
- *Is it wrong to celebrate Christmas and Easter?*
- *Does treating the body harshly make us more like Christ?*

Lesson 315

Colossians 3:2 *Set your minds on things above, not on earthly things.*

Paul's feet were on the ground, but his heart was always in heaven. Some people are so heavenly minded they're no earthly good, but this wasn't true for Paul. His heavenly thoughts enabled him to live above his circumstances, and he wanted the same for the Colossians.

Many years ago I went to a second rate zoo where I saw an eagle in a cage, sitting on the ground. A majestic bird, designed to soar, was locked in a cage and confined to earth. Christians are also designed to soar, but are often weighed down by worldliness. The more we think about things below, the more they'll pull us down. The more we think about things above, the more they'll lift us up. *Set your minds on things above, not on earthly things.*

Colossians 3:3 *For you died, and your life is now hidden with Christ in God.*

When an elderly person dies, it's not unusual for their spouse to die soon after. Over the years their union becomes so profound that whatever happens to one happens to the other. Likewise, believers in Jesus Christ are so united to him by the Spirit, that his death and resurrection become our own. We died and our *life is now hidden with Christ in God*.

There are, in fact, some advantages to being dead. Dead people are less concerned about the economy or the next election. They're not easily offended or tempted. And they're no longer plagued by the fear of death (Hebrews 2:15). *In dying he destroyed our death, in rising he restored our life.* Christian conversion is life and death. We died to the old and live to the new.

Colossians 3:4 *When Christ, who is your life, appears, then you also will appear with him in glory.*

Glory was the attribute of royalty due to their power, wealth, and beautiful homes. We can think of glory as the best life possible. When Christ returns, he'll bring the glory of heaven down to earth.

Several years ago we traveled with friends to Switzerland. We rode a cable car up to our hotel, but it was after dark, on a cloudy night, so we had little sense of our surroundings. When I opened the curtains, the following morning, I was overwhelmed by what I saw. The snow covered mountains and deep blue sky were nothing short of glorious—and so was the hotel.

These are a hint of the age to come, but we'll also have a *glorious body* (Philippians 3:21), wrote Paul. If we had to choose between a glorious place or glorious body, we might have to give it some thought. But we won't have to make that choice because, in the age to come, we'll live in a glorious place, with glorious bodies, and lots of glorious friends. *When Christ, who is your life, appears, then you also will appear with him in glory.*

Colossians 3:5 *Put to death, therefore, whatever belongs to your earthly nature: sexual immorality, impurity, lust, evil desires and greed, which is idolatry.*

One man bludgeoned a lady to death in order to steal her money. Murder for money is bad, but this was even worse. He was a pastor, and she was an elderly member of his congregation. How could someone who started out trying to be so good, turn out to be so bad?

Being good involves two parts: practicing virtue and killing sin. Many do things that are good, but also things that are bad. They steal from their job, but give to the church. They pray to God, but curse their neighbor. They neglect their kids, but help the poor. Real goodness involves more than doing good, however. It also involves killing our sinful nature.

Those who belong to Christ Jesus have crucified the flesh with its passions and desires (Galatians 5:24), wrote Paul. *For if you live according to the flesh, you will die; but if by the Spirit you put to death the misdeeds of the body, you will live* (Romans 8:13), wrote Paul again.

A military chaplain was often approached by young people about going into the armed forces. First he'd ask if they loved their country so much they'd be willing to die for it—and many were. Then he'd ask if they loved their country so much they'd be willing to kill for it. That was another question. There are many Christians who are willing to die for Jesus, but not as many who are willing to kill their sin for him. But unless we're killing sin, sin will be killing us.

Colossians 3:8 *But now you must also rid yourselves of all such things as these: anger, rage, malice, slander, and filthy language from your lips.*

As Paul preached the gospel, he often saw people change. Haters became lovers, the godless became godly, the harsh became gentle, the cruel became kind, and the angry became patient. With God's help, real change is possible.

One man read this verse and realized that he had to deal with his anger, not only because God said so, but because it was destroying his family. So he committed this verse to memory and asked his wife to pray for him. For the next several weeks, whenever he became angry, he quoted this verse out loud. It wasn't easy at first but, gradually, it became easier. Those who knew him best were amazed by the wonderful change in his life.

If Satan tempts you to exaggerate, be careful to understate. If he tempts you to laziness, be doubly industrious. If he tempts you to stinginess, be doubly generous. If he tempts you to prayerlessness, be doubly prayerful. In this way you'll spite the devil, glorify God and become deeply rooted in Christ (source unknown). One of the best proofs of the gospel are people who've been changed by it.

For Reflection and Review

- *Do you know anyone who is heavenly minded?*
- *Why is it hard to kill our sin?*
- *How much can people change?*

Lesson 316

Colossians 3:13 *Forgive as the Lord forgave you.*

Paul is echoing Jesus who taught us to pray like this: *forgive us our debts, as we also have forgiven our debtors* (Matthew 6:12). Forgiving others is one of the highest and most difficult of all moral lessons. Everyone believes in forgiveness until they're deeply hurt—then they want justice.

An elderly woman was delightful in her youth but became bitter with age. As a young lady she was engaged to be married but, three days before the wedding, her fiancé ran off with her sister. The pain was overwhelming, and she allowed it to ruin her life.

If I had the opportunity to speak to her I would've explained three things. First, forgiveness is not optional. Jesus said, *if you do not forgive others their sins, your Father will not forgive your sins* (Matthew 6:15). He didn't say this to be cruel, but kind. Until we forgive those who've hurt us, we become their prisoners. Forgiveness is the key that unlocks the door from the inside. It does more for the one who's forgiving than for the one who's being forgiven.

Second, I would've explained that forgiveness will make us more like Jesus Christ, which is the goal of the Christian life. From the cross he prayed, *Father, forgive them, for they do not know what they are doing* (Luke 23:34). It's easier to forgive others after they stop hurting you, but Jesus forgave his killers while they were still killing him. Since God's purpose is to make us like Jesus Christ (Romans 8:29), and since Jesus Christ is the most forgiving person who ever lived, God may allow us to be deeply hurt, so that we can learn to forgive deeply.

Third, I would've explained that recovery can be accelerated. Jesus said, *bless those who curse you, pray for those who mistreat you* (Luke 6:28). If you have a piece of steel that is bent, and you want to straighten it out, you have to bend it beyond straight, for it to become straight. In order to recover quickly, it's not enough to forgive the offending person, we must also bless them.

Whenever the offending person comes to mind we can pray like this: *Father, bless my friend financially; make all their dreams come true. Bless them spiritually with a deeper love for you. And bless their relationships with family and friends. And while you are at it, Father, bless me just as much.*

Praying an equal blessing for yourself will help you pray sincerely for the offending person's good, because whatever good you pray for them, you also pray for yourself. When the offending person no longer comes to mind, you know that you've recovered. The most beautiful people in the world are not those who've never been hurt, but those who've been deeply hurt and learned the art of forgiveness.

Colossians 3:18 *Wives, submit yourselves to your husbands, as is fitting in the Lord.*

I can think of at least four reasons many wives struggle with this verse. First, modern culture is more egalitarian than what we find in the Bible, so the idea of wifely submission seems unnatural to us.

Second, many wives are better leaders than their husbands, earn more money than their husbands, and supervise men at work. Why should a natural leader submit to someone with less leadership ability?

Third, some husbands are irresponsible and oppressive, making the marriage a living hell. Heartfelt submission to that kind of person is nearly impossible.

Fourth, some husbands are so unqualified to lead that following them would take the family backward in almost every way. When all these things combine, the idea of wifely submission seems almost unbearable.

A biblical example of wifely submission is *Sarah, who obeyed Abraham and called him her lord* (1 Peter 3:6). But if you read their story, you'll discover that Sarah could also be assertive. At one point she almost defied Abraham's leadership, and nearly ordered him to do what she wanted. Abraham could've put Sarah down but, instead, he obeyed God who said, *Listen to whatever Sarah tells you* (Genesis 21:12). Many have learned from experience that it's easier for wives to follow their husbands, when their husbands are willing to listen to their wives.

After many years of marriage Julene and I are still trying to sort this out, but the following example might be helpful. Every so often we'll be in the car and she'll say, *Honey, you're going to fast*. And I'll say, *Yes dear*. And she'll say, *Honey, you're going to miss your exit*. And I'll say, *Yes dear*. And she'll say, *Honey, you're going to run out of gas*. And I'll say, *Yes dear*.

I don't like to admit it but there are times when I'm going too fast, or I'm going to miss my exit, or I'm going to run out of gas. Perhaps I'm not the best driver, but it actually helps to listen to my wife. That said, there's one thing she is never allowed to do: grab the steering wheel. If two people try to steer the car, no one will enjoy the ride, and it could be fatal.

Colossians 3:19 *Husbands, love your wives and do not be harsh with them.*

Whenever I'm upset, the most natural thing in the world for me is to be harsh with my wife. But she's explained that my words can be more hurtful than I want them to be, and if I knew how hurtful they were I wouldn't say them.

Thankfully, she's been willing to overlook my harshness because I've built up an emotional bank account. Whenever I say something positive it's like making a little deposit. Whenever I say something negative it's like making a little withdrawal. As long as there's a balance, the relationship is stable. But if it gets overdrawn, things are less predictable.

A young man was getting married, and his father-in-law gave him a gift. Inside the box was a watch with words inscribed on the glass: *Say something nice to Sarah*. Whenever he checked the time, he was reminded of the easiest way to have a happy relationship.

Colossians 3:20 *Children, obey your parents in everything, for this pleases the Lord.*

Paul is stating one of the Ten Commandments given by God from the top of Mount Sinai. The first four concern our relationship with God: (1) have no other gods; (2) make no idols; (3) do not blaspheme; and (4) observe the Sabbath. The final six concern our relationship with others: (1) honor your parents; (2) do not murder; (3) do not commit adultery; (4) do not steal; (5) do not lie; and (6) do not covet.

The arrangement is significant since, generally speaking, murder is worse than adultery; adultery is worse than stealing; stealing is worse than lying; and lying is worse than coveting. But the commandment just before the prohibition of murder is to honor our parents. In fact, any child so rebellious as to curse his parents, could've been put to death (Exodus 21:17).

This may seem extreme, but honoring parents is the foundation of civilization. If children don't learn to respect their parents, they're less likely to respect their teachers, their employers, the law, or God. Authority and submission are important to God, and civilization rests on children respecting their parents.

For Reflection and Review

- *Have you ever been deeply hurt?*
- *Why is forgiveness important?*
- *Should wives always submit to their husbands?*

Lesson 317

Colossians 3:23 *Whatever you do, work at it with all your heart, as working for the Lord.*

Paul was speaking to slaves, but the idea applies to employees. If slaves were to serve their masters wholeheartedly, how much more should employees serve their employers. But Paul adds a revolutionary thought: by serving our employers we're actually serving Christ.

A friend of mine had a bad attitude at work because he thought he knew more than his boss. Then he read this verse and learned that his real boss was Jesus Christ. As a result, he became much more respectful and responsible. He also began praying for his company, and found himself enjoying his job more than ever.

Imagine this: One businessman said to another, *Guess what—I just hired a Christian!* The other said, *That's wonderful! I wish I could find a Christian to hire. They are so dependable, hardworking, and conscientious. They make the very best employees* (Del Tackett, slightly revised). If Christians saw their jobs as a way to serve Christ, they could change the world. *Whatever you do, work at it with all your heart, as working for the Lord.*

Colossians 3:24 *[Y]ou will receive an inheritance from the Lord as a reward.*

Paul was speaking to slaves who may've felt underpaid and, unlike family, weren't in line for an inheritance. To help with their discouragement, Paul reminded them of the inheritance they'd receive in the age to come. *I pray that the eyes of your heart may be enlightened in order that you may know the hope to which he has called you, the riches of his glorious inheritance* (Ephesians 1:18), he wrote.

Many years ago there was a radio program called *Missing Heirs*. Every week they'd announce the names of people who'd inherited fortunes, but didn't know it. Thousands listened weekly, and some heard their names. We can imagine their joy as they went downtown to receive their inheritance.

Now imagine you were one of them but, a mile out of town, your car broke down. You wouldn't be upset because you could walk the rest of the way. And if your shoes fell apart you wouldn't be upset, because you could go barefoot the rest of the way. And if it started to rain you wouldn't be upset, because you were extremely close to receiving your inheritance. This is why Christians have joy even in difficult times. We're on the way to receive our inheritance, and we're almost there.

Colossians 4:2 *Devote yourselves to prayer.*

Prayer is nothing more or less than talking to our heavenly Father. But words don't always come easily, so Jesus taught his disciples to pray like this: *Our Father in heaven, hallowed be your name, your kingdom come, your will be done, on earth as it is in heaven. Give us today our daily bread. And forgive us our debts, as we also have forgiven our debtors. And lead us not into temptation, but deliver us from the evil one* (Matthew 6:9-13).

These words can be said thoughtfully, in under a minute, but we don't need to stop there. We can devote ourselves to prayer, and even *pray continually* (1 Thessalonians 5:17), wrote Paul.

After seven years of marriage Anna became a widow and never remarried. *She never left the temple but worshiped night and day, fasting and praying* (Luke 2:37). The text is not explicit, but she likely prayed for the coming of Messiah. Finally, when she was eighty-four years old, she had the privilege of seeing the little Savior with her own eyes, when he was brought to the temple for his dedication. We ought to pray the Lord's Prayer, but we can also grow in prayer. *Devote yourselves to prayer.*

Colossians 4:5 *Be wise in the way you act toward outsiders; make the most of every opportunity.*

In the normal affairs of life, Christians interact with outsiders, and may be able to present the gospel. This requires wisdom and a little preparation. Telling the gospel isn't easy, which is why so few do it well. But if you're willing to memorize four easy questions, they may help you lead someone to faith in Jesus Christ: (1) Do you believe you're a sinner? (2) Do you want to be forgiven? (3) Do you believe Jesus died for you? (4) Will you receive him as your Lord?

These questions flow logically and build on each other. If you believe you're a sinner, it's logical to want forgiveness. If you believe Jesus died for you, it's logical to live for him. If someone answers *no* to any of the questions, it's not a problem. The believer's job is to present the gospel and let the other person decide. If they answer *yes* to all the questions you can simply pray with them to receive Jesus Christ. *[To] all who did receive him . . . he gave the right to become children of God* (John 1:12), wrote John. I found this helpful when my dad was on his death bed. I was able to ask him these questions and, to my surprise, he answered *yes* to each one, and prayed to receive Christ.

Colossians 4:17 *See to it that you complete the ministry you have received in the Lord.*

Paul addressed these words to a gentleman named Archippus, who is mentioned only one other time in the Bible. In the little book of Philemon, Paul referred to him as *our fellow soldier* (Philemon 1:2), suggesting he was a man of discipline. But this man of discipline apparently got distracted, because Paul had to remind him to complete the task God had given him. If this could happen to Archippus, how much more to us?

Life full of distractions, but Jesus said *seek first the kingdom of God* (Matthew 6:33, paraphrased). The kingdom of God should be our first priority, and everything else should be subordinate. Every Christian should find a way to advance the kingdom of God, and then stay on task.

One lady taught a second grade Sunday school class, for forty-three years, without missing a week. She even rescheduled surgery so as not to be absent. *It's not a duty and I'm not showing off*, she said. She simply found a place of usefulness and remained faithful.

For Reflection and Review

- *Why are authority and submission important to God?*
- *Do you look at your job as a way to serve Christ?*
- *Why is it difficult to share the gospel?*

Lesson 318

1 Thessalonians 1:1 *Paul, Silas and Timothy, To the church of the Thessalonians in God the Father and the Lord Jesus Christ.*

Paul wrote this letter to the church in Thessalonica, around AD 51, to encourage them to grow in their faith, as they waited for Christ's return. The church was mostly Gentile and was started by Paul just two years earlier.

1 Thessalonians 1:10 *Jesus . . . rescues us from the coming wrath.*

Salvation is from sin, Satan, and death, but, ultimately, from the wrath of God. Sin is more than a violation of divine law, but a personal insult to the Trinity. The Father is angry for the Son and the Spirit; the Son is angry for the Father and the Spirit; and the Spirit is angry for the Father and the Son. Every time we sin, we incite the wrath of all three members of the Trinity. *[A] fire will be kindled by my wrath, one that burns down to the realm of the dead below* (Deuteronomy 32:22), said God.

In 1874 a fire started in a Chinese coal mine that burned for over a hundred years. Over two million tons of coal was consumed ever year, causing great damage to the environment. The government spent a fortune fighting the blaze and, in 2004, finally put it out. But there is a fire that never goes out—*it burns down to the realm of the dead below.*

1 Thessalonians 2:2 *[W]ith the help of our God we dared to tell you his gospel in the face of strong opposition.*

The opposition in Thessalonica was so severe that a riot broke out. *These men who have caused trouble all over the world have now come here . . . . They are all defying Caesar's decrees, saying that there is another king, one called Jesus* (Acts 17:6-7).

Those who fiercely oppose the gospel often understand what's at stake: Jesus is a real king who demands absolute surrender (Luke 14:31-33). This is why the gospel is often resisted. But Jesus loves his people to death, and gives them eternal life. When we understand what kind of king Jesus is, we joyfully surrender and give him our allegiance.

1 Thessalonians 2:12 *God . . . calls you into his kingdom and glory.*

Paul wanted the Thessalonians to keep the end of their journey in view. God hadn't called them to an uncertain future but to his *kingdom and glory.* Even if the journey was hard, it'd be worth the trouble.

A missionary came home for a visit, and was invited to speak in church. He began by saying *I am called . . . .* But then he had a heart attack and fell over dead. He was probably going to say *I am called to China,* or wherever he was serving at the time. We're all called to serve God somewhere. But ultimately, we're called to his *kingdom and glory.*

1 Thessalonians 2:13b *. . . the word of God [is] at work in you who believe.*

When Paul preached God's word to the Thessalonians, they *accepted it not as a human word, but as it actually is, the word of God* (1 Thessalonians 2:13a). Even after Paul left the Thessalonians, his words continued to work in them, shaping their lives, and nurturing their faith.

God's word will do the same for us as we get it into our hearts. Like a vitamin taken in the morning, providing nutrients throughout the day, the word of God works in those who believe. Some say breakfast is the most important meal of the day, and morning may be the best time to read a chapter of the Bible. An excellent habit for life is to read a chapter of the Bible almost every day, and share what you learn with someone else.

1 Thessalonians 3:2 *We sent Timothy, who is our brother and co-worker in God's service in spreading the gospel of Christ, to strengthen and encourage you in your faith.*

Paul was in Thessalonica for just a few weeks before he moved on to another town. He was concerned their faith might waver, so he sent Timothy to *strengthen and encourage* them. The Thessalonians were evangelized by Paul, but Timothy followed up with them. After the work of evangelism, it's important to help new believers become established. They are *infants in Christ* (1 Corinthians 3:1), and must be cared for by those who are mature.

The person who brought me to Christ followed up extensively by making sure I was going to church, reading the Bible, and spending time in prayer. I wonder what might've happened if not for the help of my friend. He was God's agent to *strengthen and encourage* me.

1 Thessalonians 4:6 *The Lord will punish all those who commit such sins.*

Christ took the punishment we deserve (Isaiah 53:5), so we're never punished out of justice, but we may be punished out of love. *[T]he Lord disciplines the one he loves, and he chastens everyone he accepts as his son* (Hebrews 12:6), says Hebrews.

Years ago I belonged to a church with many young people who were new believers. A couple began sleeping together, and started missing church. Then they moved in together, and quit church completely. Then there was an accident that led to an amputation. Then they broke off the relationship, and started coming to church again. *Stern discipline awaits anyone who leaves the path* (Proverbs 15:10), says Proverbs. *[I]n faithfulness you have afflicted me* (Psalm 119:75), wrote the Psalmist. God *forgave us all our sins* (Colossians 2:13), but will punish us for our good.

For Reflection and Review

- *Why is God angry at sin?*
- *Who has helped you grow in your faith?*
- *Should Christians be afraid of God's punishment?*

Lesson 319

1 Thessalonians 4:11-12 *[M]ake it your ambition to lead a quiet life . . . so that your daily life may win the respect of outsiders.*

In their desire to advance the gospel, the Thessalonians were apparently too vocal, and neglected other duties. They may've been evangelizing, but were living irresponsibly. Paul wanted them to settle down and earn the respect of outsiders. Outsiders don't have to like us, but we should try to win their respect through quiet living and hard work.

1 Thessalonians 4:16-17 *For the Lord himself will come down from heaven, with a loud command, with the voice of the archangel and with the trumpet call of God, and the dead in Christ will rise first. After that, we who are still alive and are left will be caught up together with them in the clouds to meet the Lord in the air.*

The return of Christ will be the climax of history, and the Thessalonians were looking forward to it. But they were concerned about believers who had already died. Paul explained they wouldn't miss out, but would be raised with all believers to *meet the lord in the air.*

Some people think that when Christ returns, he'll take his people back to heaven. But that's not required by this passage. It was the custom, in fact, to meet people outside the city to escort them back in (Matthew 25:6, Acts 28:15). The return of Christ will be so great that believers from every age, and all around the world, will rise to meet him in the air, and escort him down to earth. This will be a day of dread for unbelievers, but a glorious day for all who belong to Christ. *Therefore, encourage one another with these words* (1 Thessalonians 4:18) wrote Paul.

1 Thessalonians 5:1 *Now, brothers and sisters, about times and dates we do not need to write to you.*

Since the return of Christ will be the climax of history, it's no surprise that many have wanted to know the date. But *It is not for you to know the times or dates the Father has set by his own authority* (Acts 1:7), said Jesus. In fact, *about that day or hour no one knows, not even the angels in heaven, nor the Son, but only the Father* (Matthew 24:36), he said.

Believers should be silent about the time of Christ's return, since Jesus himself taught that no one knows the date. And yet, dozens of dates have been predicted, most of which have passed. Whenever someone predicts the date of Christ's return, they're pretending to know more than Jesus, so they should be ignored.

Instead of telling us when he'd return, Jesus emphasized the importance of being ready. *So you also must be ready, because the Son of Man will come at an hour when you do not expect him* (Matthew 24:44), he said.

My friend worked at a bicycle store, and his boss went on vacation. Since he wasn't due back for a week, the employees closed the store during lunch, and went next door for pizza. To their surprise the boss returned early, and caught them out to lunch, when they should've been minding the store. Jesus wants us to live each day expectantly, so we won't be surprised by his return.

1 Thessalonians 5:11 *[E]ncourage one another and build each other up.*

Life is hard for everyone, but can be harder for Christians. That's why Paul made it the duty of every Christian to encourage others, and build them up in their faith. I've never known anyone who suffered from over-encouragement, but I've known many who suffered from under-encouragement.

A group of college students met weekly to hone their writing skills, and review each other's work. They were brutally honest but, twenty years later, not one of them was published. Another group also met weekly, but focused on encouragement. Twenty years later most were successful writers. *Therefore encourage one another and build each other up.*

1 Thessalonians 5:18 *[G]ive thanks in all circumstances; for this is God's will for you in Christ Jesus.*

The Thessalonians weren't to give thanks *for all circumstances*, but they were to give thanks *in all circumstances*. We don't have to be thankful for a broken leg, but we should be thankful for the one that isn't broken. We don't have to be thankful for our problems, but we should be thankful they aren't any worse.

A homeless lady was having thanksgiving dinner at a rescue mission and was beaming with joy. *I only have two teeth*, she said, *but they just happen to be opposite each other so I can chew my food.* This is the attitude Paul had in mind.

1 Thessalonians 5:23 *May God himself, the God of peace, sanctify you through and through.*

God wants every part of us, and is frequently working in a particular area. It could be our words, thoughts, deeds, habits, money, or a dozen other things. The battle will be fierce, at times, but God won't quit until we're conformed to the image of Christ (Romans 8:29).

A friend of mine struggled with a particular sin for years. As he prayed, one day, he felt a strange sensation on his head—as though God was touching it—and he lost all desire for that particular sin. This is rare, of course, but shows what God can do for his children who want to be sanctified *through and through*.

For Reflection and Review

- *How can Christians win the respect of outsiders?*
- *Why do Christians need to be encouraged?*
- *Why should believers always be thankful?*

Lesson 320

2 Thessalonians 1:1 *Paul, Silas and Timothy, To the church of the Thessalonians in God our Father and the Lord Jesus Christ.*

Paul wrote his second letter to the church in Thessalonica around AD 52, while he was staying in the city of Corinth. He wanted to encourage the Thessalonians to live responsibly in light of Christ's return, and to endure persecution.

2 Thessalonians 1:3 *. . . your faith is growing more and more.*

Paul was pleased with the Thessalonians because they were growing in their faith. This was important because faith is always growing or declining, never staying the same. This is why the Bible often commands spiritual growth. *[Be] growing in the knowledge of God* (Colossians 1:10), wrote Paul. *[G]row up in your salvation* (1 Peter 2:2), wrote Peter. *[G]row in the grace and knowledge of our Lord and Savior Jesus Christ* (2 Peter 3:18), wrote Peter again. Spiritual growth isn't optional, and doesn't happen by accident.

A master violinist was asked the secret of his success. *Planned neglect*, he said. There wasn't enough time to practice sufficiently, and keep up with the rest of his life. So he neglected everything else until he practiced his violin. He used to take care of other things first, and practice his violin second, but this resulted in mediocrity. So he began to practice his violin first, and do everything else second. This made him a master. Many have found the best time for prayer and Bible study is first thing in the morning.

2 Thessalonians 1:7-9 *Jesus [will be] revealed from heaven in blazing fire with his powerful angels. He will* *punish those who do not know God and do not obey the gospel of our Lord Jesus. They will be punished with everlasting destruction and shut out from the presence of the Lord and from the glory of his might.*

I spoke to a young man about Christ, but he had little interest. He was sure the Bible was all a matter of interpretation. *Some interpret it one way, others interpret it another way, and no one can know what it means for sure,* he said. So I read the above passage and said, *How would you interpret that?*

It's true, of course, that some passages are clearer than others, but the meaning of any passage is what the author intended to communicate to his original readers. Given this starting point, the Bible can be read and understood by ordinary people.

The clarity of the Bible can be easily shown by comparing the notes in leading study Bibles. If the scholars believe the Bible, and try to be unbiased, their notes will be remarkably similar. This shows the Bible is not a matter of interpretation, but is essentially clear in most places.

2 Thessalonians 2:4 *He will oppose and will exalt himself over everything that is called God or is worshiped, so that he sets himself up in God's temple, proclaiming himself to be God.*

The Thessalonians were concerned about the end of this *present evil age* (Galatians 1:4), so Paul informed them of the coming of the antichrist, whom he called *the man of lawlessness* (2 Thessalonians 2:3). He won't submit to God's law, or any other law.

The devil's opposition to Christ will reach its climax when this man *sets himself up in God's temple, proclaiming himself to be God.* He's the one *whom the Lord Jesus will overthrow with the breath of his mouth and destroy by the splendor of his coming* (2 Thessalonians 2:8), wrote Paul.

Many political leaders have claimed to be divine including Egyptian pharaohs, Chinese emperors, and Roman emperors. One of the worst was Antiochus IV, Epiphanes, who ruled the Seleucid Empire from 175 BC until his death in 164 BC. He was the pre-antichrist foretold by the prophet Daniel. *He will exalt and magnify himself above every god and will say unheard-of things against the God of gods. . . . He will show no regard for . . . any god, but will exalt himself above them all* (Daniel 11:36-37), he wrote.

Antiochus IV took the title *Theos Epiphanes*, meaning *manifest god*. In 167 BC he tried to destroy Judaism by burning copies of the Old Testament and by killing faithful Jews. He suddenly died of a disease a few years later. We'll see his type again when the final and ultimate antichrist comes to power.

2 Thessalonians 3:2 *[P]ray that we may be delivered from wicked and evil people.*

As Paul traveled and preached the gospel, he encountered wicked and evil people who fiercely opposed him. But God even used his opponents to advance the gospel. While Paul was under house arrest in Rome, he wrote four letters that we have in the Bible. If he hadn't been arrested, we might not have those letters.

Another hostile government opposed Christianity by limiting the size of house churches. They thought this would limit the spread of Christianity, but it caused the number of house churches to multiply, which helped even more people come to Christ. Wicked and evil people will always oppose the gospel, but God can overrule their actions for the good of his church.

For Reflection and Review

- *Is the Bible hard to understand?*
- *Why do some people pretend to be divine?*
- *Is the world getting better or worse?*

Lesson 321

2 Thessalonians 3:5 *May the Lord direct your hearts into God's love.*

Believing in God's love doesn't come easily for a number of reasons. First, we're all sinners, and God hates sin, so how can he love sinners like us? Second, we seldom feel God's love, and it's hard to believe in a love you don't feel. Third, life is hard. If God really loved us, we think he'd make it easier. For these and other reasons, we must be convinced from the Bible that God really loves us.

God is Love (1 John 4:8), wrote John. God isn't merely loving, but is love personified. The Father loves the Son and the Spirit. The Son loves the Father and the Spirit. And the Spirit loves the Father and the Son. At the heart of the universe is an all powerful love, that is the source of all other loves. The most powerful love a man ever felt for a woman, or a woman for a child, or a child for a pet, is nothing compared to the love God has for us. *We love because he first loved us* (1 John 4:19), wrote John. *God is love*, and love is from God.

Love the Lord your God with all your heart and with all your soul and with all your mind. This is the first and greatest commandment (Matthew 22:37-38), said Jesus. The bad news is that we never come close to keeping this command. The good news is that God wouldn't command us to love him any more than he loves us. If God commands us to love him with all of our heart, soul, and mind, then he must love us with all of his heart, soul, and mind. And since God is all powerful, we're the objects of an all-powerful love. Even though we never keep this command for a minute, God upholds it all the time, because God is love.

And the second is like it: Love your neighbor as yourself (Matthew 22:39), said Jesus. The bad news is that we don't even like our neighbors sometimes. The good news is that God wouldn't command us to love our neighbors more than he loves his neighbors—and we're all God's neighbors. If God commands us to love our neighbors as ourselves, then he must love us as he loves himself. We never keep this command for a minute, but God upholds it perfectly, all the time, because God is love.

For God so loved the world that he gave his one and only Son, that whoever believes in him shall not perish but have eternal life (John 3:16), wrote John. If your father was a billionaire, who gave you his affection, and everything you asked for, his love could still be doubted. But if you needed a kidney, and he gave you one of his, you could never doubt his love again, because he proved it through sacrifice. Whenever we doubt God's love, we should think about the cross.

[T]he Lord delights in those who fear him, who put their hope in his unfailing love (Psalm 147:11), wrote the Psalmist. Some people believe God loves them, but doesn't like them very much, because of their disobedience. But here we're assured that God not only loves us, but even *delights* in us.

Imagine you're a car enthusiast and recently bought an old classic. To the untrained eye it looks like a pile of junk but, because you do restoration, you can see what the car will look like when you're done—so it delights you now. If we could see ourselves the way God sees us, then we'd understand how he can delight in us even with our faults. We see the wreckage, but God sees what we'll be.

And so we know and rely on the love God has for us (1 John 4:16), wrote John. The most important time to rely on God's love is when we can't feel God's love. Relying on feelings is like picking pedals off a daisy while saying, *he loves me; he loves me not*. The love of God is objectively real, regardless of our feelings. This is important to understand when the children are sick, bills are piling up, and rain is coming through the roof.

The Apostle John described himself as the *disciple whom Jesus loved* (John 13:23). But after a lifetime of serving Jesus, John was exiled to the island of Patmos (Revelation 1:9). Instead of viewing God through the lens of his suffering, he viewed his suffering through the lens of God's love. This kind of faith brings honor to God.

2 Thessalonians 3:13 *And as for you, brothers and sisters, never tire of doing what is good.*

Following Christ often means saying *no* to ourselves, so we can say *yes* to others and to God. This isn't hard for a while but, over many years, it can be exhausting. A friend of mine made a great start in the faith, and was thinking about occupational ministry. We took classes together and he made it look easy. He was especially good at the Bible and theology.

Then he moved to another city, and I learned he quit the faith. I assumed his reasons were intellectual but, when we met for coffee, he explained that he simply got tired. He was tired of being different, tired of going against the culture, and tired of resisting temptation. So he laid down his cross and quit the faith. I wish he would've read the prophet Isaiah instead.

He gives strength to the weary and increases the power of the weak. Even youths grow tired and weary, and young men stumble and fall; but those who hope in the Lord will renew their strength. They will soar on wings like eagles; they will run and not grow weary, they will walk and not be faint (Isaiah 40:29-31), he wrote. We can expect to get tired sometimes, but God will give us strength to go on, as long as we look to him.

2 Thessalonians 3:16 *Now may the Lord of peace himself give you peace at all times and in every way.*

When Paul brought the gospel to Thessalonica it was so fiercely opposed that a riot broke out (Acts 17:5). Suddenly those who believed found themselves to be part of a persecuted minority. Their lives may've been calm before, but now they were in serious conflict. So Paul rightly prayed, *may the Lord of peace himself give you peace at all times and in every way.*

Many have found peace by trusting in God's word. *[T]he Lord blesses his people with peace* (Psalm 29:11), wrote David. *The God of peace will soon crush Satan under your feet* (Romans 16:20), wrote Paul. *And the peace of God, which transcends all understanding, will guard your hearts and your minds in Christ Jesus* (Philippians 4:7), wrote Paul again. Many have also been helped by reciting this famous prayer: *God grant me the serenity to accept the things I cannot change; courage to change the things I can; and wisdom to know the difference* (Reinhold Niebuhr). Whenever we're deep in conflict, God can give us peace.

For Reflection and Review

- *Why can it be hard to believe in God's love?*
- *How do we know for sure that God loves us?*
- *Do you ever get tired of being a Christian?*

Lesson 322

1 Timothy 1:1-2 *Paul, an apostle of Christ Jesus by the command of God our Savior and of Christ Jesus our hope, To Timothy my true son in the faith: Grace, mercy and peace from God the Father and Christ Jesus our Lord.*

Paul wrote this letter to his younger assistant, Timothy, around the year AD 64. Timothy was not an apostle, but was Paul's representative in the city of Ephesus. Timothy was dear to Paul and is mentioned in several of his letters. *Timothy, my son whom I love, who is faithful in the Lord* (1 Corinthians 4:17). And *you know that Timothy has proved himself, because as a son with his father he has served with me in the work of the gospel* (Philippians 2:22). This letter provides helpful instructions for Timothy, and for the church in Ephesus.

1 Timothy 1:15 *Here is a trustworthy saying that deserves full acceptance: Christ Jesus came into the world to save sinners—of whom I am the worst.*

Paul was nearing the end of his life, and had been a Christian for about thirty years. But even at this late stage, he felt himself to be the worst of sinners. We never know how bad we are until we try to be good, and the better we try to be, the more we know that we're not. The righteous know they are wicked, and the wicked think they are righteous.

A man walked into a bar and shot several people because he was angry. He later explained that he was a pretty good person, except when he was angry. But we're all pretty good people when nothing is bothering us. How we behave when we're upset is a better indication of what's in our hearts.

1 Timothy 1:19 *[Hold] on to faith and a good conscience, which some have rejected and so have suffered shipwreck with regard to the faith.*

Paul was describing *Hymenaeus and Alexander* (1 Timothy 1:20) who seemed to believe at first, but later *suffered shipwreck.* Christianity is a voyage to heaven, but many who embark never arrive. The ocean floor is strewn with boats that once sailed boldly. Some were dashed on rocks, others developed leaks that were never repaired.

This image was real to Paul since he was shipwrecked on his way to Rome (Acts 27:27-44). A wind of hurricane force battered the ship so badly, they passed ropes under the boat to hold it together, and threw the cargo overboard. *When neither sun nor stars appeared for many days and the storm continued raging, we finally gave up all hope of being saved* (Acts 27:20), wrote Luke. The boat got stuck in a sandbar, and was broken apart by waves but, somehow, everyone survived. Not so on the voyage to heaven. The worst storms aren't at sea, but are in the soul.

1 Timothy 2:1-2 *I urge, then, first of all, that petitions, prayers, intercession and thanksgiving be made for all people—for kings and all those in authority, that we may live peaceful and quiet lives in all godliness and holiness.*

Paul wanted Christians to pray for political leaders as a way of keeping peace in the world. Paul lived during the *Roman Peace* which lasted over two hundred years (27 BC to AD 180). This was a time of relative calm which allowed Paul to travel, and preach somewhat freely. War is hard on nations, but also on churches, believers, and missions. Since prayer is the greatest power on earth, Christians should pray for political leaders as a way of preserving peace.

Likewise, when God's people were exiled to Babylon, God told them to *seek the peace and prosperity of the city to which I have carried you into exile. Pray to the Lord for it, because if it prospers, you too will prosper* (Jeremiah 29:7). Christians are *foreigners and exiles* on earth (1 Peter 1:11), and should pray for our cities and nations. If they prosper, we too will prosper.

1 Timothy 2:5 *For there is one God and one mediator between God and mankind, the man Christ Jesus.*

When two people can no longer communicate, a third person may be needed to help mend the relationship. In a broken marriage, this may be a counselor who speaks to the husband and wife separately, on behalf of each other. A skillful counselor may even bring the marriage back together.

The relationship between God and humans was so completely broken, that it couldn't be repaired without a mediator. The mediator would have to be someone who could represent God to humans, and humans to God.

This is why it was important for Christ to be both human and divine. If he was only divine, he couldn't represent humans to God. If he was only human, he couldn't represent God to the world. Jesus was God in the presence of humans, and is a human in the presence of God. Jesus could speak to humans for God, because he is God. And he can speak to God for humans, because he's a perfect human.

Under the old covenant, people could only approach God through the priesthood. Now we go to God through Jesus Christ, our *great high priest* (Hebrews 4:14). We don't need religious professionals to represent us to God, because Jesus represents us to God. We don't need people who are better than we are to represent us to God, because Jesus is the best there is. There is, in fact, no one else who can represent us to God because *there is one God and one mediator between God and mankind, the man Christ Jesus.*

1 Timothy 2:6 *[Jesus] gave himself as a ransom for all people.*

In the case of war, ransoms were usually based on the rank of the captive. A general would bring a much higher ransom than a common soldier. But Jesus paid the highest ransom ever paid for anyone, to bring us back to God. All the money in the world couldn't do that; only the blood of Christ could do that.

For Reflection and Review

- *Why did Paul consider himself to be the worst sinner?*
- *Why is turning away from Christ compared to a shipwreck?*
- *Why is Jesus the perfect mediator between people and God?*

Lesson 323

1 Timothy 4:1 *The Spirit clearly says that in later times some will abandon the faith and follow deceiving spirits and things taught by demons.*

The church has always been plagued by false teachers. *Even from your own number men will arise and distort the truth in order to draw away disciples after them* (Acts 20:30), said Paul.

Much of the New Testament was written to combat false teaching, and the Bible remains our best defense. Christians should have two questions in the back of their minds whenever they're being taught: *What verse are we talking about?* and, *Is that what it means?* The best way for any church to avoid false teaching is for the people to know the Bible well. A good indicator of a church's strength is how well people know the Bible.

1 Timothy 4:2 *Such teachings come through hypocritical liars, whose consciences have been seared as with a hot iron.*

A seared conscience is one that is hardened against the will of God. Through chronic disobedience it has become desensitized to right and wrong, and to the impulse of the Spirit. This was true of false teachers and may be true of others. *There is a sin that leads to death. I am not saying that you should pray about that* (1 John 5:16), wrote John.

But a steak that's been seared on the outside, may have a tender spot on the inside. And those who appear to be apostate, may be only lapsed. With God's help they may, one day, return to the faith. More often than not, it's best to continue praying. *Whoever turns a sinner from the error of their way will save them from death and cover over a multitude of sins* (James 5:20), wrote James.

1 Timothy 4:7 *[T]rain yourself to be godly.*

Godliness doesn't happen by accident, any more than physical fitness happens by accident. I've never been an athlete but, in middle school, I went out for wrestling. We trained two and a half hours a day, and the last thing we did was to run stairs. We ran four flights up and down, a minimum of ten times—and that was just middle school. What would happen if all God's people trained themselves to be godly?

1 Timothy 4:8 *For physical training is of some value, but godliness has value for all things, holding promise for both the present life and the life to come.*

Some people think that godliness only pays in the life to come, but here we learn that it often pays in this life too. Sin is the way to broken relationships, financial ruin, and physical decline. But godliness often leads to health, wealth, and happiness. This is because God's way is best, but also because God is often pleased to bless our obedience. Trials and hardship will also come, but our greatest problems usually come from disobeying God, rather than obeying him.

1 Timothy 4:14 *Do not neglect your gift.*

The exact nature of Timothy's gift isn't stated, but it appears to be related to his ministry in the church. The Bible teaches elsewhere that every Christian is gifted by the Spirit to serve the church. *Now to each one the manifestation of the Spirit is given for the common good* (1 Corinthians 12:7), wrote Paul. And, *Each of you should use whatever gift you have received to serve others, as faithful stewards of God's grace in its various forms* (1 Peter 4:10), wrote Peter.

A hardware store was in business for over a hundred years, and some of its inventory was dated. Hammers, shovels, and axes that were meant to be used were never taken off the shelf. Time passed them by, and they became obsolete. In the kingdom of God it's better to wear out than to rust out.

1 Timothy 6:5 *[G]odliness with contentment is great gain.*

Adam and Eve refused to be content and plunged the world into misery. Many have followed their example and made their lives a mess. The reason God doesn't give us everything we want is to help us find our contentment in him. *[B]e content with what you have, because God has said, Never will I leave you; never will I forsake you* (Hebrews 13:5), says Hebrews.

A fifty year old man was unhappily married and asked his pastor this question: *What do you do when you have everything you ever wanted, except the one thing you want the most?* Many have asked a form of this question, and the answer depends on what you believe. If you think this life is all there is, then you go for what you want. But if this life is only preparation for eternity, then it's wise to be content.

1 Timothy 6:10 *For the love of money is a root of all kinds of evil.*

Money is so important that we can't live without it, unless we're living off someone else's money. This is why people will do almost anything for a little more money. Some will sell their bodies for money. Some will sell their children's bodies for money. Some will even sell their souls for money.

A friend of mine started working overtime because he wanted to buy a boat. He still came to church, but he was often tired from all the extra hours he was spending at work. He finally had enough money to buy the boat, but it became his new church, and he never came back.

This is why God commands us to give up some of our money for him (Luke 12:13-21). If we love God more than money, we'll give up money for God. But if we love money more than God, we'll give up God for money. And if we have to miss church in order to wax it, we probably don't need it.

1 Timothy 6:17 *God . . . richly provides us with everything for our enjoyment.*

If we have a pencil, it's a gift from God for our enjoyment. If we have a chair, it's a gift from God for our enjoyment. If we have a shirt, it's a gift from God for our enjoyment. *Every good and perfect gift is from above* (James 1:17), wrote James. The better we understand this, the more we'll want to praise God for all his wonderful gifts.

The greatest gift, of course, is Jesus Christ himself. A poor man sat down to dinner and all he had was a glass of water and a poached egg. But his heart was filled with praise and he said, *Thank you, Father, for all this, and Jesus too.* Whoever has Christ has all they need to be thankful.

For Reflection and Review

- *How does godliness improve our lives?*
- *Is there any advantage to having less stuff?*
- *Is money evil?*

Lesson 324

2 Timothy 1:1-2 *Paul, an apostle of Christ Jesus by the will of God, in keeping with the promise of life that is in Christ Jesus, To Timothy, my dear son.*

Paul wrote his second letter to Timothy around AD 67, while imprisoned in a cold Roman dungeon, near the end of his life (2 Timothy 4:6). Through this letter he also wrote to the church in Ephesus, where Timothy was serving. It was a time of persecution under Emperor Nero, and the tone of this letter is somber. This is the last known letter of Paul, and it resembles a farewell discourse.

2 Timothy 1:9 *He has saved us and called us to a holy life—not because of anything we have done but because of his own purpose and grace. This grace was given us in Christ Jesus before the beginning of time.*

If we think God saved us because of anything we have done, we don't understand grace. Since God's grace was given to us *before the beginning in time*, we shouldn't think it was due to anything we did, but to his sovereign purpose. God doesn't owe anyone anything, but freely gives to some, and not to others.

Jesus went to the pool of Bethesda where *a great number of disabled people used to lie—the blind, the lame, the paralyzed. One who was there had been an invalid for thirty-eight years. . . . Then Jesus said to him, Get up! Pick up your mat and walk. At once the man was cured; he picked up his mat and walked* (John 5:3-9).

Of all the people at the pool, that day, Jesus only healed one. When the man considered all the others he must've wondered, *why me?* That should be our response as well. Salvation is a gift of God's grace which he gives to people who don't deserve it. This should make us thankful the rest of our lives.

2 Timothy 1:10 *Christ Jesus . . . has destroyed death and has brought life and immortality to light through the gospel.*

Paul was a prisoner on death row, but wasn't afraid to die, because he had eternal life. This idea is found in the Old Testament, but isn't taught as clearly. *[T]he upright will see his face* (Psalm 11:7), wrote David. But, *Who knows if the human spirit rises upward and if the spirit of the animal goes down . . . ?* (Ecclesiastes 3:21), wrote Solomon. Thankfully, this uncertainty was clarified by the resurrection of Jesus Christ. Paul's earthly life was coming to a miserable end, but his heavenly life was just beginning.

2 Timothy 1:12 *I know whom I have believed.*

Christians ought to know what they believe, but it's even more important to know whom we believe. It's possible to know all the teachings of Christianity without knowing Christ personally. We're not saved by knowing a set of teachings, however, but by knowing Christ himself.

The criminal crucified next to Jesus said, *remember me when you come into your kingdom. Jesus answered him, Truly I tell you, today you will be with me in paradise* (Luke 23:42-43). This man didn't know a thing about justification, sanctification, or the Trinity. But he met Jesus Christ and gained eternal life through him. It's not enough to know about Christ; we must know him for ourselves. Then we can say with Paul, *I know whom I have believed.*

2 Timothy 2:2 *You then, my son, be strong in the grace that is in Christ Jesus.*

A father was teaching his little girl how to play softball, so he threw her a pitch and she missed—strike one. Then he threw her another pitch and she missed again—strike two. Then he threw her another pitch and she missed again—strike three. Because she was his daughter, however, he threw her another pitch, and then another, until she finally learned to hit the ball. God will give us as many pitches as we need as long as we stay in the game. *[B]e strong in the grace that is in Christ Jesus.*

2 Timothy 2:15 *Do your best to present yourself to God as one approved, a worker who does not need to be ashamed and who correctly handles the word of truth.*

As Paul's close associate, Timothy had the privilege of learning from the greatest Bible scholar of his day. Paul was a master of the Scriptures, and used his skill to teach God's word faithfully, effectively, and accurately. He wanted Timothy to do the same.

The minister's job isn't to amuse, or entertain, but to carefully instruct God's people, day after day, week after week, year after year. *[M]y people are destroyed from lack of knowledge. Because you have rejected knowledge, I also reject you as my priests* (Hosea 4:6), said God.

It wasn't uncommon, years ago, for churches to have a cemetery right outside their building. They wanted the pastor to see the graveyard, while he was preaching, as a reminder that he might bury one of them that week. They wanted him to know that his job wasn't to be popular, but truthful; not to make them happy in life, but happy in death. Nothing is better for a church than faithful, effective, and accurate teaching of God's word.

2 Timothy 2:19 *Everyone who confesses the name of the Lord must turn away from wickedness.*

If we confess the name of Jesus Christ, we bear some responsibility for his reputation. If we live righteously, that reflects well on him. If we live wickedly, that reflects on him too. Most people won't get their opinions of Jesus Christ from the Bible, but from those who claim to be his followers.

A young man had a father who was famous and noble. Over the years his father gave him many gifts, but the greatest gift he ever received was his father's name. He was so proud of that name that he refused to do anything that would ever tarnish it. That's how Paul felt about being a Christian.

For Reflection and Review

- *Why do you think God chose you?*
- *How can we know Christ personally?*
- *How does grace make us strong?*

Lesson 325

2 Timothy 3:5 *. . . having a form of godliness but denying its power.*

The leading religion in the world isn't Christianity, Islam, Hinduism, or Buddhism, but Formalism. People are religious by nature, because they're made in the image of God (Genesis 1:27). But most people don't take their religion too seriously. They keep the external form, but mostly want to get along, make some money, and have some fun.

This is also true of many who claim to be Christians. They claim to believe in Jesus Christ, but their lives are no different than others around them. Instead of going to a temple or a mosque, they simply go to church. They're not real Christians but formalists. They have a *form of godliness*, but without God himself.

2 Timothy 3:12 *Everyone who wants to live a godly life in Christ Jesus will be persecuted.*

Paul doesn't say *Everyone who claims to be a Christian will be persecuted* but, *Everyone who wants to live a godly life in Christ Jesus will be persecuted.* The world will punish mediocre Christians on occasion, but will always punish those who are fully committed to Christ.

Forms of persecution can be arranged on a continuum from least to greatest: (1) disapproval, (2) ridicule, (3) pressure to conform, (4) loss of opportunities, (5) economic sanctions (6) shunning, (7) alienation, (8) loss of employment, (9) loss of property, (10) physical abuse, (11) mob violence, (12) government harassment, (13) kidnapping, (14) forced labor, (15) imprisonment, (16) torture, and (17) murder.

I came to Christ just before college, and it didn't take long to discover that Jesus wasn't very popular on campus. I wanted to be popular, however, so I compromised my faith and made a few friends. But I felt wretched inside, so that summer I recommitted my life to Christ, and returned the following year a different person. I told my friends of their need for Christ, and was no longer welcomed as part of the group. One person threatened to knock me out if I mentioned Jesus one more time—and he could've done it.

I was embarrassed, at times, but remember feeling very close to Christ. *If Jesus is your greatest treasure, he will be your greatest pleasure* (John Piper). We should be less afraid of persecution, perhaps, than a total lack of it. *Everyone who wants to live a godly life in Christ Jesus will be persecuted.*

2 Timothy 3:16 *All Scripture is God-breathed.*

Paul was so convinced the Bible is God's word, that he taught every single syllable came from God's mouth. *It is easier for heaven and earth to disappear than for the least stroke of a pen to drop out of the Law* (Luke 16:17), said Jesus. A true disciple of Jesus Christ will believe in the absolute inerrancy of God's word.

One man confessed that, whenever he stays in a hotel, he looks in the night stand for a Bible. If he finds one, he rips out a certain page that condemns homosexuality because he doesn't like that part. Many Christians wouldn't think of doing such a thing, but we're all inclined to skip over parts we don't like. The Bible isn't a smorgasbord from which we pick and choose; it's the word of God by which we live and die.

2 Timothy 4:1-2 *In the presence of God and of Christ Jesus, who will judge the living and the dead, and in view of his appearing and his kingdom, I give you this charge: Preach the word.*

Since the greatest need in the world is the faithful preaching of God's word, Paul made his charge to Timothy as solemn as he could: *Preach the word*, he said. Since the faithful preaching of God's word is still the greatest need in the world, God's word to preachers hasn't changed: *Preach the word*, he says.

One preacher put it this way: *I am not here to be a cheerleader or a life coach or a motivational speaker. I am not here to be a psychologist or a political pundit. I am here for one reason: to teach the word of God* (Greg Laurie).

This kind of preacher is nothing less than a gift from God, as promised in the Old Testament: *Then I will give you shepherds after my own heart, who will lead you with knowledge and understanding* (Jeremiah 3:15), said God. A faithful shepherd with a heart for God, who teaches with knowledge and understanding, is God's gift to his people. For all such preachers, we ought to be thankful.

2 Timothy 4:7 *I have fought the good fight, I have finished the race, I have kept the faith.*

Paul looked back over his many years of ministry with a feeling of satisfaction. He fought the world, the flesh, and the devil without giving up; he finished the race without dropping out. Paul may've been thinking of the marathon race which was started in memory Pheidippides. Pheidippides ran from the city of Marathon to Athens to announce a military victory. But once he arrived, he fell over dead. The Christian life is a marathon which doesn't end until we die. But all who finish can say with Paul, *Now there is in store for me the crown of righteousness, which the Lord, the righteous Judge, will award to me on that day* (2 Timothy 4:8).

2 Timothy 4:18 *The Lord will rescue me from every evil attack and will bring me safely to his heavenly kingdom.*

Paul was on trial for his life, and he expected to die (2 Timothy 4:6). After decades of serving Christ, he was ready for heaven. This wasn't the end of his life, but the beginning of the rest of his life.

When I was growing up, the best day of the year was the beginning of summer vacation. We lived across the street from my grandparents, who lived on the lake, so I spent all summer skiing, swimming, and fishing. Every day was better than the one before, but soon it was July, then it was August, then we were back in school. Like my mother used to say, *All good things must come to an end.* But, according to the Bible, that's not true: *my salvation will last forever* (Isaiah 51:6), said God.

Some people have a five-year plan; others have a ten-year plan; but Christians have a ten-thousand-year plan. *When we've been there ten thousand years, bright shining as the sun, we've no less days to sing God's praise than when we've first begun.*

For Reflection and Review

- *Why does God allow persecution?*
- *Why should pastors teach the Bible?*
- *Why was Paul looking forward to heaven?*

Lesson 326

Titus 1:1 *Paul, a servant of God and an apostle of Jesus Christ.*

Paul wrote this letter to his coworker, Titus, around the year AD 64. Titus was working on the Island of Crete, and Paul sent instructions regarding his ministry there. Crete was known for its immorality, but Paul expected believers to demonstrate their faith through godliness.

Titus 1:16 *They claim to know God, but by their actions they deny him.*

Paul was describing false teachers on Crete who were harming the church. They had a religious vocabulary, but their lives didn't measure up to what they professed. The best indication of what we believe isn't what we say, but what we do. If a court of law had to determine whether or not you were a true Christian, and all the evidence was brought to bear, what would the verdict be? Christian profession, without Christian obedience, is a mockery of the Christian religion.

Titus 2:12 *For the grace of God . . . teaches us to say No to ungodliness and worldly passions.*

Some people think the grace of God is a license to sin. If God accepts us through faith in Jesus Christ, regardless of our sin, why not sin? This way of thinking shows a misunderstanding of grace. When we understand that God hates sin, and sent his Son to die for our sin, we no longer want to live sinfully, but righteously. We *say No to ungodliness and worldly passions.*

If you're raising a puppy, one of the first things you must teach it is the word *no.* It must be said emphatically, with the right tone, and with sufficient volume. This is how we should say it to ourselves as well. We can say *no* to sin, and *yes* to Christ. Or we can say *yes* to sin, and *no* to Christ. But we can't say *yes* to sin, and *yes* to Christ at the same time.

Titus 2:13 *[W]e wait for the blessed hope—the appearing of the glory of our great God and Savior, Jesus Christ.*

The return of Jesus Christ is the *blessed hope* of his people. And hoping for Christ's return is a good indication of spiritual health. Those who long for his return are probably in love with him, and living well before him. Those who long for other things have probably grown cold. Our greatest hope should never be for a spouse, a house, or a promotion—but for the soon return of Jesus Christ. If we are hoping for anything else, we've lost our focus.

Titus 3:4-5 *But when the kindness and love of God our Savior appeared, he saved us, not because of righteous things we had done, but because of his mercy.*

The moment we think God saved us because of something good in us, we've destroyed the gospel of grace. God didn't save us because of our faith, for that is a gift from him (Ephesians 2:8). He didn't save us because of our good works, for they're ruined by sin (Isaiah 64:6). And he didn't save us because of our good hearts, for they are *deceitful above all things* (Jeremiah 17:9). *[H]e saved us, not because of righteous things we have done, but because of his mercy.*

A lady was hospitalized for kidney failure, and the doctor told her she was going to die. She made her way to the hospital chapel, not to pray, but to curse God for taking her life. But as she made her way down the aisle, almost to the front, she fainted. When she awoke she was looking at a table with these words inscribed: *God, have mercy on me, a sinner* (Luke 18:13). Then she understood that cursing God was a bad idea, and that it wasn't too late to receive mercy. So she turned to God, through faith in Jesus Christ, and begged his pardon for her sins. Miraculously, God healed her kidney. But, even better, he saved her soul.

Titus 3:9 *[A]void foolish controversies.*

The central message of the church is the gospel of Jesus Christ. *For God so loved the world that he gave his one and only Son, that whoever believes in him shall not perish but have eternal life* (John 3:16), wrote John. The devil wants to lead the church away from this message by drawing them into less important controversies.

Abortion is an important issue, but it's not the gospel. Homosexuality is an important issue, but it's not the gospel. Political issues can be important, but they're not the gospel. The gospel will speak to these and other issues, but they're not the central message of the church.

Other controversies are simply *foolish*. I was studying the Bible with a friend at a coffee shop, when a stranger approached with another point of view. She tried to persuade us that Jesus had returned, and was living in Australia. We listened politely for a couple minutes and then I said, *Thank you very much.*

My friend wondered if we should've tried to change her mind, but I thought it was a waste of time. I could tell he was disappointed but then, providentially, the next verse in our study was, *avoid foolish controversies.*

Titus 3:10 *Warn a divisive person once, and then warn them a second time. After that, have nothing to do with them. You may be sure that such people are warped and sinful; they are self-condemned.*

Titus had a duty to maintain unity within the church, and that meant some people would have to go. The rule is like baseball—three strikes and you're out. If someone is causing trouble, one or more elders should quietly correct that person, and draw their attention to this verse. If it happens again, the same procedure should be repeated. Upon a third offense, the divisive person should be told not to return. In this way God will be honored, a sinner will be warned, and the unity of the church will be preserved.

For Reflection and Review

- *Why don't more Christians hope for the soon return of Jesus Christ?*
- *Why should Christians avoid foolish controversies?*
- *Why is God against division?*

Lesson 327

Philemon 1:1 *Paul, a prisoner of Christ Jesus, and Timothy our brother.*

This little letter was written by the Apostle Paul while he was under house arrest in Rome, around AD 61. The New Testament contains thirteen letters from Paul, arranged from longest to shortest. Philemon is last, with a mere twenty-five verses. Timothy was with Paul at this time, and is mentioned as a courtesy, or because he wrote down Paul's dictation.

Philemon 1:1b-2 *To Philemon our dear friend and fellow worker—also to Apphia our sister and Archippus our fellow soldier—and to the church that meets in your home.*

Philemon was Paul's friend, and the owner of a home where the church in Colossae met. He may've been wealthy since his home was large enough for a church, and because he had at least one slave.

We can't be certain who Apphia and Archippus were, but they may've been Philemon's wife and their son. Archippus is also mentioned in Paul's letter to the Colossians, *Tell Archippus: See to it that you complete the ministry you have received in the Lord* (Colossians 4:17).

Since the church is also mentioned, this letter was to be read to the congregation, even though it's the most personal of all Paul's letters. The main purpose of this letter was to reconcile Philemon to his runaway slave, Onesimus. The situation was sensitive, and Paul displayed extraordinary pastoral wisdom and skill.

Philemon 1:6 *I pray that your partnership with us in the faith may be effective in deepening your understanding of every good thing we share for the sake of Christ.*

Paul began his letter by reminding Philemon of the benefit he received from Paul's ministry. The nature of the partnership isn't specified, but it likely included financial support for Paul. This was helpful to Paul, but was even better for Philemon. Apart from Paul, Philemon would be lost to history but, because of Paul, there's a book in the Bible that bears Philemon's name. Paul benefitted from Philemon's partnership, but Philemon benefitted even more. Giving to ministries that do the work of Christ benefits those who give.

Philemon 1:8-9 *Therefore, although in Christ I could be bold and order you to do what you ought to do, yet I prefer to appeal to you on the basis of love.*

Paul could've used his apostolic authority to command Philemon's obedience, but he chose to use diplomacy. Paul wanted Philemon to receive back his runaway slave, without punishment, and he likely secured it through this letter.

A careful reading will show that Paul used the following diplomatic measures: By addressing the letter to the church (Philemon 1:2), Paul insured that Philemon's behavior would be judged by the Christian community. By recalling Philemon's love (Philemon 1:5), he encouraged him to love Onesimus. By calling Onesimus a brother in the Lord (Philemon 1:16), he invoked the witness of Jesus Christ. By offering to pay any debt (Philemon 1:18), he removed the demand for justice. By requesting a room (Philemon 1:22), he revealed his intention to see how things turned out. This letter is a master of diplomacy, and shows that asking a favor can be more effective than making a demand.

Philemon 1:10 *I appeal to you for my son Onesimus, who became my son while I was in chains.*

We don't know why Onesimus fled from his master, but he may've reached his breaking point. Slave owners could be harsh, and Onesimus may've felt desperate. Getting to Rome wasn't cheap, however, so he likely took some cash or goods, and fled to the most populated city in the empire.

The Bible doesn't tell us how Onesimus met up with Paul but, since Paul was under house arrest, it seems Onesimus sought him out. Onesimus wasn't a Christian when he left home, but he knew about Paul from the church that met in Philemon's house. Life as a fugitive slave would not have been easy and, with a little time to think, Onesimus may've concluded that Paul could help with his problems. The first thing Paul did was to lead him to Christ, then he wrote this letter on his behalf.

Philemon 1:12 *I am sending him—who is my very heart—back to you.*

Paul used a word for *heart* that means *internal organs*, and carries the ideas of love and affection. He also called Onesimus *my son* (Philemon 1:10), and said *He is very dear to me* (Philemon 1:16). Paul was a brilliant theologian with the heart of a pastor. He didn't just evangelize and teach people —he loved them. And people loved him back.

After serving a couple years in Ephesus Paul said goodbye to the leadership. *They all wept as they embraced him and kissed him. What grieved them most was his statement that they would never see his face again* (Acts 20:37-38). When you have a pastor who loves the church, and a church that loves their pastor, you have a little heaven on earth. *By this everyone will know that you are my disciples, if you love one another* (John 13:35), said Jesus.

Philemon 1:15 *Perhaps the reason he was separated from you for a little while was that you might have him back forever.*

Paul seemed to think that everything happens for a reason. He didn't presume to know the mind of God, but said *perhaps* this is why it happened. Christians reason this way because *God works out everything in conformity with the purpose of his will* (Ephesians 1:11). *And we know that in all things God works for the good of those who love him* (Romans 8:28). So whenever something bad happens, Christians tend to think something good will come out of it. This is the reasoning of a healthy Christian mind.

Philemon 1:16 . . . *no longer as a slave, but better than a slave, as a dear brother.*

Because Onesimus had become a Christian, Philemon wasn't receiving back a slave, but a brother in Christ. This kind of language was strikingly subversive to the institution of slavery, and probably struck a nerve with Philemon. About forty percent of the Roman empire were slaves, so slavery was fundamental to the economy, and to society.

Imagine you owned several slaves and then became a Christian. Then suppose you started a church in your house, and some of your slaves became Christians. Then suppose the Apostle Paul stopped by and said, *There is neither . . . slave nor free . . . for you are all one in Christ Jesus* (Galatians 3:28). So instead of calling you *master*, your slaves began to call you *brother*. This is how Christianity undermines slavery.

But Paul also had instruction for slaves: *All who are under the yoke of slavery should consider their masters worthy of full respect, so that God's name and our teaching may not be slandered. Those who have believing masters should not show them disrespect just because they are fellow believers. Instead, they should serve them even better because their masters are dear to them as fellow believers and are devoted to the welfare of their slaves* (1 Timothy 6:1-2).

If this is true for slaves, how much more for employees? Christianity doesn't obliterate social distinctions, but creates a culture of respect and mutual concern.

Philemon 1:18 *If he has done you any wrong or owes you anything, charge it to me.*

Onesimus may've stolen from his master and lacked the ability to pay him back. By offering to make the payment for him, Paul reminds us of Christ who paid the debt for our sins. By reconciling Philemon and Onesimus, Paul also reminds us of Jesus' work of mediation. Paul was the only person on earth who could reconcile Philemon and Onesimus. And *there is also one mediator between God and mankind, the man Christ Jesus* (1 Timothy 2:5). If Onesimus was thankful to Paul, we should be even more thankful to Jesus Christ.

For Reflection and Review

- *How do donors benefit from giving to Christian ministries?*
- *Is Christian conversion always dramatic?*
- *How does Christianity undermine slavery?*

Lesson 328

Hebrews 1:1 *In the past God spoke to our ancestors through the prophets at many times and in various ways.*

The writer of this letter isn't identified, and the church has never come to a consensus. It was written to Jewish believers around AD 67. They were being persecuted, and some were falling away. It was a difficult time for them, and much was at stake.

Hebrews 1:2 *[I]n these last days he has spoken to us by his Son, whom he appointed heir of all things, and through whom also he made the universe.*

The writer wanted to impress on his readers that Jesus is the same God who made the world (Genesis 1:1). If you knocked on the door of Mary and Joseph, a few years into their marriage, and a little boy answered the door, you'd be looking at God—not God the Father, or God the Holy Spirit, but God the Son—the second person of the Trinity. Christianity is a radical belief system that calls for a radical commitment to Jesus Christ.

Hebrews 1:3 *The Son is . . . sustaining all things by his powerful word.*

Jesus not only made the world, but is also the one who sustains it. This can be compared to a flautist who sustains a note on their flute. They can sustain the note as long as they like, or cut it off whenever they want. The note depends on the flautist for its continued existence, and the world depends on Christ for its continued existence.

The sustaining ministry of Jesus Christ can also be compared to the way a dream depends on its dreamer. The dream is filled with people, events, and conversations. The moment the dreamer awakes, however, the dream no longer exists. The world is completely real, but if Jesus stopped thinking of us, the world would cease to exist.

Hebrews 1:3b *After he had provided purification for sins, he sat down at the right hand of the Majesty in heaven.*

This is something earthly priests were never allowed to do. There were no chairs in the temple because the work of the priests was never done. They sacrificed countless animals, for hundreds of years, but were never allowed to sit down, because no amount of animal sacrifice could ever atone for sin. All the sacrificial animals could do was point ahead to the perfect sacrifice of Jesus Christ. But Jesus sat down at the right hand of God because his work of redemption was done. *It is finished* (John 19:30), he said.

Hebrews 1:14 *Are not all angels ministering spirits sent to serve those who will inherit salvation?*

The writer was concerned to show the superiority of Christ over angels because some regarded angels so highly they even worshipped them (Colossians 2:18). When the Apostle John encountered an angel, even he *fell at his feet to worship him. But [the angel said], Don't do that! . . . Worship God!* (Revelation 19:10).

God cares for us through parents, friends, and neighbors, but he also uses angels. God could do everything himself, of course, but he likes to work through his created beings. When someone is in need, he may send us to help them. And whenever we're in danger, he may send an angel help us.

A couple missionaries were walking through a jungle, on their way to a village, when they noticed a tiger was stalking them. There was nothing they could do but pray and, to their relief, the tiger turned away. Was it because of an angel? We won't know how often angels helped us until we get to heaven, but we know they're *ministering spirits sent to serve those who will inherit salvation.*

Hebrews 2:1 *We must pay the most careful attention, therefore, to what we have heard, so that we do not drift away.*

Believes don't normally fall away from Christ all at once, but gradually drift further and further away from him. Over the weeks, months, and years, the distance gradually grows until Christ is out of view. Then they fall away.

Chunks of ice floated toward Niagara Falls and, embedded in the ice, were frozen fish. Seagulls gorged themselves, as long as they dared, and flew away at the end. One enjoyed its lunch so much, however, that it didn't realize its feet had frozen to the ice. It spread its wings, like many times before, but this time it didn't work. The ice was too heavy and it plunged to its death. Many Christians gorge on sin, and hope to fly away, but it doesn't always end well. *We must pay the most careful attention . . . so that we do not drift away.*

For Reflection and Review

- *How is Jesus like a flautist?*
- *Why were there no chairs in the temple?*
- *How do believers drift away from Christ?*

Lesson 329

Hebrews 2:11 *Jesus is not ashamed to call [us] brothers and sisters.*

This was helpful to those who'd been rejected by their family because of Jesus Christ. Perhaps they were the favorite son or daughter before they believed, but then their family was ashamed of them. They needed to know that Jesus wasn't ashamed, and even called them *brothers and sisters*.

Everyone carries shame, for various reasons, and it can be destructive. A man was fired from his job but couldn't bring himself to tell his family. So he went to the library every day until the money ran out. Then he took his life. But no matter what we've done, or what's been done to us, Jesus isn't ashamed of us. The greatest person in the world puts his arm around us and calls us *brothers and sisters*.

Hebrews 2:15 *[Jesus freed] those who all their lives were held in slavery by their fear of death.*

I'm still haunted by a hospital visit I made to see a lady who was dying without Christ. She was religious, but didn't claim to know Christ savingly. I saw panic in her eyes as I explained the gospel but, strangely, she didn't want to hear it. We prayed briefly, I left, and she died.

People are afraid of death for various reasons. Fear of the unknown, fear of losing control, fear of being forgotten, and fear of being punished are just a few. But Christ has set us free from the fear of death by giving us eternal life. *[T]o live is Christ and to die is gain* (Philippians 1:21), wrote Paul. What a difference Jesus makes, especially at the end.

Hebrews 2:17 *For this reason he had to be made like them, fully human in every way, in order that he might become a merciful and faithful high priest in service to God, and that he might make atonement for the sins of the people.*

Atonement is strange word to many, but it isn't hard to understand, if we break it into syllables: at-one-ment. The sacrifice of atonement allowed God and people to be at one again. That's why the Day of Atonement was the most solemn holy day in the Old Testament. It was the only day in which the High Priest could go behind the temple curtain, into the presence of God, with sacrificial blood. But this had to be repeated every year, because the blood of animals couldn't really atone for sin. It was more like deferring payment until the real payment could be made.

Since God's holiness, justice, and majesty are infinite, an infinitely valuable sacrifice was needed. But only God is infinitely valuable, so it was necessary for God to become man, so he could be the atoning sacrifice. Therefore, *God presented Christ as a sacrifice of atonement* (Romans 3:25), wrote Paul. That's why *the curtain of the temple was torn in two from top to bottom* (Matthew 27:51) the moment Jesus died. He removed the barrier between God and mankind by his atoning sacrifice. Because of him, we're now at one with God.

Hebrews 3:1 *Therefore, holy brothers and sisters, who share in the heavenly calling, fix your thoughts on Jesus, whom we acknowledge as our apostle and high priest.*

As an effective cure to spiritual drift, we're to *fix [our] thoughts on Jesus*. This is a powerful remedy, since we can't enjoy sin without forcing Jesus out of our minds. If we're mindful of Christ watching us sin, sin loses much of it's power. As long as we're focused on Christ, sin will be less alluring.

Fixing our thoughts on Jesus will also strengthen our relationship with him. If you're poor, fix your thoughts on Jesus your provider. If you're guilty, fix your thoughts on Jesus your forgiver. If you're hurt, fix your thoughts on Jesus your healer. Since our best thoughts will always be of Jesus, we should fix our thoughts on him whenever we can.

Hebrews 3:14 *We have come to share in Christ, if indeed we hold our original conviction firmly to the very end.*

Some believers were turning away from Christ because they hadn't truly begun with him. They appeared to believe at first, but their departure showed they hadn't truly believed. Those who truly believe will never completely fall away, because they're kept by Christ himself. *[N]o one will snatch them out of my hand* (John 10:28), he said. Jesus gives us strength to hold on to him, and we hold on to him with all our strength.

A man went flying with his buddy in a small aircraft. There was a rattle in the back of the plane, so the pilot asked his friend to investigate. He discovered the door wasn't completely shut and, when he tried to close it, the door flew open and he fell out. The pilot went back to the airport filled with grief but, after he landed, he found his friend holding onto the ladder for dearest life. That's how we should hold on to Christ.

For Reflection and Review

- *How does Jesus take away our shame?*
- *How can we fix our thoughts on Christ?*
- *How do we know that we've truly believed?*

Lesson 330

Hebrews 4:9-10 *There remains, then, a Sabbath-rest for the people of God; for anyone who enters God's rest also rests from their works, just as God did from his.*

The problem with working our way to heaven is that we never know if we've done enough. How many good deeds are required? How much sorrow for sin is required? How many prayers are required? If eternal life depends on our good works, we should be exhausted, and eventually die from stress. But that's not what the Bible teaches.

Come to me, all you who are weary and burdened, and I will give you rest (Matthew 11:28), said Jesus. When he finished the work of redemption he cried out, *It is finished* (John 19:30). Since Jesus finished the work of redemption, we can never earn it, or add anything to it. If we try, in fact, we diminish his work, and reject the rest he offers. *In repentance and rest is your salvation, in quietness and trust is your strength* (Isaiah 30:15), said God. God is glorified when we put our trust in Christ, and don't try to earn our way to heaven. Christ did all the work for us so we can enter his rest.

Hebrews 4:12 *For the word of God is alive and active. Sharper than any double-edged sword, it penetrates even to dividing soul and spirit, joints and marrow; it judges the thoughts and attitudes of the heart.*

The Bible is powerful because it's the word of God. And because it's the word of God, God speaks through it. One preacher was testing the acoustics in a new auditorium and quoted a verse: *Look, the Lamb of God, who takes away the sin of the world!* (John 1:29). He didn't know it at the time, but there was a worker in rafters who was troubled by his sin. He put down his tools, looked to Christ, and was converted.

This same preacher said, *The word of God is like a lion. You don't have to defend a lion. All you have to do is let the lion loose, and the lion will defend itself* (Charles Spurgeon). We don't need to defend the word of God, so much as we need to proclaim it. God's word is powerful because God himself speaks through it.

Hebrews 4:14 *Therefore, since we have a great high priest who has ascended into heaven, Jesus the Son of God, let us hold firmly to the faith we profess.*

The priesthood is common to many religions because of the shared idea that God is too holy for ordinary sinners. We need a religious professional who can help us relate to God. A good priest is close to God, but also close to sinners, so he can help sinners be close to God. No one is closer to God than Jesus, and no one is closer to sinners than Jesus. That's why he's qualified to be our high priest.

Hebrews 4:16 *Let us then approach God's throne of grace with confidence, so that we may receive mercy and find grace to help us in our time of need.*

Approaching a king on his throne was a frightening experience because kings had the power of life and death. But the king of heaven sits on a throne of grace, from which he gives mercy to all who ask.

A soldier abandoned his post in a time of war and was brought before the king to be executed. He begged for mercy but, since he was a repeat offender, the king said he didn't deserve mercy. *But if I deserved mercy, it wouldn't be mercy*, he said. The king couldn't resist his logic, so he agreed to have mercy. We too are repeat offenders who don't deserve mercy. But we can *approach God's throne of grace with confidence, so that we may receive mercy.*

Hebrews 5:8 *[Jesus] learned obedience from what he suffered.*

Jesus never sinned (1 Peter 1:22), but had to learn obedience at increasingly difficult levels. It's one thing to pick up your toys, another to be sexually pure, and another to bear the sins of the world. Jesus learned obedience like learning to lift weights: the more he obeyed, the stronger he became. His temptation in the wilderness (Matthew 4:1-11) prepared him for his ministry, and his agony in the garden (Luke 22:42) prepared him for the cross.

The test of our obedience isn't when we get whatever we want, but when God withholds something that we want, or gives us something that we don't want. Jesus didn't want to be crucified (Luke 22:42), but he put God's will ahead of his own, and *learned obedience from what he suffered.*

For Reflection and Review

- *Does Christianity require work?*
- *Does the Bible need to be defended?*
- *Why is Jesus the best priest ever?*

Lesson 331

Hebrews 5:9 *[Jesus] became the source of eternal salvation for all who obey him.*

A ball rolled into the street and a little boy chased after it. His Father yelled *stop* and the little boy obeyed. A garbage truck ran over the ball but, thankfully, the little boy was saved. Jesus yells *stop* when he sees us running toward hell. We can listen, or keep going, but he's only *the source of eternal salvation for all who obey him.*

Hebrews 6:12 *We do not want you to become lazy, but to imitate those who through faith and patience inherit what has been promised.*

One of the best ways to grow as a Christian is to imitate what's best in others. We shouldn't try to imitate anyone perfectly, because everyone has faults. But every good person has some qualities that are worthy of imitation, and they can help us improve.

A young man asked me to study the Bible with him, which we did for about a year. I had greater knowledge, but he had greater zeal. He gained the benefit of my knowledge, and I gained the benefit of his passion. It's good to find those who can help us grow, and to imitate what's best in them. Then we'll become the kind of person someone else can imitate.

Hebrews 6:19-20 *We have this hope as an anchor for the soul, firm and secure. It enters the inner sanctuary behind the curtain, where our forerunner, Jesus, has entered on our behalf.*

The anchor is a symbol of stability, because it holds a ship in position, and keeps it from being dashed on the rocks. Instead of going down, however, the Christian's anchor goes up into heaven, where it's been secured by Jesus Christ.

There is a military exercise in which a soldier shoots a hook with a light rope to the top of a cliff. If the hook gets hold of something firm, the lightest soldier shimmies to the top. From there he tosses down a heavier rope that's been anchored to something secure. So Christ has entered heaven on our behalf and secured the way for us. He's the anchor of our souls.

Hebrews 7:25 *Therefore he is able to save completely those who come to God through him, because he always lives to intercede for them.*

The night before he was crucified, Jesus said to Simon Peter, *I have prayed for you, Simon, that your faith may not fail. And when you have turned back, strengthen your brothers* (Luke 22:32). That very night Peter denied knowing Jesus, not once or twice, but three times with a curse (Matthew 26:69-75). He went outside, wept bitterly, and might've committed suicide along with Judas Iscariot (Matthew 27:5). Because of Jesus' prayer, however, Peter recovered and brought many others to faith (Acts 2:38-41).

A young lady from an atheistic country came to Christ at the age of twenty-three. The authorities strapped her into a dental chair and began drilling her teeth until there was nothing left. When that didn't work, they put her on a starvation diet, dressed her in a thin cotton gown, and put her in a cold dark cell. Months later, she was still holding on to Christ. It's hard to imagine how a new believer could find strength to persevere under such conditions unless Jesus was praying for her. But *he is able to save completely those who come to God through him, because he always lives to intercede for them.*

Hebrews 8:10 *I will put my laws in their minds and write them on their hearts.*

The writer quoted Jeremiah (Jeremiah 31:31-34) regarding the new covenant. The old covenant was summarized on *tablets of stone inscribed by the finger of God* (Exodus 31:18). But the new covenant would be internal. *I will put my laws in their minds and write them on their hearts,* said God.

Many years ago I spoke with a friend who had a strong opinion about abortion. *I don't understand how anyone can see abortion as anything other than murder,* he said. When I asked about his opinion before he was a Christian, he said he was in favor of choice. I wasn't surprised because the same was true for me. But when I came to faith in Christ, my views abruptly changed—not because of better arguments, but because God put his law inside me. *I will put my laws in their minds and write them on their hearts.*

Hebrews 8:10b *I will be their God, and they will be my people.*

The church is the bride of Christ (Revelation 19:7), and coming to Christ is like getting married. We say, *I sinner, take thee Jesus to be my Lord and Savior, to have and to hold, from this day forward, for better for worse.* The Lord replies, *I Jesus, take thee sinner, to be my matchless bride, to have and to hold, from this day forward, for better for worse.* And we become eternally his. God becomes our God, and we become his people.

For Reflection and Review

- *Why is obedience necessary for salvation?*
- *Do you have any Christian role models?*
- *How is the new covenant different than the old covenant?*

Lesson 332

Hebrews 8:12 *I will forgive their wickedness and will remember their sins no more.*

A young man drove his car while drunk and killed a young lady. Her parents were so distraught they sued him for a dollar a week, for the next several years. Every week, as he wrote the check, they wanted him to recall what he did. In contrast, God not only forgives our wickedness, but remembers our sins no more. This is especially helpful to those with a wounded conscience.

A young lady had an affair, during her first year of marriage, and she conceived a child. Her husband forgave her, loved the child, and never brought up the affair. But she was plagued by guilt, so she went to her pastor and explained that God kept bringing her sin to mind. The pastor explained it wasn't God, but her wounded conscience, that was bringing her sin to mind. He explained that

God had forgiven her sin, so she could forgive herself. And God had forgotten her sin, so she could forget it too.

Hebrews 8:13 *By calling this covenant new, he has made the first one obsolete.*

God announced his plans for a new covenant about six hundred years before Christ. *The days are coming, declares the Lord, when I will make a new covenant with the people of Israel and with the people of Judah. It will not be like the covenant I made with their ancestors when I took them by the hand to lead them out of Egypt, because they broke my covenant, though I was a husband to them, declares the Lord.*

This is the covenant I will make with the people of Israel after that time, declares the Lord. I will put my law in their minds and write it on their hearts. I will be their God, and they will be my people. No longer will they teach their neighbor, or say to one another, Know the Lord, because they will all know me, from the least of them to the greatest, declares the Lord. For I will forgive their wickedness and will remember their sins no more (Jeremiah 31:33-34), said God.

This new covenant was initiated by Jesus Christ, the night before his death. *[H]e took the cup, saying, This cup is the new covenant in my blood, which is poured out for you* (Luke 22:20). Because we're under a new covenant, the Old Testament laws are no longer binding. *By calling this covenant new, he has made the first one obsolete.*

This is why it's no longer a sin to wear clothing made of blended fabrics, or plant a field with two kinds of seed (Leviticus 19:19). It's no longer a sin to cut the hair on the side of your head, or trim the edges of your beard (Leviticus 19:27). And it's no longer a sin to order a steak medium rare (Leviticus 19:26). These laws were given to the nation of Israel to make them distinct from surrounding nations. But under the new covenant, these and many other laws are *obsolete*.

Sundials were a wonderful invention that helped the world run on time for centuries. But the invention of the pocket watch signaled the end of the sundial. It was more portable, easier to use, and even worked at night. The sundial worked for years, but the pocket watch made it obsolete. And, *By calling this covenant new, [God] has made the first one obsolete.*

Hebrews 9:12 *He did not enter by means of the blood of goats and calves; but he entered the Most Holy Place once for all by his own blood, thus obtaining eternal redemption.*

Under the Old Covenant, the high priest entered the holiest room in the temple once a year with blood from an animal sacrifice. This was surpassed by Jesus Christ, who brought his own blood into the presence of God. He's not only our great high priest, but also our perfect sacrifice. The fact that he did it *once for all* means it's good enough for everyone, and can never be repeated.

Since we have a great high priest, as well as a perfect sacrifice, it's no longer necessary to go to a temple. Jesus, in fact, is also our temple. *For where two or three gather in my name, there am I with them* (Matthew 18:20), he said.

Jesus fulfilled the religious system of the Old Testament and also replaced it. It was fitting, therefore, that the temple be destroyed, putting an end to the priesthood and the sacrificial offerings. *Not one stone here will be left on another; every one will be thrown down* (Mark 13:2), said Jesus. This was fulfilled in AD 70, when the Romans marched into Jerusalem and destroyed the temple.

Understanding how Christ fulfills the Old Testament strengthens our confidence in both Christ and the Bible. This sort of thing would be impossible for anyone but God to orchestrate. God ordained the Old Testament religious system, then sent Christ to fulfill it. This makes us confident of both Christ and the Bible. How wonderful are his works!

For Reflection and Review

- *Should Christians feel guilty after they repent?*
- *Why is the Old Testament still important?*

- *How does Christ strengthen our confidence in the Bible?*

Lesson 333

Hebrews 9:27 *[P]eople are destined to die once, and after that to face judgment.*

The eternal destiny of every person is sealed the moment of death. There's no opportunity to repent once this life is over. The moment people die they know where they'll be forever. The word *destined*, in fact, implies the day is fixed.

A young lady was walking downtown Chicago when a window fell out of a skyscraper. She had no reason to think her life was in danger as she strolled down the sidewalk that day. Death may've been the furthest thing from her mind when the window struck her on the head and killed her.

A friend of mine witnessed to his buddy for years, but the man wanted nothing to do with Christ. They were having lunch together, one day, when the man clutched his chest and died. We don't know when the end will come, but we know it's coming soon. Everyone has a date with death; fools die unprepared.

Hebrews 10:14 *For by one sacrifice he has made perfect forever those who are being made holy.*

If you look through rose-colored glasses, everything will look rosy. Since God sees us through the blood of Christ (Romans 3:25) he doesn't see any sin. This applies to our past sins, present sins, and even future sins. We'll never be more forgiven than we are right now—even in heaven. God sees us as *perfect forever* because of Jesus Christ.

Hebrews 10:18 *[S]acrifice for sin is no longer necessary.*

At the time this letter was written, the temple in Jerusalem was still being used, and animals were still being sacrificed. Jewish Christians weren't to offer sacrifices, however, because Christ was sacrificed for them. Offering a sacrifice for sin dishonored the sacrifice of Christ, as though it wasn't enough.

Even today, many believers want to offer a sacrifice for sin. Some will fast, others will serve, and others will give money. None of these things are wrong as an act of worship, but they're all wrong if we hope they'll pay for our sins. Only Christ could pay for our sins, and he's already done it. What he wants from us is love and devotion.

Hebrews 10:25 *[Do not give] up meeting together, as some are in the habit of doing.*

When the early church began, it was so exciting that believers gathered several times a week. *Every day they continued to meet together in the temple courts. They broke bread in their homes and ate together with glad and sincere hearts* (Acts 2:46), wrote Luke. But after decades of going to church, it wasn't fun anymore, and some were dropping out.

There are good reasons for dropping out of church: the music is often dreadful, the people can be cold, the sermons can be boring, and they always want your money. It's no wonder many people choose to do something else.

But there are a few good reasons for going to church: the church is the body of Christ (1 Corinthians 12:27), and the family of God (Matthew 12:49-50). Jesus said, *I will build my church, and the gates of Hades will not overcome it* (Matthew 16:18). And, *where two or three gather in my name, there am I with them* (Matthew 18:20). Whoever is committed to Jesus Christ will be committed to what Jesus Christ is committed to. And Jesus Christ is committed to his church.

A university professor was walking to church in the rain, when a student pulled over and gave him a ride. The student asked, *Why did you decide to go to church this morning?* The professor replied, *I didn't decide to go this morning; I decided forty years ago.*

Hebrews 10:29 *How much more severely do you think someone deserves to be punished who has trampled the Son of God underfoot, who has treated as an unholy thing the blood of the covenant that sanctified them, and who has insulted the Spirit of grace?*

When a believer turns away from Christ and dies, Christian friends may comfort themselves by saying, *At least he's in heaven*. But the writer of Hebrews never said that, nor did it cross his mind. He thought those who turned away from Christ were much worse off than those who never believed. And Peter agreed: *It would have been better for them not to have known the way of righteousness, than to have known it and then to turn their backs on [it]* (2 Peter 2:21), he wrote.

Charles Templeton was a well known American preacher in the 1940's. He filled stadiums with his preaching and won thousands to Christ. But then he turned away from Christ and wrote a book entitled, *Farewell to God*. This is the worst possible fate. *If you seek him, he will be found by you; but if you forsake him, he will reject you forever* (1 Chronicles 28:9), said David.

For Reflection and Review

- *Why does God see us as perfect forever?*
- *What are some good reasons for going to church?*
- *Why is it worse to turn away from Christ than never to believe in him?*

Lesson 334

Hebrews 10:31 *It is a dreadful thing to fall into the hands of the living God.*

God is at the end of everyone's road. There's no escaping him. Whoever tries to flee from God will fall into his hands. A young man was waiting for his trial to begin when he asked permission to go to the bathroom. He stood on top of the toilet, pulled himself into the ceiling, and tried to get away. But the ceiling couldn't support his weight, and he fell into the Judge's chambers. How much worse to fall into the hands of God?

Hebrews 10:34 *You suffered along with those in prison and joyfully accepted the confiscation of your property, because you knew that you yourselves had better and lasting possessions.*

Some of the first Christians were thrown into prison and lost their homes. But they still had joy because of their *better and lasting possessions* in heaven. With the passing of years, however, they forgot about their homes in heaven, and missed their homes on earth. As a result, some were going back to their former way of life. The closer they got to heaven, the more they cared about earth.

This makes little sense, but we can fall into the same pattern if we're not careful. Since every day brings us closer to the end of our journey, our excitement should steadily increase. *[O]ur salvation is nearer now than when we first believed* (Romans 13:11), wrote Paul. Our focus should never be on what we've left behind, but on all that God has prepared for those who love him (1 Corinthians 2:9).

Hebrews 10:36 *You need to persevere so that when you have done the will of God, you will receive what he has promised.*

Perseverance is the ability to stay with a task no matter how difficult it becomes. It includes endurance, persistence, tenacity, determination, diligence, commitment, and stamina. It's absolutely essential to the Christian life.

In 1952 Florence Chadwick attempted to swim twenty-six miles from Catalina Island to the California coastline. After fifteen hours a fog set in and she doubted she could make it. She swam for another hour, and then got into the boat, just a mile from the shore. Two months later she tried again and, even through the fog, she kept on swimming. For the last several hours she never stopped thinking about the shore until she finally arrived. Satan says we'll never make it; God says we're almost there. Heaven's shore is always closer than we think.

Hebrews 11:3 *By faith we understand that the universe was formed at God's command.*

The existence of God is often argued in three different ways. First, the universe didn't always exist, and didn't create itself, so there must be a creator. Second, the world shows signs of design, which point to a designer. Third, the distinction between right and wrong point to a moral law giver. These arguments fall short of absolute proof, however, so a measure of faith is still required.

But faith is required for every explanation of the world, including atheism. To be an atheist you must believe that everything came from nothing, that non-life produced life, and that thoughtless matter produced brains. This is why it takes more faith to be an atheist than to believe in God.

Hebrews 11:6 *And without faith it is impossible to please God, because anyone who comes to him must believe that he exists and that he rewards those who earnestly seek him.*

Biblical faith isn't simply believing that God exists. *Even the demons believe that* (James 2:19), wrote James. Biblical faith is believing God exists, *and that he rewards those who earnestly seek him.* That's why many have served God at great expense. *For the Son of Man is going to . . . reward each person according to what they have done* (Matthew 16:27), said Jesus.

The repentant criminal who died next to Christ will be in heaven (Luke 23:43), but he won't have the same reward as the Apostle Paul. Our greatest opportunity isn't buying the right stock at the right price, but doing something for God every day. If we do this for sixty years, we'll have over twenty thousand good deeds for God to reward. This is reason enough to get out of bed every day.

Hebrews 11:10 *[Abraham] was looking forward to the city with foundations, whose architect and builder is God.*

As an example of faith, the writer referred to Abraham, the father of the Jewish nation. He was a wealthy man, but instead of building a house, he chose to live in a tent. Houses have foundations, tents do not. Houses are permanent, tents are not.

Abraham refused to settle down in this world because he was looking for a world that would last forever. Most people treat this life as though it were permanent, and the next as though it were brief. Abraham treated this life as though it were brief, and the next as though it were permanent. He chose to live in a tent because he was just passing through.

For Reflection and Review

- *Why do Christians need to persevere?*
- *What does it mean to earnestly seek God?*
- *Should Christians live in tents?*

Lesson 335

Hebrews 11:13 *All these people were still living by faith when they died. They did not receive the things promised; they only saw them and welcomed them from a distance.*

When people come to faith in Christ, they often have an idea of how their lives should go, and it's often a version of the American Dream. When their lives don't turn out that way, many give up on God. By one estimate, eighty percent of those who begin to follow Christ turn away from him eventually. Some are disappointed because they expected too much from this life, and not enough from the next.

But if we take a longer view we can welcome everything God has promised form a distance. We don't wait for vacation to enjoy it; we welcome it from a distance. We don't wait for retirement to enjoy it; we welcome it from a distance. And we don't wait for heaven to enjoy it; we welcome it from a distance. The best is almost here, so we can enjoy it now.

Hebrews 11:26 *[Moses] regarded disgrace for the sake of Christ as of greater value than the treasures of Egypt, because he was looking ahead to his reward.*

Christianity is a religion of deferred gratification. As long as Moses remained an Egyptian prince, the best of everything was his. But he threw it all away and sided with God—not because he was noble, but because God was a better option. Moses suffered disgrace for a little while, but is known as one of the greatest men in history.

Fifteen hundred years later, when Pharaoh was long dead, Moses stood on a mountain with Christ—very much alive (Luke 9:28-36). His faith served him well back then, and serves him well today. *He is no fool who gives what he cannot keep to gain what he cannot lose* (Jim Elliot).

Hebrews 12:1 *Therefore, since we are surrounded by such a great cloud of witnesses, let us throw off everything that hinders and the sin that so easily entangles.*

Those who've gone ahead of us watch us run the race of faith from balcony seats above. Abraham, Moses, David, and others cheer us on as we make our way to the finish line. This is the only place the Bible suggests that God's people in heaven are watching God's people on earth, but that's the idea.

Running the race of faith requires more than avoiding sinful entanglements, but getting rid of *everything that hinders*. We should review our lifestyles often to be sure that nothing is slowing our pace. Simplicity and focus are both required to finish well.

Hebrews 12:1b-2 *And let us run with perseverance the race marked out for us, fixing our eyes on Jesus, the pioneer and perfecter of faith.*

The judge stood at the finish line, at some of the ancient games, holding up the victor's crown. As the runners came down the final stretch, they were at the end of their strength. But when they saw the victor's crown, they received a burst of energy and could accelerate to the end. When our strength is flagging we need to fix our eyes on Jesus who holds a crown for each of us—*the crown of glory that will never fade away* (1 Peter 5:4), wrote Peter.

Hebrews 12:2 *For the joy set before him he endured the cross, scorning its shame, and sat down at the right hand of the throne of God.*

The crucifixion of Jesus Christ was brutal, but he endured it for *the joy set before him*. While he was on the cross, Jesus focused beyond the cross, to the glorious joy of heaven: the joy of his Father's approval, the joy of his coming kingdom, the joy of forgiving sinners, and the joy of receiving his people into paradise. Nothing helps us cope on earth, more than our thoughts of heaven (John 14:2).

Hebrews 12:5-6 *My son, do not make light of the Lord's discipline, and do not lose heart when he rebukes you, because the Lord disciplines the one he loves, and he chastens everyone he accepts as his son.*

Jewish Christians may have wondered why God wasn't treating them better. Unbelievers were doing fine, but Christians were suffering terribly. If God was their father, why wasn't he taking better care of them? Surprisingly, it's because God was their father.

Most parents don't care if the neighbor's children disobey, but if their own children disobey they need to be corrected. The word translated *chasten* actually means *to whip*, and the Lord's chastening can be severe.

Some men I know have a story like this: *I started following Christ and everything was going great. We were going to church, reading our Bibles, and sharing our faith. But then we started to party. We started missing church. Then we stopped reading our Bibles and quit church altogether. Then I lost my job, got a divorce, and lost everything. Finally, when I was at rock bottom, I turned back to the Lord.* God may have to chasten us in order to keep us, but it's always for our good.

For Reflection and Review

- *How is Christianity different from the American Dream?*
- *How does thinking about heaven help us through our troubles?*
- *Why does God chasten his children?*

Lesson 336

Hebrews 12:14 *. . . without holiness no one will see the Lord.*

In a survey given to college students, eighty-nine percent wanted to be rich, eleven percent wanted to be famous, but none wanted to be holy. No one, in fact, wants to be holy unless God gives them that desire through faith in Jesus Christ. Then he gives them what they desire.

[We've] been made holy through the sacrifice of the body of Jesus Christ (Hebrews 10:10), says Hebrews. Now we're *temples of the Holy Spirit* (1 Corinthians 6:19), wrote Paul. So *live holy and godly lives* (2 Peter 3:11), wrote Peter. God declares us holy, gives us the Holy Spirit, and helps us live a holy life.

Families often have qualities that are passed down through generations. Some families are tall, others are musical, others are athletic. God's children are different from each other in many ways, but one quality they all share is holiness—without which, *no one will see the Lord.*

Hebrews 12:28 *[W]orship God acceptably with reverence and awe.*

The New Testament gives little direction for public worship, and this allows for many styles. Some churches are formal, others are informal. Some use many musical instruments, others use no musical instruments. Some use written prayers, others use spontaneous prayers. But we're all to *worship God acceptably with reverence and awe.*

For many years I belonged to a wonderful church that enjoyed coffee and donuts before the service. One Sunday we were receiving the Lord's Supper and I saw a dear lady walking up the center aisle with her coffee in one hand and a donut in the other. When the pastor tried to give her the emblems she had to juggle her refreshments to receive the Lord's Supper. It made me wonder if it's possible to be too informal. However we choose to worship, we ought to do so *acceptably with reference and awe.*

Hebrews 13:5 *Never will I leave you; never will I forsake you.*

The feeling of God-forsakenness is very common, so the Bible repeats this promise at least four times. As we walk through life, God wants us to know that he walks with us. A young man was dying of cancer and explained to his friend that life is like a movie, except you can't skip over the bad parts. *But as I review the movie of my life, Jesus Christ is in every frame,* he said. It doesn't always seem that way but, in good times and bad, God will never leave us or forsake us.

Hebrews 13:8 *Jesus Christ is the same yesterday and today and forever.*

The changelessness of God is assumed throughout the Bible, and taught in many places. *[Y]ou remain the same, and your years will never end* (Psalm 102:27), wrote the Psalmist. *I the Lord do not change* (Malachi 3:6), wrote Malachi. And, *[God] does not change like shifting shadows* (James 1:17), wrote James.

The changelessness of God is a necessary result of his perfection. Since God is a perfect being, any change would make him less than perfect. But God's changelessness is also important because the world is always changing, which makes us feel unsettled.

A man on a boat became nauseated, so the captain told him to look at a building on the shore. Soon he regained his equilibrium and felt much better. Whenever we feel unsettled we should turn our gaze to the one who never changes. He's the only constant in the universe, and can settle our hearts when everything else is changing.

Hebrews 13:9 *It is good for our hearts to be strengthened by grace, not by eating ceremonial foods.*

Jesus put an end to the dietary restrictions of the Old Testament when he declared *all foods clean* (Mark 7:19). But after years of following these restrictions some Jewish believers felt guilty for breaking them. As a remedy, the writer wanted them to be *strengthened by grace*. They weren't accepted by God because of their diet, but because of Jesus Christ (Ephesians 2:8-9).

A young man grew up in a terrible home and, when he was twelve, both his parents died. He was adopted into a wonderful home, but his behavior was still rough. Due to the support of his parents, however, he began to change. He didn't become good in order to be accepted; he became good because he was accepted.

Jesus didn't recruit good people because they were good. He recruited bad people who became better because they were accepted by him. We're accepted buy God not because we're good, but because of Jesus Christ. *It is good for our hearts to be strengthened by grace.*

Hebrews 13:15 *Through Jesus, therefore, let us continually offer to God a sacrifice of praise.*

Jewish believers weren't to offer sacrifices at the temple anymore, because Jesus was the perfect sacrifice offered once for all (Hebrews 9:12). Instead of offering sacrificial animals they were to offer a sacrifice of praise.

Praise is easy when everything is going well, but it becomes a sacrifice when things are going badly. It's good to say, *I praise you God that I have food, and I praise you God that I have shoes, and I praise you God that I have a home.* But when we can say, *I praise you God though I have no food, and I praise you God though I have no shoes, and I praise you God though I have no home*—that's a sacrifice of praise. It's also the way to mental health.

A young pastor was having a difficult time in his first church. He was up to his eyes in student loans, his ministry was going badly, and he didn't know if he'd make it. But when his wife and child died in a car accident, he thought he'd go insane.

So late one night he drove out of town, to a lonely place, where there was no one around for miles. He got out of his car and walked up and down that lonely road praising God at the top of his lungs. This went on for quite some time and, gradually, God and the gospel came back into focus. His problems seemed less overwhelming and his mental health was restored. Praising God can be a sacrifice, but it also does us good.

For Reflection and Review

- *Why don't more people want to be holy?*
- *How can we worship God with reverence and awe?*
- *Do you ever praise God when things go badly?*

Lesson 337

James 1:1 *James, a servant of God and of the Lord Jesus Christ, To the twelve tribes scattered among the nations: Greetings.*

The author of this letter was most likely James, the brother of Jesus (Matthew 13:55). James didn't believe in his brother until after the resurrection (John 7:5, 1 Corinthians 15:7), but then became a leader of the church in Jerusalem (Acts 15:13, Galatians 2:9).

The recipients were likely Jewish Christians who'd been dispersed because of persecution (Acts 8:1, 11:19). James wrote as a pastor, to a scattered congregation, encouraging them to keep living as believers. He probably wrote around AD 45, just fifteen years after the crucifixion. If so, this may be the earliest book of the New Testament.

James 1:2-4 *Consider it pure joy, my brothers and sisters, whenever you face trials of many kinds, because you* *know that the testing of your faith produces perseverance. Let perseverance finish its work so that you may be mature and complete, not lacking anything.*

James wrote to people who were going through severe trials, but urged them to rejoice because of what it did for their character. We prefer to be comfortable, but God's design is to make us like Christ. *For those God foreknew he also predestined to be conformed to the image of his Son* (Romans 8:29), wrote Paul. This is the reason for every happiness, as well as every sorrow.

Baking soda, raw eggs, vanilla, and flour don't taste good individually. But when mixed with other ingredients, and baked for thirty minutes, they make a delicious cake. The circumstances of our lives aren't always pleasant, but the outcome will be worth it. God is at work in our pain, and this is reason to rejoice (Randy Alcorn, revised)

James 1:5 *If any of you lacks wisdom, you should ask God, who gives generously to all without finding fault, and it will be given to you.*

First century Christians needed wisdom to navigate their difficult circumstances, so James reminded them of the wisdom of prayer. We like to consult the experts, but often neglect the only one who has all the answers.

A father and son were exploring an old mine with a flashlight. They marked the intersections so they could find their way out but, deep in the mine, their flashlight failed. They crept along the walls, hoping to feel their way out but, after an hour, realized they were hopelessly lost. Then they decided to pray.

As they paused, they felt a subtle breeze which they knew could only come from outside. So they followed the breeze and found their way to safety. It would've been wiser to bring an extra flashlight, but God can give us wisdom even when we've been foolish. *If any of you lacks wisdom, you should ask God.*

James 1:6-8 *But when you ask, you must believe and not doubt, because the one who doubts is like a wave of the sea, blown and tossed by the wind. That person should not expect to receive anything from the Lord. Such a person is double-minded and unstable in all they do.*

Many Christians struggle with a split personality. They believe enough to go to church, but not enough to invite others. They have one vocabulary for Sundays, and another for the rest of the week. They believe enough to be honest, unless it will cost their job. Like someone with a foot in two boats, they're unstable in all they do.

The solution to this problem is to *believe and not doubt*, wrote James. We don't become steady in our faith by doubting, but by believing what God has said. No one knew the Bible better than Jesus, or had stronger faith than Jesus. The better we know God's word, the more convinced we'll be of it.

James 1:13 *When tempted, no one should say, God is tempting me. For God cannot be tempted by evil, nor does he tempt anyone.*

Tempting and testing are closely related and easily confused. If you find a wallet full of money, Satan will tempt you to keep it. But God is testing your faith to see if you'll return it. The same event can be a temptation and a test. Satan tempts that he may ruin; God tests that he may crown.

James 1:14 *. . . each person is tempted when they are dragged away by their own evil desire and enticed.*

First the thought enters your mind, then it sparks the imagination, then there is a sense of pleasure, then you perform the deed. That's why it's easier to resist temptation at the beginning than at the end. The longer temptation is entertained the more powerful it becomes.

The best way to beat temptation is by rejecting it at once. That's what Jesus did when he was tempted by the devil in the wilderness (Matthew 4:1-11). The temptations were powerful, but he dismissed them promptly, and emerged unscathed.

James 1:15 *[S]in, when it is full-grown, gives birth to death.*

The first time Amnon had a romantic feeling toward his half-sister, he should've put it down. But he allowed himself to become *so obsessed with [her] that he made himself ill* (2 Samuel 13:2). Eventually he raped her (2 Samuel 13:14), and was later put to death (2 Samuel 13:28-29). A sin that seemed harmless, at first, grew up and killed him. The best time to kill sin is before it kills you.

James 1:17 *Every good and perfect gift is from above.*

The smell of coffee, a gentle breeze, and a convenient parking spot are gifts to brighten our day. If we think of these as routine circumstances, we'll be guilty of ingratitude and deprive ourselves of joy. But if we believe that *every good and perfect gift is from above*, we'll give thanks to God and grow in our love for him.

For Reflection and Review

- *How can believers be joyful in trials?*
- *What's the best way to defeat temptation?*
- *Why should Christians be thankful for little things?*

Lesson 338

James 1:19 *Everyone should be quick to listen, slow to speak and slow to become angry.*

A university offered several courses on public speaking that were constantly full. They offered another course on skillful listening, but it had to be canceled due to lack of interest. We are more inclined to speak our minds, than we are to listen carefully. This is why communication often breaks down.

When two people want to communicate, but are having trouble, they should try the following exercise: The first person should hold an item (such as a pen) that gives them permission to speak, without interruption, until the second person can repeat their concerns accurately.

The second person should then hold the item (which gives them permission to speak, without interruption) until the first person can repeat their concerns accurately. When each person has listened carefully enough to repeat the other's concerns accurately, they have communicated. This is a practical way of being *quick to listen, slow to speak and slow to become angry.*

James 1:21 *Therefore, get rid of all moral filth and the evil that is so prevalent.*

We live in a world of moral filth that wants to invade our lives. But here we're told to take out the trash. This verse suits me well because I hate clutter. I like to go through the house and get rid of stuff that we don't need. I also enjoy throwing out whatever isn't helpful to my relationship with God. Some TV shows have to go. Some habits have to go. And some pastimes have to go. If we want to make room for God, we must declutter our lives.

James 1:22 *Do not merely listen to the word, and so deceive yourselves. Do what it says.*

Nothing is more common than listening to sermons, week after week, without making any improvement. Perhaps James was tired of preaching so often, and seeing so little change. He compared it to someone who looks in a mirror but doesn't clean himself up (James 1:23-24).

If you looked in a mirror and saw dirt on your face, you'd wipe it off. But many hear the word of God, or even read it, without changing a thing. We use a mirror to make ourselves presentable physically, and should use the Bible to make ourselves presentable spiritually. It's not enough to listen to God's word; we must *do what it says.*

James 1:26 *Those who consider themselves religious and yet do not keep a tight rein on their tongues deceive themselves, and their religion is worthless.*

One of the best indicators of what we believe is what comes out our mouths. It doesn't matter how often we go to church, how much we give, or how much we pray. If we don't keep a tight reign on our tongues, our religion is *worthless*, said James.

James probably got this idea from his brother Jesus. *[E]veryone will have to give account on the day of judgment for every empty word they have spoken. For by your words you will be acquitted, and by your words you will be condemned* (Matthew 12:36-37), he said.

In a court of law, few things are more incriminating than a recording of the accused person talking about their crime. On Judgment Day God will call for a transcript of every word we've ever spoken, as an indication of who we really were. A good rule to follow is this: if you wouldn't write it and sign it—don't say it.

James 1:27 *[Keep yourself] from being polluted by the world.*

The autopsy of a large turtle showed that one-quarter of its weight was plastic. Inside was a golf tee, toy beads, a rope, part of a plastic bottle, and more. Through indiscriminate feeding the turtle became a trash can. Like Jesus, we must do our work in the world, without being polluted by the world. This is a difficult task but, with God's help, it can be done.

James 2:1 *My brothers and sisters, believers in our glorious Lord Jesus Christ must not show favoritism.*

James described a rich man who came to church and was well received. A poor man also attended, but he was treated badly (James 2:2-4). This is not uncommon since rich people can enrich the church while, the poor may seem to offer little.

But the poor are precious to God and, on Judgment Day, Jesus will say, *whatever you did for one of the least of these brothers and sisters of mine, you did for me* (Matthew 25:40). If Jesus came to church in disguise, he'd probably appear poor. That's why *believers in our glorious Lord Jesus Christ must not show favoritism.*

James 2:9 *But if you show favoritism, you sin and are convicted by the law as lawbreakers.*

Favoritism doesn't seem like a serious sin, so James underscored the seriousness of all sin as a violation of God's law *For whoever keeps the whole law and yet stumbles at just one point is guilty of breaking all of it* (James 2:10), he wrote. According to James, there are only two kinds of people: those who've broken God's law, and those who haven't.

This is not to say that all sin is equally bad. Abusing children is usually worse than overeating. Murder is usually worse than anger. Stealing is usually worse than coveting. Jesus said to Pilate, *the one who handed me over to you is guilty of a greater sin* (John 19:11). There are greater sins, and lesser sins, but every sin is serious.

If you're arrested for stealing, but tell the judge you've never murdered, it will not help you. You've broken the law and are guilty. Christians shouldn't excuse themselves for lesser sins, but rely on Jesus Christ for the forgiveness of all their sins (1 John 1:9).

For Reflection and Review

- *How good are you at listening?*
- *Do all your words reflect your relationship with Christ?*
- *How do you view the poor?*

Lesson 339

James 2:14 *What good is it, my brothers and sisters, if someone claims to have faith but has no deeds? Can such faith save them?*

The gospel offers eternal life on the basis of faith alone. A good example is the criminal who was crucified next to Jesus. *[R]emember me when you come into your kingdom* (Luke 23:42), he said. *[T]oday you will be with me in paradise* (Luke 23:43), said Jesus. This man was saved by faith alone, without any works at all.

But not all faith is saving faith. *Not everyone who says to me, Lord, Lord, will enter the kingdom of heaven, but only the one who does the will of my Father who is in heaven* (Matthew 7:21), said Jesus. The good news of salvation by faith alone leads some to think they can live anyway they please and still be saved. But this is far from what the Bible teaches, as James goes on to explain.

James 2:19 *You believe that there is one God. Good! Even the demons believe that—and shudder.*

Demons know their day of judgment is coming, and tremble with fear. *What do you want with me, Jesus, Son of the Most High God? In God's name do not torture me!* (Mark 5:7), one of them begged. But many who claim to believe in Jesus Christ are less devout than demons. They sin like the devil, but with even less concern.

If your faith doesn't change the way you live, you don't have saving faith, but Satan faith. Satan believes in Jesus Christ but hasn't changed his life. And those who follow Satan's example will share in his doom. *Depart from me, you who are cursed, into the eternal fire prepared for the devil and his angels* (Matthew 25:41), Christ will say.

James 3:1 *Not many of you should become teachers, my fellow believers, because you know that we who teach will be judged more strictly.*

Since many churches were small, and met in people's homes, there were opportunities for people to teach. But not all teachers were equally qualified, and some were doing more harm than good. Those who teach *will be judged more strictly*, warned James.

Jesus gave a similar warning: *Anyone who sets aside one of the least of these commands and teaches others accordingly will be called least in the kingdom of heaven, but whoever practices and teaches these commands will be called great in the kingdom of heaven* (Matthew 5:19).

Teaching God's word is a solemn responsibility. Every Bible teacher should be one *who correctly handles the word of truth* (1 Timothy 2:15), wrote Paul. And *If anyone speaks, they should do so as one who speaks the very words of God* (1 Peter 4:11), wrote Peter. This requires careful preparation and a lifetime of study. Whoever dares to teach, must never cease to learn.

James 3:2 *Anyone who is never at fault in what they say is perfect, able to keep their whole body in check.*

James used a series of illustrations to show the surprising power of speech. A small bit can turn a whole animal (James 3:3); a small rudder can turn a whole ship (James 3:4); and a small spark can set a whole forest on fire (James 5:5).

My grandmother was enjoying a little gossip with her friend when my grandfather entered the room. Knowing they were caught in a sin, the room fell silent. After a long pause my grandfather said, *Now who should we talk about?* Sins of speech are born in hell, but heard in heaven. Many who wouldn't murder a body, murder reputations every day.

James 4:4 *You adulterous people, don't you know that friendship with the world means enmity against God? Therefore, anyone who chooses to be a friend of the world becomes an enemy of God.*

God loves the world (John 3:16), and wants us to enjoy it (1 Timothy 6:17). But when he sent his Son into the world they killed him (Luke 23:33), and still rebel against him (Romans 1:32). When Christians are too at home in the world they become worldly, and come under God's rebuke.

The problem with worldliness is that it happens so gradually we don't perceive its danger—like a boat with a slow leak. The boat belongs in the water, but if enough water gets in the boat, it'll sink to the bottom. Christians belong in the world, but if the world gets into Christians, they'll sink as well.

Demas, because he loved this world, has deserted me (2 Timothy 4:10), wrote Paul. Demas had the privilege of working with one of the greatest people of all time. But he loved the world so much that he walked away from Paul. Worldliness is any affection for this world that reduces our affection for the world to come.

There's a story of soldiers who escaped from a prison camp in a hot air balloon. But they were blown out to sea, and the balloon was losing altitude, bringing them very close to the water. So they threw out their artillery, and the balloon rose for a while, but then it got close to the water again. So they threw out everything else, and the balloon rose for a while, but then it got close to water again. So they tied themselves to the ropes and cut away the basket. The balloon rose for a while, but then it got close to the water again. But now they were close enough to shore that they were able to swim to safety. Likewise, if we hope to get to heaven, we should throw out everything that's pulling us down.

James 4:6 *But he gives us more grace.*

James wanted his readers to know that even though they failed in the past, were failing in the present, and would fail in the future—God wouldn't stop giving them grace. Grace is the undeserved favor of God through faith in Jesus Christ. Since Christ has paid for all of our sins, God will never turn his back on those who believe. No matter how badly we fail, *he gives us more grace.*

A boy got in trouble at school and his father took it seriously. The boy was very sorry, but his father told him something similar would happen again. The boy said, *Nothing like this will ever happen again.* The father said, *Yes, it will.* The boy said, *How do you know?* The father replied, *I know your dad; the problem is genetic.*

We're not sinners because we sin; we sin because we're sinners—by nature and by choice. The critical thing isn't avoiding sin completely (which is impossible) but turning back, and receiving God's forgiveness. For that, *he gives us more grace.*

For Reflection and Review

- *What are the qualities of a good Bible teacher?*
- *How should Christians view the world?*
- *Why does God keep offering grace?*

Lesson 340

James 4:7-8 *Resist the devil, and he will flee from you. Come near to God and he will come near to you.*

This is the best strategy ever devised against sin. Some people resist the devil, but don't come near to God. They're like an addict in recovery, who doesn't pray or read the Bible. Others come near to God but don't resist the devil. They're like a man who goes to church, but cheats on his taxes. Victory over sin requires offense and defense. *Resist the devil, and he will flee from you. Come near to God and he will come near to you.*

James 4:10 *Humble yourselves before the Lord, and he will lift you up.*

Never underestimate the power of humility. *God opposes the proud but shows favor to the humble* (James 4:6), wrote James. *Humble yourselves, therefore, under God's mighty hand, that he may lift you up* (1 Peter 5:6), wrote Peter.

A Gentile lady came to Jesus, seeking help for her demon possessed daughter. Even though she wasn't Jewish, she hoped that Jesus would help her. But Jesus could be rude. *[I]t is not right to take the children's bread and toss it to the dogs* (Mark 7:27), he said. In effect, he called her a dog.

After such an insult, many would walked away. But with deep humility she replied, *even the dogs under the table eat the children's crumbs* (Mark 7:28). Jesus was so impressed that he granted her request. *For such a reply, you may go; the demon has left your daughter* (Mark 7:29), he said.

Almost nothing is more important to our relationship with Christ than humility. *It is by humility that the Lord allows himself to be conquered, so that he will do all we ask of him* (Theresa of Avila).

James 4:14 *What is your life? You are a mist that appears for a little while and then vanishes.*

The Bible uses several images to illustrate the brevity of life. *My days are swifter than a runner* (Job 9:25). *Everyone is but a breath* (Psalm 39:5). *[M]y days vanish like smoke* (Psalm 102:3). *My days are like the evening shadow* (Psalm 102:11). *The life of mortals is like grass, they flourish like a flower of the field; the wind blows over it and it is gone, and its place remembers it no more* (Psalm 103:15-16).

James' original readers have now been dead for two thousand years. They'd all agree with this inscription on a tombstone: *Remember me as you pass by. As you are now, so once was I. As I am now, so you will be. Prepare for death and follow me.* Worldly wisdom says, *live longer*. Biblical wisdom says, *prepare to die*.

James 4:17 *If anyone, then, knows the good they ought to do and does not do it, it is sin for them.*

Many think of sin as a clear violation of a known command such as, *You shall not murder*, or *You shall not commit adultery*, or *You shall not steal* (Exodus 20:13-15). But here we learn about another kind of sin: not the bad things we do, but the good things we fail to do. The first can be called *sins of commission*. The second can be called *sins of omission*. It's not enough to avoid what's bad, we must also do what's good.

Jesus taught about sins of omission when he said . . . *whatever you did not do for one of the least of these, you did not do for me* (Matthew 25:45). Likewise, *If anyone has material possessions and sees a brother or sister in need but has no pity on them, how can the love of God be in that person?* (1 John 3:17), wrote John.

Everyone has an obligation to do all the good they possibly can (Matthew 25:14-30). If we don't become the best we can be, and help others as much as we can, we've failed at our vocation. We ought to develop our skills to the highest degree possible, so we can help as many people as possible. Whoever doesn't do all the good they possibly can, sins.

This idea should also make us more dependent on Christ for our salvation. When we understand how badly we've failed—not only because of the evil we've done, but also because of the good we haven't done—then we abandon all hope in ourselves, and rely only on Christ. *As it is written: There is no one righteous, not even one* (Romans 3:10).

James 5:1 *Now listen, you rich people, weep and wail because of the misery that is coming on you.*

Wealthy landowners controlled much of the Roman empire, and often oppressed the poor, to amass even greater wealth. Since their money helped them in court, the poor had little recourse. James warned the ruthless rich that vengeance belongs to God, and that he'd repay them for their evil deeds (Deuteronomy 32:35).

The love of money isn't limited to the rich, however, but is seen at every level of society. Lawyers sue innocent people, doctors do unneeded procedures, mechanics replace parts that aren't broken, and drug dealers corrupt innocent youth. All of these come under the wrath of God.

For Reflection and Review

- *Why is humility important to God?*
- *How can we be ready for death?*
- *Have you ever been cheated?*

Lesson 341

James 5:13 *Is anyone among you in trouble? Let them pray.*

It can be hard to pray when life is going well, but when we're in trouble, prayer becomes our native tongue. We don't have to read a book on prayer, take a class on prayer, or ask someone else to pray for us. When serious trouble comes, we know how to talk to God.

When I was in third grade, I walked home from school, through the neighborhood park, on a Friday afternoon. There was some construction going on, and I saw a floodlight on the ground with a sticker that said, *unbreakable glass*.

I'd never heard of unbreakable glass, and wondered if such a thing could exist. I've never destroyed anyone's property, or ever wanted to, but I picked up a piece of wood and hit the glass as hard as I could. To my dismay, the unbreakable glass shattered into a million pieces. Why did they call it *unbreakable glass?*

I quickly looked around to see if there were any witnesses, and saw a girl who was two years older than me. She asked my name, and all I could think of was *John Smith*. She said, *No you're not. You're Shane Houle, and you're in big trouble.*

I went home and prepared to die. Even if I explained myself, who would ever believe that I didn't intend to break the glass? I hit it as hard as I could with a piece of wood! All I could do was pray. So I prayed most of that night, and most of the following day.

That Sunday in church, I told God that if he'd keep my secret, I'd become his servant. Days turned into weeks, and weeks turned into months, and God kept my secret. And, several years later, he collected on my promise. *Is anyone among you in trouble? Let them pray.*

James 5:14-15 *Is anyone among you sick? Let them call the elders of the church to pray over them and anoint them with oil in the name of the Lord. And the prayer offered in faith will make the sick person well; the Lord will raise them up.*

The lack of modern medicine helped people look to God whenever they were sick. Jesus was famous for healing (Luke 4:40), and commissioned his apostles to heal as well (Matthew 10:1). Others in the church also had gifts of healing (1 Corinthians 12:9, 28, 30), so it's no surprise that James encouraged suffering Christians to call for prayers of healing. But what was the oil for?

The Good Samaritan cared for the wounded man by *pouring on oil and wine* (Luke 10:34). The prophet Isaiah spoke of *open sores, not cleansed or bandaged or soothed with olive oil* (Isaiah 1:6). The disciples also *anointed many sick people with oil and healed them* (Mark 6:13). Oil was thought to be medicinal, and was used along with prayer.

But oil is also symbolic of the Holy Spirit. *Samuel took the horn of oil and anointed [David] . . . and from that day on the Spirit of the Lord came powerfully upon David* (1 Samuel 16:13). *The Spirit of the Lord is on me, because he has anointed me* (Luke 4:18), said Jesus.

When the elders were invited to pray for the sick, they may've applied the oil medicinally, or to symbolize the Spirit's power to heal, or both. All healing is a gift from God, whether it occurs naturally or supernaturally, with or without prayer, with or without the use of medicine.

James 5:16 *Therefore confess your sins to each other and pray for each other so that you may be healed.*

Sickness can be the result of sin so, whenever illness comes, we should examine ourselves for unconfessed sin. Generally, confession should only be made to those whom we have sinned against. If we've sinned against God, we should confess to God. If we've sinned against our neighbor, we should confess to our neighbor. If we've sinned against a group, we should confess to the group. This should always be our practice, whether or not we're sick, whether or not we hope to recover.

A pastor I knew was forced out of his church by a man who then became the pastor. Some time later the man became ill, and called the former pastor to his death bed. He said the reason he forced him out was because he wanted his position. He soon died, but at least he cleared his conscience.

James 5:19-20 *My brothers and sisters, if one of you should wander from the truth and someone should bring that person back, remember this: Whoever turns a sinner from the error of their way will save them from death and cover over a multitude of sins.*

Even after we come to Christ, our sinful nature wants to lead us away from him. Since all God's people are prone to wander, we have a duty to go after strays, and bring them back to the fold.

Voyeurism got the best of King David, as he spied on Bathsheba, while she was bathing (2 Samuel 11:1-27). One thing led to another, she became pregnant, and David killed her husband to save his own reputation. Suddenly this man of God was up to his eyeballs in moral failure, and refused to come clean.

Months past, but there was no repentance or confession—just a fallen soldier enmeshed in his own sin. Finally, his friend Nathan came by and helped restore him to God (2 Samuel 12:1-13). Because of Nathan's help, David came back to the Lord.

A common theme I hear from men is that, at one time, they weren't doing well spiritually. Their train was off the track, and they were far from God. Then God sent them a Nathan, who helped them get on track, so their lives were going in the right direction again. If someone you know has wandered off, perhaps you can be a Nathan.

For Reflection and Review

- *Have you ever prayed desperately?*
- *Why was oil used for healing?*
- *Has God ever sent you a Nathan?*

Lesson 342

1 Peter 1:1 *Peter, an apostle of Jesus Christ, To God's elect, exiles scattered throughout the provinces of Pontus, Galatia, Cappadocia, Asia and Bithynia.*

This letter was written by the Apostle Peter around AD 62. It was a time of persecution, and Peter wrote to provide comfort and direction in the face of suffering. Other themes include submission, hope, and Christian duty.

1 Peter 1:4 *[You have] an inheritance that can never perish, spoil or fade.*

The word *inheritance* occurs over two hundred times in the Bible, and is a very important idea. The Promised Land was Israel's *inheritance* from the Lord (Leviticus 20:24). King David foresaw a day when *The righteous will inherit the land and dwell in it forever* (Psalm 37:34). When Christ returns he will say to his own, *take your inheritance, the kingdom prepared for you since the creation of the world.* And Paul said, *you will receive an inheritance from the Lord as a reward* (Colossians 3:24).

This was a encouragement to Christians who had lost everything for the sake of Christ. It's also an encouragement to Christians who never seem to have enough, since their day of abundance is coming.

A wealthy man lost his son in an accident and mourned the rest of his life. When the wealthy man died, his will stated that everything he owned was to be sold at auction. The first item up for bid was a painting of the wealthy man's son, which no one wanted except the family servant. As soon as it was purchased, the auction was stopped. The auctioneer explained that, according to the will, whoever got the son got everything else too. That's how it is with Christ. Whoever gets the Son gets everything else too.

1 Peter 1:8 *Though you have not seen him, you love him; and even though you do not see him now, you believe in him and are filled with an inexpressible and glorious joy.*

Despite their sorrows and hardships, the early Christians to whom Peter wrote had joy. They suffered deeply for Christ, but were excited about the age to come. Their joy was so great, in fact, that Peter described it as *inexpressible and glorious*. This isn't always our experience, but it may be at times.

A friend of mine lost his wife to cancer while their children were still young. I was surprised by an email he sent shortly after she passed. *Today, I woke up alone in bed with the strangest feeling. My heart was filled with unexplainable and unrelenting joy. I was shocked. Our circumstances are no cause for joy but the Bible says, Even though you do not see Him now, you believe in him and are filled with an inexpressible and glorious joy. While I stare in the face of the greatest loss of my life I am experiencing joy that only knowing Christ can bring.*

1 Peter 1:13 *[S]et your hope on the grace to be brought to you when Jesus Christ is revealed.*

Many Christians have mixed feelings about the return of Jesus Christ, since *God will bring every deed into judgment, including every hidden thing, whether it is good or evil* (Ecclesiastes 12:14). Nevertheless, Peter assures us that we'll receive grace when Christ returns—and he would know.

Shortly before Jesus was crucified, Peter denied him three times with a curse (Luke 22:54-62). After Jesus rose from the dead Peter may've wondered how Jesus would treat him. Would he be shunned? Would he be turned away? Would Jesus send him to hell? How happy Peter must've been when Jesus gently restored him (John 21).

That's the essence of grace, and that's what we should look forward to: not indignation, wrath, or punishment—but grace. How else could we look forward to Christ's return?

1 Peter 1:17 *[L]ive out your time as foreigners here in reverent fear.*

The Israelites had a lot of experience living as foreigners. Abraham, Isaac, and Jacob lived in the Promised Land, but they were a small group living in tents. Then they went to Egypt where they lived as foreigners for more than four hundred years. Then they traveled in the wilderness for forty years, before entering the Promised Land again. Then they were exiled to Babylon where they lived as foreigners for about seventy years. Then they entered the Promised Land again, but were often governed by foreign powers. The world wasn't nice to them, and it was hard to feel at home.

Many years ago we traveled with friends to Paris and had a wonderful time. We stayed in the best hotels and enjoyed the finest foods. We shopped in expensive stores and went to the Louvre Museum. We also went up the Eiffel tower, and saw many other attractions. But the culture wasn't quite the same, and they didn't speak our language, and soon we were ready for home again.

Even in the best of times this world is not our home (John 17:14). The culture isn't right, the language isn't right, and the gods aren't right. Longing for heaven makes us foreigners on earth. The more we long for heaven, the more we'll live *as foreigners here, in reverent fear.*

1 Peter 1:18-19 *For you know that it was not with perishable things such as silver or gold that you were redeemed . . . but with the precious blood of Christ.*

If your son was sold into slavery, and you wanted to set him free, you could purchase his redemption. Depending on his age, productivity, and the going rate, his price could be high or low. But how much is a human being worth?

A life insurance policy might put the value at a million dollars. The settlement for a wrongful death might put the value at two million dollars. If you subtract your liabilities from your assets you might be worth a hundred dollars, or less than nothing. But God put such a value on us that he was willing to shed the blood of his Son for our redemption. Since the blood of Christ is of infinite value, that's what we're worth to God.

1 Peter 1:21 *Through him you believe in God, who raised him from the dead.*

We believe in God because of Jesus Christ. Peter could've argued from the existence of the universe, to the existence of God the Creator. Or he could've argued from butterflies and daises, to God the designer. Or he could've argued from our sense of right and wrong, to God the moral law giver. These arguments are consistent with the Bible, and are helpful to some degree, but aren't how Peter's audience came to believe in God. They simply heard of Jesus Christ, and believed in God *through him*.

We don't need to believe in God before we believe in Jesus Christ. We can begin with Jesus Christ to prove the existence of God. Jesus, in fact, is the most compelling argument for God there is. The best explanation for his life, death, resurrection, teaching, miracles, and the prophecies he fulfilled is God. *Through him [we] believe in God, who raised him from the dead.*

For Reflection and Review

- *What will we inherit in the age to come?*
- *Why will we need grace when Jesus appears?*
- *How does Jesus prove the existence of God?*

Lesson 343

1 Peter 1:24-25 *All people are like grass, and all their glory is like the flowers of the field; the grass withers and the flowers fall, but the word of the Lord endures forever.*

Peter quoted the prophet Isaiah to emphasize the enduring nature of God's word compared to people. Like flowers that bloom and fade, the best and brightest come and go. But the word of God *endures forever.*

There's no lack of intelligent people who disregard God's word and persuade others it's not important. But the word of God which they despise continues to be the most influential book in the world. No education is complete without a knowledge of the Bible, because of its massive historical influence. More important by far, of course, is that it's the word of God.

1 Peter 2:2 *Like newborn babies, crave pure spiritual milk, so that by it you may grow up in your salvation.*

One of the best indicators of spiritual vitality is a craving for God's word. Peter's readers were *born again* through God's word (1 Peter 1:23), and now he wanted them to *grow up* through God's word.

A friend of mine in high school was the coolest kid in class. He was smart, funny, wealthy, and from a prominent family. He could've done almost anything, but he didn't want to go to college, learn a trade, or even get a job. He just wanted to play with his friends, and live at home with his parents. On his thirty-fifth birthday, his parents put all his possessions by the road, and changed the locks on their doors, in a desperate attempt to help him grow up.

Many who believe in Jesus Christ refuse to grow up in their salvation, but this isn't pleasing to our heavenly Father. We must feast on God's word, and do what it says, to make our Father proud.

1 Peter 2:5 *[Y]ou also, like living stones, are being built into a spiritual house.*

The temple was the dwelling place of God in the Old Testament, but the church is the dwelling place of God in the New Testament (1 Corinthians 3:16). Whenever someone comes to faith in Jesus Christ, they become a living stone, connected to all God's people throughout history.

Like the temple of God in the Old Testament, the stones are being prepared off site. *In building the temple, only blocks dressed at the quarry were used, and no hammer, chisel or any other iron tool was heard at the temple site while it was being built* (1 Kings 6:7). Christians are prepared down here, to be assembled up there. The chisel, hammer, and saw aren't always pleasant, but God is using our pain to fit us for heaven.

1 Peter 2:17 *Show proper respect to everyone.*

Christians are often despised for their faith, but Peter insists that we *show proper respect to everyone.* Christians ought to be the most respectful people in the world, in fact, because we believe everyone is made in the image of God (Genesis 1:27). To disrespect those who are made in God's image is to disrespect God himself.

One lady died in a convenience store, and the last thing she saw was people stepping over her to finish their shopping. Three times she tried to get up, but no one cared enough to help. In a culture of disrespect, Christians ought to shine, by showing *proper respect to everyone.*

1 Peter 2:24 *He himself bore our sins in his body on the cross.*

There's a certain weight to our sins which Jesus bore on the cross. *Our offenses and sins weigh us down* (Ezekiel 33:10), wrote Ezekiel. The greater our sins, the more they seem to weigh. Imagine what it would be like to carry the weight of your own sins, plus the weight of your family's sins, plus the weight of your friends' sins.

As Jesus hung on the cross he bore the sins of the world, so whoever believes in him could be saved (John 3:16). By taking our sins on himself, Jesus took them off our backs so we could be relieved of their burden. If your sins are weighing you down, you can lighten your load by giving them to Christ. *He himself bore our sins in his body on the cross.*

1 Peter 3:1 *Wives, in the same way submit yourselves to your own husbands so that, if any of them do not believe the word, they may be won over without words by the behavior of their wives.*

Some of the women in the early church were concerned for their unbelieving husbands. Instead of giving them lectures, or making them feel guilty, Peter instructed Christian wives to win their husbands to Christ through submission and godly behavior. Submission is out of style today, but most men will be less threatened by their wife's religion if it improves their marriage. A submissive and godly wife won't always convert her husband, but at least she'll improve their relationship. And many husbands have been converted through the godly submission of their wives.

1 Peter 3:3-4 *Your beauty should not come from outward adornment, such as elaborate hairstyles and the wearing of gold jewelry or fine clothes. Rather, it should be that of your inner self, the unfading beauty of a gentle and quiet spirit, which is of great worth in God's sight.*

Peter is drawing on a more extensive passage from the prophet Isaiah: *The women of Zion are haughty, walking along with outstretched necks, flirting with their eyes, strutting along with swaying hips, with ornaments jingling on their ankles. Therefore the Lord will bring sores on the heads of the women of Zion; the Lord will make their scalps bald. In that day the Lord will snatch away their finery: the bangles and headbands and crescent necklaces, the earrings and bracelets and veils, the headdresses and anklets and sashes, the perfume bottles and charms, the signet rings and nose rings, the fine robes and the capes and cloaks, the purses and mirrors, and the linen garments and tiaras and shawls* (Isaiah 3:16-23), he wrote.

Fashion isn't new, and women often focus on outward beauty rather than inward beauty. Outward beauty is praised by the world, but it isn't important to God. *People look at the outward appearance, but the Lord looks at the heart* (1 Samuel 16:7). Too much fashion can even corrupt the church.

When I was growing up, the Lord's Supper was served at the front of the church, and people got in line to receive it. Since everyone watched everyone else pass by, many of the ladies got dressed up. I was so impressed by the hair, shoes, jewelry, and makeup that, by adolescence, this was my favorite part of the service. Peter may've noticed this pattern, and wanted it to stop. Women shouldn't neglect their appearance, but neither should they flaunt it.

1 Peter 3:7 *Husbands, in the same way be considerate as you live with your wives, and treat them with respect as the weaker partner.*

Peter wanted Christian men to treat their wives respectfully, but then he called them the *weaker partner*. My wife doesn't like being called the *weaker partner* because, in some ways, she's stronger than I am. She needs less sleep, has more energy, and is able to work longer hours. But she's not as strong physically, or emotionally, so I need to be considerate in those areas. The difference between husbands and wives can be compared to coffee cups. Men are like mugs, and women are like fine china. Fine china is precious, and if you treat it like a mug it'll break. A wise husband will treat his wife like the treasure that she is.

For Reflection and Review

- *Why do some believers refuse to grow up in their salvation?*
- *Why should wives submit to their husbands?*
- *How should husbands respect their wives?*

Lesson 344

1 Peter 3:15 *Always be prepared to give an answer to everyone who asks you to give the reason for the hope that you have.*

Peter wanted Christians to know what they believed, and why they believed it, so they could answer those who asked. Volumes have been written on this subject but, first and foremost, we believe in Jesus Christ because he rose from the dead. We have eye-witness testimony from the apostles, and others, throughout the New Testament. The disciples were willing to suffer and die for their testimony (Acts 5:17-42), and never changed their story. But there's more.

In addition to the external testimony of the apostles, believers have the internal testimony of the Spirit (Romans 8:16, 1 John 5:9-11). The indwelling Spirit provides assurance to all who believe in Jesus Christ that we are God's children, and have eternal life. On the basis of the eyewitness testimony, and the indwelling Spirit, we know that Jesus Christ is *Lord of all* (Acts 10:36). This is what we believe, and why we believe it.

1 Peter 4:7 *The end of all things is near.*

This verse was written two thousand years ago, but is still true for at least three reasons. First, the end is nearer now than it was yesterday. Second, the end is near for us individually, since we're only a heartbeat away from death. Third, if Jesus doesn't return for a million years, it's still near compared to eternity.

I met a man in his forties, whose health was failing, and I offered to meet with him to explain the gospel. He put it off, assuming that he had years to live, but he died later that week. *The end of all things is near*, and may be nearer than we think.

1 Peter 4:8 *Above all, love each other deeply, because love covers over a multitude of sins.*

Peter knew his Bible well and drew on two verses from Proverbs. *[L]ove covers over all wrongs* (Proverbs 10:12), and *love covers over an offense* (Proverbs 17:9). One of the most loving things we can do for our fellow sinners is to protect their reputations. We've all done things we're ashamed of, and should simply do for others what we'd like them to do for us (Matthew 7:12). This means speaking all the good we know, and none of the bad. Some sins need to be exposed, but most do not. *Love covers over a multitude of sins.*

1 Peter 4:10 *Each of you should use whatever gift you have received to serve others, as faithful stewards of God's grace in its various forms.*

Peter knew the strength of any church depends on all the members using their god-given gifts for the good of the whole. These include serving, leading, encouraging, giving, teaching, and more (Romans 12:6-8). Broadly speaking, a spiritual gift is whatever a Christian can do for the good of the church. They can be used formally, as when a pastor gives a sermon, or informally as when someone mows the lawn. Everyone has a spiritual gift, and every gift matters.

The conductor stopped a rehearsal in the middle of a song. *Where's the piccolo?* he asked. The piccolo player thought he could quit playing and no one would notice. But the conductor noticed, and so does Jesus Christ. The health of any church depends on every believer using their gifts for the good of the whole.

1 Peter 4:12 *Dear friends, do not be surprised at the fiery ordeal that has come on you to test you, as though something strange were happening to you.*

Some of Peter's readers were surprised by the suffering they were going through. Having put their faith in God, they probably thought their lives would improve. Instead, their lives became worse. If God is good and powerful, why was he letting them suffer?

This question can be answered, but not to everyone's satisfaction. It is, in fact, the primary argument atheists use against believing in a good and powerful God. A God who allows suffering might be good, but not powerful. Or he might be powerful, but not good. But a God who's good and powerful wouldn't allow suffering, they say.

But if God has a morally sufficient reason for allowing suffering, then suffering doesn't disprove the goodness, power, or existence God. Parents buy braces to straighten their children's teeth, but aren't considered evil for the pain they inflict. The pain is for their child's good. We don't always know why God allows all suffering, but if he has a morally sufficient reason, then it doesn't disprove his goodness, power, or existence.

1 Peter 4:16 *[I]f you suffer as a Christian, do not be ashamed, but praise God that you bear that name.*

The unbelieving majority will always try to make Christians feel ashamed of their faith. Christians are mocked for attending church, shunning evil, and believing unusual things. Instead of being ashamed, however, Peter wanted believers to praise God they bear the name of Christ.

Tallison was working outside an elementary school in Armenia when the ground began to shake. He ran inside to get the children out, and then returned to be sure he got them all. Tragically, the ground shook again and the building fell on his head. From that day forward the town honored his widow by calling her *Tallison's wife*. Our greatest honor isn't *who* we are, but *whose* we are. Praise God we bear the name of Christ.

1 Peter 5:8 *Your enemy the devil prowls around like a roaring lion looking for someone to devour.*

The devil is a hungry beast, always looking for another meal. If we're not alert, we could be that meal. A lady was vacationing in Africa and viewing wildlife from the safety of a tour bus. The passengers were told to keep their windows closed at all times, but the lions looked so peaceful she didn't feel threatened. So she rolled her window down to get a better view and, without warning, one of the lions charged. She tried to roll her window up, but it was too late. The lion got a paw inside and literally ripped her face off. Satan prowls around like a roaring lion and, whenever we roll down the window of sin, we put ourselves at risk.

For Reflection and Review

- *What do we believe, and why do we believe it?*
- *Why is the end of all things near?*
- *Why doesn't suffering disprove the existence of God?*

Lesson 345

2 Peter 1:1 *Simon Peter, a servant and apostle of Jesus Christ.*

This letter was written by the Apostle Peter around AD 65, just a few years before his death. His main concerns were spiritual growth, false teaching, and waiting for Christ's return. Jesus had told Peter to *Feed my sheep* (John 21:17), which Peter faithfully did through his preaching and writing.

2 Peter 1:3 *His divine power has given us everything we need for a godly life.*

Peter was less concerned for his readers' health, wealth, and happiness than for their godliness. God doesn't promise everything we need for a *comfortable life*, but everything we need for a *godly life*. We should be less concerned for our comfort than we are for our godliness.

There's a road in England with the unusual name, *Godliman Street*. No one knows for sure but, apparently, there was man on that street with a reputation for godliness. Before the street had a name they'd say, *that's where the godly man lives*.

If a street was named in your honor, what would it be called? Would it be called *Busy-man street, Lazy-man street, Wealthy-man street* or something else? If God has given us everything we need for a *godly life*, perhaps we should be known for godliness.

2 Peter 1:3b *[He] called us by his own glory and goodness.*

Coming to Christ is like saying *yes* to the most beautiful person in the world. His glory and goodness transcend everything we've ever known, and we're powerfully drawn to him. But Jesus' beauty isn't perceived by everyone. *He had no beauty or majesty to attract us to him, nothing in his appearance that we should desire him* (Isaiah 53:2), wrote Isaiah. The beauty of Jesus isn't found in his appearance, but in his glorious goodness displayed in the cross. When God opens our eyes we're drawn to him, and want to be with him forever.

2 Peter 1:11 *. . . you will receive a rich welcome into the eternal kingdom of our Lord and Savior Jesus Christ.*

The most that we could hope for is to slink into heaven without being caught. If we think of our many sins, we'll be happy to stand in the back with any other scoundrels lucky enough to be there. But God has better plans. He's preparing a *rich welcome* for all who follow his Son.

Even now, we're *surrounded by . . . a great cloud of witnesses* (Hebrews 12:1), says Hebrews. They've already arrived, and are cheering us on as we approach the finish line. We have far more friends in heaven than we'll ever have on earth, and they're excited for us to join them. They'll give us a *rich welcome into the eternal kingdom of our Lord and Savior Jesus Christ*.

2 Peter 1:12 *I will always remind you of these things, even though you know them and are firmly established in the truth you now have.*

Peter may've led some of his readers to Christ on the day of Pentecost (Acts 2:41). If so, they'd been listening to him for about thirty-five years, and probably heard everything he had to say twice. But Peter knew an important part of preaching is reminding God's people of what they already know. It's wonderful to learn something new, but it's equally important to be reminded of the old. That's why Paul told Timothy to *Keep reminding God's people of these things* (2 Timothy 2:14).

A man in his fifties walked out his front door and promptly forgot who he was. For nearly a month he wandered around until he was found, far from home, with a full white beard. It's a terrible thing to forget what we should know, so we should thank God for those who remind us.

2 Peter 2:19 *They promise them freedom, while they themselves are slaves of depravity.*

In the name of freedom, false teachers were leading God's people into depravity. But depravity is a cruel master as many will testify. It undercuts potential, ruins relationships, and compels its victims to shameful acts—all in the name of freedom. But Jesus sets us free from our depravity, so we can be our best.

A friend of mine was going through withdrawals, and desperately prayed for money so he could buy more drugs. Since God didn't answer that prayer, he asked God to take away his craving—which he did. We can't always free ourselves, but God can set us free if we turn to him with all our hearts. This may happen instantly, or over time, but there's no freedom apart from Jesus Christ. Everlasting freedom, or eternal bondage, depend on who we serve.

For Reflection and Review

- *Why doesn't everyone find Jesus attractive?*
- *What kind of preaching do you like?*
- *Why is sin a cruel master?*

Lesson 346

2 Peter 2:21 *It would have been better for them not to have known the way of righteousness, than to have known it and then to turn their backs on the sacred command that was passed on to them.*

There have always been some who appear to receive Christ, but later walk away from him. Believing family and friends may hope for their salvation, but this verse is not encouraging. It's better never to come to Christ, than it is to walk away.

But what about the young man who comes to Christ right out of high school, and makes a good start. He prays, reads his Bible, goes to church, and shares his faith. Then he goes off to college and finds himself living in sin-city. He stumbles several times and gets back up. But, eventually, sin gets the best of him and he stops getting up. He no longer prays, reads his Bible, or goes to church. Is he still going to heaven? Was he ever really saved?

Whoever comes to Christ can never be lost. *I give them eternal life, and they shall never perish* (John 10:28), said Jesus. The reason Judas walked away from Christ is because he didn't truly believe (John 6:64). But Peter looked a lot like Judas when he was denying Jesus three times with a curse (Matthew 26:69-75). Is there a way to tell the difference between a Peter and a Judas? Not really. Sometimes Christians fall away and later return (like Peter). But those who never return were never really saved (like Judas).

The status of those who fall away can't be known unless or until they return to Christ. Either they've temporarily lapsed, or permanently apostatized. If they ever truly believed, however, they will return—even with their dying breath.

2 Peter 3:8 *But do not forget this one thing, dear friends: With the Lord a day is like a thousand years, and a thousand years are like a day.*

The alarm clock is the first sound many people hear each day. We hurry out of bed so we can start the day. Then we hurry at work because there's so much to do. Then we hurry to get home so we can do a little more. Then we fall into bed and set the alarm again.

And, with age, time only seems to accelerate. When we're five years old, a year is twenty percent of our life. When we're fifty years old, a year is only two percent of our life. Since two percent is less than twenty percent, a year seems shorter at fifty, than it does at five.

Time itself is hard to understand. The past exists only as a memory, the future exists only by anticipation, and the present is so brief it can't even be measured. Young people tend to look forward, old people tend to look backward, and the middle-aged just look frustrated.

Thankfully, God doesn't experience time the same way people do. We measure time by the sun and the moon, but God created the sun and the moon. He lives in eternity and, one day, so will we. A billion years from now, we'll still have forever to live.

I think the funniest joke in heaven will be, *What time is it?* Then we'll answer as Peter did: *With the Lord a day is like a thousand years, and a thousand years are like a day.* No more alarm clocks forever.

2 Peter 3:9 *[The Lord is] not wanting anyone to perish, but everyone to come to repentance.*

This reveals God's heart for all sinners everywhere. *For I take no pleasure in the death of anyone, declares the Sovereign Lord. Repent and live!* (Ezekiel 18:32). And *[God] wants all people to be saved and to come to a knowledge of the truth* (1 Timothy 2:4), wrote Paul.

Many years ago, a man was playing cards at a bar in North Dakota. He was cheated out of his money by a professional, so he shot him in the heart. The man was sentenced to death, but his mother took his case to the governor. The governor agreed that he might be pardoned if there was any sign of repentance. So he sent an official to the prison with a signed pardon in his pocket, in case the man repented.

But, instead of repenting, the man spoke of the terrible injustice he was going through. It was all the cheater's fault! Thirty minutes later the official left with the signed pardon still in his pocket. There is no sin God will not forgive, if we're willing to repent. *[He is] not wanting anyone to perish, but everyone to come to repentance.*

2 Peter 3:13 *[W]e are looking forward to a new heaven and a new earth, where righteousness dwells.*

The biblical vision of the age to come is not a departure from earth, but a renewal of heaven and earth. *I will create new heavens and a new earth* (Isaiah 65:17), said God. *[T]he new heavens and the new earth that I make will endure before me* (Isaiah 66:22), said God again. *[C]reation itself will be liberated from its bondage to decay* (Romans 8:21), wrote Paul.

Imagine you bought an old house, and did a thorough renovation. You raised the roof, tore out some walls, and put on some extra rooms. The former house was still there, but it was changed. The renewal of the world will be radical, but it won't be completely different.

2 Peter 3:17 *[B]e on your guard so that you may not . . . fall from your secure position.*

The Bible teaches the security of the believer, and the possibility of falling. Some overemphasize the believer's security, which can lead to careless living. Others underemphasize the believer's security, which can lead to anxiety.

Christianity is a relationship with God in which we are secure as long as we're not foolish. A person can be secure on a tenth floor balcony, if they're on the right side of the railing. But if they climb over the railing, anything can happen. God has shown us how to live so we can be secure. But if we defy his commands, we put ourselves at risk. Do not *fall from your secure position.*

For Reflection and Review

- *Are former believers lost?*
- *What does it mean to repent?*
- *Have you ever been a careless Christian?*

Lesson 347

1 John 1:1 *That which was from the beginning, which we have heard, which we have seen with our eyes, which we have looked at and our hands have touched—this we proclaim concerning the Word of life.*

Neither the writer nor the recipients are identified, but this letter is widely held to be written by the Apostle John, around AD 90, when John was an old man, and the other apostles were dead. Some who seemed to be Christians developed wrong views of Jesus, and were no longer part of the Christian community (1 John 2:19). John wrote to calm the church by providing apostolic teaching regarding the person of Christ. He also provided instruction for Christian living.

1 John 1:3 *We proclaim to you what we have seen and heard, so that you also may have fellowship with us. And our fellowship is with the Father and with his Son, Jesus Christ.*

The church of Jesus Christ isn't merely an association of likeminded people, but of those who are in fellowship with God and with each other. I have a friend who belongs to a car club that he enjoys very much. They talk about cars, work on cars, race cars, and enjoy a sense of community from their shared experience. My friend can talk about cars with anyone, but he can only have *fellowship* with his racing friends.

Christian fellowship is similar, but more profound, because the Spirit of Christ lives within every true believer. When the Spirit of Christ in us, recognizes the Spirit of Christ in someone else, there's a sense of heavenly fellowship.

Some time ago an American Christian was living in a place where Christianity was illegal. As he walked the street he was surprised to hear the person behind him whistling a Christian hymn. He slowed his pace until they were side by side; then, he began to whistle the same hymn. They didn't speak the same language, but they both stopped, locked eyes, embraced, and went their ways. All over the world there are people with the Spirit of Christ, with whom we have fellowship.

1 John 1:7 *. . . the blood of Jesus . . . purifies us from all sin.*

When we understand the justice of God, and the wickedness of sin, nothing is more important than knowing we're forgiven. John assured his readers that faith in Christ's blood, shed on the cross, is sufficient to make us clean.

A young lady lost her virginity when she was fourteen years old, and felt so dirty that she went home to shower. But no matter how long she washed, or how much soap she used, she couldn't feel clean. This feeling stayed with her until she came to faith in Christ, a few years later. Suddenly she felt cleaner inside than she could ever remember, because *the blood of Jesus . . . purifies us from all sin.*

1 John 1:9 *If we confess our sins, he is faithful and just and will forgive us our sins.*

The moment a person believes in Christ, they receive complete forgiveness (Colossians 2:13). Unfortunately, we don't stop sinning. We might not sin as badly, or as often, but *If we claim to be without sin, we deceive ourselves and the truth is not in us* (1 John 1:8), wrote John. So whenever we sin, God invites us to confess, so we can stay close to him.

When my daughter was a little girl I overheard her say to her mom, *Don't tell Daddy.* I didn't know what she had done, and I didn't care. But I wanted to hear her confession so I could pardon and restore her. God wants to do the same for us, so he invites us to come to him at any time. He even assures us in advance that he'll forgive and restore us.

The reason God forgives our sins isn't because he's nice, but because he's *faithful and just*. If I received a speeding ticket, and my older brother paid the fine, the judge couldn't make me pay it too. That would be unjust. Since Jesus paid the penalty for our sins, it would be unjust of God not to forgive us. If we truly believe in Jesus Christ we'll be troubled by our sins, and confess them, but we won't have to wonder about our standing with God.

1 John 2:1 *My dear children, I write this to you so that you will not sin. But if anybody does sin, we have an advocate with the Father—Jesus Christ, the Righteous One.*

Whenever we're in trouble with God, Jesus comes to our defense. He's our defense attorney who advocates on our behalf. We don't have to defend ourselves; Jesus speaks on our behalf.

A dear lady was at a business meeting, with many of her superiors, when she was falsely accused by one of her peers. She tried to defend herself but, the more she tried, the guiltier she seemed. Then someone spoke in her defense: *I saw everything, and she did nothing wrong.* Immediately she was cleared because someone spoke in her defense.

But Jesus comes to our defense even when we're guilty. He doesn't try to mislead the Father, but simply shows his hands, feet, and back. He gets us out of trouble because he paid the price himself. *[W]e have an advocate with the Father—Jesus Christ, the Righteous One.*

For Reflection and Review

- *What are the benefits of Christian fellowship?*
- *Why does God forgive our sins?*
- *How does Jesus keep us out of trouble with God?*

Lesson 348

1 John 2:4 *Whoever says, I know him, but does not do what he commands is a liar, and the truth is not in that person.*

The fact that God forgives us through faith in Jesus Christ will appeal to our sinful nature to keep on sinning. If Jesus paid for all our sins, why resist temptation? The logic is sound, but John insists that a true profession of faith will have a corresponding lifestyle.

A professor was having lunch with an international student who was a professing Christian. His wife was studying medicine in another country and when they finished their degrees they planned to reunite. But the student let it slip that, in his wife's absence, he was seeing a prostitute.

The professor asked how he'd respond if his wife did the same. The student replied that he'd kill his wife because that was their culture. Women had to be faithful, but men were allowed to have multiple partners. The professor asked, *What about God?* The student replied, *God will forgive because that's what he does.* It's easy to see inconsistencies in others but, whenever we do, we ought to examine ourselves.

1 John 2:9 *Anyone who claims to be in the light but hates a brother or sister is still in the darkness.*

When we come to faith in Christ, the Spirit gives us a love for fellow believers that we didn't have before. The Spirit creates a common bond that leads to genuine unity. But believers are still sinners, so conflict is still possible. Even Paul and Barnabas *had such a sharp disagreement that they parted company* (Acts 15:39), wrote Luke. If it could happen to them, it could happen to anyone.

A company was hired to build a bridge across river. They began by shooting an arrow across, with a fishline attached. On the other side, someone attached twine to the fishline, and it was pulled back. Then a cable was attached to the twine, and it was pulled to the other side again. With a little more back-and-forth, the bridge was built. If you're separated by a river of conflict, keep sending over a line. If it's ever returned, you're on your way to a bridge.

1 John 2:15 *Do not love the world or anything in the world. If anyone loves the world, love for the Father is not in them.*

John watched Jesus heal the sick, raise the dead, cast out demons, and feed the hungry. So he must've been appalled when the world rejected Jesus so violently. Instead of returning his kindness, they had him crucified. And, when he rose from the dead, they made up a story that his body was stolen (Matthew 28:13). To be at home in this kind of a world is not to love God, said John.

John wasn't saying we shouldn't love the physical world (since it was made by God), or all the people in the world (since God loves everyone). But we shouldn't be too at home in a world that hates the Father and the Son. To be in love with a world that rejects Jesus Christ, is not to love God.

1 John 2:28 *And now, dear children, continue in him, so that when he appears we may be confident and unashamed before him at his coming.*

The return of Jesus Christ will be the best and worst day for everyone on earth. Some will be received into everlasting happiness, and others sent to their eternal misery (Matthew 25:46). And many who thought they were in good standing with Christ will find out they were deceived (Matthew 7:21-23). This is why many believers have mixed feelings about the return of Jesus Christ. Instead of looking forward to the best day of their lives, they feel uncertain.

The solution that John provides is to *continue in him*. Continue in his way, continue in his word, continue in his church, and continue in his service. Then, when he appears, we'll be *confident and unashamed before him at his coming.*

1 John 3:1 *See what great love the Father has lavished on us, that we should be called children of God!*

John never lost the wonder of being a child of God. Some people are doctors, others are presidents, and others are generals. Titles are fine, but they're nothing compared to being a child of God. Our core identity isn't what we've achieved, or what other people think of us, but that we're God's children through faith in Jesus Christ.

When my daughter was small, I put her to bed one night, and said, *Baby, you're a little slice of heaven*. The next day, when her brother called her a goof, she was unfazed. *No I'm not. Dad says I'm a little slice of heaven*, she replied.

What your father says about you is more important than what others say about you. And what your heavenly Father says about you is more important than what anyone says about you. The God of heaven and earth calls you his child, and that's what you are. Like the Apostle John, we should never lose the wonder of that.

1 John 3:2 *Dear friends, now we are children of God, and what we will be has not yet been made known.*

We know that we're children of God, but we don't know how we'll appear in the age to come. The Bible gives us hints, but is surprisingly silent on this important topic. Perhaps we wouldn't understand even if God explained it. *But we know that when Christ appears, we shall be like him* (1 John 3:2b), wrote John.

Two things are clear from this. First, our sinful nature will be gone forever. The very thought of sin will be more repulsive to us than eating snake. Our words, thoughts, and deeds will all agree with God, and the struggle with sin will be a thing of the past.

Second, we'll be glorious. He *will transform our lowly bodies so that they will be like his glorious body* (Philippians 3:21), wrote Paul. This must have been a comfort to the aging apostle, and should comfort every believer who struggles with an imperfect body.

1 John 3:5 *And in him is no sin.*

The amazing thing about Christ is that those who knew him best believed he was sinless. John was closer to Jesus than anyone else (John 13:23), and he could find no fault in him. The Apostle Peter was also close to Christ and said, *He committed no sin, and no deceit was found in his mouth* (1 Peter 2:22).

We can fool some people most of the time, and most people some of the time, but it's hard to fool those who are close to us. Many leaders have an excellent public image, but their staff knows what they're really like. Jesus was just the opposite. The closer people got to him, the more perfect he seemed to them. This is the kind of Savior we need.

For Reflection and Review

- *Why shouldn't Christians love the world?*
- *How do you feel about the return of Christ?*
- *How does being God's child help your sense of identity?*

Lesson 349

1 John 3:8 *The one who does what is sinful is of the devil, because the devil has been sinning from the beginning.*

Sinners want to hear that God is forgiving, so we can sin without restraint. We like to sin, God likes to forgive, it's a perfect arrangement. But if that's our opinion, we don't belong to Christ, but are of the devil.

The view that Christians are free to sin as they please is called *antinomianism*. The opposite view is called *legalism*, and teaches that Christians are saved by faith, and by keeping rules (Galatians 2:16). More accurately, Christians are saved by grace through faith, which makes them want to live for God (Ephesians 2:8-10).

Striding Edge is a trail in Britain that runs along the ridge of a mountain. The views are spectacular, but the trail is just a few feet wide, so hikers must be careful not to fall off either side. In our passion for obedience we must not add rules to the gospel (John 3:16). And in our passion for freedom we must not ignore divine commands. We are saved by grace alone, through faith alone, in Christ alone, which makes us want to live for God alone. We must avoid the opposite dangers of legalism and antinomianism.

1 John 3:14 *We know that we have passed from death to life, because we love each other.*

A little girl sat on her Father's lap and told him how much she loved him. But when she gave him a hug, she looked over his shoulder and stuck out her tongue at her brother. That's normal family life but, according to the Bible, if you love God with all your heart you'll also love your Christian brothers and sisters. If you prefer the company of unbelievers, you haven't passed from death to life.

1 John 3:24 *And this is how we know that he lives in us: We know it by the Spirit he gave us.*

Even as an old man, John was mindful of the indwelling Spirit. When he got up in the morning, he sensed the Spirit within. And when he lay down at night, the Spirit was still with him. *The Spirit himself testifies with our spirit that we are God's children* (Romans 8:16), wrote Paul. *And if anyone does not have the Spirit of Christ, they do not belong to Christ* (Romans 8:9), wrote Paul again.

The indwelling Spirit gives a clear and conscious awareness that we are children of God. The apostles spoke of the indwelling Spirit as the common experience of all believers. Believers throughout the ages have also talked about the indwelling Spirit.

The awareness of the indwelling Spirit can't be manufactured, and isn't the same as feeling spiritual or religious. This phenomenon is unique to Christians around the world and throughout history. It's a remarkable confirmation of the truth of Christianity which only believers can understand.

A little boy was flying his kite so high that it disappeared behind the clouds. Someone asked how he knew it was still there and he said, *I can feel the pull*. The Holy Spirit puts an upward pull in our hearts, assuring us that we belong to God through faith in Jesus Christ. The Spirit comes into us the moment we believe, and remains in us throughout our lives. He is God himself, and assures us that we belong to God.

1 John 4:8 *Whoever does not love does not know God, because God is love.*

From eternity past the Father, Son, and Spirit have lived in a relationship of pure and perfect love. This divine community is partially reflected in the basic human community of husband, wife, and child. Human families are never perfect, but a loving family partially reveals what it's like to belong to God's family.

Several years ago a train accident left eleven people dead, and many others injured. As he lay dying, a man left a message to his wife and children, saying how much he love them. It was written in his own blood. He probably said *I love you* many times before, but once he wrote it in blood they could never forget it. God's love should never be forgotten, because he wrote it in blood on a cross. This is how we know that *God is love*.

1 John 4:10 *[God] loved us and sent his Son as an atoning sacrifice for our sins.*

Imagine you bought the car of your dreams and drove it to the store. You were only inside for a minute but, when you came out, you saw someone scratching your car with a key. This made you so angry that you wanted them to pay for the damage, but also to suffer for what they did.

We have two problems that are solved by the atoning sacrifice of Christ: first, we've broken God's law; second, we've made him angry. God's justice must be satisfied along with his righteous wrath. It wouldn't have been enough for Jesus to die by stabbing, stoning, or hanging—these would've been too easy. Jesus had to suffer on a cross for several hours for the wrath of God to be satisfied.

For Reflection and Review

- *If God is forgiving, why shouldn't we sin?*
- *When are you most aware of the indwelling Spirit?*
- *Why is God offended by sin?*

Lesson 350

1 John 4:16 *[W]e know and rely on the love God has for us.*

A brilliant young man, with a promising career in physics, left his job to become a missionary. The work wasn't easy but he served God faithfully. He felt the weight of his responsibility and was determined to earn God's approval. But within a few years he had a nervous breakdown that left him unable to teach, preach, or even read his Bible.

After he recovered he explained that he was trying to earn God's love, and forgot to rely on God's love. The distinction may seem subtle but it's important. The more we rely on God's love, the more stable our relationship with him will be. Settle the matter in your heart and rely on it daily: you are deeply loved by God Almighty.

1 John 5:1 *Everyone who believes that Jesus is the Christ is born of God.*

John drew on a conversation Jesus had with Nicodemus about sixty years earlier. *Very truly I tell you, no one can see the kingdom of God unless they are born again* (John 3:3), said Jesus. When people come to faith in Jesus Christ, the change is so real they become new people. *The old has gone, the new is here* (2 Corinthians 5:17), wrote Paul.

But many of the people to whom John wrote had been raised in the Christian faith. Their parents were Christians, their grandparents were Christians, and Christianity was all they ever knew. Must they be born again too?

The answer, of course, is *yes*. But those who are raised in the faith often have a less dramatic conversion than those who come from outside. Since many can't remember a time they didn't believe in Jesus, they can't remember the time they first believed in Jesus. The crucial thing isn't being able to identify the time you first believed, but that you presently believe. Because *Everyone who believes that Jesus is the Christ is born of God.*

1 John 5:3 *. . . this is love for God: to keep his commands.*

A boy was taunted by his friends when he refused to participate in their bad behavior. One of them said, *He's just afraid that if he does it, his Father will hurt him.* The boy replied, *I'm just afraid that if I do it, I will hurt my Father.* Love for God would rather die a thousand deaths than disappoint the one who loved us unto death. *[T]his is love for God: to keep his commands.*

1 John 5:10 *Whoever does not believe God has made him out to be a liar, because they have not believed the testimony God has given about his Son.*

This is like a courtroom in which a father is giving sworn testimony that another person in the courtroom is his son. You either believe the father's testimony or you don't. Whenever the gospel is preached, God takes the witness stand in the hearts of all who hear. Those who believe the gospel do so because they believe God. Those who don't believe the gospel reject the testimony of God, and make him out to be a liar.

Most Christians come to faith not because they've weighed the evidence, but because God has persuaded them. They don't need further proof because God himself has given testimony in the courtroom of their hearts. Even if the whole world disagrees they'll say with Paul, *Let God be true, and every human being a liar* (Romans 3:4).

1 John 5:13 *I write these things to you who believe in the name of the Son of God so that you may know that you* *have eternal life.*

No one has the right to tell you if you're going to heaven or not, but God has provided means of assurance so you can know with confidence where you'll spend eternity.

First, do you believe in Jesus Christ. *Very truly I tell you, the one who believes has eternal life* (John 6:47), said Jesus.

Second, do you have the Holy Spirit? *The Spirit himself testifies with our spirit that we are God's children* (Romans 8:16), wrote Paul.

Third, are you trying to live like Christ? *Whoever claims to live in him must live as Jesus did* (1 John 2:6), wrote John.

And, fourth, are you determined to believe in Christ until the end? *[T]he one who stands firm to the end will be saved* (Matthew 10:22), said Jesus.

Our faith and obedience are never what they ought to be. But, to the degree we can answer *yes* to the above questions, we are entitled to assurance of salvation.

1 John 5:20 *. . . the Son of God has come and has given us understanding.*

The more we can live without understanding, the more we have in common with beasts. Cows don't start universities, and sheep don't read Plato. But inquiring minds want to know the nature of the universe, and all that it contains.

The world is big, however, and we are small. How can we find the answers to our most important questions? Making sense of the world is like trying to understand a novel from a single word in the middle. Who is the author? What is the plot? Who are the characters? How does it end?

The only person who can fully understand the world is the one who made it. Origin, destiny, sin, salvation, meaning, and purpose are just a few things Jesus explained to help us understand the world in which we live. Mystery abounds, and we'll never understand everything, but the most important questions have been answered. *[T]he Son of God has come and has given us understanding.*

For Reflection and Review

- *Why is it important to rely on God's love?*
- *Why is rejecting the gospel like calling God a liar?*
- *How can we be sure that we're going to heaven?*

Lesson 351

2 John 1:1 *The elder, To the lady chosen by God and to her children, whom I love in the truth—and not I only, but also all who know the truth.*

The author of this letter is not identified, but is widely believed to be the Apostle John, because the style and content is similar to the Gospel of John, as well as First John. This letter was probably written around AD 90, to combat the false teaching that Jesus was not fully human. It's not clear who the recipients were, but they may've been members of a church that met in the house of a Christian lady (2 John 1:1, 13). The letter is so brief that it resembles a personal note.

2 John 1:4 *It has given me great joy to find some of your children walking in the truth, just as the Father commanded us.*

As an apostle of Jesus Christ, John defended true Christianity against false Christianity. He was so concerned for the truth, in fact, that used the word *truth* five times in the first four verses. It wasn't enough for John's readers to be sincere; they had to be sincerely right. Christianity isn't one option among many; it's the truth of God that leads to eternal life. All other ways are false.

2 John 1:7 *I say this because many deceivers, who do not acknowledge Jesus Christ as coming in the flesh, have gone out into the world. Any such person is the deceiver and the antichrist.*

If Satan can't destroy Christianity directly, he'll try to mix it with error. The error John was combating came to be known as *docetism*. It's the belief that spirit is good and matter is evil. Since Jesus was good, he couldn't have been physical, only spiritual. He may have appeared physical, but wasn't actually physical. Having spent time with Christ, however, John knew for a fact that Jesus was a physical human being.

John fought against the idea that Jesus wasn't fully human, but today it's more common to think that Jesus wasn't fully divine. The biblical doctrine of Christ was formally defined by the council of Chalcedon in AD 451. The council taught that Jesus is one person with two natures, fully human and fully divine.

These two natures weren't blended to make a third, but neither can they be separated. This means Jesus Christ is fully God and fully man forever. The idea can't be understood completely, but it's faithful to what the Bible teaches about the person of Jesus Christ.

2 John 1:8 *Watch out that you do not lose what we have worked for, but that you may be rewarded fully.*

Salvation is the gift of God to all who believe (John 3:16), and can't be earned (Ephesians 2:8-9). But all who believe in Jesus Christ will be rewarded for their service. *My reward is with me, and I will give to each person according to what they have done* (Revelation 22:12), said Jesus. John wanted his readers to keep doing their best so they would *be rewarded fully*.

The story is told of a carpenter, who was getting ready to retire, and was given his final project: a small but nice home. Since this was his final job, he did something out of character: the sloppiest work of his career. On the day of his retirement his boss surprised him with a generous gift: the key to the home he just built. Everyone who believes in Jesus Christ will have a home in heaven, but only those who serve him fully will be *rewarded fully*.

2 John 1:10-11 *If anyone comes to you and does not bring this teaching, do not take them into your house or welcome them. Anyone who welcomes them shares in their wicked work.*

Early Christian preachers traveled from place to place, depending on local believers for lodging and financial support. *We ought . . . to show hospitality to such people so that we may work together for the truth* (3 John 1:8), wrote John. But false teachers were doing the same thing, so John forbad welcoming them, lest we *share in their wicked work*. This doesn't forbid courtesy, or religious conversation, but it does forbid supporting a false religion.

Few believers give lodging to false teachers today, but many give money to schools they attended, even if those schools contradict the Bible. Any person, religion, or school that contradicts the Bible is doing a wicked work, and shouldn't be supported by Christians lest we *share in their wicked work*.

*****

3 John 1:1 *The elder, To my dear friend Gaius, whom I love in the truth.*

Like the letters of First and Second John, the author of this letter is not identified. He's widely believed to be the Apostle John, however, due to the content, and similarities with the Gospel of John. First, Second, and Third John were likely written around AD 90, and sent off together. First John was to be read in various churches, while Second and Third John each had a more specific audience.

3 John 1:4 *I have no greater joy than to hear that my children are walking in the truth.*

John was referring to Gaius, who was apparently using his home to offer hospitality to traveling missionaries sent out by the Apostle John. They returned to John with a good report about Gaius, which brought great joy to the aging apostle.

If John's greatest joy was to know that his spiritual children walked in the truth, the same is true of

Christian parents. Nothing is more important to a godly mom and dad than knowing their children will be in heaven.

A nine year old boy died of a sudden illness, and his parents were inconsolable. But as they cleaned his room they found a small New Testament in the pocket of his pants. Inside the front cover were three little words in their son's handwriting: *I love God*. Nothing in the world could've brought them greater joy, because there's no greater joy than knowing your children walk in the truth.

3 John 1:9 *I wrote to the church, but Diotrephes, who loves to be first, will not welcome us.*

As an apostle, John had the duty of guiding various churches. Most met in homes, and would've been thrilled by an apostolic visit. But Diotrephes led a church, and refused to receive John. He was spreading *malicious nonsense* (3 John 1:9) about the apostle, and excommunicated whoever disagreed with him (3 John 1:10). His dictatorial style was destroying the very church he wanted to lead.

Jesus bought the church with his own blood, and it belongs to him alone (Acts 20:28). Churches don't belong to the pastor, or to the one with the strongest personality. Good and godly leadership is a gift to any church and ought to be obeyed (Hebrews 13:17). But leaders who govern the church for themselves mislead God's people and do more harm than good.

For Reflection and Review

- *Have you ever believed a false teaching?*
- *How can we be rewarded fully?*
- *Should we always obey the pastor?*

Lesson 352

Jude 1:1 *Jude, a servant of Jesus Christ and a brother of James.*

This letter was likely written around AD 65, by the half-brother of Jesus Christ, and full brother of James. Like his brothers, Jude didn't believe in Jesus during his earthly ministry (John 7:5), but came to believe after he rose from the dead.

The recipients were probably Jewish Christians, since Jude quoted freely from the Old Testament and other Jewish sources. He wrote to combat the idea that God's free forgiveness in Christ includes the freedom to sin without restraint. Due to the subject's serious nature, the tone of this letter is severe.

Jude's letter is often overlooked because of its brevity, but it's remarkably cogent, well written, and carefully constructed. It shares much in common with Second Peter, but it's not clear if Peter relied on Jude, if Jude relied on Peter, or if both relied on a third source. This kind of sharing was commonly accepted in the ancient world.

Jude 1:1b *To those who have been called . . . .*

We should make a distinction between the *general call* of God and the *effective call* of God. Jesus spoke of the *general call* when he said *many are called, but few are chosen* (Matthew 22:14, ESV). When the gospel is preached, people are invited to come to the Savior. This is the *general call* of God to salvation.

The effective call of God is that by which he converts a sinner to himself. *And those he predestined, he also called; those he called, he also justified; those he justified, he also glorified* (Romans 8:30), wrote Paul.

God's effective call is seen in the conversion of Lydia. *The Lord opened her heart to respond to Paul's message* (Acts 16:14). Isn't said that Paul opened her heart, or that Lydia opened her own heart, but that *The Lord opened her heart*. Others were also there, but it is not said the Lord opened their hearts, only Lydia's heart.

Before you believed in Jesus Christ, you we're *dead in your sins* (Colossians 2:14), wrote Paul. Dead people can't make themselves alive, but the call of God can. Jesus went to the tomb of his dead friend and said, *Lazarus, come out! The dead man came out, his hands and feet wrapped with strips of linen* (John 11:43-44), wrote John. The word of God raised Lazarus from the dead, and raises dead sinners to life. When we understand the effective call of God, we give glory to him for our conversion, and take none of the credit ourselves.

Jude 1:1c . . . *who are loved in God the Father and kept for Jesus Christ.*

God is the one who saves, and God is the one who keeps. We must believe and obey, of course, but God is the one who keeps us for his Son. We are *kept for Jesus Christ*, wrote Jude.

Not long after I came to Christ I strayed from him and, for months, showed no evidence of being a Christian. God could've turned his back on me, the way I did on him, but he graciously called me back by the power of the Spirit. If I wasn't kept by God, I wouldn't be in the faith today.

This idea is called *preservation*, and is seen in the following verses. *I give them eternal life, and they shall never perish; no one will snatch them out of my hand. My Father, who has given them to me, is greater than all; no one can snatch them out of my Father's hand* (John 10:28-29), said Jesus.

He will also keep you firm to the end, so that you will be blameless on the day of our Lord Jesus Christ (1 Corinthians 1:8), wrote Paul. And, *[H]e who began a good work in you will carry it on to completion* (Philippians 1:6), wrote Paul again. By understanding the doctrine of preservation we give glory to God for keeping us, and take none of the credit ourselves.

Jude 1:3 . . . *contend for the faith that was once for all entrusted to God's holy people.*

The Christian faith, as taught by the apostles, was being eroded by false teachers. If believers didn't reject the false teaching, they'd soon belong to a false church. Jude rang the alarm to awaken the church to the danger it faced.

Christians should contend for the faith, but without becoming contentious. Churches have been hurt by contentious leaders who want others to agree with them on every point. *If you bite and devour each other, watch out or you will be destroyed by each other* (Galatians 5:15), wrote Paul.

It's helpful to distinguish primary doctrines such as the Trinity (Matthew 28:19), the person and work of Christ (John 1:1, 14), and the authority of Scripture (2 Timothy 3:16), from secondary doctrines such as the role and nature of angels. Everything is important, but everything isn't equally important. Contending for the faith is good; being contentious for the faith is bad.

Jude 1:4 *For certain individuals whose condemnation was written about long ago have secretly slipped in among you. They are ungodly people, who pervert the grace of our God into a license for immorality and deny Jesus Christ our only Sovereign and Lord.*

This is the heart of the problem Jude wrote to correct. The offer of forgiveness through faith in Jesus Christ was being perverted to mean that Christians can sin, without restraint, and still be saved. But, in doing so, they denied *Jesus Christ our only Sovereign and Lord.*

Jesus said, *anyone who looks at a woman lustfully has already committed adultery with her in his heart. If your right eye causes you to stumble, gouge it out and throw it away. It is better for you to lose one part of your body than for your whole body to be thrown into hell* (Matthew 5:28-29). To argue that Christians can live immorally is to deny the authority of Jesus Christ.

The heresy of antinomianism continues to flourish in many churches. Some teach that people can accept Jesus as their Savior without accepting him as their Lord. They can accept his forgiveness without accepting his commands. Other churches flatly reject Jesus' teaching on morality and condone the very behavior he condemns. But, in doing so, they deny the authority of *Jesus Christ our only Sovereign and Lord.*

For Reflection and Review

- *How has Jesus kept you in the faith?*
- *Should Christians be argumentative?*
- *What should we do if God's commands seem too hard for us?*

Lesson 353

Jude 1:5 *Though you already know all this, I want to remind you that the Lord at one time delivered his people out of Egypt, but later destroyed those who did not believe.*

Soon after the nation of Israel was delivered from Egyptian slavery, through the Red Sea (Exodus 14), they lost their confidence in God and wanted to return. God was so angry he said, *your bodies will fall in this wilderness. Your children will be shepherds here for forty years, suffering for your unfaithfulness, until the last of your bodies lies in the wilderness* (Numbers 14:32-33).

The people whom God delivered from Egyptian slavery, through the Red Sea, didn't make it to the Promised Land. Christians are in a similar position because we've been delivered from sin, through the waters of baptism, but haven't arrived in the Promised Land of heaven. If God punished the nation of Israel, who wanted to go back to Egypt, will he not punish Christians who want to go back to a world of sin?

Jude 1:6 *And the angels who did not keep their positions of authority but abandoned their proper dwelling—these he has kept in darkness, bound with everlasting chains for judgment on the great Day.*

Jude is probably referring to the fall Satan and his demons, for whom God provided no redemption. God wasn't obligated to save the fallen angels, and he chose not to. God wasn't obligated to save the fallen world either, but he chose to send Christ. Whoever defies Christ, however, will meet the same fate as the devil. *Then he will say to those on his left, Depart from me, you who are cursed, into the eternal fire prepared for the devil and his angels* (Matthew 25:41), said Jesus.

Jude 1:7 *In a similar way, Sodom and Gomorrah and the surrounding towns gave themselves up to sexual immorality and perversion. They serve as an example of those who suffer the punishment of eternal fire.*

The fire of God's judgment that fell on Sodom and Gomorrah illustrates the eternal fire of hell. *Then the Lord rained down burning sulfur on Sodom and Gomorrah—from the Lord out of the heavens* (Genesis 19:24), wrote Moses.

Sodom and Gomorrah were famous for sexual immorality. It was so extreme, in fact, that when a couple angels arrived in human form, men surrounded the house where they were staying, and demanded to have sex with them (Genesis 19:4-5). In response, God poured out his wrath in one of the most catastrophic judgments in the Bible. He didn't level the towns with an earthquake, or wipe them out with a flood, but sent fire out of heaven to consume every man, woman and child who lived there (Genesis 19:25). By God's grace a few were allowed to escape, but the rest were completely destroyed.

We can imagine burning sulfur coming out of heaven like rain, and people running for shelter. They may've run into their homes, but their homes were quickly in flames, so they had to run outside again. They may've pulled their coats over their heads, but their coats were quickly in flames, so they threw them to the ground. They may've dug holes and covered themselves with dirt, but the fire found its way into the holes and burned their flesh until they were dead.

If you want to know what hell is like think of Sodom and Gomorrah—but without being able to die. They *suffer the punishment of eternal fire*, said Jude. Day after day, week after week, month after month, year after year, century after century, millennium after millennium, throughout all eternity, *they suffer the punishment of eternal fire*.

The Apostle John picked up on this in the last book of the Bible. *Anyone whose name was not found* written in the book of life was thrown into the lake of fire (Revelation 20:15), he wrote. Heaven has a book with the names of every person who belongs to Jesus Christ, and *anyone whose name was not found written in the book of life was thrown into the lake of fire.*

If we want to know where John and Jude got this idea we must consider the words of Jesus Christ. *If your hand or your foot causes you to stumble, cut it off and throw it away. It is better for you to enter life maimed or crippled than to have two hands or two feet and be thrown into eternal fire* (Matthew 18:8), he said. The one who taught more about hell than any other person in the Bible wasn't Peter, Paul, John or Jude, but Jesus Christ himself. If we oppose the idea of hell, we're opposing Jesus Christ.

Jude 1:8 *In the very same way, on the strength of their dreams these ungodly people pollute their own bodies, reject authority and heap abuse on celestial beings.*

Having rejected the teachings of Christ and the apostles, the false teachers based their religion on *the strength of their dreams*. But dreams are a thin foundation on which to build our beliefs—especially compared to the Bible. *Scripture cannot be set aside* (John 10:35), said Jesus. If you think God has spoken to you through a dream, or some other way, but the message contradicts the Bible, then it wasn't God who spoke to you. It was the devil or your own imagination.

For Reflection and Review

- *What should we learn from those who were delivered out of Egypt?*
- *Why did Jesus emphasize hell?*
- *Should Christians be afraid of eternal punishment?*

Lesson 354

Jude 1:9-10 *But even the archangel Michael, when he was disputing with the devil about the body of Moses, did not himself dare to condemn him for slander but said, The Lord rebuke you! Yet these people slander whatever they do not understand.*

In order to win followers, the false teachers disrespected the apostles, and spoke abusively of celestial beings (Jude 1:8). Jude cited a conversation between the archangel Michael and the devil himself. Michael was speaking to the most evil being in the universe, but instead of using abusive speech he simply said, *The Lord rebuke you!* Jude's point is that Christians aren't free to use abusive speech toward anyone. This includes the wicked since they too are made in God's image (Genesis 1:27). It even includes the devil since he too was created by God.

We live in a culture of massive disrespect in which people speak abusively toward anyone they don't like. This practice is so common that we barely see the harm in it. But Jesus said, *anyone who says, You fool! will be in danger of the fire of hell* (Matthew 5:22). Sins of speech are just as serious as other sins, and bring very serious warnings.

Jude 1:11 *Woe to them! They have taken the way of Cain; they have rushed for profit into Balaam's error; they have been destroyed in Korah's rebellion.*

Jude compared the false teachers to three Old Testament characters: Cain, Balaam, and Korah. Cain was the first son of Adam and Eve, and murdered his brother Abel (Genesis 4). The false teachers were similar to Cain because they were murdering Christianity. Balaam was a false religious leader who, for money, led the nation of Israel into sexual immorality (Numbers 22-25). Through their evil teaching, the false teachers were doing the same to the church. Korah opposed the leadership of Moses, and the ground split apart and swallowed him whole, along with those who supported him (Numbers 16). The false teachers were similar to Korah because they too would go down into hell.

In a single verse Jude cited three examples from the Old Testament, which his readers probably knew. This underscores the importance of knowing the whole Bible in order to understand its various parts. The various parts of the Bible contribute to the meaning of the whole, and the whole contributes to the meaning of its various parts. But instead of learning the whole Bible, many keep returning to the parts they already know.

Even a seminary professor confessed to a colleague that he hadn't read the whole Bible. He studied Greek, Hebrew, and interpretation, but hadn't read the whole Bible. He studied systematic theology, and church history, but hadn't read the whole Bible. He became an expert in one part of the Bible, but hadn't read the whole Bible.

But here we see that to understand the various parts of the Bible, we must be familiar with the whole Bible. And to understand the whole Bible, we must be familiar with the various parts. Don't keep returning to the parts of the Bible you know until you've studied the rest.

Jude 1:12 *These people are blemishes at your love feasts, eating with you without the slightest qualm—shepherds who feed only themselves. They are clouds without rain, blown along by the wind; autumn trees, without fruit and uprooted—twice dead.*

Jude used a rapid series of metaphors to describe the false teachers. They are *blemishes at your love feasts*, he said. A love feast was a common meal that probably followed the worship service, and may've included the Lord's Supper (1 Corinthians 11:17-34). Jude was thinking of the church as the body of Christ (1 Corinthians 12:27), and the false teachers as a pimple or a mole.

Jude also compared them to *shepherds who feed only themselves*. They pretended to care for Christ's sheep, but were only in the ministry for what they could get out of it.

They were also like *clouds without rain*. The climate in Israel is dry, and every bit of moisture is needed. The presence of clouds would bring hope, and their passing would bring disappointment. The false teachers promised much, but would deliver little.

They were also like *autumn trees, without fruit*. Autumn trees should be heavy with fruit, but the fruit of the Spirit (Galatians 5:22-23) was lacking in the false teachers. They were exactly the kind of people Satan wants to lead the church.

Jude 1:13 *They are wild waves of the sea, foaming up their shame; wandering stars, for whom blackest darkness has been reserved forever.*

After a storm, many shores are covered with dirty froth and churned up debris like dead wood, dead fish, and dead weeds. The false teachers were depositing the refuse of their evil lives on the shores of their listeners.

They were like *wandering stars, for whom blackest darkness has been reserved forever*. Jude may be thinking of a shooting star that shines only briefly, then flies into oblivion. The false teachers may've seemed impressive, but would soon flame out.

Jude 1:14-15 *Enoch, the seventh from Adam, prophesied about them: See, the Lord is coming with thousands upon thousands of his holy ones to judge everyone, and to convict all of them of all the ungodly acts they have committed in their ungodliness, and of all the defiant words ungodly sinners have spoken against him.*

Jude is quoting from the book of Enoch (Enoch 1:9), which is not in the Bible. The fact that Jude quotes from an extra-biblical source has been a concern to some, but Paul also quoted from sources outside the Bible (Acts 17:28, 1 Corinthians 15:33, Titus 1:12). Quoting from an extra-biblical source doesn't imply a complete endorsement, any more than a minister quoting an author implies a complete endorsement of all that author has written.

For Reflection and Review

- *Should Christians disrespect the devil?*

- *Have you read the whole Bible?*
- *Why do some unbelievers become pastors?*

Lesson 355

Jude 1:16 *These people are grumblers and faultfinders; they follow their own evil desires; they boast about themselves and flatter others for their own advantage.*

The false teachers were experts at dividing congregations. Even today, many practice their methods of grumbling, self-promotion, and flattery. No congregation is perfect but, instead of living in harmony as the Bible commands (Romans 12:16), some complain about everything. In doing so they undermine the existing leadership, and promote themselves as better alternatives. They may even create problems in order to become the solution.

They also *flatter others for their own advantage*. Flattery is saying something to a person's face you wouldn't say behind their back. Everyone needs honest affirmation, but these people were using dishonest affirmation to win people's support. *By smooth talk and flattery they deceive the minds of naive people* (Romans 16:8), wrote Paul. And *May the Lord silence all flattering lips* (Psalm 12:3), wrote David. Honest affirmation is encouraging, but we ought to be suspicious of anyone who is overly complimentary.

Jude 1:17-18 *But, dear friends, remember what the apostles of our Lord Jesus Christ foretold. They said to you, In the last times there will be scoffers who will follow their own ungodly desires.*

Jude's readers may've been surprised that false teachers crept into the church, so he reminded them that this was foretold by the apostles. *I know that after I leave, savage wolves will come in among you and will not spare the flock. Even from your own number men will arise and distort the truth in order to draw away disciples after them. So be on your guard! Remember that for three years I never stopped warning each of you night and day with tears* (Acts 20:29-31), said Paul.

A preacher I know was invited to give a sermon while the pastor was on vacation, and used the opportunity to make terrible accusations. He also announced that he'd be starting a new church the following Sunday. About half the people followed him and the church was never the same. *I urge you, brothers and sisters, to watch out for those who cause divisions* (Romans 16:17), wrote Paul.

Jude 1:20-21 *But you, dear friends, by building yourselves up in your most holy faith and praying in the Holy Spirit, keep yourselves in God's love.*

God's love for us is constant, but we must keep ourselves in a loving relationship with him. A father may love his child deeply but, if the child doesn't love his father in return, the relationship will be strained. Instead of ignoring our relationship with God, we should try to strengthen it every day.

Many years ago I began a weight training program and nearly doubled my strength in nine months. Then I took the summer off, and lost most of what I'd gained. Likewise, the only way to grow strong spiritually is to exercise daily. Prayer, Bible study, prompt obedience, and church attendance are the building blocks of spiritual fitness. Jude reminds us to build ourselves up in our most holy faith.

Jude 1:22 *Be merciful to those who doubt.*

Some of the early Christians found it difficult to believe in a crucified Messiah whom they couldn't see. Their lives were often difficult, and some even wondered if they'd made a mistake. Faith and doubt coexist in all God's earthly people, and it's still hard to believe in a crucified Messiah whom we cannot see. This is why we should *Be merciful to those who doubt*.

Christians aren't the only ones who doubt, however. Even atheists doubt because, in order not to believe in God, they have to believe the world just happened—which is doubtful. And to reject Jesus Christ they have to believe the most credible person in history was a fraud—which is also doubtful. When it comes to faith and doubt, everyone should ask three questions: (1) What should I believe? (2) What should I doubt? And (3) How can I be ready for the hour of my death?

Jude 1:23 *[S]ave others by snatching them from the fire.*

Jude is probably referring to those who had sided with the false teachers. By believing things that were false, and engaging in immorality, they imperiled their souls. Jude didn't want faithful Christians to turn away from their wandering brothers and sisters prematurely, but to rescue them by *snatching them from the fire* of hell.

Jude is drawing on something God said about the high priest, Joshua. *Is not this man a burning stick snatched from the fire?* (Zechariah 3:2). God also said to the nation of Israel, *You were like a burning stick snatched from the fire* (Amos 4:11).

John Wesley was one of the greatest preachers of the seventeen hundreds, but nearly died as a child. When he was five years old his house caught fire late in the evening. Everyone escaped but John, who was stranded on the second floor. The house was ablaze, and the roof was about to collapse, when he was lifted out of the window by a man standing on another man's shoulders. John came to see himself as *a burning stick snatched from the fire* to serve God. When we consider the lake of fire, to which we were headed, this idea applies to every Christian, and should make us forever thankful.

Jude 1:24-25 *To him who is able to keep you from stumbling and to present you before his glorious presence without fault and with great joy—to the only God our Savior be glory, majesty, power and authority, through Jesus Christ our Lord, before all ages, now and forevermore! Amen.*

Jude concluded his letter with one of the most beautiful doxologies in the Bible. The terrible problems they were having wouldn't be the last word. God would present them *before his glorious presence without fault and with great joy.*

Even the best Christians are far from perfect but, since Jesus died for our sins, he will present us *without fault* in the presence of God. This won't happen because we're faultless in ourselves, but because our forgiveness is so complete that we're faultless in Christ. Judgment Day won't be a terror to us, but a day of rejoicing when Christ stands by our side and presents us to God *without fault and with great joy.* What an amazing Savior he is!

For Reflection and Review

- *Should Christians complain about their church?*
- *How can we overcome our doubts?*
- *When do you want Christ to return?*

Lesson 356

Revelation 1:1 *The revelation from Jesus Christ, which God gave him to show his servants what must soon take place.*

The book of Revelation was written by the Apostle John around AD 95, while he was exiled on the small rocky island of Patmos (Revelation 1:9). The church was suffering persecution, and this book is an encouragement to persevere in faith. Much of the book concerns the future, but its apocalyptic style makes it difficult to understand. It's clear, however, that the gospel will be violently opposed, and that evil will be crushed when Jesus Christ returns.

Revelation 1:7 *Look, he is coming with the clouds, and every eye will see him.*

God is identified with clouds throughout the Old Testament. *By day the Lord went ahead of them in a pillar of cloud* (Exodus 13:21). *[D]ark clouds were under his feet* (2 Samuel 22:10). *The Lord has said that he would dwell in a dark cloud* (2 Chronicles 6:1).

Jesus is also identified with clouds throughout the New Testament. *At that time people will see the Son of Man coming in clouds with great power and glory* (Mark 13:26), said Jesus. *[H]e was taken up before their very eyes, and a cloud hid him from their sight* (Acts 1:9), wrote Luke. *[We] will be caught up together with them in the clouds to meet the Lord in the air* (1 Thessalonians 4:17), wrote Paul.

Shortly after I came to faith, I was having lunch in the university cafeteria. I was looking out the window at the cloud formations thinking that Christ could return at any moment. The distant look in my eyes must've been obvious because a friend sat down and asked if I was expecting someone. I still am.

Revelation 1:12-13 *I turned around to see the voice that was speaking to me. And when I turned I saw seven golden lampstands, and among the lampstands was someone like a son of man.*

John's vision of Christ is different from anything found in the gospels. Throughout most of his life and ministry, Jesus appeared as any other man. He was so ordinary, in fact, that *even his own brothers did not believe in him* (John 7:5). A noteworthy exception was when *His face shone like the sun, and his clothes became as white as the light* (Matthew 17:2). This was brief, however, and was only witnessed by a few. Even after Jesus rose from the dead he seemed so normal that *some doubted* (Matthew 28:17).

While on Patmos, however, John had a vision of Christ in glory. He was *dressed in a robe reaching down to his feet and with a golden sash around his chest* (Revelation 1:13b). This is very interesting because Jesus died naked. Crucifixion was designed to be cruel and unusual punishment, and humiliation was part of it.

But here we see Jesus in the clothing of a high priest (Exodus 29:5), whose job was to offer sacrifices for God's people. After the sacrifice was made he'd bring the animal's blood into the temple as an offering. But Jesus *did not enter by means of the blood of goats and calves; but he entered the Most Holy Place once for all by his own blood, thus obtaining eternal redemption* (Hebrews 9:12), says Hebrews. Our high priest was also the ultimate sacrifice.

Revelation 1:14 *The hair on his head was white like wool, as white as snow.*

This may speak of the wisdom of Christ obtained through many years. Jesus died as a young man but is, in fact, eternal. Abraham lived two thousand years earlier, but Jesus said, *before Abraham was born, I am!* (John 7:58). Because he is eternal, Jesus can give eternal life to all who believe in him.

A successful lady was interviewed on television and was asked if she had any regrets. She said, *Just one—life is too short. Even if you're successful, there are only so many grains of sand in the hour glass. And when the last one falls, it's over.* But for those who believe in Jesus Christ, it's never over.

Revelation 1:14b *[A]nd his eyes were like blazing fire.*

The fire in Jesus' eyes show his holy wrath against all that is wrong in the world. When the merchants of religion were turning a profit in the temple courts, Jesus didn't take it sitting down. *[H]e made a whip out of cords, and drove all from the temple courts, both sheep and cattle; he scattered the coins of the money changers and overturned their tables. To those who sold doves he said, Get these out of here! Stop turning my Father's house into a market!* (John 2:15-16). Many only think of Jesus as *gentle and humble in heart* (Matthew 11:29), but there's fire in his eyes against all that is evil.

Revelation 1:15 *His feet were like bronze glowing in a furnace.*

The same feet that walked on water, and were nailed to a cross, will crush his opponents. *For he must reign until he has put all his enemies under his feet* (1 Corinthians 15:25), wrote Paul. The Apostle John took one look at those feet of bronze and fell on his face as though dead (Revelation 1:17). Never cross a man whose feet are like bronze.

Revelation 1:15b *[A]nd his voice was like the sound of rushing waters.*

The water's roar at Niagara Falls is so loud, it's hard to hear anything else. And the voice of Jesus Christ is so powerful, it will drown out every other voice. The Buddha will be silent before him.

Confucius will be silent before him. Muhammad will be silent before him. And every other person who presumed to speak for God will be silent before Jesus Christ.

Revelation 1:16 *His face was like the sun shining in all its brilliance.*

Jesus Christ is the light of the world (John 8:12), and will appear as such in the age to come. Those who believe in him will also *shine like the sun* (Matthew 13:43), he said. Jesus is the most glorious being in the universe, and will share his glory with us.

There's a building in California with a stainless steel exterior that reflects the sun so powerfully it can be hard to look at. Some of the neighbors have even complained that it raises the temperature in their homes by as much as fifteen degrees. In the age to come we'll be amazed by the glory of Jesus Christ, and by the glory of each other. We will *share in the glory of our Lord Jesus Christ* (2 Thessalonians 2:14), wrote Paul.

For Reflection and Review

- *How would this vision of Christ encourage persecuted Christians?*
- *What is your favorite part of this vision?*
- *How should we think of Jesus now?*

Lesson 357

Revelation 2:4 *Yet I hold this against you: You have forsaken the love you had at first.*

The second and third chapters of Revelation contain seven letters from the risen Christ to seven particular churches. They contain words of encouragement and challenge to specific congregations that can be applied to churches in every place and age.

The church in Ephesus had many good points including perseverance and discernment. They were loyal to Christ in other areas, but were no longer in love with him. This is like being in excellent physical shape but having heart disease. Jesus wanted the Ephesian church to return to their first love.

Revelation 2:5 *Consider how far you have fallen! Repent and do the things you did at first.*

After coming to faith in Christ many fall deeply in love with him. *God's love has been poured out into our hearts through the Holy Spirit* (Romans 5:5), wrote Paul. God's love will make us want to spend time with him, simply to adore him. With the press of other things, however, many allow their love for Christ to cool. But Christ's love for us never cools, and he longs to be loved in return. The more we focus on loving him, the better we'll keep his commands (John 14:23).

Revelation 2:10 *Be faithful, even to the point of death, and I will give you life.*

These are the words of Jesus Christ to the church in Smyrna. They were a poor and suffering church, that was enduring persecution. As Jesus remained faithful to the point of death for them, they were to do the same for him.

An elevator operator in a tall building enjoyed her work, even though it was routine. Then, one day, the building caught fire and many were trapped inside. She was tempted to flee, but continued making runs, up and down, saving many lives. Suddenly, the power went out and, the following day, her charred body was found on the elevator floor.

Our service to Christ can seem routine, but that can suddenly change. Whether we die heroically, or in our sleep, Christ's word is the same: *Be faithful, even to the point of death, and I will give you life.*

Revelation 2:15 *Likewise, you also have those who hold to the teaching of the Nicolaitans.*

These are the words of Jesus Christ to the church in Pergamum. They were facing opposition, and one had even been martyred. Their perseverance was commendable but, at the same time, they were tolerating false teaching, which probably included idolatry and sexual immorality (Revelation 2:14). This is not uncommon, even today.

One dear lady returned from church with tears of joy. The music was wonderful, and the preaching was powerful. But best of all, it concluded with the wedding of a man to a man—all to the singing of *Here Comes the Bride*. It's bad enough when Christians fall into sin but, when it's taught by their leaders, that church has problems.

The best safeguard against false teaching is a commitment to the inerrancy of the Bible. *All Scripture is God-breathed and is useful for teaching, rebuking, correcting and training in righteousness* (2 Timothy 3:16), wrote Paul. If a church doesn't hold to the inerrancy of the Bible (and the Bible alone) it's already teaching falsely. The second best safeguard against false teaching is a congregation that's biblically informed. The better Christians know the Bible, the less they'll tolerate false teaching.

Revelation 2:20 *I have this against you: You tolerate that woman Jezebel, who calls herself a prophet.*

These are the words of Jesus Christ to the church in Thyatira. They had a teacher who was infecting the church with false teaching that led to sexual immorality. Christians are sexual beings who often try to justify behavior that's contrary to the Bible.

When Christians fail sexually they should confess their sin to God, and God will forgive them (1 John 1:9). But if they choose to justify their sin, and refuse to turn away from it, they should be removed from the church. *Expel the wicked person from among you* (1 Corinthians 5:12), wrote Paul. The church should be full of repenting Christians, but defiant ones must be put out.

Revelation 3:2 *Wake up! Strengthen what remains and is about to die, for I have found your deeds unfinished in the sight of my God.*

These are the words of Jesus Christ to the church in Sardis. They had a reputation for being alive, but were becoming sleepy. Jesus told them to *Wake up!* since spiritual drowsiness can lead to spiritual death.

A little boy swallowed poison and his father called the doctor. The doctor told him to get his son to the hospital, and not to let him sleep, or he would surely die. On the way there the little boy began to fall asleep, so the father slapped his face repeatedly to keep him awake.

We must do whatever is necessary to wake ourselves up to God. This means getting involved in the work of Christ, so that our deeds will not be unfinished. Christ commands drowsy Christians everywhere to *Wake up!*

Revelation 3:11 *Hold on to what you have, so that no one will take your crown.*

These are the words of Jesus Christ to the church in Philadelphia. They were facing opposition, and the struggle was intense. In light of his soon return, Jesus urged them to hold on so they wouldn't lose their crown.

Years ago I went to a rodeo and watched professional bull-riders. The bulls weighed over two thousand pounds, and had the single goal of throwing the rider off as quickly as possible. The riders had to hold on for a mere eight seconds while the bull bucked, jumped, and spun with all its might. The Christian life can be just as intense, but we're never allowed to let go.

Revelation 3:15-16 *I know your deeds, that you are neither cold nor hot. I wish you were either one or the other! So, because you are lukewarm—neither hot nor cold—I am about to spit you out of my mouth.*

These are the words of Jesus Christ to the church in Laodicea, and are one of the strongest rebukes in the Bible. People like their beverages hot or cold, but not lukewarm. Lukewarm Christians are so repulsive to Jesus that he wants to spit them out of his mouth. He feels this way because his love for us is passionate. Passionate love must be returned or it will lead to frustration, and then to anger. When we understand how passionate Christ is about us, we'll begin to feel that way about him.

For Reflection and Review

- *Why do some churches disobey the Bible?*
- *How should the church treat unrepentant sinners?*
- *How can we improve the church?*

Lesson 358

Revelation 4:1 *After this I looked, and there before me was a door standing open in heaven. And the voice . . . said, Come up here.*

John was an old man, with only a few years left on earth. With little to do during his exile, he probably thought about heaven often. Suddenly, he saw an open door and heard an invitation: *Come up here*. Through John we get a glimpse of the center of the universe—the very throne of God.

[T]here before me was a throne in heaven with someone sitting on it. And the one who sat there had the appearance of jasper and ruby. A rainbow that shone like an emerald encircled the throne. . . . From the throne came flashes of lightning, rumblings and peals of thunder (Revelation 4:2-5).

In the center, around the throne, were four living creatures, and they were covered with eyes, in front and in back. The first living creature was like a lion, the second was like an ox, the third had a face like a man, the fourth was like a flying eagle.

Each of the four living creatures had six wings and was covered with eyes all around, even under its wings. Day and night they never stop saying: Holy, holy, holy is the Lord God Almighty, who was, and is, and is to come (Revelation 4:6-8).

The four living creatures seem less excited about God's wisdom, power, or love, than his holiness. Depending on a person's wealth we might say they're *rich, very rich,* or *very very rich*. By using a triple repetition, the living creatures proclaim the infinite holiness of God.

Isaiah also saw angelic creatures proclaiming: *Holy, holy, holy is the Lord Almighty* (Isaiah 6:3). If they were the same creatures John saw, they may've been proclaiming God's holiness for over six hundred years, and might be doing so today.

The holiness of God is little understood this side of heaven, but is perceived by some. *Worship the Lord in the splendor of his holiness* (Psalm 96:9), wrote the Psalmist. This is the goal of every Christ-centered worship service.

Perhaps you've been to a service where the music was spectacular, but you left uninspired. And perhaps you've been to a service where the music was barely average, but you sensed the presence of God and sang with all your heart. Whenever we sense the presence of God we begin to worship like those around his throne.

Revelation 4:10 *[T]he twenty-four elders fall down before him who sits on the throne and worship him who lives for ever and ever.*

The twenty-four elders aren't identified, but remind us of the twenty-four divisions of priests appointed to serve in the temple (2 Chronicles 24:1-19). Like the priests, they too have a sacred role to play: *They lay their crowns before the throne and say: You are worthy, our Lord and God, to receive glory and honor and power, for you created all things, and by your will they were created and have their being* (Revelation 4:10b-11).

This is like seeing a great performance and showing our approval by shouting and clapping. One of the longest standing ovations was given to the opera singer, Placid Domingo. Remarkably, it lasted over an hour. But that's brief compared to the ovation God will receive, for it will never end.

Revelation 5:11-13 *Then I looked and heard the voice of many angels, numbering thousands upon thousands, and ten thousand times ten thousand.... In a loud voice they were saying: Worthy is the Lamb, who was slain, to receive power and wealth and wisdom and strength and honor and glory and praise! Then I heard every creature in heaven and on earth and under the earth and on the sea, and all that is in them, saying: To him who sits on the throne and to the Lamb be praise and honor and glory and power, for ever and ever!*

They day is coming when all creation will be caught up in the glorious worship of God. Demons and the unconverted may be excluded here, but even they will be forced to acknowledge what can no longer be denied: *God exalted [Jesus] to the highest place and gave him the name that is above every name, that at the name of Jesus every knee should bow, in heaven and on earth and under the earth, and every tongue acknowledge that Jesus Christ is Lord, to the glory of God the Father* (Philippians 2:9:11), wrote Paul.

Worship in church can seem a little dull compared to worship in heaven. But whenever we lift our praise, we join the choir above. Even if we're small, we should see ourselves as part of the greatest congregation ever assembled. We worship the one who created the world, and died on a cross for our sins, so we could be part of his glorious kingdom. To him belongs eternal praise.

Revelation 6:16 *They called to the mountains and the rocks, Fall on us and hide us from the face of him who sits on the throne and from the wrath of the Lamb!*

At the end of this age God will pour out his wrath with such fury that people will flee to the mountains, hoping to be buried by an avalanche. This was also foretold by the prophet Hosea. *Then they will say to the mountains, Cover us! and to the hills, Fall on us!* (Hosea 10:8). It's better to have a mountain fall on your head than to face the wrath of God.

Many people go through life with a vague awareness of God's anger toward them, but never turn from their sins and live for his glory. They hope they're wrong about God's anger, and that all will go well on Judgment Day. But that day will reveal a wrath more intense than anything ever imagined, and it will never end.

Thankfully, this isn't the case for Christians. *Jesus rescues us from the coming wrath* (1 Thessalonians 1:10), wrote Paul. He bore the wrath of God on our behalf when he died on the cross for our sins (1 John 4:10). Because of Jesus Christ, we're no longer exposed to God's righteous indignation.

In the dry heat of summer, prairie fires can be a serious threat. Farmers even carry matches so, if they see a fire coming, they can burn an area around them. That way, when the fire reaches them, they can stand in the place that's already burned, and be safe from the raging flames.

Two thousand years ago, the fire of God's wrath fell on Jesus Christ, as he hung on the cross for our sins. Every lash across his back, every nail through his flesh, and every thorn on his brow was for us. If we truly believe in Jesus Christ, we are completely safe from the coming wrath. But if God poured out his wrath on Jesus Christ, what will he do to those who reject him?

For Reflection and Review

- *Have you ever sensed God's presence in church?*
- *What makes you want to praise the Lord?*
- *How are we saved from God's wrath?*

Lesson 359

Revelation 7:9-14 *After this I looked, and there before me was a great multitude that no one could count, from every nation, tribe, people and language, standing before the throne and before the Lamb. They were wearing white robes and were holding palm branches in their hands. And they cried out in a loud voice: Salvation belongs to our God, who sits on the throne, and to the Lamb.... These are they who have come out of the great tribulation.*

Before the return of Christ, the Bible predicts a time of tribulation. *There will be a time of distress such as has not happened from the beginning of nations* (Daniel 12:1), recorded Daniel. And *there will be great distress, unequaled from the beginning of the world until now* (Matthew 24:21), said Jesus.

But tribulation isn't new. In a place opposed to Christianity, fifteen university students were arrested for attending a Bible study. They were sent to a prison camp and forced to live in a shipping container. One came down with malaria but was denied medical treatment and died. The church has often suffered, in various places, but tribulation will intensify at the end of the age.

Revelation 7:14b *[T]hey have washed their robes and made them white in the blood of the Lamb.*

Even those who went through great tribulation needed their sins washed away. All their sorrow and suffering couldn't remove their sins—only the blood of Christ could do that. The blood of Christ is a miracle detergent that removes every stain without leaving a trace. The terrible sins of murder, blasphemy, and rape, are nothing compared to the blood of Christ, even if we've done them a thousand times or more.

The wickedest murderers, who repent of their murders, are no longer murderers, but faithful Christians. The wickedest blasphemers, who repent of their blasphemies, are no longer blasphemers, but faithful Christians. The wickedest rapists, who repent of their rapes, are no longer rapists, but faithful Christians. *[T]hey have washed their robes and made them white in the blood of the Lamb.*

Revelation 8:7-12 *The first angel sounded his trumpet, and there came hail and fire mixed with blood . . . The second angel sounded his trumpet, and something like a huge mountain, all ablaze, was thrown into the sea. . . . The third angel sounded his trumpet, and a great star, blazing like a torch, fell from the sky. . . . The fourth angel sounded his trumpet, and a third of the sun was struck, a third of the moon, and a third of the stars, so that a third of them turned dark.*

Trumpets were used in the ancient world to warn of a coming danger, such as an approaching army (Joel 2:1-2). John saw seven angels, with seven trumpets, announcing seven disasters coming on the world.

Whenever disaster strikes, people often ask, *Why did God let this happen?* The assumption is that people are good, and if God doesn't take care of us, he's not doing his job. But *every inclination of the human heart is evil from childhood* (Genesis 8:21), and disaster is God's way of calling us to repent. *[U]nless you repent, you too will all perish* (Luke 13:3), said Jesus.

Revelation 9:1-6 *The fifth angel sounded his trumpet, and I saw a star that had fallen from the sky to the earth. The star was given the key to the shaft of the Abyss. When he opened the Abyss, smoke rose from it like the smoke from a gigantic furnace. . . . And out of the smoke locusts came down on the earth and were given power like that of scorpions . . . . . During those days people will seek death but will not find it; they will long to die, but death will elude them.*

The Abyss is like a bottomless pit, where demons are kept. It's not an imaginary place, but a place of real misery. When Jesus confronted a legion of demons, *they begged [him] repeatedly not to order them to go into the Abyss* (Luke 8:31) wrote Luke.

The misery inflicted by the scorpion/locusts will be so great that people *will long to die, but death will elude them.* If life becomes unbearable, we assume that we can kill ourselves, but that won't always be the case. Imagine the misery of a man who tries to hang himself only to find his neck is too strong; or one who tries to overdose only to become violently ill; or one who stabs himself only to have his wound clot before he bleeds out. God is the giver of life, and can make us live as long as he wants. Everyone in hell wants to die, but they can't, because God keeps them alive.

For Reflection and Review

- *How can believers endure great tribulation?*
- *How does suffering affect you spiritually?*
- *How can we prepare for tribulation?*

Lesson 360

Revelation 9:13-21 *The sixth angel sounded his trumpet [and] . . . . A third of mankind was killed . . . . The rest of mankind who were not killed by these plagues still did not repent of the work of their hands; they did not stop worshiping demons, and idols . . . . Nor did they repent of their murders, their magic arts, their sexual immorality or their thefts.*

These people are like Pharaoh, who saw the plagues on Egypt, but refused to repent. His pride and hatred of God were so great that he rode his chariot into the sea, between the walls of water, only to drown when God withdrew his power (Exodus 14:26-28). Christians have been accused of being irrational, but nothing is less rational than opposing the Almighty.

Hardship is an alarm that turns some people to God, but not others. The same sun that melts the wax also hardens the clay. If we keep our hearts soft we'll be willing to repent whenever we are wrong. But if we choose to harden our hearts we'll have no one to blame but ourselves. *Today, if you hear his voice, do not harden your hearts* (Hebrews 4:7), says Hebrews.

Revelation 10:1-3 *Then I saw another mighty angel coming down from heaven. He was robed in a cloud, with a rainbow above his head; his face was like the sun, and his legs were like fiery pillars. . . . He planted his right foot on the sea and his left foot on the land, and he gave a loud shout like the roar of a lion.*

This mighty angel is so wonderful some believe he's Jesus Christ. But we know he's not Jesus Christ because John described him as *another mighty angel*, like the seven angels who sounded the seven trumpets. This is an angel of rank, however, and tells us something about our future.

People were created *a little lower than the angels* (Psalm 8:5), but will be exalted above the angels, just as Jesus *was made lower than the angels [but is] now crowned with glory and honor* (Hebrews 2:7), says Hebrews. Mankind was created in the *image of God* (Genesis 1:27), but that is never said of angels. Believers are called *children of God* (1 John 3:1), but that is never said of angels either. Believers are *in Christ Jesus* (Romans 8:1), but that is never said of angels either. *Do you not know that we will judge angels?* (1 Corinthians 6:3), wrote Paul. When we consider the glory of this angel, we can begin to imagine the glory God has for us.

Revelation 10:3b-4 *When he shouted, the voices of the seven thunders spoke. And when the seven thunders spoke, I was about to write; but I heard a voice from heaven say, Seal up what the seven thunders have said and do not write it down.*

So many things are revealed in Gods word that we're surprised when something is concealed. The Apostle Paul was also *caught up to paradise and heard inexpressible things, things that no one is permitted to tell* (2 Corinthians 12:4). God has revealed many things, but not everything. It's also *the glory of God to conceal a matter* (Proverbs 25:2), says Proverbs.

The Bible is not a collection of all truth, but the judge of all truth. It doesn't tell us everything we want to know, but everything we need to know. There's more to God then we'll ever know, but we ought to know what he's revealed. *The secret things belong to the Lord our God, but the things revealed belong to us and to our children forever,* (Deuteronomy 29:29), wrote Moses.

Revelation 11:3 *I will appoint my two witnesses, and they will prophesy for 1,260 days, clothed in sackcloth.*

These two witnesses are given remarkable power so that *fire comes from their mouths and devours their enemies* (Revelation 11:5). *They [also] have power to shut up the heavens so that it will not rain [and to] turn the waters into blood and to strike the earth with every kind of plague* (Revelation 11:6), wrote John.

This won't make them popular with those who refuse to repent, however, so they'll be put to death. Their bodies will be left to rot, for three and a half days, while the world sends gifts to each other. Then they'll go up to heaven in a cloud, while their enemies look on (Revelation 11:12).

These two witnesses remind us of Moses and Elijah, who did similar miracles. But they also remind us of Jesus Christ who ascended into heaven (Acts 1:9). The devil may kill us, but Christ can raise us up. *Be faithful, even to the point of death, and I will give you life* (Revelation 2:10), said Jesus.

For Reflection and Review

- *Why does hardship turn some people to God but not others?*
- *Would you rather be a Christian or an angel?*
- *Why doesn't God reveal everything?*

Lesson 361

Revelation 11:15 *The seventh angel sounded his trumpet, and there were loud voices in heaven, which said:* The kingdom of the world has become *the kingdom of our Lord and of his Messiah,* and he will reign for ever and ever.

This pronouncement seems premature since there's more conflict to come. But this is where the story is going, and the outcome is certain. The world is at war with God and won't back down until it's defeated. But it will be defeated.

The First World War (1914-1918) was considered *the war to end all wars*. It didn't turn out that way, but the real war to end all wars is coming, and Christ will be the victor. *[T]hose enemies of mine who did not want me to be king over them—bring them here and kill them in front of me* (Luke 19:27), he will say. If we don't receive Jesus as our Lord (Colossians 2:6) we'll face him as our mortal enemy.

Revelation 12:3 *Then another sign appeared in heaven: an enormous red dragon with seven heads and ten horns and seven crowns on its heads.*

This dragon is later identified as Satan (Revelation 12:9), a creature of massive power, with an appetite for destruction. *[W]oe to the earth and the sea, because the devil has gone down to you! He is filled with fury, because he knows that his time is short* (Revelation 12:12), wrote John.

The devil has been active in the world since Adam and Eve (Genesis 3:1-6), but his fury will intensify as time runs out. We should expect a decrease in righteousness, and an increase in every kind of wickedness.

There will be terrible times in the last days. People will be lovers of themselves, lovers of money, boastful, proud, abusive, disobedient to their parents, ungrateful, unholy, without love, unforgiving, slanderous, without self-control, brutal, not lovers of the good, treacherous, rash, conceited, lovers of pleasure rather than lovers of God (2 Timothy 3:1-4), wrote Paul. Under the devil's sway, people will turn into moral monsters.

Three friends murdered their buddy after a disagreement. The autopsy showed he was beaten with a board, and choked so severely that his Adam's apple was crushed. Then his head was smashed with a rock and he was left to decompose. Worst of all, the victim was only eight years old, and his killers were the same age. The world's most hateful sins are Satan's purest joy.

Revelation 13:1 *The dragon stood on the shore of the sea. And I saw a beast coming out of the sea. It had ten horns and seven heads, with ten crowns on its horns, and on each head a blasphemous name.*

This figure is thought to be the antichrist, whom the Apostle Paul also described. *He will oppose and will exalt himself over everything that is called God or is worshiped, so that he sets himself up in God's temple, proclaiming himself to be God* (2 Thessalonians 2:4). Likewise, he'll be *given authority over every tribe, people, language and nation. All inhabitants of the earth will worship the beast—all whose names have not been written in the Lamb's book of life* (Revelation 13:7-8), wrote John.

Worship belongs to Jesus Christ, but the Christ-rejecting world will worship the antichrist instead. Jesus is the rightful king of the world (Isaiah 9:6), but the antichrist will claim that honor for himself. Jesus laid down his life for the sheep (John 10:11) but the antichrist will slaughter the sheep (Revelation 13:10). He's the devil's counterfeit for the *King of kings and Lord of lords* (Revelation 19:16).

Revelation 13:11 *Then I saw a second beast, coming out of the earth. It had two horns like a lamb, but it spoke like a dragon.*

This figure is understood to be the antichrist's false prophet (Revelation 16:13, 19:20, 20:10). He will perform great signs, *even causing fire to come down from heaven to the earth in full view of the people* (Revelation 13:13). His goal is to bring glory to the antichrist so that everyone will worship him (Revelation 13:15).

Taken together, the devil, the antichrist, and the false prophet make up an unholy trinity. Like the Father, the devil remains invisible. Like the Son, the antichrist claims all authority (Matthew 28:18). And like the Spirit, the false prophet glorifies another, not himself (John 16:14). This will be a difficult time for Christians, but it will not last.

Revelation 14:9-10 *If anyone worships the beast and its image and receives its mark on their forehead or on their hand, they, too, will drink the wine of God's fury.*

The false prophet will set up an image of the antichrist, and require everyone to worship it or be put to death (Revelation 13:14-15). People will also be required to receive a mark on their right hand or forehead in order to buy or sell (Revelation 13:16-17). The mark is the name of the antichrist or the number of his name which is *666* (Revelation 13:18).

Mankind was created on the sixth day (Genesis 1:26-31), so the triple-six may represent the glory of mankind, over against the glory of God. God marks his people inwardly with the Holy Spirit (Ephesians 4:30), but the antichrist will mark his people outwardly with the *number of a man* (Revelation 13:18). The highest concern of many is the glory of mankind, but the highest concern of believers is the glory of God.

For Reflection and Review

- *Why is Jesus different here than in the gospels?*
- *Is the world getting better or worse?*
- *How does Satan imitate God?*

Lesson 362

Revelation 14:10b *They will be tormented with burning sulfur in the presence of the holy angels and of the Lamb.*

This applies to everyone who worships the antichrist and receives his mark. Pressure will be brought on Christians to conform, but they must resist no matter the cost. *I tell you, my friends, do not be afraid of those who kill the body and after that can do no more. But I will show you whom you should fear: Fear him who, after your body has been killed, has authority to throw you into hell. Yes, I tell you, fear him* (Luke 12:4-5), said Jesus.

Hell is often described as the absence of Christ, but this verse indicates otherwise. *They will be tormented . . . in the presence of . . . the Lamb* (Revelation 14:10), wrote John. The absence of Christ is what many people wish for. They don't want to worship him, they don't want to hear him, and they don't want to obey him. If hell was the absence of Christ, that would be heaven for them.

But there is nowhere that Christ isn't present, even in hell (Psalm 139:7-8). The difference between heaven and hell isn't the presence or absence of Christ, but whether he's present to bless or curse. Christ is in heaven to bless, and he is in hell to curse.

Revelation 14:11 *There will be no rest day or night.*

One of the worst things about hell will be the absence of rest. A friend of mine went without sleep for days, and thought he'd lose his mind. He laid in bed for hours, hoping to sleep, but sleep wouldn't come to him. Then he had to get up and go to work again. It's hard to go without sleep, for even a day or two, but in hell *There will be no rest day or night*. The awful descriptions of hell in the Bible should compel us to obey Jesus Christ and share the gospel with others.

Revelation 15:3-4 *Great and marvelous are your deeds, Lord God Almighty. Just and true are your ways, King of the nations. Who will not fear you, Lord, and bring glory to your name? For you alone are holy. All nations will come and worship before you, for your righteous acts have been revealed.*

These words are sung in heaven by those who are victorious over the antichrist (Revelation 15:2). The antichrist probably thought he was victorious over them, since he had put them to death. But real victory is dying in faith, not just staying alive. *Blessed are the dead who die in the Lord from now on. Yes, says the Spirit, they will rest from their labor, for their deeds will follow them* (Revelation 14:13), wrote John.

The greatest day of the believer's life is the day they go to be with Christ. *I desire to depart and be with Christ, which is better by far* (Philippians 1:23), wrote Paul. Unbelievers treat this world like it's the only one there is. Believers know it's only preparation for the world to come.

Revelation 16:1 *Then I heard a loud voice from the temple saying to the seven angels, Go, pour out the seven bowls of God's wrath on the earth.*

These are the last catastrophic judgments before the return of Christ. *The first angel went and poured out his bowl on the land, and ugly, festering sores broke out on the people who had the mark of the beast and worshiped its image* (Revelation 16:2). *The second angel poured out his bowl on the sea, and it turned into blood . . . and every living thing in the sea died* (Revelation 16:3).

The third angel poured out his bowl on the rivers and springs of water, and they became blood. . . . (Revelation 16:4). *The fourth angel poured out his bowl on the sun, and the sun was allowed to scorch people with fire. . . .* (Revelation 16:8). *The fifth angel poured out his bowl on the throne of the beast, and its kingdom was plunged into darkness. . . .* (Revelation 16:10).

The sixth angel poured out his bowl on the great river Euphrates, and its water was dried up . . . . (Revelation 16:12). *The seventh angel poured out his bowl into the air . . . . huge hailstones, each weighing about a hundred pounds, fell on people. And they cursed God on account of the plague of hail* (Revelation 16:17-21).

The catastrophic judgments coming on the earth should keep Christians from becoming too attached to this world. We should try make the world a better place, but shouldn't hold on too tightly, or be surprised when it turns against God. The goal of the church isn't to take over the world, but to preach the gospel everywhere (Matthew 28:18-20), so many may be saved. *[O]ur citizenship is in heaven. And we eagerly await a Savior from there* (Philippians 3:20), wrote Paul.

Revelation 16:16 *Then they gathered the kings together to the place that in Hebrew is called Armageddon.*

The word Armageddon only occurs here in the Bible, and likely stands for a region sixty miles north of Jerusalem, where many battles were fought. It stands for the final battle between God and his opponents: real people at a particular point in time. We should imagine massive armies, and powerful weapons, pointed toward Christ at his return.

Revelation 17:14 *They will wage war against the Lamb, but the Lamb will triumph over them because he is Lord of lords and King of kings—and with him will be his called, chosen and faithful followers.*

The world is so opposed to Christ that, when he came the first time, they put him on a cross. And when he comes a second time they'll try to kill him again. If sin was even slightly rational the world would surrender to Christ. But when they see the king in his glory, they'll turn their weapons on him. But *the Lamb will triumph over them because he is Lord of lords and King of kings.*

Revelation 18:4 *Come out of her, my people, so that you will not share in her sins, so that you will not receive any of her plagues.*

There is a time to engage the world, but there's also a time to withdraw. Jesus was such a friend of sinners that he was called a *glutton and a drunkard* (Matthew 11:19). But when the world becomes too corrupt, the church must back away, or risk corruption themselves. *Come out from them and be separate, says the Lord. Touch no unclean thing, and I will receive you* (2 Corinthians 6:17) wrote Paul.

Christians should be close enough to the world to win sinners, but not so close they win us. We must separate ourselves from the worst elements of the world, or the world will compromise our loyalty to Christ. This is not an easy balance but, it's the only way to fulfill our mission.

For Reflection and Review

- *Have you ever had a sleepless night?*
- *Why is the end of the age so violent?*
- *When should believers separate from the world?*

Lesson 363

Revelation 19:7 *Let us rejoice and be glad and give him glory! For the wedding of the Lamb has come, and his bride has made herself ready.*

Weddings are celebrated in almost every culture. They normally follow a time of engagement, in which plans are made for a lifetime of love and devotion. The long awaited day finally arrives, and the two become legally married. But this is only a faint reflection of Christ and his church. *[A] man will leave his father and mother and be united to his wife, and the two will become one flesh. This is a profound mystery—but I am talking about Christ and the church* (Ephesians 5:31-32), wrote Paul.

Now is the engagement period in which the church prepares for her wedding day. She is faithful to her groom because of their mutual love. She also grows in holiness (2 Corinthians 7:1) because she wants to please him. And we know that he will be pleased because his reaction is already recorded: *as a bridegroom rejoices over his bride, so will your God rejoice over you* (Isaiah 62:5), wrote Isaiah.

My wife was absolutely stunning on the day that we were married. Her physical beauty was striking, and no expense was spared on her gown. When I saw her walking down the aisle, she literally took my breath away.

Jesus chose an unlikely bride, but the church is getting ready. The greatest joy of the happiest couple is only a hint of what will be ours forever. *Let us rejoice and be glad and give him glory! For the wedding of the Lamb has come, and his bride has made herself ready.*

Revelation 19:11-16 *I saw heaven standing open and there before me was a white horse, whose rider is called Faithful and True. With justice he judges and wages war. His eyes are like blazing fire, and on his head are many crowns. He has a name written on him that no one knows but he himself. He is dressed in a robe dipped in blood, and his name is the Word of God.*

The armies of heaven were following him, riding on white horses and dressed in fine linen, white and clean. Coming out of his mouth is a sharp sword with which to strike down the nations. He will rule them with an iron scepter. He treads the winepress of the fury of the wrath of God Almighty. On his robe and on his thigh he has this name written: KING OF KINGS AND LORD OF LORDS.

Jesus Christ is the ultimate warrior who conquers all his opponents. *The Lord is a warrior; the Lord is his name* (Exodus 15:3), wrote Moses. This wasn't obvious when Jesus was blessing little children (Mark 10:16), or teaching people to turn the other cheek (5:39). But when he returns to execute his wrath, none will be more fierce.

His enemies will be like bursting grapes as he *treads the winepress of the fury of the wrath of God*

Almighty, and their blood will flow as high as the horses' bridles (Revelation 14:20). Whoever isn't afraid of Jesus Christ should read the end of his story.

Revelation 19:17-21 *And I saw an angel standing in the sun, who cried in a loud voice to all the birds flying in midair, Come, gather together for the great supper of God, so that you may eat the flesh of kings, generals, and the mighty, of horses and their riders, and the flesh of all people, free and slave, great and small.*

Then I saw the beast and the kings of the earth and their armies gathered together to wage war against the rider on the horse and his army. But the beast was captured, and with it the false prophet. . . . The two of them were thrown alive into the fiery lake of burning sulfur. The rest were killed with the sword coming out of the mouth of the rider on the horse, and all the birds gorged themselves on their flesh.

The hatred of sinners toward God is normally veiled, but here it's clearly evident as they gather to oppose the Lord at his return. In contrast to the *wedding supper of the Lamb* (Revelation 19:9), the birds of the air are invited to *the great supper of God [to] eat the flesh of kings* and all who oppose the Lord (Revelation 19:17-18). All the carnage of all the wars that have ever been fought will be nothing compared to the carnage at Christ's return.

Revelation 20:1-3 *And I saw an angel coming down out of heaven, having the key to the Abyss and holding in his hand a great chain. He seized the dragon, that ancient serpent, who is the devil, or Satan, and bound him for a thousand years. He threw him into the Abyss, and locked and sealed it over him, to keep him from deceiving the nations anymore until the thousand years were ended. After that, he must be set free for a short time.*

When Christ returns, the devil will be bound for a thousand years to keep him from deceiving the nations. This period is often called the *millennium* and precedes the eternal state. It's also described by the prophets as a time of great peace and prosperity.

The wolf will live with the lamb, the leopard will lie down with the goat, the calf and the lion and the yearling together; and a little child will lead them. . . . They will neither harm nor destroy on all my holy mountain, for the earth will be filled with the knowledge of the Lord as the waters cover the sea (Isaiah 11:6-9), wrote Isaiah.

The days are coming, declares the Lord, when the reaper will be overtaken by the plowman and the planter by the one treading grapes. New wine will drip from the mountains and flow from all the hills . . . . They will plant vineyards and drink their wine; they will make gardens and eat their fruit (Amos 9:11-14), wrote Amos.

They will beat their swords into plowshares and their spears into pruning hooks. Nation will not take up sword against nation, nor will they train for war anymore. Everyone will sit under their own vine and under their own fig tree, and no one will make them afraid (Micah 4:3-4), wrote Micah.

We should think of Jesus Christ ruling the world from Jerusalem, during a time of unprecedented prosperity. But paradise isn't completely restored. Children will still be born with sinful natures and, even in a perfect environment, won't be content to have Christ rule over them.

Revelation 20:7-8 *When the thousand years are over, Satan will be released from his prison and will go out to deceive the nations.*

The nations will assemble against Christ once again and, once again, they'll be defeated. *[F]ire came down from heaven and devoured them. And the devil, who deceived them, was thrown into the lake of burning sulfur, where the beast and the false prophet had been thrown. They will be tormented day and night for ever and ever* (Revelation 20:9-10). Now it's time for Judgment Day.

For Reflection and Review

- *How should the church prepare for her wedding day?*
- *Are you glad that Christ is a warrior?*
- *Why is the millennium necessary?*

Lesson 364

Revelation 20:11-15 *Then I saw a great white throne . . . . And I saw the dead, great and small, standing before the throne, and books were opened. Another book was opened, which is the book of life. The dead were judged according to what they had done as recorded in the books. . . . Anyone whose name was not found written in the book of life was thrown into the lake of fire.*

People do many things they wouldn't do if they knew they would be caught. The bad news of this passage is that every inappropriate word, thought, and deed is part of the public record. *There is nothing concealed that will not be disclosed, or hidden that will not be made known* (Luke 12:2), said Jesus. He knows what you did when you were four, and he knows what you did when you were forty. It's *recorded in the books.*

But there's another book called *the book of life.* It contains the names of every single person who belongs to Jesus Christ. Some were murderers, adulterers, thieves, gossips, and blasphemers. But they're completely forgiven because they belong to the one who paid for all their sins.

They won't be thrown into the lake of fire, but will *receive a rich welcome into the eternal kingdom of our Lord and Savior Jesus Christ* (2 Peter 1:11), wrote Peter. He'll *present [us] before his glorious presence without fault and with great joy* (Jude 1:24), wrote Jude. Even now, we are *holy in his sight, without blemish and free from accusation* (Colossians 1:22), wrote Paul.

Our greatest concern on Judgment Day won't be what we've done, or haven't done, but whether we've truly believed in Jesus Christ. *Whoever believes in him is not condemned, but whoever does not believe stands condemned already* (John 3:18), wrote John.

Revelation 21:1-3 *Then I saw a new heaven and a new earth, for the first heaven and the first earth had passed away. . . . I saw the Holy City, the new Jerusalem, coming down out of heaven from God. . . . And I heard a loud voice from the throne saying, Look! God's dwelling place is now among the people, and he will dwell with them. They will be his people, and God himself will be with them and be their God.*

The sin of our first parents strained their relationship with God, their relationship with others, and their relationship with the earth. It also got them kicked out of Eden (Genesis 3:24). But shortly after they sinned, God announced a remedy: someone would come to crush the devil's head (Genesis 3:15). When Jesus died on the cross, he defeated Satan, and opened the way for God and his people to live together again, in a place better than Eden—a heavenly city.

It'll be like Eden and Jerusalem, but better than both together. It's what Abraham was looking for as he journeyed through the Promised Land. *[H]e was looking forward to the city with foundations, whose architect and builder is God* (Hebrews 11:10), says Hebrews.

It's the city Jesus had in mind when he said, *My Father's house has many rooms; if that were not so, would I have told you that I am going there to prepare a place for you?* (John 14:2). It's the city Paul had in mind when he said, *the Jerusalem that is above is free, and she is our mother* (Galatians 4:26). And it's the place the writer of Hebrews had in mind when he wrote: *For here we do not have an enduring city, but we are looking for the city that is to come* (Hebrews 13:14). Apart from God, cities are corrupt (Genesis 11:4). But the city of God will have the best of everything, and will never be defiled (Revelation 21:27).

Revelation 21:4 *He will wipe every tear from their eyes.*

Tears begin at birth, and are common throughout childhood. But even adults have reason to cry sometimes: loss of health, wealth, beauty, reputation, opportunity, innocence, and love. *All night long I flood my bed with weeping* (Psalm 6:6), wrote David.

God may seem indifferent to our tears, but here we see he's not. The most powerful being in the universe is also the most tender. Our mothers used to dry our tears, and they were good at it. But our heavenly Father loves us even more, and he will dry our tears forever. He won't send an angel to do it, but will do it himself. Sorrow that lasted a lifetime will disappear, and purest joy will take its place.

Revelation 21:5 *He who was seated on the throne said, I am making everything new!*

Our fall into sin brought death and misery, as well as a curse on the earth (Genesis 3:17-19). As a result, everything in the world is damaged: hearts, minds, relationships, societies, and everything material. Cars that were new ten years ago, are now being sold for parts.

But Christ is making everything new. *[I]f anyone is in Christ, the new creation has come* (2 Corinthians 5:17), wrote Paul. Christ begins his work of renewal in the hearts of his people, but will not stop until the whole universe has been renewed. *[W]e are looking forward to a new heaven and a new earth* (2 Peter 3:13), wrote Peter.

A friend of mine restored an old car to better than new condition. It was still the same car but with better parts, better paint, and many improved features. The new creation will resemble the old, but will be very much improved. Imagine perfect people, in a perfect world, with a perfect God forever.

Revelation 21:8 *But the cowardly, the unbelieving, the vile, the murderers, the sexually immoral, those who practice magic arts, the idolaters and all liars—they will be consigned to the fiery lake of burning sulfur.*

The surprising thing about this list is that it begins with those who are cowardly. They're excluded from eternal life because following Christ requires courage. This is always true, of course, but especially during persecution.

Ranavalona I was queen of Madagascar in the eighteen hundreds. She was no friend of Christians, and put many of them to death. She dangled some over a cliff, and told them to renounce Christ to save their lives. Upon refusal, the rope was slowly cut until they fell to the jagged rocks below. Following Christ is scary at times, but we're never allowed to turn away (Mark 13:13). There's no place in glory for those who lack the courage to follow Jesus to the end.

Revelation 22:4 *They will see his face.*

This has been the desire of God's people since paradise was lost (Genesis 3:23-24). We're told to *seek his face* (Psalm 105:4) and that *the upright will see his face* (Psalm 11:7). All the seeking of all God's people, for thousands of years, will not be denied.

There have been times when men went off to war and didn't return for years. One soldier said goodbye to his wife who was nearly nine months pregnant. She gave birth to a girl, and often told her how wonderful her daddy was. She also showed her pictures and told her how happy she would be when she finally met her daddy.

Then one day, as she played in the yard, a handsome young man came to the gate. He looked into her eyes until, at last, she recognized him. With a squeal she jumped into his arms and said, *Oh Daddy, you are real!* To see our Father's face will be the joy by which all other joys are measured, and we'll never be apart from him again.

For Reflection and Review

- *Should Christians be afraid of Judgment Day?*
- *How will the city of God compare to a modern city today?*
- *Have you ever needed courage to follow Jesus Christ?*

Lesson 365

Revelation 22:12 *My reward is with me, and I will give to each person according to what they have done.*

The more we do for Christ now, the more we'll be rewarded then. A godly minister was near the end of his life when his friends encouraged him to relax and take life easy. *Shall I not run with all my might now that I have the finish line in view,* he asked?

(Charles Simeon). Every day is a new opportunity to store up a future reward.

Revelation 22:13 *I am the Alpha and the Omega, the First and the Last, the Beginning and the End.*

Alpha and Omega are the first and last letters of the Greek alphabet, and correspond to our A to Z. If you made a list of everything your heart desires it could run a hundred pages. But every item on the list would begin with a letter from A to Z. And yet, our greatest reward in heaven won't be what we receive from Christ, but Christ himself. He is our Alpha and Omega.

Revelation 22:16 *I am the Root and the Offspring of David, and the bright Morning Star.*

These two names for Christ have their source in the Old Testament. As the Root and the Offspring of David, Jesus is both his ancestor and his descendent. David had many descendants, but only one who was also his ancestor. Jesus existed before and after David; he is the root and the offspring—eternal in both directions.

As the bright Morning Star, Jesus signals the passing of the night. When Venus appears in the east, it means the sun will soon appear. The first coming of Christ was like the morning star; his return will be like the sun. The first coming of Christ assures us that the full light of day is nearly here.

Revelation 22:17 *Let the one who is thirsty come; and let the one who wishes take the free gift of the water of life.*

This is the last invitation in the Bible for sinners to come to Christ. It echoes the words of Jesus during his earthly ministry: *Let anyone who is thirsty come to me and drink* (John 7:37). Water is essential to life, and Jesus gives eternal life. In order to receive eternal life, we must come to Jesus Christ.

A twelve-year-old boy asked his mom to leave his room because he had to talk to God. The next morning he announced that he'd become a Christian, and was ready to be baptized. Putting our faith in Jesus Christ isn't complicated, but it does require an act of the will.

Revelation 22:18-19 *I warn everyone who hears the words of the prophecy of this scroll: If anyone adds anything to them, God will add to that person the plagues described in this scroll. And if anyone takes words away from this scroll of prophecy, God will take away from that person any share in the tree of life and in the Holy City, which are described in this scroll.*

This is a severe warning not to add or take away the book of Revelation. We find similar statements elsewhere in the Bible. *Do not add to what I command you and do not subtract from it* (Deuteronomy 4:2), wrote Moses. *Do not add to his words, or he will rebuke you and prove you a liar* (Proverbs 30:6), wrote Agur.

Churches that accept the Bible alone as their authority come to similar conclusions on most important points. But when any person, group, book, or tradition is given the same or greater authority than the Bible, the Bible's teaching will always be distorted.

There are also some who subtract from the Bible. Marcion of Sinope was a church leader in the second century, who thought the God of the Old Testament was incompatible with God and Father of our Lord Jesus Christ. So he gutted the Bible by rejecting the entire Old Testament, and many parts of the New Testament.

We may disagree with Marcion, but we're all inclined to focus on the parts of the Bible we like, and ignore the parts we don't. But *All Scripture is God-breathed* (2 Timothy 3:16), wrote Paul. It takes a whole Bible to make a whole Christian, and a whole church. Whenever you come to a verse you don't like, be sure to read it twice. God may have something to say to you.

Revelation 22:20 *He who testifies to these things says, Yes, I am coming soon. Amen. Come, Lord Jesus.*

The soon return of Jesus Christ was the hope of the early church, especially during persecution. As he wrote these words, John was sitting in exile on the island of Patmos (Revelation 1:9). When he heard Jesus say, *I am coming soon*, his heart's reply was, *Amen. Come, Lord Jesus*.

One indication you're ready for the return of Jesus Christ is that you truly want him to return. If you're engaged to be married, but aren't looking forward to the wedding, you're not ready to be married. Jesus doesn't want to return to a church that doesn't want him to return. He wants to return to a church that longs for his appearing. Like a child waiting for Christmas, the church should be waiting for the soon return of Jesus Christ.

Revelation 22:21 *The grace of the Lord Jesus be with God's people. Amen.*

John concluded with a pronouncement of grace followed by by the word *Amen*. This is the last word of the Bible, and occurs over fifty times from Genesis to Revelation. It means *it is true* and *so be it*.

Many reject the idea of truth, but if someone tells you that you've won the lottery, it matters whether or not it's true. Everyone who believes in Jesus Christ has won the ultimate lottery. To that John said *Amen*. It is true! So be it!

For Reflection and Review

- *What happens when people add to the Bible?*
- *Why is Revelation a suitable ending to the Bible?*
- *What do you think of the Bible?*

About The Author

Shane W. Houle came to faith in Jesus Christ shortly after high school and began studying the Bible almost immediately. He completed his undergraduate degree at Trinity International University, earned his master's degree at Columbia International University, and then returned to Trinity to complete his doctorate.

For many years Shane served churches in Wisconsin, where he taught and preached God's word. During this time he sensed the need for people to learn the whole Bible in a way that's easy to understand. *Learn the Bible in a Year* grew out of that need and is currently available in English, but with plans for translations into a number of languages. Shane's true passion is to teach the whole Bible, to the whole world, free of charge.

Shane has been happily married to Julene for over thirty years and, together, they have two adult children and a wonderful son-in-law. When he's not reading or writing, Shane likes to think about what he's going to read or write. Shane and Julene make their home in Colorado Springs, where they also enjoy the great outdoors.

About Bibles For The World

Bibles For The World is a catalyst for individual and cultural change through Christ and the power of God's Word. The story of the ministry's founder, Dr. Rochunga Pudaite helps explain why.

Rochunga Pudaite was born in 1927 in a tribal village in the hills of Manipur, India. He was a member of the Hmar tribe that only a generation earlier was considered among the fiercest headhunters in India. But through a missionary's brief visit in 1910, Ro's father, Chawnga, became a Christian — and dreamed that someone would one day translate the Bible into the Hmar language. Rochunga, fulfilled his father's dream…and much, much more.

Ro became the first boy from his village to go to school — in the village of Churachandpur — a dangerous hike of 96 miles. He was further educated in Calcutta and received a bachelor's degree from Allahabad University. Ro later continued his schooling in Glasgow, Scotland, and, with the help of Dr. Billy Graham and Dr. Bob Pierce, founder of World Vision and Samaritan's Purse, did his graduate work at Wheaton College near Chicago, Illinois.

Ro accomplished translating the New Testament into his native language while in graduate school, and the complete Bible in 1971. At long last, his task was finished and the Bible (published by Partnership Mission) arrived in Northeast India. There was much joy and excitement as Chawnga and others dedicated the book that had changed their people from headhunters to heart-hunters.

Ro was named executive director of the Indo-Burma Pioneer Mission in 1958, and was married in India to Lalrimawi (Mawii) Pakhuongte on January 1, 1959. Together they founded the Partnership Mission in 1968. In 1973 that ministry, which was then located in Wheaton, IL became Bibles For The World, and is now headquartered in Colorado Springs, Colorado.

Ro and Mawii started 85 village Christian schools, seven Christian high schools, two junior colleges, as well as Trinity College and Seminary, and Sielmat Christian Hospital and Research Center. God also led the pair to start churches throughout Northeast India. More than 350 churches are now a part of the Evangelical Free Church of India, the denomination they founded.

Translation and printing of Bibles, New Testaments and Scripture portions like the Gospel of John constitute one of the chief activities of Bibles For The World. Over the years, the ministry has worked with dozens of strategic partners to provide language-appropriate copies of God's Word to millions upon millions of people who would, otherwise, have little or no access.

Rochunga and Mawii also founded an extensive sponsorship program within India to help children and young people receive help that can change their lives, their families and their communities. Tens of thousands of sponsored children have received help including comprehensive Christian education in the ministry's 35 Christian schools located across northeast India, plus the College and Seminary.

For more than a half-century, Rochunga Pudaite spearheaded ministry outreaches that have touched tens, if not hundreds, of millions of people across the globe. A biography of Dr. Ro was published in 1974, *God's Tribesman*, by James C. and Marti Hefley. His life story was captured in another book by Joe Musser in 1998 called *Fire on the Hills - the Story of Rochunga Pudaite*. Dr. Ro authored many publications and books, including The Book that Set My People Free. And a major motion picture, "Beyond the Next Mountain," tells the story of how the Bible came to the Hmar people of India through Ro's efforts.

Dr. Pudaite passed away in October 2015, and his son John L. Pudaite carries on the work as president and CEO. John has a passion for reaching those people across the globe who have had little or no access to God's Word. Bibles For The World works in partnership with many missions and ministry organizations to ensure that everyone, everywhere, has the opportunity to read the Bible in his or her own language. Recent ministry efforts have included major outreaches into Nepal, China, Thailand, several African nations and many more where people are eager to read God's Word.

You can learn about the ministries of Bibles For The World at biblesfortheworld.org.

Bibles For The World
P.O. Box 49759
Colorado Springs, CO 80949

(888)382-4253 • info@bftw.org • biblesfortheworld.org

Made in the USA
Columbia, SC
04 September 2018